COMPARATIVE POLITICS

Fourth Edition

COMPARATIVE POLITICS

An Introduction
to Seven Countries

Rolf H. W. Theen
Purdue University

Frank L. Wilson
Purdue University

Upper Saddle River, New Jersey 07458

Library of Congress Cataloging-in-Publication Data

THEEN, ROLF H. W.
   Comparative politics: an introduction to seven countries/Rolf H. W. Theen, Frank L. Wilson.—4th ed.
      p. cm.
   Includes bibliographical references and index.
   ISBN 0-13-083573-0 (alk. paper)
   1. Comparative government.   I. Wilson, Frank Lee   II. Title.
JF51.T48 2000
320.3—dc21
                                                            00-029353

VP, Editorial director: Laura Pearson
Director of marketing: Beth Gillett Mejia
Assistant editor: Brian Prybella
Editorial/production supervision and interior design: Rob DeGeorge
Copyeditor: Sylvia Moore
Prepress and manufacturing buyer: Ben Smith
Electronic art creation: ElectraGraphics
Cover art director: Jayne Conte
Cover design: Bruce Kenselaar
Photo researcher: Karen Pugliano
Image specialist: Beth Boyd
Manager, rights and permissions: Kay Dellosa
Director, image resource center: Melinda Reo

This book was set in 10/11 Times by ElectraGraphics
and was printed and bound by Hamilton Printing Company.
The cover was printed by Phoenix Color Corp.

© 2001, 1996, 1992, 1986 by Prentice-Hall, Inc.
a division of Pearson Education
Upper Saddle River, New Jersey 07458

Printed in the United States of America

10 9 8 7 6 5 4 3 2 1

ISBN 0-13-083573-0

PRENTICE-HALL INTERNATIONAL (UK) LIMITED, *London*
PRENTICE-HALL OF AUSTRALIA PTY. LIMITED, *Sydney*
PRENTICE-HALL CANADA INC., *Toronto*
PRENTICE-HALL HISPANOAMERICANA, S.A., *Mexico*
PRENTICE-HALL OF INDIA PRIVATE LIMITED, *New Delhi*
PRENTICE-HALL OF JAPAN, INC., *Tokyo*
PEARSON EDUCATION ASIA PTE. LTD., *Singapore*
EDITORA PRENTICE-HALL DO BRASIL, LTDA., *Rio de Janeiro*

Contents

2   THE SOCIAL SETTING OF BRITISH POLITICS,   *16*

3   THE BRITISH POLITICAL FRAMEWORK,   *27*

4   BRITISH POLITICAL PARTICIPATION: THE CITIZEN AND POLITICS,   *43*

5   POLITICAL LEADERS IN BRITAIN,   *60*

6   BRITAIN'S POLITICAL PERFORMANCE,   *68*

27 THE JAPANESE POLITICAL FRAMEWORK, *347*

28 JAPANESE POLITICAL PARTICIPATION: THE CITIZEN AND POLITICS, *362*

29 POLITICAL LEADERSHIP IN JAPAN, *378*

30 JAPANESE POLITICAL PERFORMANCE, *386*

42 NIGERIAN POLITICAL PERFORMANCE, *529*

Preface

The study of comparative politics has moved far beyond the time when it was deemed sufficient to examine only "the great European powers." Informed citizens now require an understanding of the intricacies of Kremlin politics, the significance of military coups, the problems of political and economic development, and the importance of Confucian principles in modern China. At the same time, students need to study other ways of organizing democracy beyond their own pattern in order to understand the strengths and weaknesses of American democracy and to see how other countries have sought to deal with the universal issues of politics and to overcome their own distinctive problems.

The breadth of knowledge of foreign political systems is now so great that it is difficult to cover even the most important concepts in an introductory course. To present these issues using a topical approach usually leads to rather abstract discussion, and the student ends up with little concrete knowledge. This text examines seven countries: Britain, France, the German Federal Republic, the Russian Federation, Japan, the People's Republic of China, and Nigeria. Each country is studied individually, but from a similar viewpoint, with the goal of permitting comparisons as well as discussions of the individual countries. The countries were selected, first, because they are important in and of themselves and, second, because they illustrate some of the key issues faced by many other countries. The real understanding of these and other countries can come only through the comparison of their political patterns and experiences.

This text entailed considerable collaboration between the two authors, but each had specializations in specific countries. Professor Wilson is primarily responsible for the sections on Britain, France, and Nigeria. Professor Theen is primarily responsible for the sections on Germany and the Russian Federation, as well as the revisions of the section on China. Professors Theen and Wilson jointly authored the section on Japan. Professor James C. F. Wang authored the section on China in the first edition. We are all indebted to the many reviewers who carefully examined our manuscripts at several stages of writing and offered important corrections and useful suggestions, and we are grateful to Professor Gordon Mork for commenting on the first chapter in the section on Germany. We appreciate the suggestions and corrections from the professors and students who have used previous editions of this textbook.

We appreciate the patience and confidence of Prentice Hall's political science editor, Beth Gillett Mejia, and assistant editor, Brian Prybella. We also appreciate the excellent copyediting provided by Sylvia Moore. We also wish to acknowledge those who reviewed this manuscript at various stages and provided helpful suggestions, criticism, and comments. These include Peter Wilson and Linda L. Dolive, both of Northern Kentucky University, Andrew Milnor of the State University of New York at Binghamton, Michael J. Gorges of the University of Maryland at Baltimore, Ronald H. Hayashida of Ramapo College of New Jersey, and Hong N. Kim of West Virginia University.

Rolf H. W. Theen
Frank L. Wilson

COMPARATIVE POLITICS

Introduction

The past fifteen years have brought many dramatic changes in our world: reform in China, collapse of communism in Russia and Eastern Europe, rise and fall of military regimes, appearance and downfall of women prime ministers in major industrial democracies, renewed confidence in the democratic model of government, resurgence of ethnic nationalism in many parts of the world, and major economic changes and crises with important political consequences.

For many Americans living in a large and prosperous country, buffered from the rest of the world by thousands of miles of ocean, the impact of these events may seem remote. The communications and transportation revolutions of the last century, however, have reduced the distances that once separated us from our global neighbors. Communication satellites provide us with instantaneous coverage of sports events around the world, election results in Japan, and rioting in South Africa. Passengers can cross the Atlantic in three and a half hours by supersonic jet and, in the event of global war, missiles can cross several thousand miles in less than 90 minutes. The distances that once separated North America from its friends and adversaries in foreign countries have been bridged by modern communications and transportation.

The modern era has brought also growing interdependence between our country and other countries throughout the world. Twenty years ago, Europeans used to complain about their economies' exaggerated dependence upon the health of the American economy. It was claimed that "when America sneezed, Europe came down with a cold." In other words, a slight economic slowdown in the United States brought recession to the West Europeans, so great was their dependence upon the American economy. This remains true today, but now it is increasingly clear that the United States, too, is dependent upon the economic health and political stability of countries all over the world. Thus the economic crisis in the far east in the late 1990s has had important effects on economies around the globe.

The American economy depends heavily on foreign sources for vital natural resources and on foreign markets for the sale of certain of its goods. If these international sellers and buyers are hit by economic problems or by political instability, the effects on the American economy can be important. Political turmoil in the Middle

1

Table 1 Our Shrinking World: Transatlantic Crossing Times

1492	*Santa Maria* (sail)	72 days		
1620	*Mayflower* (sail)	66 days		
1820s	*Savanah* (sail—assisted by steam engine)	16 days		
1850s	*Persia* (steamship)	8 days	1 hour	45 minutes
1910s	*Lusitania* (steamship)	4 days	11 hours	42 minutes
1930s	*Normandie* (steamship)	3 days	22 hours	7 minutes
1940s	Lockheed Constellation (piston airplane)		14 hours	
1960s	Boeing 707 (jet airplane)		6 hours	30 minutes
1970s	*Concorde* (supersonic jet)		3 hours	33 minutes

East threatens American oil supplies—as was demonstrated during the early stages of the Iraqi invasion of Kuwait in 1990. Weather conditions and the efficiency of farm production in Russia, Argentina, and Australia have important effects on midwestern farmers in the United States who hope to sell their wheat and other grains abroad. This in turn affects domestic food prices, since greater foreign demand for American agricultural exports means higher food prices in the United States.

As our economy has grown and become more highly developed and specialized, interdependence between our economy and foreign economies has increased. It seems likely that this interdependence will continue in the years to come. Even a large country endowed with natural resources, such as the United States, cannot expect to achieve autarchy, or a state of self-sufficiency, without enormous economic dislocations and a sharp drop in the standard of living.

In the past, the United States counted on its isolation from critical areas of conflict and its neutrality to eliminate foreign threats to its security. Now, interdependence is also the rule in national security. After two world wars, Americans have learned that democracy in the United States cannot be secure if other democracies are threatened by aggression and imposed dictatorships. In the absence of an international framework to assure world peace and order, American national security depends today upon the security and stability of countries around the world.

Interdependence among contemporary countries throughout the world affects traditional notions of national sovereignty. Until recently, international practices and law assumed that a state had "absolute and perpetual" power to act independently within its borders. Now even the mightiest countries find that they must take into consideration the attitudes and reactions of other countries as they make policy decisions. Efforts to maintain good economic relations with trade partners place additional restraints. World reactions to a country's policies also place restraints on sovereignty. The desire for tourists, foreign investments, and export/import opportunities may lead a country's leaders to pursue democratization or to observe human rights despite their own disinterest in such values. International organizations, such as the United Nations, the International Monetary Fund, and the World Trade Organization, place limits on a country's independent action. Among the most important of these international bodies is the European Union, whose members include the major economic and political countries of western Europe.

With the shrinking of effective distances in the modern world and the growing global interdependence, it is of great importance that Americans have a better understanding of what is going on elsewhere on our small planet. Political events halfway around the world can have important consequences for Americans. Changes in the Chinese political leadership after the death of Mao Zedong, for example, not only opened up a vast new market for Coca-Cola, but also affected America's security by increasing the ideological distance between China and the Soviet Union. Violence between Catholics and Protestants in Northern Ireland concerns Americans because of the potential effects of this turmoil on an important ally and also because Irish Americans are torn by the emotions of a centuries-old conflict in their ancestral homeland. These foreign political developments need to be understood by informed citizens.

The study of comparative politics offers help in gaining this understanding. The *subject matter* of comparative politics includes the political forces, processes, institutions, and performances of foreign countries. In short, comparative politics is concerned with political experience in other cultural and historical settings. From the study of comparative politics comes the understanding of the historical and social background, the political groups and parties, and the political institutions that produce the events we read about in the newspapers.

Comparative politics also has a specific approach or method in gathering political knowledge. As the name implies, the comparative study of politics is based on the *comparison* of political experience in different countries in the hope of identifying and explaining similarities and differences from one country to another. In effect, the world is the laboratory that provides a variety of experience from which political scientists can hope to build a better understanding of the nature of politics. A broad, worldwide examination of political experience permits generalizations and the identification of tendencies and perhaps even continuities.

Through the study of comparative politics, we can even achieve a better understanding of our own political system. For example, a student of American political parties would not recognize that these parties are disorganized, poorly disciplined, and difficult to distinguish from each other without comparisons with parties in other democracies—such as Britain or France, where political parties are highly organized, disciplined, and distinct from each other. In short, the study of politics in other settings can help us to gain a better understanding of the workings of our own political system through comparison and explanation of the differences and similarities that we discover. Such comparisons will also help us to acquire an informed, critical perspective on our own political system through the development of reference points outside the American political experience.

Through examination of foreign political experience, we can also find ideas for solving political, social, and economic problems in our own

society. Foreign experience can provide models for policy and institutional changes, and it can also alert us to dangers or problems that might confront our political system. There are many instances in our political history where Americans have borrowed institutions or policies developed in other countries. For example, American reformers relied heavily on the experience of the British civil service and the Prussian bureaucracy in setting up our civil service system. More recently, national health reform in the United States benefited from examining the experience of other countries. Proposals for strengthening the American party system almost inevitably are based on European party experience. In short, a better understanding of politics abroad can help in perfecting and adapting American political institutions and policies.

As an introduction to the study of comparative politics, we will examine the political systems in seven countries: Britain, France, Germany, Russia, the People's Republic of China, Japan, and Nigeria. These seven countries have been selected, first of all, because they are among the countries most frequently discussed in our daily newspapers. They include some of the most important world powers, past and present, countries that have left their political, economic, and cultural imprint on the world today.

Political experience is so diverse in today's world that it is difficult to find a country whose politics is "typical" of politics elsewhere. But these seven countries do permit us to introduce many of the crucial questions necessary for understanding politics elsewhere. Four of our countries are Western-style democracies. By *Western democracies,* we mean political systems where the principal public officeholders are selected through regular, competitive, and free elections in which there is a possibility of those in power being replaced by an alternative set of leaders.

Most democratic states are found in the more advanced industrialized countries, although India and Costa Rica provide examples of successful democracies in preindustrial or developing settings. The four examples of Western democracy illustrate the diversity of democratic experience. Britain has long been regarded as the epitome of parliamentary democracy, and its "Westminster"

WHAT IS A STATE?

When Americans use the word "state," they are usually referring to one of the subunits of the United States of America: California, Indiana, Texas, or New York. In political science, however, "state" refers to a country-wide political entity like Britain, Canada, France, Nigeria, or the United States of America. It encompasses the formal political institutions such as legislatures, executives, civil services, and courts. It is used in preference to the term "nation" because many states are multinational in that they are made up of several ethnically different peoples. For example, French Canadians would be willing to see themselves as part of the Canadian state but would probably reject the notion of their making part of a Canadian nation; they are their own nation or people.

---

parliamentary system has been copied in numerous countries. France has a long but turbulent history of democracy with problems similar to those facing the southern European democracies such as Italy and Spain. Its political system had an important impact on the emergent political institutions of its former African and Asian colonies. Germany and Japan are rare instances of the establishment of stable democratic regimes in countries with long histories of authoritarianism. Japan also provides an example of successful implementation of "Western democracy" in an "Eastern" setting.

Until recently, there was an important alternative model for organizing politics in many countries: the communist model. To a large extent, communist political and economic structures were based on Marxist-Leninist ideology and practices developed in Russia after 1917. These distinctive patterns set the communist countries apart from the other countries. At their maximum, communist countries numbered no more than 16, but they ruled nearly half the world's people. In spite of the common ideological basis, the different settings and historical legacies produced different political organizations and practices, epitomized by the contrasting approaches of the former Soviet Union and China.

During the 1980s, new tensions and economic problems brought many communist states to the brink of collapse.[1] At the end of the last decade, most of these countries underwent dramatic, even revolutionary changes.[2] Most of the East European countries repudiated the communist model and sought to move toward the West European democratic and free enterprise societies. The Soviet Union split into several countries, and Rus-

sia experienced disorder as it sought new political and economic forms.[3] Only a few countries, notably China, resisted this tide of change, although that resistance required the violent suppression of reformers in the tragic events of 1989 in Beijing's Tienanmen Square.

Communism as a form of government and economic structure appears to be on the wane as we move into a new century. It is still important to understand how it worked and why it collapsed. More important is the need to look at the different ways that Russia and China have responded to the needs to change from communism to other political and economic forms.

Finally, Nigeria offers a glimpse of the complex political problems confronting the Third World. It is easy to find certain political similarities among Western democratic countries and among the communist states. But there are economic and political differences between the prosperous semifeudalism in Saudi Arabia, the operational parliamentary democracy in India despite enormous economic problems, and the extreme poverty and political disorder in Ethiopia. Nigeria may not be typical, but it offers an example of a Third World country struggling with economic and political development and vulnerable to pressures from outside forces.

A common political format in the Third World is military rule. For this reason, Nigeria offers a good example of non-Western political experience: it has faced seven military coups or attempted coups since 1966, and the military remains a key political force even as Nigeria tries once again to move to civilian government. Nigeria also offers an illustration of the violence and turmoil that can result from the coexistence

THREE WORLDS?

The term "Third World" is a cold war term that was first used in the 1950s to describe those developing countries that declined to ally with either the Western industrial democracies (the First World) or the Soviet bloc (the Second World). Usage evolved so that by the 1960s the term referred more broadly to countries that were economically or politically "underdeveloped." To refer to these countries as "underdeveloped" seemed demeaning and to talk of them as "developing" often seemed too optimistic. The term "Third World" seemed a more neutral way of referring to the many countries seeking political and economic development. The Third World always contained a wide variety of political and economic approaches including socialist and free enterprise economies and traditional oligarchies, civilian dictatorships, and military political regimes. What really set them apart from other political systems were their weak economies and their political turbulence and instability. A decade after the end of the cold war and the disappearance of the "Second World," the term Third World is still widely used.

within a single state of several hostile ethnic groups. Nigeria's ordeals in the transition from colonial dependence to an independent country are similar to those of other former colonies.

In presenting an introduction to comparative politics, we look separately at these seven countries for a brief but integrated view of their political experiences. By examining them separately, we realize that we will be deemphasizing the comparisons that should be a part of "comparative" politics. The advantage of this country-by-country approach is that it provides an overall view of the political process that is needed to make intelligent cross-national comparisons. To avoid neglecting comparisons, we will make frequent reference to American experience. And as we go from one country to the next, the countries presented first will be used as a basis for comparisons that will make the politics of the countries presented later more understandable.

As we look at each separate country, we will ask many of the same questions. This will help readers to make their own comparisons and to draw their own conclusions. As we will discover, however, the questions and emphasis will have to change from one country to the next. In the section on France, we will have to devote a great deal more attention to its very active political party system than when looking at Nigeria, where parties have been outlawed periodically. However, within these limitations, the study of each country will look at the following subjects:

1. History and political culture
2. The social setting of politics
3. The political framework
4. Political participation: Citizens and politics
5. Political leadership
6. Political performance

In the section on each of the seven countries, these themes will be explored in six chapters. We attempt to draw comparisons among the various countries because it is often only through comparisons that we can understand the underlying political institutions and phenomena. As a reader, you are encouraged to compare the countries by rereading chapters dealing with specific subjects across countries as well as reading the chapters within individual country studies. This comparative analysis will enable you to understand basic concepts and theories of politics as well as to understand the nature of politics in the separate countries.

NOTES

[1]Zbigniew Brzezinski, *The Grand Failure: The Birth and Death of Communism in the Twentieth Century* (New York: Charles Scribner's Sons, 1989).

[2]See Ralf Dahrendorf, *Reflections on the Revolution in Europe* (New York: Random House, 1990).

[3]Carol R. Saivetz and Anthony Jones, eds., *In Search of Pluralism: Soviet and Post-Soviet Politics* (Boulder, CO: Westview, 1994).

Part I: Britain

Chapter 1

British History Enshrined

"... a nation with only its past to live for."

John Fowles
Daniel Martin

Each year at the opening of Parliament, the members of the House of Commons, Britain's most powerful legislative body, are summoned to the Lord's chamber to stand and listen to the Queen's speech from the throne. An officer of the House of Lords—known as Black Rod—goes to the House of Commons to convene its membership to this special session. But as Black Rod reaches the chamber of the House of Commons, the door is slammed in his face and bolted shut. Only after a brief conversation through the peephole assures the Commons of Black Rod's peaceful intentions do the members of Commons follow the Royal Mace and their bewigged and berobed Speaker to the Bar of the House of Lords to hear the Queen's address.

For over three hundred years the distinguished members of Parliament have annually repeated this ritual. It reminds members of the time when King Charles I and a band of armed men sought to arrest six members of the House of Commons.

Of course, the royal threat to Commons has long since disappeared, but tradition perpetuates the memories of the struggles to limit the monarch's power and to maintain the independence of the House of Commons.

Such traditional ceremonies are found in all branches and levels of British government; they make British politics more colorful than similar political events in other countries. But these ceremonies do more than simply attract tourists: They evoke historical memories that add legitimacy to the overall political system. They impress public officeholders with the dignity and responsibility of their positions. These historical traditions and ceremonies more or less consciously stimulate patriotism and national unity. British television gives extensive coverage to the pageantry (and foibles) of the royal family. Marriages and births in the royal family, visits to foreign countries, and even the ordinary activities of the monarch's family focus public attention on the glory and history of the country. Even though they are nonpolitical, such royal events elicited in the past feelings of patriotism and satisfaction with the political system.[1] The royal families' continuing scandals eroded some traditional awe

6

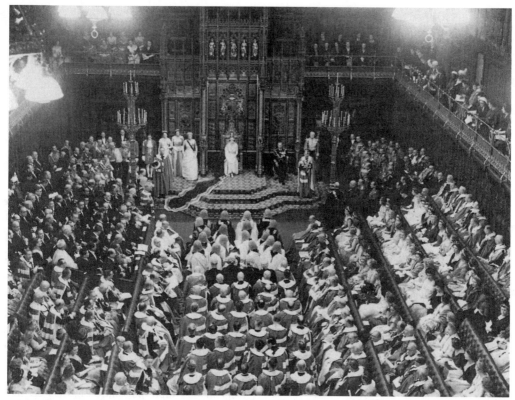

The Queen's annual speech from the Throne is the equivalent to the American president's state of the union address. The Queen, however, does not write her own speech. It is prepared by the Government and given her to read. (*Photographer/Source:* British Information Services)

for the monarchy in the 1990s. The tremendous public mourning of Princess Diana's death in 1997, although sometimes tinged with resentment against other members of the royal family, demonstrated again the emotional ties between the monarchy and the British people.

The lasting political consequences of historical practices are illustrated in the floor plan of the House of Commons. Unlike most legislative bodies British members of parliament (MPs) sit facing each other, with the government party in benches on the right side of the speaker's seat and the opposition on the speaker's left. This spatial arrangement of benches is an accident of history. When Commons first met it used a small chapel in Westminster. Typical of English medieval churches, the pews were arranged on two sides facing toward a central aisle that led from the altar to the door. Later, permanent quarters for Commons were established, but the seating pattern was retained. Many historians and political scientists believe that the physical separation of the chamber into two seating areas contributed to the development of the two-party system, one of the most significant and often-praised features of British politics.

This careful preservation of tradition is characteristic of the British pattern of political development (Table 1–1). Modern British democracy is the product of at least seven hundred years of gradual evolution. We may designate as the beginning of democratic evolution the year 1215, when King John was compelled by his barons to sign the Magna Carta, guaranteeing them certain privileges. While the Magna Carta's immediate effect legitimated the power of an independent aristocracy, it has come to symbolize the limitation of the king's powers and the supremacy of

Table 1–1 Important Landmarks in British History

1066	Norman conquest of England, the last successful invasion of the British Isles
1215	King John signs the Magna Carta
1265	First Parliament meets
1536	Act of Union binds England and Wales
1542	Henry VIII assumes title of King of Ireland
1642–1649	Civil War ends in execution of Charles I and establishment of a military dictatorship under Oliver Cromwell
1660	Restoration of the monarchy under Charles II
1688	The Glorious Revolution deposes James II for attempting to reimpose Catholicism on England
1689	Bill of Rights accepted by William and Mary on their coronation assures political supremacy of Parliament
1707	Act of Union binds Scotland to England
1721–1742	First prime minister: Sir Robert Walpole
1832	Great Reform Act extends suffrage to middle classes
1867	Reform Act further extends right to vote
1911	Powers of the House of Lords abridged
1918	Right to vote extended to most women
1945–1951	Postwar Labour government enacts sweeping social and political reforms

law. Thus, the nobility, along with the Church, checked the monarch's exercise of power. Conflict over power between the aristocracy and the monarch and among various factions within the aristocracy produced the long and costly War of the Roses (1455–85).

Weakened by this civil war, the aristocracy's ability to check the monarch declined and the Tudor era (1485–1603) marked the high point of monarchical power. However, even during this period, religious dissidents and the growing influence of Parliament prevented royal abuses of power. The seventeenth century was a high point in the struggle between Parliament and the monarch. The Puritan Revolution (1642–49) culminated in the trial of King Charles I by Parliament and his subsequent execution for treason. After a dozen years of military dictatorship under Oliver Cromwell and his son, England restored the monarchy when Parliament invited Charles II to assume the throne. But the power of Parliament was again demonstrated by the Glorious

Revolution of 1688–89 in which the monarch, James II, was deposed because of his Catholicism. Parliament later assured its inalienable supremacy over the monarch in the Bill of Rights, which William and Mary accepted as they assumed the throne in 1689. The Bill of Rights included some guarantees of individual freedoms, but it was more important as a contract between the Crown and Parliament limiting the powers of the Crown.

The confirmation of Parliament's supremacy did not mean the advent of democracy, since the nobility, the wealthy, and the Church of England dominated Parliament. It was only in the nineteenth century that the first steps were taken to make the House of Commons a truly representative legislative body. Originally, the membership of Commons included two knights from each county and two citizens elected by a highly restricted portion of the middle-class population of each borough. In the nineteenth century, however, the Industrial Revolution caused rapid changes in population distribution. Certain boroughs, called "rotten boroughs," lost most of their populations but retained representation in Commons. New industrial centers and cities that had experienced very rapid population growth had little or no representation. The result was extreme malapportionment of seats in the House of Commons. While hundreds of thousands of people living in new industrial centers like Manchester, Leeds, Birmingham, and Sheffield had no representatives in Commons, 51 boroughs with a combined total of less than 1500 voters sent more than 100 representatives to sit in Commons.[2]

The Great Reform Act of 1832 corrected some of these inequities, abolishing most of the rotten boroughs, granting certain industrial centers their first representation in Commons, and increasing the representation of other cities. The Reform Act also enfranchised middle-class males, thus doubling the size of the electorate, but the eligible electorate still amounted to only 4 percent of the total population. In 1867 another Reform Act was passed, reducing property requirements for the vote and extending the vote to the lower middle class, rural tenant farmers, and some urban workers; the size of the electorate thus doubled again. In 1872 the secret ballot was introduced, freeing voters from possible intimidation. Further reforms in 1884 and 1885 corrected malrepresentation due to uneven distribution of seats relative to population.

Then, after World War I, the Representation of the People Act of 1918 granted universal suffrage to males over 21 and to women over 30. In 1928 a new law lowered the minimum voting age for women to 21. The Representation of the People Act of 1948 adjusted the distribution of seats according to population shifts and established the principle of one citizen–one vote by abolishing procedures that had permitted certain upper-class citizens to vote as many as three times in each election. Finally, in the 1960s, Parliament lowered the voting age to 18.

It is difficult to specify the exact date of the emergence of British democracy, since the evolutionary process continues today, but a convenient reference point is the adoption of the Parliament Act of 1911. This law established the supremacy of the House of Commons over the House of Lords; in the event of conflict between the two houses, the decision of Commons (whose membership is determined by popular elections) would ultimately prevail over that of the Lords (whose membership was based on aristocratic birth). Thus, seven centuries after the Magna Carta, gradual political changes had resulted in a representative, parliamentary democracy within the framework of a constitutional monarchy.

TWO MYTHS ABOUT BRITISH POLITICAL DEVELOPMENT

The continued existence and operation of medieval political institutions sometimes leads to the conclusion that the extent of political change in Britain is limited. It is true that many of the most important political institutions—such as the monarch, Parliament, the court system, and common law—had developed during medieval times. But these institutions have changed radically several times over the centuries so that their current functions and basis for popular acceptance are completely different from earlier periods. This can be illustrated easily in the case of the monarchy. The monarch's role changed from that of a feudal overlordship legitimized by military strength and dynastic claims during medieval

times, to a royal absolutism based on a purported "divine right" to rule during the Tudor period (1485–1603), to a monarchy ruling with the consent of Parliament after the Revolution of 1688–89, to a limited constitutional monarchy legitimized by the monarch's acceptance of limits on his or her political role during the eighteenth and nineteenth centuries, to finally a ceremonial figurehead in a parliamentary democracy legitimized by tradition and by the monarch's total abstention from politics in the twentieth century.[3]

In a like manner, other medieval institutions persist today, often still bearing the paraphernalia of bygone days. But their tasks in today's democratic regime are much different from their functions in the autocracies of the past. While institutions continue and their outward forms remain imbued with the past, their actual performance has changed completely to accommodate the needs of a modern industrial democracy.

A second widely accepted myth about British political history is that these changes were accomplished peacefully. In fact, there was a good deal of violence associated with British political development until the nineteenth century. The War of the Roses (1455–85), which resulted in the consolidation of royal power, was a costly blood-letting of the aristocracy. The Civil War (1642–49) asserted parliamentary supremacy over the monarch in struggles on the battlefield as well as in the halls of Westminister Palace. The Restoration of the monarchy in 1660 was furthered by military force. The unions of Scotland and especially of Ireland with the English Crown were accomplished and maintained by violence. The eviction of small farmers from what once had been common lands during the "enclosures" of the eighteenth century entailed "massive violence exercised by the upper classes against the lower."[4]

Even in the nineteenth and twentieth centuries, violence often accompanied political change in Britain. The movement that ultimately resulted in the Great Reform Act of 1832 gained impetus from a bloody riot in 1819. The Chartist movement included strong undercurrents of violence and near-violence. Women found recourse to violence in seeking the right to vote: in 1912 Emmeline Pankhurst, a suffragette leader, and her associates used arson and window-smashing to further their causes, claiming, "The argument of the broken window pane is the most valuable argument in politics."[5] Finally, there was the long and violent struggle to keep Ireland in the union and the bloodshed necessary to achieve Irish home rule in 1921. Only in comparison with the even more tumultuous and violent changes in France, Germany, Italy, and Spain can one claim that even recent political change in Britain has been peaceful or orderly.

EVOLUTIONARY POLITICAL CHANGE

There remain far more evident links with the past in Britain than in most other European democracies. Other countries abandoned old institutions and experimented with new political forms; Britain, in contrast, tinkered with existing institutions to make them fit the needs of an evolving society and state. Over the past three hundred years, while revolution and political turmoil shook and divided neighboring countries, Britain's political institutions evolved gradually and rather peacefully, with leaders of nearly all political forces demonstrating a concern for maintenance of the links with the past rather than urging an abrupt rupture with tradition.

There is no single factor that accounts for the relatively peaceful evolution of modern British politics. Some historians have pointed to Britain's geographic setting: "a great deal of what is peculiar in English history is due to the obvious fact that Great Britain is an island."[6] Its borders are well defined and protected from foreign invasion and the consequent political disruptions. Unlike France, Germany, Russia, and others, which sometimes had internal political change forced upon them by military defeats, Britain has not faced military invasion since 1066. Insulated by the seas from the political turmoil and conflict on the continent, Britain could develop at its own pace.

Also important in explaining Britain's pattern of development is the absence of political absolutism since the seventeenth century. By that time the powers of the monarch were limited, but by no means inconsequential. The restrictions on the monarch's powers prevented royal authoritarianism, while the residual royal prerogatives served as obstacles to the perpetuation of a new absolutism by Parliament, prime ministers, or military figures.

Another partial explanation is that much social discontent took the form of religious rather than political dissent. Conflict between Protestants and Catholics had strong political overtones but assumed a theological character.[7] The Methodism of John Wesley, Puritanism, Congregationalism, and other "nonconformist" religions diverted social unrest into religion, thereby reducing possible sources of support for political dissent. As Walter Bagehot noted, even the most miserable and discontented did "not impute their misery to politics."[8]

Religious and political grievances often led the seriously discontented to emigrate. In North

---

HOW RELIGION DEFLECTED SOCIAL CONFLICT

A novelist recently described well how religious divisions in Britain deflected the social and political tensions of the Industrial Revolution:

. . . people were going to their various churches. Girls in their best dresses were in hope of making passes at the lads. The boys were ogling the girls, whom they only saw on Sundays. Old ladies thought of meeting a sister, a son or a daughter from over the hill, and men of a deal to make en route to the church. But they were isolated in their sects. Methodists would not speak to Baptists, who would not murmur a word to Anglicans, who would impale or burn Papists if they could. The members of one denomination would not so much as pass the time of day with another, even if they lived next door. They moved through a place that was filling up with mills and smokestacks. This was transforming their lives, yet they were more interested in the trivial points of doctrine that divided them.

Glyn Hughes, *The Rape of the Rose* (New York: Simon & Schuster, 1993), p. 197.

America, Australia, New Zealand, and elsewhere these discontented people were able to build new societies conforming to their religious and political beliefs. The empire thus provided a safety valve for social and political discontent in the same way that the western frontier offered escape to American dissidents during the nineteenth century.

Another reason for the evolutionary nature of British politics was the ability of those holding power to recognize growing demands for change and to respond to them. In doing so, they both deflected demands for more radical change and preserved their own political power. The political philosopher Edmund Burke stressed the importance of maintaining tradition and social hierarchy in order to have stable and effective government, but he also argued that the best way to do so was through ongoing change to adapt the existing political and social institutions to an evolving society.

In practice, the Conservative party, long the most important and successful political party, was particularly adept at this. Driven by a powerful will to rule, the Conservatives were quick to accept and enact reforms proposed by others. In many cases the Conservatives, though they represented the most privileged sectors of the population, took the initiative in carrying out far-reaching social and political reforms before they had even been proposed by supposedly more reform-minded sectors of society. The Conservative party's interest in reform was not simply a means of perpetuating its hold on political power, but also an outgrowth of British aristocratic notions of *noblesse oblige,* or the responsibility of the governing class to concern itself with the general well-being of all people. As a result of this philosophical commitment to the social duties of the upper class, Conservative governments often led the way in social reform. For example, the Conservative government of Benjamin Disraeli (1874–80) enacted a series of innovative social reforms, including legal protection of the right to strike, definition of workers' rights, establishment of sanitation services, slum clearance and reconstruction, and regulation of food and drug standards. These are not isolated instances.

Furthermore, the willingness of liberal forces to negotiate and compromise their demands for change complemented the propensity of the conservative forces to accept change. The "practical good sense of the British workingman" led the working class to use its political strength to encourage reform rather than to promote revolt.[9] In Britain few have advocated violent revolution to achieve their ends. Rather than insist on rapid change, the socialist and liberal forces have adopted a gradualist approach to their social and political goals. The Fabian Society, long the voice of radicalism and socialism in Britain, illustrated this commitment to evolutionary development in its emblem—the turtle—symbolizing the belief that the British road to socialism was one of slow but steady progress through reform. Thus, at the leadership level there has been agreement (or "elite consensus") between those favoring radical change and those representing the status quo, an agreement that change should occur through compromise within the existing order.

On the part of the population there has rarely been much interest in political agitation. This is partly attributable to general political apathy and the availability of other outlets for social discontent (the dissenting religions and, later, the labor movement). Another explanation is broad popular confidence in the country's political leaders. Among the few mass political movements prior to the twentieth century was the Chartist movement (1838–50). The Chartists advocated universal suffrage to achieve democracy and social equality. To promote their goals, they organized strikes and demonstrations and circulated petitions. The widespread support of the Chartists is attested to by their submission of a petition bearing over 3 million signatures—a tremendous accomplishment in the nineteenth century. Chartism eventually died out when general prosperity and new factory reform laws improved conditions for the working class. Thenceforth, mass working-class activities were directed toward economic issues by the trade union movement and remained on the margins of politics until the twentieth century.

Thus, change in British politics has more often resulted from the acquiescence of powerful and privileged groups than from mass action. This pattern of gradual reform from above, rather than revolt from below, has developed into a tradition of peaceful coexistence and even cooperation

BRITAIN

among sectors of society with different values—a tradition that continues to affect British political life. For example, the Conservative party, because of its concern for the needs and interests of the lower classes, continues to enjoy the confidence and electoral support of a sizable sector of the working class. Walter Bagehot noted this phenomenon of deference toward social betters and wrote that in England the "numerical majority . . . is ready, is eager to delegate its power of choosing its ruler to a certain select minority. It abdicates in favour of its elite and consents to obey whoever that elite may confide in."[10] Even today, at least one-third of the working class regularly votes for the Conservative party, the direct descendant of the aristocratic party of old. With support from all sectors of society, the Conservatives have dominated British politics, heading the government for over 75 years since 1891.

By no means do all elements of the lower classes manifest this social and political deference. However, even among those sectors of the lower classes that are more motivated by egalitarian and secular democratic values, the tradition of accommodation rather than violent class conflict affects contemporary political behavior. The British aristocracy and lower classes, as well as business groups and labor unions, work together quite readily to resolve their differences without trying to destroy their opponents. Each side has a variety of viewpoints and interests to defend, and each recognizes the other's right to exist and to defend its interests. Both sides emphasize accommodation and compromise. This tradition of mutual forbearance is solidly rooted in a history of cooperative adjustment of interests and demands by rival classes or groups.

There are good reasons to question whether or not the deference to social betters, facilitating evolutionary change during the nineteenth century, still operates in the modern industrial society of Britain in the 1990s.[11] Much of the remaining deferential attitudes appear to have succumbed in the 1970s to the multiple assaults of student and worker activism and to a new wave of populism calling for greater genuine citizen involvement in politics.[12] Deference and other similar political values may nonetheless explain the evolutionary nature of past British political history. New studies of Britain's political culture reveal a greater concern for the broad principles of liberty and equality.[13] These attitudes now are more important in shaping public responses to government actions than is deference.

Even with the decline of deference, history has produced political attitudes that contribute to the willingness of Britons to accept the basic political order and to work within the system for change. The value placed on tradition, the acceptance of a hierarchical society, the willingness to compromise, and the strong emotional attachment to political institutions and symbols all characterize Britain's historical legacy of political attitudes. Together with more modern political attitudes, such as the predisposition to be informed about politics and take part in the political process, these traditional attitudes give Britain a political culture conducive to the success of liberal democracy.

A "CONSERVATIVE REVOLUTION"

When we examine the troubled pasts of France, Germany, Russia, and China, there will be a temptation to minimize the degree of British political change in the past two centuries. The contrast with others is striking: During the twentieth century, France has experienced five different regimes—the Third Republic, Vichy France, a postwar Provisional Government, the Fourth Republic, and the Fifth Republic. Germany during the same time has experienced six regimes—Imperial Germany, the Weimar Republic, the Nazi dictatorship, the postwar occupation government, the Federal Republic, and the reunited Germany. In contrast, Britain has had a single regime; not since 1688 has there been a regime change in Britain.

However, the various social, political, and economic changes that swept over Europe in the eighteenth and nineteenth centuries did not miss Britain. Indeed, some of them, such as the Industrial Revolution, appear to have originated in Britain. But Britain's uniqueness was the ability of the existing social and political order to accommodate these changes without violent breaks with the past. One historian notes:

The true "miracle of modern England" is not that she has been spared revolution, but that she has assimilated so many revolutions—industrial, economic, social, political, cultural—without recourse to Revolution.[14]

Britain has had drastic and far-reaching change but it has not had a Revolution. It has undergone "conservative revolution" in the sense that revolutionary change came in Britain through compromise among contending social forces. The result was adaptation of existing forms rather than their coercive replacement by disorder and generalized violence. The revolutionary violence that beset Britain's continental European neighbors served as a warning of the dangers of excessive rigidity. All social forces, conservative as well as liberal, used the threat of revolution to urge reform. In effect, the fear of revolution motivated change designed to avoid revolution.

The length of political development facilitated the avoidance of explosive revolutionary change in Britain.[15] The various forms of revolution—political, industrial, economic, social, cultural—took place sequentially, one after another, rather than simultaneously. The early issues of defining the nation's identity (who it includes and what are its frontiers) and of establishing the basic political institutions (where decision-making power and political authority are located) were settled by the seventeenth century; the economic revolution of industrialization came in the eighteenth and nineteenth centuries; political revolution and democratization followed in the late nineteenth and early twentieth centuries; and finally the social revolution erupted in the move toward an egalitarian society in the twentieth century.

Since these transformations happened one at a time rather than all at once—as in the French revolution of 1789—they were more easily managed without recourse to revolution. There was a modern state already legitimized to cope with new demands for change. In contrast, countries that began modernization late often faced simultaneous demands for political, economic, and social change. Faced with multiple demands for radical change, these late modernizing countries often found it impossible to direct change in nonviolent channels. For them, the results were often catastrophic social disorder, as in Russia and China or in the Germany of the 1920s and 1930s.

HISTORICAL LEGACY: ASSET OR LIABILITY?

For many years, historians and political scientists probed Britain for clues to its success in providing stable democratic government. Most scholars determined that this success derived from Britain's unique historical development. They attributed contemporary democratic stability in Britain to the gradual evolutionary course of change. The search for compromise and consensus among contending social forces provided a political culture and political traditions that contributed to the successful operation of modern democracy. The British developmental pattern was unique and could not be applied to other countries. But the legacy of history was clearly an asset for British political leaders as they sought to confront contemporary demands for adaptation. Long and honored traditions seemed to assure that whatever the problems and however serious the apparent challenges of the present, "there will always be an England."

But a glorious history can also have disadvantages. When Britain faced economic and political problems in the 1970s, the idea that "there will always be an England" produced complacency that impeded the search for solutions to very real new problems. The attachment to a past as a world power and especially a colonial empire hindered adaptation to a more modest situation in the postwar world. Immigration into Britain of people from former colonial areas bred racial intolerance and violence. The absence of fundamental social reform left Britain with an archaic and unproductive aristocracy and with glaring social and economic inequalities that fomented class conflict. The traditional problem-solving strategy of pragmatic compromise—the seeming explanation for the past success of British politics—came under criticism when applied to contemporary politics, condemned as unprincipled "muddling through" and as ineffective in meeting the multiple challenges of the last half of the twentieth century. Finally, and most tragically, three hundred years of near-continuous fighting in Ireland left a legacy of heroes, slogans, and battle tactics for modern terrorists in Northern Ireland: "For you see, in Ireland there is no future, only the past happening over and over."[16]

Many of these problems still remain to be solved. It is no doubt an exaggeration to blame Britain's past for its contemporary malaise. Britain's history, like that of most other countries, passes on to its present political leaders both challenges in the form of unsolved problems and resources in the form of past successes and emotion-laden historical symbols that can unite and mobilize the population. But how these historical assets and liabilities are used, and the balance sheet for history's contribution to the present, depend largely on the leadership's perceptions of the problems and resources of this legacy and on its skill in using the strengths from the past to solve contemporary crises. Current problems may have taken some of the luster from Britain's glorious past, but few in Britain advocate a break with this past through radical change or revolution.

NOTES

[1]Tom Nairn, *The Enchanted Glass: Britain and Its Monarchy* (London: Radius, 1988).

[2]Kenneth MacKenzie, *The English Parliament* (Harmondsworth, England: Penguin, 1965), p. 95.

[3]Keith Thomas, "The United Kingdom," in *Crises of Political Development in Europe and the United States,* ed. Raymond Grew (Princeton, NJ: Princeton University Press, 1978), pp. 56–59.

[4]Barrington Moore, Jr., *Social Origins of Dictatorship and Democracy: Lord and Peasant in the Making of the Modern World* (Boston: Beacon, 1966), p. 29.

[5]George Dangerfield, *The Strange Death of Liberal England, 1910–1914* (New York: Capricorn, 1961), p. 170.

[6]Lewis Namier, *England in the Age of the American Revolution,* 2nd ed. (London: Macmillan, 1961), p. 7.

[7]Antonia Fraser, *Faith and Treason: The Story of the Gunpowder Plot* (New York: Nan A. Talese/Doubleday, 1996).

[8]Walter Bagehot, *The English Constitution* (Ithaca, NY: Cornell University Press, 1963), p. 249.

[9]Samuel H. Beer, "The British Political System," in *Patterns of Government: The Major Political Systems of Europe,* 3rd ed., ed. Samuel H. Beer et al. (New York: Random House, 1973).

[10]Bagehot, *The English Constitution,* p. 247.

[11]Dennis Kavanagh, "Political Culture in Great Britain: The Decline of the Civic Culture," in *The Civic Culture Revisited,* ed. Gabriel A. Almond and Sidney Verba (Boston: Little, Brown, 1980), pp. 124–176.

[12]Samuel H. Beer, *Britain Against Itself: The Political Contradictions of Collectivism* (New York: Norton, 1982).

[13]William L. Miller, Annis May Timpson, and Michael Lessnoff, *Political Culture of Contemporary Britain: People and Politicians, Principles and Practice* (Oxford, England: Oxford University Press, 1998).

[14]Gertrude Himmelfarb, *Victorian Minds* (New York: Knopf, 1968), p. 292.

[15]Cyril E. Black, *The Dynamics of Modernization: A Study in Comparative History* (New York: Harper & Row, 1966).

[16]Leon Uris, *Trinity* (Garden City, NY: Doubleday, 1970), p. 751.

Chapter 2

The Social Setting of British Politics

Among the explanations offered for Britain's relatively peaceful evolution into a modern democracy is the homogeneity and unity of the British people. The absence of deep divisions in British society, according to some observers, is an important reason for the avoidance of civil war and mass political violence in Britain. Insularity and compact size supposedly fostered this social harmony. In fact, this viewpoint ignores important social cleavages or divisions that have always been a part of British society. Britain avoided social revolution *despite* important cleavages in society.

Social class divisions were only one of several sharp cleavages in British society; other important social cleavages with political consequences included religion, nationality, and region. In Britain these cleavages did not produce revolution, but they did find reflection in politics through the party system, electoral alignments, and conflict over specific policies.[1] For an understanding of contemporary British politics, it is essential to look at the continued political impact of two of these social cleavages: social class and nationality.

CLASS STRUCTURES

One of the most striking anomalies of British politics is the flourishing of one of the oldest and best developed class structures alongside a democratic government. Elsewhere in Western democracies, the titled aristocracy has virtually disappeared and the remaining nobility lacks any political role. In Britain, the medieval nobility still exists. While Britain's aristocracy is small numerically, it still retains its glamour, prestige, and, through the House of Lords, some remnants of its political power.

The class structure descends from this narrow, aristocratic social elite to the much larger middle and working classes. In the past, the hierarchy was rigid and exploitative as the upper classes profited from the labor of underpaid and harddriven working classes. In the last half of the nineteenth century, the class system seemed ripe for a revolt by the oppressed working class. Novelists such as Charles Dickens described the misery of the workers. Karl Marx sought a scientific explanation of the "passion of capital for an unlimited and reckless extension of the working day" that held children and adults in virtual bondage to their employers.[2] The exploitative relations between classes appeared to be like a zero-sum game where one class could better itself only through decreasing the benefits to other classes. With this perspective, it was logical for Marx and his disciples to call for the workers to rise up, throw off their chains, and destroy the oppressing classes.

Today, very few Britons share the notion of inevitable class conflict despite the continued presence of class differences. The sense of belonging to a social class or the sense of class identity is declining. In 1990, over half the Britons polled declared that they did not feel that they belonged to any social class.[3] Some studies report, however, that the level of working-class identification is still high in Britain, where more people identify themselves with the working class than elsewhere in Europe.[4] British miners, factory workers, and even government paper shufflers take pride in their working-class identification. But the tendency to view life or politics in terms of class conflict and to interpret that conflict in terms of "us versus them" is much less widespread than it was fifty years ago.

A variety of factors helped defuse class tensions in Britain. The aristocracy has long been an open one compared to the more closed upper classes found elsewhere in Europe. It absorbed capable, upwardly mobile people into its ranks. Its members often supported reforms, and some became outspoken advocates of radical social change. A recent example of upper-class supporters of radical reform include a hereditary lord who for many years gave the British Communist party its only seat in Parliament through his membership in the House of Lords. In the past and today, there is much greater upward class mobility than might be expected. In the last twenty years, the expansion of the middle class through the growth of services and the contraction of the industrial sector has facilitated the upward movement of the working class. This mobility promoted integration of the lower classes and social harmony and stability.

Parliament enacted moderate reforms that helped defuse class tensions by attacking the worst aspects of working-class oppression—child labor laws, maximum workdays legislation, minimum wage standards, and the like. Other government actions sought to reduce the insecurity inherent in the economic cycles of a free enterprise economy, such as social security, disability and unemployment insurance, and various health programs. In many cases, the British government was among the first to undertake such programs.

In the meantime, the workers' movement was integrated into the political system through its association with the Labour party. Through that party, the working class was assured representation in Parliament and sometimes in government. It could work to achieve its aspirations from within the system. With a political party serving as their political voice, the trade unions concerned themselves with seeking better salaries and working conditions in negotiations with management rather than with seeking radical change through political pressures on government.

Another reason for the failure of class conflict to take more explosive forms is the growing complexity of social class structures in modern industrial societies. The pyramid-shaped social structure with the narrow elite at the top dominating the much larger lower classes at the base of the social pyramid is too simplistic for modern society. The distinction between employee and employer/owner has broken down as even top-level administrators are employees of firms owned by faceless institutional stockholders; factory workers who are the prototypical working class often earn more money than "white-collar" middle-class employees such as salespersons, clerks, and teachers; the middle class is no longer the nineteenth-century bourgeoisie of independent shop and factory owners but employees of vast organizations in which they feel as helpless as do the typical, proletariat blue-collar workers. Given the erosion of class identity and fragmentation of old class structures, former notions of class solidarity and class conflict do not have much meaning in Britain at the beginning of the twenty-first century.[5]

Finally, and perhaps most important, social class tensions have cooled as economic prosperity has continued through most of the postwar period. The economic pie has expanded, and workers' benefits in salaries and access to consumer goods have grown with it. There are still large differences between the benefits enjoyed by the workers and those from more privileged classes, but the differences are now in degrees of benefits rather than in having or not having. Someone from the upper middle class may drive a Jaguar while the worker makes do with an old Ford. There is, of course, considerable difference between these cars, but both the working- and middle-class persons have vehicles. It is no longer a question of the working class having to do without while the privileged monopolize the available consumer benefits.

This leveling of society relaxes class tensions and provides incentives for workers to stay within the system rather than to seek radical change. The leveling process is furthered by mass communications—especially television. Nationwide television programs promote a national life-style and value system. This tends to destroy the distinctive life-styles of the various classes and thus reduces the sense of "apartness" that once reinforced class lines. Tax structures also encourage this leveling process through progressive income taxes, capital gains taxes, and inheritance taxes that take from the rich to finance social welfare benefits distributed to all those in need. Studies of income distribution in Western democratic countries indicate that Britain is among the most equal societies in terms of current earnings after taxes.[6] The movement toward moderating the gap between the earnings of the very rich and the poor helped to ease potential social tensions.

While objective class distinctions are becoming less clear, the structuring of society along social class lines remains well defined. This is due in part to the continued presence and indeed often the veneration of a medieval hereditary aristocracy. As a result, Britain remains wedded to social class in a more highly structured and visible way than most democracies. It is nonetheless surprising that the percentage of Britons who believe that class conflict is real in their country rose from 60 percent in the early 1960s to 81 percent in the mid-1990s.[7] Perhaps this is a lingering legacy of the class confrontations of the 1980s during the Thatcher years.

Perhaps a more important source of the perpetuation of class lines is an education system that for many decades supported an elitist and deferential society. Not until 1879 was public primary education assured to all, and it was 1944 before universal secondary education was provided. There are two sets of schools offering primary and secondary education: state-funded schools and the exclusive private "public" schools.

This educational system perpetuates social class divisions. The British state education system is still one of the least equitable in Western Europe. More students leave school early: nearly 70 percent have left by the time they are 17 years old (compared to 44 percent in France and 15 percent in Germany); the amount of annual spending per student in Britain is only one-third the figure in France and one-fourth the German figure.[8]

Higher education is still dominated by Oxford and Cambridge. In the past, graduates of these

---

BRITISH "PUBLIC SCHOOLS"

The so-called public schools are in fact private, elite schools—often boarding schools. They have provided Britain with its political, social, and economic elite since the fifteenth century; the two oldest and most prestigious are Eton (founded in 1440) and Winchester (founded in 1382). Eton alone has provided eighteen prime ministers. Despite the elitist nature of the public schools, few efforts have been made to reform them. Those who defend the public schools point to the self-discipline and commitment to public service they supposedly instill in their pupils. The social and political influence of the public schools has diminished in recent years as the state-sponsored school system has produced well-educated young people who have moved into prominent positions. But most government and business leaders still come from the public schools. Labour's victory in 1997, despite its populist and modernist pretenses, resulted in a cabinet where most of the ministers came from public schools.

two universities accounted for the most prominent politicians and nearly all the senior civil servants. Their dominance seems likely to wane in the future as able and civic-minded young people graduate from the newer universities (referred to as the "Redbrick" universities, in contrast to "Oxbridge"). In addition, the London School of Economics (founded in the nineteenth century) has particular political significance, since many of the Labour party's leaders were educated there. The number of new universities has quadrupled since 1939; the number of students has grown even more rapidly. But the proportion of young people attending universities is lower in Britain than in most other industrial nations.

The Political Manifestations of Social Class

The political consequences of social class are modest in contemporary Britain. Some British citizens see themselves as belonging to a given social class, but there is little evidence of significant class conflict. Thus, Marxist predictions that society would polarize along class lines and that class conflict would intensify have not been fulfilled in Britain. What class-based politics exists takes the thoroughly un-Marxian forms of labor union activities and voter alignments with political parties.

Nevertheless, social class does shape some political attitudes and behavior, and more so in Britain than in other modern industrial democracies.[9] The voters' class identification is one of the major determinants of their decision on which party to support. Most who identify with the working class vote for the Labour party, and most who regard themselves as middle or upper class vote Conservative (see Table 2–1). The alignment along class lines is by no means perfect. Expected class loyalties may be overridden by current events or the personalities of party leaders. Thus, Margaret Thatcher's Conservatives in the 1980s were able to draw strong support from the working classes usually loyal to Labour, and Tony Blair's New Labour drew important support from middle-class voters in the 1997 election.

There are signs that the class basis for party support may be declining as the awareness of

Table 2–1 Class Differences in Voting Behavior: Britain 1997

	Conservative	Labour	Liberal Democrat
Middle Class	42%	31%	21%
Lower Middle Class	26	47	19
Skilled Workers	25	54	14
Semiskilled and Unskilled Workers	21	61	13

Source: David Butler and Dennis Kavanagh, *The British Election of 1997* (New York: St. Martin's, 1997), p. 246.

class declines and as new cleavages—such as national identity—override class considerations.[10] Once the impact of class on the voting decision was much stronger in Britain than it was in the United States, France, Germany, and other Western democracies;[11] it is no longer clear that that is still true.

The other political manifestation of class is the trade union movement. Trade unions represent the working class in negotiations with government leaders, bureaucrats, and other interest group representatives over proposed policies. This is class conflict in the sense of competition for influence in policy making, but it is obviously of very low intensity. Strikes represent a somewhat higher level of union-led class conflict. Union leaders use strikes as a means of achieving economic advances in the form of higher salaries or longer vacations, rather than for political purposes. The avoidance of political strikes and the unions' resolve to keep strikes nonviolent have kept even this variety of class conflict at low levels of intensity in Britain. However, strikes can manifest growing worker unrest and can be a means of intensifying class conflict.

During the 1970s, labor unrest increased as the economy continued to grow at a relatively slow pace and as rapid inflation cut into the pocketbooks of salaried workers. Unauthorized "wildcat" strikes gave evidence of growing worker discontent and dissatisfaction with the results of the trade union leadership. Most of this labor unrest was channeled into economic rather than political action. The strikers wanted higher wages and better benefits, not changes in government policy.

Worker unrest continued into the early 1980s, but the Conservative government of Margaret Thatcher took advantage of public disgust with the radicalism of the unions to pass several laws designed to reduce trade union power. The economic crisis, high unemployment rates, and membership decline in trade unions weakened the labor movement. There were fewer strikes, but some of those that did occur were exceptionally bitter and even violent. The most serious labor disturbance was the long coal miners' strike in 1984–85, which ended in defeat for the miners.

Arthur Scargill, head of the National Union of Mineworkers, used a class warfare rhetoric during the coal miners' strike in 1984. But such class conflict imagery is rarely used in Britain today (and in the coal miners' case resulted in a split of the union). With rare exceptions, British unions avoid the terminology of class conflict and instead battle for material advantages for their workers. This contrasts sharply with the ideological and class-warfare approach of French union leaders; antiregime appeals are unattractive to the British working class. What British workers protested was the failure of wages to keep up with inflation and the government's seemingly heavier hand in controlling wages than in limiting price increases. Political and trade union leaders were successful in keeping worker discontent focused on moderate economic objectives rather than permitting a frontal confrontation of classes with important political ramifications.

Many trade union leaders and members expected the Labour government of Tony Blair to repeal some of the anti-trade-union legislation passed under Thatcher. Such changes are coming slowly if at all. On other fronts, the Blair government has responded to union calls for acceptance of the European Union's Social Charter (a far-reaching set of commitments to enhance the role of workers and their unions) and to adopt a minimum wage. The unions remain a vehicle of class representation, but in Britain they are by no means a force in the class war envisioned by classical Marxist thinkers.

ETHNIC DIVERSITY AND CONFLICT

The proper name for modern-day Britain is the United Kingdom of Great Britain and Northern Ireland. It is the union of three nations inhabiting the island of Great Britain and the peoples of the northeastern six counties of the island of Ireland.[12] This amalgam of nations is symbolized by the national flag, the Union Jack, which is the overlapping of the crosses of St. George, St. Andrew, and St. Patrick, the patron saints of England and Wales, Scotland, and Ireland. These peoples once had separate political units. Their unification under the English crown was achieved through conquest, although this occurred long ago: Wales in 1536, Ireland in 1542, and Scotland in 1707.

The overwhelming numerical superiority of the English often leads observers to overlook the ethnic diversity of the United Kingdom (see Table 2–2). Since the English make up over 80 percent of the total population, there is a tendency to equate Britain with England. But the various nationalities in Britain still identify themselves first

Table 2–2   Population by Region in the United Kingdom

	1990 Population	Percent of Total Population	Percent of Total Land Area
England	47,838,000	83.3%	53.8%
Wales	2,881,000	5.0	8.6
Scotland	5,102,000	8.9	32.0
Northern Ireland	1,589,000	2.3	5.6
	57,410,000	99.5%	100%

Source: Whitaker's Almanack 1993 (London: Whitaker, 1992), p. 119.

as English, Scottish, Welsh, or Irish rather than as British.[13] While most have political loyalty to Britain, they still feel themselves distinct from other nationality groups in the United Kingdom. A Scot or a Welsh person would be offended if a foreigner labeled him or her as English.

Britain was viewed as a highly homogeneous nation until the late 1960s when the Irish in Northern Ireland, the Scots in Scotland, and the Welsh in Wales asserted demands for greater autonomy and respect for their cultural traditions. In Northern Ireland, the Irish manifested their ethnic cleavages in violence; the Scottish and Welsh manifested theirs in the electoral growth of nationalist parties. Scottish Nationalists advocating autonomy for Scotland won nearly 30 percent of the Scottish vote, and Welsh separatists won nearly 11 percent of the Welsh vote in the October 1974 House of Commons election.

In Scotland and Wales, nationalist parties pushed for greater local self-government and some even advocated complete separation from Britain. As a partial gesture to meet some of these demands, the Labour Government of James Callaghan pushed legislation through Parliament granting limited "devolution" of some authority over Scottish and Welsh affairs to local assemblies. But these laws had to be "ratified" by separate referenda in Scotland and Wales, with the stipulation that the yes-vote must be at least 40 percent of the registered voters for final approval to be accorded later by Parliament. When the chance came in 1979 to vote for modest steps toward regional autonomy, voters showed great caution. A bare majority of votes were cast in favor of a Scottish parliament, but this was only 32.9 percent of the registered voters, well below the 40 percent goal. In Wales, an overwhelming four to one negative vote rejected the even more modest proposals for regional autonomy.

After these defeats, Scottish and Welsh nationalists regrouped slowly. By the mid-1990s, nationalist feelings again were running strong. Despite government subsidies, Scotland and Wales lagged behind the economic recovery experienced by the rest of Britain. The Scots and Welsh believed that greater autonomy would allow them to address these economic problems. In the past, there were fears that independence in Scotland or Wales would leave their small

economies at risk. By the 1990s, the European Union offered an answer to those fears: even small states could be members and enjoy the benefits of access to a vast European market. In Scotland, the Oscar-winning film *Braveheart,* based on a thirteenth-century conflict between the Scots and English, renewed pride and hope for yet another triumph over England.

During the long build-up to the 1997 general elections, the Labour party pledged to offer Scotland and Wales a new chance to create legislative assemblies. Labour won those elections and the Conservative party, which opposed any devolution to Scotland and Wales, failed to elect a single MP in either Scotland or Wales. Within a few months of the Labour victory, referendums were held in both areas to approve creation of new assemblies with limited but important powers of self-rule. In Scotland, voters approved by a three to one majority the creation of a Scottish assembly and granted it powers of taxation.[14] In Wales, the measure won narrow support with those favoring a Welsh assembly, taking a mere 50.3 percent of the vote but a sufficient margin for the approval of the measure.

The new assemblies in Scotland and Wales were elected in 1999 and began operation in 2000. (See Table 2–3.) Their authority includes housing, education, health, cultural affairs, and local government. (See Table 2–4.) More important than their actual powers, however, the Scottish and Welsh assemblies have symbolic victories in parts of the United Kingdom conquered by the English centuries ago.

There remain many important questions to resolve about the relations between these as-

Table 2–3 Elections to the Scottish Parliament and Welsh Assembly, May 1999

	Seats in Scotland	Seats in Wales
Conservative party	18	9
Labour party	56	28
Liberal Democrats	17	6
Scottish Nationalists	35	-0-
Welsh Nationalists	-0-	17
Others	3	-0-
Total	129	60

Table 2–4 Powers of British Legislative Bodies

Scottish Parliament	Welsh Parliament	British Parliament
Criminal and civil law	Health	All powers enjoyed by regional bodies
Police	Education	*plus* the following powers for all of
Health	Training policy	the United Kingdom:
Education	Housing	Foreign policy
Training policy	Planning	Defense and national security
Housing	Economic development	Fiscal, economic, and monetary
Planning	Financial assistance to industry	system
Economic development	Tourism	Border control, immigration
Financial assistance to industry	Local transportation	Drug policies
Tourism	Environment	European Union policy
Local transportation	National heritage	Energy policy (coal, gas, etc.)
Environment	Agriculture, forestry, fisheries	Transportation policy
National heritage	Arts	Social security
Agriculture, forestry, fisheries		Employment legislation
Arts		Abortion
		Broadcasting
		Equal opportunity policies

semblies and the national government in London. Some argue that the Scotch and Welsh MPs should no longer be able to vote on domestic matters affecting only England. Others would create similar assemblies in the various regions of England. In any case, these new assemblies are major constitutional changes that will have wide ranging effects over the next decade. If the Scottish Nationalist party has its way, the creation of the new assembly will be only the first step on the road to an entirely independent Scotland.

The Troubles in Northern Ireland

The most critical threat to British national unity is the conflict between Catholics and Protestants in Northern Ireland. Northern Ireland is made up of the six northern counties (most of the province of Ulster) of Ireland. When the almost uniformly Catholic south obtained independence in 1921, predominantly Protestant Ulster, most of whose inhabitants were fiercely loyal to Britain, insisted on the partition of Ireland and the continued union of Northern Ireland to the United Kingdom. Over the objections of the Irish, the island was finally partitioned, Ulster remaining a part of Britain and the rest of Ireland gaining independence.

Today Northern Ireland continues to be a major problem for the British political system. The conflict there is essentially a cultural division between the Protestant majority and the Catholic minority. About 60 percent of the population in Northern Ireland is Protestant with 40 percent Catholic; of course the Irish Catholics contend that their minority status is due only to their "unnatural" separation from the rest of the island of Ireland. The Protestants are descendants of Scottish and English immigrants who colonized Northern Ireland in the seventeenth and eighteenth centuries when others from Britain were colonizing America; the Catholics are Irish whose ancestors were dispossessed by the colonists.

There is also a social and economic element in the conflict. Relative to the rest of Britain, Northern Ireland is industrially underdeveloped, and there is considerable economic discontent among both Protestants and Catholics. The Catholics allege economic discrimination in the form of lower salaries and lower-quality public services, such as council (public) housing. However, it is the religious aspect of the conflict that most deeply affects politics. When class loyalty and ethnic loyalty conflict, the ethnic bond usually takes precedence: The Protestant worker joins middle-class Protestants to fight "popery"—

rather than joining the Catholic worker in a struggle against middle-class exploitation of the proletariat. Indeed, the militancy and extremism of the proletariat on both sides has caused the situation to be described as "the war of the proles": Catholic workers fight Protestant workers.

Unlike Scotland and Wales, Northern Ireland has had its own parliament and regional government, and considerable local autonomy. The Protestant two-thirds of the population was able to control the Northern Irish government and used its ascendancy to assure continued political, economic, and social dominance over the Catholic minority. In the 1960s, a moderate Catholic civil rights movement, inspired by the civil rights movement in the United States, pressed for an end to discrimination. However, reforms were slow in coming, and those that were instituted at the end of the 1960s were branded as insufficient by key sectors of the Catholic community and as excessive by some Protestants. In 1968 Catholic civil rights demonstrations and counter-demonstrations by Protestants led to rioting.

Once open conflict began, both sides revived the tactics and organizations of earlier confrontations. The memory of martyrs from earlier battles, celebrated in folklore and annual parades, provided models for today's militants. The Irish Republican Army (IRA), a militant Catholic nationalist group that had led the battle for Irish independence in the first few decades of the twentieth century, was revitalized. Growing rapidly in numbers and in activity, the IRA sought an end to British rule in Northern Ireland and the reunification of all Ireland. When the IRA began to perpetrate bombings and assassinations, the Northern Irish police proved unable to keep order. Furthermore, the police force was part of the problem, since it was virtually all Protestant and consequently distrusted by most sections of the Catholic community. Over 15,000 British troops were sent to Ulster, but they too failed to restore order. Most Catholics viewed the troops as agents of British domination and protectors of the Protestants.

In 1972 the British government moved to end the violence by dissolving the overtly anti-Catholic Ulster government and appointing a British governor to rule over Northern Ireland. At first the British governor made headway by adopting a more conciliatory attitude toward the Catholics and freeing many Catholics being held in "preventive detention" without trial as suspected terrorists. The Protestants, fearing a British sellout of their interests, reacted by mobilizing their own irregular army, the Ulster Defense Association (UDA). The UDA began taking reprisals against Catholics for IRA terrorism, but ultimately clashed with British troops. In addition, rival groups within the Protestant and Catholic communities fought among themselves. By the middle of 1998, the conflict had claimed the lives of some 3,250 people.

The British government has attempted to find a basis for a compromised settlement to the crisis in Northern Ireland. To prevent the reemergence of Protestant political dominance that might be used against the Catholic minority, the British have insisted political power be shared among both communities. But Catholic extremists reject this as insufficient, and Protestant extremists regard any such power sharing as a violation of the will of the majority. A number of efforts were made to organize new Northern Irish assemblies and governing bodies to promote Catholic and Protestant cooperation during the 1970s and early 1980s, but these efforts were thwarted by extremists from both camps.

During the 1980s, new efforts to resolve the conflict in Northern Ireland were made. This time the British government joined with the government of the Republic of Ireland to propose a settlement. Extremists on both sides rejected these efforts. For the Protestant extremists, the role of the Irish government was unacceptable; for Irish Nationalists, the Irish government's accceptance that no change was possible without an agreement by the majority of the people in Northern Ireland was anathema. By the early 1990s, little progress had been made toward building on the Irish-British accord.

In the mid-1990s, a cease fire among the antagonists brought hopes for some progress. But the IRA broke the cease fire in 1996 with bomb attacks on the British mainland and British European military bases. The United States offered its services as a mediator through former Senator George Mitchell. Eventually, the IRA renewed its cease fire and its political party, Sein Fein, was allowed to participate in the negotiations. Slow progress began, and in April 1998, the various parties reached an accord. The agreement calls for the creation of a Northern Irish assembly. The Northern Irish Assembly will have powers like those of the Scottish and Welsh assemblies and will gradually take over policy making currently coming out of London. The accord also includes acceptance of the principle that the status of Northern Ireland will not change without the consent of a majority of its residents. This involves revisions of the Irish constitution to eliminate absolute claims for Northern Ireland. Other points in the agreement call for reform of the Northern Irish police force, agreements for early release of prisoners held on charges related to the conflict, and the disarming of extremists on both sides of the dispute. Despite the opposition of both Catholic and Protestant extremists, the agreement was overwhelmingly approved by simultaneous referendums in May 1998 in both the Republic of Ireland (94 percent "yes" votes) and Northern Ireland (71 percent "yes"). In June 1998, an Assembly was elected with a comfortable majority of moderates and parties committed to the settlement agreement.

As positive as these steps are, there remain concerns about the peace process. These were driven home within weeks of the 1998 ballots when the annual "marching season" began. The marching season is a summertime series of parades by Protestant militants to celebrate military victories over their Catholic neighbors centuries ago. Traditionally, the parade route goes through Catholic neighborhoods accompanied by the beating of drums. They have often been the cause of violence between marchers and Catholics in the neighborhood. The Protestants did not alter the tradition in 1998 and faced police and military barricades to prevent them from following the usual routes. The result was extraordinary tensions, violent confrontations, and bombings. These events demonstrate the difficulties that lie ahead for those who work for peace in Northern Ireland. There are still extremists on both sides who prefer violence to accommodation.

The hopeful sign is the rallying of the overwhelming majority of people in Northern Ireland to a peaceful resolution of their conflict. The current agreement offers the best chance for peace in over 30 years. But the legacy of a conflict rooted deep in 350 years of mistrust and enmity will be difficult to overcome.

The New Ethnicity: Racial Tensions in Britain

In Scotland and Wales, tensions between ethnic communities rarely involved violence or acts of hatred. Britain's greatest danger of ethnic violence comes not from these old ethnic tensions but from a new ethnicity produced by the immigration into Britain of large numbers of racially different peoples. This change in nonwhite population is recent and dramatic. In 1951, the nonwhite population of the United Kingdom was 74,000 people or 0.2 percent of the total population; in 1991 nonwhites totaled 3.0 million or 5.5 percent of the inhabitants. Now most of these immigrants are British citizens; many of them are second- and even third-generation residents of Britain.

The immigrants have come from former British colonial areas, especially from India, Pakistan, and the West Indies. Attracted by the hope of a good job, these peoples added a new element of racial diversity. These newcomers have not integrated easily with the native Britons.[15] They have brought with them well-developed cultures that they have sought to maintain in their new home. Their presence is made more obvious by their heavy concentration in London and a few other large industrial cities.

Buffered by its insularity, Britain earlier had only to contend with the diversity of its own indigenous peoples. The rapid influx of nonwhite immigrants gave the government the new challenge of promoting racial understanding and tolerance among people who in the past did not have much contact with people of different colors. This has not been an easy task. Resentment against immigrants is especially strong among native manual workers who find themselves competing with the immigrants for jobs, housing, and social welfare benefits. Accustomed to viewing Britons as superior to other races of people—white as well as nonwhite—many people in Britain resent the new immigrants.

One consequence of the rapid growth of the nonwhite population was Parliament's adoption of a series of laws designed to slow immigration, especially of nonwhites. While white persons with family ties in Britain can enter freely, there is a quota restricting the entrance of dependents of nonwhites already settled in Britain. In a more positive action, successive governments have worked to promote racial tolerance through a series of laws barring racial discrimination and establishing a Committee on Racial Equality and a Race Relations Board. But British legislation on race relations has not gone as far as in the United States, where civil rights laws require equal treatment regardless of race. As in the United States, however, British efforts are hindered by the difficulty of changing prejudice through legislation. Government posters urging racial harmony are commonplace but so, unfortunately, are antiblack graffiti scrawled on walls.

The rapid growth of the nonwhite population, its concentration in industrial centers, and the immigrants' resistance to assimilation created animosity among the indigenous people with whom they competed for jobs and social services. When the economy worsened in the late 1970s and many native Britons found themselves out of work, there was a tendency to blame the immigrants for unemployment. Racial hatreds mounted despite government efforts to promote tolerance. The immigrants suffered too from the economy's problems. They lived in deteriorating council (public) housing, their children went to overcrowded schools, and they faced overburdened social service providers. With unemployment very much higher among the immigrants than in the general population, social unrest rose in nonwhite neighborhoods. By the 1980s, the tensions exploded into riots in Brixton, Tottenham, and Birmingham. These were not racial riots, since participants and victims were nearly all black. But they did reflect the economic unrest and frustration with discrimination felt by nonwhites in Britain.

The political consequences of racism have been limited. So far, the nonwhite vote has not been an election factor except in a very few districts. The Labour party has presented a number of nonwhite candidates, and nine now serve in the House of Commons. But race has not emerged as an important element in voting decisions, nor has there been much of a backlash among native white voters. Unlike in France, where an anti-immigrant National Front posed a serious challenge, the British National Front proved to be an electoral failure. The major parties have avoided demaguery on the immigration issue.

After centuries of isolation from regular contact with other racial groups, the British now face the challenge of learning to live harmoniously with an increasing number of nonwhite immigrants. For the government, the task of balancing conflicting claims from natives, immigrants, and people abroad wanting to immigrate will continue to be difficult. At the same time, the government must avoid pushing native whites toward extremist backlash groups, promote the integration and acceptance of immigrants already in Britain, and accommodate requests for immigration from dependents of those already there.

CONCLUSION

Most Western democracies are pluralist societies in the sense that their governments permit diverse social forces representing various sectors of society to develop and act autonomously. There are therefore present in these countries independent labor unions, business groups, civic action movements, political groupings, churches, and racial associations that seek to promote the interests of the various categories of society. Since the free interaction of these social forces is tolerated, and sometimes fostered by government, social conflict is a normal aspect of this social pluralism. The free competition of social forces is simply a reflection of the variety of conflicts and cleavages within the society. The open expression of tensions produced by these social divisions in Britain permits the government to perceive potential problems, to respond to the needs of special sections of society, and to prevent the deepening of social cleavages. The consensus on the political and socioeconomic structures produced by centuries of conflict and compromise helps keep conflict at manageable levels. It is only when this consensus breaks down, as it has in Northern Ireland, that democratic stability is endangered.

In general, the social cleavages in Britain are moderate and manageable. The slow growth of the economy has kept economic shortage from aggravating social cleavages. The political effects of the class structures are reduced by the integration of the working class into the political and social systems. National sentiments are present among the Scots and Welsh, but both these peoples seem to attach greater importance to the benefits they derive from the union with England than they do to possible benefits from greater self-rule. Only in Northern Ireland, where two polarized groups confront each other, is the social fiber severely shredded. There three centuries of violence and hatred fuel modern terrorism and prejudice and pose serious problems for contemporary political leaders.

NOTES

[1] Seymour M. Lipset and Stein Rokkan, "Cleavage Structures, Party Systems, and Voter Alignments: An Introduction," in *Party Systems and Voter Alignments: Cross-National Perspectives,* ed. Seymour M. Lipset and Stein Rokkan (New York: The Free Press, 1967), pp. 1–64.

[2] Karl Marx, *Capital: A Critique of Political Economy* (New York: Random House, 1906), p. 326.

[3] *British Politics Newsletter* 22 (Fall 1990): 10.

[4] Samuel H. Barnes, Max Kaase, et al., *Political Action: Mass Participation in Five Western Democracies* (Beverly Hills, CA: Sage, 1979), p. 127.

[5] Jan-Erik Lane and Svante O. Ersson, *Politics and Society in Western Europe,* 2nd ed. (London: Sage, 1991), pp. 89–96.

[6] Ibid., pp. 92–93.

[7] *The Economist,* 27 September 1997.

[8] *The Economist,* 16 February 1991.

[9] Bernadette C. Hayes, "The Impact of Class on Political Attitudes: A Comparative Study of Great Britain, West Germany, Australia, and the United States," *European Journal of Political Research* 27 (January 1995): 69–91.

[10] See Samuel H. Beer, *Britain Against Itself: The Political Contradictions of Collectivism* (New York: Norton, 1982), pp. 79–103. See also Richard Rose and Ian McAllister, *Voters Begin to Choose: From Closed-Class to Open Elections in Britain* (London: Sage, 1986).

[11] Robert A. Alford, *Party and Society* (Chicago: Chicago University Press, 1963), and Paul R. Abramson, "Social Class and Political Change in Western Europe: A Cross-National Longitudinal Analysis," *Comparative Political Studies* 4 (July 1971): 131–155.

[12] On the multinational character of modern United Kingdom, see Richard Rose, *The Territorial Dimension in Government Under the United Kingdom* (Chatham, NJ: Chatham House, 1982).

[13] See Richard Rose, *Governing Without Consensus: An Irish Perspective* (Boston Press, 1971), pp. 42–73.

[14] James Mitchell, David Denver, and Hugh Bochel, "The Devolution Referendum in Scotland," *Parliamentary Affairs* 51 (April, 1998).

[15] Zig Layton-Henry, *The Politics of Immigration: "Race" and "Race" Relations in Postwar Britain* (London: Blackwell, 1993).

Chapter 3

The British Political Framework

We have made, or rather have stumbled on a constitution which . . . has two capital merits: it contains a simple efficient part which, on occasion, and when wanted, can work more simply and easily, and better, than any instrument of government that has yet been tried; and it contains likewise historical, complex, august, theatrical parts, which it has inherited from a long past.[1]

As long as humans have recorded history, we have sought to define "good" government and to identify the conditions that would permit its existence. Plato outlined the ideal state in his *Republic;* Aristotle sent his students out to make comparative studies of existing governments in a search for the best form; Montesquieu proposed the creation of ideal government through a system of checks and balances; Locke urged government based on a social contract with citizens in order to pursue collective political goals. For most of these political thinkers, the way to create ideal government was to establish a good set of political institutions and provide them with the proper powers and restraints. In short, to have a good democracy, what was needed was a constitution establishing a set of appropriate institutions—a parliament or legislature, an executive, and a system of courts—and defining the relationship among them.

John Stuart Mill, however, had noted that behind liberal government there must be a liberal society, and the rise of fascism in the 1920s and 1930s proved his point. In Italy, Germany, and other European democracies, well-drafted democratic constitutions were no protection against despots and extremists. Democratic institutions could not assure genuine democracy in countries lacking appropriate social and economic features and supportive political attitudes. After World War II, the new regimes of Eastern Europe established a facade of democratic institutions behind which Communist party dictatorships operated freely. Thus, particular institutions in a given country do not determine a state's nature, nor does a well-designed constitution have much meaning when it is not in harmony with the social and political environment.

As a result, political scientists have reexamined the importance of political institutions in shaping the political process. While there are still examples of important overall political changes resulting from the particular set of constitutional provisions, in many other cases it is not the constitution that shapes the government, but the cumulative practices of government that forge the institutions and the real constitution. Britain is an excellent example of a political system in which the political setting and practices produce the constitution and political institutions. The changing society and ideas have molded an absolute monarchy into a modern constitutional democracy.

As we shall see, the British conserve old institutions, giving them new tasks or simply permitting them to exist without new functions for the dignity and legitimacy they give to the governmental process. In other countries, constitutional reforms have imposed new institutions and relationships in conscious efforts to shape political practices through "constitutional engineering." Sometimes this is successful, as in the political changes brought about by the constitution of the Fifth Republic of France. But in Britain, the general trend has been the opposite, with political practice adapting existing institutions and relationships without abandoning them.

THE CONSTITUTION

Unlike most other Western democracies, Britain lacks a written constitution that systematically outlines government procedures and institutions. The British constitution is made up of a series of customs, traditions, historical documents, and acts of Parliament that have never been codified or assembled in a single document. That the constitution has never been written out or formally adopted in no way detracts from the respect of the British people for their constitution. Nor does its unwritten status reduce its effectiveness in organizing government action and in setting limits on the exercise of power.

The unwritten nature of the British constitution provides the advantage of avoiding a break with the past before a set of constitutional principles was adopted. The cumulative nature of the British constitution preserves historical unity and continuity. Written constitutions usually include rather difficult procedures for amending them in

---

PARLIAMENTARY SYSTEM OF GOVERNING

Britain and most other European democracies use a *parliamentary system.* This system deemphasizes the separation of powers that is so important in the American presidential system. In the parliamentary system, the legislative branch (or parliament) is viewed as the supreme voice of the people. The executive powers are divided between a head of state and a head of government. The head of state may be a constitutional monarch, as in Britain, or a president elected by the parliament and electors chosen by the state governments, as in Germany. He or she is the symbol of the state, carrying out largely ceremonial tasks, such as signing into law (without right of veto) measures adopted by parliament, convening and disbanding parliament, and receiving foreign dignitaries.

In all of these activities, the head of state usually acts under the direction of the *government.* The government is composed of a head of government (prime minister, premier, or chancellor) and a cabinet of ministers. It is this body that collectively exercises the principal executive responsibilities. The members of the government are named by the parliament, usually from among its members, and they serve only so long as they retain the confidence of the parliament. The executive is thus dependent upon the continued support of parliament. If the parliament votes to condemn the government (a motion of censure), or if it refuses to pass a measure deemed important by the government (a motion of confidence), the government must resign. It may even be necessary for a government to resign without a formal vote against it if it senses that it lacks a stable majority in parliament. When the government resigns or is ousted, there may be efforts to form a new coalition in parliament to support a new government. Another way out of such a governmental crisis is for the head of state (usually acting upon the advice of the outgoing head of government) to dissolve parliament and call for new elections. After the election, a government is selected by the new parliament.

CONSTITUTIONAL CHANGE IN BRITAIN

The British Constitution is changed most commonly by the passage of an act of Parliament. Such a change does not require a special majority or ratification by any other body. But the Constitution can also be changed simply by the recognition of a new political situation. A recent example came in the 1970s. Until then, it was generally "understood" that a government that lost a major vote in the House of Commons should resign or call new elections. Then in the 1970s, there were several gov-

ernments with narrow majorities who lost several key votes. The government did not resign; it did not call for elections. Nor was there clamor from the opposition parties or the press for such actions. As a result, the old constitutional principle was replaced by a new constitutional reality that allowed a government to ignore defeats of major bills if subsequent votes in parliament revealed that it still had the support of a parliamentary majority.

---

order to limit frivolous change. But these complicated procedures can hamper rapid adaptation to changing needs.

The British constitution is remarkably easy to change when necessary. For example, during World War II the normal 5-year limit on the life of a parliament was extended by a simple act of Parliament in order to avoid the inconvenience of a national election during the war. Once the war was over, and the exceptional circumstances gone, the rule of general elections at least once every 5 years was reactivated. The constitution can also be changed by new practices and informal understandings. In the past several decades, it has become accepted as constitutional principle that the prime minister must be chosen from among those sitting in the popularly elected House of Commons rather than from the aristocratic House of Lords. No law was passed to this extent; it simply became clear to all that a democracy required a prime minister who had contested and won election to public office.

This flexibility can sometimes produce confusion. In addition, the absence of a court with the power to determine the constitutionality of acts of Parliament and actions of the executive adds to the potential for confusion. Occasionally, the constitution is changed simply by the unchallenged violation of what was once believed to be constitutional principle.[2]

In actual practice, there is little division in Britain over the content of its unwritten constitution. A general consensus exists at the level of the political leadership and the informed public

about what is and what is not permitted by the constitution. Those in power are in fact restrained from violating constitutional principles by the threat of public outcry and the fear of sanction by the voters in the next election. The gradual evolution of the British constitution, generally through compromise and accommodations, has developed its broad acceptance.

In the last few years, there has been a lively debate in Britain about the actual codification of the constitution. Some contend that a written constitution is needed to assure protection of civil rights, to clarify the powers (or lack of powers) of such traditional institutions as the monarchy and the House of Lords, and to define Britain's relationship to the European Union. Not only is there no consensus on what a new constitution should include, but there is also no agreement that there is a need for one.[3]

A CONSTITUTIONAL MONARCHY

Over the centuries, conventions, traditions, and political struggles have transformed the British political structures from an absolute monarchy to a *constitutional monarchy* with a parliamentary structure. This same evolutionary process democratized the constitutional monarchy through the competitive election of members of the Commons by universal suffrage.

A century ago, Walter Bagehot, in a classic treatment of the English constitution, distinguished between two aspects of the British

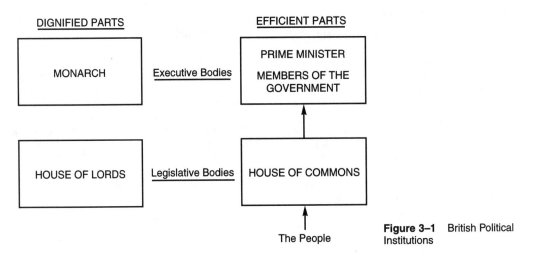

Figure 3–1 British Political Institutions

government: the dignified parts (those institutions and practices that excite and preserve the reverence of the population) and the efficient parts (those institutions and practices actually responsible for the conduct of government); see Figure 3–1. Chief among the dignified elements is the monarch. More than any other modern state, Britain has preserved the traditions and institutions of its monarchical past, while placing them in a democratic context. There are other constitutional or democratic monarchies, but Britain alone has maintained not only its monarchy, but also a full-blown titled aristocracy, elaborate ceremonies, and mass adulation. As the soon-to-be-deposed King Farouk of Egypt said in 1951, "There will soon be only five kings left—the Kings of England, Diamonds, Hearts, Spades, and Clubs."[4]

In the 1990s, there were new concerns about the survival of this ancient monarchy. The royal family's marital scandals and the very high public costs of maintaining a grand monarchy have reduced public support to its lowest levels since opinion polls began. Instead of being a source of national pride, the royal family has become the daily object of amusement or titillation in the tabloid press. As recently as the mid-1980s, 77 percent of Britons felt that the country would be "worse off" without the monarchy; in 1996, only a third expressed that opinion.[5] In the past, only a handful of extreme leftists called for the end of the monarchy; now there are more voices from all over the political spectrum calling for its end. Yet even with royal scandals, a critic of the monarchy had to

admit that a strong majority (66 percent) of Britons in the mid-1990s still affirmed their preference for the indefinite continuation of the monarchy.[6]

In theory and in law, all acts of government are performed in the name and by the authority of "Her Most Excellent Majesty Elizabeth the Second": She promulgates laws, negotiates treaties, selects a prime minister and a cabinet, names other political and religious leaders, and grants pardons. In actual practice, the Queen exercises virtually no political power whatsoever. All the acts performed in her name are actually undertaken by the prime minister and the cabinet. In fact, the political prerogatives of the Queen are less extensive than those of the ordinary citizen. She does not have the right to take a partisan position, she cannot express her own political views. Even the conduct of her personal life is subject to approval by the government that is in theory subordinate to her.

The monarch's political role is thus strictly limited. Any temptation to exceed these limits is effectively countered by the knowledge that the monarch's interference in politics would certainly lead to a public reaction that would endanger the very existence of the monarchy. A monarchy can be democratic only so long as the unelected monarch completely abstains from interfering with the actions of elected leaders.

The monarch does have the right to be informed on all actions of government and the right to advise the prime minister in private. Some recent monarchs have exercised these rights, but there is no evidence that Queen Elizabeth has done so during her 45 years as monarch. By abstaining from political involvement, Queen Elizabeth has kept the monarchy above political controversy. Practical-minded Americans wonder why the British put up with the bother and expense of a Queen who seems to do nothing. But the monarch does serve a useful role in relieving the prime minister from many of the ceremonial duties required of a chief of state: receiving ambassadors, making public appearances, paying state visits to foreign countries, and inaugurating artistic, industrial, or scientific works of national significance. Most important, the monarch personalizes the state, embodies national unity, and links the present with a glorious past. In so doing, the monarch is an important political symbol producing strong emotional or affective ties in the general public.[7] These affective sentiments contribute to a sense of patriotism and to a willingness to accept political rule by less glamorous prime ministers and members of Parliament. As one analyst wrote, the Queen was "a historical figure whose presence not only gave pleasure to her people but identity and confidence too."[8]

PARLIAMENT

The British Parliament traces its origins back more than seven centuries. Its long history lends dignity and legitimacy to its proceedings. In addition to its historical trappings, Parliament is also the main forum for the clash between modern political parties over contemporary issues. This combination of history and modern politics makes Parliament a lively place with remarkable contrasts: For example, the bewigged and befrocked Speaker of the House of Commons presides with supreme dignity over the session while the prime minister and other party leaders may casually prop their feet up on the table where the Mace—symbol of royal authority—is placed, in order to relieve the tedium of a long debate. Likewise, the traditional line on the carpet—originally traced centuries ago to keep sword-bearing members out of sword's reach of each other—contrasts dramatically with the raucous cries of "Order, order," when a careless modern member accidentally crosses the line while addressing the House.

Technically speaking, Parliament refers to three distinct elements: the monarch, the House

Table 3–1   The Stages of a Bill
in the British Parliament

House of Commons

1. Deposition of a bill
2. First reading (A formality to put the bill on the public record)
3. Second reading (The major debate on the general principles)
4. Committee stage (Clause-by-clause examination of the bill by one of the eight standing committees)
5. Report stage
   Floor debate
   Consideration of amendments
6. Third reading
   No floor debate
   Vote on the bill as amended by the House

House of Lords

Steps are similar to those in House of Commons, but the procedures are much more informal.

Final Stages

1. When the Commons and Lords versions are the same:
   a. Promulgation of the law by the Queen's Royal Assent (last refused in 1707)
2. When the Commons and Lords versions differ:
   a. Consideration of the Lords' amendments
   b. "Money Bills" (those raising or spending money) cannot be amended or delayed by the Lords. They become law through the Royal Assent regardless of the action of the Lords.
   c. Other Bills may be presented for the Royal Assent if they have been approved by Commons in two consecutive sessions (at least 12 months) regardless of the disapproval of the Lords.

Source: David F. Roth and Frank L. Wilson, *The Comparative Study of Politics,* 2nd ed. (Englewood Cliffs, NJ: Prentice-Hall, 1980), p. 360.

of Lords, and the House of Commons. Together they exercise sovereign legislative power with the Queen affixing the Royal Assent to legislation passed by the two chambers of Parliament (Table 3–1). In practice, the monarch's role is symbolic, since the monarch has not refused the Royal Assent since 1707. The House of Lords' powers also have been reduced sharply since the beginning of the nineteenth century. In terms of real political power, Parliament is now the House of Commons.

The House of Commons

The House of Commons is made up of 659 elected members of Parliament (MPs), each of whom represents a geographic constituency.[9] Commons must approve all legislation and treaties. If there is a difference on legislation adopted by Commons and the House of Lords, the House of Commons is now dominant and empowered to override the House of Lords when necessary. While it is the Queen who formally names the prime minister and the cabinet of ministers, in fact, the prime minister is leader of the majority party in the House of Commons. He or she must be able to count on the support of the majority in the House of Commons in order to stay in power. Commons can force the resignation of the government by passing a motion of censure. While tight party discipline usually makes censure unlikely, the House of Commons' power to oust the government is a real one exercised as recently as 1979.

Despite Parliament's theoretical supremacy over the government, the prime minister and cabinet usually have ascendancy over their supposed parliamentary masters. Some comparisons with the very powerful American Congress will illustrate the limited power of the British Parliament. In the United States, each house of Congress sets its own agenda, whereas in Britain the government controls the subjects to be debated and the length of the debate. The opposition is granted time to debate issues of its choosing, but the legislative agenda is set by the government. The American president can suggest legislation to Congress, but the president personally cannot introduce bills for congressional debate and vote. To introduce a bill on the floor of Congress, the president must find sponsors among members of Congress. Then the president's bill may be replaced in committee by another bill, or it may be completely changed by the committee's amendments. American presidents are thus not assured of ever getting Congress even to vote on their proposals. In Britain, virtually all legislation is introduced by the government, and successful amendments usually have the approval of the appropriate minister. Bills introduced by individual MPs ("private member bills") rarely are discussed and even more rarely adopted. On the other hand, prime ministers know that Parliament will vote on their bills with their wording—and they can nearly always count on the bills being passed.

The ascendancy of the government over Parliament is due to the presence of *party government* in Britain.[10] Typically, when a single party wins a majority in the House of Commons, its leaders become the government. The government can count on the loyal support in Parliament of their disciplined party members, thus assuring it a majority on virtually all procedural and substantive votes. MPs usually vote in Parliament according to their party's position even if this conflicts with their own preferences or with the interest of their constituents. This discipline permits the government to dominate Parliament and to enact its programs. Parliament, of course, retains the ability to reassert its mastery over the government, but it chooses not to out of discipline and concern for effective government.

For some observers, Parliament has lost much of its power and purpose with its abilities to control legislation limited by the government and its capacity to control the government reduced by the presence of disciplined party majorities. One former minister writes that the House of Commons "is no longer a power, but a place where things happen. There are people in it who can do things, but it has itself ceased to be an authority."[11] Even in this reduced state, Parliament still has important functions that it does fulfill. Perhaps the most important is its role in linking the citizens with the state. The MPs serve as intermediaries between their constituents and the state, thereby aiding individuals and groups with particular grievances to cut through the normal red tape in seeking redress from the government. Constituents seem to prefer MPs who are interested in their needs and who can relate to their problems rather than someone who is more interested in national or international affairs.

Parliament still has important influence over legislation. Even though the government can control the legislative process, it is usually responsive to criticism from "backbenchers" (those MPs who do not hold government or party leadership

The Palace of Westminister, along the banks of the Thames River, is the seat of the British Parliament. The term "Westminister system" refers to the parliamentary structure of government developed here and widely imitated in other countries. Houses of Parliament London, England. (*Photographer/Source:* British Tourist Authority)

positions). It often modifies proposed bills and sometimes withdraws them in response to pressure from the backbenchers. This pressure is usually exerted behind the scenes in party meetings or in private sessions, but it nevertheless constitutes an important parliamentary influence over legislation.

Much of the potential power of the House of Commons is limited in practice by the strength of party ties. Members from the same party usually vote in solid-party blocs for or against a bill in accordance with the party leadership's decision. MPs who vote against their party fear that their party will deny them access to leadership positions or even the opportunity to run for re-election under the party's label. Thus, individual MPs must often vote against their conscience or even against constituency interests in the cause of party cohesion. The willingness of MPs to do

so shifts policy-making power from the House of Commons to party and government leaders.

There are indications of some slight increase in MP independence. Several key issues over the past two decades have cut across party lines rather than between parties. Most important, issues of European unity and Britain's role in the European Union have caused divisions within parties as much as between Conservative and Labour parties. In addition, a new generation of MPs more independent and more insistent on their rights has been willing to break party discipline in order to force the government to pay attention to backbench opinion in Commons.[12] They are more conscious of the importance of caring for the specific needs of their constituents and are able to see electoral advantage in doing so.[13] The Commons has revised the committee structures against the will of ministers to create new select committees.[14] Unlike the older standing committees, the select committees are specialized and deal with specific areas of public policy. They oversee specific ministries, and permit more expertise to develop among committee members.

The debate on the floor of the House of Commons permits the airing of different viewpoints on current issues. It allows the opposition to criticize government policies and to present alternatives in a public forum. The opposition controls the agenda in Commons on "Opposition days" and can challenge government performance through public debate on a topic of the opposition's choice. In addition, the opposition can force debate on a given issue by filing a motion of censure. A censure motion has priority over other legislative business and must be debated. Even if the motion is doomed to failure by the presence of a disciplined majority, as it usually is, the debate on the censure motion permits the opposition to criticize the government and forces the government to defend its conduct in office before the public.

Each week during "Question Time," MPs from all parties can pose questions to the prime minister and other ministers regarding their policies or performance.[15] Questions permit backbenchers to force ministers to give personal attention to specific matters of concern to the MP. With many of these questions designed to embarrass or criticize a minister, Question Time is often an important parliamentary check on the exercise of executive power by the Parliament. That this questioning can be an effective restraint on the government is attested to by former prime minister Harold Wilson:

> . . . no prime minister looks forward to "PQs"—Parliamentary Questions—with anything but apprehension; every prime minister works long into the night on his answers; and on all the notes available to help him anticipate the insistent and unpredictable supplementary questions that follow his main prepared answer. . . . If Britain ever had a prime minister who did not fear Questions, our parliamentary democracy would be in danger.[16]

There are new threats to the power of the House of Commons. Among the most important, and one shared by other members of the European Union, is the shift of policy-making decisions from national parliaments to EU institutions in Brussels. These shifts contribute to the discomfort of many British MPs about losing control over policies that their constituents count on them to monitor. With democratic controls over the EU still very weak, national parliaments, and notably the House of Commons, are seeking ways to exert their own control over EU decisions.

In the view of some analysts, this is only part of the challenge to the House of Commons' place in British politics.[17] The public's interest in Commons seems focused on the spectacular whether it be the weekly Question Time or the latest scandal involving an MP. Referenda, such as those in 1997 approving devolution in Scotland and Wales or those in 1998 to endorse the settlement in Northern Ireland or the election of a mayor in London, suggest the transfer of ultimate authority out of the Commons. The courts have become less passive and have challenged and implicitly revoked legislation enacted by Parliament.

In comparison with the powerful and independent U.S. Congress, the British Parliament appears weak and subordinate to the executive. But parliaments in France, Germany, and most other democratic countries have had their powers eclipsed by the growth of executive powers. The British Parliament's role in initiating legislation has declined, but the House of Commons remains an important partner in the legislative process with amendatory and veto powers and an important forum for debate of government policies and opposition alternatives. Commons remains above all an effective check on executive power. This was illustrated in the most dramatic way by the ouster of a prime minister as recently as 1979 and by the effectiveness of a key group of MPs in imposing their Euroskeptic views on Prime Minister John Major in 1996–1997.

The House of Lords

The House of Lords plays a much less important political role. Until 1999, its membership was composed of titled nobility who inherited their positions, life-time peers (named by the government, usually to honor achievement), law lords,

Table 3–2 Composition of the House of Lords, 1998

Basis of Membership	
Hereditary peers	650
Life peers	514
Total	1,164

Party Affiliations	
Conservatives	475
Labour	171
Liberal Democrats	69
"Cross benchers" and others	449
Total	1,164

Source: Figures from author's files.

and "lords spiritual" from the Church of England. (See Table 3–2.) During the twentieth century Parliament curtailed the powers of the House of Lords. It no longer has the ability to block legislation passed by Commons, though it can delay most legislation for a year (financial legislation for only a month). Since the Lords do not have to worry about reelection, they can debate important but controversial issues that most politicians would prefer to avoid. Thus, the House of Lords has conducted useful and intelligent debates of issues such as legislation on homosexuality and on the death penalty. Because their legislative agenda is less charged, the Lords can devote greater time to the tedious but important review of highly technical passages in proposed legislation. This remoteness from the real world of politics sometimes makes the House of Lords appear irrelevant. For instance, in 1979, while the country was paralyzed by a series of crippling strikes, the Lords debated the reality of unidentified flying objects and the impact on religion of the belief in such phenomena.

The party balance in the House of Lords heavily favors the Conservatives. Consequently, Labour governments tend to face greater problems in dealing with the House of Lords than do Conservative governments. However, the Lords generally avoid confrontation with the government, whether it is Conservative or Labour. They recognize that at best they can only delay legislation, not block it. They usually feel that they have the greatest chance of improving the legislation through amendments or language changes if they avoid outright clashes with the government. They also fear that direct conflict with the government may well result in legislation that would eliminate what little power the House of Lords still has.

In 1999, the Labour government enacted legislation to reform the House of Lords. The reform calls for the elimination of hereditary peers from the House of Lords. The chamber continues to exist with its current powers but its membership and voting rights are restricted to the lifetime peers, those named in recognition of their contributions to British society. For an interim period, 92 hereditary peers will continue to serve in the House of Lords. In addition, the government intends to appoint a large number of Labour life peers to compensate for the current party balance that so strongly favors the Conservative party. The government hinted also at future changes in the House of Lords that might alter the selection process or the powers of the Lords.

A legislative chamber with its membership unelected and largely composed of men and women who serve because of hereditary rights is clearly an anomaly in a modern democracy. The House of Lords has had only limited powers, since the elected House of Commons can override its actions by a simple majority vote. Over the years, it has often performed useful tasks, but few Britons regret or oppose the Labour government's reform proposals.

THE GOVERNMENT

The prime minister, the cabinet of ministers, other ministers who head governmental departments but who are not members of the cabinet, and the junior and assistant ministers constitute the *government.* A typical government includes around ninety people. Most of these people are members of the House of Commons; a few are from the House of Lords; only rarely is a nonmember of Parliament chosen as a member of the government.

The *prime minister* is formally selected by the Queen but, in fact, the Queen designates the leader of the party with a majority in the House of Commons. The general public never gets a chance to vote directly for the prime minister; in the general elections voters elect only the members of Parliament. But because both major parties have made known their choices for prime minister, the outcome of the election determines the naming of the prime minister. If Conservatives win a majority in the Commons, for example, the Conservative party leader will become prime minister.

The prime minister selects the other members of the government and enjoys considerable leeway in making these choices. There are some important informal limits. Except during rare experiences with coalition governments, the prime minister chooses only members of his or her own party who are also serving in Parliament. In addition, prime ministers usually try to balance various factions within their party and to include potential rivals in order to reduce the chance of revolt within their own parties. These selections are not subject to formal ratification or investiture votes, although prime ministers generally try to avoid antagonizing their supporters by unpopular appointments. Prime ministers can also dismiss ministers at their own discretion without consulting Parliament.

From the members of the government, the prime minister selects about twenty to twenty-five of the most important ministers to form the *cabinet*.[18] The cabinet meets weekly to discuss major issues and to collegially set government policy. The guiding principle is the *collective responsibility* of the cabinet to Parliament and the people. Cabinet decisions are collective in the sense that all members are presumed to have assented to the decision. The government stands accountable collectively for its policy decisions and a vote by Parliament to censure its action brings the resignation of the entire government. Under the convention of collective responsibility, the deliberations of the cabinet are secret, and all cabinet members are responsible for all decisions regardless of whether or not they supported the position in cabinet discussions. Ministers who are not able to support the government's decisions on all issues are expected to resign; if they indicate public opposition to a cabinet decision and fail to resign, they are usually dismissed by the prime minister. In addition, the ministers are

individually responsible for the management of their own departments and for the detailed administration of policies relevant to that department. Thus, the Minister of Housing is accountable to Parliament for the administration of the government's housing policies.

Ministers who fail to implement their policies or to prevent abuses by the bureaucracy under their control may bring their own individual resignations without causing the downfall of the whole government. Collective and individual responsibility are important principles of British parliamentary government because they establish clear lines of accountability for government action. Unlike in the United States—where a president might blame failures to act or bad decisions on Congress, the cabinet members, or the bureaucracy—in Britain the cabinet stands permanently vulnerable to removal from office by adverse votes in the House of Commons should its performance be deemed unsatisfactory.

While the decisions of the government are regarded as collective, the prime minister generally plays a leading role and sets the tone for the entire government. Since prime ministers can appoint and dismiss their cabinet colleagues, they have greater influence over the decisions of the cabinet. The prime minister sets the agenda for cabinet meetings and determines (usually without a formal vote) the collective decision of the cabinet. The real source of prime ministerial power is the prime minister's ability to count on the cooperation of a loyal majority in Parliament that will support the government's actions and legislative program with a minimum of delay and change. In this sense British prime ministers are more powerful than American presidents, who must constantly struggle to get their programs through a powerful and independent Congress.

The role of the prime minister is so preeminent that some observers regard the British system now as a "prime ministerial government" rather than as a collective "cabinet government."[19] Those who make this argument see prime ministers as free to act largely as they please. Some see them as responsible alone for all major governmental decisions, with department ministers and the cabinet as a body involved in actually making only the secondary decisions. They point to the fact that prime ministers have sometimes committed their governments to certain actions or policies without consulting the full cabinet. A recent example is the near exclusive control over economic policies held by Margaret Thatcher, in league with her Chancellor of the Exchequer (Minister of the Treasury) during the 1980s.[20]

Others challenge this view of excessive prime ministerial powers, arguing that "cabinet government" still prevails. They point to the very real limits placed on prime ministers by the overwhelming tasks of their job and by their colleagues. They point out that prime ministers have often been forced to give up desired legislative proposals because of opposition within the cabinet or within the party. The need to maintain cabinet and party unity, both essential if the prime minister wishes to stay in power, leads the prime minister to seek cooperation and compromise rather than to exercise personal dominance over the cabinet and party. In the view of these observers, the powers of government are still in the collective hands of the cabinet rather than in the hands of the prime minister alone.

Only exceptional leaders can dominate the political process and then only for limited periods. Margaret Thatcher, a very powerful prime minister, was eventually ousted by her colleagues and replaced with the much less active John Major.

The contrast between Margaret Thatcher and John Major illustrates the dynamics of the balance of power between prime ministers and their cabinet members and between the prime ministers and their parliamentary supporters. Thatcher was a powerful leader who firmly imposed her will on her party and her cabinet. Prime Minister Major stressed collegiality and the search for consensus within the cabinet and among his parliamentary supporters. The cabinet began to play a larger role in the decision-making process than had been the case under Thatcher. But even such conciliatory leadership styles did not spare Major from serious dissent within his party over the sensitive issue of Britain's further involvement in the European Union. Indeed, John Major's prime ministership may have been undermined by his more open style, which came to be viewed as weakness.

Tony Blair's leadership style suggests that he will develop into a strong prime minister. He has reshaped his party in and out of parliament to give him and his supporters unusual latitude and strength for Labour party leaders and prime ministers.

In comparison with American presidents, British prime ministers enjoy strong control over the legislative process. But British prime ministers must consult and deliberate with their cabinets more regularly and more meaningfully than American presidents are obliged to do with their

The prime minister is the key political leader in Britain. Tony Blair was named prime minister in 1997 after the Labour party's election victory. He is a strong leader who exercises considerable control over both his fellow ministers and the Labour party. (*Photographer/Source:* Fiona Hanson/AP/Wide World Photos) cabinets. They must solicit their colleagues' advice, and prime ministers who systematically ignore this advice soon find their positions untenable. Memoirs of former prime ministers and cabinet members reveal a good deal of give and take in these meetings, with prime ministers occasionally forced to withdraw favored proposals due to a hostile cabinet reception. Prime ministers have accumulated additional power as they have sensed themselves increasingly visible to the public and as the growing complexity of modern government has augmented the need for a coordinator. Nevertheless, they remain only *primus inter pares* (first among equals) in relation to their fellow ministers. These ministers serve at the will of the prime minister, but they are much more independent political forces than are American cabinet secretaries.

With a strong party uniting the executive and parliamentary action, some express concern about the effectiveness of democratic controls over the actions of the government. The only formal restraint on the government is the House of Commons' ability to force the government to resign through a vote of censure. But this has happened only once in the past sixty-five years, and then it was the result of the government's loss of its parliamentary majority through by-elections rather than a revolt by Parliament against executive excesses. The most effective restraints are informal controls that, though not legally binding, limit the government's ability to abuse power.

One such informal control is its need to retain the confidence of the party's backbenchers. Backbenchers rarely flout party discipline to vote against the government in Parliament, but dissenters can and do work within the party to undermine leaders who act peremptorily. This respect for the party's unity is reinforced by the recruitment pattern for prime ministers and ministers. In the United States, the president and cabinet may be individuals with little or no political experience or commitment to a party. In Britain, those who become prime ministers and cabinet ministers have spent most of their lives working for their party. The typical prime minister has had more than 20 years of prior experience in the House of Commons. Such leaders are unwilling to jeopardize the party they have spent years building by engaging in some adventure or by

abusing the power they hold because of their party leadership positions. They recognize that leadership must be responsive and responsible if divisions are to be avoided.

Another informal restraint is the anticipated response of the public, which restrains government in two ways. First, the government knows that it must face the electorate at least once every 5 years, and it recognizes that the opposition will use any apparent abuse of power to discredit the government and its party. Second, in a democratic system, governments must count on the public's voluntary acquiescence in the enforcement of the laws. The government must evaluate probable reactions to proposed legislation by powerful sectors of public opinion. Hostile reactions to a new policy by the press, labor unions, or the sectors most directly affected by the policy may undermine the government's public support.

Americans are preoccupied with establishing formal institutional restraints on the abuse of power, such as the separation of powers and the system of checks and balances. The British are no less concerned with misuse of political power, but they have located the means of protection in informal rather than formal institutional restraints. There is no evidence of any serious abuse of power by the British government, despite the informal nature of restraints on its powers.

A CENTRALIZED DEMOCRACY

Another example of the American concern for institutional restraints on the exercise of political power is found in the federal structures dividing power between a national government and individual state governments. The constitutional guarantees of states' rights are designed to check the potential abuse of power supposedly inherent in the concentration of power at the center. Indeed, Americans sometimes seem to believe that without this federal structure democracy is impossible.

Once again, Britain has developed an effective democratic system without these institutional checks on power. The British government is highly centralized in that the national government has all power and has the discretion to grant or withdraw prerogatives and power to local

---

CENTRALIZED GOVERNMENT

In a centralized state, all political power resides in the hands of the national government; there are no reserved rights for the territorial sub-units. The regional, district, county, and local governments exercise only those prerogatives that are granted them by the national authorities. In many instances, these local governments are simply administrative agencies for the national government with few real independent powers. The concentration of political power at the national level promotes uniformity and equity in the delivery of government services. But there are often complaints that the national government is insensitive to local needs and that overcentralization produces rigidity and stifles innovation at the local level.

Britain and France have succeeded in combining democracy with highly centralized government for over a century without the concentration of power in the hands of the central government menacing liberty and democracy. Protection against abuse of power is found not so much in this or that political framework, but in the will and behavior of those who hold leadership positions.

---

authorities. Despite this centralization of political power, the all-powerful national government does not seem inclined to abuse its powers.

As we have already seen, Britain is a union of several peoples: English, Scots, Welsh, and the peoples of Northern Ireland. The various nations have distinct geographic boundaries, but they lacked separate political institutions until very recently. The establishment of the Scottish and Welsh assemblies and the revival of the Northern Irish assembly mark important steps toward decentralization in Britain. The details of what these assemblies will and will not be able to do remain to be determined in practice. Some talk about continuing this decentralization by creating similar assemblies in the various regions of England. At this point, this seems unlikely.

The Local Authorities

The pattern of local government in Britain is extremely complicated.[21] For one thing, the structures of local government vary from one part of Britain to another. England and Wales have one set of structures; Scotland another; Northern Ireland yet another; and the greater London metropolitan area has its own. Next, even in the same part of the country, the powers of individual local governments vary from one community to the next. Political responsibilities are granted for all local governments by Parliament. Sometimes these grants are general for all local authorities; other times Parliament grants certain powers to specific local governments that are not given to the others.

A major reform in 1972 established a two-tier system of local government. The broader layer is made up of county councils (regional authorities in Scotland) providing major governmental services such as education, social services, police and fire protection, and highways. The lower level is made up of a greater number of smaller district councils responsible for local services such as recreation, housing, garbage collection, and street cleaning. At both levels, the members of the councils are elected by the general public to 4-year terms. The councils in turn elect their presiding officers or mayors.

In general, the local authorities administer policies established by the national government. Central control over local authorities is assured by the supervision of the government's ministers and through the allocation of government funds for specific purposes. The various ministries verify the performance of local authorities through visits of inspectors and auditors. The extent of the financial dependency of local authorities is evident in the fact that over half of the funds needed by local government come in the form of central government grants. In addition, the *ultra vires* rule ("beyond authority" rule) bars local authorities from doing anything that has not been authorized by Parliament.

These limits on local government are not entirely unsatisfactory from the standpoint of

DEMOCRACY AND DECENTRALIZATION

Americans believe that decentralization is necessary for democracy; Britons have long felt that centralization and democracy are compatible. Advocates of decentralization often assume that it will bring greater citizen control over decisions that affect citizens' lives. But there are some reasons to question this assumption. It is not at all clear, for example, that decentralization would lead to greater citizen participation. The public's interest in local government is lower than its interest in national politics—as suggested by the fact that voter turnout for local-level elections is much lower than for national elections. Very few people attend county or district council meetings or can name their locally elected councilors. This disinterest insulates locally elected officials from their constituents and makes them less, rather than more, responsive to the public when com-

pared to national political figures who are more visible to their electorate.

In addition, local governments may be more vulnerable to the influence of special interests than is the national government for two reasons: First, the lower levels of public interest may increase the local officials' susceptibility to blackmail in the form of certain groups threatening to mobilize their supporters against uncooperative officeholders. Second, at the national level, government is protected against excessive pressure from any single group by the large number of groups and by the fact that many have conflicting interests that the government can use to offset interest-group pressures. At the local level, however, officeholders may find it more difficult to refuse the demands of a firm that dominates its economy.

elected local officials. New services or programs taken on their own initiative would have to be financed by raising local taxes (taxes on nonagricultural property called "rates"). The "rates" are not popular and efforts to raise them are always politically risky. Local authorities do have some real means to resist the central government. In practice, local authorities often can delay or even alter the application of unwanted policies.

In a formal sense, British local authorities appear to be more autonomous and more powerful than their counterparts in other centralized or unitary states.[22] There are no central government agents, such as the French prefectural corps, to oversee the British local authorities. There is a long tradition of local control over schools and the police, vital governmental functions reserved for the central governments in France and other unitary states. Despite this apparent autonomy, British local authorities lack the political weight of their counterparts in France. There is no equivalent in Britain to the great prestige and political influence of French mayors. Nor do British local officials play the brokerage role between the central government and the citizens as their French colleagues do. Finally, British local governments have had many reforms imposed on them by the

central government with little or no opportunity to respond. Even in other highly centralized states, notably France, such sweeping reforms of local government would not have been possible.

Decentralization in a Unitary State

During the early 1970s and again in the 1980s, Conservative governments cut the powers of local governments. In 1972, for instance, the central government cut the number of locally elected officials by one-third. Other centrally directed changes stripped local authorities of many of their powers. Some were the result of specific restrictions on the powers of local authorities; others came as past responsibilities of local governments were sold off to private enterprise: city buses, local airports, public utilities, and council housing. Severe limits were also placed on local government expenditures. Illustrative of the style of these reforms was Thatcher's abrupt abolition in 1984 of the Greater London Council, a body dominated by the Labour opposition party.

When in opposition, the Labour party called for decentralization and greater powers for local democracy. Once in office, however, Labour has shown less interest in devolving new responsibilities to local authorities. Indeed, the Blair government continued to monitor local budgets very closely and to prevent local governments from increasing expenditures or local rates. In part, this was a means of countering expected criticism of Labour for allowing taxes and expenditures to rise. But it also reflected fundamental reservations on the part of national Labour leaders about the wisdom of returning financial powers to local governments. One important local reform is the establishment of an elected leader for London. The government submitted a referendum to Londoners in May 1998 for approval of a directly elected mayor. It was endorsed by a strong majority and the mayor was elected in 2000. Other cities may also seek such an officer to replace the present ceremonial, appointed mayors. It remains to be seen if such city leaders would be able to become effective advocates for local rights.

In the last analysis, Britons do not seem to mind the centralization of their state. They do not see it as an impediment to democracy. Public-opinion polls suggest that in abstract Britons support decentralization. But they do not want to give local authorities more power. Indeed, a poll in 1998 showed that 70 percent of Britons did not care whether local or national officials ran public services as long as they were run well.[23]

CONCLUSION

> The one thing that saved England from the fate of other countries was not her insular position, nor the independent spirit nor the magnanimity of her people . . . but only the consistent, uninventive, stupid fidelity to that political system which originally belonged to all the nations that traversed the ordeal of feudalism.
>
> Lord Acton

The persistence of traditional political institutions dating back nearly a thousand years makes Britain particularly attractive for tourists. These quaint political institutions and practices, however, have important value beyond their picturesqueness. The durability of these institutions through the centuries adds to the public's respect for their current decisions and actions. They confer *legitimacy* on the political system—or the sense that the political system in place not only

has political power, but *ought* to have this power. They contribute to the public's willingness to accept the authority of the decisions emerging from these institutions.

It is remarkable that these feudal institutions provide the framework for a highly successful democratic government. This has been possible because the procedures of these institutions and the power relationships between them have changed apace with the times, permitting their democratization and their continued relevance for modern political challenges. This conservation of traditional institutions through gradual change and compromise has helped create and perpetuate a political style based on accommodation and adjustment rather than on conflict and radical revolution.

Political scientists often debate the effects of particular political frameworks on the overall nature of politics in a given country. Some argue that the social setting, the prevailing political culture (the pattern of political attitudes and values), and the behavior of political actors have much greater effects on the shaping of the political system than do the particular political institutions present in the country. Others insist that the nature of the institutions can affect and in certain cases even determine the political culture and behavior. In Britain, it appears that the relationship between institutions on the one hand and political culture and behavior on the other is one of interdependency. The practices and power relationships of British political institutions have evolved gradually and harmoniously with the democratization of political attitudes and behavior.

NOTES

[1]Walter Bagehot, *The English Constitution* (Ithaca, NY: Cornell University Press, 1963), p. 65.

[2]Philip Norton, *The Constitution in Flux* (Oxford, England: Martin Robertson, 1982).

[3]For a review of the debate, see Dawn Oliver, "Written Constitutions: Principles and Problems," *Parliamentary Affairs* 45 (April 1992): 135–152.

[4]Kingsley Martin, *The Crown and the Establishment* (London: Penguin Books, 1963), p. 11.

[5]*The Economist,* 23 May 1993 and 9 March 1996.

[6]Stephen Haseler, *The End of the House of Windsor: Birth of a British Republic* (London: I. B. Tauris, 1994).

[7]For an interesting analysis of the role of the monarch, see Tom Nairn, *The Enchanted Glass: Britain and Its Monarchy* (London: Radius, 1988).

[8]Richard Rose and Dennis Kavanagh, "The Monarchy in Contemporary Political Culture," *Comparative Politics* 8 (July 1976): 548–576.

[9]See Andrew Adonis, *Parliament Today,* 2nd ed. (Manchester, England: Manchester University Press, 1993).

[10]Richard Rose, *The Problem of Party Government* (London: Macmillan, 1974).

[11]Richard H. S. Crossman, *The Myth of Cabinet Government* (Cambridge, MA: Harvard University Press, 1972), p. 18.

[12]Philip Norton, *Dissension in the House of Commons, 1974–1979* (London: Oxford University Press, 1980).

[13]Bruce Cain, John Ferejohn, and Morris Fiorina, *The Personal Vote: Constituency Service and Electoral Independence* (Cambridge, MA: Harvard University Press, 1987).

[14]Michael Jogerest, *Reform in the House of Commons: The Select Committee System* (Lexington, KY: University of Kentucky Press, 1993).

[15]Mark Franklin and Philip Norton, eds. *Parliamentary Questions* (New York: Oxford University Press, 1993).

[16]Harold Wilson, *The Governance of Britain* (London: Weidenfeld and Nicholson, 1976), p. 132.

[17]Jane Einer, "The Most Powerful Woman in the World," *Philadelphia Inquirer Magazine,* 7 June 1987, p. 41.

[18]Peter Hennessy, *Cabinet* (London: Basil Blackwell, 1986).

[19]Crossman, *The Myth of Cabinet Government,* pp. 51–58.

[20]Anthony King, ed., *The Prime Minister,* 2nd ed. (London: Macmillan, 1987).

[21]J. A. Chandler, *Local Government Today,* 2nd ed. (Manchester, England: Manchester University Press, 1996).

[22]Harold F. Alderfer, "European Local Political Structures," in *Comparative Local Politics: A Systems-Function Approach,* ed. Jack Goldsmith and Gil Gunderson (Boston: Holbrook Press, 1973), pp. 136–149.

[23]*The Economist,* 9 May 1998.

Chapter 4

British Political Participation: The Citizen and Politics

The past two decades have brought major changes in the patterns of interaction among peoples as a result of a veritable revolution in communications technology. Improved and expanded telephone services, electronic mail, facsimile transmission, and interactive television link people more closely to each other and to government and social institutions than ever before. This revolution has affected many social activities such as business, recreation, and individual shopping. So far, however, it has had only limited impact on the patterns of democratic political participation that were established early in the twentieth century. But many of the new technologies offer important opportunities for changing political participation and are likely to bring changes in the ways in which people and groups behave in politics.

Political participation is not only affected by these technological advances; attitudes and values about politics are also changing. This has led to new forms of political participation, and many contend that we have already seen a broadening of the repertoire of political actions.[1] In Britain and elsewhere, the new forms of political action—often unconventional and even disrup-tive—necessitate adjustments in the polity and especially in the traditional political actors: individual citizens, political parties, and interest groups.

THE INDIVIDUAL IN POLITICS

As in other Western democracies, British citizens are expected to be interested in the political process, informed about issues and parties, and capable of deciding rationally between contending candidates at election time. However, in Britain, as elsewhere, these expectations are often not met by the majority of the citizenry. Political participation is voluntary and spontaneous, and the level of public involvement depends upon the interest and motivation of the individual citizen. The level of political interest is generally low (see Table 4–1). For the majority of Britons, voting is the only political act. Britons usually turn out heavily for elections; for example, 71 percent voted in the 1997 House of Commons election. (This figure is high by American standards but low in comparison with France, Germany, and most other European democracies.) Other

Table 4–1   Levels of Political Interest in Four Democracies, 1993

Interest in Politics	Britain	Germany	France	U.S. (1996)
Very interested	14%	17%	10%	32%
Somewhat interested	40	40	29	52
Not much interested	31	31	37	16
Not at all interested	15	11	23	16

Source: Britain, France, and Germany from *Euro-Barometer, Trends, 1974–1993,* pp. 161–164; United States from 1996 American National Study, Center for Political Studies, University of Michigan.

political activities—if there are any—are undertaken only on rare occasions and usually for brief periods of time. One expert in British politics suggests that the proportion of the adult population actively participating in politics today is scarcely any larger than it was before the democratization of Britain during the nineteenth century.[2]

The low level of political involvement is not unique to Britain; it is as low in Germany and lower in France. Indeed, it is quite normal that there be a small group of politically interested and involved citizens and a much larger group of citizens with only marginal political interest. This is in fact desirable even for democracies presumably based on the public's involvement. Very high rates of participation are generally accompanied by intense political feelings symptomatic of severe social crisis. Large masses are politically mobilized only when they feel threatened.

The usual image of a peaceful historical development of British democracy, as we have seen, is exaggerated. Some see signs of a new era of disruptive citizen action. There is a growing tendency for Britons to indicate that they will use unconventional means of participation to press their political views. In the last twenty years Britain's usually quiet political scene has been disturbed by protest movements that brought large numbers of sometimes unruly demonstrators into the streets of the cities. Yet the extent of political protest and street politics in Britain is still far lower than in France or Germany.

It is relatively easy to mobilize citizens who feel their interests are at stake for the excitement of protesting in the streets. It is much more difficult to attract even a handful of citizens willing to commit themselves to a long and often boring effort to produce alternative policies.

VOTING

Voting bears closer examination since it is the only political act for most Britons.[3] Table 4–2 summarizes the various British elections. The most important election, and the only national election, is for the membership of the House of Commons. Voter turnout for this election is generally very high, with about 75 percent of the eligible voters typically voting (see Table 4–3). This is in sharp contrast to the poor turnout in recent

---

POPULAR SOVEREIGNTY

One reason for the increase in political involvement on the part of the general population is the widespread acceptance, in principle if not always in fact, of *popular sovereignty* as the basis of legitimate political power. Popular sovereignty is the doctrine that the right to rule belongs to the people and that those who govern derive their authority from the people. With very few exceptions, rulers no longer claim to rule by divine or hereditary rights. The general acceptance of the principle of popular sovereignty in both democratic and dictatorial regimes lends support to the norm of mass political participation: If political power is derived from the people, the people should be involved in politics to exercise their sovereignty.

Table 4–2 Elections in Britain

Type	Frequency	Electing Body
European Parliament elections	Every 5 years	Entire electorate
General elections		
(House of Commons)	Every 5 years or earlier	Entire electorate
Municipal elections[a]		
Borough councillors	$1/_3$ elected each year (3-year terms)	Entire electorate
Aldermen	$1/_2$ elected every 3 years (6-year terms)	Borough Councillors
Mayors	Every year	Councillors and Aldermen

[a]Municipal elections in the administrative counties are conducted somewhat differently.

American presidential elections. At the polls, British voters encounter a much less complicated ballot than do Americans. In the United States, the voter must be prepared to vote for candidates from a long list of public offices—the president, a senator, a member of Congress, a state assembly representative, a state senator, judges, and so on—and to make decisions on a number of complicated propositions. In Britain, the voter in a general election must make only one decision: which party's candidate to support for the House of Commons.

The British electoral system for the House of Commons election and all other elections is "the first past the post" plurality system. There are 659 districts of approximately equal population—one district for each member of Commons. No primary elections are held, candidates being nominated by the local party units. The candidate winning the largest number of votes, whether or not it constitutes a majority of the votes cast, is elected. There is some discontent about the effects of this plurality system since it produces the underrepresentation in Commons of smaller parties—especially the Liberal Democratic party. For example, in the 1992 election the Liberal Democrats received 16.8 percent of the vote, but they won only 7.1 percent of the seats in the House of Commons because their candidates often did well but came in behind the Conservative or Labour candidate. The Liberal Democrats urge that the plurality system be replaced by proportional representation. It does appear unfair that the Liberal Democrats are consistently underrepresented in Parliament. Systems of proportional representation are now used in European Parliament elections (starting in 1999) and in elections for the new assemblies in Scotland, Wales, and Northern Ireland. Tony Blair's Labour government set up a special committee to explore reforming the electoral system for House of Commons elections. It seems likely that there will be some changes, but few expect the committee to endorse a "pure" system of proportional representation for general elections. The current "first-past-the-post" system benefits the Labour party

Table 4–3 Percentage of Eligible Electorate Voting in Britain, France, Germany, and the United States

British House of Commons Elections		French National Assembly Elections		German Bundestag Elections		U.S. Presidential Elections	
1997	71.2%	1997	70.0%	1998	82.3%	1996	49.0%
1992	77.0	1993	68.9	1994	79.1	1992	55.2
1987	76.0	1988	65.8	1990	77.8	1988	50.0
1983	72.6	1986	79.5	1987	84.3	1984	53.0
1979	76.0	1981	70.4	1983	89.1	1980	52.6
1974 (Oct.)	72.8	1978	82.8	1980	88.7	1976	53.3
1974 (Feb.)	78.7	1973	80.9	1976	91.0	1972	54.5
1970	71.5	1968	80.0	1972	91.2	1968	61.0

ELECTORAL SYSTEMS

There are two basic electoral systems or rules for tabulating election results: the "first-past-the-post" plurality system, and proportional representation. The *plurality system* is familiar to Americans as the basis of all our legislative elections. The country is divided into territorial districts of roughly equal population with each district selecting one representative for the legislative body. The candidate receiving the largest number of votes is elected. Suppose four candidates sought a legislative seat in a given district: candidate A received 27.0 percent of the votes cast; candidate B, 26.9 percent; candidate C, 23.1 percent; and candidate D, 23.0 percent. Candidate A would be elected even though he or she outdistanced candidate B by only a few votes and even though the vote for A fell far short of a majority of those voting.

In *proportional representation,* the districts are larger, and each district elects several representatives. Each party presents a list of candidates for these legislative seats. After the election, the seats are distributed according to the proportion of the vote going to each party list. Suppose a district has twenty representatives. When the votes are counted, party A with 25 percent of the vote would get 25 percent of the seats or five seats that would be filled by the top five names on its list of candidates; party B with 20 percent of the vote would get four seats; party C with 20 percent would also get four seats; party D with 15 percent of the vote would get three seats; and so on.

Proportional representation has the advantage of more accurately and equitably reflecting the election preferences of the voters in the legislative body. It assures representation even for minority views. Some argue, however, that proportional representation encourages numerous small parties and therefore renders difficult the task of building majority coalitions in parliament. It is widely used in democratic systems including Germany, Belgium, the Netherlands, and the Scandinavian countries.

whether or not it wins the election. Whatever system is proposed, there will be a national referendum to approve the shift. If Britain does move toward a system of proportional representation, it will come at a time when other democracies, notably Japan and Italy, are moving away from proportional representation because of the instability it has caused in their political systems.

Until recently, referendum measures, whereby specific policy proposals are presented to the voters for their approval or disapproval, have been avoided in Britain. The reason stemmed from the constitutional principle that it was Parliament and not the people that controlled sovereign power. During the 1970s, several referendums were held, always with the stipulation that the outcomes were advisory to Parliament in order to preserve the constitutional principle of parliamentary supremacy. Three of the referendums were regional in that they took place in only part of the country, Similar referendums were held again in 1997 and 1998 in the same areas: Scotland, Wales, and Northern Ireland. The only national referendum

was in 1975 when voters approved membership in the European Community. There have been suggestions that other issues also should be submitted as referendums, and it is likely that the referendums of the 1990s will be used as precedents for additional experiments in the future. This would be a logical extension of the gradual shift of sovereign power from the monarch to Parliament, and now to the people—in fact if not yet in constitutional precept.

Considerable research has been devoted to determining how the citizen decides how to vote. The central concern of such research is to ascertain how logical voters are as they make voting decisions. Clearly, the low levels of political interest and information among citizens raise doubts about the degree of rationality they exercise in voting. Uninformed and uninterested voters will have a poor chance of selecting candidates who support their policy preferences. The choice is simplified for the British voter by the relative homogeneity and unity of the political parties. In the United States, a voter would not be able to tell much by knowing the party of a candidate because Democrats vary from very conservative to very liberal, and Republicans are equally diverse. In Britain, the party label means more, and voters who elect a Conservative candidate can be assured that that candidate will always support the positions of the Conservative party. Thus in Britain the personality of the individual candidate is rarely a factor in voting. Voters select their candidates on the basis of party and, occasionally, on the basis of the party's prime ministerial candidate.

In the past, many British voters selected a party and voted regularly for that party throughout their lives. They often did so even when their party's positions differed from their personal positions on given issues. There appears, however, to be growing volatility in partisan choice among British voters.[4] This means that voters switch from one party to another, decreasing the influence of past habits in determining current voting preference; voters appear increasingly swayed by their judgment of party leaders and their issue positions. For example, Labour's victory in 1997 came in spite of a thriving economy provided by Major's outgoing Conservatives. Voters seemed to think it was "time for a change." More important, voters admired Tony Blair's personal attributes and his success in imposing himself on his previously divided party, especially when contrasted with John Major's seeming ineffectiveness and his divided party.[5]

Some voters clearly are swayed by the position of parties on specific issues. Notably, immigration policy and European integration are issues that do not correspond to the usual Conservative/Labour split. Voters with strong opinions on these issues often break with their normal party. The presence in Britain of clear distinctions between a party in government and a party in opposition makes it easy for voters who are dissatisfied with the overall performance of the current government to show that dissatisfaction by voting for the opposition. Their votes for or against the incumbent government may thus represent rational decisions to affirm or reject the previous performance of one set of candidates, whether or not they can relate their own specific issue positions correctly with those of a party.

WOMEN IN POLITICS

British women won the right to vote in a protracted and sometimes violent struggle. The Suffragette Movement peaked in 1910–14 when militant suffragettes accelerated their efforts to win equal rights and, especially, the right to vote for women. The suffragettes' tactics included rallies, demonstrations, window-smashing campaigns, heckling of public speeches by government ministers, attempts to destroy the mail, burning slogans on golf greens, hunger strikes, random arson of houses and churches, and even a few bombings. World War I delayed their victory until 1918, when all women over 30 years of age were granted the right to vote; men could vote at 21. Formal political equality was achieved in 1928, when the age of eligibility was reduced to 21 for women as well.

Despite formal legal emancipation, women remain politically second-class citizens.[6] Though more than half the electorate is female, women are less likely than men to become involved in politics. In recent years, women have begun to demonstrate greater interest in politics and a greater desire to participate. They are among the sections of society that are providing new, previously inactive participants to the political scene.

The percentages of women in public office reflect the fact that politics remains a predominantly male pursuit. Women made broad gains in the 1997 general elections,[7] so much so that some dubbed 1997 as the "year of the woman." The number of women elected to Commons was the highest ever: 120 women MPs, exactly double the number in the outgoing parliament. But women still accounted for only 18.2 percent of the House when women make up over half the electorate and about that same share of party members. In comparison with 1992, the number of women candidates did not increase significantly. What accounted for the increase in women's presence in Commons was the Labour party's decision to select women candidates for half of all winnable, vacant seats. In addition to the large number of women in Commons, Tony Blair named 5 women as members of his 22-member Cabinet. They were appointed to important ministries, often far from the ministries

DO WOMEN MAKE A DIFFERENCE?

The increasing number of women in politics—as members of parliament and as political leaders—raises questions about their impact on the policy process. Is there a specific set of issues that women leaders are more likely to champion? Do women politicians have distinctive political styles?

In Britain, for example, Margaret Thatcher, the country's first woman prime minister, served in that key post longer than anyone else in this century (1979–1990). She was a very powerful and effective leader in pursuing her goals. She clearly did not fit the stereotype of a self-effacing, consensus-seeking woman leader. Furthermore, her policy agenda did not include issues usually thought of as emanating from the women's movement. Indeed, British women's movements frequently found themselves at odds with her policies. Nor did Thatcher open new opportunities for women: she was the only woman in her government.

It is not clear that there is any set notion of a women's agenda or viewpoint on broad political issues or any agreement on a set of issues as particularly important to women. What appears most important is that larger numbers of women in Parliament and political leadership positions helps to legitimize these institutions in the eyes of both women and men.

For more on this subject see Pippa Norris, "Women Politicians: Transforming Westminister?" *Parliamentary Affairs* 49 (January 1996): 89–102.

typically thought of as of special interest to women.

Women are active in all British political parties, but they have not often served as candidates for Parliament. For example, in 1997 the Conservatives nominated only 67 women as candidates out of nearly 650 nominations; the Labour party nominated 155 women; and the Liberal Democratic party presented 139 women candidates. The number of women candidates presented has grown from an average of about 5 percent in the elections between 1964 and 1974[8] to 19 percent of the major party candidates in the 1997 election. Women frequently account for a high proportion of the volunteer campaign workers in Britain but, even when they outnumber men as party workers, they are less likely to assume positions of party leadership. For example, a study of a local Conservative party unit in England revealed that women accounted for 57 percent of the members, but only 25 percent of the officers.[9]

The small number of women in politics is attributable, by and large, to socialization patterns rather than overt sex discrimination. National party leaders are anxious to recruit more women candidates, but the local constituency parties, even those where women compose the majority of the membership and the leadership, usually select male candidates. There is little evidence of noteworthy voter antagonism to women candidates for public office. In the two general elections of February and October 1974, which gave the opportunity to evaluate voter reaction to women candidates, there were 39 instances where the same party presented a man in one 1974 election and a woman in the other 1974 balloting in the same district. This permitted an assessment of the impact of gender on voting. There was no indication that the sex of the candidate had any effect on the voting patterns among voters for Conservative and Labour party candidates, and only a possible marginal tendency to favor male candidates in the smaller Liberal party electorate.[10] Thus, it is not fear that voters will automatically reject women candidates that accounts for the small number of women candidates and officeholders. The real obstacle to presenting more women candidates is to be found in the local party candidate selection committees that nominate the candidates.[11]

Many Western democracies are experiencing a period of transition in which the role of women in society is being reassessed. This is true of Britain. There is an active women's movement promoting equal rights,[12] and both major parties have shown a sensitivity to the need to promote social and political equality for women. However, because the scarcity of women in politics is the product of people's attitudes and women's self-restraint rather than overt discrimination, changes will probably be gradual and slow. It is one thing to eliminate legal barriers to participation; it is quite another to change the attitudes of men and women toward their social and political roles.

INTEREST GROUP POLITICS

Political activity by interest groups is especially prevalent in the political processes of Britain and other Western democracies. Interest groups promote the specific interests of their memberships, which may or may not be compatible with those of the public or the nation as a whole. They are generally free to act as they please within broad legal limits—designed to prevent bribery and corruption, rather than to restrain group political activities. In Britain, such groups can and do openly oppose governmental policies they find distasteful, seeking to influence officials and, if necessary, public opinion. When Americans think of interest groups, they usually conjure up images of well-heeled lobbyists wining and dining legislators in order to win their support on bills affecting their clients' interests. Such legislative lobbying is unusual in Britain because of the disciplined voting of MPs. It makes little sense to pressure MPs who vote as the party decides, so British interest groups seek other channels of influence.[13] They develop contacts in the ministries and government departments. They devote special attention to party leaders who are in positions to influence the party's stands.

Group politics in Britain takes several forms: electoral support or campaign contributions can be traded for a legislator's support of the group's interest; informal contacts between group representatives and government officials can be established; or formal participation in policy making can be attempted. While it would be inaccurate to conclude that interest groups control politics, they do strongly influence the nature and implementation of policy. Political leaders, who are accountable to the electorate, generally determine the general direction and outline of policy. But groups, accountable only to their clientele, actively influence the specific details

of policy. Group political action is also a way of increasing the individual's political efficacy. In league with others, citizens feel greater effectiveness and, indeed, are likely to be more effective. Consequently, groups emerge freely to champion small and large causes as the need arises. For example, in the 1980s some citizens became concerned when they discovered that hundreds of hedgehogs were falling into the pits under cattle guards and perishing. They organized themselves into the British Hedgehog Preservation Society and successfully urged local governments to install concrete escape ramps to permit the hedgehogs to climb out from under the grids.

Since World War II, interdependence between government and important interest groups has grown rapidly. As the government's role in managing the economy and directing society has increased, its need for information and cooperation from those it regulates has also increased. For example, in operating the National Health Service, Britain's national health program, the government must have information on medical needs and resources that often can be supplied only by the medical practitioners themselves. This gives medical professionals some control, since they usually interpret the needed data in a way that supports the interests of their own group. They can threaten to sabotage unwanted policies through noncompliance—in order to shape policy in ways that better respond to the needs of their members. Thus, the government's role in society has grown enormously, but it is now increasingly dependent upon the cooperation and voluntary compliance of the powerful groups it seeks to regulate.

In order to win cooperation from affected interest groups, the government beginning in the early 1960s and through the 1970s formed advisory bodies, including civil servants and representatives from affected interests, to discuss policy proposals and policy implementation. These policy advisory boards were known as "quangos"—quasi-autonomous, non-governmental organizations. The result was a "neocorporatist" pattern of policy making where interests often had direct roles in making and implementing policy. The government needed information and cooperation from the interest groups; the interest group traded their information and their willingness to persuade their members to accept new government policies for the opportunity to influence the policies as they were formulated. The interdependence led to significant interest group influence in the policy process, especially during the 1970s.

Margaret Thatcher sensed that such neocorporatist collaboration of government and affected interest groups was decreasing the autonomy and power of government. She dissolved many of the boards and quangos where interest groups had policy-making power and strove generally to reduce interest group influence. Even business interests close to her Conservative party found that their ability to influence policy during Thatcher's eleven years as prime minister was less than it had often been under Labour governments. This was characteristic of the strong, independent, and personal leadership that was a central feature of Thatcher's political style.

Thatcher failed in her objective of eliminating quangos. Her government and those that have followed have found it useful to have semi-official forums for consultation between government and interest groups affected by public policy. Above all, governments have found that these bodies assist in the implementation of public policies. By soliciting their advice, involving them in policy deliberation, governments find that quangos gain "a stake" in the policies and often assist government in implementing what otherwise would be difficult for a government to impose on interest groups and those they represent. As a result, in 1997 there were some 5,681 quangos doing business with some part of the government or civil service.

The political situation of the trade unions was particularly weakened during the past twenty years. In part, the unions suffered because of Conservative party dominance until 1997.[14] Thatcher, in particular, launched attacks designed to reduce the political influence of trade unions. British trade unions have also been affected by the general decline of unions in all industrial democracies as the number of blue-collar jobs has decreased and as the remaining workers have shown less commitment to their unions. Membership has dropped and the Trades Union Congress (TUC) has lost political influence even in the Labour party. Even with the return of a

Labour government in 1997, trade unions hve not recovered their political clout. Tony Blair has loosened the Labour party's ties to the trade union movement and done little to reverse the Thatcher legislation restricting trade union activities. As a result, the labor movement is seeking new ways to influence government policy.[15]

There have also been broad changes in interest group lobbying during the past decade. First, there has been a rapid increase in groups designed to advocate particular interests in government policy making. Increasingly, large firms and specific interests approach government directly and individually rather than through their peak associations. Second, smaller British firms and interest groups are now imitating American groups by turning to professional political consultants, law offices, or public relations firms to serve as their advocates with the state.[16] Third, interest groups have further developed their contacts with appropriate civil servants in the government departments that deal with issues that concern their members. Fourth, while the British have always been good joiners, they are even more willing now than in the past to form local and national groups to press their viewpoints on government. Fifth, interest groups are shifting some of their attention from London to Brussels as the European Union increases in importance over many formerly "domestic" economic and social issues. Lobbying in Brussels is vigorous and more American-like than what has been traditionally accepted in Britain and other European countries. Lobbying techniques and perspectives used in Brussels are finding their way into politics in London.

Finally, all groups pay more attention to Parliament than in the past. Even small groups can sometimes affect government through their contacts with the House of Commons. An example of successful parliamentary lobbying came in 1993 when the National Federation of Sub-Postmasters feared that a change in government policy might affect their jobs. They mobilized citizens in small towns and villages to defend the very existence of their branch post offices, which in many cases were the only evidence of the existence of these tiny communities. Members of Parliament found their mail boxes jammed with letters protesting the demise of sub-post offices. The result was that the government rewrote its regulations to calm fears that the branch post offices would disappear and with them the identity of small towns and villages. Parliament is still far from the principle target of interest group actions but it is no longer ignored.

The sheer number of groups attempting to influence policy in Britain is overwhelming. Some groups represent very narrow interests; some are concerned only with local policies; some are active only intermittently, as issues of concern to them arise; some have only fleeting existences contingent on the prominence of a specific issue. Other groups are much more active in politics, attempting to influence policy in many issue areas at the national and local levels. Some of these highly political groups are based in particular sectors of society, such as pensioners, veterans, ethnic groups, or such broader sectors as automobile drivers, taxpayers, or gun owners.

Despite these changes, groups based on occupational interests (such as labor unions, business groups, and professional associations) are among the most politically active, especially since governments have become more involved in regulating economic and social affairs. Table 4–4 lists the major occupation-based interest groups in Britain. The groups listed are the national organizations (sometimes called "peak" associations) that federate the many smaller associations based

Table 4–4   Major Occupational Interest Groups in Britain

Labor Unions

Trades Union Congress (TUC) (linked to Labour party) 7,200,000 members
National Union of Teachers 290,000 members

Employers Associations

Confederation of British Industry (CBI), (close to the Conservative party) 12,000 member companies
British Employers' Confederation
Association of British Chambers of Commerce

Farmers Associations

National Farmers Union (NFU) 106,000 members

in particular regions or industries. For example, the Trades Union Congress (TUC) includes the Transport and General Workers' Union, the Amalgamated Engineering Union, the National Union of Mineworkers, and others.

The diverse nature of these peak associations gives the strength of numbers. But this diversity also reduces their ability to speak with one voice since member groups often have divergent or even opposed views. This has been true in important issues such as involvement in the European Union, where some industries and some trade unions stand to gain and lose from further integration. As a result, the peak associations are sometimes unable to present a clear trade union or business position to government.

Several of the major peak associations have close ties with political parties. In Britain, business and farm interests have informal links with the Conservative party, maintained by Conservative members of Parliament who are business people, industrialists, or professionals who remain friendly with employers' associations or are even members. Such ties are useful to the interest groups, especially when the Conservatives are in power. The Conservative party and business groups remain formally autonomous, but political cooperation between them is frequent.

The Labour party is a political offshoot of the trade union movement and remains closely and formally tied to the TUC. Members of unions affiliated with the TUC are automatically members of the Labour party. The trade unions are a principal source of funding for the Labour party. However, the trade unions continue to lose members. As recently as 1985, the trade unions included over half of all British workers; that figure is now down to 26 percent of the work force.

As the trade unions have lost members and as their public image has varied, the Labour party has sought more independence from the unions. The TUC and other affiliated unions still have half of the votes at Labour party conferences, but those conferences are no longer as influential in setting policy and electing leaders than they were in the past. The unions once provided 80 percent of the party's income; they now provide less than half the Labour party's revenues. With Labour back in power since 1997, the government has consciously separated itself from its friends in the union movement to emphasize its independence. Blair has also shown little interest in responding to unions' calls to reverse Thatcher's anti-union reforms from the 1980s.

The power of interest groups in Britain and other Western democracies raises important questions for democratic regimes. Where broadly defined policies are passed by elected bodies and then interpreted and applied by bureaucrats and interest group representatives, important policy-making powers are in the hands not of elected officials directly accountable to the voters, but of anonymous group leaders and unaccountable bureaucrats serving in quangos and similar bodies. This situation often leads to regulation of society and the economy by the very groups supposed to be the objects of regulation. As an illustration of the regulated regulating themselves, the British Medical Association (BMA) sits on key governmental committees that define national medical policies and regulate the activities and fees of BMA doctors.

A second concern is that much group activity takes place behind closed doors. Negotiations and compromises between interest groups and government are facilitated by secret meetings. But such secrecy is detrimental to democratic control by the public, since it is difficult for the voter to attribute to any individual or group the details of policies worked out in secret sessions. A third problem is that some sectors of society are unable to participate in this process on an equal footing. The advantage lies with established and well-organized groups. Those elements of society that for a variety of reasons find it difficult to organize—the poor, ethnic minorities, the elderly, the young, consumers—find access to the decision-making process difficult or impossible.

Finally, there is the question of the accuracy with which the leaders of interest groups reflect the attitudes of their memberships. It is often alleged, and correctly, that union leaders do not accurately convey the political feelings of their members, and that employers' associations do not know the attitudes of those they represent on any given issue. The problems involved in ascertaining the representativeness of group spokespersons are great. Who is to know, for instance, whether the Royal Automobile Club is correctly reflecting its members' views in urging a new highway?

Interest groups are likely to continue to be prominent participants in the democratic political process. Governments need their information and cooperation, and citizens in Britain, France, Germany, and other Western democracies believe that their governments *ought* to consult groups affected by public policies. Group involvement in politics may also be seen as increasing the representativeness and responsiveness of government by supplementing individual representation by legislators with the functional representation of specific interests by groups. Given the low levels of individual political participation, group politics may be a means of making democracy work despite the inactivity of the masses. In this sense, groups serve as substitutes for individual participation and at least foster political involvement among those interested in and affected by governmental policies.

POLITICAL PARTIES

Political parties are usually the most important political actors in Western democracies. They organize the competition between alternative sets of leaders that makes possible a democratic choice for the electorate. Through their role in the electoral process and their efforts to adapt their positions to the needs and interests of the people, the parties help to link the government with the citizens. Because of the importance of political parties, the effectiveness, strength, and stability of the political party system often have an important effect on the overall stability of democratic states.

In the United States, the link between party and government is weak because of the lack of organization and discipline of American parties and because of the frequent division of power between a president of one party and a congressional majority of the other party. American voters thus have difficulty in attributing blame or praise to the Republicans or the Democrats for past faults or accomplishments. In contrast, in Britain, the presence of party government—where a disciplined party controls a majority in the legislature and also forms the executive—

facilitates the voters' task of judging between the parties. Each British party presents a fairly clear platform at election time. One party usually wins a majority of the seats in the House of Commons and thus singlehandedly controls the government. The leader of the majority party becomes the prime minister, and the cabinet is made up of parliamentarians from the same party. The minority party becomes "Her Majesty's Loyal Opposition" and chooses a "shadow government" of individuals who would likely become ministers if the minority party should win control of Commons.

The opposition challenges government policy and explains to the public how its action would differ from that of the incumbent government. The leader of the opposition, the person who would become prime minister if the majority changes, receives a government salary. Thus, the distinction between government and opposition in Britain is obvious, and confrontation between the two parties is institutionalized. The government can be held accountable for its decisions and action; it cannot evade responsibility by claiming that the legislature refused to cooperate. If the government fails to perform its duties adequately, the voters can turn to the opposition for a viable alternative.

The Conservative and Labour parties have dominated British politics since 1924. (See Table 4–5 for recent election results.) The Conservative party tends to represent the interests of the middle and upper social classes, whereas the Labour party defends the interests of the working and lower-middle classes. However, these class lines are not rigid; a large number of "working-class Tories" usually vote Conservative. And an important sector of the middle and upper classes regularly votes Labour. Both parties attempt to attract voters from all socioeconomic classes, especially those that normally vote for their opponent. Conservatives make special efforts to woo the working-class vote, and the Labour party devotes special attention to the middle class. Thus while there are clear differences in the class backgrounds of the constituencies of the two British parties, it would be inaccurate to label them class-based parties since both seek and receive support from all classes.

The Conservative Party

The Conservative party (also known as the Tory party) has dominated British politics through most of the twentieth century.[17] For much of the time since World War II, the Conservatives have advocated social and economic policies that are just right of Center. For a decade, however, while the party was led by Margaret Thatcher (1979–90), it moved more to the right. Thatcher introduced a strident brand of "neoliberalism"[18] and launched a decade-long battle against government economic intervention and the social welfare state. Under her government, most of the industries that had been owned by the government were privatized by selling full ownership to private individuals and institutions. She was less successful in cutting back on social welfare programs, largely because of the popularity of public education, the National Health Service, and

Table 4–5 Political Parties in British General Elections

	Percentage of Vote			Seats Won in House of Commons			Percentage of Total Seats		
	1987	1992	1997	1987	1992	1997	1987	1992	1997
Conservative party	42.3	41.9	30.7	375	336	167	57.7	51.7	25.3
Labour party	30.8	34.2	43.2	229	291	418	35.2	41.6	63.4
Alliance—Liberal-Democrats	22.8	17.9	16.8	22	20	46	3.5	3.1	7.0
Plaid Cymru (Welsh National party)	0.4	2.3	2.5	2	4	6	0.3	0.6	0.9
Scottish Nationalist party	1.0			3	3	4	0.5	0.5	0.4
Others	3.0	6.0	6.8	16	16	20	2.5	2.5	3.0

economic benefits for the less advantaged portions of the population.

In foreign policy matters, Thatcher's Conservatives took a hard line against the Soviet Union. She developed a close, personal relationship with the U.S. President Ronald Reagan and perpetuated Britain's "special relationship" with the United States. Thatcher supported the European Union but recognized that a reluctant Britain could often win concessions from its EU partners.

Thatcher's neoliberal social and economic views represent an important current in the Conservative party's traditions[19] but by no means the only such current or even the dominant one. Indeed, even during the decade that Thatcher was prime minister there was never a "Thatcherite" majority in the Conservative party, in her Government, or among Conservative voters. What made Thatcher such an effective prime minister was her assertive leadership style. By the force of her personality and her persistence, she was able to persuade her colleagues in Parliament and in the Conservative party to acquiesce to her views.

Ultimately, Thatcher's abrasive style in dealing with her fellow Tories wore thin. In 1990, she withdrew from the election for Conservative party leader when it became clear that she would be defeated and stepped down as prime minister. The Conservative party has a history of eliminating party leaders who cannot win elections. Polls at the time suggested that a Thatcher-led Conservative party would be defeated in the next general elections. This tradition of seeking winning leaders, coupled with the Conservative MPs' fatigue with Thatcher's rough style, brought down the "Iron Lady."

John Major was elected Conservative party leader and named prime minister after Thatcher withdrew from the 1990 leadership contest. He subsequently led his party to an electoral victory in the 1992 general elections. Major proved to be more pragmatic than Thatcher. He did not reverse many of the Thatcher policies but he administered them with greater compassion and with a willingness to seek accommodations with those who opposed him. At first, his leadership was welcomed by party members and leaders. However, by 1993, he faced serious divisions within his party over how far Britain should proceed with

European integration. Much of this opposition was generated by Thatcher, who attacked her successor from her seat in the House of Lords. The apparent division of the Conservative party not only weakened Major's position but undermined the party's support among the general electorate.

In the past decade, the party's membership has declined to an estimated 400,000 members. The membership is aging—some observers put the average age of the Conservative party members at over 60 years. A local Tory constituency party had to disband its "young wives club" when it turned out that its chairwoman-elect was 65 years old. The aging membership and stagnating local leadership reduce the effectiveness of local party units in mobilizing support for elections.

Midway through the 1990s, the Conservative party faced internal division and public disinterest. Above all, the Conservatives were divided over Britain's involvement in the European Union. A number of key Conservative MPs were strong opponents of further engagements in Europe. These "Euroskeptics" did not want Britain to withdraw from the EU, but they opposed many of the EU's new initiatives, including social programs and the single European currency. Other Conservatives remained advocates of a strong and positive presence for Britain in the EU. Major was unsuccessful in bridging these differences leaving the appearance that the Conservatives were fielding a prime minister who was weak and ineffective.

Losses in by-elections and divisions in the party ultimately eroded the party's majority in the House of Commons. Major retained his majority in the House of Commons only due to the support of Northern Irish Unionists, and that support was uncertain as the government pushed for a negotiated settlement in Northern Ireland. Personal scandals hit a number of prominent Conservative politicians and forced their resignations from government. Public opinion polls showed Major to be the least popular prime minister since polling began sixty years ago.

General elections in 1997 produced a historic defeat for the Conservative party. Never in the twentieth century had the party polled such a small percentage of the vote; never had it elected as few MPs as it did in 1997. The party lost all its seats in Scotland and Wales and became essentially an "English" party in a union where separate nationalities were becoming more important. It was an unusual defeat in that the Conservative party's policies were popular and they were giving Britain exceptional economic strength at a time when other west European countries were struggling with economic stagnation. The reasons for the Conservative defeat were multiple. Among the most important was the party's long tenure in office. After the party's 18 years in office, people were ready for a political change. As often happens when a political party holds power for a long time, its leaders are vulnerable to charges of greed and malfeasance in office. The Conservative party was tarnished by numerous personal and financial scandals involving its MPs and leaders. Finally, the Conservatives' claim to be the "natural" party of government was undermined by serious internal divisions and outright conflict between various party factions. Of course, it is also important to note the popularity of the Labour leader and his revitalized party. "New Labour" offered a very attractive alternative to Conservative rule for the first time in over 20 years.

John Major was discredited by the devastating defeat and immediately stepped down as party leader. Several of the party's most effective potential leaders were eliminated since they had failed to win reelection to Parliament. Eventually, the party elected William Hague as its new leader. Hague is a "Euroskeptic" and Thatcherite. Many Conservatives and others believe that he is not a leader who can rebuild the Conservative party and regain the public's confidence. He has announced reforms of the party's organization but these have built little enthusiasm either among the party loyalists or the public in general. The extent of the Tories' defeat makes quick recovery unlikely. Furthermore, the Blair Labour government has picked up many of the successful and popular policies of their Conservative predecessors. This leaves little room for the party to maneuver as it seeks to redefine itself to the public.

The Tories have a long history of responding well to needs for change in order to rewin public confidence and support. Driven by a "will to govern," the Conservatives have proven able to make difficult adjustments quickly and effectively. Tory party leaders who seem unable to do this are disposed of without mercy. At the present, the Conservative party's prospects seem dim, but the next

general election is not due until 2002, long enough for the party to make changes and for the Labour government to make mistakes.

The Labour Party

Labour's election victory in 1997 was spectacular. It marked the successful recovery from a period of errors in political judgment and decline that dated back to the 1970s. At that time, the party's internal divisions and doctrinal confusion resulted in the ouster of a Labour government by a vote of censure, the only successful such removal of a government in the twentieth century.

In the late 1970s, the party moved sharply to the Left and advocated profound economic changes toward socialism, a withdrawal from the European Community, and unilateral nuclear disarmament. While its parliamentary leaders took more moderate positions, the rank-and-file membership and several highly visible leaders took positions that were far from the mainstream of British political traditions. The party underwent internal "democratization" but that process led to the increased power of radicals who dominated local party units. It decreased the influence of more moderate national leaders and members of parliament.

The party seemed to be the captive of the "loony" Left. The influence of the far Left minority in the party frightened voters who otherwise might have voted for a moderate leftist party. In addition, factional disputes within the party over program and organizational matters led the public to question the ability of Labour to form a cohesive government. Moderate voters who had supported Labour in the past deserted the party. In 1983, Labour's share of the vote fell to 27.6 percent of voters, the lowest result since the 1930s. Even within the party, decay had set in. The number of members declined and those who remained became less active (a phenomenon that had facilitated the takeover of many local party units by a handful of radicals).

Most of the next ten years were spent trying to regain voter confidence. Under the leadership of Neil Kinnock, the Labour party worked to expel its radical fringe groups and to reassure voters of its moderation and unity. The party abandoned talk of new nationalizations and accepted many of the Thatcher economic reforms. It promised to show greater attention to the needs of the disadvantaged and to increase government spending on education and social programs. It shifted back to support of the European Union and aligned its defense outlooks with those of other NATO members. However, the task of winning back its lost electorate was not easy. The party's policy shifts and the continued presence of some radical voices within the party's hierarchy left voters wondering who, if anyone, really controlled the Labour party. By 1992 Labour still trailed the Conservative party, with only 34.2 percent of the vote in that year's national election.

After the 1992 elections, a new Labour party leader was chosen, John Smith. After Smith's death in 1994, Tony Blair became party leader. Blair continued the efforts of Kinnock and Smith to bring the party back to the center. He also increased efforts to distinguish the party from the trade unions. The Labour party's origins early in this century were as the political branch of the trade union movement. Much of its membership comes from individuals who join trade unions and as a result become members of the Labour party. Blair and his predecessors have tried to reduce the voice of the trade unions in the Labour party while retaining the money and activists that come from the trade union movement.

The Labour party needed to assert its distinctiveness from the trade unions and to develop its own identity. In Chapter 2 we discussed the waning influence of social class on voting behavior; a party based solely in any one class is unlikely to win the votes needed for parliamentary majority. In addition, Labour's "natural" constituency in working-class voters has eroded as the economy has shifted away from traditional blue-collar industries, as the ability of trade union leaders to deliver the votes of their members has declined (in national elections during the 1980s, fewer than half of trade union members voted for Labour), and as new issues with little relevance to class lines have become the more important political questions.

Labour has begun to champion new causes: environmentalism, equal rights for women, civil liberties, education, and quality-of-life issues. It has endorsed increased integration into Europe and

sees the EU as a way of achieving social changes that cannot be obtained in Britain alone. But the British Labour party, like left-of-center parties elsewhere in Europe, has not yet been able to define a distinctive identity that accords with a changed economic situation and the post–Cold War world. It is a difficult challenge to make this shift to attract the needed new voters while retaining the loyalty of the traditional party supporters who may not see their place in a changing Labour party.

Tony Blair has proven effective in gaining greater freedom from the trade union movement. He has worked to eliminate language in the party's program that suggested it supported public ownership of business and industry. Blair has achieved party unity on the often divisive issue of European integration. Indeed, by the mid-1990s, the Labour party was more unified and more capable of governing than at any time in the last thirty years. The contrast between a unified and moderate Labour party and a divided and wavering Conservative party increased Labour's support in the public.

The Labour party's vision of socialism was always contested within its ranks, and it has been widely interpreted as dictated by electoral needs.[20] Under Tony Blair, the party has moved far from the social-democratic model that prevailed until 1979 and much to the right of the party's position during the early 1980s.[21] Some contend that Blair's "New Labour" is really nothing more than "Tory Lite." In fact, in many ways the Labour party's positions differ substantively and in style from those of the Tories. The differences are more stylistic when dealing with economic and budgetary matters. There the Labour government seems more concerned with administering with greater humanity the policies of previous Conservative governments than with changing these policies. But Blair's government has taken a sharply different road on European issues, constitutional changes, and social policies compared to those practiced by the Conservatives during the 1980s and 1990s.

Now that Labour is back in government, what seems to preoccupy Blair is avoiding confirming the image of Labour as a "tax and spend" party. This leaves many traditional Labour constituencies unsatisfied, notably the trade unions, teachers, and local government officials. But it is a wise course for Blair to follow in the desire to translate his 1997 landslide into a lasting Labour era in power. Labour's vote in 1997 was well below a majority of the voters. It cannot count on the continuation into the future of the special conditions that produced a Labour landslide of 418 seats with a vote of just 43 percent of the voters. Labour must turn its present advantage into a solid and durable electoral base.

Liberal Democrats

The Liberal Democratic party is in part a relic from the last century and in part a product of the polarization of the Conservative and Labour parties in the 1970s and early 1980s. The bulk of its membership and its local base comes from the old Liberal party, which shared dominance of the party system with the Conservatives until after World War I. At that time, the Labour party emerged as one of the two key parties and the Liberal party was relegated to minor party status. It experienced a resurgence in the 1970s as the Conservative and Labour parties foundered on some difficult economic and social issues. It gained even greater strength when the Right wing of the Labour party quit Labour in protest of that party's move to the Left. The resulting Social Democratic party linked itself for election purposes with the old Liberal party.

The Liberals and Social Democrats hoped that a more centrist position would attract moderate voters who were disaffected by the shift to the political extremes by Thatcher's Conservatives and the Left-moving Labour party. The "Alliance" did well in by-elections (elections to replace MPs who die or resign) and local elections. But in national elections, the Alliance was tripped up by the simple plurality electoral system. In 1983 and 1987, the party won over 20 percent of the vote but failed to elect more than a small handful of MPs.

The Liberal Democratic party was formed by a fusion of the Liberals and most of the Social Democrats after the 1987 election loss. The hope was to give more cohesion to this "centrist" grouping. The new party found firm leadership in Paddy Ashdown and greater clarity of program

and purpose. It appeared to be moving to a popular standing that would allow it to hold enough seats in parliament to deny a majority to either Labour or the Conservatives in the 1992 elections. But voters seemed to fear the uncertainty of a "hung parliament" and Liberal Democratic voting support dropped to only 18 percent of the vote in 1992.

With a similar percentage of the vote, the Liberal Democrats did much better in 1997, electing 46 MPs. Despite Labour's overwhelming majority, the Blair government courted support from the Liberal Democrats. Most dramatic was the appointment of the Liberal Democratic party leader, Paddy Ashdown, to join Labour leaders on a Cabinet committee reviewing constitutional reforms. Ashdown also enjoyed several private meetings with Prime Minister Blair. Other Liberal Democrats were invited to meet in one-on-one meetings with other members of the government. In Britain, such efforts at bipartisanship are very unusual. For the Liberal Democrats to benefit from their new privileged position, the Labour government will need to remain popular. And the Liberal Democrats will need to broaden their program to appeal to more voters. Too often they appear as interested only in changing the electoral system to introduce proportional representation. While such a reform would benefit the Liberal Democrats, it is not a popular issue or a broad enough platform for a major party.

British Political Parties and Democracy

Britain's political party system is remarkably durable. The same parties that dominated politics at the start of the twentieth century continue to be the major actors at the end of the century. Of course, they have changed much over the years: Their doctrines are substantially different; they have completely different organizational structures and strategies. In many ways, their changes have promoted and reflected the democratization of Britain.

Many political scientists see political parties as the keys to successful, stable democracy. Britain is often cited as an example to support those claims. Indeed, Britain's parties have

---

PARTY GOVERNMENT AND ACCOUNTABILITY

Contemporary, representative democracy is based on political parties. Political parties offer choices and conduct periodic elections. Thereby parties provide the linkage between people and government otherwise impossible in large societies. Where parties provide clear policy alternatives and disciplined parliamentary majorities, voters can be assured of the accountability of government to their wishes. In Britain, the competition between two parties has created a clear pattern of government and opposition. One party governs; its discipline and unity provide voters with a party to reward or blame based on their judgment about the government's performance. Voters can vote against policies and governments that they do not like by voting for the opposition party. This clear line of accountability between election and government through parties is referred to as *party government*. Britain is one of the countries that comes closest to the ideals of party government that provide for responsible government. American parties, lacking discipline and clear policy differences and operating in a political system that divides power, are much less successful in achieving party government. Voters are thus less able to hold elected officials accountable for their actions in government.

---

promoted effective democracy at times when party systems in other countries contributed to the failure of democracy. Political party chaos and failure brought dictatorship in Germany in the early 1930s, in France in 1940,s and in Italy in the 1920s.

The strength of British parties, with their vigorous but orderly competition and their effectiveness in recruiting and training able political leaders, has been an important source of stability for the entire political system over the past hundred years.

CONCLUSION

In most parts of the world, democratic and nondemocratic countries are experiencing a political-participation explosion caused by the entry into politics of many new actors placing additional demands on government. In Western democracies, such as Britain, this explosion poses important problems since democratic leaders feel obliged by philosophy, and also by fear of electoral sanctions, to try to respond to these demands. However, the new participants—the young, women, immigrant populations, nationality groups, neighborhood action committees, and environmentalists—are not easily absorbed by existing interest groups and parties. New participants aroused to political action by current issues, these activists often are completely unorganized or involved in groups with only a fleeting existence. Their political action may take the forms of protests or demonstrations that mobilize thousands for a brief political fling, but not for the sustained political battles in fact needed to change existing practices and policies. The problem is to direct these participants into channels where their involvement will be more satisfying both in terms of achieving needed policy changes and also in giving interested citizens a sense of political efficacy.

The new issues—such as nuclear power, European integration, immigration and racial relations, and regional interests—cut across the major parties and interest groups. These traditional political forces have their basis in older economic and social cleavages that appear at times to be no longer relevant to the current issues and social divisions. However, new parties and groups reflecting the new concerns have not yet been able to emerge as major political actors; the privileged positions of the existing parties and interest groups—derived from the electoral system and their institutionalized positions in politics—prevent newer parties and groups from breaking into the system. In any case, the major British parties and interest groups have succeeded in adapting to changing priorities and needs for decades, and it seems possible and even likely that they will continue to do so, thus providing constructive channels of participation for most politically interested Britons.

NOTES

[1]Samuel H. Barnes, Max Kaase, et al., *Political Action: Mass Participation in Five Western Democracies* (Beverly Hills, CA: Sage, 1979).

[2]Richard Rose, *Politics in England,* 4th ed. (Boston: Little, Brown, 1986), p. 181.

[3]Geraint Parry et al., *Political Participation and Democracy in Britain* (Cambridge, England: Cambridge University Press, 1992), pp. 42–47.

[4]Russell Dalton et al., eds., *Electoral Change in Advanced Industrial Democracies* (Princeton, NJ: Princeton University Press, 1984).

[5]Early analyses of the 1997 election include David Butler and Dennis Kavanagh, *The British General Election of 1997* (New York: St. Martin's, 1997) and Anthony King, et al., *New Labour Triumphs* (New York: Chatham House, 1997).

[6]Anna Coote and Polly Pattulo, *Power and Prejudice: Women and Politics* (London: Weidenfeld and Nicolson, 1990), and April Carter, *The Politics of Women's Rights* (White Plains, NY: Longmans, 1988).

[7]Joni Lovenduski, "Gender Politics: A Breakthrough for Women," *Parliamentary Affairs* 50 (October 1997): 708–719.

[8]R. N. Punnett, *British Government and Politics,* 5th ed. (Chicago: Dorsey, 1988), p. 137.

[9]Ibid., p. 127.

[10]David Butler and Dennis Kavanagh, *The British General Election of October 1974* (London: Macmillan, 1975), p. 345.

[11]Jorgen S. Rasmussen, "Women's Role in Contemporary British Politics: Impediments to Parliamentary Candidature," *Parliamentary Affairs* 36 (Summer 1983): 300–315.

[12]Paul Byrne, "The Politics of the Women's Movement," *Parliamentary Affairs* 49 (January 1996): 333–342.

[13]Wyn Grant, "Pressure Groups," in Lynton Robins and Bill Jones, eds. *Half Century of British Politics* (New York: St. Martin's, 1997).

[14]Jens P. F. Thomsen, *British Politics and Trade Unions in the 1980s: Governing Against Pressure* (Aldershot, England: Dartmouth, 1996).

[15]David Marsh, *The New Politics of British Trade Unions: Union Power and the Thatcher Legacy* (London: Macmillan, 1992).

[16]Kevin Moloney, *Lobbyists for Hire* (Aldershot, England: Dartmouth, 1996).

[17]Jorgen Rasmussen, "British Conservatives: A Dominant Party in Crisis," in Frank L. Wilson, ed., *The European Center-Right at the End of the Century* (New York: St. Martin's, 1998).

[18]Europeans and others use the term "liberal" to refer to the free enterprise, capitalist views that Americans associate with the political Right. The use of "liberal" to refer to left-of-center politics is unique to North America.

[19]Earl A. Reitan, *Tory Radicalism: Margaret Thatcher, John Major, and the Transformation of Modern Britain, 1979–1997* (Lanham, MD: Rowman & Littlefield, 1998).

[20]Steven Fielding, ed., *The Labour Party: Socialism and Society Since 1951* (Manchester, England: Manchester University Press, 1997).

[21]David Butler and Dennis Kavanagh, *The British General Election of 1997* (New York: St. Martin's, 1997), pp. 46–67.

Chapter 5

Political Leaders in Britain

Democracy means government by the people, but in practice some people are more politically engaged than others. Those individuals who are actively engaged and achieve positions of responsibility in the political framework make up the political elite. The word *elite* often carries negative connotations of rule by a closed circle. But this need not be the case. The relative openness and responsiveness of the political elite are of vital importance in democracies, which claim to provide government by and for the people. This chapter will examine three parts of the political leadership: the elected political leaders, the civil servants, and the military.

The scope of influence for members of the political leadership is influenced by the political context in which they operate. The limited scope of government in liberal democracies such as Britain means that the political leadership must share important decision making with a number of autonomous, nonpolitical bodies: unions and private management help set wages and prices; churches and social clubs help establish moral and ethical codes; educators and parents' groups help determine education policy; banks, insurance companies, and other private financial

groups help regulate the economy; and so forth. This is true in Britain. The pluralist nature of British society dictates a plurality of leadership, of which the political leadership is usually the most important. Nonpolitical leaders can make social and economic decisions that have wide-ranging effects. For example, a private firm's decision to close unprofitable textile factories or shipyards can have important economic and political effects on the regions in question. The political leadership's ability to control politics is thus limited not only by the difficulty of imposing controls on large and complex societies but also by the fact that many decisions are made by autonomous groups beyond its control.

The setting is not only pluralist but also competitive, in that officeholders regularly confront rivals who wish to replace them. In Britain the competition between alternative sets of leaders is highly institutionalized. The leader of the opposition and the shadow government offer a credible substitute for the existing government. Some critics see a good deal of overlap among the various elites, especially between the business elite and the Conservative-party leadership. But the various elites have different goals and clienteles to defend. There is no evidence to suggest a conspiracy among the elites to exercise political power in their own narrow interests. The very multiplicity and open competition of these elites make such connivance unlikely.

ELECTED NATIONAL OFFICIALS

I grew so rich that I was sent,
By a pocket borough into Parliament.
I always voted at my party's call,
And I never thought of thinking for myself at all.
I thought so little they rewarded me,
By making me the ruler of the Queen's Navee![1]

As is true of all good satire, there is an element of truth in this verse from the Gilbert and Sullivan operetta *H.M.S. Pinafore.* The character in the operetta was patterned after a real-life First Lord of the Admiralty, Sir William H. Smith, and the jesting comments about wealth and party loyalty remain potential points of criticism about the recruitment of contemporary British public officials.

The political leaders are heterogeneous in that they come from a wide variety of social backgrounds but they are by no means a faithful reflection of society as a whole.[2] The national elected officials tend to be male, wealthy, upper middle class, and highly educated. As is the case in many countries, family ties often are very useful for aspiring politicians. The children of past political leaders often become leaders in the next generation because of family contacts and because they have learned from the experiences of their parents. It is not surprising, then, that of the 20 twentieth-century prime ministers, six have fathers who were once in Parliament and seven have children who later served in Parliament.

Among the most significant inequities in the composition of the British political elite is the lack of women. Women make up approximately 52 percent of the total population but account for only 18.5 percent of the MPs (members of Parliament) elected in 1997 and only a few of the ministers. Yet these limited achievements were touted as historic breakthroughs. The presence of women in national politics is growing slowly. The Labour party now requires constituency parties to prepare women-only short lists of nominees for parliamentary seats in Conservative-held marginal districts. These quotas assisted women to increase their presence in national politics in 1997. The prevalence of party positions over personal agendas that is so much a part of British parliamentary tradition may very well limit the ability of women MPs to bring women's issues to greater prominence even as their numbers increase.

As might be expected, the House of Commons is composed of well-educated professionals or business people. The Conservative party tends to attract as MPs more business executives, lawyers, and farmers, while the Labour party tends to attract educators, blue-collar workers or trade union officials, and white-collar workers. There is a greater number of MPs from modest, working-class backgrounds than is the case in the U.S. Congress. The reason is the closer tie between the Labour party and British trade unions. Many of the Conservative MPs are graduates ("old boys") of the private boarding schools, while few Labour MPs have such exclusive and elitist training. The majority of MPs in both parties have university degrees, but most Conservatives have their degrees from Oxford and Cambridge while most Labour MPs have degrees from less prestigious "red-brick" universities.

In Britain the political careers of national leaders often begin with election to local offices.[3] The next stage is usually election to the House of Commons. Almost invariably, leaders serve long apprenticeships in Parliament before moving into ministerial positions. In the United States, the president's cabinet frequently includes non-politicians, members of the opposition party, or even individuals the president has never met. Such recruitment of outsiders is alien to the British political system.[4] British cabinet ministers are almost always veteran members of the House of Commons or the House of Lords and are never from the opposition party (except in wartime coalitions). Cabinet ministers are usually also party officers with long histories of service to the party. Prime ministers are always members of Commons, with an average of 15–20 years of parliamentary service prior to selection as a prime minister. They also have usually had several years of experience as ministers in varying posts during previous governments. They are party loyalists who have earned the position of party leader through years of devoted party work.

NOMINATION OF CANDIDATES FOR THE HOUSE OF COMMONS

In the United States, candidates for virtually all public offices are nominated through primary elections. Primary elections were introduced as a means of enhancing democracy by giving citizens a direct voice in the choice of candidates. In practice, primary elections have often failed to achieve this democratic goal due to low voter turnout and the likely dominance of the primary elections by the more dedicated voters but not from representative samples from the two parties. In recent years, Americans have complained frequently and loudly at election times about the poor candidates that emerged from the primaries to be their choices in the general elections. It is not unusual for American parties to find themselves "stuck" with candidates that differ from the party's overall philosophy or particular policy positions. They can do nothing about it, and it muddles choices for voters who cannot count on a Democratic candidate representing the viewpoints of the Democratic party or on a Republican candidate to reflect the dominant trends of the party.

In Britain, the approach is different. There are no primary elections; parties select their own candidates in meetings of party committees in each constituency. The national party headquarters often establish guidelines for the selection process. For example, the Labour party requires its constituent parties to include women in its lists and sometimes insists that only women be listed. The national parties also control the use of the party's label: no one can claim to be a Conservative or Labour party candidate without the approval of the respective national party.

Each party dominates the choice of its candidates, and voters are then given the opportunity of choosing between the candidates selected by the parties, another aspect of the principles of party government described in Chapter 4. The strength of British parties in the nomination process means party discipline and loyalty are stronger among their elected MPs, party distinctions are maintained, and voters' choices are clearer and easier to make.

There has been a tendency over the past few years for parties to select younger, less experienced leaders.[5] John Major, Tony Blair, and William Hague all are examples of the search for younger, more telegenic leaders in an era when the party's image is shaped by its leader. But none was a newcomer or an outsider; Major and Blair had both served over 10 years in Commons prior to their selection as their parties' leaders.

The top-level leaders tend to have remarkably similar social, as well as political, backgrounds. Conservative ministers tend to be products of British public schools, and especially of Eton. They have usually graduated from Cambridge or Oxford and are upper middle class or upper class in social background. The Thatcher cabinet in 1986 illustrates these tendencies: fifteen out of twenty-two ministers were "old boys" from the elite, residential public schools; another two were from private schools in London; twenty were university graduates, and all but five of them were from Oxford or Cambridge.[6] When Labour is in power, the ministers are generally products of

government-run schools. The typical Labour minister attended a less prestigious university than either of the Oxbridge schools. The Labour ministers' social backgrounds are more mixed than those of Conservatives; some come from working-class and labor union backgrounds, many from the middle class, and a few from the upper class.

In the last twenty years, there has been a subtle shift in the kinds of people seeking seats in Commons.[7] Whereas in the past many amateur politicians sought office as a fitting climax to careers in other fields, today more and more people see parliamentary service and politics as appropriate careers in themselves. They tend to take their parliamentary duties more seriously than did earlier MPs and devote more time to building personal followings based on service to their constituents.[8] This change in recruitment patterns may well affect the overall political system. For example, career MPs often assert their independence from party leaders in ways that amateur MPs avoided. Part of the explanation for the revival of Commons is found in the presence of this new type of career politician in that body.

The leadership-development process and the similarity of leaders' backgrounds result in a group who share experiences and outlooks. They have worked together in the party for years; they have collaborated in Parliament; they may even have served together in a previous government. Many have social ties from university and boarding school days. This phenomenon fosters teamwork and unity and contributes to the gentility often noted in British politics. However, it may also stifle initiative and innovation. Too much inbreeding may accentuate the already unrepresentative nature of leadership and inhibit bold departures from established policies and practices by either party.

Critics of British democracy often point to the social background of the political leaders as evidence of the fact that the "little people"—the poor, minority groups, the less educated—do not have a voice in British politics. It is clear that the social backgrounds of the leaders are not representative of the population as a whole, although, in comparative terms, the British elite includes more individuals from modest working-class origins than is the case in the United States. Despite the predominance of the wealthy and the highly educated in the British political elite, there is no evidence that this means that the poor are unrepresented in government. Often their interests are championed ably by leaders from the most affluent sections of society, even from the titled aristocracy. There is little evidence to suggest that their social backgrounds make any difference in the conduct or policy preferences of political leaders. The entry into the political leadership of large numbers of individuals from more modest backgrounds would not necessarily mean any change in the attitudes or behavior in office of the leadership. Indeed, individuals from modest social backgrounds who succeed are often the least tolerant of other disadvantaged individuals who have not been able to improve their lot.

Leadership Styles and Skills

In Britain, leaders from both major parties have usually demonstrated a pragmatic approach to government. Leaders who appeared ideologically committed in intraparty debates while out of power generally became pragmatic once in positions of national leadership. In the past, the existence of broad consensus among political leaders from all parties on major policy orientations and the ways to achieve them encouraged a moderate, nonideological approach.[9] In the late 1970s the continued economic malaise and government's seeming inability to correct it brought criticism of this consensus between the parties. As a result, both the Conservative and Labour parties chose more ideologically committed leaders with more radical approaches to the economic problems. In office, these leaders, too, accepted pragmatic compromise of their principles rather than rigid adherence to ideology.

The parliamentary system of government originally connoted a collective form of leadership in which a cabinet of ministers shares power. In Britain the principle of the "collective responsibility" of the government derives from this notion. While individual ministers are held accountable for their personal conduct and the actions of their departments, the whole cabinet is collectively responsible for decisions made by the government. Thus cabinet decisions must be accepted and publicly defended by all ministers, even those who strenuously opposed them in the privacy of cabinet meetings. If a minister cannot defend a decision, he or she is obligated to resign. While this practice seems strange to Americans accustomed to accounts of disagreements in the president's cabinet, the doctrine of collective responsibility does keep the lines of political responsibility clear. The public knows that the entire cabinet is accountable for all acts of government.

The growing powers of the prime minister have enhanced the personalist nature of leadership in Britain. Voters increasingly see the prime minister and a few other top leaders as embodiments of the government and the ruling party. Thus leaders with unattractive images reflect unfavorably on the government and the party. Though the prime minister is not directly elected, there is evidence suggesting that voters often cast their ballots for the candidate of the party whose leader they would like to see as prime minister. Elections are sometimes won or lost on the basis of the impressions made by the leaders. However, the personality of the party leader is not as important as in American politics. Thus, Margaret Thatcher's Conservatives won the 1979 election even though polls showed that most voters viewed her rival James Callaghan as a more desirable prime minister. Indeed, too heavy a reliance on the personality of the party leader may well cost a party the election.

The British political leader must be concerned with maintaining a solid standing in the public eye because of the electoral implications of declining public approval. Moreover, the leader's ability to control his or her own party and retain the confidence of colleagues in government depends on a favorable public image. Prime ministers whose standings in public opinion polls fall often experience challenges within their own parties. An unpopular leader is likely to be an electoral liability who may find it difficult to persuade colleagues to support or follow his or her guidance. Indeed, it was such a concern among Conservative MPs about Margaret Thatcher's public standing that produced her political demise in 1990.

Above all, leadership styles in Britain, as in other Western democracies, reflect the electoral preoccupations of the leaders, whose tenure depends upon maintaining sufficient public confidence to win the next election. The prevailing pragmatism reflects the public's general lack of interest in abstract political ideologies and concern with specific issues. Personalism follows from the voters' growing tendency to focus attention on the top political leader. And leaders' concern for public opinion and image consciousness stem from recognition of their dependence on public support in and between elections to maintain the confidence and cooperation of colleagues.

BUREAUCRATS AND POLITICIANS: WHO'S IN CHARGE?

The bureaucracy must be subject to the political leaders in a democracy if the people are truly to retain control of their government. Elected officials subject to the voters' sanctions must control the unelected and thus democratically irresponsible bureaucrats. But it is unrealistic to expect bureaucracies to have no say in policy making. It is also undesirable, since bureaucrats represent not only their own interests but also the interests of the clientele they serve. For example, governmental social workers often defend the interests and needs of their clients, the poor and disabled. However, if the lines of democratic responsibility are to be maintained, it must ultimately be an elected official who regulates the bureaucracy's actions.

In Britain the burden of controlling the civil service falls on a comparatively few politically responsible leaders. This situation contrasts with that of the United States, where each federal department has many—sometimes as many as several hundred—top-level political appointees who oversee the permanent bureaucrats. In the typical British government department, there are only three or four political leaders: the minister and a couple of parliamentary secretaries, all of whom are MPs. The rest of the managerial positions, including the permanent secretary, deputy secretaries, and the minister's private secretary, are all career civil servants removable only on grounds of malfeasance in office. The American principle of control has been to staff all policy-making positions in the administration with politically reliable appointees to assure that the civil service implements the president's policies. The British have based their approach to political control of the administration on the principle that civil servants will be neutral and will faithfully execute the policies of whatever government is in place.

Even the top-level political leaders in Britain have little time to supervise their civil servants. As elected members of Parliament as well as members of the government, they have multiple demands on their time: attendance at parliamentary sessions and committee meetings, public appearances and speeches, party leadership obligations, and the need to tend to their own parliamentary constituencies.

Despite this lack of political personnel in supervisory positions, the British civil service remains loyal to the political leadership. Political neutrality and responsiveness to political control are firmly established as norms of the civil service, which explains the British bureaucracy's impressive record of political control and accountability. There have been some abuses, particularly involving bureaucrats' selective use of information to justify a given course of action to a minister. However, the civil service's general record of nonpartisanship and acceptance of political direction is good.

The social backgrounds of senior civil servants tie them more closely to the Conservatives, through "old boy" networks and general social attitudes, than to the Labour party. Thus the key test of the bureaucracy's submissiveness to political leadership occurs when Labour assumes power. Its performance has been surprisingly good. Labour governments have found civil servants not merely willing to follow political guidance but almost eager to cooperate in meeting Labour's objectives. For example, when the Labour government came to power in 1974, Labour ministers arrived at their Whitehall offices on the day of their appointment and found that the civil servants had already drawn up proposals to implement the policies they had advocated during the election. The proposals were ready for submission and the cabinet was able to act on some of them the next day.[10] Similar cooperation was found when the Labour ministers came to their offices in 1997 after almost 20 years of Conservative dominance. In the powerful ministry of the Treasury, the civil servants who had loyally served Conservative ministers for the past 18 years lined the stairs to warmly applaud the arrival of their new Labour minister.

Some former ministers, especially those from Labour governments, have complained about uncooperative civil servants.[11] The complaints usually do not involve allegations of political bias; rather, they assert that the civil servants in a given department develop a "departmental policy" or viewpoint, which they then seek to persuade ministers from both parties to accept: Bureaucrats use their longer experience in the department to give credibility to their positions; they flood the minister with minor matters that might have been decided elsewhere to prevent the minister from pushing a new and unwanted policy; they withhold information from the minister or selectively give him or her information that will support the departmental viewpoint. An example of this was the withholding of information by civil servants in the energy department about an accident in a nuclear power station at the time the energy minister was deciding on expansion of the plant. The civil servants feared that the news might prejudice the decision against expansion and thus counter "the department's policy" in favor of fur-

ther growth of the nuclear power capacity.[12] In addition, the long tenure of civil servants in a single department sometimes gives them tunnel vision, in that they are unable to see new approaches to problems they have dealt with in one way over the years. They have little incentive to be creative, since any credit for innovation would go to the minister and any failure would reflect poorly on their careers.

While civil servants are apolitical, they are very ready to defend the prerogatives and interests of the bureaucrats against challenges from both Conservative and Labour governments. Some recent examples demonstrate this resistance to change. In the 1970s, the bureaucrats effectively sabotaged a major reform of the civil service. One critic noted that the civil servants "tore the heart" out of the reforms while all the time maintaining that the changes were being implemented.[13] Even Margaret Thatcher's strong leadership faced a battle in overcoming bureaucratic resistance to her goals of cutting the size of the civil service. Eventually, she succeeded—briefly—in reducing the number of bureaucrats but only at the cost of sacrificing other civil service reforms that she felt important.[14] Now, the Blair government faces a battle with the bureaucracy over its practice of appointing non-civil service advisers to assist ministers in developing perspectives different from those of the civil servants, views that sometimes are frozen in long-standing "departmental policies."

The problem of maintaining political control over the burgeoning government bureaucracies is one shared by all modern states, democratic or not. Governments have tried a variety of means to exercise this control, ranging from the American practice of flooding the top levels of the administration with political appointees to the Soviet technique of elaborate, parallel bureaucracies that check on each other. Britain's approach has been to rely on civil servants to accept the norm of subservience to political leaders. This norm appears to be well established in Britain, and it seems effectively to deter civil servants from favoring one party's policies over the other's. But it does not deter the civil servants from defending *their* own corporate interests: their jobs, their lines of authority, their expertise. In an era when the bureaucracy's size and cumbersomeness have become key political issues, the bureaucrats' resistance to internal reforms becomes a clear challenge to the political authority and preeminence of the elected leaders.

UNQUESTIONED CIVILIAN MASTERY OF THE MILITARY

The military hero, traditionally pictured on a white horse rushing to the aid of his troubled country, often plays an important part in politics. In many countries, the military is the most important political actor, periodically challenging and overthrowing the civilian government. Not so in Britain. The most recent military intervention in British politics occurred in the seventeenth century, when the revolt of the army brought about a military dictatorship under Oliver Cromwell. The king was executed; unsympathetic members of Parliament were purged; ultimately Parliament was expelled and the Puritan army became the government of England. Although the interregnum lasted only 12 years, it left in the British a deeply ingrained mistrust of political action by the army and a strong antimilitarism.

The primary domestic political activity of the British military is to convey its needs and interests to the government. As in the United States, there is a military lobby pressing for greater defense expenditures or to support strategic military priorities, but it is neither as visible nor as powerful as the military-industrial complex in the United States. This circumstance in part reflects the nature of the British political scene; interest groups rarely devote much attention to Parliament since party discipline assures Parliament's acceptance of government proposals. No doubt the military does argue its needs—as indeed it should—within the ministry of defense and related ministries. But most commentaries on interest group politics in Britain do not list the military among the most active and powerful pressure groups.

The British military's lack of politicization is especially surprising in light of the developments of the last 50 years. Once a world power of the first order, Britain is now dependent upon other nations for its defense. Britain's navy, long the world's most powerful, has slipped to the rank of a second-rate power. Britain's nuclear weapons program has been curtailed, and other important military procurement programs were precipi-

tously canceled by politicians. There are far too many high-ranking officials for the military tasks at hand. The army's long involvement in controlling urban guerrilla warfare in Northern Ireland has also tested the traditional norm of civilian mastery of the military. Despite these numerous grounds for discontent and politicization, the British military has not become a major political actor.

An indication of the military's political aloofness is the near-total absence of former military figures in the political world. It is not unusual in other countries for retired officers to pursue political careers; examples are Eisenhower in the United States and de Gaulle in France. However, in the past 300 years, there has only been one British prime minister with a military background, and that was over 150 years ago.

The most important restraint on the British military has been parliamentary control of the army and navy. Members of Parliament recognized early that the military was potentially a weapon the monarch might use against them. As a result, budgetary controls over the military were imposed as a means of assuring not only civilian control but also Parliament's independence from the monarch. Another important factor in the control of the military is Britain's historical reliance on the navy, rather than a land army, as its primary means of defense. It is harder for a navy deployed on the seas to intervene in domestic politics than it is for an army based in the heart of the country.

More important than formal and legal restraints on the military is the impact of a 300-year-old tradition of political uninvolvement. The socialization of military officers informally instills the norms of civilian supremacy and abstention from political action. The informed restraints imposed by such values and orientations make it virtually unthinkable for a British officer to defy civilian authority and seek public support for a political act.

POLITICAL LEADERSHIP IN BRITAIN

Democracies need strong leaders as much as do any other kinds of government. In democracies, however, the leaders need to be accountable to the citizenship. A balance between effective leadership and democratic accountability is sometimes difficult to obtain. The British have been more successful than other democracies in recruiting and bringing to the fore political leaders who are capable and effective but who also observe the niceties of democracy. Britons are not afraid of strong leaders. Indeed, weak or ineffective leaders are generally despised by the public. In part, that was the reason for John Major's downfall. Unable to control his own followers, unclear in his vision, and unable to impose those values he did have, Major soon lost the confidence of his party and the electorate in general. In contrast, Tony Blair's success is due in large part to his effective leadership as he imposed his ideas on what had long been a divided and squabbling party. Blair's leadership, at least so far, has not led to significant concerns about his responsiveness to the democratic controls of his fellow MPs and the public's attitude.

NOTES

[1] W. S. Gilbert and Arthur Sullivan, "When I was a lad . . . ," *H.M.S. Pinafore.*

[2] Pippa Norris and Joni Lovenduski, *Political Representation and Recruitment* (Cambridge, England: Cambridge University Press, 1994).

[3] Dennis Kavanagh, *British Politics: Continuities and Change,* 2nd ed. (Oxford, England: Oxford University Press, 1990), p. 71.

[4] In 1964, Prime Minister Harold Wilson named five non-members of Parliament to his government. Except during wartime, this was unprecedented. Since 1964, no other non-parliamentarians have been named to the government.

[5] Donley T. Studlar, *Great Britain: Decline or Renewal* (Boulder, CO: Westview, 1996), pp. 94–97.

[6] R. M. Punnett, *British Government and Politics,* 5th ed. (Chicago: Dorsey, 1988), p. 139.

[7] Anthony King, "The Rise of the Career Politician in Britain—and Its Consequences," *British Journal of Political Science* (July 1981): 452–485.

[8] Bruce E. Cain, "Blessed Be the Tie That Unbinds: Constituency Work and the Vote Swing in Great Britain," *Political Studies* (March 1983): 103–111.

[9] On the development of this consensus, see Samuel H. Beer, *British Politics in the Collectivist Age* (New York: Knopf, 1965). See also Geoffrey Smith and Nelson W. Polsby, *British Government and Its Discontents* (New York: Basic Books, 1981), pp. 89–101.

[10] Harold Wilson, *The Governance of Britain* (London: Weidenfeld and Nicholson, 1976), pp. 42–43.

[11] Richard Crossman, *The Diaries of a Cabinet Minister,* 3 vols. (London: Hamilton, 1975–1977) and Brian Sedgemore, *The Secret Constitution: An Analysis of the Political Establishment* (London: Hodder and Stoughton, 1980).

[12] Smith and Polsby, *British Government and Its Discontents,* p. 152.

[13] Peter Kellner and Lord Crowther-Hunt, *The Civil Servants: An Inquiry Into Britain's Ruling Class* (London: Macdonald, 1980).

[14] Geoffrey K. Fry, "The Development of the Thatcher Government's 'Grand Strategy' for the Civil Service: A Public Policy Perspective," *Public Administration* 62, no. 3, (1984): 322–335.

Chapter 6

Britain's Political Performance

Democracy in Britain evolved during times when the sphere of governmental activity was limited generally to providing for national defense, maintaining domestic order, providing a currency, and minor policing of the economy. During the twentieth century, government's role has vastly expanded as people have come to expect more and more from the state. Sixty or 70 years ago, an economic recession was viewed as the product of natural economic cycles; now it is viewed as the result of government mismanagement of the economy. In the past a drought was thought of as a natural disaster; now the government is often held responsible, if not for its occurrence, at least for coming up with steps to mitigate its impact. In Britain now, as elsewhere, people expect the state to protect them not only against internal and external threats to their lives but also against unemployment, inflation, illness, accident, polluted air, inadequate housing, and so forth. They also expect government action to protect equal rights and freedom. Those who study how people vote—and the politicians who seek the votes—feel that voters choose between parties on the basis of how well the government has met these multiple expectations.

This trend toward greater government involvement seems irreversible. It occurs whether conservatives or socialists are in office. Thus, between 1951 and 1977, public spending in Britain (and in the United States) increased in real terms 23 out of the 26 years.[1] Even conservative leaders who proclaim their intent to reduce government's role—such as Margaret Thatcher or Ronald Reagan—have failed to reverse the trend. They can and do redirect government action to benefit different portions of society and shift government involvement from the national to the local level. But they have little success in actually reducing the level of government involvement in society. The reason is that while everyone talks about eliminating government involvement in general, few want government to stop those activities that further their own economic or ideological interests. Over the long run, the large industrial populations of modern democracies such as Britain, faced with decreasing natural resources, can only expect government's role to increase. This causes concern among those interested in the future of Western democracy. Democracy emerged as a limited form of government, but as the limits on government's role are progressively removed government becomes much more pervasive and powerful. Furthermore, citizens place greater demands on government, and they also seem more willing to mobilize to protest inadequate performance in meeting these demands.

The overloading of government threatens its effectiveness and efficiency.[2] It also undermines its legitimacy as citizens complain about growing government expenditures and apparent failures despite high costs to meet new expectations. At the same time, the insistence on greater government action to assure human rights and economic equality for immigrants and Northern Irish Catholics provides additional danger to political stability. This chapter evaluates Britain's performance in economic matters, the extent of political stability or instability, and the state of human rights.

A MANAGED ECONOMY AND WELFARE

A woman whose husband was in prison was struggling to support herself and her eight children. The rent was in arrears so a social security officer came to investigate to see if the woman qualified for supplementary benefits such as money for rent and food. The children were scruffy, the house was damp, and there was no hot water. This brought in the school-care people. Prison welfare officers were called in connection with the father's situation. One child was ill and the regular health visitor became involved. The water drains failed and this was the concern of a public health inspector.[3]

This summary of one London family's problems and government's role in solving them illustrates the extent of the government's involvement in British society. Even before World War II, the social and economic activities of government had begun to grow. Wartime needs considerably furthered the expansion of government, and the postwar government of Clement Attlee enacted a series of major political, social, and economic reforms establishing a managed economy and welfare state.

A Troubled Economy

For the next 30 years, government played a major role in managing the economy and in assuring welfare protection for its citizens. A broad con-

sensus on the appropriateness of such government action existed among political leaders of all major parties and the public in general. By the middle of the 1970s, however, this consensus began to break down as citizens questioned the government's ability to promote economic growth and control the growing costs of social welfare benefits. Britain's economy had not kept pace with the rapid growth that other West European industrial democracies had experienced since the end of World War II. In the mid-1950s, Britain ranked in the ten richest industrial countries of the world with a per capita gross national product greater than that of West Germany and five times that of Japan. By the end of the 1970s, it ranked in the mid-twenties and had fallen far below the per capita GNP of both Germany and Japan.

In seeking to reverse this economic decline, Margaret Thatcher attacked the old social and economic consensus.[4] She contended that excessive social welfare benefits were draining the country's economic strength. Thatcher Conservatives further claimed that high taxes and government economic entanglement had paralyzed individual initiative. In effect, the claim was that the social welfare state destroyed private enterprise and had produced Britain's economic decline.

So frequently is this explanation of the effects of the social welfare state used that it has been dubbed the "British disease" and is widely accepted as a self-evident fact. But there are reasons to question whether the social welfare state is the real cause of Britain's decline. If it is indeed "creeping socialism" that has caused Britain's economic problems, we could expect that other countries with extensive welfare systems and government economic involvement would experience economic problems similar to those of Britain. Most other West European democracies have social welfare programs that are as sweeping and as costly as those in Britain, and yet these countries have prospered. Many also have public sectors— those parts of the economy controlled directly by the government such as the civil service and nationalized enterprises—that are as large or larger than Britain's public sector.

These countries have all done much better than Britain and as well economically as have countries with smaller public sectors; all of these industrialized democracies have thriving economies. British workers receive less in unemployment benefits than do workers in all other industrial countries, but it is British workers, not the more highly insured French, German, or Danish workers, who are accused of avoiding work because of unemployment protection. British trade unions are powerful, but labor unrest cannot be blamed for the economic problems.

In spite of the weakness of its logic, the social welfare state explanation guided Thatcher's economic policies from 1979 to 1990. The Thatcher government sought to reduce the role of the state in the economy and to dismantle social welfare benefits. Public housing was sold to its tenants; publicly owned enterprises were privatized; government economic regulations were greatly reduced. There was less success in reducing social programs such as the public health service that proved popular in spite of their high costs. The results were generally positive in that Britain's economic statistics were comparable to those of other European democracies. By the beginning of the 1990s, however, the seeming gains of the Thatcher era were reversed by Britain's worst economic recession since the worldwide depression of the 1930s. Britain's economy was plagued by the same problems that it had encountered in the 1970s: unemployment, inflation, high interest rates, imbalance of international payments, and little or no economic growth.[5]

Despite these problems, the British economy rebounded more quickly than did most other European economies. By the mid-1990s, British unemployment was half that in Germany or France; economic growth was slightly more rapid than that in most other European countries. Inflation, on the other hand, remained more of a problem, compared to other EU economies. Britain had not yet pulled its per capita gross domestic product up to the levels of the leading European countries. In comparison with major economic rivals, Britain has low labor costs that allow it to attract new businesses interested in establishing themselves in the European Union.

Underlying these signs of economic success, however, there is much public concern about the economy. The thriving economy should have been an asset for the Conservatives in the 1997 elections. But voters were skeptical of the Conservative government's economic achievements and of the government's ability to continue them in the future. New job opportunities are often lower-paid positions than those that people held in the past. Parts of the country, especially areas where heavy industries once sustained the economy, still face high and chronic unemployment problems.

The new Labour government of Tony Blair continued the basic economic policies inherited from its Conservative antecedents. One important change was the granting of autonomy to the central bank in setting interest rates and monitoring the currency supply. In doing so, Britain followed other European countries. As the 1990s progressed, there were concerns among some British economists that another recession might hit at the end of the decade. Their concerns came from weakening of traditional markets in Asia as a result of that region's economic crisis. There was also concern that the strength of the British pound compared to other major world currencies made British goods more expensive in international markets. Another concern was the impact of Britain's self-exclusion from the new European monetary system and single currency (the euro). Investors looking for places to establish businesses within the European Union might be discouraged from choosing Britain because of its lukewarm attitude toward the EU and its refusal to use the euro.

During the second half of the twentieth century, Britain's economic growth has been slower than most other countries. To some extent this reflects a deliberate choice of life-style that places other values higher than economic expansion. Thus, the British have protected the beautiful rolling fields, criss-crossed by hedgerows and trees, of their rural settings because of their esthetic value rather than flattening and extending the fields for more economical farming. Workers prefer remaining in their neighborhoods, where they have established friendships and families, to moving away to areas where jobs pay more. Even in times of great economic adversity, Britons have remained loyal to these values and to the broader value of democracy.

Britain and the European Union

The European Union (EU) began in the early 1950s as a means of coordinating economic actions among West European countries. The initial members included France, West Germany, Italy, Belgium, the Netherlands, and Luxembourg. Britain was invited to join in the negotiations that created the European Coal and Steel Community, the first of the organizations that now form the European Union.[6] For a variety of political and economic reasons, the British declined to participate. Many Britons did not feel a part of continental Europe and still oriented their perspectives to the broader world and the far-flung British Empire, even as that empire was breaking up.[7] In the mid-1950s, the six members of the European Coal and Steel Community decided to broaden their economic cooperation by creating the European Economic Community (EEC), more popularly known as the European Common Market. Again, Britain was invited to join but declined.

With its principal base of operations in Brussels, the Common Market began to impose itself on the economic policy making of its member countries. The Common Market did away with all tariffs between its members and erected a common external tariff for goods coming into the Common Market from all the rest of the world. In addition, the Common Market established uniform policies for certain economic activities such as transportation, nuclear energy, and agriculture. The Common Agricultural Program was especially well developed and eventually assumed all government policy making on farming and agricultural subsidies.

Both the Common Market and the earlier Coal and Steel Community were enormously successful. They achieved cooperation in the efforts to rebuild the devastated post-World War II economies of their member countries. More important, they expanded markets for enterprises within its member countries and thereby stimulated an exceptional era of economic growth and prosperity.

Britain's response to the growing success of the EEC was the creation of a rival organization, the European Free Trade Area (EFTA). It sought to achieve some of the advantages of a free trade area but without the entanglements that the EEC brought. EFTA was almost an immediate failure. By the end of the 1950s, Britain sought to join the EEC. Negotiations were long and difficult with Britain seeking many special exemptions. Eventually, French President Charles de Gaulle announced that France would veto Britain's admission to the Common Market. Throughout the 1960s, the Common Market continued to thrive and Britain sought off and on, but always unsuccessfully, to renew negotiations for its membership.

It was not until 1973, after de Gaulle's death, that Britain was able to win membership into the European Community (EC)—as the Common Market was then called. However, it achieved this goal at an inauspicious moment: the European Community almost immediately faced its first recession due to the energy crisis of the 1970s and emerging, rival economies in Asia. As a result, Britain was paying rather heavy costs in making the economic shifts to the EC standards at the same time that the benefits of membership were declining due to the worldwide economic crisis. There was considerable pressure within Britain to withdraw, but a 1975 popular referendum confirmed the will of the British people to continue as part of the EC.

During the 1980s, Prime Minister Margaret Thatcher sought successfully to win concessions for Britain in the amount of membership dues. She fought hard for the British point of view and national interests. Of course, all countries sought to achieve advantages for themselves in EU activities, usually discretely and quietly. What made Thatcher different was her single-mindedness and her blatant threats and badgering. The result was that Britain gained a reputation as a "bad partner" in the EC. The public bickering with the EC also fostered internal opposition to the EC in the United Kingdom, especially among Conservatives. After Thatcher's forced resignation, her successor John Major inherited these problems. His prime ministership was characterized by efforts to renew Britain's reputation as a good member of the European Union (EU)—as it became known in 1994. This was difficult when his own party backbenchers forced him to have Britain "opt out" of key EU programs such as the Social

Table 6–1   Support for the European Union, 1998

Is your country's membership in the EU a good or a bad thing?

	A Good Thing	A Bad Thing	Neither Good nor Bad	Don't Know
Britain	41%	19%	30%	10%
France	51	13	30	6
Germany	41	13	36	10

Source: Eurobarometer, No. 49, on the web, European Commission, Brussels.

Charter and the single currency. But these concessions were not enough; Major had to fend off continued attacks on the EU and Britain's role in it from the "Euroskeptics" in his own party. This internal division within the Conservative party was an important factor in its loss of public confidence and in its crushing defeat in the 1997 elections.

Labour Prime Minister Tony Blair has moved gradually to reintegrate Britain into the mainstream of the EU. His movements toward Europe are slow because Britons as a whole are among the least supportive of European integration (see Table 6.1). Blair accepted the EU's Social Charter with its mainly symbolic commitments to trade unions and the disadvantaged. Blair continued to keep Britain out of the single currency, but he facilitated the use of the euro by British firms who found it advantageous.

The frequent reverses in Britain's stance toward European integration remains an important hindrance to British efforts to provide leadership within the European Union. As a result, Britain has had to sit by while the French and the Germans provide the initiatives and new ideas for the Union. It will take Blair—and successive prime ministers—many years to win a key role in EU for the United Kingdom.

SOCIAL WELFARE
AND HUMAN DEVELOPMENT

Social welfare is not a new concern for the British government. As early as 1908 the British government enacted an old age pension program, and in 1911 it passed the National Health Insurance Act providing governmental assistance to meet the medical needs of the poor. However, welfare programs enacted since World War II now provide government-sponsored services from the cradle to the coffin.

Attempts to reduce the gap between the wealthy and the poor have included progressive taxation and the providing of necessary social services to all. A major share of the government's receipts comes from a steeply progressive income tax: the higher the income, the greater the tax rate. In addition, estate taxes help to minimize the inheritance of wealth. The government spends heavily on social services targeted toward lower-income groups far more than toward the wealthy: These services include housing, health care, education, and old age pensions. Thus, income is redistributed by taxing the wealthy to aid the poor.

Through such programs, Britain reduced inequality of income distribution and was among the most equal Western democratic societies in the 1970s. In 1938 the wealthiest 10 percent of the population received after taxes 34.4 percent of all personal income; by 1977 that after-tax share of the same group had dropped to 22.3 percent.[8] During the 1980s, however, this trend was reversed and the number of Britons earning less than the average national income grew sharply as the number of very poor increased (see Table 6–2). Between 1977 and 1991, the share of national income controlled by the poorest 10 percent shrank from 4.2 to 3 percent while the share of the wealthiest 10 percent grew from 22 to 25 percent.[9] Social benefits to aid the disadvantaged in Britain have fallen below those in other West European countries.

One of the most successful and popular of Britain's social services is the National Health

Table 6–2 British Population with Income Less Than Half the National Average Income

	Estimated Number	Percentage of Population
1961	5,000,000	10%
1977	3,000,000	5
1991	11,000,000	20

Source: Financial Times, 3 June 1994.

Service (NHS). Founded in 1948, the NHS provides complete medical, dental, and eye care at no charge. Patients may choose their own doctors, and the doctors receive remuneration based on the number of patients on their "panels." Drugs, eyeglasses, and other personal medical supplies are subsidized. The cost of operating the system came to $71.2 billion in 1997.[10] Under the NHS, medical expenses in Britain absorb a smaller portion of gross national product than in the United States, France, or Germany. Although medical costs have risen more slowly in Britain than in the United States, rapid inflation of NHS costs during the 1980s and 1990s forced some reductions in service and the imposition of modest charges for certain medical services.

When Labour returned to power in 1997, they promised reform of the NHS. Specifically, Blair's government proposed to shorten waiting time for appointments with specialists and for nonemergency surgery. Cost pressures are also to be addressed, and that may mean additional cuts in services. Because the public tends to trust the Labour party more than the Conservatives in social welfare issues, the Blair government may be able to make some needed changes in the NHS without angering and frightening the voters. The ability of any government to make major changes in the health program is limited by the fact that Britons regard free access to quality medical care as a basic right.

One of Thatcher's most successful social reforms was the promotion of private home ownership. By the mid-1980s, nearly two-thirds of all British households owned their homes. In part, this came from the sale of council housing to occupants with generous discounts (55 percent) for families occupying the unit for 15 years or more.

As a result, mortgage payments ended up being little more or even less than the council housing rental fees. In addition, government housing subsidies were redirected from the construction or maintenance of council housing to assisting families to purchase their own homes. However, mortgage defaults, declining property values, and homelessness have become major policy problems in the 1990s.

As in the United States, benefits for the long-term unemployed, the disabled, single parents, the elderly, and the disadvantaged have become major political issues. There is much greater tolerance of such programs in Britain than in the United States. The notion of the welfare state has positive connotations for most Britons. But, as in the United States, Britain faces growing concerns about welfare program costs, especially as programs, even popular ones have sky-rocketed in costs. For example, the costs of caring for the disabled increased by four times in the past 20 years.[11] Again, the challenge for the Labour government is to find ways to provide support for the needy without increasing taxes. As in the United States, Blair is pushing a welfare-to-work program to address the problems of many of Britain's needy.

Over the past fifty years or so, the growing social benefits have contributed to overall political stability in Britain by integrating the working class into the society, alleviating some of the worst effects of persisting economic inequality, and providing a sense of security about the future to those with modest means. Some now suggest that the growing costs of maintaining these social welfare programs may be destabilizing elements. High taxes, bureaucratic controls, chronic government deficit spending, and the general overloading of government caused by social programs may lead to social disintegration and political instability. Clearly, the consensus that once supported such programs has broken down, at least among political leaders; Conservatives are sharply critical of welfare programs but recognize that their popularity makes them difficult to reduce. Labourites are favorable to their maintenance but know that rising costs are difficult to meet and may ultimately undermine public support for them.

CHALLENGES TO STABILITY

Britain is the epitome of democratic stability in the eyes of many, including the overwhelming majority of its own citizens. Much of this pride is derived from satisfaction with the past and present political forms. The legitimacy of the British political system is virtually unchallenged. Britons take special pride in the effectiveness of their political institutions: Asked what they like about their country, many spontaneously mention these institutions. They acknowledge that their anachronistic blend of democracy and monarchy is a special form of democracy that only they can make work, but they regard it as more successful than "purer" forms of democracy. There is general satisfaction with the political system's performance in managing conflict and policy making.

Economic stagnation and public discussion of the possible decay of British democracy have eroded somewhat the very high levels of confidence that Britons usually express about their political institutions. Nevertheless, the public's evaluation of the political system still remains overwhelmingly positive. Even those with grievances generally do not deem it appropriate to express them through unconventional or violent means. Another sign of legitimacy is the absence of an antiregime party. A 1990 public opinion poll found only 6 percent of the British insisting on radical social changes through revolutionary action, 62 percent wanted social improvement through gradual reforms, and 25 percent thought that present institutions ought to be defended against any major changes.[12] With a majority favoring gradual change and only a small handful supporting revolutionary change, public attitudes appear conducive to the maintenance of political stability.

The strength of British political institutions is attested to first by their durability: Parliament had its origins over 700 years ago; the House of Commons emerged as a separate chamber by the middle of the fourteenth century. The cabinet dates back to the fifteenth century and assumed its modern form by the early eighteenth century. The significance of age in these institutions is not simply that they have survived, but that they and other ancient structures continue to prove their utility by adapting to modern circumstances.

British political institutions were capable of incorporating new participants and responding to new political demands during the era of rapid social and economic development. The durability of traditional structures, including such anachronisms as the House of Lords and the monarchy, provides the British regime with powerful political symbols that unite Britons and link the present with a glorious past. In so doing, they enhance the stability of the regime.

Britain's institutions are by no means rigid, despite the years of tradition they embody. Confronted with a crisis, the regime has proved highly flexible. During World War II, for example, all parties consented to suspend partisan politics and elections for the duration of the war. More recently, in 1976–79, the political system quickly adjusted to the absence of any majority party by providing stability through a governing minority party. This flexibility contributes to the strength of British political institutions, allowing them to evolve in response to new needs while retaining the traditions and grandeur that convey legitimacy.

The process of recruiting political leaders in Britain tends to favor individuals with leadership skills well suited to the management of conflict. The leaders who gain the top party and government posts have served long apprenticeships in the party and in Parliament and are skilled in compromise and accommodation. They have already proven that they are sensitive to needs for change and capable of making the required adaptations. British leaders are particularly skillful at balancing contending party and interest group viewpoints in pursuit of a consensus.

Tension among Immigrants and the Northern Irish

The levels of unrest in Britain seem generally manageable by the political system. There are, however, important areas of social unrest, and two of these deserve extended analysis: racial tensions produced by the influx of immigrants, and the situation in Northern Ireland.

The growing numbers of Asian and West Indian immigrants in large British cities have created racial tensions and in some cases a climate conducive to political extremism. Racial incidents and racist graffiti threatening non-whites with violence evidence the intensity of antiminority feelings. Britain escaped the political extremism engendered by racial antagonisms that we will find later in this book in France and Germany. It has not avoided frequent but isolated episodes of violence by individuals and groups of young toughs against minorities.

Since the early 1960s, both major parties have supported limits on immigration and more recently on asylum rights. This is no longer a "solution" since the racial minorities are well implanted and already account for over 5 percent of the total population. Many "immigrants" are second- or third-generation residents and citizens. Nonwhites in Britain confront higher rates of joblessness and poverty than among the population in general. Feelings of exclusion, discrimination, and economic despair fueled major riots among nonwhites in the early 1980s. Labour and Conservative governments have tried to respond to these problems with legislation barring racial discrimination in housing and employment and promoting a British version of affirmative action programs.[13]

The economic distress of old industrial centers among both immigrant and indigenous populations remains a potential problem for political order. Thus, the problems of easing racial tensions—of providing jobs, better housing, and government services for racial minorities and the whites they displace, and of combating urban crime—are important to the assurance of British political stability. At present, the threat is still minimal, but these kinds of problems, if not resolved, can fuel extremism, violence, and political instability.

The most serious current challenge to British stability is the conflict in Northern Ireland. For over 30 years Protestants and Catholics have been on the verge of civil war, and the authorities have been unable to prevent bombings, assassinations, and other forms of violence. But the strife and violence in Northern Ireland appear to have little impact on the British political unit as a whole, for three reasons. First, Northern Ireland is geographically isolated from the rest of Britain, remote from the areas of densest population and from the center of political power. Attempts by

Catholic extremists to enlarge the area of conflict by bombings or other acts of terrorism in London and other cities have failed. Second, since conflict has been restricted to Northern Ireland, only 2.6 percent of the total population is in a position to be directly affected by it.

Third, the rest of Britain considers the conflict a Northern Irish rather than a British problem. Most Britons do not understand why Irish Catholics and Protestants cannot get along. Both Catholics and Protestants elsewhere in Britain are dismayed and puzzled by the conduct of their coreligionists in Northern Ireland; to them, the behavior of both sides in the conflict is "un-British" and therefore baffling. Often expressed is the sentiment that the conflict simply reflects the Irish temperament, which the English, Welsh, and Scots have never really understood.

The predominant feeling in Britain, then, is aloofness from the conflict in Northern Ireland, accompanied by a sense of frustration. This feeling was well expressed by Roy Jenkins, who as home secretary had to deal with Northern Irish problems: "Despite the many attributes of the English, a peculiar talent for solving the problems of Ireland is not among them."[14] The conflict is acceptable, or at least understandable, to the bulk of the people as a peculiarly Irish problem. Thus Britain as a whole continues to enjoy the solid political stability that is characteristic of the British political tradition.

HUMAN RIGHTS

Britain lacks a constitutional document that is equivalent to the American Bill of Rights. There is a British "Bill of Rights" that dates back to 1689, but it defines the rights of Parliament in relationship to the monarch rather than specifying individual rights and liberties. Despite the lack of formal constitutional guarantees, Britain has a long tradition of respect for individual rights and the law that assures these basic freedoms. These rights are jealously guarded by an independent judiciary, a free press, and a Parliament whose opposition members are ready to seize on human rights' violations as a means of criticizing the government. In addition, Britain has signed the European Declaration for Human

Rights, which enumerates a long list of freedoms, and has accepted the right of individuals to appeal to the European Court of Human Rights. This means that any British citizen who feels the government has abridged his or her rights and has not given this individual's case adequate attention in the British courts may appeal to the European Court of Human Rights. The decision of this international court is then binding on the British courts.

There is public debate in Britain now over the advisability of a constitutional document specifically stating basic human and political rights. The concern underlying those advocating a Bill of Rights is not about what has happened so far but about what a Parliament might do sometime in the future. In general, those seeking a Bill of Rights appear worried about possible encroachments on human rights as government continues to increase its impact on the personal lives and activities of individual citizens and groups. A bill of rights would define those rights and liberties that would be inviolable as government's influence expands. The proposals face political opposition from both the Right and the Left, based on different priorities about the political and social rights that ought to be protected.

There is also a constitutional issue at stake since the existence of a bill of rights would place limits on the absolute sovereignty of Parliament, and thus go against a basic principle of Britain's unwritten constitution. In effect, it is part of the British legal tradition that rejects the American principle of judicial review whereby courts can invalidate laws that fail to comply with the constitution.

As a way to avoid this constitutional limit, the Labour government announced plans in 1997 to incorporate the principles of the European Convention of Human Rights into British law. Courts, however, will not be able to invalidate existing or future acts of Parliament that conflict with terms of the Convention. Instead, judges will be directed to interpret British laws so that they comply with the Convention.[15] In practice, however, the European Court of Human Rights becomes an international court of appeals to which Britons who feel that their rights have been abused may turn. That court in effect invalidates British laws that conflict with its decisions.

Parliament may suspend human rights in national emergencies. This has happened on a number of occasions in the protracted conflict in Northern Ireland. A 1973 law allowed the preventive detention without trial of individuals suspected of terrorists acts; a 1975 law permitted the government to bar the entry into Britain of anyone coming from Ireland who was suspected of being a terrorist; a new law passed in 1988 lifted the right of individuals accused of terrorism to refuse to testify against themselves; and at the end of 1988 the government barred British journalists from broadcasting interviews with known terrorists. All of these involved restrictions on basic rights, but they were viewed as necessary to fight terrorists who use these rights to carry out acts of violence on other citizens.

While Parliament has carefully monitored these laws to prevent abuse of the special powers, the troubles in Northern Ireland produced several most unfortunate violations of human rights. Eager to control terrorists bombings, the government sometimes neglected the rights of the accused. In the 1970s, the European Court of Human Rights found that the British army had used inapproprite methods of interrogation in investigating Irish nationalist terrorism. Between 1989 and 1991, Britain's own appeals courts overturned the convictions of 16 accused terrorists who had been found guilty of terrorist bombings in three separate trials during the 1970s. In each case, the courts found that the convictions were tainted by forced confessions or by testimony by expert government witnesses who concealed evidence that cast doubt on the guilt of the accused.

Another area of potential human rights abuse is the Official Secrets Act of 1911. The government designed the act to deal with spies and saboteurs, but it has occasionally used the act to censor the press and control political dissidence. Even without such abuses, the British tradition of governmental secrecy is at odds with the needs of a democratic public to monitor the actions of its government. This may be in the process of changing. The Labour government introduced legislation to establish a "right to know" or freedom of information law. When enacted, it will greatly diminish the British government's former

JUDICIAL REVIEW

One of the early innovations in the evolution of the American political system was the assertion of the right of judicial review by the United States Supreme Court in the celebrated decision *Marbury vs. Madison* (1803). In this key decision, the Court declared its right to invalidate laws passed by Congress that violated the Constitution. It was a uniquely American notion derived from the distinctly American principle of a separation of powers among three equally important branches of government. In Britain and most other European democracies, judicial review was slow to develop because there the notion is that parliament is supreme. Thus, the executive and the judiciary must accept the decisions and laws of parliament. Parliament alone and by its actions determines what is and is not "constitutional."

After World War II, judicial review emerged as a new feature of European parliamentary regimes. Constitutional courts in France, Germany, and elsewhere acquired the right to review legislation to assure its compliance with their constitutions. In Germany and some other constitutional courts (but not in France), the courts acquired also the power to defend citizens against violation of their civil liberties. In Britain, however, the sovereignty and absolute power of Parliament restrained the develop-

ment of judicial review. It is only now beginning to emerge, more as the result of Britain's international obligations than because of a conscious decision to adopt judicial review.

The two international trends promoting acceptance and use of judicial review in Britain and other European countries are the powers of two European supranational courts. European Union members ceded by treaty the right of the European Court of Justice to review their national laws for compliance with EU laws and treaties. The ECJ has the power of judicial review since it can void national laws that violate EU laws and treaties. National courts also can refer to EU laws to void their own countries' laws that are incompatible with the Union's treaties. Then there is the European Court of Human Rights. All EU countries and many other European countries have signed a convention obligating them to observe a broad range of human rights. They have also accepted compulsory jurisdiction for the European Court of Human Rights to review national governments' actions in alleged cases of human rights abuse. Decisions by the European Court must be accepted and observed by those who have signed the convention—including Britain, France, and Germany.

use of secrecy to control the flow of information about its acts and issues of public policy.

The British government's overall performance in human rights has been exemplary. Faced with a long guerrilla war in Northern Ireland and terrorism that has sometimes spread beyond the affected province, the government's response generally has been moderate. The real threat to human rights in Britain today comes not from the government but from individual citizens. Certain people refuse to accord equal treatment to their fellow citizens because of religious intolerance (especially in Northern Ireland) or racial prejudice (especially toward nonwhites). There are laws to deal with such discrimination and the government has made conscientious efforts to enforce them, but it is not easy for a democratic

government to overcome the prejudices of its people as they deal with each other.

A MODEL DEMOCRACY?

> In the study of comparative politics, England is important as a deviant case, deviant because of its success in coping with the many political problems of the modern world. Just as Alexis de Tocqueville travelled to America in 1831 to seek the secrets of democracy, so today one might travel to England in search of the secrets of stable representative government.[16]

This statement was made over 35 years ago by a respected American observer of the English political scene. The intervening years have been

Table 6–3   Public Satisfaction with Democracy in Britain

	Extent of Satisfaction with Performance of Democracy in Britain				
	Very	Fairly	Not Very	Not at All	No Reply
1973	7%	37%	34%	20%	2%
1978	6	45	28	12	9
1983	12	49	20	12	7
1988	10	37	37	13	3
1993	6	42	32	14	6
1997	8	55	18	7	11

Source: Eurobarometer: Trends 1974–1993, pp. 33–34 and Eurobarometer 48 (Fall 1997) from the European Union web site.

difficult ones for British democracy. Many of the presumed strengths of its political system either have disappeared or have been eroded. The supportive deferential political culture has given way to new political attitudes much less accepting of tradition and hierarchy. The much-vaunted two-party system has faced the twin threats of internal decay of the main parties and of strong electoral challenges from third parties. Governmental stability, long thought to be a particularly important virtue of British democracy, has been challenged by the indiscipline of MPs and the narrowness of governmental majorities in Commons. Violence and terrorism related to the conflict in Northern Ireland have shattered the presumably normal calm of British politics. The abilities of the government to govern, to manage the economy, and to finance the needed social programs have been called into serious doubt.

Predictions about the demise of British democracy, however, have been premature. The best evidence of the strength of the British political system has been its ability to encounter problems—such as the economic, social, and political challenges of the 1970s and 1980s—and adapt to them. Britain appears to have done so. That does not mean that current governments are always competent or popular. Democracy rests on the willingness of citizens to be critical of those who hold power. It is such criticism of current leaders and policies that explains the mixed pattern of public attitudes about how British democracy performs, as shown in Table 6–3. However, beneath such skepticism about how democracy may function at given point in time, there is a broad reservoir of public support for Britain's basic institutions and political values.

A major challenge for the British over the next decade will be the adjustments of mind and economic structures to an increasingly interdependent world. Over the past decade, Britain has placed itself on the margins of the efforts to unite Europe. In its reluctance to join in the venture, Britain risks missing out on the growing political, social, and economic benefits of the growing cooperation among members of the European Union. Few can question the uniqueness of Britain's past, but its future lies in better adaptation to the world around it. That adjustment will be difficult in a country where children are still taught to recite by memory Shakespeare's praise of British insularity:

> This precious stone set in the silver sea
> Which serves it in the office of a wall
> Or as a moat defensive to a house,
> Against the envy of less happier lands.[17]

NOTES

[1]Richard Rose and Guy Peters, *Can Government Go Bankrupt?* (London: Macmillan, 1979).

[2]See Richard Rose, ed., *Challenge to Governance: Studies in Overloaded Politics* (Beverly Hills, CA: Sage, 1980).

[3]*Christian Science Monitor,* 4 April 1970.

[4]Dennis Kavanagh, *Thatcherism and British Politics: The End of Consensus?* (Oxford: Oxford University Press, 1987).

[5]Stephen Wilks, "Economic Policy," in *Developments in British Politics 4,* ed. Patrick Dunleavey et al. (New York: St. Martin's Press, 1993).

[6]On Britain and European Unification, see Stephen George, *An Awkward Partner: Britain in the European*

Community, 2nd ed. (Oxford, England: Oxford University Press, 1994).

[7]John Darwin, *The End of the British Empire* (London: Blackwell, 1991).

[8]*The Economist,* 10 November 1979.

[9]*Financial Times,* 3 June 1994.

[10]*The New York Times,* 10 December 1997.

[11]*The Economist,* 28 March 1998.

[12]*Eurobarometer Trends 1973–1993,* p. 48 (7 percent had no reply).

[13]Zig Layton-Henry, *The Politics of Immigration* (London: Blackwell, 1993).

[14]Cited by Richard Rose, *Governing Without Consensus: An Irish Perspective* (New York: Basic Books, 1971), p. 42.

[15]*The Economist,* 25 October 1997.

[16]Richard Rose, *Politics in England* (Boston: Little, Brown, 1964), p. 1.

[17]William Shakespeare, *Richard the Second,* Act II, Scene I.

BRITAIN: SELECTED BIBLIOGRAPHY

Andrew Adonis, *Parliament Today* (Manchester, England: Manchester University Press, 1993).

Samuel H. Beer, *Britain Against Itself: The Political Contradictions of Collectivism* (New York: Norton, 1982).

Samuel H. Beer, *Modern British Politics: Parties and Pressure Groups in the Collectivist Age* (New York: Norton, 1982).

Vernon Bogdanor, ed., *Politics and the Constitution: Essays on British Government* (Aldershot, England: Dartmouth, 1996).

Ian Budge, et al., *The New British Politics* (London and New York: Longman, 1998).

S. E. Finer, *The Changing British Party System, 1945–1979* (Washington: American Enterprise Institute, 1980).

Justin Fisher, *British Political Parties* (London: Prentice-Hall, 1996).

Leonard Freedman, *Politics and Policy in Britain* (White Plains, NY: Longman, 1996).

Wyn Grant, *Pressure Groups, Politics and Democracy in Britain* (London: Philip Allan, 1989).

Bill Jones and Dennis Kavanagh, *British Politics Today*, 6th ed. (Washington, D.C.: CQ Press, 1998).

Grant Jordan and Jeremy Richardson, *Government and Pressure Groups in Britain* (Oxford, England: Oxford University Press, 1990).

Dennis Kavanagh, *British Politics: Continuities and Change,* 2nd ed. (Oxford, England: Oxford University Press, 1990).

Anthony King, et al., *New Labour Triumphs: Britain at the Polls* (Chatham, NJ: Chatham House, 1998).

Joni Lovenduski and Pippa Norris, eds., *Women in Politics* (Oxford, England: Oxford University Press, 1996).

Philip Norton, *The British Polity,* 3rd ed. (New York: Longman, 1994).

Philip Norton, *The Commons in Perspective* (London: Blackwell, 1985).

Jorgen S. Rasmussen, *The British Political Process: Concentrated Power Versus Accountability* (Belmont, CA: Wadsworth, 1993).

Richard Rose, *Do Parties Make a Difference?* 2nd ed. (Chatham, NJ: Chatham House, 1984).

Anthony Sampson, *The Essential Anatomy of Britain* (New York: Harcourt Brace, 1993).

Donley Studlar, *Great Britain: Decline or Renewal?* (Boulder, CO: Westview, 1996).

Part II: France

Chapter 7

Historical Background to Contemporary French Politics

[The French] view their own past as an epic unmatched in the history of Western civilization. The past is a warehouse stocked with treasures ready to be displayed whenever useful . . . France secretes, constantly reshapes and feeds on its own past.[1]

Unlike the British, who honor their history by perpetuating traditional institutions and practices in their modern politics, the French have repeatedly restructured their governing institutions since 1789 through a series of revolutions. This does not mean that history's impact on contemporary France is any less important than that of history in Britain, for, as one historian noted, "Frenchmen remained traditionalists even when they were being most progressive and revolutionary."[2] Living in a country embellished by the traces of a long and rich history, the French are accustomed to thinking in historical terms. They not only take pride in the cultural and political accomplishments of the past, they seek solutions to current problems from historical precedents. A graphic example of this search for historical solutions can be seen in the "Events of May 1968," the period of intense student/worker rebellion that nearly toppled the regime. In the

midst of a modern revolt provoked by youthful students and workers—who distrusted anyone over 30—left-wing political leaders proposed to face the crisis with a strategy last used by the Left to fight demagoguery in 1877! The irony of this proposal—although apparent to foreign observers—no doubt went unnoticed by the young rebels, who themselves were consciously drawing on the Paris Commune of 1870–71 and earlier revolutionary episodes as models for their revolt.

In contrast to the thousand years of continuity in British history, French history is marked by its discontinuity and numerous disruptions. During the same 200-year-period that Americans have lived under a single Constitution, the French have gone through five democratic republics, three monarchies, two empires, one fascist regime, and several provisional governments (see Table 7–1). In addition, frequent civil disturbances threatened and sometimes toppled the various regimes. Instead of uniting the French, as history does the British and Americans, history divides the French. In the United States, no one seriously questions the value of the American Revolution, but in France the virtues and excesses of the

Table 7–1 Some Important Landmarks in French History

1789–1794	French Revolution abolishes the monarchy and establishes the First French Republic.
1799–1815	Rule of Napoleon Bonaparte.
1815–1830	Restoration of the Bourbon monarchy.
1830–1848	July 1830 Revolution forces the abdication of Charles X and establishes the monarchy of Louis Philippe.
1848–1851	Revolution of 1848 establishes the Second Republic.
1851–1870	Coup d'état of Louis Napoleon overthrows the republic and establishes the Second Empire.
1870–1940	Defeat in the Franco-Prussian War brings the collapse of the empire and establishment of the Third Republic.
1940–1944	Defeat by Germans leads to the fascist Vichy Republic of Marshal Pétain and Pierre Laval.
1944–1946	Provisional government of Charles de Gaulle.
1946–1958	Fourth Republic.
1958	Revolt of military and settlers in Algeria precipitates fall of the Fourth Republic and establishment of the Fifth Republic.
1968	Student and worker revolt ("The Events of May") nearly topples the Fifth Republic.
1981–1986	Election of first Socialist president and parliamentary majority in 45 years, bringing important social and economic reforms.

French Revolution of 1789 remain a topic of discussion. And there is still widespread disagreement. Even tourist guidebooks betray the authors' biases for or against events now over 200 years past.

In attempting to simplify this troubled past, many observers point to two major political patterns that presumably have alternated throughout the past 200 years: an authoritarian pattern found in the monarchical, imperial, and Vichy regimes, and a democratic pattern characterized by the five republican regimes. Some go so far as to claim that these two patterns reflect two separate Frances: Red France (the France of the Revolution) and Black France (the France of the old

monarchy and the Church). These two Frances are seen coexisting in the same geographic boundaries but each having its own distinctive historical traditions and symbols and its own partisans. Each rejects compromise and accommodation with the other in preference to waiting its turn to rule in its pure form. Thus the French philosopher Ernest Renan writes:

> According to the old Hebrew legend, Rebecca, feeling the two children she was bearing struggling within her, was told on inquiring of the Lord that "two nations were struggling in her womb." In the womb of our country, as in Rebecca, two peoples are struggling, each of which wants to smother the other.[3]

This dichotomization of French history, however, greatly overstates the degree of political difference between the "two Frances." The typical French citizen was usually unaffected by the changes from one type of regime to the next.[4] The same individuals enforced the law and collected the taxes; the same laws remained on the books. Despite major political changes when the type of regime shifted from authoritarian France to democratic France, the routine of government continued without interruption and the disruption in the lives of the general citizenry was minimal or nonexistent.

The dichotomization into Red and Black France leads to even greater distortion by neglecting the commonalities of the two regime types. While the top governmental structure varied from monarchs to emperors to presidents and prime ministers, the day-to-day conduct of government by the administration and local governments went unchanged. Even at the top, the form of government changed little in its basic nature. The features usually associated with authoritarian eras—such as centralization, nationalism, glorification of the state, and bureaucracy—can be found unchanged or even reinforced in the democratic republics. And democratic features such as political pluralism and a concern for equality and liberty can be found in French authoritarian regimes. The two Frances in fact share traditions, beliefs, and practices. For these reasons, this chapter will avoid the usual division of the historical legacy and will emphasize the common heritage that all French regimes find in the past.

THE CONCEPT OF THE STATE

The French concept of the State has remained relatively constant during the 300 years since Louis XIV as absolute monarch pronounced: *"L'Etat, c'est moi."* ("I am the State.") The French think of the state as a political entity apart from the divisions and conflicts of everyday politics. It is distinguishable from the current government that reflects these partisan divisions and that may be captured by narrow and selfish interests. Aloof from the petty squabbles of self-seeking groups and individuals, the state represents the overall public interest, the Rousseauian notion of a general will that can command the unanimous support of the people. The state thus represents the *general interest* in its pure form as opposed to the attenuated versions that might be forthcoming from specific governments.

The state is not, however, simply an abstract entity. It is embodied in the administrative services of the *bureaucracy.* The French bureaucracy was already well developed by the time of the 1789 Revolution. Modernized by Napoleon, it has continued without major reform through revolution and counterrevolution to the present. The pervasive power of the Napoleonic civil service led observers of later democratic regimes to complain that while the Republic was above the surface, the Empire still prevailed below, through the bureaucracy where the government actually came in contact with the people. Imbued with the doctrine of the state's sanctity and convinced that they were better aware of the citizens' interests than the citizens themselves, civil servants then and now attempted to foresee and to take care of everything through regulation.

The integrity and unity of the state necessitated a high degree of *centralization* of power, rather than decentralization through a federal structure or through autonomous local-level authorities. Already under the autocratic monarchy of the prerevolutionary ancien régime, French government was highly centralized.[5] The Jacobins, who controlled the First Republic, furthered the state's centralized authority by breaking up the old provinces into new administrative units known as departments. Napoleon consolidated centralization of the state by instituting a system of centrally appointed prefects who would represent the state and assure its dominance over local officials. The state came to represent the unity of the nation opposed to the tendencies toward separation or splitting off often present in outlying regions. The supremacy of the state assured uniformity of law and standards throughout the country and promised equality of governmental services to all. This system of state superiority through prefectoral control has continued to the present, maintaining the political control of the central government over the most important tasks of government, from police duties to education, while permitting regional differences in culture, culinary preferences, dress, folkways, and even language.

Another feature of the French state is its strong involvement in the social and economic life of the nation. Already under the prerevolutionary monarchy, the state regularly intervened in agriculture, commerce, and the crafts. The Revolution only eliminated the feudal aspects of this interference. Succeeding regimes maintained the interventionist approach to the economy. Of particular importance were the state's efforts, not always successful, to promote industrialization.[6] Indicative of the continuity of such economic intervention by the state is the fact that price controls on bread, first established during the Revolution of 1789, continued in effect without interruption until *1979.*

Thus, for the French, the state is supreme, rising above the turmoil of mundane political squabbles to embody the general will and the lofty aspirations of the people as a whole. While sometimes betrayed by the actual holders of power, the state has represented the potential greatness of the people. The glorification of the state justified the insistence on rigid central government and the power of bureaucrats supposedly serving the state's interests. Whether the current regime was democratic or authoritarian, few seriously considered undermining the integrity and supremacy of the glorified state.

NATIONALISM

The exaltation of the state had its foreign dimension as well. Prior to the Revolution, eighteenth-century Enlightenment thinkers were convinced that all people everywhere were potentially French and that they really wanted to be French.[7] The prerevolutionary pride in French cultural achievements was supplemented by revolutionary

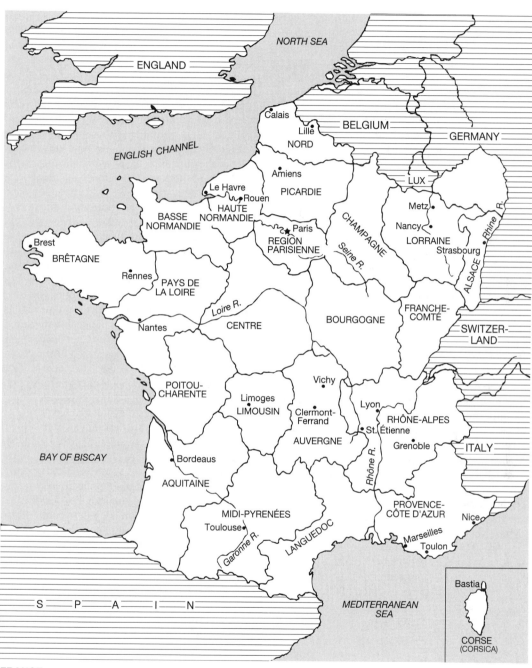

NORTH SEA

ENGLAND

BELGIUM

GERMANY

Calais

Lille

NORD

LUX

ENGLISH CHANNEL

Amiens

Le Havre

Rouen

PICARDIE

Metz

Nancy

LORRAINE

Strasbourg

HAUTE
NORMANDIE

BASSE
NORMANDIE

CHAMPAGNE

ALSACE

Rhine R.

Brest

BRÊTAGNE

Paris

RÉGION
PARISIENNE

Seine R.

Rennes

PAYS DE
LA LOIRE

FRANCHE-
COMTÉ

Loire R.

Nantes

CENTRE

BOURGOGNE

SWITZER-
LAND

Vichy

POITOU-
CHARENTE

Limoges

LIMOUSIN

Lyon

RHÔNE-ALPES

Clermont-
Ferrand

St. Étienne

BAY OF BISCAY

AUVERGNE

Grenoble

ITALY

Rhône R.

Bordeaus

AQUITAINE

PROVENCE-
CÔTE D'AZUR

Nice

MIDI-PYRENÉES

Toulouse

LANGUEDOC

Marseilles

Toulon

Garonne R.

S   P   A   I   N

MEDITERRANEAN
SEA

Bastia

CORSE
(CORSICA)

FRANCE

expansionism after 1789: the Revolution should be exported to bring the liberty and equality achieved in France to other oppressed peoples in Europe. Indeed, the Revolution produced modern mass-based nationalism by replacing the mercenary armed forces of the past with popular armies mobilized by the desire to spread the Revolution and French culture to other peoples. The calling up of all able men to defend the Revolution was a major step toward modern warfare and provided a precedent for using nationalism as a means of generating mass support for the foreign objectives of the state.

French nationalism manifested itself in the messianic fervor of the revolutionary era, in the expansionist imperial eras of the two Napoleons, in the refusal to surrender to the Prussians that sparked the Commune riots in 1870–71, in the Third Republic's seeking revenge for the defeat by the Prussians, in the "civilizing mission" of French colonialism, in the jingoism of the 1930s, in de Gaulle's search for the reaffirmation of French *grandeur* in the 1960s, and in current efforts to protect the French language from international use of English.[8]

Pride in France's contribution to the cultural, political, and scientific legacy of the modern world promoted French nationalism. This sense of pride was well captured by Charles de Gaulle when he proclaimed that France could not be France without *grandeur* (greatness). While it is possible to see a movement of nationalist support from the Left of the political spectrum at the time of the Revolution to the Right in the twentieth century, all political tendencies in fact try to wrap themselves in the mantle of nationalism. Gaullists on the Right and Communists on the Left, and the various parties between, all claim to defend French national interests and the cause of French nationalism against various external threats such as the Soviet Union, the United States, or the supranational European Union.

POLITICAL PLURALISM

Another legacy of the past affecting contemporary politics is France's extreme political pluralism. Unlike the British pattern of politics, which for more than a century has been distinguished by two large political camps, the French political system has always had a large number of small political factions competing for public office. The French political spectrum runs from fascists, monarchists, and Bonapartists (who wish to restore the Napoleonic Empire) on the far Right to anarchists, Trotskyites, and Maoists on the far Left. Even during the French Revolution of 1789 there was no united revolutionary movement but, instead, a large number of loose factions, which eventually turned on each other with the same violence they had directed earlier at the monarchy.

Many of these political groups have elaborate ideologies that shape their political actions and interpretations of the world: communism, socialism, fascism, liberalism. Others profess vaguer principles of political action, such as anticommunism, anticlericalism, or anti-Gaullism, which prove to be equally firm obstacles to interparty cooperation despite their relative lack of rigor. These political belief systems often persist as guidelines for action long after the problems that inspired them have lost their political significance. For example, division over the Catholic church's role in politics continued to cause political cleavage long after the issue had been resolved by the curtailment of the church's influence. Thus political disputes of the past are perpetuated even though issues and personalities change.

French political leaders have often shown great skill in compromising their ideological beliefs when circumstances have demanded it. But compromise is not considered as heroic or desirable a style of political action as loyalty to abstract principles and ideologies. Fidelity to ideological principles thus hinders compromise and may ultimately undermine those compromises that are successfully negotiated. Under the Third and Fourth Republics, for example, the coalition governments were based on delicate compromises among several parties. Most were eventually overthrown when one or more of the parties involved responded to the promptings of its ideological convictions.

AUTHORITARIAN PATTERN OF POLITICAL POWER

Patterns of authority are shaped by the reciprocal expectations of governors and the governed about each others' responsibilities and behavior. Such a pattern sets the norms for this relationship and establishes what each "ought" to do in relation to the other. An authoritarian pattern stresses the integrity of the state, the need for the government to govern and the citizens to obey, the rejection of political controversy in favor of a search for the general will, the exercise of power by a relatively small group of leaders with only a limited role for the citizens, and a paternal concern by the governors for those they govern.

In the French notion of the state discussed earlier, there are several authoritarian elements: the supremacy of the state, its aloofness from the contention of divisive and self-serving interests, and its identity with the general will. The bureaucracy that serves this state puts these authoritarian notions into practice. Neither the concept of the state nor the performance of the bureaucracy changes much as the regime shifts from the "democratic" or Red France to the "authoritarian" or Black France historical models. These authoritarian features prevail under both patterns, even the supposedly democratic. Authoritarian patterns in local government continue as well under both regimes. At the grassroots level of politics, political controversy is avoided and the rule of a paternalistic "indispensable man" as mayor prevails.[9]

The same concept of power explains both the authoritarian political structures and the democratic structures that have alternated in France. The different structures simply switch reliance on the indispensable man from the local to the national level. Under the authoritarian pattern, a single aloof and indispensable leader rules at the top; under the democratic pattern, local notables, aloof and indispensable to their constituents, are chosen to negotiate with other such delegates at the national level. In both cases, the citizen's role beyond obedience is minimal. Reinforced by authority relations in the home and schools,[10] this pattern of political authority persists through both democratic and authoritarian regimes and contributes, through its apartness from citizens, to what some have labeled a stalled or stalemate society.[11]

The persistence of the authoritarian pattern even under "democratic" regimes does not mean that democracy cannot function in France. Under the democratic republics, free expression of political differences, multiple parties competing for public office, and open and free elections to determine who holds the key political positions assure the voters the means to express their preferences and to control their political leaders by threatening them with ouster from office in the next election. But French democracy coexists with an authoritarian bureaucracy and with an authoritarian style of leadership at both the local and national levels of politics. It is perhaps proper to describe French democracy as a mildly authoritarian brand of democracy.

A PROPENSITY FOR REVOLT

Coexistent with this usual authoritarian power relationship is a tendency for the French citizen to resist the government and to revolt periodically. A prominent French political thinker explained this seeming paradox between authoritarianism and revolt: "Resistance and obedience are the two virtues of the citizen. By obedience he guarantees order; by resistance he guarantees liberty."[12] This is, in essence, a tradition of *revolt against tradition* and dates back at least to the Revolution of 1789, a revolt against the tradition embodied in the monarchy.[13] Once established, this "right" of revolt has justified yet further revolts.

While the French routinely accept rule by aloof governors in both authoritarian and democratic garb, they retain the right to protest vigorously against specific actions they view as detrimental to their interests. At times this protest explodes spontaneously into a more general revolt. There is a long string of such popular uprisings. Successful or not, they become historical precedents that future generations will draw upon as patterns for future revolts. Many of these events—especially the Revolutions of 1789 and 1848, the Paris Commune of 1870–71, and the events of May 1968—are imbued with a mystique of revolutionary camaraderie, spiritual uplift, and glamour that make them highly attractive. Thus, when discontent rises there is always the temptation to recreate a glamorous past by patterning a new revolt on the episodes of an earlier time.

The most recent such instance was the student/worker revolt in May 1968. In the spring of that year, student riots and a general strike provoked the most serious political crisis to confront the Fifth Republic and brought France to the brink of civil war. Student unrest had a number of causes: seriously overcrowded university facilities, archaic university procedures, aloof professors, restraints on freedom of political expression, limited guest hours in dormitories, and uncertain job prospects for graduates. The French students were also clearly influenced by the student unrest and rioting that beset most Western democracies at the end of the 1960s.

The violence of the police in dealing with the students prompted the labor unions to call a general strike for May 13. In Paris on that day, a procession of 600,000 workers, students, teachers, and other sympathizers marched through the Latin Quarter. The purpose of the demonstration was to express support and sympathy for the students, but it was clear from the workers' placards that the unions were using the occasion to make their own demands. Spontaneous strikes broke out during the next week, followed by the occupation of factories by their workers. Eventually 10 million people took part in the strikes, and at the same time university and many high school students occupied their campuses.

Leaders of both the communist union and the noncommunist unions attempted to limit the strikers' claims to economic issues, rather than actively politicizing the strikes. In spite of their efforts, however, the strikes rapidly assumed a political flavor at the grassroots. Thus, when union leaders presented strikers with the agreement reached between government and management, the strikers rejected it. The reason for rejection was not unsatisfied economic demands, but political demands for the resignation of President de Gaulle.

The strikes, student riots, and occupations of factories, universities, and public buildings continued for over three weeks. The rebels claimed that "imagination was in power" and that "power was in the streets." It was a remarkable political-cultural event: Art students covered city walls with bold posters; students occupied their classrooms, sleeping on the floors, turning lecture halls into debating centers or emergency hospitals, and taking time out to learn traditional revolutionary songs; even theater companies and soccer teams put aside their regular routines to debate political issues. Unable to gain control of

the mounting rebellion, de Gaulle fled the country only to be persuaded by his prime minister and military leaders to return.

The beginning of the end of this "psychodrama" came when de Gaulle dissolved the National Assembly and called for new elections. This act shifted the focus of conflict from street politics and strikes to electoral politics. The strikes quickly ended, student rioting abated, and order was restored as politicians and social leaders concentrated on the election. In the elections held in June 1968, the overwhelming victory of the Gaullists and the defeat of all left-wing forces—including those even remotely associated with the crisis—marked the final chapter of this episode.

The romantic attraction of revolution in France explains the intensification of conflict to the point of endangering the regime.[14] Many participants consciously patterned their vocabulary, goals, and actions on past revolutionary eras: the Revolution of 1789, the Revolution of 1848, the Paris Commune of 1871, and the General Strike of 1936. Present-day events provided the opportunity to experience firsthand the romance and glory of revolution, which could otherwise be experienced only through books. The implication of this argument is that France will always be vulnerable to periods of rapidly accelerating social conflict and near-revolution because serious conflict has been manifested thus in the past. The Events of May belong to a long history of glorious revolutionary episodes that will doubtlessly incite similar ventures in the future.

ORIGINS OF THE FIFTH REPUBLIC

The political system that emerged in France after World War II—the Fourth Republic (1946–58)—was very similar to the Third Republic, although some efforts were made to remedy certain problems that had led to paralysis and ineffectiveness before the war.[15] As in most parliamentary systems, the premier and cabinet needed a majority to stay in office. The French parliament was presumably all-powerful, but there were so many parties that it was difficult to form durable coalitions to keep a government in office or to pass

---

FRANCE'S FIVE REPUBLICS

The current regime in France is known as the French Fifth Republic. This is because there have been five rather different republican regimes since the French Revolution in 1789. The term "republican" in France connotes not only democratic government but also a regime headed by elected officials, usually presidents, rather than hereditary monarchs.

The First Republic was founded in the chaos of the Revolution. Ongoing battles between revolutionaries and counter-revolutionaries and among the revolutionaries themselves prevented the First Republic from acquiring much real existence or even established institutions. It was essentially dead even before Napoleon Bonaparte declared his own imperial regime. The Second Republic had a similar fate. It was a product of the Revolution of 1848 but was gone by 1851 when Bonaparte's nephew Louis Napoleon declared a new imperial regime.

The Third Republic was the longest lasting French republic. But it was always an interim regime without even a constitution of its own. It emerged literally by default when the royalist majority in parliament could not agree on whom to make king. Nor was it very successful. It endured because there was no agreement on a replacement and because its fragility helped prevent it from doing much to provoke opposition to it. The Third Republic lasted until 1940 when France's defeat by Nazi Germany installed collaborationists in the so-called Vichy regime.

After World War II, a new republic, the Fourth, developed through awkward and unwieldy compromises among the French resistance victors. Hopes of avoiding political stalemates that so often had characterized the Third Republic were dashed as the Fourth Republic reproduced a system with most of the institutional characteristics and faults of the Third Republic. The Fourth Republic collapsed under the pressures of its failure to resolve France's colonial dispute. When challenged by a military coup, there were very few French citizens interested in defending it against whatever was offered as a replacement. The war hero Charles de Gaulle offered his services in the midst of a military coup on condition that he be allowed to rewrite the constitution. The Fifth Republic came into being in January 1959.

---

controversial legislation. The weakness of the executive was compounded by the numerous, poorly disciplined, and ideologically based political parties. Because of the divisions within and between parties, the parliament, which was very powerful on paper, in fact was able to exert its powers only in a negative way by blocking proposed reforms and by overthrowing governments. The result was instability, with twenty-seven separate governments in the twelve years of the Fourth Republic.

The issue that eventually brought about the fall of the Fourth Republic was the question of Algerian independence.[16] Algeria had been more than a typical imperial colony. Most French regarded it as an integral part of France, and large numbers of French citizens had emigrated to Algeria with government encouragement. Alongside the indigenous population of 9 million Algerians lived some 1.2 million Europeans, mostly of French extraction. In 1954, Algerian

rebels began an armed struggle to achieve independence. The French military, called in to control the revolt, soon came to believe that the civilian regime in Paris was hindering its ability to conduct the war by its internal divisions, its instability, and its general incompetence.[17] In France, the colonial war in Algeria became increasingly unpopular. Politicians wavered between negotiations with the rebels and military actions. The public itself split between those wanting to end the war even at the cost of an independent Algeria and those defiantly insisting on keeping Algeria French.

Eventually it was the French population in Algeria—fearful that the government would capitulate to calls for Algerian independence—that precipitated an insurrection that toppled the Fourth Republic. On May 13, 1958, rebellious French civilians seized public buildings in Algiers and set up a "Committee of Public Safety" to govern in place of the Paris-appointed officials.

The military and the police joined with the rebels instead of defending the Parisian government. The French rebels in Algeria threatened to drop paratroopers on Paris if their demands that Algeria remain a part of France were not met.

With the regime crumbling amid threats of military revolt and civil war, the leaders of the Fourth Republic turned to General Charles de Gaulle, leader of the wartime Resistance movement and an outspoken critic of the regime, to prevent further chaos. De Gaulle appeared to be the only person capable of averting anarchy and civil war. On June 1, 1958, the National Assembly invested de Gaulle as premier and voted full powers to him. The National Assembly also granted de Gaulle the authority to revise the constitution. Instead, de Gaulle and his supporters drafted an entirely new constitution, duly ratified by the voters in a special referendum at the end of 1958. On January 1, 1959, the Constitution of the Fifth French Republic took effect, putting an end to the Fourth Republic.

Once in power, de Gaulle proceeded to do exactly what those who had made possible his ascent to power had feared the old regime would do: Within a year he had announced that Algeria would be allowed its self-determination. De Gaulle won overwhelming public endorsements for Algerian independence in two referendums. Diehard advocates of a French Algeria formed a Secret Army Organization (OAS) and resorted to terrorism. They made several attempts to assassinate de Gaulle. In Algeria, the military and the French settlers organized two abortive uprisings, but the decision to terminate colonial rule held, and in 1963 Algeria became an independent state.

The end of the Algerian war marked the consolidation of the Fifth Republic. The new Republic was a combination of France's two historical patterns, providing effective executive government with democratic controls. These two patterns have always had considerable common ground and overlap. The Fifth Republic openly unites similar traditions that in the past have been wrongly viewed as separate alternatives, thus confirming the old and overused French adage *le plus ça change le plus c'est la même chose* ("the more it changes, the more it is the same thing").

The Fifth Republic has proven successful. Many thought that it was so closely tailored to the needs and personality of its founder, Charles de Gaulle, that the Fifth Republic would not survive him. It is now more than 40 years old—the second-longest-lived polity in France since the Revolution of 1789. It has acquired a legitimacy and effectiveness that no previous regime has succeeded in obtaining. But France continues to look back on its revolutionary past, sometimes with regrets but more often with pride. An example of the continued relevance of revolutionary divisions was seen when the French commemorated the execution of Louis XVI a few years ago. Mock trials and lengthy, often impassioned debates in the media and in classrooms reexamined whether the king should have been executed 200 years earlier. In the United States, such a preoccupation with history and its old divisions is difficult to understand. No one in the United States marked the bicentennial of the execution of Benedict Arnold and there certainly was no debate over the wisdom of that act. But Europeans, and the French in particular, relive the past and in doing so bring its divisions into the present.

NOTES

[1] Sanche de Gramont, *The French: Portrait of a People* (New York: G. P. Putnam's Sons, 1969), p. 65.

[2] David Thompson, *Democracy in France Since 1870,* 5th ed. (London: Oxford University Press, 1969), p. 36.

[3] Cited by Roger Soltau, *French Political Thought in the 19th Century* (New York: Russell and Russell, 1959), p. 486.

[4] See Theodore Zeldin, *France 1848–1945: Politics and Anger* (London: Oxford University Press, 1979), for an excellent social history of this period. He demonstrates the lack of impact of political change and ideology on the typical citizen.

[5] Alexis de Tocqueville, *The Old Regime and the French Revolution,* trans. Stuart Gilbert (Garden City, NY: Anchor Books, 1955), pp. 32–60.

[6] J. H. Clapman, *Economic Development of France and Germany 1815–1914* (Cambridge, England: Cambridge University Press, 1966) and Richard F. Kuisel, *Capitalism and the State in Modern France: Renovation and Economic Management in the Twentieth Century* (Cambridge, England: Cambridge University Press, 1981).

[7] Crane Brinton, *The Americans and the French* (Cambridge, MA: Harvard University Press, 1968), p. 45.

[8] Mort Rosenblum, *Mission to Civilize: The French Way* (New York: Harcourt Brace Jovanovich, 1986).

[9] Mark Kesselman, *The Ambiguous Consensus: A Study of Local Government in France* (New York: Knopf, 1967), p. 161. See also Sidney Tarrow, *Between Center and Periphery: Grassroots Politics in Italy and France* (New Haven, CT: Yale University Press, 1977), pp. 205–232.

[10]William A. Schonfeld, *Obedience and Revolt: French Behavior Toward Authority* (Beverly Hills, CA: Sage, 1976).

[11]Michel Crozier, *The Stalled Society,* trans. Rupert Sawyer (New York: Viking, 1973).

[12]Alain [Emile Chartier], *Elements d'une doctrine radicale* (Paris: Gallimard, 1933), p. 281.

[13]Charles Tilly, *The Contentious French* (Cambridge, MA: Harvard University Press, 1986).

[14]Frank L. Wilson, "Political Demonstrations in France: Protest Politics or Politics of Ritual?" *French Politics and Society* 12 (Spring-Summer 1994): 41–64.

[15]On the Fourth Republic, see Frank Giles, *The Locust Years: The Story of the Fourth Republic, 1946–1958* (New York: Carroll & Graf, 1994).

[16]See Tony Smith, *The French State in Algeria: 1945–1962* (Ithaca, NY: Cornell University Press, 1978).

[17]See John Stewart Ambler, *Soldiers Against the State: The French Army in Politics* (Garden City, NY: Anchor Books, 1968).

Chapter 8

The Social Basis
of French Politics

Throughout its history, important social, cultural, and political cleavages have plagued France. These divisions separate the population into various social or ideological "families" having few contacts with each other. Each section of society has sought to fight for its rights and privileges against real or imagined threats coming from the other groups. Each advocates its own view of the way society and politics ought to be organized. Overall, there seems to be no consensus or agreement on the social and political framework acceptable to all these various families. Many observers blame the failure of successive political regimes since 1789 on the political tensions generated by such internal divisions in French society.

Historians now question how much these social divisions actually affected the population at large in the nineteenth and early twentieth centuries.[1] Conflict over the various social perspectives and their political consequences filled the newspapers of the time and agitated the political elite, but such discord seems likely to have been of little interest to the population in general, whose knowledge of the society's political divisions was limited. Much the same appears to be the case today. Social issues divide the political

elite, but public opinion surveys indicate that the public itself is much less divided by these issues. By the 1980s, even the politicians in the mainstream parties come to share broad socioeconomic and political consensus. However, in the past decade, the consensus between moderate leftist and center-right parties has been challenged by a new political force that rejects that consensus: the National Front (FN). The positions it advocates are often extreme but its voters, now about 15 percent of the vote in national elections, are more supportive of the general protest orientation and malaise represented by the FN than of its specific policy proposals. Thus, at the level of the mass population, there appears to be much greater consensus on political and social issues than would seem to be the case if we listened only to the rhetoric of the political leaders.

Although the popular basis for social divisions in France has been exaggerated, a number of important social cleavages have political consequence, chief among them social class, religion, and ethnicity. The political elite remains attached to these divisions in that they serve as rallying points for their supporters even if the general public is no longer, if it ever was, deeply interested in these old conflicts. Thus, the traditional social cleavages continue to have political impact even though the social and economic conditions that originally produced them have disappeared.[2]

SOCIAL CLASS DISTINCTIONS

Among the most important divisions in French society are those dividing the French into socioeconomic classes. The French have a more powerful sense of class membership than do Americans. Most see themselves as belonging to the working class, the middle class or, less frequently, the upper class. Differences between these social classes have been important and highly visible. The working class has had a living style sharply different from that of the middle class (or the bourgeoisie).

The differences can be illustrated by looking at eating habits. The middle class is responsible for the fine French cuisine that has won worldwide acceptance: rich sauces and superb cuts of meats, accompanied by vintage wines. The working class family dines more modestly on a less expensive cut of meat (the *bifteck*), french fries, and a *vin ordinaire*. These class differences are found also in family organization, manner of dress, preferred leisure activities, favorite spectator sports, educational levels, and political behavior.

In the years since World War II, many of these class differences have diminished as modern communications have created more uniform national culture and life-styles, supplanting the once-distinctive class and regional patterns. The economic prosperity of the postwar years has decreased the economic distress of the working class. The expanded access to consumer goods, for example, is impressive: In 1958, 71 percent of households in France had *none* of three major consumer goods: refrigerator, washing machine, or television; in 1978, 71 percent of the households had *all* three.[3] There has also been some equalization in levels of income between the industrial worker and the white-collar worker. From 1967 to the mid-1980s, there was a steady reduction in the gap between income of the rich and the poor as a result of increased wages for workers, social benefits, and progressive income

tax policies. But since the mid-1980s, as in Britain, the United States, and many other industrial democracies, the gap between the poor and the rich began to expand again.[4] This trend toward greater inequality continued into the mid-1990s under both conservative and Socialist governments. Unskilled workers and some low salary white collar workers have suffered most as income inequality has increased.

Despite the recent growth in inequality and high unemployment in the 1990s, French citizens from all social backgrounds believe that class distinctions are gradually giving way to a more uniform society. These improvements in interclass relations have limits. In comparison with other industrial countries, France has one of the most unequal distributions of wealth. This is reinforced by tax structures that hit the poor more heavily than the wealthy. Over 60 percent of the government's revenue comes from indirect taxes, such as the value-added taxes, which are regressive in that they have a relatively greater impact on the poor than on the wealthy. Progressive income taxes are weakened by loopholes and widespread evasion. Other taxes that are used by many countries to redistribute wealth from the rich to the poor—such as inheritance, property, and capital gains taxes—are minimal. Even the Socialist governments took only modest steps in the direction of tax reform and income redistribution.

Class lines are more rigid in France than in Britain and other modern industrial societies. While the standard of living for the worker has improved, the opportunity for workers and their children to move into the middle or upper classes is very limited. The children of blue-collar workers largely grow up to be workers, and those of middle-class parents remain in the middle class. The lack of social mobility is due in part to the educational system.

Access to higher education is much greater now for people from all social backgrounds in France. With nearly 45 percent of young people between the ages of 20 and 24 enrolled in full-time education, France has more students in higher education than any OECD country except the United States and Canada.[5] The opening of higher education to the masses, however, has not been followed by improved job opportunities for those who complete a university education.

Enrollments in universities have soared and the number of children from families of modest means receiving degrees has also increased dramatically. But the large number of university degrees awarded has diluted the value of the degree. As a result the children of well-to-do families, who "inherit" prestige and other social assets that offset the devaluation of a university degree, still end up getting the best jobs, thus perpetuating inherited class lines.[6]

A further limit on the benefits of expanded university access is the existence of a parallel system of higher education known as the *grandes écoles*.[7] These specialized schools, including the École Nationale d'Administration (ENA) and the École Polytechnique, train the people who ultimately go on to dominate leadership positions in politics, society, and business. These schools virtually assure their graduates of prominent positions in society throughout their lives, however much or little they may do in the future. In most other countries, after graduation it is the individual's own accomplishments that determine his or her future; but in France this is not the case. As one critic—himself a product of a grande école—points out, the diploma from one of these prestige schools is "a long distance rocket that barring accident will propel you until retirement."[8] For those who are trained elsewhere, access to elite positions is much more difficult and precarious.

Theoretically, the grandes écoles are open to all qualified young people whatever their social background, since admission requires passing highly competitive entrance examinations. But applicants from modest social backgrounds generally are ill prepared for the style and content of the examinations. The Socialists tried to open up the elitist ENA to people of more modest backgrounds by reserving ten places in each entering class for individuals who have worked previously in trade unions, community associations, or local government.

Yet the real problem is not so much *who* gets into these elite schools but what the schools *do* to them. Even admission into the grandes écoles of additional lower-class students would be unlikely to change their elitist nature. The workers' children are apt to acquire the same values and attitudes as their more privileged fellow students and thus no better reflect the working class than the middle-class elite. It is true that this elite system of schools is not unique to France; we found the same in Britain in the "public" schools and "Oxbridge." But in Britain the elite schools are private institutions, and the state has worked to reduce their influence through improvements in the state-run schools. In France, the elite schools are state-run, and all educational reforms have avoided any challenge to the preeminence of these grandes écoles.

Political Manifestations of Class Divisions

Social class divisions are reflected in the voting patterns in France. The working class is more likely to vote for the leftist parties and the middle and upper classes tend to support the Center-Right government parties (Giscardians and Gaullists). Table 8–1 illustrates this class impact on the vote by showing how various occupational categories divide their votes among the principal parties. In recent years, the nature of class has altered from specific class identifications, salary levels, and occupations. Class is now manifest in type of employment (work in the public sector or for private firms), the individual's perceptions of social rank, and property ownership. When redefined in these terms, the impact of social class on voting decisions remains significant.[9]

The relationship between social class and voting choice, however, is not as strong in France as it is in Britain. With the exception of the Communist party, which draws the majority of its votes from the working class, other French parties draw upon several occupations or classes for their political support. Other factors such as the voters' degree of religious commitment or geographic location are more important than the voters' class identities in predicting electoral choices.

The class conflict in France is particularly evident in the action of trade unions. A long history of mutual suspicion and dislike results in class confrontation between workers and management in much of French industry and business. A comparative study of French and British workers in the same industry found that the French workers had a much higher sense of class deprivation and felt much more strongly that the class distinctions were unjust and inequitable than did British

Table 8–1 Impact of Class Background on Voting Preferences on First Ballot of the 1997 National
Assembly Election

	Far Left	Communist	Socialist	Moderate Conservatives	Ecologists	Far Right
			Indicated Vote for:			
All voters	2.5%	10%	26%	31%	7%	15%
By occupation:						
Farmers	0	3	29	54	0	4
Small business owners and shopkeepers	0	8	15	30	8	26
Professionals & business people	5	7	29	30	13	4
White-collar workers	3	10	31	23	10	14
Blue-collar workers	2	15	28	19	8	24
No profession & retired	0	6	17	44	8	12
By type of employment:						
Self-employed	0	6	17	44	8	12
Employed in public sector	3	13	32	22	10	12
Employed in private sector	3	10	28	24	9	19
Unemployed	6	8	32	17	9	15
Retired, housewives, students	2	9	23	39	5	14

Source: "Le Profil des électeurs au premier tour des élections législatives," *Revue Française de Science Politique* 49 (June-August 1997): 463.

workers.[10] To some extent, this greater sense of class confrontation is due to the attitudes of French labor unions. Competition among several unions encourages union leaders to take more extreme positions. Furthermore, the prominence of the communist union, the CGT, gives the labor movement an antisystem and anticapitalist orientation that is not found in Britain or Germany. While they struggle to improve their members' salaries and working conditions, the radical unions are also seeking to replace entirely the existing society at some future date. They want to create an atmosphere of social unrest that will hasten this change. In Britain and Germany, trade unions serve to integrate the working class into the existing society; in France they work to avoid the workers' integration into the system because that would make them less likely to rise up eventually to overthrow that system. If salaries and working conditions are good in a plant or industry, the French unions agitate against some other real or imagined grievance to maintain a social climate of class tension and conflict.

But trade union ideologies do not alone explain the working-class sense of class confrontation. Unlike Britain, France does not have a tradition of accommodating social class grievances to eliminate sources of grievance. Instead, what reforms have occurred in France have been won through militant political activity by the workers and their allies. One French observer notes:

There is hardly a single achievement of the workers—wages, paid holidays, social security, length of workweek, and tempo of work rate—that has not been torn from their private or state employers at the end of a serious crisis. How could workers not be tempted to join labor unions committed to confrontation rather than concertation?[11]

Because the unions' ultimate focus is on overall social change, there is a greater tendency toward political strikes than is the case in Britain, Germany, or elsewhere. The general strike that paralyzed France during the Events of May 1968 illustrates the explosiveness of an effective general strike. Such mass action is rare, but trade unions frequently call their workers off the job for a "day of action" in pursuit of this or that political objective. This focus on political action comes not only from the unions' desire to change society, but also from the French workers' conviction that the state operates in cooperation with management and the privileged sectors of society. This contrasts with the attitude of British workers, who see the state as neutral in social conflict. French workers see the state as the source of any solution to economic inequality and social injustice, whereas British workers see the solution coming naturally through economic expansion. With such attitudes widespread among French workers and with French unions committed to radical social and political change, it is hardly surprising to find signs of important class confrontation in the factories and in the negotiations between workers and the government.

THE RELIGIOUS CLEAVAGE

Despite the fact that most French are at least nominally Roman Catholic (87 percent), a division among Catholics themselves has been the source of social tensions. One of the oldest and deepest cleavages in French society is between those who sought to reduce the political and social role of the Roman Catholic church (the anticlericals) and those who defended the church's place in French society (the clericals). With roots in the Revolution of 1789 and even earlier, the religious cleavage reflects the long battle over the church's political power in France, which was not definitively decided until the final separation of church and state in 1905.

The fluctuations in the church's political power can be summarized in the history of the Pantheon, one of the many beautiful monuments attracting tourists to Paris. The Pantheon was originally designed as an abbey. Completed just as the Revolution began in 1789, it was turned into a temple of fame to hold the remains of revolutionary heroes. In 1806 under the more conservative Napoleon, the Pantheon became a church and the bodies of revolutionary greats were moved elsewhere. The bodies were returned briefly during the revolution of 1848 and then

removed again as the clericals regained influence under Napoleon III. After the establishment of the Third Republic, the Pantheon became and has remained the temple of fame for revolutionary and literary greats.

Even after the formal separation of church and state in 1905 and the exclusion of the church from active politics, anticlerical forces, generally on the Left, attacked remaining areas of church influence, such as in parochial schools. Clericals, generally on the Right, often contested the democratic parliamentary system as a whole because of the republicans' past violent attacks on the church; to support the republicans was to aid the enemies of the church.

Since World War II, changes in the Roman Catholic church and in French society have eased the tensions between clericals and anticlericals.[12] The active role of many practicing Catholics in the wartime Resistance movement served to integrate Catholics into the political system and to demonstrate to often suspicious anticlericals that Catholics could be devout and democratic at the same time. The church no longer condemned the Left as heretical, and the left-wing parties reduced their dogmatic anticlericalism. The only significant political issue left over from the old conflict is the question of state financial aid to church schools. Among the general public, this issue seems to stir little interest, since a compromise was reached in 1960 allowing state aid for private schools that conform to state-dictated educational programs and standards. Political elites on the Left still pledge the elimination of subsidies to church schools and even talk of the nationalization of all private schools. Conservatives are equally determined to defend what they insist is the freedom to choose parochial or other private schools and for the state to make that choice financially attractive through public subsidies to private schools. The issue of whether or not to provide public funds to private schools is not an unusual one to Americans. But in the United States it lacks most of the ideological content of the French battles over secular education. In addition, the issue is played out in the courts in the United States; in France, church-state relations bring politics into the streets.

While the general public seems content with the status quo of modest state subsidies to private schools, governments periodically reopen the church-state cleavage by trying to decrease or increase the subsidies. When that happens, defenders of public schools or advocates of private education mobilize huge demonstrations to support their positions. Usually, the government retreats from the divisions and tensions. For example, in 1984, the Socialist government, motivated by its ideological convictions, tried to eliminate state subsidies. Massive demonstrations that brought millions into the streets forced the government to withdraw its legislation. Nine years later, a conservative government tried to increase public financial support to private education. It too was compelled to drop the idea as a result of massive protests.

Now in the 1990s, new church-state tensions are emerging as a result of the growing Islamic population. Islam, with 3 million adherents, is now the second-largest religion in France, more numerous than the Protestants and Jews. New religious tensions have emerged. Some are based on disputes among Muslims over varying degrees of commitment to Islamic principles; others come from indigenous French people who resent the continued attachment of North Africans to "alien" religions. This new religious division is complicated by the ethnic issues that underlie it, as we shall see later in this chapter.

Aside from such symbolic outbursts, the most important political manifestation of the religious cleavage is in voting behavior. For nearly a century or more, the single best indicator of likely partisan preference has been the voter's level of religious conviction.[13] The more faithfully the individual practices Catholicism, the more likely he or she will vote for right-wing parties (see Table 8–2). This religious impact on voting behavior reflects the intensity of feelings engendered by the long struggle between the anticlerical republican forces on the Left and the church-supported conservatives. For a devout Catholic to vote for the Left was for many years tantamount to apostasy, or at the very least to disobedience. In 2000, the parish priests no longer tell their parishioners how to vote from the pulpit, but the strong association between religious practice and voting makes the level of religious dedication a better predictor of partisan ties than social class identity or any other factor.

There is some evidence suggesting that the influence of religion on voting choice is declining.[14] In part, this is due to the overall decline of the level of religious commitment among the French. There are simply fewer devout Catholics today than there were twenty-five years ago. In addition, those Catholics who do remain loyal to the church seem less closely tied to the parties of the Right and Center than before. The church no longer plays as central a role in shaping values, including political orientations, as it once did. Left-wing parties have put aside their traditional

Table 8–2   Religion and Vote Preference in France

	Percentage Voting on First Ballot of 1997 National Assembly Election for a Candidate of:					
	Far Left	Communist	Socialist	Moderate Conservatives	Ecologists	Far Right
All voters	2.5%	10%	26%	31%	7%	15%
By religious commitment:						
Regularly practicing Catholic	0	2	14	58	6	7
Occasionally practicing Catholic	5	4	22	43	6	12
Nonpracticing Catholic	0	11	28	27	7	18
Other religions	0	11	32	29	7	13
No religion	5	20	32	12	9	17

Source: "Le Profil des électeurs au premier tour des élections législatives," *Revue Française de Science Politique* 49 (June-August 1997): 464.

mistrust and begun courting the votes of loyal Catholics. They have also welcomed practicing Catholics into their ranks. Despite the slight loosening of the linkage between religious practice and electoral choice, religion still provides the most reliable predictor of likely voting choice. The closer the voter's attachment to the Catholic Church, the more likely he or she is to vote for the Center-Right; the more distant the relationship to the Catholic Church, the more likely the voter is to support a party of the Left.

ETHNIC DIVISIONS

Since 1789, nearly all French regimes have suppressed regional and ethnic differences in the cause of the uniformity and equality provided by a highly centralized state. There nevertheless is still a diversity of peoples within the boundaries of France. In a country very proud of its national language and almost defiant in its efforts to preserve that language, it is surprising to find a number of other languages. But about 35 percent of the French speak a regional language as well as French, or sometimes in preference to French. This linguistic pluralism is the result of the incorporation into France centuries ago of a number of different nationalities. Several of the nationalities remain distinct even after centuries of attempts to integrate them; these hardy groups include the Alsatians, Basques, Bretons, Catalans, Corsicans, and Occitanians.

While the nationalities have preserved their customs, folkways, and sometimes their language, they are for the most part loyal to the French state. In contrast to the situation in Britain, where people identify themselves as Scots, Welsh, or English rather than as British, in France the overwhelming majority of the ethnic minorities identify themselves as French rather than as some other nationality.

In recent years, some elements within all the minority nationalities have pressed for greater respect for the distinctive traits and languages of their ethnic group. In many cases, the motive for this renewed awareness of national distinctions is the fear of the possible loss of these unique features as a national, homogenous French culture is developed through modern communications and migration patterns. Television and the movement of people from their birthplace to other parts of France seem to endanger the survival of distinctive Breton or Alsatian or Occitanian cultures. Often an underlying cause of the unrest among these nationality groups is their economic discontent. The pattern of economic growth has been uneven; areas nearest Paris and the growing European markets have experienced the most rapid growth. Most of these ethnic groups are located in peripheral areas along the frontiers. With the exception of the Alsatians, who find themselves well situated to benefit from the economic expansion of the European Union, the other ethnic groups feel isolated from the economic development of France in recent years. This economic discontent is a source of unrest itself, but it also reinforces fears of cultural extinction, since the young people living in these distressed areas are compelled to leave their home regions to find work in areas where it will be more difficult to maintain their unique cultural heritage.

Renewed ethnic assertiveness has had only minimal impact on French politics. Unlike the situations in Scotland and Wales, the French national minorities have not succeeded in developing political parties capable of cutting into the electoral support of the major parties. There are several ethnic-based political movements in each area, and they have occasionally run candidates in national and local elections. But none has so far had any electoral success at all.

The only two ethnic groups with movements that have attracted large followings are the Bretons[15] and the Corsicans. Many Bretons and Corsicans favor greater autonomy in the form of control over local matters; much smaller groups from both minorities advocate total separation from France and the creation of independent Breton and Corsican states. While their electoral efforts have been unsuccessful, Breton and Corsican nationalists have used other forms of political pressure to seek greater autonomy for their regions and greater respect for their unique cultural contributions. Small terrorist groups among both Bretons and Corsicans have even used violence through bombings and kidnappings to press their demands.

In recent years, it has been Corsicans who have pressed their demands with the greatest fervor. The island of Corsica has been a part of France since 1768 and generally well integrated into the French nation. The national government subsidizes the Corsican economy with payments of approximately $5,000 for each of the island's 250,000 residents.[16] At the end of 1996, a public-opinion poll showed that over 90 percent of Corsicans were opposed to independence. A small group, however, advocates independence and have pressed their cause with violence. Since 1996, a string of terrorist bombings and shootings have disturbed Corsica and occasionally the mainland. In one day in early 1997, 58 bombs were set off at post offices, tax bureaus, and other government buildings in Corsica. At the end of the 1990s, the average number of Corsican terrorist bombing incidents averaged 500 a year.[17]

There have been some steps to provide regional governments greater powers. To help defuse violence in Corsica, it was one of the first such regions to gain new powers. Other concessions have included greater respect for the cultural heritage of Corsicans and other nationalities. But the gains have been more symbolic than real: The Corsicans got a university; the Bretons got some television programs in their language; the Alsatians were allowed to use their dialect in state-run nursery schools; smaller ethnic groups, such as French Jews, were given libraries, museums, and theaters to promote their distinctive cultural expressions. While the state has been willing to spend more for ethnic minorities to preserve their cultures, it has conceded little real power to the ethnic communities.

New Ethnic Cleavages

Since World War II, France has experienced a new wave of immigrants who are changing the ethnic composition of the nation. The immigrants came, first from southern European countries such as Italy, Spain, and Portugal and later from Northern Africa, to fill the labor shortage caused by the rapidly growing French economy. Others came seeking refuge from conflict in former French colonies in North Africa or Indochina. More recently, France has received many refugees from the social and economic strife of central and southern Europe. Some of these peoples came presumably for short periods; many

remained and now have families born and raised in France. By the mid-1990s, the immigrant population reached nearly 5 million or nearly 9 percent of the total population. The impact and presence of the immigrants are especially noticeable in the impoverished areas around large industrial cities such as Paris, Lyons, and Marseilles. There the immigrant population often exceeds 15–20 percent of the regional population.

Initially, the immigrants were welcome assets in meeting shortages of unskilled labor. However, by the 1980s, France began to have unemployment problems. The numbers of immigrants had grown. There were also problems of assimilation. It had been easy to assimilate the first wave of immigrants from southern Europe. Later immigrants, especially Muslims from Northern Africa, had no interest in assimilation. It soon proved difficult for a people who believed that everyone secretly wanted to be French to abide the presence in its midst of immigrants who rejected French culture and perpetuated their own "alien" traditions and beliefs. To us in North America who are experiencing similar challenges in absorbing large numbers of recent immigrants, the problem is familiar. But Americans have the advantage of having worked with the challenges of diversity since the first colonists arrived. What makes the French problem more critical is the newness of the challenge of dealing with a multiethnic society.

The growth of immigrant populations in cities coincided with new problems of urban decay, crime, and drug abuse. The native French came to associate these problems with the presence of the immigrants. The French have long prided themselves on their racial tolerance, and indeed, their attitudes conveyed to public opinion pollsters suggest that they are more tolerant than the British. But there are deep-seated suspicions and stereotypes about immigrants, especially those from North Africa, that are often not admitted to pollsters. By the mid-1980s, racial relations had become very tense. While France had been spared the rioting of immigrant populations that had hit British cities, nasty incidents involving individuals and small groups had become commonplace in many parts of France.

Public opinion became openly hostile to the immigrants. The major parties, however, avoided

---

IMMIGRATION AND ASSIMILATION

France has long welcomed immigrants and especially political refugees. But the welcome has usually been conditioned on the immigrants' acceptance of French cultural values. Earlier immigrants found assimilation easier than have the North Africans who make up a large part of the recent wave in immigration. The North Africans are visibly different in appearance. They maintain ties with their homelands; they continue to speak Arabic, and they retain their Muslim religion. The result is often a clash between North Africans desiring to maintain their heritage and the native French expecting immigrants to assimilate. For example, a few years ago, three North African girls were barred from attending public school when they came to class wearing the traditional Muslim scarf over their heads and part of their faces. School administrators insisted that the wearing of the scarves violated the usual bar against wearing religious symbols in schools. The debate over this issue was passionate, largely because of a deeper motive of using public schools as a means of assimilating new immigrants into French culture. After the issue was debated pro and con in the national press, the courts ultimately supported the schools' position against allowing the scarves to be worn in the classroom.

---

the issue. Both conservative and leftist governments tried to stem new immigration and tried to encourage the voluntary departure of those already in France through bonuses for workers who agreed to return to their homelands. Both Right and Left political leaders tried to encourage nondiscrimination and racial understanding.

The failure of the major parties to respond to the changing public mood offered opportunities for extreme right-wing groups. One, the National Front, emerged as a powerful political force bent on exploiting the racial issue. With a platform calling for the compulsory repatriation of immigrants, the National Front won over 10 percent of the vote in the 1986 National Assembly elections and 15 percent on the first ballot of the 1997 parliamentary election. The presence of this challenge from the National Front has led the mainline parties of the Left and moderate Right to take harder lines on immigration issues in efforts to undercut support for the far Right. The government has adopted tighter rules on naturalization (the process of becoming a French citizen), cracked down on radical fundamentalism among the Muslims in France, and imposed ever stricter limits and controls on new immigration.

The major challenge is to foster tolerance among peoples in an increasingly diverse population. There are laws to bar discrimination, but they are not easy to impose when many individuals are intolerant. This is a major obstacle in a country where nearly half the population admits to feeling "very" or "fairly" racist.[18] As a result, this new ethnicity is likely to be a continuing source of political conflict through the coming decade. As in Britain, the French face the difficult challenge of learning to live with a racially diverse population after centuries of relative racial homogeneity.

A STALLED SOCIETY?

It has long been fashionable to claim that multiple social cleavages, rigid class structures, educational elitism, and, most importantly, unresponsive bureaucrats have blocked social change in France. Thus the distinguished French sociologist Michel Crozier contends that France has become a "stalled society" and Stanley Hoffmann wrote of a "stalemate society."[19] To be sure, Hoffmann at least noted signs of a break in this stalemate, but others have adopted his terminology to insist on the static nature of French society.

Conflicting with this image of a stalled society is evidence that French social structures have proved highly adaptive and dynamic in the postwar years.[20] They have supported rapid economic change and development. From the late 1950s through the mid-1970s, France had on average the highest economic growth rate in Western Europe and a higher rate than any other industrial country except Japan. The society tolerated without major disruption the change from a commercial and industrial structure dominated by small shopkeepers and small owner-operated industry into a complex, consumer-oriented, mass society. The social structures were flexible enough to adapt to the transformation of the economic base from a largely peasant country to a modern industrial power. In the process, the farm population dropped from 26.7 percent of the total population in 1954 to 9.3 percent 20 years later. Some 2 million people from families once involved in farming were successfully integrated into the industrial and commercial sectors in less than two decades. For the most part, these social changes were achieved with a minimum of social unrest or disruption. In contrast to the crisis-induced change that is characteristic of "stalemate societies," the postwar social changes in France were planned and directed by the government, not precipitous actions taken in emergencies.

Yet there remain important problem areas in society, and these illustrate the dilemma of social change in France. The working class is poorly integrated into the political and social system, a situation that does not appear to have changed under Socialist leadership. Management for its part resists programs to involve the workers in the system because it fears worker infringement on the absolute independence of the owners. It prefers a divided and weakened labor movement to one that might become a partner with management in promoting productivity. In such an environment, government efforts to promote social integration are vain. For example, both labor and management fought government proposals for a very modest profit-sharing program. In this case the government did prevail, but in other government efforts to reform work conditions labor and management have combined to block meaningful reform.

Decentralization of the highly centralized state is another issue that has received much attention but little action until recently, and the Socialist efforts at decentralization are still modest and by no means assured of success. While public

opinion supports the general idea of decentralization, the intensity of interest is low. There are enormous political obstacles at the local as well as the national level to any reduction of central political control. For example, leaders in Nice on the Mediterranean coast favored decentralization in abstract, but when they learned that the capital of the new decentralized government structures would be located in Marseilles, they fought ardently against decentralization. Rather than see additional prestige and political importance go to a rival city, the politicians of Nice preferred no decentralization. Recalling battles between the two cities in ancient history, the mayor of Nice scornfully declared that his city would never accept rule by "the Phoenicians."

The educational system is in disarray and serves to perpetuate the advantages of the already privileged. One of the great achievements of the postwar era has been the rapid growth of the universities to provide educational opportunities to ten times the number of students as before the war. But the rapid expansion came at the cost of reduced quality and devaluation of the diploma. Student resentment over inadequate facilities and job opportunities was a principal cause of the Events of May 1968, which nearly shattered the regime.

When faced with social unrest provoked either by the government's inability or unwillingness to change or by the nature of the changes it is pursuing, the government uses what has been described as a "feather quilt strategy."[21] It absorbs the blows from the discontented, even when they take the form of low-level violence, without modifying its approach. The government simply waits for the dissidents to tire and to dissolve because of their internal divisions. The "feather quilt strategy" works well because of the low degree of mass interest in most of these social issues. Periodically, unrest becomes more general and turns to revolt, as in May 1968, thus tearing the quilt and scattering the feathers; then the regime is shaken clear to its foundations. France has a strong tradition of such revolts, as we saw in Chapter 7. The danger for the state—and the hope for those committed to social change—is that the various discontented groups will call upon the romance of past revolts to take collective action

again in order to right contemporary social
wrongs.

NOTES

[1]Theodore Zeldin, *France 1848–1945: Politics and Anger*
(London: Oxford University Press, 1979).

[2]Stanley Hoffmann, *Decline or Renewal: France Since
the 1930s* (New York: Viking, 1974), pp. 111–144.

[3]INSEE figures in *Les Dernières Nouvelles d'Alsace,* 22
May 1979.

[4]Centre d'Etudes des Revenus et des Coûts, *Les Français
et leur revenus: Le Tourant des années 80* (Paris: CERC,
1989).

[5]*The Economist,* 18 September 1993.

[6]Hoffmann, *Decline or Renewal,* p. 463.

[7]See Ezra N. Suleiman, *Elites in French Society: The Politics of Survival* (Princeton, NJ: Princeton University Press,
1978). See also Michalina Vaughan et al., *Social Change in
France* (New York: St. Martin's, 1980), pp. 12–62.

[8]Alain Peyrefitte, *Le Mal français* (Paris: Plon, 1977),
p. 320.

[9]Michael Lewis-Beck, "Class, Religion, and the French
Voter: A 'Stalled' Electorate?" *French Politics and Society*
16 (Spring 1998): 43–51.

[10]Duncan Gallie, "Trade Union Ideology and Workers'
Conception of Class Inequality in France," *West European
Politics* 3 (January 1980): 10–32.

[11]Peyrefitte, *Le Mal français,* p. 376.

[12]See William Bosworth, *Catholicism and Crisis in Modern France* (Princeton, NJ: Princeton University Press, 1962).

[13]Duncan MacRae, Jr., *Parliament, Parties, and Society
in France, 1946–1958* (New York: St. Martin's, 1967),
pp. 244–260.

[14]Guy Michelat and Michel Simon, "Religion, Class, and
Politics," *Comparative Politics* 10 (January 1977): 159–184.
See also Daniel Boy and Noona Mayer, eds., *The French Voter
Decides* (Ann Arbor: University of Michigan Press, 1993).

[15]Patrick Gaillou and Michael Jones, *The Bretons* (Oxford, England: Blackwell, 1996).

[16]*The New York Times,* 15 January 1997.

[17]*The Economist,* 14 February 1998.

[18]Eurobarometer, No. 48, Fall 1997.

[19]Michel Crozier, *The Stalled Society,* trans. Rupert Swyer
(New York: Viking, 1973), and Stanley Hoffmann, "Paradoxes
of the French Political Community," in *In Search of France,*
ed. Stanley Hoffmann et al. (New York: Harper Torchbooks,
1965).

[20]See John Ardagh, *France Today* (Harmondsworth, England: Penguin, 1987).

[21]Suzanne Berger, *Peasants Against Politics* (Cambridge,
MA: Harvard University Press, 1972), pp. 237–238.

Chapter 9

The French Political Framework

The French lack, apparently, the gift of governability. . . . They love the notion of creating a state on the best rational principles, but they are temperamentally incapable of allowing it to work. The state is an intellectual glory, but is also the enemy.[1]

The French are reputed to view their country from two viewpoints. On the one hand, they see the *pays réel*—the real country—in a very positive way as the essence of France, worthy of respect and sacrifice on the part of its citizens. On the other hand, they view the *pays légal*—the legal country in the sense of its formal governmental institutions and leaders—with cynicism and contempt; citizens are justified in sabotaging or evading its acts since it discredits the *pays réel*. With such a dichotomy between the French people's attitude toward the country's abstract nature and its concrete reality, even the best drafted constitutions in France face skepticism and opposition.

The public's ambivalent attitude toward the state makes it difficult to find an appropriate political framework that can long endure. As we have seen, France has had a long series of different political frameworks in the past two centuries. Unlike in the United States, where the American

Revolution resulted in a consensus on the form of government, the French Revolution divided the French; no consensus on the framework of government emerged. The average life span for a constitution in France is around 15 years. Over 100 years ago, the transitory nature of French political frameworks was already the object of a popular joke: a Parisian bookseller explains to a potential customer that he cannot sell him a copy of the French constitution because he does not deal in periodical literature.

Despite the frequent change in regime, two basic patterns have prevailed and succeeded each other. The democratic pattern featured a powerful elected parliament dominating politics and a correspondingly weak political executive. This pattern was found in the Third and Fourth Republics and earlier democratic regimes. The authoritarian pattern, found in the monarchies, the empires, and the Vichy era, emphasized the power of the executive. The legislature, when it still existed, was left with little or no power to check the executive's actions.

The current regime, the Fifth Republic established in 1958, attempts to blend these two patterns by increasing executive power but retaining

CONSTITUTIONAL ENGINEERING: A SUCCESS STORY

For political scientists, one of the interesting aspects of recent constitutional developments in France is the use of constitutional reform to alter long-standing political features and practices. In Britain, we saw that the process was the opposite: Evolving political practices have reshaped and redefined traditional political institutions. In contrast, the drafters of the French Constitution hoped to change certain patterns of behavior and practices thought to be undesirable. The success of this "constitutional engineering" illustrates that the relationship between political institutions on the one hand and political attitudes and social setting on the other is complex. If it is true that sometimes well-engrained political attitudes and social structures determine the nature and operation of political institutions (as is the case to a great degree in Britain), it is also true that political institutions can shape and even radically transform established political attitudes and behavior.

the democratic controls of an independent legislature and free elections. After 40 years, this constitution enjoys broader support than have most earlier political frameworks. It has worked well in both crises and in normal times. Its institutions have worked to correct some of the political problems of previous French regimes. Indeed, there is now a broad consensus in support of the institutions of the Fifth Republic. Only fringe parties on either extreme question its value and then only by suggesting minor amendments rather than wholesale revision.

THE CONSTITUTION OF THE FIFTH REPUBLIC (1958)

When the Fourth Republic ground to a halt, Charles de Gaulle agreed to come back to power on condition that he be authorized to change the constitution. The drafters of the new constitution intended to use the new framework to alter long-standing features of French democratic practice and behavior. To correct for the past weakness of the executive, the Constitution of the Fifth Republic granted extensive independent power to the president and to the government (the prime minister and council of ministers). To respond to the past problem of a seemingly overpowerful parliament, the new constitution reduced the legislature's areas of competence and limited its power to oust the government through censure and votes of no-confidence. In response to the chronic and excessive pluralism of the French

party system, the constitution included an electoral system that encouraged party coalitions and later added a system of presidential elections that forced parties to combine in order to elect a president.

In general, these efforts at "constitutional engineering" have succeeded in eliminating the problems they were designed to treat. The establishment of a powerful, popularly elected presidency has eliminated governmental instability; the electoral devices have contributed to the simplification of the party system. On balance, the institutions of the Fifth Republic do seem to have achieved the drafters' objective of finding a more effective framework for democratic government.

A Mixed Presidential–Parliamentary Structure of Government

To correct the governmental instability of past French democracies, the drafters of the Fifth Republic's constitution sought to mix the parliamentary and presidential political frameworks. The result is a hybrid with elements of both these basic organizational patterns (see Figure 9–1). The parliamentary elements include the presence of a prime minister and cabinet of ministers who are accountable to parliament and who can be ousted by a vote of censure in the National Assembly. The presidential elements include a popularly elected president who appoints the prime minister and enjoys a variety of other constitutional prerogatives and powers. The mixed system results in a dual executive—a president and a

THE FRENCH MIXED PRESIDENTIAL-PARLIAMENTARY SYSTEM

Since 1962, France has had a mixed system including both a popularly elected president with his own mandate and a prime minister and government accountable to the National Assembly. The mixed system has the merit of providing strong presidential leadership along with parliamentary government. It has worked well, although the president's powers are generally reduced when he is from the opposite political party from the majority in the National Assembly. The overall success of the mixed presidential-parliamentary system has led many newer democracies, such as Russia, Poland, and other former communist states, to pattern their constitutions on the French constitution.

prime minister—sharing responsibility in the direction of the government. So far, this mixed system has worked well in providing effective and stable government. The rotation of short-lived cabinets that weakened and discredited the Third and Fourth Republics has ended. For example, there were 27 prime ministers during the 12 years of the Fourth Republic; during the first 40 years of the Fifth Republic, there were only 16 prime ministers. In addition, the presence of a powerful president gives added stability and continuity to

government under the Fifth Republic. As indicated in Table 9–1, the continuity of the French executive compares favorably with experience in other Western democracies.

The President

In the introduction we noted that one of the disadvantages of the presidential form of democracy is that there is a tendency for the powers of the president to grow, sometimes to the point that the

Figure 9–1   Basic Institutions of French Government

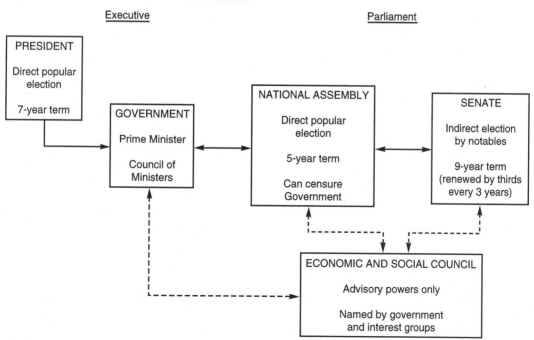

Table 9–1   Number of Chief Executives, 1959–99

France	5 Presidents
	16 Prime ministers
Britain	8 Prime ministers
Germany	6 Chancellors
United States	9 Presidents

president exercises personal and uncontrolled power. The trend for the growth of presidential power is certainly in evidence in Fifth Republic France, although it has not reached such a point as to compromise the basic democratic nature of the regime.

The constitution provided for a presidency tailored to the political style and philosophy of its first occupant, Charles de Gaulle. As a war hero and the person who incarnated the resistance to the German occupier and the liberation of France to his own people, de Gaulle believed, and many French also believed, that he was aloof from the normal partisan political passions that sometimes immobilized the French state. The constitution therefore called for the president to be an arbiter whose primary charge is to ensure "by his arbitration, the regular functioning of the governmental authorities, as well as the continuity of the state" (Article 5). The president should intervene when narrow and self-interested groups threaten to divert government from the general interest or paralyze its action.

In practice, the president's role has been much more than that of an aloof and neutral arbiter who intervened only to prevent impasse or to decide among competing interests. Furthermore, presidential power has grown under each of the presidents. By the beginning of the 1980s, the supposedly mixed French system was clearly very much more "presidential" than it was "parliamentary."[2]

There are several explanations for the growth of presidential power. First, in efforts to correct for the weaknesses of previous French presidents, the constitution grants substantial power to the president. He is elected for a 7-year term with the possibility of reelection. The president has the power to appoint and dismiss the prime minister and members of the cabinet. He presides over the meetings of the Council of Ministers; he controls the agenda of these meetings and thereby controls the discussion and action of the government. He can require parliament to reconsider legislation it has passed. He can dissolve the National Assembly and call new elections at his discretion. He may propose a referendum on any question he desires to have people vote on. He has the right to declare a state of national emergency and to rule by decree. In addition, since the president ordinarily names and controls the Council of Ministers, he benefits from the extensive grants of power accorded this institution.

Second, the popular election of the president accords additional political weight to the presidency. Originally, the president was elected indirectly by an electoral college of local and national officials; in 1962 a referendum replaced this indirect election with the direct election of the president by universal suffrage. This greatly increased the political stature of the presidency. Popular election permits presidents to claim that they represent the nation as a whole. As one president put it, "I have legitimacy from the free election." All other elected officials come out of relatively small electoral districts; the president alone can claim a national constituency.

In addition, the dynamics of a national election force the president to be a powerful political leader and not just an aloof arbiter. The need to develop a national electoral majority leads the president to build a broad-based political party or coalition. Once elected, if the president harbors any interest in reelection, and all have so far, the president must continue after the election to exert leadership over his political supporters. To maintain the appearance of a president above the parties, he generally controls his party through intermediaries rather than through his own efforts. This partisan leadership position makes it unlikely that the president can fulfill the role of an aloof arbiter stipulated by the constitution. He is indeed the principal political leader and, as such, is very clearly a partisan leader rather than a neutral referee.[3]

The election process contributes to the growing political role of the president in another way. To get elected, the president has to make a number of campaign pledges on what he will do once in office. After the election, the president's sense of obligation to fulfill his campaign pledges leads

---

DIVIDED GOVERNMENT IN FRANCE AND THE UNITED STATES

In the United States, we have "divided government" when the presidency is controlled by one party and the majorities in Congress by the other. In general, divided government poses few problems in the United States because party discipline is loose: members of Congress vote their consciences rather than along party lines. Furthermore, differences between parties are usually not great on most policy matters. A skillful president from one party usually can develop a compromise position that will be supported by a broad, bipartisan majority. The American political depolarization is well illustrated by the personal friendship and frequent political cooperation between a committed Democratic liberal like Senator Ted Kennedy and a conservative Republican like Senator Orrin Hatch.

In France, however, party discipline is very tight with most deputies always voting as directed by their party group; party differences are greater, if not in actual policy positions then in the emotional distance between them. Party polarization in France is so great that instances of cross-party friendships are unusual and bipartisan policy cooperation is practically nonexistent. As a result, during "cohabitation" in France the president usually withdraws from day-to-day policymaking and the parliamentary elements of France's mixed constitution prevail, at least in domestic politics. One observer correctly noted the situation: "Cohabitation never became cooperation, but it was reasonably close to peaceful coexistence."[4]

---

him to take an active and directing role in politics. French voters regard the presidential election as the most important electoral contest, the one that determines the political future of the country. The president is therefore impelled to lead the policymaking process.

A third factor in the growth of presidential power in France has been the presence of a sympathetic majority in the National Assembly. In addition, the presidential majority generally has been cohesive and disciplined in parliamentary voting. Unlike the situation in the U.S. Congress, where presidents cannot rely automatically on legislative support even from legislators of their own party, French presidents can count on their supporters to give them a legislative majority on virtually all their major proposals.

All of these powers are contingent upon the presence of a sympathetic majority in the National Assembly. But the election sequence makes it likely that there will be times when the president does not have that parliamentary majority. Then the president faces a hostile majority and must assume a more modest role based more on the constitutional model of an arbiter rather than on the activist role that has evolved in practice.

For many years, the issue of how to resolve a situation when the president did not have a supporting majority in the National Assembly was hypothetical. The first test of the French system's ability to deal with divided partisan control came in 1986 when a conservative parliamentary majority headed by Jacques Chirac faced the challenge of governing with a Socialist president, François Mitterrand. The first "cohabitation" proved to be difficult and tense since Mitterrand and Chirac were contenders in the next presidential election. A second experience with cohabitation came in 1993 when again a conservative prime minister, Edouard Balladur, had to govern with Socialist President Mitterrand. It was less contentious, but in practice, cohabitation still led to a temporary reduction in the powers of the president. The third episode of cohabitation began in 1997 when a newly elected Socialist majority in the National Assembly faced a conservative president, Jacques Chirac. The Socialists selected their leader Lionel Jospin as prime minister.

In all three eras of cohabitation, the president lost the ability to control the composition of the cabinet. The president still presided over weekly meetings of the cabinet, but real decisions were made elsewhere by supporters of the government. The president no longer had much influence over domestic politics although he could and did publicly warn the government—often with partisan motivations—about their policies and practices. The president continued to assert the primacy of the presidency in foreign and defense policy making. Since these policies reflected a general consensus, there was no real showdown on the president's powers in foreign and defense matters. These eras of cohabitation demonstrate that the powers of the president, strong as they have been under the Fifth Republic, can only be exercised fully if there is a supportive majority in the National Assembly.

In the first two experiences with cohabitation (1986–88, 1993–1995), the reduction in presidential powers was only temporary. The same is likely to be true of the present era of cohabitation. The dynamics that produced the powerful presidency in earlier years bring a resumption of presidential primacy once there is harmony between the president and the National Assembly majority: a popular election, the cohesion and discipline of the parties, and the ambitions of the individuals who become president. The presidency attracts the top politicians. Once they are in that office, even those who in the past advocated reduced presidential powers—as Mitterrand had done—have acted to extend their powers and prerogatives. As long as the president is popularly elected and is seen as the pinnacle of politics, and as long as the most ambitious politicians seek that post, the presidency will be the seat of major policy decisions. There are likely to be occasional eras of cohabitation, but they will be the exception and short-lived rather than a new direction in the evolution of the institutions of the Fifth Republic.

The Constitution of the Fifth Republic clearly solved the chronic weakness of the executive branch of government during earlier French democracies. Some critics, however, raise the complaint that this constitutional engineering has created an even bigger problem of an overly powerful, even potentially dictatorial presidency. At times, the president's actions in ignoring parliament—due to his assurance of a majority vote there—or in abusing government control over radio and television news coverage, give credence to these charges of arbitrary rule. But the French presidency is still far from dictatorial. French presidents are more powerful than their predecessors in earlier democratic regimes; they are more powerful than American presidents, who must contend with an independent Congress and who lack the support of strong political parties. But they are probably no more powerful than British prime ministers or German chancellors when they are backed by firm parliamentary majorities. In the last analysis, much of the power that the French president has acquired has resulted from the voluntary acquiescence of the National Assembly to presidential leadership.

Perhaps the most threatening constitutional power the president possesses is the ability to rule by decree in the event of a national emergency. The terms of Article 16 defining the conditions of a state of emergency are vague, and there is no way to challenge the president's interpretation of what constitutes a national emergency. So far, presidents have avoided using these powers. The emergency powers have been used only once, in 1961 during the threatened military coup by disgruntled military leaders opposed to granting Algeria independence. While some argued that the state of emergency lasted longer than necessary, few criticized de Gaulle's use of the emergency clause or the decrees issued during that period.

Another controversial feature of the French presidential role is the president's ability to propose referendum issues to the electorate. Presidents can thus consult the people directly on issues of their choice. Many French are suspicious of the referendum, not so much because of an alleged threat to the sovereignty of parliament that leads many British political figures to oppose referendums, but because in past French experience, referendums and plebiscites were devices used by authoritarian leaders to give the appearance of democracy to their regimes. In practice, use of the referendum has been risky for presidents. De Gaulle resigned when the public rejected his 1969 referendum, thus setting an awkward precedent for later presidents who may lose referendums. Since then, there have been only two referendums, and while the presidents' position prevailed low turnout or narrow victories have embarrassed rather than strengthened the presidents who proposed them. Clearly, earlier fears that the referendum procedure would be used excessively or abusively as a plebescite on the president have proved to be unfounded.

A powerful presidential system such as that of the French Republic poses the danger that a demagogic and ruthless leader may somehow get himself or herself elected and then rule dictatorially. But this same danger is difficult to avoid in any type of political system if the emerging leaders lack genuine commitment to democracy or if the people are not vigilant. Leaders in France who have had serious chances of winning the presidency thus far have been individuals with firm democratic attachments. Even de Gaulle, whose concept of himself as the embodiment of the French nation led to doubts about his democratic convictions, resigned promptly in 1969 when the electorate rejected his referendum proposal.

The Prime Minister and Council of Ministers

The mixed presidential-parliamentary system produces an often awkward pattern of relationships between the two executives, the president and the prime minister.[5] Under normal circumstances, the president selects a prime minister and the Council of Ministers, collectively known as the government. The ministers head government departments such as economy, defense, education, and industry, with the prime minister serving as coordinator and director under the leadership of the president. The government directs the state's administrative structures and handles the daily conduct of government affairs.

The constitution of the Fifth Republic provided the Council of Ministers with important new powers. The government can handle many issues through decrees issued on its own authority or on the basis of broad grants of decree powers given it by parliament. It can control the parliamentary agenda and give priority to questions it deems important. It can insist that parliament vote on its proposals without making any amendments. It is protected from parliamentary sanctions by a difficult censure procedure; the motion of censure must be signed by a tenth of the members of the National Assembly (who lose the right to sign another censure motion for the duration of that session). Voting is personal with no proxy votes accepted on censure motions.

The development of a powerful and cohesive majority coalition has buttressed the position of the government. On nearly all issues, the government can count on the loyal support of a comfortable majority in parliament. The cohesion of the majority is even more impressive on censure motions: Since 1962 members of the government majority have voted for censure only three times, and in these cases the defectors were very few in number and had no effect on the outcome of the vote. The only time the National Assembly ousted a government by censure was in 1962, before the consolidation of the present party coalitions.

These constitutional and political developments have made French governments more effective and more durable. Under the Fourth Republic the average government lasted for only a few months; since 1959, prime ministers have served an average of 2.5 years. In addition, presidential leadership added still more continuity to governments. Despite the fact that the prime minister of the Fifth Republic acts often as the agent of the president rather than on his or her own initiative, the position is still much more powerful than that of premier in the Fourth Republic, who faced continual threats to the very life of the government.

With a variety of means to control parliament's agenda and actions, the government is in a strong position to press its legislative programs through parliament. When an issue is politically sensitive, the prime minister may simply make the measure a vote of confidence. Under the constitution, when the government declares a bill to be an issue of confidence, that measure is deemed to be passed by the legislative body without a vote taking place. In order to block the legislation, opposition groups must censure the government and vote it out of office. The opposition parties may try to censure the government. So far when this has happened, the majority has backed the government rather than risk dissolution and new elections. While deputies may not like the measures forced through by the government, they are reluctant to oust the government. A variety of other procedures permit a government, even a minority government, to govern as long as there are not enough deputies in the National Assembly sufficiently opposed to it that they will vote for censure (see Table 9–2).

The relationship between the government and the president is complex, due to the mixed

Table 9–2   The Stages of a Bill in the French Parliament

NATIONAL ASSEMBLY

1. Deposition of a bill
    Projets de loi (Introduced by the government)
    Propositions de loi (Introduced by a member of parliament)
2. Consideration by the Economic and Social Council of all legislation dealing with social or economic issues
3. Action by parliamentary committee
    Consideration of amendments and alternative texts
    Preparation of a report on the legislation and amendments
4. Floor debate
    General discussion
    Discussion of each article
    Final vote on the whole text
5. Second consideration of all or part of the bill upon the request of the government or a member of parliament

SENATE

Steps 1–5 Repeated

FINAL STAGES

1. When the National Assembly and Senate versions are the same:
    a. If the constitutionality is challenged, the Constitutional Council renders a decision.
    b. Signature by the prime minister
    c. Signature and promulgation of the law by the President of the Republic
    d. Publication of the law
2. When the National Assembly and Senate versions differ:
    a. Consideration of changes made in the second chamber by the first chamber to adopt the bill. If approved, bill goes through final stages described above.
    b. When differences remain, a joint committee (*navette*) is appointed to work out differences. The revised legislation must then be approved by both houses before going through the final stages.
    c. If agreement cannot be reached, the government may ask the National Assembly to decide the fate of the bill or it may simply let the bill die.
    d. If differences are resolved, step 1 as above.

presidential-parliamentary nature of French government. The constitution assigns the government the responsibility of determining and conducting the nation's policies. In practice, the growth of presidential power has meant that the president and his staff determine the major programs and reforms that are proposed by the government. The extent to which the presidential staff intervenes directly in a specific policy decision varies with the minister concerned and with the importance of the issue at hand. Presidents can count on the government to reflect accurately their own priorities and preferences in the conduct of state affairs.

In most parliamentary democracies, such as Britain or Germany, the governments are accountable only to their parliaments, which select them and can oust them through censure. In France, under the mixed parliamentary-presidential system of the Fifth Republic, the government has dual accountabilities. On the one hand, the president appoints the prime minister and other members of the government; he can also dismiss them at his own discretion. The government is not even required to seek a vote of investiture from the National Assembly although many governments have done so voluntarily. On the other hand, the National Assembly can oust the government through a vote of censure. It can also attempt to make life very difficult for the government by slowing or obstructing its legislative proposals. Despite the dual accountabilities in theory, so far the government's main accountability in practice has been to the president. The president's firm majority in the National Assembly has given him the ability to select and remove governments without much concern for parliamentary reaction. As we have already suggested, when the president lacks a majority in parliament, the president either has to sacrifice some control over the government and its policies, or resign.

Even with the presidents selecting the prime ministers, there has occasionally been major friction between the two executives. Popular and independently minded prime ministers can threaten presidential primacy. Even President de Gaulle, who benefited from enormous popular support, felt compelled to replace ambitious prime ministers with lesser-known figures. The problem is that the dual nature of the French executive, with a powerful president and a highly visible prime minister responsible for the day-to-day conduct of government, leads to conflict between these two leaders even if they share the same political philosophy and partisan ties. This problem is of course much more acute during eras of cohabitation when they come from different political parties.

Parliament

The French parliament has two chambers. The *National Assembly* is the more powerful body, with its membership elected directly by the people for 5-year terms. Members of the Senate are elected indirectly by an electoral college made up of local elected public officials; senators serve 9-year terms. The government is accountable only to the popularly elected National Assembly; the Senate cannot censure the government. Both chambers act on all legislation. When there are differences between the texts adopted by the two houses or when one chamber adopts and the other rejects them, the prime minister can convene a joint committee to find a compromise settlement. If this fails, the government can ask the National Assembly to decide the issue alone. This procedure permits the supremacy of the popularly elected National Assembly, but the important discretionary powers of the government cannot be overlooked. When the government finds it in its interests, it can let the Senate block a piece of legislation by not convening a joint committee; when it wants the proposal passed, it can ask the National Assembly to override the Senate's action.

As in Britain, where there is criticism of the aristocratic House of Lords, there are periodic attacks on the unrepresentative French Senate. The electoral college that elects the Senators overrepresents rural and small-town interests; more than one half of the members of the electoral college come from towns and villages with less than 1500 inhabitants, where less than a third of the French population lives. This often gives the Senate an entirely different political composition than the popularly elected National Assembly, and this results in conflicts between the two chambers. An attempt to reduce the Senate's powers failed in a 1969 referendum, and there has been little interest since in reforming or eliminating the Senate. The Socialists have often been upset by the delays and obstruction their reforms encountered in the Senate. In case of clashes between the Senate and the National Assembly, the constitution allows the executive and the National Assembly to prevail over the upper chamber. That limited power of the Senate reduces the desire to abolish or further weaken the chamber even if it sometimes stands in opposition to the presidents and their National Assembly majorities.

Until the beginning of the Fifth Republic, the Palais Bourbon, where the French National Assembly meets, was the very heart of French politics. There laws were written and governments made and unmade. Parliamentary debate was lively, even tumultuous, with the fate of the nation in the hands of the deputies. The galleries were filled with lobbyists, who sometimes brazenly used hand signals to direct friendly deputies on the floor on how to vote, and with journalists and foreign diplomats interested to see whether the government would survive another day of parliamentary action. Nowadays, parliamentary debate is usually lower keyed and attracts much less interest because the seat of political power is now located in the Elysée presidential palace and the prime minister's residence at Matignon, not in the Palais Bourbon. Even the questioning of ministers ("interpellation"), a lively part of the British House of Commons' agenda, lacks excitement in France. The questions are routine and ministers take pride in avoiding responses to the embarrassing ones.

This shift of power from the legislature to the executive is by no means unique to France. It can be observed in Britain, Germany, the United States, and other Western democracies. The increased needs for technical expertise in drafting legislation and for expeditious handling of diplomatic and military matters have shifted lawmaking initiative to the executive. The development of disciplined parties has also reduced the legislature's ability to control the executive as long as the executive maintains the support of a majority.

These trends present elsewhere were accentuated in France by the deliberate effort of the constitutional drafters to reduce the powers of parliament. Most French citizens felt that past parliaments had used their extensive powers in a negative and destabilizing manner. Reaction to the excesses of parliamentary powers under the Third and Fourth Republics led to restrictions on parliament under the Fifth Republic.[6] These restrictions included a reduction in the scope of parliament's lawmaking powers. The constitution specifies parliament's areas of competence, with all issues not specifically assigned to parliament considered as regulatory matters that the government can handle by decree. In certain important legislative fields, the government can request authorization from parliament to legislate by decree, with only the broad outlines being specified by parliament. Even parliament's traditional control of the purse strings is limited by a constitutional provision barring it from increasing government expenditures or decreasing revenues.

The government controls the legislative agenda and can insist on priority treatment for its proposals. It can avoid votes on amendments it opposes by forcing parliament to vote on its text without any parliamentary amendments (known as the "package vote"). It can also declare a proposed law to be a matter of confidence and engage its responsibility in parliament; in such cases the legislation is considered as adopted even though no vote is taken.

Change in the party system reinforced the effect of these constitutional reforms in reducing parliamentary power. First, parties are fewer in number and they have been able to form more durable coalitions than was the case under the Fourth Republic. Second, parties are more disciplined than in the past in the sense that members of a party feel the obligation to vote together on most issues.[7] Because of the presence of a disciplined and coherent majority, the government can count on firm parliamentary support for its action and its legislative program.

In recent years, reforms have strengthened the French parliament. It is now a full-time parliament that meets year-round. Deputies are now limited in the number and kinds of other elected mandates that they hold thus allowing them more time to devote to parliamentary duties. Deputies and senators can more easily challenge the legality of legislation through the Constitutional Council. New resources including more office space and funds for assistants increase the capabilities of members of parliament. Parliamentary committees, especially those in the National Assembly, are more active and powerful. Parliament is more active and more efficient but its pursuit of greater powers is at best only partly and gradually successful.[8]

Despite the curtailment of its powers under the Fifth Republic, parliament still retains the ability to make life difficult and even impossible for any government. For most of the Fifth Republic it has chosen not to do so because of agreement between the majority in parliament and the government. Thus, a major part of the explanation of the decline of parliament's influence under the Fifth Republic is parliament's self-denial, in that it does not use the powers that it still has. Parliament could force the government to consider its amendments by voting down government-imposed package votes; it could throw out the government through censure. It can exercise these controls but it chooses not to because the majority accepts, albeit sometimes grudgingly, the dominance of the executive.

The reduced powers of the French parliament have sometimes led political analysts to discount parliament's role in French politics. This is an error since parliament still exercises important controls over legislation. Parliamentary committees have grown in influence over the last decade and often play an important part in reshaping legislation. Many bills introduced by the government are modified by amendments; some emerge out of parliament radically changed from the government's original text.

Parliament also affects legislation before it is introduced through the discreet influence of committee leaders or key members of the majority. Pressure from parliamentarians often results in government modifications of its proposed legislation in the drafting process, before it is submitted to parliament. While the parliament rarely rejects outright a government bill, the government frequently withdraws proposals it has already introduced when they receive a hostile reception. In addition, the National Assembly can reassert control over the government if the majority coalition breaks down. Finally, the National Assembly remains a powerful center for political discussion. As such, it has the ability to bring issues and ideas to the forefront of political debate.[9]

Paradoxically, the overall decline of parliament has in some ways permitted French deputies to express viewpoints on important policy issues which in the past were excluded from parliamentary consideration. During the Fourth Republic, the fragility of executive power and the tenuous nature of the government coalition often resulted in informal agreements among top political leaders to bypass parliamentary discussion of complicated or emotion-laden issues. These issues were handled by the bureaucracy or, more frequently, simply ignored. Now, with a disciplined majority and a powerful executive, parliamentary discussion of complex and explosive issues can be permitted since it will not topple the government nor disturb intricate legislative proposals. As an example, under the Fourth Republic, the long-range economic plans were depoliticized. The plans were not submitted to parliament for fear that parties would act as voices for special interests and disrupt the carefully balanced economic plan. Under the Fifth Republic, the greater control that the executive had over the parliamentary process and the security of the majority coalition encouraged the government to allow full parliamentary debate on the various 5-year economic plans.

Even in the area of executive-decree laws as authorized by the Constitution of the Fifth Republic, the National Assembly has not been as passive as is often believed. One study points out that, contrary to general impressions, executive-decree laws have been used less frequently during the Fifth Republic than during the Third or Fourth Republics.[10] Nor have the decree laws of the Fifth Republic exceeded the importance or scope of those issued during earlier regimes. Parliamentary debates on the decrees and on the subsequent enabling acts have been lively and often effective in modifying the implementation of the decrees.

Parliament's loss of power in the Fifth Republic is relative. It is far less powerful than the parliaments of the Third and Fourth Republics, but most analysts agree that these powerful but unmanageable legislatures were largely to blame for the political instability that characterized these regimes. It is not clear if the parliament of the Fifth Republic is any less powerful than legislatures in other Western democracies (with the exception of the unusually powerful U.S. Congress). It has ousted a government by censure. It would have rejected the 1980 budget on two or three occasions had the government not made it a measure of confidence and thus avoided a vote (the British House of Commons has never given a budget such a hostile and threatening reception). The French parliament is clearly not the "rubber-stamp" type of legislative body found in authoritarian regimes.

The Constitutional Council

In the last two decades, the Constitutional Council has gained new prominence in French politics. The council is composed of nine justices serving nine-year terms: three each appointed by the president of the republic, the presiding officers of the Senate, and those of the National Assembly. In addition, all former presidents have the right to sit on this body but no one has so far exercised that right. When created in 1958, the council had a relatively modest role of assuring the regularity of elections and the constitutionality of major legislation.

Expansion of the role of the council began in the early 1980s when it emerged as the most potent source of opposition to the Socialist reforms.[11] Socialist control of the presidency and

National Assembly assured them of the ability to force through whatever legislation they wanted, but the Constitutional Council remained dominated by jurors named by earlier conservative presidents and parliamentary leaders. Opposition deputies and the conservative president of the Senate referred controversial reforms to the council to delay or block them. The Council's workload increased dramatically. The Council proved more willing to void legislation than in the past. It ruled that nearly half of the measures brought to it were at least partially unconstitutional. Over time, the Socialists used their appointment powers to name their friends to the council. By 1986, the council had a majority favorable to the Socialists. Thus, when the Conservatives returned to power that year, they found the council an obstacle to their efforts at undoing earlier Socialist reforms.

Beyond the actual voiding of legislation, the presence of the Council and its activism had deterrent effects on the legislative process. Anticipated reaction of the Council has become a prominent concern of governments as they consider draft legislation.

The notion of judicial review is well established in the United States but it lacks depth in Europe. In Europe, the tradition has been the supremacy of the popularly elected parliament as the manifestation of popular sovereignty. In the last two decades, there has been a growing tendency for European courts to review the constitutionality of their government's actions and their parliament's laws. This is especially true in countries that introduced constitutional courts after World War II such as Germany, Italy, and, after 1958, France. But it has also happened in Britain where normal courts have begun to assert the supremacy of a constitutional law, especially in the area of human rights.

The French experience with judicial review differs from the others in several ways. First, access is limited with the French Constitutional Council only handling questions referred to it by the president, the presiding officers of parliament, or by the joint appeal of sixty deputies or senators. Second, the council can only deal with laws before promulgation; it cannot reverse laws already in force as can the courts of other countries. Third, the courts in other countries have

emerged as potent defenders of individual civil liberties; the French Council has not dealt with human rights issues except in a most indirect manner. Fourth, the French Council has become a highly partisan body with controversy swirling around its actions while the other constitutional bodies have developed reputations for independence and impartiality.

Public reaction in France to the Constitutional Council's new assertiveness was initially favorable. Citizens saw the council as a more neutral body guaranteeing continuity and constitutional regularity in times of rapid political change. But the increasingly apparent partisan nature of the Council began to erode its public support. As a result, the Constitutional Council exercised judicial self-restraint in the last few years. Indeed, in the last half of the 1990s, the Council's political impact has been much less than it was during the 1980s and early 1990s.

The Reshaping of French Political Institutions

In contrast to the gradual evolution of British political institutions in harmony with political traditions, the present French regime is the product of deliberate efforts to correct constitutional failures of the past and to change traditional practices. This experiment in constitutional engineering has succeeded in providing a framework for a stable government; the 1958 Constitution seems to have eliminated the worst problems of past French democracies. But that constitution introduced new problems. It fostered the development of a very powerful presidency without adequate concern for controlling its possible excesses. It has left open the question of resolving differences between a president of one political tendency and a National Assembly from a hostile political camp. It has created a dual executive with an inherent propensity for rivalry between the two executives. So far, none of these potential problems has posed serious difficulties, and the regime has survived several potential crises that might well have toppled an unsound constitution. The constitution permitted the resolution of crises such as the turmoil of decolonization, the near revolt of May 1968, the passing of the charismatic leader for whom the constitution was designed, the transfer of power from conservatives to socialists, and three experiences with the cohabitation of a president from one political camp and a hostile majority in the National Assembly. The successful handling of these crises has strengthened the constitution by increasing its legitimacy and demonstrating its adaptability. This in turn makes it more likely that the constitution will survive future crises.

THE ONE AND INDIVISIBLE REPUBLIC

Observers have often commented on the presence of important social and regional divisions in France and the difficulties that they create for the political system. To preserve national unity in the face of cultural diversity, first the monarchs of the prerevolutionary ancien régime and then the various regimes since 1789 have sought to impose rigid centralized rule from Paris. All major political decisions emanate from Paris. Local governments serve more to implement the decisions made by the central government than to solve local problems through their own initiative. The high degree of centralization in France is only slightly exaggerated by an anecdote about a Third Republic minister of education: Supposedly this official delighted in pulling out his pocket watch and telling visitors that at that moment every 8-year-old in France was studying page so-and-so of a specific textbook.

Centralization not only promotes national unity in a diverse society, it also assures equality. Government policies and services are presumably uniform throughout the country with the result that citizens in one part of the country are treated in the same way and provided the same services by the government as elsewhere. The urge for equality is powerful in France and reinforces centralization even at the cost of stifling local initiative and innovation. Not long ago, the minister of education terminated an innovative experiment in a Paris suburban public school involving special techniques and equipment with the explanation that "it is difficult to accept that teaching in one school should be very different from that in other schools."

Decentralization

The Socialist government adopted a major reform in 1981 to decentralize French government. The principal feature of the reform was the reduction in the power of the centrally appointed prefects. Prior to the reform, the prefects were the principal agents of the national government, one appointed by the prime minister for each of the 96 departments. Working under the supervision of the minister of interior, the prefects controlled the police and maintained public order. They coordinated and supervised the administration of the affairs of state within their departments. In addition, they were charged with exercising control or tutelage over locally elected officials. They could invalidate actions by local officials who failed to comply with central guidelines; in extreme cases they could dismiss local-level governments for malfeasance. After the decentralization reform, the prefects were stripped of most of these powers. At present, the president of the popularly elected general council (*conseil général*) is to exercise most executive functions in the department. The prefects are to serve only as liaisons between the local government units and the national government.[12]

There are some reasons for hesitancy in hailing these new reforms as major transformations of French politics. To a large extent, they have only formalized changes under way for several decades. In practice, the prefects were never as powerful as they were reported to be. They worked cooperatively with local governments and only very rarely used the coercive power at their disposal. Even without the old powers, the prefects are likely to be very influential links between central and local governments. The prefects' strategic intermediary position, their contacts with the central bureaucracy, and their skills in negotiating and bargaining continue to make them key political actors.[13]

Government at the Local Levels

Each department has a popularly elected general council with powers to legislate on certain limited issues such as roads, public housing, and some welfare services. The council elects a president from among its members. The president serves as the chief executive of the department, setting the agenda for the council, preparing the budget, and representing the department in negotiations with the central government. The general council also votes on the departmental budget. The centrally appointed prefects no longer have the power to propose the budget, but they do exercise audit control over expenditures and thus deter, as in the past, improper departmental expenditures. The ability of the general councils to use their new freedom to control their budgets is also reduced by limited taxation powers and the absence of increased national funds for the departmental level.

At the local level, there are more than 36,000 communes or municipal governments in France. This is an exceptionally large number for the size of the country. France has more communes than are found in Belgium, Holland, Italy, Luxembourg, and Germany combined, even though these countries have a total population three times larger than France. Each French commune elects a municipal council for a 6-year term; the council in turn elects a mayor for the duration of its mandate. Once elected the mayor dominates local government, with municipal councilors clearly relegated to secondary roles of greater or lesser importance according to the desires of the mayor.

Although local governments' powers are circumscribed by central controls and lack of independent finances, the mayors are important political figures who can and do influence the futures of their communities. The mayors serve as brokers mediating between individuals at the local level and the central government.[14] They compete with each other for resources offered by the central government and seek to adapt centrally decided policies to local situations. Although they work primarily through the prefecture and administrative channels to implement governmental programs and seek support for local projects, they can also seek political support for their positions through contacts with parliamentarians. These contacts with national politicians are facilitated by the possibility of holding multiple elected mandates. Thus many members of parliament also serve as mayors and/or members of a general council. In contrast to the limited influence of British mayors, French mayors are important political figures with more

influence than might be expected in a state as centralized as France.

In addition to the 1981 shift in power to the departments' general councils, there were earlier efforts to reduce centralization through the creation of 21 regions in 1958. Originally designed to help in economic planning and regional development, they have only slowly accumulated other responsibilities. Both local and central authorities have resisted shifting any of their authority to the new regional bodies. Each region has an assembly elected directly by the people. There is also a regional economic and social council, whose members are designated by labor unions, business groups, farmers' associations, and family and cultural associations. The executive officer of the region is the president of the regional assembly. The scope of activities for these regions is narrow, the most important act being the approval of the region's budget. But the funds available for regional governments are small. Most subnational expenditures are controlled by local governments; regions have less than 5 percent of the funds available to local governments to carry out their activities.

Nearly everyone in France complains about excessive centralization and about its supposed social and political consequences.[15] But there is usually stiff opposition to concrete proposals for decentralization, both from national politicians who wish to preserve their control and from local politicians who prefer the familiar pattern of relations to experimentation with new ones. There is thus a strong coalition of local and national politicians, reinforced by the powerful centralized state bureaucracy, that opposes decentralization as a threat to its established privileges and practices. Few political leaders dare to confront this coalition, and even fewer succeed in even temporarily overcoming it. It was a defeat in a referendum on regional reform that brought an end to Charles de Gaulle's political career.

Public interest in decentralization is somewhat ambivalent. Opinion surveys show overwhelming support for it when phrased in general terms, but public reaction to specific proposals is much less positive. Indeed, important reservations surface in the general public as well as within the political elite on the issue of decentralization whenever it appears that such decentralization may foster different qualities or levels of government services. Such efforts, which might facilitate greater responsiveness to local needs, would infringe upon the principle of equality that the French insist upon so strongly.

CONCLUSION

In contrast to the gradual evolution of traditional political institutions observed in Britain, the French have frequently made abrupt changes in their political institutions. The current institutions have worked well over the past 40 years and have won broad public acceptance. The presence of a powerful executive has modified some political practices that in the past hindered the smooth operation of French democratic regimes. But the viability of these institutions must remain in doubt in a country where there is a tendency to change the constitutional order when there is a crisis.

The changes of the Fifth Republic have helped to control some of the institutional problems encountered by earlier French democracies. There remain other challenges coming from the behavior of key political actors: a citizenry that guards its privilege of periodic revolt against the powers that be; the high degree of polarization between the majority and opposition political groupings; an aloof and ponderous bureaucracy that resists reform; and political elites at national and local levels that often seem to prefer customary power relationships to efforts at rationalizing and decentralizing political authority. In the following chapters we will look at these problems, which so far have resisted change under the new constitutional order.

NOTES

[1] Anthony Burgess, "Le Mal Français: Is There a Reason for Being Cartesian?" *New York Times Magazine,* 29 May 1977, p. 52.

[2] On the growth of presidential power see François Goguel, "The Evolution of the Institution of the French Presidency, 1959–1981," in Fred Eidlin, ed., *Constitutional Democracy: Essays in Comparative Politics. A Festschrift in Honor of Henry W. Ehrmann* (Boulder, CO: Westview, 1983), pp. 49–61 and Ezra N. Suleiman, "Presidential Government in France," in *Presidents and Prime Ministers,* ed. Richard Rose and Ezra N. Suleiman (Washington: American Enterprise Institute, 1981).

[3] On professional powers, see Robert Elgie, "The French Presidency: Conceptualizing Presidential Power in the Fifth Republic," *Public Administration* 74 (Summer 1996): 275–291.

[4] Stanley Hoffmann, "The Institutions of the Fifth Republic," in James F. Hollifield and George Ross, eds., *Searching for the New France* (New York and London: Routledge, 1991), p. 48.

[5] Robert Elgie, *The Role of the Prime Minister in France, 1981–1991* (New York: St. Martin's, 1993).

[6] For a full discussion of these limitations, see Philip M. Williams, *The French Parliament, 1958–1967* (London: George Allen and Unwin, 1968) and William G. Andrews, *Presidential Government in France: A Study of Executive-Legislative Relations* (Albany: State University of New York Press, 1983).

[7] Frank L. Wilson and Richard Wiste, "Party Cohesion in the French National Assembly, 1958–1973," *Legislative Studies Quarterly* 1 (November 1976): 467–490.

[8] See the useful chapter on parliament in William Safran, *The French Polity,* 5th ed. (New York: Longman, 1998), pp. 221–263.

[9] See Frank R. Baumgartner, "Parliament's Capacity to Expand Political Controversy in France," *Legislative Studies Quarterly* 12 (February 1987): 33–54.

[10] William G. Andrews, "The Constitutional Prescription of Parliamentary Procedures in Gaullist France," *Legislative Studies Quarterly* 3 (August 1978): 465–506.

[11] Alec Stone, *The Birth of Judicial Politics in France: The Constitutional Council in Comparative Perspective* (Oxford: Oxford University Press, 1990).

[12] Vivien A. Schmidt, *Democratizing France: The Political and Administrative History of Decentralization* (Cambridge, England: Cambridge University Press, 1990).

[13] John Longlin and Sonia Mazey, eds., *The End of the French Unitary State? Ten Years of Regionalization in France* (Ilford, England: Frank Cass, 1995).

[14] Sidney Tarrow, *Between Center and Periphery: Grassroots Politicians in Italy and France* (New Haven, CT: Yale University Press, 1977).

[15] For a widely shared view of the adverse consequences of centralization in France, see Michel Crozier, *The Stalled Society* (New York: Viking Press, 1973).

Chapter 10

Political Participation: The French Citizen and Politics

To participate is to lose some of one's freedom; it means abandoning the normally comfortable, sheltered position of the critic; it means running the risks of emotional commitment; it means submitting to the constraints of someone else, to the group or unit in whose decision-making process one participates.[1]

Many observers believe that successful representative democracy requires a delicate balance of two levels of political involvement: (1) some informed citizens who are actively involved in politics to assure democratic control over government and (2) many less-informed citizens whose political involvement is less intense but nonetheless passively supportive of the existing system.[2] This balance would permit orderly government, since too many participants would overcharge the representative bodies and create chaos. Others criticize this viewpoint as excessively elitist; they have fewer concerns about overloading democracy with too much citizen participation.[3] Whether mass participation is viewed positively or negatively, France is often the example of a modern democracy with an unusually active citizenry ready to press its demands on government by direct action.

A closer look at the role of France's citizens in politics will suggest that this activist image of the French is probably exaggerated. Levels of political interest seem no higher among them than among other democratic populations. Even their reputation for excessive protest is exaggerated.

Nevertheless, mainstream parties in France are now under pressure. They have failed to convince voters that they are responsive to new issues, notably immigration and urban blight. As in many democracies, the major French parties have been tainted by scandals as their leaders have sought financial means to support ever more expensive electoral campaigns and as some of their politicians have used their access to government at the local and national levels for personal enrichment. This crisis in the party system is a major cause of concern as France begins the new century.

THE INDIVIDUAL IN POLITICS

Foreign visitors often come away with the impression that the French are very highly politicized. They see political posters everywhere, slogans painted on buildings, and frequent street demonstrations. Despite such visible indications of great political activity, studies of French political behavior suggest that the French are no more interested in politics than people in other Western democracies. A study of French political attitudes quotes the following as an example of the feelings of politically uninterested people in France:

> So far as I'm concerned, everything's fine; I'm not married and I'm looking for a suitable wife. . . . I'm putting all my efforts into improving my position. . . . As for the general state of France, I'm not really interested, I couldn't care less. Who cares about political debates? The housing situation's bad? Well, let them sort it out then, it's nothing to do with me.[4]

For those who are interested in political involvement, the forms of possible political action vary greatly. The range includes joining a political party or interest group, participating in political meetings or rallies, taking part in political demonstrations, standing as a candidate for elective office, and so forth. In France, there is an unusually large number of opportunities to serve in elected offices. There are many small communities, each with its own elected municipal council providing some 470,000 local elected offices. (In contrast, in Britain there are only 24,000 municipal councilors.) With so many elected positions, about 14 people out of every 1000 French voters serve in an elected capacity, and at least an equivalent number run for public office every 6 years. Parties actively seek to recruit citizens in their ranks for sustained political activity.

The French notion of party membership is more than the simple self-identification with a party that Americans claim as Democrats or Republicans. Party membership in France involves paying regular dues, accepting the obligation to attend meetings, and propagating the party's ideals through distributing tracts, putting up posters, and organizing rallies. For this reason, the French refer to the rank-and-file party members as *militants,* not because of their radicalism but because of their active commitment to their parties. The major political parties together claim to have approximately 2 million members; active party members are considerably less than that number, perhaps half.

Many French citizens are sporadically involved in politics when they feel their interests endangered and mobilize to fight for a certain cause. For example, residents in areas where the government proposes to build an airport may become very deeply involved in the political battles over location and safety measures. Parents may mobilize to urge the installation of traffic lights to protect children on their way to school. University students, concerned about the lack of employment opportunities, may organize to demand government action to create new jobs.

These movements are usually ad hoc in that they produce their own temporary organization rather than developing out of ongoing political groups or parties. There are some problems with this kind of specific, issue-related political participation: Those who become involved often do so with great emotional intensity; they are protesting government action or inaction they feel seriously damages their immediate interests. This may lead to confrontation and violence, as has happened, for example, with farmers' demonstrations. Furthermore, when the government decision goes against the interests of those who are mobilized, as it must from time to time, the participants are disillusioned, embittered, and unwilling to trust "democratic procedures" in the future.

We noted earlier a trend toward protest politics in Britain. In France, protest politics is the norm, not the exception.[5] The Events of May 1968, when student rioting and general strikes nearly overthrew the regime, are the most recent manifestation of a long tradition of spontaneous protest and revolt. In addition to major revolutionary or near-revolutionary actions, there have been numerous less spectacular but nevertheless disruptive protests. Indeed, there has rarely been a period in French history when some spontaneous or organized protest was not underway. Seen from the outside, at times there appear to be few French citizens who are not protesting in one way or another.[6]

The proclivity of the French to protest is founded in their attitudes toward political participation and authority. An intense desire to safeguard their individual prerogatives and independence tends to make French citizens reluctant to participate in conventional civic action. By avoiding involvement, furthermore, the French retain their right to protest or oppose whatever decision is finally agreed upon.

There is in the French a certain desire to resist authority, to oppose *le pouvoir*. This impulse to oppose, which is often combined with a strict egalitarianism, has always been an important factor in French politics, especially among those ideologically on the Left. On the other hand, the French are also prone to accept a superior authority, and they look to the strong leader to make decisions in normal times as well as during crises. This ambivalence was well described by Alexis de Tocqueville over a century ago:

> Undisciplined by temperament, the Frenchman is always readier to put up with the arbitrary rule, however harsh, of an autocrat than with a free well-ordered government by his fellow citizens, however worthy of respect they be. At one moment he is up in arms against authority and the next we find him serving the powers-that-be with a zeal such as the most servile races never display. So long as no one thinks of resisting, you can lead him on a thread, but once a revolutionary movement is afoot, nothing can restrain him from taking part in it.[7]

A more recent French observer notes that the French have "a begging bowl in one hand and a Molotov cocktail in the other."[8]

VOTING

Voting is the only political act for the vast majority of French citizens. All citizens 18 years and older are eligible to vote. Until recently election turnout was generally high: usually in excess of 80 percent. However, in the last decade the voter turnout rate has declined sharply. In the 1997 National Assembly elections, for example, turnout was only 70 percent. Analysts are unsure of the cause of this decline. It may be due to disgust with the parties and their leaders; it may be the result of the lessened policy differences between the Left and Right; it may be complacency in a political world that seems to have little effects on citizens' lives. It is a cause for concern in France even though the French turnout rate still far exceeds the 50 percent or fewer voters who turn out in the United States.

French citizens have frequent opportunities to go to the polls (see Table 10–1), but each time they go they must make only a single decision: a vote for a presidential candidate in presidential elections, a vote for a deputy in National Assembly elections held on a different date, and so on. Before the election, each voter receives a packet in the mail that includes a statement from each candidate and slips of paper, each with a candidates name, that serve as the ballots. Voting is secret with booths available for the voters' use. In practice, many voters do not use the booths; they bring the ballot of their candidate that came in the mail and place it in the envelope without using the booth.

The presidential and National Assembly elections are the two most important elections because they determine who controls national politics. The president is elected for a 7-year term in a direct election. If no candidate receives an

Table 10–1   Elections in France

Type	Frequency	Electing Body
National elections:		
Presidential	7-year terms	Entire electorate
National Assembly	5-year terms	Entire electorate
Senate	$^1/_3$ elected every 3 years for 9-year terms	Electoral college of 104,000 locally and nationally elected officials
Referendum	At initiative of the president (8 since 1958)	Entire electorate
Local elections:		
Regional assemblies	6-year terms	Entire electorate
General councils	$^1/_2$ elected every 3 years for 6-year terms	Entire electorate
Municipal councils	6-year terms	Entire electorate
Mayors	6-year terms	Municipal councilors in each town

Table 10–2 Hypothetical Example of a District's Results in a National Assembly Election

First Ballot		Second Ballot
Republican candidate	29%	49%
Socialist candidate	29	51 *Elected*
Communist candidate	17	Withdrew, supported Socialist
Gaullist candidate	15	Eliminated, supported Republican
Eight other candidates	10	All eliminated

absolute majority, a run-off election is held 2 weeks later between the two leading candidates. The 577 deputies in the National Assembly are elected for 5-year terms.

There has been controversy surrounding the rules for organizing these elections. During most of the Fifth Republic, the election has been based on electing a single member from each district in a two-ballot system. However, in 1985, the Socialist government of the time introduced a system of proportional representation (PR) for National Assembly elections. After the conservative victory in 1986, a two-ballot majority system was readopted and remains in use today.

Under the present electoral laws, it takes an absolute majority of votes to win on the first ballot. Having a majority occurs in about a third of the districts. If no candidate has a majority, a runoff is held one week later. All candidates with fewer than 15 percent of the registered vote (or about 18 to 20 percent of the votes cast) on the first ballot are eliminated; other candidates may withdraw. In most cases, the second ballot involves a duel between the strongest candidate on the Right and the strongest candidate on the Left. In those cases where more than two candidates

are present on the second ballot, a simple plurality is sufficient for election. An example from a recent election will illustrate (see Table 10–2).

This two-ballot system has won wide support among the general public. It is relatively straightforward and easy to understand. Its runoff procedures encourage similar parties to coalesce and reduce the political impact of marginal or extremist parties. It also facilitates the winning of solid parliamentary majorities to support government coalitions. But, as with Britain's plurality system, it leads to distortions of public support. A comparison of the results from the 1997 election under Table 10–3 provides a comparison of election outcomes using the existing two-ballot majority system with the projected results using the system of proportional representation used in 1986. Note especially the impact of the two-ballot system on an isolated party such as the National Front. Instead of the 77 seats PR would have given the party, the FN in fact elected only a single deputy in 1997. Note also that the victorious Left under the two-ballot system would not have had a majority of deputies under proportional representation. Despite these inequities, it is unlikely that France will go back to proportional

Table 10–3 Effects of Alternative Electoral Systems in France

Party	1997% of Vote	Actual Seats Won in 1997	% of Seats in National Assembly	Projected Seats under PR	Projected % of Seats in Assembly with PR
Communists	9.9%	35	6.0%	36	6.2%
Socialists	31.9	275	47.7	220	38.1
Gaullists and Giscardians	30.9	244	42.3	222	38.5
National Front	15.3	1	0.2	77	13.3

Source: Projected electoral outcome from SOFRES, reported in *Le Monde*, 5 June 1997.

representation. The major parties, those who control parliament, are the beneficiaries of the two-ballot system. They are unlikely to introduce a system that will reduce their representation and increase the representation of a far Right party that they believe is undemocratic.

The Socialists had adopted proportional representation in 1985, as their popularity waned, in an effort to stem party losses. When the conservatives returned to the two ballot system in 1986 it was, at least in part, to assist them in fending off threats from the far Right. Indeed, there is a long history of changing the electoral rules in France with the party in power trying, often unsuccessfully, to rig the system to help it stay in power. Thus, between 1871 and 1999, there have been 11 different electoral systems for 38 national legislative elections. Such manipulations of the basic procedures of democracy do little to build citizen confidence.[9]

In the case of Britain, we suggested that voters could render a rational judgment on the performance of the incumbent government by voting for or against the government's party candidate. In France, such a clear-cut choice between the currently governing party and an alternative governing party was absent for many years.[10] It is only in the past 20 years that voters came to see the left-wing parties as an acceptable and viable alternative government.

Personality factors seem to have a greater importance in France than they do in Britain. Often, the personality of leading party figures and even the personalities of specific candidates influence how the voters will vote. For example, when Charles de Gaulle was president, most voters claimed to base their decision to vote for a legislative candidate on that candidate's support or opposition to de Gaulle. More recently, François Mitterrand's popularity spilled over to the Socialist party in general, electing Socialist National Assembly majorities in 1981 and 1986. As we saw in Chapter 8, French voters are influenced by socioeconomic and especially religious cues. While the class influence is less developed than in Britain, a recent comparative study of voting behavior in France and the United States demonstrated the much greater effect of socioeconomic and religious cleavages in structuring the vote in France.[11] Other studies do not ignore the impact of these social divisions but see voting also strongly influenced by the voter's self-identification with

the Left or Right and their seeking to elect candidates reflecting that attachment.[12]

WOMEN IN POLITICS

In France, traditional femininity, not feminism, has been the rule.[13] There was no French counterpart of the British suffragette struggle, and the right to vote was not granted to women until 1945. Even then female suffrage came about not in response to demands by women but as one of the Liberation reforms promulgated by the Provisional Government of Charles de Gaulle. Similarly, equal rights for wives vis-à-vis their husbands were achieved late. Until 1965 women needed their husband's permission to apply for passports, open bank accounts, or conduct other financial affairs. In divorce cases, infidelity on the part of the wife was much more readily accepted as grounds for a divorce than was identical behavior by the husband.

Since their enfranchisement, French women continue to play a much less important part in politics than do men. Women first held junior minister positions in the Popular Front government formed in 1936, before they had even been granted the right to vote. However, the number of women in the government has never been large. A woman, Edith Cresson, was named prime minister in 1992 but was removed in less than a year. Her short tenure was not due to her gender but to a series of errors, a bad economy, and strong unpopularity with the public. After the 1997 Socialist victory, Prime Minister Lionel Jospin named women to 30 percent of the ministries in his government, a record for France.

In the national Assembly, women remain underrepresented. In 1997 the percentage of women deputies rose to 11 percent, the highest ever for France. This was due largely to the Socialist party's success and its commitment to have women for at least 30 percent of its candidates. Even this success, however, leaves France at the bottom of the 15 member countries in the European Union, with the share of women exceeding only those in the Greek parliament. At every level of government, women remain underrepresented in France (see Table 10–4).

The scarcity of women in elected positions is due to the infrequency with which women are

Table 10–4   Women in French Politics. Women Elected Officials as Percentage of Total Officeholders[a]

	1946	1956	1967	1988	1997
Deputies in					
National Assembly	5.4%	3.1%	2.2%[c]	5.7%	11.0%
Senators	3.6	1.9[c]	1.8[b]	2.8	5.6
General Councilors	N/A	0.8[c]	2.3	4.0	7.0
Mayors	N/A	1.0[d]	1.8[e]	4.1	8.0
Municipal Councilors	N/A	2.4[d]	4.4[e]	14.1	17.1[f]

[a]In 1988, women made up 53% of the electorate.
[b]1962. [c]1958. [d]1959. [e]1971. [f]1993.
Sources: Compiled by the authors.

nominated to elected office by the major parties. In the 1997 elections, women candidates made up only 23 percent of the total. In all elections, women candidates often represent minor parties and have little chance of winning. Far fewer women candidates are nominated by the major parties, and they often run women candidates in districts where the party has no chance of winning. Before the 1997 elections, the Socialist and Communist parties set a quota of 30 percent women in their lists of candidates. They did not quite reach these goals, but the newly elected Socialist group of deputies included 17 percent women. The parties of the Right did not have such quotas and ended up with only a handful of women in their elected ranks.

There are counterparts to American women's liberation movement in France, but they have won neither the influence nor the following the American movement has enjoyed. Women's movements in France have encountered several difficulties. Organizing women for joint action has been hampered by the lack of a tradition of women's clubs or sororities, which provided American and, to a lesser extent, British women with a sense of solidarity. Those women's groups that have emerged in France had their appeal limited due to their association with particular political currents, usually on the far Left. In addition, traditional values on women's roles in the home and community are still well established and change is resisted by many women.

There is little evidence to suggest that the small number of women in politics is due to systematic political discrimination against women. The nature of social organization limits the role of women in society as a whole, not just in poli-

tics. Political activity is a luxury requiring time commitments away from the home or the job that many French women simply cannot afford. Women are rarely found in the liberal professions or leadership positions in business or industry that permit free time for politics. Instead, they are occupied with household activities, childbearing, or outside jobs that give little spare time for political activities.

Growing numbers of women are rebelling against these traditional roles, insisting upon recognition of their rights to political and social involvement on an equal footing with men.[14] Recent studies show that French women define their political opinions independently and do not conform to the usual stereotype of simply following the political beliefs of their husbands or fathers. They have seen major increases in their involvement in elected and appointed public offices. From time to time since the mid-1970s, governments have included a ministry for women's affairs. The growing importance of women in politics is evidenced by the fact that even when the conservative parties held power, the government pushed through a liberalized abortion law despite the opposition of the Catholic hierarchy in a still heavily Catholic country.

INTEREST GROUP POLITICS

As in Britain and other Western democracies, interest groups play an active part in French politics. Organized groups, such as labor unions, employer's associations, farmers, and special interest groups, are involved in influencing policy making and implementation at all levels of

Table 10–5   Major Occupational Interest Groups in France

Labor Unions

Confédération Générale du Travail (CGT)
  Linked to Communist party
  600,000 members
Confédération Française Démocratique du Travail (CFDT)
  Leftist orientation
  450,000 members
Force Ouvrière (FO)
  Moderate leftist orientation
  400,000 members
Fédération d'Education Nationale (FEN)
  Leftist orientation
  450,000 members

Employers' Associations

Mouvement des Entrepreneurs de France (Medef)
  1,000,000 firms
Confédération Générale des Petites et Moyennes
  Entreprises (PME)
Centre des Jeunes Dirigeants d'Entreprise

Farmers' Associations

Fédération Nationale des Syndicats d'Exploitation
Agricole (FNSEA)
  Favorable to the Center-Right
  600,000 members
Centre National des Jeunes Agriculteurs (CNJA)
  Linked to FNSEA
  60,000 members
Mouvement de Défense de l'Exploitation Familiale
(MODEF)
  Linked to Communist party
  100,000 members
Confédération Nationale Syndicale des Travailleurs—
Paysans (CNSTP)
  Linked to Socialist party
  80,000 members

government and in virtually all major areas of government action. From neighborhood protection associations and parent-teacher organizations to veterans' groups, environmentalists, and labor unions, groups seek to pressure government in order to shape policy to meet the needs of their clienteles.

Among the most important of these interest groups are the major occupation-based associa-

tions listed in Table 10–5. As in Britain, these groups are peak organizations, linking at the national level many regional and industry-based unions or associations. Smaller groups with narrow interests to defend are often very influential in the shaping of policies that affect them.

Legislative lobbying, important during the Fourth Republic (1946–58) when parliament had considerable power and independence, is less important now because of the greater political power of the executive. As a result, French interest groups direct their efforts toward building contacts with ministers and senior civil servants in those government departments concerned with issues affecting their members.[15] Many observers have felt that the strong Fifth Republic executive is aloof from interest groups, but in fact government officials seek the opinions of affected interest groups even if they do not always follow their advice. Most interest groups leaders, both those favorable to and those opposed to the governing parties, seem to feel that they are able to influence policy decisions to a greater or lesser degree.

In France, there is a strong state tradition that often leaves interest groups appearing as self-interested advocates of narrow interests clashing with a government committed to the "general will." This served as an important limitation on the influence of groups in public policymaking. In the 1970s, it inhibited the development of the neocorporatist patterns of interaction between the state and large interest confederations that characterized German politics and to a lesser extent pre-Thatcher politics in Britain. Of course, French interest groups have learned to cast their own viewpoints in ways that try to persuade officials that the groups' positions are in the overall national interest. This is a time of change in French interest group politics. With the European Union increasingly the locus for economic policy-making, French interest groups have focused greater attention to the EU institutions in Brussels. As they have done so, new tactics and organizations have become more important players than the traditional peak interest group associations. French interest group politics in Paris as well as Brussels have begun to shift away from the central action of the large occupational interest groups listed in Table 10–5 and toward more independent action by individual firms and even by professional lobbying agencies.

In general French interest groups often feel that their interests are ignored by the state. As a consequence, they are often left only with the option of expressing disapproval of government policies through street demonstrations. As a result, politics looks turbulent. Groups that in other countries never engage in street politics—dentists, truck drivers, pharmacists, small business owners—routinely demonstrate in the streets of Paris. The policy effects of such demonstrations are limited but they do allow disgruntled citizens a way of expressing their dissatisfaction with government policies affecting their interests.[16]

A major source of weakness for French interest groups is their usual divided organizations. This is illustrated by the ineffectiveness of the labor unions. Their weakness stems from their internal divisions. Although all are leftist in orientation, their ideological differences often prevent joint action. These unions expend a great deal of effort competing with each other for members in the same companies. They cannot assure the loyalty of their followers who might shift to another union if the leadership of one joined the government in supporting an unpopular policy. In addition, a large proportion of the eligible work force remains nonunionized. Less than 10 percent of the work force is unionized in France, compared to more than 28 percent in Britain and 43 percent in Germany. Since the unions and other interest groups are poorly organized and cannot assure that their members will respect their leaderships' agreements with government and each other, the value of linkages with them is diminished in the eyes of the government.

POLITICAL PARTIES

Ideally, in democratic states, political parties offer the electorate choices between differing sets of leaders, philosophies, and policy options. Indeed, electoral competition between two or more parties is an essential aspect of the Western democratic process.

Tables 10–6 and 10–7 list the major parties in France and show their electoral strength in recent elections.[17] The most striking difference in the party system in France compared to the British, German, and American systems is the larger number of parties in France. But there is a subtler and more important difference between French parties and the others. In France, parties represent the full political spectrum—from Trotskyites and Maoists on the far Left to neofascists on the far Right; in Britain, Germany, and the United States, the parties have converged at the Center.

The major French parties are grouped into two loose coalitions: the Left, and the Gaullist and Giscardian coalition. In contrast to the large number of parties in the past, these two durable blocs have dominated French politics since the mid-1960s. Parties remaining outside of one of these coalitions increasingly have been isolated from effective political roles.

The Parties of the Left

The Left has two main components: the Socialist Party (PS), now the strongest party in France, and the French Communist Party (PCF). There

Table 10–6 Political Parties in France (Results of Recent National Assembly Elections)

	1978	1981	1986	1988	1993	1997
The Left						
Communists (PCF))	20.6%	16.2%	9.7%	11.3%	9.2%	9.9%
Socialists (PS)	22.6	37.5	31.6	37.5	17.6	25.5
Left-wing Radicals (MRG)	3.3		0.3		0.9	
Various leftists	6.2	1.9	2.4	0.3	3.6	7.7
Total for Left:	52.7	55.6	44.0	49.1	31.3	42.1
The Center-Right						
Gaulists (RPR)	22.6%	20.8%	41.0	40.4	20.4	16.8
Union for French Democracy (UDF)	21.5	19.2			19.1	14.7
Various rightists	2.4	2.8	3.8	0.6	8.4	4.7
The Far Right						
National Front (FN)	nil	0.4	9.8	9.8	12.4	15.0
Total for Right:	46.5	43.2	54.6	50.8	60.3	51.2

Table 10–7   Recent Presidential Elections in France

| | | 1981 Ballot | | | 1988 Ballot | | | 1995 Ballot | |
		First	Second		First	Second		First	Second
Party:									
RPR	Chirac	18%		Chirac	20%	46%	Baladur	19%	
							Chirac	21	53%
UDF	Giscard	28	48%	Barre	17		No candidate		
PS	Mitterrand	25	52	Mitterrand	34	54	Jospin	23	47
PCF	Marchais	15		Lajoinie	7		Hue	9	
FN	No candidate			LePen	14		LePen	15	
Others		14			8			13	

are other smaller parties—notably the Movement of Left-wing Radicals (MRG) which, despite its title, is actually more moderate than the Socialists. These smaller parties have allied themselves with the Socialists or been pushed to the margins of politics.

The Socialists   The Socialist party (PS) was first founded in 1905, but in many ways the current party is the creation of François Mitterrand. Following years of decline, the party was revived and redirected after 1972 under his leadership.[18] With new leaders and ideas, he turned the party into a powerful political machine and nearly tripled its electoral strength over the next decade. In 1981, Mitterrand won the presidency and his party took 37.5 percent of the vote and an outright majority in the National Assembly. Since that time, the PS has remained the single largest party in terms of vote and size of parliamentary delegation.

Until the mid-1980s, the PS stood apart from other European socialist parties because of its attachment to fundamental socialism and to the overthrow of what it saw as an oppressive capitalist society. It continued to use the classic Marxist terminology of class warfare while even the radical elements of the European left-wing parties, such as the left wing of the British Labour party, shunned that rhetoric as outdated. After it came to power in 1981, however, the Socialist party forgot most of its past radicalism.

There were a number of important reforms reflecting Socialist values: nationalization of a number of private industries and banks, shorter work week, decentralization, and new labor relations laws. But by 1984, the Socialist government and its party tempered its reforms. Indeed, in the next few years, the PS seemed to come to an acceptance of the existing socioeconomic order. When the PS returned to power in 1988, its government continued programs of denationalization and limited its economic interventions. The Socialist government's policies resembled closely those of the conservatives. Even the party's rhetoric was toned down and denunciations of "monopolistic capitalism" disappeared from PS publications and speeches.

In 2000–2001, the PS continues to advocate a free market economy with some adjustments to protect the unfortunate from the dangers of capitalism. The Socialists no longer talk of nationalizations and accept a limited role for government in economic planning. In the 1997 election campaign, the Socialists again promised major changes in socioeconomic policies to combat chronic double-digit unemployment: massive job creation programs; expansion of public transportation; reduction of the workweek to 35 hours with no loss of pay; new social benefits; an end to and possible reversal of the privatization of public corporations like Air France, France Télécom, and Thomson electronics; relaxation of immigration laws; and so on. Once in office, however, the Socialist government's actual conduct has been more moderate. The Socialists have enacted legislation to press for a 35-hour work week to be phased in over several years and with many of the details yet to be agreed upon. They raised the minimum wage but much less than expected. The French Socialists found their economic reforms confined by the realities of observing European Union rules and international economic competition. The challenges of meeting EU limits on budget deficits have limited the PS's ability to fulfill its promises of protecting public sector jobs and maintaining existing social welfare benefits.

The Socialist party does show some greater humanitarian concerns than its conservative rivals. It advocates "solidarity" with those who are underprivileged through protecting and even expanding their state social benefit programs. They propose crime prevention programs based on social changes rather than through more vigorous law enforcement. They express greater tolerance for France's new racial minorities and are more moderate in their positions on immigration. When the PS regained control of government in 1997, however, actual policy changes on sensitive issues such as immigration and law-and-order were limited because the Socialists' electorate also harbors resentment toward immigrants and fear the deterioration of their quality of life due to rising crime and drug use.

In foreign and defense policies, the PS was a firm supporter of the Western cause during the Cold War. Unlike the British Labour party, the PS never went through an era of pacifist neutralism. The Socialist party continues to support the French independent nuclear weapons force and the missiles to deliver those weapons. Socialist governments have led efforts to enhance the defense cooperation of European Union states in ventures in Bosnia and elsewhere. For example, Socialist President François Mitterrand took the lead in developing a joint Franco-German infantry battalion. Military and foreign policy cooperation between France and the United States has usually been better under Socialist-led governments than under Gaullist governments.

After a devastating defeat in the 1993 National Assembly elections, Lionel Jospin rallied the party from despair to a respectable showing in the 1995 presidential elections and election

victory in the 1997 legislative elections. The party's victory in 1997, however, hides some underlying parties. The Socialists won in 1997 not because the Left's political support expanded but rather because the Center-Right parties were crippled by the National Front's strength and its election tactics. The PS has not found the key to regaining the former left-wing voters who now support the far Right. Unlike Blair's "New Labour" in Britain, Jospin's Socialist party did little to broaden his electoral base with a campaign platform that sounded more "traditional left" than modern.

For a durable revival, the PS must find ways to expand its electoral base. At the grassroots, the PS still lacks active members, and those remaining are no longer as enthusiastic as when the party was advocating a more dramatic and ideology-driven change in society. Even the 1997 victory has not revived grassroots followers. Factionalism within the party remains important, and it is not clear that Jospin has the skills that Mitterrand demonstrated in holding the diverse tendencies together.

After three years in office, Jospin's government remains more popular than any government in the past decade. But gnawing problems of unemployment, social unrest, and international economic competition remain formidable tasks that the government has not yet addressed. It will have to do so in the presence of a Gaullist president, Jacques Chirac, who can be expected to take advantage of the government's errors to criticize and eventually even to dissolve the National Assembly at a time when the Socialist government is most weakened.

The Communists   The French Communist party (PCF) once had the largest membership and tightest organization of any party in France. From 1946 to 1956, the PCF had the support of one out of every four French voters, polling more votes than any other single party. In 1958 under the new Fifth Republic, the PCF vote total fell but then stabilized at 20 to 22 percent of the vote through the 1970s. But by the 1981 election, the party's share of the vote fell to 16.2 percent and plummeted by 1997 to only 10 percent of the vote. The Communist party's loss in electoral support is matched by declines in its party's membership, its labor union, and its newspapers.

Unlike other West European Communist parties, the PCF has changed little in response to the collapse of communism in the Soviet Union and Eastern Europe. It remains an orthodox Marxist-Leninist-Stalinist party when Communist parties elsewhere are modifying their doctrine, adopting new strategies, and even changing their names. The PCF's failure to respond to the events in Eastern Europe since 1989 is not the main explanation for the PCF's collapse. Most of its electoral decline had occurred by the time of the revolutionary changes in the East after 1989.

In part, its decline can be traced to the rise of a strong Socialist party. Many voters supported the Communist party in the 1950s and 1960s because that party seemed to be the party of the Left. In the 1970s and 1980s, however, Mitterrand's Socialists preempted the Communist claim as the standard bearer of the Left. As a result, a large number of voters who had once voted Communist began voting for the Socialists. By the end of the 1970s, the Socialists stood as the largest and most effective party of the Left and drew away a substantial portion of the PCF's electorate.

Another important reason for the PCF's decline was its inability to adopt a consistent stand and political strategy in the 1970s and 1980s. At times, the PCF moved toward moderation and "Eurocommunism." At other times the PCF insisted on a doctrinal purity that was not even found in Moscow. The PCF pressed on occasion for an alliance of the Left with the Socialist party; then it would attack the PS as its main enemy and rival. The Communists accepted three ministries in Mitterrand's 1981 government, left it in 1984, and then returned as a supporting party in 1988 for a series of Socialist minority governments. These sharp reversals in party strategy and especially the off and on affair with the Socialists led to the disaffection of many PCF activists, especially those from intellectual circles.[19] The party was riven with unparalleled internal conflict that demoralized even those who were not alienated by the sudden shifts in political posture.

The fate of the PCF is very much uncertain at the turn of the century. The party has new leadership with Robert Hue as general secretary. His efforts to reform the party, however, come late, as he admits. "We're 20 years too late; it has cost us dearly."[20] Caught between a large "old guard" committed to preserving the PCF of the past and a small body of reformers, Hue's ability to bring change has been limited during his first five years as party leader. The PCF still talks in Marxist terms and proudly displays the hammer and sickle emblem of old-style communism. While formally committed to bringing privatized firms back under the state's control, the PCF has toned

---

EUROCOMMUNISM

During the 1960s and 1970s, most Communist parties in Europe went through an era of dramatic changes. Pressured by electoral needs to look less like tools of the Soviet Union, these communist parties moderated their doctrines, reduced authoritarian controls within their parties, and charted an independent course in foreign policy matters. No longer could they be seen as only clones of the Kremlin as they publicly criticized Soviet leaders for their abuse of civil liberties, economic failures, and undemocratic practices.

These changes, known as "Eurocommunism," enabled communist parties to better compete for voters no longer inspired by the "triumph of socialism" in the USSR. The larger Communist parties in Europe, notably those in Italy and Spain, pioneered in these reforms. The French Communist party lagged behind and when it did move toward Eurocommunism, it did so hesitantly and without conviction. By the end of the 1970s, the PCF had largely returned to its old practices and doctrines. As a result, when communism toppled in Eastern Europe and the Soviet Union at the end of the 1980s, the PCF was poorly situated to respond to the new situation that confronted communist parties everywhere. Even with a leadership change in the 1990s, the PCF has remained out of touch with the French population and with changes that have elsewhere, notably in Italy, allowed former Communist parties to succeed.

down its backing of nationalization. The PCF remains ardently anti-European Union, which it labels a monopoly capitalist club. Its tardy reforms have left it besmirched with the now admitted excesses of the Stalin's communist movement.

In 1997, Hue did reach an electoral agreement with the Socialists despite important differences in the two parties' policy positions. This allowed the PCF to retain a presence in the National Assembly. The PCF delegation provided Jospin with the votes necessary to form a government. Jospin's cabinet includes three communist ministers. Cooperation between the two parties, essential to the preservation of the Socialist government, has been good despite continued policy differences. For example, the PCF did not withdraw its support or its ministers when the Socialist government agreed to participate in the EU's single currency despite the PCF's vigorous opposition to the EU in general and the single currency in particular.

The PCF's survival as a meaningful political force is now dependent upon its cooperation with the Socialists. The two-ballot electoral system encourages their electoral alliance since both parties need each other's votes for second-ballot run-offs. The PCF is experiencing trouble in maintaining its own electorate. Its most natural base of support, the industrial working class, continues to diminish in size and political cohesion. In the past, the PCF also drew support from voters who were alienated from society and the polity; those disgruntled voters now are more likely to vote for the Far Right. As the party continues to lose voters and its suburban working class bastions, it risks losing even more seats in Parliament. At present, it barely has enough deputies to qualify for a recognized group in the National Assembly. If it loses its visibility in Parliament, it will become even more a fringe party that is increasingly a relic of the past than a consequential political force.

The Moderate Conservative Parties

Although the Socialists control the government at this time, the usual pattern of government in France over the last 50 years is a coalition of Center-Right parties. This coalition is composed of the Gaullist Rally for the Republic (RPR) and various centrist groups linked until 1998 in a Union for French Democracy (UDF). For most of the Fifth Republic, these parties have formed the governing coalition. So long did they hold uncontested power that they were known as the "majority" and as the "ex-majority" between 1981 and 1986 after they had become in fact the minority. As the Conservatives have won political support by their appearance as the "natural party of government" in Britain, so has the Gaullist-UDF coalition in France.

The Gaullist Party   The largest party in this coalition is the Gaullist RPR. The Gaullists defend the legacies of the era when Charles de Gaulle was president: the political institutions of the Fifth Republic as established by de Gaulle; national independence in foreign, defense, and economic policies; resistance against alleged threats to French national sovereignty coming from the United States or efforts to further European unification; and "participation," a vague ideal of involving citizens in making the political, social, and economic decisions that affect their lives.

The Gaullist philosophy makes it difficult to place the party on a Left-Right political spectrum. On the one hand, the Gaullists support political options traditionally associated with the Right: law and order, strong executive power, independent military strength, and French nationalism. They draw support from social groups usually aligned with the Right: the middle class, faithful Catholics, and voters in the north and east of France. On the other hand, the Gaullists are committed to a modernist philosophy of change and adaptation alien to the traditional French Right. During the Fifth Republic, the Gaullists completed decolonization; enacted major university, agricultural, and economic reforms; and pressed for fundamental changes in the free enterprise system to provide for the "association" and "participation" of workers in the profits and decisions of industry.

Through most of the Fifth Republic, the Gaullists advocated strong government action to direct the economy. This set them apart from other conservative groups which favored more classical free enterprise. When the Center-Right returned to power in 1986, the new Gaullist prime minister, Jacques Chirac, adopted a Thatcherite economic policy. His government reduced the role of the state and sold a number of state-owned banks and enterprises to private shareholders. Even with these steps, the Gaullist party remains attached to an active economic role for the state that sets it apart from more traditional conservatives.

The RPR backs a strong state. Most of the generous welfare state benefits enjoyed by the French were initially enacted by Gaullist governments. Even now as the Gaullists adopt a more neo-liberal stand, they defend the state's social and economic roles and insist on centralization. This is far from the British Conservative party's calls for a diminution of the state in society and economics. The RPR takes strong positions against further immigration and calls for stern measures to combat the deterioration of law and order in urban areas. Its position on these social issues, however, is not as extreme as that of the Far Right National Front.

The Gaullists advocate a strong and independent voice for France in international politics. They support France's independent nuclear force and its missile delivery system. One issue that divides Gaullists is France's role in the European Union. De Gaulle was a hesitant supporter of European unification and above all saw efforts to unite Europe as ways to pursue narrowly defined French goals. More recent Gaullist leaders are more positive about France's participation in the European Union. President Chirac is a strong advocate of the EU and worked diligently to achieve the creation of a single European currency. The 1992 referendum on the Maastricht Treaty illustrates the divisions of Gaullists on this issue. The treaty called for expanded powers for the EU, including the single currency. Chirac, then prime minister, endorsed the referendum calling for a "yes" vote to ratify the treaty. The yes position prevailed but narrowly. Analyses of the results showed that voters identifying with the Gaullist party voted "no," two to one against ratification. Gaullist divisions over Europe reflect the persistence in the party of many supporters who still yearn for the nationalist orientation that de Gaulle gave to his party four decades ago.

The RPR claims over 800,000 members and a powerful party organization. From 1958 to 1978, the RPR was France's largest party with more voters and deputies than any other party. The first

two presidents of the Fifth Republic, Charles de Gaulle (1959–1969) and Georges Pompidou (1969–1974) were closely associated with the Gaullist party, as were all prime ministers from 1958 to 1976. The influence of the Gaullist party declined after the death of Georges Pompidou in 1974, when the Gaullists lost the presidency to their ally Valéry Giscard d'Estaing. After the Socialist victory in 1981, the Gaullists regained leadership of the Center-Right coalition. Their party's organizational strength and their leaders' ambitions make the Gaullists the heart of the conservative opposition coalition. In 1995, the Gaullist party regained control of the presidency with the election of Jacques Chirac.

The current RPR acknowledges its Gaullist heritage, but it is more than anything else the creation of Jacques Chirac, President of the French Republic. From the mid-1970s until Chirac's election in 1995, Chirac dominated the RPR. He has been a perennial presidential candidate with unsuccessful campaigns in 1981 and 1988, and again a candidate in 1995. In 1995, he faced a strong competitor from within his own Gaullist party: Edouard Balladur, prime minister since 1993. The competition caused rifts within the Gaullist party but the RPR pulled together to unite in support of Chirac for the second ballot.

Despite Chirac's victory in the 1995 presidential election, his continued leadership of the Gaullist party was called into question when he called early legislative elections and then oversaw an unsuccessful campaign. The 1997 defeat undermined his leadership of the party and left him in a situation of long-term cohabitation with the Socialists. Chirac pulled away from active leadership of the RPR as a means of saving what little influence he had under cohabitation. He assumes the posture of a neutral and benevolent president and left the management of the RPR to others. The other Gaullist leaders welcomed this since they held Chirac responsible for the election debacle. The RPR is now led by Michèlle Aliot-Marie, elected in 1999 over the candidate preferred by Chirac. The party's leadership is struggling to rebuild the party's organization and the morale of its supporters in the aftermath of the 1997 defeat.

In the early 2000s, the once dominant RPR is in crisis.[21] Its electoral base is threatened by the growth of a powerful Far Right; it does not know how to define its relationship with that extremist party. Its members are demoralized and demobilized. It lacks a clear leadership with Aliot-Marie the formal leader, but Chirac is intervening more and more. Many of its other leaders are tainted by corruption and in some cases facing embarrassing trials for misuse of state funds. However, it would be wrong to count the RPR out. Many have done so in the past. It was not supposed to survive once de Gaulle left power; it was thought likely to fail as the vision of its founder faded after his death; it was deemed certain to fail if it ever lost hold on government. It has survived these past crises and seems likely to overcome the present problems. Parties rarely die, especially one like the Gaullist party that responds to the political aspirations of a large portion of the population.

The Union for French Democracy
By the end of the 1990s, it became difficult to know what to call the group of small, conservative parties that long allied themselves with the Gaullists. From 1978 until 1998, they were linked in the Union for French Democracy (UDF). It was a means of assembling the various supporters of President Valéy Giscard d'Estaing in a single political movement. While the UDF persists as a political body, its member parties suffered heavily in the defeats in the 1997 National Assembly elections and the 1998 regional assembly elections. Several of its components have withdrawn and gone their own way. These parties, sometimes labeled "centrists," still have similar policy concerns and appeal to exactly the same voters. These political realities will keep them loosely together in the future despite current efforts at asserting their own identities.

The UDF itself continues under the presidency of François Bayrou, the former leader of the Christian democratic party known now as the Democratic Force. Also still in the UDF is the Radical party, a gross misnomer for an essentially conservative party. The Liberal Democracy party, the new name for what was until 1997 the Republican party, is closest to the legacy of former President Giscard but it has cut its ties with the UDF. Originally, the UDF was primarily a voice for its several constituent parties with a handful of direct members of its own. It is now building its own independent existence as the other parties defect.

The loose confederation of parties and leaders that makes up the UDF coalition is a major source of weakness. More important, the absence of a major UDF candidate in the 1995 presidential election relegated the party to the sidelines of that crucial political contest. With French politics so focused on the president and presidential campaigns, parties without viable presidential candidates lose credibility and impact. The UDF parties do not have such a candidate at the present. They will need to develop one before the next presidential elections if they hope to remain key political actors.

The RPR-UDF Coalition
Despite internal differences and occasional tensions between Gaullists and the others, the Gaullist-Giscardian coalition has remained remarkably cohesive, permitting it to control politics for over 25 years. There are periodic feuds, and the bitter ones in the late 1970s and the early 1980s contributed to their 1981 defeats. In opposition, they reforged their unity and were successful in winning back the confidence of the voters in 1993. Some observers believed that the large parliamentary majority won that year would bring more manifestations of the coalition's internal divisions. However, Gaullist-UDF unity prevailed in the mid-1990s.

Policy and political style differences between the RPR and the UDF parties are small. The so-called "centrists" groups are in fact quite conservative in their economic outlooks. In the past, they differed with the RPR over the Gaullists' hesitations about European unification and the Gaullists' preference for strong state intervention in the economy and society. These differences are now muted as the RPR leadership is more supportive of the European Union and as Gaullists have adopted a more market-oriented economic perspective. The UDF parties were once more concerned with the sometimes heavy-handed, confrontational approach of Gaullists in issues of political style. That distinction has faded over time as Gaullist rule has become more consensual and as the UDF has taken increasingly hardline positions on issues such as immigration, urban decay, and crime. There are few differences between those who vote for the Gaullist RPR and those who vote for the UDF; when their electorates are broken down by socioeconomic, religious, and demographic factors, they are virtually identical. The continuing distinctiveness between these two groups are based on historical divisions and personal rivalries. The separate identities of the RPR and UDF-centrists made sense when de Gaulle was still around. But 30 years after his death, the differences among the groupings of the Center-Right are marginal at best.

The two-ballot electoral system works to keep the two elements of the coalition together. Often, the two groups run a single slate of candidates in national elections, as they did in 1986, 1988, 1993, and 1997. When the Gaullists and Giscardians run separately, electoral support is quite evenly divided. (See Table 10–6 on page 123.) Center/Right voters seem equally willing to support either Gaullist or Giscardian candidates, depending upon whichever party has the coalition's candidate in their district.

Despite this near electoral parity, the Gaullists usually appear as the leaders of the coalition. The Gaullists have several advantages. Their party has a stronger organization and a large corps of activists. The Gaullist party is more coherent than the often squabbling mini-parties that make up the Giscardian UDF. Most important, the Gaullists have been more successful in developing leaders with presidential capabilities who then become automatic leaders of the Center/Right. Thus the two leading candidates from the moderate Right for the 1995 presidential elections were two Gaullists: Balladur and Chirac.

At the turn of the century, the Center-Right is clearly in crisis. The defeat in 1997 left the parties demoralized and disoriented. The task of renewing the confidence and commitment of the party rank-and-file is a major challenge, especially for the UDF parties as they self-destruct with multiple schisms. The one advantage that the Center-Right has is the continued presence of President Jacques Chirac in the Elysées Palace. If Chirac can overcome the anger of his party leaders and followers for the failed election of 1997, he is in a position to provide leadership and an alternative program. He is able to take advantage of any failures of the PS to call new elections at

a time inconvenient for the Socialists. But that will take some time and some miscalculations on the part of the Left.

Above all, the parties of the Center-Right are confused and divided about how to deal with the emergence of a strong Far Right (FN) that has cut into their electorate. Up until now, the mainstream parties have regarded the FN as too extreme, antidemocratic, and racist for them to deal with. In the 1997 elections, the RPR-UDF would have had a comfortable majority if the FN had not run as strongly as it did on the first ballot and then deny the traditional Center-Right their voters' support on the second ballot. In 1998 regional elections, the FN's strong showing forced Center-Right regional leaders to either cooperate with the FN or lose their hold on regional politics. The moderates called for regional leaders to refuse cooperation with the FN. Such cooperation with an extremist party might legitimize a party that most mainstream politicians and the voting public as a whole regard as undemocratic. Not all regional RPR and UDF leaders followed the calls of their national leaders. Some regional leaders, especially from the UDF, formed coalitions with the FN even at the cost of expulsion from their parties. What strategy to adopt toward the FN remains the key issue for the Center-Right as it enters the new century. To ignore the FN, the mainstream parties run the risk of losing more voters to this extremist party. To adopt the FN's stands on race, immigration, and law and order would risk the loss of the majority of the RPR and UDF voters who reject the extremist positions. To form a second ballot coalition with the FN would be equally dangerous in terms of alienating moderate voters. The dilemma is a real one and is unlikely to be quickly resolved.

Other Parties

Over the past 40 years, French politics has been dominated by exchanges between the two coalitions of the Left and the Center-Right. There are, however, numerous smaller parties seeking to be active in French politics. For most of them, their only impact on politics comes in the form of small press releases occasionally reported in the national newspaper of record, *Le Monde*. Two minor parties have had important presences in recent elections: the National Front and the Ecologists.

The National Front On the Far Right of the political spectrum, the National Front has emerged as an important political force. During the first 28 years of the Fifth Republic, political movements from the Far Right had little consequence. Indeed, it was believed that one of the major accomplishments of the Gaullist era was the incorporation of the often antidemocratic French extreme Right into moderate and democratic parties. This achievement is cast into doubt by the stunning rise of the far rightist National Front (FN) of Jean-Marie Le Pen.[22]

Le Pen is an open admirer of the Vichy collaborator leader Marshal Pétain. His party advocates a slightly diluted dose of right-wing extremist themes intertwined with the populist rhetoric of the 1990s. It criticizes the press and electronic news media, the erosion of traditional virtues, the decline of public order and the rise in violent crimes, the aloof bureaucracy, big government, and the plight of the common citizen facing a distant, unresponsive state. The FN has also exploited French nationalist concerns about the European Union. With the mainstream parties of both Left and Right in full support of European unification, the National Front can raise nationalist fears and complaints about the EU's policies and failures. Finally, the FN can claim to have "clean hands" as political leaders of the PS, RPR, and UDF have become embroiled in financial scandals.

Most important, the National Front skillfully exploits popular resentment against the large number of immigrant workers. In its strongly law-and-order and antiforeigner rhetoric, the National Front makes little attempt to disguise its appeal to the racist sentiments of many French citizens against the primarily North African and Middle Eastern immigrants. The main parties, with only a few temporary lapses, have refused to exploit these sentiments. That has left the field open to the National Front.

The National Front is strongly influenced by the personality and politics of its leader, Jean-Marie Le Pen. However, it would be wrong to see it only as Le Pen's leadership.[23] It remains primarily a national party with only minor success

as the local elections. For example, a year after Le Pen won 15 percent of the vote in the 1995 presidential elections, his party's candidates in local elections managed to win less than 7 percent of the vote. At the national level, the FN's voter support is impressive. In 1997, FN candidates for the National Assembly took 15 percent of the vote, outpolling the Communist party and the UDF's separate total and nearly equalling the RPR vote. The isolation of the FN prevents it from turning this electoral strength into legislative seats because in France's two-ballot electoral system no party is willing to ally with a political pariah like the FN. In 1997, the National Front elected only one deputy to the National Assembly. But it was able to use its position as a spoiler, and it can claim responsibility for the Center-Right's defeat in the 1997 National Assembly elections.[24]

The National Front has developed a broad electorate drawing voters from both Right and Left. Many of its leaders are former RPR and UDF politicians. But National Front electoral support is very diverse. It has attracted unskilled workers from the Left who feel that their job security is undermined by the large numbers of immigrants. It wins support from small business owners increasingly threatened by a changing and international market. It is successful among many voters who once supported the Center-Right but who have become disillusioned with mainstream leaders and their supposed neglect of urban decline and crime. The FN's appeal is especially strong in urban areas heavily populated with immigrants: Paris, Lyons, Marseilles, Nice, Strasbourg, and Toulon.

For a decade, mainstream politicians expected the National Front to wither up and disappear because of its intimate association with Jean-Marie Le Pen. If Le Pen did not self-destruct through his own excesses, observers felt that there would be no one who could maintain the party when he retired or died. That is not happening; nor is it likely to do so with a new set of aspiring leaders ready to assume leadership when Le Pen steps down. It poses a long-term threat to French democracy. Its racism and antisemitism are alarming. But it is also worrisome to watch the few National Front local governments in action. For example, in the southern city of Orange, the newly elected FN mayor purged the library, removing books that portrayed the Revolution of 1789 in a favorable light. Also removed were books with stories of Northern Africa, books with illustrations showing races mixing, books authored by critics of the National Front. In their places, the new mayor placed antisemitic books on purported Jewish conspiracies, fascist classics, and recent books denying the Holocaust.[25]

Like the Communist party in the 1950s and 1960s, the National Front is largely isolated on the political extreme. There have been some coalitions between the FN and Gaullists or Giscardians at the local and regional levels. And there are some natural affinities on some policy and political matters. With few exceptions, however, the moderate conservative parties have refused all political contact with the National Front. They regard it as an extremist party whose goals and tactics are undemocratic. The dilemma for mainstream parties, and especially the RPR and UDF, is how to respond to this political challenge. For the mainstream parties, to simply ignore the FN and its threat does not work; to pick up the FN's positions helps to legitimize the FN and anger their traditional voters.

While racial tensions from the growing numbers of immigrants have mounted in many European countries, only in France have they been translated into a political movement. A National Front in Britain organized a few marches but could not translate that into electoral support; neo-Fascist groups in Germany have greater visibility because of their violent clashes with immigrants and police, but their voting share is usually less than a third of that of the French National Front's. The greater success of the French FN can be explained at least in part by its leader's effectiveness. Le Pen has proven to be an attractive leader despite his extremism. He has been skilled in the use of the media that he condemns.

The FN faced division in the late 1990s with one of its leaders, Bruno Mégret, breaking away to form a new party. Mégret opposed Le Pen's all-out battle against the Center-Right and advocated efforts to build a coalition with the Gaullists and UDF. His party ran a separate list in the 1999 European elections. The new party drew some voters from the FN, but the schism seemed to drive voters away from both Far Right parties. As a result, the future of the National Front seems uncertain as the new century begins.

The Ecologists   The environmental movement in France has not been as important as it is in Germany. Certainly, the German Greens have had a much greater impact on electoral politics than have the French ecologists. Part of the reason is the electoral system. In Germany, a party that receives at least 5 percent of the vote will get deputies in the Bundestag; in France the threshold for participation on the second ballot is 15 percent of registered voters. As a result, in 1993 when the French ecologists recorded their highest ever record for a national election, 7.6 percent, only a handful of ecology candidates were able to stand in the run-off elections and none was elected. In the 1997 elections, some ecology candidates allied themselves with the Socialist party. As a result, a handful of Greens were elected to parliament even though the vote total for environmental candidates dropped to only 5.3 percent.

The French environmental movement is divided and this affects its political effectiveness. Often two ecology candidates oppose each other on the first ballot. The divisions among the French Greens are over different approaches to the environmental issues, the kinds of political links they should have with mainstream parties, and especially personal rivalries. Even with the election successes in 1997 and a Green party member in the government, the French environmentalists remain a fringe party with little effect on the political process.

The French ecologists seem most successful in local elections and in elections that "don't count," such as by-elections and European parliamentary elections. Their presence has encouraged the mainline parties, especially the Socialists, to give greater heed to environmental issues in order to ward off potential defections to the ecologist parties.

Parties and Political Stability

The French party system contributes friction and instability to the overall political scene. Some attribute this instability to the large number of parties, arguing that multiparty systems are inherently unstable and two-party systems are inherently stable. However, the number of parties alone is not the crucial factor; other democratic states—The Netherlands, Sweden, Canada, and others—have stable party systems despite the presence of more than two parties. Much more germane to the relative stability of party systems is the degree of ideological or emotional polarization among parties. Where parties are polarized, whatever their number, the party system is likely to be unstable.

The degree of polarization between parties is much greater in France than in Britain. The intensity of partisan feelings makes interparty cooperation and friendship difficult. In the past, the polarization came from the sharply different views of society represented by the Left and Right. These differences are now less dramatic. In 1981, the Socialist party offered French voters a choice of a new society, one based on doctrinaire socialism. Once in office, the PS found that practical domestic politics and international influences made it necessary to temper and eventually abandon that doctrine. By the end of the 1980s, the once-radical Socialists had signed on to the consensus around a market-driven economy. They retreated also on social issues. Differences between Left and Right had virtually disappeared on most issues of substance. Party polarization nevertheless continued. It was based more on style, discourse, and personal grudges between politicians on the Left and Right. It is now more of an emotional polarization than an ideological one. But it is just as strong an impediment to multiparty cooperation. This is why periods of divided government—cohabitation—are so tense in France.

Moderation of the Socialist party's agenda and consensus on many constitutional, economic, and social matters does open up more options for French voters. The Socialists' moderation in their doctrine and policy positions is helping to reduce polarization—at least on public issues. Personal rivalries reflecting past battles still remain strong. However, the cumulative effect of declining polarization made the second experience with cohabitation between Mitterrand and Balladur a much less hostile relationship. From 1958 to 1981, the Gaullist coalition ruled often by default in the absence of a realistic alternative. Now

French voters can choose between a slightly left-of-center Socialist party and a slightly right-of-center RPR-UDF coalition. Such a viable choice for voters is important from the standpoint of democratic accountability.

The French parties have suffered recent losses in membership and challenges in moving from the old party barons who dominated politics for over 20 years to new leaders. There are several issues—such as European unification, domestic order, environmentalism, and immigration policies—that divide parties internally. Furthermore, the whole notion of political parties is under review as the membership-based political machines of the past are giving way to parties run by specialists who adapt the parties to public opinion and manipulate the media. Parties no longer need militants to pass out brochures or paste up posters; they need public relations experts, pollsters, professional campaign managers. These new techniques permit parties to do without the mass memberships they once sought but they require new financial resources that are difficult to acquire.

As is the case in most other western democracies, French parties have been discredited by scandals. In France, as elsewhere, a more independent and critical press has pored over the lives and activities of politicians. Although uninterested in the kind of titillating personal peccadillos that have preoccupied the American press, the French press has found illegal campaign contributions (needed to fund the new media-based parties), bribery of public officials, and the diversion of public resources to private use and gain. Such scandals have weakened the public's attachment to the mainstream parties and help to account for the frequent swings in voter support in France over the past 25 years.

Above all, the health and stability of the French party system is menaced by the rise of an undemocratic and extreme-rightist National Front. The major parties—PS, RPR, UDF—all face threats to their electorates from this movement. But the FN has the advantage of being able to avoid blame for current problems—unemployment, weakening family ties, urban decay, drug trafficking, crime—because they are out of government. They can and do exploit these concerns in extremist ways that responsible parties in government cannot consider. As parties of the Left and Right confront these problems—and fail to resolve them—the FN stands to continue its rise.

CONCLUSION

In contrast to the more or less orderly nature of political participation in Britain, the French proclivity to political protest and periodic revolt gives an unpredictable and destabilizing element to French politics. For example, in the early spring of 1968, political observers commented in French newspapers that the public seemed bored with political issues and unwilling to become involved in politics. A few weeks later, student riots and a general strike provided the most serious political crisis to confront the Fifth Republic and brought France to the brink of civil war. The disorder paralyzed the country's economy and brought normal political and social life to a virtual standstill. During the Events of May 1968, some 10 million people took part in strikes whose motives were more political than economic. Students occupied their schools; workers occupied their factories or offices. Everywhere, people engaged in long debates over political and social reform. Marches organized by opponents and supporters of the regime each brought nearly a million people into the streets of Paris.

This explosion of political involvement was short-lived; eventually people tired of political debates and left their schools and factories for the comforts of home. The government called for new parliamentary elections, which directed political participation into more usual—and safer—channels. In the elections, the majority of the voters reacted against excesses during the events and voted against any party even remotely sympathetic to the student and worker uprising.

The Events of May 1968 are often cited as an example of a new form of political participation, one that is likely to trouble Western democracies as they confront the value and social changes inherent in advanced stages of development. However, the Events seem more a product of the French tradition of revolt dating back to the Revolution of 1789 than a prototype for a revolt in other democracies. They do provide a dramatic illustration of the potential for revolt in French people. When other channels of participation appear blocked or ineffective, the French may draw on their long tradition of revolt to take to the streets again. Indeed, the glamour and romance associated with May 1968 and earlier revolts could make additional episodes of mass rebellion in France more likely.

NOTES

[1]Michel Crozier, *The Stalled Society,* trans. by Rupert Swyer (New York: Viking, 1973), p. 67.

[2]See, for example, Gabriel A. Almond and Sidney Verba, *The Civic Culture: Political Attitudes and Democracy in Five Nations* (Boston: Little, Brown, 1965).

[3]See Jack Walker, "A Critique of the Elitist Theory of Democracy," *American Political Science Review* 60 (June 1966): 285–295, and Peter Bachrach, *The Theory of Democratic Elitism* (Boston: Little, Brown, 1967).

[4]E. Deutsch et al., "Les Familles politiques en France," cited in *French Politics,* ed. Martin Harrison (Lexington, MA: D. C. Heath, 1969), p. 134.

[5]Frank L. Wilson, "Political Demonstrations in France: The Politics of Protest or Ritual Politics?" *French Politics and Society* 12 (Spring-Summer 1994): 23–40, and Charles Tilly, *The Contentious French* (Cambridge, MA: Harvard University Press, 1986).

[6]Stanley Hoffmann, *Decline or Renewal?: France Since the 1930s* (New York: Viking Press, 1974), pp. 111–144.

[7]Alexis de Tocqueville, T*he Old Regime and the French Revolution,* trans. Stuart Gilbert (Garden City, NY: Doubleday, 1955), pp. 210–211.

[8]Maurice Druon, cited by Alain Peyrefitte, *The Trouble with France* (New York: Knopf, 1981), p. 248.

[9]Byron Criddle, "Electoral Systems in France," *Parliamentary Affairs* 45 (January 1992): 108–116.

[10]Philip E. Converse and Roy Pierce, *Political Representation in France* (Cambridge, MA: Harvard University Press, 1986).

[11]Roy Pierce, *Choosing the Chief: Presidential Elections in France and the United States* (Ann Arbor: University of Michigan Press, 1995).

[12]Daniel Boy and Noona Mayer, *The French Voter Decides* (Ann Arbor: University of Michigan Press, 1993). See also Michael Lewis-Beck and Andrew Skalaban, "France," in Mark Franklin, et al., eds., *Electoral Change: Responses to Evolving Social and Attitudinal Structures in Fifteen Countries* (Cambridge, England: Cambridge University, 1992).

[13]See John Ardagh, *France Today* (Harmondsworth, England: Penguin, 1987), pp. 330–342.

[14]Dorothy McBride Stetson, *Women's Rights in France* (Westport, CT: Greenwood Press, 1987).

[15]Frank L. Wilson, *Interest-group Politics in France* (Cambridge, England: Cambridge University Press, 1987).

[16]Wilson, "Political Demonstrations in France."

[17]On French parties, see John Frears, *Parties and Voters in France* (New York: St. Martins, 1991).

[18]D. S. Bell and Byron Criddle, *The French Socialist Party*, 2nd ed. (London: Oxford University Press, 1988). For recent developments, see William Safran, "The Socialists, Jospin, and the Mitterrand Legacy," in Michael Lewis-Beck, ed., *How France Votes* (Chatham, NJ: Chatham House, 1999).

[19]See Jane Jenson and George Ross, *The View From Inside: A French Communist Cell in Crisis* (Berkley: University of California Press, 1985).

[20]*The Economist,* 22 November 1997.

[21]Frank L. Wilson, "The French Right in Search of Itself," in Frank L. Wilson, ed., *The European Center-Right at the Turn of the Century* (New York: St. Martin's, 1998).

[22]Harvey G. Simmons, *The French National Front: The Extremist Challenge to Democracy* (Boulder, CO: Westview, 1996).

[23]Edward DeClair, *Politics on the Fringe: The People, Politics, and Organization of the French National Front* (Durham, NC: Duke University Press, 1999).

[24]James G. Shields, "La Politique du pire: The Front National and the 1997 Legislative Elections," *French Politics and Society* 15 (Summer 1997): 21–36.

[25]David Zane Mairowitz, "Fascism à la Mode: In France, the Far Right Presses for National Purity," *Harper's Magazine,* October 1997, pp. 59–63.

Chapter 11

Political Leaders in France

Prior to World War II, critics of the Third Republic claimed that an industrial-financial oligarchy of "200 families" dominated French politics behind a democratic facade. The power of the 200 families, who were purported to turn public policy to further their own ends, was no doubt greatly exaggerated. But the political leadership of France in that period did indeed seem more closed and elitist than in other democracies. For some observers, this continues to be the case. There is considerable overlap among the various economic, political, and social elites, suggesting to some the presence of a ruling elite.[1] The state's role in creating an exclusive and narrow elite through the *grandes écoles* that dominates politics, business, and the bureaucracy is widely and correctly criticized.[2] Such features of French elites detract from the pluralist character usually attributed to leaderships in Western democracies.

Of course, there is still considerable pluralism in France among autonomous sets of leaders— from politics, business, labor, religions, the bureaucracy, and others seeking influence over public policy. And the top political leaders must win office in open and competitive elections. There is cooperation, too: Some collaboration of the various sets of political, economic, and social elites is useful for effective government. But too much collaboration threatens democracy. A French sociologist described well the balance needed for democratic political leadership:

> A unified elite means the end of freedom. But when the groups of the elite are not only distinct but become a disunity, it means the end of the state. Freedom survives in those intermediate regions, which are continually threatened when there is moral unity of the elite, where men and groups preserve the secret of single and eternal wisdom and have learnt how to combine autonomy with cooperation.[3]

It may well be that French political leaders are more elitist than those in Britain, although such comparisons are always impressionistic and difficult to demonstrate factually. But France's political leadership still probably falls in that intermediate area between unified elites and chaos where democracy can operate.

ELECTED NATIONAL LEADERS

The elected political leaders in France tend to be better educated, richer, more often from Paris, and overwhelmingly more often male when compared to the general adult population. This is not unusual; political leaders in all types of political systems are never a good reflection of the society as a whole. There are more blue-collar workers in the French political elite than we find in the United States. But working-class presence in the leadership ranks is less widespread than in Britain, where close ties between the Labour party and the trade union movement bring many workers into Parliament. In France the unions lack such political influence, and fewer of their members are nominated to public office even by the working-class parties of the Left. Deputies with business backgrounds are also less common in France than in Britain or the United States. This is due to a mutual mistrust of politicians and business people even in conservative parties. Gaullist and Giscardian party leaders do not want to give substance to the Left's claims that the Center-Right parties are too closely tied to business interests, and this means avoiding recruitment of a lot of business people to elected or party leadership positions.

During eras of cohabitation, when the president's party does not have a majority in the National Assembly, this changes. The prime minister then is by necessity a political rival to the president as was the case after 1997 when the Gaullist president Jacques Chirac faced a government headed by a Socialist prime minister, Lionel Jospin. Most decision-making powers shift under cohabitation to the prime minister, and the president then stands as a very prominent critic of the actions of the government.

The diversity of backgrounds that French politicians have compared to the parliamentary grooming of British political leaders may reduce some of the danger of inbreeding. This diversity of occupational backgrounds in French political leadership, however, is offset by the fact that the leaders from all major parties, the senior civil service, and prominent business figures have all come from the same elite *grandes écoles* such as the National School of Administration (ENA), and the Polytechnic School. Their educational training is the same; many were classmates; most share similar outlooks on society and the state.

In the United States, training in the law is often seen as a way to a political career. In France, however, there are nearly twice as many medical professionals as there are lawyers and many more school teachers than these professions combined. The importance of the medical professions (doctors, pharmacists, veterinarians) in French politics comes from a tradition of political involvement by doctors and pharmacists and their role as local notables with political and social influence in the small villages. Left-wing parties often recruit schoolteachers to political action. In France this phenomenon is attributable to the old battle against church-run schools and suspicion of private schools. Another important source of political leaders is the civil service, which is free from the strictures against partisan involvement found in Britain and to a lesser degree in the United States. On the whole, occupational groups well represented in parliament tend to be those whose practitioners can afford to take leaves of absence for full-time political activity without damaging their careers.

There are significant differences between the types of people recruited to politics by the Center-Right Gaullists and Giscardians and by the leftist communists and socialists. Both Left and Right, however, draw their leaders from the upper classes. The socialists and communists recruit their leaders from the intellectual branch of the upper class: teachers, writers, and scholars; the Gaullists and Giscardians recruit among the economic elite: business people and landowners. Neither Left nor Right is representative of the general public nor of its electorate. Critics see the resulting political conflicts within the political elite as reflecting more the struggle of various factions of the dominant classes than the real conflict of interests in society.

In Britain, political careers usually follow a pattern of lengthy apprenticeship in Parliament before appointment to ministerial rank. In France, the situation under the Fifth Republic is somewhat different. While leaders may be drawn from similar socioeconomic backgrounds, the extent of their prior shared political experience is much more limited. Even when a single party has had a majority in the National Assembly (as in

1968–73 and 1981–86), the governments were based on a coalition of parties whose leaders conducted separate and competing partisan activities. Furthermore, under the Fifth Republic, the Council of Ministers has frequently included individuals with little or no prior political experience. These outsiders have generally been senior civil servants, but they have also included diplomats, professors, and intellectuals. Even at the level of prime minister, outsiders with little political experience have been selected. Georges Pompidou was a political unknown when de Gaulle selected him as prime minister in 1962, and he went on to become president. Similarly, Edouard Balladur was more a behind-the-scenes aide than a party leader when he was selected as prime minister in 1993.

The selection of politically inexperienced outsiders as members of the government, and even as prime ministers, reflects the primacy of the president in the Fifth Republic. All five presidents have preferred good administrators and technicians to potential political rivals as top ministers, and especially as prime minister. Politically ambitious prime ministers can threaten the delicate division of powers between the president and the prime minister required by the mixed presidential-parliamentary system. The relationship between the two executives requires the president to be preeminent and the prime minister to take the blame for failure and give credit for success to the president.

In any case, the long-term close political collaboration characteristic of the top leadership in Britain is lacking in France, which may detract from the cohesion and cooperation of French governments. Indeed, there does appear to be greater internal conflict and tension in French than in British governments.

LEADERSHIP STYLES AND SKILLS

Many of France's political leaders have been intellectuals as well as politicians. Americans would think it strange to regard the president as an expert on literary or philosophical matters. But Georges Pompidou edited an anthology of French poetry just before he was elected president. His successor, Valéry Giscard d'Estaing, while president, gave an hour-long televised interview on the literary achievements of the celebrated nineteenth-century French novelist Gustave Flaubert.

A consequence of the prominent political role of intellectuals is a concern for ideology and correct doctrine. French politicians are much more

---

THE CUMUL

An unusual feature of French political leadership is the practice of holding several elected mandates at the same time, a practice known as the *cumul*. In the United States and most other democracies, members of the national legislature are not allowed to hold other elected positions. In France, however, politicians are allowed to hold more than one elected mandate. Until recently, it was not unusual to find deputies or senators with three or four other mandates beyond their parliamentary seat. An individual may have been a deputy in the National Assembly and at the same time mayor of a large city, member of a department's general council, or member of a regional council. A 1985 reform tried to limit this practice but *cumul* remains important. In 1996, 93 percent of the National Assembly deputies held at least one other local or regional elected office. After the 1997 elections over a fourth of the deputies were also mayors of large cities or presidents of departmental or regional councils.[4] Many others held additional locally elected positions.

The *cumul* is an important means of developing political leadership. The very fact that aspiring leaders hold two or more elected mandates makes them "notables." They are also able to build links between the national government and local governments in a very centralized political system. However, the practice of *cumul* may face additional legal limits. Longer parliamentary sessions also make it more difficult for deputies to handle multiple mandates. But it is unlikely that the *cumul* will disappear entirely.

attached to their ideologies than are political leaders in Britain, Germany, or the United States. In nearly all cases, this attachment reflects a sincere desire to reshape society according to their ideological models. In office, however, French leaders have proved pragmatic. Gaullists have championed ideological views of nationalism and anticommunism in their doctrine but pursued moderate policies of European unification and international accommodation while in power. The Left is reputed to be even more burdened by its ideological baggage. But President François Mitterrand engaged in more pragmatic adjustments to political reality than blind implementation of the Socialist party's ideology, which he had earlier helped to shape.

The notion of the collective responsibility of government ministers, a basic principle of British parliamentary government, is much less developed in France. During the Third and Fourth Republics, loose, multiparty coalitions did not contribute to a disciplined and united government. Under the Fifth Republic the collective action and responsibility of the Council of Ministers has begun to become established because of the ministers' dependence on the president and their obligation to support and defend his actions. This is less a matter of genuine collective decision making, however, as it is presumed to be in Britain, than it is a well-functioning hierarchical structure committed to the collective defense of the president. Under the Fifth Republic, the collective responsibility of the government has been furthered by the president's willingness to dismiss any minister who voices public opposition to his policies.

The nationalization of politics and political leadership has promoted the personalization of political leadership. In the past, the electorate's most immediate contact with the political world was through local officials and the local member of parliament. Now, thanks to national media systems and especially to television, voters can more readily see and hear national leaders discussing national issues. The leaders who receive the greatest exposure on the media are the top-level officials and their rivals in the opposition. Increased visibility has tended to enhance national leaders' political power and to broaden the gap between the top strata and subordinate levels of leadership.

The central position of the president in French politics since 1958 also contributes to the personalization of political leadership in the president and the several rivals for that position. Charles de Gaulle was a leader who dominated French politics for 30 years. He was viewed by many French citizens as having saved France after its defeat in 1940 by the Nazis. Called back to power in 1958 at a time of national crisis and political collapse, de Gaulle's authority was charismatic.[5] His sense of mission and personal mystique led many to believe that he alone could save France from the new threat in 1958 of military rule and civil war. De Gaulle's personal style permeated his regime: his sense of mission, flexibility, aloofness, paternalism, scorn of "intermediaries" (such as parties and interest groups), regal bearing, self-concept as savior of France, and, above all, the personal mystique that he used to win support from French citizens in all walks of life. Many of the French perceived even legislative elections as opportunities to vote for or against de Gaulle through the medium of candidates pledged to follow or to oppose him. Since de Gaulle's resignation in 1969, the charismatic aspect of leadership has dissipated, but the president remains the central figure in French politics.

The presidents who have succeeded de Gaulle—Georges Pompidou, Valéry Giscard d'Estaing, François Mitterrand, and Jacques Chirac—attempted to play more modest roles but often were caught up in the same pomp and aloofness that characterized de Gaulle's rule. The powers of the president grew under every president, so that by the time Mitterrand was elected in 1981 presidential powers and prerogatives far exceeded those exercised by de Gaulle. Critics complain that the presidential powers are so extensive that the president is now an elected monarch. Mitterrand had pledged to reduce the president's powers—while he was in opposition. Once in the presidency, he enjoyed fully the powers, prerogatives, and perquisites of the office. Many referred to him as monarchical; some even saw him as a benevolent old uncle.

The French attitude toward authority—described earlier as shunting power to strong and remote leaders—contributes to the elitist nature of the political leadership. In the past, the French have put up with authoritarian leaders for long periods, and then revolted and thrown out the whole regime. Between revolts the leaders continued to rule despite their involvement in scandals or their aloofness and authoritarianism. Now, under the Fifth Republic, prestigious and powerful leaders are eliminated by elections rather than riots. In 1981, for example, the French elected a Socialist president over an incumbent who had become too aloof from popular feelings. Between 1986 and 2000, control of the National Assembly shifted back and forth from the Left to the Right several times. Leaders are now allowed significant powers, but the electorate seems ready to hold them accountable for their actions. This reflects a healthier attitude toward political authority than traditionally found in France.

CONTROLLING THE BUREAUCRACY

In 1931, a French critic of the Third Republic wrote: "Republican France has in reality two constitutions: one . . . is official, visible, and fills the Press—it is parliamentary; the other is secret, silent . . .—the Napoleonic constitution which hands over the direction of the country to the administrative corps."[6] Since these words were penned, the challenge of assuring democratic mastery of the bureaucracy by the elected officials has continued to be a major problem. France has a vast and highly centralized bureaucracy. There are nearly three million people working for the state. The largest single category is made up of school teachers since the public schools are all run by the national government. The key to the government's control over this vast army of civil servants is a corps of approximately 5,000 senior civil servants mainly located in Paris and mainly graduates of *grandes écoles*. Their responsiveness to directions from the elected political leaders is the key linkage between the people and those who administer government policies at the grass roots.

For years the rapid rotation of ministers in the short-lived governments of the Third and Fourth Republics hindered the ability of politically accountable leaders to control the civil service. Under the Fifth Republic ministerial tenure has lengthened, but the rising power of the bureau-

cracy in its modern form, technocracy, remains a problem. The practice of recruiting ministers from the bureaucracy rather than parliament has led to the colonization of government by technocrats and the politicization of the civil service.[7] The reduction of parliament's powers has increased the bureaucrats' contempt for deputies, whom they regard as uninformed, petty politicians, and, worst of all, as powerless.

The French civil service adheres much less strongly than its British counterpart to the norm of political nonpartisanship. To correct for this the French have a more extensive layer of politically appointed leaders. Each minister selects a cabinet of personal advisers.[8] The members of the cabinets, civil servants borrowed from other ministries and younger politicians favored by the minister, form a body of advisers that compensates for the lack of innovation endemic in bureaucracies. They also help the minister master the bureaucratic structures and control the bureaucrats who serve under him or her. In addition, the office of the president has a large staff of senior civil servants and political protégés. Both presidents and ministers have used their cabinets to bypass the bureaucracies, to avoid bureaucratic sabotage, and to develop innovative ideas.

Until 1995, the formal limit on the number of cabinet members was ten although most ministers had many more and one prime minister had eighty. A 1995 reform set the limit at only five per ministry. However, enterprising ministers have found ways to increase that number through "temporary" assignments. Widespread use of ministerial cabinets demonstrates how important ministers feel that such independent and politically loyal aides are in providing their own directions and control over the bureaucracy they are supposed to lead.

Among the most important elements in seeking government control over the bureaucracy has been the presence during much of the Fifth Republic of a dominant party and a solid majority coalition. As Ezra Suleiman points out:

> . . . ministers are more able to exert greater influence in the administrative and political spheres—not because of the diminished role of parliament or the ministers' relatively longer stay in office, but because they have had the support of a dominant political party.[9]

With the presidency and parliament in the hands of a cohesive and durable majority, the government can in fact govern. Freed from the necessity of fighting for its existence on a daily basis, the government has the energy and time to oversee the administration of its policies. There has been bureaucratic obstruction, of course. The government has usually been able to overcome such resistance when it was determined to do so. For example, it forced through important reforms affecting education, agriculture, and foreign affairs. It was able to do so not only because of the strong executive leadership, but also because of the political base provided by the majority parties' strength in and out of parliament.

One of the critical tests of the bureaucracy's obedience to political leadership came with the Socialist victory in 1981. After over two decades of conservative rule, the bureaucrats, inherently conservative in outlook, faced the obligation to work with a Socialist government bent on enacting major changes. The Socialists replaced some senior civil servants, but the changes were modest, bringing new people more than ideological supporters of the Socialist party. The bureaucracy posed no obstacle to the Socialist reforms. Since then, political power has shifted to the Conservatives and then back to the Socialists. There have been few personnel changes, but the civil servants have proved loyal to whichever political force has been in power.

Cases of overt bureaucratic obstruction are rare. Usually the blocking tactics are most effective in preventing changes directed at the civil service structures and procedures rather than at policy content itself. A more prevalent danger is that the range of policy options open to ministers will be restricted by unimaginative thinking, lack of rigorous and open-minded analysis of alternatives, and unsympathetic treatment from permanent officials in their ministries. Of course, an alert, imaginative, and dynamic minister can demand—and probably elicit—better treatment from bureaucrats. All too often, however, ministers are preoccupied with other concerns or they simply lack the intellectual and technical abilities to tell whether officials are performing as they desire.

Ministerial skills are not always the primary criterion of choice: party factions must be represented and balanced; senior deputies must be rewarded; political debts must be paid. In France the pool of potential ministers is somewhat larger than it is in Britain because ministers can be selected from outside parliament. But the pressure to balance factions and parties, reward the faithful, and pay political debts operates to limit choice. Thus, by ministerial default, policy-making powers often slip from the hands of the politically accountable leaders into those of the bureaucrats.

The French bureaucracy is highly centralized but also compartmentalized. The various strata and divisions are often insulated from each other, and the whole system is prone to stalemate because of centralization and lack of communication.[10] To avoid the stalemate, informal relations have developed to provide the essential communications between politicians and bureaucrats and among otherwise isolated bureaucrats. For example, old boy networks made up of the alumni of the elite *grandes écoles* facilitate communication between bureaucrats, politicians, and business people. The accumulation of multiple elected mandates permits politicians to serve as links between various levels and parts of government. This enhances politicians' powers and also helps the system avoid stalemate. In effect, the French bureaucratic system produces a high degree of interdependence between civil servants and politicians at all levels of government. Although this assures political leaders of important roles in the administration of laws, the highly personalized nature of the politicians' involvement does not make this a good means of assuring democratic control.

THE MILITARY: DEPOLITICIZATION OF A POLITICAL ARMY

Alongside France's long democratic tradition is the willingness of French citizens to look to the "man on the white horse" to rescue France from its troubles. For example, when the Third Republic became mired in scandal and inaction in the late 1880s, a war hero, General Georges Boulanger, swept across the country winning multiple seats to Parliament. With his followers in the streets, Boulanger was poised to seize power.

At the crucial moment, however, he chose to spend the evening with his mistress. The masses milling in the streets clamoring for Boulanger went unmobilized and the coup collapsed. However, France has not always been so lucky. Other "men on white horses" have taken power legally or illegally—Napoleon Bonaparte, Louis Napoleon, and Marshal Philippe Pétain, for example.

Recently the tradition of the politicized military has been manifested in the form of quasi-military coups, the first of which occurred in 1940 at the time of France's defeat by Germany. As the legal civilian government capitulated and transformed itself into the Vichy regime, General Charles de Gaulle, a little-known junior minister and second-level military leader, fled France against the orders of his civilian masters and established a "provisional government" in London. However laudable de Gaulle's action—which stirred the resistance and hopes of the defeated French people—it was an instance of political insubordination by a military leader. The only thing that distinguished de Gaulle's action from a typical coup was that it took place in exile and created a government that controlled little territory. Only a few French colonial territories initially accepted his leadership. Ultimately, de Gaulle's action was legitimized by success, and his triumphal return to France vindicated his act of insubordination.

Again in 1958, de Gaulle came to power as the result of a near-coup. The French army in Algeria joined a revolt of French colonial settlers to prevent compromise with the Moslem Algerian freedom fighters. The rationale for de Gaulle's 1940 action served as a precedent: The army declared that the corrupt and bungling governments of the Fourth Republic were betraying French national interests by considering independence for Algeria; therefore action must be taken to defend France from its politicians. There is no evidence that de Gaulle personally incited the revolt, but some of his supporters were actively involved. The military and civilian rebellion in effect vetoed the leadership of the Fourth Republic and thrust de Gaulle upon the politicians.

To be sure, de Gaulle enjoyed considerable independent popularity in France, but his return to power was made possible by illegal action and insubordination on the part of the army in Algeria. Once again, the quasi-coup was legitimized by the overwhelming popular approval accorded the new Fifth Republic. A referendum on its new constitution was approved by nearly 80 percent of the voters; only the communists and a small handful of leftists campaigned against it.

A number of developments since 1945 had politicized the French army.[11] In contrast to the relatively peaceful dismantling of the British Empire after World War II, the French became entangled in long and debilitating colonial wars in Indochina and Algeria. Involved in guerrilla wars for 15 years, the French army had become isolated from the nation. By the late 1950s, the army's new techniques of psychological warfare led it to take political action, first in the colonial territory in question and ultimately in the homeland.[12] The shift from trying to win the hearts and minds of Algerian Muslims through skillful propaganda, to political action to shape French public opinion and persuade political leaders in Algeria and Paris through the same tactics was an easy one. The military felt betrayed by the civilian governments that rotated in and out of office with alarming frequency during the Fourth Republic. It accurately sensed the public's withdrawal of legitimacy from the Fourth Republic, and as a result was encouraged to take political action. A poll taken in early 1958 revealed the low degree of legitimacy accorded the civilian leadership: Only 8 percent of those polled said they would oppose or even withhold approval of a military coup; only 13 percent would oppose a communist coup.

Once it had become politicized, it was not easy to depoliticize the French army. When de Gaulle decided to grant independence to Algeria, the military acted against him. When the military commander of Algiers, General Massu, was dismissed in 1960 for publicly opposing de Gaulle's offer of self-determination to Algeria, a right-wing civilian revolt took place in the colony. While the army itself remained loyal in this crisis, it was the public expression by a military figure of opposition to the government's policy that triggered the revolt.

A year later, in April 1961, the army was more directly involved in an attempted coup led by four retired generals opposed to Algerian independence. The chief sources of military support for the revolt were the elite paratroop units stationed in Algeria and the French Foreign Legion. In the face of threatened paratroop attacks on Paris, de Gaulle appealed for public help. The revolt was quelled by the rallying of public support for de Gaulle, and the resistance of loyal military units in Algeria to the efforts of the insurgents to expand their control. In subsequent months right-wing extremists known as the Secret Army Organization (OAS), led by former General Salan, who had been involved in the abortive coup, engaged in acts of terrorism in Algeria and France. But the threat of military rebellion was ended.

The Fourth Republic's inability to act and declining public acceptance had fatally undermined its efforts to control the military. In contrast, the Fifth Republic's demonstration of effectiveness and legitimacy achieved the depoliticization of the military. De Gaulle's regime made effective decisions and commanded overwhelming popular acceptance. The very policy that the army had rejected—independence for Algeria—was sustained by the broadest popular consensus. The principle of Algerian self-determination was approved by 75 percent of French voters in the referendum of January 1961, and 90 percent of the voters in April 1962 ratified the actual grant of independence to Algeria.

Perhaps the most important factor in reestablishing military loyalty to civilian leadership was the failure of the Algerian revolt. The leading figures in the revolt were tried and condemned to death or long prison terms (although no executions were actually carried out and all the conspirators in prison had been pardoned by 1968). Thus the decisive defeat of 1961 supplanted the 1940 and 1958 precedents of successful military intervention. Such a defeat is unlikely to stimulate further efforts at forceful military intervention in politics.

At present the French military is involved in only the lowest-level political action. No longer as influential in Gaullist circles or in parliament, the army pursues its interests through the appropriate channels. And it is not very successful there. There are indications of malaise in the military stemming from economic causes: insufficient appropriations for favored weapons, low pay, low social status. The firm attachment of de Gaulle and later presidents to their own strategic concepts and disdain for interest group intermediaries appear to have led to the exclusion of the military from the reorientation of French defense priorities after 1962. Some see France's continued nuclear program as a sop to the generals. But there is little substance to such arguments. Presidents from the Left and Right continue to assert France's need for its own independent nuclear capability on the grounds of international power relations. Indeed, at times military leaders have seemed to want to reduce the nuclear budget commitment to favor other military equipment and programs.

There were some fears in the late 1970s that the military would not tolerate a left-wing government that included Communists. However, there were no military challenges to civil masters when Mitterrand came to power in 1981 and chose a cabinet that included three Communist ministers. In short, after experimenting for 20 years with an active political role, the French army now has adopted the role of "the Great Mute"—one in which the military stays out of politics. At the end of the twentieth century, it is difficult to conceive of any situation that would again bring the French army back into politics.

NOTES

[1]Pierre Birnbaum, *The Heights of Power: An Essay on the Power Elite in France* (Chicago: University of Chicago Press, 1982).

[2]Ezra N. Suleiman, *Elites in French Society: The Politics of Survival* (Princeton, NJ: Princeton University Press, 1978).

[3]Raymond Aron, "Social Structures and the Ruling Class," *British Journal of Sociology* 1 (June 1950): 143.

[4]*Le Monde*, 4 June 1997.

[5]Stanley Hoffmann, *Decline or Renewal?: France Since the 1930s* (New York: Viking, 1974), pp. 63–110.

[6]Daniel Halevy, cited by David Thomson, *Democracy in France Since 1870*, 5th ed. (New York: Oxford University Press, 1969), p. 55.

[7]Anne Stevens, "Politicization and Cohesion in the French Administration," in *Conflict and Consensus in France*, ed. Vincent Wright (London: Frank Cass, 1979), pp. 68–80.

[8]John Gaffney, "Political Think Tanks in the U.K. and Ministerial Cabinets in France," *West European Politics* 14 (January 1991).

[9]Ezra N. Suleiman, *Politics, Power, and Bureaucracy in France: The Administrative Elite* (Princeton, NJ: Princeton University Press, 1974), pp. 285–315.

[10]Michel Crozier, *The Stalled Society* (New York: Viking, 1973).

[11]See John Stewart Ambler, *Soldiers against the State: The French Army in Politics* (Garden City, NY: Doubleday, 1968).

[12]George A. Kelly, Lost Soldiers (Cambridge, MA: MIT Press, 1966).

Chapter 12

French Political Performance

While poets, foreign and native, wax eloquent in their praise of France's virtues, French social critics are fond of bemoaning their country's maladaptation to the modern world. They call it a troubled country, a "stalemate" or "stalled" society and refer to the problem as *le mal français*—the French sickness.[1] They claim that the country's social divisions, its citizens' lack of civic responsibility, and its overcentralized and overbureaucratized political system have blocked progress and prevented needed social and political change. One writer drew the analogy between French society and "an ungaited horse, each of whose legs is proceeding at a different cadence."[2]

Such views of a sick and blocked French political system are unfair and inaccurate. In fact, over the past fifty years France has experienced remarkable social and economic change. In some cases, changes have been imposed by external forces such as the European Union and growing international economic interdependence. Other changes have been made by far-sighted political leaders able to legislate change through the institutions of the Fifth Republic.

A RETREAT FROM THE PLANNED ECONOMY

For many years, the French economy was regarded as one of the weakest among major industrial countries. However, since 1960 the French economy has changed dramatically and become one of Europe's, indeed the world's, strongest economies. This was also a time of great economic transformation in France, with a substantial portion of the rural population leaving small and unprofitable farms for work in industry. The French government has always played a major role in stimulating and directing this economic transformation. In the 1980s, the government's role increased during the early years of Socialist rule and then decreased under both conservative and socialist leadership. Despite these changes, the role of the state in managing the French economy remains important.

Agricultural Policy

Agriculture remains a very important part of the French economy and society. It accounts for approximately 10 percent of GNP and about 4 percent of the working population. However, French agriculture has been plagued with serious problems. The basic difficulty is that there are still too many farmers working farms that are too small. Under the Fifth Republic the government directed several important reforms that have aided farmers to consolidate their holdings and adjust to changing markets and techniques.[3]

Today, nearly all farm policy—for France and other European states—is made in Brussels by the European Union. The French Ministry of Agriculture, however, administers these policies. While the French farmers have been the chief beneficiaries of the European Union's farm price supports and subsidies, they still have a number of grievances. The farmers direct their complaints, often in very theatrical ways, to their national government with the expectation that the government will then champion their cause in Brussels. Not long ago, angry farmers chased the minister of agriculture across a muddy field and the minister had to be rescued by helicopter. During the 1990s, French farmers organized frequent disorderly demonstrations throughout the country and in Brussels to protest trade negotiations and other policies that would diminish protection and subsidies for farmers. Such protests keep agricultural policy a central issue in France.

Economic Policies

From the prerevolutionary times of Colbert to the Mitterrand years, the French state played an important part in developing and directing the economy. The state generously subsidized mining, banks, railroads, and heavy industry. Later, important parts of the economy were brought under direct ownership by the state: part of the automobile industry, all public utilities, much of the defense industry, tobacco, telecommunications, and over half of the banks and insurance firms. In addition, the government established five-year economic plans in the 1960s and 1970s to guide economic development. To achieve these plans, the state influenced the private sector through investment policies, subsidies, and economic planning.[4]

Economic performance over the last 45 years has been very positive. From the mid-1950s through the end of the 1970s, France's rate of economic growth was the highest in Western Europe, exceeding even the German economic record. During this period, the economy was transformed from one based largely on agriculture and small industry into a modern industrial state renowned for its achievements in such sophisticated fields as nuclear energy, automotive engineering, aircraft and missiles, and telecommunications.

The role of the state in the economy has long been a center of political controversy. Unlike in the United States, where conservatives call for less government economic intervention, French conservatives have accepted a large role for the state in economic matters: promoting new industries through subsidies, currency and exchange regulation, price controls, and economic planning.[5] It was such an active state role that helped France recover so quickly from the devastation of World War II and to become a strong participant in the world economy. However, for much of the period since 1945, there has been a wide division between the moderate conservatives, with their Keynsian or managed capitalism economic policies, and the Left, which has advocated much greater government control over the economy through socialism: nationalization of private industry, state economic subsidies to ensure full employment, control over investments, and mandatory economic planning. Rooted in ideology, the debate over the economic role of the state was highly divisive in politics and economics.

The culmination of this debate came in the 1980s when the Socialists came to power with a commitment to a fundamental break with "monopolistic capitalism" and to creating a new society and economy based on socialist principles. Between 1981 and 1984, the French Socialist government sharply increased state intervention into the economy. They expanded the public sector by nationalizing nearly all privately owned banks and eleven major industrial groups. With these new publicly owned firms, the government then controlled about 30 percent of the nation's industry. Beyond nationalizations, the Socialists took an active role in the rest of the economy by directing investment, controlling prices and wages, and regulating employment reductions in the public and private sectors.

While other countries were cutting public expenditures and reducing public employment, the

Socialists in France substantially increased social welfare benefits. New programs were created and old programs were administered with greater generosity. The government created thousands of new posts in public employment and increased the minimum wage level. It imposed a new, wealth tax and reduced taxes for lower income families, in contrast to the British and American efforts to decrease taxes especially for the middle and upper income categories.

The results were initially positive—unemployment dipped and the economy grew more rapidly than before and more rapidly than did the economies of many of France's neighbors. Disposable income grew, spurring consumer spending. But inflation also increased at a time when other countries' rates were decreasing. Government indebtedness expanded. Most important, the attempt to prod the French economy seemed to benefit trade competitors more than it helped the domestic economy. The increased consumer spending was for imported goods, such as Japanese videocassette recorders. The expected stimulus of domestic production did not occur.

In effect, France suffered from an economic policy that was not in harmony with its trading partners. The French government inflated its economy in anticipation of a worldwide economic recovery that did not take place. The difficulties of Mitterrand's economic policies did not necessarily prove the failure of a socialist alternative so much as they demonstrated the problems of following independent economic programs in an increasingly interdependent international economy. But people, including many on the Left, concluded that socialist policies were ineffective in economics at the end of the twentieth century. Most of all, people on all points of the political spectrum came to recognize the limits of a single government in controlling its economy when it is so dependent on the economies of other countries.

After less than two years, the Socialist government began to retreat from its initial economic strategy. A new policy of "rigor" stressed reduction in inflation, decreased public deficits, and defense of the franc. The policy of economic rigor closely resembled the economic policies followed by conservative governments in France and elsewhere.

One lesson learned during this period was that the change of ownership from private hands into public hands did not have the dramatic effect on the overall economy hoped for by Socialists. The government found that newly nationalized industries had to operate the same as privately owned firms. They had to be concerned with profitability; managers had to be able to make their decisions free from political considerations; public firms had to be able to reduce employment; they had to be as firm with unions as were competing private firms. Most important, the Socialists found that nationalizations did not mark a rupture with capitalism. Indeed, during their years in government, the Socialists seemed to rediscover the virtues of free enterprise. From 1983 to 1986, the Socialists gradually eased many of the economic controls they had earlier championed.

When the Conservatives returned to power under Chirac in 1986, they aggressively attacked the mechanisms of state economic control. They eliminated most currency controls on the franc. They dropped government controls on laying off excess workers. They lifted price and wage controls and reduced controls on investment. They introduced a sweeping program to sell off most of the publicly owned industries. This meant denationalizing not only the firms the Socialists had nationalized in 1981, but also firms brought under public ownership by de Gaulle in 1945, and some enterprises, such as television networks, that had always been state-owned.

Pressed by international competition and European Union policies, the French moved toward a broad political consensus based on a more limited role of the state in its economy than had ever been the case before. State economic planning and industrial policies designed to focus state economic investments on promising industries came to an end. The sector of the economy owned and run by the state, once among Europe's largest, shrank in size. By the 1990s, France's commitment to economic *dirigisme* that had thrived under the Left and Right for centuries was reduced but not eliminated. France has not moved as far toward the neo-liberal, free enterprise models of the British and Americans, but it is much less involved in managing its economy than ever before in its history.

In 2000, the French economy shows mixed performance. Its international balance of trade is strong; inflation is low; the economy continues to grow although slowly; and the government deficit is down. On the downside, however, unemployment is very high at nearly 12 percent of the adult population. Many of the unemployed are young people trying to enter the workforce or semi-skilled or unskilled workers who have been without jobs for long periods of time. The Socialist victory in the 1997 National Assembly elections owed much to the failure of the Center-Right to reduce unemployment. The Socialist government of Lionel Jospin hopes to cut into unemployment by creating more public sector jobs and by reducing the work week to 35 hours. After three years of the Jospin government, there was little indication that these measures would in fact reduce unemployment. By 1998, unrest among the jobless brought demonstrations and the occupation of state job centers by the unemployed. The inability of either the Left or the Right to resolve this problem has produced public malaise in a country where such malaise may turn to revolt.

Social Welfare and Human Development

Since World War II, France has developed an extensive system of social benefits, largely through the efforts of Conservative and Centrist governments. Government programs include unemployment and disability insurance, retirement benefits, health and hospitalization insurance, subsidized housing, subsidized public transportation, and direct family payments based on the number of children irrespective of income.[6] These benefits have received broad political support.

The programs are costly, amounting to nearly one-fourth of the gross national product. Despite the extent and costliness of the benefits, there has been little discussion of a welfare state mentality in France like that which has preoccupied the British. In part, this is because the French economy has performed well and there has been no need to look for domestic causes of economic lethargy. It is also due to the format of French welfare programs. Unlike in Britain, where medicine was "nationalized" by creating a National

Health Service, in France doctors and many hospitals remain private operations, with the government paying for services through an insurance program rather than providing the services directly. The same is true in housing. In Britain, government-owned council housing once made up nearly a third of all dwellings. In France, government-owned housing accounted for less than 1 percent of total dwellings, but the government provides households with generous subsidies for housing provided by nonprofit associations (HLMs—moderate price housing associations sponsored by the government) and private landlords.

The method of financing French programs is different from Britain's. Nearly all British welfare programs are funded directly out of general state revenues; they are paid for with receipts from income, inheritance, and national sales taxes. In France, most of the programs are funded through employment taxes as a sort of insurance program. Both employers and employees pay a hefty percentage of salaries into social security funds. These funds are then used for retirement and disability benefits and for medical and dental care reimbursements. They also fund some educational and medical research and construction programs. One advantage of these taxes is that they tend to be less visible than income taxes. Workers are aware that part of their pay is deducted for the social security program, but few recognize that when the employers' share is added in the total cost, employment taxes amount to about a third of their income. The disadvantage is that when unemployment soars, as it has in the 1990s, welfare programs lose much of their revenue. Also, as the elderly and retired population grows, the burden on active workers increases. As a result, the French welfare programs have experienced deficits and cutbacks in the mid-1990s.

French social-welfare programs provide services and benefits for all, usually without any test of the individual's own means to afford them. The benefits tend to be more important to people of modest means in that the value of social benefits amounts to a much greater percentage of their total income. But the goal of these programs is not redistribution of wealth from the rich to the poor. For example, the generous system of family payments based on the number of children provides increasingly large payments as the number of children goes up without regard to family income. It is not so much a policy to provide assistance to needy people as it is one to encourage families to have more children in order to correct a too low birth rate.

Some of the programs are controversial. For example, the government met an acute housing need in the 1970s by subsidizing construction of huge apartment tower complexes. These housing developments soon contributed to overcrowded neighborhoods, with rising delinquency and crime. They also failed to meet the growing public desire for ownership of single-family units. Social welfare programs are also costly. As in other countries, these costs have grown rapidly and the prospect of paying for them out of declining employment taxes as the population ages poses a real challenge. The programs often involve complex and cumbersome bureaucracies to implement them. But most of the programs are very much appreciated by the public. Neither Conservatives nor Socialists talk much of reducing benefits, of imposing user fees, or of eliminating programs. The social benefits are too popular for politicians to risk attacking them. In addition, political leaders remember that chief among the substantive complaints that fueled the tumultuous Events of May 1968 was a reduction in social security benefits.

The social welfare state has helped to integrate less advantaged people into the capitalist system. Trade unions have pushed for these benefits and have been drawn into the system to promote them and administer them. The programs reduce some of the uncertainties of a free enterprise system by providing for medical emergencies, income protection in case of disability, and retirement benefits. Coupled with government programs to mandate a 35-hour work week and five weeks of annual paid vacation for all workers, the social welfare state promotes domestic tranquility by giving all a clear stake in the existing system.

There will continue to be changes. In recent years, both Conservative and Socialist governments have worked to shift the pattern of benefits to favor the least advantaged portions of the population in the cause of national "solidarity." Such an orientation may be expected to continue in the future as a way of controlling rising costs. But there will be no broad retreat from the popular and stabilizing welfare state.

FRANCE AND THE EUROPEAN UNION

France was among the founding members of what is now the European Union. The French saw economic integration as a way to prevent excessive economic rivalries in Western Europe and as a way to bind Germany into a European community so that the Germans would never again take up arms against its neighbors. From its inception in 1953 to the initiation of a single European currency in 1999, the European Union has grown in its economic duties. By now, virtually all economic policy for France is set, not in Paris, but in Brussels and the other locations of EU institutions.

The European Union is what it is today because of the French. Since the early 1960s, French presidents and German chancellors have worked in tandem to set the direction for European unification. The French have never been embarrassed about seeking their own national interests through European integration. The EU's very generous farm subsidies and protected agricultural markets have benefitted above all French farmers as a counter to the advantages that Germany's industries have gained through the EU. The French are obstinate in getting their way when they feel that important national interests are at stake in the EU—although in recent years they have been able to better disguise such obstinacy than have the British. More important, French leaders have also been creative and progressive in pushing for further unification of Europe. Nevertheless, there is much ambiguity among French political and economic elites about the EU.[7]

The French government was among the most committed to the creation of the single European currency, the euro. Important political and economic sacrifices were made by French leaders to see this important step succeed. While the political elite from the mainstream parties of the Left, Center, and Right have all strongly supported the European Union, there are many citizens in

Table 12.1   Public Attitudes Toward the European Union, 1998

Country:	Britain	France	Germany	All 15 EU Members
As a result of membership,				
country has benefitted	36%	44%	33%	44%
has not benefitted	43	37	44	35
don't know	20	20	22	21

Source: Eurobarometer 49, Spring 1998.

France who are uneasy about European integration. A 1992 referendum on the Maastricht Treaty that expanded EU competencies passed very narrowly: 51 to 49 percent. Fears about the loss of national sovereignty and rising French nationalism underlie these concerns. They are important reasons for increased support for the extremist National Front.

While there are French citizens who have qualms about European unification, most see it as a chief reason for their country's overall economic health during the past half century. Mainstream parties on both the left and right support European unification and continue to press for greater responsibilities for the European Union. In this they continue to be supported by most French citizens. A 1997 poll showed that the French have more confidence in the institutions of the European Union than they do in their own government.[8] As seen in Table 12.1, French support for the EU is strong compared to other member countries. (See also Table 6.7, p. 72.)

As the EU continues to have growing powers and responsibilities, its impact on France increases. The obvious effects are the increased amount of public policy that is "made in Europe" rather than "made in France." However, policy making and politics in Brussels is also affecting the nature of national politics in Paris. Interest group politics has changed with a greater orientation toward Europe and the adoption by interest groups of tactics better suited to the EU policy makers than to national policy makers. The French parliament is at last making greater efforts to oversee the actions of the EU. French regions turn to Brussels now nearly as often as they do to Paris in seeking resources. In short, French domestic politics are becoming "Europeanized."

UNCERTAIN STABILITY

In the past, France has had difficulty sustaining both democracy and stability. Its frequent changes of regime—an average of one every 15 years—have made for a history of turmoil. Some believe that the Fifth Republic, combining as it does elements of the authoritarian and democratic varieties of previous French experience, may bring new stability. After more than 40 years, it is appropriate to assess the Fifth Republic's success in providing stable government by looking at prevailing public attitudes, the strength of political institutions, and the extent of socioeconomic unrest.

The attitudes of French citizens toward the present regime and toward power and authority in general are seen as an important source of potential political instability. The French often distinguish between the nation or fatherland (*la patrie*) and the government. The nation is considered worthy of respect and honor, while the government is thought to be made up of "weak, stupid, selfish, ambitious men. It is the duty of the citizen not to cooperate with these men . . . but to hinder them, to prevent them in every possible way from increasing their power over individuals and over families."[9]

Ambivalent attitudes toward authority tend to foster protest rather than positive participation in the political system. Authoritarian attitudes are reflected in the aloof and often arbitrary rule of French political leaders. The compatibility of these political authority patterns with the authoritarian structure of homes, schools, and other social groups should lead to stability. However, the French citizen's impulse to defy authority and revolt against the powers that be—also expressed in homes, schools, and social groups as well as in the political sphere—obviously threatens stability. Paradoxically, the proclivity to revolt is not reflected in a desire for revolutionary change. A 1990 poll found only 6 percent of the French advocated revolutionary action to change society; 69 percent preferred moderate reforms; and 21 percent wanted little or no change but greater efforts to defend the status quo against subversive elements.[10]

With respect to the legitimacy of current political institutions, there is conflicting evidence. On the one hand, public opinion polls indicate fairly broad acceptance of the institutions of the Fifth Republic. For example, a poll taken in 1988 indicated that 63 percent of the public had such confidence.[11] There is no longer any significant challenge to the legitimacy of these institutions. Prior to 1981, the Socialist and Communist parties pledged major changes in the constitution, especially in order to reduce the powers of the president.

Once in power with a Socialist president and parliamentary majority, the Socialists and Communists ceased their calls for reducing presidential powers. The rotation into power of the long-time leftist opposition seems to have completed the process of creating a broad consensus supporting the presidentialism of the Fifth Republic.

No doubt, much of the support for the institutions is based on their successful operation even in times of stress. The political institutions established in 1958 proved sufficiently flexible and durable to manage a variety of social and political conflicts that would strain the abilities of the strongest political institutions: an attempted military coup, terrorist attacks by right-wing extremists opposed to Algerian independence, other tensions and disorders accompanying decolonization, the riots and general strike of May 1968, and the succession crisis provoked by the sudden resignation of the charismatic leader for whom the institutions were created. The regime proved able to handle each threat within the framework of its established institutions. Only once, at the time of the 1961 military putsch, was it thought necessary to invoke the emergency provisions of the constitution.[12] And even then the special

powers of decree were used sparingly. It can be argued that, given the French proclivity to sporadic revolt, the institutions of the Fifth Republic are well designed to control such periods of disruption while retaining the democratic elements of popular control through free elections. Certainly the challenges thus far encountered have proved the political institutions' strength and value in crisis situations.

At times, it seems that everyone in France is protesting something or other.[13] But since protest is commonplace and traditional, high levels of unrest are expected and tolerable. In contrast to the relatively tranquil political scene in Britain, France is accustomed to conflict and crisis. If London or even Bonn were to experience in a year the number of political protests, rallies, and demonstrations that occurs in Paris during a typical 2- or 3-month period, it would be a sign of serious instability. In France, such activity is normal.

French political leaders have had considerable experience dealing with such protests, and there is a special police force trained in crowd and riot control—the CRS (Compagnies Républicaines de Sécurité). Furthermore, groups that engage in political protests and demonstrations do not necessarily hope for positive outcomes as a result of their actions. They are frequently content simply to manifest their unhappiness publicly. Some see the extent of protest in France as a positive element, claiming that the expression of social tension in a traditional and readily controlled format reduces the likelihood that it will build to dangerous levels. As Stanley Hoffmann argues, "The protest movement is both the safety valve of a society divided by deep conflicts and the traditional French form of democracy."[14]

Despite the superficial turbulence of political activity, there is a surprising amount of continuity. The basic public laws that govern the lives of individuals persist as regimes rise and fall. People visiting France cannot avoid seeing stenciled on public buildings the words *Défense d'afficher—loi du 29 juillet 1881* ("Post no bills—law of July 29, 1881"). The law remains in effect even though the regime that enacted it and two subsequent regimes have disappeared. Continuity is also assured by the persistence of the bureaucracy, whose nature and modes of operation have changed very little despite changes of regime. Taxes are collected and governmental services performed in familiar ways even if the regime crumbles and is replaced by an entirely different political order. Because of these elements of continuity and stability, the surface political turbulence that characterizes France may have little direct impact on the average French citizen.

The mixed nature of the evidence elicits caution in assessing French stability. The Fifth Republic has been more stable in many ways than preceding regimes. It has brought strong but democratically responsible leaders willing to abide by the electorate's decisions. There has been a slow emergence of consensus on the institutions and their operation. It is, however, the public attitudes toward political power that provoke important reservations about the stability of the regime. Perhaps stability must always be in question in a country like France, whose citizens feel they have a right to revolt and periodically assert this right by rising up against the existing powers.

HUMAN RIGHTS

The French have claimed a special interest in the defense of civil liberties ever since the Declaration of the Rights of Man at the height of the Revolution of 1789. This revolutionary document still serves as the constitutional basis for civil rights, reinvoked as it is in the preamble of the Constitution of the Fifth Republic. France has also accepted the European Convention of Human Rights. Citizens who feel that their rights have been abridged by government action in France and who have exhausted all French channels of appeal may take their complaints to the European Court of Human Rights. Decisions by that body are binding on the government and citizens of France.

In general, the state of human rights in France is very positive.[15] The availability of newspapers expressing every possible political belief from the extreme Left to the extreme Right attests to freedom of the press; freedom of assembly and speech is also evident in the presence and free activity of political parties representing all these political tendencies. The regular incidence of political demonstrations without fear of police repression attests to freedom of dissent. The rule of law and freedom from arbitrary arrest are assured by an independent judiciary. A variety of influential bodies—such as the League for the Rights of Man, and the Movement Against Racism and for Friendship among Peoples—monitor the government's performance in the area of civil rights.

Despite this positive overall condition of human rights, there are some problem areas. First, while political dissent is tolerated in most instances, the government on occasion has acted forcefully to repress groups thought to be dangerous to the public order. It can dissolve political organizations, ban publication of certain newspapers, and jail those who attempt to evade these controls. These repressive measures were used in the early 1960s against extreme right-wing elements who opposed the granting of independence to Algeria. They were used again in the late 1960s and early 1970s against extreme left-wing groups involved in the Events of May 1968. As recently as 1982, the Socialist government banned several groups—both on the far Left and far Right—suspected of political violence.

After 1981, the Socialist government abolished the death penalty and dissolved a special State Security Court used to try terrorists and other extremists outside normal judicial structures. The police's power to stop anyone with or without cause for "identity checks" was restricted, and new controls were placed on the use of wiretaps and listening devices by law enforcement bodies. These restrictions on the police came at a time when the French were troubled by rising drug use and crime. Clearly, there was a large group of citizens in favor of stern approaches to these problems and the Socialist reforms seemed to run counter to the desire for more "law and order." Among the law enforcement forces, there has continued to be uneasiness with these new rules and occasional abuses. In general, however, there is now a better respect for human rights in French law enforcement than in the past.

Another problem over the years has been government attempts to control the electronic news. Until the 1980s, French radio and television were government monopolies. Unlike the renowned independence of the British Broadcasting Corporation, the French state-owned radio and television system acquired a reputation for clear bias in favor of their political masters. Television news gave uneven and even distorted coverage of opposition groups while carefully and favorably covering activities of the government of the time.

There is now, however, hope that overt government intervention in television and radio will decline. Under Mitterrand, the government's monopoly over radio was abandoned. Numerous private stations have emerged and their impact has grown. While most have limited budgets and very small news staffs, these private stations offer the potential, and in some cases the reality, of broadcasting independent, and even critical voices over the airwaves. Then the government permitted the creation of privately owned, independent television stations and in the mid-1980s sold the largest state-owned television channel to private investors.

The impact of privatization in both radio and television is important. It has decreased overt government manipulation of news. But the government's presence is still felt through its supervision of these private stations. In addition, the shift to private hands may have reduced government control, but it also increased the influence of economic and social forces. Stations find it difficult to find sponsors for documentaries or controversial programs. They may be pressured to eliminate "bad" news or to support the status quo by the powerful private interests that now own them or pay for the advertising.

The assurance of broad access to a wide range of political views and to independent news coverage is a problem in all democracies. It has been a particularly thorny one in France. The shift of some radio and television to private hands will not eliminate the danger of news control, but it will shift that control out of the hands of government officials. The biases of the future will be less due to government news management than to the built-in economic and social biases of a consensual, free enterprise structure.

At the start of the twenty-first century, the greatest danger to civil liberties in France lies in the treatment of the large non-European immigrant population. In Chapter 8, we discussed the very rapid growth in the number of immigrants and the intolerance that the immigrants have found among native French people. In general, the government has encouraged tolerance and equal treatment of people regardless of their race or national origin. But the public is very hostile, and governments of both the Left and Right have given in to public pressures by adopting new limits on immigration, more difficult requirements for naturalization, and limits on gaining political asylum in France. In addition, the state has acted to control Islamic religious practices as the numbers of Muslims have increased and the state has feared the rise of "imported" Islamic fundamentalism.[16]

More menacing than the state's actions against immigrants are those of the citizenry in general. Racial intolerance is rising and France's much vaunted notions of equality are tested by individual discrimination against foreigners. While France has avoided the major problems of Germany and Britain, there are frequent although isolated episodes of racially motivated violence against foreigners. The appeal of the far right National Front demonstrates the strength of anti-immigrant sentiments among the French. Respect for the rights of immigrants and non-Europeans in France will be the major human rights issue for a long time to come.

The guaranteeing of human rights requires a vigilant public to counteract the natural tendencies of governments to abuse their powers. France has had its problems in human rights, but the overall picture is very good. The French citizen is assured of a full range of liberties. France prides itself on being the country that pioneered the defense of the rights of citizens. It certainly can take pride in the positive condition of the civil liberties guaranteed in theory and accorded in practice to its people.

CONCLUSION

At the beginning of the twenty-first century, France has a very different political system than it did at the start of the twentieth century or even 50 years ago. After decades of political instability and deadlock, the Fifth Republic established in 1958 has provided political order and efficacy within a democratic framework. It may well be that images of a sick or stalemated political system were accurate descriptions of the past, but such is no longer the case, even if French social critics seem to ignore the changes. Over the past 40+ years the political system has performed smoothly and endowed the executive with sufficient power, within reasonable democratic limits, to resolve many of the past divisions and problems.

The political system has overseen the transformation of a once-rural society into an industrial one accommodating massive population shifts from farming to industrial and service occupations. The social divisions of the past based on socioeconomic differences and ideologies have largely been overcome. The French economy has proved to be one of the most successful in Europe, with a growth rate that continues to be among Europe's strongest. The elusive consensus on political structures seems finally to have been attained with no major party advocating constitutional changes and virtually no public support for such reforms. All this suggests that the popular image of a sick or stalemated society is not an accurate description of contemporary France. Certainly there are still problems to resolve, but the prospect of successfully facing them is good. French society and politics, far from blocked, are as dynamic as those of other Western democracies.

If there is still concern about the French polity, it comes from the failure of representative bodies, especially political parties, to change in response to the new social, technological, and attitudinal milieu. The old divisions of Left-Right seem no longer relevant; a population more interested in what's on the television than on engaging in political activities, as well as new ethical expectations, are factors challenging the way things were in French political parties. Citizens seem alienated from the major democratic parties even as new parties such as the National Front offer only radical and undemocratic options. A large part of the public's disdain for the current political order is due to a series of major political and economic scandals involving the mainstream parties and their leaders that exposed parties on both the Left and Right to corruption charges.[17] This is of critical concern because French parties, as is true in other advanced democracies, rely on the parties to link the people with the political process. Stale-

mate and instability are gone, but concerns about the future of the French political order are still important in an era of change when society and attitudes are in such flux.

NOTES

[1]For examples see Michel Crozier, *The Stalled Society,* trans. Rupert Swyer (New York: Viking, 1973), and Alain Peyrefitte, *The Trouble With France* (New York: Knopf, 1981).

[2]Sanche de Gramont, *The French: Portrait of a People* (New York: Putnam, 1969), p. 460.

[3]John Ardagh, *France Today* (Harmondsworth, Eng.: Penguin, 1987), pp. 208–213.

[4]Peter A. Hall, *Governing the Economy: Politics of State Intervention in Britain and France* (London: Oxford University Press, 1986).

[5]William J. Adams and Christian Stoffaës, eds., *French Industrial Policy* (Washington: The Brookings Institution, 1986).

[6]Douglas E. Ashford, "In Search of the Etat Providence," in James F. Hollifield and George Ross eds., *Searching for the New France* (New York: Routledge, 1991).

[7]Alain Guyomarch, Howard Machin, and Ella Ritchie, eds., *France in the European Union* (New York: St. Martin's, 1998).

[8]*Eurobarometer* 48, Fall 1997.

[9]Lawrence Wylie, *Village in the Vaucluse* (New York: Harper & Row, 1964), p. 207.

[10]*Eurobarometer, Trends 1974–1990,* March 1991, p. 39.

[11]SOFRES, *L'Etat de l'opinion, cles pour 1989* (Paris: Seuil, 1989), p. 204.

[12]The president of the republic is authorized by Article 16 of the constitution to take whatever measures he feels are necessary to respond to grave and immediate threats to the institutions of the republic, the independence of the nation, or its fulfillment of international commitments.

[13]Frank L. Wilson, "Political Demonstrations in France: The Politics of Protest or Ritual Politics?" *French Politics and Society* 12 (Fall 1994).

[14]Stanley Hoffmann, "Protest in Modern France," in *The Revolution in World Politics,* ed. Morton A. Kaplan (New York: John Wiley & Sons, 1962), p. 79.

[15]See William Safran, *The French Polity,* 5th ed. (New York: Longman, 1998), pp. 303–322.

[16]See A. G. Hargreaves, *Immigration, "Race" and Ethnicity in Contemporary France* (London: Routledge, 1995).

[17]Yves Mény, "The End of the Republican Ethic in France?" in Donatella Della Porta and Yves Mény, eds., *Democracy and Corruption in Europe* (London: Pinter, 1997).

FRANCE: SELECTED BIBLIOGRAPHY

John Ardagh, *France Today* (Harmondsworth, England: Penguin Books, 1987).

Daniel Boy and Noona Mayer, *The French Voter Decides* (Ann Arbor: University of Michigan Press, 1994).

Alistair Cole, *French Politics and Society* (London: Prentice Hall Europe, 1998).

Philip E. Converse and Roy Pierce, *Political Representation in France* (Cambridge, MA: Harvard University Press, 1986).

Edward DeClair, *Politics on the Fringe: The People, Policies, and Organizations of the French National Front* (Durham, NC: Duke University Press, 1998).

Henry Ehrmann and Martin Schain, *Politics in France,* 5th ed. (New York: HarperCollins, 1992).

John Frears, *Parties and Voters in France* (New York: St. Martin's, 1991).

Julius W. Friend, *The Long Presidency: France in the Mitterrand Years, 1981–1995* (New York: HarperCollins, 1997).

Paul Godt, *Policy-Making in France: From de Gaulle to Mitterrand* (London: Pinter Publishers, 1989).

Charles Hauss, *Politics in Gaullist France: Coping with Chaos* (New York: Praeger, 1991).

James Hollifield and George Ross, eds. *Searching for the New France* (New York: Routledge, 1991).

Andrew Knapp, *Gaullism Since de Gaulle* (Aldershot, England: Dartmouth, 1994).

John Laughlin and Sonia Mazey, eds., *The End of the French Unitary State? Ten Years of Regionalization in France* (Ilford, England: Frank Cass, 1995).

Michael Lewis-Beck, ed., *How France Votes* (Chatham, NJ: Chatham House, 1999).

Roy Pierce, *Choosing the Chief: Presidential Elections in France and the United States* (Ann Arbor: University of Michigan Press, 1995).

William Safran, *The French Polity,* 5th ed. (New York: Longman, 1998).

Ronald Tiersky, *France in the New Europe: Changing Yet Steadfast* (Belmont, CA: Wadsworth, 1994).

Frank L. Wilson, *Interest-group Politics in France* (Cambridge, Eng.: Cambridge University Press, 1987).

Theodore Zeldin, *The French* (New York: Vintage Books, 1984).

Chapter 13

German History
and Political Culture

From the end of World War II in 1945 to October 3, 1990, Germany was a divided country. In the name of the Third Reich—the empire proclaimed to last a thousand years—Hitler waged total war against Germany's neighbors and their allies. The result was Germany's total defeat and the postwar partition of the country into its Western regions with a population of 50 million people, which evolved into the Federal Republic of Germany (FRG), and its Eastern regions with 17 million people, which eventually became the German Democratic Republic (GDR). Parts of Germany's former territory were annexed by Poland[1] and the USSR.[2] Thus, one price Germany paid for the aggressive nationalism that gave birth to World War II was the loss of its national unity, which had existed only since 1871. Like China, Korea, and Austria (until 1955), Germany emerged from the war as a divided country.

Viewed from a historical perspective, however, the lack of national unity resounded with echoes of the past, recalling Friedrich Hölderlin's description of Germany as a "chronically torn and divided" country.

The Germans are one of the oldest people in Europe—in a sense older even than the English.

But they achieved national unity very late in their history. While there had been a German people for a thousand years, they had lived in a state of national unity for less than 75 years (1871–1945). Prior to 1871, when France and Great Britain were already powerful nation-states, Germany, in the words of the Austrian statesman Metternich, was little more than "a geographical expression."

In 1945, after World War II, the short-lived unified German state that had been forged by the skillful diplomacy of Bismarck and the force of Prussian arms ceased to exist. From 1945 to 1949 there was no "German" political system, as the four principal wartime allies—the United States, France, Great Britain, and the Soviet Union—took over and placed what had been Germany under military rule, carefully controlling "German" politics even at the local level. When the division of Germany was formalized by the proclamation of the Basic Law of the FRG and the Constitution of the GDR in 1949, two German states emerged. Although the difficult and problematic relations between these two political entities were "normalized" to a degree by a treaty concluded in 1972 and numerous

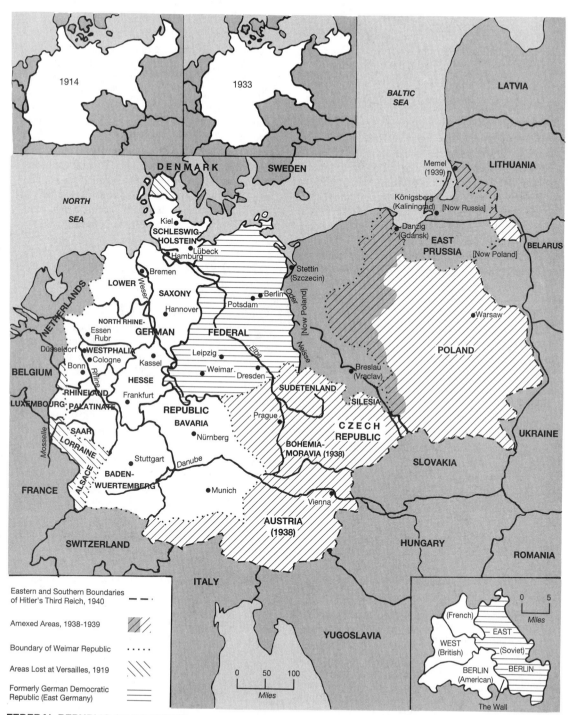

1914

1933

BALTIC
SEA

LATVIA

LITHUANIA

Memel
(1939)

Königsberg
(Kaliningrad)   [Now Russia]

BELARUS

NORTH
SEA

DENMARK   SWEDEN

Danzig
(Gdansk)

EAST
PRUSSIA   [Now Poland]

Kiel
SCHLESWIG-
HOLSTEIN

Lübeck
Hamburg

Bremen

Stettin
(Szczecin)

LOWER

SAXONY

Hannover

Berlin

Potsdam

[Now Poland]

Warsaw

POLAND

NORTH RHINE-

Essen
Ruhr

GERMAN

FEDERAL

Düsseldorf
WESTPHALIA

Bonn   Cologne

Kassel

Leipzig

Weimar

Dresden

Elbe

Oder

Neisse

Breslau
(Vraclav)

SILESIA

UKRAINE

BELGIUM

LUXEMBOURG

RHINELAND

PALATINATE

Rhine

HESSE

Frankfurt

REPUBLIC

BAVARIA

SUDETENLAND

Prague

CZECH
REPUBLIC

SLOVAKIA

NETHERLANDS

Weser

SAAR

LORRAINE

Mosselle

ALSACE

Stuttgart

Danube

BADEN-
WUERTEMBERG

Nürnberg

Munich

BOHEMIA-
MORAVIA (1938)

Vienna

AUSTRIA
(1938)

HUNGARY

ROMANIA

FRANCE

SWITZERLAND

ITALY

YUGOSLAVIA

Eastern and Southern Boundaries
of Hitler's Third Reich, 1940   — — —

Amexed Areas, 1938-1939

Boundary of Weimar Republic   · · · ·

Areas Lost at Versailles, 1919

Formerly German Democratic
Republic (East Germany)

0   50   100

Miles

0   5

Miles

(French)

EAST

WEST
(British)

(Soviet)

BERLIN
(American)

BERLIN

The Wall

FEDERAL REPUBLIC OF GERMANY

subsequent agreements, Berlin, the former capital of Germany, remained a divided city. Surrounded by East German territory, its Western sectors were closed off from the GDR-controlled part of Berlin and the rest of the GDR by the infamous Berlin Wall, erected on August 13, 1961.[3]

Thus, in spite of the "normalization" treaty of 1972, the problem of the divided Germany continued to fester in the heart of Europe, causing untold human suffering, preventing the unification of families, inhibiting normal contacts among people of the same nation, and complicating East-West relations. Surely one of the paradoxes of German history and politics is that although as a people the Germans are very old, they have been a unified nation for a relatively brief period only, and until the unification of the two Germanies in 1990 they lived in separation in the two youngest states in Europe.

CONTINUITY AND DISCONTINUITY IN HISTORY

In a comparative study of political systems, Germany stands out from other major nations because its long history does not present us with a consistent and definite political pattern. Unlike the English, the French, or the Russians, who have spent most of their history as subjects of a single centralized state, the Germans during most of their past lived under some vaguely defined empire or owed allegiance to a multitude of princes, bishops, and knights, being "citizens" at one time of more than 300 sovereign political entities.

The German people came into being during a 250-year period of consolidation between approximately A.D. 750 and 1000, followed by four more centuries of further expansion—first southward, then northward and eastward. Cities located in the middle of Germany today were frontier posts a thousand years ago. The eastward movement of the Germans is also reflected in the clearly Slavic origin of many "German" family names found scattered all over Eastern Europe—testimony to the assimilation of the non-German natives of these regions and proof that the Nazi notion of the supposed purity of the so-called Aryan race was a myth.

The eastward advance of the Germans was finally stopped in 1410, when the army of the German Order of Teutonic Knights was defeated by the Poles (with the aid of Russian Cossacks) in the historic Battle of Tannenberg. But by that time the Germans had succeeded in carving out the province of East Prussia, which was to become Germany's largest, most vigorous, creative, and powerful state—a state destined, as we shall see, to play a fateful role in the unification, as well as the destruction, of Germany. But six centuries of consolidation and expansion failed to produce a unified German state. This is one reason why it is difficult to discern a definite political pattern in the long history of the German people.

THE FIRST GERMAN EMPIRE (800–1806)

Charlemagne, or Karl der Grosse, accomplished during his reign what the Romans had failed to achieve, namely, to bring the numerous German tribes *(Stämme)* under unified political control. With the crowning of Charlemagne in A.D. 800 in Rome by the pope, the First German Empire, the so-called Holy Roman Empire of the German Nation, was established. However, the original political conception of the empire as developed by Charlemagne—the idea of a unified secular government ruling with the support and blessing from a universal church—was not realized in practice. In 842 the empire was divided into the West Frankish Empire, which became France, and the East Frankish Empire, which became Germany.

One of the most important developments during the more than thousand-year history of the First German Empire was the gigantic struggle between church and state for political supremacy. The political recovery of the papacy in the eleventh century posed a threat to the power of the emperor. The popes succeeded in finding allies among the German princes, who were also interested in preventing the aggrandizement of imperial power. Given this conflict of interests, the stage was set for the great confrontation.

The dramatic showdown between Pope Gregory VII and Emperor Henry IV ended with the capitulation of the emperor at Canossa in 1077. These events were to have a major impact on the future political evolution of Germany, marking, as they did, the beginning of the fateful tension in German history between central political authority and the local power of the princes—a tension that ultimately resulted in the destruction of that authority and left to the German people the unfortunate legacy of an extreme *particularism or separatism.*[4]

The imperial campaigns against the papacy—in the course of three centuries German armies invaded Northern Italy forty times (that is, on the average every seven to eight years) in an attempt to enforce the emperor's will on the pope—made the emperor increasingly dependent on his vassals, forcing him to grant all kinds of concessions to the princes, who in this way acquired the right to maintain their own courts, have their own armies, build castles, coin money, and collect taxes. The church-state conflict thus contributed directly to the increasing fragmentation of Germany into a bewildering array of independent states under the rule of princes, whose rights and privileges were ultimately codified in the Golden Bull granted by Emperor Charles IV in 1356.[5]

This extreme particularism proved to be a legacy from which the Germans were unable to extricate themselves peacefully. In 1789, the year of the French Revolution, Germany consisted of 320 separate states. It was left to a foreign conqueror, Napoleon, to reduce this number by amalgamating many of the smaller states into larger units. After the defeat of Napoleon by the allied armies of Europe in 1813, the Congress of Vienna (1815) settled the question of the political future of Germany by establishing 39 states within the framework of a loose confederation *(Bund),* with Austria being the permanent president of the *Diet* (federal assembly).

In addition to the territorial fragmentation of Germany and the fact that for centuries the imperial power in the First German Empire was virtually monopolized by the Hapsburgs—a dynasty of emperors for whom the interests of Germany were at best of secondary importance—the emergence of an effective centralized political authority in Germany was further complicated and impeded by religious differences. In the sixteenth century the Protestant Reformation initiated a long period of religious conflict that sapped the vitality of German society. Stirred to rebellion by

Martin Luther's doctrines concerning the rights and duties of the individual conscience against the corruption of the Catholic church, the peasants rose against the nobles in an attempt to throw off the yoke of feudal servitude—which was as oppressive in Germany as serfdom was in Russia. In the Peasants' War of 1524–25 and subsequent conflicts, in which Luther staunchly backed the princes, some 100,000 peasants lost their lives in a terrible slaughter.

The Treaty of Augsburg in 1555 settled the conflict temporarily and established the important principle *cujus regio, ejus religio* (the religion of the ruler determines the religion of the people), but it failed to contain the dynamic of the conflict. In 1618 religious wars broke out again, with religious zeal soon to be joined by political opportunism as the main reason for the conflict. For 30 long years—an entire generation!—Protestant and Catholic princes fought to prevent the emergence of an effective imperial power for fear that the losing denomination might be eliminated by a victory of the other side. In their struggle against the German Catholic states, the Protestant princes of Germany not only received aid from Protestant Denmark and Sweden, but also from the notorious Cardinal Richelieu, the chief minister of Catholic France, whose policy it was to prevent the unification of the German states. Thus, during the Thirty Years' War (1618–48) Germany became the battlefield for a gigantic military contest between Austria and Spain (the Hapsburgs, in other words) on the one hand, and France, Sweden, and the maritime powers (the Netherlands and England) on the other.

The barbarity of this terrible war, fought in part by mercenaries, was extraordinary. Arson, murder, and rape were the order of the day. Entire villages were plundered, destroyed, or totally deserted. Berlin lost half of its population, and the city of Chemnitz lost 80 percent of its inhabitants. It is a measure of the savagery of this war that cannibalism and polygamy were officially condoned in an attempt to combat hunger and depopulation.

According to the available estimates, the population of Germany decreased from 30 million to 20 million. The losses of material wealth to all classes were catastrophic. Among the unfortunate consequences of the war was the even greater domination of the peasants by the landlords and the increased dependence of the landlords on the state. Another crucial consequence was that Germany failed to develop a counterpart to the rural and mercantile middle class that produced the Puritan Revolution in England in the seventeenth century and the French Revolution in 1789. Many historians have argued that the savage bloodletting of the religious wars dissipated the energy and vitality of the German people to such an extent that for centuries thereafter any thought of revolution by the masses against their rulers became impossible.

Thus, the Protestant Reformation, which began with a strong impetus in the direction of individualism and occasioned a profound revolution in German thought and language, in the end turned out to be a major contributing factor in the development of a political tradition characterized by a highly deferential attitude toward authority and uncritical support of the state. The ultimate result of the Reformation was the creation of a state-controlled religion and church. Both Lutheranism, by encouraging passive obedience to authority, and Calvinism, by spreading the idea of active obedience and service to the state, contributed in important ways to the growth of authoritarianism in German politics and to the increasing centralization of state power—albeit for the time being not yet at the level of a unified German state, but at the level of the numerous individual German states.

THE RISE OF PRUSSIA

From 1648 to 1806 two historical developments interacted to shape the future course of German history: (1) the political decline of Austria, which held the imperial crown; and (2) the ascendance of Prussia, which aspired to replace Austria as the dominant German state.

Prussia developed from the territory conquered in the thirteenth century by the German Order of Teutonic Knights and subsequently colonized by German settlers. When the political fortunes of the Order declined after the Battle of Tannenberg in 1410, West Prussia came under the jurisdiction of Poland, leaving East Prussia cut off from the rest of Germany—a development that created the "corridor" problem that was to become so important and fateful in German–Polish relations. In 1618 Prussia, which meanwhile had become a duchy, was inherited by a member of the Hohenzollern family who ruled Brandenburg, the territory located between the Oder and Elbe Rivers. It was this unification of Brandenburg and East Prussia that created the nucleus of the future Prussian state and thus became the cradle of a host of problems that ultimately affected all of Europe and, indeed, the world. During subsequent years the domain of the Hohenzollern family increased through territorial acquisitions. In 1660 Frederick William, the "Great Elector" of Brandenburg, invaded Poland, captured Warsaw, and ended Poland's nominal overlordship over East Prussia. His son, Frederick William I, became the first "King in Prussia" (1701).[6]

The succession of a remarkable line of strong, competent, and ruthless monarchs (Frederick William the Great Elector, Frederick William I, and Frederick II, known as Frederick the Great) was a major factor in the development of an extraordinary administrative apparatus by 1700.[7] Thus, in contrast to Great Britain, in Prussia the establishment and development of a strong administrative apparatus, a civil service renowned for its efficiency and incorruptibility, preceded the creation of a parliament, to say nothing of the recognition of parliamentary supremacy that was achieved in England in 1689.

Under the leadership of such rulers as Frederick William I, Prussia was turned into a model absolute monarchy. The potential powers of the estates vis-à-vis the king were neutralized. The parliamentary assembly of the estates, that is, the high social classes—nobility, clergy, and townsmen—were effectively turned into an instrument of the Crown. An enormous standing army was created, which rendered the estates and local institutions impotent. The nobility was accorded social preeminence in the Prussian state, as well as relative freedom from taxation and immunity from billeting. Although the members of the Prussian nobility, the so-called *Junkers,* were deprived of their independence, they enjoyed a near-monopoly of offices in the government, both at the national and the local level.

Moreover, it became accepted practice and tradition for the elder sons of the Prussian nobility to run the family estates and for the younger sons to enter the civil service and the army, in particular its officer corps. It was to Prussia that the German people owed not only the legacy of an efficient civil service, but also a unique militarist tradition and the idea of the authoritarian state—a state presumably capable of taking care of all the needs of its citizens and thus entitled to unquestioned obedience and loyal support.

With the reign of Frederick the Great (1740–86), the process of Prussia's territorial and political aggrandizement through military conquest began in earnest. A skilled administrator, a talented military leader, and an unprincipled aggressor, Frederick the Great embarked upon a coldly calculated course of conquest, beginning with Silesia in 1740. The twin pillars of the Prussian state, the army and the civil service, having been honed to perfection, were now ruthlessly used to seize and control non-Prussian lands. Silesia and Saxony were annexed. Poland was partitioned (with Austria and Russia), and the western and eastern parts of Prussia were once again united. Thus Prussia did not slowly evolve into a national community during the course of a long peaceful existence, but rather as the result of abrupt and rapid growth due to military expansion and annexation.

Frederick the Great, in other words, was the German equivalent of Cardinal Richelieu in France and the Tudors in England. What made the German variant of the Machiavellian prince so dangerous and fatal was that in Prussia (and later on in Germany from 1871 to 1945) the army dominated the civilian politicians and ministers. Moreover, for the Prussian army and in particular for its Junker-dominated officer corps, the object of service and duty was not the nation or parliament, but rather the Prussian king. As we shall see, this peculiar nexus between the Prussian aristocracy and its supreme landlord and warlord, the king, was cleverly exploited by Adolf Hitler—with disastrous consequences for the German people and the world.

STABILITY, UNION, AND LIBERTY: THE GERMAN DILEMMA

In contrast to France and Great Britain, where the main phases of the struggle for liberty occurred within states that had already achieved national unity, or the United States, where liberty and union were thought of as "one and inseparable," in Germany both national unification and liberty seemed to be out of reach, given the authoritarian rule of the princes and the extreme fragmentation of the country into numerous independent states. The pursuit of one goal seemed to preclude the other, and thus the choice between national unification and liberty always proved to be a difficult one and was frequently attended by tragic consequences.

The particularism of the German states militated against the development of a broadly based popular movement against authority. Instead of writers and politicians like Hobbes, Locke, Milton, Burke, Bentham, and J. S. Mill in England, or Montesquieu, Rousseau, and Voltaire in France, Germany produced a large number of philosophers who sought refuge in the realm of metaphysics—men like Herder, Schlegel, Fichte, Schelling, and Hegel, who endorsed authority and nationalism, conceived of freedom as duty, and, in the case of Hegel, elevated the Prussian state to the supreme achievement and the end of the historical process. These men idolized the *Volk* (a kind of tribal notion of the German people) and envisaged the future as belonging to the Germans.[8]

Thus, the political and institutional development of Prussia was paralleled and reinforced by an authoritarian and nationalist tradition in German philosophy and political thought—a tradition that triumphed over the liberal elements in German society and culture. However, in spite of the authoritarianism and absolutism in politics, the German people developed a great culture in the second half of the seventeenth century, with a humanistic tradition in science, poetry, and music. And a significant part of this culture was political and liberal in outlook: Among its outstanding representatives were the poets Friedrich von Schiller and Johann Wolfgang von Goethe; the writer, critic, philosopher, linguist, and statesman Wilhelm von Humboldt; and later in the nineteenth century the philosophical anarchist Max Stirner and the poet Heinrich Heine. As a matter of fact, while authoritarianism continued to hold sway in German politics, German culture increasingly embraced a liberal outlook and humanist values. Kant and Lessing belonged to the Freemasons, a secret fraternal order, and Mozart and Beethoven made no secret of the fact that they were sympathetic to the French Revolution.[9] Kant was a great admirer of Rousseau and readily admitted that it was Rousseau who straightened him out.

But this tremendous enthusiasm for the rights of the individual was eventually suppressed—in part, at least, because many German liberals were repelled by the excesses of the French Revolution. The Reign of Terror in France caused some German sympathizers of the French Revolution to have second thoughts, and after Napoleon's conquest of Germany few Germans were inclined to advocate the ideals of 1789. In point of fact, the intense and passionate nationalism that swept through Germany during the late eighteenth and early nineteenth centuries was in large measure a reaction to the humiliating defeat by Napoleon's armies. In the context of the time, therefore, any attempt to propagate "liberty, equality, fraternity" was quickly branded as unpatriotic.

And thus it was that, in contrast to England and France, Germany was to have no revolution. The great revolutionary wave of 1789 found Germany in a state of national weakness, its universities decaying, its population virtually stagnating. Economically, politically, and intellectually Germany was unprepared for revolution. Initially welcomed as an opportunity to weaken the international position of France, the French Revolution was soon suppressed by the German rulers, especially in Prussia, with all the ruthlessness and force of which reactionary governments are capable.[10]

Nevertheless, the idea of constitutional government slowly made headway in Germany as well. Half a century later, when another revolutionary wave came to Germany from France, the people living in the western states compelled their rulers to appoint liberal ministers. The demands for a constitution were accepted, and a Rhineland liberal was appointed as prime minister of Prussia. In the end, however, the Revolution of 1848, too, was a failure in Germany.[11] The German middle class valued stability above all else and was prepared to sacrifice liberty whenever stability or its own economic interests and nationalist aspirations were at stake.[12] The peasants

proved to be equally conservative—in part, no doubt, because their situation had substantially improved since the Thirty Years' War, and because most of the remaining vestiges of feudal oppression had been abolished just prior to the Revolution of 1848.

THE TRIUMPH OF PRUSSIA: UNIFICATION FROM ABOVE

The Congress of Vienna (1815) took a step in the direction of German unification by creating the German Confederation (1815–66), under the perpetual chairmanship of Austria. But under the influence of the Metternich System[13] and with the consent of Prussia, the German Confederation became an instrument in the struggle against the movement for unification and constitutionalism. Its "parliament," whose members were appointed by the princes, proved to be incapable of providing effective government. Among other things, this body was hampered by the unanimity rule and by its dependence on the individual states for the execution of its decisions.

The Frankfurt Parliament, a child of the Revolution of 1848, was also a failure. It was a remarkably liberal body and drew up an excellent constitutional instrument. But Austria objected to the very idea of constitutional monarchy, and the Prussian king contemptuously refused to become the first constitutional monarch of a united Germany when he was offered the opportunity. In so doing he sealed the fate of German liberalism in the nineteenth century. The failure of the carefully planned, judicious, and conciliatory effort by the German liberals to create a German nation under a constitutional government was a blow from which they never recovered.

Nevertheless, in spite of the political failure of German liberalism, the new ideological currents inspired by the French Revolution and the Revolution of 1848 were not entirely without effect even in Prussia, the citadel of reaction. The Rhenish aristocrat Baron vom Stein, imposed upon the king of Prussia by Napoleon in 1807, made a serious effort "to build a nation through reform," aiming to bring about political education and democratization, the active "participation of the people in legislation and administration," as well as "an informed and intelligent public opinion."[14] Although vom Stein, who—to the great consternation of Napoleon— turned out to be not only the hoped-for competent reformer but also a German nationalist, was dismissed after slightly more than a year of service, his municipal reforms initiating self-government for the German towns and cities were not revoked. More important, perhaps, vom Stein had set an example for future generations of German politicians. Also noteworthy is the fact that the united Prussian diets *(Landtage)* convened in 1847 and 1848 refused to do the king's bidding— resulting in their dissolution and the imposition of a constitution by the king. Thus, although Prussian authoritarianism triumphed in the end, the immediate prehistory of the forceful unification of Germany under Prussian hegemony is not entirely without auspicious episodes and promising points of departure.

The end of these promising beginnings came in the 1860s, when Otto von Bismarck, the descendant of a 400-year old Junker family in Brandenburg, came to power as prime minister of Prussia and decided to reverse Prussia's evolution toward constitutional government. Confronted with a parliamentary majority which refused to sanction the government's proposed military reforms, Bismarck, the "mad Junker," cowed the Prussian Diet into submission, collected taxes illegally, and pushed through his entire program against the opposition of the *Landtag.* This confrontation was the great divide in modern German history. If ever there was a time for a liberal revolution in Germany, this was it: only a full-fledged revolution could have changed the course of events against the concerted opposition of the Crown, the army, and the civil service. Although the liberals continued to push for a constitutional monarchy, a division of powers between king and parliament, and liberal legislation, there was still no revolution. The German people dutifully paid their taxes, and a few years later the *Landtag,* by now a conservative body elected in wartime, pardoned Bismarck's illegal actions in connection with the collection of taxes and voted official congratulations on the victorious conduct of the wars of aggression

against Denmark (1864) and Austria (1866)— a portent of things to come in the twentieth century.

Like Hitler later in *Mein Kampf,* Bismarck gave ample warning of what was in store for the German people and their neighbors. In his famous "Blood and Iron Speech" of 1862, a kind of funeral oration over genuine parliamentary institutions in Germany, he practically announced the forthcoming aggressive wars against Denmark, Austria, and France (1870):

> Germany does not look to Prussia's liberalism, but to her power. . . . Since the treaties of Vienna, our frontiers have been ill-designed for a healthy body politic. The great questions of our time will be decided, not by speeches and resolutions or majorities (that was the mistake of 1848 and 1849), but by blood and iron.[15]

In achieving the unification of Germany, Bismarck used manipulation, diplomacy, and force. It is important to recognize, however, that for him the unification of Germany was not an end in itself but a means for the aggrandizement of the Prussian monarchy. His motto was: "Our solution is not union at any price, but the prerogative of the Prussian Crown by every means."

The German nation which came into being in 1871, then, was not based on the free and spontaneous integration of the various groups and social classes making up German society, but on the acknowledgment by these groups and classes of their political impotence and on their submission to the Iron Chancellor's policies of political suppression and social and economic concessions. Moreover, the manner in which German unification came about meant that henceforth national success and glory in the minds of many Germans came to be associated not with democratic political institutions and processes, but with the decisive action and determined will of a powerful political leader. Finally, the Bismarck solution to the problem of German unity meant that for decades to come the political elite involved in ultimate national decision making was neither elected nor, in any way, representative of various walks of life, but rather was a remarkably homogeneous elite whose members came from the ranks of the Prussian dynasty and aristocracy, men with predominantly military training.[16]

THE SECOND GERMAN EMPIRE (1871–1918)

After the defeat of Austria in 1866, the impotent German Confederation was replaced by the North German Federation, which had many of the characteristics of a genuine state and constituted an important step in the process of the formation of the Second German Empire. Through the vehicle of the Customs Union *(Zollverein)* and the Franco-Prussian War of 1870, the South German states were drawn into increasingly close economic, military, and political relations with Prussia, culminating ultimately in permanent union with the North German Federation, which after this expansion changed its name to German Empire in December 1870. Thus the Second German Empire was born. On January 18, 1871, after the victorious campaign against France lasting only a few weeks, the coronation of King William as German Emperor took place in the magnificent Hall of Mirrors in Versailles before the princes and military leaders of Germany assembled on the soil of France, which for so long had opposed the unification of Germany.

In formal terms Imperial Germany was "an eternal alliance" of the king of Prussia, in the name of the North German Federation, with the kings of the southern states for the purpose of protecting the territory, laws, and interests of the German people. It was a federation of dynasties, not a federation of peoples. As a matter of fact, Bismarck regarded the separatism of the various dynasties as the "indispensable cement" holding together the different parts of the empire.

Although the Second German Empire clearly was not a unitary or centralized state in view of its federalist features, it was a peculiar kind of federation. First of all, the federation was clearly dominated by Prussia—through the king of Prussia, who as German emperor was the presiding officer of the federation; through the imperial chancellor, who was usually simultaneously the prime minister of Prussia; through Prussia's dominant position in the Federal Council *(Bundesrat),* the upper house, which was the center of the

Constitution of Imperial Germany; through the Prussian-dominated civil service; and through the sheer weight of its population (80 percent).

Second, the federation of the Second German Empire was characterized by parliamentary impotence. The freely elected Reichstag engaged in unrestricted debate and sometimes confronted the government with embarrassing questions, but it could not oust the government. Deprived of any real power, the Reichstag came to be perceived as a *Schwatzbude,* a place for gossip and empty debate, in the eyes of many Germans. This unfortunate circumstance, coupled with the fact that the era of imperial Germany coincided with a period of growth, prosperity, and expansion, was a major factor in habituating the German people to look to the executive, not the parliament, for political results—and later on, during the dark days of the Weimar Republic, for salvation.

The federation was also peculiar because the states were not treated equally in terms of representation in the Federal Council and in terms of the powers they relinquished to the federal authority. Bavaria, Saxony, and Württemberg, for example, were granted quasi-military autonomy during peacetime. Furthermore, initially the federation was dependent for its revenue on periodic contributions from the states. Finally, a unique feature of imperial Germany was the fact that the Reich had to rely on the civil servants of the various states for the administration of federal laws—an arrangement that gave rise to a sort of diplomatic procedure to ensure the uniform execution of the law. Only in the areas of foreign affairs, mail and telegraph service, finance, and military affairs did the imperial government have its own civil service.

The imperial system established by Bismarck was in essence an all-German federation with a Prussian soul. The Iron Chancellor had no compunction about manipulating the political parties against one another and conducting politics by guile and outright deception. He freely invoked the danger supposedly posed by the French, the Poles, or the socialists. Particularly vicious was his attack on the Catholic church and the Catholic Center party in the infamous *Kulturkampf* (1873–78), the "struggle for civilization," as it was called.[17] Although Bismarck eventually realized the futility of his attack on the Catholics,[18] he had set the terrible precedent of a state-sponsored and orchestrated campaign against a minority accounting for no less than one-third of the population of Germany.

With the establishment of the Second German Empire, the majority of the German people at last achieved nationhood—but at the cost of subordinating liberty and sacrificing popular sovereignty. The priorities of the Germans, as it turned out, were precisely those listed in Hoffmann von Fallersleben's *Song of the Germans* (1840): "Unity and Law and Freedom/For the German Fatherland."

THE WEIMAR REPUBLIC
AND THE THIRD REICH

During the 1850s and 1860s Germany experienced rapid industrial growth and economic development. A far-flung railway network was built—made to order for a new type of warfare, the *Blitzkrieg,* which depended on the ability of the German army to move troops and material rapidly between Germany's eastern and western frontiers. In 1846 the Krupp gun foundries were established in Essen, which soon manufactured rifled guns with a range never before attained. By 1860 Krupp supplied the Prussian army with breechloaders. In the mid-1890s the German navy occupied seventh place among the navies of the world; by 1914 it was second only to the British navy.

Still in the state of infancy as a nation, Germany's new leaders—William II and his entourage—nevertheless thought the country was ready to embark upon *Weltpolitik,* to pursue policies having worldwide objectives and ramifications, to engage Germany politically on a scale which even the ambitious Bismarck had studiously sought to avoid. The closing decade of the nineteenth century saw an almost frenzied effort on the part of Germany to make up for lost time. Determined to have its "place in the sun," to control an extensive colonial empire of its own, Germany developed political ambitions in the Far East, the Near and Middle East, the Pacific, and North Africa. Members of the Pan-German League had dreams of a German-dominated Central Europe that would include the Benelux

countries, Poland, Hungary, Austria, Serbia, Romania, and parts of Switzerland. When war came in 1914, all the German political parties—with some individual exceptions, notably among the Social Democrats—supported it. Concluding the *Burgfrieden* of August 4, 1914, a political truce for the duration of the war, they united in solid support behind the government in the war effort.

World War I, which according to the calculations of the German generals was to last six weeks, not only resulted in the collapse of the imperial regime in 1918, but also gave the German people their first taste of total mobilization and pushed the country in the direction of a planned economy.[19] Although William II did not abdicate until the end of the war, he had long before ceased to be the emperor in all but name, as the Supreme Command of the Army, in particular General Erich Ludendorff, took over in the course of the war. The true state of affairs was revealed after the war by the centrist leader Matthias Erzberger in a statement to the Reichstag on July 25, 1919: "For four years," he said, "Germany has had practically no political government but a military dictatorship."[20]

When the fortunes of war turned against Germany to such an extent that even the Supreme Command could no longer ignore them, the generals forced the civilian political leadership to negotiate an armistice. After the armistice had been negotiated, however, they refused to assume any responsibility for it. Adroitly stepping aside, they let the Social Democrats, the largest party in the revived Reichstag, preside over the liquidation of the old and the creation of the new order, thus saddling the civilian leadership and the Reichstag with the awesome problems of the impoverished country and the terrible onus of the armistice and the Peace Treaty of Versailles. Because Germany was defeated in World War I with her troops still on foreign soil and because the German public had been led to believe in the invincibility of German arms until the very end, the generals in the minds of many Germans remained associated with victory (which they had not achieved) and the postwar civilian political leaders came to be associated with defeat (for which they bore no responsibility).

The insidious myth of the "stab in the back" was put into circulation—the idea that Germany, in spite of the victories of her generals on the battlefield, had lost the war because the nation's will to fight had been undermined by a conspiracy of socialists, Jews, and democrats at home. "Like Siegfried stricken down by the treacherous spear of Hagen," Field Marshall Hindenburg wrote, "our weary front collapsed."[21] Thus, the circumstances attending the birth of the Weimar Republic (1919–33), named after the city in which its constitution was drawn up, were anything but auspicious. As a matter of fact, the Weimar Republic had many of the characteristics of an illegitimate and unwanted child. It certainly suffered from a crisis of legitimacy from the very beginning and thus, like German social democracy during the period preceding the unification of Germany, was crippled from birth.[22]

The Weimar Republic was Germany's first experiment with democratic government at the national level. Its constitution, adopted on July 31, 1919, was extremely liberal and provided for a federal and democratic government. It was based on universal suffrage, including women, the voting age being 20. The Reichstag, the lower house of parliament, emerged as a powerful institution. But throughout the 14 years of the Weimar Republic the power of the Reichstag was frequently nullified by the extreme fragmentation of its members, who were elected by a system of proportional representation.

The Weimar Constitution also gave considerable powers to the executive and provided for rule by decree under certain circumstances. The chancellor was made responsible to the Reichstag, but he was appointed and could be dismissed by the president, who was elected directly by the people and thus enjoyed as much of a popular mandate as the Reichstag. The notorious Article 48 of the Weimar Constitution gave the president emergency powers, including the right to suspend civil liberties and to rule by decree. For several years before 1933, when the National Socialists (Nazis) came to power, Germany was ruled virtually by presidential decree.[23] For all practical purposes, therefore, the republic had effectively ceased to function before Hitler took over—the Nazis, needless to say, having contributed in a major way to the immobilization of the Reichstag that led to the emergence of government by decree in accordance with Article 48.

With the advantage of hindsight, it is possible to identify a number of structural factors in the 1919 constitution that contributed to the downfall of the Weimar Republic—for example, the electoral system based on proportional representation, the emergency powers clause (Article 48), the popular mandate of the president, and the provisions concerning the popular initiative and referendum. But these factors alone hardly explain the failure of the Weimar Republic. Given different historical circumstances, the constitutional framework established by the 1919 constitution might well have succeeded. As it turned out, however, a number of other factors combined with these structural weaknesses to complicate Germany's first experiment in democracy. First of all, it was a stupendous distance from the Prussian-dominated imperial regime to the exceedingly liberal Weimar system—especially considering the fact that the Weimar government was run by a highly reactionary bureaucracy. Second, the Social Democratic party, until 1932 the largest and strongest party—which because of its commitment to democracy and the republic should have, and perhaps could have, carried the Weimar Republic—failed the test of leadership. Third, the establishment of the Weimar Republic cut short the course of the November Revolution of 1919.

As a result, there was no expropriation of the Junker class, the big industrialists, or the bourgeoisie; the general staff and the officer corps of the army were left intact as a kind of state within a state; and the civil service and the judiciary were essentially left untouched. Furthermore, aside from the onus of the dictated Treaty of Versailles and the reparations question, which poisoned the political atmosphere both within and around the Weimar Republic, the post-imperial German government was subjected to international opprobrium and condemnation at the very moment when it had made every effort to meet the norms expected and insisted on by the victor powers—a time, we might add, when it needed all the support it could get at home and abroad.

Nevertheless, in spite of these terrible handicaps the Weimar Republic might have stabilized and successfully dealt with the problems confronting it, had it not been for the ruinous inflation of 1923, which hit the working class very hard and financially wiped out the middle class,[24] and the economic crisis of 1930, triggered by the stock market crash on Wall Street, as well as the subsequent large-scale unemployment in Germany. In spite of the substantial prosperity of the years 1924–29, it was this conjunction of events, precipitated at least in part by external developments, which gave the *coup de grâce* to the Weimar Republic. Between May 1928 and September 1930, the Nazi vote increased from 800,000 to 6.4 million. Clearly, the economic crisis and the resulting fear and uncertainty multiplied the desire of the German people for a new order. For a people accustomed to a stable executive, the very concept and practice of coalition government—inherently unstable—had little attraction, especially during a period of prolonged crisis. Confronted with a series of seemingly endless economic and political problems, the Germans lost whatever little faith they may have had in the efficacy of parliamentary government and looked for a leader—first Hindenburg, then Hitler—to bring them salvation.

Between February 1919 and January 1933 there were no less than twenty-one cabinets in the Weimar Republic, their average life being about 8 months. The twenty-second cabinet under the Weimar system was not to be. On January 30, 1933, Adolf Hitler became the new chancellor with Hindenburg's consent, after the aging field marshall had been convinced by his entourage that the German people wanted to be ruled by the *Führer* (literally leader or guide) and been persuaded that von Papen and others would pull the strings in the background. The actual course of events, however, was very different. Within a few months Hitler transformed what was left of the Weimar Republic into a totalitarian dictatorship that sought to obliterate any meaningful line of distinction between the state and society. The state was elevated above everything and the individual reduced to nothing. This formula reduced all of culture to one purpose: to serve the interests of the mythical Volk and its Führer and to contribute to their glorification. The cultural break with the past found symbolic expression on May 10, 1933, when thousands of books were burned in Berlin.

The main ideas of the Nazi movement were developed in Hitler's book *Mein Kampf (My Struggle)*, written in 1924 in prison. Extolling war as eternal and inevitable in the pursuit of *Lebensraum* (living space) for the Germans, this programmatic book argued that it was the destiny of the German people to become a *Herrenvolk*, that is, to subjugate or exterminate all other nations and turn itself into the master race. By definition Germans were regarded as superior to all other people—especially to the Jews, who were classified as *Untermenschen* (subhumans) and were the first, but not the last, category of peoples later to be designated for extermination. Before it was all over, some 6 million Jews had been systematically slaughtered (over half of them infants and teenagers), hundreds of thousands of Germans had been tortured and murdered, and millions of German soldiers and a half-million German civilians had died in the war (which in addition took the terrible toll of another 60 million lives). Indeed, as one historian has put it, from 1933 to 1945, Germany went "berserk."[25]

In large measure, the Nazi regime owed its "success" to the ambiguity of its appeal: It promised law and order to the middle class; stable jobs, higher wages, and better positions to the workers; higher prices to the peasants; elimination of the trade unions to big business; and radical reforms to left-wing extremists. Cleverly playing on the widespread resentment of the "dictate" of Versailles, unscrupulously exploiting the economic difficulties and continuing crisis, as well as the general dissatisfaction with the political leadership of the Weimar Republic, the Nazis found it relatively easy to recruit a mass following by mobilizing the frightened and malcontent middle class, especially its lower strata, the unemployed, and all those who were eager for "action." As a matter of fact, the Nazis encountered no particular difficulties in cultivating and gaining the cooperation of various experts belonging to the older generation—people like Alfred Hugenberg, a prominent politician and the founder of a press empire, and Hjalmar Schacht, the financial wizard who endowed Hitler and his followers with an air of respectability. Beginning in 1930 Hitler also received important financial and press support from big business. As a matter of fact, it has been argued that it was the industrialist barons and big bankers who saved Hitler after his popular support had begun to decline in the subsequent elections of November 1932.[26]

Without ever formally abolishing the Weimar Constitution, Hitler simply suspended it and ruled by decree, thus bringing about the de facto end of the Weimar Republic and constitutional government. Using the burning of the Reichstag building as a pretext, he inaugurated a reign of terror against opponents and political allies alike, in a transparent attempt to eliminate any potential sources of challenge to his rule.

The Reichsrat, the upper chamber that traditionally perpetuated the separatism of the various German states, was abolished in 1934. The *Länder* (state) governments and parliaments were also liquidated—their functions being absorbed by the central Ministry of the Interior and by the infamous *Gauleiter,*[27] that is, the governors or regents appointed by Hitler. When Hindenburg died on August 1, 1934, Hitler fused the presidency and the chancellorship into one office, and thus the dual executive of the Weimar Republic was transformed into one amalgamated all-powerful executive office in the Third Reich. Not content with his designation as Reichskanzler—which to him sounded too much like a civil servant—Hitler assumed the title of Führer, signifying presumably his special and unique relationship to the German Volk.

The Reichstag was permitted to lead a nominal existence—after it had voted for its suicide in the Enabling Act on March 23, 1933, which shifted legislative power to the executive. Civil liberties had been eliminated earlier, on February 28, 1933, the day after the Reichstag fire. Other important steps on the road to the establishment of unchecked rule by Hitler included the prohibition of all political parties—except the Nazi movement, which was incorporated into the state; Hitler's deal with the officer corps of the army, resulting in the fateful personal oath of the German generals to Hitler; the *Gleichschaltung*[28] of the courts; the purge of the civil service (with the Nazis taking over approximately 80 percent of the top positions), the police, and the security forces; and the control of the press. Within 18 months the liberal Weimar Republic was turned into a totalitarian dictatorship.

The institutional vehicle for the execution of the Führer's will was the Socialist German Workers Party (*Nationalsozialistische Deutsche Arbeiterpartei* or NSDAP) and its member groups and affiliated associations.[29] At the height of its power, the NSDAP ranks included some 9 million dues-paying members. Modeled after the Communist party of the Soviet Union (CPSU), its top leadership paralleled the government agencies of the Third Reich. As in the case of the CPSU, there was a considerable degree of personnel overlap in the highest echelons of the party and state structure.

An all-powerful secret police apparatus was created, which soon applied to the conduct of terror the professional expertise, efficiency, and ingenuity the world had come to expect of German science, industry, and public administration. Again following the example of the Bolsheviks, a new kind of serfdom was instituted for peasants and workers. Membership in the Nazi-sponsored unions was made compulsory, and all strikes were outlawed. Concentration camps were organized to house all those who found it difficult or impossible to live with the new order or who came under suspicion for one reason or another. At first the camps were filled with Germans—primarily Jews, Social Democrats, Communists, and Catholics. Later new *categories* of people targeted for persecution, slave labor, or extinction were added. After Hitler embarked on his military ventures, the concentration camps literally became human stockyards for the various categories of "subhumans"—Russians, Poles, Balts, gypsies, and more Jews—defined by Nazi ideology. At the Nuremberg Trial of War Criminals it was estimated that some 8 million people entered the 50 concentration camps. Of this number fewer than 600,000 survived to bear witness to the horrors perpetrated by the Nazis against their helpless victims in Auschwitz, Treblinka, Buchenwald, Bergen-Belsen, Dachau, and all the other concentration and death camps.

Having subdued German society, the Nazi regime embarked upon the acquisition of additional living space for the Germans and the unification of German minorities scattered throughout Eastern Europe. Drunk with his own rhetoric and perhaps a victim of his party's propaganda, which confidently proclaimed: *"Heute gehört uns Deutschland, morgen die ganze Welt"* ("Today Germany belongs to us, tomorrow the entire world"), Hitler was ready to unleash his hordes on Europe and the rest of the world. In

1936 he rearmed the Rhineland; in 1938 he engineered the *Anschluss,* that is, the seizure of Austria, and destroyed Czechoslovakia. Next on his agenda was the solution of the Polish corridor problem, which became the pretext for a savage attack on Poland in September 1939. In the subsequent campaigns against France, the Benelux countries, Denmark, and Norway, success seemed to be Hitler's handmaiden. It was not until he had attacked the Soviet Union, had contemptuously treated as "sub-humans" the Russian population—some of whom initially welcomed his troops as liberators—and had failed to make use of the large number of Soviet defectors who wanted to fight against the Communists, that the tide began to turn against him. When under the onslaught of the Western Allies and the Soviets the last remnants of Hitler's once-proud armies surrendered unconditionally, the Führer was no longer among the living. He had committed suicide in the bunker of the Reich Chancellery in Berlin because, as Goebbels put it, the German people had failed and did not deserve the Führer. Nevertheless, the lie was broadcast that the Führer had fallen "fighting at the head of his troops." And thus, appropriately, the regime that began with a lie when Hitler took the oath of office, and which perfected the technique of the "big lie" under the tutelage of Goebbels, also ended with a lie.[30]

GERMANY SINCE 1945

For nearly half a century—from 1945 to 1990—Germany existed as two separate and very different states: the Federal Republic of Germany or West Germany (FRG), which evolved into a democratic society and political system, and the German Democratic Republic or East Germany (GDR), which developed under a communist dictatorial regime. From the perspective of German history, it can be argued that the FRG, in many respects but also with important modifications, represents the continuation of the ill-fated Weimar Republic, Germany's first attempt at democratic government. The GDR, by contrast, followed a very different trajectory of development, one that was much more in line with the traditional pre-Weimar pattern of authoritarian government in

Germany and, more specifically, with the totalitarian regime of Nazi Germany.

Although both states claimed to be democracies, neither owed its existence to an indigenous popular movement for democracy; in fact, their respective political systems were installed by the victorious allies that controlled their respective territories when the war ended. But while citizens in the FRG increasingly identified themselves with their liberal democratic republic, there was substantial opposition to the communist regime in the GDR from the outset. On June 17, 1953, East Germans staged the first revolt in communist Eastern Europe, which was brutally squelched by Soviet tanks and soldiers. Before the erection of the Berlin Wall on August 13, 1961, millions of East Germans fled to the West. The majority of GDR citizens, however, accommodated themselves to the regime as best they could.[31] Although relations between the two German states were normalized to some extent in the 1970s, the consolidation of the communist regime in the GDR turned out to be more apparent than real. When Mikhail Gorbachev initiated a reformist policy in the USSR and let it be known that the communist regimes in Eastern Europe were left to their own devices, political opposition once again came to the surface in East Germany. In October 1989, forty years to the month after the establishment of the GDR, the first successful democratic revolution took place in Germany. It was a remarkable and significant revolution for a number of reasons: It was peaceful, it led to the unification of East and West Germany in 1990, and it made possible the democratization of 16 million Germans who had lived under an oppressive regime. As we will see, it was significant in yet another respect: It revealed the full extent to which the two parts of Germany—capitalist West Germany and "socialist" East Germany—had grown apart and developed differently in the course of only four decades. The unification of Germany, which resulted in the bringing together of two societies in one state, has confronted the new, united FRG, with an enormous and exceedingly difficult challenge—one which has shaped its domestic and foreign policy agenda ever since and is likely to continue to do so for years to come. Leaving aside the historical problem of regionalism and the postwar phenomenon of multiculturalism due to the influx of millions of foreigners and German-descended refugees into Germany, the FRG now has to deal with the fact that some 16 million East Germans, approximately one-fifth of its total population, have been socialized in a very different political system. Since October 3, 1990, Germany is politically unified once again, but it is far from having a unified political culture.

NOTES

[1]As a result of the territorial changes following World War II, Poland moved westward, as it were, acquiring the territory east of the Oder and Neisse rivers, including the Silesian industrial basin, Pomerania, and the southern part of East Prussia. Poland received these lands as "compensation" for territorial losses it sustained as the result of the annexation of formerly Polish territories in the East by the Soviet Union.

[2]The USSR annexed the northern part of East Prussia, thereby obtaining direct access to the Baltic Sea.

[3]The Western sectors of Berlin were under the jurisdiction of the Allied Control Council and technically not governed by the FRG government in Bonn. The former Soviet sector of Berlin became the de facto and openly proclaimed capital of the GDR—in clear violation of the Four Power Agreement on Berlin.

[4]Gordon A. Craig, *The Germans* (New York: G. P. Putnam & Sons, 1982), pp. 16–17. The phenomenon of particularism is more accurately captured by the German term *"Kleinstaaterei"*—that is, the advocacy of numerous small states.

[5]Konrad Müller, ed., *Die Goldene Bulle Kaiser Karls IV* (Bern: Lang, 1957).

[6]The title was changed to King of Prussia in 1772, when Prussia—in the course of the First Partition of Poland—acquired West Prussia (excluding Danzig and Thorn) and achieved formal equality with Austria.

[7]For comparison: the British Civil Service was not established until 1852, the United States Civil Service not until 1883!

[8]For a useful discussion of these thinkers, see R. D. Butler, *The Roots of National Socialism* (New York: E. P. Dutton, 1942).

[9]Beethoven's enthusiasm for the French Revolution eventually waned. After completion of the "Eroica" (1804), he wished the French out of Vienna.

[10]See J. Droz, *L'Allemagne et la révolution française* (Paris: Presses Universitaires de France, 1949).

[11]See Karl Grievant, "Ursachen und Folgen des Scheiterns der Deutschen Revolution von 1848," *Historische Zeitschrift* 170 (October 1950): 495–523.

[12]Although the Revolution of 1848 failed, German liberalism was not totally without influence during the formative years of the German Empire. See Gordon Mork, "Bismarck and the 'Capitulation' of German Liberalism," *Journal of Modern History* 43, no. 1 (March 1971): 59–71.

[13]The "Metternich System" refers to the policies pursued by Count K. W. Metternich in his attempt to maintain the status quo established at the Congress of Vienna in 1815.

[14]Cited in Hugo Preuss, *Staat, Recht und Freiheit* (Tübingen: J. C. B. Mohr, 1926), p. 30.

[15]See Lothar Gall, *Bismarck: Der weisse Revolutionär* (Frankfurt: Verlag Ullstein GmbH, 1980), pp. 256–257.

[16]See Otto Butz, *Modern German Political Theory* (Garden City, NY: Doubleday & Co., 1955), p. 12.

[17]On Bismarck, see Lothar Gall, *Bismarck: Der weisse Revolutionär.*

[18]See R. Lill, *Die Wende im Kulturkampf: Leo der XIII., Bismarck und die Zentrumspartei, 1878–1880* (Tübingen: Niemeyer, 1973).

[19]See Leo Grebler and Wilhelm Winkler, *The Cost of the World War to Germany and Austria-Hungary* (New Haven, CT: Yale University Press, 1940), and Albrecht Mendelssohn-Bartholdy, *The War and German Society* (New Haven, CT: Yale University Press, 1937).

[20]Cited in K. S. Pinson, *Modern Germany: Its History and Civilization,* 2nd ed. (New York: Macmillan Co., 1966), p. 318.

[21]Paul von Hindenburg, *Out of My Life,* vol. II (New York: Harper & Brothers, 1921), p. 275.

[22]I have borrowed this phrase from R. W. Reichard, *Crippled from Birth: German Social Democracy, 1844–1870* (Ames: Iowa State University Press, 1969).

[23]It should be noted that Article 48 was resorted to rather frequently throughout the entire existence of the Weimar Republic—although theoretically this Article gave decree-making powers to the president only in truly extraordinary circumstances. On the Weimar Republic, see Hagen Schulze, *Die Deutschen und ihre Nation: Weimar, Deutschland 1917–1933* (Berlin: Severin and Siedler, 1980).

[24]The price of a magazine in April 1923 was 200 marks, in July, 2,000; in September, 150,000; in October, 4 million; and in November, 8 million marks. When in November 1924 a new currency was established, it was exchanged at the rate of 1 Rentenmark to 1 trillion old marks. The national elections of 1924 clearly reflected the political consequences: the Nationalists and the Communists, both determined opponents of the Weimar Republic, registered heavy gains at the expense of the Social Democrats; the Nazi party received almost 2 million votes and the Communists became the fourth largest party. The close correlation between economic conditions and politics is also illustrated in the 1928 elections, held at a time of economic prosperity: the extremist parties all lost heavily and the Nazi vote declined to 800,000 (Pinson, *Modern Germany,* p. 388).

[25]Ibid., p. 479.

[26]See the controversial study by David Abraham, *The Collapse of the Weimar Republic: Political Economy and Crisis* (Princeton: Princeton University Press, 1981). For another viewpoint on the role of big business, compare Henry Turner, *German Big Business and the Rise of Hitler* (New York: Oxford University Press, 1985).

[27]Named after the "Gaue" (administrative regions with which the Nazi Party crisscrossed the *Länder*).

[28]*Gleichschaltung* was a political slogan used by the Nazis during the seizure of power. It refers to the extensive or total elimination of social and political pluralism, the political co-

ordination or bringing into line of all institutions and organizations, and the elimination of opposition.

[29]The member groups included the SA (storm troopers in brown uniform), the SS (elite guard in black uniform), the youth organizations for boys (Hitler Youth) and for girls (BDM), the Nazi German Student Federation, and the Motor and Flying Corps (NSKK). The affiliated organizations included the Nazi unions for civil servants, lawyers, teachers, professors, physicians, and the German Labor Front.

[30]The literature on the *Third Reich* is very extensive, indeed vast, by now. See, among others, William L. Shirer, *The Rise and Fall of the Third Reich* (New York: Simon and Schuster, 1960); Allan Bullock, *Hitler: A Study in Tyranny* (New York: Harper & Row, 1962); George L. Mosse, *The Crisis of German Ideology: Intellectual Origins of the Third Reich* (New York: Grosset & Dunlap, 1964); F. L. Schuman, *The Nazi Dictatorship: A Study in Social Pathology and the Politics of Fascism* (London: R. Hale & Co., 1936).

[31]Between August 13, 1961, when the borders of East Germany were sealed through the erection of the Berlin Wall, and February 1989, more than 600 East Germans were killed by GDR police and border guards while trying to escape.

Chapter 14

The Social Setting
of German Politics

Because of the profound social changes that have taken place in Germany since 1945, both East and West, an examination of the underlying social and economic bases of contemporary Germany is particularly important for an understanding of German politics. As a result of the outcome of World War II, the eastern part of Germany, or the German Democratic Republic (GDR), fell under the influence of the USSR and developed as an authoritarian "socialist" state[1] on the Soviet model. The Western part, or the Federal Republic of Germany (FRG), by contrast, was controlled by the United States, Britain, and France; as a result, it developed as a democratic capitalist or bourgeois society—a society, however, whose capitalism has always been substantially moderated by a strong social welfare orientation.

POPULATION

With an estimated total population of 82 million in December 1997, the Germans are the largest national group in all of Europe.[2] As is apparent from Table 14–1 the FRG, with a population density of 230 inhabitants per square kilometer, is the most heavily populated large state in Europe. Of the world's important industrial states it is the fourth largest in area and the second most densely settled; only Japan has a higher population density. Although only slightly smaller than the state of Montana and smaller than France, the FRG is the twelfth largest country in the world in terms of population and the largest in Europe. Before reunification, the FRG ranked ninth among European nations (not counting the former Soviet Union) in size of territory. The combined area of the two postwar German states placed Germany in fourth place—after France, Spain, and Sweden.

The population of the FRG is highly urbanized. But urbanization in Germany is mainly a postwar phenomenon. Approximately one-third of its inhabitants today live in large cities of more than 100,000. In the central Ruhr area, the most industrialized part of Germany, population density reaches over 5500 persons per square kilometer. But the majority of Germans live in villages and small towns. The western part of Germany is more densely populated than the five new states in the east that until 1990 formed the GDR, where only 15.5 million people (about

172

Table 14–1 Population Density in Selected Countries, 1997

Countries/Area	Area (1000 sq. km)	Population (in million)	Density (per sq. km)
FRG	357	82	230.1
Belgium	30	10.1	333.8
France	547	58.6	107.8
Great Britain	244	58.9	241.4
Italy	301	57.5	190.9
Netherlands	41	15.6	460.9
China	9,572	1,227.7	128.3
India	3,166	967.6	305.7
USA	9,363	267.8	28.6
Russia	17,075	147.2	8.6
Japan	377	126.1	333.8
European Union	3,236	374.2	115.6

Source: 1998 Britannica Book of the Year (Chicago: Encyclopedia Britannica, 1998), pp. 555, 672, 748.

one-fifth of the population) live on approximately 30 percent of the territory of the FRG. Of the 19 cities with more than 300,000 inhabitants, only three are located in the eastern part of Germany.

One important characteristic of the FRG is its polycentric structure. Unlike France, Great Britain, or Japan, there is no single center of socioeconomic, political, or cultural affairs. To be sure, the central government, the national parliament, and the intricate apparatus engaged in the conduct of the far-flung and complex foreign relations of the FRG are now centered in Berlin and Bonn, the former FRG capital. But a number of key federal agencies are located in other cities—for example, the Federal Constitutional Court (in Karlsruhe), the Deutsche Bundesbank (central bank) in Frankfurt, the Federal Intelligence Service (in Pullach near Munich), and so forth. The capitals of the 16 constituent federal states play an important role in domestic policy making and public administration. Nongovernmental activities, too, are decentralized and dispersed throughout the country. Many of the great financial, industrial, commercial, and mass-media conglomerates have their headquarters in Frankfurt, Cologne, Munich, and Hamburg. In short, Bonn never attained the status and place of prewar Berlin, which was not only the capital and seat of government of Germany, but also a European cultural center. Once again the capital of united Germany and the seat of government, Berlin will almost certainly regain its former status as the

cultural center of Germany. According to present projections, it will be a metropolitan area with a population of 8 million.

The urbanization of Germany can be traced back to the last quarter of the nineteenth century—a period during which Germany experienced a surge of economic development, becoming one of the world's great industrial powers within one generation. During the post-World War II period, West Germany, thanks to the Marshall Plan and the energy and industriousness of its people, surprised the world with the so-called *Wirtschaftswunder* (economic miracle). Recovering unexpectedly quickly from the devastation of the war, Germany—in spite of its territorial amputation—once again joined the ranks of the leading industrial states. Today the FRG is the largest industrial power in Western Europe and the third among the Big Seven, after the United States and Japan.

In terms of age structure the German population, both east and west, shares some of the characteristics of the population of the former USSR. Because of the large losses of males during the two world wars, there was an imbalance in the ratio of males and females—especially older age groups. But in the decades since 1945 this imbalance has begun to correct itself. In 1992 the ratio of males to females was 48.38 to 51.62, but this ratio also reflects the significantly higher life expectancy for women as compared to men in the FRG.[3] Another important demographic factor is the aging of the German population. In 1950, 66.1 percent of the FRG population were under 45 years of age and 32 percent under 25 years; in 1992 these age groups accounted for only 58.3 percent and 29 percent, respectively. To the political scientist these demographic facts are of interest because there is a fairly strong correlation between age and conservative political views. Moreover, in the past the large number of women voters has given a slight advantage to the Christian Democratic Party (CDU). Finally, aging populations mean greater demands on social security and old age pension systems, creating—especially during a time of economic recession—an explosive political issue.

The population of the FRG is further characterized by a high degree of geographic mobility. But much of this movement was intraregional rather than interregional, and thus it did not have a substantial effect on regional political alignments. In the aftermath of unification, there has been a substantial interregional movement—especially from east to west and from west to east.

In both the western and the eastern parts of Germany, the farm population has declined significantly during the postwar period. During the 1960s the West German government pursued a policy of promoting the consolidation of small farms, which resulted in the elimination of almost one-third of all farms under 40 acres in size. In the GDR the collectivization of agriculture did away with individual ownership and small-scale farming. In 1950 the agricultural sector still accounted for 25 percent and 28 percent of employment respectively in West Germany and East Germany. By 1992 the labor force in agriculture had declined to 3 percent of the total labor force.[4]

SOCIAL STRUCTURE

Prior to 1918—that is, before the collapse of Imperial Germany—the nobility played a dominant role in German politics and society. At that time German society was characterized by a rather rigid class structure, which included the nobility, the privileged stratum of civil servants, the bourgeoisie, a growing working class (proletariat), and the peasants. Since 1918 there have been significant changes in this traditional class structure.

The nobility has lost its place of preeminence to an industrial grand bourgeoisie, and the upper middle class consists primarily of top managers in private enterprise, high officials, highly paid lawyers and doctors, and big farmers. Class distinctions have become much less rigid and, generally speaking, less significant.

Some observers of the German political scene have used the designation of "leveled-out middle-class society" (*nivellierte Mittelstandsgesellschaft*) to describe West Germany, pointing out that, with the exception of the top elite, the outward life-style and external appearance of all social classes have become remarkably similar.[5] All things considered, however, substantial differences always remained between the top and bottom of the social structure. Similarly the former GDR, supposedly a more egalitarian society, had a stratified social structure not unlike that of its capitalist neighbor to the west. But there were also important differences suggesting that, after the unification of Germany, two "societies" existed within one state, presenting Germany with the problem of integrating two different social structures.

As is apparent from Table 14–2, in 1990, the year Germany was unified, 89.2 percent of all the gainfully employed in former West Germany derived their livelihood from some form of dependent employment—as workers, salaried employees, or civil servants, and 10.8 percent were self-employed. Salaried workers represented the largest contingent of the labor force, followed by the workers, the self-employed, and the civil servants, who might also be added to the salaried employees. These figures indicate a substantial change in the employment structure of West Germany: Between 1950 and 1990 the number of self-employed and assisting family members decreased by over 60 percent, while the salaried employees and civil servants more than doubled their number—a change that reflected the transformation of West Germany's economic structure and the growing importance of its tertiary sector (services). In the new federal states (the former GDR), by contrast, workers accounted for the majority (52.3 percent) of the labor force, followed by salaried employees (44.5 percent), and self-employed or assisting family members (3.2 percent).

Table 14–2 Labor Force of West Germany and East Germany by Professional Status, 1990 (in percent)

Professional Status	West Germany	East Germany
Salaried employees	43.3%	44.5%
Civil servants	8.5	—
Wage earners (workers)	37.4	52.3
Self-employed and assisting family members	10.8	3.2

Source: Based on Statistisches Bundesamt, ed., *Daten Report 5: Zahlen & Fakten über die Bundesrepublik Deutschland 1991/1992* (München/Landshut: Verlag BONN AKTUELL, 1992), pp. 99, 101 [hereafter cited as *Daten Report 5*].

As indicated in Table 14–3, the 1990 white-collar employees (salaried employees and civil servants) constituted the largest contingent of the male labor force in West Germany (44.4 percent), followed by almost as many workers (44.0 percent). The self-employed accounted for 11.1 percent of the male labor force, and assisting family members for 0.5 percent. In the female labor force, white-collar employees constituted an even larger contingent (62.9 percent), followed by wage earners (27.6 percent). The self-employed accounted for 5.3 percent and assisting family members for 4.2 percent. It should perhaps be noted that in West Germany the proportion of civil servants and self-employed was more than twice as high for males as for females.[6]

In East Germany, by contrast, wage earners accounted for almost two-thirds of the labor force, salaried employees for less than one-third, and less than 4 percent of the male labor force were self-employed or assisting family members. In the female labor force in East Germany, salaried employees, with nearly 61 percent, were clearly dominant, followed by workers (nearly 37 percent); only 2.5 percent of the female labor force were self-employed. Clearly, one of the important differences in the labor force of West Germany and East Germany in 1990 was the much higher proportion of workers and the much smaller proportion of self-employed in the labor force of East Germany.

Problems of social inequality ultimately pose a challenge to any political system. In the case of Germany, these problems assumed a special urgency and extraordinary magnitude at the time of unification because of the significant difference in the prosperity of the populations of former West Germany and the new federal states that for four decades had developed under the communist regime of the GDR. But the initial difference in the levels of prosperity of the western and eastern parts of united Germany is only one problem. The introduction of a market economy in the new federal states in the east and their integration in the West German economy not only led to an increase in the prosperity of these states, but also to an increase in the social inequality of their population and the development of a more differentiated social structure.

The inequality in living conditions connected with belonging to the different social classes expresses itself, among other things, in differences

Table 14–3 Labor Force by Profession and Sex in West Germany and East Germany in 1990 (in percent)

Profession	West Germany		East Germany	
	Male	Female	Male	Female
Salaried employees	33.4%	58.2%	30.4%	60.6%
Civil servants	11.0	4.7	—	—
Wage earners (workers)	44.0	27.6	65.8	36.9
Self-employed and assisting family members	11.6	9.5	3.8	2.5

Source: Daten Report 5, p. 100.

in income and level of education, which in turn constitute crucial resources for the individual in shaping his or her life. In addition to the smaller proportion of homemakers not gainfully employed in eastern Germany and the presence of a disproportionally large number of unemployed and part-time workers, the structure of the labor force, as we have seen, differed above all in terms of the larger proportion of workers and the smaller number of white-collar employees. Most important and urgent, however, were the significant differences in income levels. In the summer of 1991, households in the eastern part of Germany had slightly less than half of the need-adjusted per capita income available to them compared to the households in the western part.[7] In October 1992, the differences in monthly gross incomes of wage earners and salaried employees in comparable lines of work in the west and east ranged from 46.5 percent to 28.1 percent. In short, in the best case (construction industry), workers in the east earned 28.1 percent less than their counterparts in the west. In the worst case (raw material and producer goods industry), they earned 46.5 percent less. In the fall of 1992, workers and salaried employees in the east, on the average, earned only 61 percent of what their counterparts in the west earned for comparable work.[8]

These and other factors explain why the Germans living in the eastern part of the FRG view themselves as disadvantaged and inferior compared to their counterparts in the west. As Figure 14–1 illustrates, in 1991 there were major differences in the self-perception of Germans living in the west and those living in the east with respect to their belonging to different social classes. Studies of the subjective classification of Germans in the west and east into lower and worker stratum, middle stratum, upper middle, and upper stratum produced the familiar onion shape of a middle class society for the west and the typical pyramidical shape of a wage earner (worker) society for the east.

Thus, almost two-thirds of the Germans in the west identified themselves as belonging to the middle class, while nearly as many Germans in the east regarded themselves as members of the lower or working class and only 37 percent as members of the middle class. In the east, only 2 percent identified themselves as part of the

Western Germany	
Upper and Upper Middle Stratum	13%
Middle Stratum	62
Lower and Wage Earner (Worker) Stratum	25
Eastern Germany	
Upper and Upper Middle Stratum	2
Middle Stratum	37
Lower and Wage Earner (Worker) Stratum	61

Figure 14–1. Subjective Social Class Identification in Western and Eastern Germany, 1991 (in percent) (*Source:* Based on *Daten Report 5*, p. 539.)

social elite, while in the west as many as 13 percent did. These are dramatic differences, indeed, which can hardly be explained solely on the basis of the differences in the socioeconomic structure of the population. The available evidence suggests that in their subjective classification within the social class structure of the united Germany, Germans in the east compare themselves first and foremost with Germans in the west and subordinate themselves to them because they feel relatively deprived and underprivileged.[9]

It should come as no surprise that there were also major differences in the perception of the two populations with respect to the fairness and justice of their society, based on the existing system of distribution. While more than two-thirds of the Germans in the west indicated that they were receiving their fair share or more, more than three-fourths of the eastern Germans expressed their conviction that they were receiving less than their fair share. Indeed, every third German in the east indicated the belief that he or she was receiving "much less" than was fair.

Interestingly enough, in a 1991 survey a majority of Germans in the west (64 percent) and in the east (58 percent) indicated their belief that social inequality is a necessary price for the guarantee of adequate motivation for performance and achievement. And a majority of Germans both in the west and in the east disagreed with the proposition that income should not be based solely on an individual's performance, but rather on a family's requirements for a decent life. In short, in spite of their "socialist/communist" past, the Germans in the east, it turns out, do not reject the idea of an achievement society. Yet in overall terms, studies in the early 1990s have shown a startling difference in attitude to "their" society between Germans in the west and in the east. When asked in 1991 whether they regarded the social differences in their country "on the whole as just," nearly half (48 percent) of the Germans in the west, but only 15 percent in the east, responded in the affirmative.[10]

Clearly, as the difficult task of "unification" began, Germans in the west and in the east differed significantly in their perception, legitimation, and acceptance of the existing social inequality. Since 1990 the recognition has dawned on many, if not most, Germans that the solution of this problem will require considerable time. Meanwhile the perception and consciousness on the part of Germans in the east that, as a group, as "Ossies" (East Germans), they are far below their counterparts in the west, as well as their collective conviction that they are underprivileged and their general perception that wealth is distributed unfairly in Germany, constitute sources of potential conflict.

While progress has been made toward socioeconomic equalization in the eastern and western states, wages in the east are still about 25 percent lower than in the west. Major differences remain in the standard of living and the quality of life. What is more, western and eastern Germans have not come together psychologically. As recent surveys indicate, the majority of Easterners have become disenchanted with "western" capitalism and have come to regard German unification as a "hostile takeover" of their country by the West. In their view, unification resulted in "colonialism in one country." Indeed, some argue today that eastern and western Germans have

grown further apart in the years since unification than they had during their separation between 1945 and 1990. To this day, western Germans are far more likely to travel and spend a vacation outside of Germany than in the eastern part of their country. More important, even in the city of Berlin, Germany's new capital, the East-West divide continues to exist: Only 4 percent of the city's marriages involve German couples from opposite sides of the former Berlin Wall. This does not augur well for the integration of "Ossies" and "Wessies" (West Germans).

The issue of socioeconomic insecurity, it should be noted, is not a new issue in the FRG. Long before unification, people in West Germany had become disillusioned with the Sozialstaat (social welfare state), calling into question how "social" their state really was. By 1971 the majority of West Germans had come to feel that the state benefited primarily the rich.[11] And there was ample evidence to support this perception. Between 1970 and 1978, for example, the income differential between the highest-paid group (self-employed) and the lowest-paid group (social security pensioners) more than doubled. A 1978 study of the distribution of wealth in West Germany revealed that, on a per capita basis, white-collar workers had nearly twice as many capital assets (land, stocks, bonds, securities, savings and life insurance assets) as did manual workers; civil servants had nearly 5.5 times as many capital assets; and the capital assets owned by the self-employed were over 40 times as great as those of the manual workers.[12] Moreover, although the expansion of social services to manual workers and white collar employees in the postwar period has gone far in the direction of economic leveling, the FRG's army of public officials (*das Beamtentum,* or "officialdom," as the Germans often call it contemptuously), continues to enjoy many special privileges, ranging from unparalleled job security (civil servants are employed for life and cannot be dismissed) to special car insurance rates, low-cost loans, and so on.[13]

RELIGION

The religious structure of Germany has traditionally played an exceedingly important role in its politics, not only in terms of the ratio between Protestants and Catholics, but also in terms of their regional distribution. Prior to 1945 Catholics were a minority in Germany nationally, being outnumbered by Protestants about two to one. However, in predominantly Catholic regions such as Bavaria, Rhineland-Palatinate, and Silesia (now part of Poland), the Catholics wielded a great deal of political influence. As a result of the loss of Germany's eastern territories, which were 80 percent Protestant, and the division of Germany, involving once again predominantly Protestant territory, the Catholics achieved near-numerical parity with the Protestants in West Germany. Politically this was a most significant development because it put an end to the traditional preeminence of the Protestants in political elites, as well as to the minority status of the Catholics in Germany.

Today more than 55 million people in Germany are members of a Christian church. Of these, over 28 million belong to the Protestant (Evangelical) Church; about 27 million are Roman Catholic; and a minority of Germany's inhabitants belong to other Christian denominations. While the religious landscape in Germany includes many other faiths, Protestants and Catholics account for approximately two-thirds of the population. Following the historical pattern, Protestants predominate in the north and the east. Catholics are in the majority in the south and west. Thus, the states of Rhineland-Palatinate, Saarland, and Bavaria are predominantly Catholic. In the largest state, North Rhine–Westphalia, and in BadenWürttemberg, Catholics and Protestants are about equally strong. In the other states the Protestants are in the majority. As a result of reunification, the balance between Protestants and Catholics shifted once again in favor of the Protestants, who accounted for 47 percent of the population of the GDR, while only 7 percent were classified as Catholic (and 46 percent as unaffiliated or other).

Aside from the effects of the population migration after 1945 (especially the influx of expellees and refugees), the present distribution of Catholics and Protestants goes back to the Reformation—a period of history that also accounts for the special relationship between church and state in Germany. After decades of religious wars, the Peace of Augsburg in 1555 gave regional rulers or princes the right to determine the religious denomination of their subjects. This prerogative was substantially limited by the Peace of Westphalia in 1648, which ended the Thirty Years' War and helped create a situation in which ultimately people chose their religious faith regardless of the ruler's. Nevertheless, the relationship between church and state in Germany has always been a very special and close one. For centuries after the Reformation, for example, the Protestant temporal rulers also tended to be the leading bishops of their regions. Even the attempt in the Weimar Constitution of 1919 to bring about the separation of church and state failed to break the historical ties completely. The Basic Law of 1949 essentially took over the provisions of the Weimar Constitution concerning church-state relations, incorporating Articles 136–139 and 141 of the earlier document.[14]

As Article 137 of the Weimar Constitution made clear, there is no state church in Germany. Likewise, according to the Basic Law, the state occupies a position of neutrality with respect to all religious groups and creeds. In other words, the state recognizes the autonomy of the churches and all other religious groups. At the same time, the established churches in the FRG are not private associations in the strict and ordinary sense. They are corporate bodies whose special status is regulated by public law.[15] More specifically, the relationship between the churches and the state is spelled out in a number of agreements and concordats.[16]

The churches in the FRG are well positioned to defend their interests in the political arena. They have high-ranking representatives in the nation's capital. They benefit from the guarantee of their property by the state and are legally entitled to financial allocations from it. A portion of the salaries of the clergy, for example, is paid by the state, which also contributes to the construction and maintenance of certain church facilities. The churches are authorized by law to impose taxes on their members. These taxes, as a rule, are collected by the state and local authorities for the churches. The members of the clergy are for the most part trained at state universities, where the churches have traditionally been involved in theological appointments. The employees of the established churches in the FRG, finally, enjoy the status of civil servants, with all the attendant privileges.

Certainly from an American perspective, the relationship between church and state in the FRG is unique and different. Churches in the FRG enjoy a very special status—a status which reflects the fact that the state has left to the churches certain traditional and historically rooted privileges—for example, with respect to the church tax, religious instruction, and social services.

In view of the far-ranging privileges of the churches, de facto separation between church and state in the FRG is at best limited. Rather than conceptualizing the church-state relationship in the FRG as an imperfect form of separation, it is perhaps more appropriate and enlightening to envisage it as a form of partnership—one in which the state recognizes the fundamental principle of the separation of church and state, does not identify itself with any particular religious denomination, and treats all religious groups equally; a partnership in which the churches recognize certain limits to their autonomy set by the legal order of the state and are willing to share their public responsibilities with other groups and organizations in a pluralistic democratic society. If thus far there has been little public support for the abolition of the traditional privileges of the churches in the FRG, it is in part because there is general recognition—both among politicians and the broad public—that the manifold sociopolitical and welfare activities of the churches constitute an important, necessary, and desirable element in the present German social order.

Prior to 1918 the Evangelical church in Germany was accustomed to seek the exercise of political influence through its role as the established and recognized state church, as a political ally of the ruling interests. The Catholics (then a definite minority), by contrast, sought to further their political interest through the organization of a special religiously based political party, the Center party (*Zentrumspartei*). The establishment of the CDU (Christian Democratic Union) in 1945, which brought Protestants and Catholics together in one party, created an entirely new situation— one in which there is much greater distance between the churches and the union of Protestants and Catholics in a common political party. Both

major churches have been active in the political arena, seeking to influence public opinion on controversial issues and to inject Christian values and standards into the political debate and process. The Evangelical church, in particular, has addressed the nation on numerous occasions in a series of position papers and statements. The most influential one of these was the famous *Ost-Denkschrift,* which dealt with the FRG's relationship to its eastern neighbors.

While Catholics and Protestants in Germany, as elsewhere, are still likely to disagree on a good many specific issues, there is little hostility between the two denominations. Greater religious, cultural, and ethnic tolerance is one of the most attractive features of postwar German society. In the aftermath of the Nazi horrors, there were few Germans who were inclined to support extreme forms of intolerance. Moreover, the modern middle-class life and relative affluence of the majority of the population following the economic recovery contributed to the erosion of the religious divisions of the past. Although Catholics are still underrepresented in cultural, educational, and business elites, their integration in the FRG has been remarkably successful. One index of the greater tolerance between the two major religious faiths is the increase in interdenominational marriages. At the turn of the century, less than 10 percent of the marriages in Germany fell in this category;[17] by 1987 nearly 40 percent of the marriages entered into by Protestant women and about 31 percent by Catholic women in West Germany were interdenominational.[18] There is little doubt that the emergence of interdenominational labor unions and political parties during the postwar period was a major factor in facilitating the integration of the Catholics and in overcoming religious barriers at the level of the individual.

Both surveys and statistical data based on official church records show a decline in religious belief. In the year 1987 alone, the Evangelical church in the West lost 140,638 members and the Catholic Church, 81,598.[19] Prominent church leaders and theologians have openly questioned the relevance of the church to the modern world.[20] On the other hand, the long-term prospects of the major churches, especially in the Western part of the FRG, are not necessarily dismal. There, in spite of the exodus of church members at the end of the 1960s and the beginning of the 1970s, 89 percent of the population belong to some religious community.

In the eastern part of Germany, on the other hand, church membership is the exception rather than the rule. The majority of the population in the east (64 percent) does not belong to a church. Reflecting the historical dominance of the Protestants in the east, there is also an important difference in regard to the balance between the two major established churches: 27 percent of the adult population belong to the evangelical church, 6 percent to the Catholic church. Considering that in 1950 approximately 80 percent of the population in the east belonged to the evangelical church and 10 percent to the Catholic church, it is clear that the evangelical church in particular suffered enormous losses in membership during the four decades of communist rule.

Thus, in terms of church and religion, there are significant differences between Germans in the west and in the east. In the west, 92 percent of all parents had their children baptized in 1991; for the east, the comparable figure was 36 percent. In the west, those who attend church regularly (24 percent) and those who never attend church (21 percent) were in the minority. The majority of adults (54 percent) in the west indicated that they attend church at least once a year or more. In the east, those who never attend church were in the majority (60 percent). Whereas in the West 66 percent of the population said they believe in God, only 25 percent did so in the east. In the east, one out of two adults advocated a distinctly atheistic position; in the west only 10 percent claimed to be atheists.[21] As might be expected, lack of interest in religion was especially pronounced among the younger generations that were born and grew up in the GDR. Considering these facts, the conclusion is inescapable that four decades of communist rule produced, among other things, a fundamental break in the life and tradition of Christianity in this part of Germany.

EDUCATION

With the memory of German culture and education under the Nazis still vivid and fresh, and under the influence of the United States, the framers of the Basic Law did not assign significant powers or extensive jurisdiction in the realm of culture and education to the federal government. Reverting to the pre-Weimar pattern, the Basic Law (Article 30) by implication recognized the cultural sovereignty of the states (*Länder*). More specifically, all cultural matters (issues relating to schools and education, science and art) were made the responsibility of the states, to be administered by the ministers (or senators) for education. The necessary coordination of the various school systems and other institutions was to be achieved through joint agreements concluded by the states. A Permanent Conference of the State Ministers for Education now meets on a regular basis to discuss issues of common concern.

Only in a limited number of educational policy areas—state supervision of the schools, religious instruction, and private schools—does the Basic Law stipulate a uniform nationwide regulation. It was not until May 1969 that the power of the federal government to issue framework legislation was extended to include issuing guidelines governing the running of the university system and other institutions at the upper level of the educational system. Later, a joint Commission for Educational Planning and Promotion of Research was established by the federal government and the states. In 1973 it produced a General Plan for Education, which outlined the development of the entire education system up to 1985—a plan which has since been updated.

In the GDR, by contrast, a highly centralized system of education developed. Following the example of the Soviet Union (and also Nazi Germany), the East German regime subordinated all spheres of culture, including education, to political and economic considerations. Education was highly politicized, as, indeed, was sports. The core institution in the "uniform socialist system of education" of the GDR was the general education polytechnical high school, which in a 10-year program laid the foundation for all forms of higher education and vocational training. In accordance with the State Treaty on Currency, Economic and Social Union, the integration of the former GDR educational system into the educational system of West Germany began on September 1, 1990.[22]

Historically the educational system has been a major factor in the creation of a highly stratified society and the perpetuation of the traditional elitist class structure. Although under this system a basic education was made available to all, advanced education—i.e., attendance at a *Realschule* (6-year intermediate or general high school), a *Gymnasium* (9-year academic high school preparing students for the university), or a university—for the most part was the prerogative of the middle and upper classes. In 1989, for example, only 26.9 percent of the children enrolled in a *Realschule* or *Gymnasium,* the two major tracks leading to higher or advanced education, came from a working class background—compared to 51.6 percent for the children of the self-employed, 55.4 percent for the children of salaried employees, and 61.3 percent for the children of civil servants.[23]

Gradually, however, educational opportunities have been expanded. On the basis of a constitutional amendment adopted in 1969, the national government has become more involved in educational policy and reform. The main thrust of the changes in the educational system is the introduction of a new institution, the *Gesamtschule*—a single comprehensive school that merges the traditional three tracks of the educational system, i.e., the *Hauptschule* (general school), the *Realschule,* and the *Gymnasium.* The idea behind this innovation is to have children from all social backgrounds attend the *Gesamtschule* at least until the age of 16. Students at that point can go on to vocational training and full-time employment, or continue in the *Gesamtschule* for three additional years of study, thus qualifying themselves for admission to a university. Clearly, the *Gesamtschule,* like the American high school, is an institution that is conducive not only to greater equality of opportunity but also to a higher level of social mobility.

This arguably democratic and much-needed educational reform has proved to be very controversial in the FRG, running into opposition not only from conservative politicians but also many *Gymnasium* teachers. Generally speaking, the Social Democratic Party (SPD), currently the party in power, and the Free Democratic Party, the coalition partner of the CDU/CSU at the national level, have supported the *Gesamtschule* and other educational reforms, while the Christian Democratic Party (CDU/CSU) has opposed this innovation in German education. The opposition of the former ruling party at the national level notwithstanding, the *Gesamtschule* has been introduced in all the states, including the new eastern states, at least on an experimental basis. By 1992 close to 500 integrated *Gesamtschulen* were in operation—the overwhelming majority of them (about 80 percent) in SPD-governed states. In the same year, these schools, including private integrated schools, had an enrollment of 493,000 students.[24] Another significant change in German education is the dramatic increase in the number of students in academic tracks. Whereas in 1950 only 18 percent of all Germans had some educational experience beyond the *Hauptschule,* this figure has increased to more than 45 percent.

ISSUES CONFRONTING GERMAN SOCIETY

On January 29, 1983, the eve of the fiftieth anniversary of Hitler's seizure of power, mass demonstrations took place in West Germany. Thousands of people jammed the streets of the FRG's great metropolitan centers: Hamburg, Cologne, Munich, and Frankfurt. These demonstrations followed numerous serials and documentaries about the seizure of power by Hitler broadcast on television in the FRG during the preceding weeks. Recalling the events of January 30, 1933, the demonstrators carried banners proclaiming: "Fascism: Never Again!" On the day of the anniversary, Chancellor Helmut Kohl addressed a rally at the old Reichstag building in Berlin—a building that once housed the German parliament and that became the site of a remarkable exhibition entitled "Questions to German History."[25]

Within a few decades after the end of World War II, the Germans living in the western part of the FRG had reason to be proud and grateful. Their country was rebuilt. They lived in a modern and very affluent society. They enjoyed the benefits of a stable government committed to the advancement and preservation of basic human rights, constitutionalism, social welfare, and progress. The government, moreover—unlike Germany's first democracy, the Weimar Republic—was recognized as legitimate by the overwhelming majority of citizens and succeeded in developing a viable political party system. Although certain vestiges of the past remained—a relatively high degree of socioeconomic stratification; limited social mobility; male domination of the socioeconomic, political, and cultural elites; inequities in access to educational opportunities—public policy had gone far in attempting to deal with these issues and, generally speaking, was ahead of society in this respect.

Germans living in the eastern part of Germany—that is, in the former GDR—by contrast, did not fare as well. Although they enjoyed the highest standard of living in the communist world, they had not attained the level of prosperity achieved in West Germany. It is only after the unification of the two Germanies in 1990 that the disparity between the two German states has become fully apparent. The legacy of communist rule in the eastern part of Germany includes a rundown and antiquated infrastructure and major environmental problems, as well as a different work ethic. The united Germany is therefore confronted with a host of problems arising from the need to integrate the 16 million citizens of the former GDR, to reduce regional differences in wealth, employment, education, and standard of living. In the years ahead, the politics of socioeconomic and cultural integration will occupy an important place in the agenda of the German government.

For the time being, the period of economic boom seems to be over. In recent years, the FRG has faced the problem of high unemployment. In 1988, for example, over 2 million workers were without a job, and unemployment reached 8.4 percent in 1989. Unification has further aggravated an already serious unemployment problem. With the closing of many plants in the eastern part of Germany, unemployment among former GDR citizens is very high (16 percent in the first quarter of 1993), and the costs of reducing unemployment in the east are staggering. While this still falls considerably short of the abysmal situation in 1930, when unemployment stood at over 30 percent and some 6 million hungry and jobless workers helped swell the ranks of Hitler's

followers, it is nevertheless cause for concern. No less prominent and responsible a politician than Helmut Schmidt, the former chancellor, has drawn an explicit parallel between the present situation and the last years of the Weimar Republic. Stable and popular government may very well prove increasingly elusive in the years ahead—especially since shrinking tax revenues, triggered by the economic recession, will force the FRG government, regardless of which party or coalition is in power, to restrict what in the FRG is commonly called *"das soziale Netz,"*—the elaborate "net" of social services Germans have come to take for granted. The social and economic integration of the former GDR, with its neglected infrastructure and serious environmental problems, confronts the FRG with a difficult political agenda whose solution will require years, if not decades. The problems are so daunting that they will tax even the wealth and financial strength of the FRG.

Another potentially explosive issue is the presence of some 7.4 million foreigners (as of 1997) in the FRG—mostly Turks, Yugoslavs, Italians, Greeks, and Spaniards—who together account for 7.3 percent of the total population. During the years of prosperity when the German economy expanded rapidly and there was an acute manpower shortage, these "guest workers" were welcomed as a much-needed addition to the labor force.[26] Unable to speak fluent German and to function effectively in a demanding work environment, they all too often ended up with the most menial jobs. With the development of widespread unemployment, they came to be viewed as competitors for scarce jobs and as an unwanted burden on the state's treasury.[27] According to a poll taken in the fall of 1982, two-thirds of the citizens of the FRG felt the immigrant workers should return to their own countries.

During the 1970s and 1980s pressures mounted on public officials to find a solution. As anyone who has traveled in West Germany in recent years can attest, many houses, subway trains and stations, park benches, and shop windows were defaced with inscriptions such as: *"Türken raus!"* ("Turks, go home!") or *"Wir brauchen keine Ausländer"* ("We don't need foreigners.") There were an increasing number of attacks on foreigners, producing statistics that, in the words

FOREIGNERS IN GERMANY (DECEMBER 31, 1997)	
Country/Continent of Origin	
Turkey	2,107,000
Former Yugoslavia	721,000
Italy	607,000
Greece	363,000
Africa	305,000
Poland	283,000
Bosnia-Herzegovina	281,000
Croatia	206,000
Austria	185,000
Portugal	132,000
Spain	131,000
Iran	113,000
United States	110,000
Others	1,821,000
Total	7,365,000
	(Total = 9% of FRG population)

Source: German Information Center, *Quick Facts about Germany,* www.germanyinfo.org/facts/quick.htm

there is no question that these acts of violence against foreigners were perpetrated by a relatively small group of extremists, including neo-Nazis, and were condemned by the majority of Germans both in the east and the west, they met with the passive approval of some Germans, including local residents. The scale of the violence, along with other factors, suggests that, especially in the crisis-ridden eastern part of the country, Germans, in particular the young, are by no means immune to appeals by political extremists. In contrast to the Weimar Republic, however, the spectrum of political parties is not as diverse and includes a democratic right wing; moreover, the over-whelming majority of citizens in Germany, both east and west, supports the idea and practice of democratic government.

NOTES

[1]There is a world of difference between the authoritarian "socialism" in the former Soviet Union and the socialism in such countries as the FRG, Denmark, Norway, Sweden, or other countries in Western Europe that have preserved the traditions of European social democracy.

[2]German Information Center, *Quick Facts about Germany,* www.germany-info.org.facts.htm. (1/19/1999).

[3]See CIA, *The World Factbook 1993,* p. 145.

[4]*Stat. Jahrb.* BRD, p. 113.

[5]On the social structure of the FRG, see Wolfgang Littek, "Sozialstruktur," in eds. K. Sontheimer and H. H. Röhring, *Handbuch des politischen Systems der Bundesrepublik Deutschland* (Munich: R. Piper & Co. Verlag, 1978), pp. 556–573.

[6]These figures are based on Statistisches Bundesamt, ed., *Daten Report 5: Zahlen & Fakten über die Bundesrepublik Deutschland 1991/1992* München/Landsberg: Verlag BONN AKTUELL, 1992), pp. 98–101 [hereafter cited as *Daten Report 5*].

[7]Ibid. p. 538. The adjustment included the differential size and age structure of the households.

[8]*Stat. Jahrb.* BRD, p. 603.

[9]*Daten Report 5,* p. 539.

[10]Ibid., p. 544.

[11]Manfred Koch, *Die Deutschen und Ihr Staat* (Hamburg: Hoffman & Campe, 1972), p. 45.

[12]Karl Roemer, ed., *Facts about Germany* (Gütersloh: Lexikothekverlag, 1979), p. 227; H. Mierheim and L. Wicke, *Die personelle Vermögensverteilung in der Bundesrepublik* (Tübingen: J.C.B. Mohr, 1978), pp. 250ff.

[13]See Wilhelm Bleek, "Berufsbeamtentum," in K. Sontheimer and H. H. Röhring, ed., *Handbuch des politischen Systems der Bundesrepublik Deutschland* (Munich: R. Piper & Co., 1978), pp. 556–573.

[14]See Articles 4 and 140 of the Basic Law. For the text in English translation, see H. Finer, *The Major Governments of*

of Gerhart Baum, the former minister of the interior, "should fill every democrat with great worry."[28]

After the unification of Germany in 1990, the collapse of the Soviet Union in 1991, and the war in the former Yugoslavia, the situation became even worse, due to the large influx of refugees and asylum seekers. Having taken in 887,000 asylum seekers during 1990–1993 and nearly a quarter of a million in the first six months of 1993, Germany effectively adopted a zero-immigration policy. The Bundestag amended the Basic Law and thereby restricted the right of asylum that it had previously extended generously and with pride to almost all applicants.

Before the government succeeded in defusing the situation, Germany experienced the worst outbreak of violence against foreigners since the end of the Third Reich. While most of the incidents took place in the eastern part of the country, where unemployment was highest, especially among the young, they occurred in the western part of the country as well. There was large-scale destruction of property and loss of life. Although

Modern Europe (Evanston: Row, Peterson & Company, 1960), pp. A18–A36.

[15]See "Kirchenrecht und Staatshoheit," in Otto Model and Carl Creifelds, *Staatsbürger-Taschenbuch* 20th rev. ed. (Munich: C. H. Beck'sche Verlagsbuchhandlung, 1982), pp. 762–791.

[16]Most of these agreements were concluded at the state *(Land)* level. The important exception is the famous *Reichskonkordat* of 20 July 1933, concluded between Hitler and the Vatican, which remains in force today in accordance with a ruling of the FRG Constitutional Court of 26 March 1957.

[17]M. R. Lepsius, "Sozialstruktur und soziale Schichtung in der Bundesrepublik Deutschland," in R. Löwenthal and Hans-Peter Schwarz, ed., *Die Zweite Republik* (Stuttgart: Seewald Verlag, 1974), p. 264.

[18]*Stat. Jahrb.* BRD, p. 61.

[19]Ibid., pp. 84–85.

[20]See, for example, the address by Karl Rahner to the West German Synod in 1974, reported in *Kölner Stadt-Anzeiger,* 27 May 1974.

[21]*Daten Report 5,* pp. 602–611.

[22]See Karl Schmitt, "Education and Politics in the German Democratic Republic," *Comparative Education Review* 19 (50): 31–50.

[23]*Daten Report 5,* p. 86.

[24]By comparison, 1.5 million students were enrolled in the *Hauptschule,* 1.4 million in the *Realschule,* and 2.0 million in the *Gymnasium. Cf.* Statistisches Bundesamt, ed., *Datenreport 1994: Zahlen und Fakten über die Bundesrepublik Deutschland* (Bonn: Bundeszentrale für politische Bildung, 1994), pp. 51, 53.

[25]See *Fragen an die deutsche Geschichte: Ideen, Kräfte, Entscheidungen von 1800 bis zur Gegenwart* (Bonn: Deutscher Bundestag, 1981).

[26]By 1972 foreign workers accounted for 11 percent of the FRG labor force—a figure that represented a ten-fold increase since 1962. See L. J. Edinger, *Politics in West Germany* (Boston: Little, Brown and Company, 1977), p. 58.

[27]Constituting 7.2 percent of the total population of the FRG, foreigners accounted for 12.5 percent of the unemployed in 1988. See *Stat. Jahrb.* BRD, p. 105.

[30]Associated Press, January 30, 1983.

Chapter 15

The Political Framework of Germany

When the Basic Law (*Grundgesetz*) was drawn up in 1948–49, it was envisaged as giving "a new order to political life for a transitional period."[1] The framers of the Basic Law deliberately avoided calling the instrument that established the FRG a constitution in order not to complicate the hoped-for eventual reunification of Germany.[2] A new German constitution, they thought, would be and should be drafted by a National Assembly consisting of representatives of all Germans, not merely of those living in the occupation zones of the Western Allies. To emphasize the provisional nature of the Basic Law, the framers proposed ratification by the state parliaments rather than through a direct vote by the citizens of the Western occupation zones. Similarly, the designation of Bonn as the capital of the FRG was regarded as a temporary and expedient measure; Bonn was not viewed as the permanent capital.

The political order created by the Basic Law, in short, was to be a strictly provisional one. If since its adoption in 1949 it has evolved into a more permanent political arrangement, this was not by design, but due to a variety of factors, not least of all to the progressive deterioration of U.S.–Soviet relations in the late 1940s and 1950s and the Cold War, which rendered any thought of the reunification of Germany along liberal democratic lines an idle dream.[3] As a consequence, the Basic Law became a constitution in all but in name.

Compared with Germany's first attempt at democratic government, the Weimar Republic, the FRG in many respects presents a sharp contrast. While the Weimar Republic was characterized by a great deal of political turbulence, the politics of the FRG, especially during the first two decades of its existence, were distinguished by a great deal of continuity and stability. The first chancellor of the FRG, Konrad Adenauer, for example, was in office from 1949 to 1963—that is, for a longer period of time than all twelve chancellors of the Weimar Republic combined. For 20 years, moreover, the FRG—like postwar Japan—was in effect ruled by a single conservative party—though in coalition with a number of other parties. It was not until 1969 that the FRG was faced with its first experience of a full-scale political turnover.

So only in the third decade of its existence were the inherent difficulties of coalition politics added to the political agenda of the FRG. While in the Weimar Republic a multitude of political parties—including several regional, special-interest, and extremist parties—vied for parliamentary representation and political power,[4] only three major parties have emerged in the FRG, all of which strongly support the political order established by the Basic Law. Finally, in contrast to the Weimar Republic, the FRG benefited from an expanding economy and growing prosperity, as well as increasing international respect and prestige—important forms of support that contributed to the acceptance and legitimacy of the new fledgling government.

In view of the success of the Bonn regime, however, it is well to remember in retrospect that in 1949 the prospects of Germany's second experiment in democratic government were anything but bright. The initial reaction of Germans to the end of the Nazi regime and the occupation of Germany by the victorious Allies was more or less total indifference to politics on a mass scale.[5] During the immediate postwar years the vast majority of Germans were completely preoccupied with problems of physical survival, the restoration of their own lives, and the reunification of their families—to the extent to which this was possible. In 1945 Germany, in the words of the historian Friedrich Meinecke, was "a burned-out crater of power politics."

In Berlin alone an estimated 260 million cubic feet of ruins had to be cleared away before reconstruction could begin. More houses had been destroyed in the capital than had ever existed in Munich, one of Germany's great metropolitan centers. There was hunger, despair, and demoralization everywhere. And after the capitulation the economic system broke down completely. In the streets of the burned-out cities German women and girls were selling themselves to Allied soldiers for a few cigarettes (the prevailing currency at the time since money had become worthless), candy bars, and food. For a while the daily food intake averaged only 800 calories— approximately one-third of the normal requirement. Millions were disabled, widowed, or orphaned by the war. The housing situation was indescribable in 1945—and for years the housing shortage was made worse by the steady stream of expellees from the eastern territories. In his 1949 New Year's Eve address, Theodore Heuss, the first federal president, spoke of an endless catalog of German hardships and needs.

Although under these circumstances one can hardly blame the Germans for their lack of interest in public life, in particular politics, and their almost total retreat into their own private lives, their reaction to the postwar years nevertheless posed a severe problem for those trying to cope with the prevailing chaos and create a viable democratic order amidst the ruins of post-Nazi society. In 1949 there was a good deal of skepticism with respect to the prospects of the Bonn government, whose problems of establishing "legitimacy" in the eyes of the German people were complicated by the FRG's self-proclaimed provisional character and the division of Germany.

THE BASIC LAW

The constitutional instrument that became the basic for the creation of the FRG—the Basic Law—contains many provisions reflecting the effort of the Parliamentary Council[6] (the drafters of the new document) to draw realistic conclusions from the past and to avoid the kinds of mistakes that had contributed to the downfall of the Weimar Republic. The delegates recognized that the destabilizing strife of multiparty politics as practiced in the Weimar Reichstag, the resulting instability of the executive, and the excessive involvement of the public in popular initiatives and referendums all contributed to the political turmoil on which Hitler and his Nazi followers were able to capitalize.

A presidential system based on the separation of powers and modeled after the U.S. government was briefly considered as an alternative to a parliamentary system. But this idea was quickly abandoned. For one thing, at that time Europe had had very little experience with presidential government. For another, after the experience with Hitler and the Nazi regime few delegates were willing to support the creation of a political system that called for the concentration of a great deal of power in the hands of one person and institution. Instead, the delegates decided in favor of a variant of the parliamentary system that would be tailormade to deal with the particular problems of German politics and history.

In the new parliamentary system devised in 1948–49, both the presidency and the popularly elected legislature—the two most powerful institutions of the Weimar system—were retained. However, their power was substantially curtailed. The presidency was stripped of almost all independent political power, deprived of its former basis for claiming a popular mandate,[7] and virtually reduced to a figurehead role. The lower house of the legislature (renamed *Bundestag,* or Federal Diet) was greatly restricted in its power to overthrow the government or cabinet (the chancellor and ministers). To deal with the problem of instability of the executive, the Basic Law provides for a "constructive no-confidence vote." In practice this means that the Bundestag can overthrow a chancellor through a no-confidence vote only if it is first able to agree on a successor.

The popular initiative and referendum were abolished at the national level. In the redistribution of powers, two traditional political institutions gained significantly: the upper house of the legislature (*Bundesrat* or Federal Council) and the federal chancellor (*Bundeskanzler*). As a matter of fact, the political position of the chancellor is so dominant in the West German polity that the FRG has been described as a "chancellor democracy." At the same time, the "emergency powers" are very circumscribed in the Basic Law—again clearly a reaction to the experience with respect to Article 48 of the Weimar Constitution.

The political system created by the Basic Law is in many respects unique because it includes a variety of checks and balances grafted onto a parliamentary system of government. The FRG, for example, has a powerful Federal Constitutional Court, which rules not only on the constitutionality of legislation and administrative acts, but also on basic questions of constitutional interpretation. It has far-reaching powers for dealing with disputes between the federation (*Bund*) and the states (*Länder*), between the states themselves, or between supreme organs of the government or their subdivisions.[8] Thus, the Federal Constitutional Court—handling for the most part constitutional complaints by individuals and recognized legal entities in the FRG[9]—is qualitatively different from its historic predecessors and in many respects unique when compared to similar institutions in other countries. Like the Supreme Court in the United States, it has emerged as a major factor in the politics of the FRG.

The provisions of the Basic Law dealing with civil liberties also deserve special emphasis. First of all, they occupy a conspicuous place at the very beginning of the Basic Law (Articles 1–19). Unlike the Weimar Constitution, the Basic Law does not treat civil liberties as a kind of afterthought to be elaborated by subsequent legislation, but rather spells them out in comparatively great detail in a section that precedes the provisions concerning the machinery of government. Second, they constitute an impressive and comprehensive Bill of Rights—all the more remarkable because Germany, unlike Great Britain, France, or the United States, does not have a strong tradition with respect to civil liberties. In German legal and political thought the emphasis has been on defining the obligations of the citizens to the state rather than on the individual's rights as a citizen and human being vis-à-vis the state. The Germans did come to accept the idea of a state based on the rule of law (*Rechtsstaat*); but the concept of natural law (*jus naturale*)—the idea of certain fundamental laws that are higher than, and antecedent to, the establishment of the state—was slow in gaining acceptance.

The Basic Law, then, is a remarkable departure from traditional German legal and constitutional thought. It explicitly recognizes certain inalienable rights, makes their observance binding on the legislature, the executive, and the courts (Article 1, paragraph 3), and grants that, in the case of a conflict of conscience, these rights take precedence over the duties of the individual to the state. Accordingly, the Basic Law (Articles 4 and 12a), for example, explicitly recognizes the right to conscientious objection to military service. The Basic Law, furthermore, is unique in that it affirms the superiority of international law (*jus gentium*), whose "general rules," according to Article 25, "form part of the federal law . . . , take precedence over the laws and directly create rights and duties for the inhabitants of the federal territory."

While the Weimar Constitution spoke of the fundamental duties of the citizen, there are only fundamental rights listed in the Basic Law. That document, moreover, makes it abundantly clear that these fundamental rights are absolute and unconditional as long as they are not used to subvert the constitutional order of the FRG. In short, the

Basic Law stipulates clearly that there are some things that are beyond the authority of the state. Thus, for example, the fundamental rights enumerated in the initial section of the Basic Law cannot be suspended in an "emergency"—as happened under Hitler. Moreover, two key articles in the Basic Law cannot be amended in any way: Article 1 obligates "all state authority" to respect and to protect the dignity of man, stipulates the existence of inviolable and inalienable rights, and declares that the fundamental rights enumerated in the Basic Law are binding on all government organs; Article 20 sets forth the basic organization of the FRG as a "democratic and social federal state," recognizes the sovereignty of the people, guarantees elections, and subjects all government agencies to the Basic Law and the rule of law. These strong guarantees of the Basic Law, however, were weakened by the emergency legislation passed in 1968—over the opposition of the trade unions, the FDP, and fifty SPD deputies.

Perhaps even more impressive than the significance attached by the framers of the Basic Law to the guarantee of civil liberties is the fact that the vast majority of Germans living in the FRG have also come to think of civil liberties as being of utmost importance. In a survey conducted 20 years after the establishment of the FRG, only a small number of citizens indicated their willingness to consider giving up freedom of speech (2 percent), free elections and competitive political parties (3 percent), or freedom of assembly (10 percent) in exchange for the unification of their country. While it is a difficult and precarious enterprise to draw definite conclusions from this type of data, these figures nevertheless do seem to suggest that the great majority of FRG citizens attached greater value to their civil liberties than to national unity.[10]

BUND AND LÄNDER: FEDERALISM IN THE FRG

One of the important considerations in organizing political power in a political system is the division of governmental responsibilities among various layers of government: national, state or regional, and local. In the United States, the Constitution provides for a federal structure in which the powers of the national and state governments are carefully delimited. The autonomy of state governments in conducting their own affairs permits greater responsiveness to sectional or regional needs and encourages experimentation and innovation. These advantages of the federal structure are to some extent offset by its disadvantages: lack of uniformity and standardization; the likelihood of inequities—with some of the states providing greater or better services than others; and the increased costs of government arising from the duplication of political institutions, administrations, and services in fifty states. Another of the often cited advantages of federalism—that it protects democracy against threats of authoritarian abuse of power through the dispersion of power—is questionable, since most democratic governments have centralized political structures.

The creation of a federal state in the Western occupation zones in 1949 was a response that complied with the Allied order to the Parliamentary Council to organize West Germany along federal lines. Likewise it was a reaction to the fact that, as a result of the Nazi regime, the idea of a centralized, unitary state had been thoroughly discredited. But most important, it was a solution that reflected the prevailing political forces in the Western zones at the time—a solution, moreover, which affirmed a tradition with deep roots in Germany's past. Throughout German history the federal or, more precisely, confederal state had been the most prevalent form of state organization: Confederalism was both the fruit of the efforts undertaken at various points in history to unify the German nation and a measure of the difficulties which this endeavor had historically entailed.[11] But in contrast to Switzerland and the United States, confederalism (and later federalism) in German history developed less as the result of rational considerations, planning, or decisions than as a function of political compromises, historical coincidence, and the attempt to contain the aspirations first of Austria, then of Prussia, to achieve hegemony. Confederalism in the German-speaking parts of Europe, therefore, was "more of a historical by-product, a necessity that could not be circumvented, than a constructive organizational principle of compelling force."[12]

In modern times, the idea of confederalism developed in the German territories in response to the conflict between the growing aspirations for national unity and the particularist orientations of the various German principalities-turned-states, especially after the final collapse of the Holy Roman Empire in 1806. Both the *Rheinbund* (1806–13), a confederation of over thirty German principalities, duchies, grand duchies, and kingdoms under the protectorate of Napoleon I, and the *Deutsche Bund* (1815–66), the German Confederation established by the Congress of Vienna, incorporated the beginnings of a federalist organization for the German states. Similarly, the draft constitution adopted by the National Assembly in 1848, the so-called Frankfurt Parliament, envisaged a federalist solution to the problem of political organization in Germany; and the North German Confederation (*Norddeutscher Bund*) of 1867–70 was a model for, and precursor of, the future German federal state.

Thanks to the genius of Bismarck, finally, the principle of confederalism was fused with the principle of (Prussian) hegemony in the Second Empire—resulting in the structural perversion of the formally confederal state. The dominant position of Prussia in the Reichsrat or upper house, the comparative weakness of the Reichstag or lower house, the reserved rights of the southern states, and the privileged position of Bavaria all distorted the federal structure and led to the emergence of a kind of pseudofederalism in practice. Nevertheless, the state governments were able to preserve a degree of integrity and independence by retaining control over most direct taxes.

The idea of federalism suffered a significant setback in Germany as the result of the collapse of the Second Empire and the emotional mood for unity that prevailed both at the beginning of World War I and at its end. The introduction of the parliamentary system of government under Allied pressure in October 1918 necessarily reduced the power of the Reichsrat and thus significantly undermined the ability of the various state governments to influence national policy. This decision thus not only predetermined the constitutional structure of the Weimar Republic to a significant extent, but also contributed directly to the centralist bias of the Weimar Constitution. The threat to the unity of Germany—less than 50 years old at the time—posed by the disillusionment with the Reich, separatist movements in the Rhineland supported by France, and the idea of a Danube Confederation to consist of Bavaria, Czechoslovakia, and Austria[13]—made the idea of a unitary state all the more attractive.

Thus the key question before the National Assembly in Weimar was whether Germany was to be organized as a federal or as a unitary state. In advancing the model of a decentralized unitary state, the draft constitution—written by Hugo Preuss, state secretary of the interior and professor of public law at the University of Berlin—reflected the mood of the majority of the delegates. In spite of the energetic protests of the state governments, the centralists ultimately prevailed. Although in terms of formal structure the Weimar Republic was a federation, it was a polity destined to evolve in the direction of a decentralized unitary system.

The dynasty-based states of the Bismarck Reich were downgraded to "Länder" (literally: lands) and stripped of many of their former powers. The legislative prerogatives of the central government were greatly extended and, perhaps most important, the administrative jurisdiction of the Länder was curtailed in favor of the evolution of a growing central administrative apparatus. Increasingly, the Länder became dependent on funds provided by the central government in Berlin. The continued political dominance of Prussia, which after 1918 still had more inhabitants than all the other Länder combined, made a political equilibrium practically impossible. As a result, the Weimar Republic turned out to be a pseudo-federation—a polity in which the effective functioning of federal institutions was greatly weakened.[14]

In the Third Reich, finally, the Nazis were quick to drop any pretense of federalism. Since the Nazi ideology, which stood for an all-powerful party, a leader state, and the unconditional subordination of the individual and all groups, rejected the principle of the separation of powers, the remnants of federalism in Germany became a logical target. The *Gleichschaltungsgesetz* (Coordination Law) of March 31, 1933, effectively destroyed what remained of the federalist structure of the Weimar Republic and, together with the *Ermächtigungsgesetz* or "enabling legislation" of March 24, 1933, and the law on the new organization of the Reich of January 30, 1934, established the "legal" basis for the emergence of the totalitarian unitary state.

The Modern FRG Political Structure

The political structure of the FRG represents in many respects a compromise: first of all, between the various conceptions of the four Allied powers that controlled Germany after the war; and, second, between the different conceptions of the political parties recognized by the Allied authorities in 1949—conceptions that reflected the views of the members of the Parliamentary Council. With the sole exception of the KPD (Communist Party of Germany), none of the political parties opposed in principle the idea of a federal structure for postwar Germany. The conceptions of the Allies, on the other hand, reflected a much greater degree of division. Historically opposed to a strong and unified Germany, France, itself a centralistic unitary state, initially pursued an extreme policy of decentralization with respect to postwar Germany; the USSR declared itself opposed to any "forced federalization of Germany";[15] Great Britain prepared plans for a decentralized unitary state; and the United States, finally, advocated a federal state on the American model.

In the end, the Western occupation zones of Germany were reorganized as a *federative* state. The traditional German Länder were reestablished or reorganized to form the constituent "states" of the FRG—with the important exception of Prussia, whose destruction was one of the few things the Allies were able to agree on after the war. This approach reflected the political reality of continuing particularism in the southern part of Germany (Bavaria) and recognized historical traditions in the case of Hessen and Baden-Württemberg. But it posed problems elsewhere, particularly in the north, where former regional orientations and loyalties had been effectively destroyed by a century of Prussian hegemony. In the British occupation zone, therefore, artificial states had to be created. Only in the case of the two city-states—Hamburg and Bremen, the American enclave in the British occupation zone—did the territorial reorganization of the

northern part of postwar Germany coincide with historical tradition. The former Hanseatic city of Lübeck was incorporated into the state of Schleswig-Holstein. Similarly, the state of Rhineland-Palatinate (see map on p. 157) was created as an artificial unit after the war—from the former Bavarian province of Palatinate, Rhenish Prussia, and part of Hessen. The former Länder of Oldenburg, Braunschweig, and Schaumburg-Lippe—together with the remaining territory of the Prussian province of Hannover—came to constitute the new Land of Niedersachsen (Lower Saxony). North Rhine—Westphalia, the largest state in terms of population, was formed from the three northern administrative districts of the former Prussian Rhine province and the former Prussian province of Westphalia, as well as the old Land of Lippe.

Of particular interest is the case of the Saarland. Part of the French occupation zone, this area was organized as a formally independent state, but in effect was closely linked to France in terms of customs regulations, currency system, and other economic ties. As a result of a plebiscite, the Saarland reverted to the FRG politically in 1957—followed by its complete economic integration in 1959.

Thus—with the exception of Bavaria, by far the largest state in terms of territory, and the city-states of Bremen and Hamburg, by far the smallest and most heavily populated states (not counting West Berlin), whose traditional territorial boundaries remained largely intact—the constituent states of the FRG were established in a rather arbitrary manner.[16] As Table 15–1 shows, the constituent units of the FRG also vary greatly in terms of size, population, and population density.

Before the unification of Germany, the FRG consisted of eleven states, including West Berlin (see note 16). In the GDR, five states were formed initially partly along traditional lines; but in 1952 they were abolished and replaced by fourteen districts as part of the East German regime's drive to centralize its administrative framework. After the first free election in the former GDR on March 18, 1990, the parliament restored the five states. On October 3, 1990, the former GDR became part of the FRG and East Berlin and West Berlin were merged. The five former states of the GDR

Table 15–1   FRG Länder (States): Area and Population, 1991

Land	Area in Square Kilometers	Population in Thousands	Density per Square Kilometer
Baden-Württemberg	35,751	10,002	280
Bavaria	70,554	11,596	164
Berlin[a]	889	3,446	3,876
Brandenburg[b]	29,053	2,543	88
Bremen	404	684	1,691
Hamburg	755	1,669	2,209
Hessen	21,114	5,837	276
Lower Saxony	47,364	7,476	158
Mecklenburg-West Pomerania[b]	23,598	1,892	80
North Rhine-Westphalia	34,071	17,510	514
Rhineland-Palatinate	19,846	3,821	193
Saarland	2,570	1,077	419
Saxony[b]	18,338	4,679	255
Saxony-Anhalt[b]	20,443	2,823	138
Schleswig-Holstein	15,731	2,649	168
Thuringia[b]	16,251	2,572	158

[a]Former East Berlin and West Berlin combined.
[b]New states (former GDR).
Source: Stat. Jahrb. BRD, p. 50.

and a united Berlin thus became part of the federal structure of the united Germany.

Judged from the vantage point of the American model of federalism, the FRG emerges as a political order that in a good many respects is distinctly different. Thus, for example, in the FRG legislative power is largely exercised by the Bund, the federal government, while most administrative powers are exercised by the states, reflecting a kind of functional separation of powers.[17] Only in certain specified areas—for example, the foreign service, the federal finance administration, the federal railways, the federal postal services, federal waterways and shipping, and the federal defense forces—did the Basic Law call for direct federal administration with its own administrative structure.

In recent years, disenchantment with big government and bureaucracy has led to the partial or total privatization of telecommunications, the postal service and savings banks, the railway system, and Lufthansa, the state-operated airline. In the case of Germany, privatization, which is also going on at the state and local level, has been especially difficult because of the opposition of the public employees in these sectors of the economy, who did not want to lose their civil service status.

While the Basic Law merely stipulates that each state must have its own constitution, which "must conform to the principles of republican, democratic and social government based on the rule of law, within the meaning of this Basic Law," in fact much of the legislation passed by the states follows the example and parameters of so-called federal "framework laws." Moreover, through the Bundesrat—the Federal Council—the Länder ministers participate directly in the formulation of federal legislation.

Up to now it has not proved possible to reorganize the territory of the FRG into more balanced Länder units—a restructuring suggested in 1948 by the Allies and envisaged in Article 29 of the Basic Law. Only in the case of Baden–Württemberg did such restructuring take place. Subsequent efforts to reorganize the territory of the FRG along more equal and rational lines have failed—not so much because of strongly developed identities of the existing states as because of the resistance of individual politicians and firmly entrenched bureaucracies at the Länder level. As a result, relatively large and small states, predominantly rural and highly urbanized states, and rich and poor states coexist together. The great discrepancy in the economic and tax base of the different Länder of the FRG has given rise to a complicated system of revenue sharing between the states in order to create greater economic equalization throughout the FRG.

THE POLICY-MAKING INSTITUTIONS

In considering the policy-making institutions of the FRG, it is well to remember that, by comparison with countries like Great Britain or the United States, the institutional framework of the FRG is still comparatively young. Moreover, a number of factors combined to delay or slow down the development of stable political patterns in the FRG—for example, the assumed provisional character of the FRG during its initial history and the fact of continued Allied occupation (the FRG did not regain virtually full sovereignty until 1955!). Both the absence of a strong parliamentary tradition and the pronounced authoritarian leadership style of Konrad Adenauer, the first FRG chancellor, resulted in a decision-making process clearly dominated by the executive during the FRG's initial 14 years. After Adenauer's resignation as chancellor in October 1963, a different balance between the executive and legislative institutions gradually developed. The more assertive role of the Bundestag in national decision making and the changing role of the Bundesrat in recent years are among the most interesting and significant developments in the constitutional evolution of the FRG.

In taking the measure of the major policy-making institutions of the FRG, moreover, it should be remembered that, unlike Great Britain or France, the FRG is not a unitary state but rather a federation, in which the constituent states play an important role in national decision making, both within and outside the framework of the Bundesrat. The states, as a matter of fact, existed as viable and important political units before the establishment of the FRG in 1949. Today they not only reflect the regional diversity of the FRG, but also perform an important function in the balanced distribution of state power, both through their key role in the administration of federal law and through their direct role in national decision making in the Bundesrat.

Without exception, all of the major policy-making institutions in the FRG—the Federal Diet (Bundestag), the Federal Council (Bundesrat), and the Federal Government (*Bundesregierung*)—that is, the chancellor and the cabinet—have antecedents in the German political tradition, but they also reflect novel aspects and approaches. The same is true of the Federal President (*Bundespräsident*), who is the ceremonial head of state but lacks much effective political power.

We turn now to a discussion of the legislative institutions—the Bundestag and the Bundesrat. The executive institutions (the federal chancellor and cabinet), as well as the federal president, will be examined in greater detail in Chapter 17.

THE BUNDESTAG

Prior to reunification, the Bundestag consisted of 496 deputies, who were directly elected, and 22 delegates from West Berlin, who were indirectly elected. In the general election of 1990, the first all-German election in 58 years, in which West Germans and East Germans chose a single legislature, 662 Bundestag deputies were elected—319 representing the Christian Democratic Union/Christian Social Union (CDU/CSU), 79 representing the Free Democratic Party (FDP), the coalition partner of the CDU/CSU, and 239 representing the Social Democratic Party of Germany—that is, the opposition. The remaining 25 deputies (17 from the PDS, ex-SED, and 8 from the East German Greens) benefited from a once-only special electoral provision laid down by the Federal Constitutional Court in gaining representation in the Bundestag.

It was clearly the intention of the framers of the Basic Law to make the Bundestag the center of policy making. The 662 deputies or members of the Bundestag are the only political officials in the FRG to be directly elected. In the constitutional structure of the FRG, therefore, the Bundestag is the institution with the strongest political mandate. The authority and legitimacy of all other elected political officials and institutions are based on a mandate derived from indirect election. Moreover, under the Basic Law primary responsibility for the framing of legislation is vested in the Bundestag, which also elects and controls the federal government, elects half of the members of the Federal Constitutional Court (*Bundesverfassungsgericht*), and plays a key role in the supervision of the bureaucracy and the military.

During the years of 1949–63, the Bundestag stood very much in the shadow of the powerful first FRG chancellor, Konrad Adenauer, and functioned within the framework of what was called "chancellor democracy." Only in the post-Adenauer period did the Bundestag begin to function in accordance with its formal position in the constitutional framework of the FRG. The Bundestag faced the initial problem and difficult task of establishing its credentials as a vital and respected institution in the political framework of the FRG. Viewed from the perspective of the evolution of constitutionalism in Germany, the significance of the Bundestag lies in the fact that it breaks with the traditional structure of "negative parliamentarianism"—to use Max Weber's phrase—and marks the effective adherence of Germany to modern parliamentarianism.[18]

Because of the central role that the Bundestag, in accordance with the Basic Law, plays in the formation of the federal government and its continued existence, the Bundestag belongs with those parliamentary systems that fuse the legislative and executive functions and powers. In practice, of course, the liberal idea of parliament—rationally discussing questions of public policy with a view to the common good and acting as a body in the public interest—turns out to be a fiction in the case of the FRG, as elsewhere. Instead, the governing majority constitutes the effectively functioning unit, with its leadership taking over the key positions in the government (for example, the cabinet posts through appointment by the chancellor) and its political program serving as the basis for the legislative program of the federal government.

The function of checking the power of the governing majority is largely performed by the opposition. However, the vertical separation of powers between the Bundestag and the Bundesrat and the open process of the formation and dissemination of political opinions in general also contribute in important ways to the balancing of power. The result is a political system with complex relationships between the cabinet, the governing majority, and the opposition, as well as between the Bundestag, the Bundesrat, and the federal and state governments—relationships which cannot be encompassed in any concept of confrontation between legislative and executive. Taking the long view, moreover, the FRG has been a political system in which cooperation and coordination have played a more important role than confrontation, a system in which the political parties have aspired to codetermination rather than total control.

In view of the traditional place of Berlin in German history and culture, it comes as no surprise that the question of relocating the capital in Berlin was immediately raised when reunification became a realistic possibility. Shortly after unification it was decided that Berlin would be the capital of the united Germany; in 1991 the decision was made to relocate the government of the FRG in Berlin over a period of 10 years.

The deputies or members of the Bundestag constitute an important part of the political elite in the FRG. Almost all cabinet members (the ministers), all state secretaries (the political assistants of the ministers) and, most important, the chancellor are selected from its ranks. An examination of the socioeconomic and educational background of the Bundestag membership, therefore, should provide important insights into the prevailing values and patterns of the dominant elite culture and help to identify the leadership qualities held in high esteem by the FRG "selectorates," the relatively small groups of party leaders at the various levels of the political system who control the nomination process and thus play a decisive role in the recruitment of Bundestag members.

Important changes have taken place in the social composition of its members. Nearly half of the members of the first Bundestag were wage earners—manual workers and lower-level white-collar employees. By 1969, twenty years later, this group accounted for less than 15 percent of the deputies. Even the election victories of the SPD—something of a "people's party"—in 1969 and in subsequent years did not reverse this trend. In the twelfth Bundestag (1990–94), manual workers accounted for no more than 1.2 percent of the deputies—less than the share of housewives.[19] By contrast, two other groups have become increasingly prominent: civil servants and representatives of interest groups. These two occupational groups together have accounted for over 60 percent of the Bundestag members since the 1980s. Compared to their proportion in the population at large, they are greatly overrepresented and wield more political power and influence than any comparable group in the U.S. Congress or the British Parliament.

Parallel careers in the civil service and parliament have long been a characteristic of German politics. Unlike in Great Britain or the United States, where civil servants cannot run for public office without first resigning from the civil service, German civil servants may serve in parliament without losing their status as civil servants. As a matter of fact, there are powerful incentives for civil servants to run for public office. Any government employee who is a candidate for public office at the national, state, or local level, receives a 6-week leave of absence (at full pay) to participate in the election campaign. If his or her bid is successful, the leave of absence is extended to the end of the legislative term, with the civil servant continuing to receive full pension credit and "normal" promotions in the civil service while serving as a legislator. The civil servants in the Bundestag, therefore, become eligible for double retirement benefits—from the civil service and from parliament. Prior to a ruling by the Federal Constitutional Court in 1975, moreover, they even had their civil service salaries continued while serving in the Bundestag (or in state parliaments).

In addition to strong material incentives, the disproportional strength of the civil servants in the Bundestag also reflects an important trait or bias of German political culture—the tendency to equate politics and administration and to regard legal and administrative experience as the best preparation for political office. "The delegate conferences of the parties," in the words of an astute observer of German politics, "are inclined to impute to civil servants a special political competence, which has always led to an

overrepresentation of civil servants in the history of German parliaments."[20] It is thus for good reason that some commentators have referred to the Bundestag as a parliament of "administrative advisers" and described the civil servants in the Federal Assembly as the "fourth party" in parliament.[21]

The second most important group in the Bundestag is composed of the representatives of trade unions and other interest groups (21.9 percent in 1990–94), leaving manual workers, farmers, housewives, business people, and professionals decidedly underrepresented. In recent years, moreover, there has been a pronounced tendency toward an increase in the number of "professional politicians," that is, full-time party officials—a group which by 1980 accounted for more than 20 percent of the total Bundestag membership.[22] Perhaps even more significant is the fact that it is precisely these professional politicians who have by far the best prospects of becoming members of the elite political leadership. As of 1980, 49 percent of the professional politicians in the Bundestag held positions of political leadership, while the corresponding figure for the Bundestag membership as a whole was only 32 percent.[23]

Since 1949 the Bundestag, as a matter of fact, has become increasingly less representative of the FRG population as a whole. One indication is the steady increase in the educational level of the Bundestag deputies. By 1976, 95 percent of the deputies had received an education beyond the traditional 8-year *Volks-* or *Grundschule,* and close to one-third had earned a doctorate. This trend is likely to continue, since the younger, highly educated deputies with administrative training and management skills enjoy the highest success in reelection. As a result, the members of the Bundestag have become a more homogeneous professional elite, set apart from the general population by educational level and social background—a development which, no doubt, has contributed importantly to consensus politics at the elite level. On the other hand, this aspect of the political evolution of the FRG also illustrates the increasing difficulties faced by members of socially disadvantaged groups in gaining access to the decision-making institutions of the FRG.[24]

The smallest unit of the Bundestag is the individual deputy, who is guaranteed independence, immunity, and indemnity. As a rule, deputies are also members of a political party, whose general philosophy they share, whose political programs they endorse, and to which they owe loyalty because it nominated and supported them as candidates. In practice this means that the individual deputy exercises independence and freedom of action for the most part within the working groups and political circles of his or her party.

The parties in the Bundestag are organized into *Fraktionen,* groups or caucuses of parliament members belonging to the same party. If there are independent deputies who lack formal party affiliation, they are given "visiting rights" entitling them to join a Fraktion. The size of a party's Fraktion plays an important role because it determines the strength of its representation on the committees, its share of committee chairmanships, the assignment of clerical staff, the allocation of office space, and its representation on the powerful executive bodies of the Bundestag: the Council of Elders (*Ältestenrat*) and the Presidium.

Composed of the president of the Bundestag, who is a member of the largest Fraktion, the three vice presidents, and the twelve to fifteen representatives of all Fraktionen, the Council of Elders functions essentially as a steering committee, setting the agenda of the Bundestag, scheduling debates, establishing time limits, assigning committee chairmanships to each party in proportion to its strength in parliament, and playing a key role in determining the budget of the Bundestag. The Bundestag Presidium, which consists of the president and the vice-presidents, takes care of general administrative matters, such as the recruitment of clerical staff and research personnel, the physical facilities of the Bundestag, and the like. It is charged with the responsibility of promoting the work of the Bundestag and presiding over its sessions.

Another important organizing instrument of the Bundestag are the parliamentary committees, which play a more important role than their counterparts in Great Britain or France, but are not as significant or powerful as committees in the U.S. Congress. For one thing, they lack the large independent staffs of U.S. congressional committees and they cannot shelve or reject bills; they subject them to careful scrutiny, hear testimony and, if necessary, propose amendments to the plenary session of the Bundestag, but they must pass bills on to the full body. Both the composition and the leadership of the committees reflect the overall strength of the parties in the Bundestag. In contrast to the U.S. Congress, therefore, the German Bundestag follows a practice that gives the opposition its share of committee chairmanships.

Party discipline plays an important role in the Bundestag. Most votes tend to be straight party votes; deputies of the various parties follow the instructions of their parliamentary leader, the chairman of their Fraktion, or accept the outcome of the vote of a party caucus taken prior to an upcoming bill. There are few bills on which the deputies do not receive binding instructions from their party leadership. If a deputy finds it impossible to support his party on a particular and crucial issue, he is free to leave his Fraktion and join another, without losing his mandate during the current legislative term.

Institutionally, the Bundestag is the most important organ in the legislative process. Without its vote, no law can come into being. Along with the Bundesrat and the federal government, it has the right to initiate legislation. It also plays a decisive role in the issuing of statutory rules and orders, which it authorizes and whose repeal it can demand at any time. In actual practice, of course, the comprehensive jurisdiction of the Bundestag in legislative matters is a fiction—given the complexity of legislation in a modern industrial and social welfare state and the time pressures on the Bundestag created by the relentless dynamic of social change and technological progress. Consequently, as in parliaments elsewhere, the executive and administration have come to play a key role in the preparation of legislation.

Among the most important functions of the Bundestag is the election of the federal chancellor. In contrast to the procedure followed in the Weimar Republic, the Bundestag no longer elects individual ministers but only the chancellor, who then appoints the ministers of his cabinet. It goes without saying that the appointment of the cabinet ministers is not left solely to the discretion of the chancellor; it is rather the outcome of complex political negotiations between the chancellor and the leadership of his party.

Another vital function of the Bundestag is the control of the federal government and of the bureaucracy or administrative apparatus of the state. To this end, deputies have the right to subject individual members of the cabinet to oral questions in a regular "question hour" (limited to 60 or 90 minutes, usually at the beginning of a plenary session)—a practice borrowed from British parliamentary procedure.[25] Such questions may range from the registration of complaints by individual citizens through their deputies—often with an eye to the likely or predictable press coverage—to basic concerns about the general direction of government policy. One measure of the emancipation of the Bundestag from domination by the executive is the dramatic increase in the number of questions addressed to members of the cabinet by Bundestag deputies.

The practice of the question hour was extended in 1965 by the adoption of a so-called current hour (*Aktuelle Stunde*) in order to accommodate the interest, both inside and outside the Bundestag, in the discussion of urgent current political issues in parliament. This procedure involves a request by a group of deputies—usually from the opposition[26]—for a question period set aside specifically for the debate of an especially urgent issue. During the fifth and seventh Bundestag terms in particular deputies made extensive use of this new control device.[27]

In addition, deputies may submit written questions to the government, which can be answered in writing and entered into the record of the Bundestag. A "small inquiry" (requested by at least 15 deputies) does not require parliamentary debate; a "major inquiry" (submitted by at least 30 deputies) requires a full-scale parliamentary debate.

Like the U.S. Congress, the German Bundestag has the power to investigate specific areas of government activity. It can subpoena any government or state official and, upon the request of one-fourth of the Bundestag deputies, an investigating committee must be established. However, the composition of such committees reflects party strength in the Bundestag as a whole—a severe drawback to the potential effectiveness of an investigation of the government. The weak tradition with respect to parliamentary investigation in Germany, the inadequate staffing of Bundestag committees, the cultural deference to the executive, and the traditional awe of the state bureau-

cracy limit the use and effectiveness of this control instrument.

The ultimate control device available to the Bundestag, as to other genuine parliaments, is the formal vote of no confidence in the government (the chancellor and cabinet). Generally speaking, in a parliamentary system the tenure of the political executive depends on its ability to retain at least the passive support of the majority of the lower house of parliament. The loss of this support is either expressed by the refusal of the lower house to pass a major bill initiated by the executive, or by its approval of a motion of censure or no confidence against the government. Whenever a lack of confidence is expressed in one of these ways, the government is generally expected to resign.

The requirement or practice according to which the tenure of the government is dependent on the support of a majority in the legislature is based on sound logical and practical reason: It helps to avoid political stalemate and prolonged political immobility. Cabinet responsibility to the lower house of parliament, therefore, makes good sense and in fact defines the outer limits of executive power and discretion. If for any reason a cabinet loses the requisite support in parliament, its political position becomes untenable and it is ultimately forced to resign—whether it is required to do so by formal legal rules or by constitutional practice and tradition. This explains why, for example, the Swedish and Dutch cabinets have always resigned when confronted with the loss of support in parliament—even though they are not legally required to do so.[28]

The provisions of the Basic Law governing the positive or constructive no-confidence vote in Germany stipulate that, if the Bundestag tries to oust a chancellor and his cabinet and fails, the chancellor may ask the president to dissolve the Bundestag, setting the stage for new elections.[29] Because of the inherent difficulty of this process, the no-confidence procedure has been used only three times: once unsuccessfully against Chancellor Willy Brandt, and once successfully against Chancellor Helmut Schmidt. In the aftermath of the breakup of the SPD-FDP coalition government of Helmut Schmidt, a "stage-managed" vote of no-confidence was used by the new CDU/CSU–FDP coalition to enable the new chancellor, Helmut Kohl, to call for new elections at an early date. Whether the constructive no-confidence vote will ever make the contribution to political stability in Germany envisaged by the framers of the Basic Law remains to be seen. One of its obvious disadvantages is that it forces the party leaders to conspire behind the back of a reigning chancellor in order to reach agreement on a possible successor—a kind of throwback to the early days of constitutionalism.

The Bundestag has become increasingly assertive and independent—a development that augurs well for the future of democracy in Germany. The provisions of a parliamentary reform bill passed in 1969 require the government to submit preliminary drafts of proposed legislation to the Bundestag, advance drafts of its annual reports on the economy and the "state of the nation," as well as other important information. Public committee hearings have become much more common since 1965. Since 1970 the Bundestag deputies have enjoyed greatly improved research facilities, reference services, an enlarged parliamentary staff, and generally better working conditions. Television coverage of important Bundestag sessions has brought its proceedings closer to the public—a trend likely to increase with the spread of cable television.[30]

The 1990 Bundestag Election

In the first all-German general election to be held since 1932, Chancellor Helmut Kohl was not only reelected for his third term, but became the first chancellor of a united Germany. His CDU/CSU–FDP coalition did well in both West and East Germany. It won 43.8 percent of the vote (44.3 percent in West and 41.8 in East Germany). The FDP, led by Otto Lambsdorff and Foreign Minister Hans-Dietrich Genscher, won 11 percent of the vote (10.6 percent in West and 12.9 percent in East Germany)—its best showing in decades. The SPD, on the other hand, did poorly in the first all-German election in nearly two generations. Nationwide it won only 33.5 percent of the vote (35.7 percent in West and 24.3 percent in East Germany). The Greens did not win the required 5 percent of the vote to be represented in the Bundestag. Two other minor parties—the PDS, the

ex-SED (Socialist Unity Party of Germany), and the East German Greens, representing the political groups that were instrumental in bringing about the peaceful revolution in the GDR—won representation in the Bundestag, but only because of a special electoral provision for the 1990 election.

The 1994 Bundestag Election

In 1994 Germany experienced a veritable election marathon. In addition to the second national election to the Bundestag since unification, elections to the European parliament, and the election of a new president by a special Federal Assembly consisting of an equal number of representatives of the Bundestag and the federal states, there were eighteen state parliament and local government elections. At the national level (our focus here), the ruling CDU/CSU–FDP coalition suffered a major defeat at the polls, barely managing to stay in power with 48.4 percent of the vote (compared to 54.8 percent in 1990). This means that, during his unprecedented fourth term, Chancellor Helmut Kohl only had a majority of ten seats in the Bundestag (compared to 134 in 1990). Various explanations have been given for this election outcome, ranging from ennui with the present coalition, disenchantment over the pace, difficulty, and cost of unification, to high unemployment, increased taxes, rising state debts, crime, the problem of refugees and foreigners in Germany, and, above all, the government's (mis)handling of the economy.

The results of the 1994 Bundestag election are summarized and compared with the 1990 election in Table 15–2.

In the 1994 Bundestag, 177 of the 672 deputies (26.3 percent) were women—5.6 percent more than in the 1990 Bundestag. Of the political parties represented in the Bundestag, the Alliance 90/Green delegation had the proportionally highest number of women (29 of 49); the FDP delegation had the proportionally smallest number (9 of 47). Following the narrow election victory of his party, Helmut Kohl was reelected by a landslide as chairman of his party, but when the Bundestag voted on his election as chancellor he received only 338 votes—one vote more than he needed. This means that three members

Table 15-2 Comparison of the 1990, 1994, and 1998 Bundestag Elections

Party	1990		1994				1998			
	Percentage of Vote	Number of Seats	Change Percentage	Percentage of Vote	Number of Seats	Change Number	Change Percentage	Percentage of Vote	Number of Seats	Change Number
CDU	36.7%	268[a]	-2.5%	34.2%	244[b]	-24	-5.8%	28.4%	198	-46
CSU	7.1	51	+0.2	7.3	50	-1	-0.6	6.7	47	-3
FDP	11.0	79	-4.1	6.9	47	-32	-0.7	6.2	43	-4
Total	54.8	398	-6.4	48.4	341	-57	-7.1	41.3	288	-53
SPD	33.5	239	+2.9	36.4	252[c]	+13	+4.5	40.9	298[d]	-46
Alliance 90/ Greens	3.8/1.2	8	+2.3	7.3	49	+41	-0.6	6.7	47	-2
PDS	2.4	17	+2.0	4.4	30	+13	+0.7	5.1	36	+6
Total	40.9	264	+7.2	48.1	331	+67	+3.9	47.6	345	+44

[a]Includes 8 "overhang mandates."
[b]Includes 12 "overhang mandates."
[c]Includes 4 "overhang mandates."
[d]Includes 13 "overhang mandates."

Note: "Overhang mandates" (*Überhangmandate*) come into being when a party wins more seats in the "first ballot" voting than it would be entitled to under strict proportional representation. These additional seats are called "overhang" mandates. The Bundestag ordinarily has 656 members, but its membership increases if there are "overhang" mandates. Thus, the Bundestag elected in 1994 had 672 members, and the Bundestag elected in 1998 has 669 members.

of his ruling CDU/CSU–FDP coalition voted against him.

The 1998 Bundestag Election

The 14th Bundestag election on September 27, 1998, was unique in that, for the first time in the history of the FRG, a change of government was brought about by the direct votes of the German electorate. The election resulted in the worst showing of the Christian Democratic Party since the first election in 1949, when it gained the support of 25.2 percent of the voters. Its permanent coalition partner, the CSU, too, lost ground in this election, gaining only 47 seats in the Bundestag—the lowest number since 1949. Nearly 50 million voters (82.2 percent) of the eligible electorate took part in the election, which, in addition to the six parties represented in the Bundestag, was contested by thirty-four minor political parties and movements. With the defeat of the CDU/CSU-FDP coalition, Germany joined France, Great Britain, and Italy—all of which by the time of the German elections were ruled by left-of-center parties, Spain being the only exception of a major West European country differing from this pattern.

The defeat of the conservatives in Germany did not come as a surprise. Their electoral fortunes had been in decline for a number of years, as reflected in the 1994 national elections (see Table 15–2). Public opinion surveys conducted prior to the elections indicated the growing disenchantment of German voters with the policies of the Kohl government, especially in the new eastern states, which have continued to experience high unemployment.

For Helmut Kohl, the "unity chancellor," who headed the CDU for 27 years and served as head of government for 16 years, i.e., longer than any German chancellor, it was a bitter defeat. As it turned out, he suffered defeat not only in the national election, but also lost his direct mandate in Ludwigshafen to SPD-candidate Doris Barnett. In spite of his electoral defeat, Chancellor Kohl will be remembered by Germans and other Europeans as an exceedingly capable leader, determined to promote European integration and cooperation. His achievements in this regard were recognized in December 1998, when he was

given the title of "Honorary Citizen of Europe"—the highest award of the European Union, given by the heads of state and heads of government of the EU member states. Chancellor Kohl was only the second person, besides Jean Monnet, to receive this honor.

Unfortunately, Chancellor Kohl's extraordinary political career came under a cloud in the fall of 1999, a few weeks after he had been voted one of the top ten "greatest Germans" of all time by his people—alongside Luther, Goethe, and Einstein. At the center of Germany's biggest political corruption scandal since 1949, Kohl admitted accepting $1 million in unreported party donations and thus violating a strict party-financing law. The subject of a criminal investigation, he was forced to resign as honorary chairman of the CDU and, if found guilty, may have to serve a five-year prison sentence. At the time of this writing, the full dimensions of the scandal are still unfolding, engulfing other members of the CDU/CSU and threatening to bring down the party which has dominated German politics since the establishment of the Federal Republic in 1949. The ramifications of this scandal and others involving SPD politicians are so far-reaching that the entire party system faces an uncertain future. According to the Federal Criminal Office, 2,400 cases of corruption were investigated in 1998—twice as many as in 1995. Thus, Germany, it would seem, is following the example of France and Italy.

Kohl's successor, Gerhard Schröder, has had his eyes on the post of chancellor since 1982, when reportedly one night he went to the chancellery building, shook the fence surrounding it, and yelled: "I want to get into this place." He is a seasoned politician, who joined the SPD at the age of 19 and most recently served as minister president of the state of Lower Saxony. At age 54, he represents a new generation of politicians and sees himself as a modernizer. Self-confident and very ambitious, he has been something of a maverick in the highest echelons of the SPD. Like President Clinton and Prime Minister Blair in their respective political arenas, he is likely to steer a middle course between the traditional social democratic doctrines of the Left and the free-market-oriented ideology of the Right. As Table 15–2 indicates, his "Red-Green" coalition has a comfortable margin of 57 votes in the 669-member Bundestag. It stands to reason that on a good many issues the PDS will also support his government.

THE BUNDESRAT

The Bundesrat (Federal Council), the second chamber in the FRG parliament, incorporates the federative principle on which the FRG is based and thus serves as a political counterweight to the Bundestag. It is not elected, however, and thus lacks a mandate equivalent to that of the Bundestag. It is composed of ministers of the state governments or their delegates, who are appointed and recalled by the state governments. Although the power relationship among the political parties is generally not reflected directly in the Bundesrat, this unique constitutional organ nevertheless frequently becomes the arena of party politics. The government and the Bundestag as a rule pursue a similar political course—a reflection of the fact that the government has majority support in the Bundestag—and enjoy a very close day-to-day working relationship. The Bundesrat, however, assuming the requisite difference in the political complexion of its membership from that of the Bundestag, becomes the likely instrument in the hands of the parliamentary opposition for attempts to block or impede the policies of the ruling majority or coalition.

Including the representatives of Berlin, the Bundesrat has 69 members. Every state has at least three votes; states with more than 2 million inhabitants have four votes, states with more than 6 million inhabitants have five votes, and states with more than 7 million inhabitants have 6 votes. Every state is entitled to as many Bundesrat members as it has votes. Accordingly, the composition of the Bundesrat is as shown in Table 15–3.

The Bundesrat members are delegates of the state governments and as such are bound by the instructions of their respective state cabinets—except when they serve as members of the *Vermittlungsausschuss,* a mediation committee consisting of sixteen members of the Bundesrat (one from each state) and sixteen members of the Bundestag.[31] Bundesrat members cannot cast sep-

Table 15–3 Composition of the Bundesrat by States and Number of Members, 1990

Länder (States)	Number of Members
Baden-Württemberg	6
Bavaria	6
Berlin	4
Brandenburg	4
Bremen	3
Hamburg	3
Hessen	5
Lower Saxony	6
Mecklenburg–Western Pomerania	3
North Rhine-Westphalia	6
Rhineland-Palatinate	4
Saarland	3
Saxony	4
Saxony–Anhalt	4
Schleswig-Holstein	4
Thuringia	4
Total	69

arate votes; instead, the members from a given state must vote as a bloc. According to the Bundesrat's own rules of procedure, a Bundestag mandate is incompatible with membership in the Bundesrat. Members of the Bundesrat typically carry a number of different responsibilities; they are not only members of their respective state governments but, as a rule, also members of their state parliaments. Furthermore, many of them hold important positions in leading organs of their party. Taken together, these multiple responsibilities constitute a considerable workload for members—a circumstance that has not always had a positive effect on their activity in the Bundesrat.

The Bundesrat is an autonomous chamber. It chooses its own president from among the minister presidents, the "prime ministers," of the states in accordance with an annual rotation system established in 1950, thus allowing each state to have a hand in the presidency of the Bundesrat on a regular basis[32] and it determines its own rules of procedure. The president convenes the Bundesrat and chairs its plenary sessions. If for any reason the federal president cannot carry out the duties of his office, the Bundesrat president takes his place and becomes head of state in the FRG. The establishment of a regular rotation system for the election of the Bundesrat president has tended to depoliticize this office, complementing the essential role of the Bundesrat as the institution representing the interests of the states.

Generally speaking, the deliberations of the Bundesrat are public. Like the Bundestag and parliamentary bodies in general, the Bundesrat has found it desirable and necessary to form committees, whose membership may include other members or delegates of the state governments. For the most part, the structure of the sixteen Permanent Committees of the Bundesrat has evolved to correspond to the ministries of the federal government. It is in these committees, in which each state has one vote, that the bulk of the work of the Bundesrat is done. To deal with urgent and confidential issues involving the European Union, the Bundesrat, according to the Basic Law (Art. 52), can also form a "Europe Chamber" (*Europakammer*), consisting of 16 Länder representatives, with the right to make independent decisions for the Bundesrat. This chamber, established in 1988, is formed only at the express request of the Bundesrat president. In February 1993, furthermore, the Länder, in order to achieve better coordination of their various interests in European integration, established a special conference for Land ministers specializing in this policy sphere.

The Bundesrat elects three vice presidents (by a rotation system, with the outgoing president always becoming the first vice president) and two secretaries—again for one-year terms. The president and the vice presidents form the Presidium, which advises the president. There is also a permanent advisory body (*Ständiger Beirat*), which advises the president and assists in the preparation of the sessions. It is composed of plenipotentiaries of the states who are stationed in Bonn, or civil servants who have been authorized to represent the various states in the capital.

Formal decisions are made by the Bundesrat in regular plenary sessions by an absolute majority vote. In the case of impeachment proceedings against a federal president, and when voting on amendments to the Basic Law, however, a qualified two-thirds majority is required. Plenary sessions for the most part serve largely a ratification function—the necessity for extensive debate

having been obviated by thorough preparatory work in the sixteen Permanent Committees of the Bundesrat.

In terms of prestige and public interest, the Bundesrat is clearly overshadowed by the Bundestag—a fact reflected in the inaugural addresses by most of the Bundesrat presidents over the years.[33] Nonetheless, the actual constitutional role and political significance of the Bundesrat is far greater than its public image suggests. Although its position in the legislative process and constitutional framework generally is not as strong as that of the U.S. Senate or the much earlier Federal Council (Bundesrat) of the Second German Empire of 1871, the FRG Bundesrat nevertheless is more powerful than the House of Lords in Britain or the upper house in France or Italy.

The power of the Bundesrat, as well as its specific function and competence, are mainly based on Article 50 of the Basic Law, according to which "the Länder shall participate through the Bundesrat in the legislation and administration of the Federation." Accordingly, the Bundesrat plays an important part in the legislative and executive power of the Federation. As a matter of fact, by virtue of its overall constitutional authority, the Bundesrat is the most important constitutional organ of the Federation after the Bundestag. More specifically, the power and authority of the Bundesrat derive from the principle that it must give its consent to any law affecting the interests of the states. In 1997 almost two-thirds of all laws fell into the category of *consent* laws.

In the case of laws for which Bundesrat approval is not mandatory, the Bundesrat has the right of objection. This objection, however, is not absolute; it can be overruled by the Bundestag. Before the Bundesrat can exercise its right of objection, a mediation committee (consisting of thirty-two members, sixteen members from each chamber) must be convened. In most cases, mediation committees succeed in working out acceptable compromises.

Finally, the Bundesrat has the right to initiate legislation, but it does not make very frequent use of this right. The Bundesrat also has the power to initiate impeachment proceedings against the federal president and plays an important role in the determination of violations by the Länder in the execution of federal laws. Last, but not least, the Bundesrat plays a key role in the administration of federal law. Thus, for example, general administrative rules may be issued by the federal government only with Bundesrat approval.

The Bundesrat is a unique institution in terms of its structure and functions. Based on the single-will doctrine, a state cannot have two contradictory wills and, therefore, the votes of the representatives of each of the constituent states must be cast as a bloc. While the Bundesrat has some of the attributes of a second chamber, it lacks one of the essential requirements, namely, independence; its members are not directly elected but are appointed, and they are subject to binding instructions by their respective Land governments. Moreover, because the representation of the Länder is effected through appointed members of the state governments (council principle) rather than through representatives elected by the people or by the Länder parliaments (senate principle), we have the unique situation of the attribution of legislative functions to representatives of the executive in a parliamentary system.

THE FEDERAL CONSTITUTIONAL COURT

Our discussion of the political framework of the FRG would be incomplete without mentioning the Federal Constitutional Court. This institution, for which there is no counterpart in German political life and experience prior to the establishment of the FRG, is the guardian of the Basic Law. Not only the highest court of the land, it is a constitutional body independent of all other constitutional organs, such as the Bundestag, the Bundesrat, the federal president, or the federal government, and is equal to them in status.

The jurisdiction of the Federal Constitutional Court is set forth in Article 93 of the Basic Law. The Court rules in disputes between the federation and the states, in cases involving the rights and duties of the supreme federal organs, in disputes between the states, in disputes involving public law within a state (unless recourse to another court exists), and in disputes involving the

compatibility of state law with the Basic Law or with other federal law. In addition, the Federal Constitutional Court rules on complaints about the scrutiny of elections by the Bundestag and the compatibility of statutory law with the Basic Law, as well as cases involving the rights and duties of FRG citizens arising under Article 25 of the Basic Law from public international law (Article 100). Finally, since 1969 individual citizens of the FRG, as well as communes (municipalities) or associations of communes, have the right to turn to the Federal Constitutional Court with a constitutional complaint if they feel that their rights under the Basic Law have been violated by public authority or that their right to self-government has been infringed and recourse to a state constitutional court is not available.

Looking at the actual caseload of the Federal Constitutional Court, we see that constitutional complaints account for the overwhelming majority of cases. Of the over 35,000 cases considered by the Federal Constitutional Court by 1976, over 33,000 were constitutional complaints.[34] Cases involving the standardization of legal norms in the FRG constitute the second largest category. Most surprising, perhaps, is the very small number of disputes between the federation and the states—only ten during the first 25 years of the Court's existence.

Within these broad areas of jurisdiction, the Federal Constitutional Court acts only if cases are brought before it by certain bodies or organs, such as the federal government, the state governments, the Bundesrat or the Bundestag, the lower courts, or—in the case of constitutional complaints—by individuals or communes. Since it assumed its work in 1951, the Federal Constitutional Court has overturned some important laws and put a restrictive interpretation on interstate treaties. While it has not sought explicitly to shape the direction of political action of the various state bodies, it has nevertheless had a major impact on the evolution of politics in the FRG. Clearly the Federal Constitutional Court has played a major role in giving substance to the fundamental rights guaranteed in the Basic Law.

Situated in Karlsruhe, the Federal Constitutional Court consists of two senates, each of which has eight judges. Half of the judges are elected by the Bundestag, the other half by the

Bundesrat.[35] The term of office is 12 years. Judges must be at least 40 years of age and may serve until age 68, but cannot be reelected. While serving on the Federal Constitutional Court, judges may not be members of the Bundestag, the Bundesrat, the federal government, or a corresponding institution at the state level. The only professional activity regarded as compatible with the position of a judge on the Federal Constitutional Court is that of a law school professor.

Not surprisingly, the Federal Constitutional Court has become the most political court in the FRG, representing, as it does, a major constitutional innovation clearly marking Germany's departure from the continental legal tradition that rejects the principle of judicial review and limits the role of judges to the mere administration of the law (legal positivism). While Germany's other state and national courts are administratively subordinated to their respective ministries of justice, the Federal Constitutional Court, as a constitutional organ, is completely independent. It has its own budget and, like the Bundestag and Bundesrat, negotiates directly with the Ministry of Finance and the relevant parliamentary committees. Justices of the Federal Constitutional Court cannot be impeached by the FRG parliament; they can only be removed by the federal president at the request of the Federal Constitutional Court itself. Since it began functioning in 1951, the Federal Constitutional Court has not only established itself as the supreme arbiter of the Basic Law, but has recognized certain fundamental principles, such as democracy, the rule of law, and federalism, as having a higher legitimacy than constitutional or ordinary legal provisions, thus clearly abandoning the traditional legal positivism prevalent in German history prior to 1949. Fiercely independent, it has not hesitated to make use of its power. During the first four decades of its existence, it struck down laws and regulations in close to 800 cases involving the constitutionality of legislation at the state and federal level. More than half of the Basic Law's articles have now been interpreted by the Federal Constitutional Court in more than 2,000 cases. According to a survey conducted in 1994, the court enjoys more trust than any other public institution.[36]

The political framework of the FRG also includes an elaborate court system. This system, along with the role of the major political parties, the civil service, and the executive, will be discussed in Chapter 17.

NOTES

[1] See the Preamble to the Basic Law, in Guido Goldman, *The German Political System* (New York: Random House, 1974), Appendix C, p. 157.

[2] As a matter of fact, the Parliamentary Council that drafted the Basic Law was convened under Allied pressure. German political leaders were reluctant to proceed with the establishment of a separate German state because they rightly feared that such a development would result in the permanent division of Germany. In the end they yielded to an Allied ultimatum. See K. S. Pinson, *Modern Germany: Its History and Civilization,* 2nd ed: (New York: Macmillan Co., 1966).

[3] On the history of the establishment of the FRG, see P. H. Merkl, *The Origin of the West German Republic* (New York: Oxford University Press, 1963); K. Niklauss, *Demokratiengründung in Westdeutschland. Die Entstehung der Bundesrepublik von 1945–1949* (Munich: Piper, 1974); and J. F. Golay, *The Founding of the Federal Republic of Germany* (Chicago: University of Chicago Press, 1958).

[4] Between 1919 and 1933 a total of seven major political parties and many small splinter parties were represented in the Reichstag. See Hagen Schulze, *Die Deutschen und ihre Nation.* Weimar: Deutschland 1917–1933 (Berlin: Severin und Siedler, 1982), pp. 67ff.

[5] According to a national survey conducted in 1949, only 51 percent of the population in the Western occupation zones were in favor of the creation of the FRG; 23 percent opposed it, 13 percent were undecided. See Institut für Demoskopie, *Jahrbuch der öffentlichen Meinung, 1947–1955,* vol. I (Allensbach: Verlag für Demoskopie, 1956), p. 161.

[6] The Parliamentary Council, convened on September 1, 1948, to draft the Basic Law, consisted of 65 delegates, elected by the Landtage (state parliaments) and each representing approximately 750,000 inhabitants, as well as five observers from West Berlin. State (Land) representation among the delegates was based on each state's share of the total population. In terms of party affiliation, the breakdown is as follows: Social Democrats (SPD)—27; Christian Democrats and Christian Socialists (CDU/CSU)—27; Free German Party (FDP)—5; Center Party—2; German Party—2; and Communist Party of Germany (KPD)—2.

[7] Under the Constitution of the Weimar Republic, the president was elected directly by the people—an arrangement that enabled him to claim a popular mandate, if need be, against the popularly elected legislature (*Reichstag*). Under the Basic Law, the president is elected indirectly, by an absolute majority of the Federal Assembly, a special organ consisting of the members of the lower house (*Bundestag*) and an equal number of members selected by the *Landtage* (state parliaments), using the proportional system, in accordance with their political party composition at the time.

[8] On the Federal Constitutional Court, see D. P. Kommers, *Judicial Politics in West Germany: A Study of the Federal Constitutional Court* (Beverly Hills, CA: Sage Publications,

1976) and H. Saecker, *Das Bundesverfassungsgericht. Status—Funktion—Rechtsprechungsbeispiele* (Munich: Beck, 1975).

[9]Between the beginning of the activity of the Federal Constitutional Court in 1951 and December 1976, constitutional complaints accounted for 94.2 percent of the total case load. See Werner Billing, "Bundesverfassungsgericht," in ed. K. Sontheimer and H. H. Röhring, *Handbuch des politischen Systems der Bundesrepublik Deutschland* (Munich: R. Piper & Co., Verlag, 1978), p. 136.

[10]Institut für Demoskopie, *Jahrbuch der öffentlichen Meinung, 1968–1973*, vol. 5 (Allensbach: Verlag für Demoskopie, 1975), p. 227.

[11]On federalism as a principle of state organization and the history of the concept, see Ernst Deuerlein, *Föderalismus: Die historischen und philosophischen Grundlagen des föderativen Prinzips* (Bonn: Bundeszentrale für politische Bildung, 1972).

[12]Heinz Laufer, *Das föderative System der Bundesrepublik Deutschland* 3rd ed. (Munich: Bayerische Landeszentrale für politische Bildung, 1977), p. 21.

[13]The idea of a Danube Federation was proposed by Kurt Eisner, the Bavarian prime minister, to Thomas Masaryk, the president of the new Czechoslovak state, and to Karl Renner, the state chancellor of Austria. Nothing came of this idea—in part because of massive pressure from the Reich government in Berlin, which even threatened to use military force. (See Laufer, *Das föderative System*, p. 33.)

[14]Ibid., pp. 32–37. See also Hagen Schulze, *Die Deutschen und ihre Nation*, pp. 90ff.

[15]Declaration by the Soviet foreign minister, Molotov, on March 22, 1947.

[16]Strictly speaking, West Berlin was not part of the territory of the FRG and, therefore, not one of its *Länder* (states). De facto, however, it was regarded and treated as a state.

[17]See P. H. Merkl, "Executive-Legislative Federalism in West Germany," *American Political Science Review* 53, no. 3 (September 1959): 732–741.

[18]The first formal attempt to overcome the tradition of "negative parliamentarianism" was made in the Weimar Constitution of 1919. While affirming the principle of popular sovereignty, this constitution, however, did not grant the central political position to the Reichstag, that is, to the lower house, which is the hallmark of modern parliaments, and assigned important powers to the president of the Reich, creating in effect a dual executive (president and chancellor plus cabinet).

[19]*Daten Report 5*, p. 178.

[20]Klaus von Beyme, *Das politische System der Bundesrepublik Deutschland* (Munich: R. Piper & Co. Verlag, 1981), p. 133. On this point, see also Gerhard Loewenberg, *Parliament in the German Political System* (Ithaca, NY: Cornell University Press, 1967), p. 46.

[21]Rolf Zundel, "Ein Parlament der Regierungsräte," *Die Zeit*, no. 48 (November 28, 1969): 12.

[22]See Heino Kaack, "Zur Struktur der politischen Führungselite in Parteien, Parlament und Regierung," in *Handbuch des deutschen Parteiensystems*, H. Kaack and R. Roth, ed. (Opladen: Leske Verlag & Budrich GmbH, 1980), p. 215.

[23]See Table 8 in ibid., p. 214.

[24]This phenomenon of the increasing unrepresentativeness of parliamentarians and the growing "access" difficulties of nonelite groups is by no means confined to the FRG, but is generally found in Western democracies—for example, in the United States, Great Britain, and Italy. See Robert D. Putnam, *The Comparative Study of Political Elites* (Englewood Cliffs, NJ: Prentice-Hall, 1976), pp. 22–23.

[25]P. Schindler, "Die Fragestunde des Deutschen Bundestags," *Politische Vierteljahresschrift* 7 (1966): 407ff.

[26]During the Seventh Bundestag (1972–76), for example, 69 percent of the questions came from the CDU/DSU Fraktion, 27 percent from the SPD, and 4 percent from the FDP.

[27]See Klaus von Beyme, *Das politische System*, p. 158; K. Sontheimer, "Fragestunde/Aktuelle Stunde," in eds. K. Sontheimer and H. H. Röhring, *Handbuch*, pp. 200–202.

[28]In 1967, finally, Sweden, too, adopted the formal constitutional requirement that the tenure of the Cabinet is contingent upon the confidence of the majority in parliament (*Riksdag*). In the Netherlands the Cabinet is not legally required to resign—even if it loses the support of parliament (*Tweed Kamer*).

[29]For details, see Article 68 of the Basic Law.

[30]For a discussion of the plans for the introduction of cable TV—the subject of a long and acrimonious debate—see the article by H. A. Griesser, in *Die Welt*, April 30, 1983, Supplement, p. 1.

[31]On the Bundesrat, see Dr. Gebhard Ziller, *Der Bundesrat* (Düsseldorf: Droste-Verlag, 1979); F. K. Fromme, *Gesetzgebung im Widerstreit: Wer beherrscht den Bundesrat? Die Kontroverse seit 1969* (Stuttgart: Verlag Bonn Aktuell GmbH, 1980); Heinz Laufer, *Der Bundesrat: Untersuchung über Zusammensetzung, Arbeitsweise, politische Rolle und Reformprobleme* (Bonn: Bundeszentrale für politische Bildung, 1972).

[32]The autonomy of the Bundesrat was tested during the election of its very first president by Adenauer's attempted and unsuccessful intervention. See Laufer, *Das föderative System*, pp. 52–53.

[33]See Alois Rummel, *Föderalismus in der Bewährung. Antrittsreden und Amtsperioden der Bundesratspräsidenten 1949–1974* (Stuttgart: Verlag Bonn Aktuell GmbH, 1974).

[34]See Werner Billing, "Bundesverfassungsgericht," in K. Sontheimer and H. H. Röhring, ed., *Handbuch*, p. 136.

[35]In the case of the Bundesrat, the vote is by two-thirds majority of the plenum. The Bundestag election takes place through a twelve-member electoral committee elected proportionally from the Bundestag, again by two-thirds majority vote.

[36]General Social Survey (ALLBUS), 1994, pp. 104–123.

Chapter 16

Political Participation:
The German Citizen in Politics

When the FRG was established in 1949, many observers of German politics were highly skeptical about the prospects of Germany's second experiment with democratic institutions. There were sound reasons for their skepticism at the time. In 1949 it was impossible even to imagine the miraculous economic recovery of Germany—on both sides of the Iron Curtain, but especially in West Germany. No one could have predicted the era of stable politics and comparatively rapid economic recovery that was so instrumental in preparing the ground for the consolidation of the FRG. As a matter of fact, the evident lack of popular enthusiasm with which Germans of the Western occupation zones greeted the establishment of the FRG seemed to confirm the worst fears of many German and foreign political leaders: that the FRG would suffer the same fate as the Weimar Republic and fail because of lack of popular support.

Such skepticism was justified in 1949. The Germans were still faced with the historically unresolved problem of creating a link between their sense of national identity in terms of ethnicity, language, and culture, and their commitment to a particular form of government and political system. In 1949 this was an especially difficult problem because of the officially proclaimed provisional character of their new state and the division of their country. During the initial years of the FRG's existence, the West Germans were asked by their political leaders to perform the unlikely feat of developing a strong identification with liberal democratic values without becoming unduly attached to the FRG as a state—the assumption being that eventually all Germans would be reunited in a single democratic entity. At the same time, the West Germans somehow had to make sense out of the claim put forth by their "provisional" government that the FRG—in spite of the existence of another German state on German territory and because of the lack of free elections in this "other Germany"—was the sole legitimate successor of the German Reich and the only legitimate voice and representative for all Germans.

The apolitical stance on the part of the majority of Germans during the postwar period was not only a reaction to the Nazi regime and the consequence of the general disenchantment with politics; it also reflected the lack of a well-established tradition of democratic participation. Here we are dealing with an important aspect of the basic discontinuity of German history: The succession of four so completely different and even contradictory political systems and social orders as those of imperial Germany, the Weimar Republic, the Nazi regime, and the FRG within a single century militated against the development of a stable tradition of democratic values, modes of behavior, and procedures.

The mass retreat by postwar Germans into their own private lives enhanced the freedom of the political elites, but it also limited the degree of political participation in Germany's new democratic order and impeded the development of a strong identification of the citizens with this new order. For many years after the war, the German people's experience of "nationalism" under the Nazi regime and the fact of the division of Germany combined to create a powerful obstacle to a sense of national identity.

In time, however, the awareness of common ethnic, cultural, and historical bonds linking Germans on both sides of the Iron Curtain became progressively weaker. In the case of many West Germans, it receded so far in their consciousness that the existence of Germans on the other side of the border—Germans who were vividly perceived as "our brothers and sisters" only a few decades ago—was all but forgotten. Increasingly, the GDR was perceived as *Ausland,* a foreign country, by the citizens of West Germany, in particular by its young people. Correspondingly, to the extent to which citizens of the FRG rediscovered a German national community and a sense of national identity, they came to identify themselves with the FRG.

Thus, public opinion polls registered a steady decline in the priority Germans assigned to the question of reunification. Furthermore, FRG citizens tended to draw an increasingly sharp distinction between their society and the GDR. According to a 1971 study, FRG citizens described their country as a society allowing a great deal of personal freedom (88 percent), with good social welfare and health programs (78 percent), as a generally progressive social order (80 percent). By contrast, the GDR was perceived as militaristic (81 percent), as a country in which the influence of the state on the liberty of the individual was excessive (81 percent), and as a society in which people did not trust each other. When

questioned about "our national interests," more than two-thirds of the respondents mentioned only the FRG and made no reference to the GDR at all.[1]

A 1981 survey also found that the perception of the GDR as a foreign country among young people changed dramatically as the result of two or more visits to the GDR; some 71 percent of respondents in this "visitors" group indicated that the GDR was "not a foreign country." When advocates of reunification among the young were questioned about the conditions under which, in their view, reunification should take place, none preferred "a communist system, similar to the GDR"; 32 percent chose "a libertarian-democratic system, obliged to remain neutral, similar to Austria"; and 67 percent chose "a libertarian-democratic system in alliance with the Western world, similar to the FRG." Only one-third of the young people surveyed, however, believed in the possibility of reunification on the model of the FRG; almost half regarded the attainment of a neutral reunified Germany as most likely; and 27 percent envisaged the possibility of reunification under communist rule as most likely.[2]

Sad as the progressive weakening of West German identity with the GDR was in many respects, the growing identification with the institutions and political framework of the FRG among its citizens augured well for the future of that system. From the standpoint of democratic values, it was certainly encouraging to learn from the 1981 study that "the possibility to express one's opinion freely and to offer criticism" was the element of life in the FRG most valued by the young people surveyed. As the responses in the survey made clear, some 35 years after the end of the war, the young citizens in the FRG had become firmly attached to the libertarian-democratic order of their society and come to regard the preservation of this order as more important than the reunification of their divided country.

The foreign policy of the FRG in the 1970s reflected this changing mood of the public. Through a series of treaties with Poland, Czechoslovakia, and the USSR, the FRG "normalized" its relations with its neighbors in the East. The end result of this new *Ostpolitik* (policies toward the East) initiated by the Brandt government was the explicit recognition of the postwar territorial status quo in eastern Europe—that is, the acceptance of the annexation of former German territories east of the Oder and Neisse Rivers by the USSR and Poland, as well as the postwar border with Czechoslovakia. With the de facto recognition of the GDR in 1972, the FRG clearly resigned itself to the more or less permanent division of Germany and abandoned a long-standing principle of its foreign policy. But the Ostpolitik marked not only a sharp departure from the foreign policy pursued by the West German state during its formative period; it also reflected the growing independence of the FRG in international relations. With the Ostpolitik, the FRG came of age. For our purposes here, it is important to recognize that the Ostpolitik contributed significantly to the legitimacy of the Bonn regime in the eyes of its citizens, as well as to the development of greater identification with, and commitment to, the FRG as a specific kind of political system.

Public opinion polls notwithstanding, when unification became a possibility in 1989 and a reality in 1990, few Germans spoke out against it. The whole country was seized by a euphoria: Families were reunited, travel barriers came down, and there were endless celebrations. Initially, at least, there was overwhelming support for unification—even at the cost of a substantial retreat in economic development.

VOTING AND ELECTIONS

Reacting to Germany's experience with the institutional structure and procedures of the Weimar Republic, the framers of the Basic Law for the most part were afraid that excessive popular participation in politics could lead to instability. Given this basic posture, it is not surprising that the formal constitutional rules they designed for a "representative democracy" in postwar Germany accorded only a minimal, limited, indirect, and intermittent role to the citizens in the determination of public policy and in the selection of public officials. Beyond the exercise of their right to vote, the majority of FRG citizens do not avail themselves of the opportunities for active political participation in the political process on a regular basis.

There is every reason to believe that such an arrangement was rather consonant with the prevailing attitude of Germans in the immediate postwar years. A comparative study of the political attitudes in five nations found that in the Germany of 1965, "norms favoring active political participation are not well documented." The authors of the study, Almond and Verba, concluded that the orientation of FRG citizens to their political system was "still relatively passive—the orientation of the subject rather than of the participant."[3]

To function properly, however, a democratic system of government requires a certain amount of public discussion, active participation, and constructive criticism on the part of the citizens—a kind of involvement in public affairs which, for the most part, has been conspicuously lacking in the German political experience. Germans have been notorious for their submissive attitude toward all sorts of authority, for their inclination to observe rules and regulations, for their *Gehorsamkeit* (obedience). Only in Germany, it seems, can one observe pedestrians obeying traffic signals on totally deserted street corners with no traffic in sight! Only about Germans could the—possibly apocryphal—story be told that Marxist revolutionaries, attacking government buildings in Berlin in a putsch attempt in 1918, refused to step on the lawns because there were signs saying "Keep off the grass!"

In regard to political participation, the FRG presents us with a curious paradox. On the one hand, cross-national studies suggest that the level of political interest among West Germans is relatively high—higher than among Americans, the English, or Italians. On the other hand, relatively few Germans show an inclination to become actively involved in politics for a prolonged period of time. While there is a large public with a high degree of political awareness, only a small component of the population is politically active.

On the other hand, voting participation is very high in the FRG—especially by American standards. While only about 50 percent of eligible voters in the United States cast ballots in national elections, close to 90 percent of eligible voters in the FRG typically take part in national elections. Prior to unification, voting participation in Bundestag elections ranged from 78.5 percent in 1949

```
VOTING PARTICIPATION IN
NATIONAL ELECTIONS IN THE FRG

1948                          78.5%
1953                          85.8
1957                          87.8
1961                          87.7
1965                          86.8
1969                          86.7
1972                          91.1
1976                          90.7
1980                          88.7%
1983                          89.1
1987                          84.3
1990                          77.8
1994                          79.0
1998                          82.2
```

Source: www.inter-nationes.de/d/frames/presse/
sonder/e/wahl10-e.html

subnational elections in other advanced industrial countries, ranging—during 1990–92—from a high of 83.2 percent in Saarland to a "low" of 65.1 percent in Saxonia-Anhalt and averaging 71.4 percent overall.[5]

Even in the elections to the European Parliament, certainly perceived as a "politically distant" institution by many voters, FRG citizens managed a turnout of 62.3 percent in 1989, a margin of participation that still puts American voters to shame.[6] What explains this extraordinarily high level of participation by the FRG electorate?

In assessing this dimension of the political behavior of German citizens, it is important to remember, first of all, that a high margin of participation in elections is a traditional German characteristic. As is apparent from Table 16–1, as far back as 1871, with only 19.4 percent of the population eligible to vote, some 52 percent of the eligible voters cast a ballot. In 1912, with the franchise having been expanded only slightly (to 22.2 percent of the population), voting participation among those eligible reached over 84 percent.

The consistently large turnout over the years and the absence, in FRG politics, of highly divisive issues of the kind likely to mobilize even apathetic voters, suggest that voting participation in Germany is largely independent of specific issues, events, and candidates. Given the German voters' low estimation of the political efficacy of

to 91.1 percent in 1972. In the first all-German election in 1990, voting participation declined to 77.8 percent, due in part to lower rates of participation in the new states, which, with the exception of Berlin, averaged 73.9 percent. Among the 16 federal states, participation ranged from 85.2 percent in Saarland to 70.6 percent in Mecklenburg-Western Pomerania.[4]

In elections to the state parliaments too, the turnout has been significantly higher than in

Table 16–1 Expansion of Suffrage in Germany and Voting Participation in Selected Elections, 1871–1990

Year	Eligible Voters		Voting Participation		Valid Ballots Cast as Percent of Population
	Absolute Number (Thousands)	In Percent of the Population	Absolute Number (Thousands)	In Percent of Eligible Voters	
1871	7,656	19.4%	4,148	52.0%	9.4%
1890	10,146	21.7	7,702	71.5	14.6
1912	14,442	22.2	12,251	84.2	18.3
1919	37,362	63.1	30,525	83.0	49.9
1930	42,958	68.9	35,226	82.0	53.7
1949	31,208	68.4	24,496	78.5	50.4
1976	42,058	68.5	38,166	90.7	
1990	60,437	76.1	46,996	77.8	

Source: Dietrich Nohlen, "Wahlen/Wahlrecht," in eds. Kurt Sontheimer and H. H. Röhring, *Handbuch des politischen Systems der Bundesrepublik Deutschland,* 2nd ed. (Munich: R. Piper & Co. Verlag, 1978), p. 636; *Stat. Jahrb.* BRD, p. 99.

the act of voting and their general sense of political impotence, most observers of German politics agree that FRG citizens turn out at election time because they consider it their civic duty to vote. The fact that voting takes place on Sundays and that registration is not required is also conducive to high turnouts. Although it is difficult and precarious to make generalizations about any nation, it is probably correct to say that one of the virtues (or vices!) of the Germans is a highly developed sense of duty. When linked to a good and worthwhile purpose, this cultural trait can be a great asset; but when placed in the service of a bad cause, it can lead to disaster.

In any event, if FRG citizens stream to the ballot box on election day, it is not because they believe that their vote will make a difference in the selection of the ruling elite or in the determination of governmental policy. Survey research conducted in the FRG suggests that, at least during the 1950s–70s, political participation in the FRG, including voting in national and state elections, was extensive rather than intensive.[7] But this has changed. Measured by such indications as interest in politics, party identification, and attitude toward party affiliation, FRG citizens have become increasingly more politicized. A continued high standard of living, more leisure time, and progressively higher levels of education have resulted in greater "quality" and intensity in the process of political participation in the FRG.

The development of the political party system in the FRG in many respects surpassed even the most optimistic hopes and expectations of the founders of the Bonn Republic. With the exception of the Communist party (KPD), the German party (DP), the Center party (ZP), and a few other small political groupings, the political parties licensed by the Allied occupation authorities in 1949 prospered and succeeded in developing strong and growing support among the electorate. During the 1950s and 1960s, most of the smaller parties disappeared from the political scene, their members in many cases being absorbed into the major parties. Although at least three parties have been continuously represented in the German parliament, and although the composition of the twelfth Bundestag even included seven parties, the FRG has increasingly moved toward an effective two-party system, evolving farther in that

direction than any other country in continental Europe.

In a clear departure from the political pattern of the Weimar Republic, splinter movements and special interest parties, extremists of the Left and Right, have been singularly unsuccessful in competing with the electoral appeal of the major political parties. For the first time in German history, a party system has developed in which one political party—in free and competitive elections—was able to win an absolute majority of the seats in parliament.[8] As is apparent from Table 16–2, since 1949 the electoral strength of the two major parties, the Christian Democratic Union/Christian Social Union (CDU/CSU) and the Social Democratic Party (SPD), has increased substantially and has never fallen below 81 percent. Indeed, between 1961 and 1983, all of the parties represented in the Bundestag were mainstream political parties.[9]

The Bundestag is elected by a personalized system of proportional representation. Half of the Bundestag deputies are elected by a plurality vote in single-member districts, the other half by proportional representation from state party lists. Every FRG voter accordingly votes twice—once for a district candidate (direct mandate) and once for a party (indirect mandate). The vote for the party is more important because it determines the ultimate percentage of Bundestag mandates a party will receive. The direct mandates (the seats won in the district elections) are then deducted from the total number of a party's mandates. However, in order to be "proportionally" represented in the Bundestag, a party must win a minimum of three direct mandates in district elections or receive at least 5 percent of the vote. Furthermore, if a party wins more district mandates than it is entitled to on the basis of the party list vote, it retains these seats and the Bundestag membership is increased accordingly. Thus the FRG election system is a modified system of proportional representation.

An important aspect of political participation in the FRG has been the cooperation of various parties in coalitions. Although the CDU/CSU won absolute majorities in 1953 and again in 1957, all governments formed in the FRG since 1949 have been coalition governments. During the fifth legislative period (1965–69), the

Table 16–2   Composition of the Bundestag by Party Representation, 1949–98

Year of Election	Total Seats	CDU/ CSU	SPD	Combined Seat Percentage: CDU/ CSU and SPD	FDP	DP	BP	ZP	KPD	Others[a]
1949	402	139	131	68%	52	17	17	10	15	21
1953	487	244	151	81	48	15		2		27
1957	497	270	169	88	41	17				
1961	499	242	190	86	67					
1965	496	245	202	90	49					
1969	496	242	224	94	30					
1972	496	225	230	91	41					
1976	496	243	214	92	39					
1980	497	226	218	90	53					
1983	520	255	202	86	35					28
1987	519	234	193	82	48					44
1990	662	179	239	84	79					25
1994	672	294	252	81	47					79
1998	669	245	298	81	43					83

[a]This category includes: In 1949—Association for Economic Reconstruction, 12; German Conservative Party and German Imperial Party, 5; without party affiliation, 2; Emergency Association, 1; and South Silesian Voters Association, 1. In 1953—BHE (Refugee party). In 1983: Greens (Green Front), an environmentalist group, 28 seats. In 1984 and 1987—Greens and Alternative List—for Democracy and Environmental Protection (AL) in West Berlin. In 1990—Alliance 90/Greens: 8 seats, and PDS (Party of Democratic Socialism): 17 seats. In 1994—Alliance 90/Greens: 49 seats, PDS—30 seats. In 1998—Alliance 90/Greens: 47 seats, and PDS—36 seats.

Note: Figures for the first nine Bundestag terms (1949–84) do not include the 22 representatives from West Berlin; figures for the tenth and eleventh terms include the representatives from West Berlin. Beginning with the twelfth term, figures are for Germany after unification.

Source: Otto Model and Carl Creifelds, *Staatsbürgertaschenbuch* (Munich: C. H. Beck'sche Verlagsbuchhandlung, 1982), p. 109; *Stat. Jahrb.* BRD, p. 99; www.inter-nationes.de/d/frames/presse/sonder/e/wahl10-e.html; www.statistik-bund.de/wahlen/ergeb98/d/bunu.htm. Column 5 calculated.

CDU/CSU and the SPD formed the so-called Grand Coalition, with a total of 447 seats. The year 1969 marked the beginning of the period of true equality between the SPD and the CDU/CSU. For the first time the SPD formed a successful coalition (with the FDP) that, after 20 years as the dominant party in government, made the CDU/CSU the opposition party. Thus began a long period of SPD-FDP government, but with a thin margin (and briefly during the sixth Bundestag, no margin) over the CDU/CSU opposition.

As it turned out, FRG citizens grew to approve of the impressive performance of the German party system within two decades after 1949. In 1951, 22 percent of the voters surveyed in West Germany still preferred a single-party system, but by 1968 only 7 percent expressed such a preference. During the same period, the number of those who preferred a competitive multiparty system increased from 61 percent to nearly 82 percent. These survey results would seem to indicate that a growing number of West Germans were inclined to endorse a competitive multiparty system as their first preference. Furthermore, survey research findings also indicate that most voters in the FRG had developed a rather clear and well-defined "cognitive map" for making political choices.[10] Taken together, these developments suggested a promising future for democracy in West Germany.

Because of their key role in providing political leadership in the FRG, the three traditional "system parties"—the CDU/CSU, the SPD, and the FDP—which have been continually represented in the Bundestag since 1949—will be discussed in more detail in Chapter 17. There are, however, a number of other parties or movements that have been instrumental in raising the level of political participation in the FRG even though they have not enjoyed great success at the polls: We shall turn to them next.

MINOR POLITICAL PARTIES AND MOVEMENTS

Since 1956 the Federal Election Law in West Germany has required a political party to win a minimum of three direct mandates or at least 5 percent of the indirect vote in order to qualify for representation in the Bundestag. Until the election in March 1983, no other parties besides the "big three" succeeded in overcoming this hurdle— clearly designed to keep splinter parties out of the Federal Diet and thus effectively out of national politics. But in that 1983 election the Greens, Germany's newest political movement, received 5.6 percent of the vote and won 28 seats in the Bundestag, thus becoming the first left-wing opposition group to gain representation in the Federal Diet since the Communist party won 15 seats in 1949. A collection of environmentalists, opponents of nuclear power and nuclear weapons, and other social activists, the Greens may be seen as the successors of the protest movement of the 1960s, known collectively as the APO (Extra-Parliamentary Opposition). When they first organized themselves into a political party in 1979, they threatened to redefine the role of political opposition in West Germany by resorting to various forms of parliamentary obstructionism. Their appearance in the Bundestag produced some change in the atmosphere of politics in the FRG. Their platform embraced many issues that found active support at the national level: the advocacy of peace; protection of the environment; the right to abortion; equality of women; the end of discrimination against homosexuals and foreigners; the advocacy of human rights for prisoners; unlimited freedom of opinion and the press; an end to the concentration of the mass media in the hands of the few; better housing; and even "schools that are fun."

In the aftermath of their failure to clear the 5 percent hurdle in the 1990 election, the "realists" staged a takeover and pushed out the "fundamentalists." As a result, they succeeded in entering the coalitions of two state governments in the west (Lower Saxony and Hesse) and one in the east (Brandenburg). After the 1990 election they also merged with the eastern German civil rights groups New Forum and Alliance 90.

Other small parties in the FRG, which have not succeeded in qualifying for representation in the Bundestag, include the All-German Party (DP/BHE), a refugee party; the German Peace Union (DFU), an advocate of the neutralization of the FRG; the Bavarian Party (BP), with an extreme federalist program; the National Democratic Party (NPD), a neo-Nazi party that enjoyed some success in the 1960s and, after winning 4.3 percent of the vote, disintegrated; and, more recently, the Republikaner, an extremist right-wing group, which received 2.1 percent of the vote in 1990. Parties on the left have included the former Communist Party of Germany (KPD), founded in 1919 by Karl Liebknecht and Rosa Luxemburg, which, outlawed in 1956 by the Federal Constitutional Court as unconstitutional, then dissolved. A new German Communist Party (DKP) was founded in 1968, with a new program, which carefully avoided any overt anticonstitutional tendencies and declarations. Other left-wing groups have included the Maoists, the Communist Party of Germany/Marxists-Leninists, and the Communist League—West Germany. What all these groups have in common is that they have not enjoyed any significant support among the voters.

Another left-wing party that entered the political scene in 1990, the PDS (Party of Democratic Socialism), the successor to the SED, the GDR's former ruling party, was able to enter the Bundestag in 1990, due to special rules for that election. Although, like the CSU in Bavaria, a primarily regional party in terms of electoral appeal, the PDS has been more successful at the polls than was initially expected—reflecting the disillusionment of many Germans living in the new eastern states with the realities of unification. Having gained 17 seats in the 1990 election, it increased its representation in the Bundestag to 30 seats in 1994, and 36 seats in 1998. Six of the seats in the 1998 Bundestag were won outside the new eastern states—in Baden-Württemberg, Bavaria, Hessen, Lower Saxony, and North Rhine-Westphalia (2). In terms of its declared aspirations, the PDS is an internationalist party working for peace and security, social justice and democracy, not only in Germany and Europe but throughout the world.

CITIZEN INITIATIVES

In contrast to the United States and other Western countries, where the spontaneous formation of groups for the pursuit of shared political goals has long been a common occurrence, similar activities by citizens in the FRG are a relatively new development. Only since the beginning of the 1970s have such "citizen initiatives" become politically important. In recent years, however, they have served as the common denominator of all sorts of citizen activities and actions, directed as often as not against political and administrative decisions. They have also become a key concept in an as-yet diffuse, but nevertheless significant general movement for greater participation and democratization.

The rapid spread of citizen initiatives throughout West Germany in the 1970s, involving a variety of political issues, reflected two simultaneous developments: (1) the heightened political consciousness of German citizens that resulted from, among other things, the student protest movement of the 1960s, and (2) the diminished success of the major political parties as voices for many FRG citizens who were members of minority groups or who felt compelled to speak out on their behalf. Given the potentially anarchistic tendencies of movements such as citizen initiatives, it is not surprising that the remnants of the APO saw in them very promising points of departure for their own activities, which in some cases involved violations of the Basic Law and occasionally the use of force. In East Germany, citizen initiatives such as New Forum, Democracy Now, and the short-lived Round Table played an important part in bringing down the communist regime in 1989.

It lies in the nature of movements like the citizen initiatives that precise information about them is difficult to generate. Since they normally do not give rise to permanent organizations and are formed spontaneously on an ad hoc basis to attain specific goals or oppose specific political or administrative decisions, their number is subject to considerable fluctuation and difficult to determine. According to available estimates, several thousand citizen initiatives existed by the late 1970s. The greatest number of participants in citizen initiatives were attracted by demonstrations against the construction of nuclear power plants and the deployment of new U.S. missiles in the FRG and other European countries. Most (about one-sixth) were concerned with environmental issues of one kind or another; the others (in order of frequency) focused on kindergarten facilities, playgrounds, traffic, schools, city development and restoration, marginal groups such as immigrants and the economically disadvantaged, cultural questions, and questions relating to youth affairs.

The membership of citizenship initiatives ranges from very small groups concerned with local issues to initiatives that mobilize hundreds of thousands of people. The social group most strongly represented in the initiatives are the Akademiker (university-educated persons), while workers are for the most part conspicuously absent. The citizen initiative is thus essentially a middle-class phenomenon in FRG politics. This fact—together with the movement's rapid development and demonstrated capacity to mobilize enormous numbers of people—suggests that in the perception of the middle-class citizen, not all is well in the FRG with respect to democratic decision making. The prominent role citizen initiatives have come to play in recent FRG politics also suggests that legitimate interests have been and continue to be inadequately represented by established popular parties. Given this fact, it seems likely that citizen initiatives will continue to play an important role in German politics in the foreseeable future.[11]

INTEREST GROUPS

One of the most important forms of political participation in developed political systems is the activity of interest groups. Germany is no exception in this respect. As a highly organized society, the FRG is characterized by an intricate network and structure of interest groups. Survey data suggest that FRG citizens are more inclined to rely on interest groups as a means of influencing governmental policy than are Americans, Britons,

Italians, or Mexicans.[12] In his encyclopedic study of the FRG political system, Thomas Ellwein estimated that there were at least 200,000 citizens' associations in West Germany.[13] Many, of course, pursue primarily nonpolitical goals and/or engage in political activity only intermittently. The point is that the organization of special interests has a long tradition in German history—a tradition that antedates the establishment of an independent sovereign German state and, in the case of some occupational associations, professional guilds, and economic interest groups, reaches back to the medieval corporate guilds.

The modern descendants of these guilds and associations exercise important regulatory and other state functions: They enforce the compulsory membership of all those who want to practice a certain profession; they recruit new members and supervise their training; they license them upon the completion of a rigorous apprenticeship and thus maintain professional standards. Virtually all skilled craftsmen and legal and medical professionals are organized into guilds and chambers, which are hierarchically structured from the local to the national level and wield considerable economic and political power. As a matter of fact, these associations enjoy a quasi-governmental status; their spokespersons at the national level are part of the larger political elite in the FRG, who deal directly with the ministerial bureaucracies and are regularly consulted by the federal government in matters of policy affecting their membership.

In the FRG, as elsewhere, political parties and interest groups do not exist independently or separately side by side; rather they are interconnected in numerous ways. Almost all members of the Bundestag parties belong to one or several associations.[14] More important, a significant number of Bundestag deputies are representatives of occupational or professional interests.[15]

The traditional pattern of an exceptionally pronounced integration of interest groups, political parties, and the government in Germany has continued to develop in the FRG. During the late 1960s this pattern was institutionalized in the so-called *Concerted Action:* A regular conference brought together approximately 50 top representatives of the government, the business community, labor, and the *Council of Experts,* to discuss economic problems of common concern and to set general guidelines for wage increases, price increases, and government spending and taxation, in an attempt to create optimum conditions for noninflationary economic growth. The practice of "concerted action" broke down in the late 1970s—as the consensus between labor, business, and the government disintegrated under the increasing strain due to the economic recession—but the future may very well see a revival of such mechanisms.[16] In any event, informal contacts between government, business, and labor have continued.

In addition to recruiting Bundestag deputies and being regularly consulted by the government, interest groups exert influence in the politics of the FRG through representatives who are appointed to the numerous permanent commissions and consultative bodies in the various ministries and other state agencies. This practice reflects the government's desire to tap the expertise of the interest groups and to gain their cooperation and support for the implementation of public policy. The many regular formal and informal contacts between the government and interest groups in Germany have led some political scientists to describe the FRG as a "neocorporatist state."[17] Here, neocorporatism means the close cooperative relationship between the government and a few compulsory, hierarchical associations accorded recognition by the state as the virtually monopolistic representatives of their particular interests.

In the FRG, the focus of interest group activity is on the executive rather than on the Bundestag. Normally interest groups in Germany will "lobby" in the Federal Diet only if they fail in their efforts to influence the executive. Generally speaking, interest groups in the FRG have been more successful as veto groups than as promoters of specific policies. German interest groups, finally, benefit from the elaborate system of special administrative courts, which frequently affords them the opportunity to defend or advance their interests through the support of their members in key legal cases involving principles with more general implications for their membership.

Major Interest Group Organizations

The major interest alignments in the FRG are formed by business, labor, agriculture, and the churches. The pattern of organization is basically similar. The numerous local and state organizations are represented at the national level by one or more umbrella organizations. Thus, for example, business interests in the FRG are organized in a large number of employer associations at the state and local level. These business groups have their own national offices, and are also represented by three umbrella organizations, all of which maintain large offices and staffs in or near the capital. These are the BDI *(Bundesverband der Deutschen Industrie)* or Federation of German Industry, the most influential voice for business interests in the FRG, which represents about 40 individual industry associations and a total of more than 90,000 firms; the BDA *(Bundesvereinigung Deutscher Arbeitgeberverbände)* or Federation of German Employers' Associations—the only organization on the employers' side to include all branches of the national economy, bringing together nearly 400 member associations and representing some 47 trade associations; and the DIHT *(Deutscher Industrie und Handelstag)* or German Industrial and Trade Conference, established as far back as 1861, which represents the interests of small businesspeople and craftsmen, and functions as the national umbrella organization for some 70 chambers of industry and commerce in the FRG and some 40 German foreign chambers of commerce.[18]

Labor, of course, is another important constellation of interests. Labor in the FRG is organized into sixteen separate trade and industrial unions, with a combined membership of close to 8 million in 1990. By the end of 1991, its membership increased to 11.8 million, due to the influx of workers from eastern Germany. By the end of 1996, however, membership had declined to slightly over 9 million. The national umbrella organization for labor unions is the DGB *(Deutscher Gewerkschaftsbund)* or German Trade Union Federation. Established in 1949, it was, in part at least, a response to Allied pressure to dissociate the labor unions from the political parties. The establishment of a single unified trade union federation, it was thought, would end the fragmentation of the German labor movement so prevalent during the Weimar Republic, and shift its major focus and concern from the preoccupation with radical social and economic change to more pragmatic objectives, such as higher wages and improved working conditions.

This calculation proved to be correct. Within a few years after its establishment, the DGB ceased to advocate the Marxist goals (central economic planning and the nationalization of the most important industries) incorporated in its 1949 political program. Instead it turned to the pursuit of collective bargaining and of workers' participation or "codetermination"—the latter a scheme to give workers equal representation on a company's board of directors with the management and stockholders. Thus, the DGB accepted the market economy and the existing political order as the framework for the gradual improvement of the workers' situation. In its 1981 Program of Principles, the DGB demanded full employment, the humanization of work, the extension of codetermination, the participation of workers in profit sharing, the expansion of the system of social security, and the expansion of training programs for its members.[19]

In addition to the DGB there is a special association for white-collar employees—the DAG *(Deutsche Angestellten-Gewerkschaft)* or German Salaried Employees Union, which had a membership of 600,000 in 1990. Another major association representing labor interest is the DBB *(Deutscher Beamtenbund)* or Federation of German Civil Servants, with a membership of 800,000 in 1990. While the work of an individual usually determines his or her membership in a particular union or association, this is not always the case. The ranks of the DGB, for example, now include many civil servants and white-collar workers. Of the three-fourths of the civil servants who belong to unions, about half belong to the DGB and the other half to the DBB. The DAG likewise has not been a particularly successful competitor of the DGB for members among the white-collar employees. The majority of white-collar workers belong to the DGB. The DAG has been more successful in recruiting members among high-level employees in private enterprise.[20]

By the mid-1970s only about 40 percent of the labor force in West Germany belonged to unions. The growth of organized labor thus did not keep pace with the expansion of the labor force in the FRG, which was largely due to the massive influx of women and foreign ("guest") workers during the postwar economic boom. Nevertheless, organized labor in the FRG represents a major political force that no politician can afford to ignore or overlook.

Thus far trade unions in the FRG have been much less militant in the pursuit of their interests than their counterparts in other European countries or in the United States. Although guaranteed in the Basic Law, compared to other leading industrialized nations the FRG has had few major strikes and enjoyed a considerable measure of labor peace. Because of their moderate policies the labor unions accordingly deserve a good share of the credit for the high degree of political stability the FRG has enjoyed during the first three decades of its existence.

In more recent years "young Turks" among the union officials have attempted to radicalize the members of their unions by charging that the economic prosperity and stability of the FRG was bought at the expense of workers and by offering dogmatic solutions (income equalization; nationalization of industries, banking, trade) that hold out the promise of far-reaching socioeconomic change. Thus far, however, these efforts have been singularly unsuccessful. This is a reflection of the widespread perception, among the rank and file, of unions as effective, representative, and responsive. German workers in the west have shared in the prosperity of the FRG. And trade union leaders in West Germany are satisfied and comfortable with the integration of organized labor into the political process and system. Interelite bargaining, rather than public "actions" such as strikes, has become their preferred political style—a style that has been very instrumental in supporting the existing political order. The large influx of new members from the east has not changed this style, but has had a major impact on the agenda of the trade unions. Because of the high level of unemployment in the east, for example, contemporary labor issues in the west have, in some cases, been pushed aside.

If interest groups in the FRG were to be ranked according to internal cohesiveness and unity of purpose, the organizations representing agricultural interests would undoubtedly be among the top. At the national level, farmers in the FRG are organized into three associations: the Association of Agricultural Chambers, the DBV or German Farmers' League, and the DRV, an association of agricultural cooperatives and banks. Membership in the corporate units of the Association of Agricultural Chambers is compulsory for all agricultural proprietors. Most farmers also belong to the other two organizations representing farm interests. All three of these organizations and the German Agricultural Society or DLG, an association of farmers and scientists for the promotion of German agriculture, are linked together in the Central Committee of German Agriculture.[21]

Agricultural interests in the FRG are closely identified with the CDU/CSU. Since 1949 about 10 percent of the FRG deputies have been farmers; a very cohesive political group, they have dominated the Agricultural Committee in the Bundestag. For many years the agricultural lobby in Bonn was very successful in obtaining tax concessions, price supports, and state subsidies. In more recent times, however, its power has declined— especially its relative position vis-à-vis the other major interest groups. The dramatic decline in the number of farmers has resulted in a drastic erosion of its membership base. Plans within the framework of Common Market agreements call for a further reduction of the German farm population. Within the context of a highly competitive export-oriented and export-dependent economy, the agricultural sector in the FRG, as the long-time recipient of large state subsidies and confronted with a continuing decline in the farm population, is likely to face an uphill political struggle in the years ahead—especially during a period of economic recession and large-scale unemployment.[22]

Prior to unification, over 90 percent of the citizens of the FRG belonged—in almost equal proportion—to the two great churches of Germany: the Protestant or Evangelical church and the Catholic church. This fact in and of itself made the two churches important factors in public life. It comes as no surprise, therefore, to find that, both by custom and by law, the two historic German churches have played a key role in public affairs of the FRG. This role has become anchored in constitutional provisions and other legal requirements, in all of the federal states, that call for the participation of the clergy in the formulation and implementation of social and cultural policies. The clergy, for example, has a voice in public education, including the selection of professors of theology at German universities; it is represented on the supervisory boards for radio and television in the FRG, as well as on various advisory commissions at the federal and state level; in Bavaria, members of the clergy are even appointed as representatives in the upper house of the state parliament. Thus separation of church and state in Germany effectively does not exist. On balance, the churches as institutions and religious leaders as elites have exerted greater influence and have been more extensively involved in the process of public policy formation than in most advanced industrial societies.[23]

While the Basic Law recognizes religion as a private matter and guarantees its free exercise by the individual, the organized expression of religion is regarded as a public affair and therefore subject to legal regulation. The church organizations in the FRG accordingly are special institutions of public law. For our purposes it is important to know that, although the churches themselves claim a special position and do in fact enjoy a privileged status among interest groups in the FRG, their role in the political system is very similar to that of other interest group associations.

The Evangelical or Protestant church (*Evangelische Kirche*) in the FRG today consists of twenty-four Land churches, whose boundaries do not coincide with the boundaries of the federal states. The Land churches vary not only in terms of size, but also in denomination: There are Lutheran, United, and Reformed churches. Their common national umbrella organization is the EKD (*Evangelische Kirche in Deutschland*) or Evangelical Church in Germany. Unlike the Roman Catholic church, the EKD has been less concerned with the advocacy of the interests of its members than with more general political issues—for example, reunification, civil liberties, educational reform, codetermination in industry, the extension of the welfare state, the improvement of East-West relations, and the like. (In the late 1960s and early 1970s the EKD played a key role in setting the stage for the discussion of the Brandt government's Ostpolitik). The EKD has even taken a position on such highly controversial issues as the legitimate use of violence, cautiously endorsing revolutionary action as consistent with Christian principles when directed against an oppressive regime not permitting change by democratic and peaceful means.

Because of the uniformity of its doctrine, the organization of the Catholic church is far less complicated. It follows purely territorial principles that reflect historical developments. Like the Land churches of the Protestant church, the boundaries of the dioceses and archdioceses of the Catholic church, therefore, do not coincide with the modern territorial division of the FRG. Following unification, the Catholic church in the FRG, as of the end of 1990, is organized into 25 bishoprics. There is an apostolic administrator for the new federal states. Germany's archbishops and bishops consult together in the German Bishops Conference, which has a secretariat in Bonn.

Traditionally, the German Catholic church has been more concerned with the pursuit of specific interests of its members than has the Protestant church. Major issues for the Catholic church and in particular its leadership have been the advocacy of state support for separate Catholic and Protestant schools, stricter divorce laws, the continued prohibition of abortion except in urgent medical cases, more restrictive legislation on pornography, and so on. But in all of these areas the Catholic church has been fighting a losing battle in recent years. Bidenominational schools, attended by both Catholic and Protestant students who share the same classes but receive separate religious instruction by representatives of their faith, have become the prevailing postwar pattern of education in the FRG. On the issue of "separate but equal" schools, the established leadership of the Catholic church has found itself increasingly isolated from the younger clergy and its lay members, as the inefficiency and differential quality and standards of this system became increasingly a public issue.

The religious complexion of the FRG today, of course, is far more intricate than is suggested by the foregoing discussion. In addition to the two major churches, there are numerous smaller organizations. Among these are the so-called "free churches," such as the Methodists and the Evangelical Community (joined in 1968 as the Evangelical Methodist church); the Alliance of Free Evangelical Congregations (Baptists); the Old Catholic church, which broke away from the Roman Catholic church in the 1870s over the issue of papal infallibility; the Mennonites; the Quakers; and the Salvation Army. There are also more than 61,000 Jews in the FRG, organized into about seventy congregations. Their umbrella organization is the Central Council of Jews in Germany.

Due to the massive influx of foreign workers, finally, both the Greek Orthodox Church and Islam (1.7 million members) have become important new additions to the religious spectrum in the FRG.

NOTES

[1]Erich Kitzmüller, Heinz Kuby, and Lutz Niethammer, "Der Wandel der nationalen Frage in der Bundesrepublik Deutschland," *Aus Politik und Zeitgeschichte.* Supplement to *Das Parlament,* 25 August 1973, p. 24.

[2]*Frankfurter Allgemeine,* 29 July 1983, p. 3.

[3]Gabriel Almond and Sidney Verba, *The Civic Culture* (Boston: Little, Brown and Company, 1965), pp. 312, 313.

[4]*Stat. Jahrb.* BRD, p. 99.

[5]*Daten Report 5,* p. 179.

[6]*State Jahrb.* BRD 1989, p. 77.

[7]On political participation in the FRG, see E. Hübner, *Partizipation im Parteienstaat. Bürgerbeteiligung in Parteien und Wahlen* (Munich: Ehrenwirt, 1976). For the early history of the FRG, see J. Steiner, *Bürger und Politik. Empirisch-theoretische Befunde über die politische Partizipation in Demokratien unter besonderer Berücksichtigung der Schweiz und der BRD* (Meisenheim am Glan: A. Hain, 1969).

[8]In the Bundestag elections of 1953 and 1957, the CDU/CSU won 244 of 487, and 270 of 497 seats, respectively.

[9]Thus, for example, the electoral support of the CDU/CSU increased from 35 percent in 1949 to a high of 54 percent in 1957 with an average of 48.8 percent for the years 1953–83. The SPD increased its electoral support from 33 percent in 1949 to 46 percent in 1972 with an average of 40.1 percent for the years 1953–1983.

[10]H. D. Klingemann, "Testing the Left-Right Continuum on a Sample of German Voters," *Comparative Political Studies* 5 (1972): 93–106.

[11]On citizen initiatives in the FRG, see R. Gronemeyer, *Integration durch Partizipation* (Frankfurt/M: Fischer-Taschenbuch-Verlag, 1973); P. C. Mayer-Tasch, *Die Bürgerinitiativbewegung* (Reinbek: Rowohlt, 1976); H. Zillessen, "Bürgerinitiativen im representativen Regierungssystem," *Aus Politik und Zeitgeschichte.* Beilage zur Wochenzeitung *Das Parlament,* 23 March 1974; see also K. Sontheimer and H. H. Röhring, eds., *Handbuch des politischen Systems der Bundesrepublik Deutschland* (Munich: R. Piper & Co., Verlag, 1978), pp. 67–71.

[12]G. A. Almond and S. Verba, *The Civic Culture* (Princeton, NJ: Princeton University Press, 1963), p. 218.

[13]See Thomas Ellwein, *Das Regierungssystem der Bundesrepublik Deutschland,* 4th rev. ed. (Opladen: Westdeutscher Verlag, 1976), p. 133.

[14]H. J. Varain, "Parteien und Verbände in der Bundesrepublik," *Geschichte in Wissenschaft und Unterricht* 10 (1959): 748ff., and, by the same author, *Interessenverbände in Deutschland* (Cologne: Kiepenheuer and Witsch, 1973); E. Reigrotzki, *Soziale Verflechtung in der Bundesrepublik* (Tübingen: J. C. B. Mohr, 1956), p. 178.

[15]According to one estimate, approximately one-third of the Bundestag deputies in 1957-1961 represented professional interests. See G. Loewenberg, *Parliament in the German Political System* (Ithaca, NY: Cornell University Press, 1966), p. 113.

[16]On the "Concerted Action," see H. Adam, "Die Konzertierte Aktion in der Bundesrepublik." WSI-Studien zur Wirtschafts- und Sozialforschung, no. 21, Cologne, 1972; Uwe Andersen, "Konzertierte Aktion," in Sontheimer and Röhring, *Handbuch,* pp. 331–340.

[17]Gerhard Lehmbruch, "Liberal Corporatism and Party Government," in *Trends Toward Corporatist Intermediation,* Philippe Schmitter, ed. (Beverly Hills, CA: Sage Publications, 1979), pp. 147–188.

[18]For basic information on the major interest group associations and their umbrella organizations, see Sontheimer and Röhring, *Handbuch,* pp. 260–265, and Model/Creifelds, *Staatsbürger-Taschenbuch,* pp. 764 ff., pp. 840 ff. On the role of business, see G. Braunthal, *The Federation of German Industry in Politics* (Ithaca, NY: Cornell University Press, 1965). See also Jürgen Weber, *Die Interessengruppen im politischen System der Bundesrepublik Deutschland* (Stuttgart: Kohlhammer, 1977); Ulrich von Alemann/Rolf G. Heinze, ed., *Verbände und Staat. Vom Pluralismus zum Korporatismus—Analysen. Positionen, Dokumente* (Opladen: Westdeutscher Verlag, 1979).

[19]On the trade unions in the FRG, see W. Abendroth, *Die deutschen Gewerkschaften* (Heidelberg: W. Rothe, 1955); D. Schuster, *Die deutschen Gewerkschaften seit 1945* (Stuttgart: Kohlhammer, 1973); Frank Deppe et al., eds., *Geschichte der deutschen Gewerkschaftsbewegung* (Cologne: Pahl-Rugenstein, 1978); Manfred Wilke, *Die Funktionäre. Apparat und Demokratie im Deutschen Gewerkschaftsbund* (Munich: Piper, 1979); and C. W. Witjes, *Gewerkschaftliche Führungsgruppen. Eine empirische Untersuchung zum Sozialprofil, zur Selektion und Zirkulation sowie zur Machtstellung westdeutscher Gewerkschaftsführungen* (Berlin: Dunker und Humblot, 1976).

[20]On the civil service, see Heiner Geissler, ed., *Verwalteter Bürger—Gesellschaft in Fesseln, Bürokratisierung und ihre Folgen für Staat, Wirtschaft und Gesellschaft* (Frankfurt/M.: Ullstein, 1978); Ulrich Lohmar, *Staatsbürokratie—Das hoheitliche Gewerbe. Deutsche Aspekte eines neuen Klassenkampfes* (Munich: Goldmann, 1978); Hubertus Zumer, *Schlankheitskur für den Staat* (Stuttgart: Seewald 1979), Daten Report 5, pp. 183–188.

[21]On the German Farmers' League, see Paul Ackermann, *Der Deutsche Bauernverband im politischen Kräftespiel der Bundesrepublik* (Tübingen: Mohr, 1970).

[22]The profound changes that have taken place in agriculture in the FRG are frequently obscured by the concept of "structural change in the countryside"—a concept that conceals the fact that, within the span of one generation, half of the agricultural enterprises in the FRG ceased operation.

[23]On the role of the churches, see E. G. Mehrenholz, *Die Kirchen in der Gesellschaft der Bundesrepublik* (Hannover: n.p. 1969); H. Maier, "Die Kirchen," in R. Löwenthal/H. P. Schwarz, ed., *Die Zweite Republik* (Stuttgart: Seewald Verlag, 1974); W. Huber, *Kirche and Öffentlichkeit* (Stuttgart: Klett, 1973).

Chapter 17

Political Leadership
in Germany

There is no question that stable and, on the whole, capable political leadership has played a crucial role in the political evolution of the FRG. In view of the extraordinary political stability the FRG has enjoyed since 1949, it is not surprising that there has been a tendency to overlook the profound changes that have taken place in the social composition and style of its political leadership compared to previous German regimes. Generally speaking, access to the political elite, that is, the policy-making stratum at the national level, is much more open in the FRG today than it was once in Germany, or is now in many other countries. No longer are political leaders recruited virtually exclusively from a relatively small number of aristocratic families as in imperial Germany, nor do they have to be members of the "Aryan" race and accept the dictates of a narrow and rigid ideology as during the Nazi period. Personal wealth is not nearly as important an asset for gaining access to the policy-making elite in the FRG as it tends to be in the United States. And, unlike France or Great Britain, top policy makers in West Germany are not the graduates of a few select universities and schools.

Gender, education, skill, organizational affiliations, experience, and resourcefulness tend to be the major determinants of upward political mobility in the FRG today. In 1969, Willy Brandt, the illegitimate son of a saleswoman, was elected federal chancellor after having previously been the mayor of West Berlin—a kind of political career that would have been unthinkable in imperial Germany.

Equally important is the fact that leadership groups formerly denied acceptance in earlier regimes (for example, the military in the Weimar Republic, or labor leaders and the Catholic clergy in imperial Germany) have been effectively integrated into the political system. Political leadership and policy making in the FRG are shared between elected officials, the leaders of interest groups and political parties, the civil service and the military, and between national and regional (state) officials. Before discussing the federal chancellor, the main center of executive power in the FRG, and the federal president, we turn to an examination of the major political parties that have been so instrumental in providing political leadership in the FRG.

THE CHRISTIAN DEMOCRATIC UNION (CDU)/CHRISTIAN SOCIAL UNION (CSU)

The Christian Democratic Union (CDU) was founded in 1945 by two groups: by Catholics determined to transcend the ideological appeal and membership limitations of the all-Catholic Center party, which had existed prior to 1933; and by Protestants, liberals and conservatives who, prior to the Nazi takeover, had belonged to one of several Center or right-of-Center parties. The CDU is dedicated to the democratic organization of public life in the service of the German people, imbued with a sense of Christian responsibility and in accordance with Christian moral precepts on the basis of individual freedom.

The CDU has been an extremely heterogeneous party, retaining and/or developing quite different complexions in the various regions of the FRG. As a matter of fact, at the time of its founding, the CDU was so heterogeneous that many observers predicted this political conglomeration would not last very long. For many years, the CDU did not attempt to work out a set of fundamentals or a basic and detailed political program. As a Christian-Democratic alliance, it sought to bring about the political unification of the members of all Christian denominations; as a "people's party" *(Volkspartei),* it sought to represent all groups and segments of the German people. It was not until 1978, more than a generation after its establishment, that the political goals of the CDU were summarized more or less systematically and comprehensively in the *Program of Principles.*[1]

The CDU committed itself to "social progress" and a "just peace for all nations of the world," and "peace with the Soviet Union on the basis of an accommodation free of aspirations of hegemony." A strong supporter of the NATO alliance, the CDU/CSU for many years proclaimed the unification of Germany as the "supreme goal of German policy."

In terms of socioeconomic policy, the CDU's commitments included adherence to the principle of a "free social market economy," personal freedom, property, equality of opportunity, social progress for all, codetermination for employees, and a greater role for students, parents, and teachers in education, and greater citizen participation.[2]

The CDU's "sister party," the Christian Social Union (CSU), was also founded in 1945. Its initial membership came primarily from the former Bavarian People's Party, which was one of the parties represented in the parliament of the Weimar Republic. The CSU is an organizationally independent party that exists and operates only in the state of Bavaria, where the CDU has no party organization and leaves the field to the CSU. Likewise, the CSU does not maintain a party organization outside of Bavaria, leaving the field to the CDU. The goals of the CSU are largely identical with those of the CDU, but they reflect the special interests of the state of Bavaria, especially in economic and cultural matters. In national politics, the CSU has been a close political partner of the CDU since 1949, with both parties forming the CDU/CSU parliamentary bloc (Fraktion) in the Bundestag.[3] The CSU is without question the most cohesive and homogeneous component of the CDU/CSU. Since 1957 the CSU has consistently demonstrated greater electoral appeal in Bavaria than the CDU has been able to muster in any of the other federal states.[4] In recent years, the CSU has greatly increased its membership; today it organizes a greater number of Bavarians than the SPD, which in other regions of Germany is the classic membership party.[5] Thanks to its electoral appeal and its homogeneity as a voting bloc within the CDU/CSU Fraktion in the Bundestag, the CSU has been able to exert considerable influence on national politics through its dominance of the right wing of the CDU/CSU.

The election defeat of 1969, which for the first time forced the CDU/CSU into the role of an opposition party, also led to basic changes in its membership. The organizational apparatus of the party was tightened and strengthened, new forms of management were introduced, public relations work was improved, and the party lost its character and structure as a party of dignitaries, becoming increasingly a membership party (1998 membership: 625,800). Traditionally, the party was particularly strong among independent craftsmen, merchants, and other entrepreneurs, as well as farmers. In more recent years the share of these groups in CDU/CSU membership (and in the overall West German population) has declined. Workers continue to be underrepresented. The influx of new party members has come primarily from white-collar groups and civil servants.

Thus far the CDU/CSU has clearly been the most successful political party in the FRG in terms of electoral support at the national level. In all Bundestag elections except two, it has emerged as the strongest parliamentary party—the sole exception being the seventh legislative period (1972–76) and the fourteenth Bundestag election in 1998. From 1953 to 1961 the CDU/CSU had an absolute majority in parliament—an unprecedented political feat for a German political party in free elections. In nine out of fourteen legislative periods, the CDU/CSU has elected the chancellor, the key figure in the FRG political system. Without a doubt, the CDU/CSU has exerted a decisive influence on the political evolution of the FRG. Under its leadership, West Germany experienced the "economic miracle," rebuilding its wartorn economy, developing a strong free market system, and evolving in the direction of a social welfare state—an orientation that won even greater impetus and prominence when the SPD took over the reigns of power beginning in 1969.

Under the leadership of the CDU/CSU, the FRG joined the West European Community and became an integral part of NATO. It also played a major role in institutionalizing the deep-seated religious-denominational conflict in Germany, effectively removing it from the political arena. Perhaps its most dramatic and greatest triumph was the achievement of German reunification under the capable leadership of Chancellor Helmut Kohl and Foreign Minister Hans-Dietrich Genscher. In the fall of 1999, however, the CDU/CSU was shaken by revelations that Helmut Kohl and other leading figures in the party were involved in a far-flung financial scandal.

THE SOCIAL DEMOCRATIC PARTY (SPD)

Founded in 1869 by A. Bebel and W. Liebknecht as the Social Democratic Workers' Party, united in 1875 with the General German Workers'

Association established by F. Lassalle in 1863, outlawed from 1878 to 1890 by Bismarck's Anti-Socialist Laws, the SPD has historically represented the German workers' movement. Of all the political parties in Germany, the SPD can claim the longest continuous history and strongest traditions. With 34.8 percent of the seats, it was the most powerful party in the Reichstag in 1912. In November 1918, it was the SPD politician Philipp Scheidemann who proclaimed the free German republic to forestall the proclamation of a socialist republic by the communists. Friedrich Ebert, the chairman of the SPD, became the first president of the Weimar Republic in 1919 and held that office until 1925. Later, the SPD, under the leadership of Otto Wels, was the only party in the Reichstag to vote unanimously against Hitler's Enabling Act in 1933. During the Nazi era, the SPD fought against Hitler as a banned and underground organization. In 1945 it was reestablished by Kurt Schumacher. A long-time SPD politician, Schumacher was a member of the Reichstag during 1930–33 and a concentration camp inmate for more than 10 years under the Nazis. In the Soviet occupation zone, the SPD was forced into unification with the Communist party in 1946, becoming part of the combined Socialist Unity party of Germany (SED), the ruling party of East Germany; the SPD was subsequently prohibited altogether in the GDR.

The SPD stands for parliamentary democracy and social justice secured by law. Its fundamental position was outlined in the *Godesberg Program of Principles* adopted in 1959, which emphasizes freedom, justice, and solidarity as basic political values. Until 1959 the SPD was—at least formally—committed to the *Heidelberg Program of 1925,* which still proclaimed the "struggle for the liberation of the working class" as an objective of the party, reflecting the Marxist past of the SPD's heritage. In more recent times, however, the SPD has developed increasingly into a reform-oriented integration party, actively seeking the support of population segments outside the working class. In the Godesberg Program of Principles of 1959, the SPD accordingly renounced the concept of a narrow ideological party and embraced the idea of a more broadly based party dedicated to the idea of a reform-oriented socialism. That program acknowledged the framework of a market economy, "to be adapted to the constant structural changes in a systematic way," with the state exercising the function of maintaining order.

In addition to full employment and expanded codetermination for workers and employees, the SPD has sought the establishment of curbs on large-scale economic power and the protection of private ownership of the means of production—as long as such protection does not interfere with a just social order.[6] For many years the SPD has consistently advocated an extension of the social security system, as well as expanded educational opportunities in order to make it possible for all people "to develop their talents and abilities without hindrance." In an important party document promulgated at the Mannheim Party Congress in 1975, the SPD defined in broad outline the parameters of its economic and political program for the years 1975–85 and affirmed "freedom, justice and solidarity" as its basic values.[7]

It was the SPD, under the leadership of Chancellor Willy Brandt, which was the collective architect of the Ostpolitik, the new set of policies toward Eastern Europe and the USSR, which at the beginning of the 1970s opened up an era of improved East-West relations and made possible the so-called détente between the superpowers and, subsequently, their respective allies. Segments of the SPD wavered in their support of the Western Alliance—largely over the issue of the stationing of new missiles in Europe, in particular the deployment of Pershing II and cruise missiles wanted by NATO and scheduled for the end of 1983 in accordance with the NATO two-track decision of 1979. Along with disputes over economic policy, it was this issue that greatly complicated the position of Chancellor Helmut Schmidt and thus was instrumental in bringing an end to more than a decade of SPD rule, shattering the 8-year-old government of a very popular chancellor in October 1982.

With 774,431 members in 1998, the SPD, by a considerable margin, is the largest political party in the FRG. Its position of preeminence in terms of absolute party membership, however, has been declining. As is apparent from Table 17–1, in 1968 the SPD accounted for nearly two-thirds of the total membership of all parties

represented in the Bundestag, but by 1979 its share had steadily declined to slightly over one-half—a loss of more than 12 percentage points, or more than 1 percent per year. During the same period, the CDU and CSU registered corresponding gains in membership development—at an equally steady pace.

The changes in the social structure of the SPD reflect its transformation from a political party consisting predominantly of workers to a more broadly based *Volkspartei* (people's party). In 1930, workers accounted for approximately 60 percent of the total membership of the SPD; that figure had dwindled to 45 percent in 1952, and to 22 percent in 1977. During the same period, the number of white-collar employees in the SPD increased from 10 percent in 1930 to 24 percent in 1977, and the number of civil servants from 4 to 13 percent.[8] Self-employed persons account for only a small share. Pensioners and housewives, on the other hand, constitute more significant segments of the SPD party membership (a total of 24 percent in 1977). And at times, young voters still in school have accounted for a significant share of the SPD membership (7 percent in 1973, for example).

As Germany's oldest political party, the SPD has had comparatively little influence on the evolution of German politics as a ruling party in the twentieth century—either in the prewar Reich or in the postwar FRG. Always afflicted with the distrust of the bourgeois or establishment parties, at times forced into an existence of illegality and underground activity, the SPD has not had a great deal of opportunity to leave its mark. During the postwar period, the SPD had to content itself with the role of opposition party for 20 years before assuming power in coalition with the FDP in 1969—after acquiring its initial experience in governing in the Grand Coalition with the CDU/CSU (1966–69). During its reign in the 1970s, the SPD was faced with the difficulty of ruling against an increasing majority of CDU/CSU-governed states in the Bundesrat.

The electoral fortunes of the SPD in recent years and its relative decline in terms of membership since the late 1960s suggest that the SPD has not managed its transition from a working-class party to an integration party altogether successfully. The SPD by now includes a large

Table 17–1 Membership and Electoral Strength fo Bundestag Parties, 1968–91[a]

Year/Election	SPD Number of Members	SPD Percent of All Parties	SPD Percent of Total Votes	SPD Number of Seats	CDU/CSU Number of Members	CDU/CSU Percent of All Parties	CDU/CSU Percent of Total Votes	CDU/CSU Number of Seats	FDP Number of Members	FDP Percent of All Parties	FDP Percent of Total Votes	FDP Number of Seats	Members per 1,000 Eligible Voters
1968	732,446	63.7%		202	360,159	31.3%		245	57,034	5.0%		49	27.1
1969 BTE			42.7%	224			46.1%	242			5.8%	30	27.1
1969	778,945	64.0		224	380,187	31.2		242	58,750	4.8		30	28.6
1970	820,202	63.1		224	422,459	32.5		242	56,511	4.4		30	30.4
1971	847,456	62.0		224	465,530	34.0		242	53,302	3.9		30	31.8
1972				222				248				26	
1972 BTE			45.8	230			44.9	225			8.4	41	
1972	954,394	61.9		230	529,919	34.3		225	57,757	3.7		41	35.7
1973	973,601	60.6		230	569,306	35.5		225	63,205	3.6		41	37.1
1974	957,253	56.9		230	653,294	38.8		225	70,938	4.2		41	38.7
1975	998,471	55.6		230	723,075	40.3		225	74,032	4.1		41	41.1
1976 BTE			42.6	214			48.6	243			7.9	39	
1976	1,022,191	53.8		214	798,443	42.0		243	79,162	4.2		39	43.3
1977	1,006,316	52.7		214	824,187	43.1		243	79,539	4.2		39	43.3
1978	997,444	51.9		214	840,996	43.9		243	80,928	4.2		39	43.4
1979	998,000	51.6		214	852,029	44.1		243	83,000	4.3		39	43.4
1980 BTE			42.9	218			44.5	226			10.6	53	
1983 BTE			38.2	202			48.8	255			6.9	35	
1984	916,485	48.2		202	914,621	48.1		255	71,183	3.7		35	43.1
1990 BTE			33.5	239			43.8	303			11.0	79	
1991	928,000	45.9		239	941,500	46.6		303	151,000	7.2		79	33.4

[a]Membership figures for CSU used to calculate total CDU/CSU membership in 1970, as well as membership figures for FDP and SPD in 1979, are based on interpolation. BTE = Bundestag Election. Membership figures are as of the end of the year. The first entry for 1972 reflects changes in party affiliation ("defections") of Bundestag deputies.

Source: H. Kaack and R. Roth, eds., *Handbuch des deutschen Parteiensystems*, vol. 1, pp. 82–83; Otto Model, Carl Creifelds, eds., *Staatsbürgertaschenbuch*, p. 109; *Stat. Jahrb.* BRD 1982, pp. 83, 85; *Stat. Jahrb.* BRD 1993, pp. 99, 100; *Daten Report 5*, p. 182.

segment of members who do not (or no longer) support the idea of far-reaching change and the establishment of a new order. Some critics have argued that the SPD has ceased to be a reform party[9] and instead has become a party in which the nonworking-class elements have come to exercise a disproportionately large influence. Given the opposition within its own ranks, especially from the Young Socialists (Jusos) and the Study Group for Employee Questions—that is, the left wing; given the changed socioeconomic and professional structure of its membership; given its decline in electoral appeal at the national level; and given the pressure on the SPD from the Left—that is, from the Greens, the identity problem of the SPD (working-class versus integration-party orientation) is likely to continue for some time to come.[10] Even after unification, SPD membership increased to only 920,000 in 1991, before declining once again. Nevertheless, in the 1998 Bundestag election, the SPD won a decisive victory and returned to power.

THE FREE DEMOCRATIC PARTY (FDP)

The FDP was founded by Theodor Heuss and Reinhold Maier in 1945 and constituted as a federal party in 1948, bringing together the state associations formed by liberal groups of various orientations in all of the Western occupation zones during 1945–47. The FDP continues the traditions of German liberalism, which had its origin in a bourgeois reaction to the late phases of absolutism and was shared by quite a number of parties before World War II. Historically the FDP has reflected the division of German liberalism into a left-liberal and a national-liberal wing; party cohesion, therefore, has been a major problem for the FDP.

The freedom and dignity of the individual are central to the political philosophy and concept of society endorsed by the FDP. It follows that tolerance and a state based on the rule of law (Rechtsstaat) constitute fundamental elements in the political outlook and conception of the FDP. The preservation of the rights of the citizen vis-à-vis avoidable intervention by the state is a prominent theme, for example, in the Freiburg

Theses (1971), the *Kiel Theses* (1977), and the decisions of the FDP Federal Party Congress of 1978. Accordingly, the FDP has been a voice of caution, warning against "overreaction" on such issues as the formulation of criminal law, dealing with terrorism, and the qualifications required for entry into the civil service. The FDP seeks greater humaneness in economic life and the equality of men and women in politics and in the economy, as well as in work, education, and family life.

The FDP also advocates greater citizen participation in administration and favors the introduction of "citizen demands" at the level of the local community. Having laid claim to the heritage of the great democratic revolutions in America and France at the end of the eighteenth century, the FDP seeks the democratization and liberalization of state and society. In particular, the FDP aspires to bring about an end to the "imbalance of advantage and the concentration of economic power resulting from the accumulation of money and wealth and the concentration of the ownership of the means of production in a few hands."[11] Furthermore, the FDP has advocated an educational system that meets the demands of the economy, of modern technology, and of the state, while at the same time enabling all citizens to examine critically their life situation and expectations for the future and to take an active part in shaping their lives in a democratic process. Over the years the FDP has been an advocate for those who are limited in their ability to perform and produce, for the old, and for the economically disadvantaged. Among other measures, the FDP has strongly supported the expansion of the system of incentive measures designed to encourage savings and to make an accumulation of a modest degree of wealth possible for all citizens. In contrast to the SPD and the CDU/CSU, the FDP, in the Theses *"Free Church in a Free State"* (1974), has advocated the mutual independence of church and state.

In terms of membership, the FDP is by far the smallest of the political parties traditionally represented in the Bundestag. Its membership has fluctuated a great deal—ranging from 53,302 in 1971 to an estimated 151,000 in 1991. The change in coalition partners (from the SPD to the CDU/CSU) at the national level in 1982—a development foreshadowed by a similar change at the state level during the preceding years—proved costly for the FDP. In the election in March 1983, it received only 6.9 percent of the votes and 34 seats in the Bundestag—its worst showing in over 10 years. In the first all-German election in 1990, however, the FDP won 11 percent of the total vote (10.6 percent in West Germany and 12.9 percent in East Germany)—a vote that reflected the popularity of Foreign Minister Hans-Dietrich Genscher, who played a major role in setting the stage for German reunification.

Organized in state associations that match the federal states of the FRG, the FDP has a comparatively small party apparatus. It maintains contacts with industrial, agricultural, and professional groupings, but has only limited connections with the German Trade Union Federation (DGB). Historically the self-employed, white-collar employees, and civil servants have dominated the membership of the FDP, with workers accounting for only 5 percent. As might be expected, the electoral strength of the FDP and its electorate have varied with its coalition preferences (see Table 17–2).

Until the 1998 election and the formation of the SPD-Alliance 90/Greens coalition, the FDP has been the third but pivotal party which—with the exception of the years 1953–61, when the

Table 17–2 Social Composition of Party Membership in the FRG, 1984 (in Percent)

Social Group	CDU	CSU	SPD	FDP
Workers	10.1%	14.8%	27.6%	5%
Salaried employees	28.1	22.9	25.6	30
Civil Servants	12.4	12.5	10.9	14
Self-employed	24.9	28.6	4.5	19
Pensioners	4.7	4.7	8.1	12
Housewives	11.1	5.2	12.1	11
Those still in school or professional training	6.5	6.3	8.5	9

Source: Wolfgang Rudzio, *Das politische System der Bundesrepublik Deutschland: Eine Einführung* (Opladen: Leske Verlag + Budrig GmbH, 1987), p. 161.

CDU/CSU won an absolute majority—has always been necessary for the formation of a coalition government. In its role as a coalition partner with the CDU/CSU until 1966 and with the SPD during 1969–82, the FDP has served a corrective function—exerting at times a disproportionately great influence on national policy. During its short-lived phase as the opposition party (1966–69), the FDP developed a progressive action program, but in more recent years it has increasingly moved away from its earlier reform positions.

THE FEDERAL GOVERNMENT: CHANCELLOR AND CABINET

The federal government in Germany consists of the federal chancellor *(Bundeskanzler)* and his cabinet—the federal ministers appointed and dismissed by the federal president, upon the proposal of the chancellor. In addition to his key role in determining the composition of the federal government, the chancellor also sets forth, and is responsible for, the general policy guidelines of the federal government. "Within the limits of these guidelines," according to Article 65 of the Basic Law, "each Federal Minister shall conduct the affairs of his department autonomously and on his own responsibility."

In the constitutional theory and practice of the FRG, this provision has come to mean that the federal chancellor cannot bypass a minister and deal directly with a department or a civil servant within the ministry or interfere in the daily affairs and routines of a ministry. However, if the policies pursued by a ministry violate the chancellor's general guidelines, the chancellor has the authority to dismiss the minister in question, or to effect the repeal of a particular policy by means of a direct order.

The chancellor is enjoined by the Basic Law to "conduct the affairs of the Federal Government in accordance with rules of procedure adopted by it and approved by the Federal President." The chancellor himself is nominated by the federal president and elected by the Bundestag. In practice, however, the president's right to nominate the chancellor has become a mere formality due to the predetermination of the chancellor by the election results, in the case of a general election, or by the coalition agreements preceding a general election campaign, or a no-confidence vote in the Bundestag.[12] The reduction of the number of parties and the clear-cut election outcomes have resulted in giving the voter considerable influence on the election of the chancellor. Generally speaking, in the case of general elections the chancellor has been determined by the election results—either directly or indirectly; only in the four cases where a new chancellor has come into office between election periods has the chancellor been elected without the participation of the electorate—that is, by the Bundestag.

Usually the strongest party in the Bundestag supplies the chancellor, but not always—for example, in 1969 and 1976. Because of the strong position of the chancellor within the constitutional framework set up by the Basic Law, the opposition parties have designated "chancellor candidates" since the early 1960s. While this practice is not provided for in the Basic Law, it makes good sense in view of the fact that the chancellor is clearly the key figure in the political system of the FRG.

Only the chancellor is responsible to the Bundestag; the cabinet ministers, in turn, are responsible to him alone. In the FRG, in contrast to the Weimar Republic, there is no individual ministerial responsibility. While federal ministers may be subjected to questions by FRG deputies, the Bundestag cannot remove individual ministers through a no-confidence vote without ousting the chancellor and his entire cabinet. The position of the chancellor himself is made more secure by the provision that a parliamentary majority against him is not sufficient to remove him from office; the parliamentary opposition must also be able to marshal a majority of votes in favor of a new chancellor (the "positive" or "constructive" no-confidence vote).[13]

The provisions in the Basic Law defining the position and authority of the chancellor reflect, on the one hand, the desire of the framers of the Basic Law to exclude any misuse of power and, on the other, to concentrate governmental power in the office of the chancellor. A close reading of Articles 62–69 of the Basic Law reveals three competing and, in a sense, contradictory principles:

1. The *chancellor principle,* according to which the chancellor determines the general policy guidelines and is responsible for them to the Bundestag.
2. The *department principle,* according to which each federal minister is autonomous within his or her own sphere and responsible to the chancellor.
3. The *collegial principle,* according to which differences of opinion between the federal ministers are to be decided by the federal government.

These formal provisions, however, can merely define the parameters within which the exercise of the powers of the chancellor tends to move. The actual authority and power of a particular chancellor depend on a number of extraconstitutional factors—his own personality and popular appeal, the relative strength of his party or coalition in the Bundestag, the level of economic prosperity, international developments during his term of office, and so on.

Konrad Adenauer, the first FRG chancellor, enjoyed great popularity and had a very forceful personality, as well as a distinctly authoritarian style. He clearly dominated his cabinet and frequently bypassed the Bundestag; disdainful of committee work and decision making, he preferred to rely more on top civil servants than on the ministers in his cabinet. His forceful and authoritarian leadership style gave rise to the description of the FRG as the "chancellor democracy"—a polemical slogan first used in the 1950s but quickly adopted by social scientists to describe rather accurately the FRG's actual constitutional-political evolution in the early years.[14]

Observers of politics in the FRG generally agree that the structural principles underlying the federal government clearly favor the position of the chancellor. His "guideline authority" is generally interpreted and accepted as the decisive leadership function that shapes policy. His position of preeminence is further underlined by the *Rules of Procedure of the Federal Government,* which stipulate, among other things, that all plans and measures affecting the policy guidelines of the chancellor must be submitted to him for approval; that the chancellor has the authority to determine the portfolio, or the functions and sphere of jurisdiction, of the ministries; that in cases of doubt the decision of the chancellor must be obtained; and that the federal ministers are bound by the rule of solidarity in terms of the chancellor's policy guidelines when making statements in public.[15]

To assist the chancellor in his various duties is the responsibility of the Chancellor's Office, which is the real "nerve center" of the federal government. With its steering, coordinating, and control functions, this office is the chancellor's chief instrument for influencing the decision-making process in the federal government, the Bundestag, and the chancellor's own administration. The Chancellor's Office has a staff of approximately 500 and is thus larger than the staffs of the British prime minister or the French premier, but smaller than the White House staff. Headed by a cabinet minister without portfolio or a senior civil servant with the rank of state secretary, the Chancellor's Office is organized into six departments, which correspond roughly to the structure and most important divisions of the cabinet and provide liaison between the chancellor and the federal ministries. Since collectively these departments duplicate or "mirror" the federal government in miniature, they are referred to as *Spiegelreferate* ("mirror sections").[16] Due to their regular access to the chancellor on an almost daily basis, the key officials of the Chancellor's Office are among the most important and influential people in the government of the FRG. It was through this office that Konrad Adenauer virtually ran his party and established firm control over the bureaucracy, and it was the unmasking of a high-ranking official in this office as an East German spy that led to the resignation of Chancellor Willy Brandt in 1974.

While the Basic Law invests the chancellor with the power to form his government by proposing the composition of his cabinet to the federal president, in practice he is never entirely free to do so. In selecting his ministers, the chancellor usually has to satisfy the demands made by his own party (no easy thing to do, given the heterogeneity of the CDU/CSU and the range of factions in the SPD), meet the demands of the coalition party (usually specific demands for choice ministries), and consider the qualifications of available and likely candidates in terms of the requirements of the job.

Like his counterpart in France and Great Britain (and, to a lesser extent, his opposite number in the U.S. Cabinet), the typical FRG minister is a successful politician with extensive experience in parliament, in the party hierarchy, or in his profession.[17] The most common avenues to ministerial office in the FRG are (1) a successful career in the party hierarchy, (2) a successful occupational career (in business, interest group administration, or the free professions), (3) a successful career in the civil service or in local and state government, and (4) recognized expertise in science, economics, education, or another important field. Generally speaking, while most federal ministers in the FRG have been competent in their sphere of responsibility, political considerations have frequently tended to outweigh the criterion of qualification in the selection of ministers.

The number of cabinet posts in the FRG has been slightly larger than in the United States, but smaller than in Great Britain, France, or Russia.

The size of the cabinet is a product of bureaucratic tradition as well as of "coalition arithmetic." The number of ministries in the FRG has varied from fifteen to twenty. While ministers do not have to be members of the Bundestag (or of a political party for that matter), they usually are. As a matter of fact, over the years the Bundestag has become an important training ground for federal ministers—a function that was enhanced by the introduction of the institution of the parliamentary state secretary (modeled after the British parliamentary secretary) in 1967.[18]

Including the federal chancellor, the 1998 FRG Cabinet has 20 members—five of them women. With the exception of the Foreign Affairs Office, the SPD controls all of the classic and most powerful ministries—defense, finance, interior, and justice. One cabinet member is without party affiliation. Assuming that the coalition holds, the Schröder administration is in a relatively strong position with a majority of 57 votes in the Bundestag.

Born in 1944, Germany's new chancellor, Gerhard Schröder, is the first FRG chancellor without direct memory of World War II. He grew up in a family of six, without his father, who died in the war. His family being "as poor as church mice," he put himself through school and studied law. A member of the SPD since 1963, he rose quickly in the party hierarchy, becoming the federal chairman of the Young Socialists (Jusos) in the SPD in 1978 and a member of the SPD Party Council in 1979. From

INSTITUTIONAL, PARTY, AND GENDER REPRESENTATION IN THE 1998 CABINET

Institution	Party	Gender
Chancellor's Office		
Federal Chancellor	SPD	M
Chief of Chancellor's Office	SPD	M
State Minister for Culture	SPD	M
State Minister for Reconstruction and Affairs of the New States	SPD	M
Foreign Affairs Office		
Minister and vice-chancellor	Alliance 90/Greens	M
State Minister	SPD	M
State Minister	Alliance 90/Greens	M
Ministries/Ministers:		
Interior	SPD	M
Justice	SPD	F
Finance	SPD	M
Economics and Technology	Unaffiliated	M
Nutrition, Agriculture and Forestry	SPD	M
Labor and Social Affairs	SPD	M
Defense	SPD	M
Family, Senior Citizens, Women, and Youth	SPD	F
Health	Alliance 90/Greens	F
Regional Planning, Construction, Housing, and Transportation	SPD	M
Environment, Conservation and Reactor Safety	Alliance 90/Greens	M
Education and Research	SPD	F
Economic Cooperation and Development	SPD	F

1980 to 1986 he served as a member of the Bundestag. In 1986 he became a member of the national executive committee of the SPD and in 1989 a member of its presidium. Having left the Bundestag in 1986, he became a member of the *Landtag* (land parliament) of Lower Saxony and was elected as chairman of the SPD-Fraktion. In 1990 he became minister-president of Lower Saxony, forming a coalition of the SPD and the Greens. He served in that capacity until he once again won a Bundestag mandate in September 1998 and became FRG Chancellor a month later, winning 351 votes of the 666 votes cast in the Bundestag. He stands for justice and social responsibility. His goal is to create a modernized society in which all have equal opportunities.

The election of Gerhard Schröder marks the first direct transfer of political power from the ruling coalition to the opposition as the result of a general election in the history of the FRG. All previous changes of government were the result of the rise and fall of ruling coalitions in the Bundestag—e.g., through the formation of the Grand Coalition in 1966, the subsequent breakup of that coalition and the formation of the SPD/FDP coalition in 1969, and the formation of the CDU/CSU-FDP coalition in 1982 and the use of the constructive no-confidence vote, which unseated Chancellor Helmut Schmidt and brought Chancellor Helmut Kohl into power.

THE FEDERAL PRESIDENT

The federal president is the ceremonial head of state of the FRG. Following Bagehot's classic distinction on the British constitution, the federal president thus represents the "dignified part" and the chancellor, the "efficient part" of the German constitutional system. When conceptualizing the office of the federal president, the framers of the Basic Law sought to eliminate the tragic problems created by the dual executive in the Weimar Republic. Accordingly, in the Basic Law the federal president was clearly subordinated to the chancellor and the Bundestag in regard to his policy-making role. Moreover, his overall constitutional position was substantially weakened.

To begin with, the federal president is not directly elected and thus cannot claim a popular mandate. Instead, he is elected every 5 years by a special Federal Assembly consisting of all Bundestag deputies and of an equal number of deputies elected by the state parliaments on the basis of proportional representation according to party. After public discussion of the candidates, the election itself is held without debate and is secret—which makes it difficult for party leaders to enforce discipline in cases where party politics are involved—as they were in 1969 in connection with the election of Gustav Heinemann, the first Social-Democratic federal president. According to a poll published in January, 1999, 52 percent of western Germans and 59 percent of eastern Germans think the president should be elected by a popular vote.[19]

In addition to extensive representative functions, the federal president signs treaties with foreign countries, accredits and receives envoys; he signs all laws, certifies their enactment in accordance with the prescribed procedure, and promulgates them in the *Bundesgesetzblatt* (Federal Legal Gazette); he appoints and dismisses federal judges, civil servants, and officers and noncommissioned officers; and he exercises the right of pardon. Upon the proposal of the chancellor, he appoints and dismisses federal ministers. Whether the federal president is a mere "state notary" or has real power—to refuse to promulgate laws (ones that he finds unconstitutional) or to reject appointments (of, in his view, unsuitable persons)—is in dispute. According to his oath of office, the federal president must preserve and defend the Basic Law.

If the Bundestag is unable to produce a majority for the election of a chancellor, the federal president can appoint a chancellor elected by a minority or dissolve the Bundestag. Likewise, if a chancellor is refused a vote of confidence by the Bundestag and the majority fails to elect a new chancellor, the federal president can dissolve the Bundestag or declare a state of legislative emergency in accordance with Article 81, enabling the chancellor and his cabinet to govern without majority support in the Bundestag for a period of up to 6 months. Here too, the powers of the federal president are circumscribed. A state of legislative emergency can be declared only at the request of the federal government and with the consent of the Bundesrat. It is largely because of this possible role of the federal president in a parliamentary crisis that the case has been made for keeping politically inexperienced persons out of this office.

The federal president is assisted in his work by the Office of the Federal President, headed by a high-level civil servant with the rank of state secretary. The office is divided into seven departments, including Protocol and Foreign Affairs; Constitutional Questions; and Liaison with the Supreme Federal Agencies—to mention some of the more important ones. In contrast to the Weimar Republic, the federal president himself cannot take part in cabinet meetings. However, he is represented by his state secretary or the secretary's deputy.

For the duration of his term of office, the federal president is expected to be politically neutral, that is, nonpartisan. This expectation has generally been met by the men who have held the office. Only one federal president, Walter Scheel (1974–79), attempted to enlarge the powers of the office; Scheel's actions met with the determined resistance of the Bundestag and the chancellor.[20]

OTHER POLICY-MAKING INSTITUTIONS

The activity of the major political parties, the chancellor and his cabinet, the Bundestag and Bundesrat, as well as the federal president, involve the more visible aspects of political leadership and policy making in the FRG. However, our discussion of the policy process would be incomplete without a consideration of the role of the state administration (bureaucracy), the judicial system, and a variety of planning bodies. Like other modern polities, the FRG has an elaborate court structure and a highly developed bureaucracy at the local, state, and national levels, which play an important role in the implementation and adjudication of policy. In the case of Germany the civil service and the judiciary are of particular importance because these two institutions survived the frequent regime changes relatively intact. This fact, no doubt, is part of the reason why—both at the level of the elites and the masses—Germans have expressed greater confidence in dealing with the courts and the bureaucracy than with other governmental institutions.[21]

While technically competent and efficient, these two institutions have nevertheless failed Germany at crucial points in its history. Their ambivalent or even hostile stance was an important contributing factor in the downfall of the Weimar Republic, and their more or less wholesale capitulation to Hitler greatly facilitated his rapid consolidation of power after 1933. While the Western Allies were fully intent upon reorganizing and "democratizing" both the civil service and the judiciary in 1945, nothing—with the exception of the disqualification of Nazis from top-level leadership positions—was actually done. The Allied reform plans were postponed, in part because—in the aftermath of the fall of Czechoslovakia and the Berlin Blockade—foreign policy considerations soon came to prevail over plans for internal reform. More than five decades after its establishment, the FRG still faces the challenge of a fundamental reorganization of the civil service and the judiciary, a task rendered much more difficult in the meantime by the firm (re)entrenchment of these two "castes" in the political system of the FRG.

In 1996, according to government statistics, employees in the public service numbered about 5.2 million, including 4.2 million full-time employees.[22] At that time nearly one out of every eight Germans was employed by the state. Not quite half of these state employees have the coveted status of *Beamter* or *Beamtin*—that is, public official for life. By far most of the employees in the public service (nearly 60 percent) work at the state level; approximately one-third at the local level; and about 11 percent at the national

level. Of the civil servants with life tenure, about 80 percent are employed at the state level, 12 percent at the local level, and 8 percent at the national level. It is estimated that about 20,000 civil servants are employed in the federal ministries, close to one-seventh of these in decision-making positions.

Both law and custom confer special privileges and obligations on civil servants at all levels in the political system of the FRG. In exchange for loyalty, obedience, and the willingness to make a long-term commitment to the state (including forgoing the right to strike),[23] the civil servant is given extraordinary job security, a generous salary, excellent benefits, including superb retirement pay, and special privileges running the gamut from lower insurance rates for automobiles to preferential interest rates for home mortgages and loans.

In recent years the civil servants have been subjected to a great deal of criticism. Their privileged position and the antiquated reward structure have been questioned on a number of grounds. The "structural disorganization" of the state administration in the FRG is the focus of many reform proposals, but thus far little actual progress has been made. The German system of state administration is also frequently criticized for its peculiar combination of hierarchical organization and decentralized structure. According to the charges made by critics, the system of administration that has developed in the FRG is so complex and fragmented that it inhibits large-scale reforms and intelligent policy planning.

It is precisely the failure of the system of state administration to come to grips with the wide-ranging problems of a modern society that has provided the impetus to the development of various planning bodies at the national and state level. Initiated in the early 1960s, partly in response to proposals made by the EEC, the focus to begin with was on economic and financial planning. Later on, planning was extended to education, land use, and regional development. In 1969 a special planning department was set up in the Chancellor's Office to coordinate the work of planning officials in the various ministries, to facilitate the formation of "project groups," and thus to encourage more systematic work and interministerial cooperation. However, this promising development suffered a serious setback in the early 1970s—largely due to the lack of support by the political leaders. The effective use of centralized planning, even under the best of circumstances (that is, with strong support from the political leadership) faces enormous difficulties in the FRG because of its highly fragmented institutional structure, which makes uniform implementation exceedingly difficult.

If life in the FRG for the most part seems highly regulated and predictable, this is in part because most Germans tend to be very law- and regulation-minded. Rules and regulations, whether grounded in custom or in law, play an enormous role in German life, especially in the rural areas and in small towns. In spite of some relaxation, store hours, for the most part, continue to be strictly regulated. If a German forgets to stock up for the weekend before Saturday noon, he or she is out of luck (and so is the family!). Given the maze of rules and regulations, it is no surprise that the judicial system in the FRG plays an enormously important role in the life of the citizen.

Unlike Great Britain or the United States, the FRG belongs to the continental legal tradition, which stresses the importance of, and relies on, comprehensive legal codes. In that tradition, the judge is viewed as an administrator who applies the relevant provisions of the legal code to a particular case, not as an independent actor in the judicial process. Accordingly, unlike the Anglo-American concept of law and justice, this tradition does not recognize the principle of *stare decisis,* legal precedent or judge-made law. In the continental legal tradition, the state is viewed as the sole source of law. Consequently, there is no basis or place for the recognition of common or natural law, which plays such a crucial role in the Anglo-American legal tradition.[24] In retrospect it is easy to see how this kind of legal positivism, by elevating the state above society and recognizing it as the only source of law, contributed to the statism that was the hallmark of the Nazi era and to the ignominious capitulation of the legal profession to Hitler.

As in other European states, the court system and the state bureaucracy in the FRG are hopelessly intertwined. Out of a total of 22,134 judges in 1995, only 510 served at the federal level.[25]

Judges are civil servants—comparable in terms of salaries, promotion criteria, rank, and tenure to civil servants in the higher service.[26] Since advancement depends on the recommendation of superiors in the judicial hierarchy, few judges are inclined to rock the boat by demonstrating an independent point of view or by showing personal initiative. An encouraging sign, however, is the pronounced difference in attitude of the younger judges. Younger judges in the FRG as a group are much more strongly committed to social change and reform.[27] On the other hand, the civil service ordinarily does not attract the more independent-minded, brilliant, and ambitious students.[28]

On January 1, 1990, there were 665 courts of first instance with jurisdiction in civil and criminal cases, and 194 specialized courts of first instance with jurisdiction in cases involving labor law, administrative law, financial law, and social insurance law in West Germany—all under the control of the states. There were only eight national courts—all of them high courts of appeal. Unlike the United States, there is a uniform body of law throughout the FRG and a common set of procedural rules that all regular courts follow.

Aside from the absence of a separate system of state and federal courts, the FRG also differs from the United States because of its elaborate system of specialized courts, already mentioned. On the other hand, the FRG judicial system is fairly unique among European countries and similar to that of the United States in that it has accepted and institutionalized the principle of judicial review—an entirely novel concept in German philosophy and in the continental legal tradition. The function of judicial review is exercised by the Federal Constitutional Court—a uniquely independent institution (see Chapter 15).

NOTES

[1]Earlier statements of principles include the *Hamburg Program* (1953) and the *Berlin Program* (1968), which was further developed at the Düsseldorf Party Congress in 1971.

[2]H. J. Kleinsteuber, "Christlich-Demokratische Union," in K. Sontheimer and H. H. Röhring, eds., *Handbuch des politischen Systems der Bundesrepublik Deutschland* (Munich: R Piper & Co. Verlag, 1978) pp. 163–166. See also H. Putze, *Die CDU* (Düsseldorf: Droste, 1976).

[3]The political partnership of the CDU/CSU was temporarily threatened after the elections in 1976, when forces in the CSU leadership attempted to dissociate the CSU from its sister party. The attempt ended in failure because of the resistance of opposition groups within the CSU and the determined refusal of the CDU, which threatened to build up a CDU organization in Bavaria.

[4]The electoral appeal of the CSU increased from 29.2 percent of the total votes in Bavaria in 1949 to 60 percent in 1976. In 1990 it received 51.9 percent of the vote; in 1998 it fell below the 50 percent mark.

[5]On the CSU, see A. Mintzel, *Die CSU—Anatomie einer konservativen Partei* (Opladen: Westdeutscher Verlag, 1975); T. Waigel, "Das neue Profil der CSU," *Politische Studien 26* (July–August 1976): 405ff.

[6]The nationalization of the means of production advocated by the Marxist wing of the SPD was rejected by the majority of the SPD at the party congress in Hannover in 1973.

[7]Cited in Sontheimer and Röhring, *Handbuch,* pp. 541–542.

[8]Ibid., p. 542, and H. Kaak/R. Roth, ed., *Handbuch des deutschen Parteiensystems,* vol 1 (Opladen: Leske Verlag + Budrich GmbH, 1980), p. 95.

[9]W. D. Narr et al., *SPD—Staatspartei oder Reformpartei?* (Munich: Piper, 1976), p. 235.

[10]On the SPD, see H. J Brauns et al., *Die SPD in der Krise* (Frankfurt/M.: Fischer-Taschenbuch-Verlag, 1976); H. Heimann, *Theoriediskussion in der SPD. Ergebnisse und Perspektiven* (Frankfurt/M.: Europäische Verlagsanstalt, 1975); S. Miller, *Die SPD vor und nach Godesberg* (Bonn-Bad Godesberg: Verlag Neue Gesellschaft, 1976); J. Raschke, *Innerparteiliche Opposition. Die Linke in der Berliner SPD* (Hamburg: Hoffmann und Campe, (1974).

[11]Cited in H. J. Kleinsteuber, "Freie Demokratische Partei (FDP), in Sontheimer and Röhring, *Handbuch,* p. 217.

[12]Since 1949 the right of the Federal President to nominate the Chancellor has been exercised in such a way that the nomination was not made until the election of the Chancellor candidate was assured.

[13]On the no-confidence mechanism, see L. C. Mayer and J. H. Burnett, *Politics in Industrial Societies: A Comparative Perspective* (New York: John Wiley & Sons, 1977), pp. 166 ff, and Klaus v. Beyme, "Misstrauensvotum," in Sontheimer and Röhring, *Handbuch,* pp. 193–195.

[14]A. Heidenheimer, "Der starke Regierungschef und das Parteiensystem: Der 'Kanzler-Effekt' in der Bundesrepublik," *Politische Vierteljahresschrift,* 1962, pp. 241–262; K. D. Bracher, "Die Kanzlerdemokratie," in R. Löwenthal and H. P. Schwarz, eds., *Die zweite Republik* (Stuttgart: Seewald Verlag, 1974), Karlheinz Niclauss, *Kanzlerdemokratie: Bonner Regierungspraxis von Konrad Adenauer bis Helmut Kohl* (Stuttgart: Verlag W. Kohlhammer, 1988).

[15]W. Hennis, "Richtlinienkompetenz und Regierungstechnik," *Recht und Staat,* no. 300/301 (1964): 7–47; G. Loewenberg, *Parlamentarismus im politischen System der Bundesrepublik Deutschland* (Tübingen: Wunderlich, 1969), pp. 265 ff.; Otto Model and Carl Creifelds, *Staatsbürger-Taschenbuch,* 20th ed. (Munich: C. H. Beck'sche Verlagsbuchhandlung, 1982), pp. 123–127.

[16]In the past these departments were (1) Law and Administration; (2) Foreign and Inner-German Relations; (3) Internal Affairs; (4) Economic, Financial, and Social Policy; (5) Planning; (6) Intelligence Services. More recently, departments dealing with Culture and (after unification) with Eastern Reconstruction have been added.

[17]As in the United States and most other countries, the cabinet has remained a predominantly male domain. Since 1961 usually one woman and at times two or three women have been included in the cabinet. The twenty-member cabinet appointed in 1990 included four women.

[18]For basic data of the FRG ministers, See Volker Ronge's essays "Bundesminister" and "Bundesministerien" in Sontheimer and Röhring, *Handbuch,* pp. 82–96.

[19]Die Woche, January 13, 1999, as cited in *The Week in Germany,* January 15, 1999.

[20]On the federal president, see H. J. Winkler, *Der Bundespräsident, Repräsentant oder Politiker?* (Opladen: Leske, 1967), and, by the same author, "Bundespräsident," in Sontheimer and Röhring, *Handbuch,* pp. 96–98.

[21]See Gabriel A. Almond and S. Verba, *The Civic Culture* (Princeton, NJ: Princeton University Press, 1963), pp. 189ff.

[22]*Stat. Jahrb.* BRD 1997, pp. 109, 531.

[23]According to prevailing legal interpretation, civil servants in the FRG do not have the right to strike.

[24]As noted in Chapter 15, the provisions in the Basic Law concerning the rights of the individual constitute an important departure from traditional German legal philosophy.

[25]*Stat. Jahrb.* BRD 1997, p. 364.

[26]Depending on educational qualifications upon entry (secondary school, intermediate school, high school, or university level), civil servants are employed and promoted in four career tracks: simple, intermediate, elevated, and higher service *(einfacher, mittlerer, gehobener, and höherer Dienst),* ranging in responsibilities from custodial and messenger work to decision-making. See Wilhelm Bleek, "Berufsbeamtentum," in Sontheimer and Röhring, *Handbuch,* p. 52.

[27]Manfred Riegel, "Political Attitudes and Perceptions of the Political System by Judges in West Germany." Paper presented at the Ninth World Congress of the IPSA, Montreal, 1973, p. 11.

[28]N. Luhmann and Renate Mayntz, *Personal im öffentlichen Dienst* (Baden-Baden: Nomos-Verlagsgesellschaft, 1973), pp. 56 ff.

Chapter 18

German Socioeconomic
and Political Performance

The government of the FRG began its existence under less than auspicious circumstances, and during the first decade of its history it was confronted with the seemingly insurmountable task of reconstruction. While much of the credit for rebuilding Germany must be given to the efforts of nongovernmental agencies, institutions, and groups, to outside assistance in the form of Marshall Plan aid, and, above all, to the hard work of countless individuals, the gigantic task could not have been accomplished without an effective governmental system to provide overall direction and coordination.

If today most Germans—especially those of the older generation in the west—have developed a strong sense of identification with the government of the FRG, it is in part because they associate that government with the successful rebuilding of their country. Beyond reconstruction, however, most Germans also associate their present political system with an unprecedented era of prosperity and stability. Furthermore, while more than 50 years ago Germans were widely regarded as international outcasts (especially in Europe), today the FRG and its citizens are respected members of the international community.

That this is so is to a large extent the result of the successful, and even impressive, performance of the political system of the FRG.

SOCIOECONOMIC PERFORMANCE

Although the FRG is notably poor in raw material resources of its own,[1] it is one of the leading industrial nations in the world. In per capita gross domestic product (GDP), the FRG (not including the new states) in 1991 ranked behind Japan, but led the EEC countries, Canada, and the United States. The reunification of West and East Germany, among other things, resulted in a substantial decrease in the per capita GDP and posed a formidable challenge even to the powerful economy of the FRG. With the new states in the east included, Germany in per capita gross domestic product in 1996 ranked behind not only the United States, Japan, and Canada, but also France, Italy, the Netherlands, and the United Kingdom.[2] For years the German mark (DM) has been one of the most stable and sought-after currencies in the world. Like Japan, the FRG is living proof that a country does not have to be

---

WORLD MARKET SHARES OF SELECTED COUNTRIES, 1992–1997 (IN PERCENT)

	1992	1993	1994	1995	1996	1997
USA	14.3%	16.0%	15.7%	15.4%	15.5%	16.4%
Germany	12.2	10.9	10.8	11.1	10.7	10.0
Japan	9.8	10.6	10.4	9.8	8.8	8.6
France	6.7	6.2	6.0	6.0	5.9	5.8
United Kingdom	5.3	5.1	5.0	5.0	5.1	5.1
Italy	5.0	4.6	4.6	4.6	4.7	4.4
China	2.8	3.3	3.6	3.8	3.8	4.2
Russia	1.3	1.4	1.7	1.6	1.5	1.4

Source: DIHT (Association of German Chamber of Industry and Commerce), at www.diht.de/aktuell/diht0540.htm

---

blessed with natural resources to be successful in terms of economic production. Today the FRG is one of the world's largest producers of iron, steel, coal, cement, chemicals, machinery, ships, and vehicles. Among the important assets of the FRG in gaining its position of prominence among the leading industrial nations have been a high standard of technology, a highly skilled and disciplined labor force, and an efficient productive sector. One of the present challenges facing the FRG is to create these high standards and levels of discipline in the relatively backward and less efficient economy it inherited from the former East Germany.

The economy of Germany is critically dependent on foreign trade. After the United States, it has the second largest foreign trade turnover in the world. More specifically, Germany is both import- and export-dependent. In 1990, prior to unification, imports and exports accounted for 22.7 percent and 26.5 percent, respectively, of the FRG's gross social product—measures comparable to GNP.[3] Furthermore, Germany is not only dependent in terms of foreign trade volumes and trading partners, but also in terms of products and industries—for example, oil, electronics, and medical technology, which involves such a giant as the Siemens Corporation with over 400,000 employees. While the export strength of the FRG has been the envy of many countries—West Germany has had an export surplus since 1952—the FRG's close link with the economies of the rest of the world also makes its own economy highly

vulnerable to disturbances in world trade. In an economy in which—prior to unification—one out of every four gainfully employed persons worked for exports, employment, standard of living, profits, and investments are highly dependent on world trade. Consequently the FRG has a vital interest in a stable world economy, free trade, and an orderly monetary system.

With respective estimated growth rates of 2.9 and 3.1 percent in 1998, the countries belonging to the European Union (EU), along with the countries that are part of the North American Free Trade Agreement (NAFTA) were the mainstays of the world economy. In 1997, 73 percent of total German exports went to European countries, 10 percent to North America (NAFTA), and 10.5 percent to the Asia/Pacific region. Even with the downturn in exports to the troubled Asian countries, Germany achieved an estimated 9 percent increase in exports in 1998 and, as in prior years, continued to have a trade surplus since imports increased at an estimated rate of only 7 percent. Part of the explanation for the strong performance of the German export economy in recent years lies in the depreciation of the German mark vis-à-vis the U.S. dollar in 1997 and the decrease in commodity prices, especially crude oil, in 1998.

In 1997, when the world economy as a whole grew by close to 19 percent, German exports increased by only 12.4 percent, resulting in a decrease in Germany's world market share (see Box above). Among the reasons for this was the relatively weak representation of German exporters

Table 18–1   FRG Trading Partners (Imports and Exports), 1996

Country of Origin/Destination	Share of Total Imports (in %)	Share of Total Exports (in %)
1. France	10.0%	10.9%
2. Netherlands	8.6	7.4
3. Italy	8.2	7.4
4. United States	7.3	7.8
5. Great Britain and Northern Ireland	6.8	8.0
6. Belgium-Luxembourg	6.3	6.2
7. Japan	5.1	2.7
8. Switzerland	4.1	4.9
9. Austria	3.8	5.6
10. Spain	3.3	3.6
Total	**64.1**	**64.5**

Source: Stat. Jahrb.BRD 1997, p. 308.

in innovative and rapidly growing markets (with the exception of East Central Europe) compared to the United States. On the other hand, because of its weaker market position in Asia, the German economy in 1998 was less affected by the crisis in Asia than were the economies of the United States or Japan.[4]

Table 18–1 shows the extent to which the economy of the FRG is intertwined with the leading industrial countries in Europe, the United States, and Japan. The ten most important trading partners account for nearly two-thirds of Germany's imports and exports. Although its world market share has decreased since 1992, Germany's export position remains strong. In 1998, when the "red-green" coalition of the SPD and Alliance 90/Greens took over the reins of power from the Kohl Administration, inflation was at an all-time low (0.9 percent) since unification. By the end of November 1998, Germany's trade surplus reached the highest level since the record year of 1989. High unemployment, on the other hand, continued to be a major problem as the Kohl era came to an end. In December 1998, seasonal unemployment rose by over 250,000, bringing total unemployment to nearly 4.2 million. For Germany as a whole, this meant an unemployment rate of 10.9 percent (9.3 percent in the western states, and 17.4 percent in the five new eastern states), compared to 4.3 percent in the United States. Benefiting from its central location in the largest open market in the world, its well-

established position to the EU-countries, and its proximity to the emerging economies in Central and Eastern Europe, the prospects for the German economy continue to be good, especially considering that its productive reinvestment (more than one-fifth of Germany's GDP) is much higher than in most of the industrialized countries, including the United States.[5]

The theoretical concept on which the development of the West German economy is based is the concept of a "social market economy," which is a composite of a number of socioeconomic models developed by various writers and which is frequently described as "neoliberalism." In the case of the FRG, the so-called *Ordoliberalismus* of the Freiburg School—a liberalism that stands for competition and the preservation of private ownership of the means of production, but permits state regulation—was particularly influential. The foremost exponent of this school, Walter Eucken, advocated the view that, from the perspective of the diffusion of power necessary to secure the liberty of the citizen, a competitive economic system and a liberal democracy are dependent on each other.[6] In Eucken's view, the political freedom of the citizen cannot be guaranteed in a centrally planned economic system.

The concept of the social market economy was shaped by the basic perspectives of neoliberalism, but it also differs in important respects. In its concept of competition, for example, it is a good deal more realistic; it places much greater emphasis on social policy; and, finally, it goes much farther in embracing the idea of state direction of essential macroeconomic processes. Despite criticisms, the basic framework and parameters of the social market economy came to be accepted by all the major parties, including the SPD.[7]

If the FRG has enjoyed an extraordinary degree of labor peace compared to other industrial countries in the world,[8] one important reason must be sought in the fact that its citizens benefit from a remarkably comprehensive social security network. Employees enjoy extensive protection against potentially deleterious financial effects and hardships resulting from old age or illness, accidents, unemployment, the bankruptcy of employers, the costs connected with retraining programs, and the like. Far from being charity, this multifaceted program of social security measures—which also includes allowances for every child,[9] rent supplement payments, state premiums to low income groups to encourage and reward regular savings, and a variety of social benefits for the needy—is paid for by contributions to the different social insurance programs, many of which are mandatory and involve employers and employees alike. Basically the intricate network of social security measures in the FRG combines the principle of insurance with the ideal of communal assistance, assuring communal help to the insured who are in need and raising the necessary funds to cover claims from membership dues. The total of public and private expenditures for social security amounts to approximately one-third of the national product—which, of course, is a staggering sum.

If one looks at the end use of the gross national product in the FRG, one finds a picture broadly comparable to that found in other Western industrialized countries—for example, Britain, France, Italy, or the United States. As might be expected, private consumption accounts for the largest share of the GNP—57.6 percent in 1996, followed by gross investments (21.5 percent), government expenditures (19.6 percent), and net foreign balance, that is, exports minus imports (1.3 percent).[10] Over the years the share of private consumption has remained fairly constant, government expenditures have tended to increase, and gross investments have declined.[11]

In looking at the rise in state expenditures, however, one must take into account the staggering amount of transfers of public funds to private households, which in 1996, for example, amounted to over DM 661 billion or 37 percent of total state expenditures.[12]

One of the challenges facing the unified Germany is to integrate the East German labor force of nearly 9 million into a single economic system—no small problem considering the differences in standards, training patterns, and work ethic that developed in the half century since the end of World War II in the separate German states. And this is not the only problem. The population of the former GDR must also be integrated culturally, psychologically, and politically. Integrating the population of the new states has proved much more difficult, protracted, and expensive than had been anticipated at the time of unification. High unemployment and the many other problems facing Germans, especially young people, in the east have generated anger and despondency. They look with envy at their prosperous countrymen in the west and, with justification, regard themselves as second-class citizens. Yet, unlike the people in the other former communist countries now embarked on the difficult road to a market economy and a democratic order, they are the beneficiaries of large-scale financial infusions from the federal government in Bonn—to the tune of approximately $490 billion in net transfers between 1991 and 1997—a sum which is equivalent on average to 4.25 percent of the West German GDP annually. These staggering financial transfers not only helped to close the gap in the standard of living, but produced investment-driven growth in the east averaging more than 7 percent per annum between 1992 and 1995.[13]

In spite of these prospects, there is little question that the abrupt transfer of the West German order to the eastern states, which was rather successful on the constitutional, institutional, and legal levels, resulted in large-scale destruction and a severe crisis in the sphere of economics, including a drop in industrial production of 65 percent during 1990–91 and the loss of 2 million jobs in manufacturing and 750,000 in agriculture. The "shock therapy" approach to economic restructuring in the eastern states produced open unemployment of 17.5 percent and hidden unemployment of 30–35 percent. While, thanks to the large-scale financial assistance from the FRG government, the virtual collapse of the economy in the east did not lead to mass poverty, the Germans in the east clearly went through an extraordinary trauma. Between 1989 and 1992, the east German birthrate declined by 60 percent and the marriage rate by 65 percent. As Jurgen Kocka, a professor of history at the Free University of Berlin, has observed: "Declines of this magnitude are extremely rare in history. Only the Great Wars offer similar examples."[14]

Generally speaking, the FRG—whether governed by the CDU/CSU or by the SPD—has pursued remarkably enlightened policies with respect to the rights and welfare of the workers. Not only have the dependently employed citizens in the FRG shared in the economic prosperity of their country, they have also become increasingly involved in economic decision making directly affecting them—at least at the enterprise level.

The idea of worker codetermination, which goes back to legislation adopted in 1920 providing for the election of worker representatives in all companies, received a major impetus during the postwar period. In 1952 the FRG, then a mere 2 years old, enacted legislation giving important codetermination rights and representation in the management to workers in the large mining and steel enterprises. Legislation enacted that year extended codetermination rights in social welfare and personnel matters, as well as the right to be heard in business policy decisions, to almost all firms. In 1972 and 1976 these rights were further extended by legislation. As a result, workers in almost all larger enterprises enjoy various forms of management codetermination rights—rights that are legally secured and have become the norm in German industry.

Thus, for example, since 1952 one-third of the members of the Supervisory Council of every corporation in the FRG, by law, have been elected labor representatives. In the case of the large mining and steel companies with more than 1000 employees, the owners and labor each have half of the seats in the Supervisory Council and must agree on one additional neutral member. Furthermore, the Executive Board, which makes day-to-day decisions, must include a Labor Director

with equal rights who can be appointed only with the approval of the labor representatives in the Supervisory Council. In other large industrial enterprises with more than 2000 employees, the provisions of the Codetermination Act of 1976 apply; this act calls for full numerical labor and management parity in the Supervisory Council. In a tie vote, however, the decisive vote is that of the chairman, who can be elected only with the approval of the owners. On the other hand, one of the representatives of labor must be a staff member with managerial functions.

This system may not be perfect, but it has basically worked well in helping to create a relatively cooperative relationship between labor and management. It has made management more sensitive to the interests, needs, and perspectives of labor, and it has made the labor leaders more aware of the problems of management. Whatever its shortcomings and imperfections may be, it certainly is a progressive system of labor-management relations at the enterprise level and represents a vast improvement over the situation prevailing in Germany in the early days of this century, when the power of owners and management vis-à-vis the workers was almost unlimited.[15]

The socioeconomic policy of the FRG has been enlightened and progressive in yet another respect. The model of the social market economy has always included an active role for the state in the management of the economy—especially at times when economic growth and stability are jeopardized by unfavorable business cycle developments. The Stability and Growth Act of 1967, for example, commits the federal government, as well as the governments of the states, to manage the economy over the business cycle and to secure stable prices, high employment, and external economic balance, as well as steady and adequate economic growth.

In the FRG, however, it is not only the state that is shouldered with the difficult responsibility of reconciling these partly contradictory goals. The employer associations, the labor unions, and the autonomous German Federal Bank *(Deutsche Bundesbank)* also share in the responsibility of managing the economy. The Germans have developed a successful system of procedures for bringing these diverse interests, groups, and institutions together in a cooperative relationship. The Business Cycle Council, which consists of the federal ministers of economics and finance, one member from each state government, and representatives of the communes and communal associations, and which may also include representatives of the German Federal Bank, normally holds consultations twice a year and seeks to develop a coordinated approach to economic policy. Its counterpart, the Financial Planning Council, a body with similar composition, has the responsibility of coordinating the financial planning of the federation, the states, and the communes, that is, the revenue and spending plans of the central, regional, and local authorities. Since the 1960s the federal government and the states are obligated by law to develop financial plans several years in advance in order to make possible the balancing and reconciliation of government revenues and expenditures with the changing requirements and capacity of the national economy.[16]

Another important and interesting practice with respect to macroeconomic management of the economy is the in recent years inoperative Concerted Action—that is, the regular consultations between representatives of the state, the trade unions, and employer associations for the purpose of achieving agreed-upon economic policy objectives. In 1963, furthermore, the so-called Council of Experts, a panel of five economic experts, was set up. Known as the "five wise men" in popular parlance, these experts assess overall economic developments every fall. Their findings, evaluations, and recommendations become an important input into economic decision making. Thus, for example, the Annual Economic Report presented every January by the federal government to the Bundestag and Bundesrat, among other things includes a discussion of the findings of the Council of Experts.[17]

POLITICAL STABILITY

In every polity the policymakers not only have to cope with the necessity of adapting the political system to the changing internal requirements of the society, but also to the constantly changing international environment. This is an inherently difficult task because it is not always possible to foresee and accurately predict politically significant changes in the domestic political arena and in the international environment. Moreover, even if such domestic and international changes could be accurately anticipated, the policymakers would still be faced with the unpleasant fact that as often as not they have little or no control over such developments. While this is a problem common to all states, but especially to highly developed industrial societies, it is even more acute in a country that is as deeply involved in international affairs and as dependent on a stable international environment as is the FRG.

Given the uncertainties of the international environment, competent political leadership, the development of a flexible political style, and consensus on domestic political issues at the elite and mass level were crucial and even imperative for the success of the postwar government of the FRG. In view of the political divisiveness and instability of the Weimar Republic, the emergence of elite consensus and mass support was particularly important for the viability of the new regime. The political performance of the Bonn Republic suggests that these essential conditions for political stability did in fact come about.

Until the late 1960s the FRG enjoyed a remarkable degree of domestic peace and political harmony. Given the widespread political indifference of the masses, the policy-making elites, usually operating within the framework of coalitions, found it relatively easy to agree on the main directions and priorities in both domestic matters and foreign affairs. For many years opinion polls and election results provided evidence of a strikingly low level of political conflict. Within the context of growing economic prosperity, socioeconomic cleavages in the FRG did not give rise to bitter political conflicts between the workers and their employers, between the well-to-do and the less affluent. "Class consciousness" in the Marxian sense was and is much less pronounced in the FRG than in countries like Britain, France, or Italy. Until fairly recently, sharp divisions in public opinion and lack of consensus among the policy-making elites were almost unknown; if they developed—as, for example, in the case of the disagreement over the *Ostpolitik,* they were the exception rather than the rule.

Berlin, November 11, 1989. Peaceful sit-in
by hundreds of Berliners on top of the
Berlin Wall near the Brandenburg Gate.
(*Photographer/Source:* AP/Wide World Photos)

Until the 1970s political relationships in the
FRG seemed to rest on firm and broad consensus both at the elite and mass level. Unlike the
Weimar Republic, the rules of the new constitutional order found wide acceptance among both
the elites and the masses. Over the years, the citizens of the FRG developed a rather pragmatic
attitude toward their political system, identifying
with it on a practical-rational rather than emotional level and preferring the role of spectator
(consumer) rather than that of active participant
(producer). In addition to the general satisfaction
with the performance of their government, the
force of habit also promoted the institutionalization of the new regime.

Yet it would be a serious mistake to accept the
exceptional political stability of the FRG during its
first two decades of existence and its remarkably
good performance during the more trying 1970s

and 1980s as a permanent feature in German politics. In the world of politics few things, if any,
may be regarded as permanent or taken for
granted. Like other liberal democratic regimes
with deeper historical roots and thus presumably
stronger foundations, the FRG in recent years has
seen itself confronted with a range of domestic
political problems and foreign policy issues that
may yet test its mettle as a polity—that is, test its
capacity to adapt its institutions and processes to
a less favorable environment and more formidable
issues and challenges than have existed in the past.

As a result of the slowdown in economic
growth beginning in the 1970s, the Bonn regime
was no longer in a position to satisfy the expectations of its citizens in regard to the further expansion (or even maintenance at current levels) of
the network of social security measures, to which
large segments of the population of the FRG had

grown accustomed. Cutbacks in government services and support programs began under the SPD government of Helmut Schmidt and continued, at an accelerated pace, under the CDU/CSU government of Helmut Kohl. FRG citizens were faced with a rapid rise in living costs during the 1970s. Perhaps most important, for the first time in its history the FRG was confronted with a large-scale unemployment problem. In mid-1983, for example, unemployment, seasonally adjusted, came to 2.35 million or about 9 percent of the labor force.[18]

As we have seen, the problem of unemployment was greatly exacerbated by the unification process beginning in 1990, with the unemployment rate averaging 16.1 percent and rising as high as 18.2 percent in the new eastern states in 1997. In the western states, unemployment averaged 8.6 percent for the period 1990–1997 and rose as high as 10.1 in 1996.

Increasingly, citizens of the FRG have had to recognize that over the years they have placed responsibilities for the general welfare on the federal government and various other public authorities, which may well be beyond their collective powers—especially during a time of economic recession. As presently constituted, the state authorities at the various levels cannot deliver everything that is expected of them.

Political unification in 1990 has presented the FRG with a range of problems that will test its mettle as a polity committed to the values of social democracy. The attempt to transfer the West German model to the new states has run into unanticipated difficulties and met with massive resistance on the part of the population in the east. This should not come as a surprise, considering that these Germans lived under communism for 45 years (32 years longer than under the Nazis!) and that their attitudes toward the state were shaped—to a greater extent than in the case of the Germans in the west—by the paternalist traditions of Prussia. The result is a significant difference in the attitude structure between the two populations. Survey research shows that the desire for a comprehensive role of the state is much stronger in the east than in the west.[19]

In addition to facing the challenge of closing the gap between the values, attitude structures, and socioeconomic and political preferences of the two German societies now living under one political roof, the FRG is also confronted with other problems. First, ways must be found to bring Germans from the east into the political elite of united Germany. Four years after unification, there were very few eastern Germans in positions of authority—at the level of senior civil servants, permanent state secretaries, or elected prime ministers of state governments.

Second, the unification of Germany may well lead to a realignment in the party system. During 1945–94, the FRG was under CDU/CSU rule for 29 years and under SPD rule for 13 years. With the exception of four years, the FDP was a partner in the ruling coalition and thus the pivotal party. With support for the traditional mainstream parties on the decline (from 70 percent before unification to 60 percent in 1994) and the presence of the PDS and the Greens, there may well be changes in the German party system. One such change was the emergence of the Alliance 90/Greens party as a coalition partner of the SPD at the national level in the aftermath of the 1998 Bundestag election. While "red-green" coalitions are not a novelty at the regional level in German politics, this is the first time that "the Greens" were able to enter a ruling coalition at the national level. Another change was the surprisingly strong showing of the PDS in the 1998 election and its electoral appeal outside the five new eastern states: Six of its 36 seats were won in five western states. The PDS is thus no longer an exclusively regional party and, without the benefit of special exemptions, it succeeded in making the transition from a "Gruppe" (group) to a Fraktion in the Bundestag—a status it has never had before.

Third, united Germany is a single country consisting of "sixteen tribes" and a federal government in Bonn and beginning in 2000, Berlin, which—after Switzerland and Belgium—is the most decentralized government in Europe. The most basic feature of the FRG before unification was consensus politics—more specifically, consensual federalism. This system involved, among other things, "revenue sharing"—a system of redistributing income from the rich to the poor states designed to support the consensus. In 1990 this system was temporarily suspended since the inclusion of the much poorer eastern states would have resulted in its bankruptcy. Instead, the federal government took over financial responsibility for the new states in the east. With the reactivation of the "financial equalization" system in 1995, a number of former "recipient" states in the west became "donor" states—as the lion's share of the money in the system—some DM12-15 billion—flowed to the new and much poorer states in the east. According to OECD data, the financial transfers (in descending order of magnitude) will come from Baden-Württemberg, North Rhine–Westphalia, Hesse, Bavaria, and Hamburg, and go to Berlin, Saxony, Saxony-Anhalt, Thuringia, Brandenburg, Mecklenburg-West Pomerania, Bremen, Lower Saxony, Saarland, Rhineland-Palatinate, and Schleswig-Holstein.[20] Unification thus may well have the effect of weakening the coherence of the states—there are 16 now instead of eleven—and putting additional strains on consensual federalism in the FRG, perhaps pushing it in the direction of a more competitive federalism. In any event, in the years ahead, Germany will have the opportunity to prove that it is indeed a nation, not merely a collection of provinces, as some have argued.

HUMAN RIGHTS

As has been discussed earlier, the Basic Law guarantees extensive (but not unlimited) individual rights, on the one hand, and also obligates legislative, executive, and judicial agencies at the federal, state, and local levels to take all necessary measures for the protection of the constitutional order and the public welfare.

The question of the proper balance between a "free democratic basic order" and a "constitutional order"—two key concepts in the Basic Law—has long been a subject of political and legal debate. Generally speaking, the record of the FRG in regard to the observance of constitutional norms and human rights has been very good. The prolonged and intense discussion in the 1960s triggered by the passage of laws and constitutional amendments concerning the powers of the government in emergency situations indicates that a good many Germans no longer were willing to sacrifice personal freedom and the right to privacy for internal security. Even in dealing with the wave of terrorism in the 1970s—bank

robberies, kidnappings, murders, and attacks on key government and business leaders—the government of the FRG showed remarkable restraint and was careful to observe legal procedures and respect constitutional rights.

While thus far there have been relatively few public controversies involving the alleged violation of basic rights by the state, two cases or issues became political causes célèbres. One was the *Spiegel* affair in 1962, which involved a police raid on the premises of the newsmagazine *Der Spiegel* and the arrest of two of its editors for the alleged illegal procurement and unauthorized publication of secret defense documents. Franz Josef Strauss, who was the minister of defense and was responsible for ordering the raid, figured prominently in an exposé of corruption of government officials in connection with military contracts and purchases. The government's action was roundly condemned by the press, by the opposition in the Bundestag, and by a large segment of the ruling CDU/CSU; the minister of justice, who had not been informed, resigned in protest, and his party, the FDP, made its continued participation in the government coalition contingent upon the resignation of Strauss. The case formally ended with the resignation of Strauss and the quashing of the indictment by the Federal Appeals Court. But the affair has not been forgotten. In the foreseeable future any FRG government is likely to think twice about using such heavy-handed tactics against the press.

The other controversy involves the question of "radicals" in the public service. This controversy entails, first of all, the question of whether communists, neo-Nazis, or other political radicals should be allowed to enter the civil service, which in the FRG, among other things, includes all teachers from the elementary school to the university. The Basic Law (Article 3, §2) prohibits discrimination against anyone on the basis of political views. On the other hand, can the existing constitutional order be preserved if teachers use or misuse their civil service positions to indoctrinate school children with Marxist-Leninist or Maoist ideas and slogans? Clearly no state can be expected or can afford to support, as it were, seditious activities directed against itself. Yet how far should the requirements for internal security be allowed to infringe on civil liberties?

In 1972 the FRG government and the state governments took a hard line in this matter with the enactment of an executive order, barring radicals engaged in subversive activities from public employment. This action by the federal government, which was taken as an interim measure to deal with the problem until formal legislation could be passed by the Bundestag and Bundesrat, did not solve the problem. The question that now arose was: What should be the basis for determining whether a particular individual was engaged in seditious activities? Was membership in a radical organization now or at some time in the past a sufficient reason for excluding an otherwise qualified individual from public employment?

In practice the 1972 decree was not uniformly implemented—despite a 1975 ruling by the Federal Constitutional Court.[21] In SPD-governed states mere membership in radical organizations was not regarded as sufficient cause for disqualification. Individuals holding leadership positions or offices in such organizations, on the other hand, were dismissed. In CDU-governed states, by contrast, mere membership led to dismissal or exclusion. The number of individuals involved, however, was never very large. Between 1972 and 1975, for example, only about 300 FRG citizens were denied public employment and only about 50 out of almost 3.7 million public employees were dismissed from their jobs.[22]

Legislation submitted by the federal government in 1975—designed to create guidelines consistent with the ruling of the Federal Constitutional Court—was vetoed by the Bundesrat. A year later, the federal government issued a new set of guidelines incorporating most of the ideas contained in the proposed 1975 legislation, which now apply to federal employees. At the state level, more and more governments in the late 1970s have failed to implement the 1972 decree, as often as not honoring it, as it were, in the breach.

As in all other states there are unresolved problems in the area of human rights in the FRG. There is evidence, for example, that in the FRG, as in the United States, socially disadvantaged groups are less likely to benefit from the rule of law than their more affluent and better educated fellow citizens. Significant inequalities continue to exist with respect to educational opportunity—which, in the eyes of many observers, is the key to the full enjoyment and exercise of constitutional rights.

Another problem area is the status of minorities—especially women and foreign workers. By custom and tradition German society has tended to keep women out of public affairs. Their place in the scheme of things was defined by the three Ks: *Kinder* (children), *Küche* (kitchen), and *Kirche* (church). While this perception of the role of women has been slow to change, there has been a significant increase in the political awareness and activity of women in the FRG. In 1972, Annemarie Renger became the first woman to be elected president of the Bundestag. From 1972 to 1976 she thus held—in terms of protocol—the second highest office in the FRG. At least one woman has served as a cabinet member in all but one government in the FRG since 1949. Prior to the election in 1994, four women held cabinet positions. The Greens, the newcomers to the Bundestag, were led by Petra Kelly, a very able and dynamic young woman. The 1998 Cabinet headed by Chancellor Gerhard Schröder included five women.

Yet women remain definitely underrepresented in the political elites at many important levels. Thus, for example, women, who in 1992 made up 52 percent of the population, accounted for only 26 percent of the membership of the three mainstream parties and only 20.5 percent of the deputies in the Twelfth Bundestag elected in 1990.[23] This, however, was a significant improvement since 1980, when women accounted for only 8 percent of the Bundestag deputies. Legal discrimination and significant income differentials between men and women in both nonmanual and manual work constitute another important dimension of the problem. What is encouraging, however, is the increase in the political awareness of women and the fact that the women now entering the world of politics hold university degrees and are highly qualified.

Foreign workers today constitute the most visible and problematic minority group in the FRG. Welcomed—though never without misgivings by some Germans—during the years of economic boom, they are tolerated, but not really accepted by significant segments of the population. Whereas in 1957 there were only 110,000 of these "guest workers" in the FRG, their ranks swelled to 2.9 million in 1991—about 17.3 percent of the labor force.[24] At a time of large-scale unemployment, their presence is resented by many Germans, especially by those who are out of work. Their cultural, socioeconomic, and political integration poses an enormous problem, which defies solution in the short run. In many of the large metropolitan centers like Hamburg, Frankfurt, and Munich, foreign workers account for one-fifth or more of the labor force and as much as one-half of the manual labor force. In some metropolitan centers of Western Germany—for example, Frankfurt—half of the newborn children are descendants of foreign workers. It is not difficult to see that the situation of this minority is pregnant with an enormous potential for social unrest.

The overall presence of foreigners in Germany is much greater—7.4 million, or 9 percent of the total population in 1998.[25] The preferred destination of asylum-seekers (256,112 in 1991 alone) and other refugees, Germany during 1989–93 took in an average of 830,000 immigrants a year—a figure that is proportionately comparable to the number of immigrants taken in by America during the peak immigration years in the early part of the twentieth century. With a foreign population of about 6.5 million (7.8 percent of the population) in 1994, the FRG became the closest thing to a melting pot in Europe. Concentrated for the most part in the major cities of western Germany, foreigners in 1990 accounted for more than one-fourth of the population of Offenbach and Frankfurt, and close to one-fourth of the population of Munich and Stuttgart. The cities with the largest number of foreigners included Berlin (West)—312,200; Munich—259,000; Hamburg—194,500; Cologne—159,400; and Stuttgart—115,600.[26]

The issue of the presence of foreigners in Germany has simmered for a long time. In the more recent past, there has been a significant and troubling increase in the number of acts of violence against foreigners. In 1991 Germany, both west and east—but especially east—experienced an explosion of xenophobia, and a wave of violence against foreigners. Right-wing extremists attacked refugees and refugee dwellings. Most Germans were horrified and condemned these acts, others—too many—remained silent, and some—even worse—applauded these acts of violence.

The FRG government capitulated to mounting pressure to deal with the issue of foreigners in Germany, especially in the aftermath of two state elections—in 1992 in Baden-Württemberg and Schleswig-Hostein, in which the campaign focused on the asylum issue—elections in which the established parties lost a sizeable percentage of their electoral support to right-wing fringe parties advocating "Germany for Germans." Joining France and the Benelux countries in the Schengen Treaty, a "secret" pact designed to restrict the influx of foreigners, Germany in effect abandoned its liberal asylum policy, amended Article 16 of the Basic Law, and in effect endorsed the concept of "Fortress Europe."

This is certainly not the only case in which government policy has been determined by the actions of a relatively small number of political extremists. What needs to be pointed out is that the overwhelming majority of Germans have been appalled by these acts of violence, have demonstrated en masse against them, and have done a great deal to help foreigners. Research on the attitude of Germans to foreigners suggests that there has been no increase in "hostility to foreigners." While a substantial number of Germans (34 percent) feel that greater assimilation by foreigners in terms of their life-style would be desirable, the majority (especially among the better educated) is in favor of their continued presence in Germany, regards their contributions to German life and society as valuable, and is not opposed to intermarriage. Furthermore, survey studies undertaken in 1990 suggest that since 1980 Germans had become more, rather than less, tolerant in their attitudes toward foreigners.[27]

Recognizing the importance of addressing the issue of integrating the "foreign" residents of Germany, the Schröder Administration, shortly after assuming the reins of power, moved quickly to propose legislation to deal with the burning issue of citizenship and naturalization—legislation that would constitute the most thorough revision of German laws on citizenship in more than eight decades. If adopted, dual citizenship would become much easier to obtain, and approximately 4 million of Germany's 7.4 million legal aliens would become eligible for German citizenship in the near future. The CDU/CSU immediately announced a petition campaign to enlist public support against "this harmful and senseless policy."

The principle on which the German concept of citizenship is based is called *jus sanguinis,* i.e., the law of descent or parentage (literally: the law, or right, of the blood). It is the traditional basis for determining citizenship in all of northern, central, and eastern Europe, in the Islamic countries, as well as Japan. In the United States, Canada, and Australia—all countries that were colonized by immigrants from Europe—the principle determining citizenship, by contrast, is called *jus soli,* i.e., the law of the birthplace (literally; law, or right, of the soil. In response to a major influx of European and non-European residents of their former colonies after World War II, Britain and France have also recognized the principle of *jus soli.* Whether Germany will follow their example remains to be seen. German tolerance for foreigners notwithstanding, the issue of extending citizenship to them remains highly controversial.[28]

REUNIFICATION

At midnight on October 2, 1990, the German Democratic Republic, or East Germany, ceased to exist. With the beginning of the next day, five new, but at the same time historic, *Länder* (states)—Brandenburg, Mecklenburg–West Pomerania, Saxony, Saxony-Anhalt, and Thuringia—became part of the reunified Germany. In a tectonic geopolitical change, the unnatural division of the most populous country in the heart of Europe came to an end. On October 3, 1990, the East German parliament, the so-called *Volkskammer* (People's Chamber), voted itself out of existence. The flag of the Federal Republic of Germany was hoisted on the Reichstag building in Berlin, where the Bundestag, in an enlarged session including 144 members of the East German parliament, met in historic session.

The reunification of Germany was the product of many factors, ranging from the most mo-

mentous changes in international relations in Europe since the end of World War II, the reform course being pursued by the Soviet regime under Gorbachev in 1989, and the changed image of Germany and the Germans in Europe to the fortuitous presence of politicians in all the key countries who had the requisite courage and far-sightedness to make reunification possible. When it came in the fall of 1990, it was almost anticlimactic. Reunification was not a discrete event, but rather a process which began with Gorbachev's declaration in the fall of 1989 in East Berlin that the regime in the German Democratic Republic, like those elsewhere in Eastern Europe, was on its own. It was a process for which some of the essential prerequisites were created by the *Ostpolitik*—the policy of rapprochement and reconciliation with the East—launched in 1969 by Willy Brandt. It was a process, moreover, which was a foregone conclusion after the Berlin Wall came down in November 1989, but which was greatly facilitated by the skillful diplomacy of FRG Foreign Minister Hans-Dietrich Genscher and Chancellor Helmut Kohl. It was a process, finally, that was the product of a unique kind of cooperation between the four victorious allies of World War II. Thanks to these circumstances, reunification occurred peacefully and with the consent, rather than against the will, of Germany's neighbors.

As we noted in our discussion of the political framework of the FRG, the Basic Law was conceived as an instrument for a "transitional period." According to Article 146, the Basic Law "shall become invalid on the day that a new constitution, chosen by the German people in a free decision process, takes force." Had the two Germanies come together as two sovereign states, that day could have come in 1990. Instead, the leaders involved in making the arrangements for unification chose to extend the Basic Law to the former GDR and to "join" it to the FRG on the basis of Article 23, which allowed for the accession of the (reconstituted) former GDR states to the FRG.[29] Considering the circumstances at the time, this was a logical and expedient decision, but it was also a decision that effectively deprived the 16 million Germans in the east of a fundamental right by forcing them to live under a constitutional order in whose determination they had no part or voice.

The *fait accompli* of reunification presents the FRG government with a series of difficult economic, social, and political problems. The integration of the former GDR into the FRG has not been an easy undertaking. The scale of the problems that need to be addressed—from serious environmental problems and a grossly neglected infrastructure to acute social problems and inequities—have taxed even the powerful German economy. It is no wonder that, within a few months, the initial euphoria over reunification gave way to more sober and realistic assessments of the problems involved.

In political terms, at least initially, reunification was a boon to the government of Helmut Kohl, the first "unity" chancellor, who entered his third term with few potential challengers or successors in sight. Having received a clear mandate to govern the country after reunification, the CDU/CSU-FDP coalition could look to the future with confidence.

That confidence was at least partly shattered as the complexity and sheer magnitude of the tasks lying ahead became more clearly apparent. Difficult as the integration of the GDR's command economy into the FRG's social market economy proved to be in terms of structural, legal, financial, and many other considerations, perhaps the greatest challenge involved the human factor—the "dismantling of the wall in people's heads," as it has been called. The overnight introduction of a new legal system, a new tax system, and a service sector—very underdeveloped and neglected in the GDR economy—required extensive training programs. The *Mittelstand* (small or medium-sized private enterprises), the backbone of the FRG's economy, was nonexistent before unification, and so were the values and infrastructure that go with it. And if the environmental problems in the new states pose a nightmare whose full dimensions are not yet fully recognized, so does the peculiar malaise that has gripped the Germans in the east as a society.

The collapse of communism produced cataclysmic demographic consequences everywhere, but nowhere as severe as in the former GDR. Birth rates and marriage rates have collapsed and

death rates have risen sharply. According to Nicholas Eberstadt, the well-known demographer, "Eastern Germany's adults appear to have come as close to a temporary suspension of childbearing as any large population in the human experience." In 1992, the birth rate was 55 percent lower than in 1989, and further declining. During the first five months of 1993, eastern Germany's birth rate was under 5.1 per 1,000—over 60 percent fewer than during the same period in 1989, and less than half the extremely low birth rate in western Germany. And the greatest decline was in births to married women between 25 and 34 years of age. What is more, there has been an equally precipitous decline in the marriage rate: In 1992 it was 62 percent below the level of 1989—more than twice the decline experienced in war-torn Berlin.[30] These rates are without precedent, and they provide a measure of the trauma and hopelessness experienced by the people of eastern Germany in the aftermath of unification.

PROSPECTS FOR THE FUTURE

While the political sky over the FRG is by no means cloudless, there are nevertheless many reasons for a hopeful and reasonably optimistic assessment of the future. The Bonn Republic, originally conceived as a strictly provisional solution, not only acquired characteristics of permanence on its own, but in 1990 succeeded in achieving reunification after 45 years and thus ceased to be "a former country in the middle of Europe." When thinking about Germany, many Americans immediately think of the "economic miracle," and the postwar economic recovery of western parts of Germany was, indeed, a kind of miracle. But the political development and performance of the FRG, even before the achievement of reunification, was every bit as miraculous—if not more so, as one observer has correctly pointed out.[31] Germany's institutions and procedures thus far have worked remarkably well, and there has been no major threat to the democratic order. In view of the ability and resourcefulness the Germans have demonstrated in dealing with difficult economic and political problems in the past, there is every reason to believe that they will be able to address the problems that lie ahead with confidence, intelligence, and success.

NOTES

[1] The FRG's shortages are particularly critical with respect to mineral raw materials—bauxite, copper, manganese, titanium, rock phosphate, tin, and wolfram. Iron ore, nonferrous metals, petroleum, rubber, and sulfur are also in short supply.

[2] CIA, *Handbook of Economic Statistics, 1997* (Washington, DC: U.S.Government, 1997), p. 16.

[3] *Daten Report 5*, p. 279.

[4] "Competitiveness of German Industry in 1998," DIHT (Association of German Chamber of Industry and Commerce), at http//:www.diht.de/aktuell/diht0540.htm (1/25/99).

[5] "The Week in Germany," January 15, 1999, at www. germany-info.org/gnew/wkh_01_15_99.htm (1/19/99).

[6] See Walter Eucken, *Grundsätze der Wirtschaftspolitik* (Tübingen: J. C. B. Mohr, 1968).

[7] See Walter Eucken, *Grundsätze der Wirtschaftspolitik* (Tübingen: J. C. B. Mohr, 1968). In spite of some reservations and differences in emphasis and interpretation, the SPD accepted the existing economic order in its *Godesberg Program* of 1958.

[8] While in 1971 and 1978 the German economy lost more than 4 million, and in 1984—more than 5 million workdays due to strikes, during the other years this figure was much lower and well below that of the other leading industrial countries. In 1996, for example, only 98,135 workdays involving 165,721 workers were lost due to strikes. (*Stat. Jahrb. BRD* 1997, p. 127).

[9] This is a federally financed program, established by the Federal Child Endowment Act, to assist families with the upbringing and education of children. As of 1978, this program provided an allowance of DM 50 per month for the first child, DM 100 for the second and DM 200 for each additional child. Ordinarily child allowances are paid to age 18, but if the child is still being educated or is involved in vocational training (which in the FRG involves mandatory attendance of a vocational school), benefits may continue to age 27 and in some cases even longer.

[10] *Stat. Jahrb, BRD* 1997, p. 675.

[11] Ibid.

[12] Ibid., pp. 683, 684.

[13] Beginning in 1995, however, the GDP growth rate in eastern Germany began to decrease, falling from 9.9 percent in 1994 to 1.6 percent in 1997. ("Economic Facts on Germany," at www.germany-info.org/facts/germecon.htm).

[14] *The Economist,* "A Survey of Germany," 21 May 1994, p. 10.

[15] On worker co-determination, see F. Vimar, *Mitbestimmung am Arbeitsplatz. Basis demokratischer Betriebspolitik* (Neuwied: Luchterhand, 1971) and, by the same author, *Politik and Mitbestimmung: Kritische Zwischenbilanz— intergrales Konzept* (Kronberg: Athenäum-Verlag, 1977);

D. Schneider, R. Kuda, *Mitbestimmung—Weg zur industriellen Demokratie* (Munich: Deutscher Taschenbuch-Verlag, 1969).

[16] On financial planning, see K. Gresser, *Probleme der mehrjährigen öffentlichen Finanzplanung* (Berlin: Duncker and Humblot, 1974); H. Schatz, *Politische Planung im Regierungssystem der Bundesrepublik Deutschland* (Göttingen: Schwartz, 1974): A. Zunker, "Finanzplanung," in K. Sontheimer and H. H. Röhring, eds., *Handbuch des politischen Systems der Bundesrepublik Deutschland* (Munich: R. Piper & Co., Verlag, 1978), pp. 185–187.

[17] On the Council of Experts, see R. Molitor, ed., *Zehn Jahre Sachverständigenrat* (Frankfurt/M.: Athenäum-Verlag, 1973); Uwe Andersen, "Sachverständigenrat," in Sontheimer and Röhring, *Handbuch*, pp. 536–539.

[18] *DIW Wochenbericht,* June 23, 1983, p. 321. *Stat. Jahrb. BRD 1997,* pp. 123–124; "German Economy: Comparative Information," at www.germany-info.org/facts/intro.htm. (1/19/1999).

[19] *Daten Report 5,* pp. 641–644.

[20] *The Economist,* "A Survey of Germany," 21 May 1994, p. 29.

[21] While essentially upholding the 1972 decree, the Court ruled that mere membership in a radical organization was not a sufficient basis for disqualification from the public service in the absence of other "anticonstitutional activity."

[22] On the "radicals controversy," see "Radikale im öffentlichen Dienst," in *Beilage zur Wochenzeitung Das Parlament,* no. B 27, 1973; see also "Extremistenbeschluss und demokratische Verfassung," in ibid., no. B 50, 1973.

[23] *Daten Report 5,* p. 176, 182.

[24] *Stat. Jahrb. BRD,* p. 116.

[25] "Quick Facts About Germany," at www.germany-info.org/facts/quick.htm (1/19/99).

[26] *Daten Report 5,* p. 57.

[27] Ibid., pp. 612–623. On this subject, see also Klaus Grosch, "Foreigners and Aliens," in Susan Stern, ed., *Meet United Germany: Perspectives 1992/1993* (Frankfurt am Main: Frankfurter Allgemeine Zeitung Information Services/Atlantik-Brücke, 1992), pp. 133–151.

[28] *The Week in Germany,* 8 and 15 January 1999; "German Society: Citizenship and Naturalization," at http://www.germany-info.org/facts/cit.htm. (1/19/99).

[29] Article 23 of the Basic Law was repealed by Article 4, Section 7 of the August 1990 Unity Treaty between the FRG and the GDR.

[30] "Eastern Germany: Living and Dying in a Barren Land," *The Economist,* 23 April 1994, p. 54.

[31] R. Löwenthal, "Prolog: Dauer and Verwandlung," in eds. R. Löwenthal and H. P. Schwarz, *Die zweite Republik* (Stuttgart: Seewald Verlag, 1974), p. 9.

FRG: SELECTED BIBLIOGRAPHY

John Ardagh, *Germany and the Germans* (London: Penguin Books, 1991), new revised edition.

Kendall L. Baker, Russell J. Dalton, and Kai Hildebrandt, *Germany Transformed: Political Culture and the New*

Politics (Cambridge, MA: Harvard University Press, 1981).

Hanna Behrend, ed., *German Unification: The Destruction of an Economy* (East Haven, CT: Pluto Press, 1995).

Karl Dietrich Bracher, *The German Dilemma: The Relationship of State and Democracy* (New York: Praeger Publishers, 1975).

Gerard Braunthal, *Parties and Politics in Modern Germany* (Boulder, CO: Westview Press, 1996).

David P. Conradt, *The German Polity* 6th ed. (New York and London: Longman, 1996).

Werner Conze, *The Shaping of the German Nation: A Historical Analysis* (New York: St. Martin's Press, 1979).

Ralf Dahrendorf, *Society and Democracy in Germany* (New York: Doubleday Anchor Books, 1969).

Immanuel Geiss, *The Question of German Unification, 1806–1996* (London and New York: Routledge, 1997).

Alfred Grosser, *Germany in Our Time: A Political History of the Postwar Years* (New York: Praeger Publishers, 1971).

Hans Hahn, *Germany in the 1990s* (Atlanta, GA: Rodopi, 1995).

Stephen E. Hanson and Willfried Spohn, *Can Europe Work?: Germany and the Reconstruction of Postcommunist Societies* (Seattle, WA: University of Washington Press, 1995).

G. Hirschfeld and L. Kettenacker, eds., *The "Führer State": Myth and Reality* (Stuttgart: Kett-Cotta, 1981).

Ursula Hoffman-Lange, ed., *Social and Political Structures in West Germany: From Authoritarianism to Postindustrial Democracy* (Boulder, CO: Westview Press, 1991).

Harold James and Marla Stone, eds., *When the Wall Came Down: Reactions to German Unification* (New York: Routledge, 1992).

Nevil Johnson, *Federalism and Decentralization in the Federal Republic of Germany* (London: H. M. Stationary Office, 1983).

Nevil Johnson, *State and Government in the Federal Republic of Germany: The Executive at Work,* 2nd ed. (New York: Pergamon Press, 1983).

Jane Kramer, *The Politics of Memory: Looking for Germany in the New Germany* (New York: Random House, 1996).

Hermann Kurthen, Werner Bergmann and Rainer Erb, eds., *Antisemitism and Xenophobia in Germany After Unification* (New York: Oxford University Press, 1997).

James McAdams, *Germany Divided: From the Wall to Reunification* (Princeton: Princeton University Press, 1993).

Laurence McFalls, *Communism's Collapse, Democracy's Demise?: The Cultural Context and Consequences of the East German Revolution* (New York: New York University Press, 1995).

Stephen Padgett, ed., *Parties and Party System in the New German Polity* (Aldershot: Dartmouth, 1993).

Peter E. Quint, *The Imperfect Union: Constitutional Structures of German Unification* (Princeton, NJ: Princeton University Press, 1997).

Gerhard Ritter, *The Sword and the Scepter: The Problem of Militarism in Germany* (Coral Gables, FL: University of Miami Press, 1969–73), 4 vols.

Sabine Von Dirke, *All Power to the Imagination: The West German Counterculture from the Student Movement to the Greens* (Lincoln, NB: University of Nebraska Press, 1997).

David Schoenbaum and Elizabeth Pond, *The German Question and Other German Questions* (New York: St. Martin's Press, 1996).

Susan Stern, ed., *Meet United Germany: Perspectives 1992/ 1993,* 2 vols. (Frankfurt/Main: Frankfurter Allgemeine Zeitung GmbH Information Services/Atlantik-brücke, 1992).

Philip Zelikov and Condoleeza Rice, Germany *Unified and Europe Transformed: A Study in Statecraft* (Cambridge, MA: Harvard University Press, 1995).

Part IV: The Russian Federation

Chapter 19

Russian History and Political Culture

In a legal sense, the Russian Federation, or Russia, is a very young and new state. No sovereign Russian state has ever existed in the geographic space now occupied by the Russian Federation. As presently constituted, both in terms of territory and population, the country we now call Russia is a new political configuration that is still very much in flux and thus lacks at least some of the attributes commonly associated with the concept of the state—for example, a fixed relationship between a political community and territory, sovereignty, and the monopoly of the legitimate use of physical coercion. In a very real sense, the Russian Federation, although recognized by the international community as a full-fledged state, is still involved in the process of *"state building."*

Technically speaking, the Russian Federation came into being in the aftermath of the abortive right-wing coup attempt on August 19, 1991, which, along with other factors, led to the collapse of the Soviet Union in December of that year. More specifically, the Russian Federation was established on December 26, 1991, when its predecessor, the Russian Soviet Federated Socialist Republic (RSFSR), voted to change its

official name to the Russian Federation. But actually Russia's march to independence began earlier, on June 20, 1990, when the RSFSR declared its independence from the Soviet Union in a nonbinding resolution on sovereignty, including the right to veto Soviet law. This day is now celebrated as Independence Day in Russia.

In a cultural, historical, and political sense, Russia is very old—even by European standards. Before the establishment of the Russian Federation, Russia existed as the RSFSR—the largest and most important republic of the Union of Soviet Socialist Republics (USSR)—a totally artificial political construct created by the Bolsheviks in 1922 for the purpose of legitimizing the continued existence of part of the former Russian Empire. Prior to the October Revolution of 1917, a large part of the territory that is now the Russian Federation was part of the Russian Empire established by Peter the Great in the eighteenth century, and, earlier, of Muscovite Russia, which dates back to the fifteenth century. And before the Muscovite state there existed the Kievan state, which traces its beginnings back to the ninth century. In short, a Russian state has existed in various territorial and ethnic configurations for over a thousand years.[1]

That long history has left a deep—some would say indelible— imprint on the psychology, political culture, and traditions of the Russian people. In order to understand Russia's development in the twentieth century and its situation today, therefore, it is necessary to have at least a rudimentary understanding of its history.

One of the important things to remember about Russian history is that for many centuries the Russian people have been part of an empire. Every Russian has been taught that Kiev, now the capital of Ukraine, was the cradle of Russian civilization, the "Mother of Russian cities," in the words of the *Russian Primary Chronicle*. For this reason, as a people, Russians have found it difficult, and in many cases even impossible, to understand themselves and their place in the world outside, and apart from, the existence of an empire. In short, Russian national consciousness has always included other people, non-Russians, who have been part of the empire. If, in the aftermath of the collapse of the Soviet empire the Russian people have suffered a serious and peculiar identity crisis, it is precisely for this reason. In an interview in 1991, the literary critic Yuri Burtin addressed this issue: "We cannot separate the Russian Republic from the center. We look back in history, and the center is somehow ourselves. Even Boris Yeltsin seems to see Russia's future as the heart of a remade Soviet Union, not something separate from it."[2] According to the philosopher Alexander Tsipko, the problem is that the leaders of the Russian Federation claim to speak in the name of Russian history and the Russian Empire, but "they fail to understand that without today's Ukraine, there cannot be a Russia in the old, real sense of the word."[3] And it is not only Russian intellectuals who have difficulty in conceiving of Russia without, or apart from, the empire. As Len Karpinsky, the former editor of *Moscow News,* has put it: "The problem here is that millions of Russians are convinced that, without Ukraine, it is impossible to speak not only of a great Russia, but any kind of Russia at all."[4]

As a number of Russians have pointed out, Russia has a unique cultural identity that is not Russian in a national or monoethnic sense

(russkiy), but Russian in a supranational (or imperial) sense *(rossiyskiy)* and that this identity was shaped by more than three centuries of interaction of Slavic and Turkic cultural traditions.[5] In this connection, we should note that in the official name of postcommunist Russia—*Rossiyskaya Federatsiya* (Russian Federation)—the more inclusive supranational version of the word Russian is used. In short, today, as in the past, the idea of a supranational political community is central to the Russian conception of statehood— a conception that reflects the fact and the recognition that the Russian Federation, like the RSFSR and the Russian Empire, is a multinational state.

Russia constitutes an illustration par excellence of the thesis—persuasively argued by Arnold Toynbee with regard to England and all other modern European states—that national history is not an "intelligible unit of historical study."[6] Toynbee's singular insight into the nature of the historical process explicitly recognizes that nation-states exist not only in space but also in time; in terms of their historical development and interaction political systems are seldom, if ever, the discrete units they appear to be on maps. Their behavior and evolution can rarely be fully fathomed by reference to intrinsic factors alone; frequently they are the product of forces that emanate from wider causes and extend across centuries.

In the study of Russia especially, the historian's perspective cannot be ignored. In a sense, ever since the October Revolution in 1917 we have witnessed the spectacle of a new type of revolutionary regime locked in deadly combat with the Russian past—a gigantic contest that ended in the collapse of the Soviet Union and the formation of the Russian Federation in 1991. While a good many vestiges of the Soviet political order have survived in postcommunist Russia, there is no question that the Russian people are trying to find the way back to their past. But what is this past? Both the history of Soviet Russia and the brief postcommunist period illustrate that, as François Guizot has observed, national traditions of long standing are not easily abolished, that even the most extreme revolutionary regimes cannot entirely break with the past and in the end are shaped by them to a significant extent.[7]

THE IMPACT OF HISTORY

The Russian Federation, like the Soviet Union that preceded it, did not begin its existence on a *tabula rasa.* As the legal "successor" to the Soviet Union, it inherited not only more than three-fourths of the territory and slightly over half of the population of the USSR, but also a host of pressing political and socioeconomic problems, cultural values and dispositions shaped by centuries of history, a very difficult political and historical legacy, as well as a dramatically different political environment: Along with Russia, fourteen other "successor states" gained their independence. Situated northwest, west, southwest, and south of the Russian Federation, they constitute what Russians now call the "near abroad."[8] With the exception of the three Baltic states (Lithuania, Latvia, and Estonia), the other twelve successor states have joined the Commonwealth of Independent States (CIS), an organization in which the Russian Federation plays the leading role. In addition, the political legacy inherited by the Russian Federation from the USSR included a diaspora of 25–30 million ethnic and acculturated Russians who, as a result of the collapse of the Soviet Union, found themselves living outside Russia in the "near abroad"—as minority groups. Furthermore, for two years after its establishment the Russian Federation operated under a constitution adopted in 1977 and with a "parliament" consisting mostly of old-style, hardline communists elected when the Soviet Union still existed.

There are many other aspects of the legacy inherited from the Soviet Union by the Russian Federation. But even this short list suggests the impact of the most recent history immediately preceding the establishment of the Russian Federation. What about the influence of Russia's centuries-long history before the October Revolution and the establishment of the Soviet Union?

To begin with, there is the peculiar historical relationship of Russia to Europe and, in a larger sense, to the West—a relationship perhaps best characterized as ambivalent.[9] Searching for explanations of this ambivalence, we discover that almost from the very beginning of recorded Russian history, which dates back to Kievan Rus in the ninth century, the main contacts with the outside world developed by the emerging Russia were not with Western Europe, but with the Byzantine Empire, located in the area now occupied by Turkey.

During the Kievan period the idea of Russia's uniqueness and sense of being different from Europe was least developed; royal marriages between the Kiev Court and various courts in Europe were frequent and began to diminish only after the schism between Eastern and Western Christianity became final in 1054.[10] Nevertheless, the "Byzantine connection" in Russian history meant the growing isolation of Russia from the mainstream of European history for a number of centuries—a development reinforced by the Mongol invasion, which destroyed Kiev in 1240 and resulted in the domination of Russia by the Tatars for 200 years (with the exception of the principality of Novgorod and the part of Russia controlled by Poland).

As a result, such signal movements as the Renaissance and the Reformation were to have virtually no impact on Russia. Eventually, Russia's Byzantine heritage would include Orthodox Christianity (instead of Roman Catholicism); the Cyrillic alphabet (instead of the Latin alphabet used in Western Europe); the institution and concept of the *czar*—a kind of God-Emperor, combining in his person both supreme spiritual authority and supreme secular power. As a matter of fact, Russia laid explicit claim to the religious and political heritage of Byzantium. After Constantinople—the capital of the Byzantine Empire—had been conquered by the Turks in 1453, the Grand Dukes of Moscow adopted the Byzantine double-headed eagle as their insignia and assumed the title of czar. Moscow was officially proclaimed the "third Rome"—the idea being that, as a result of the fall of Constantinople (the "second Rome"), Moscow had now become the sole remaining repository of the true Christian faith and henceforth would remain the center of orthodoxy. This doctrine played an important part in the formation of the Muscovite state, imbuing it with a strong and growing sense of messianism[11] and reinforcing Moscow's isolation from the West. The profession of *pravoslavie,* the true, Orthodox Faith, became the ultimate test of belonging to the Russian kingdom.

As the result of its isolation from Europe, the Mongol invasion, and the subsequent formation of the centralized state of Muscovy (Moscow), Russia did not take part in the intellectual and spiritual movements that laid the foundation for the modernization and secularization of Europe. When the West came to Muscovy in the fifteenth century, it found a civilization ill-equipped to cope with the vastly more advanced world of Europe. The result was a profound crisis of identity. Like the underdeveloped countries in our time, the emerging Russia was forced into a search for national identity in what was then an essentially European world. And as in the case of many underdeveloped countries today, the Russian reaction to Europe was marked by a great deal of ambivalence.

It was, however, not until the seventeenth century that a far-reaching process of selective Westernization began in Russia, a process which—though superficial in many respects—in some ways went deeper and was more successful than the Westernization of Japan two centuries later. It was also a process that called forth an enormously powerful reaction in Russia. The reign of Peter the Great, which was marked by an unprecedented policy of forced Westernization, now constitutes the great divide in Russian history. This fact is reflected in Russian historiography, which distinguishes Russian history in terms of a pre-Petrine and a post-Petrine period. The forced selective Westernization of Russia under Peter the Great made the question of Russia's relationship to the West into the central and most crucial issue of a national debate that has gone on ever since. Perhaps future historians will come to look upon the Russian Revolution of 1917 and its aftermath as merely one chapter in this debate—and not necessarily the concluding one. Disagreement over the question of Russia's relationship to the West has divided Russians for centuries, including during the Soviet period, and it continues to divide them today.

THE POLITICAL TRADITION

The impact of history is reflected not only in the evolution of Russia's relationship to the West and in the Russian attitude structure toward the West, but also in the development of Russian political institutions and practices. Here, generally speaking, it is important to recognize that the political culture of Russia, especially during the Moscow period (1462–1696), developed in almost direct opposition to the Latin West.

The long Mongol domination, coupled with the Byzantine inclination toward autocracy and the ever-present threat of invasion from both the West and the East, resulted in the introduction of "oriental despotism"—to borrow Wittfogel's phrase[12]—in Russia and ultimately in the formation of a highly centralized bureaucratic empire, which at least in part was a response to the inherently difficult problem of organizing the vast Russian territory. After throwing off the Tatar yoke in the course of the fifteenth century, the Russian czars pursued their own kind of "manifest destiny," a policy of territorial aggrandizement on an unprecedented scale. As a result of this policy, Russian territorial expansion is estimated to have averaged 50 square miles a day for a period of 400 years.[13] The original principality of Moscow, consisting of a few thousand square miles, by 1917 had grown into a huge empire occupying one-fifth of the earth's land surface.

The price paid for this enormous effort of "gathering the Russian lands" was the total subordination of the interests of the individual and even entire social classes to the state. Summarizing modern Russian history from the sixteenth to the mid-nineteenth centuries, the distinguished prerevolutionary Russian historian V. O. Kliuchevsky wrote: "the expansion of state territory, which strained beyond measure and exhausted the resources of the people, only increased the power of the state without elevating the self-consciousness of the people. . . . The state swelled up, the people grew lean."[14]

As a result of having been cut off from contacts with Western Europe for a number of centuries and without the benefit of the liberating effects of the Renaissance and Reformation, Russia developed a framework of political institutions and practices centered around the autocracy, which was increasingly at variance with the patterns found in Western Europe as time went on. From the standpoint of political evolution, perhaps more so than in any other respect, Russia followed a path of development that differed greatly from that of Western Europe.

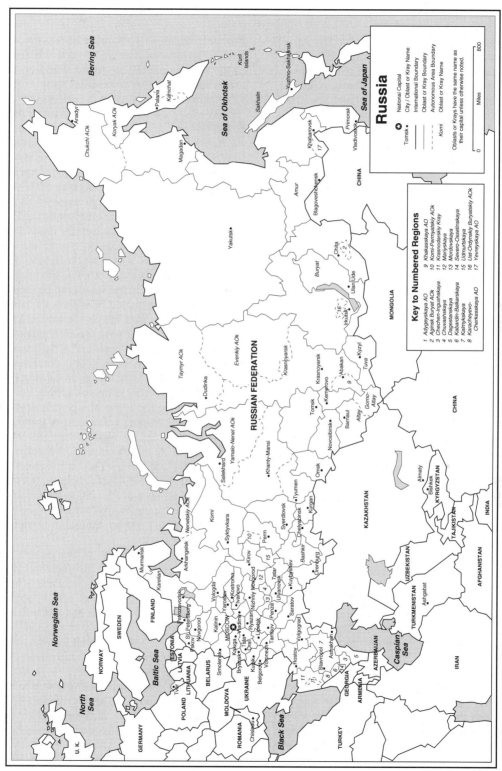

RUSSIAN FEDERATION

Russia

- ⊛ National Capital
- Tomsk • City / Oblast or Kray Name
- International Boundary
- Oblast or Kray Boundary
- Autonomous Area Boundary
- *Komi* Oblast or Kray Name

Oblasts or Krays have the same name as their capital unless otherwise noted.

0   Miles   800

Key to Numbered Regions

1 *Adygeyskaya AO*
2 *Aginsk Buryat AOk*
3 *Chechen-Ingushskaya*
4 *Chuvashskaya*
5 *Dagestanskaya*
6 *Kabardin-Balkarskaya*
7 *Kalmykskaya*
8 *Karacheyevo-Cherkesskaya AO*
9 *Khakasskaya AO*
10 *Komi-Permyatskiy AOk*
11 *Krasnodarskiy Kray*
12 *Mariyskaya*
13 *Mordovskaya*
14 *Severo-Osoetinskaya*
15 *Udmurtskaya*
16 *Ust-Ordynskiy Buryatskiy AOk*
17 *Yevreyskaya AO*

RUSSIAN FEDERATION

251

Western thought, for example, already during the early Middle Ages had developed the theoretical foundations that ultimately led to the separation of church and state. There is nothing comparable in Russian thought. On the contrary, following the Byzantine concept of *symphonia,* Russian thought centered around the idea of the fundamental unity and harmony of church and state. Autocracy or *caesaropapism,* the concentration of ecclesiastical authority in the hands of the emperor, became the accepted pattern of political authority in Russia—a pattern not widely questioned and challenged until the nineteenth century. Western political thought after the Middle Ages involved, among other things, the progressive secularization of political ideas. In Russia, the secularization of political thought did not occur until the nineteenth century—and even then much of it continued to move in an essentially religious mold.

In the West, the marriage of Greek and Roman thought gave birth to the idea of natural law, a concept of immense significance for the development of political institutions and practices in the West because it resulted ultimately in limiting and circumscribing the power of the state over the individual. In Russia, by contrast, the idea of natural law never acquired comparable significance and influence. Moreover, the Russian Orthodox Church, unlike the Western Church, never developed an independent body of canon law. As a result, in Russia all law was regarded as emanating from the czar-autocrat, who was perceived as the only and universal source of law. The gigantic struggle between spiritual and secular authority, between pope and emperor, which left such an indelible imprint on the history of the West and ultimately resulted in limiting the spheres of authority of both church and state, did not occur in Russia. Russia entered the twentieth century with a powerful autocracy and a church that was in effect just an instrument of the state.[15]

To make a long story short, whether one examines the religious-cultural, economic, or more narrowly political aspects of Russian life, one finds that the state played an enormous role in the development of Russian society and history even before 1917—a role that was by far greater than that played by its counterpart in Western European countries. As a matter of fact, the state loomed so large in Russian life that this aspect of the Russian experience found reflection in a theory that the state was the chief agent in Russian history. This resulted in the development of the so-called state school of Russian historiography. The basic argument of this perspective on the Russian past was that, unlike its counterpart in Western Europe, the Russian state was not the product, but rather the creator, of social classes. This fact did not escape the attention of Russian revolutionaries in the nineteenth century,[16] as well as such twentieth-century revolutionaries as Trotsky and Lenin, and fundamentally determined their approach to revolution.[17]

But the state in Russia, historically speaking, is unique not only because of its dominant position in Russian life. It also stands out because of its separation from the rest of society, its "alien" character in the eyes of the people, and its basic lack of support among virtually all segments of society. The dominant position of the Russian state and the fact that it was widely perceived as an alien force in Russian life, as an "abstract entity" without real roots in the soil of Russia,[18] go far in explaining the apparently paradoxical coincidence of liberalizing reforms from above and the development of an organized revolutionary movement from below during the reign of Alexander II (1855–1881). These attributes of the Russian state before 1917 also help us to understand why a number of Russian revolutionaries, Lenin included, came to look upon the state both as the chief target and an important instrument of revolution.[19]

Before discussing some of the factors and events leading to the Russian Revolution in 1917, let us summarize some of the salient characteristics of the autocratic political system against which Lenin had declared war and of the Russia he proposed to overturn. You will then be in a better position to judge for yourself to what extent the Russian Revolution succeeded in producing a "break with the past."

First of all, there is the indisputable fact of Russia's relative political backwardness. At the turn of the century, when constitutional government was already well established in most European countries, Russia was still ruled by an absolute autocrat. The principle of rule by divine right was even explicitly enshrined in Article I of the *Fundamental Laws of the Russian Empire,* promulgated in 1802: "The Emperor of all the Russias is an autocratic and unlimited monarch. God himself commands that his supreme power be obeyed out of conscience as well as fear."

Second, lacking representative institutions and a constitutional framework, political power in Russia remained highly personalized. Without exception, all higher governmental organs—for example, the State Council, the Committee of Ministers, the Senate, and the Holy Synod—were creatures of the czar-autocrat, without any real independent political power. The czar personally selected, appointed, and dismissed his ministers, who were "servants" in the literal Latin sense of the word. Since the higher organs of government were not elected, they could not claim to have a mandate and functioned in a purely advisory capacity to the czar. The Committee of Ministers was merely a conference of ministers convened on an ad hoc basis for the purpose of coordinating policy. Generally, the czar dealt with them directly and on an individual basis in areas of policy and on issues falling within their jurisdiction. Frequently, however, the czar relied for advice on a coterie of personal favorites who had been placed in high offices or made use of parallel channels of executive power, both informal and formal. To an American observer, the extraordinary concentration of power in the executive, to the detriment of legislative and judicial organs, is perhaps the most striking feature of the czarist political system. A foreign diplomat serving in St. Petersburg during the reign of Catherine the Great captured the essence of Russia's autocratic system very well when he said that "the whole of Russian government could be located between her brow and the back of her head."[20]

Third, czarist Russia was a highly centralized bureaucratic empire, governed by a "gigantic administrative machine,"[21] a veritable army of bureaucrats, set apart from the population by elaborate uniforms and ranks, *chinovniki* (rank-holding officials) who for the most part looked to St. Petersburg for instructions and more or less dutifully, if inefficiently and often obstreperously, carried out whatever orders they received from their superiors. The huge Russian Empire, stretching from the Baltic Sea to the Pacific, was divided into provinces or *guberniia,* each ruled by a governor, who was appointed by the Ministry of Internal Affairs in St. Petersburg and, along with a host of other officials in the provinces, acted as an agent of the central government. Prior to 1861, there was no genuine local government and, with the sole exception of Finland, no meaningful degree of autonomy for the non-Russian nationalities within the Russian Empire. Political centralization, in short, went hand in hand with the development of the empire and the huge bureaucracy that administered it.

Fourth, the absence of a strong legal tradition and a constitutional basis of government, combined with extreme centralization of political power, led to a pattern of political coercion involving, on the one hand, the strict subordination of local authorities to the central organs of government, and, on the other, the use of centrally controlled police power for political purposes. Judicial autonomy was frequently subverted in order to achieve political purposes.

Civil liberties, as known in the West, were practically nonexistent. Prior to 1905, political parties were prohibited. This fact in and of itself explains a great deal about Lenin's political program and the origin of Bolshevism.[22] From the very outset, the conditions prevailing in czarist Russia forced what eventually became the Bolshevik party into a pattern of illegality and underground existence, resulting in the development of a mentality from which that party, in a sense, never recovered.

Beyond the prohibition of political parties, autocratic Russia featured official censorship of all publications and an internal passport system designed to control the movement and residence of the people. There was also a powerful secret police, the *Okhrana,* with a far-flung network of informers throughout Russia. In addition, the Russian Orthodox Church, controlled by the state through the Holy Synod and such trusted and influential advisers to the czar as Konstantin Pobedonostsev, served as another control instrument vis-à-vis the population, including governmental officials, who were required to attend communion at least once a year and to present written evidence of their attendance to their superiors.

THE COMING
OF THE REVOLUTION

The nineteenth century, a "century of inward revolution" to quote Berdyaev,[23] saw not only the development of a revolutionary movement in Russia, but also serious efforts at reform on the part of the autocracy. In the aftermath of the Era of the Great Reforms of the 1860s—which abolished serfdom, established the rudiments of local self-government (the so-called *zemstvo* movement), and gave Russia a new judicial system, but left the central institution of Russian political life, the autocracy, intact—Russia was destined to illustrate the validity of Alexis de Tocqueville's thesis that "the most dangerous time for a bad government is when it attempts to reform itself." In 1861, Alexander II, who had agreed to a "revolution from above in order to avoid one from below," told Bismarck that constitutional government was "not in accord with Russia's political tradition," that constitutional limitations of the czar's autocratic power would undermine the belief of common men and women throughout the empire who "still regarded the monarch as their 'paternal and absolute God-given ruler'."[24] On another occasion, in a conversation with an advocate of constitutional reform in 1866, the Czar-Liberator remarked that if he were to sign a constitution today, Russia would fall to pieces tomorrow.[25] It is one of the great ironies of history that he later changed his mind and was in the process of arranging for the publication of the Loris-Melikov "constitution" when revolutionaries assassinated him, ushering in an era of severe repression and reaction under Alexander III.

The chief architect of this reaction was Pobedonostsev, who was Director General of the Most Holy Synod of the Russian Orthodox Church for 25 years, a senator for almost 40 years, a member of the State Council for 35 years, a member of the Committee of Ministers for 25 years, and the tutor of the new czar, Alexander III (1881–94).[26] Though a legal scholar by training (Pobedonostsev taught civil law at Moscow University), he denounced all parliamentary forms of government, the idea of popular sovereignty, the separation of church and state, the jury system, and even universal education. To save Russia from these modern "evils," he revived the old reactionary formula of "orthodoxy, autocracy, and nationality."

To Alexander III, as well as to his mentor, Pobedonostsev, government and autocracy were synonymous. "The whole secret of Russia's order and progress is at the top, in the person of the monarch . . . ," Pobedonostsev wrote to the future Alexander III on October 12, 1876. "The day may come when flatterers . . . will try to persuade you that it would suffice to grant a so-called constitution on the Western model, and all difficulties would disappear and the government could live in peace. This is a lie, and God forbid that a true Russian shall see the day when this lie will become an accomplished fact."[27] Toward the end of his career, Pobedonostsev wrote to the successor of Alexander III, Nicholas II, in a letter of March 21, 1901, about the "insane longing for a constitution, that is, the ruin of Russia." To the end of his life, he remained convinced that the idea of democracy and the principle of the sovereignty of the people constituted what he called "the great falsehood of our time."[28]

In tutoring the last two czars, Pobedonostsev evidently did extremely thorough work. It was not until the Revolution of 1905, coming on the heels of Russia's ignominious defeat in the Russo-Japanese war of 1904–05, that some minimal constitutional concessions were extracted from a most reluctant and unwilling czar. At that point in time, a national parliamentary assembly, the State Duma, came into existence and political parties were legalized—a fact, incidentally, to which Lenin in terms of his politics never really responded. But the State Duma, the first constitutional plant in Russian soil during the modern period, did not prosper. Based on a very limited franchise (2.4 percent of the population), it overrepresented the upper classes and underrepresented the peasants. The czar retained the sole power to initiate legislation. He appointed half of the upper house, the State Council, which had veto over the State Duma. In addition, the czar himself had the power to veto decisions of the Duma and to dissolve it. Ministers remained responsible to the czar, who also retained control of two-thirds of the state budget. The first two Dumas were dissolved; the third Duma was more conservative, due to a change in the electoral law that gave still greater representation to the upper classes. The fourth Duma was likewise dominated by conservative nationalists.

In short, Czar Nicholas II never reconciled himself to the status of a constitutional monarch and never fully accepted the fact that his will was not above the law. He proved to be incapable of making the transition from an autocrat to a constitutional monarch—and Russia's experiment with constitutional government ended in failure. No genuine parliamentary and constitutional tradition developed, and the autocracy survived virtually intact until it was destroyed in the February Revolution of 1917.

For the ancien régime of Russia the 1905 Revolution was the beginning of the end. Although we frequently think of the Russian Revolution in terms of the dramatic events of the year 1917, the revolutionary wave that ultimately swept away the czarist autocracy actually began in 1905. As a matter of fact, the events of 1905—a series of violent outbreaks, strikes, political assassinations, and the mutiny on the battleship Potemkin in the Black Sea, immortalized in Eisenstein's classic film—foreshadowed what was to come rather accurately.

Twelve years after the "great rehearsal," as Lenin called the 1905 Revolution, it was again a disastrous war—this time against Imperial Germany—that proved to be the midwife of revolution. As the result of military defeat, peasant unrest, workers' strikes and demonstrations, the demoralization and ineffectiveness of the army, and—perhaps most important—the practically universal hostility toward the monarchy by the educated classes, the "revolutionary wave" once again crested, to use Lenin's vivid metaphor. The reign of the Romanov dynasty, which had ruled Russia for three centuries, and the autocracy, the central political institution in Russian life, simply collapsed and disintegrated.

In the ensuing anarchy of the "dual power" of two self-proclaimed governments—the Provisional Government under Kerensky, created by the Duma, and the Petrograd Soviet of Workers' and Soldiers' Deputies, a throwback to the traditions of 1905—the Bolshevik party under Lenin's leadership, after an abortive coup attempt in July 1917, was able to muster the requisite discipline and organization to pick up power in October of that year.[29] The government that Lenin overthrew,

therefore, was not the autocracy or the government of the czar, but rather the Provisional Government set up in March 1917. Although the role of Lenin in the revolution was without question a major and decisive one, it was in conquering the anarchy of the revolution and in creating the highly authoritarian Soviet state out of the revolutionary chaos prevailing in Russia in 1917 that Lenin demonstrated the full measure of his genius as a politician.

CONCLUSION

In assessing the impact of Russian history and political culture as part of the background against which the Soviet political system evolved and postcommunist Russia is evolving, we must, no doubt, consider the seemingly overwhelming continuity in the autocratic pattern of Russian politics—the sheer cumulative weight of centuries of autocratic politics in a society that for several centuries has had to live with the persistent challenge of an economically and technologically superior West on its doorsteps, a society that, as we have seen, developed a very ambivalent attitude and response to the West, and to this day is searching for the answer to the question raised by Gogol in that curious passage in *Dead Souls:* Whither Russia?

Perhaps no other leading figure personifies this basic unresolved problem in Russian history and this schizophrenic ambivalence with regard to the challenge from the outside as clearly and as tragically as Pobedonostsev who, in the words of his biographer, was both "a Muscovite Russian nationalist and a Westerner."[30] Fluent in several European languages, deeply steeped in European and American literature, a frequent traveler to Western Europe, Pobedonostsev played a major role in the modernization of Russia's judicial system in 1864 and advocated changes in the Russian economy to bring it in line with the patterns already evident in Europe. On the other hand, he was vehemently opposed to the introduction of Western ideas and practices in the realm of politics. As the person most responsible for torpedoing the constitutional designs of Count Loris-Melikov and others who sought to close the gap between state and society in Russia in 1881,

Pobedonostsev thus symbolized one of the great unresolved issues in modern Russian history: the issue of how to cope with the West, which persistently challenged the fundamental precepts of the Russian state and posed a constant threat to the basic fabric of Russian society.

Although one may violently disagree with Pobedonostsev, one has to grant that there was something very Russian in his outlook. Perhaps the best way to look at him is to regard him as the personification of the fact that notions of legality, constitutionality, and democracy were basically alien to the prevailing Russian historical tradition. It is important for us to recognize that this same quality of "Russianness" also characterized the Russian radical movement. In the context of nineteenth century Russian history, this means that there was an anti-Western or, more precisely, an anti-European quality about the Russian conservative or reactionary mentality as well as the Russian radical mentality. As one Western historian has put it, the members of the Russian intelligentsia "believed themselves resolutely opposed to autocracy in principle, yet in many cases the objection was to an autocracy which served the existing social system rather than to autocracy as such."[31]

There is today no czar on the throne of Russia. But we may well raise the question of whether the October Revolution really did break the pattern of autocratic rule in Russia. While it is easy to point to the obvious differences between the czarist autocracy and Soviet totalitarianism, it is important to recognize the continuity between some of the policies pursued by Soviet government and the policies recommended by Pobedonostsev.

Similarly, the "democratization" of the Russian Federation notwithstanding, President Yeltsin has exhibited a distinctly autocratic style of leadership, frequently ignoring or violating the provisions of the 1993 Constitution of the Russian Federation which bears his personal imprint—and this in spite of the fact that this constitution gives him extraordinary powers that are difficult to reconcile with any meaningful definition of democracy. Not surprisingly, his countrymen have frequently referred to him as "Czar Boris."

Certainly until the death of Stalin, who more than any other leader shaped the basic contours

and the essence of the Soviet political system, the politics of the Soviet Union moved in an essentially autocratic mold. Stalin's heroes were Ivan the Terrible and Peter the Great, whom he regarded as "progressive czars." Ivan's secret police, the *oprichnina,* served as the model for Stalin's NKVD.[32] Stalinism, among other things, involved the wholesale glorification of the historic Russian state, the reintroduction of a modern-day equivalent of Peter the Great's Table of Ranks, and the personalization of political power in the form of an autocratic style of leadership, accompanied by an extreme and grotesque leadership cult.[33] Ideology notwithstanding, Stalin embarked on an intense process of state building—a process that, as in czarist days, entailed the binding of the peasant to the land and the creation of new social classes.

But in the end, the totalitarian state created by Stalin did not survive its architect. After his death on March 5, 1953, the Soviet Union experienced an era of reform politics under Nikita Khrushchev. While limited and not successful, this first wave of reforms set the stage for what was to come in the 1980s and 1990s. After the neo-Stalinist interlude under Brezhnev, the "children of Khrushchev," with great determination and vigor, embarked on a new struggle for reform under Gorbachev. The pursuit of reform, as it turned out, led to truly revolutionary changes in Soviet cultural, socioeconomic, and political life. The fissures that had developed in the Stalinist state and party structure during the post-Stalin era grew into ever-widening cracks, and ultimately that structure crumbled under the impact of ethnic conflict, a rapidly deteriorating economy, growing social problems, a serious crisis of confidence in the Communist Party, and the system's failure to address even the most salient issues confronting Soviet society in the 1980s. The reforms under Gorbachev—in particular democratization (including the introduction of free, multicandidate elections), the abolition of the monopoly position of the Communist Party, and the implementation of a new information policy *(glasnost)*—rewrote the rules of politics in the largest country on earth. Acquiring a dynamic of its own, *perestroika,* which had begun as an effort at reform, i.e., within-system change, turned into a full-blown revolution that ultimately led to the collapse of central power in the Soviet state and the migration of power from Moscow to the republics. Although this revolution is far from having run its course, it is perhaps not premature to say that in time its significance may well eclipse that of the October Revolution in 1917. For the first time in history, the common people, the masses, have become meaningful and autonomous participants in the political process. Overcoming their fear nurtured by centuries of oppressive rule, they finally spoke out, airing their grievances against the regime, crying out for help, and most importantly, demonstrating that they have in fact made the transition from subjects to participants in politics. It was the people who forced the pace of change and who played a crucial role in overcoming the forces of reaction behind the coup attempt in August, 1991. This fact augurs well for the future and suggests that the resurrection of an all-powerful centralized state is unlikely.

At the same time, there is no question that many serious problems lie ahead. The political agenda of every political unit now taking shape on the territory of the former Soviet Union is replete with difficult issues. Not only will they have to deal with their own problems, but they will have to find a new modus vivendi and develop effective ways of addressing the issues they face in common. They will have to find the way back to their own history, fill the spiritual void left by the long decades of Soviet rule, learn how to live and function in a competitive market environment, and overcome their own deeply ingrained conservatism.

The October Revolution of 1917 in many respects led to the isolation of Russia and its subject people from the rest of the world. The Revolution of 1991 promises just the opposite. The regime spawned by the Bolshevik victory in 1917 sought to destroy the Western state system. Most, if not all, of the political systems now taking shape in the former Soviet Union endeavor to build bridges to the rest of the world—and especially the Western world. Let us hope that these endeavors will find an appropriate response on the part of the governments and peoples of the West.

For Russia, the disintegration of the Soviet Union, inter alia, has resulted in a multidimensional identity crisis with not only socio-economic and political, but also cultural, demographic, and ecological components. Alone among the peoples of the former union republics of the USSR, the Russians have lost their identity as a people because they, above all, considered the multinational Soviet Union as their state. Since Russian "national" consciousness and identity for centuries has been based on territory, the multinational state, and the multiethnic empire, the Russians are now confronted with the problem of finding a new sense of national identity, negotiating the difficult transition to a secular nation-state and, because of the multiethnic character of the Russian Federation, developing a viable form of federalism—something with Russia has long needed, but never had.[34]

NOTES

[1]On the history of the Russian state, see Michael T. Florinsky, *Russia: A History and Interpretation,* 2 vols. (New York: Macmillan Company, 1960).

[2]Cited in Vera Tolz, "The Democratic Opposition in Crisis," *Report on the USSR* (May 1991): 3.

[3]*Komsomol'skaya pravda,* January 14, 1992.

[4]*Moscow News,* no. 51, 1991, p. 8.

[5]Vera Tolz and Elizabeth Teague, "Russian Intellectuals Adjust to Loss of Empire," *RFE/FL Research Report* 1, no. 3, p. 7.

[6]Arnold Toynbee, *A Study of History,* vol. 1 (New York and London: Oxford University Press, 1963), p.11.

[7]François Guizot, *Essai sur l'histoire de France* (Paris: J. L. L. Brière, 1823), p. 17.

8At times, especially when responding to protests from Baltic Leaders, Russian politicians have excluded the Baltic states from the concept of the "near abroad," which is frequently defined as Russia's exclusive sphere of influence.

[9]For a discussion of this relationship in Russian thought, see Alexander von Schelting, *Russland und Europa im russichen Geschichtsdenken* (Bern: A. Francke AG Verlag, 1948).

[10]Ibid., p. 14.

[11]On this point, see Emanuel Sarkisyanz, *Russland und der Messianismus des Orients: Sendungsbewusstsein und politischer Chiliasmus des Ostens* (Tübingen: J. C. B. Mohr [Paul Siebeck], 1955), pp. 186ff.

[12]Karl A. Wittfogel, *Oriental Despotism: A Comparative Study of Total Power* (New Haven, CT: Yale University Press, 1959).

[13]A. Brückner, *Die Europäisierung Russlands* (Gotha; 1888), p. 9.

[14]V. O. Kliuchevskii, *Sochineniia,* vol. 3 (Moscow, Gosudarstvennoe izdatel'stvo politicheskoi literatury, 1958). p. 12.

[15]On the Russian Orthodox Church, see Ernst Benz, *The Eastern Orthodox Church* (New York: Doubleday & Company, 1963), especially pp. 163ff.; on Byzantine thought, see

Ernest Barker, *Social and Political Thought in Byzantium* (Oxford: Clarendon Press, 1961).

[16]See, for example, P. Tcatschoff [P. N. Tkachev], *Offener Brief an Herrn Friedrich Engels* (Zurich: Typographie der Tagwacht, 1874), p. 6, and V. Figner, *Memoirs of a Revolutionist* (New York: International Publishers, 1927), pp. 75–76.

[17]On this point, see R. H. W. Theen, "The Idea of the Revolutionary State: Tkachev, Trotsky, and Lenin," *Russian Review* 31, no. 4 (October 1972): 383–397.

[18]See, for example, Sir Donald MacKenzie Wallace's description in *Russia on the Eve of War and Revolution* (New York, Vintage Books, 1961), p. 12, and Robert C. Tucker, "The Image of Dual Russia," in Cyril E. Black, ed., *The Transformation of Russian Society: Aspects of Social Change Since 1861* (Cambridge: Harvard University Press, 1960), pp. 587–605.

[19]See R. H. W. Theen, *Lenin: Genesis and Development of a Revolutionary* (Philadelphia and New York: J. B. Lippincott Company, 1973), pp. 115ff.

[20]Cited in R. C. Tucker, "Ruling Personalities in Russian Foreign Policy," in *The Soviet Political Mind* (New York: Frederick A. Praeger, 1963), p. 147.

[21]I have borrowed this phrase from Wallace, *Russia: On the Eve of War and Revolution,* p. 4.

[22]For the sake of history, it must be stated that Lenin did not change his political program or his conception of the party when political parties were legalized in Russia in 1905.

[23]Berdyaev, *The Origin of Russian Communism,* p. 22.

[24]W. E. Mosse, *Alexander II and the Modernization of Russia* (New York: Collier Books, 1962), p. 112.

[25]Ibid., p. 113.

[26]On Pobedonostsev, see R. F. Byrnes, *Pobedonostsev: His Life and Thought* (Bloomington: Indiana University Press, 1968).

[27]Tsentrarkhiv, *Pis'ma Pobedonostseva k Aleksandru III,* vol. I (Moscow: "Novaia Moskva," 1925), pp. 53, 54.

[28]K. P. Pobedonostsev, *Reflections of a Russian Statesman* (Ann Arbor: University of Michigan Press, 1965), pp. 32ff.

[29]Adam Ulam has argued that the Bolsheviks "did not seize power" but simply "picked it up." See Adam B. Ulam, *The Bolsheviks* (New York: The Macmillan Company, 1965), p. 314.

[30]Byrnes, *Pobedonostsev,* p. IX.

[31]Hugh Seton-Watson, *The Russian Empire* (Oxford: Clarendon Press, 1967), p. 538.

[32]The Soviet secret police had different names: Cheka (1917–22), GPU (1922–23), OGPU (1923–34), NKVD (1934–38), NKVD-MKGB (1938–45), MVD/MGB (1945–54), and KGB (1954–91).

[33]On Stalin, see Robert C. Tucker, *Stalin in Power: The Revolution from Above, 1928–1941* (New York: W. W. Norton and Company, 1990).

[34]On the national identity crisis of postcommunist Russia, cf. Rolf H. W. Theen, "Quo Vadis, Russia? The Problem of National Identity and State-Building," in Gordon B. Smith, ed., *State-Building in Russia: The Yeltsin Legacy and the Challenge of the Future* (Armonk, NY: M. E. Sharpe, 1999), pp. 41–80; B. P. Kurashvili, *Kuda idet Rossiia?* (Moscow: Prometei, 1994); Tim McDaniel, *The Agony of the Russian Idea* (Princeton: Princeton University Press, 1998).

Chapter 20

The Social Setting
of Russian Politics

In trying to understand the politics of the Russian Federation, it is important to recognize that it is in many respects a unique country. Even after the disintegration of the Soviet Union, its Russian component, now the Russian Federation, is still by far the largest country on earth. Stretching almost from the Baltic Sea in the west to the Pacific Ocean in the east, from the Arctic Sea in the north to the Caspian Sea, Kazakhstan, China, and Mongolia in the south, the Russian Federation occupies nearly 6.6 million square miles (17.1 million square kilometers)—about three-fourths of the territory of the former USSR. It is thus more than twice as large as Brazil or almost as large as China and Australia combined. Canada, the second largest country in the world, has a territory of 3.85 million square miles—56 percent of the territory of Russia (see Table 20–1). In contrast to the formation of most other empires, Russian territorial expansion took the form of the annexation of contiguous territory, the incorporation of various "borderlands" in the west, south, east, and north. As a consequence of this process of expansion, extending over several centuries, the Russian Empire came into being, which as a result of the October Revolution in

1917 was transformed into the Union of Soviet Socialist Republics. As presently constituted, the Russian Federation has 12,514 miles of land frontiers and 23,396 miles of coastline, bringing it into direct or relatively close land or sea contact with more than a dozen nations, including the two most populous countries, China and India, and the most industrialized nation in Asia, Japan. Finally, across the Bering Sea, only 56 miles separate the Russian Federation from the United States of America—until the mid-1980s its chief political, military, and ideological antagonist.

THE SOCIOECONOMIC STRUCTURE BEFORE 1917

Prior to the 1917 Revolution, Russia was a highly stratified and, by Western standards, a very backward country. Its social class structure was based on legally established estates: the nobility, the town inhabitants, and the peasantry. The nobility, which was exempt from taxation, compulsory military service, and corporal punishment, was stratified into fourteen different ranks. Further, the nobility was distinguished in terms of three

Table 20–1   The World's Largest States in Terms of Territory

Rank	Country	Area in Square Miles	Population	Density per Square Mile
1	Russian Federation	6,592,800	146,861,000	22.3
2	Canada	3,849,674	30,677,000	8.0
3	China	3,696,100	1,242,980,000	336.3
4	United States	3,615,215	270,262,000	74.8
5	Brazil	3,300,171	161,760,000	49.0
6	Australia	2,966,200	18,725,000	6.3
7	India	1,222,243	984,004,000	805.1
8	Argentina	1,073,400	36,125,000	33.7
For comparison:				
	USSR	8,649,800	291,062,000	33.6

Source: 1999 Britannica Book of the Year (Chicago: Encyclopedia Britannica, 1999), pp. 756–760. Population data are estimates for mid-1998.

additional categories: the hereditary nobility, which before the abolition of serfdom in 1861 possessed the further privilege of owning serfs; the personal nobility, whose members held their title for life, but could not pass it on to their children; and the merchants, whose privileges were contingent upon the payment of legally specified amounts, as well as membership in the two highest guilds, thus requiring in essence a certain degree of wealth. The taxable estates consisted of the town inhabitants—small shopkeepers or artisans, in short, the lowest stratum of the merchants (but without the privileges of the wealthy members of their class), and the great mass of the rural inhabitants, the peasantry, by far the majority of the population. Being under the jurisdiction of ecclesiastical rather than civil authority, the clergy was not included in any of these estates. There were also some other groups—the Cossacks and Jews, for example—who were not regarded as members of any of these estates; instead, special provisions were made for them.[1]

The structure of the estates in Russia was not as rigid as that in Western Europe. Title and status of nobility in Russia could be acquired through conferral by the czar or through the attainment of a certain rank in the state service.[2] In addition, one could enter the lower ranks of the nobility by virtue of a university degree or the accumulation of the necessary wealth required to join one of the merchant guilds that entailed nobility status. Because of the relative ease of entry

into the Russian nobility, this class or estate is perhaps more accurately described by the term "gentry." It is also useful to conceptualize it as a service nobility, that is, a class specifically created to serve the interests of the state.

By far the majority of the Russian population before 1917 was engaged in agriculture and was largely illiterate. As is apparent from Table 20–2 the peasantry accounted for the vast majority of the population at the turn of the century. In actual fact the peasantry was much more heterogeneous than was commonly thought at the time. In addition to regional differences with respect to religion and education, the peasantry was

Table 20–2   Population of the Russian Empire by Estates in 1897

Nobility[a]	2,193,000
Clergy	588,900
Merchants	281,100
Town inhabitants	13,386,300
Peasants	96,896,500
Cossacks	2,928,700
Jews	5,215,805

[a]Includes all ranks and *chinovniki*, i.e., state officials not belonging to the nobility.

Source: N. A. Troinitskii, ed., *Obshchii svod po imperii resul'tatov razrabotki dannykh pervoi vseobshchei perepisi naseleniia proizvedennoi 28 ianvaria 1897 goda* (St. Petersburg: Tsentral'nyi statisticheskii komitet, 1905), vol. 1, pp. 160–161; vol. 2, p. xvi.

characterized by significant differences in wealth. There were rich peasants with substantial land-holdings—the class on which the government based its "wager on the strong" after the Revolution of 1905; there were peasants with medium-size and small landholdings; and there were landless peasants who were essentially agricultural hands.[3]

Two factors that figured importantly in the breakup of the old social order of prerevolutionary Russia were rapid population growth and industrialization. During the nineteenth century the population of Russia tripled, reaching 125.6 million for the Russian Empire as a whole in 1897. Of this total, 16.8 million, or 13 percent, lived in cities and towns. The 1897 census, the only comprehensive census ever conducted in Imperial Russia, also revealed that only 21 percent of the population could read or write. As might be expected in the case of a traditional society, the literacy rate was higher for men (29 percent) than for women (13 percent) and significantly higher for the urban than for the rural population (45 percent and 17 percent respectively).[4]

At the turn of the century, the Russian working class—on which Lenin, at least in the realm of Marxist theory and Bolshevik propaganda, so confidently based his hope for revolution—was still very small. While reliable statistics are difficult to come by (in part because the official classification categories used in czarist Russia did not recognize those engaged in industry and commerce), it is estimated that in 1913 wage and salary workers accounted for 16.7 percent of the population, that is, 23.3 million, but industrial workers included in that figure made up only 1.41 percent (2.3 million) of the total population.[5] By comparison, in the United States industrial workers accounted for 11.6 percent of the population in 1910.

In spite of its relative backwardness, however, there is no doubt that by the turn of the century Russia was well on its way to becoming industrialized and modernized. The 1890s especially saw a great upsurge of industrialization sponsored by the state and carried out largely with the assistance of Western European technology and investments. There was a large influx of capital from Britain, France, Belgium, and Germany. The British invested heavily in textiles and oil;

Table 20–3 Average Annual Rates of Growth of Industrial Output, 1870–1913 (in Percent)

Period	Russia	U.S.	Britain	Germany
1870–1884	—	4.65%	1.98%	4.22%
1885–1889	6.10%	8.75	4.56	5.15
1890–1899	8.03	5.47	1.80	5.44
1907–1913	6.25	3.52	2.72	3.90

Source: A. Gerschenkron, "The Rate of Growth in Russia," *The Journal of Economic History,* 7 (1947): supplement, p. 156.

Franco-Belgian interests owned more than half of the mines in Russia at this time. Oil production increased so rapidly that by 1901 Russia produced more oil than the United States. After 1890 the average annual growth rates for industrial output began to surpass those of the United States, Britain, and Germany (see Table 20–3).

However, as in the past, the economic development of Russia followed a curious pattern. In response to the real or perceived military interests and needs of the state, the government typically induced a rapid upsurge of economic growth, usually with the assistance of foreign capital and technology. But in the process it imposed such a heavy burden on the peasants that the rapid spurt would fizzle out in a few years because of the exhaustion of the population.[6] What is important in regard to this pattern is the dominant role of the state in economic development, the long-established nexus between military considerations and economic policy, and the continuity of a tradition according to which the interests of society were always eclipsed by those of the state. It was the military needs of the expanding Muscovite state that dictated the establishment of serfdom in the seventeenth century and the binding of all classes through compulsory service to the state. Similarly, the famous reforms of Peter the Great in the early eighteenth century were primarily motivated by the desire to bolster Russia's military power. In the nineteenth century, finally, in the aftermath of Russia's defeat in the Crimean war (1854–56) and its diplomatic defeat at the Congress of Berlin in 1878 (which deprived Russia of its victory in the

Russo-Turkish War of 1877), a reluctant czarist government once again embarked on the road to selective modernization and development in an attempt to enhance its military position vis-à-vis Western Europe.

Thus, time and again the interests of the Russian people were sacrificed to the interests of the Russian state. The energies and resources of Russian society were sapped and consumed by the process of "internal state-building" with such regularity and over such extended periods of time that the exploitation of society by the state became a historical pattern in Russia.[7] Unfortunately, although undertaken "in the name of the people," the Russian Revolution of 1917 did little to change the dominant position of the state vis-à-vis society. On the contrary, as part of yet another "revolution from above," undertaken by Stalin in 1929 in anticipation of a second inevitable world war, a new kind of serfdom was imposed on the people of the Soviet Union under the name of collectivization—a revolution which, within the space of a decade, resulted in the forceful conversion of approximately 25 million individual peasant farms into about 200,000 collective farms under state control, ushering in an era of state dominance over society that was unprecedented even in the annals of Russian history.[8] As a recent essay makes clear, the pattern of "state-building" and the eclipse of the interests of society continued after Stalin's death and was part of his legacy to the Russia of our time.[9]

Whether the result of state sponsorship or the initiative of private entrepreneurs, the sociological consequences of industrialization in Russia were similar to those observed earlier in Western Europe and in the developing countries today. The growth of industry brought with it urbanization and the large-scale migration of people from the villages to cities and towns. It resulted in the formation of new social classes: factory workers, managerial and professional personnel—groups which could not be easily integrated into the official social structure of czarist Russia. As the nineteenth century drew to a close, the growing diversity of the population resulting from the new occupational groups generated by industrialization and the development of previously weak social classes (a prosperous, land-owning peasantry, industrial working class or proletariat, and a middle class) added to the already considerable socioeconomic and cultural heterogeneity of czarist society, producing additional stresses and strains for the regime, which clung desperately to the anachronistic idea of absolutism at a time when the country was in the midst of an extremely rapid socioeconomic and cultural transformation.

ETHNIC AND RELIGIOUS DIVISIONS

Our cursory examination of the social cleavages of czarist Russia would be incomplete without a brief discussion of the national, religious, racial, and linguistic groups that contributed to the great cultural diversity of the czarist Empire, but also provided a measure of vertical integration with respect to the various divisions of czarist society based on estates, class, and occupation.

At the time of the October Revolution, the Russian Empire was the product of nearly four centuries of continuous expansion—a process frequently described by Russian historians as "the gathering of the Russian lands." However, most of the borderlands into which the dynamic state of Moscow expanded were inhabited by non-Russian peoples. Almost from its very inception, therefore, the history of the Muscovite state involved the subjugation of indigenous populations and dominion over non-Russian nationalities. The 1897 census revealed that more than half of the population of Imperial Russia consisted of non-Russians (see Table 20–4).[10]

Closely associated with nationality was religion—another important dimension of social cleavage. The multinational structure of the population of czarist Russia meant the coexistence of a large number of different religious traditions. Of course, accompanying these different religions were the attendant political tensions and strains which would especially occur in a polity whose autocratic government, prior to its secularization toward the end of the eighteenth century, had for some 200 years made concerted efforts to convert Jews, Moslems, and other non-Christians to the Russian Orthodox faith.

With respect to religion the diversity of the Russian Empire was, indeed, enormous. The

Table 20–4 Population of the Russian Empire by Nationality in 1897 (in Percent)[a]

Slavs	
Russians	44.32%
Ukrainians	17.81
Poles	6.31
Belorussians	4.68
Turkic peoples (Tatars, Uzbeks,	
Kazakhs, and others)	10.82
Jews	4.03
Finnish peoples	2.78
Lithuanians and Latvians	2.46
Germans	1.42
Caucasian Mountain peoples	
(*gortsy*)	1.34
Georgians	1.07
Armenians	0.93
Iranian peoples	0.62
Mongolians	0.38
Others	1.03

[a]Nationality identification based on language claimed as native tongue.

Source: Richard Pipes, *The Formation of the Soviet Union* (Cambridge, MA: Harvard University Press, 1964), p. 2.

Russians (or Great Russians), Ukrainians, Belorussians, and Georgians, for example, were predominantly Russian Orthodox. Among the Ukrainians and the Belorussians, however, there was a sizable Roman Catholic minority. Most of the Roman Catholics among the Ukrainians were Uniats, who preserved an Eastern ritual. Poland and Lithuania were overwhelmingly Catholic. According to the 1897 census, the population of the Russian Empire included 1.5 million Roman Catholics, including Uniats, who spoke Russian, Ukrainian, or Belorussian. In Armenia, Christianity had been a state religion since the fourth century. The Armenian church had developed its own distinctive church architecture and differed in many important respects from the Russian Orthodox church.

The remaining Christian churches important in terms of their membership were the Lutherans (strongest in Estonia and Latvia), the Baptists, and the Old Believers, who broke off from the official Russian Orthodox Church in the seventeenth century. The incorporation of the Turkic peoples of Central Asia and parts of European

Russia brought the Russian Empire into direct and intimate contact with Islam. The Jews, finally, who came to Russia primarily from Europe, brought with them yet another distinct heritage with respect to language, religion, and way of life.

In examining the czarist regime's treatment of the national minorities, one looks in vain for a consistent policy. If there was a basic pattern, it was that of attempted Russification. Thus, the Ukrainians were refused recognition as a distinct ethnic group and their language was treated as a mere local dialect. The Belorussians (also known as White Russians) and Poles were also subjected to various forms of Russification. Nationalism was identified with Russian Orthodoxy, leading to various forms of discrimination against, and persecution of, any dissenting groups—from the Old Believers and Roman Catholics to Protestants, Moslems, and Jews. Russian became the only language officially recognized and accepted throughout the Russian Empire.

The case of the Jews illustrates perhaps most clearly the extremes of discrimination and religious persecution under the czars. In 1783 and 1791 under Catherine II, Jews were restricted by law to the Pale of Settlement, that is, exclusive residence in designated areas in western and southern Russia. In 1794 they were subjected to discriminatory taxation at twice the prevailing rate. During the first half of the nineteenth century, the czarist regime pursued a policy of assimilation. In 1804 Jews were admitted to schools without restriction and granted eligibility for university degrees. Beginning in 1827 they were drafted into the Russian army. In preparation for their eventual closing, Jewish schools were placed under Russian control. In 1844 the dissolution of the Jewish autonomous communities *(kahals)* was decreed, and in 1850 Jews were prohibited from wearing their national dress.

There was a brief respite during the reign of Alexander II (1855–81). But during the last two decades of the nineteenth century the persecution of Jews under the czars reached its height. In 1882, they were prohibited from settling in rural areas—even within the pale; they were de facto excluded from the legal profession in 1889. In the 1880s and 1890s they were also subjected to quotas in secondary and higher schools and to disfranchisement. Worst of all, they were victimized by a series of pogroms condoned and in some instances even instigated by the authorities.[11]

The vicious anti-Semitism of this period was a manifestation and a measure of the militant nationalism that inspired the policies of the czarist government in the closing decades of the nineteenth century. In a transparent attempt to mobilize the national sentiments of the Great Russians as a weapon against the increasing social unrest in the Empire, the czarist regime resorted to a concerted policy of minority repression and Russification. This chapter in the history of czarist nationality policy coincided with the most severe governmental reaction, which deprived even the Great Russians of many rights they had been granted during the Great Reforms under Alexander II. It should be pointed out, however, that in pushing the policy of Russification to its limits, the advocates of aggressive Russian nationalism did not have the support of the nobility as a whole or even the higher levels of the bureaucracy. The more reactionary legislative proposals, which reflected the thinking of such highly placed anti-Semites as Pobedonostsev, Count Dmitri Tolstoy, the Minister of Internal Affairs and Chief of Gendarmes, and Mikhail Katkov, the highly influential publicist, were enacted into law over the opposition of the State Council, an assembly of high officials and large landowners appointed by the czar.

SOCIOECONOMIC AND ETHNIC DIMENSIONS OF POLITICS

Marxism-Leninism, the official ideology of the Soviet Union, postulated a world view according to which the historical development of mankind proceeds in definite sequential stages—from primitive communism throughout slavery, feudalism, capitalism, and socialism to communism. Prior to the establishment of socialism, the basic fact of human existence and the essence of history is class struggle, that is, the natural antagonism between the workers (the proletariat) and those who exploit them (the capitalist class or bourgeoisie). The outcome of this struggle is foreordained. In the end, the workers will be victorious, free themselves from the domination of their expropriators, the bourgeoisie, emerge as the new ruling class, and set up the first genuine majority government in history, the so-called dictatorship of the proletariat. Under socialism, so the doctrine goes, all exploitation of man by man—and, therefore, the class struggle—will come to an end, the social relations among men will be governed by the principle of equality, and a classless and stateless society will be established. The traditional state—being itself the product of class struggle, according to Marxism-Leninism—will be superfluous in the postrevolutionary society; with the disappearance of social classes and the class struggle, the state—in the words of Friedrich Engels, the intellectual comrade-in-arms of Karl Marx—will "wither away."[12]

A second important precept of Marxism-Leninism from the perspective of the political evolution of the USSR has to do with nationalism. Marx and Engels shared, albeit in modified form, the illusion of J. G. Herder and J. J. Rousseau that the emancipation of the nations would lead to the elimination of the national conflicts. "The victory of the proletariat over the bourgeoisie," Marx declared in 1847, "is at the same time the victory over the national and industrial conflicts which today place the nations in hostile opposition to one another."[13] In *The Communist Manifesto,* Marx postulated the disappearance of the hostile confrontation of nations as the result of the elimination of the class struggle within nations. He thus logically subordinated national to social emancipation, arguing at one point that "Poland, therefore, must be liberated in England, not in Poland."[14]

Except in the realm of ideology and propaganda, the Soviet Union never came close to the ultimate goal of a classless and stateless society, one in which equality prevails and all traces of nationalism have been eliminated. As a matter of fact, many Soviet citizens developed a high degree of skepticism with respect to the possibility of ever achieving the end goal, that is, what in Soviet parlance was called *full communism.* When questioned about the ultimate goal of communism, a Soviet friend told one of the authors during a visit in Moscow: "Full communism is like the horizon—a remote, imaginary line that is constantly receding."

Official Soviet doctrine dealt with the discrepancy between theory and practice through the modification of theory, as well as the veiling and embellishment of practice. Generally speaking, the official view held that there was no longer any class struggle in the Soviet Union, that all class antagonisms had disappeared, and that only class differences still persisted—differences that would disappear with the attainment of full communism. More specifically, the Stalin Constitution recognized two nonantagonistic classes in the USSR: the proletariat and the peasantry. The intelligentsia, by contrast, was considered a mere "social layer" whose members were recruited from the ranks of the proletariat and the peasantry. The Brezhnev Constitution of 1977, in Article I, declared the USSR to be "a socialist state of the whole people" (also translated as ". . . state of all the people") and described the present-day USSR as "a developed socialist society," which was said to be "a logically necessary stage on the path to communism." While the 1977 Constitution thus stopped short of proclaiming the arrival of communism and the achievement of a classless society, it explicitly stated that "having fulfilled the tasks of the dictatorship of the proletariat, the Soviet state has become a state of the whole people." Moreover, in the Preamble, it described the USSR as "a society of mature socialist social relations" and "a new historical community of people—the Soviet people—[which] has come into being on the basis of the drawing together of all classes and social strata and the juridical and actual equality of all nations and nationalities and their fraternal cooperation."[15]

The idea of egalitarianism, one of the important revolutionary ideals that inspired Soviet political practice under Lenin, was one of the casualties of the reign of Stalin, who regarded industrialization and economic development as much more important than the achievement of an egalitarian society. In 1931, Stalin attacked the "leftist" practice of wage equalization[16] and five years later the famous principle of payment "from each according to his ability, to each according to his work" was duly enshrined in Article 12 of the "Stalin" Constitution of 1936. The realization of the Marxist principle of payment "from each according to his ability, to each according to his need" was relegated to the indefinite future.

The differences in social status, cultural levels, and life-style between the various social groups in the USSR were very considerable. There existed, for example, a definite hierarchy of occupations in the perception of Soviet citizens: Doctors, scientists, and engineers were held in higher popular esteem than factory managers, army officers, or party secretaries. In terms of material rewards, however, the order was reversed: party secretaries, factory managers, and army officers ranked higher than doctors, scientists, and engineers.[17]

While one rarely encountered the kind of conspicuous consumption in the Soviet Union that is typical of the wealthy in the United States, there was a privileged class of high-level party and state officials, successful artists and writers, managers of important industrial enterprises, top scientists, and others, who not only received substantially higher incomes than the average Soviet citizen, but also had access to better and more spacious housing (a very scarce resource in the USSR), private transportation, restricted consumer outlets (special stores not open to the general public), domestic servants, restricted beaches and vacation facilities, foreign travel, imported furniture, special hospitals and medical services, and so forth.[18] In the words of a Soviet observer: "Many of the privileges Russia's upper crust arrogate to themselves would not be tolerated for a moment under the most unrestrained capitalist economy . . . No Rockefeller, and not even a Rothschild, could get away with the kind of disdainful high-handedness taken for granted here."[19]

Thus it was not the absence of affluence and privilege that accounted for the relative invisibility of inequality in the Soviet Union, but the practice of throwing a veil over wealth and elite life-styles; of carefully compartmentalizing Soviet society by means of walls, fences, guards, police forces, and a controlled press; of concealing inequalities of income as a matter of government policy.[20] While in the 1970s differentials between manual, nonmanual and white-collar workers declined, the differences in access to scarce goods and services constituted major barriers in Soviet society and contributed to its social stratification.

But while income inequalities did exist in the Soviet Union, they were not as extreme as those

Table 20–5 Changes in the Social Structure of the Soviet Union, 1928–77 (in Percent of the Population)

Group	(1913)	1928	1939	1959	1970	1977	1987
Manual and nonmanual workers	17.0%	17.6%	52.5%	68.3%	78.4%	84.3%	88.0%
Collective farmers and cooperative craftsmen	—	2.9	47.2	31.4	21.5	15.7	12.0
Individual peasants and craftsmen	66.7	74.9	2.6	0.3	0.03	—	—
Merchants (bourgeoisie)	16.3	4.6	—	—	—	—	—

Source: The USSR Economy: A Statistical Abstract (London: 1957), p. 19; *Voprosy ekonomiki*, 1961, no. 1, pp. 58ff; *Narodnoe khoziaystvo SSSR v 1969 g* (Moscow: 1970), p. 30; *Narodnoe khoziaystvo SSSR v 1975 g* (Moscow: Finansy i statistika, 1976), p. 9; *Narodnoe khoziaystvo za 60 let* (Moscow: Statistika, 1977), p. 8; *The USSR in Figures for 1987* (Moscow: Finansy i Statistika Publishers, 1988), p. 176.

prevailing in capitalist countries like the United States. According to one study, in the United States the maximum income in 1960 was 11,000 times the minimum and 7,000 times the average income, while the maximum income in the Soviet Union was only 300 times the minimum and 100 times the average income.[21] However, since many goods and services in Soviet society were effectively removed from the market on a more or less permanent basis or were available only in special stores for the privileged, income inequalities as such were not nearly as significant there as they tend to be in a country like the United States. While income was important in the Soviet Union as elsewhere, it frequently was not as important as "access" and the special privileges and perquisites conferred by high office and status.

What was much more important in Soviet society was the inequality in political power, which—along with occupation, education, and wealth—was a major determinant of social status and frequently a precondition for the achievement of economic power and the attainment of at least a degree of wealth. In the absence of a propertied class such as exists in the United States and in the presence of demonstrable differences in social status and political power, the Soviet Union demonstrated the fallacy of the Marxist theory that social inequalities are always based on property.

The Bolshevik seizure of power in 1917 entailed not only a radical political transformation but also a massive social upheaval. For nearly three-fourths of a century, the Communist party

(CPSU) was involved in a large-scale attempt to bring about the far-reaching social and institutional changes dictated by the objective of rapid industrialization and economic development. As a result of this deliberate all-out effort at social engineering, Soviet society, especially during the 1930s, experienced an enormous increase in social mobility[22] and fundamental changes in class structure (see Table 20–5). Between 1928 and 1939 the manual and nonmanual labor force almost tripled, a new class of collective farmers and cooperative craftsmen was created, and two former social classes—the merchant class or bourgeoisie and the independent peasants and craftsmen—disappeared. As the requirements for skilled manpower increased, a premium was placed on education, which became the single most important channel of upward mobility.

In the field of education, the Soviet regime had every reason to be proud of its accomplishments. By 1939 mass illiteracy had been eradicated. In 1959 the literacy rate stood at 97.8 percent and most non-Russians in the USSR by the 1990s were able to read and write Russian in addition to their native language. Universal compulsory education was introduced beginning in 1930–31 and higher education became available to increasing segments of the population during the years of Soviet rule. Higher education became increasingly important in the Soviet Union, not only as a means for achieving higher social status, but also as a virtual prerequisite for the attainment of high political office. Thus, by 1967 fully 97.6 percent of the party secretaries at the republic, *oblast,* and *krai* level had a complete higher education, 1.4 percent had an incomplete higher education, and only 1 percent had no more than a complete secondary education.[23]

Unlike its czarist predecessor, the Soviet regime did a great deal to encourage and promote the languages and cultures of many of the national minorities. The political platform of the Bolsheviks before the 1917 Revolution included a "new deal" for the non-Russian nationalities, a program that advocated the equality of nations and languages, the right of nations to national self-determination, including the right to secession and the formation of an independent state. But the right to national self-determination and secession was limited by the crucial caveat that it had to be reconcilable with the interests of the proletariat in the class struggle. Furthermore, from the very beginning the Bolsheviks, following the example of Lenin, were adamantly opposed to the formation of a proletarian party along national lines.

The political practice that evolved after 1917 showed very quickly that the right to self-determination and secession existed only on paper, that the Bolshevik regime was determined and prepared to use armed force to keep the nationalities of the former Russian Empire together under the aegis of the new Soviet state. And while in some sense there was equality of languages in the USSR in formal terms, in actuality Russian was the *lingua franca,* the officially recognized and accepted language, in the Soviet Union—in much the same way as it was under the czars.

The results of the 1979 census showed that, although the Russians continued to lose ground in terms of their share of the population, their language had gained in significance.[24] As far as the "equality of nations" was concerned, one only had to study the nationality composition of the decision-making bodies and high-level organs of the CPSU and the Soviet government to dispense with this notion. The nationality policy that evolved from the original Bolshevik platform was one that granted many of the major nationalities a degree of cultural autonomy, but not political equality or independence.

Soviet propaganda claims notwithstanding, the "national question" was not solved in the USSR.

The Soviet Union, like the Russian Empire before it, remained a multinational state par excellence, consisting of more than 200 different ethnic groups of very diverse size. As before, the Russians remained the dominating nation, constituting by far the largest ethnic group. But, as is apparent from Table 20–6, long-term demographic trends and extremely great disparities in the growth rates of the different nationalities were slowly but surely working to alter the ethnic balance of the population of the USSR.

The 1979 census data showed an increase in the populations of all fifteen nationalities that enjoyed union republic status. But the crucial demographic factor was the enormous differential in the growth rates of the populations. The Latvians, for example, increased by only 0.6 percent during 1970–79, while the Tadzhiks increased by 35.7 percent, that is, almost 60 times as much. The growth rate of the three Slavic nationalities (Russians, Ukrainians, and Belorussians) and the three Baltic nationalities (Lithuanians, Latvians, and Estonians) continued to be under the national average, resulting in the decrease of the Slavic share of the population from 76.2 percent in 1959 and 74 percent in 1970 to 72.2 percent in 1979 and a corresponding decline in the Russian share from 54.6 percent in 1959 and 53.4 percent in 1970 to 52.4 percent in 1979.

The growth rates of the five Central Asian nationalities (Uzbeks, Kazakhs, Tadzhiks, Turkmen, and Kirghiz), by contrast, were three to four times the national average. In 20 years the population of the Tadzhiks, Turkmen, and Uzbeks more than doubled. By 1979, the five Central Asian nationalities numbered nearly 26 million, constituting close to 10 percent of the total population of the USSR, as compared to 6.22 percent in 1959. The growth rates of the other Moslem nationalities were not quite as startling, but in 1979 the total Moslem population of the Soviet Union came to 43 million. This means that the Moslem population of the Soviet Union increased by 25 percent from 1970 to 1979, whereas the non-Moslem population grew by only 5 percent during the same period.

With the imbalance in the growth rates of the nationalities expected to continue, the Russians were faced with the prospect of losing their majority status and becoming a minority—even

Table 20–6 Nationality Composition of the Soviet Population and Growth Rates, 1959–89 (in Percent)

Nationality	Share of Population				Average Annual Rates of Growth		
	1959	1970	1979	1989	1959–1970	1970–1979	1979–1989
Russians	54.6%	53.4%	52.4&%	50.6%	1.1%	0.70%	0.5%
Ukrainians	17.8	16.9	16.2	15.4	0.8	0.40	0.4
Belorussians	3.8	3.7	3.6	3.5	1.2	0.50	0.6
	76.2	74.0	72.2	69.5			
Uzbeks	2.88	3.80	4.75	5.8	4.0	3.40	3.0
Kazakhs	1.73	2.19	2.50	2.8	3.5	2.40	2.2
Tajiks	0.67	0.88	1.11	1.5	4.0	3.50	3.8
Turkmen	0.48	0.63	0.77	0.9	3.9	3.20	3.0
Kirghiz	0.46	0.60	0.73	0.9	3.8	3.10	2.9
	6.22	8.10	9.86	11.9			
Azerbaijani	1.41	1.81	2.09	2.4	3.7	2.50	2.2
Armenians	1.33	1.47	1.58	1.6	2.3	1.70	1.1
Georgians	1.29	1.34	1.36	1.4	1.7	1.10	1.1
	4.03	4.62	5.03	5.4			
Lithuanians	1.11	1.10	1.09	1.1	1.2	0.80	0.7
Latvians	0.67	0.59	0.55	0.5	0.2	0.07	0.7
Estonians	0.47	0.42	0.39	0.4	0.2	0.10	0.1
	2.25	2.11	2.03	2.0			
Moldavians	1.06	1.12	2.03		1.8	1.10	
Other nationalities	10.24	10.05	8.85				
USSR	100.00	100.00	100.00		1.3	0.90	

Source: Ann Sheehy, "The Nationality Composition of the Population of the USSR According to the Census of 1979," *Radio Liberty Research Bulletin,* March 27, 1980 (RL 123/80): 13–14. CIA, Directory of Intelligence, *USSR: Demographic Trends and Ethnic Balance in the Non-Russian Republics* (Washington, DC: National Technical Information Service, 1990).

though by far the largest minority. Given the manpower shortage and the concentration of the industrial base of the Soviet Union in the Russian Soviet Federated Socialist Republic (RSFSR) and the western republics, the dramatic shift in the population balance would have confronted the Soviet regime with difficult problems and political choices in the years ahead. To quote the well-known Soviet dissident Igor Shafarevich, a mathematician by profession: "Of all the urgent problems that have accumulated in our life, the most painful seems to be that concerning relations between [sic] the various nationalities in the USSR. No other question arouses such explosions of resentment, malice, and pain—neither material inequality, nor lack of spiritual freedom nor even the persecution of religion."[25]

The validity of this analysis was confirmed within a decade. During the 1980s the nationality issue, in all its explosiveness, manifested itself in the Baltic republics, Belorussia and the Ukraine, the Caucasus, central Asia, and even the Russian Republic—itself a federation of different nationalities. In the era of reform politics, for which Gorbachev initially served as the catalyst, it was precisely this issue that added a special kind of volatility to the already existing political turbulence in the Soviet Union, producing large-scale violence among non-Russian nationalities and between Russians and non-Russians. Although the Soviet Union was confronted with many serious problems, it was the nationality issue that called into question the continued existence of the Union of Soviet Socialist

Republics in its traditional configuration as a federal state.

THE RUSSIAN FEDERATION

As a result of the disintegration of the Soviet Union and the emergence of Russia as an independent state, the position of the Russians in terms of ethnic balance has fundamentally changed. Ethnic Russians constitute 81.5 percent of the population in the Russian Federation. The other major ethnic groups are the Tatars (3.8 percent), Ukrainians (3.0 percent), Chuvash (1.2 percent), Bashkirs (0.9 percent), Belarusians (0.8 percent), and Moldavians (0.7 percent), with other nationalities accounting for 8.1 percent. In the twenty-one federal republics that had emerged by December 1993, when the new Russian Constitution was adopted, Russians accounted for the absolute majority in ten republics and the majority group in two republics.

In terms of religion, Russians are predominantly Eastern Orthodox, but there are also Jews, Muslims, Protestants, and Roman Catholics. The religions in the twenty-one federal republics and autonomous areas include Sunni Muslims (in Bashkortostan, Chechnya, Ingushetia, Dagestan, Kabardina-Balkaria, North Ossetia, and Tatarstan), Buddhists (in Buryatia and Kalmykia), Shia Muslims (in Dagestan), believers in a mixture of Eastern Orthodoxy and shamanist-animist beliefs (in Tuva and Komi), and Eastern Orthodox (in Chuvashia, Karelia, Mari-El, Mordvinia, North Ossetia, Sakha [Yakutia], and Udmurtia).

Russians account for 86 percent of the urban population, Tatars for 4 percent, Ukrainians for 3 percent, Chuvash for 1 percent, and others for 7 percent of the urban population. In terms of Russia's rural population, the distribution is as follows: Russians, 71 percent; Tatars, 5 percent; Ukrainians, Chuvash, Bashkirs, and Chechens, each 2 percent; and others 16 percent. In addition to political issues arising from rural-urban, ethnic, and religious cleavages, the Russian Federation also has to deal with the problem of the 25–30 million ethnic and acculturated Russians living outside the territory of Russia.

Since becoming an independent state, Russia, like the other successor states, has faced enormous economic dislocations and serious political turmoil. In the absence of political consensus about the direction and/or pace of economic reform, politics have remained conflictual: Diametrically opposed political forces have struggled for dominance of the state, seeking to control both power and policy. During its initial existence as an independent state, Russia, so old in many ways, is not only a society in great flux, but still faces the task of state-building.

Difficult even under the best of circumstances, this task has been greatly complicated by the fact that, in Russia's case, the crucial nexus between the introduction of new political institutions and an improvement in the standard of living has not materialized, at least not for the great majority of Russians. On the contrary, living conditions have deteriorated significantly. Privatization and marketization, among other things, have undermined and eroded the basic services and amenities that the Soviet system provided for its citizens, resulting in increased unemployment and homelessness, as well as the deterioration of the housing situation. While life expectancy more than doubled from 32 years in 1917 to 65 in the mid-1960s and the infant mortality rate decreased to 25 deaths per 1,000 under the Soviet regime, by 1996 life expectancy for men had decreased to 57 years, and Russia's "natural" population growth rate—births minus deaths—was negative (–5.4 percent).

While Russians today enjoy greater choice and higher quality in consumer goods, their effective purchasing power has decreased and they have to spend a greater proportion of their income for food (over 50 percent in 1994) than under Soviet rule (approximately one-third in 1989). Rampant drug abuse and increased alcoholism; prostitution; a serious decline in the level of public health; outbreaks of polio, cholera, diphtheria, AIDS, malaria, hepatitis, and tuberculosis are indicative of the extent to which the health care system has collapsed since the demise of the Soviet Union. A continuing long-term threat to the quality of life in Russia is the environmental damage perpetrated by the Soviet regime in its pursuit of military power and economic development— from the dumping of toxic wastes without adequate environmental protection and the sinking of nuclear submarines in shallow waters to the diversion of water for irrigation of cotton fields in Turkmenistan and Uzbekistan, causing the shrinkage of the Aral Sea to one third of its original size, and the pollution of Lake Baikal, the world's largest lake.

NOTES

[1]Robert A. Feldmesser, "Social Classes and Political Structure," in Cyril E. Black, ed. *The Transformation of Russian Society* (Cambridge, MA: Harvard University Press, 1960), p. 238.

[2]Lenin's father, I. N. Ulyanov, became a member of the hereditary nobility because of his state service in the field of education.

[3]The best study of the Russian peasantry before the Revolution is G. T. Robinson, *Rural Russia Under the Old Regime* (New York: Macmillan, 1961).

[4]Data based on M. T. Florinsky, *Russia: A History and an Interpretation,* vol. 2 (New York: Macmillan, 1960), p. 1235.

[5]Warren Eason, "Population Changes," in Black, *Transformation,* p. 88, and Frank Lorimer, *The Population of the Soviet Union* (Geneva: League of Nations, 1946), p. 22.

[6]See Alexander Gerschenkron, "Problems and Patterns of Economic Development," in Black, *Transformation,* pp. 42–72.

[7]For a discussion of this pattern, see R. C. Tucker, "Swollen State, Spent Society: Stalin's Legacy to Brezhnev," *Foreign Affairs,* Winter 1982, pp. 413–435.

[8]That the peasants perceived collectivization as a new form of serfdom is illustrated by the fact that they immediately revived the old Russian term *barshchina,* which described the most oppressive form of serfdom under the czars.

[9]Tucker, "Swollen State, Spent Society," pp. 413–435.

[10]If anything, the census figure of 55.7 percent underestimates the non-Russian population since the census used language, not nationality, as the criterion. Russian, the lingua franca of the Empire, was considered by many non-Russians as their native tongue. Consequently, they were classified as "Russians" in the census. Allowing for this fact, the non-Russians probably accounted for close to 60 percent of the population of the Russian Empire in 1897. See Richard Pipes, *The Formation of the Soviet Union* (Cambridge, MA: Harvard University Press, 1964), p. 2.

[11]For a comprehensive treatment of the subject see S. M. Dubnow, *A History of the Jews in Russia and Poland,* 3 vols. (Philadelphia: The Jewish Publication Society of America, 1916–1920).

[12]Friedrich Engles, "Herrn Eugen Dühring's Umwälzung der Wissenchaft ("Anti-Dühring"), in K. Marx/F. Engels, *Werke,* vol. 20 (Berlin: Dietz Verlag, 1968), vol. 20, p. 262.

[13]Ibid., vol. 4, p. 416.

[14]Ibid., vol. 4, p. 417.

[15]Robert Sharlet, ed., *The New Soviet Constitution of 1977: Analysis and Text* (Brunswick, OH: King's Court Communications, Inc., 1978), pp. 73ff..

[16]J. V. Stalin, *Works,* vol. 13 (Moscow: Foreign Languages Publishing House, 1955), p. 58.

[17]P. H. Rossi and A. Inkeles, "Multi-dimensional Ratings of Occupations," *Sociometry* 20, no. 20 (1957): 247.

[18]See Mervyn Matthews, *Privilege in the Soviet Union* (London: George Allen & Unwin, 1978), and Hedrick Smith, *The Russians* (New York: Quadrangle, 1976), especially chapter 1.

[19]"An Observer," in *Message from Moscow* (New York: Alfred A. Knopf, 1969), p. 109.

[20]See Isaac Deutscher, *The Unfinished Revolution* (New York: Oxford University Press, 1967), p. 58.

[21]G. E. Lenski, *Power and Privilege* (New York: McGraw Hill, 1966), pp. 312–313.

[22]Two other important factors contributing to increased upward mobility were the purges under Stalin and the enormous manpower losses caused by World War II.

[23]Ellen Mickiewicz, *Handbook on Soviet Social Science Data* (New York: The Free Press, 1973), p. 167.

[24]Ann Sheehy, "The National Composition of the Population of the USSR According to the Census of 1979," *Radio Liberty Research Bulletin,* March 27, 1980 (R1 123/80): 2.

[25]Igor Shafarevich, "Separation or Reconciliation? The Nationalities Question in the USSR," in Alexander Solzhenitsyn et al., *From Under the Rubble* (Boston: Little, Brown, 1975), p. 88.

Chapter 21

The Political Framework
of the Russian Federation

The Russian Federation is one of 15 successor states that gained their independence as the result of the disintegration of the Union of Soviet Socialist Republics (USSR) in December 1991. Among these states the Russian Federation, or Russia, is unique because it is the successor not only of a former union republic—the Russian Soviet Federated Socialist Republic (RSFSR)—but also of the Soviet Union. It is Russia, in short, that emerged as the legal successor of the USSR and laid claim to the assets of the former Soviet Union (FSU)—from its seat in the U.N. Security Council and its embassies in foreign countries to its army, navy, and air force, its nuclear weapons, its governmental bodies, including the central ministries and state committees, its banks, and so on.

Historically speaking, the Russian Federation is the descendant of the Russian Soviet Federated Socialist Republic, which was established on November 7, 1917, and became a part of the USSR on December 30, 1922. In terms of territory, population, industrial output, and many other measures, the RSFSR was by far the most important of the 15 union republics that made up the USSR (see Table 21–1). Even after the dismemberment

of the Soviet Union, its successor, the Russian Federation, remains by far the largest country on earth.

Before we examine the political framework of the Russian Federation, it is necessary to become acquainted with the Soviet political system. For in spite of the collapse of the USSR in 1991, many vestiges of the Soviet political order have survived and continue to complicate the political evolution of postcommunist Russia.

THE SOVIET POLITICAL SYSTEM

In terms of its formal structure, the USSR was a federal state in which political power was divided between a central, federal or All-Union government in Moscow, which exercised jurisdiction throughout the territory of the USSR in areas defined in Article 73 of the Constitution, and its constituent units, the 15 union republics. The political-administrative subdivisions of the USSR reflected one of two principles: nationality or territory. The nationality-based subdivisions consisted of union republics, autonomous republics, autonomous oblasts, and national areas

Table 21-1 Successor States of the Former Soviet Union: Territory, Population, and Nationality

Republic	Territory in Thous. Sq. Mi.	Population In Thous.	Population Rank	Titular Nationality in Percent	Russian (in Percent)	Other Name	Other (in Percent)
Russia	17,076	149.3[d]	1		82%	Tatar	4%
Kazakhstan	1,048	17.2	4	40%	38	German	6
Ukraine	233	51.8	2	73	22	Jewish	1
Turkmenistan	188	3.9	11	72	9	Uzbek	9
Uzbekistan	174	22.1	3	71	8	Tajik	5
Belarus[a]	80	10.4	5	78	13	Polish	4
Kyrgyzstan[b]	77	4.6	9	52	21	Uzbek	13
Tajikistan	55	5.8	7	62	8	Uzbek	24
Azerbaijan	33	7.6	6	83	6	Armenian	6
Georgia	27	5.6	8	70	5	Armenian	9
Lithuania	25	3.8	12	80	9	Polish	8
Latvia	24	2.7	14	52	34	Beloruss.	5
Estonia	17	1.6	15	62	30	Ukrainian	3
Moldova[c]	13	4.5	10	64	13	Ukrainian	14
Armenia	12	3.5	13	93	2	Azeri	3

[a]Formerly Belorussia   [b]Formerly Kirghizstan   [c]Formerly Moldavia   [d]Estimates for mid-1993

Source: David T. Twining, *The New Eurasia: A Guide to the Republics of the Former Soviet Union* (Westport, CT: Praeger, 1993); CIA, *The World Factbook 1993* (Washington, DC: U.S. Government, 1993).

(redesignated in 1987 as autonomous areas); the territorial subdivisions, based on considerations of administrative expediency, consisted of territories *(krai),* regions *(oblast),* districts *(raion),* cities, towns, settlements, and villages. The union republics constituted the highest form of recognition, or the highest political-administrative status, a nationality could attain in the Soviet Union. Autonomous republics, autonomous oblasts, and national (later autonomous) areas represented lower levels of nationality recognition.

The 15 union republics were supposedly equal in terms of legal rights but varied greatly in regard to size, population, ethnic composition, and economic significance. The ethnically more heterogeneous republics were subdivided into autonomous republics (a total of twenty), autonomous regions (a total of eight), and national areas (a total of ten). These units varied in size and significance, but they were all based on the existence of relatively homogeneous nationality groups and represented different degrees of recognition of these nationalities. As is apparent from Table 21-2, two of the subdivisions—the

national area and territory *(krai)*—were unique to the RSFSR, the largest union republic. In the smaller union republics—Lithuania, Latvia, Estonia, Moldavia, and Armenia—districts were the only subdivisions.

But in spite of its formal organization as a federal state, the USSR functioned like a unitary state. In practice the central government in Moscow had power in all important matters throughout the Soviet Union. Soviet "federalism" was part of an elaborate facade of democracy, behind which was concealed the reality of a strong, centralized, and would-be totalitarian state. A rudimentary knowledge of the nature of Soviet federalism and its basic framework, the territorial-administrative structure, is important not only for understanding the Soviet political system, but also because it became the point of departure for the process of "sovereignization" that resulted in the disintegration of the USSR in 1991.

The territorial-administrative structure constituted the basic framework for the organization of both state and party organs. Soviets of People's Deputies existed at every level of the territorial-

Table 21–2   Nationality and Territorial Subdivisions of the Union Republics, 1987

Republics	Autonomous Republics	Autonomous Oblasts	Autonomous Areas	Territories	Oblasts	Districts
RSFSR	16	5	10	6	49	1,834
Ukraine					25	480
Belorussia					6	117
Uzbekistan	1				12	155
Kazakhstan					19	222
Georgia	2	1				65
Azerbaijan	1	1				61
Lithuania						44
Moldavia						40
Latvia						26
Kirghizia					4	40
Tajikistan		1			3	45
Armenia						37
Turkmenistan					5	44
Estonia						15
Total	20	8	10	6	123	3,225

Source: *SSSR: Administrativno-territorial'noe delenie soiuznykh respublik na 1 ianvaria 1987* (Moscow: Izdatel'stvo "Izvestiia sovetov deputatov trudiashchikhsia," 1987, p. 14.

administrative structure, from the highest level—the USSR Supreme Soviet, that is, the national "parliament"—to the lowest level, the village or rural Soviet.

As both the Constitution and the standard national reference work in the Soviet Union made clear, Soviet state administration was based on "the strictest subordination of lower organs to the direction and control of higher organs; the acts of higher organs are binding on lower organs."[1] As a result, in spite of the mobilization efforts by the CPSU and the great fanfare in Soviet propaganda about local participation, the organs of local government were effectively reduced to a purely administrative function; their role in decision making was for the most part negligible, especially since all finance in the USSR was centralized and the union republics received all of their funds from Moscow.

One peculiar feature of Soviet federalism was the explicit right of each union republic to secede from the USSR. ("Each Union republic retains the right freely to secede from the USSR"—Article 72 of the 1977 Constitution.)[2] During most of the history of the Soviet Union, this provision

remained a dead letter. Attempts to assert republic autonomy in the early days of the Soviet federation were stopped by the Red Army. Only under Gorbachev did Article 72 acquire real meaning and importance. By November 1990, 14 of the 15 union republics, 11 of the 20 autonomous republics, 3 of the 5 autonomous oblasts, and 4 of the 10 autonomous okrugs had adopted declarations of sovereignty and/or independence, and the Supreme Soviet of the fifteenth republic—Kirghizia—approved the first reading of a declaration of state sovereignty on October 31, 1990. These declarations produced a grave constitutional crisis and called into question the continued existence of the Soviet federation in its Stalinist configuration.

Basic Institutional Structure

In terms of its basic organizational framework, the Soviet political system created by Stalin consisted of three parallel institutional structures or hierarchies: (1) the CPSU, headed by the Politburo and the Central Committee; (2) the executive structure, headed by the USSR Council of

Ministers (the bureaucracy); and (3) the parliamentary structure, that is, the Soviets at the various levels of the territorial administrative structure, nominally headed by the USSR Supreme Soviet, but actually supervised by its presidium.

The *decision-making function* in the USSR was largely concentrated in the party. But while the CPSU was clearly in command and virtually monopolized the decision-making process, it did not actually govern the country directly. The function of *implementing* party decisions and running the country on a day-to-day basis was largely the responsibility of the ministerial hierarchy, a formidable bureaucracy also directly involved in managing the Soviet economy. The raison d'être of the parliamentary structure in the USSR consisted primarily in the *legitimization function,* that is, legitimizing the decisions of the party and the implementation of these decisions by the bureaucracy. Like the Soviet Constitution, the structure of the Soviets was an important part of the "Potemkin village" aspect, the democratic facade of the Soviet Union, behind which was concealed a system that in most respects remained profoundly undemocratic—at least by European and American norms.

The power relationship between the party, the bureaucracy, and the Soviets did not remain constant over time, with most of the significant changes occurring in the relationship between the party and the bureaucracy. The important point to remember is that, throughout most of the history of the USSR, the CPSU was the center of political decision making in the Soviet Union.

The Government

The actual administration and legal enforcement of policy was the responsibility of the government, which basically consisted of two structures: (1) a system of so-called Soviets [Councils] of People's Deputies, theoretically "the power organs" that were elected and organized on a territorial basis; and (2) a system of state administration or "executive" bodies, consisting of ministries, state committees, commissions, and administrations that were appointed by and theoretically responsible to the Soviets.

The USSR Supreme Soviet

Prior to the reorganization of the Soviet political system under Gorbachev, the USSR Supreme Soviet, according to the Constitution, was "the supreme body of state power in the USSR" (Article 108). Unlike the lower-level Soviets, all of which were unicameral, it consisted of two chambers or houses with equal rights: the Council of the Union *(Sovet Soiuza)* and the Council of Nationalities *(Sovet Natsional'nostei).* Following a constitutional change in 1979, the number of deputies in each house was fixed at 750. Thus, before the reorganization in 1989, the USSR Supreme Soviet, the national parliament, consisted of 1,500 deputies—much too large a body for effective work.

The Council of the Union was elected from 750 election districts with equal populations (Article 108). The election to the Council of Nationalities was more complex. It is here that the nationality-based subdivisions of the USSR came into play. As the name suggests, this chamber of the USSR Supreme Soviet was specifically created to grant recognition and give representation to various nationalities in the USSR. However, by far not all of the nationalities (not even all the major ones) were granted the territorial recognition entitling them to representation in the Council of Nationalities on an equal basis. In any event, for the purpose of elections to the Council of Nationalities, each union republic was divided into thirty-two districts and thus was entitled to thirty-two seats in the Council of Nationalities. In addition, each autonomous republic was entitled to eleven seats, each autonomous oblast to five, and each national area to one seat (Article 110)—a formula that yielded 750 deputies. In 1989 this formula was changed to reduce the size of the Supreme Soviet.

Unlike Western legislatures, the deputies to the USSR Supreme Soviet were not full-time professional legislators. The Supreme Soviet met only twice a year for sessions lasting 3 to 5 days. Consequently, the recruitment pool and thus the professional range of the deputies could be and was much broader than that found in Western legislatures. Supreme Soviet deputies were elected for a term of 5 years (4 under the 1936 Constitution). In addition to a broad spectrum of the Soviet population from all walks of life, their ranks also included the most important political figures in the Soviet Union: the central party leadership, members of the CPSU Central Committee, and powerful regional party secretaries.

Legislation was passed by a simple majority vote in both houses, which usually met separately. If there was disagreement, a conciliation committee was formed, consisting of the same number of deputies from both houses. If this committee failed to agree, the Presidium of the USSR Supreme Soviet had the power to dissolve the Supreme Soviet and order new elections. In practice, this never proved necessary.

Between sessions of the USSR Supreme Soviet—which prior to the transformation of the Supreme Soviet into a bona fide standing parliament under Gorbachev was most of the time—supreme state power in the USSR was exercised by the 39-member Presidium of the USSR Supreme Soviet, described as the "continuously functioning agency of the USSR Supreme Soviet" in the Constitution (Article 119). Subject to later ratification by the Supreme Soviet, the Presidium was empowered to take any action that did not violate the Constitution: it could promulgate edicts and resolutions, reorganize the ministerial system, remove and appoint members of the USSR Council of Ministers.[3] The Presidium was also authorized by the Constitution (Article 121) to take action in regard to the declaration of war, general or partial mobilization, the formation of the USSR Defense Council,[4] the appointment and removal of the supreme command of the Soviet Armed Forces, and so forth.

The chairman of the Presidium of the USSR Supreme Soviet was generally considered to be the Soviet head of state—until the 1960s a largely ceremonial post without any real power and usually held by an elderly Politburo member. Beginning in the 1960s, however, the men who held the position—Leonid Brezhnev (1960–64), Anastas Mikoyan (1964–65), and Nikolai Podgornyi (1966–77)—were powerful men in the Politburo.

The USSR Council of Ministers

According to the Soviet Constitution (Article 128), the USSR Council of Ministers—the USSR government—was "the supreme executive and administrative body of state power in the USSR."

Besides the initiation of legislation, the functions of the Council of Ministers included supervising the vast state bureaucracy, and policy execution.

In spite of the explicit emphasis in the Soviet Constitution on the executive and administrative role of the Council of Ministers, a great deal and perhaps most Soviet legislation actually emanated from the USSR Council of Ministers.[5] The Council of Ministers had the power to issue decrees and orders. Both were supposedly issued pursuant to existing laws (Article 133), but again practice at times diverged from theory. Frequently the Council of Ministers issued decrees and orders that anticipated laws to be enacted at a later date. In any event, whether in accordance with this provision of the Soviet Constitution or not, the execution of decrees and orders of the Council of Ministers was "mandatory throughout the USSR" (Article 133).

As of August 1982, the USSR Council of Ministers consisted of 64 ministries, 20 state committees, and 4 other agencies with ministerial status. In addition, 17 agencies were attached to the Council of Ministers without having ministerial status. Finally, the chairmen of the union republic Councils of Ministers were ex officio members of the USSR Council of Ministers. Thus, the full Council of Ministers had a minimum of over 100 members—a body much too unwieldy to play an effective role in the decision-making process.[6]

Under Gorbachev, the size of the Council of Ministers was reduced. At the end of 1990, this important government organ consisted of 36 ministries, 20 state committees, 6 commissions, and 4 bureaus. In addition, the membership of the Council of Ministers included 15 other members. Nevertheless, much of the resistance to the fight for reform and against bureaucracy came from powerful ministries and state committees.

As in the case of the USSR Supreme Soviet, there was a smaller body within the USSR Council of Ministers, the Presidium of the Council of Ministers, which—in the language of the Soviet Constitution—functioned "as a permanent agency of the USSR Council of Ministers" (Article 132). This arrangement, no doubt, was necessitated by the fact that the Council of Ministers throughout much of its history met only every 3 months or so.

There were two types of ministries: (1) the All-Union Ministry, which had jurisdiction in its particular area of responsibility throughout the USSR; and (2) the Union-Republic Ministry, which operated through corresponding ministries in the 15 union republics. In 1982, at the end of the Brezhnev era, there were 32 All-Union and 32 Union-Republic Ministries. The state committees were similarly divided into All-Union and Union-Republic institutions. The distinction between ministries and state committees seemed to be a function of the responsibilities of institutions. Normally a ministry had a narrower legal jurisdiction and responsibility—say, for a particular branch of the Soviet economy like the chemical industry—than a state committee, whose jurisdiction generally extended to a number of branches and affected a number of ministries (such as the USSR State Committee for Science and Technology).

In Western parliamentary and presidential systems, cabinet ministers are frequently political leaders who may hold a number of different portfolios over time. In the Soviet Union, by contrast, transfer of a minister from one ministerial post to another was practically unknown. The vast majority of the ministers and state committee chairmen were professionals, with a high degree of specialization, who had risen through the ranks. Almost invariably ministers were members of the CPSU Central Committee. Again unlike their Western counterparts, Soviet ministers did not need to be members of the Soviet "parliament," that is, the USSR Supreme Soviet, and they were prevented from being members of the Presidium of the USSR Supreme Soviet (to which the Council of Ministers was responsible when the Supreme Soviet was not in session) by a rule observed since 1938.

The Police and the Courts

Following the example of Karl Marx, Soviet constitutional theory and practice did not recognize the principle of the separation of powers. In the Soviet Union, law was viewed as the expression of the will and the power of the ruling class; justice was perceived as class justice. Before Gorbachev, law was regarded as an instrument in the hands of the CPSU to be used for political purposes and to be subordinated to party policy. Given this vantage point, it is not surprising to find that the judiciary played no significant role in national policy making (with the exception of policy making regarding the more narrow technical and procedural, as opposed to the substantive, aspects of law). Moreover, if one looks at the role of the courts and law in Soviet society, one discovers that they were weak with respect to adjudication and strong with respect to enforcement.

The large scope of court and police jurisdiction over the individual in the Soviet Union was an important aspect and reflection of the enormous scope of the state in Soviet society—a society that traditionally had placed great emphasis on the collective as opposed to the extraordinary emphasis on the individual in liberal societies. However, we should remember that Russia and the Soviet Union followed the continental European legal tradition, which has never put as pronounced an emphasis on individual rights and liberties as the legal tradition in England, the United States, and other common law countries.

An important instrument in the party's effort to enlist law in the construction of socialism was the procuracy, an enormous, highly centralized bureaucracy with nationwide scope. It was headed by the Procurator General, a very powerful official, who was appointed for a 5-year term by the USSR Supreme Soviet and who usually was a member of the CPSU Central Committee. The Procurator General, in turn, appointed his subordinates at the various levels of the territorial-administrative structure down to the level of the region, with the lower-level procurators appointing their subordinates for 5-year terms. Like the secret police, the procuracy operated independently from local government organs. Besides the institution of criminal proceedings and the supervision of the preliminary investigation process, the procuracy was responsible for the observance of legality throughout Soviet society.[7]

In a very real sense, the procuracy was what Peter the Great, who first introduced this institution in Russia, designed it to be, namely, "the eyes and ears of the government." In the case of the Soviet Union, the procuracy acted primarily as the legal watchdog for the CPSU.

The Soviet court structure paralleled the structure of the Soviets. At the top of the judicial hierarchy was the USSR Supreme Court, formally appointed by, and responsible to, the USSR Supreme Soviet. The next level was comprised by the Supreme Courts of the 15 union republics, and so forth. The lowest level of the court structure was made up of the People's Court. The Supreme Court, whose judges were selected for a 5-year term, was mostly a court of appeal; it took cases of first instance only in very exceptional circumstances.

The significance of the courts and the rule of law in Soviet society, furthermore, were diminished by the traditional lack of a clear presumption of innocence and the absence of a strong and independent legal profession. Another important factor was Soviet legal procedure, which placed great emphasis on the pretrial investigation, thus detracting from the intrinsic importance of the court trial itself.

While it is easy to point out various shortcomings of the Soviet legal system from the standpoint of Western norms and standards, there is no question that the development of the Soviet legal system was one of the most significant consequences of the de-Stalinization of the Soviet Union.[8] In particular under Gorbachev, great emphasis was put on the creation of a law-governed state during 1988–89.

THE POLITICAL REFORMS OF GORBACHEV

Five years of "restructuring" *(perestroika)* under Gorbachev during 1985–90 failed to revitalize the Soviet system. Nevertheless, the second half of the 1980s will go down in history as a seminal period of serious, far-reaching, and even radical reform efforts. Indeed, there is little question that the pursuit of *perestroika* undermined the foundations of the Soviet system—already weakened by economic and political stagnation—to such an extent that it became the victim of a curious and unexpected implosion.

In assessing the reform efforts of Gorbachev, it is important to realize that the initial concern of his administration was the pursuit of acceleration of socioeconomic growth and development, a goal that suggested a change in the pace rather than the direction of development. A year into his administration, however, he concluded that more fundamental change was needed. The unsuccessful pursuit of economic reform led to the realization that restructuring of the economy was impossible without political reform. Increasingly aware of the scope and depth of the malaise afflicting Soviet society, Gorbachev launched a new information policy *(glasnost),* advocated new thinking in foreign and domestic policy, stressed the importance of social justice, and, most important, called for the democratization of Soviet society as the indispensable prerequisite for restructuring of the Soviet system.[9]

The policy of *perestroika* produced dramatic changes not only in the Soviet Union, but also in international relations. In foreign policy, it resulted in the disengagement of the USSR in Afghanistan, Central America, Africa, and Southeast Asia. It directly contributed to the rapid collapse of the communist regimes in Eastern Europe and made possible the reunification of Germany—developments that were inconceivable before Gorbachev. In domestic policy, it resulted in the establishment of a new legislative system, consisting of the USSR Congress of People's Deputies and a smaller Supreme Soviet elected from its membership—the first standing parliament in Soviet history. Furthermore, under Gorbachev the Soviet parliamentary system evolved into a presidential one—a development that, among other things, involved a fundamental change in party-state relations.[10] Finally, abolition of the monopoly position of the Communist party, far-reaching personnel changes in the Soviet political elite at all levels, election reforms, a comparatively free flow of information, and a much greater measure of cultural freedom transformed the political atmosphere and made possible the emergence of the first open political opposition in the Soviet Union since the 1920s and, eventually, the development of a multiparty system.

The institutional structure of the Soviet political system underwent a series of changes under Gorbachev. Through constitutional amendment, the new Congress of People's Deputies, consisting of 2,250 members, was made the new "supreme organ of USSR state power." Elected for a five-year term, it elected the 542-member Supreme Soviet, renewing one-fifth of its membership every year. Like its predecessor, the new Supreme Soviet consisted of two chambers: the Council of the Union and the Council of Nationalities. As far as the executive was concerned, the centerpiece of political restructuring was the development of a strong executive presidency, which by the end of 1990 had concentrated greater legal and constitutional powers in the hands of Gorbachev than Stalin enjoyed at the height of his power. Unfortunately, these truly tectonic changes, coupled with a rapid deterioration in economic performance and ethnic unrest, produced the kind of political turbulence that made sustained reforms of any kind virtually impossible.

Gorbachev's pursuit of increasingly radical and, indeed, revolutionary political changes, which developed into a far-reaching attempt to dismantle the Stalinist system, put him on a collision course with the institutional pillars of that system and the elites spawned by it. Moreover, mounting ethnic strife, the independence movements in both the non-Russian republics and the Russian Republic, and Gorbachev's indecisiveness and ineptness in coping with the growing economic problems and the explosive nationality issues, undermined his position and resulted in the de facto shift of power from the central government to the republics. Thus, paradoxically, the rise in the constitutional (and potentially, indeed, dictatorial) powers of the Soviet president was accompanied by the development of a power vacuum at the center.

In response to the growing and increasingly evident political impotence of the central government in Moscow, more and more republics embarked on the road to independence. The Baltic republics were the first to declare their independence from the Soviet Union. Infected with the "Baltic virus," the other republics, one after another, joined the "parade of sovereignties." Gorbachev's efforts to stem the tide of nationalism through a new union treaty ended in failure. When on December 1, 1991, over 90 percent of the population of Ukraine voted for independence, the fate of the Soviet Union was sealed. The ensuing constitutional crisis led to the political collapse of the USSR and the creation of the Commonwealth of Independent States. Even before December 25, 1991, when Gorbachev resigned as president of the USSR and handed the launch codes for the Soviet nuclear missiles over to Russian President Yeltsin, the demise of the USSR was a fait accompli.

THE COMMONWEALTH OF INDEPENDENT STATES

A few weeks before the formal establishment of the Russian Federation on December 26, 1991, Russia was joined by the two other Slavic republics of the former Soviet Union—Ukraine and Belorussia (now called Belarus)—in the establishment of the Commonwealth of Independent States (CIS), a supranational organization that was to assume joint responsibility for military, strategic, and nuclear issues, as well as foreign and economic affairs, customs and immigration policies, transportation, communications, environmental questions, and crime control. Together, the three Slavic republics that founded the CIS represented 73 percent of the population of the former USSR and 80 percent of its territory. They also were in control of most of its military and economic assets.

At a meeting on December 21, 1991, in Alma-Ata, as the capital of Kazakhstan was then called, all the other former union republics of the USSR joined the CIS, with the exception of the three Baltic republics and Georgia, which became a member in 1993. Today the CIS—in which the Russian Federation is as dominant as its predecessor, the RSFSR, was in the Soviet Union—includes all the republics of the former Soviet Union, with the exception of Latvia, Lithuania, and Estonia. Contrary to the expectations of many observers in 1991, the CIS not only survived but developed into an important instrument in Russia's increasingly determined drive to achieve the economic, political, and military reintegration of the former Soviet "space." By the end of 1994, Russia, in spite of its continuing domestic problems, had not only made remarkable progress toward the attainment of this objective, but had been successful in gaining tacit de facto recognition of the "near abroad" as its exclusive sphere of influence.

More recently, however, the CIS has run into difficulties, increasingly becoming an institutional fiction that creates merely "an illusion of commonality in the post-Soviet space."[11] Instead of contributing to the integration of its member states, it has become a divisive factor in their relations. With the possible exception of Belarus and Kazakhstan, the non-Russian successor states, it turned out, had no interest in the resurrection of the former Soviet Union in any form. Instead, they have formed alliances excluding Russia and entered into partnerships with other, economically stronger countries. In the grip of nationalism and determined to preserve their sovereignty, they fear Moscow's ultimate intentions and resent its heavy-handedness in dealing with the states of the "near abroad." Given its own continuing problems, Russia has been unable to offer any meaningful incentives to lure the CIS member states into a closer pattern of cooperation.[12]

THE POLITICAL SYSTEM OF THE RUSSIAN FEDERATION

The circumstances in which the Russian Federation began its political existence were anything but auspicious. Not only did the collapse of the Soviet Union produce unprecedented dislocations in the economy of Russia and the other former Soviet republics, it also confronted the Russian people with a serious identity crisis. Whereas the disintegration of the USSR made it possible for the other republics to regain their political independence and to reaffirm their sense of national identity, and thus was seen in a positive light, the effect in the Russian Federation was quite different. Its own independence notwithstanding, the emergence of the former Soviet republics on Russia's periphery as independent states and the resulting disintegration of the Soviet Union were perceived by many in the Russian Federation as a negative development, entailing the "loss" of territory and peoples that had—in some cases for centuries—been part of the Russian Empire. Thus, in the case of Russia, the end of the Soviet Union did not contribute to an enhanced sense of national identity but, on the contrary, detracted from it. The problem is that the Russian people never developed a sense of statehood based on national or ethnic identity. Before the process of "nation-building" was completed, Russia embarked on the process of territorial expansion that led to the formation of the Russian Empire. Thus, the Russians never developed a national identity, except as the dominant part of a greater Russian empire. Unlike the peoples of Europe (and the "near abroad"), where national consciousness based on ethnic identity has become the norm, the "national" consciousness of the Russians, even in modern times, has been based first and foremost on territory and the state—in short, the empire.[13]

Furthermore, the disintegration of Soviet central authority in Moscow and the independence movement involving the former union republics did not stop at the borders of Russia. From the very outset, the Russian Federation has faced the problem of centrifugal political forces within its own territory. Correctly perceiving the weakness of the federal government in Moscow, the republics and regions in the Russian Federation increasingly asserted their authority and power vis-à-vis the federal government. If they were initially very successful in pursuing this course, it was in no small measure due to the fact that they were able to exploit the political rivalry between the Russian parliament and President Yeltsin.

Among other things, the Russian Federation inherited from its predecessor, the RSFSR, its first constitution, adopted on April 12, 1978, as well as a parliament dominated by communists elected in 1990. Thus, for the first two years of its existence, the Yeltsin government was politically handicapped because it had to operate within the framework of a constitution dating back to the Soviet era and with an increasingly hostile parliament. Between mid-1991, when Russia's drive for independence began, and the end of 1993, that Constitution was amended more than 300 times. The rivalry between the executive and the legislative branches ended in the dissolution of parliament in the fall of 1993 and a subsequent armed confrontation—a confrontation that included the bombardment of the Russian White House, the seat of the Russian Parliament, and resulted in the death of over 150 people.

The circumstances in which the Russian Federation began its political existence were inauspicious in another respect. The collapse of the

Soviet Union did not sweep aside the old institutional structure and the Soviet ruling class, the infamous *nomenklatura.* On the contrary! Through the privatization of state property, many members of the *nomenklatura,* who previously had managed but now owned this property, became its new proprietors. Having succeeded in translating their former political power into economic wealth, they now have a new basis for exerting political influence in post-Communist Russia.

The 1993 Constitution

On December 12, 1993—within two and a half months after the executive branch of their government had liquidated the legislative branch—Russians went to the polls. By a narrow margin and in a controversial election,[14] they adopted a new Constitution and elected representatives to a bicameral Federal Assembly. The Constitution clearly reflects President Yeltsin's determination to reverse the trend toward increased local and regional autonomy, to regain central control over the republics and regions, and to establish a powerful executive. The elections to the lower house of the Federal Assembly, the State Duma, ended in the victory of the antireform parties. Contrary to the preelection polls and everyone's expectations, Vladimir Zhirinovsky's ultranationalist (and misleadingly named) Liberal Democratic Party of Russia won 23 percent of the popular vote, while Russia's Choice, the liberal reformist electoral bloc, won only 16 percent. Although this was the first true multiparty election in Russia in over seventy years and obviously a crucial election, voter turnout was very low—barely exceeding the required 50 percent of the electorate.[15] Thus, the present Constitution of Russia was not only endorsed by a minority, but may have been adopted in violation of the rules.

The Constitution consists of a preamble and 137 articles, followed by a short section containing concluding and transitional provisions. The preamble affirms the multinational character of the Russian Federation and "a common destiny on our land," asserts human rights and freedoms, civil peace and concord, calls for the preservation of "historically established state unity," recognizes "the equality and self-determination of peoples," and speaks of "reviving the sovereign

statehood of Russia" and "the immutability of its democratic foundations." The preamble also acknowledges "responsibility for our Homeland to present and future generations" and recognizes Russia as "part of the world community."[16]

The Constitution itself devotes 16 articles to the constitutional system, describing Russia as a "democratic federative rule-of-law state with a republican form of government." In the longest section (48 articles) and in prominent place, the Constitution sets forth an impressive Bill of Rights, acknowledging the inalienable character of basic human rights and freedoms. Subsequent sections deal with the federative structure and the key institutions of the Russian Federation: the President, the Federal Assembly (the State Duma and the Federal Council), the Government (Cabinet and Prime Minister), and the Judiciary. The Constitution, finally, devotes four articles each to local self-government and procedures for amending and revising the Constitution.

The Constitution recognizes 89 subjects, or components, of the Federation: 21 republics, 6 krays, 49 oblasts, 2 cities of federal significance (Moscow and St. Petersburg), 1 autonomous oblast, and 10 autonomous okrugs. The republics, the autonomous oblast, and the autonomous okrugs are nationality-based units of the Russian Federation; the krays and oblasts, as well as Moscow and St. Petersburg, are purely administrative or territorial components in the Russian federal system. Thus, like federalism in the former Soviet Union, Russian federalism reflects the national-territorial principle. The resulting "unevenness" in the state structure of the Russian Federation poses a serious problem and is likely to produce continuing political conflict between the republics, which enjoy the highest level of autonomy in the Russian Federation, and the regions (oblasts), which aspire to "equal rights." In addition to the provisions of the 1993 Constitution, the nature and character of federalism in Russia are also shaped by three federation treaties between the federal government and (1) the republics, (2) the regions (oblasts) and krays (territories), and (3) the autonomous okrugs and the autonomous oblast (Birobijan), concluded in March 1992.

Prior to the adoption of the 1993 Constitution, the differences in status between the republics and the regions, as well as the other components of the Russian Federation, were of considerable significance. In the treaty signed in 1992, the republics insisted on their recognition as "sovereign states"—with the right to their own independent foreign policy and foreign trade, their own banking system, and ownership of their land and mineral wealth. The rights of the regions, by contrast, were much more restricted. These differences in status were eliminated by the 1993 Constitution.

It should be noted that in 9 of the 21 nationality-based republics, Russians account for an absolute majority of the population, and in 3 they are the largest ethnic group. In only 5 republics does the titular nationality group constitute an absolute majority, and in 3, the largest ethnic group.[17] In one republic—Bashkortostan, the titular nationality, the Bashkirs, are not only outnumbered by the Russians, but also by the Tatars.

The State Duma

The new Russian parliament created by the 1993 Constitution, called the Federal Assembly, has two chambers—the State Duma and the Federation Council. The State Duma is elected for a term of four years[18] and consists of 450 deputies, who work on a full-time professional basis. Apart from teaching, scientific, or other creative activity, deputies cannot be involved in state service or any other paid activity. The political prerogatives of the State Duma include:

- Confirmation of the chairman of the Government of the Russian Federation (i.e., the prime minister), nominated by the president; if the Duma turns down his nominations for prime minister three times, the president can dissolve the Duma
- Initiation of impeachment proceedings by the Federal Council against the president by charging him with treason or another "serious crime"; this requires a two-thirds majority and the concurrence of the Constitutional Court that the charge is valid
- Right to vote no confidence in the government
- Right to appoint and remove from office the chairman of the Central Bank of the Russian

Federation, the chairman of the Comptroller's Office, and the commissioner of human rights
- Initiation and adoption of federal laws
- Declaration of an amnesty

Unless otherwise stipulated by the Constitution, ordinary federal laws are adopted by a majority of the deputies of the State Duma and the Federal Council; federal constitutional laws require a two-thirds majority of the State Duma and a three-fourths majority of the Federal Council. The right of legislative initiative is vested in the president of the Russian Federation, the Government of the Russian Federation, the Federation Council, members of the Federation Council, members of the State Duma, and legislative (representative) organs of components of the Russian Federation. In matters under their jurisdiction, the Constitutional Court, the Supreme Court, and the Superior Court of Arbitration of the Russian Federation also have the right of legislative initiative.

The powers of the State Duma are quite limited. Its main function is to draft and adopt legislation, but, as we have seen, it shares the right of legislative initiative with other state organs and the president—an arrangement that could very well lead to a new "war of laws" between the president and the legislature, thus recreating the situation that existed before the adoption of the new Constitution. Legislation involving taxation and federal budget expenditures requires the approval of the government before it becomes effective. Legislation passed by the Duma can be vetoed by the Federal Council and the president. A veto by the Federal Council can be overturned only by a two-thirds majority in the Duma; a veto by the president requires a two-thirds majority in both the Duma and the Federal Council.

The Federal Council

The Federal Council consists of 178 deputies—two representatives from each of the 89 components of the Russian Federation, one each from the representative and executive organs of state power. The prerogatives of the Federal Council include:

- Decisions on changes of the borders between the members of the Federation
- Approval of presidential declarations of martial law and a state of emergency, as well as the use of military force outside the borders of the Russian Federation
- Final say in the impeachment of the president
- Upon nomination by the president, confirmation of the appointment of the judges of the Constitutional, Supreme, and Higher Arbitration Courts, as well as appointment and dismissal of the prosecutor-general
- Power to veto legislation passed by the State Duma
- Power to override a presidential veto (together with the State Duma)
- Right to schedule presidential elections

The pattern of intergovernmental relations set up by the Constitution gives local authorities a substantial amount of discretion, including the right to pass their own laws and levy their own taxes—the price local leaders demanded for their support of the Constitution and the continued territorial unity of the Russian Federation, which had been called into question by some of them and rejected by others. Through their membership or representation in the Federal Council, which has significant policy-making authority in cooperation with other federal organs, local and regional leaders are potentially able to exert considerable political influence. As in the former Soviet Union, the republics of the non-Russian nationalities, in addition to equal representation in the Federal Council, also enjoy cultural autonomy, including the right to separate legislative organs, flags, and language.

The President

The president of the Russian Federation is the head of state. Limited to two consecutive four-year terms, the president has extensive powers. Charged with the responsibility of guaranteeing the Constitution and human and civil rights and freedoms; safeguarding the sovereignty, independence, and state integrity of the Russian Federation; and ensuring the coordinated functioning

and collaboration of the organs of state power, the president has the power to determine the basic guidelines of the state's domestic and foreign policy. More specifically, the president's powers include the following:

- Appointment of the chairman of the Government of the Russian Federation (the prime minister), with the consent of the State Duma
- The right to chair sittings of the Government of the Russian Federation
- Dismissal of the Government of the Russian Federation
- Formation of the Security Council of the Russian Federation (headed by the president)
- Appointment and removal of key officials, including deputy prime ministers and federal ministers, the chairman of the Central Bank, justices of the Constitutional Court, the Supreme Court, and the Superior Court of Arbitration, and the General Prosecutor (with the consent of the Federal Council)
- Appointment and dismissal of the high command of the Armed Forces, and diplomatic representatives of the Russian Federation
- Appointment and dismissal of plenipotentiary representatives of the Russian president
- Formation of the Administration of the President of the Russian Federation
- Dissolution of the State Duma
- Power to propose, sign, promulgate, and veto legislation
- Power to issue edicts and directives whose implementation is mandatory throughout the territory of the Russian Federation
- Declaration of martial law and a state of emergency
- Power to decide questions of citizenship, political asylum, and pardons

Thus, the 1993 Constitution created a political system that is dominated by the president, who has substantial power to manage, if not control, the State Duma and, if necessary, to govern independently of it. Indeed, the political system created by the new Constitution is so strongly executive-oriented that it could easily lead to presidential abuse of power and deteriorate into a dictatorship. It is no coincidence that Vladimir Zhirinovsky, the leader of the extremist ultranationalist Liberal Democratic Party, strongly endorsed the 1993 Constitution.

Modeled after the Fifth French Republic, the Russian Federation is a variant of the semipresidential form of government, comparable in some respects to the Weimar Republic. In formal terms, the 1993 Constitution set up a divided, dual, or bipolar executive: the directly elected president and a prime minister who, along with his Cabinet, is responsible to the State Duma. De facto, in terms of actual political power, however, the Russian political system has a unipolar executive consisting of several levels, including the government (in the narrow European sense, i.e., the prime minister and the Cabinet), the Security Council, the Presidential Administration, and the president's appointed representatives in the various subjects of the Russian Federation—an executive, moreover, which has for the most part behaved as though Russia is in a permanent state of emergency. Making use of his power to issue decrees, President Yeltsin made the so-called "power ministries"—defense, internal affairs, justice, state of emergency, and civil defense—directly subordinate to his office. Moreover, he repeatedly interfered in the legislative process, ignored constitutional procedures, and neutralized the constitutional rights of the Federal Assembly through the use of his decree power. By resorting to an autocratic leadership style, limiting the powers and autonomy of the Russian parliament, and preventing the diffusion of political power and the development of constitutional counterweights to his authority, President Yeltsin effectively impeded and delayed the institutionalization of democracy in Russia. Before judging Russia's first president too harshly, however, let us remember that democracy is a new plant in Russia's soil.

Although Yeltsin had repeatedly stated that he would remain in office until the scheduled presidential election in June 2000, he gave up the presidency on the eve of the new millennium. In his resignation statement he spoke of the painful difficulties involved in "jump[ing] from the grey, stagnating, totalitarian past into a bright, rich and civilized future." He acknowledged his naïveté in believing that this transition could be undertaken "in one fell swoop" and asked the Russian people for forgiveness for the mistakes and failures that had occurred during his presidency.

The Government

The Government consists of the chairman (the prime minister) and the deputy chairmen of the Government of the Russian Federation and the federal ministers. The prime minister is appointed by the president with the consent of the State Duma. If the Duma rejects three candidacies for prime minister, the president dissolves the Duma and schedules new elections.

The prime minister is responsible for developing proposals for the structure of the federal organs of executive power, the nomination of deputy chairmen, and the definition of basic guidelines for the activity of the Government and

TENURE OF RUSSIAN PRIME MINISTERS		
1992–1999		
Yegor Gaidar	— 15 Jun 1992–14 Dec 1992	183 days
Viktor Chernomyrdin	— 14 Dec 1992–23 Mar 1998	5 years +
Sergey Kiriyenko	— 23 Mar 1992–23 Aug 1998	154 days
Viktor Chernomyrdin	— 23 Aug 1992–10 Sep 1998	19 days
Yevgeny Primakov	— 10 Sep 1998–12 May 1999	245 days
Sergey Stepashin	— 12 May 1999–9 Aug 1999	89 days
Vladimir Putin	— 9 Aug 1999– ?	?

the organization of its work. The powers and responsibilities of the Government (the prime minister and cabinet) include:

- Drafting of the federal budget
- Implementation of a unified fiscal, credit, and monetary policy
- Implementation of a unified state policy in the spheres of culture, science, education, health, social security, and ecology
- Administration of federal property
- Implementation of measures to ensure the defense of the country, state security, and the realization of the foreign policy of the Russian Federation
- Implementation of measures to ensure the rule of law, civil rights and freedoms, the protection of property, the maintenance of public order, and the struggle against crime
- Power to issue decrees and directives that are mandatory in the Russian Federation

The prime minister and the cabinet are responsible for the day-to-day administration of the country. The Government may be dismissed by the president or it may be forced to resign by a no-confidence vote in the State Duma, which requires a simple majority vote and the consent of the president. If a no-confidence vote by the State Duma is repeated within three months, the president has no choice but to dismiss the Government.

Since mid-1992, i.e., in seven years, Russia has had six different prime ministers, one of whom, Viktor Chernomyrdin, served for more than 5 years and later was reappointed for 19 days. Between March 1998 and May 1999—in less than 14 months!—Russia had four different prime ministers. The dismissal of Yevgeny Primakov in May 1999 came as a surprise to many since he had considerable support in the State Duma and a popular approval rating of 72 percent, compared to 2 percent for President Yeltsin. His replacement, Sergey Stepashin, made his career in the military and the security services, eventually becoming the director of the domestic secret service, later the minister of justice, and then minister of internal affairs.

After less than three months in office, Stepashin was replaced by the current prime minister, Vladimir Putin, who also made his career in the secret service and, among other things, worked as a spy for the KGB in former East Germany. Unlike his predecessors, Putin was not only nominated as prime minister, but also annointed by President Yeltsin as his preferred successor in the presidency. Thanks, for the most part, to his vigorous pursuit of the war in Chechnya, Putin quickly became the most popular politician in Russia. When President Yeltsin resigned on December 31, 1999, Putin, as specified by the Constitution, became acting president. This astute political maneuver by Yeltsin and his entourage, which moved up the date for the presidential election by three months, gave Putin an enormous advantage as a candidate for the presidency. As expected, one of the first official acts by Putin in his new capacity was to grant Yeltsin immunity from criminal prosecution.

The prime minister of Russia has major responsibilities for the economy—an area in which the last three prime ministers and the current prime minister have had no experience. More generally, he is responsible for the vast bureaucratic apparatus of the Russian Federation, which includes about two dozen ministries; over a dozen state committees; and about two dozen federal commissions, services, agencies, inspectorates, and other federal executive organs. In addition to the ministers, the Russian cabinet includes a number of first deputy prime ministers and deputy prime ministers, who assist in the supervision and coordination of policy. While the Constitution formally vests executive power in the "government" and charges it with the implementation of federal laws and policies, the prime minister and the cabinet, like the State Duma, are subject to presidential interference and control. Unlike in other parliamentary systems, Russian ministers may not simultaneously hold legislative seats and are subject to presidential approval. Given the president's ability to influence and even control the composition and the actions of the prime minister and the cabinet, the distinction between the "presidency" and the "government" is rather meaningless. President Yeltsin has never assumed responsibility for failed policies, preferring instead to blame social, economic, and political problems on the actions, or lack of actions, of "incompetent" prime ministers (whom he nominated) and ministers (whom he approved).

The Judiciary

Under the 1993 Constitution, the court is the only institution that has the right to exercise justice in the Russian Federation. More specifically, judicial power is the prerogative of constitutional, civil, administrative, and criminal courts. A special provision in the Constitution prohibits the creation of emergency courts. Justices enjoy immunity and may not be removed, except in cases and in accordance with procedures established by federal law. Ordinarily cases in all courts are open and the examination of criminal cases in absentia cannot take place unless permitted under federal law.

The judicial structure at the federal level consists of the Constitutional Court, the Supreme Court, the Superior Court of Arbitration, and the General Prosecutor. As we have seen, the justices of these courts, as well as the General Prosecutor, are appointed by the President, with the consent of the Federal Council. Justices must be 25 years of age and have a higher legal education and at least five years of experience in the legal profession.

The Constitutional Court of the Russian Federation consists of nineteen justices, who hear cases—brought by the President, the Federation Council, the State Duma, one-fifth of the members of the Federation or the deputies of the State Duma, the Government, the Supreme Court, or the Superior Court of Arbitration, or organs of legislative and executive power of the components of the Russian Federation—relating to compliance with the Constitution of:

- federal laws and normative enactments (of the President, the Federation Council, the State Duma, or the Government)
- the constitutions of republics and the charters of the components of the Russian Federation and laws and other normative acts issued by them concerning matters within federal jurisdiction or joint jurisdiction of federal organs and organs of state power of components of the Russian Federation
- treaties between the Russian Federation and its components

- international treaties of the Russian Federation that have not yet entered into force

In addition to resolving jurisdictional disputes involving the federal organs of state power and the organs of state power of its components, the Constitutional Court has the power of judicial review and interprets the Constitution. Finally, it becomes involved in any attempt to remove the President from office, by ruling on the observance of established procedure in the presentation of the charge.

The Supreme Court of the Russian Federation is the highest judicial organ for civil, criminal, administrative, and other cases within the competence of the courts of general jurisdiction. It is also responsible for judicial oversight of their activity within the procedural forms established by federal law and for clarification on questions of judicial practice.

The Superior Court of Arbitration of the Russian Federation has similar powers and responsibilities with respect to economic disputes and other cases within the jurisdiction of courts of arbitration. Like the Supreme Court, it exercises judicial oversight over the activity of the lower courts and provides clarification on questions of judicial practice.

The office of the General Prosecutor of the Russian Federation is a single centralized system, in which lower-level prosecutors are subordinate to higher-level prosecutors and to the General Prosecutor. Like the justices of the Constitutional Court, the Supreme Court, and the Superior Court of Arbitration, the General Prosecutor is appointed by the Federal Council upon nomination by the President. Prosecutors of components of the Russian Federation are appointed by the federal General Prosecutor with the consent of the components of the Russian Federation.

Local Government

The 1993 Constitution clearly breaks new ground in regard to local government. Article 12 explicitly recognizes and guarantees the principle of local self-government, acknowledging it as independent within the limits of its powers. This principle was completely unknown in prerevolutionary Russia and expressly rejected in Soviet constitutional theory and political practice, which operated on the basis of the Leninist concept of "democratic centralism." The placement of the brief section on local government at the very end of the Constitution, after the section on the judiciary, may be seen as the symbolic expression of the exclusion of the local government institutions from the rest of the state structure. In the language of Article 12: "Organs of local self-government do not form part of the system of organs of state power."

NOTES

[1]*Bol'shaia Sovetskaia Entsiklopediia* (Moscow: Izdatel'stvo "Sovetskaia Entsiklopediia," 1975), p. 656.

[2]Robert Sharlet, *The New Constitution of 1977: Analysis and Text* (Brunswick, OH: King's Court Communications, 1978), p. 97.

[3]How far-reaching the power of the Presidium was in this respect was illustrated in October 1964, when N. S. Khrushchev was replaced as Chairman of the Council of Ministers, by A. N. Kosygin—all without convening the USSR Supreme Soviet.

[4]The existence of this body was revealed in 1976 when the Soviet press indicated that the chairmanship of this body was one of Brezhnev's responsibilities.

[5]It is difficult to make an accurate calculation because not all Soviet legislation was published.

[6]A new law on the Council of Ministers, published in Pravda, July 6, 1978, increased its membership to 109 (all male!).

[7]See Articles 164–168 of the 1977 Constitution.

[8]For details on the Soviet legal system, see Robert Conquest, ed., *Justice and the Legal System in the USSR* (New York: Praeger, 1968).

[9]See Rolf H. W. Theen, "Perestroika vs Reform: The Radicalization of Gorbachev," *The World & I,* 4, no. 3 (1989): 246–272.

[10]See Rolf H. W. Theen, "Party-State Relations Under Gorbachev: From Partocracy to 'Party' State?" in Mel Gurtov, ed., *The Transformation of Socialism: Perestroika and Reform in the Soviet Union and China* (Boulder, CO: Westview Press, 1990), pp. 59–86.

[11]Konstantin Zatulin and Andranik Migranian, "SNG posle Kishineva: nachalo kontsa istorii," *Sodruzhestvo NG,* no. 1 (December 1997), pp. 1–2.

[12]On the CIS, cf. Paul Kubicek, "End of the Line for the Commonwealth of Independent States," *Problems of Post-Communism,* March–April (1999), pp. 15–24.

[13]Rolf H. W. Theen, "The Appeal of Autocracy and Empire: A Threat to Russian Democracy," *The World & I,* 9, no. 9 (September 1992): 583–609.

[14]Only 54.8 percent of the eligible voters took part in the elections and the referendum on the new Constitution; 58.4 percent of the voters endorsed the Constitution. In seventeen republics and regions, voting participation was under the required quorum. In four republics a majority voted against the Constitution. In Chechnya neither the referendum nor elections took place.

[15]There were widespread allegations of irregularities and fraud after the elections. See Vera Tolz and Julia Wishnevsky, "Election Queries Make Russians Doubt Democratic Process," *RFE/RL Research Report* 3, no. 13 (April 1, 1994): 1–6.

[16]The Russian text is in *Argumenty i fakty,* no. 45 (November 1993), pp. 7–12. An English translation can be found in *FBIS-SOV-93-216,* November 10, 1993, pp. 18–37.

[17]At time of the last census in 1989, the basis for these figures, Chechnya and Ingushetia were still a single Soviet autonomous republic. The population distribution in these two republics has not yet been determined. In the Chechen-Ingush republic existing in 1989, Russians accounted for 23.1 percent of the population.

[18]In the section on concluding and provisional provisions, the 1993 Constitution stipulated that the first Federal Assembly would serve only two years, to coincide with the remainder of Boris Yeltsin's term as president.

Chapter 22

Russian Political Participation: The Citizen in Politics

The idea of political participation has always been central to Western concepts of democracy. Communist theory, too, extolled the importance of the role of the citizen in politics and the virtue of active political participation by the masses. If one examines the regular calendar of events and the political routine of communist regimes, one finds many occasions—special events, holidays, and elections, for example—which provided the citizen with opportunities to become involved in the political system. The form, substance, and extent of political participation, however, was always carefully controlled in communist systems.

POLITICAL PARTICIPATION IN CZARIST RUSSIA

There is little doubt that Russian society was ready to become involved in politics at the turn of the century. When the news flashed across Russia in February 1917 that the czar had abdicated, not only the leaders and activists of the various political parties and revolutionary groups were prepared to take part in the establishment of a new social and political order, but also thousands of soldiers, peasants, workers, white-collar groups, students, Moslems, Jews, and so on. There was literally an outburst of political activity—with people sending letters and telegrams to the Duma and the Soviet, composing political programs, and becoming active on the local level. Like so many other things during this turbulent period, political participation was "in the air."[1] In a perceptive essay dealing with the reasons for the breakdown of the czarist autocracy, George F. Kennan has pointed to the failure of the czarist regime to broaden the base of political participation through the establishment of a parliamentary institution at the national level during the nineteenth century as the most calamitous error.[2] We might add that it was precisely the failure of the czarist regime to create opportunities for political participation that drove hundreds of talented and educated young men and women into the revolutionary movement—which was the only alternative they had.

POLITICAL PARTICIPATION
IN THE USSR

While the tsarist regime did not make any pretense of being a democracy, the Soviet Union made every effort to conceal its authoritarian nature behind a facade of democratic structures and processes. As a matter of fact, Soviet propaganda tirelessly proclaimed the USSR as the most democratic country on earth, basing this claim on the unparalleled participation of its citizens in politics. But if Soviet citizens did, indeed, become involved on a large scale, it was in ceremonial forms of mass participation, i.e., through the channels created for them by the regime, not through their own channels. These channels included "the nucleus of [the Soviet] political system,"[3] the CPSU, which between 1921 and 1990 enjoyed a de facto—and after the adoption of the 1977 Constitution also a de jure—monopoly position as the single party. They included, furthermore, the mass organizations, such as the Komsomol (Young Communist League) and the trade unions, as well as a large number of other organizations, whose memberships ran into the millions. All of these organizations, and many others like them, were subordinated to the CPSU and directed by its leaders. Their purpose—to use the language of Lenin and Stalin—was to function as "transmission belts" for the implementation of party policy. If there was mass participation in the Soviet Union, it was "controlled mass participation"—with the accent on "controlled."[4]

The Soviet regime was not interested in genuine and spontaneous political participation—certainly not on a mass scale. Accordingly, the CPSU did not aggregate group interests or develop policy alternatives; rather it sought to control group interests through indoctrination, and it imposed policy on the government by *diktat*. Organizing, at the height of its power, approximately 10 percent of the adult population, the CPSU served as the recruiting ground for political leaders at all levels and played a key role in the vertical and horizontal integration of elites. In the strict (and certainly in the Western) sense of the term, the CPSU was not a political party, one of whose main purposes it is to compete for political power in free, fair, and competitive

elections. It had much more in common with a military organization designed to conduct warfare, first against the tsarist autocracy and then against traditional and backward Russia—all in the name of the vision of an ideal social order dictated by communist ideology. Rather than serving as a link between society and the state, the CPSU sought to control both in an attempt to maximize its theurgical might.

In a very real sense, the CPSU was the physical manifestation of an "ideology in power,"[5] which operated in a system in which the distinction between state and society had become virtually meaningless. In such a system, there was no room or function for a viable autonomous civil society. On the contrary, all social organizations were subject to the approval and careful control of the CPSU, which played a decisive role in the selection of their leaders and the direction of their programs and activities. Large and successful public organizations were co-opted by the state and transformed into state organizations. Even the Russian Orthodox Church acquired a semi-official status and was allowed to engage only in activities compatible with the political goals and objectives of the Soviet regime. Although the 1977 Constitution, in Article 52, recognized the separation of church and state, the Russian Orthodox Church was not free to appoint senior-level officials, but had to obtain approval from the CPSU.

SOVIET ELECTIONS

In modern times the electoral process has come to be regarded as the touchstone of mass participation in politics. Communist regimes are no exception in this regard. Following the example of the Soviet Union, all of them made elaborate provisions for the election of local, regional, and national officials. In deference to the universal appeal of the idea of democracy and out of concern for their legitimacy at home and abroad, communist regimes erected complex edifices of formal constitutional arrangements and democratic institutions that were, indeed, impressive at first glance. However, only the form, not the substance or spirit, of democracy was adopted in the communist world. Yet democratic forms alone are not sufficient. As John Stuart Mill recognized long ago, behind a liberal constitution and a liberal government there must be a liberal society.

Ever since the adoption of the Stalin Constitution of 1936—"the only thoroughly democratic constitution in the world," to quote Stalin[6]—the citizens of the Soviet Union enjoyed the right of universal suffrage. The restrictions on suffrage and the indirect election system previously in effect were abandoned; voting was extended to all citizens 18 years of age and older, regardless of social origin, race, religion, or occupation.[7] However, the principle of direct elections was never extended to the "real government" of the USSR, the CPSU, in which the members or delegates of all higher bodies were chosen by the next lower party body instead of by the rank and file members—at least insofar as the formal provisions were concerned.[8]

Democracy is a complicated system of dealing with the multitude of issues and problems that arise in the life of a society—especially a complex, modern society. It is difficult to reduce the essential requirements of democracy to a single proposition. But perhaps of all the rights that are important to a free citizen in a democracy, the most crucial one is the right to organize an opposition. On this right hinges the citizen's ultimate ability to seek redress against an arbitrary, unjust, oppressive, ideologically unacceptable, or incompetent government. Before the political reforms under Gorbachev, this right was explicitly prohibited by the USSR Constitution. Article 6 of the 1977 Constitution recognized the CPSU as "the leading and guiding force of Soviet society," as "the nucleus of its political system and of all state and public organizations." Article 50 guaranteed Soviet citizens the right to free speech, but only "in accordance with the interests of the people and for the purpose of strengthening and developing the socialist system." Similarly, the right to association was preceded by the caveat that this right may be exercised by Soviet citizens only "in accordance with the goals of communist construction." Clearly, these provisions, seen from a Western perspective, turned the elections into a farce. In the context of Soviet politics, they effectively reduced political participation to supportive activity for the CPSU, the sole recognized and "legitimate" political party in the USSR.

What is more, the CPSU did not take the one step that might have endowed Soviet elections with a modicum of respectability, namely to offer the electorate a choice of candidates—albeit candidates who were members (or supporters) of the same, that is, the one and only, political party. Although the legal provisions governing the nomination of candidates for political office seemingly permitted multiple-candidate elections, even such limited choice was denied to the Soviet voter. The CPSU did not hold primary elections; instead it selected the one candidate whose name appeared on the printed ballot on election day. One can well imagine the perplexity and consternation of the young Soviet citizen who, voting for the first time, read the instruction on the ballot: "Cross out all but one name"—and found that only one name appeared on the ballot.[9]

One of the most discussed aspects of Soviet elections is the enormous turnout of voters on Election Day. Whereas in the United States a turnout in the vicinity of 50 percent in a national election is considered a good turnout, Soviet election officials regularly reported close to 100 percent participation by eligible voters. If we are to believe the official statistics published after every election to the Supreme Soviet of the USSR and the Supreme Soviets of the fifteen union republics, the Soviet electorate, indeed, compiled an enviable record. For over four decades more than 99.9 percent of the eligible Soviet voters faithfully cast their ballot. Between 1937 and 1979 the lowest participation figure was 99.94 percent—in 1966. Near perfection was reached in the elections of March 4, 1979, when the Central Electoral Commission of Uzbekistan reported that only 14 voters out of a total electorate of over 7 million had failed to cast a ballot.[10] According to *Pravda* (which translates as *The Truth*), then the leading national newspaper of the Soviet Union, 174,920,221 voters out of a total of 174,944,173 registered voters, that is, 99.99 percent, took part in the elections to the Supreme Soviet. Only one republic reported a participation percentage below this figure: Estonia—99.98 percent.[11]

Needless to say, these claims were difficult to believe for anyone who was familiar with life in the Soviet Union and had been in Uzbekistan. Nothing in the Soviet Union—from transportation and communication to organization and record-keeping—worked that well! There is every reason to believe that these impressive figures were considerably inflated by election officials who were under some pressure to report a turnout of close to 100 percent.[12]

ELECTION REFORM AND DEMOCRATIZATION

If elections in the past amounted to little more than a ritual in the "shadow dance" of Soviet democracy, they acquired a completely new role and meaning under Gorbachev. In a dramatic break with the past, contested elections at the national level were held in the Soviet Union for the first time since 1917 on March 26, 1989. If there were any doubts about the readiness of Soviet citizens for meaningful political participation, they were surely laid to rest by these elections which, in the words of TASS news analyst Igor Yefimov "awakened the population from a long political slumber."[13] When given the opportunity, the majority of Soviet voters were quite prepared "to throw the rascals out." Major establishment figures were rejected by the electorate, including a Politburo member in Leningrad, the party-backed candidate running against Boris Yeltsin in Moscow, the first party secretary and mayor in Kiev, as well as a large number of regional party leaders. All in all, the elections amounted to a resounding vote of no-confidence in the Communist party. They also demonstrated the crumbling of the traditional ideological dogmas and the growing role of nationalism and religion in Soviet politics. In a broader sense, the elections went a long way toward legitimizing genuine politics in the largest country on earth.

As promising as these developments were, they did not assure the development of democratic institutions and practices. During 1990 the Communist party recovered from its initial disorientation and demoralization in the wake of the 1989 elections. Although clearly suffering from a "crisis of confidence,"[14] the CPSU showed signs of adjusting to the changed circumstances. The strength of the conservative elements in the party was demonstrated by the formation of a separate Communist party of the Russian Republic (RSFSR) in the summer of 1990 and the systematic attack on the political reforms of Gorbachev. By the end of 1990, leading reactionaries called for the end and, indeed, reversal of *perestroika,* including the dismantling of parliamentary institutions.

The political reforms under Gorbachev resulted in both the intensification and broadened scope of political participation. Not only was the monopoly of the Communist party effectively challenged and legally ended in March 1990, but the "awakening of the Soviet population from a long political slumber" led to the sudden emergence of independent trade unions, youth organizations, and a multitude of "informal" groups, creating a vastly different political climate and much broader opportunities for citizens to become involved in politics. As a result, the traditional framework for political participation was not only greatly expanded, but qualitatively transformed by the emergence of innumerable groups and organizations concerned with environmental, religious, ethnic, and local issues.

POLITICAL PARTICIPATION IN THE RUSSIAN FEDERATION

When in the transitional period under Gorbachev thousands of independent social organizations sprang up like mushrooms in the political landscape of the Soviet Union, they were viewed by many observers as the shoots of an emerging civil society. This grassroots activism reflected the wide-ranging interests and social complexity of Soviet (and Russian) society, on the one hand, and the ability of independent political activists to organize these interests into politically effective groups, even against the concerted opposition of a hostile state. After the collapse of the Soviet Union, however, it became increasingly apparent that the foundations for a civil society in Russia remain tenuous at best. Indeed, as the Soviet Union collapsed and Russia gained its independence, the divisions in Russian society proved to be so numerous and deep that no political consensus on the direction of political and economic reform emerged—let alone a political coalition willing and able to support the implementation of a concerted program to deal with the daunting problems of Russia.

Specifically, for a number of reasons—the legacy of a state-dominated society, the lack of an integrative national identity, the absence of an established infrastructure linking society with state power, to mention a few—no effective representative political party system developed in Russia. What is more, no political center emerged. On the contrary, the democratic movement, which was instrumental not only in bringing down the communist regime and in defining the political agenda during the transition period, but also in helping Boris Yeltsin become the first popularly elected president of Russia, disintegrated into a number of factions. By the time of the 1993 elections and the referendum on the 1993 Constitution, no unified democratic movement existed. Instead, that election marked the political advance of the political forces on the right and the left of the political spectrum—forces equally opposed to democracy and the rule of law. In assessing the prospects for democracy in Russia, it is well to remember that these forces acted as godfather to the 1993 Constitution: They were instrumental in its adoption; without their support of the referendum, the Constitution would not have received the necessary majority endorsement.

The emergence of hundreds of political parties and political movements in the aftermath of the abolition of the monopoly of the CPSU led to organizational divisiveness and made the unification of the opposition more difficult. With the "common enemy"—the Soviet Union—out of the picture, and in the absence of consensus on the goals and priorities of the new Russian state, let alone the methods to be used for their achievement, the democrats found themselves without a basis for continued organized cooperation. This dilemma found reflection in the 1993 elections to the State Duma, whose composition is discussed later in this chapter.

Political party formation in the Russian Federation began as a response to the communist regime; its main focus was the destruction of that regime. Without a firm social base and well-defined social interests, without the challenge of coalition-building in anticipation of new elections, and without an established tradition of multiparty politics, Russian political parties in the post-Soviet period sought to redefine themselves

in terms of issues. The result was a split along issue lines—in particular three issues: economic reform, Russian nationalism, and the construction of the Russian state. Perhaps the most important impediment to the development of a coherent political party system was the fact that political parties became operative before the crisis of legitimacy of the new Russian state had been resolved.[15] The issues of national identity and construction of the new state not only proved to be highly divisive, but also produced a shift in the political spectrum. It stands to reason that as long as these issues remain unresolved, political parties will not succeed in building a constructive political center.[16] Nevertheless, given the lack of institutionalized independent political participation in Russia's past, the transformation of unstructured political activity at the grassroots level into political party activity, no matter how nascent and tenuous, constitutes a necessary and potentially important step toward democracy.

Russian Elections

One of the surprising developments in post-Communist Russia is the speed and the degree to which elections have come to be accepted. As we have seen, already in 1989, before the collapse of the Soviet Union, Soviet voters demonstrated their understanding of the power of the ballot box in the first free election in the history of the USSR. Within five years after its establishment, the Russian Federation adopted a new Constitution by national referendum and held two parliamentary elections (in 1993 and 1995), as well as a presidential election (in 1996) and numerous regional and local elections. Considering the history of election under Soviet rule, it comes as no surprise that Russian electoral practice is far from meeting Western democratic norms. There have been many irregularities and forms of outright fraud, such as the purchase and sale of signatures and signature lists required for registration by candidates and parties, the pressuring of members of the military and state employees to sign candidate registration lists, raising money by selling space on party lists to potential candidates, and so forth. There is reason to believe that the referendum on the new Constitution and the first parliamentary election in 1993 were attended by widespread fraud and falsification. In the 1995 election, too, there were numerous violations of the electoral law. According to a member of the Liberal Democratic Party (LDP), close to half of his colleagues in the LDP fraction in the State Duma, had paid an average of $1 million each for their places on the LDP party list. In spite of these shortcomings, the outcome of the constitutional referendum and the outcome of the elections have been accepted by both the parties and the people. Hundreds of international observers from the Council of Europe, the European Union, and the Organization for Security and Cooperation in Europe (OSCE) concluded that the parliamentary elections in 1995 and the presidential elections in 1996 met the fundamental standards of democracy.

The State Duma

Half of the 450 deputies of the State Duma, the lower house of the Russian Assembly, are directly elected in single-member districts. The other half of the deputies are elected through proportional representation and are assigned seats from the lists of the successful parties. As in Germany, a party must win at least 5 percent of the national vote in order to claim its share of the seats based on proportional representation. However, there are no "overhang mandates" as in Germany. State Duma deputies serve four-year terms and have no term limits. Candidates for the State Duma must be Russian citizens, 21 years of age, and otherwise qualified to vote. Unless they are directly nominated by a party, they must collect signatures from 1 percent of a district's electorate to run for a district mandate; if they run for a seat allocated by proportional representation, they must be placed on a party list, and the party must submit the number of signatures required for registration. Running unopposed in an election for a Duma seat is prohibited by the Constitution. State Duma deputies are prohibited from holding office in the executive or judicial branch of the government. Although the State Duma is elected by popular vote and thus has a direct mandate, it is the less powerful of the two chambers making up the Federal Assembly.

On June 25, 1999, President Yeltsin signed a new election law that governed the parliamentary

elections held in December 1999. While the new law did not change the basic rules for elections to the State Duma, it introduced a number of significant changes in an attempt to address election fraud, including ballot rigging and "dirty techniques," the candidature of individuals with criminal records, etc. In accordance with a ruling by the Constitutional Court in 1998, the new law also contains a new interpretation of the "five-percent rule" that limits parliamentary representation to parties winning at least 5 percent of the national vote. According to the new law, the five-percent threshold remains in effect only if the parties that clear this hurdle together win at least 50 percent of the national vote. If that is not the case, parties and political groups that received 3 percent of the national vote are also seated in the Duma until the required 50 percent requirement is met. Four days after the new law was adopted, Vladimir Putin, the director of the Russian Federal Security Service announced that the Security Service would play a major role in the upcoming elections in order to ensure compliance with the electoral law and to keep criminals from penetrating into positions of power.

The 1999 Duma Election

On December 19, 1999, the third election to the Russian parliament, the State Duma, was held in post-communist Russia. The turnout, still high by American standards, was 60.1 percent—down 2.4 percent from 1995. This figure includes those who voted against all parties (3.3 percent—compared to 2.8 percent in 1995). In addition, 1.2 percent of the votes cast were ruled invalid—down 0.7 percent from 1995. In the 1995 Duma election, 43 parties were listed on the ballot, only four of which received enough votes (5 percent minimum) to qualify for proportional representation. This vote fragmentation—the average vote for a party was only 2.3 percent!—resulted in an enormous election bonus for the parties that did qualify for seats based on proportional representation. In the 1999 election, after the disqualification of two parties, 26 parties were on the ballot, six of which cleared the 5 percent hurdle and thus qualified for proportional representation in the Duma. The average party vote in 1999 was 3.8 percent. However, independent candidates and parties which did not qualify for proportional representation won 132 seats by securing direct mandates—ten fewer than in 1995.[17]

The final results of the election, as announced by the Central Elections Commission on December 29, 1999, for the major parties were as follows:

the votes cast for other movements representing women, it appears unlikely that a women's party will be able to clear the 5 percent barrier in the foreseeable future. In the present Duma, 13 deputies seated from party lists and 19 from single member districts are women—for a total of only 32. There is a slight chance that this number

Table 22–1   1999 Parliamentary Election Results

Party	Vote in %	PR Seats	Direct Mandates	Total
Communist Party of Russia (KPRF)	24.29	67	46	113
Unity* (MEDVED)	23.32	64	8	72
Fatherland All Russia (OVR)	13.33	36	30	66
Union of Rightist Forces (SPS)	8.52	24	9	33
Zhirinovsky Bloc (Liberal Democratic Party of Russia)	5.98	17	0	17
Yabloko (Apple)	5.93	16	5	21

* The full name of this party is Inter-Regional Movement Unity. Its nickname "Medved" means "bear."

Source: "1999 Russian Parliamentary Election Results" (RFE/RL) at www.rferl.org/elections/russia99/results/index.html.

The parties that did not qualify for proportional representation in the Duma but won direct mandates include Our Home-Russia (NDR) with 7 seats, the All-Russian Political Movement in support of the Army (DPA), and the Russian All People Unity Party (ROS) with 2 seats each. Finally, the Spiritual Legacy Party (DN), the Bloc of General Andrei Nikolaev and Academician Svyatoslav Fedorov (AN/SF), the Congress of Russian Communities and Movement of Y. Boldyrev (KRO-DYB), the Party of Pensioners (PP), the Russian Socialist Party (RSP), and the Women of Russia (ZhR) each won 1 seat direct mandate. Independent candidates not affiliated with any political party won 106 direct mandates (nearly 24 percent of the total Duma membership, or 47 percent of the direct mandate seats).

While in the 1995 Duma women accounted for some 11 percent of the deputies, only about 7 percent of the members of the 1999 Duma are women. The Women of Russia won only 2.04 percent of the party list vote. Even if one adds

might increase since a number of the high-ranking candidates who were elected will give up their seats to work in other positions, especially in the executive.

It is both interesting and significant that the new Duma includes a rather large number of politicians who were dismissed from office by former President Yeltsin—e.g., all five former prime ministers in the Yeltsin Administration: Yegor Gaidar, Viktor Chernomyrdin. Sergei Kirienko, Yevgenii Primakov, and Sergei Stepashin. Two former first deputy prime ministers, one former deputy prime minister, and two high-ranking ministers (finance and justice) also won Duma seats. Finally, former Yeltsin confidant and bodyguard Aleksandr Korzhakov and former Soviet prime minister Nikolai Ryzhkov are also among the newly elected deputies, and the first session of the 1999 Duma, if tradition is followed, will be opened by the oldest deputy, Yegor Ligachev, who was among Gorbachev's key opponents.

The 1999 parliamentary election was important because it resulted, for the first time, in a major victory of the centrist parties, thus strengthening the position of Acting President and Prime Minister Putin, who at the time of the election still enjoyed great popularity because of his handling of the war in Chechnya. While the Communists remained the largest party, their hard-line allies suffered significant losses. Although it remains to be seen how many factions will emerge in the new Duma, there is a reasonable chance that Putin will have a small majority of supporters—at least until the presidential election scheduled for March 26, 2000. On the other hand, if and when he proceeds to address the problems confronting his country, the new Duma quite likely may prove to be quite fractious and come to resemble the 1993 Duma more than its immediate predecessor, in which bloc voting played a major role.

The Federation Council

Unlike the U.S. Senate, the Federation Council, which represents the 89 "subjects" or subdivisions of the Russian Federation, is not directly elected by the people. Only in 1993, when President Yeltsin had dissolved the regional legislatures in the aftermath of the armed attack on the Russian White House, did Russians have the opportunity to elect the members of the Federation Council by direct vote. In that election, nearly 500 candidates competed for the 178 seats of Russia's upper house. The Federation Council consists of two representatives from each of Russia's 89 subdivisions—one from the regional legislature and one from the regional executive. Like the U.S. Senate, the Federation Council, therefore, is based on the principle of equal geographical representation. However, in Russia's case half of the members of the Federation Council are regional governors and the other half are heads of the regional legislatures. The electoral law governing the composition of the Federation Council became the subject of a major political battle in the fall of 1995, centering on the issue of how regional governors and legislative leaders in the regions would be selected. For the most part, regional governors had been appointed by President Yeltsin, thus virtually assuring his control over the upper house. Eventually, however, it was decided that the executive and legislative leaders of Russia's regions had to be elected by popular vote by December 1996.

Unlike the State Duma, the Federation Council is a part-time institution. Like the U.S. Senate, it ratifies treaties (in cooperation with the Duma) and has the power to impeach the president by a two-thirds vote—if impeachment proceedings are initiated by at least one-third and supported by at least two-thirds of the State Duma deputies and if there is a ruling by the Constitutional Court that the correct procedures for bringing impeachment charges have been observed. It also approves presidential appointees to Russia's three high courts, the appointment of the Prosecutor-General, border revisions within the Russian Federation, and the deployment of the military outside of Russia.

Presidential Elections

The president of the Russian Federation is elected by popular vote and may serve two four-year terms. Candidates for the office of president must be Russian citizens and meet a 10-year residence requirement. The presidential election consists of a two-round process. The first round involves the selection of the two top candidates, who then compete in a runoff election. One of the interesting innovations has been the introduction of the "protest vote," which allows Russians to vote "none of the above" in the presidential election. If the winner of the runoff election does not receive more votes than the total of the protest vote, new elections must be called within three months. Whether contenders for the presidency who have lost in the first round are eligible to run a second time in the new elections is not clear. Russian presidential elections involve a much shorter campaign period, with "media campaigns" being limited to one month prior to election day. Moreover, on paper at least, financial contributions to presidential campaigns are subject to strict limits.

President Yeltsin's first term as president began in June 1991, when the RSFSR still existed and the Russian Federation had not yet come into being. Five years later, in June 1996, post-communist Russia had its first presidential election, which was initially contested by no

THE 1996 PRESIDENTIAL ELECTION (FIRST ROUND)

Candidate	Vote (in %)
Boris Yeltsin	35.3%
Gennady Zyuganov	32.0
Aleksandr Lebed	14.5
Grigory Yavlinsky	7.3
Vladimir Zhirinovsky	5.7
Svyatoslav Fedorov	0.9
Mikhail Gorbachev	0.5
Martin Shakkum	0.4
Yuri Vlasov	0.2
Vladimir Bryntsalov	0.2
"Against all candidates"	1.5

Source: Rossiyskaya gazeta, June 22, 1996

fewer than 78 candidates, nominated by 94 organizations. In the end, only 11 candidates met all the requirements. As indicated in Box 22-1, in the first round Yeltsin was the front runner, with a little over one-third of the vote, followed closely by Gennady Zyuganov, the leader of the Communist Party, and—with less than 15 percent of the vote—by Alexander Lebed, the general who was instrumental in negotiating the cease-fire in Chechnya. In the second round, with 67 percent of the eligible citizens voting, Yeltsin, endorsed by Lebed and Fedorov, won with 53.7 percent of the vote—against 40.4 percent for Zyuganov. In this round, almost 5 percent of the voters made use of the "protest vote."

NOTES

[1] See Marc Ferro, "The Aspirations of Russian Society," in Richard Pipes, ed., *Revolutionary Russia* (Garden City: Doubleday, 1969), pp. 183–208.

[2] George F. Kennan, "The Breakdown of the Tsarist Autocracy," in Pipes, *Revolutionary Russia,* pp. 7ff.

[3] Art. 6. See Robert Sharlet, *The New Soviet Constitution of 1977: Analysis and Text* (Brunswick, OH: King's Court, 1978), p. 78.

[4] J. N. Hazard, *The Soviet System of Government,* 5th ed. (Chicago: University of Chicago Press, 1980), pp. 56ff.

[5] I have borrowed this phrase from Bertram D. Wolfe's *An Ideology in Power: Reflections on the Russian Revolution* (New York: Stein and Day, 1969).

[6] I. V. Stalin, *Sochineniia,* vol. I (XIV) (Stanford: Hoover Institution on War, Revolution and Peace, 1967), p. 165.

[7] For the constitutional history of the USSR, see the essay by John N. Hazard in F. J. M. Feldbrugge, ed., *Encyclopedia of Soviet Law,* vol. I (Leiden: A. W. Sijthoff, 1973), pp. 151–154. The first two Soviet constitutions, the RSFSR Constitution of 1918 and the USSR Constitution of 1923, can be found in J. H. Meisel and E. S. Kozera, *Materials for the Study of the Soviet System* (Ann Arbor: George Wahr Publishing Company, 1953), pp. 57–59, 79–91, 152–168.

[8] See "Rules of the Communist Party," in Hazard, *The Soviet System of Government,* especially pp. 297ff.

[9] This form of ballot was in use in the USSR since 1937.

[10] *Pravda,* March 7, 1979, p. 1.

[11] See Ibid., pp. 1, 3–8, for a summary of the election results.

[12] See Friedgut, *Political Participation in the USSR,* pp. 113ff.

[13] FBIS, *Soviet Union: Daily Report,* 89/057, March 27, 1989, p. 39.

[14] *Izvestiia,* March 22, 1989.

[15] See Giovanni Sartori, *Parties and Party Systems: A Framework for Analysis* (Cambridge, England: Cambridge University Press, 1976), pp. 16–17.

[16] For additional information, see Marcia A. Weigle, "Political Participation and Party Formation in Russia, 1985–1992: Institutionalizing Democracy?" *Russian Review* 53 (April 1994): 240–270.

[17] Some of the figures for the 1999 election are preliminary; final tabulations were not available in all cases at the time of this writing. Among other things, the available data are incomplete because only 216 of the 225 single-member district seats were filled on December 19, 1999. In eight districts, the elections were declared invalid, and there were no elections in Chechnya.s

Chapter 23

Political Leadership
in the Russian Federation

Political leadership is one of the most important concepts in political science and sociology. It is the diametrical opposite of "dominion," "control," or "command." All of these concepts signify the existence of a power relationship. But political leadership connotes a special type of power that is based on the consent of, and accountability to, those who are being led. Consent must be constantly renewed and regained by the leader or leaders through appropriate actions and performance consonant with the interests of the governed, that is, those who have entrusted the political leadership of their society to a particular individual or group of individuals.[1]

In the Western democracies, a free press, a host of autonomous interest groups, and political parties play an important role in the crucial nexus between the masses and the elite by assisting the public in a variety of ways in the articulation and aggregation of interests and the translation of these interests into effective political demands. Russian political culture, by contrast, has traditionally been characterized by the virtually total lack of an effective demand structure vis-à-vis the government or the political elite. In this respect, unfortunately, the October Revolution brought little

change. In short, the interface between the political elite and the masses in the USSR was characterized by the conspicuous absence of a viable interest group structure and was, therefore, qualitatively different from that found in Western societies.

POLITICAL LEADERSHIP IN THE SOVIET UNION

The "legitimacy" on which the Soviet regime was based derived neither from the performance of the kind of political leadership that was based on genuine trust nor from the freely given consent of the Soviet population. The relationship between the ruling elite and the masses in the Soviet Union was described much more accurately by the terms dominion, control, or command. One of the truly tragic aspects of the Russian Revolution is that in Lenin's thought prior to 1917, and in the political practice of the communist regime after the October Revolution, the Marxian concept of the "dictatorship of the proletariat" became transformed into a "dictatorship *over* the proletariat"—a development foreseen by Leon Trotsky in 1904. "The dictatorship over the proletariat," Trotsky wrote in his famous pamphlet *Our Political Tasks,* "[means] not the self-activity of the working class which has taken into its hands the destinies of society, but a 'powerful, commanding organization,' ruling over the proletariat and, through it, over society, thus presumably securing the transition to socialism."[2] It is difficult to imagine a more accurate description of the Soviet political system.

In terms of decision-making power at the national, regional, and local level, the CPSU was by far the most important institutional actor on the political stage in the Soviet Union. More specifically, we should note the emergence of a party-dominated central political bureaucracy in the Soviet Union, a power elite that was in firm control of the key positions throughout Soviet society and that exercised virtually monopolistic decision-making power in all significant spheres of social life.[3] The decisions of this power elite were frequently arbitrary and autocratic, free of any effective control by the people or the rank-and-file membership of the CPSU.

The Communist Party of the Soviet Union

Using party membership structure as the basis for differentiation, Maurice Duverger has distinguished between *mass parties* and *cadre parties.* The mass party, according to Duverger, regards the recruitment of members as a fundamental goal and activity; it relies on democratic financing, relatively small contributions from a large membership instead of large donations from a few individuals; it aims at quantity rather than quality. Its basic strategy is to seek political influence through a large membership.

The cadre party, by contrast, is characterized by a relatively small membership. It seeks to capitalize on the influence, prestige, special skills, and expertise of individuals. It is therefore highly selective and exclusive in its membership. Its emphasis is on quality rather than quantity of membership. To quote Duverger: "What the mass party secures by members, the cadre party achieves by selection." In terms of party organization, the cadre party corresponds to caucus parties; it tends to be more decentralized and less cohesive than the mass party.

In terms of Duverger's distinction between cadre parties and mass parties, the CPSU, historically speaking, shared characteristics of both, without ever becoming a pure example of either type. But because of its cell-based structure the CPSU was never a pure type of cadre party, and although it acquired many characteristics of a mass party, it never fully divested itself of the elitist character and the emphasis on certain "qualities" on which Lenin insisted. The unique character of the Leninist party was recognized by Duverger in his concept of the *devotee party,* that is, a party conceived of as the elite.[4]

As a matter of fact, the kind of party Lenin organized, directed, and bequeathed to the Soviet Union after his death in 1924 was a new type of party, sui generis in many respects. Its objective, unlike that of Western socialist parties, was never to win election in open competition with other parties but to fight its way to power—if necessary, by deception and violence. In its role as the vanguard of the proletariat, the raison d'être of Lenin's party before the revolution lay in conducting warfare against the czarist autocracy. After the Revolution of 1917 its chief purpose was to lead a resolute battle for the total reconstruction of Russian society. In short, the CPSU was originally conceived by Lenin as a fighting organization, militant in its outlook, conspiratorial and secretive in its organization, and selective in its membership. Thus, the CPSU was to resemble an army more closely than a political party.

Membership of the CPSU

On January 1, 1990, the CPSU, which at the time of the 1917 Revolution commanded a membership of only 24,000, claimed 18,856,113 members and 372,104 candidate members, for a total membership of 19,228,217.[5] This means that approximately 10 percent of the adult population (20 years old and older) of the Soviet Union held membership in the CPSU.

With the exception of the RSFSR, by far the largest of the 15 union republics, all 14 non-Russian union republics had their own party organizations—at least in nominal terms; the party organizations in the Russian Republic were

Table 23–1   Composition of the CPSU by Nationality (January 1, 1990)

Nationality	Party Membership[a]		Population[b]	
	In Absolute Numbers	In Percent	In Absolute Numbers	In Percent
Russian	11,183,749	58.2%	147,072,000	50.6%
Ukrainian	3,113,560	16.2	44,136,000	15.4
Belorussian	747,261	3.9	10,030,000	3.5
Uzbek	499,250	2.6	16,686,000	5.8
Kazakh	416,829	2.2	8,138,000	2.8
Azerbaijani	375,925	1.9	6,791,000	2.4
Georgian	338,502	1.8	3,983,000	1.4
Armenian	304,558	1.6	4,627,000	1.6
Lithuanian	148,377	0.8	3,068,000	1.1
Moldavian	120,598	0.6	3,355,000	1.2
Tajik	93,881	0.5	4,217,000	1.5
Kirghiz	86,857	0.4	2,531,000	0.9
Turkmen	82,979	0.4	2,718,000	0.9
Latvian	76,483	0.4	1,459,000	0.5
Estonian	58,654	0.3	1,029,000	0.3
Other	1,580,754	8.2	26,860,000	0.9
Total	19,228,217	100.0	286,700,000	

[a]Includes members and candidate members.
[b]Population figures are based on 1989 census.

Source: Izvestiia TsK KPSS, No. 4 (April 1990), p. 113; CIA, Directorate of Intelligence, *USSR: Demographic Trends and Ethnic Balance in the Non-Russian Republics* (Washington, DC: Central Intelligence Agency, 1990).

administered directly from Moscow. In 1990, a separate party organization was finally established for the RSFSR as well. But it should be emphasized that the CPSU was never perceived—let alone administered—as a federation of independent party organizations.

As is apparent from Table 23–1, the CPSU was dominated by Russians who, along with the Ukrainians, Belorussians, and Georgians, were overrepresented in terms of numbers. Constituting 50.6 percent of the Soviet population, the Russians accounted for 58.2 percent of the CPSU membership. Even more pronounced was the domination of the CPSU membership by Slavs: Russians, Ukrainians, and Belorussians together accounted for 69.5 percent of the Soviet population on January 1, 1990, but for 78.3 percent of the CPSU membership. By contrast, some nationalities—in particular the Uzbeks, Moldavians, Tajiks, Kirghiz, and Turkmen—were greatly underrepresented. Soviet party statistics also allow us to infer that certain groups (Russians,

Belorussians, and Armenians) figured importantly in party organizations outside their respective union republics and that some of the indigenous nationalities (especially the Kazakhs, Moldavians, Latvians, Kirghiz, and Estonians), were not strongly represented in the party organizations in their own republics. Indeed, in Latvia and Kazakhstan, the indigenous or titular nationality accounted for less than half of the membership of the republic party organization. (See Table 23–2.)[6]

What most likely explains the variation in party membership from nationality to nationality were varying levels of education among the different national minority groups. There was a high correlation between party membership and advanced education. By January 1, 1990, 35 percent of all CPSU members had a complete higher education, and 58 percent an incomplete higher, or a complete or a partial secondary education, leaving only 7 percent of the total party membership with merely an elementary education.[7]

Table 23–2   Composition of CPSU by Union Republic (January 1, 1990)

Union Republics	Republic CP Membership in Absolute Numbers	Republic CP Membership as Percent of Total CPSU Membership	Titular Nationality[a]	Nationality Representation in CPSU as Percent of Republic CP Membership
RSFSR	10,438,851	57.83%	Russians[b]	107.14%
Ukraine	3,294,038	18.28	Ukrainians	94.52
Kazakhstan	842,417	4.68	Kazakhs	49.48
Belorussia	697,608	3.87	Belorussians[c]	107.12
Uzbekistan	664,520	3.69	Uzbeks	75.13
Azerbaijan	401,526	2.23	Azerbaijanis[d]	93.62
Georgia	400,662	2.22	Georgians	84.49
Lithuania	199,917	1.11	Lithuanians	74.22
Moldavia	199,796	1.11	Moldavians[e]	60.36
Armenia	199,751	1.11	Armenians	152.47
Latvia	177,409	0.98	Latvians	43.11
Kirghizia	154,650	0.85	Kirghiz	56.16
Tajikistan	126,881	0.70	Tajiks	73.99
Turkmenistan	115,008	0.64	Turkmen	72.15
Estonia	106,295	0.58	Estonians	55.18
Total	18,019,329[f]	99.88		

[a]Dominant nationality in the republic or nationality after which the republic was named.
[b]Also called Great Russians.
[c]Also called White Russians.
[d]Also called Azeris.
[e]Also called Moldovans.
[f]This total differs by 1,208,888 from the total given for the membership of the CPSU as a whole on January1, 1990, in *Izvestiia TsK KPSS*, no. 4 (April 1990): 113.

Source: Calculated from data in *Izvestiia TsK KPSS*, no. 2 (February 1990): 91; no. 3 (March 1990): 116; no. 5 (May 1990): 60–61.

If one looks at party membership in terms of social class structure, it becomes clear that the CPSU was not a "workers' party" in the ordinary sense of the term. Adopting the categories used in official Soviet publications and statistics, we find that the Soviet population consisted of: (1) *rabochie,* that is, manual workers engaged in material production—a category that included workers on state farms; (2) *kolkhozniki,* that is, collective farm workers; and (3) *sluzhashchie,* that is, secretarial, administrative, and executive personnel. This last group formed the largest single contingent within the CPSU. Constituting only 26.2 percent of the total labor force in 1987, it accounted for no less than 53.8 percent of the CPSU membership in 1990. The workers and peasants, by contrast, who together constituted close to 75 percent of the total population, were represented by only 46.2 percent of the CPSU

membership during the same year. By 1981 the CPSU had become very much of a "middle-aged party"—an observation that is even more apropos with regard to the top echelons of the Soviet leadership, as we shall see.

The significance of this aging process becomes apparent when one correlates the age structure of the CPSU with the age structure of Soviet society (see Table 23–3). In considering CPSU policy with regard to the admission of members of the younger generations, we should also take into account the official policy of strengthening the *Komsomol* (Communist Youth League), the youth organization adjunct of the CPSU, and the increased role of the Komsomol as a gateway to CPSU membership—a policy reflected in an amendment to the Party Rules governing the admission of new members adopted by the Twenty-third CPSU Congress in 1966,

Table 23–3 Party Representation by Age Group, 1977

Age Group	Absolute Numbers	Percentage of Population	Total CPSU Members in Age Group	Percent of Age Group in CPSU
18–25	37,265,000	14.30%	929,408	2.50%
26–30	19,010,000	7.30	1,729,738	9.00
31–40	33,520,000	12.86	4,134,166	12.30
41–50	33,745,000	12.95	4,229,078	12.50
51–60	22,505,000	8.63	2,897,398	12.90
Over 61	32,355,000	12.42	2,074,688	6.40
Total	178,400,000	68.46	15,994,476	8.96

Source: "KPSS v tsifrakh," *Partiinaia zhizn',* no. 21 (November 1977): 31. Population data and extrapolations are based on U.S. Bureau of the Census, International Population Reports, Series P-91, no. 24, *Projections of the Population of the USSR and Eight Subdivisions, by Age and Sex: 1973 to 2000* (Washington, DC: U.S. Department of Commerce, 1975), p. 15; and Series P-91, no. 23: *Estimates and Projections of the Population of the USSR by Age and Sex: 1950 to 2000* (Washington, DC: U.S. Department of Commerce, 1973), p. 21.

providing that young people up to and including the age of 23 could join the CPSU only through the Komsomol.[8]

Historically speaking, the percentage of women in the CPSU was low. In 1920, for example, only 7.4 percent of the CPSU members were women. But in the subsequent decades the percentage of women in the CPSU more than quadrupled. As of January 1, 1990, they accounted for 30.2 percent of the total membership of the CPSU. Considering that they constituted 52.7 percent of the Soviet population in 1989, they were still very much underrepresented (as they tend to be in other political systems). There was some improvement under Gorbachev. In the Central Committee elected in 1990, women accounted for 33 of the 412 members (8.0 percent). Among them were a Politburo member, a member of the Central Committee Secretariat, a USSR minister, a regional *(oblast)* secretary, and two district *(raikom)* secretaries.

Structure of the CPSU

The machinery of the state consisted essentially of two main types of organizations: public or mass organizations and state organizations. The CPSU, the trade unions, and the governing bodies of the Soviets, all of which were, at least in a formal sense, elected, were examples of public organizations. State organizations—whose

personnel, by contrast, was appointed and, within certain limits defined by law, was endowed with legal authority—included such bodies as the ministries and the state committees attached to the Council of Ministers structure. Both the public and the state organizations were organized into two formally separate but related power hierarchies and operated on all levels of the national-territorial structure: The 15 union republics[9] and the other 38 nationality-based subdivisions (autonomous republics, autonomous oblasts, and autonomous areas); and the purely territorial subdivisions (krays and oblasts, cities and urban districts, and rural districts).

In addition to these territorial levels, the CPSU also operated on still another level of organization, that of the *primary party organization,* reflecting the "production principle" or a functional basis of party organization. Primary party organizations existed in factories, schools, state, and collective farms, as well as various governmental, cultural, scientific, and educational institutions.

At every level of the territorial-administrative structure of the Soviet Union and wherever work and other activities took place, the CPSU was represented and provided political leadership. The growing complexity of Soviet society found reflection in the structure of the CPSU. In addition to the hundreds of thousands of primary party organizations in state enterprises, collective farms, military units, and so on, the territorial-administrative subdivisions of the Soviet Union alone accounted for over 52,600 in 1987.[10]

In contrast to the formal governmental structure of the USSR that sought to project the facade and decorum of a federal system and thus provided for a certain amount of decentralization of authority, the CPSU did not claim to be federal in character. The basic principle of the organizational structure of the party was "democratic centralism"—a principle of organization that in practice involved a heavy emphasis on the word *centralism*. More specifically, democratic centralism meant:

> Election of all leading Party bodies, from the lowest to the highest; periodic reports of Party bodies to their Party organization and to higher bodies; strict Party discipline and subordination of the minority to the majority; the obligatory nature of the decisions of higher bodies for lower bodies; and collective spirit in the work of all organizations and leading Party bodies and the personal responsibility of every communist for the fulfillment of his or her duties and Party assignments.[11]

The principle of democratic centralism was duly enshrined as the basic principle of Soviet political organization in Article 3 of the 1977 Constitution and extended to include all state organs as well. The concept of democratic centralism also formed part of the basis for the Soviet claim that the USSR represented a new kind of state, a "state of all the people." The Preamble of the 1977 Constitution was quite candid in acknowledging that it was a state in which "the leading role of the Communist Party—the vanguard of all the people—has grown."

The Twenty-eighth Party Congress in 1990 demonstrated that the Leninist legacy of centralization in the party had not yet been overcome. In response to the centrifugal tendencies among the Communist parties in the republics, changes were introduced in the party rules, effectively expanding the autonomy of the republican parties and giving their first secretaries ex officio membership on the Politburo. Yet in granting these concessions, Gorbachev refused to abandon the Leninist principle of centralization, stopping well short of federalization—which may have been the only way to save the Communist party from becoming totally irrelevant.

The Leading Party Organs

Theoretically, the apex of the CPSU was the All-Union Party Congress, a body that during the early years of Soviet power was, indeed, an important decision-making body. At that time it met on an annual basis and consisted of a relatively small number of delegates—a number that, however, grew from 104 in 1918 to 825 in 1923. Subsequently, a substantial increase in its size (5,002 delegates at the Twenty-sixth CPSU Congress in 1981) and a decrease in the frequency of its meetings (once every 5 years, according to Rules of the CPSU, as amended in 1971) combined to bring about the progressive decline in its actual significance and authority. Increasingly, the Party Congress became an institution in which the central political bureaucracy, above all, was represented.[12]

Of greater importance in policy making than the party congress was the Central Committee, an organization, that, according to the party rules, met at least once every six months. The Central Committee elected in 1981 consisted of 317 full (voting) members and 151 candidate (nonvoting) members, by far the largest Central Committee ever elected. Under Gorbachev, the long-term trend toward increased size was reversed. The Central Committee elected in 1990 had 412 members, candidate membership having been abolished. Consisting of leading representatives of all walks of life, the Central Committee was a kind of Who's Who in the USSR, indicating elite status for various groups, but, above all, for the political, or power, elite. In the Central Committee elected in 1990, for example, party and government officials accounted for 48.6 percent; white-collar workers, 19.4 percent; military officers, 4.1 percent; and representatives of public organizations, 1.9 percent, leaving only 25.7 percent of the delegates to represent workers and peasants.[13] According to the party rules, the Central Committee managed party affairs between sessions of the party congress. In practice, of course, this was impossible because of its large size and the infrequency of its meetings. Actually, the day-to-day management of party affairs—an enormous task—was handled by the Politburo and the Secretariat in the name of the Central Committee.

Throughout much of the history of the USSR, effective political power was concentrated in the

Politburo (called Presidium of CPSU Central Committee from 1952 to 1966). The Politburo came closest to being the equivalent to the "cabinet" in a Western parliamentary system, at least in terms of the decision-making process and the exercise of power. Unlike the cabinet members in a Western parliamentary democracy, however, the members of the Politburo, as a rule, did not have specific governmental responsibilities for a governmental office or ministry.[14] Generally speaking, their position could be effectively challenged only from within their own ranks.

The size of the Politburo (or Presidium until 1966) ranged from 36 (25 voting and eleven nonvoting) members to 16 (11 voting and 5 nonvoting) members. Prior to the de facto "federalization" of the Politburo in 1990, which resulted in the representation of all the union republics for the first time in history,[15] this key decision-making body in the CPSU was almost totally dominated by Russians. Before the appointment of Yuriy Andropov as general secretary after the death of Leonid Brezhnev in 1981, the Politburo had become a veritable gerontocracy, with an age range of 50–83 years and an average and median age of 70 years. The Politburo elected in 1990, with an age range of 45–64 and an average and median age of 54 years, was much younger.

In dealing with a wide range of issues, they had at their disposal an enormous staff agency, the central party apparatus, under the direction of the Secretariat of the CPSU Central Committee, which was the nerve center of the CPSU. One measure of the importance of the Secretariat is the fact that all men appointed to the post of general secretary of the CPSU, the most powerful position in the Soviet political system, beginning with Stalin, were chosen from its ranks. The key role of the Secretariat in the CPSU was clearly illustrated in the fall of 1988, when its reorganization (and emaciation) by Gorbachev spelled the beginning of the end for the CPSU as the engine in the Soviet political scheme of things.

Supervising and controlling some 443,192 primary party organizations at the base of the party and an intermediate party hierarchy consisting of nearly 4,500 party committees,[16] the Secretariat ran the vast party machine. More clearly than any other structure within the CPSU or the political system in general, therefore, the central party apparatus embodied a vertical integration and control function that, together with the horizontal interlacing of key posts with the party apparatus (involving the "elected" leading party organs), assured the CPSU effective control of the leadership positions throughout the USSR and enabled its leadership to aspire to the more or less total control of Soviet society.

The Nomenklatura System

One of the important characteristics of the central political bureaucracy created by Stalin was the degree to which it was politicized and self-selected. The mechanism most directly involved in this was the *nomenklatura* system—a system of great interest to the political scientist because it illustrated how a complex and highly bureaucratized but essentially monocratic political system coped with the problem of elite selection or recruitment.

The term *nomenklatura* originally referred to a list of key positions, the appointment to which was directly or indirectly controlled by the secretaries of the CPSU at the various levels of the political and territorial-administrative structure of the Soviet political system. As it developed under Stalin, the system was an extreme form of political clientelism, a phenomenon found in all political systems. Among modern variants of political patronage systems it was unique because of its scope: It encompassed all important positions in the Soviet Union—whether in the party, the government, the military, the trade unions, the press, agriculture or industry, science, education, sports, or the world of arts. In the case of the Soviet Union, the nexus between the system and the elite it produced was perceived as being so close that the term *nomenklatura* in time became a byword for the ruling elite.

Through its exclusive or joint control over the personnel appointments to all key positions in Soviet society via the basic or the registration and control nomenklatura, the CPSU gained a preponderant institutional advantage which, among other things, enabled it to claim for itself "the leading role" in Soviet society. Thus, at the highest level, that of the CPSU Central Committee (in reality the Politburo and Secretariat), the system encompassed 300,000 or more positions.[17] At all levels, perhaps more than 2 million positions were involved.[18]

Clearly, the elaborate nomenklatura system in the USSR brought with it the institutionalization of an elitism that was totally at variance with the professed egalitarian goals of the CPSU for Soviet society. The vision of a society in which the state would be administered by all, a society in which "everybody would become a 'bureaucrat' for a time so that, therefore, nobody could become a 'bureaucrat'," a society in which those who administer the state would be paid the same wage as workers, would be elected, and would be subject to recall at any time, a society, finally, in which the state would be needed only "temporarily" by the proletariat and would ultimately "wither away," as Engels had predicted—that vision, so vividly depicted by Lenin in The State and Revolution[19] proved to be a pipe dream. Considering the unprecedented scope of the state in Soviet society, one is tempted to argue that the USSR represented in many respects the very opposite of Lenin's dream.

The Party in Disarray

The Gorbachev reforms, as we have seen, began as an attempt to restructure the existing system essentially within its Stalinist contours. The CPSU was to play the star role in this endeavor, which began very much like many of the previous major campaigns so characteristic of the Soviet regime. Before long, however, Gorbachev came to realize that the CPSU, and not just the middle echelons of the government bureaucracy, was a large part of the problem. The party proved to be impervious to any attempt to change its way of thinking and modus operandi, leading Gorbachev to conclude that socioeconomic and political reforms could not be achieved as long as the CPSU remained the major institutional force in Soviet society.

While continuing to pay lip service to the ideological formula of "the leading role of the party," Gorbachev quietly engineered a major change in party-state relations that involved a shift of power from the party to the state and a reduction in the party's functions, especially in the economy. As the scope of the political reforms in the Soviet Union widened, the CPSU lost first its de facto, then its de jure, political monopoly. A multiparty system came into existence—and for the first time since the early 1920s, the CPSU faced actual political competition. To add to the problems of the party, as *glasnost* transformed the political atmosphere, it found itself the target of innumerable attacks in the mass media, especially in connection with the campaign against corruption in high places. As Gorbachev rewrote the rules of Soviet politics, the CPSU found itself ill-prepared to cope with real democratization. The organizational changes in the party apparatus introduced by Gorbachev further disoriented the CPSU, which for decades had no need or incentive to be flexible, resourceful, or responsive. The elections in the spring of 1989, already conducted under the new rules, proved to be a traumatic experience for the CPSU, including a good many well-known establishment figures in high posts.[20] As the image and credibility of the CPSU declined as a result of continued poor performance and the onslaught of the mass media, the party faced a steady and increasing stream of defectors. Nationwide, it lost approximately 10 percent of its members (nearly 2 million) between 1986 and 1991. Polls taken in 1990 indicated that, in terms of popular appeal and confidence, the CPSU came in a poor third behind the Russian Orthodox Church and the environmentalists.

POLITICAL LEADERSHIP IN THE RUSSIAN FEDERATION

From the extreme of single party rule and the seemingly unchallengeable dominance of a well-entrenched political elite, the Russian Federation in 1991 plunged into a situation that thus far, it would seem, has defied all attempts at political leadership. Instead of a stable political framework dominated by a single monopolistic ruling party, the political landscape of postcommunist Russia included a multitude of political groups, movements, parties, and informal associations, as well as a communist constitution adopted in 1978, with more amendments than original articles. The Russian two-tier parliament—the Supreme Soviet and the Russian Congress of People's Deputies—consisting predominantly of old-style hardline communists elected in 1990, after

Anti-Communist Demonstration in Moscow, March 10, 1991, attended by 500,000 people. The signs read: "The leopard cannot change its spots—The CPSU was and is the oppressor of the freedom of the peoples" and "We support Yeltsin's policy." (*Photographer/Source:* AP/Wide World Photos)

initially endorsing a program of economic and political reform, soon proved to be at loggerheads with President Yeltsin, whom it had earlier supported in their common struggle for independence from the Soviet Union. Before long, the legislative and executive branches of the Russian Federation were embroiled in a bitter political struggle that made any concerted effort at the pursuit of economic and political reform impossible. Ultimately, this confrontation ended in the dissolution of the Russian parliament by military force—a development that in and of itself called into question Russia's progress toward "democratization."

Be that as it may, the bloody suppression of a minority of resisting deputies on October 3 and 4, 1993, made new parliamentary elections urgently necessary. The new parliament, as it turned out,

was to be elected on the basis of a new constitution, which likewise had to be approved by the voters of Russia on December 12, the day of the elections and the referendum on the new constitution. The adoption of a new constitution was necessary because of the patently undemocratic character of the old one and the need to overcome the political gridlock produced by the mutual blocking of the parliament (the former Russian Congress of People's Deputies and the Supreme Soviet) and the executive (the President).

In response to the announcement of the new parliamentary elections, 140 parties, movements, and organizations registered with the Russian Ministry of Justice and thus acquired the right to draw up lists for the elections. As it turned out, 35 parties and electoral associations succeeded in collecting the necessary number of signatures and

Table 23–4 Political Forces in the Council of the Russian Federation, January 1994

Political Affiliation	Number of Seats (Approximate)[a]	Percent
Proreform democrats	48	28.1%
Russia's Choice	40	
Yabloko[b]	3	
Party of Russian Unity and Accord	4	
Russian Movement for Democratic Reform	1	
Moderate Reformers	23[c]	13.5
Centrist opposition to the government	36[d]	21.1
Communist and socialist opposition	20	11.7
Communist Party of the Russian Federation	15	
Agrarian Party	3	
Socialist Workers' Party	1	
Labor Party	1	
Extreme nationalists	2	0.01
Cossacks' Movement in Kuban	1	
Russian National Council	1	
Subtotal	199	
Otherss	42	25.0
Total	241[e]	

[a]Numbers are approximate since most candidates did not identify their party affiliation; political sympathies imputed from speeches and other secondary information.
[b]Yabloko-Boldyrev-Lukin Bloc.
[c]Many are close to Minister Viktor Chernomyrdin.
[d]Many are close to the Civic Union.
[e]The total number of deputies is 178; only 171 were elected in December 1993.

Source: Russkaya mysl', January 6–12, 1994.

presented their lists with approximately 4,000 candidates for registration. After examination of the signatures, the Central Electoral Commission recognized only 13 lists, including 11 political parties, 7 movements, and 7 associations.

These 25 political parties, movements, and associations formed 13 electoral blocs, falling roughly into four political orientations or camps: Democrats, Communists-Nationalists ("Red-Browns"), Centrists, and Independents.

In the 1993 elections to the lower house of the Federal Assembly, the State Duma, the democrats did not do very well, while the electoral appeal of the nationalists and communists proved to be surprisingly strong. The Liberal Democratic Party of Russia, led by the flamboyant and extremist Vladimir Zhirinovsky, received nearly 23 percent of the popular vote.

In Russia's upper house, the Council of the Federation, the distribution of political forces was

significantly different. As is apparent from Table 23–4, the centrist opposition to the government was not as strong, the nationalists and communists were not as strong, and the proreform democrats, together with the moderate reformers, accounted for over 40 percent. In assessing the balance of the political forces in the Russian Assembly, it should be remembered that the State Duma has very limited powers, while the Federal Council is by far the more powerful of the two chambers in the Russian parliament. One important political development reflected in the outcome of the 1993 elections was the diminished strength of centrist groups, which had played a more prominent role in Russian politics in late 1992.

The real center of power in the political system of the Russian Federation is the president and his apparatus. Ever since Russia gained its independence from the former Soviet Union and became a sovereign state, the executive has consisted of two parts: the government (prime minister and cabinet) and the presidential apparatus. Instead of relying (and depending) on the agencies of the government, the president of Russia has developed his own executive administrative apparatus through which he can implement his policies. More specifically, two institutions were established to increase the president's power: the Administration of the President, which advises the president on all political questions and is in charge of all presidential appointments, including regional cadres, and the Security Council, which supervises security, defense, and foreign policies. The government, under the leadership of the prime minister, was given the difficult task of running the economy.

Reflecting the persisting instability of Russian politics, there was a great deal of personnel change in the Yeltsin administration. Generally speaking, the supporters of radical reform, who played a key role in Yeltsin's rise to power and in his administration during 1991–92, were replaced by more conservative politicians, personified by Prime Minister Viktor Chernomyrdin. As the government's political course became increasingly conservative, especially in the aftermath of the 1993 elections, the reformers found themselves in opposition to the government and became increasingly critical of the president.

The structure and makeup of the cabinet is similar in many respects to the Council of Ministers during the Soviet era. In September 1994, the cabinet, in addition to Prime Minister Chernomyrdin, consisted of half a dozen deputies, twenty-four ministers (including one without portfolio), ten committee chairmen, the chairmen of the intelligence and counterintelligence services, the Central Bank of Russia, and a few other high-level officials.

The presidential apparatus under Yeltsin, it should be noted, within a very short time, experienced almost exponential growth. In November 1994, already it reportedly had reached some 40,000—a number several times higher than the staff of the Central Committee of the CPSU in the Soviet period.[21] In addition to the prime minister, the Security Council included among its permanent members such key officials as the minister of internal affairs, the defense minister, the

foreign minister, the minister of justice, the minister of civil defense, and the directors of the intelligence services. A number of commissions of the Security Council supervise such policy areas as the struggle against crime and corruption, defense security, ecological safety, economic security, information security, scientific and technical questions of the defense industry, foreign policy, and science. Attached to the president's office are numerous councils, administrations, services, agencies, and offices—in short, a huge bureaucracy. In response to the persistent criticism of the mushroomlike growth of the presidential apparatus in the Russian press, President Yeltsin ordered his administrative staff cut by one-third.[22]

While, especially in the aftermath of the 1993 elections, the prime minister succeeded in claiming more powers for the government, Yeltsin remained committed to a strong presidential administration. This commitment was reflected in his determination to maintain control over the "power ministries": defense, internal affairs, and the successor agencies to the former KGB. In addition, in February 1994 he set up a new Administration for the Federal Civil Service to ensure presidential control over all important appointments in federal executive bodies. Tucked away in the presidential apparatus is the Council for Cadre Policy, headed by such high-level politicians as Sergey Filatov and Vladimir Shumeyko. To the student of Soviet politics, many of the postcommunist structures set up by Yeltsin seem quite familiar: They underscore the fact that, in the face of many changes, a great deal of the past, including the former Soviet ruling class, the *nomenklatura,* has survived. Given the continuing lack of consensus concerning the future political and economic course of Russia among top decisionmakers, the present "dual" executive may well lead to a power struggle between the president and the government.

Designated by the 1993 Constitution as the head of state, the president of the Russian Federation has far more extensive powers than the ceremonial duties usually associated with this office in parliamentary systems. One reason is that Russia, like the French Fifth Republic, has a hybrid political system that combines elements of the presidential and the parliamentary systems. In Russia's case, the balance of power clearly lies with what is in effect an "executive presidency," with considerable control over the government, i.e., the prime minister and the cabinet, as well as important prerogatives in domestic and foreign policy, including the power to nominate and appoint key officials.

First and foremost among these prerogatives is the president's power to issue decrees *(ukazy)*, which have binding force throughout the Russian Federation, providing they are in accordance with the Constitution and federal law. President Yeltsin made extensive use of his power to issue decrees, circumventing the State Duma on numerous occasions. In the first seven months of 1996, for example, he issued 591 normative decrees, i.e., an average of nearly 85 per month, or almost three per day. By resorting to his decree-making power so frequently instead of working with the Russian parliament, President Yeltsin effectively diminished the stature of the State Duma and even marginalized its place in the Russian political system.

While the decree-making powers of the Russian president are in theory extraordinary, they are limited in practice by the ability and/or willingness of the bureaucracies at the federal, regional, and local levels to carry them out. Historically, implementation has been the Achilles' heel of politics in Russia—whether under the czars or the Soviet regime. Evidently this pattern has not changed in post-communist Russia. Faced with bureaucratic inertia, obstinacy, resistance and sabotage, President Yeltsin, in mid-1996, felt compelled to issue a decree requiring the faithful execution of all decrees. Four months later, he issued a follow-up decree, requiring concrete measures for the implementation of decrees to be taken within one month of their issue.

In his relations with the regions, the president, on the basis of the Constitution, can use "reconciliatory procedures" if there are conflicts between the federation and any of its 89 "subjects." He also has the power to suspend acts of the regional executives if, in his judgment, they violate the Constitution or federal law. This suspension remains in effect until there is a ruling by the appropriate court. In his relations with the Federal Assembly, too, the president has, as it were, judicial review powers. In addition to his other formal powers vis-à-vis the State Duma and the Federation Council, the president can return proposed laws on the grounds that they are legally flawed or were not passed in accordance with the required procedures. Since he has both decree and veto power, the Russian president has enormous influence on legislation. However, in spite of his extraordinary powers, President Yeltsin did not provide the kind of political leadership Russia needed to deal with its daunting problems. On the contrary, by not respecting the primacy of law and resorting to an autocratic leadership style, he undermined the still weak legal and constitutional structure of the Russian Federation, thus adding to the uncertainty about the future of democratization in Russia. Unfortunately, still in its infancy, the political party system, too, has thus far failed to provide much-needed leadership. As a consequence, the Russian ship of state has had to negotiate the treacherous waters of transition politics without the steady guidance of an experienced captain and without the benefit of a national consensus about its course and ultimate direction.

With President Yeltsin at the helm, Russia became—to borrow the language of Larry Diamond—"an electoral democracy," i.e., "a civilian, constitutional system in which the legislative and chief executive offices are filled through regular, competitive, multiparty elections with universal suffrage,"[23] but no more. Whether this system will survive and evolve into a genuine democracy is still very much in doubt. Much will depend on whether a non-authoritarian solution to Russia's economic crisis will be found. Encouraging is the fact that the system survived the financial crisis in August 1998 which culminated in the meltdown of Russia's financial system. Another positive development is a major de facto shift of power from the president to the government, the parliament, and the regional executives in the aftermath of the crisis—a change in the distribution of power, however, which is as yet without a constitutional basis.

Unfortunately, the repercussions of the August 1998 crisis not only resulted in a major reconfiguration of the political forces in Russia, but also called into question—for the first time since 1993—whether elections would remain "the only game in town" for attaining political office. During and after the crisis, Moscow was, once again, flush with rumors about impending coup attempts, leading President Yeltsin to warn that "we have enough forces to stop any plans for taking power."[24] A peaceful transition of power from President Yeltsin on the basis of a fair, free, and competitive election—an unprecedented event in Russia's more than thousand-year history!—would have enhanced the prospects for the recognition of constitutionalism and the rule of law, as well as for the consolidation of democracy. President Yeltsin's decision to resign and the circumstances surrounding his resignation illustrate the extent to which politics in Russia continue to be personalized.

NOTES

[1]The concept of political leadership as defined here is based on Weber's distinction between rational-legal, traditional, and charismatic types of authority. See Max Weber, *The Theory of Social and Economic Organization* (Glencoe: The Free Press, 1947), pp. 328ff.

[2]L. Trotskii, *Nashi politicheskie zadachi* (Geneva: Izdanie rossiiskoi sotsial-demokraticheskoi rabochei partii 1904), p. 102.

[3]For the concept of the central political bureaucracy, I am indebted to Jacek Kuron and Karol Modzelewski, *Monopolsozialismus: Offener Brief an die Polnische Vereinigte Arbeiterpartei* (Hamburg: Hoffmann und Campe Verlag, 1969). The concept is developed at length in Rolf H. W. Theen, "Party and Bureaucracy," in Gordon B. Smith, ed., *Public Policy and Administration in the Soviet Union* (New York: Praeger, 1980), pp. 21ff.

[4]Maurice Duverger, *Political Parties: Their Organization and Activity in the Modern State* (London: Methuen & Co., 1955), pp. 62ff. Citations on p. 64.

[5]*Izvestiia TsK KPSS,* no. 4 (April 1990): 113.

[6]For useful data on future demographic developments, see CIA, *Directorate of Intelligence, USSR: Demographic Trends and Ethnic Balance in the Non-Russian Republics* (Washington, D.C.: Central Intelligence Agency, 1990).

[7]*Izvestiia TsK KPSS,* no. 4 (April 1990): 114.

[8]By 1980, 73 percent of the new CPSU members were recruited from the Komsomol. See Bohdan Harasymiw, *Political Elite Recruitment in the Soviet Union* (New York: St. Martin's Press, 1984), p. 85.

[9]The CPSU had central committee organizations in the fourteen non-Russian union republics. Party affairs of the largest republic, the RSFSR, until 1990, were administered directly by the central, All-Union party apparatus in Moscow.

[10]*SSSR: Administrativno-territorial'noe delenie soiuznykh respublik na 1 ianvaria 1987 goda* (Moscow: [Izdatel'stvo "Izvestiia sovetov narodnykh deputatov SSSR"], 1987), p. 10.

[11]*Rules of the Communist Party of the Soviet Union* (Moscow: Novosti Press Agency Publishing House, 1986), p. 12.

[12]See Boris Meissner, "Parteiführung, Parteiorganisation und soziale Struktur der KPdSU," *Osteuropa,* nos. 8–9 (August–September 1976): 646; nos. 9–10 (September–October 1981): 767–768.

[13]*Pravda,* July 5, 1990, p. 4.

[14]Occasionally senior ministers were members of the Politburo—for example, during World War II and the immediate postwar period, as well as following Stalin's death.

[15]*Izvestiia TsK KPSS,* no. 7 (July 1990): 70–81; no. 8 (August 1990): p. 7.

[16]See "Statisticheskiye dannye po KPSS na 1 ianvaria 1990 g." *Izvestiya TsK KPSS,* no. 4 (April 1990): 115. Note: The RSFSR did not have its own party organization until July 1990.

[17]See Theen, "Party and Bureaucracy," pp. 131–166.

[18]See Harasymiw, *Political Elite Recruitment,* p. 185. On the nomenklatura system, see also Bohdan Harasymiw, "Nomenklatura: The Soviet Communist Party's Recruitment System," *Canadian Journal of Political Science,* no. 4 (December 1969): 493–512; John Löwenhardt, "Nomenklatura and the Soviet Constitution," *Review of Socialist Law* 10, no. 1 (1984): 35–55.

[19]Lenin, *PSS,* vol. 33, pp. 60, 101–102, 109.

[20]See Rolf H. W. Theen, "Democracy Soviet Style," *The World & I* 4, no. 6 (June 1989): 96–103.

[21]Reported by Boris Fedorov, former minister of finance, in *RFE/RL Daily Report,* no. 208, November 2, 1994.

[22]Ostankino Television, November 1, 1994.

[23]Larry Diamond, *Developing Democracy: Toward Consolidation* (Baltimore: Johns Hopkins University Press, 1999), p. 10.

[24]As quoted in Bill Powell and Evgeniia Albats, "Summer of Discontent," *Newsweek* (International edition), January 19, 1999.

Chapter 24

Russian Political Performance

The performance of a political system is crucial in creating the essential prerequisites for the maintenance of political stability and the necessary conditions for the continued adaptability and development of the system as it is confronted with perpetually changing circumstances, both at home and abroad. In the final analysis, the viability of a given set of political institutions and processes depends on their success in coping with the salient socioeconomic and political problems that confront them in a particular political setting.

The Soviet political system, Russia's predecessor, is a case in point. Its performance, even when measured against its own promises, was mixed at best. In terms of the original goals of the Russian Revolution—the attainment of a classless and stateless society, the achievement of socioeconomic equality, and material abundance, and the emergence of the "New Soviet Man"—the Soviet system clearly failed. As a matter of fact, by the early 1980s, Western observers spoke of a "reversal" of the revolution[1] and a "farewell to communism."[2] Similarly, the Soviet system was not successful in achieving "the highest standard of living in the world" by

the 1970s—a goal proclaimed in the Third Program of the CPSU adopted in 1961. On the other hand, in terms of the achievement of overall economic growth, the development of science and technology, the advancement of education, or the accumulation of military power and political influence in international politics, it was quite successful. Certainly the leading position of their country in space technology, its overall economic development and modernization, and, above all, its victory over Nazi Germany in the Great Patriotic War were sources of pride for many Soviet citizens. The imbalance in the development of the Soviet economy was no secret to Soviet consumers and a source of constant frustration and irritation. Soviet critics caustically described their country as belonging with the Third World, as "an Upper Volta with missiles." But aside from the permanent shortage of a wide range of consumer goods, the frequent "bottlenecks" in the supply and distribution of many products (which Soviet citizens learned to live with), the slowly but steadily rising standard of living in the post-Stalin period resulted in a Soviet version of the "revolution of rising expectations." One of the most serious problems of Gorbachev's reform program was its failure to fulfill these expectations. What about the performance of the political system of the Russian Federation?

SOCIOECONOMIC PERFORMANCE

Declining economic growth was one of the important problems confronting Gorbachev when he became general secretary of the Soviet Union in 1985. Indeed, as we have seen, it was the pursuit of economic reform which, among other things, led to the dramatic political changes that ultimately resulted in the collapse of the Soviet Union.

If the economic problems facing Gorbachev in 1985 amounted to a major challenge and called for extraordinary political leadership, the problems encountered by President Yeltsin and the fledgling Russian Federation after the collapse of the Soviet Union were even more daunting. When the USSR disintegrated at the end of 1991, the resulting dislocations sent the economy into a tailspin. The implosion of the Soviet Union, in short, entailed not only political disintegration, but also the breakup or paralysis of economic relationships and command structures essential to the functioning of the centrally planned economy of the former Soviet Union. This process, it should be noted, had begun earlier, when Gorbachev began to dismantle the Stalinist system, but it was greatly intensified when the USSR broke up into fifteen successor states, each determined to pursue "independence" and "sovereignty" at any cost.

In pursuing marketization, privatization, and democratization, the Yeltsin regime initially opted for the "shock therapy" approach, i.e., it embraced a strategy designed to solve Russia's problems by means of a "quick cure." Launched in January 1992 under the leadership of Yegor Gaydar, this strategy involved the abrupt tightening of the money supply by sharply reducing government borrowing from the central bank, pegging the ruble to the American dollar, and securing substantial amounts of foreign aid to support the stabilization effort, decontrolling prices, and privatizing state-owned assets. Seeking to reduce the first quarter 1992 state deficit to zero (from 21 percent of gross domestic product, according to

the International Monetary Fund), the Gaydar government slashed defense expenditures and state-financed investments, as well as subsidies to industries and consumers. If local governments wanted to subsidize basic food items and services, they had to find their own financial resources. Indexation of the income of state employees and pensioners to the cost of living was abolished, and almost all prices were decontrolled.

Initially, shock therapy seemed to work. Although the decontrol of prices in January 1992 led to a 300 percent jump in prices within a month, by August monthly inflation was down to 9 percent—the lowest level in 1992. But in 1993 Russia suffered from the degree of high inflation shock therapy was supposed to eliminate; indeed, Russia was faced with the threat of hyperinflation. In the absence of an adequate and effective social safety net, there were increasing fears of large-scale unemployment; people with fixed incomes, especially pensioners, found it increasingly difficult to make ends meet.

In the end, shock therapy failed in Russia because stabilization at the macroeconomic level did not produce the hoped-for changes at the microeconomic level: manpower reductions in unprofitable enterprises; flexible and rational decisions by enterprise managers, who would declare bankruptcy rather than seek state subsidies as they always had in the past; a flexible labor market, allowing laid-off workers to move from unprofitable and closed enterprises to profitable ones; and managerial sensitivity to price and market signals. Most of all, the well-entrenched paternalism toward workers, inculcated and cultivated by more than seven decades of socialism, militated against factory closures and large-scale layoffs.

There were political reasons for the failure of shock therapy in Russia as well. As has already been mentioned, prior to Yeltsin's dissolution of the old parliament and the attack on the White House in October 1993, the Russian President and his team of reformers faced an increasingly hostile legislature. As the resistance to radical economic reform on the part of the managers became increasingly clear, opposition galvanized in the Supreme Soviet among antireform extremists (including communists) and proreform

Table 24-1   Income Structure of the Population of the Russian Federation, 1993

Group	Monthly Income in Rubles	Percentage of Population	Change Compared to 1992 (in %)
I	Under 25,000	34–35%	– 2–5%
II	25,000–50,000	29–30	– 4–5
III	50,000–150,000	24–25	+ 5–6
IV	Over 150,000	10–14	– 2–3

Source: Based on data in N. Khubulava, "My i nashi dokhody," *Argumenty i fakty,* no. 44 (November 1993): 1.

centrists who were opposed to the reform pace. As a result, the government was forced into financial bail-outs of bankrupt enterprises. By the fall of 1993 the Supreme Soviet was prepared to push the state budget deficit to 25 percent of the gross national product. In short, in the case of Russia, the shock therapy approach proved to be not only economically impractical but also politically unacceptable and unrealizable. The macroeconomic stabilization called for by this strategy did not last because after 1992 growing political opposition made the requisite fiscal and monetary control and discipline impossible. Another factor contributing to the failure of shock therapy was that the hoped-for and necessary massive foreign assistance did not materialize.

If the Russian economy was the recipient of "therapy," the consumer in postcommunist Russia was the victim of "shock." Measured in average statistical terms, which tell only part of the story, a large part of the population of the Russian Federation experienced a precipitous decline in their standard of living, continuing a pattern that had already begun during Gorbachev's perestroika. But the repercussions of the pursuit of marketization by means of shock therapy were by no means uniform for all the population groups. In the words of N. Khubulava, a researcher in the Central Scientific Research Institute of Economics in the Russian Ministry of Economics, one of the results has been the "continuation of the stratification of society into poor and rich."[3] In 1994, the ratio of the top 10 percent of the highest to the bottom 10 percent of the lowest wages and salaries in the Russian Federation was 26:1. In the United States, this ratio in 1991 was 14:1; in Sweden, 11:1; and in China, 3:1.[4] In September 1993, one fourth to one-third of the Russian population (37–49 million people!) had an income at or below the subsistence level. The income structure of the population is summarized in Table 24–1.

In response to an inquiry from a reader concerning the likely fate of the most disadvantaged stratum (Group I), Khubulava, in a follow-up article, indicated that this group can be divided into three subgroups. The first (approximately 6.5–7 percent of the population) consists of the poorest of the poor—pensioners, invalids, and other recipients of public assistance, with incomes of up to 15,000 rubles per month.[5] The second subgroup (18–18.5 percent of the population) is composed of people with monthly incomes of 15,000–20,000 rubles. These are mainly people trying to run small businesses—street trade, individual labor activity, and the like. The third subgroup (9–9.5 percent of the population) is made up of people with incomes of 20,000–25,000 rubles. This is a comparatively active part of the population, consisting of people who, all the same, have not yet succeeded in linking up with the market economy.[6]

One measure of the degree of indigence of the first group is the fact that even the Russian citizens in Group II (with a monthly income of 25,000–50,000 rubles) had to spend 88–90 percent of their income for food. As before, this group includes some representatives of the state budget sector—scholars and scientists, as well as people working in education, health care, culture, the arts, and others.

The third group, with incomes ranging from 50,000 to 150,000 rubles per month, consists of people working in joint-stock companies and commercial organizations, associations, joint enterprises, companies, exchanges, and the

Table 24–2 Monthly Income by Sector,
September 1993

Sector	Thousands of Rubles
Average for the entire economy	80.9
All of industry including:	87.0
Gas	237.2
Oil extraction	221.1
Agriculture	50.5
Construction	116.5
Transportation	121.2
Healthcare, sports, and social security	63.1
Education	57.2
Culture and art	46.4
Science and scientific services	50.3
Credit and insurance	159.3
Administrative organs apparatus	86.7
Average-size pension	26.5

Source: Argumenty i fakty, no. 45 (November 1993): 1.

majority of scientists and representatives of the world of culture and the arts. In this category, expenditures for food amount to 35–38 percent of total income.

The fourth group, made up of people with incomes of over 150,000 rubles per month, is extremely diverse. It consists of people who were able to adjust quickly to the new economic circumstances. In this group, which includes people with incomes of 1.5 million rubles per month and more, expenditures for food consume only 5–7 percent of total income.[7]

As it apparent from Table 24–2, there were significant income differentials between sectors. In some branches of industry, the average wage in the fall of 1993 was 320,000 rubles per month; in the oil and gas industry in Tyumen Oblast, a worker could earn as much as 500,000 rubles per month. By contrast, the highest salary in the state service was only 80,000 rubles per month.[8] The phenomena of income differentials and poverty are not new to Russia. In 1988, three years before the Soviet Union collapsed, 41 million people (14 percent of the Soviet population) lived below the poverty line.[9] While the pursuit of reform in postcommunist Russia during 1992–94 did not produce the catastrophic famines and

massive suffering that occurred at times under the Soviet regime, there was a substantial increase in the percentage of the population living at or below the poverty line.

According to the data provided by Khubulava, in the fall of 1993 more than one-third of the population of Russia (34–35 percent) fell into this category. Restructuring of the Russian economy, at least in the short run, produced a worsened situation for most consumers. Although in the major cities previously scarce or unavailable goods are in abundant supply, the decline in real wages and continuing inflation put them out of reach for most consumers. Indeed, reversing the pattern established during the Soviet period, many families were forced to spend a larger share of their income for food and to reduce their consumption of higher-priced meat, fish, milk, vegetables, and fruit, in favor of more bread and potatoes.[10]

While the advocates and opponents of "shock therapy" are still debating whether Russia had too much shock or too little, there is no question that the stabilization program pursued by Gaydar, well-intended though it was, given the economic and political conditions of Russia, did not work. In fact, it brought Russia close to hyperinflation: consumer prices rose 2,500 percent in 1992 and 847 percent in 1993. In 1994, to the surprise of many observers, the Chernomyrdin government made an attempt to return to the stabilization program. During the first half of 1994 inflation was held to below 90 percent, giving Russia a chance to reduce the increase in the consumer price index to 245 percent for the year. But this remarkable achievement was accompanied by steep declines (25–30 percent) in industrial production compared to the first half of 1993, as well as a significant rise in unemployment. In November 1994, Russia's gross domestic product was still declining by 16 percent compared to 1993, and its industrial production by 23 percent.[11] Nevertheless, the very austere anti-inflationary draft budget for 1995 submitted by the government to the State Duma on October 27, 1994, suggested that the Yeltsin administration was determined to stay the reform course. On November 14, 1994, the State Committee for the Defense Industry announced the speed-up of the privatization of 60 percent of Russia's nearly 2,000 defense plants and organizations.[12]

Unfortunately, the large-scale privatization of major state assets in Russia—more so than in other communist successor states—benefited primarily insiders, members of the former Soviet ruling class (the *nomenklatura*), and the mafia. If the deleterious consequences of "shock therapy" undermined the legitimacy of democracy in Russia, "nomenklatura privatization," probably more than any other single factor, destroyed what was left of it. Russians perceived correctly that only a small minority had profited from privatization and marketization, while the majority had to cope with a declining standard of living. According to the Russian Ministry of Labor and Social Affairs, in 1998 70 percent of all social transfer payments were made to the wealthiest 30 percent of Russian households. Given the bitter experience of Russia since 1992, it comes as no surprise that "the words 'democracy,' 'reforms,' and 'liberal' and the concepts and names associated with them have been discredited."[13]

Even before the conflict over Kosovo, Russian attitudes toward the United States, the West, and such institutions as the IMF had undergone a significant change. In the aftermath of the financial crisis in August 1998, Russians were much more inclined to accept government intervention in the economy and in social life, to believe in theories of a Western conspiracy against Russia, to blame the West and the IMF for the economic malaise of their country, and to follow those who advocate the idea of a special and unique path for Russia. Disenchanted with privatization, the market, democracy, and the whole "liberal experiment" of the Yeltsin regime, they feel that the dislocations they have suffered and the sacrifices they have made in pursuit of "economic reform" have been in vain. From their point of view, the only tangible result of the promised transition to a market economy and democracy has been the economic and political take-over of the country by thieves, criminals, members of the mafia, and corrupt politicians.

POLITICAL STABILITY

Although the Russian Federation continues to face enormous economic problems and challenges, the situation is not altogether bleak or utterly hopeless. As the data cited suggest, the formation of a new middle class is under way. In its present configuration, this new class can hardly be compared with its counterparts in the West. It does not yet play an integrating role; on the contrary, it is at present (and probably in the foreseeable future) an incipient new social class, whose economic behavior is likely to be perceived as being conducive to social disintegration. Much of the behavior of this class is, indeed, undesirable and—by the standards of the Western world—unacceptable. But, in part because of more than seven decades of Soviet rule, Russia did not produce the kind of middle class that emerged in Western industrial societies. And even if such a class existed in Russia today, it would be too "civilized" to be able to initiate the transition to a private market economy successfully. As one student of the transformation process in Russia has pointed out, "it is precisely the special sociopsychological attributes of the new Russian middle class distinguishing it from those in Western Europe that enable it to fulfill the role of the dynamic pacemaker of the private economy."[14] Still highly heterogeneous at this point in time, this new social stratum, it would seem, is nevertheless being welded into a social class by the conflict with its political and administrative opponents. In short, its growing political solidarity is the product of its struggle for economic survival. When judging the self-serving and frequently immoral behavior of this class, it should be kept in mind that, in seeking to either suppress or to exploit the reforms, its political opponents, including the authorities, are no less guilty of the violation of legal and moral norms.[15]

In assessing the prospects for the success of Russia's emerging new middle class, it is important to bear in mind that the formation of this class is likely to occur in a much shorter period of time than was the case in the West, where the emergence of the middle class, because of very different historical conditions, required several centuries. While the collapse of the Soviet Union undoubtedly released an enormous potential for political conflict, it also triggered the dissolution of its segmented social structure. Captivated as we are by the seemingly endless political turbulence in Russia during the process of its transformation, we frequently forget or overlook that, prior to its disintegration, the Soviet system, its shortcomings notwithstanding, had reached a rather high (though, admittedly, unbalanced) level of industrial development and produced a fairly sophisticated mix of "human capital." If this incipient new middle class has already made its imprint on post-communist Russia, it is not only because—having been prevented from achieving material prosperity and professional independence by more than seven decades of Soviet rule—it is highly motivated, but also because it is highly qualified, well educated, and professionally experienced. Russia's "human capital," in short, may have to be retrained to function in the condition of a market economy, but it does not have to be created.

A NEW RULING CLASS?

Part of the political reality of postcommunist Russia is that state employees, teachers, and university professors have suffered a decline in their social status. Aside from pensioners, they find themselves at the bottom of the income scale. As might be expected, this has made many of these members of the intelligentsia bitter opponents of the new course. Among other things, they are indignant about Article 43 of the new Constitution, which, while endorsing the basic right to free preschool, basic general, and secondary vocational education, does not extend this guarantee to higher education. This is viewed as a barrier to upward mobility and a means of assuring the self-perpetuation of the new upper strata capable of paying for a privileged education. It goes without saying that the alienation of this segment of the intelligentsia does not augur well for the future since, it would seem, a new democratic elite should develop, above all, from members of these professional groups.

Another source of concern is the fact that, unlike some of the former communist states in Eastern Europe, Russia has not had an elite change. The levers of power at the national, regional, and local level are, for the most part, controlled by members of the old Soviet elite—in short, by products of the nomenklatura system. Indeed, the argument has been made that "there are more and more reasons to speak of the transformation of the communist nomenklatura, which has accepted some outsiders in its ranks, into a new ruling class."[16]

The "survival" of large segments of the Soviet nomenklatura in Post-Communist Russia should come as no surprise. Along with the operators of the Soviet shadow economy, the Russian "mafia," only the members of the old nomenklatura had the necessary capital and political access to establish viable "private" enterprises. As the power structures of the Soviet Union weakened or collapsed, more and more members of the Soviet ruling elite sought to transform their political power into economic power, in other words, property. Having failed in their attempt to prevent the introduction of market reforms by relying on their monopoly of political power, they availed themselves of the opportunities of "privatization"—using their position, access, and influence to defeat their competitors in the struggle for property.

Whereas in China, and to some extent in Hungary and elsewhere in Eastern Europe, privatization occurred under state supervision, in Russia it began when the Soviet Union was already in an advanced state of disintegration, during a period of the weakening of state authority and political decentralization. The collapse of the Soviet empire disrupted the relations among the former Soviet union republics and had devastating economic consequences. The bitter power struggle between the friends and foes of reform—that is, the executive under President Yeltsin and the Supreme Soviet—not only made any political consensus impossible, but also led to uncertainty, unpredictability, and inconsistency with respect to the future of Russia and the fate of economic reform. The resulting contradictions in legislation were an open invitation for the penetration and expansion of criminal elements into business and politics. From the extreme degree of regimentation under Soviet rule, Russia plunged into the extreme of *bespredel* (literally, boundlessness): a state of anarchy, lawlessness, and "anything goes." Whatever the ethical dimensions of this state of affairs, there is no question that it constitutes fertile soil for the illegal accumulation of capital in the hands of potential entrepreneurs.

One of the effects of the unsuccessful coup in August 1991 was that it triggered a massive exodus of significant segments of the old elite, the nomenklatura, into the private economy. While these members of the nomenklatura did not become sudden converts to the market economy because they valued its intrinsic social merits, they nevertheless found it attractive because they could see the handwriting on the wall: The disintegration of the old Soviet order, the reduction of the state and party apparatus, the prohibition of the old-style Communist Party and other mass organizations affiliated with it, and the downsizing of the army posed an acute threat to their socioeconomic position and status. Before long, the number of defectors from the old nomenklatura ran into the hundreds of thousands. As the Soviet order collapsed, they found themselves almost ideally positioned to take advantage of the opportunities of the "transition" period. Within a relatively short period, they not only succeeded in demonstrating their acumen for management in the new conditions, but also developed a very different attitude toward the market economy. With the exception of the directors and managers of state industrial and agricultural enterprises, as well as conservative elements in the administrative bureaucracy, significant segments of the old nomenklatura have assumed a new socioeconomic and political role: They are now self-interested defenders of the market economy. Given their unique advantages in terms of personal connections to the relevant bureaucrats in the central and regional structures and their inside knowledge of the old system, including, in many cases, the criminal underworld, the "nomenklatura-privatizers" have proved most successful. To quote a Russian student of the subject:

> By the way, the manner of privatization practiced by the nomenklatura, proves to be by far the most successful. With the support from the ministries and the enterprise directors, which of course is not given without self-interest, numerous small enterprises have come into being, which organize production and sell it at free market prices, using in so doing the cheap manpower which the—in this regard privileged—state supply system puts at their disposal.[17]

Historically, the emergence of the middle class has always preceded the development of capitalism, and the existence of democracy is not a prerequisite for the formation of the middle class. As we have seen, there are at least some indications that Russia may follow this pattern. But the road from the planned economy to a market economy is likely to be difficult. For the time being, part of Russia's trade is handled through the market economy, but production for the most part still does not respond to market laws and signals. Russia, in short, has the beginnings of capitalism in trade and commerce, but it does not (yet) have industrial capitalism.

One of the main problems facing Russia is the lack of an effective legal system—an absolute prerequisite for a market economy, especially in a country where the respect for laws is low and the consciousness of law and justice is not highly developed. While a number of important framework laws on the protection of private property, consumer protection, and so on have been adopted, the Russian Federation thus far has not succeeded in breaking with the tradition of weak and ineffective implementation that was characteristic of both Soviet and prerevolutionary Russia.

PRESIDENTIAL-DEMOCRACY?

The 1993 Constitution was tailor-made for President Yeltsin; it was not designed to serve the long-term interests of the Russian Federation. It stands to reason, therefore, that his departure from the political arena may well trigger a battle for a new constitution and initiate a period of potentially great and prolonged political instability. Even if the constitutional order is not called into question in the foreseeable future, there are other problems.

The 1993 Constitution, as we have noted, reduces parliamentary supervision of the executive to insignificance. It is a document in which the principles of the constitutional order were dictated by the current political objectives of the executive. Thus, the 1993 Constitution not only continues the long tradition of executive dominance in Russian (and Soviet) politics, but is also unlikely to contribute to the democratization and long-term political stability of Russia. It should be noted that the Yeltsin administration has shown no sign of according a substantial political role to other institutions apart from the executive. In all probability, the unexpectedly strong showing of extremist forces in the December 1993 elections further undermined the idea of parliamentarianism in Russia. If we add to this the provisions of the 1993 Constitution and, some promising developments notwithstanding, that Russia still has no genuinely independent judiciary, that the press (with the consent of many journalists) is still used as an instrument of state propaganda, and that President Yeltsin has issued a number of decrees whose constitutionality is doubtful,[18] it becomes clear that the future of democracy in the largest country on earth is by no means assured.

Indeed, one of the chief dangers for Russian democracy arises precisely from the 1993 Constitution because it gives virtually authoritarian powers to the president. Even allowing for the circumstances that led to the confrontation between President Yeltsin and the old Russian "parliament" (the Supreme Soviet) and for the evident need for a strong executive during the period of transition politics, legitimate questions can be raised about the extent of presidential powers. As one observer has put the issue:

> Yeltsin's supporters assert that he is a democrat and that this is an extraordinary and transitional period. But even if one assumes that he is motivated only by what is good for Russia, should his successors, who may be less benign, have the unchecked power this Constitution accords a Russian President?[19]

Finally, it is by no means certain that the 1993 Constitution will be observed by the members of the Russian Federation. The republics of the Russian Federation whose constitutions violate the 1993 Federal Constitution—such as Yakutia (Sakha), Tatarstan, and Tuva—have not taken the necessary steps to modify them. What is more, on December 24, 1994—that is, after the adoption of the new federal Constitution—Bashkortostan adopted its own new constitution, some provisions of which violate the new Constitution of the Russian Federation. Indeed, when the final draft of that Constitution was published, the chairman of Bashkortostan's parliament let it be known that the republics would not surrender their sovereignty, regardless of the provisions of the new federal Constitution.[20] In the case of Tatarstan, a bilateral power-sharing treaty was signed between Russia and Tatarstan. While this treaty was a compromise and fell short of

recognizing the state sovereignty of Tatarstan, it nevertheless set a precedent and granted Tatarstan more privileges than those enjoyed by the other republics under the 1993 Constitution.[21] Thus, in the words of an astute Western observer: "The likely prospect for 1994 and 1995 is one of increasing powerlessness and instability of the center, with Russians struggling to survive in an increasingly regional framework"[22]—a prediction which proved to be valid beyond 1995.[23]

The regional framework of the Russian Federation is as diverse as Russia is large. In the 21 republics that make up the Russian Federation, the forms of government range from presidential autocracy (Kalmykia) to pure parliamentary rule without a president (Mordvinia). Some of the republics have experienced the same confrontation and mutual paralysis of the executive and the parliament that led to the political crisis in the fall of 1993 at the federal level.

There is a considerable range in the interpretation of sovereignty among the republics. Some have been engaged in the conduct of their own foreign policy, including the conclusion of treaties with states that are not part of the Russian Federation. The Republic of Tuva has developed close ties with Mongolia. The political party landscape is equally diverse. In a number of the republics, National People's Fronts are calling for the resurrection of their own non-Russian and pre-Russian traditions. In Kazan, for example, the anniversary of the subjugation of the Tatars to Russian rule by Ivan the Terrible in 1552 is now observed as a national day of mourning. Such demonstrations notwithstanding, new (or renewed) ties to Moscow have been forged. In the long run, however, the attempts of the federal government in Moscow to bind the regions to the center will be successful only if it is able to overcome its own political paralysis.

HUMAN RIGHTS
IN THE SOVIET UNION

Russia does not have a strong tradition with respect to the observance of human rights. Unfortunately, the Russian Revolution of 1917, despite its lofty ideals, did not improve this aspect of Russian life. On the contrary, the Soviet Union left to Russia an unenviable and probably unparalleled record of human rights violations. Indeed, in few, if any, areas of Soviet life was the discrepancy between theory and practice, ideological facade and political reality, as great as in the sphere of human rights.

The Soviet Union was always in the forefront of the nations advocating the drawing up of various human rights conventions. It signed and ratified the most important United Nations conventions on human rights,[24] as well as other international conventions of the ILO and UNESCO.[25] The Soviet Union also became a signatory to the Helsinki Accords—that is, the Final Act of the Conference on Security and Cooperation in Europe (CSCE), on August 1, 1975, which obligates all members to respect basic human rights, in particular those of "freedom of thought, conscience, religion or belief, for all without distinction as to race, sex, language or religion.[26] In addition, like earlier Soviet constitutional documents, the 1977 Constitution of the USSR, the last Soviet constitution, was studded with "guarantees" of the fundamental rights of Soviet citizens, including a "Bill of Rights" far more extensive and detailed than those commonly found in the constitutions of other states.[27]

But this impressive list of rights and freedoms was counterbalanced by the duties of the Soviet citizen, enumerated in the same chapter of the 1977 Constitution. Prior to the greater emphasis on the rule of law under Gorbachev, the elaborate "Bill of Rights" in the Soviet Constitution was practically negated by the provision that "the exercise of rights and liberties by citizens must not injure the interests of society and the state" (Article 39). In actual fact, the fundamental human rights guaranteed by the Soviet Constitution could be exercised only if, and as long as, they promoted "socialism" and the interests of the Soviet state, as defined by the CPSU, the sole legitimate political party of the Soviet Union (Article 6). The cause of human rights in the Soviet Union made a major advance when this article was revised and the Communist Party's legal monopoly of political power was abolished. In October 1990, the USSR Supreme Soviet approved a Law on Public Associations, which in fact legalized a multiparty system.

In practice, the position of the Soviet citizen with respect to human rights was not an enviable one. While the full-scale terror of the Stalin period was not revived, the Soviet leadership dealt harshly with individuals and groups who took Soviet constitutional guarantees at their face value or used the various international conventions signed and ratified by the USSR as a yardstick for measuring actual political practice in the Soviet Union.[28] Under Article 70 of the RSFSR Criminal Code (and analogous articles in the criminal codes of the other 14 union republics), "anti-Soviet agitation and propaganda," the circulation of "slanderous fabrications which defame the Soviet state and social system," and the circulation, preparation, or keeping of (slanderous) literature constituted a state crime, punishable "by deprivation of freedom" for up to 7 years, with or without additional exile for a term of 2 to 5 years."[29] It was this article under which Andrei Sinyavsky (Abram Tertz) and Yuli Daniel (Nikolai Arzhak) were tried and sentenced in 1966, becoming the first writers in the history of not only Russian but of world literature to be held criminally responsible in a court of law explicitly for what they had written.[30]

Prior to the legal reforms under Gorbachev, in addition to Article 70, Article 190–1 of the RSFSR Criminal Code (and its equivalent in the other union republics)—which prohibited the dissemination of deliberately false fabrications slandering the Soviet state and social system—turned the constitutional guarantees of free speech into a farce. Freedom of the press was effectively eliminated through a multitier system of censorship.[31] The constitutional guarantee of "freedom of assembly, mass meetings and street processions and demonstrations" was nullified by the provision in the criminal codes prohibiting the "organization or active participation in group activities, violating the public order" (Article 190–3), "participation in anti-Soviet organizations" (Article 72), and the "organization of mass disorders" (Article 79)—entailing a penalty of deprivation of freedom for a term of 2 to 15 years. Similarly, the constitutional guarantee of freedom of association was in effect negated by the organizational monopoly of the CPSU. In short, the only legitimate alternative open to the Soviet citizen who was intent upon exercising freedom of speech and assembly was to come out in support of the government and to march in officially sponsored parades (May Day, Anniversary of the Revolution, and the like).

Fundamental to the understanding of the treatment of human rights by the Soviet regime is the realization that this regime did not view a person as a free entity who is primordial to the state, but as a particular historical product of definite social relations and political goals. In the Marxist-Leninist perspective, the full freedom of the individual was relegated to the future—which is why the education of the New Soviet Man was regarded as the prime task of the Soviet state. The 1977 Soviet Constitution, therefore, did not recognize universal human rights, it did not recognize the concept of natural law and the existence of inalienable rights. Instead it proclaimed that "the Soviet people, guided by the ideas of scientific communism"—that is to say, by, through, and for the party—"establish the rights, liberties and duties of citizens . . . and proclaim them in this Constitution" (Preamble).

In the Marxist-Leninist view, in short, the individual had no meaning, no raison d'être, and no rights apart from the state. The state was antecedent to any rights, including fundamental rights, and was superior to the citizens of the USSR not only in terms of sovereignty, but also in a qualitative and value sense. For this reason, and because by definition the Soviet state, as a "socialist state of all the people," always represented and carried out the interests of the people, there could not be any legitimate challenge to the state on the part of a citizen or a group of citizens.

HUMAN RIGHTS
IN POST-COMMUNIST RUSSIA

If the observance of human rights suffered from too much state power and interference under the Soviet regime, it can be argued that in postcommunist Russia the problem has been the very opposite: a state too weak and too disorganized to be able to protect human rights—assuming that this would be one of its political priorities. Human rights, it seems, are a luxury of Western civilization few societies can afford, least of all Russia in its present state. Even if Russia were a country with a strong tradition of respect for human rights, their observance would probably become one of the first casualties in the prevailing conditions of social and economic anarchy and political instability.

Eight years into independence, many citizens of the Russian Federation are dispirited, disenchanted, hopeless, and indifferent to political life. In the 1993 election and the referendum on the new Constitution, nearly half of the electorate failed to vote. Much of the country seems to be in the grip of nostalgia of one sort or another: for the order of the Stalin period, for the slowly but steadily rising standard of living of Brezhnev's rule, for the days of military glory and superpower status, for the lost empire that for centuries was its identity. With a diaspora of 25–30 million of their countrymen living in what are now "foreign lands" or the "near abroad," with the collapsed economy, the threat of nuclear accidents, ecological nightmares, the day-to-day uncertainty, and no sense of direction, it is no wonder that large segments of the Russian population yearn for the security of the Soviet past. But in the case of Russia, in particular, nostalgia for the past is no fertile soil for democracy and the observance of human rights. One measure of the depth of Russia's present crisis is the degree to which the intelligentsia, which served as the self-appointed conscience of the people and the defender of human rights in both prerevolutionary and Soviet Russia, has seemingly become insignificant.

It should be noted, however, that the 1993 Constitution no longer serves as an instrument for the limitation of human rights and the control of political dissent, or, more generally, the enforcement of conformity by all citizens. Unlike the constitutions of the Soviet era, the 1993 Constitution of the Russian Federation explicitly links human and civil rights and freedoms to the "recognized principles and norms of international law" and affirms categorically that "basic human rights and freedoms are inalienable" (Article 17). Moreover, these rights are recognized as belonging to all persons, not only to citizens. All in all, the new Constitution, in its human rights provisions, spelled out in 48 provisions (placed prominently near the beginning), is on a level with those found in modern democratic constitutional states.[32]

The problem is that Russia has not been able to develop the kind of political culture that is necessary to support the now existing constitutional framework. As has already been mentioned, even President Yeltsin, whose personal imprint is clearly visible in the new Constitution, has violated its provisions on a number of occasions. Furthermore, even if the political leadership of Russia were determined to observe the provisions of the new Constitution, it would not succeed: the rights guaranteed by the Constitution exceed the present (and likely future) capacity of the government. Many of the provisions, especially those relating to the guarantee of housing, social security, health care, education, and "a decent environment," are clearly beyond its reach.[33]

Moreover, the Russian Federation has yet to develop an effective system of law enforcement. Widespread crime and corruption at all levels of the government, the army, and the police have followed in the wake of the collapse of the Soviet Union. Today Russia is "a kind of strategic capital of organized crime from where all the major operations are launched."[34] Its mobsters are into everything, from arms sales (including nuclear material) and banking (including drug-money laundering) to drug traffic, prostitution, and so on. Corruption is rampant and the government seemingly helpless—unwilling or unable to deal with the problem. No wonder that many Russians have become completely disillusioned with "democratization" and the "market." Having earlier been bombarded with Soviet propaganda about the evils of Western democracy and capitalism, they are now gaining first-hand experience about the excesses of capitalism.

It is in these conditions that President Yeltsin and his team during 1992 and most of 1993 tried to create, simultaneously, a market economy and a democratic political system, as well as a civil society to support both—a virtually impossible task, especially considering that the continuing problems with the economy and the nostalgia for the past exhibited by many Russians put a potentially lethal weapon into the hands of his opponents. As a result, President Yeltsin and his supporters faced a difficult choice: Adhere to the norms of democracy and risk that Russia will become a victim of the anarchy that increasingly reigned supreme, or "act decisively," that is, postpone the establishment of a civil society to the indefinite future. But the choice of a transitional regime involving some variant of "guided democracy" or "enlightened authoritarianism," with the focus on the concentration of power in the executive this would entail, also meant the possibility and danger of a drift into dictatorial or iron rule—the traditional mode of "government" in Russia, a return to Russia's "habits of the heart."[35]

As it turned out, such an authoritarian government was written into the 1993 Constitution, which bears President Yeltsin's personal imprint and reflects the political culture of both of the elite and the people. In the aftermath of the 1993 parliamentary election, President Yeltsin increasingly abandoned the pursuit of democratization and turned to the national-patriotic forces for political support. During 1994 he pursued a hardline course of protecting Russian national interests vis-à-vis the CIS countries and the West aimed at the reconstitution of a "sustainable empire." The war against Chechnya not only turned the political spectrum in Russia upside down, but also made clear that Russia, at least for the time being, had reversed course and returned to its historical moorings. In domestic politics, this meant the pursuit of the consolidation of power by the center vis-à-vis the regions and republics; in foreign policy, this meant a determined effort to salvage the empire—albeit in a different form and guise. Unfortunately, little progress has been made in dealing with Russia's first and foremost problem: The transformation of ethnic diversity into civic loyalty as the defining element of Russian identity.

As Russia approached the end of President Yeltsin's second term in office, it remained a country of paradoxes, combining dynamic changes with continuity and inertia, successes in some areas with crisis, collapse and stagnation in others, democratic institutions with a highly authoritarian presidency, and the explicit recognition and guarantee of human rights in the Constitution with the persecution of individuals trying to exercise those rights. After nearly a decade of independence, the institutional foundations of political pluralism in Russia—the rule of law, the acceptance and observance of a democratic constitution by the government, the elites, and society, a popularly elected legislature, an independent judiciary, and civilian control of the military—remain very much in flux.

While Russia has had numerous elections, including one presidential and 3 parliamentary elections, they have not produced a change of power at the national level or a significant change in the nature and composition of the new ruling elite. According to data of the Institute of Sociology of the Russian Academy of Sciences, more than 75 percent of the political elite and 61 percent of the economic and business elite come from the ranks of the former Soviet nomenklatura. The corresponding figures for the regional and local elites are even higher since they were less affected by the transformation process.[36] In view of this high degree of elite continuity, it comes as no surprise that the second term of President Yeltsin was marked by a gradual restoration of the ancien regime—including increasing restrictions on the media, the establishment of a new media ministry,[37] the enlistment of the security services to enforce election rules in 1999, and much greater tolerance of fascists and antisemites—leaving the future of Russia very much in doubt.

Furthermore, in the case of Russia, the elections have thus far not encouraged the development of an effective multiparty system; the electoral process in 1996 and 1999 was less free, fair, competitive and transparent than it was in 1990. Even more disturbing is the fact that, in the aftermath of the August 1998 crisis, the certainty of elections once again became a subject of discussion. While the 1999 parliamentary election was in fact held, the all-important presidential election scheduled for June 2000 was derailed by President Yeltin's resignation—a clever and self-serving political maneuver that not only allowed his chosen successor, Vladimir Putin, to become acting president and to gain an enormous advantage in the presidential election (now moved up to March 2000) but also revealed the continued existence of a mindset among the governing elite that focuses on the importance of holding on to power by any means rather than on the acquisition of the legitimate right to rule through free, fair, and competitive elections. This does not augur well for the future of democracy in Russia. A peaceful transfer of power in the presidential election originally scheduled for June 2000, on the other hand, would have been unprecedented in Russia's more than thousand-year

history and perhaps would have marked the beginning of constitutionalism and the rule of law.

NOTES

[1]Ronald J. Hill et al., "The USSR: The Revolution Reversed?" in Leslie Holmes, ed., *The Withering Away of the State* (London: SAGE Publications, 1981), pp. 197–222.

[2]Günther Wagenlehner, "Abschied vom Kommunismus: Zu Fragen der Ideologie auf dem XXIV. Parteitag," *Osteuropa*, 31, no. 9–10 (September–October 1981): 769–781.

[3]N. Khubulava, "My i nashki dokhody," *Argumenty i fakty*, no. 44 (November 1993): 1.

[4]G. Valyuzhenich, "Chtob vam zhit' na odnu zarplatu" [Interview with Russian Minister of Labor G. Melik'yan], *Argumenty i fakty*, no. 47 (November 1993): 4.

[5]At the end of 1993, the minimum amount of state assistance given to the needy was 8,000 rubles per month (ibid).

[6]N. Khubulava, "Bednyye my, bednyye . . . ," *Argumenty i fakty*, no. 45 (November 1993): 1.

[7]These data were taken from the two articles by Khubulava, cited above.

[8]"Paradoks: zarplata rastet, zhiznennyy uroven' padayet," *Argumenty i fakty*, No. 45, (November 1993) p. 1.

[9]Rene Ahlberg, "Armut in der Sowjetunion," *Osteuropa* 40, no. 12 (December 1990): 1159–1174. See also Mervyn Matthews, *Poverty in the Soviet Union: The Life-Styles of the Underprivileged* (Cambridge: Cambridge University Press, 1986), and Nick Eberstadt, *The Poverty of Communism* (New Brunswick, NJ: Transaction Books, 1988).

[10]In the Soviet period, the proportion of income spent for food declined from 53.8 percent in 1940 to 31.7 percent in 1980 for industrial workers and from 67.3 percent to 35.9 percent for collective farmers during the same period. See Roger A. Clarke and Dubravko J. I. Matko, *Soviet Economic Facts* 1917–81, 2nd ed. (London: Macmillan Press Ltd., 1983), pp. 51–52.

[11]*The Economist*, November 19, 1994, p. 120. The figure cited is for the third quarter 1994.

[12]*Interfax*, November 14, 1994.

[13]"What Went Wrong in Russia? The Roots of the Economic Crisis," *Journal of Democracy*, April 1999, pp. 68–69.

[14]Rene Ahlberg, "Soziale Aspekte des Transformationsprozesses: Sozialstruktur und Marktwirtschaft in Russland," *Osteuropa* 44, no. 5 (May 1994): 435.

[15]See L. A. Belyayeva, "Sredniy sloy rossiyskogo obshchestva: Problemy teniya sotsial'nogo statusa," *Socis*, no. 10, 1993.

[16]Liliya Shevtsova, "My umudrilis' otvratit' narod ot demokratii eshche do togo, kak ona nastupila," *Literaturnaya gazeta*, December 12, 1993, p. 11.

[17]Belyayeva, "Sredniy sloy rossiyskogo obshchestva," p. 19.

[18]For example, in appointing Anatoliy Chubays, chairman of the State Committee for the Management of State Property, as deputy prime minister, and in giving former Minister for Nationalities and Regional Affairs Sergey Shakhray special status in the government, President Yeltsin exercised

prerogatives that, under the 1993 Constitution, belong to the prime minister.

[19]Margot Light, "Democracy Russian-Style," *World Today,* no. 12 (December 1993): 231.

[20]*Kommersant-Daily,* November 9, 1993.

[21]Elizabeth Teague, "Russia and Tatarstan Sign Power-sharing Treaty," *RFE/RL Research Report* 3, no. 14 (April 8, 1994): 19–27.

[22]Peter Reddaway, *International Herald Tribune,* January 10, 1994.

[23]On this issue, cf. Vladimir Shlapentokh, Roman Levita, Mikhail Loiberg, *From Submission to Rebellion: The Provinces Versus the Center in Russia* (Boulder, CO: Westview Press, 1997).

[24]Along with all other members of the UN General Assembly, the USSR became a signatory to the International Covenant on Civil and Political Rights and the International Covenant on Economic, Social and Cultural Rights of December 16, 1966, after it had earlier (December 10, 1948)—along with the East European communist countries, Saudi Arabia, and the Republic of South Africa—abstained in the vote on the Universal Declaration of Human Rights.

[25]Among these are: (1) The International Convention on the Elimination of All Forms of Racial Discrimination (1965); (2) The International Convention on the Political Rights of Women (1953); and (3) a number of ILO Conventions dealing with forced labor (1930), freedom of association (1948), equal pay for men and women (1951), and discrimination in employment and profession (1958). It might be added that the Soviet Union was quite willing, in fact eager, to put its signature to all sorts of substantive declarations and covenants on human rights, but steadfastly refused to agree to any procedures for verifying compliance with such covenants—using the principle of noninterference in internal affairs as justification.

[26]For the text of the Final Act of the CSCE, see *State Department Bulletin,* September 1, 1975, pp. 323–349.

[27]For the text of the 1977 Soviet Constitution, see Robert Sharlet, *The New Soviet Constitution of 1977: Analysis and Text* (Brunswick, OH: King's Court Communications, 1978), especially pp. 89–96 (Articles 39–69).

[28]The best known of these were the groups set up during 1976–77 in Moscow, Kiev, Latvia, Lithuania, Tbilisi, and Armenia to monitor Soviet compliance with the Helsinki Accords.

[29]See H. J. Berman, *Soviet Criminal Law and Procedure: The RSFSR Codes* (Cambridge, MA: Harvard University Press, 1966), p. 180.

[30]For the relevant documents, see Max Hayward, *On Trial: The Soviet State vs. "Abram Tertz" and "Nikolai Arzhak"* (New York: Harper & Row, 1967).

[31]See Peter Hübner, "Aspekte der Sowjetischen Zensur," *Osteuropa* 22, no. 1 (January 1972): 1–24.

[32]For the text of the 1993 Constitution, see Foreign Broadcast Information Service, *Daily Report: Eurasia,* FBIS-Sov-93-216, November 10, 1993, pp. 18–37.

[33]For a commentary, see Klaus Westen, "Die Verfassung der Russischen Foederation," *Osteuropa* 44, no. 9 (September 1994), especially pp. 813–819.

[34]Luciano Violante, chairman of Italy's parliamentary committee of inquiry into the mafia, cited in David Remnick,

Lenin's Tomb: The Last Days of the Soviet Empire (New York: Vintage Books, 1994), p. 537.

[35]On the "temptation of a superpresidential system," cf. Sergei Moiseev, "Iskushenie superprezidentskoi sistemy," *Pro et Contra,* Vol. 3 (Summer 1998), at: http://pubs.carnegie.ru/p&c/Vol3-1998/3/05moiseev.asp.

[36]See Sergei Khenkin, " 'Partiia vlasti': rossiiskii variant," *Pro et Contra,* vol. 1 (Fall 1996), at http://pubs.carnegie.ru/p&c/Vol1-1996/1/03henkin.asp.

[37]On July 7, 1999, President Yeltsin set up a Ministry of the Press, Television and Radio Broadcasting, and Mass Media Communications, which was immediately dubbed "Minpravdy" in Russia and thus compared with George Orwell's "Ministry of Truth."

RUSSIA: SELECTED BIBLIOGRAPHY

David Bender and Bruno Leone, eds., *The Breakup of the Soviet Union: Opposing Viewpoints* (San Diego, CA: Greenhaven Press, 1994).

Timothy J. Colton and Robert Legvold, eds., *After the Soviet Union: From Empire to Nations* (New York: W. W. Norton & Company, 1992).

Robert V. Daniels, *The End of the Communist Revolution* (London: Routledge, 1993).

Robert V. Daniels, ed., *Soviet Communism from Reform to Collapse* (Lexington: D. C. Heath, 1995).

Karen Dawisha and Bruce Parrot, eds., *The End of Empire? The Transformation of the USSR in Comparative Perspective* (Armonk, NY: M. E. Sharpe, 1997).

Harry Eckstein et al., *Can Democracy Take Root in Post-Soviet Russia? Explorations in State-Society Relations* (Lanham, MD: Rowman & Littlefield Publishers, 1998).

Michael Ellman and Vladimir Kontorovich, eds., *The Destruction of the Soviet Economic System: An Insider's History* (Armonk, NY: M. E. Sharpe, 1998).

Marshall I. Goldman, *What Went Wrong with Perestroika* (New York: W. W. Norton & Company, 1992).

Barbara B. Green, *The Dynamics of Russian Politics: A Short History* (Westport, CT: Greenwood Press, 1994).

Stephen Handelman, *Comrade Criminal: Russia's New Mafiya* (New Haven, CT: Yale University Press, 1995).

Bohdan Harasymiw, *Political Elite Recruitment in the Soviet Union* (London: Macmillan Press, 1984).

Erik P. Hoffmann and Robin F. Laird, eds., *The Soviet Polity in the Modern Era* (New York: Aldine Publishing Company, 1984).

Ilpyong Kim and Jane Shapiro Zacek, eds., *Establishing Democratic Rule: The Reemergence of Local Governments in Post-Authoritarian Systems* (Washington, DC: In Depth Books, 1993).

Charles King and Neil J. Melvin, eds., *Nations Abroad: Diaspora Politics and International Relations in the Former Soviet Union* (Boulder, CO: Westview Press, 1998).

David Lane, ed., *Russia in Flux: The Political Consequences of Reform* (Brookfield, VT: Edward Elgar Publishing Company, 1992).

John Lowenhardt, *The Reincarnation of Russia: Struggling With the Legacy of Communism, 1990–1994* (Durham, NC: Duke University Press, 1995).

Martin Malia, *The Soviet Tragedy: A History of Socialism in Russia, 1917–1991* (New York: The Free Press, 1994).

Mervyn Matthews, *Privilege in the Soviet Union: A Study of Elite Life-Styles under Communism* (London: George Allen & Unwin, 1978).

David Remnick, *Lenin's Tomb: The Last Days of the Soviet Empire* (New York: Random House, 1993).

T. H. Rigby and Bohdan Harasymiw, eds., *Leadership Selection and Patron-Client Relations in the USSR and Yugoslavia* (London: George Allen & Unwin, 1983).

Lilia Shevtsova, *Yeltsin's Russia: Myths and Reality* (Washington, DC: Carnegie Endowment for International Peace, 1999).

David K. Shipler, *Russia: Broken Idols, Solemn Dreams* (New York: Times Books, 1983).

Vladimir Shlapentokh, et al., *From Submission to Rebellion: The Provinces Versus the Center in Russia* (Boulder, CO: Westview Press, 1997).

Konstantin Simis, *USSR: The Corrupt Society: The Secret World of Soviet Capitalism* (New York: Simon and Schuster, 1982).

Gordon Smith, ed., *State-Building in Russia: The Yeltsin Legacy and the Challenge of the Future* (Armonk, NY: M. E. Sharpe, 1999).

Hedrick Smith, *The New Russians* (New York: Random House, 1990).

Wista Suraska, *How the Soviet Union Disappeared: An Essay on the Causes of Dissolution* (Durham, NC: Duke University Press, 1998).

Roman Szporluk, ed., *National Identity and Ethnicity in Russia and the New States of Eurasia* (Armonk, NY: M. E. Sharpe, 1994).

Vladimir Tismaneanu, ed., *Political Culture and Civil Society in Russia and the New States of Eurasia* (Armonk, NY: M. E. Sharpe, 1995).

David T. Twining, *The New Eurasia: A Guide to the Republics of the Former Soviet Union* (Westport, CT: Praeger, 1993).

Stephen White et al., *How Russia Votes* (Chatham, NJ: Chatham House Publishers, Inc., 1997).

Daniel Yergin and Thane Gustafson, *Russia 2010 and What It Means for the World* (New York: Vintage Books, 1995).

Part V: Japan

Chapter 25

Japan's History
and Political Culture

Japan, or Nippon (literally, "Land of the Rising Sun"), differs from all the other countries discussed in this volume in that it is actually an archipelago consisting of more than 3,000 islands stretching some 2,000 miles off the coast of northeast Asia. Four of the islands—Honshu, Hokkaido, Kyushu, and Shikoku—account for 98 percent of the country's land area. All in all, Japan is slightly smaller than California or one and one half times as large as Britain.

In terms of ethnic divisions, Japan's population of about 126 million[1] is remarkably homogeneous. The Japanese account for 99.4 percent of the population. The only significant and distinct ethnic minority group consists of some 600,000 Koreans, who were brought to Japan as laborers between 1910 and 1945. Japan is as highly urbanized as the United States. In 1995, only slightly more than one-fifth of the population in both countries was classified as rural.[2] Most Japanese observe both Shinto and Buddhist rites. About 10 percent belong to other faiths, most of them being members of the "new religions," which incorporate elements of Shintoism, Buddhism, Taoism, and Christianity. A small pro-

portion of the population (about 1 percent) is Christian.[3]

The terrain of Japan is mostly rugged and mountainous: more than two-thirds of the land is forest and woodland, and only 13 percent is arable; irrigated land accounts for 9 percent of the land use; permanent crops, meadows and pastures—for another 2 percent. Japan has many dormant and some active volcanoes and in any given year experiences approximately 1,500 seismic occurrences (mostly tremors). Because of its geological environment, Japan is prone to suffer from so-called *tsunami,* great sea waves produced by submarine earth shifts or volcanic eruptions.

Compared to the other industrial giants, Japan is not well-endowed with respect to natural resources. Thus, for example, only about 3 percent of the required iron ores are mined in Japan itself. In terms of this important industrial input alone, Japan is dependent on imports—from Australia, India, Malaysia, the United States, Canada, and the Philippines. In energy sources too, Japan depends heavily on imports. In 1995, for example, it produced primary energy equivalent to 2,230,000 barrels of oil per day, but consumed

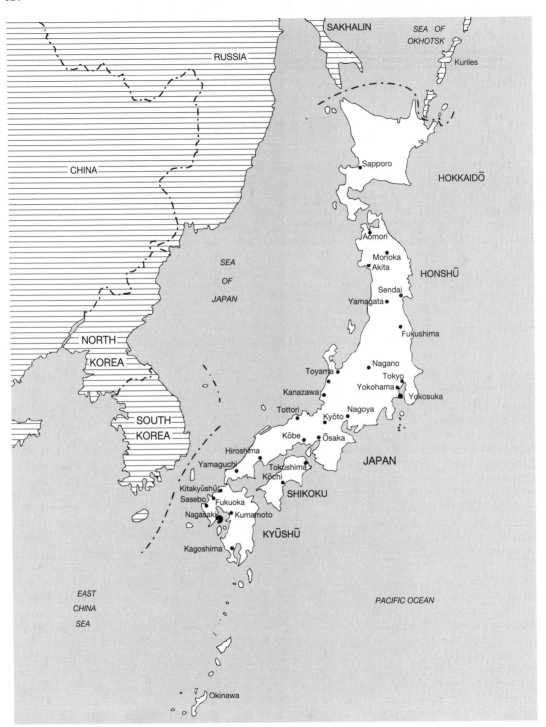

JAPAN

energy equivalent to 9,945,000 barrels per day, more than four times as much.[4] With acute shortages of major industrial raw materials and fossil fuels, the Japanese economy, like that of Germany, is dependent on imports. In 1991, for example, fuels and other energy sources accounted for 23.3 percent of total imports; raw materials for 14 percent. Thus, more than one-third of the total imports of Japan in 1991 consisted of basic economic inputs, including petroleum, bauxite, cobalt, manganese, chromium (100 percent each), platinum group metals (98 percent), copper (92 percent), and primary energy (80 percent). Of the United States, the European Economic Community (EEC), the USSR, and Japan, Japan in 1991 was the least self-sufficient in terms of fuels and raw materials, while the USSR was the most. With a few key exceptions—primary energy, petroleum, and iron ore—the profile of Japanese net imports as a share of consumption is remarkably similar to that of the EEC.[5]

Awareness of the comparatively disadvantageous position of Japan with respect to natural resources makes its economic performance even more impressive. With only 2.3 percent of the world's population in 1992, Japan accounted for 10 percent of the world's gross national product (GNP)—a performance that put Japan in third place behind the United States and the EEC (23 percent). In terms of other aggregate data, too, the performance of Japan has been outstanding. In 1989 this East Asian island nation led the developed world in real economic growth, but by 1996 had fallen behind China, South Korea, Singapore, Indonesia, India, Thailand, Philippines, and Pakistan in Asia. In terms of total GDP, Japan ranked third (after the United States and China) and, as Table 25–1 indicates, it also ranked third in terms of per capita GDP (after Luxembourg and the United States).

Japan is of great interest to the student of comparative politics not only because of its intrinsic importance as an economic superpower that has overtaken Germany and Canada in terms of GNP, is closing the gap in per capita GNP that still separates it from the United States, and is able to compete successfully with the leading industrial states, especially in a number of high-technology areas. Japan is the only example of a highly industrialized "mature" society in Asia. It is often

Table 25–1 Comparative Economic Performance, 1996

Country	Real Growth in %	Per Capita GNP in 1996 US
Luxembourg	NA	$33,200
United States	2.4%	28,500
Canada	1.5	20,800
Japan	3.7	23,800
Germany	1.4	20,000
France	1.5	21,700
United Kingdom	2.1	20,100
India	6.5	1,500
Singapore	7.0	22,900
China (Taiwan)	5.7	13,200
South Korea	7.1	12,800
Russia	–6.0	4,500
China (PRC)	9.7	3,200

Source: Central Intelligence Agency, *Handbook of Economic Statistics, 1997* (Washington: U.S. Government Printing Office, 1997) pp. 16, 17, 18, 20.

looked upon as a successful model for development, whose experience perhaps foreshadows what may happen in other Asian countries now undergoing industrialization, secularization, and democratization. If, indeed, there are Chinese and Indian paths to modernization, there is also a Japanese path—and it has arguably been the most successful thus far. Indeed, it is sometimes argued that the future political landscape of Asia is likely to depend on the outcome of the competition between these different patterns of modernization.

From this perspective, the historical significance of Japan lies in the fact that it was the first non-Western country to achieve modernization. Moreover, within four decades after it embarked on the road to political modernization and industrialization, it successfully challenged the Russian Empire with technically advanced weapons. Japan's victory in the Russo-Japanese War of 1904–05 not only effectively checked the continuous territorial expansion of the Russian Empire for the first time since Ivan the Terrible and helped trigger the 1905 revolution, but also sent shock waves through Asia. For the first time since the sixteenth century, an Asian country had inflicted military defeat on a major European power. As a result, a "thrill went through Asia"—and due note was taken of the fact that Japan's method of assimilating European techniques to fight Europe had proved successful.[6]

THE HISTORICAL BACKGROUND

Modern Japanese political history is usually dated from 1867–68, that is, from the Meiji Restoration that ended the Tokugawa Shogunate (1603–1867), the most effective and lasting system of national government in Japanese history. Like China, Japan has a very ancient culture, one that existed for many centuries in isolation and without an effective central government. Chinese sources of the first century A.D. refer to Japan, the Empire of Wo (Japanese: *Wa*), as consisting of more than 100 separate states. These states became eventually unified under the Yamato Court, with the *tennō* (emperor of heaven) at its center.

The Yamato Court reached its peak in the early fifth century and then went into rapid decline—in part the result of the breakaway of the Korean states that had been under the control of Japan, which deprived the court of substantial revenues (tribute). It was during the declining years of the Yamato Court that Buddhism was introduced from Korea—an event of great importance for the cultural and political development of Japan.

The multifaceted problems of the Yamato Court led to reform efforts by the imperial family—efforts inspired by the ideas of Taishi Shotoku, the crown prince who became the new ruler. Shotoku established Buddhism as the state religion, adopted Chinese administrative institutions, and promulgated a code of 17 government articles, sometimes referred to as the "17 Articles Constitution" of 604. The constitution set forth the ideals of the state, conceptualized as consisting of three human elements (the ruler, his ministers, and the people), and clearly defined their respective rights and duties; it stipulated rules for human conduct; and it provided a theoretical foundation for the position of the emperor and Son of Heaven as the absolute and divinely legitimated sovereign. It thus established the pattern of a centralized state, headed by a single ruler, and set the important precedent of a kind of basic law for the nation.

For a variety of reasons, however, the actual authority of the imperial house deteriorated substantially and, especially beginning in the ninth century, was increasingly undermined by the rising influence of feudal and aristocratic systems, more or less effectively controlled by various warrior groups, especially after the latter part of the twelfth century. It was not until 1603, after a period of protracted civil violence called the "warring states" period, that Ieyasu Tokugawa established the political ascendancy of his house and succeeded in laying the foundation for a more effective national government and more central control. Even this system, however, was a far cry from a modern centralized political system. Between 1603 and the Meiji Restoration in 1867–68, Japan, in effect, went through a long period of "centralized feudalism"—a delicately balanced system in which prime political authority was exercised by a shogun (a military governor), who shared power with more than 250 feudal lords (*daimyō*) controlling approximately three-fourths of the national territory. The contours of the modern Japanese political system emerged from the relatively rapid disintegration of this peculiar system of "centralized feudalism" in the mid-nineteenth century—a process which reflected not only domestic factors, but also Japan's response to an increasingly competitive international environment.

THE MEIJI RESTORATION AND THE BIRTH OF THE MODERN STATE

Les extremes se touchent (extremes meet), the French say. This adage aptly characterizes Japanese civilization under the Tokugawa Shogunate, precariously balanced as it was between seemingly polar opposites: the moral ideal of the warrior *(samurai)* with its emphasis on Spartan rigor versus the undisguised indulgences of the Floating World; the official isolation from the outside world versus the intense curiosity about and interest in *yogaku* (Western learning) and *rangaku* (Dutch learning); the personal, hereditary ties of the Japanese feudal order versus the clearly apparent contours of bureaucratic administration in the more than sixty clan fiefdoms into which

Tokugawa Japan was divided; the separation between economic power and political power—which made it possible for the generally despised class of merchants to prosper, while the traditionally more prestigious and superior warrior and peasant classes suffered increasing hardships; and the holy but powerless sovereign, surrounded by elaborate ritual and ostensibly revered as the source of all authority, versus the shoguns who actually controlled power and ruled the country with the help of their officials, soldiers, and spies.[7]

This uneasy equilibrium of extreme opposites, maintained with great difficulty by the shogun, explains why the appearance of Commodore Perry's black ships in 1853–54 could become the fuse for the subsequent explosive transformation of Japanese society. Japan had been under external pressure to end its isolation and open itself up for commerce since the end of the eighteenth century—from the Russians in the north and later from the British, who came to East Asia from the south. Furthermore, the British subjugation of China in the Opium Wars (1839–42) and the dispatch of a joint Anglo-French fleet to Canton (1857) to force the Chinese to open their markets to Western commerce were object lessons that were not lost on Japan.

Not by preference or free choice, but in the face of massive naval strength, the Japanese decided to act on the recommendations of American missions in the 1850s: The long era of isolation was ended, and henceforth Japan would participate in international trade and diplomacy. Once the concept of a competitive international society had been adopted, a widespread consensus emerged concerning the necessity of building national strength in order to avoid falling behind in this competition. A rapid and far-reaching process of selective Westernization got under way almost immediately.[8]

The series of events that led to Japan's successful response to the challenge of the West is known as the Meiji Restoration. In many respects, the designation "restoration" is a misnomer: Mutsuhito, who ascended the imperial throne in 1867 at the age of 15 and adopted the reign name of Meiji (literally, "enlightened rule"), did not regain the absolute powers claimed by his eighth-century ancestors, who had ruled by right of divine descent. In short, there was no "restoration" of an emperor with total power over the

state. On the contrary, the Meiji Restoration resulted in the establishment of yet another powerful oligarchy, military in origin and character, and divided by regional loyalties. Led by Koin Kido, Takamori Saigo, Kaoru Inoue, Tosimichi Okubo, Tomomi Iwakura, Hirobumi Ito, Aritomo Yamagata, Masayoshi Matsukata, and Shigenobu Okuma—men who were capable of rising above the limitations of sociocultural background and education—this new ruling group launched and guided Japan on the precarious path to modernization. If the modernization of Japan in the second half of the nineteenth century proved to be uniquely successful, it was due in no small measure to the capable leadership of these men, who at a critical point in its history subordinated their regional interests, class privileges, and loyalties to national considerations, recognizing the paramount importance of a powerful and industrialized Japan.

At the same time, the Meiji Restoration was more than a palace coup. Although it was not attended by a massive shift in the basis of political power, protracted civil violence, a reign of terror, or the sudden appearance of new elites, its long-term implications and consequences were profoundly revolutionary. The complex four-level system of social stratification, consisting of samurai, peasant, artisan, and merchant—part of the legacy of Japan's feudal past—was abolished, along with the special rights and privileges of the samurai, the traditional land tenure system, and the Tokugawa fiefs. The feudal structure of clan power was destroyed and political decision making was centralized. The military power of the feudal lords (daimyō) was broken and replaced by a modern conscript army under the command of the central government. In 1871, feudalism was declared officially abolished; the approximately 300 fiefs were turned into 72 prefectures and 3 metropolitan districts—a number later reduced by one-third. Mass publication and modern industrial technology were introduced, as well as a professional bureaucracy to serve the rapidly growing needs of the state.

When the leaders of Japan in the 1870s and 1880s developed the country's modernization strategy, they studied the American and European experience, in general finding the example of Germany to be most relevant. Nevertheless, the modernization of Japan did not follow the patterns observed in Europe. For one thing, the role of the state was much greater and more critical in the modernization of Japan than in any European country. Moreover, there was a close connection between modernization and considerations of military power.[9] In these respects, there are some interesting parallels in the modernization patterns in Japan and in Imperial Russia and, more recently, the Soviet Union. However, in contrast to the policies adopted in the Soviet Union, the Japanese permitted and even encouraged a far-flung network of small entrepreneurs who operated within the framework of traditional artisan and family relationships. For another, while the Japanese adopted Western techniques of machine production and followed the example of the West in the codification of civil and criminal law, they kept their socioeconomic organization largely intact. It was in part for this reason that the successful industrial modernization in Japan was not accompanied by a democratic revolution; in this important respect, the course of Japanese history differed from that of Europe.

As elsewhere, the modernization process in Japan produced a good deal of stress and tension. Even if pre-Meiji Japan had been a more unified society not burdened with the legacy of its feudal past and had faced a less complex international environment, the scope, rapidity, and success of the Japanese drive for modernization alone would have produced considerable tension and conflict, both internally and externally. In the case of Japan, the tensions and conflicts that developed were severe both at home and abroad. While a consensus emerged about the necessity of national unification in the face of foreign military superiority, the pursuit of this goal proved to be divisive. The debate over the problem of modernization, in particular over the abandonment of Japan's long-standing policy of isolation from the outside world, polarized Japanese society into those who were determined to resist foreign demands and influence, if necessary by force of arms, and those who perceived the country's future to require its opening to the world and its participation in international trade and commerce.

The polarization and ambiguity of Japanese society during the mid-nineteenth century were reflected in the growing antagonism between the Imperial Court in Kyoto and the Tokugawa shogun; in the extremism and prolonged violence during the closing years of the Tokugawa era; and in the contradictions and conflicts of the Meiji era, expressed most graphically in a series of armed revolts, the last and greatest of which took place in 1877 and was led by Takamori Saigo, who had played a key role in the formation of the new government.[10]

A pattern of psychological polarity and abrupt changes in behavior, however, was woven into the fabric of Japanese culture long before the policy of isolation was abandoned in 1854.[11] The fascination with the accomplishments of other cultures and civilizations was usually followed by the equally intense repudiation of foreign influence, leading once again to seclusion and self-imposed isolation. Beginning in the sixth century A.D., the Imperial Court began to assimilate many features of Chinese civilization, and later on the Portuguese and Dutch were given an enthusiastic reception. But in every case there followed a period in which there was intense emphasis on Japanese identity and uniqueness. In this century, there have been sharp reversals in Japanese attitudes toward the United States and other foreign countries.[12] Japan, indeed, is a nation that has demonstrated an intense need for the preservation of its own separate identity, on the one hand, but has been driven by a variety of circumstances into prolonged periods of contact with foreign cultures, on the other.

If the confrontation of Japan with the technologically superior West in the nineteenth century evoked a uniquely successful response, part of the reason is that the assimilation of Western ideas and techniques was facilitated by prior historical experience, in particular by the fact that for more than a thousand years Japan had intermittently borrowed a great deal of its higher culture and technical skills from China. The selective adoption and adaptation of foreign cultural elements was nothing new in the history of Japan. The descendants and cultural heirs of generations of Sinophile Japanese, inspired by the example of their ancestors, easily became ardent proponents of Westernization—and in so doing conformed to the ways of their forefathers. One of the unique aspects of Japanese modernization, therefore, is that among the motivations that prompted and sustained it was also a peculiar ideological conservatism.

Another interesting characteristic of Japanese modernization has to do with the way it was effected. As has been indicated, the Meiji Restoration took the form of a reactionary *coup d'état,* carried out by young samurai who wished to "revere the emperor" and "drive out the barbarians." It was this group, whose members had little practical experience in government and administration, that launched the industrial modernization of Japan. The purpose of opening up the country to foreign trade and the influx of Western technology was to enable Japan to resist and ultimately to repel foreign influence. Massive and rapid as the process of modernization was in the case of Japan, the pattern was highly selective, focusing as it did on industrial and military technology but leaving the traditional, distinctively Japanese social hierarchy and organization largely intact.

This had two important consequences. First of all, the maintenance of the traditional patterns of deference in the relations between the various ranks and classes in society made it possible for a relatively small group of determined leaders to carry out a fundamental reorganization of the military and economic institutions within a single generation—and to interpret these sweeping changes as traditional in motivation. Second, the maintenance of social discipline through the renewed cultivation of traditional values, myths, and symbols made possible rapid institutional transformation. At the same time, it was the radical institutional changes, engineered and guided by a group of progressive leaders dedicated to building the strength of the country, which undergirded the ideological stability of Japan. The pattern of modernization in Japan thus turned out to be the very opposite of that observed in China, where rapid and frequently violent ideological changes developed against a background of a relatively impervious institutional structure.

SOCIOECONOMIC DEVELOPMENTS IN MEIJI JAPAN

The feudal lords and the samurai who overthrew the shogunate in 1867 and carried out the sweeping institutional changes collectively referred to as the Meiji Restoration were by no means advocates of popular sovereignty and democracy in the Western sense. Motivated, in the case of the feudal lords, by long-standing clan enmities against the Tokugawa regime, and in the case of the samurai by growing dissatisfaction with their declining social and economic status, they were deeply concerned about the threat to Japan's security posed by the West. Accordingly, fear of the West decisively shaped the contours of Japanese nationalism and Japan's response to the challenge of modernization, resulting in a highly instrumental concept of Westernization. Generally speaking, Westernization in Japan proved to be less disruptive than in China and elsewhere because the Japanese were much more successful in maintaining their spiritual and political independence.

The new ruling oligarchy proceeded from the view that Western strength was a function of (1) national unity, which itself was perceived as the product of constitutionalism; (2) industrialization, which was seen as the source of economic and material strength; and (3) a well-trained, modern national military establishment. It is this analysis of the sources of Western power that served as the point of departure for the major policies enacted during the Meiji period.

Thus, the Japanese military establishment was fundamentally reorganized and a European-style army was established—a process that not only deprived the samurai of their traditional monopoly of military service, but also entailed the successful transition from a system of traditional deference hierarchies based on status and social origin to one based on officeholding. As a consequence, the military became a very important channel for upward mobility: The sons of peasants, through professional accomplishment, could now attain a status previously reserved to hereditary samurai. Ironically, with the large influx of peasants into the new imperial army, this institution became an important channel for the expression of the interests and sentiments of the rural population, and thus in a way a potential democratic force.

In terms of industrialization, the Japanese during the Meiji era wrote the first chapter in what was to become a remarkable success story. As a matter of fact, a good many prerequisites for economic development had been created during the three centuries of Tokugawa rule—an economic system encompassing the whole country, a rather effective network of transportation and communications, and a measure of consciousness with at least some common elements. To these beginnings, the Meiji regime added modern means of transportation and communications, a modernized school system, including compulsory primary education, newspapers and other publications, a streamlined financial system, and a modern taxation and production system. By the time of World War I, thanks to the development of modern industry and transportation, Japanese manufactures were able to compete successfully with European and American products everywhere in the Far East. During the interwar period, the Japanese developed and expanded their commercial operations and penetrated markets all over the world. Along with a competitive civilian economy, there rapidly emerged a powerful industrial base capable of supporting a modern army, navy, and air force. Indeed, by the turn of the century Japan had emerged as a major military power and, like Germany, was prepared to pursue the building of an empire.

POLITICAL DEVELOPMENTS IN THE MEIJI ERA

In political terms, the Meiji era was characterized by a great deal of experimentation. During this period a limited number of educated Japanese became acquainted with the political ideas and systems of the West. Not surprisingly, a good many of them, including the members of the ruling oligarchy, showed a distinct preference for the authoritarianism of the Prussian state and the ideas championed by the Austro-Prussian school of constitutional law. In the perception of the ruling elite, the Prussian model seemed to fit more harmoniously into the traditions of Japan and offer the best guarantee of the development of national unity and strong leadership. On the other hand, among the dissidents, the liberal ideas of the West found a stronger echo.

The rapid and massive assimilation of Western ideas and techniques led inevitably to internal tensions and contradictions. The creation of a modern state presupposed, among other things, the successful completion of the nation-building process—that is, the replacement of local and regional with national loyalties. In particular, the goal of a strong, unified state required the prop-

agation of new loyalties among the masses, which had remained inarticulate and powerless in traditional Japan and thus effectively outside the political process. Utilizing a revival of Shinto, the state cult, the Meiji regime elevated a bureau of Shinto to the highest position in the new political hierarchy and tried to undermine the influence of Buddhism through renewed emphasis and greater prominence of national deities. Samurai loyalty, the traditional heritage of the ruling class, was integrated in public education as a value for the masses. The Imperial Rescript on Education (1890) set forth the basic lines of Confucian and Shinto ideology, which came to define and undergird the moral content of Japanese education. Loyalty to the emperor, whose exalted position was perceived from the perspectives of Confucianism and Shintoism, became the center of the new citizen's political outlook.

The Meiji era was a seminal period in Japanese history. It continued the crucial transition from reliance on the sword as the weapon for settling political disputes to reliance on the written and spoken word, which during the preceding two centuries, under the "Pax Tokugawa," had slowly transformed the samurai into administrators. After 1877, armed revolts were replaced by political party movements. In the 1870s, adherents of the "liberal" perspective organized the first political parties in Japan, responding to the rise of popular political movements that were themselves reflections of the struggles and conflicts within the Meiji regime. The "liberals" not only challenged the political dominance of the ruling oligarchs, but also voiced demands for limited suffrage, more representative government, and a national assembly. Thus, the Meiji period was crucial not only in defining the political agenda of the nation for years to come, but also in setting the tone and style of political competition. Indeed, the authoritarian and the liberal traditions, which have dominated modern Japanese politics, have their source in the Meiji period.[13]

THE MEIJI CONSTITUTION OF 1889–1890

The crowning achievement of the Meiji regime, in many respects, was the Meiji Constitution. Drafted and ratified in secret, promulgated as a token of imperial benevolence in 1889 and put into effect in 1890, some 2,550 years after the legendary founding of the Japanese state, it constituted the legal basis and framework of government and politics in Japan until 1945. Although not particularly conservative by the standard of the time, it contained a good many undemocratic features and reflected a balance of imperial power and constitutional forms inspired by the example of Germany. While representing an overture to modern government and constitutionalism, the Meiji Constitution clearly betrays the overriding concern of its authors with the maintenance of effective control and leadership.

Thus, in 1884, five years before the Meiji Constitution was promulgated, a European-style peerage was organized as a counterweight to the popularly elected Diet. The government leaders, military commanders, and former feudal lords (daimyō) were given titles and thus qualified for a seat in the House of Peers. In 1885 a cabinet system was set up, followed in 1888 by the establishment of a privy council designed to judge and safeguard the Constitution. Rights and freedoms were granted "except as regulated by law." Amendments could be made only upon imperial initiative. Under the Constitution, the emperor was "sacred and inviolable"; he was commander of the military; and he could dissolve the Diet at will. Clearly, the legislative and judicial organs were subordinated to the executive, which could always claim to represent the will of the emperor.

The Constitution having taken the form of a benevolent grant of the emperor, the government created by it rested on what the Japanese call *kokutai*—a theory of the state which viewed the emperor, as the successor of an unbroken line of divinely descended ancestors, as the embodiment of the Japanese state, and thus placed him at the very center of the concept of the state. The theory of kokutai regarded the emperor as the ultimate source and sole repository of all power—legislative, executive, judicial, administrative. As a lineal descendant of the sun goddess, the emperor also had supreme spiritual authority, being the central figure in Japan's State Shinto cult.[14] Viewed from this perspective, the theoretical thrust of the Meiji Constitution is in the direction of an extreme and—for modern times—even unique degree of political centralization.

Thus, in theory the "restoration" of Imperial power in Meiji Japan went very far indeed. But as so often in life, and especially in politics, there was considerable divergence between theory and practice. The theory of kokutai notwithstanding, in practice the real powers of the emperor were dispersed among those who were supposed to serve him—the prime minister and the cabinet, military leaders and administrators, the bicameral legislature, the dual system of judicial and administrative courts, and the increasingly professional and elitist bureaucracy.

In reality, the role of the emperor was in many ways similar to that of the institution of the monarchy in Britain. The emperor served as an important basis and source of legitimacy, from time to time supporting, justifying, and legitimizing the institution of government in general, as well as specific government policies, through ritual and the divine aura of the imperial house. Furthermore, he served as an important symbol of national identification and continuity. In fact, in the case of Japan, it can be argued that the modern state, to a considerable extent, was built on the traditional symbol of the emperor and imperial power.

Clearly, the purpose of the Meiji Constitution was not to establish a democratic system of government; on the contrary, it was designed to make possible the continuation of authoritarian rule in modern form. The real intent of the Constitution was revealed in the limitations it placed on the legal powers of the Diet, in the almost total lack of local autonomy, in the division of legislative authority between the bicameral legislature and the cabinet, which in emergency situations could rule by executive order and decree, and in the Constitution's failure to address the most important reality of Japanese politics, viz. the traditional and continuing excessive reliance on clan loyalties, as well as family and local ties. In these respects, the Constitution proved to be very much the creature of its framers, who had a high personal stake in the perpetuation of authoritarian rule.

Nevertheless, the Meiji Constitution also contained a number of democratic provisions in the area of popular rights and representation. More specifically, the Constitution gave much greater scope to political dissent than had existed previously; citizens enjoyed greater freedom of association and religious belief than ever before. Jointly with the House of Peers, whose members were appointed, the elected Diet had the power to initiate and pass legislation, approve the national budget, in particular increases in military spending, levy taxes, and subject ministers to questioning. Most important, from the outset the Meiji leaders found the Diet more intractable than they had anticipated; in spite of their power of dissolution, their resources for bribery, and their capacity for intimidation, they experienced considerable difficulty in manipulating and controlling the Diet. Before long it became apparent that the Constitution had in fact changed the political landscape and altered at least some of the rules of the game of politics.

The long-term significance of the Meiji Constitution lies in the fact that it had a number of unanticipated consequences. As time passed, the importance of clan loyalties declined, the traditional social hierarchy became less rigid, and the electorate was expanded through the reduction of the tax qualification in 1900 and 1920 and the establishment of universal male suffrage in 1925. The political process became more complex and competitive. Gradually, a slow process of liberalization got under way that ultimately resulted in a significant transformation of the institutions created by the Meiji Constitution. Thus, although deliberately designed to serve as an instrument for the perpetuation of authoritarian rule in a modernized Japan, the Meiji Constitution, it turned out, also created a legal and institutional framework conducive to the emergence of political liberalism.

POST-MEIJI JAPAN, 1890–1945

The years immediately following the adoption of the Meiji Constitution were characterized by an intense struggle for power between the government leaders and the party leaders in the Diet. The first cabinets sought to establish the principle that the government represented the emperor's will, that it should remain aloof from the parties, and that it was the duty of the Diet to approve the proposals and requests of the government. The party leaders, on the other hand, determined to expand their power and patronage, fought for cab-

inets responsible to the Diet. This contest was an important aspect of the larger struggle between the authoritarian tradition in Japanese politics and an emerging parliamentary tradition with pro-toliberal elements.

Vying for position and power in post-Meiji Japan, in addition to the Meiji oligarchs and their successors, as well as the party leaders, were a number of other important groups: the increasingly powerful, professionalized, and distinct military, who at times were powerful enough to break a Cabinet; the higher stratum of the civil service (bureaucracy); the *zaibatsu,* the big business magnates, who cooperated with both the civilian and the military oligarchs, rewarded government officials with sinecure positions when they retired from public service, and after World War I began to develop close alliances with the most important conservative parties, becoming an important source of campaign funds for them; and the modernized hereditary nobility created in 1884, many of whose members held influential posts at the Imperial Court, in the House of Peers, or on the Privy Council, an important advisory body to the emperor.

Against the background of frequent changes in the political roles and allegiances of these leadership groups, the growing differentiation of the civilian and military leadership along functional lines and away from clan lines, the increasing professionalization and social diverseness of the bureaucracy, the close association of the zaibatsu with the government and later with the major conservative political parties, and the expanding franchise (from 500,000 voters in 1890 to 14,000,000 in 1925), the party leaders gradually increased their power vis-à-vis the civilian and military leaders, the bureaucracy, and the nobility. The years 1924 to 1932 in particular gave rise to the hope that eventually liberalism would triumph in the great struggle between the authoritarian and the liberal forces in Japanese society—a struggle of which the Meiji Restoration was but an expression.

However, there was to be no "liberal" triumph. While the expansion of the electorate and the rise of the political parties, among other things, resulted in the widening of political participation and a broader base for the conduct of public affairs, the parties themselves remained rather conservative in their ideologies, self-centered and narrow in their perspectives, insensitive to large segments of public opinion, and frequently even irresponsible. But in the mid-1920s the Japanese political parties were only a little over 30 years old and thus, as political institutions go, still in their infancy. They did not differ substantially from Western political parties at a comparable stage of development. Moreover, given the centuries-long authoritarian tradition in Japan, it was a foregone conclusion that "liberalism" would first be embraced as an instrument in the struggle for power, rather than as an end in itself. Nevertheless, at the University of Tokyo liberal ideas were championed by Dr. Sakuzo Yoshino, the organizer of student and intellectual circles called *Shinjinkai* (new Peoples Associations), a name that symbolized the determination of its members to break with tradition. Professor Tatsukichi Minobe, one of Japan's most distinguished constitutional theorists and legal scholars, in 1910 advanced the so-called *organ theory,* the idea that the Emperor was not the sole source of sovereignty, but merely one, though the highest, organ of the state. It is indicative of the political realities of the 1920s and 1930s in Japan that both men eventually were forced to resign from their positions. Professor Minobe, then a member of the House of Peers, was violently attacked for his 25-year-old theory in the Diet, driven out of public and academic life, and subjected to personal assault.

These events foreshadowed the authoritarian resurgence that was to come in the years between 1932 and 1945. Faced with widespread economic problems at home and abroad, corruption and irresponsibility in the zaibatsu-dominated Diet, the threat of "subversion,"[15] and the prospect of declining influence in world affairs due to an ineffective foreign policy, Japan once again returned to its mainstream political traditions. With military and ultranationalist forces in ascendance, the "liberal" interlude came to an end. The steady deterioration and rapid disintegration of the country's democratic institutions suggest something about the fragility of their structure and the shallowness of their roots.

After a series of plots, assassinations, revolts, and attacks on leading statesmen, the major political "players"—the party leaders, the zaibatsu,

Table 25–2 Japanese Losses in World War II

Casualties (military and civilian)	1,800,000
Civilians (killed, wounded, or missing)	668,000
National wealth	25%
Residential housing	20%
Industrial capacity	30%
Shipping	80%
Thermal power-generating capacity	47%
Prewar territory (some only temporarily)	46%

Source: Robert E. Ward, *Japan's Political System* (Englewood Cliffs, NJ: Prentice-Hall, 1978), p. 17.

the elder statesmen *(genro),* and imperial advisers—made an unsuccessful attempt to salvage the situation, turning for support to the emperor, the imperial court, and even the military. But in the end they were forced to capitulate and to accommodate themselves to the dominant role of the military. Thus, within a surprisingly short time, parliamentary government fell under the blows of terrorism and the nationalist ambitions of junior military officers.

Japan's pursuit of empire and its involvement in World War II resulted not only in defeat and enormous human and material losses (see Table 25–2), but also brought with them the increased regimentation of society. Higher taxes, massive conscription, government regulations affecting peasants and industrial workers, consumers and producers had an impact on the lives of virtually all the people. The political parties were dissolved to form the "Imperial Rule Assistance Association." Thus, ironically, by increasing political awareness, interest and involvement in government and politics, the return to authoritarianism helped pave the way for the far-reaching democratic reforms imposed by the Supreme Commander for the Allied Powers (SCAP) after the war.

DEMOCRACY IN MODERN JAPAN

It is sometimes argued that the imposition of democratic reforms by the Allied Powers is the only real reason for the development of democracy in postwar Japan. While the role of the Allied Powers no doubt was a major one, it alone can hardly explain the successful emergence of democratic government in modern Japan. Indeed, the "miracle" of "Japan's transformation in less than a century and a half from a full-fledged feudal land into a firmly based, exemplary democracy"[16] calls for a more cogent explanation.

In trying to find the answer to this problem, it is important to recognize that the Japanese cultural and political heritage is very complex and, along with a strongly entrenched authoritarian tradition, also included a number of democratic impulses and elements. Thus, while Japanese feudalism gave rise to such ideal values as the absolute obedience of the inferior status groups and granted unlimited authority to the superior lords, it also emphasized the legal nature and mutuality of feudal rights and obligations. Moreover, in reality a highly complex structure of interrelationships emerged between lords and followers. To be sure, one looks in vain for any concept of inalienable rights, but from their Confucian heritage the Japanese derived a strong sense of the importance of ethics as the basis for government, which was conducive to the development of relatively high standards of honesty and efficiency in political administration.

Furthermore, along with the problem of modernization or Westernization, it is the great struggle between the authoritarian and the anti-authoritarian tradition that has been a central theme in modern Japanese history. While the Meiji leaders of the mid-nineteenth century did not seek to establish a democratic polity in the Western sense and regarded democracy as neither appealing nor necessary, but rather perceived it as a means to an end—the establishment of a strong centralized Japan—they did in fact introduce certain democratic institutions that fundamentally changed the nature of Japanese political development. Devastated, defeated, and demoralized, postwar Japan was able to look back to its prewar democratic experience. In a tradition-conscious society, this greatly facilitated the acceptance of democratic institutions imposed by a foreign power.

In the difficult enterprise of building a democratic government and society, the Japanese political experience and heritage had other valuable things to offer. In contrast to other non-Western countries, most of whom had to overcome divisions based on religion, ethnicity, and/or language, Japan brought to the problem of modernization and nation-building a strongly developed sense of unity—a product of its relative isolation, its extraordinary homogeneity, and its centuries-long tradition of political centralization. As one Western scholar has pointed out, the sharp conflict between the Japanese ideal of uniform and centralized political rule and the feudal realities of local autonomy and class divisions created internal tensions in nineteenth-century Japan that opened the door to the introduction of changes, including the development of democratic ideas and concepts.[17]

In developing the important concept and practice of power sharing, the Japanese could draw on their own long tradition of group leadership—the institution of the *genro* (elder statesmen) being just one example. Indeed, among modernizing nations Japan is unique because of the absence of a single leader. Finally, modernization and political development in Japan were facilitated by an effective bureaucracy, the presence of a highly developed entrepreneurial spirit, and a high level of literacy. The Japanese cultural heritage and political tradition were by no means devoid of elements conducive to modernization and democratization when a Western-style democracy was imposed by General Douglas MacArthur at the end of World War II.

The political culture that has evolved in Japan since 1945 recognizes, on the one hand, the importance of consensus as the traditional guiding principle of political life, but, on the other, has given rise to increasingly pervasive conflicts in Japanese politics—conflicts between individual politicians, between interest groups and political parties, between small and large business, and between politicians at the local and the national level. In short, the political culture of contemporary Japan contains both a "competition-conflict-fragmentation dynamic" and a dynamic that seeks to contain and constrain conflict through negotiation, consultation, and coordination. Taking issue with the view of Japanese politics as highly centralized and integrated, a recent study suggests that the postwar Japanese political system is best understood as a form of "bargained distributive democracy," in which political power is horizontally "fragmented and pluralistic" and the style of political competition reflects "native cultural preferences" . . . best described as "an amoral groupism." In this Japanese style of political competition, "conflict is endemic, [and] potentially very intense," at times defying any attempt at resolution through customary mechanisms. At the same time, such conflict takes place within the context of a political culture that places a high value on the routinization and institutionalization of political processes, conflict reduction, and compromise.[18]

NOTES

[1]This figure is an estimate made by the (Japanese) Statistics Bureau at www.stat.go.jp/1602.htm. (2/9/1999).

[2]"Britannica World Data," in *1998 Britannica Book of the Year* (Chicago: Encyclopaedia Britannica, 1998), pp. 631, 735.

[3]Ibid., p. 631.

[4]Meyers *Enzyklopaedisches Lexikon* (Mannheim/Vienna/Zurich: Lexikonverlag: 1980), vol. 13, p. 64; CIA, *Handbook of Economic Statistics,* (Washington, DC: U.S. Government Printing Office, 1993), 1997, pp. 91, 92.

[5]CIA, *Handbook of Economic Statistics,* 1993, p. 140.

[6]A. Lobanov-Rostovsky, *Russia and Asia* (Ann Arbor: George Wahr Publishing Company, 1951), pp. 235ff.

[7]See Edwin O. Reischauer, "Japanese Feudalism," in Rushton Coulborn, ed., *Feudalism in History* (Princeton: Princeton University Press, 1956).

[8]For an insightful discussion of the emergence and nature of modern Japanese nationalism, see Masao Maruyama, *Thought and Behaviour in Modern Japanese Politics* (London: Oxford University Press, 1969), pp. 135ff.

[9]When the spuriousness of the Tokugawa slogan *sonno-joi* (Revere the Emperor! Drive out the Barbarians!) was exposed in the 1850s, it was replaced by the slogan *fukokukyohei* (Rich country, strong arms).

[10]On the modernization of Japan and the Meiji era, see Marius B. Jansen, *Changing Japanese Attitudes Toward Modernization* (Princeton, NJ: Princeton University Press, 1965); Donald Shively, ed., *Tradition and Modernization in Japanese Culture* (Princeton, NJ: Princeton University Press, 1974); George M. Beckmann, *The Making of the Meiji Constitution* (Lawrence: University of Kansas Press, 1957).

[11]See Ruth Benedict, *The Chrysanthemum and the Sword* (Boston: Houghton Mifflin 1946), and Robert N. Bellah, *Tokugawa Religion: The Values of Pre-Industrial Japan* (Glencoe, IL: The Free Press, 1947).

[12]The recent much-discussed book by Akio Morita and Shintaro Ishihara, *The Japan That Can Say "No": The New U.S.–Japan Relations Card* (Kobunsha: Kappa-Holmes, 1989), translated by the U.S. Department of Defense, among other things, is a modern manifestation of this cultural trait. Excerpts were published in *Congressional Record* 135, no. 159 (November 14, 1989): E3783–E3798.

[13]See Robert E. Ward, *Japan's Political System* (Englewood Cliffs, NJ: Prentice-Hall, 1978), p. 11.

[14]Ibid., pp. 11–12. On present-day conceptions of kokutai, see Edwin O. Reischauer, *The Japanese Today: Change and Continuity* (Cambridge, MA: Harvard University Press, 1988), pp. 241, 243.

[15]Under the peace preservation laws of 1928, a special police corps was set up to investigate "dangerous thoughts." Similar laws passed earlier declared labor unions to be subversive and thus illegal and made it a crime to advocate a basic change in the political system. See Frank Langdon, *Politics in Japan* (Boston: Little, Brown, 1967), pp. 43, 48; Reischauer, *The Japanese Today,* p. 97.

[16]Reischauer, *The Japanese Today,* p. 231.

[17]Ibid., p. 233.

[18]Bradley Richardson, *Japanese Democracy: Power, Coordination, and Performance* (New Haven and London: Yale University Press, 1997), pp. 7–8, 240 ff.

Chapter 26

The Social Setting
of Japanese Politics

The transformation of the Japanese polity from a military dictatorship in 1945 into a "democracy" within a relatively short period of time, when viewed against the background of the history of Japan, in particular its political tradition, constitutes no less of a "miracle" than the economic recovery and development of Japan and its emergence as a leading technological and financial power, "the Asian challenge," as it came to be called in the 1990s. Even a superficial examination of the contemporary political system in Japan, however, reveals that, although inspired by the classical Western models, Japanese democracy has developed into a distinctive style of government and politics. A parliamentary democracy in structure and form, the modern Japanese polity has evolved into "a highly centralized system, overseen by a powerful bureaucracy and carefully regulated according to detailed law codes and myriad bureaucratic rulings."[1] Accordingly, modern Japan offers many striking contrasts and unique features in its constitutional structure and political processes—reflections of the historical and cultural forces that have shaped its development over the centuries. Japan indeed is a country in which "the historical legacy is evident not

so much in the forms of government, which are completely western in outward appearance, but rather in the spirit that moves the machinery of government."[2]

In addition to historical factors and cultural traditions, a political system also expresses and mirrors the particular social characteristics of the population—ethnic and religious composition, social and class structure, literacy and education, social and political mobility, wealth and income distribution, degree of urbanization, and so on. The social characteristics of a population have important implications for the power structure in a political system and help define the political agenda of a government. In postwar Japan, for example, private interests and the government have been merged in a unique relationship involving a degree of complexity and intimacy not commonly found in the Western democracies.

POPULATION AND ECONOMY

Growing at a rate of 0.4 percent and outpacing earlier projections, the Japanese population reached 125,506,492 in mid-1995.[3] As is

Table 26–1 Population Growth, Selected Industrial Countries, 1960–93 (Million Persons at Midyear) and Rate of Growth (1993 Estimate)

Country	1960	1970	1975	1980	1985	1990	1995[a]	Rate
Japan	94.1	104.3	111.6	116.8	120.8	123.5	125.5	0.32
United States	180.7	205.1	216.0	227.8	238.5	249.9	263.8	1.02
Germany[b]	72.5	77.8	78.6	78.3	77.7	79.4	81.3	0.26
France	45.7	50.8	52.8	53.9	55.2	56.7	58.1	0.46
United Kingdom	52.4	55.6	56.2	56.3	56.6	57.4	58.3	0.27
Italy	50.2	53.7	55.6	56.5	57.1	57.7	58.3	0.21

[a]Figures for 1995 are estimated.
[b]Includes the population of both eastern (former GDR) and western (former FRG) areas.

Source: Central Intelligence Agency, *Handbook of Economic Statistics, 1989* (Washington, DC: U.S. Government, 1989), pp. 44–45; ibid., 1993 ed., p. 32; Central Intelligence Agency, *The World Factbook 1995* (Washington, DC: U.S. Government, 1995), pp. 145, 159, 211, 215, 440, 443.

apparent from Table 26–1, the population of Japan is not quite half as large as that of the United States, but considerably larger than the population of Germany or even the combined populations of France and Britain. In terms of population dynamics, Japan ranks ahead of Britain, Germany, and Italy, but behind the United States and France.

Like Italy, France, and Germany among the industrial countries, and Korea among the East Asian nations, Japan is ethnically exceptionally homogeneous. With only a small minority (0.6 percent), consisting of Koreans, Chinese, and Americans,[4] Japan has had the rare and important advantage of not having to contend with the problems of ethnic politics, which have complicated the process of modernization and political development in so many other societies. Among the politically important consequences of ethnic homogeneity, reinforced by geographical isolation, history, and language, have been the development of a strong nationalism, an intense sense of ingroup identification against the foreign outsider, and the desire and ability to present a united front to the outside world.

But if it has been spared the divisiveness of ethnic conflict, Japan has faced other problems. First and foremost among these is population pressure—a problem, as it turns out, that predates modern Japan. Already during the Tokugawa shogunate (1600–1868), Japan had to support an increasing population for some 200 years.[5] As it

entered the modern period, Japan experienced rapid population growth. In 1872, when the first modern registration system was adopted, the population was reported at about 35 million. During the next 50 years, it increased by 65 percent, reaching 56 million in 1920; by 1936, it stood at 70 million. In short, the Japanese population doubled in 64 years! While not as explosive as the population growth experienced by some of the less developed countries in the twentieth century (see Table 26–2), this population increase put a severe strain on the available resources. The problem in a nutshell, to quote an American expert, is that "Japan is land-poor, resource-poor, and overpopulated."[6]

During World War II, Japan experienced setbacks in its population growth. However, in the postwar years Japan had its version of the baby boom. With the birth rate exceeding that of the prewar period, Japan added more than 17 million people to its population between 1945 and 1955. This was more than the total population of Argentina in 1950, or more than three times the population of Switzerland.[7]

If population growth in Japan during the postwar period proved to be more dynamic than had been predicted, this was not due to rising birth rates. As a matter of fact, after the initial postwar marriage boom, birth rates decreased sharply from 25.6 births per 1,000 population during 1950–52 to 16.8 in 1961 and 11.0 in 1990—a rate below that of the United States, France, and the

Table 26–2   Population Growth, Selected Less Developed Countries, 1960–95
(Million Persons at Midyear)

Country	1960	1970	1980	1985	1990	1995[a]
Iran	21.6	28.9	38.8	46.6	57.0	64.6
Mexico	38.6	52.2	68.7	76.6	85.1	94.0
Nigeria	51.1	49.3	65.7	74.7	86.6	101.2
Pakistan	50.4	65.7	85.2	99.3	114.8	131.5
Philippines	28.6	38.7	50.9	57.6	64.4	73.3
South Korea	24.8	32.2	38.1	40.8	43.2	45.5
Thailand	27.5	37.1	47.0	51.8	56.2	60.3

[a]Figures for 1995 are estimated.

Source: Central Intelligence Agency, *Handbook of Economic Statistics, 1990* (Washington, DC: U.S. Government, 1990), p. 51; ibid., 1993 ed., p. 33; Central Intelligence Agency, *The World Factbook 1995* (Washington, DC: U.S. Government, 1995), pp. 202, 232, 279, 313, 324, 338, 414.

United Kingdom. The population increase reflected, above all, a dramatic improvement in public health care, which resulted in an even more rapid decrease in the death rate as well as a lower infant mortality rate. Indeed, in 1995 Japan led not only the United States, but also France, Germany, and the United Kingdom in terms of high life expectancy and low infant mortality. Contrary to earlier expectations, Japan at present seems to be headed for a major population decline. With an estimated total fertility rate (TFR) of only 1.39 in 1998, it was well below the 2.1 TFR required to maintain the population at its present level and thus joined the European countries, most of which (Italy, Spain, and Germany in particular) also have remarkably low birth rates and face the prospect of population decline in the foreseeable future. With Japan's under-19 population at its lowest level since the 1920s and its male labor force already shrinking, it seems certain that demographic factors will play an important role in Japanese politics in the twenty-first century. If predictions of a population decline by half (or even more) in the next century are at all accurate, Japan's exclusive culture, which thus far has allowed only a trickle of immigrants, will come under enormous pressure once again, especially if the present negative net migration rate (−36 migrants/1,000 population in 1998) continues.[8]

Since about 1950 there have been some important qualitative changes in the population of

Japan. Whereas in the prewar period the average age of the population declined (due to the increasing proportion of the population under the age of 15 and the decreasing number of old people over 65), these trends were reversed in the postwar period. As a result, in the more recent past Japan has had to deal with the problems of an aging population, the problem of generating employment for a rapidly growing working age group, the provision of increased social services—in short, issues familiar to the student of Western political systems.

Age-related issues are likely to become even more important in the years ahead. Today Japanese men and women have the longest life expectancy in the world, and the Japanese population is aging at a faster rate than any other nation. While earlier in this century, Japan was a country with a relatively young population (the average age in 1920 was 26.7!), today 18.5 million Japanese—almost 15 percent of the population—are 65 or older. If current demographic projections are correct, in the year 2000 Japan will become the country with the highest proportion of senior citizens. What is more, sometime during the first quarter of the next century, Japanese who are 75 and older will outnumber senior citizens in the 65–74 age group.[9]

As is apparent from Table 26–3, among the major industrialized nations of the world Japan has the highest population density. In Western Europe, only the population of the Netherlands

Table 26–3 Population Density, Selected Countries, 1997

Country	Area (Sq mi)	Rank	Population	Rank	Density (Sq mi)
China	3,696,100	3	1,227,740,000	1	332.2
India	1,222,559	7	967,613,000	2	791.7
United States	3,679,192	4	267,839,000	3	72.9
Indonesia	741,101	16	199,544,000	4	269.3
Brazil	3,286,488	5	159,691,000	5	48.4
Russia	6,592,800	1	147,231,000	6	22.3
Japan	145,883	61	126,110,000	8	864.5
Germany	137,847	62	82,143,000	12	596.0
United Kingdom	94,241	79	58,919,000	19	625.1
France	210,026	49	58,616,000	21	279.1
Canada	3,849,674	2	30,287,000	33	8.5
Netherlands	16,163	134	15,619,000	56	1,193.6
Belgium	11,783	139	10,189,000	73	864.4

Source: 1998 Britannica Book of the Year (Chicago: Encyclopaedia Britannica, 1998), pp. 555 ff., 756–760.

is more densely settled. In Asia, such countries as Bangladesh, Singapore, South Korea, and Taiwan have higher population densities. But among the seven countries with the largest populations, Japan has the highest density; only India is a close second. Land, therefore, is an extremely valuable commodity in Japan. Real estate prices in Tokyo are so high that only very wealthy individuals or companies can afford to become property owners.

More than two-thirds of the land in Japan is forest and woodland; arable land accounts for only 13 percent of the total. Although, relatively speaking, more fortunate than Brazil, Indonesia, China, or Russia in terms of agriculturally usable land, Japan is not in a strong position. (See Table 26–4.) Indeed, the figures cited for population density are misleading: In the case of Japan, population density in 1990 came to an astounding 6,520 persons per square mile when measured against the available arable land—one of the

Table 26–4 Land Use, Selected Countries, 1995 (In Percent)

Country	Arable Land	Permanent Crops	Meadows & Pastures	Forest & Woodland	Other
Brazil	7	1	19	67	6
Indonesia	8	3	7	67	15
China	10	0	31	14	45
Russia	8	0	5	45	42
Japan	13	1	1	67	18
USA	20	0	26	29	25
Netherlands	26	1	32	9	32
United Kingdom	29	0	48	9	14
Germany	34	1	16	30	19
Nigeria	31	3	23	15	28
France	32	2	23	27	16
India	55	1	4	23	17

Source: Central Intelligence Agency, *The World Factbook 1995* (Washington, D.C.: U.S. Government, 1995).

Table 26–5   Japanese Foreign Trade,1997

Commodities	Exports	Imports
Total amount in billion $	421 (f.o.b.)	339 (c.i.f.)
Manufactures (%)	96	54
Including (%):		
Machinery	50	
Motor vehicles	19	
Consumer electronics	3	
Other products (%)	4	
Fossil fuels (%)		16
Foodstuffs and non-fossil raw materials (%)		28

Source: Central Intelligence Agency, *The World Factbook 1998* (Washington, D.C.: U.S. Government, 1998), at www.odci.gov/cia/publications/factbook/ja.html.

highest rates in the world. With crop yields among the highest in the world, agriculture in Japan accounts for only 2 percent of the gross national product. The principal crops are rice, sugar beets, vegetables, fruit, and animal products. With shortages of wheat, corn, and soybeans, Japan is only about 50 percent self-sufficient in food production—in spite of the world's largest fish catch.

These economic realities are reflected in the import-export structure of Japan. As is apparent from Table 26–5, Japan basically exports manufactured goods (97 percent) and imports manufactures, food and non-fossil raw materials (54, 28, and 16 percent respectively). In 1996, 39 percent of Japanese exports went to the East Asian Rim and Oceania, 29 percent to the United States, Canada and Mexico, 16 percent to Western Europe, 5 percent to China, 4 percent to OPEC, 3 percent to Latin America, and 1 percent to South Asia. In the same year, 19 percent of Japanese imports came from the United States, 10 percent from Canada and Mexico, 14 percent from the European Union, 12 percent from China, and 13 percent from OPEC. In spite of growing domestic economic difficulties, Japan continued to run an export surplus with most of its major trading partners, which in 1996 amounted to nearly $62 billion.[10]

In spite of its lack of natural resources and fossil fuels, Japan during the early 1970s became the third largest industrial economy in the world,

with a GNP in 1989 of $1,914.1 billion and a per capita GNP of $15,600—the third highest among the major industrial nations. During the postwar period, the performance of the Japanese economy was nothing short of spectacular. During the 1960s it grew at an average annual rate of 10 percent, and during the 1970s and 1980s at the rate of 5 percent. Indeed, Japan's success in industrial development is a unique and remarkable achievement. Even before World War II, the Japanese had achieved undisputed economic primacy in Asia. By 1954 Japan regained prewar economic levels and in 1969 it overtook West Germany as the second largest noncommunist economy. In the 1960s Japan became the world's third-largest producer of crude steel and aluminum, the sixth-largest exporter, and the biggest shipbuilder, exceeding the production of its four closest competitors combined. By 1980, Japan produced more automobiles than the United States. With the demise of the Soviet Union, Japan became the second largest economy in the world—a place, however, which it lost to China in 1993.

Keeping unemployment and inflation rates at the lowest level among the major industrial countries and continuing to accumulate huge trade surpluses, the Japanese have been in a position to invest extensively in foreign countries, becoming one of the foremost financial powers in the world. Relatively small expenditures for national defense, a strong work ethic, stable labor-management relations, and good cooperation between government and industry have been important factors in the outstanding performance of the Japanese economy.

Beginning in the 1990s, however, the Japanese economy, for a variety of reasons, ran into major difficulties. Industrial production growth rates started to fall and were in negative territory in 1992 and 1993. Labor productivity decreased dramatically between 1991 and 1994. While relative labor costs in Japan in 1996 were lower than in Germany (the world's highest!) and the other EU countries, they were higher than in the United States and Canada, more than twice as high as in South Korea, and more than three times as high as in Hong Kong, Singapore, and Taiwan. In overall terms, the GDP growth rate of Japan declined from 4.3 percent in 1991 to –0.2 percent in 1993, before achieving a moderate recovery during 1994–1996.[11] During 1997, however, the GDP once again declined by 0.7 percent and in the fall of 1998 the Economic Planning Agency in Japan reversed its forecast from 1.9 percent growth to 1.8 percent decline. This contraction marks the first time that Japan has registered economic decline two years in a row since 1955, when the Japanese government first began to release GDP figures. One reason for the decline in the world's third largest economy is the financial meltdown in Asia, which has sharply reduced the demand for Japanese goods and services. But most economists also emphasize structural problems in the Japanese economy; a significant drop in personal consumption, the single largest component of the economy, as well as a decline in the domestic demand for new goods and services; the poorly supervised banking industry, which—in the aftermath of falling land prices in the early 1990s—ended up with an estimated $570 billion in failed or risky loans; widespread and large-scale corruption reaching into the highest levels of officialdom involving the Bank of Japan and the Ministry of Finance, arguably the most powerful institution in Japan; a decline in the demand for new housing; and a reduction in new investment.

SOCIAL VALUES, STRUCTURE, AND HIERARCHY

Considering the rapid and extensive changes that have taken place in Japanese society during the modern period, it would appear, at first glance, that Japan was extraordinarily successful in making the transition from a traditional and pre-industrial society to a modern one. Indeed, Japan's uncommonly swift transformation from a feudal sociopolitical regime to a modern nation-state, the abolition of the traditional class structure, and the introduction and rapid takeoff of industry might well be cited as evidence of the validity of such a view. It is precisely the success of the modernization of Japan, however, which has tended to obscure the fact that, under the country's modern exterior, a good many elements of traditional Japan have survived. Social behavior in Japan, in other words, continues to reflect both traditional and modern values, which as

often as not coexist in an uneasy balance in individuals and groups.

Geographic location, territory, and population are among the given factors for any political system. Although, generally speaking, they are slow to change, they are far from immutable. In the case of modern Japan, the territorial factor has not been constant. One of the consequences of World War II was that Japan was reduced to about 46 percent of its prewar territories.[12]

Generally speaking, however, the impact of geographic location and territory on political systems tends to be of a long-term and relatively constant nature. By contrast, it is the character and changing cultural, socio-economic, and demographic configuration of the population which in large measure determine not only the power structure and the rules of political competition, but also define the capacities and limitations of political systems, as well as their agenda—i.e., the most important problems they must address and attempt to solve.

Although hybrid in its distant historical origins, the Japanese population is unique among major nations because, for practical purposes, it has become 99 percent ethnically "pure." This circumstance has been an important advantage in Japan's transition from a traditional to a modern society, sparing it the turmoil of ethnic conflict, which has complicated the politics of so many countries today. The Japanese, moreover, have not had to confront some of the other important problems of political integration commonly found in multiethnic societies. For many centuries, they have had a common language and shared a common history and culture. Unlike most other non-Western societies, therefore, the Japanese did not have to overcome the debilitating political effects of religious, tribal, and linguistic divisions. Reinforced by racial homogeneity and geographic isolation, these attributes of the Japanese people were conducive to the development of an exceptionally strong sense of group identity against the outside world and against foreigners, frequently leading in modern times to extreme forms of nationalism.

Like the other East Asian nations, China in particular, the Japanese, in their pursuit of modernization, also benefited from their strong sense of unity and ancient traditions of political centralization, which remained strong even in the face of the feudal realities of local autonomy and class divisions. Indeed, throughout East Asia the centralized state was regarded as the highest ideal and embodiment of civilization. The Meiji Restoration of 1868 was an example of conservative and selective modernization, which sought to combine the pursuit of national power and technical development with the cultivation of traditional values, using the "restoration" of imperial rule as justification for the elimination of feudal political and social divisions.

Although during much of its past Japan has succeeded in presenting a strong and united front to the outside world, it has by no means been free of domestic cleavages. On the contrary, sectionalism has played an important role in the political history of Japan. For many years after 1868, the new political system established by the Meiji regime was perceived by its opponents as one dominated by "domain-cliques" *(hanbatsu)*. Even today, the basis of political support of most politicians is regional in nature. While clan affiliations no longer play a major role in Japanese politics, regional differences in economic interests, culture, language, and traditions persist.

One of the important differences between American (or, more generally, Western) and Japanese culture is the much greater emphasis on the group in Japanese society. While Western "individualism" may well be a much-exaggerated ideal or myth, group affiliations are clearly more important for the Japanese than for Westerners in general and Americans in particular. The group consciousness of the Japanese is reflected in their tendency to use institutional affiliation rather than universal attribute as a means of identifying their position in society. Thus, instead of saying that a person is a salesman or a lawyer, the Japanese will tend to identify his social position by saying that he belongs to a certain company or firm. Likewise, in the academic world it is not a person's degree that is of primary importance, but rather the institution from which the person was graduated.[13]

This extraordinary group consciousness has been conducive not only to the emergence of strong institutions, but also to the development of extremely stable and highly emotional bonds between the individual and the institution with which he or she is affiliated. While the attributes of the individual are not unimportant, it is institutional affiliation, or the "frame" of the individual's existence, that matters most; the individual's sense of identity is secondary.

Thus it comes as no surprise that the antagonism that frequently characterizes the relationship between Western companies and their employees is largely absent in Japan. To the Japanese, his company *(kaisha)* is the community to which he belongs, which gives him identity and defines the social context within which he lives, and whose authority extends to all aspects of his existence, including his private life. While an individual may belong to several groups, there is always one primary group that is preferred and has claim on the person's loyalty. In short, the Japanese find it "rational" to pursue self-interest through institutions and groups.

The group orientation prevalent in Japanese society and fostered by government policy has important social, economic, and political consequences. It has resulted in a unique lifetime employment pattern, very different labor-management relations than those found in the United States—relations characterized, above all, by a much more solicitous attitude on the part of the employer toward employees, a vertically rather than horizontally based group structure, and the institutionalization of the social order on the basis of seniority based on length of service or age rather than merit.

Because of the high degree of cohesion and solidarity, the primary group that serves as the individual's frame tends to become a closed world. Within the group, an intricate system of ranking evolves, which defines the hierarchial relationship of the members to each other. This ranking order is a deeply ingrained aspect of how the Japanese communicate and interact with members of their group and also governs their behavior toward outsiders. Even differences based on occupation, status, or class are normally subordinated to distinctions based on vertical ranking. The result is not only the development of firm personal links between bosses and subordinates, but also great reluctance on the part of most Japanese to ignore or try to change this vertical ranking system.

The prevailing pattern of social stratification in Japan, therefore, does not follow horizontal lines—stratification by class or caste—but vertical lines (stratification by institution or group of institutions). This form of social organization emphasizes the unitary aspects of social groups and is conducive to the development of vertical schisms, thus encouraging sectionalism. It also determines the nature of political competition and affects the conditions of political stability. Thus, for example, political battles in Japan are not fought among contenders standing in a vertical relationship to each other, but by contenders occupying parallel positions. If labor unions in Japan have developed along different lines than in Western countries, one important reason must be sought in the group structure. Labor-management relations tend to be compartmentalized as "in-house" problems. The very nature of Japanese society thus prevents labor problems from having the kind of national impact they frequently have in Western political systems. On the other hand, a disadvantage of the social stratification system in Japan is that it inhibits cooperation between equally competing groups and makes stability the function of the dominant position of one power over all the others.[14]

Generally speaking, hierarchy is much more important in Japan than in the United States, where the sense (or ideal) of equality is more widespread and accepted. Although there are some groups in Japan whose members are equals, most groups consist of leaders and followers—a continuation of the cultural pattern of the traditional family, or *ie*. A reflection of their long history of power based on heredity and aristocratic rule, as well as their relatively recent feudal past, the Japanese accept differences in rank and status as something natural and unavoidable. But while hierarchy is taken for granted and status is very important, the Japanese do not have a highly developed sense of class, and actual class differences in Japan are not very pronounced. Most Japanese do not identify themselves in terms of class; when asked to do so, nine out of ten describe themselves as belonging to the middle and especially the upper middle class—a perception that is fairly realistic. With respect to income distribution, Japan is similar to the United States in regard to the middle income brackets, but not in regard to the upper and lower income groups. In overall terms, income inequality is not as pronounced in Japan as in the United States. Indeed,

Japan, along with Sweden and Australia, is one of the three industrialized democracies with the least income spread between rich and poor.

Our discussion of the role of values, structure, and hierarchy in Japanese society would be incomplete without reference to the dramatic change that has taken place in the basis for hierarchical status in Japanese society—away from the reliance on class and hereditary authority prevalent before the Meiji Restoration of 1868. With the adoption of the Western idea of universal education and its gradual implementation in practice, heredity as the primary basis for determining hierarchical status was increasingly undermined. Today, with few exceptions, it is education, not family background or class, that determines the functions of the individual in society. Formal educational achievements and rigorous examinations have become extremely important—indeed, decisive—in qualifying individuals for prestigious positions. The Japanese emphasis on educational achievement, perceived as excessive by many critics, has resulted in a higher degree of social mobility than is found in the United States or Western European countries.

It should also be noted that in recent years many Japanese values and traditions—from the work ethic to stable and lifetime employment—have come under pressure and even open attack. Like their international competitors, some major Japanese companies have been forced to "downsize" their work force. In a recent best-seller, *Blueprint for a New Japan,* Ichiro Ozawa, the key figure behind the dramatic upheaval in Japanese politics that began in mid-1993, has made the case for a more rational, more individualist, and more Western Japan—a Japan that would take a more vigorous stance in global affairs and emerge as a responsible world military power in partnership with the United States. Clearly, Japanese society has entered a period of self-examination and reorientation, which may well lead to important political changes in the future.

SOCIAL CLEAVAGES

As elsewhere in the world, the division of the population between urban and rural inhabitants is of fundamental social and political

Table 26–6   Urbanization of Japan, 1920–95

Year	Percent Rural	Percent Urban
1920	81.9%	18.1%
1940	62.1	37.9
1960	36.5	63.5
1975	24.1	75.9
1985	23.3	76.7
1990	22.6	77.4
1995	22.4	77.6

Source: Robert E. Ward, *Japan's Political System* (Englewood Cliffs: Prentice-Hall, Inc., 1978); p. 45; *1990 Britannica Book of the Year* (Chicago: Encyclopaedia Britannica, 1990), p. 764; ibid., 1994 ed., p. 766; ibid., 1998 ed., p. 631.

significance. It is in the cities that industrialization first begins to break down the traditional social relationships, presenting the political system with new and different problems. Generally speaking, the urban component of a population is more receptive to change and innovation than its rural counterpart. Thus, it is the city that tends to produce the pressures for social change.

Although Asia has more than its share of old cities,[15] large-scale urbanization has been relatively slow in coming to this part of the world. Even in modern times, Asian societies have been predominantly agrarian, with the majority of their inhabitants living and working in the countryside. In 1998 in India, for example, only 25.7 percent of the population were classified as urban; in Indonesia, 30.9 percent; in China, 26.4 percent; and in Thailand, only 18.7 percent. Japan, and to a lesser extent the two Korean states, are the great exception to this general picture.[16]

Not only is Japan the most highly urbanized country among the major nations in Asia, but it is unique because of the extraordinary speed of its urbanization. As Table 26–6 illustrates, urbanization in Japan developed a simply astounding dynamic in the twentieth century, doubling between 1920 and 1940 and again in the next 35 years. By 1996, 77.6 percent of the Japanese population, a higher percentage than in the United States (76.4 in 1996), were classified as urban. Among the major industrialized countries, only the United Kingdom (89.4 percent in 1996) and Germany (86.1 percent in 1996) are more highly urbanized.

Although the statistical measures used by the Japanese slightly exaggerate the urban component of the population, it is clear that during the past few decades Japan has experienced intense urbanization. By 1975, 57 percent of the total population lived in "densely inhabited districts," in areas with a population density of 4,000 or more inhabitants per square kilometer (1,544 per square mile). Indeed, today considerably more than half of Japan's population is concentrated in the so-called Tokaido Corridor—a megalopolitan belt that includes the Tokyo, Osaka, and Chukyo metropolitan regions, as well as Shizuoka, and stretches from Tokyo to Kobe. The Tokyo Metropolitan Region alone accounts for approximately one-fourth of Japan's population, and Tokyo, one of the world's largest cities, approached a population of 12 million in 1975.

With the rapid process of urbanization has come a fundamental and equally dramatic change in the employment characteristics of the Japanese population. In 1920, 53.6 percent of the total labor force of just under 27 million were employed in agriculture, fishing and forestry—that is, in the primary or rural industries, 20.7 percent in the secondary industries (construction, manufacturing and mining), and 23.8 percent in the tertiary or service industries (communication, finance, government, services, trade).[17] By 1997, the labor force had grown to 67.2 million. Of this total, only 6 percent were employed in the primary industries, 33 percent in the secondary industries, and 61 percent in the tertiary industries.[18] Thus, in less than seven decades, a dramatic change had occurred in the occupational characteristics of the Japanese labor force. By 1997, only one of every seventeen Japanese in the total labor force was engaged in a rural occupation, one-third were employed in manufacturing, mining, and construction, and 61 percent were employed in the service sector of the economy.

As elsewhere, these fundamental changes in the occupational profile and characteristics of the population and the underlying and profoundly unsettling urbanization process produced startling changes in the attitudes, values, and behavior of the Japanese. They have played and continue to play an enormous role in enhancing the capability of Japan and its place in international affairs. Indeed, they have been instrumental in the emergence of the "Japanese superstate."[19]

If the national mentality of Japan at the end of World War II was that of a "twelve-year old," as General Douglas MacArthur put it, the Land of the Rising Sun lost little time in going through adolescence. In its "adult" stage, peacefully and firmly, though by no means perfectly, integrated in the international community in the aftermath of World War II, Japan has not only developed into an economic superpower whose foreign trade performance poses a challenge—some would argue, a threat—to other industrialized countries, but into a society worth emulating. Previously perceived as backward, semi-feudal and undemocratic, it is today regarded by many as a model of superefficiency and success, as the most advanced example of postindustrial society, as a country which, as it were, has beaten the West at its own game—or, as some observers have suggested, is playing a new and different game.

If democracy has become firmly established in Japan, it is in part because this imported institution has accommodated native values and come to reflect the structural characteristics of Japanese society. In contrast to the West, where the emphasis is on the individual and the autonomous self, Japanese society, its political system included, stresses the interpersonal self—that is, the individual as part of a network of social relations. While the uniquely Japanese *ie* (family) system has been undermined, it has nevertheless survived as a social custom.[20] Indeed, some theorists have argued that the Japanese principle of group formation based on kinship lineage and the structural patterns of the *ie* society are compatible with industrialization and modernization. On the other hand, the traditional Japanese emphasis on consensus rather than competition in politics appears to be incongruent with pluralism. Japanese democracy, therefore, has a number of unique characteristics—especially in the corporate world. The emergence of citizens' movements in the 1960s focusing on antiwar, antinuclear, environmental pollution, community, and other issues suggests that in Japan, as elsewhere, the established political parties and labor union movements have failed to address all the problems of concern to the citizens. Since these citizens' movements cut across party and company lines, their appearance signals perhaps that the political activity of citizens in the modern sense may become an increasingly important aspect of Japanese politics.

As the first non-Western society to achieve a high level of industrialization, Japan has been widely regarded as the most successful model of noncommunist modernization. Certainly in Asia a number of countries have sought to emulate the example of Japan—with varying degrees of success. It is, however, by no means a foregone conclusion that the Japanese pattern can be easily repeated elsewhere. There are not many potential national communities in the non-Western world that, like the Japanese, have the advantage of ethnic and religious homogeneity, the cultural predispositions that facilitate the introduction of universal education, and the historical experience in borrowing from other civilizations and adapting foreign values without losing their own cultural identity in the process. In short, although some components of the Japanese modernization pattern may work in other cultural contexts, the trajectory that has propelled Japan within such a short time into the front ranks of the industrial democracies is not likely to be repeated.[21]

NOTES

[1]Edwin O. Reischauer, *The Japanese Today* (Cambridge, MA: Harvard University Press, 1988), p. 260.

[2]Warren M. Tsuneishi, *Japanese Political Style: An Introduction to the Government and Politics of Modern Japan* (New York and London: Harper & Row, 1966), p. 22.

[3]Central Intelligence Agency, *The World Factbook 1995* (Washington, DC: U.S. Government, 1985), p. 215. Earlier projections called for the population to stabilize at around 100 million in 1970, or peak at 113 million in the year 2000. See Ardath W. Burks, *The Government of Japan* (Westport, CT: Greenwood Press, 1982), p. 41, and Tsuneishi, *Japanese Political Style*, p. 13.

[4]In 1975, Koreans accounted for 86 percent of the minority groups in Japan, Chinese for 6 percent, and Americans for 3 percent. See Robert E. Ward, *Japan's Political System* (Englewood Cliffs, NJ: Prentice-Hall, 1978), p. 42.

[5]Burks, *The Government of Japan*, p. 40.

[6]Jerome B. Cohen, "International Aspects of Japan's Economic Situation," in *Japan Between East and West* (New York: Harper, 1957), p. 108.

[7]See Burks, *The Government of Japan*, pp. 40–41.

[8]Central Intelligence Agency, *The World Factbook 1995* (Washington, DC: U.S. Government, 1995), pp. 145, 159, 440, 443; ibid., 1998 ed., at www.odci.gov/cia/publications/factbook/ja.html (2/13/99).

[9]"Japan Insight: Population Aging and Longevity" at www.jinjapan.org/insight/html/in_persctive/in_persctive.html.

[10]Central Intelligence Agency, *Handbook of International Economic Statistics 1997* (Washington: U.S. Government, 1997), pp. 138, 144, 147–148, 157; *1998 Britannica Book of the Year* (Chicago: Encyclopaedia Britannica, 1998), pp. 840–841; for slightly different data, see (Japanese) Ministry of Finance, "Foreign Trade Statistics," at www.jef.or.jp/news/wp1996/fig1/fig/1-8.gif (2/14/99).

[11]Central Intelligence Agency, *Handbook of International Economic Statistics 1997* (Washington, DC: U.S. Government, 1997), pp. 28, 33, 46, 50–51.

[12]As a result of World War I, Japan lost its territorial acquisitions overseas—its small empire in Korea, Formosa (Taiwan), Manchuria, and southern Sakhalin, as well as parts of its integral territory—the Kuril Islands and, until 1968 and 1972, respectively, the Ogasawara (Bonin) and Ryukyus (Okinawa) islands, which were under the administrative control of the United States.

[13]Chie Nakane, *Japanese Society* (Berkeley: University of California Press, 1970), pp. 2–3. The subsequent discussion is mainly based on this source, pp. 3–103. See also Takeshi Ishida, *Japanese Society* (New York: Random House, 1971), especially pp. 7–16, 37–112.

[14]On the significance of group orientation, see also Reischauer, *The Japanese Today,* pp. 128ff.

[15]Archeological finds date the beginnings of Peking (or Beijing) as far back as the twelfth century B.C. Tokyo, formerly called Edo (Estuary Gate), began as a village in the twelfth century A.D.

[16]*1990 Britannica Book of the Year* (Chicago: Encyclopedia Britannica, Inc., 1990), pp. 762–766.

[17]Ward, *Japan's Political System,* p. 46.

[18]Central Intelligence Agency, *The World Factbook 1998* (Washington, DC: U.S. Government), at www.odci.gov/cia/publications/factbook/ja.html.

[19]Herman Kahn, *The Emerging Japanese Superstate: Challenge and Response* (Englewood Cliffs, NJ: Prentice-Hall, 1970).

[20]See Tadashi Fukutake, *The Japanese Social Structure: Its Evolution in the Modern Century,* translated and with a foreword by Ronald P. Dore (Tokyo: University of Tokyo Press, 1982), pp. 123ff.

[21]See Gavan McCormack and Yushio Sugimoto, eds., *The Japanese Trajectory: Modernization and Beyond* (Cambridge: Cambridge University Press, 1988).

Chapter 27

The Japanese
Political Framework

In the aftermath of World War II, American occupation forces directed the drafting of a new constitution for Japan. With only one occupying power to oversee the process, those writing the constitution faced fewer problems than in Germany. Indeed, the Japanese constitution was prepared during a six-week period in early 1946 under the direction of General Douglas A. MacArthur, Supreme Commander for the Allied Powers in Japan. MacArthur initially had charged the interim Japanese cabinet to revise the Meiji Constitution to achieve the kind of democratic processes American leaders felt essential. He had clear ideas of how that constitution should handle such sensitive issues as the role of the emperor and human rights. By early February 1946, MacArthur was dissatisfied with the Japanese attempts at revision and impatient to get a new constitution in place. He directed the writing of a new document by American occupation officials. It was prepared in six days, translated into Japanese and delivered to reluctant Japanese cabinet officials, who were cajoled into accepting the American draft as their own. The draft was endorsed by the emperor, and the Diet adopted the new constitution as amendments to the Meiji

Constitution in November 1946. The new constitution took effect on May 3, 1947.

The constitution drew upon the earlier Meiji Constitution adopted in 1890, which was based on the study of European regimes, especially the Prussian model. It was a Western import into the rich Eastern cultural setting of Japan. At times, the process of copying the West was artificial. Thus, in order to create a basis for an aristocratic upper legislative chamber, the Japanese mandated the creation of princes, marquis, counts, viscounts, and barons. They attempted with only some success to graft this Western notion of nobility onto the existing feudal society. Western in inspiration, the Meiji constitution shielded antiquated political and social structures from forces for change. The 1947 Constitution brought even more of the West to Japan as the occupation forces tried to change feudal social structures and shape the new regime in a way that would prevent the military despotism that had emerged in the 1930s.

While technically the postwar constitutional process involved simply amending the Meiji Constitution, in fact it involved the adoption of a new constitution. This time the model was the British parliamentary system. Unlike the constitutional engineering in postwar Germany where the object was to correct the problems that had appeared in Weimar Germany, the 1947 Japanese Constitution simply imported the practices and institutions of the successful British regime.

The preamble to the Constitution states: "We the Japanese people . . . do proclaim that sovereign power resides with the people." In fact, the people were not involved in the process of drafting the constitution and the role of their elected representatives was only minimal. Even more so than in Germany, the Japanese found themselves with a constitution written for them by the foreign powers who had defeated them militarily. Occupation censors assured that there was no discussion of the constitution's American parentage until after the formal end of the occupation in 1952. But there were real concerns that once the occupation was ended, the Japanese people or leaders might reject this foreign import. These worries proved unfounded.

The Constitution of 1947 has won wide acceptance among people and leaders from all points on the political spectrum, a small segment of ultra-conservatives excepted. Democracy may have been imposed by the "iron will" of the occupiers, but the liberation it offered from oppression by militarists and nationalists in the past was welcomed, often eagerly, by the Japanese people. Recent scholarship suggests that part of

the acceptance of this "foreign imposed" constitution may come from the different "readings" of the constitution in English and Japanese.[1] The Japanese reading is much more compatible with the cultural and political experiences of Japan than is suggested in the English version.

A deeper concern is about another important but unintended effect of the constitutional drafting period. The occupation forces and their constitutional process and content reinforced the strength of an already well-entrenched bureaucracy. The postwar search for political stability and economic recovery was privileged over the need to democratize. This legacy of an already powerful imperial bureaucracy made still stronger remains one of the principal challenges to bringing political reform to modern Japan.[2]

In the last few years, the political system has come under attack as a result of widespread corruption of political leaders and their parties. Many Japanese have come to believe that they have a first-rate economy and third-rate politics. Political reform has been high on the political agenda. A number of important constitutional changes have been discussed but virtually none implemented. In part, resistance to change comes from the sanctity of the Constitution and hesitation about changing a document that has gained acceptance. More important, though, in understanding resistance to constitutional change is the fact that politicians, bureaucrats, and private

---

A PACIFIST CONSTITUTION

Unlike Germany's foreign-imposed Basic Law which has been amended some forty times over its lifetime, Japan's American-drafted constitution marked its fiftieth anniversary in 1997 without a single amendment. Over the years, public opinion polls showed that the Japanese did not want to change their constitution. Many appreciated its guarantees of civil rights and the democratic practices that have emerged under it. But many also feared that any amendment would open the way to modifying Article 9—the celebrated peace clause. Article 9 repudiates the possession of "war potential" and Japan's "right to belligerency." This clause is

seen as a bulwark against any return to the militarism of the past.

At the start of the new century, the Japanese constitution remains unamended. The public now seems open to the idea of constitutional change. A 1997 poll showed 45 percent of the public supporting amendments with only 37 percent opposed.[3] However, much of the talk of constitutional change focuses on adjusting Article 9 to support Japan's new position as a world economic power rather than addressing other parts of the constitution that have created the domestic political problems of the 1990s.

interests have adjusted to make the system work to their benefit and they have become entrenched defenders of the status quo.

THE EMPEROR

Among the most sensitive issues addressed in the new Constitution was the role of the emperor. The Japanese imperial dynasty is the oldest in the world; it claims descent from a mythological sun goddess of 660 B.C. The direct descent of the emperor is well established from early in the sixth century A.D. In spite of his status as a divinity incarnate, the emperor's political powers have been largely formal throughout most of the dynasty's two-thousand-year history. Only in times of political instability had the emperor played an important role in politics.[4] In fact, one of the few acts directly involving the emperor in politics during this century was his laudable role in arranging Japan's surrender in 1945.

Many foreigners and a few Japanese felt that the emperor was a war criminal who ought to be tried or at least purged along with others responsible for governing Japan during the war. In fact, wartime leaders used the emperor as a "shield against criticism of their wrongful and illegal acts" while ruling themselves.[5] The emperor's personal involvement in politics was minimal until his intervention in bringing the war to an end. The terms of surrender left the emperor in place, with his ultimate status to be determined by the Japanese at a later date. The Americans believed that his powers during the war had been largely symbolic: "an object of veneration rather than . . . a political authority."[6] More important, they felt the emperor could provide continuity and legitimacy for both the occupation government and the new Japanese regime they wanted to see constructed.

In early 1946, when the status of the monarchy was still uncertain, Emperor Hirohito publicly renounced the once divine nature of his monarchy. The new Constitution shifted sovereignty from the throne to the people and established a strictly symbolic role for the emperor:

The Emperor shall be the symbol of the State and of the unity of the people, deriving his position from the will of the people with whom resides sovereign power.

Table 27–1 Public Attitudes Toward the Emperor, 1986

What are your feelings toward the emperor?	
Reverence	33%
Affection	22
Nothing	40
Antagonism	2
Other, don't know	3
Do you feel a closeness toward the royal family?	
Yes	51%
No	37
Other, don't know	12
What do you think of the imperial system?	
Support the present system	84%
Abolish the present system	9
Increase emperor's powers	4
Other, don't know	3

Source: Adapted from Foreign Press Center, *Facts and Figures of Japan: 1987 Edition* (Tokyo: Foreign Press Center, 1987), pp. 18–19.

The stipulation that the crown is bestowed by the will of the people makes it clear that even though the emperor's claim to the throne comes from his lineage, his right to the throne comes from the people. The political tasks remaining for the emperor are symbolic acts such as formally appointing the prime minister who is elected by the Diet or appointing the chief judge of the Supreme Court who has been designated by the government or receiving ambassadors from abroad. What remains important is that the

> . . . Emperor today stands as symbol, not of some irrational "superiority" of the Japanese race, but rather as a projection of their own pride in their own achievements as a modern people; not as a reminder of the terrors of war and humiliation of defeat but rather as symbol of Japan's purity of intent to lead the world in working for peace.[7]

The emperor does continue to play an important part in stressing the continuity and unity of modern-day Japan. As in Britain, there is little hostility to the monarchy except among a small handful on the left fringe of politics. Table 27–1 shows that there are many Japanese who are not as closely and emotionally attached to the emperor as the British appear to be to their royal family. However, the widespread mourning and emotional trauma of Hirohito's death in 1989 revealed a greater depth of attachment to the emperor, or at least to Hirohito, than indicated by the polls.

The Japanese emperor has even fewer political powers than the British monarch. While the queen is the head of state in Britain, the emperor is only a "symbol" of the Japanese state. The Japanese situation explicitly acknowledges that sovereignty resides in the people, while the British still cling to a constitutional myth of the sovereignty of the crown. Postwar occupation reforms in Japan eliminated the titled nobility that still adds glamour and prestige to the British monarchy. The emperor lacks the British queen's potential discretionary powers if there is no clear majority in Parliament. Like the British monarch, the emperor can become a discreet and knowledgeable advisor to the prime minister. Despite Hirohito's long tenure (1926–1989), his political involvement was minimal even in this kind of behind-the-scenes advisory role. He devoted his attention instead to marine biology. After his death, the new emperor, Akihito, has continued his private interests rather than develop greater political interests. As in Britain, the popularity and very existence of the monarchy increasingly depend on the absolute political neutrality of the royal family.

THE DIET

The 1947 Constitution is based on the British pattern of parliamentary democracy. It designates the Diet, or parliament, as "the highest organ of state power" and "the sole law-making organ of the State." In effect, it is the political institution that embodies the sovereign public. In its first two decades of operation, the Diet clearly did not achieve its political potential. A large and disciplined conservative majority simply ratified the decisions reached by the cabinet or party bodies. In a setting where they felt condemned to ineffectiveness, the opposition parties vented their frustration with protests and obstruction on the floor of parliament.[8] Only in the last twenty years, with the growing influence of opposition parties and increased maneuvering among factions of the ruling party, has the Diet emerged as a more significant political institution.

The Diet has two chambers, both directly elected by the citizens: the House of Representatives and the House of Councillors. The House of Representatives is the larger and more influential chamber. It is made up of 500 deputies elected to four-year terms. In practice, the government usually dissolves the House of Representatives before the normal expiration of the legal term, with general elections taking place on average every 30 months since 1947. The House of Councillors is a smaller body with only 252 members. Members of the House of Councillors serve six-year terms, with half the members elected every three years. The House of Councillors cannot be dissolved prematurely. The longer term and security from dissolution was designed to allow this chamber the ability to take a longer-range view of issues before the Diet, free from the prospect of immediate elections.

The two chambers have similar powers and responsibilities. However, the House of Representatives is given the final word should there be differences between the two chambers. Both houses are supposed to elect the prime minister, but if the Councillors disagree to fail to designate the same person as named by the Representatives, the decision of the House of Representatives becomes the decision for the whole Diet. The same is true when the texts of proposed legislation differ in the two houses. If efforts to resolve the differences fail, then the House of Representatives can resolve the issue by passing its version of the legislation for a second time with a two-thirds or greater majority. On budget measures and treaties, the failure of the House of Councillors to adopt bills passed by the Representatives within 30 days leads to the automatic passage of the measure even without the Councillors. In practice, this is rarely needed. In addition, only the House of Representatives has the power to censure the government and force its resignation. Further evidence of the greater influence of the House of Representatives is found in the tradition of drawing the majority of the members of the cabinet, and always the prime minister, from that chamber. By tradition, generally only three of the 20 cabinet posts are allotted to Councillors.

Roll call voting in the Japanese Diet requires deputies to file past the Speaker's podium to cast their votes. In this 1989 vote on the budget, the opposition party—usually seated on the Speaker's left in the empty banks shown in this picture—boycotted the vote over procedural and policy matters. (*Photographer/Source:* AP/Wide World Photos)

As in Britain, France, and Germany, the Japanese periodically question the role of their second chamber, the House of Councillors. The absence of a distinctive electorate or representative basis makes the chamber simply a less important reflection of the House of Representatives. To counter this, the House of Councillors has tried to define areas of special competence and influence. It has recently created new committees that are different from those existing in the House of Representatives. It has also sought to stress the advantages of its long-range view of issues. Finally, defenders of the current bicameralism stress the importance of a second house to check potential abuses of power.

The Diet meets less frequently than do European parliaments: about 80 days a year, which is only half as often as the British or Italian legislatures.[9] As a result, a considerable amount of the legislative work is carried out by the standing committees. The committees generally parallel the responsibilities of specific ministries. They exercise oversight over these ministries and conduct the substantive discussion of legislation within their competence. Party strength on the committees is determined by the overall party balance in the chamber. Even when one party has a majority, it has become customary in the last decade or so to allocate several committee chairs in the House of Councillors to figures from the opposition party. In the House of Representatives, the dominant party has usually kept all committee chairs for its own members. In general, the committees do not report legislation to the Diet as a whole unless it has the support of both government and opposition parties. Because of the parliamentary framework, these legislative committees lack the power of their counterparts in the U.S. Congress. But they have become increasingly important forums for the detailed discussion of pending legislation.

The bureaucracy has a major presence in the Diet. Many members of the Diet, as many as one in four,[10] are former senior civil servants who bring the perspectives and values of their bureaucratic background and attachments into the legislative bodies. In addition, active bureaucrats play key roles in initiating and drafting legislative proposals that are then introduced by the government. They are also able to get friendly legislators to introduce amendments and parliamentary questions reflecting their views. In recent years, the bureaucracy's general decline in influence has been offset in the Diet by the decline of the LDP's once strong, centralized party policy bodies with agendas of their own.

As in other parliamentary systems, question time is an important opportunity for Diet members to get explanations of government action from the government. Interpellation in Japan is often lively. Opposition members hope to stump the government with a "bomb question"—one that is unexpected and that the minister cannot answer.[11] Ministers often assign their junior ministers to try to find out from opposition members who have indicated they have questions what the substance of the question will be in order to prepare an effective response. When they are not able to get that information and are unable to answer, the session often comes to an embarrassing standstill. Since these sessions are televised, parliamentary questions are important checks on the government and the bureaucracy.

Major legislation is still nearly always introduced by the government. Only a few private bills are enacted into law. On the other hand, most of the government's proposals are eventually enacted. Over the years, 80 percent of the cabinet's legislation has been adopted. However, there is a growing tendency for legislators to develop areas of policy interest and expertise. This gives them more influence over policies that in the past were simply dictated by the government and bureaucracy.[12]

In comparison to the government-dominated proceedings in Britain, France, and Germany, the Japanese legislators exercise more control over the legislative process. Party discipline in voting on measures before the Diet is as effective in Japan as in these other parliamentary systems. However, individual members of parliament often have more influence than is the case in the highly disciplined parties in Western Europe. During the long years of LDP dominance, its deputies were able to bargain for pork barrel legislation to benefit their constituents and financial backers. In addition, there was extensive involvement of interested LDP Diet members in the drafting stages of much of the government's legislation. Since 1993, when power slipped from a solid LDP majority into the hands of a loose and undisciplined coalition government, party discipline among government supporters has been much less certain. This has led to even greater involvement of Diet members and their party leaders in shaping public policy.

The influence of the Diet is due to the acceptance among Japanese citizens and political leaders that major policy should draw broad support from all political groups. As a result, even when the government has a secure majority, it generally avoids ramming unpopular policies through the Diet against strong resistance from opposing parties. Such a course of action would damage the legitimacy of the policy and of the government. This means that even opposition Diet members have a subtle influence in shaping policies that emerge from the LDP-dominated parliament. The government shies away from proposing policies that might provoke sharp resistance from within its ranks or from opposing parties. The emphasis on building a consensus is strong and prevents the use of party discipline to push through controversial measures.

The search for consensus has been useful in building broad support for the government and its policies. But the cost has been that Japanese policy has been more reactive than forward looking. Major policy changes come only when there is a crisis that requires a response.[13]

The lower house of the Diet has the power to oust the prime minister and government through a vote of no-confidence. This has happened four times, in each case only because the LDP's discipline failed to hold. In the most recent case, in July 1993, a motion of no-confidence forced the resignation of the government of Kiichi Miyazawa. Prime Minister Miyazawa exercised his option of dissolving the House of Representatives and called for new elections. In the subsequent elections, the LDP lost its Diet majority for the first time in 40 years.

Over the past decade, the political role of the Diet and its members has expanded. The Diet has improved visibility as the result of the televising of its sessions. Diet members have increased capacity as a result of the growth of the parliamentary staff. The Diet has improved stature now that the confrontational politics of the 1950s and early 1960s has given way to more consensual politics. In the past, tensions were often very high. Unable to affect legislation by normal processes, opposition members would obstruct the process by stalling votings, occupying the speaker's chair, or otherwise blocking legislative procedures through extralegal protest. On occasion, the police had to be called in to separate brawling members. Over the last 20 years, there has been much less of this kind of obstructionist opposition as both government and opposition parties have moderated their ideological stances and sought consensus.

This is a time of flux in Japanese legislative politics.[14] The "1955 regime" that came into being with the merger of the Liberal and Democratic parties into a durable and dominant parliamentary majority seems to have ended. The once dominant Liberal Democratic party lost its majority and, for a few years, even a governing coalition. The new forms of legislative action are still emerging. They appear to have familiar features: the still very prominent role of the LDP, a weak and disorganized opposition, a strong bureaucracy, and compulsion to seek consensual rather than confrontational politics.

THE PRIME MINISTER

Despite the important role of parliament, the prime minister and cabinet play the key roles in Japanese politics. The prime minister is a member of the House of Representatives designated chief of government by a resolution passed by both houses of the Diet. If there is a disagreement between the two chambers, the choice of the House of Representatives prevails. When the LDP has a parliamentary majority, the selection of the prime minister is made by the Liberal Democratic party when it selects its president. The president of the LDP is elected by the LDP Diet members plus the LDP prefectoral sections—a body of about 450 people. The party president becomes the candidate of the majority party in parliament,

thus assuring election by the Diet when the LDP has a majority. Elections for LDP president are held every two years and over the last two decades an informal rule has emerged barring more than one reelection. That means that the prime minister normally serves at most four years. The process of selecting the prime minister contributes to weak leadership. When the LDP has been in power, the selection of the LDP president (who then becomes prime minister) has been dominated by behind-the-scenes factional politics.

The process of building a coalition to win the LDP presidency has been compared with diplomatic negotiations among foreign countries:

> There are telephone calls, and face-to-face meetings that take place between people who know each other well, or have been arranged by intermediaries. In this process, who met whom, when, and under what circumstances, who were the intermediaries, who is going to meet with whom, all are pregnant with meanings. . . . They may send up trial balloons by holding press conferences in the office of the faction, or in a train while traveling from one place to another. They may send out false information in an effort to increase suspicion among factions and individuals and thus separate them.[15]

Intraparty conflict is minimized by the tendency of party faction leaders or party "barons" to reach a preliminary accord on which one of them should become prime minister. The rivalry is also eased by the fact that the prime minister's relatively short term assures the sharing of the position among the factions over time. In addition, respect for seniority eases intraparty tensions in that parliamentary tenure and party service narrow the candidates to only a few each time the LDP chooses a new leader. The selection by the party barons of very senior politicians means that the prime minister is often older than national leaders in other countries.

There are some negative consequences from these efforts to reduce LDP in-fighting over the prime ministership. It means that there is considerable turnover of prime ministers. A widely repeated joke is that in Japan one discards popular singers after one year, prime ministers after two. In the 1980s, six individuals held the position of prime minister. Between 1947 and 2000,

Table 27–2   Japanese Prime Ministers, 1990–2000

Name	Party of Prime Minister	Dominant Party in Government Coalition	Date Installed
Toshiki Kaifu	Liberal Democratic Party (LDP)	LDP	August 1989
Kiichi Miyazawa	LDP	LDP	November 1991
Morihiro Hosokawa	Japan New Party	ex-LDP parties	August 1993
Tsutomu Hata	Renewal Party	New Frontier Party	April 1994
Tomiichi Murayama	Social Democratic Party of Japan (SDPJ)	LDP	June 1994
Ryutaro Hashimoto	LDP	LDP	January 1996
Ryutaro Hashimoto	LDP	LDP	October 1996
Keizo Obuchi	LDP	LDP	July 1998
Yoshiro Mori	LDP	LDP	April 2000

24 different men held the position of prime minister, with an average term of well under three years. In the 1990s, prime ministerial instability increased. Seven different men in eight different government coalitions served as prime minister with an average length of term of only 15 months. (See Table 27–2.)

In 1993, the LDP lost its parliamentary majority for the first time in decades. At that time, a coalition of the Social Democratic party, the Japan Renewal party, the Komeito party, and three other small parties formed a majority and after lengthy negotiations on all ministerial duties selected Morihiro Hosokawa as prime minister. He remained in office for less than a year and was replaced by Tsutomu Hata. Prime Minister Hata lacked a majority in the Diet and was soon replaced by the Social Democrat Tomiichi Murayama. Murayama's government, however, was dominated by the LDP.

Murayama's situation was similar to that of many Japanese prime ministers. Whether it is the factional politics of the LDP or the complicated coalition negotiations of the other parties, the selection process contributes to weak prime ministerial leadership. They are usually beholden to the factional or party leaders whose support enabled them to win the post. These "symbolic" prime ministers have short careers and always have to contend with shifting factions and coalitions.[16] The real holders of power remain in the background, thereby escaping public accountability.

While theoretically free to select their own ministers, prime ministers in fact must select a cabinet that balances the party factions or coalition partners. They must include rivals and even those who opposed them prior to their election. In LDP governments, there are two informal rules that govern the selection of ministers and other key officials that effectively limit prime ministerial power. The first is the seniority rule that calls for posts to be assigned on the basis of tenure. Typically, politicians are in their fifth to seventh term in parliament when they receive a cabinet portfolio. The second rule accords each faction its equitable share of the ministries. As a government is being formed, each faction draws up a list of its members for the use of the prime minister designate. The list ranks faction members by seniority, and the prime minister draws from these lists to fill the cabinet posts.

The short experience of the non-LDP governments since 1993 suggests two problems. First, the multiparty coalition with as many as six partners representing a wide range of political programs makes for very complicated negotiations on the composition of the government and its policies. Second, the governments of Prime Ministers Hosokawa and Hata suffered from the lack of experienced ministers to place in key positions. The LDP dissidents who joined these governments lacked ministerial experience and so did the leaders of the other coalition partners who had languished in opposition for 40 years. The bureaucracy took advantage of inexperienced ministers and the weakness of these governments to assert even more power than usual over the policy process after 1993.

Unlike the powerful prime ministers in Britain and chancellors in Germany, Japanese prime ministers are not able to dominate the policy process during the short period of time they hold office. Rather than leading the policy debate, Japanese prime ministers tend to react to proposals by others within their government or in the bureaucracy.[17] However, prime ministers are then able to play an important if not critical role in shaping the actual content of the change.

In the mid-1990s, reform to strengthen the office of prime minister was discussed. Among the proposals was a suggestion that the prime minister might be directly elected or ratified by a popular plebiscite. This and other institutional reforms were soon shelved due to an unwillingness of the public and top politicians to tinker with the constitution. However, a more subtle shift may bring prime ministers more power. In the past, prime ministers were more the products of factional politics and not always the most powerful figures. Since the collapse of the old 1955 system, prime ministers seem to be more "political" in that they have agendas and sometimes non-factional power bases of their own. Clearly, the collapse of the LDP's monopoly on power and the weakening of its party structures, open new opportunities to ambitious, younger, and more public-oriented leaders.[18]

THE CABINET AND POLICY MAKING

The prime minister presides over a cabinet of about twenty ministers. The ministers are drawn from the membership of the Diet, with only a handful coming from the House of Councillors and an occasional nonparliamentarian. In the Japanese political culture, it is regarded as poor taste to be too openly ambitious for political office and especially to appear to compete openly with those with more seniority. The notion that all senior party leaders should have a turn in government ministries leads to the rapid turnover of ministers. On average, the minister of finance serves 16 months; other ministers average less than 12 months in their positions.[19] Such short tenure leaves ministers dependent upon civil servants for information and assistance in policy making. Few are in office long enough to carry major legislative programs from conception through adoption to implementation alone.

As in other parliamentary systems, key policies are set by the collective decision of the prime minister and other ministers in cabinet meetings. The Japanese cabinet meets twice a week to discuss and decide major issues. In practice, discussion is relatively limited since most contentious issues have already been resolved in preliminary meetings among the relevant ministers, party leaders, and their civil servants. Cabinet meetings do not produce free-ranging discussions of all the issues before the nation. Instead, ministers usually intervene only in discussions affecting their own portfolios. Voting in cabinet meetings is rare, since decisions are consensual and unanimous.

The government is responsible for its action and inaction before the Diet. The House of Representatives has the power to force a government to resign by passing a motion of no-confidence. A simple majority vote against the government in the House of Representatives on such a motion of no-confidence forces the government to step down or dissolve the House. In practice, there are fewer no-confidence motions introduced in Japan than in France or Britain. In the first 40 years, there were only 32 no-confidence votes. Four were successful—the most recent in 1993—and brought the dissolution of the House of Representatives.

There are more important informal restraints on the exercise of power by the cabinet. Factional considerations limit the range of policy options for most governments. Government parties play a greater role in influencing policy than do majority parties in Britain, France, or Germany. The LDP's Policy Research Council has specialized sections for most policy domains. The interaction of the party officials, Diet members, bureaucrats, and representatives of the ministers usually determines policy well before it arrives before the cabinet for a formal decision. Networks of interested politicians, bureaucrats, and interest groups are thus very influential in policy making and impose limits on the policy options cabinets can realistically consider.

Studies of Japanese public policy stress the diversity of styles and patterns of policy making within the existing insitutional framework.[20] Sometimes the process is very open to participation from a variety of social and political forces; at other times it operates behind closed doors with the participation of only a handful of key actors. In some cases, personalities and personal networks play an important part, but in others broad social forces are more important in determining the outcome. In some issue areas, the Diet plays a major part in the decision; in others, it has little influence at all. The heterogeneity of the policy process is not unusual, but it illustrates the adaptability of institutions that is needed to respond to the wide variety of different demands made on the governments of modern industrial democracies.

Within the government, between the government and its parliamentary supporters, and even between the government and opposition, there is always an emphasis on consensus and accommodation. The citizenry seems to expect that nothing should be done until a broad agreement has been reached on all sides. The result is that "Harmony is treasured to the point where the principle of majority rule becomes diluted."[21] It is furthermore very difficult to respond to public demands for major reforms. This has been the case over the past five years as public calls for electoral and constitutional reform to remedy the cancer of political corruption have gone unanswered by a political elite that can only act on the basis of consensus.

The current Japanese constitution was based on the British parliamentary model. In operation, it has developed as a strikingly different regime from that which served as its model. Japanese political and cultural traditions, as well as the impact of the long-term dominance of the regime by a single but faction-ridden party, have all given the Japanese parliamentary system its particular pattern and style. Indeed, the ability to accommodate these old traditions and new political realities may be the reason why this foreign constitution has survived so well.

BUREAUCRATIC POWER?

One of the big questions about contemporary Japanese politics is the strength and autonomy of the civil service. The Japanese bureaucracy is

a comparatively small one: 3.9 percent of the total population instead of 7.3 percent in Britain or 11.2 percent in France. Instead, its strength comes from a long tradition of bureaucratic government in Japan's past. As one commentator notes, "Historically, the bureaucratic system was the sole authority around which society was constructed."[22] With roots that predate the Meiji era, the strong bureaucracy was another of the legacies of the past that Japan struggled to accommodate in its adaptation of western democracy. The Confucian pattern of the past was confirmed in conscious decisions by postwar American occupying forces who wanted to preserve Japan's economic structures and to use the bureaucracy to carry out their own policies.[23]

In the first three decades of Japanese democracy, there was considerable evidence to support claims that the unelected bureaucracy in league with large business interests dominated Japanese politics. Elected political leaders seemed to have only minimal influence and provided a democratic façade for bureaucratic government.[24] It is not uncommon for ministers to reply to questions in parliament by saying: "Since this is an important issue, I must turn the floor over to the Government officials [i.e., the civil servants]."[25] The Ministry of International Trade and Industry (MITI) and the Ministry of Finance were seats of major political power with politicians reduced to handing out small goodies to their supporters. Others argued that the long-term dominance of the governing Liberal Democratic party (LDP) allowed the party to develop institutions to counteract the sway or more often the inertia of the bureaucracy. By the mid-1970s, the MITI had declined in influence but the Ministry of Finance remains a key factor in Japanese public policy making. These historical and institutional problems were aggravated by the regular shifting of the politically accountable ministers who were supposed to provide for public accountability.

Whether or not one accepts extreme positions on the extent of bureaucratic power, it is clear that the Japanese bureaucracy exercised great sway over the economic and social agendas of Japan for many years. In the 1990s, the bureaucracy lost public standing as a result of its entanglement in the web of scandal that pervaded Japanese politics. In the mid-1990s, a series of disasters shook people's confidence in the bureaucracy's effectiveness. The civil service attempted to cover up a minor accident in a nuclear power plant. In January 1995, a major disaster destroyed much of the port city of Kobe, leaving six thousand fatalities. The quake itself was accepted as a part of living in an earthquake-prone area. But the public condemned the failure of the state to be prepared to manage such a predictable crisis. Later that same year, a radical religious sect, the Aum Shinrikyo, released deadly sarin gas in Tokyo subways. The ensuing investigation demonstrated the ineptitude of the police, customs agencies, and others in not better monitoring this radical group. In 1996, there was a scandal suggesting that ministry of health officials allowed the use of HIV contaminated blood. Above all, the multi-billion dollar failure of Japanese banks, the economic collapse of the late 1990s, and the seeming inability of the state to address much less overcome these crises further shook public respect for the bureaucracy. As a result, the issue of bureaucratic reform has been one of the principal democratic concerns of the past decade. Once acclaimed as the source of the postwar Japanese success, the bureaucracy had become the scapegoat for the failures of the 1990s.

While bureaucratic reform is often discussed, it became more difficult to achieve in the 1990s.[26] Party instability, shifting and short-lived coalition governments, and the decay of the LDP's structures gave additional influence to the bureaucracy and deprived reformers of the political strength to confront this powerful adversary. The proposed reforms in the bureaucracy have been modest: some call for reduction in the number of ministries and agencies; others call for breaking up the larger and most powerful ministries; and some advocate minor steps toward decentralization of what is still one of the most centralized political systems in the world. Even these small reforms have elicited strong opposition from the civil service and its supporters. None had been carried out by the end of the twentieth century. The Japanese bureaucracy remains very often a power to itself with little accountability to the ministers who can be held accountable to the voters for the bureaucracy's behavior.

THE SUPREME COURT

The postwar constitution established an independent judiciary system. At the peak of the judiciary is the Supreme Court. The chief judge and 14 other judges are designated by the Cabinet. Their appointment is confirmed by the electorate in the first House of Representatives election after their designation and then every subsequent 10 years. In practice, no judge has been voted out of office since the establishment of the constitution in 1947.

The Supreme Court serves as an appellate court. It also has explicit power of judicial review—the power to rule on the constitutionality of laws passed by the Diet. However, the Court has used this power with great circumspection. In fact, in over 50 years, it has ruled fewer than ten laws to be unconstitutional. In a sense this reflects the British tradition that served as a pattern for the current constitution. The Court acknowledges the supreme power of parliament and has therefore avoided broad use of judicial review.

The Court has also had its problems in enforcing its decisions. For example, the Supreme Court ruled several times in the 1980s that the existing apportionment of seats for the House of Representatives failed constitutional requirements of fairness and equity. Despite these rulings, the Diet moved very slowly toward redefining electoral districts to better reflect the size of their current populations. While the Court declared the exiting malapportionment to be illegal, it did not take the steps that might force resolution of the issue. It might, as requested by several of the plaintiffs, declare the most recent Diet election to be null and void because of malpportionment. Or it might, as did the U.S. Supreme Court in the 1960s, order lower courts to do the redrafting of electoral districts themselves when the political authorities failed to act in response to the Courts rulings. The lack of enforcement powers and enough legitimacy for it to compel acceptance leaves the Japanese Supreme Court a weak and mainly ineffective defender of constitutionalism. Government ministers and bureaucrats are able to act "in the shadow of the Constitution" without fear of repudiation.[27] As a result, the Japanese Supreme Court looks like a powerless body unable to force compliance with its rulings even

---

"DESCENT FROM HEAVEN"

The influence of the Japanese bureaucracy is heightened by the common practice of senior civil servants moving into high-paying, top-level jobs in private business. The practice is known as *amakudari* or "descent from heaven." Civil servants may retire early, receive generous pensions, and accept work in the private sector for very large salaries. These practices produce powerful "old boy networks" that provide business enterprises with experts on government policies and procedures. Some even contend that civil servants prepare for such lucrative positions by shaping their decisions while still in public service to the benefit of likely future employers.

In addition to the career benefits for bureaucrats, *amakudari* produces close ties and collaboration between business interests and the civil service and undermines the control of the Diet and other elected politicians over public policy. "Descent from heaven" practices also lead to corruption and the failure of proper government oversight. Many point to the cosy relations between former civil servants who had taken jobs in the banking industry and their former colleagues in the bureaucracy overseeing banks for the catastrophic banking crisis that hit Japan in the last half of the 1990s.

There is a similar practice in France known as *pantouflage,* derived from the French word for "soft slippers," as in a restful retirement. Senior civil servants take early retirement from their public duties and then move into high-ranked positions in private business or trade associations that lobby their former colleagues in state positions. The results are similar to those in Japan: close collaboration between special interests and the state; failure of appropriate government surveillance of industrial and business activities, and civil service corruption.

For further information on *amakudari,* see Ulkrike Schaede, "The Old Boy Network and Government-Business Relationship in Japan," *Journal of Japanese Studies* 21 (No. 2, 1995): 293–317.

---

when the issue is one that most Japanese citizens acknowledge as among the essential changes needed in contemporary Japanese politics.

The Supreme Court has emerged as a major advocate of civil liberties; it has even expanded the definition of these rights—as, for example, its role in protecting citizens from environmental hazards. It was the Court rather than the Diet that established the principle that the polluter must pay. In general, however, the trend seen in European democracies toward greater judicial activism has not developed in Japan.

LOCAL GOVERNMENT

The 1947 constitution said little about local government other than to leave its definition to subsequent laws to be passed by the national parliament. It established the principle of local autonomy but did not prescribe a division of responsibilities between local and national authorities. The powers and responsibilities of local government are thus those delegated by the central government. Where the central government acts, its policies supersede local government policies. One of the chief responsibilities of local government is the enforcement of national laws. The Japanese system is thus a unitary one, with the key powers held by the central government. The importance of the central government's control is demonstrated by the fact that 70 percent of local government revenues come from the national government. This is reinforced by the centralized nature of parties as well. As one observer noted:

> . . . the solution to many local problems came to rest on the decisions of the central government. In this way, the present system of party politics shifts the burden of solving many problems in a variety of areas to the National Diet, or to the central government.[28]

The national ministry that oversees local governments is called the Local Autonomy Ministry, but in spite of its name that ministry has slowly strengthened its control over local governments.

The unitary system in Japan is similar to the highly centralized British state and still centrally dominated French state. Nor is there any pressure for decentralization as even these unitary European states have experienced in the past two decades. Centralization, which was heightened during the Meiji era, was seen as a way of building the strong state necessary to face the challenges from the outside world of Western barbarians. The unitary state was simply one more dimension of the nationalistic glorification of the state and the Japanese people that was to prevail over the next 75 years.[29] Then the loss of World War II brought political changes, but these did not include any insistence on decentralization or federalism.

There are two layers of local government: prefectures and municipalities. There are 47 prefectures including those of 3 large metropolitan areas: Tokyo, Kyoto, and Osaka. Prefectural governments deal with regional economic development; highways and other major public works with impact beyond a single municipality; and the regional coordination of education standards, police, municipal governments, and the state administration. However, in many of these issues, the central government is also involved either as a policy maker or as a source of funds. The involvement of the central government leads to limits on local autonomy even while in principle it is exalted.

Each prefecture has an assembly elected by the people to serve terms of four years. There is also a popularly elected governor in each prefecture. This creates an unusual blend of presidential and parliamentary procedures in local politics. Thus, the governor has the "presidential" prerogative of vetoing unwanted legislation passed by the assembly. But governors are also subject to "parliamentary" motions of no-confidence and have the "parliamentary" power to dissolve the assembly. When there are conflicts between the governor and the assembly, they are usually resolved through negotiations. In extreme cases, the assembly may pass a no-confidence motion. Such a motion requires a three-fourths majority in the assembly, with at least two-thirds in attendance. When a no-confidence motion is passed,

the governor must dissolve the assembly for new elections or resign. Such incidents are rare; the more common pattern is the dominance of local politics by the governors. The Japanese prefectures are like the French departments at their weakest.[30]

There are 3,200 municipalities. Municipal governments are charged with the construction and administration of local parks, hospitals, health and welfare facilities, local public utilities, and local environmental protection. Each municipality elects a mayor and an assembly. With directly elected assemblies and mayors, municipal governments face the same kind of potential problems in the event of discord between the mayor and the assembly. However, party divisions in local government are less well defined than at the national level. As a result, crises between mayors and their assemblies are very rare.

There has been little public interest in decentralization in Japan. In contrast to the efforts in many European countries to achieve decentralization, in Japan there were efforts in the 1970s and early 1980s to further centralize the regime. The relatively compact size of the country has limited interest in decentralization. In addition, while the formal power structure is centralized, there is considerable room for local initiative and adaptation of centrally defined policies. The clientele relations between national party figures and local politicians and constituents assist in easing tensions from the unitary system. Thus, centralization and local autonomy seem to coexist harmoniously. Finally, there is no tradition of local autonomy to serve as a basis for separatist movements, with the exception of Okinawa.

AN END TO "KARAOKE" DEMOCRACY?

In the mid-1990s, as Japan's political institutions were under attack for their failure to deal with ingrained corruption, policy stagnation, and instability, observers described the political pattern as "karaoke democracy." The reference was to the karaoke stage, found now even in many American bars and restaurants, where people come to sing or lip-sync to recorded music. The singers come and go, but the music is limited to a small, rarely changed, and frequently repeated repertoire.[31] Some saw a break with this established pattern of LDP-dominated politics with the transfer of political power from the LDP to its rivals after 1993. Indeed, there was talk of a "regime shift" in Japan in the 1990s.[32] Despite brave talk of political reform, the major change was that of the electoral system. And, as is often the case, changes in the electoral system do not correct fundamental institutional or systemic problems. They persist under the new election rules. That seems to be the case in Japan. Even the change in singers on a karaoke stage is limited. Politicians sometimes have changed parties but they are the ones who emerged earlier and continue to be prominent actors as the 1990s come to an end. At the beginning of a new century, the LDP is back in power. The constitution is still unchanged. Policy stagnation has contributed to Japan's worst economic decline since World War II and to a possibly devastating crisis in the banks and other financial institutions.

Amidst these challenges, the political institutions remain intact. In general, constitutions that are engineered to solve past political problems do not work well. It is especially surprising that a constitution imposed on the Japanese people by a foreign conqueror has lasted so long and become so popular in a country proud of its own legacy. However, several factors account for the success of this new constitution.

First, while foreign-inspired, the constitution built on previous Japanese practices. Thus, the constitution redesigned the Meiji Constitution the Japanese had earlier imported from the West. Most important, it preserved the institution of the emperor and gave him the role of aloof symbol that he had often held in the past. The presence of the emperor gave a sense of continuity with the past while new institutions were developing. In addition, the structures introduced by the new constitution were sufficiently flexible to allow traditional Japanese practices such as deference to seniority, personal ties, clientelism, and even long-term dominance of a single party within an overall setting that remains democratic.

Second, the new political system won broad support as it provided for the rapid economic recovery of a country devastated by the war. As in West Germany, the economic success of democracy gave legitimacy to the regime. The development of an extensive social welfare system added support from people of all walks of life to the institutions that had provided for their economic security.

Finally, the success of new political institutions reflect the Japanese skill in identifying desirable features in other countries and then perfecting them in their own setting. Just as the Japanese are masters at developing and applying technologies invented elsewhere, they have proved adept in importing Western democracy and adapting it to their own historical and cultural traditions. In doing so, they have broken with some Western European principles, but they have proved the viability of Western liberal democracy in the non-Western setting. Indeed, the Japanese model of democracy may be more applicable in other non-Western countries than the "pure" European democracies.

NOTES

[1]Kyoko Inoue, *McArthur's Japanese Constitution: A Linguistic and Cultural Study of Its Making* (Chicago: University of Chicago Press, 1991).

[2]John O. Haley, "Consensual Governance: A Study of Law, Culture, and the Political Economy of Postwar Japan," in *The Political Economy of Japan*, vol. 3 (Stanford, CA: Stanford University Press, 1992), pp. 51–53.

[3]Tomoaki Kawauchi, "How the Japanese View Their Pacifist Constitution," *Japan Echo*, August 1997, pp. 47–49.

[4]John Whitney Hall, "A Monarch for Modern Japan," in Robert E. Ward, ed., *Political Development in Modern Japan* (Princeton, NJ: Princeton University Press, 1968), p. 41.

[5]Ryosuke Ishii, *A History of Political Institutions in Japan* (Tokyo: University of Tokyo Press, 1980), pp. 122–126.

[6]Akio Watanabe, *Government and Politics in Modern Japan* (Tokyo: International Society for Educational Information, 1988), p. 9.

[7]Hall, "A Monarch for Modern Japan," p. 62.

[8]Hans Baerwald, *Japan's Parliament: An Introduction* (Cambridge, England: Cambridge University Press, 1974).

[9]Kent E. Calder, *Crisis and Compensation: Public Policy and Political Stability in Japan, 1949–1986* (Princeton, NJ: Princeton University Press, 1988), p. 203.

[10]J. A. A. Stockwin, "Reforming Japanese Politics: Highway of Change or Road to Nowhere?" in Purnendra Jain and Takaski Inoguchi, eds., *Japanese Politics Today: Beyond Karaoke Democracy?* (New York: St. Martin's, 1997), p. 79.

[11]Jun-ichi Kyogoku, *The Political Dynamics of Japan* (Tokyo: University of Tokyo Press, 1987), p. 186.

[12]Gerald L. Curtis, *The Japanese Way of Politics* (New York: Columbia University Press, 1988), pp. 114–116.

[13]Calder, *Crisis and Compensation*.

[14]Minoru Nakano, "The Changing Legislative Process in the Transitional Period, in Jain and Inoguchi, eds., *Japanese Politics Today*.

[15]Kyogoku, *The Political Dynamics of Japan,* pp. 192–193.

[16]Morita Minoru, "Self-Centered Statecraft Under a Symbolic Prime Minister," *Japan Echo* 18, no 3 (1991): 28–38.

[17]Kenji Hayao, *The Japanese Prime Minister and Public Policy* (Pittsburgh: University of Pittsburgh Press, 1993).

[18]Timothy Hoye, *Japanese Politics: Fixed and Floating Worlds* (Upper Saddle River, NJ: Prentice Hall, 1998), pp. 74–75.

[19]J. A. A. Stockwin, "Parties, Politicians and the Political System," in J. A. A. Stockwin et al., *Dynamic and Immobilist Politics in Japan* (Honolulu: University of Hawaii, 1989), p. 43.

[20]Pempel, *Policy and Politics in Japan.* See also Calder, *Crisis and Compensation,* and T. J. Pempel, ed., *Policymaking in Contemporary Japan* (Ithaca, NY: Cornell University Press, 1977).

[21]Takeuchi Yasuo, "The Weakness of Japanese Democracy," *Japanese Echo* 18, no 3 (1991): 37.

[22]Takashi Inoguchi, "Japanese Bureaucracy: Coping With New Challenges," in Jain and Inoguchi, eds., *Japanese Politics Today,* p. 106.

[23]John W. Dower, *Embracing Defeat: Japan in the Wake of World War II* (New York: W. W. Norton, 1999).

[24]Karel van Wolferen, *The Enigma of Japanese Power* (New York: Knopf, 1989).

[25]*The New York Times,* 5 May 1996.

[26]Lonny E. Carlile, "The Politics of Administrative Reform," in Lonny E. Carlile and Mark C. Tilton, eds., *Is Japan Really Changing Its Ways? Regulatory Reform and the Japanese Economy* (Washington, DC: Brookings Institution Press, 1998).

[27]J. Mark Ramseyer and Frances McCall Rosenbluth, *Japan's Political Marketplace* (Cambridge, MA: Harvard University Press, 1993), pp. 150–151.

[28]Kyogoku, *The Political Dynamics of Japan,* p. 178.

[29]Ibid., p. 22.

[30]David Williams, *Japan: Beyond the End of History* (London: Routledge, 1994), pp. 21–24.

[31]Takashi Inoguichi and Purnendra C. Jain, "Introduction," in Jain and Inoguichi, eds., *Japanese Politics Today,* p. 2.

[32]T. J. Pempel, *Regime Shift: Comparative Dynamics of the Japanese Political Economy* (Ithaca, NY: Cornell University Press, 1998). See especially pp. 136–168.

Chapter 28

Japanese Political Participation: The Citizen and Politics

The construction of the new Narita International Airport near Tokyo took over two decades. The project was opposed by its neighbors so vehemently that construction was delayed for years.[1] After the completion of the facility, continuing demonstrations delayed the completion of rail and highway links between Narita and Tokyo for another decade. In the meantime, foreign visitors arriving at Narita and anticipating the well-ordered society for which Japan was so reputed, were surprised to find the new airport surrounded by barbed wire, multiple posts for checking identification papers, and lengthy traffic delays into the city.

This ability of Japanese citizens to oppose what they perceive to be autocratic actions by their government is a recently acquired skill. As in Germany, Japanese citizens have had to learn to take part in the new democratic political opportunities open to them since 1947. Earlier opportunities for political involvement had been limited. After more than 50 years, it appears that the Japanese have learned the art of political participation well. There is much evidence that the Japanese have learned the rights and duties of democratic citizens in a relatively short period.

A set of effective and responsive interest groups has emerged to assist citizens in expressing their views and in translating their views into policies. In contrast, the Japanese party system is in turmoil. The party system that was long dominated by the Liberal Democratic party provided both strength and challenges to the emerging democratic order in Japan. The party system that emerged in the mid-1950s and lasted for more than 40 years is now very much under pressure. The future shape of the emerging new party system and the ability of Japanese parties to fulfill the linkage between state and citizen were still very much uncertain as the twentieth century ended.

THE INDIVIDUAL CITIZEN IN POLITICS

There is an extensive system of clientelism or patron-client politics in Japan. These networks of political ties link elected and party officials with citizens. Party notables provide benefits to their constituents, such as assistance in winning government contracts or in avoiding bureaucratic delays, in exchange for political support in the form of votes and financial contributions. In some cases, political support is exchanged simply for the prestige of the presence of a political notable at a supporter's wedding or funeral. The client relations in Japan differ from those found in many Third World countries. In other settings, the patron is often a powerful landlord or traditional communal leader who can extract political support by virtue of social or economic position. In Japan, the contemporary politician is

> . . . more a supplicant promising to deliver more pork barrel than his competitor. Ties of sentiment based on family, marriage, school relationships, favors to be repaid and so on are crucial to forging bonds between politician and voter. . . . But politicians who prove themselves to be ineffective in providing what the Japanese like to call a "pipe" from the center to the locality to serve local interests find these ties of sentiments to be fragile indeed.[2]

These individualistic clientele relations have been found among all parties and in all parts of Japan, but they were best developed in the rural bastions of the Liberal Democratic party. Although this clientelism resembles on the surface the once-important American urban political machines, in fact it is based on historical Japanese political practices. The clientele relations represent another example of Japan's blending of its traditional culture with Western political

democracy. Of course, such a clientelist system leads to inefficiency. At its peak, approximately 30 percent of the Japanese budget went to such particularistic benefits as opposed to about half that much in Britain or the United States.[3] It also affected the "efficiency" of voting since voters were encouraged to look at election alternatives in these material terms rather than in terms of policy options.

Clientele politics once provided the core of political party life. Now they are weakened because of excesses and political changes. Clientelism produced massive corruption that tainted the reputations of parties and politicians during the late 1980s and early 1990s.[4] Corruption, graft, and scandal contributed to a crisis of the party system that is not yet resolved. This in turn facilitated changes in the electoral system that have reduced the need for clientelist relations. Finally, the economic crisis of the late 1990s raised questions about whether Japan could still "afford" the extra costs imposed on the state by clientelist politics. Traditions of pork barrel politics and the blending of economic and political elites, however, will die only slowly, especially in a country like Japan where clientelism is so deeply ingrained in its culture.

Other social changes are affecting traditional patterns of citizen political action. The persistence of the historical sense of community in many small and medium-size cities and towns long provided for extensive citizen participation

---

PATRON-CLIENT POLITICS

In its use of clientelism, Japan's political parties follow a pattern that is at once in harmony with its historical culture and a common form of party politics in many parts of the world. Patron-client relations are not unique to Japan. They characterized the big-city political machines in the United States in late nineteenth and early twentieth centuries. They are often found in Third World countries, as we shall see is the case in Nigeria. Clientelism is often criticized for the dependency and subordination it imposes on the clients and for its propensity to use public resources for particularistic goals or for individual payoffs.

In Japan clientelism corresponds to histor-

ical patterns of vertical and hierarchical social relations. These highly personalized relations allow individuals at the bottom of the hierarchy to use their connections to obtain attention to their concerns by individuals much higher in the system. Such access gives citizens the sense of political competence, a sense that they can affect what those who govern do as it relates to their personal needs. These deep cultural roots are likely to mean that clientelism will reappear in Japan as the new party system emerges in the next decade. It will probably have different features than those that prevailed until the political shifts of the 1990s. But clientelism is likely to persist.

in local politics. In the last two decades, rapid economic growth and change has affected traditional life patterns in these communities. One result has been "a decided trend toward greater citizen participation, activism, and dialogue in local government."[5] In another form, the same community orientation leads the Japanese to engage in politics through groups.[6] They seem more likely to affiliate with groups than are citizens of other democracies.[7]

One aspect of this increased participation has been the growth in citizen movements at the local and regional level. Many citizens, unhappy with the usual political organizations such as parties and interest groups, have joined new and more specialized political action groups. These groups grew very rapidly in number and importance during the 1970s. They have continued to play important political roles both at the local and national levels. At times, these new citizen action groups have advocated such vague notions as "the right to sunshine, the right to an unobstructed view, or the right to see and hear."[8] At other times, they pursue specific goals that have not been addressed by established parties and groups. Many have championed the environment or consumers' rights. Occasionally, as in the case of the airport protests, they have developed into major challenges to decisions by the national government.

They are particularly effective at the local level in influencing political decisions. At the national level, these citizen movements are more frequently successful in simply expressing the sentiments and usually the opposition of their members to the government's activities. The protests that plagued the Tokyo airport are extreme examples of this opposition. Other causes, such as environmental movements and protests against high speed train corridors,[9] have mobilized large numbers. In less dramatic incidents, the citizen movements have served as a means of expressing the tensions and uncertainties related to the very rapid economic growth and social change Japan has experienced in the last quarter of a century.

VOTING

As in most democracies, voting is the most common, and frequently almost the only, political act of the Japanese citizen. Voting turnout in Japan is low compared to European countries but much higher than in U.S. elections. In most Diet elections, approximately 70 percent of the eligible voters take part. Unlike the situation in Western Europe and the United States, where national elections attract more voters than local contests, participation in Japanese local elections is even higher than the turnout in national elections. This reflects a long tradition of voting in local elections and the strength of personal and friendship ties between local politicians and their voters. In recent elections, both national and local, turnout has declined. For example, in the 1996 national Diet elections, voter participation dropped to only 59.7 percent, a postwar record low turnout. In part, this is due to general disgust with the corruption of the major parties and their leaders. It is also due to the weakened partisan attachments as the transformation of the party system undermines old voter-party loyalties and tries to build new ones.

The question of why Japanese voters select the parties they do is much less clear than in other democracies. Japan lacks the social, regional, religious, and ethnic cleavages that tend to structure the voting decision in Western Europe and North America.[10] Prior to 1996, there were some differences between the LDP and the Japan Socialist party along occupational lines (see Table 28–1). Even these loose alignments are unclear now with the major recent changes in the party system and especially the collapse of the leftist Socialist party. Japanese voters are less strongly

Table 28–1 Composition of Votes on the Basis of Occupation, 1986

	Liberal Democratic Party	Japan Socialist Party
Farmers	28%	9%
Manufacturers and merchants	24	11
White-collar workers	30	51
Blue-collar workers	18	28

Source: Adapted from Scott C. Flanagan et al., *The Japanese Voter* (New Haven, CT: Yale University Press, 1991), p. 80.

attached to a political party than are voters in other democracies. They tend to be more interested in the personalities of specific candidates than do voters in Europe. There is some evidence that Japanese voters are "issue voters," who base their election choices on the parties' position on key issues. The issues that seem most potent in structuring the vote are corruption and money politics[11] and perceptions of the ability of the party to manage the economy.[12]

As in Europe, election campaigns are relatively short, with usually only three to five weeks of formal campaigning. There are a number of restrictions on campaign practices that are common in other democracies. For example, door-to-door canvassing is barred; posters and billboards are limited; and radio and television time for parties is relatively restricted. Japanese elections are nonetheless among the most expensive in the democratic world. Prior to electoral reform in the mid-1990s, competition between factions of the same parties as well as competition between parties produced enormous election costs. Some assert that Japan is "the most expensive political system on earth."[13] The large sums were used to finance the patron-client political networks and payoffs that were part of the political scene prior to 1995. By 1996, new laws were in place limiting campaign expenses and contributions. But the problems of money politics continued. One newspaper editorial reported that it had seen candidates in the 1996 elections "peddling favors" rather than engaging in policy debates.[14] It remains to be seen if the electoral system and party changes in the late 1990s will result in a decline of these costs.

THE ELECTORAL SYSTEM

There are two national elections: one for the House of Representatives and the other for the House of Councillors. Since the terms of office for the two chambers differ in length, these elections are usually held separately. Occasionally, the dissolution of the House of Representatives is timed so that the new elections for the lower chamber can take place at the same time as the councillors are elected. House of Councillors elections take place every three years when half the membership is elected.

Until recently, the electoral system for the House of Representatives was based on multi-member districts of usually three to five seats per district. Unlike the multimember districts in most systems of proportional representation, however, the Japanese system presented candidates as individuals rather than as party lists. Each voter cast a single vote and the candidates with the largest votes were elected. Large parties, such as the Liberal Democratic party (LDP) could and did present several candidates. As a result, competition was often as much between LDP candidates as between the LDP and other parties. This tended to reduce discussion of issues and instead focus campaign rhetoric on competitive promises for more money or projects for the district. For example, in a district with three seats, two small parties might each present only one candidate while the much larger LDP would have three candidates. The LDP, even if it had enough votes to win all three seats, might risk dividing its vote among its three candidates in such a way that one or more of the other parties' candidates would be elected. This meant that the campaign was complicated for the large parties and required careful organization of their voters to maximize their seats. It also opened up the process to factional struggles within the party and to involvement by business interests who promised help and money to organize the vote. The result was massive corruption in all of the major parties but especially in the LDP.

A second problem was malapportionment of electoral districts coming from recent population shifts. Unlike the United States, where electoral boundaries must be redrawn every 10 years in accordance with the latest census, there is no such requirement in Japan. This results in a bias favoring rural districts, which in general tend to be more conservative. Even after some changes, the ratio in voters to seats was still three times greater in some of the larger urban districts compared to the smallest rural districts in the early 1990s.

After years of acrimonious debate on the subject of electoral reform and reapportionment, the Diet finally enacted electoral reform in 1994 and 2000. In the first reform, the new rules for House of Representative elections established 300 single-member districts with a simple majority vote as in the United States and Britain. An additional

200 deputies were elected from party lists through proportional representation on a regional basis. The 2000 reform reduced the number of representatives from 500 to 480, with all twenty cuts coming from among those representatives previously elected by proportional representation. As a result, 300 seats are elected under single-member district, plurality rules and 180 under proportional representation. Both the 1994 and 2000 reforms were designed to make it harder for smaller parties to win seats in the House of Representatives and to foster a two-party system.

The electoral system used for House of Councillors elections is somewhat different. Of the total membership of 252 councillors, 100 are elected in a national proportional representation system. There is only one district for these 100 seats, and candidates are elected in proportion to their parties' strength. As a result, even candidates from small parties are able to win election to the House of Councillors. The other 152 members are elected in 47 prefectural districts ranging in size from 2 to 8 seats.

In both House of Representative and House of Councillor elections, citizens cast two votes: one for a specific representative from their district and a second for a party list. Candidates can run both in single member districts and as part of party lists. The reforms for both houses also included public subsidization of election campaign costs. Limits on the cost of the campaigns and on raising other funds were also implemented.

The 1994 electoral system has been used only a few times: in 1996 and 2000 for the House of Representatives; in 1998 for the House of Councillors. It will take several more elections before we can assess the effects of the new electoral rules. In defining the electoral districts, some of the malapportionment was remedied. As for the effects on the parties, the first elections suggest that hopes for a simplification in the party system by reducing the number of parties or creating two blocs of parties were unlikely to be achieved through electoral reform alone. Party factionalism has declined in the LDP and virtually disappeared in the Socialist party along with the near disappearance of that party in its entirety. The hope for greater discourse on issues did not materialize since most of the competition was between LDP candidates and former LDP members with little disagreements over public policy.

WOMEN IN POLITICS

The cultural values of the East persist most clearly in relations between men and women. To a Westerner accustomed to a society striving for equality between the sexes, men in Japan appear still solidly male chauvinist and women seem oppressed and submissive. One observer notes:

> . . . husbands frequently treat their wives with disdain. Women are usually meek and long-suffering in their dealings with their menfolk, and girls hide shyly behind a screen of simpering. Social life, insofar as it exists, has little place for the married woman. A double sexual standard, which leaves the man free and the woman restricted, is still common.[15]

The 1947 constitution pressed toward equality between men and women, barring political, economic, or social discrimination on the basis of sex, requiring mutual consent for marriages and equal rights for both marriage partners, and granting women full political rights alongside men. Progress toward these goals, however, has been slow.

The Japanese women's movement has not been a powerful one. Women still cling to traditional values and most have ignored feminist politics. The largest and most active women's groups have been those motivated by traditional values of family and household that seek to support the role of women as housewives. Furthermore, Japanese women do not see politics as a vehicle for changing their social roles.[16] Even modest effort to press for equal rights has engendered broad public opposition in the press and elsewhere, as if the very survival of Japanese culture were at stake.[17] What victories are won by women are usually partial at best. For example, women pressed successful court cases in the 1970s to end the practice of requiring women to quit work when they marry or reach marriageable age. But informal pressure still works to force many Japanese women to quit most jobs when they marry or approach 29 years of age.[18]

Deep-seated cultural patterns leave Japanese women politically behind their counterparts in

Western democracies. Unlike European women, whose political interest is now as high as that of men, Japanese women are still less likely to show political interest or to identify with a political party. However, differences in voting rates have virtually disappeared as Japanese women have become accustomed to the right to vote. For the first few years after their enfranchisement, Japanese women tended to turn out for elections at much lower rates than did men. By the mid-1970s, that difference had disappeared, and women actually voted slightly more than did men. However, women still seem to regard political activity as part of the man's world.

As in Western Europe, the contemporary Japanese women's movement emerged out of the radical student groups or peace movements of the 1960s. Sensing that women's issues were neglected or openly scorned by the student organizations, women organized their own movements. This gave the new women's groups a leadership corps, but the radical positions they adopted generally limited their appeal to a small audience. Thus, in the early 1980s, the Japanese women's movement could claim only 2,000–3,000 members.

Women have become very prominent in local politics and community affairs. They are involved in local government and community citizen and volunteer groups. This is particularly the case among women born after World War II, who have grown up with the right to vote and with improving images of community roles for women. An estimated 10 percent of suburban women are now involved in volunteer activities such as consumers' groups, parent-teacher associations, and the like.[19] The step from local politics to national politics is a short one and it is already being made by many Japanese women.

However, the movement toward expanding opportunities for women in national politics has been slow. The number of women elected to the House of Representatives increased by 50 percent in 1996, but that still provided a total of only 23 women out of a total of 500 Representatives (4.3 percent). The figure in the House of Councillors was higher: 13.9 percent. So far, with little competitive pressure to do so, Japanese party leaders show little interest in recruiting women for national politics. In the 1996 election, women candidates made up less than 3 percent of the LDP nominees. An example of a failed sensitivity to recruiting women can be seen in the late 1980s. The Socialist party selected a woman as its leader, Takako Doi. In response, the LDP prime minister brought two women into the national cabinet to offset any advantage that the Socialists might gain from their woman leader. After the next election when Doi's party did not significantly increase its strength in the next national elections among women voters, the LDP prime minister promptly dismissed the women ministers.[20] Despite limited opportunities, in public opinion polls Japanese women tend to express greater satisfaction with government and society than do men.[21]

Takako Doi stepped down as leader of the Democratic Socialist party in 1991 after her party suffered electoral reverses in local elections. She faced challenges during her stint at leadership based on her gender. Other politicians, including those in her own party, seemed more concerned with her appearance and apparel than with her political ideas.[22] After the 1993 elections, however, Doi was selected as the first woman president of the House of Representatives. While the position is more ceremonial than powerful, it does place a woman politician in a highly visible public office. Doi continued in that post after the 1996 elections and shortly thereafter resumed leadership of the weakened Social Democratic Party of Japan.

Most recent governments have included two or more women cabinet members. Heartening as such progress is, the political and social positions of women in Japan remain well behind what is found in Western democracies. It is likely that change will continue, but not without frequent reversals.

INTEREST GROUP POLITICS

Over the past 50 years, an extensive set of well-organized interest groups have emerged in Japan to advocate a variety of interests ranging from environmental protection to the owners of Korean pinball machine *(pachinko)* parlors.[23] As in West European democracies, the most important and most powerful groups tend to be those based

Table 28–2 Major Occupational Interest Groups
in Japan

LABOR UNIONS

Japanese Trade Union Council *(Rengo)*
  Umbrella organization encompassing most trade
  unions
  7.9 million members
National Confederation of Trade Unions
  affiliated with the Japanese Communist party
National Trade Union council
  mainly railroad workers

EMPLOYERS' ASSOCIATIONS

Japan Federation of Economic Organizations
(Keidanren)
  Links 121 trade associations and approximately
  913 individual firms
Japan Chamber of Commerce and Industry *(Nissho)*
Japan Federation of Employers *(Nikkeiren)*
Japan Committee for Economic Development
 (Doyukai)

FARMERS' ASSOCIATION

National Federation of Farmers *(Nokyo)*
  Close to the LDP
  5 million members

on occupation (see Table 28–2). In the past, most
interest groups formed close alliances with specific political parties. However, the fluidity of the
party system in the past decade has weakened the
partisan linkages between parties and interest
groups.

Japanese business interests have been particularly effective in gaining influence in government policy making. There is close interaction
between the business community, the bureaucracy, and the Liberal Democratic party in the
formulation of economic and industrial policies.
Indeed, the relationship among these three groups
is so intimate that some have given the process
the label of "Japan, Inc." Representatives from
business and financial associations are invited
members of key economic policy advisory bodies such as the Economic Advisory Council, the

Council on Industrial Structures, and the Council
on Financial Policies.

As a result, the business groups enjoyed insider status, giving them extensive control over
government policies that affect their interests.
Business trade associations and cartels were relied upon by the bureaucracy and government to
negotiate on pending statutes and to implement
policies.[24] Outside groups, even those representing large numbers of people, could protest and
complain, but they could do little to influence
policy or prevent its implementation. This collaboration permitted Japan's extraordinary economic growth in the 1980s. It also contributed to
the financial scandals and economic stagnation
that rocked Japan in the 1990s.

Business ties to politics are in flux as a result
of the recent changes in Japanese politics. Many
large enterprises were caught up in the financial
scandals of government officials in the early
1990s. Furthermore, all business interests have
been affected by the economic crises of the late
1990s and have fewer resources to engage in the
level of money politics that prevailed earlier. With
their privileged ally, the LDP, in chaos and sometimes out of power, business interests have
searched for new ways of influence. One of the
main approaches has been for business to
strengthen already strong ties with senior civil
servants. But even with these ties, business no
longer is as powerful a political voice because of
growing internal divisions. Export-oriented industries have different public policy interests than
do those businesses committed to protecting their
economic niche by tariffs and other protectionist
policies; new technology-based industry has different interests than do heavy industries; growing industries differ in their desires for public
policies than do declining industries; financial institutions have different policy concerns than do
those to whom they loan. These divisions reduce
the ability of business to exercise its influence on
Japanese politics compared to its effectiveness in
shaping economic policies up until the mid-
1980s.

The Japanese trade union movement has faced
several challenges to obtaining a voice in politics. A strong sense of paternalism among employers in the private sector and long-term or even
lifetime employment weakened the ability of

unions to mobilize workers. In addition, the major unions represented all-out opposition to the existing capitalist system politics. With a strong Marxist flavor until the mid-1980s, the trade unions' activities were more often political than focused on wages, benefits, and protection of their members. Japan had among the higher strike rates for industrialized democracies in the 1960s and 1970s. The highly political and often extremist views of the Japanese trade union leaders excluded them from participating in dialogues with government and business over public policy affecting the economy and their members. In addition, the unions were divided into two rival confederations. Part of the division was based on different political party loyalties. Another source of division was between the more militant unions that recruited primarily among government employees and the less activist unions based in the private sector where workers felt more vulnerable.

In 1989, the two major trade unions came together in a single organization, the Japanese Trade Union Council or Rengo. At about the same time, the unions moderated their tone and sought a more constructive role in the policy process and in the workplace.[25] The strike rate has dropped to among the lowest in industrialized democracies. For example, from 1979 to the early 1990s, the level of participation in strikes fell in Japan by over 200 percent, the greatest drop of all industrialized countries.[26] In its first few years, Rengo flourished as a result of its newly found unity and also because of a prosperous economy. Union voices were strong and earned greater respect among government policy makers. Rengo expanded its contacts with the center-right political groups that had long dominated Japanese politics. It redirected its focus on workplace issues of wages and working conditions. The center of union activity shifted from national politics to the individual plant and enterprises. Rengo retained a full political agenda as a voice for political reform. Rengo, along with Keidanren, the largest business association, was among the principal advocates of the electoral reforms.

At the national level, labor now has seats alongside other economic actors in discussions of economic policy. The chief advances have been at the local level where salaries and work conditions improved through the more cooperative stance of the unions. But a national law brought a significant gain for Japanese workers in terms of their hours on the job. Japanese workers once worked on average 400 hours more per year than did workers in other advanced democracies. By the mid-1990s, under the new law, Japan's working level had fallen to approximately the same as for workers in the United States and Britain but still higher than among continental European democracies.[27]

The slowing of political reform and the economic crisis of the late 1990s reduced the influence of Rengo both in politics and in the workplace. The level of unionization is low— around 25 percent of eligible workers belong to a union. As in other industrial countries, Japanese labor has been further weakened by a continuing decline in the number of union members.

Interest groups are important actors in Japanese politics and they will remain so in the future. At the present, however, their strategies and alliances are in flux as a result of broader political, economic, and social changes under way in Japan. This is truly an unusual era and its consequences are far-reaching for all political actors. No doubt the extensive system of interrelationships between interest groups, political parties, and bureaucrats will continue and be important factors in shaping public policy. But the new relationships, when they become clear, are likely to be different from those that dominated Japanese politics from before 1955 to 1995. Many of the old actors will still be around but the ways in which they interact are likely to be different.

POLITICAL PARTIES

One of the principal characteristics of liberal democracies is the central importance of competitive elections between two or more independent political parties. Japan has always had more than one political party, but the free competition among the parties led to government by one of these parties for over forty years: the Liberal Democratic party (LDP). That party dominated Japanese politics in a way not found in other democracies. Only in the last few years have the

Table 28–3 Election Results for House of Representative Elections in Japan, 1983–93

Party	1983		1986		1990		1993	
	Percent	Seats	Percent	Seats	Percent	Seats	Percent	Seats
Liberal Democratic party (LDP)	45.8%	250	49.4%	300	46.1%	275	36.6%	223
LDP dissidents	2.4	8	1.8	6	–0–	–0–	20.4	103
Japanese Socialist party (JSP)	19.5	112	17.2	85	24.4	136	15.4	70
Democratic Socialist party (DSP)	7.3	38	6.4	26	4.8	14	3.5	15
Communist party of Japan (JCP)	9.3	26	8.8	26	8.0	16	7.7	15
Komeito	10.1	58	9.4	56	8.0	45	8.1	51
Other	5.7	19	6.8	13	8.7	26	7.8	34

other parties had a place in government and then their success was due more to schisms in the LDP than to a shift of public support to the long-time opposition parties. Japan thus still has a dominant party system where one party is so clearly stronger than its rivals that it is able to control national politics (see Table 28–3). Other parties operated freely, contesting elections and holding seats in the Diet. These minority parties were able to win local elections, but they lacked the ability to win control of the national government. The party system was well established and unchanged since the merger of the old Liberal and Democratic parties into the LDP in 1955. Known as the "55 system," this configuration of parties and political practices dominated Japanese politics from 1955 to 1993.

By the middle of the 1990s, the party system was changing its form and membership. A new electoral system was at work; new parties had

---

THE 55 SYSTEM

In 1955, the Liberal and Democratic parties unified into the Liberal Democratic party (LDP). In doing so, the parties consolidated the political pattern that had been emerging since the end of the war: the dominance of the center-right, now unified into a single party and an ineffectual left-wing Socialist party doomed to perpetual opposition at the national level. From 1955–1993, the LDP controlled a majority of the seats in the House of Representatives and provided all prime ministers. This was a dominant or hegemonic single party system where other parties could compete but not win in national politics. Some referred to the pattern as a "one and a half party system" with the Liberal Democrats as the one party and the Socialist party as the feckless half party.

The 55 system developed its own set of party practices: strong factionalism, clientelism, and gerontocracy. It featured close ties between business and finance leaders, the bureaucracy, and the LDP to ensure the state's assistance in rebuilding the economy and expanding Japanese trade abroad. Eventually, the 55 system brought policy stagnation, unresponsiveness to pressures for political and economic reform, political corruption, and public disillusionment with the parties and the political system. Party and political changes at the end of the 1990s have weakened many of the features of the 55 system, but it is not at all clear that its essential features will not survive.

Table 28–4　1996 House of Representative Election Results

	Percent of vote*	Seats in House of Representatives
Liberal Democratic party (LDP)	38.6%	239 (35.7%)
New Frontier party (NFP)	28.0	156 (28.0%)
Democratic Party of Japan (DPJ)	10.6	52 (13.4%)
Japanese Communist party (JCP)	12.6	26 (12.9%)
Social Democratic Party of Japan (DSPJ)	2.2	15 (4.3%)
Sakigake	1.3	2 (1.2%)
Others	2.3	1 (0.6%)
Independents	4.4	9 (4.4%)

*In single member districts

emerged and old ones changed their appearance. While the LDP remained the principal party, it now faced new and more formidable opposition as shown in the results of the 1996 House of Representative elections (see Table 28–4).

The Liberal Democratic Party

The Liberal Democratic party was formed in 1955 by the merger of two conservative parties—the Liberals and the Democrats. Even before their merger these parties had dominated Japanese politics; in their unified form, the LDP has continued to do so. Since 1958, the Liberal Democrats have gained between 36.6 and 57.8 percent of the popular vote in elections to the lower house. This has been enough to give it a majority in nearly every Diet. Twice in the 1970s, it lacked an absolute majority in the Diet but was able to continue its hold on government due to the divisions of the opposition and informal alliances with tiny LDP dissident parties. Not until 1993, when a deeply divided LDP scored its worst ever result of only 36.6 percent of the vote, was the LDP forced out of government by a shaky coalition of other parties. In the 1996 elections, the LDP's strength went up slightly and since then it has again exercised political control through a variety of weak coalition governments.

In a way, the Liberal Democratic party was within itself its own multiparty system. The party had a number of well-organized and competing factions. It was accurate to view the LDP as a "coalition of factions"[28] Five or six factions

dominated the life of the party. Their negotiations and coalitions determined the party leader, who became prime minister, and the composition of the government. Each faction was headed by a powerful leader who used his faction to win a share of power for his followers and to wrangle for his turn as prime minister. These factions were based less on ideological differences than on personal cliques behind prominent LDP leaders. The factions were highly organized and activity within the factions was more lively than party activity.

The party's strength came not so much out of its formal membership but out of its ability to draw in large numbers of supporters through patron-client political networks. Liberal Democratic politicians exchanged favors in the form of jobs, government contracts, or assistance in dealing with the bureaucracy for political support from those who receive these benefits. The client networks were strongest in the rural areas and small towns, where a strong sense of community binds citizens and their local politicians.

The personalized nature of clientelism means that citizens relate more to the individual personalities than to the party as an institution or as a set of policy positions. The LDP reflects this in its lack of a clear-cut party doctrine or program. The party means different things to different people and at different times. Its major orientation is toward conservative economic and social policies. But the LDP built Japan's extensive social welfare system and gave the state a leading role in developing and directing the economy.

Above all, the party seems to value compromise and accommodation over attachment to a clearly defined party doctrine. In adjusting to political variations within the party and to opinion shifts in the general population, the Liberal Democrats have preferred pragmatism to principle. The Liberal Democrats' pragmatism and their ability to provide rewards to large numbers of supporters accounts for the durability of such a coalition of factions.

The LDP has its political base in the farm population, which still accounts for about 10 percent of the work force. It also has strength among Japan's small and medium-sized commercial and industrial enterprises. However, the dominance of the party is based on its ability to appeal to a broad range of voters regardless of social and demographic categories. It is the wide appeal cutting across all segments of society that has provided the electoral basis for the LDP's political dominance.

At the end of the 1990s, the LDP remained the single most important party in Japan. But its 40-year hegemonic position had ended. Governments have been formed without the LDP's participation. In other cases, the LDP has had to allow leaders from other parties to take the key position of prime minister even when the LDP has made up the largest part of the parliamentary majority. Fundamentally, however, the LDP today still stands as the principal party in Japan, if no longer a hegemonic one. Less has changed than has remained the same; one analysis suggests that these were "changes . . . required in order for things to remain more or less the same."[29] The LDP factional disputes continue and reduce the authority of the party's president and, when the party rules, the power of the prime minister. The party's association with financial scandals and the economic crises of the 1990s have weakened the LDP but not destroyed it as a political party. But its survival as the major political party is due less to its own abilities than to the divisions and inadequacies of its opponents.

The New Parties of the Center-Right

The principal opposition to the LDP is provided by several splinter groups that have broken with the LDP. Since the mid-1990s, these parties have come and gone. They have allied with each other, with parties of the left and right, and with the LDP. They have changed names several times, with such innovative titles as "the New New Party." But their electoral appeal is to the same voters who have supported the LDP in the past.

Above all, these new parties have failed to define clear alternatives to the LDP. Their basic economic, political, and social positions are essentially the same as those of the LDP. Originally, their differences with the LDP lay in their support for greater political and economic reform. After a few token economic changes and the change in the electoral rules, these parties lost their reform agendas and even their interest in change. They are more than anything vehicles for the ambitions of the political leaders that head them.

The Japanese party system is very unstable at the present with no clear alternative yet to emerge on the center-right to the LDP. This is demonstrated by Table 28–5. It shows the dramatic shifts in party delegations between the elections in October 1996 and two years later—without any elections taking place. The principal development was the collapse of the New Frontier party with its elected members going back to the LDP or to some other center-right party. The New Frontier party was led by Ichiro Ozawa. In the 1996 election, it appeared to establish itself as the principal center-right rival to the LDP when it took 28 percent of the vote and won 156 seats in the House of Representatives. But Ozawa's leadership was erratic and by 1998 the New Frontier party was virtually gone. It no longer had a presence as such in the Diet.

At the end of the 1990s, the two largest non-LDP center-right parties were the Democratic Party of Japan (DPJ) and the Liberal party. Both have their origins among leaders and voters who in the past supported the LDP. Many of their Diet members and supporters were part of the New Frontier party that contested the 1996 elections and then collapsed. The Democratic party is headed by Naoto Kan. The political positions of the Democrats are very close to those of the LDP. Its once important focus on political and economic reform has diminished. It is a strong voice of criticism to the LDP's attempts to redress the economic crisis but it does not offer a clear alternative view.

Table 28–5 Shifts in Party Alignments in the Japanese House of Representatives, 1996 to 1999

Party	Representatives elected in October 1996	Representatives in the Diet as of the Middle of 1999	Gain or Loss
CENTER-RIGHT			
Liberal Democrats	239	266	+27
New Frontier party	156	–0–	–156
Democratic Party of Japan	52	93	+41
Liberal party	–0–	39	+39
Sakigake	2	2	–0–
New Komeito and Reformers Network	–0–	52	+52
CENTER-LEFT			
Japanese Communist party	26	26	–0–
Social Democratic party	15	14	–1
OTHERS			
Independents	9	6	–3
Other parties	1	2	+1
Vacancy		1	+1
Totals	500	500	

In the 1998 House of Councillors elections the Democratic party emerged as the largest opposition party to the LDP. Its success deprived the LDP of a majority in that chamber of the Diet. As a result, the LDP prime minister stepped down. In the ensuing struggle to choose a new prime minister, the Democratic party leader Naoto Kan was the candidate elected in the House of Councillors. But the LDP's Keizo Obuchi was elected in the House of Representatives. (When the two chambers differ on the choice of the prime minister, the more powerful House of Representatives' selection prevails.) The Democrats continue to lead a shaky majority against the LDP in the House of Councillors and occasionally slow or block LDP legislation.

The Liberal party is headed by Ichiro Ozawa. It is another remnant of the New Frontier party. Ozawa and his followers are mainly LDP dissidents. They have tried to establish a distinctive identity by allying with the liberal tradition in Western Europe, presenting their party as the Japanese equivalent to the British Liberal party or the German Free Democratic party. Its electorate is composed of voters with similar social and economic backgrounds to the LDP and the Democratic party. Early in 1999, the Liberal party formed a loose coalition with the LDP in order to shore up the

shaky Obuchi government, especially in the House of Councillors where the LDP lacks a majority of its own. The Liberal party's future in this coalition is uncertain especially given the unpredictability and ambitions of its leader, Ichiro Ozawa.

Another party of the center-right represents an entirely different political tradition and is not composed of LDP dissidents, the Komeito. The Komeito, known earlier in English as the "Clean Government party," is the political branch of the Buddhist Soka Gakkai sect. The political program of the Komeito is not clear-cut although usually more to the right than to the left of center. In recent years it has opposed liberalization reforms that have reduced the state's role in the economy. But the party defies placement on a left-right scale and has been very opportunistic in seeking allies. In the 1970s, the party flirted with the Communists and then returned to a more conservative stance. At the end of the 1970s, it tried to form an alliance with a small center-left party. Then, at the end of the 1980s, the Komeito sought closer ties with the ruling LDP. More recently, the party dropped its own identity and joined in the New Frontier party for the 1996 elections. When the New Frontier party fell apart after 1996, the Komeito reappeared and has tried to reassert its own distinctive identity.

Despite all these various strategies, the Komeito has usually polled no more than 8–10 percent of the overall vote. The Komeito has two groups of voters: the key support comes from the Soka Gakkai religion; other support comes from more disparate groups of voters dissatisfied with the status quo for a variety of economic, political, and cultural reasons. The religious link is at once its best asset and its biggest liability. The Komeito gains a large and highly loyal body of follows from its links with Soka Gakkai. But its association with a minority religious group hinders its attractiveness to the Shinto majority in Japan. As a result, the party has both strong supporters and strong opponents.

The Parties of the Left

The Social Democratic Party of Japan (SDPJ) is the new name adopted by the Socialist party in the early 1990s. The change in name was symbolic of a new and presumably more moderate approach to politics. Between its reorganization after World War II and the mid-1980s, the Socialist party had strong ideological positions based on Marxism and pacifism. Long divided over ideological disputes and unable to present a credible alternative to the LDP because of its extremist positions, the Socialists have been in steady decline from the mid-1960s to the present. Until the mid-1960s, the Socialist party usually attracted about one-third of votes in national elections. By 1996, the SDPJ's share of the vote was only 2.2 percent.

The old Socialist party advocated a doctrinaire socialism until the mid-1980s. It also championed antiwar and antinuclear causes during the 1950s and 1960s. The party gained more of its support from popular sympathy for its peace and antinuclear stands than from public interest in its radical socioeconomic programs. The JSP's hostility to Liberal Democratic rule, its use of obstructionist and almost violent tactics in the Diet, and its ambivalence about postwar political institutions made it an antisystem party for much of its first 30 years. However, when the JSP governed in towns and cities, the actual practice of its members was more pragmatic than hard-line socialist. Indeed, the JSP built personal client networks at the local level based on material exchanges, just as the LDP did at all levels of politics.

The Socialist party also has an extensive system of factions. Unlike the LDP, the SDPJ has not been able to maintain its unity. The party split into two roughly equal parties early in the 1950s and then reunited in 1955. It split again between moderate and radical factions in 1960 with the creation of the Democratic Socialist party (DSP). Even now, the party is plagued by disagreements within its ranks over key issues such as defense policies, policy toward Korea, and nuclear energy.

In 1986, the JSP began important modifications in its style and doctrine. A new party program, "The New Declaration," gave the party a social democratic stance very similar to that found in the moderate left-wing parties in the German Federal Republic and Scandinavia. Under the leadership of Takako Doi, the Socialists moved toward moderation and pragmatism. In 1991, the party changed its name to the Democratic Socialist Party of Japan. These changes do not appear to have won the Socialists many new voters. Indeed, the 1993 election results represented an all-time low figure for the Socialists. It came at a time when the SDPJ might have expected good returns since the LDP was in such political trouble. However, the anti-LDP vote went elsewhere.

Already in decline, the SDPJ lost nearly all of its remaining support when it joined the LDP in a coalition government. The SDPJ leader, Tomiichi Murayama, became prime minister but the government was clearly controlled by the LDP. For many of the long-term supporters of the Socialist party, this seemed like an act of treason. The party had already abandoned most of its Marxist doctrine but to ally with its long-term and often bitter rival, the LDP, was too much for the core Socialist voters to bear. From an already record low 15.4 percent share of the vote in 1993, the Socialists virtually dropped out of the political scene in the 1996 election with only 2.2 percent of the vote. Some of its deputies ran for election under the Democratic party label with little success; some ran as Socialists; others simply pulled out of politics.[30] It was a resounding defeat of what had long been Japan's second most important party.

In the aftermath of the 1996 election defeat, Takako Doi returned as party leader. But she was not able to renew the dynamism that she brought the party in the 1980s. Prospects for a revival of the Socialist party seem slim. It has always lacked a solid base in the working class. Japanese voters seem much less motivated by class considerations in making voting decisions than are voters in Britain or even in France. Voters seeking ways to oppose the LDP now have other, apparently more attractive options.

One of these options for voters committed to leftist values is the Communist party. The Japanese Communist party (JCP) moderated its policies in the 1960s and 1970s at about the same time some European communist parties were doing the same thing.[31] The JCP dropped Marxism-Leninism and the doctrine of the "dictatorship of the proletariat." It distanced itself from the Soviet Union's foreign and domestic policies well before the fall of Russian communism. The JCP was never successful in attracting a large electorate; in 1993, the JCP received just 7.7 percent of the vote. However, it is now in place to pick up leftist voters who are disaffected from the Socialist party. In the 1996 election, the JCP scored a 40-year high at the polls when its candidates took 12.6 percent of the vote. With a young and dynamic leader, Kazuo Shii, the Communist party may continue to pick up voters looking for a progressive option in Japanese politics. However, it is likely to remain on the political margins in a country as conservative as postwar Japan has become.

THE POLITICAL PARTY SYSTEM AND JAPANESE DEMOCRACY

The Japanese political parties have never become a source of stability and strength for democracy. In the first 25 years of Japanese democracy, the party system was characterized by extreme polarization between the dominant LDP and the permanent JSP opposition. Unable to affect legislation and harboring a vision of an entirely different society, the JSP expressed that opposition in antisystem conduct. Since it could not outvote the LDP in the Diet, it tried to prevent the Diet from operating by obstructing its procedures. The result was high tension and polarization between the two parties.

In the next 20 years, this polarized dualism eased due to two changes. First, the direct confrontation between the LDP and the JSP was lessened by the emergence of intermediary parties: the Democratic Socialists, Komeito, and the New Liberal Club. Rarely did any of these smaller parties exceed 10 percent of the vote, but they did occupy the political center and reduce tensions between the Liberal Democrats and the Socialists. Second, both the LDP and later the JSP backed away from some of their more extreme positions. The LDP sought accommodation on sensitive issues such as defense. The JSP moderated its hostility to Japan's defense alliances and later moved toward social democracy. The result of these two processes has been a reduction in political tensions and polarization.

Moderation of politics, however, did not bring the alternation in power between rival political groupings. By the end of the 1980s, a crisis in the party system was spreading. Factionalism, scandal, and inept leadership decreased public support not just for one party but for the overall party system. When change came in the 1990s, it did not bring clear political alternatives to voters or new options to disgruntled or alienated citizens. The Socialists self-destructed just at the time when they may have been able to make headway against a discredited LDP. The new opposition parties were essentially LDP dissidents whose differences from the LDP and among themselves were more based on personality rivalries than on policy agendas. At the end of a decade of party transformation, an unreformed and unrepentant LDP remains the key political actor. It is in position to reclaim political hegemony over an even more divided and weakened opposition than it faced in the years between 1955 and 1990.

This is not what Japanese voters seem to want. Disaffection with the political parties is evident in continuing declines in voter turnout for national elections. A search for options beyond the existing parties can be seen in the victories of independent and non-partisan candidates in recent local and provincial elections.

CITIZENS AND POLITICS

More so than anywhere else, Japan has succeeded in blending Western democracy with non-Western cultural traditions and historical patterns. In Britain or France, traditions of political participation were slow and homegrown historical developments.[32] In Japan, democracy was imposed and the Japanese have had to learn to be effective citizens in the aftermath of this foreign inspired political change. Prior to 1945, the Japanese had "no experience with the concepts and practices of democracy."[33] As a result, Japanese political culture and patterns of participation differ from those in liberal democracies of the West. They draw on Shintosim, Japanese versions of Buddhism and Confucianism, and other cultural values to make democracy different from elsewhere. They build on the traditional Japanese leader-follower relationships. Clientelism gives many citizens a sense of political competence in being able to influence decisions that affect their livelihoods. The Japanese aversion to political conflict and their eagerness for consensus are values that often limit the open clash of ideas that we in the West see as the essence of politics.

Westerners may resent the slowness of the Japanese in offering women equal political and economic opportunities; they may point to the inefficiencies and vulnerability to corruption of the vast clientele networks that long dominated Japanese politics. But the Japanese still find ways for citizens to perform the key democratic goals: holding government accountable to the public for its actions and inactions and limiting government infringement of basic rights and liberties. The Japanese success in building this kind of citizen political involvement offers hope and perhaps even an alternative model for other non-Western societies searching for ways to adapt democracy to local cultural values.

NOTES

[1]David E. Apter and Nagayo Sawa, *Against the State: Political and Social Protest in Japan* (Cambridge, MA: Harvard University Press, 1984).

[2]Gerald L. Curtis, *The Japanese Way of Politics* (New York: Columbia University Press, 1989), p. 222.

[3]Matthew Soberg Schubert and John M. Carey, *Presidents and Assemblies: Constitutional Design and Electoral Dynamics* (Cambridge, England: Cambridge University Press, 1992), p. 169.

[4]Jean-Marie Bouissou, "Gifts, Networks and Clienteles: Corruption in Japan as a Redistributive System," in Donatella Della Porta and Yves Mény, eds., *Democracy and Corruption in Europe* (London: Pinter, 1997).

[5]Kishimoto Koichi, *Politics in Modern Japan: Development and Organization,* 3rd ed. (Tokyo: Japan Echo, 1988), p. 150.

[6]Kent E. Calder, *Crisis and Compensation: Public Policy and Political Stability in Japan, 1949–1986* (Princeton, NJ: Princeton University Press, 1988), pp. 183–186.

[7]Sidney Verba, Norman H. Nie, and Jae-on Kim, *Participation and Political Equality: A Seven Nation Comparison* (Cambridge, England: Cambridge University Press, 1978).

[8]Taketsugu Tsurutani, *Political Change in Japan: Response to Postindustrial Challenge* (New York: David Mckay, 1977), pp. 53–58.

[9]Margaret A. McKean, *Environmental Protest and Citizen Politics in Japan* (Berkeley: University of California Press, 1981 and David Earl Groth, "Media and Political Protest: The Bullet Train Movements," in Susan J. Pharr and Ellis S. Krause, eds., *Media and Politics in Japan* (Honolulu: University of Hawaii Press, 1996).

[10]Scott C. Flanagan et al., *The Japanese Voter* (New Haven, CT: Yale University Press, 1991), p.16.

[11]Ibid., pp. 381–384.

[12]Yakushiji Taizo, "Japan's Political Change Toward Internationalization: Grafted Democracy and Political Recruitment," in Glenn D. Hook and Michael A. Weiner, eds., *The Internationalization of Japan* (London: Routledge, 1992).

[13]Bouissou, "Corruption in Japan," p. 135.

[14]*Asahi Evening News,* 21 October 1996 as quoted in Michael Gallagher, "The Political Impact of Electoral System Change in Japan and New Zealand, 1996," *Party Politics* 4 (No. 2, 1998): 203–228.

[15]Edwin O. Reischauer, *The Japanese Today: Change and Continuity* (Cambridge, MA: Harvard University Press, 1988), p. 175.

[16]Sumiko Iwao, *The Japanese Woman: Traditional Image and Changing Reality* (New York: Free Press, 1994), pp. 214–216.

[17]Karel van Wolferen, *The Enigma of Japanese Power: People and Politics in a Stateless Nation* (New York: Alfred A. Knopf, 1989), p. 173.

[18]Ibid., pp. 172–173.

[19]Iwao, *The Japanese Woman,* p. 243.

[20]Peter R. Moody, Jr., *Tradition and Modernization in China and Japan* (Belmont, CA: Wadsworth, 1995), p. 329.

[21]Timothy Hoye, *Japanese Politics: Fixed and Floating Worlds* (Upper Saddle River, NJ: Prentice Hall, 1998), p. 169.

[22]Iwao, *The Japanese Woman,* pp. 228–233.

[23]Ronald J. Hrebrenar and Akira Nakamura, "Japan: Associational Politics in a Group-Oriented Society," in Clive S. Thomas, ed., *First World Interest Groups: A Comparative Perspective* (Westport, CT: Greenwood Press, 1993), pp. 203–209.

[24]Chalmers Johnson, *Japan: Who Governs? The Rise of the Developmental State* (New York: W.W. Norton, 1995).

[25]Toru Shinoda, "Hesei Labour Politics: A Long and Winding Road," in Purnendra Jain and Takashi Inoguichi, eds. *Japanese Politics Today* (New York: St. Martin's, 1997).

[26]T. J. Pempel, *Regime Shift: Comparative Dynamics of the Japanese Political Economy* (Ithaca, NY: Cornell University Press, 1998), p. 152.

[27]Ibid., p. 153.

[28]Kishimoto, *Politics in Modern Japan,* p. 92.

[29]Peter Mair and Tomokazu Sakano, "Japanese Political Realignment in Perspective: Change or Restoration?" *Party Politics* 4 (No. 2, 1998): 178.

[30]Junko Kato, "When the Party Breaks Up: Exit and Voice Among Japanese Legislators," *American Political Science Review* 92 (December 1998): 857–870.

[31]Peter A. Berton, "Japanese Eurocommunism: Running in Place," *Problems of Communism* 35 (July–August 1986): 1–30.

[32]Curtis H. Martin and Bruce Stronach, *Politics East and West: A Comparison of Japanese and British Political Culture* (Armonk: W. E. S. Sharpe, 1992).

[33]Edwin O. Reischauer and Marius B. Jansen, *The Japanese Today: Change and Continuity* (Cambridge, MA: Belknap Press, 1995), p. 231.

Chapter 29

Political Leadership in Japan

The modern history of Japan, unlike that of China, is not dominated by powerful leadership figures: Sun Yat-sen, Chiang Kaishek, Mao Ze-dong, and Deng Xiaoping have no counterparts in Japan in terms of historical stature. Few people, other than specialists, are familiar with the names of the Japanese leaders who played a key role in such a momentous endeavor as the Meiji Restoration in the nineteenth century. Even in the post-war period, a high profile and name recognition have not been characteristic of the prime ministers who were instrumental in transforming war-torn Japan into the—until 1993—second most powerful economy of the world. What explains the comparative anonymity of Japanese leaders? Is it true that "Japanese soil" is incapable of "growing a charismatic leader?"[1]

CULTURAL DIMENSIONS OF POWER AND LEADERSHIP

For an answer to this question, we again have to turn to the history of Japan and its unique culture. Whereas the Chinese concept of power and leadership was based on the ideal of a single supreme ruler, the modern Japanese idea of power and leadership was a product of feudal pluralism and reflects a continuing belief in the importance of primary relationships.[2] Generally speaking, in both Japanese tradition and modern practice, there is much less emphasis on leadership and on individual leaders than in the United States. While in the United States and other Western countries leadership is usually associated with the demonstrated abilities, successful performance, and other personal attributes of the individual, in Japan the emergence of a brilliant leader tends to be perceived as "living testimony to the power and dignity of the organization" he represents. Given the importance of leadership in any society, it is not surprising to find that, along with other important components of the political system, Japanese leadership has a number of "unique qualities inherited from earliest times" and "is a flower no less indigenous to the soil of Japan.[3]

As seen from a Japanese perspective, among the unique qualities of the Japanese leader is the ability to feign unawareness and pretend ignorance of what is going on, while actually being in complete command of the situation and delegating responsibility to subordinates. In short, "the successful leader in Japan's group-oriented society is the one who can activate the group's energy to the fullest, reserving only the final decision-making power for himself."[4] A second quality of Japanese leadership is the ability of the leader to help subordinates in their career advancement. This ability is crucial for the leader's rise to power and success in maintaining his position. In contrast to the United States, where there is a great deal of horizontal mobility in the labor force, employment in Japan centers around a particular company or bureaucracy rather than around a profession or line of work. The employment pattern in Japan thus deemphasizes job specialization and horizontal mobility and emphasizes the vertical rank concept.

The usual practice in Japan is for an individual to spend his entire career in one company or bureaucracy and to rise through the ranks. In such a structure of career advancement, which focuses on the group rather than the individual, leaders and followers exist in a relationship of mutual dependence. The lower ranks are dependent on the help and protection of the leader or leaders (if there are factions) for their career advancement, while the leader or potential leader is dependent on the support of his subordinates. Assistance, protection, and generosity on the part of the leader generates support and loyalty on the part of the followers. As the subordinates in the group advance in rank with the help of the leader, his support structure becomes more powerful and he is pushed higher in the rank order.

This pattern of career development, which prevails not only in corporate Japan but also in the government bureaucracy, the underworld, and the Japanese guilds, rewards loyalty, teamwork, group orientation and identification, and sensitivity and submissiveness by subordinates to the wishes of leaders. If elderly men in Japan, after 30 or more years of loyal service in the ranks, are selected for top leadership positions for which they would not qualify on the basis of strict merit considerations in the West, the reason is not to be found so much in Japanese respect for age and experience as in the social power which these men have accumulated during their long careers within the group.

To generalize, this particular aspect of Japanese leadership is a good example of the political clientelism characteristic of the politics of many traditional societies, where political power is a function of the existence of intricate networks linking the members of the power elite (patrons) at the various levels with their followers (clients). It is interesting and significant that Western and Japanese scholars have perceived parallels between the political clientelism of Japan and the nomenklatura system in the former Soviet Union.[5]

The third quality of Japanese leadership represents another aspect of political clientelism, the ability of the leader to surround himself with a "protective wall" of trusted and competent followers who are prepared to link their political fortunes to those of the leader. In short, a Japanese leader must have the ability and skill to form and maintain his own faction; only as a successful faction leader can he hope to succeed in the competition with other candidates for the top leadership position.

The fourth quality of leadership in Japan is the ability to influence subordinates without articulating instructions, or the mysterious power to teach others without saying a word. In short, a successful Japanese leader must not only be skilled in human relations, but must have extraordinary communication abilities. He must be able to motivate his subordinates and exercise authority without appearing to do so.[6] In fact, ever since the days of the Tokugawa regime, one of the intriguing aspects of Japanese politics has been the systematic denial by the powerholders that power is exercised.[7]

Thus, the Japanese approach to power and leadership differs in a number of important ways from the conceptions of the leadership role found in other cultural settings. Unlike Western political leaders, who are expected to demonstrate their own "personal style," their decisiveness and forcefulness, their determination, control, and acumen for decision making, and even their dominance, Japanese leaders, both symbolically and in actual political practice, are expected to be sensitive to the feelings of their subordinates, to treat them as junior associates rather than as underlings. In Japan it is consensus building, not decision-making ability and authority per se, which is the mark of a good leader. Moreover, a successful Japanese leader is expected to demonstrate a sense of responsibility for those working under him and to become involved in their private lives to an extent that might be considered inappropriate in the West. Thus, for example, it is common for superiors in business and government to be asked by their subordinates to act as go-betweens in marriage arrangements. The cultural norms dictate that, in return for such benevolence, those in inferior positions will reciprocate with demonstrations of loyalty and respect for their superiors. In short, the traditional concepts of *on* (benevolence by the superior) and *giri* (reciprocal sense of loyalty and duty from the inferior) have survived in modern Japan and continue to influence social and political behavior in the form of a "benign paternalism" in the relationship between leaders and followers.[8]

INDIGENOUS ROOTS
OF DEMOCRATIC LEADERSHIP

While the political history of Japan does not include experience with the ideas and practices of democracy as understood in the West, it nevertheless contained many valuable political assets which facilitated the transition from a feudal order to a democracy. Aside from a strong ethical basis for government, which had its source in their (borrowed) Confucian heritage, and the derivative high standards of honesty and efficiency in public administration, the Japanese were able to draw on a long tradition of group leadership.

The practice of sharing power in the group rather than entrusting it to a single individual was established as early as the thirteenth century. In the Kamakura period, the exercise of power was shared through the existence of a variety of councils in Kamakura, through the system of paired deputies in Kyoto, and through the practice of a "co-signer" who functioned as a counterpart to the Hojo regent in Kamakura. Power sharing became even more pronounced during the Tokugawa regime, where decision-making power was centered in the "council of elders" and the "council of junior elders." Below this level there existed a system of paired officials, or administrative positions held by groups of four men. The members of the top councils, as well as the groups below them, followed a rotation system

in assuming the responsibilities of officers in charge.

In Meiji Japan, the practice of power sharing and group leadership was continued. The *genro* (elder statesmen) acted as a group and took turns in the execution of administrative tasks. Even the responsibilities of the office of prime minister, created in 1885, were shared among the members of the group. Indeed, the practice of power sharing was expanded and, as the functions of government increased, the sharing of power and leadership among individuals gradually evolved into power sharing among institutions. In the political system set up by the Constitution of 1889, the balance of power shifted away from the genro and their successors to the civil bureaucracy, the Diet, the military, big business, and the general public.[9]

Thus, even during the period of rapid socioeconomic and political change, Japan did not produce a leader equivalent to Turkey's Kemal Atatürk or Indonesia's Sukarno. The Japanese political tradition, it would appear, is not conducive to the emergence of a charismatic leader, let alone the veneration of dictatorial power. Even General Tojo, whose power on the eve of the attack on Pearl Harbor was greater than that of any Japanese leader in half a century, was a group leader, not a dictator. Expressed in positive terms, the tradition of group leadership, shared decision making, consensus building, and many other intrinsic features of Japanese life contributed in important ways to the development of a full-fledged democratic system.

THE ELUSIVENESS OF POWER
AND LEADERSHIP

In view of Japan's samurai tradition, its history of imperial conquest, its surprise attack on Pearl Harbor, and its recent industrial and trade policies, it is difficult for Westerners to believe that the Japanese have never developed a positive image of decisive executive power or identified leadership with independent decision-making power. But the fact is that "even the word 'leader' has had to be imported into Japan and naturalized imperfectly as *riida*—or even more implausibly as *wan man riida*."[10] In contrast to the

American concept of a successful top executive, the ideal Japanese leader is "warm" and "unassertive"—a consensus builder, rather than an aggressive and independent decision maker.[11] When occasionally Japanese prime ministers— for example, Shigeru Yoshida, Nobusuke Kishi, and Yasuhiro Nakasone—have violated this cultural norm by trying to establish a position of dominant leadership or by being too assertive, they have been severely criticized and, in the case of Shigeru Yoshida, Japan's first important postwar prime minister, removed as head of his party.

While the emphasis on cooperation, consensus, and group identity is of central importance for an understanding of Japanese society, some native interpreters of Japanese culture have called attention to the fact that the cultural identity of the Japanese is more complex. Along with the values of cooperation and group identity that define the individual's relationship to their group and are derived from the ideal of the family system, the individual's social behavior also reflects awareness of the need to engage in faction building and competition—values that play an important role in the individual's orientation to the outside world and are traced back to the village.[12]

It is because the Japanese are so extraordinarily conscious of the boundaries separating their primary group from the "outside" that they are inclined to treat people quite differently, depending on whether they belong to their primary group or not. In so doing, their behavior may well range from great sensitivity and extreme refinement to unexpected insensitivity and outright rudeness. The sharp distinction drawn by the Japanese between in-group members and "outsiders" has frequently been used to explain their sometimes inconsiderate and callous behavior in crowd situations and as tourists. In a penetrating study of Japanese culture, largely based on interviews with first-, second-, and third-generation Japanese-Americans and U.S. specialists on Japan, Ruth Benedict attributed the extraordinary brutality shown by the Japanese in war to this ingroup–out-group syndrome.[13]

The thesis of the cultural singularity of Japan, first advanced by Lafcadio Hearn[14] and popularized in the United States by Ruth Benedict, reflects not only a widespread outside perspective on Japan, but is also consonant with the self-image of the Japanese, with their strong belief in the special uniqueness of their culture, with their sense of being ultimately different from all other peoples, being "neither East nor West but all alone."[15] It comes as no surprise that the belief in their cultural uniqueness has led some Japanese writers and politicians to promote the idea of Japanese racial superiority. When Prime Minister Nakasone, in September 1986, caused an international uproar with his statement that the United States was a less "intelligent" society than Japan because of its black and Hispanic minorities, he was voicing a view shared by many Japanese. Indeed, a special genre of literature, called *nihonjinron* ("theorizing on the Japanese") exists in Japan. It not only emphasizes that the Japanese culture is unique and different, but also claims that the Japanese way of life and modus operandi is superior to what the rest of the world has to offer.[16] A government-sponsored report published in the 1970s evinced this spirit in its confident prediction that Japanese forms of social and economic management would become universally accepted "in all advanced industrial societies" if their further development would be determined by rational considerations.[17]

But while at various points in their history the Japanese have laid claim to world leadership—asserting their moral superiority over the Chinese, regarding their country as the ancestor of all others, proclaiming the emperor as "the sole true Son of Heaven and sovereign of the world, destined to rule all within the four seas as lord and master," and now holding up Japan as the model to the industrial world—political leadership and the exercise of power within Japan have remained highly elusive and therefore difficult to assess. Its numerous virtues notwithstanding, one of the major problems with the Japanese style of political leadership has been its tendency to diffuse responsibility to a point where accountability for the exercise of power, or the failure to exercise it, becomes virtually impossible.

If the paternalistic style of politics in Japan and the strong emphasis on consensus building have the advantage of developing a sense of common purpose and increasing the morale and cohesion of the group, they also have the tendency of fostering indecisiveness and vague compromise, ambiguity, policy drift, and a lack of accountability. The problem is compounded by the Japanese practice of making a formal act or ritual out of apology and the assumption of responsibility. It is not uncommon, for example, for a superior official to resign in the case of a major failure or problem in his company or department—even if he was not legally or morally responsible in any way and had no control over the event. Thus, the head of Japan Airlines resigned when, due to pilot error, one of the company's planes was involved in a crash. Not too long ago, the cultural norms of Japan would have dictated suicide on the part of the leader assuming formal responsibility for a "failure" of this magnitude. While such sense of responsibility by a superior is admirable and, if acted upon, brings honor to the official involved, it produces only a symbolic solution. The point is that such a ritual does not address the actual problem or assign real responsibility.

Thus, modern Japan, it seems, continues in the tradition of the political system created by the Meiji Constitution—a system in which the ruling oligarchs, behind the façade of an institutional structure resembling the parliamentary systems of the monarchies in Europe, retained the reins of power in their hands and shielded their activity from criticism through their close identification with the Emperor. In an oft-quoted passage, Masao Maruyama described how the Meiji system obscured the all-important issue of the locus of political leadership and political responsibility: "An uncertain sharing of responsibility was preferred so that no person could be pointed out as bearing the ultimate responsibility for decisions." The "Emperor-state system" of the Meiji era, he observed, obviously carried within it "the danger of developing into a colossal system of irresponsibility."[18]

While there is considerable justification for the view that Japanese politics follow cultural dictates (as they do elsewhere!), we should also be aware that Japanese culture has not developed independently of politics. The most common perspectives of Japanese and foreign scholars seeking to explicate "inscrutable Japan" have focused on its social and/or cultural aspects, deemphasizing or even ignoring the impact of politics. However, a good case can be made for the argument that "if there is one nation whose predominant social and cultural idiosyncrasies can be traced back to political decisions that can clearly be seen in isolation from other influences, it is Japan."[19]

The fact that political power in Japan has tended to be elusive, indeterminate, and diffuse does not mean that power and leadership have played a minor role in Japanese history. On the contrary, one of the important characteristics of power in Japan is its pervasiveness—the counterpart to its being "out of focus." Throughout Japanese history, the great cultural imports—Buddhism in the sixth century, Confucianism and the Chinese model of state administration, and medicine, astronomy, and Christianity from Portugal—were the result of deliberate political decisions and were allowed only in carefully measured and limited doses. After opening itself up first to Chinese and later to Portuguese influences, Japan retreated once again into isolation. In the modern period, Japan yielded to pressure from the West, but again it was highly selective in its cultural borrowing: it became "modernized but not westernized."[20] The leaders of the Meiji Restoration in the nineteenth century, which launched Japan on its successful trajectory of modernization, found it useful to justify their policies in the name of the reestablishment of the ancient institution of imperial rule. In short, throughout history political elites in Japan have sought to protect their country against the corrosive and subversive influence of foreign cultures. If even today, in the words of one recent study, Japan finds itself "in the world but not of it,"[21] one important reason is the control which its political elites throughout history have exercised over the development of culture. Indeed, Japan is a country in which political power not only has penetrated culture to an extraordinary extent, but has operated in the guise of culture.[22]

POLITICAL LEADERSHIP IN THE POSTWAR PERIOD

In spite of the diffusion of political power in Japan, it is possible to identify certain individuals who occupy leadership positions in the political system. As has already been noted, the emperor, his title notwithstanding, has purely symbolic functions and no powers relating to government. He appoints the prime minister and the chief judge of the Supreme Court. But these appointments are designated by the Diet and the Cabinet. The other "acts in matters of state" performed by the emperor "on behalf of the people"—such as the convocation of the Diet, the dissolution of the House of Representatives, proclamation of the general election of members of the Diet, the promulgation of amendments of the constitution, laws, cabinet orders and treaties—are carried out "with the advice and approval of the Cabinet."

Real political power, such as it is in Japan, is in the hands of the state bureaucracy, the members of the Liberal Democratic party, and the opposition who make up the National Diet. Given the nature of Japanese party politics, this means that power is wielded by professional politicians. At the highest level, political leadership and executive power are vested in the Cabinet, consisting of the prime minister and about 20 ministers and other officials. The first Cabinet installed by Prime Minister Obuchi on July 30, 1998, included a chief Cabinet secretary, twelve ministers with portfolios, and seven directors general in charge of eight central government agencies. Their age ranged from 37 to 78. Including the prime minister, the average age of the first Obuchi cabinet was 60.4 years. The second Obuchi Cabinet,

installed on January 14, 1999, had the same age range, but was slightly smaller and younger (59.6 years). It included a new Ministry for Financial Reconstruction, but had only four central agencies (defense; economic planning; environment; and management and coordination). The political experience of the Cabinet members ranged from twelve terms in the Lower house or Diet (in the case of Prime Minister Obuchi) to one term in the Upper House (in the case of the minister of education). On average, the ministers had served 6.8 terms in the Diet. The minister of education was a first-term member of the Upper House. Of the seven agency directors, three had political experience in the Upper House, three in the Lower House, and one had no political experience. Personnel continuity notwithstanding, the reshuffle of Prime Minister Obuchi's Cabinet in January 1999 illustrated, inter alia, the continuing importance of factions in Japanese politics and the shifting political coalitions within the LDP and the Japanese Diet.[23]

The exercise of informal power in Japan is rarely the subject of public scrutiny and therefore poses no particular problem. Although omnipresent and ultimately unavoidable, it is subtle and difficult to locate. The same cannot be said of the exercise of formal power. The officially designated leader finds himself in an unenviable position as the focal point of severe and constant

---

THE FIRST OBUCHI CABINET (JULY–JANUARY 1999)

Ministries	Agencies
Agriculture, Forestry and Fisheries	Economic Planning
Construction	Environment
Education	Hokkaido Development
Finance	Japan Defense
Foreign Affairs	Management and Coordination
Health and Welfare	National Land
Home Affairs	Okinawa Development
International Trade and Industry (MITI)	Science and Technology
Justice	
Labor	
Post and Telecommunications	
Transport	

Source: "The First Obuchi Cabinet," at www.bekkoame.or.jp/~jneuffer/files/Cabinets/Obuchi1.html (2/16/99).

tension. While accepting the use of informal power and leadership as something natural, the Japanese evidently are uncomfortable when power is exercised by officially designated leaders.

The officials who are formally in charge of the country—the prime minister and his Cabinet—are given extensive powers under the Constitution. In actual practice, however, they are not allowed to exercise these powers. Clearly designated, formal and explicit leadership is not a positive value in the Japanese scheme of things. Genuine political leadership, as understood in the West, invites deep mistrust and continuous sabotage on the part of the political elite. In spite of the explicit provisions in the Constitution (Articles 65–75) granting broad powers to the prime minister and the Cabinet, Japan's head of government and his ministers in actual practice do not enjoy the unambiguous right to rule. As a matter of fact, in Japan no individual or elite group has this right. The very idea of an uncontested leader being clearly in charge violates the widespread practice and tradition of power sharing and threatens the existing diffusion of power.

However, the available evidence would seem to indicate that it is not so much the public which resents the idea of uncontested political leadership, as it is the members of the various elites, who evidently fear that the emergence of a strong leader would pose a threat to their position in the system. Japan has produced its fair share of gang leaders, interest group bosses, and politicians who had both the desire and the potential of becoming strong national leaders—Nobusuke Kishi, Hayato Ikeda, Kakuei Tanaka, and Yasuhiro Nakasone. Individualism, decisiveness, and the pursuit of effective leadership, moreover, are not traits many Japanese find objectionable in a national leader or popular hero. On the contrary, Prime Minister Nakasone, who sought to bring the powers of his office more in line with those of his foreign counterparts, was held in high esteem and was very popular among the people. But he was greatly disliked and distrusted by perhaps the majority of the members of the LDP, his own party, in the National Diet. He also faced strong resistance to his proposed policy adjustments by the bureaucracy. Had the political and bureaucratic elites accepted his explicit style of leadership, they would have condoned the principle of unambiguous central political leadership—and this, they clearly were not prepared to do.

Perhaps the fundamental problem of political leadership in Japan has to do with the fact that— the Constitution of 1947 notwithstanding—the right to rule has not been clearly established. In particular, no consensus concerning this vital question has emerged among the various elites, whose members continue to be ambiguous about the question of who among them should be entrusted with the leadership function. While not necessarily insisting on their right to rule, the various elites have not been eager or willing to confer the political leadership function on anyone else.

While the issue of legitimacy has been raised only by leftist intellectuals disenchanted with Japan's role as a servant of "monopoly capitalism," it can nevertheless be argued that the political system in Japan—particularly so far as the Japanese elites are concerned—has had and continues to have a serious "legitimacy problem." As one astute observer has put it: "The Japanese System seeks to be self-validating. It is itself the 'divinity,' supplying its own closed system of faith and self-justification. And since a political system cannot legitimise itself, the Japanese System can by definition never be legitimate."[24]

The fact that the question of the right to rule has never been definitively settled in Japan affects virtually every facet of political life in this island nation, which has attained international preeminence in spite of weak national leadership. Both the powers granted to him under the Constitution and his place at the center of the "three rings of power"—the National Diet, the Liberal Democratic party, and the ministries of the national government—would appear to endow the prime minister with unparalleled power. But each of these relationships also entails limitations on what the prime minister can actually do in practice. In his capacity as president of the party, the prime minister is in a position to exert considerable influence; but at the same time, he is expected to defend and promote the party's interests. Faction-ridden as the LPD is, this is no easy task. As a member of the Diet, the prime minister, along with his Cabinet, can bring pressure to bear and exert influence from within, but ultimately he and his cabinet are accountable to the Diet. Finally, while the prime minister and the Cabinet supposedly direct and supervise the national ministries and central agencies, they are no match for the skill and experience of the professional bureaucracy.[25]

If foreigners frequently are perplexed, frustrated and annoyed by the evident lack of response on the part of the Japanese government to a variety of issues, the reason in many cases has to be sought in the very structure of the political system. The existence of effective and responsible government in Japan is, to a considerable extent, a myth. In its present form and configuration, the Japanese political system seems to lack the instruments necessary to effect fundamental changes in overall policy.

Even though the need for political reform has been widely recognized in Japan, including within the political elite, for some time, comprehensive change in the political system has thus far eluded the efforts of all would-be reform politicians. Coming in the aftermath of the brief tenure of two prime ministers committed to reform, the alliance between the former ruling party and the left-wing Social Democrats, as well as the election of Tomiichi Murayama, a socialist who in 1993 formally opposed the U.S.–Japan security pact, as the new prime minister, was a measure of the disarray in the former ruling party. The LDP, it appears, was more interested in settling political scores (above all, with "defector" Ichiro Ozawa) than in serving as the vehicle of much-needed reform. It will, indeed, take extraordinary leadership to pull the political system of Japan out of its present quagmire. Meanwhile political control, to a large extent, remains in the hands of the powerful bureaucracy that is determined to conduct business as usual and is poised to resist any attempt to bring about genuine political reform.

NOTES

[1]C. Nakane, *Japanese Society* (London: Pelican, 1970), pp. 70–71.

[2]Lucien W. Pye, with Mary W. Pye, *Asian Power and Politics: The Cultural Dimensions of Authority* (Cambridge, MA: Harvard University Press, 1985), p. 183.

[3]Mitsuyuki Masatsugu, *The Modern Samurai Society: Duty and Dependence in Contemporary Japan* (New York: AMACOM Book Division, 1982), p. 206.

[4]Ibid., p. 207.s

[5]For an interesting comparative analysis of clientelism in the USSR and Japan, see Shugo Minagawa, "Political Clientelism in the USSR and Japan: a Tentative Comparison," in T. H. Rigby and Bohdan Harasymiw, eds., *Leadership Selection and Patron-Client Relations in the USSR and Yugoslavia* (London: George Allen & Unwin, 1983), pp. 200–228. See also Karel van Wolferen, *The Enigma of Japanese Power: People and Politics in a Stateless Nation* (New York: Alfred A. Knopf, 1989), pp. 300–301.

[6]The discussion of the qualities of Japanese leadership is largely based on Masatsugu, *The Modern Samurai Society,* pp. 206–213.

[7]See van Wolferen, *The Enigma of Japanese Power,* pp. 304–305.

[8]Edwin O. Reischauer, *The Japanese Today* (Cambridge, MA: Harvard University Press, 1988), pp. 156–158.

[9]For a more detailed discussion, see ibid., pp. 234 ff.

[10]Lewis Austin, *Saints and Samurai* (New Haven: Yale University Press, 1975), p. 128.

[11]Pye, *Asian Power and Politics,* p. 171.

[12]Seizaburo Sato, Shumpei Kumon, Yasusuke Murakami, "Analysis of Japan's Modernization," *Japan Echo* 3, no. 2 (1976), cited in Pye, *Asian Power and Politics,* p. 170.

[13]Ruth Benedict, *The Chrysanthemum and the Sword: Patterns of Japanese Culture* (Boston: Houghton Mifflin, 1946).

[14]Lafcadio Hearn, *Japan: An Attempt at Interpretation* (London: Macmillan Company, 1905).

[15]Miwa Kimitada, "Neither East nor West But All Alone," in Harry Wray and Hilary Conroy, ed., *Japan Examined: Perspectives on Modern Japanese History* (Honolulu: University of Hawaii Press, 1983), pp. 384–389.

[16]For a discussion of this literature, see Peter N. Dale, *The Myth of Japanese Uniqueness* (New York: St. Martin's Press, 1986).

[17]Nakawa and Ota, *The Japanese-Style Economic System* (Tokyo: Foreign Press Center, 1980), cited in van Wolferen, *The Enigma of Japanese Power,* p. 16. For a recent critique of American management from a Japanese perspective, see Akio Morita and Shintaro Ishihara, *The Japan That Can Say "No": The New U.S.-Japan Relations Card;* Translated by the U.S. Department of Defense (Kobunsha: Kappa-Holmes, 1989).

[18]M. Maruyama, "Japanese Thought," *Journal of Social and Political Ideas,* April 1964, p. 44.

[19]Van Wolferen, *The Enigma of Japanese Power,* p. 18.

[20]Edwin O. Reischauer, "Not Westernization But Modernization," in Wray and Conroy, ed., *Perspectives on Modern Japanese History,* pp. 369–375.

[21]Van Wolferen, *The Enigma of Japanese Power,* pp. 408ff.

[22]Ibid., pp. 245ff.

[23]"Cabinet Lineups, 1996–1999" at www.bekkoame.or/jp/~jneuffer/files/cabinets.html (2/16/99).

[24]Van Wolferen, *The Enigma of Japanese Power,* p. 297.

[25]For further discussion see Charles F. Bingham, *Japanese Government Leadership and Management* (New York: St. Martin's Press, 1989), p. 17ff.

Chapter 30

Japanese Political Performance

"An ordered, but free society."

At the beginning of the 1990s, Japan stood as the epitome of a successful democratic economy. Its economic strength was second only to the United States, and many Americans and others around the world looked to Japan for the keys to economic success. While the European and American economies had struggled during the 1980s, the Japanese economy continued healthy. Between 1982 and 1990, the annual increase in Japan's gross domestic product was 4.2 percent, well above the comparable figures in Britain, France, Germany, and the United States.

The brilliance of Japan's economic achievement was equaled in importance by the success of its political system. A once authoritarian regime had been replaced by an effective democracy. Japan stood as the best example of the successful implantation of Western democratic traditions in a non-Western setting. It achieved this through adapting Western democratic principles to accommodate its own rich historical legacies. The result is a "Western" democracy that is not alien to the Japanese experience. After 55 years, Japanese democracy has acquired firm support among

its public and has proved able to adapt to meet the changing demands of its society. Despite Japan's economic and financial problems in the last years of the century, it would be wrong to underestimate the dramatic economic progress that Japan experienced from 1950–1995.

THE JAPANESE ECONOMIC MIRACLE

Few can ignore the dramatic economic progress in Japan over the past few decades. As in Germany, Japan began the postwar era impoverished and devastated. With 10 million people unemployed and critical shortages of food and energy resources, Japan was on the brink of economic disaster at the end of World War II.[1] From a country struggling to recover from a devastating war through the sale abroad of cheap toys and trinkets, it has progressed to the second or third most powerful economy in the world. No longer relying on its skill in efficiently producing the innovations of others, Japanese industry now leads in many of the most important fields of high technology and modern industrial manufacturing.

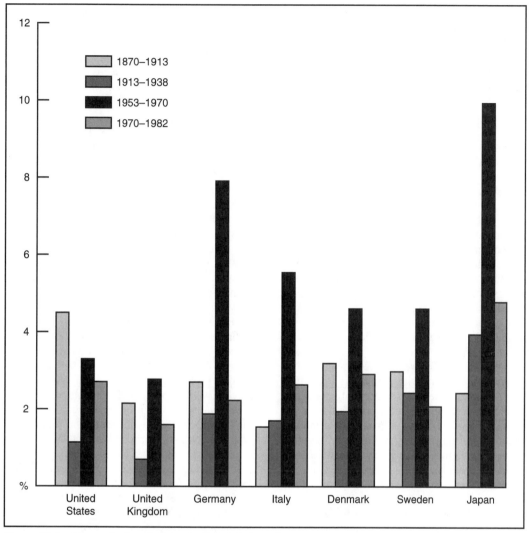

Figure 30–1 Economic Growth Rates for Selected Countries (*Source:* Takafusa Nakamura, *Economic Development of Modern Japan* [Tokyo: Ministry of Foreign Affairs, 1985], p. 7)

These accomplishments are widely recognized in an era when Japanese microchips, automobiles, videocassette recorders, and cameras dominate the quality market for these goods. What is less frequently recognized is the long-term nature of Japan's economic boom. Rapid economic development began under the Meiji era in the nineteenth century and has continued to the present. During most of this 125-year period, Japan's economic growth rate has exceeded that of all other major countries. As Figure 30–1 shows, Japan's average annual rate of economic growth exceeded that of all the countries for a century, except for the United States during the first period, 1870–1913. Between 1953 and 1972, Japan's rate of economic growth averaged nearly 10 percent annually, a phenomenal sustained rate of progress.

To a large degree, this unusually rapid growth is the result of the "late development" effect.

Benefitting from advancements in other countries, Japan was able to borrow technology developed elsewhere. In doing so, it was able to build an entirely new economic base founded on the latest technological breakthroughs while more mature economies added a few new facilities to a continuing set of industrial plants based on older techniques. The rapid rate of growth during the 1950s and 1960s was also the result of rebuilding an economy shattered by war. Japan's accomplishment was nonetheless very impressive. Although economic growth in Japan has slowed during the last two decades, it remains higher than for most other industrial nations. The slowing of its growth suggests its economic maturity rather then any fundamental problems with the economy.[2]

Alongside Japan's economic growth, there is also the strong commitment of Japanese employers to their tradition of protecting their employees. Employment is often an informal lifetime commitment on the part of both employer and employee. This provides job security for many Japanese that cannot be found elsewhere in the capitalist world. The factory also becomes a community with employers providing not only employment but a range of social and cultural opportunities to their workers. As a result of the special nature of employee/employer relations, the patterns of economic change in Japan differs from elsewhere in the industrial world. The obvious result is that Japanese unemployment rates have been much lower than elsewhere.

The 1990s have brought needs for the Japanese to adjust to international economic changes. In the event, Japanese responses were not always timely or well conceived. Japan faced the need to modernize its factories, to make them more efficient, and to increase worker productivity in order to compete with competition from newly industrializing countries in Asia and elsewhere. In addition, the population was aging more rapidly than in other countries, producing new sets of challenges for Japanese industry, business, and government. The new challenges weakened traditions of lifetime employment and contributed to a massive crisis in the banks and financial enterprises by the late 1990s. Not only did the economy stop growing but unemployment became a problem for the first time since the days immediately after the end of the war.

At the beginning of the 1990s, Japan was seen as a model to other industrial democracies of techniques to improve productivity and spur economic growth; by the end of the decade it was viewed as an example of failure to respond to economic change. Japan did have lessons for other industrial states on how to improve their economies. But many of the features are intimately linked with Japanese traditions—such as the special sense of community that often develops in Japanese factories—that cannot easily be transplanted into other settings. Nor should everything be adopted elsewhere.

Some of the most admired features of the Japanese economy worked as well as they did because of its long-term economic boom rather than any particular strength of the Japanese methods of management and production. When that boom slowed in the early 1990s, the very practices that were lauded a few years earlier were now seen as having deleterious effects. For example, "relational contracting," which involves enterprises buying from domestic friends rather than importing less expensive comparable goods from abroad, is widespread and accounts for some of the difficulty foreign producers encounter in trying to penetrate the Japanese market.[3] Employers who protect their workers' jobs end up trying to protect their markets from competition coming from more labor-efficient producers outside Japan.

Japan is an economically strong country, but its citizens lag behind other countries in the enjoyment of their wealth. Much of the wealth remains in the hands of a few very powerful corporations. The Japanese save more than many other peoples, at a rate twice as high as in the United States. But their homes are small and cramped. The average living space per household in Japan is 920 square feet, compared to an average in the U.S. of 1,693 square feet per household. By the mid-1980s, over 40 percent of the dwellings in Japan still lacked a flush toilet. The Japanese are the world's leading manufacturers of automobiles, but fewer Japanese own cars than is the case in other industrial democracies (see Table 30–1). This pattern of self-restraint is easing and the acquisition by Japanese households of

Table 30–1 Private Automobiles in Selected Countries (1993)

	Number of People for Each Private Vehicle
Britain	2.5
France	2.5
Germany	2.0
Japan	3.2
Nigeria	152
Russia	n.a.
China	673.4
United States	1.8

Source: Quid 1995 (Paris: Robert Laffont, 1995), p. 1803.

consumer products is rising. During the 1970s, for example, the percentage of Japanese homes with telephones increased from 25 to 77 percent. New housing is bringing some relief to the acute shortage of living space. In the 1980s and especially the 1990s, this trend toward a greater distribution of consumer goods expanded to cover a wide range of household and personal products. In response to slower expansion of international markets, the Japanese government encouraged greater domestic consumption. At the end of the 1990s, the state took a larger role in promoting consumerism in order to counter the economic recession that Japan was then experiencing. The government tried tax breaks and finally the issuing of special cash certificates that could be used to purchase consumer goods. But long traditions of modest purchases coincided with fears about the economic future and kept most Japanese from really entering the consumer society.

State-Assisted Capitalism

Japan has often been portrayed as a paragon of successful capitalism. Government expenditures as a percentage of gross national product are relatively low compared to other industrial democracies. As a result, taxes are also low. The bureaucracy is small in comparison to other industrial countries. Private industry is widespread and the public sector is small. Many of the industries that are (or have been) nationalized in European democracies—such as the railroads,

electric power, telecommunications, and steel—are already privately owned in Japan.

Despite these facts, the Japanese government is a major actor in the economic realm. For over a century, it has promoted economic growth by protecting its own industries and producers from international competition. While tariffs often appear no higher than those of other countries, other restrictive practices are encouraged by the government. For example, as the American sport of baseball spread in popularity in Japan, Japanese manufacturers of baseball bats convinced the government to bar imported American bats because they failed to meet Japanese quality standards. Apparently, Americans could export their national sport but not the bats needed to play it. While this example is not very important in the broad scheme of international trade, it is illustrative of the Japanese government's willingness to intervene into the economy and to restrict trade to assist the growth of its own industries.

Even more important in terms of the government's role in the economy has been Japan's extensive industrial policy. An industrial policy involves the government in establishing priorities for industrial development. Once priorities are established, the government promotes the achievement of these goals through investment incentives and direct and indirect subsidies to private firms. Government collaborates with private economic actors—entrepreneurs, investors, banks—to establish favored areas for economic development. The Japanese government has pursued such industrial policies over many decades. In doing so, it was able to encourage investment in certain economic sectors where the government thought Japan could develop a competitive edge or in strategic areas of high technology. Not all aspects of the industrial policy have succeeded, but the Japanese government has not left key decisions on economic investment in the unseen hands of free market forces. Instead, it has actively directed Japan's economic recovery and expansion through close collaboration and cooperation with influential economic decision makers outside of government.

Japan's industrial policies have varied, with outright subsidies among the least important elements. The government has facilitated collaboration among industries in research and product

---

THE MINISTRY OF INTERNATIONAL TRADE AND INDUSTRY

The key agency in developing and administering Japan's industrial policy has been the Ministry of International Trade and Industry (MITI). Although MITI has a relatively small staff, it has been the primary government body involved in directing the Japanese economy. MITI's small size aids its cohesion and influence over the economy. Working hand-in-hand with the well-organized associations of private industries, MITI has served as an "economic

general staff" for the country.[4] It assisted in deciding on areas for economic growth, on restructuring declining industries, and on international trade policies and strategies. MITI's influence in the last 20 years is less than what it was in the 1950s and 1960s. The Ministry of Finance and the Economic Planning Agency exert control over economic policy as well. But MITI remains an important state influence on the capitalist structures in Japan.

---

development. It has aided in planning moves away from inefficient product lines or production facilities. The government coordinates its public works efforts with the needs of industry. It has provided guidance to managers and private firms to assist them in making appropriate investment decisions.

It is difficult to see Japan's economic miracle without acknowledging the role of government in this achievement. Free enterprise is predominant in Japan, but the government has not left many of the major economic options to the chance of the market. It has played and continues to have a major role in economic matters.

The End of the Japanese Economic Miracle

After only a few years of being the model for economic success for the world, Japan's economy was in disarray. Throughout the 1990s, Japan experienced economic slowdown and then even a few years when the economy actually shrank. For example, in 1999, economists expected the Japanese economy to shrink by 2.2 percent. At the same time, the financial structures were hit by a deep crisis based on overextended loans to enterprises that were no longer able to repay their debts. The financial crisis was produced by bad debts amounting to over a trillion dollars, or 17 percent of the nation's gross national produce. By the end of the decade, Japanese unemployment, long among the lowest in the world, reached record postwar levels and exceeded that of the United States. Numerous Japanese banks and financial institutions faced collapse with huge unsecured and failing outstanding loans.

The state's response to this economic chaos was confused and inadequate. Indeed, the crises were as much political as economic in their origins and especially in their prolongation through an entire decade.[5] Prime ministers came and went, each trying new approaches to the economic crisis. Governments tried tax increases and tax cuts; both seemed to increase the budget deficits to record levels with little effect on the overall economy. Above all, the government struggled with calls for deregulating the economy. Although capitalist in basic form, the Japanese economy has always had many formal and informal regulations that have impeded the operation of free market forces. The state actively intervened in many aspects of the economy from financial controls, to subsidies, to import levies and quotas, and impediments to the free flow of capital in and out of Japan. In the eyes of many economists inside and outside of Japan the key to economic recovery lay in lifting many of the state's extensive economic regulations. Such liberalization of the economy would allow for more competitiveness in the international economy, less rigidity, and greater economic rationality.

Removal of these regulations is politically difficult. They have long histories that reflect traditional values. They incorporate restrictions that were helpful in early stages of economic modernization that no longer are needed but which those who benefit from them do not want to lose. Many of these regulations are there because powerful interests placed them there to protect specific industries or enterprises. These special interests remain powerful forces with important influence in the LDP and with other center-right parties. These parties are as unwilling now as before to alienate these political allies and financial supporters. The result is a decade of talk about deregulation and many pledges by parties and enterprises to reduce regulation but very little significant change. Two observers note:

> Overall, the result has been to chip away at some public restraints on the market while leaving intact the private restraints on competition that are especially important in markets for manufactured goods.[6]

With all its problems at the end of the 1990s, Japan's economy is still the second largest in the world. Its people remain prosperous and content despite a decade of economic stagnation. Eventually, Japan will recover from its economic malaise of the 1990s. As it does, it may find the courage and political determination to undertake the economic reforms that will allow the economy to be more competitive without the current system of state regulation and protection. When that happens, it will benefit the Japanese people themselves as much as those foreigners whose goods and services will be able to penetrate the Japanese market.

The Politics of Economic Success

The economic prosperity that Japan has experienced throughout the postwar era has contributed to popular support for the democratic regime. It has brought legitimacy to a political formula originally imposed by foreign conquerors. As in Germany, economic success has built a reservoir of support for the regime that will permit it to weather current and future economic and political crises. Even for those groups which still feel disfavored, there is hope from the continuing economic miracle that their fate will change as well. In such a prosperous setting, it is difficult for political dissidence to develop broad support.

The determined pursuit of economic ends has granted an exceptional amount of political power to the bureaucracy. The Japanese often complain that the LDP may reign but it is the bureaucracy that rules.[7] The power of the bureaucracy and business interests assure economic prosperity at the cost of "government for the people."[8] Some critics refer to the country's political system as

simply "Japan, Inc." because of the close collaboration of business, bureaucrats, and politicians.[9]

It is also possible to see a much greater role for politics and politicians.[10] Democracy is praised for its role in Japan's economic miracle, but democracy is also discredited for the venality of its politicians and the continuing prominence of powerful bureaucrats who are able to block political and social reforms. Transformation of political institutions and in the political party system begun in the mid-1990s brings the hope that the old patterns of state-economic interactions—both those that perpetuated the state's dominance over the economy and those that brought corruption—will evolve for the better. These political changes will be supported by international competition and political forces that also press for economic reform in Japan.

THE SOCIAL WELFARE STATE IN JAPAN

On first impression, it would seem that Japan has not seen the rapid expansion of welfare programs that has occurred in other countries. Government expenditures in Japan are significantly lower than in other industrial democracies. Social security benefits, for example, account for 11.9 percent of GDP in Japan compared to 30.9 percent in France, 27.6 in Germany, and 21.3 in the United States.[11] Japan provides a minimal welfare safety net for the impoverished. In the United States, approximately one in ten families receives some welfare benefit such as aid to dependent children or food stamps; in Japan fewer than one in a hundred receive welfare.[12] The explanation for this difference is found not only in the number of poor but in the screening processes in Japan that send the needy first to relatives and then assist only some of those who are unable to find family assistance. Over time, Japan's aging population is likely to vastly increase the country's expenditure on welfare and social security programs.

The Japanese government directs a vast system of social security programs. It also provides a mandatory national health insurance program to provide universal access to medical services. A basic pension plan provides retirement benefits for those not covered by private plans. There is an extensive state-sponsored program of childcare facilities for working parents. Beyond the social

Table 30–2   High School Graduates in Selected
Countries in 1996

Country	Ratio of Graduates to Population at Usual Age of High School Graduation
France	85
Germany	86
Japan	99
Russia	88
United States	72

Source: OECD, *Education at a Glance, OECD Indicators*
(Paris: Organization for Economic Cooperation and
Development, 1998).

welfare programs of the state are the extensive
social benefits provided by employers. Until
recently, as much as a third of the population enjoyed the virtual assurance of lifetime employment. This reduced fears of unemployment—and
limited need for government programs to provide
pay or retraining programs for those who lose
their jobs. Finally, it is important to note the continued strong influence of the family in Japanese
society. As a result, family-provided social services, notably for the aged and single mothers,
are also important. The overlapping of multiple
private and public programs of social welfare
often leads to confusion and bureaucratic red
tape.

Japan's education system receives high praise
for both its overall quality and its availability to
citizens from all walks of life (see Table 30–2). It
is "one of the most single-mindedly meritocratic"
educational systems in the world.[13] Until the age
of 15, students of all abilities attend the same
schools, thus narrowing social class differences
and distinctions. Students then go on to a three-
year secondary education with varying programs
according to the students' interests and abilities.
Retention is high, with over 90 percent of students continuing in school until the age of 18
years. There are some 500 universities for students desiring to go on to higher education, and
nearly 40 percent of young people of college age
do go on to university or college.

At the university level, issues of equal access
to education reappear. Graduates of the University of Tokyo and two or three other prestigious
universities are virtually assured of successful
careers while graduates of other institutions
of higher education enjoy much less secure
prospects.

Among Japan's achievement is the overall
economic equality of its citizens. Even though
the country has been governed constantly by conservatives, the pattern of income distribution reflects more equality than is the case in most of
Western Europe and the United States. The gap
between the share of national income received by
the richest 30 percent and that received by the
lowest 30 percent of the population is smaller
than in most other industrial democracies (see
Table 30–3). The result is that Japan does not
have the large underclass of impoverished citizens that is found on the welfare rolls of countries like the United States, France, Germany, or
Britain.

Table 30–3   Distribution of Income in Selected Countries

Country (year of data)	After-tax Distribution of Income		
	Wealthiest 30%	Middle 40%	Poorest 30%
Japan (1994)	47.8%	36.5%	15.7%
Britain (1995)	54.0	33.8	12.2
France (1989)	51.2	36.7	12.1
Germany (1994)	49.6	37.0	13.4
United States (1994)	55.3	34.4	10.3

Source: Luxembourg Income Study cited in *The New York Times,* 26 October 1998.

AN OVERSTABLE STATE?

The Japanese place high value on harmony and consensus in their personal and social lives. This tends to place limits on the open competition that is the hallmark of democratic politics. This helps explain the 40-year hold on politics by the LDP and the disconcert felt by citizens when the first non-LDP governments proved so divided and weak. As a result, the first experiments with governments without the LDP did not bring the political and social reforms that many had expected and hoped for. To return to the Karaoke analogy, the faces of the singers changed but their voices, words, and motions remained the same.

A healthy democracy needs a political party system that offers two or more viable coalitions and the occasional shift between the "ins" and "outs." Without real competition for power, the governing party often develops overly cosy and illicit relations with powerful economic interests. This happened repeatedly during the past 45 years when Liberal Democrats found themselves embroiled in bribery and influence peddling. For many years, voters tolerated these excesses because they felt there was no viable alternative offered by the Socialist opposition. The 1993–94 experiments with non-LDP governments were made possible by the defection of reformers from the LDP and the voters' willingness to give them a try in bringing about eagerly awaited reforms. The failure of the Hosokawa and Hata governments not only ruined hopes for alternation in power but also deepened popular cynicism about politics and politicians.

The absence of rotation in and out of power brings policy stagnation and runs the risk of leaders becoming unresponsive to the need for change. As a result, the Japanese policy process is characterized above all by its resistance to change unless provoked by crisis.[14] Then change tends to come in the form of buying off or compensating all sides rather than more fundamental attacks on the root of the problem. The views of opposition groups are often incorporated into the settlement, but this cooptation of their platforms further removes their chance of bringing a real change in politics. One positive development has been the greater influence and success of opposition parties and "non-partisan" candidates in local and regional politics. From these grassroots political bases, the opposition parties can continue to serve as alternative voices and critics of the government at all levels.

The encompassing consensus on politics and economics tends to smother opposition groups. The recent moderation of Rengo, the newly unified trade union movement, and opposition parties interest in collaborating with the LDP only add to the problems of trying to build a legitimate and viable opposition.

One good sign is the near absence of any interest in the revival of Japanese nationalism. Contempt for inferior foreigners and strident Japanese nationalism brought the catastrophes of World War II. There is still the possibility that foreign resentment of Japanese economic success and trade imbalances will lead to "Japan bashing," which may well provoke a nationalist response. Indeed, there were signs of such a reaction in Japan in the 1990s as Japanese nationalists capitalized on American and European resentment of Japan's success in penetrating their markets. But nationalism now lacks the broad appeal and the militaristic dimension that it had in the past.

Japan is far from resuming its prewar militarism even if it resents the hostility of other countries. The postwar constitution includes a provision (Article 9) renouncing war and barring the raising of an army. It kept Japan from taking part in the United Nations action against Iraq, even though Japan was among the countries most vulnerable to the loss of oil from the Persian Gulf. This episode and growing economic power have reopened debate in Japan on amending the constitution to allow the military role that its economic status requires. It is an issue that cuts across party lines with supporters and opponents in all parties—even in the once very pacifist Socialist party. The public is also divided, although the majority oppose changing the constitution.

Even as Japan's economic influence has made it an international actor, it has moved slowly and hesitantly in accepting a larger role in world politics. This hesitation comes from the reluctance to appear in any way like the "old" prewar Japan and is part of the rejection of nationalism that comes from guilt over the excesses of earlier militarist nationalism. It comes also from recognition of the apprehension Japan's neighbors in Asia would display if Japan attempted to wield political power in the region commenserate with its economic power.

The prospects for immediate political and economic change appear slim. The tradition of consensus is strong, and few of the areas where the need for reform is most pressing are likely to achieve a consensus in the near future. The non-LDP governments have been too weak to carry through major reforms. When the LDP returned to power it was unrepentant, unchanged, and uninterested in reforming the political system. Too much political stability may seem an unlikely source of concern. However, there is a need for a country to change, and when the political system becomes stagnant and unable to respond to needs for change, political and social problems accumulate. Over the long run, the failure to address the major problems now confronting Japan may strain what has so far been a fairly successful democracy.

Japan's major weakness is its resistance to change. The political system promotes inertia rather than initiative and innovation. This is clearly evident in the debates at the end of the 1990s over how to deal with Japan's economic crisis. There were no novel approaches among the factions of the LDP or even among its rivals on the center-right or left. As a result, the economic crisis was prolonged by the near permanent political dilemma of stagnation of ideas and absence of will to change.

HUMAN RIGHTS

The postwar constitution includes guarantees of a broad range of civil liberties and political rights. The record of the government in observing and protecting these rights has been outstanding. A number of active human rights advocacy groups speak out in cases where civil liberties are abused by the government or by individuals. Court proceedings in criminal cases are fair and assure protection of the rights of the accused. However, the Japanese courts have not emerged as major defenders of human rights. This reflects a generally lower profile for the judiciary in Japanese society

than is the case in the United States or Britain.[15] The courts are largely immune to direct influence from the government, but they do respond to the prevailing social consensus.

The press is free to criticize the government, but there is no tradition of penetrating investigative reporting such as is found in the United States. There are three major daily newspapers, all of which purport to be politically independent. They more frequently reflect the orthodox consensus rather than challenge it with serious questioning of government policies or actions. Television and radio include a mix of state-owned and state-operated stations and private stations. The public stations, such as NHK—the national television company—give equal coverage to candidates from government and opposition during campaign periods.

Civil liberties advocates direct what criticism they have of Japanese human rights at some relatively minor problems. Japan is one of the few industrial countries to use capital punishment and this is deplored by civil rights groups. Another criticism is of the large number of people confined to mental institutions. There are 330,000 people in Japanese mental institutions, compared to less than 120,000 in the United States, which has a population twice that of Japan's.[16]

There is also criticism of unofficial discrimination against the few ethnic minorities in Japan: Koreans and two indigenous minorities, the Ainu and Burakumin. Most of the Koreans are descendants of people brought to Japan as forced laborers during the Japanese colonial rule of Korea prior to World War II. Even though they have lived in Japan for all of their lives, many still are denied citizenship. They must register as aliens and file fingerprints with public authorities. Only those Koreans who accept Japanese names and undergo a lengthy official investigation of their backgrounds are eligible for citizenship. Other Koreans may not vote or become civil servants, and they are subject to deportation if they break the law. In addition, there is often job discrimination and social barriers for Koreans as well as for the Ainu and Burakumin. Recently, immigrant workers from other Asian countries, notably Chinese and Filipinos, have encountered similar discrimination. Such discrimination is illegal but difficult for the government to prevent.

The Japanese problems with ethnic discrimination are not as severe as those of West European countries with large populations of recent, racially distinct immigrants. But the number of immigrants in Japan is much lower than in Western Europe.

Perhaps the most serious limit on civil liberties are the subtle ones coming from a tradition-bound society. Traditions are still important and they lead to real restrictions on the freedom of certain groups. Women, for example, still find themselves restricted in their social and political activities by traditional roles, even though laws have established their formal equality.[17] Official policies to promote equal employment opportunities and equal pay have been difficult to enforce. In a country where tradition stresses conformity with the collective good, the individual who dissents from the status quo faces important psychological and social pressures to keep quiet. As we have seen, dissent is present, but it comes at an important cost in social acceptance. Thus, while formally free to dissent, there is a powerful sociopolitical consensus that silences its critics.

These comments should not, however, discount the very positive record of human rights that Japan has achieved in the past 50 years. The restraints of tradition and social pressure are common in many countries widely acknowledged to be leading examples in observing civil liberties. In a comparative sense, Japan's record of respecting human rights ranks with the highest.

CONCLUSION

A decade ago, Japan was often set as a model for transforming the principles of western democracy into reality in a non-Western society. An Asian country with traditions and values far different from the Judeo-Greco-Roman culture of the West, Japan had established a stable democracy. It had also built the second strongest economy in the world. In doing so, of course, the Japanese had made modifications to fit their own culture and traditions. Yet at the start of the century, Japan's politics and economics are now reviled as examples of what can go wrong in democratic, capitalist societies. The truth lies between these two extreme judgments. Japan's

search for political and economic consensus slows response to needed changes. But democracy as a set of values and practices seems ingrained in the attitudes of the political elites and in the expectations of the people. Egalitarian values are also strongly implanted and achieved better than in most other developed democracies. Democracy in Japan, however, may continue to lack the possibility of real alternation in power between rival parties or coalitions. It may build links to the voters through material payoffs through patron-client relationships and thus avoid the linkage between parties and people on major public issues. Japan's polity is nonetheless perceived as democratic and open by the Japanese and by others even if it has its own peculiarities.

At a time when there is a need for models of successful democracy in many parts of the world, Japan might seem an appropriate model for Eastern Europe or parts of the Third World. However, there are reasons to doubt that Japan's experience can be transferred to other settings. The economic miracle came out of particular social and economic settings—such as the preexisting economic base, a high level of education, a strong sense of community, a favorable international economic climate—that are not readily reproduced in other settings.

The Japanese model of democracy builds on deep historical traditions that are peculiar to Japan. It thrives in a setting of relative cultural and socioeconomic homogeneity that is not found in most of the countries hoping for democratization. It reflects a particular blend of individualism and community values that are not widely found in other countries. The political success is also based on an ability to avoid the heavy costs of defense and foreign involvements. Japan gets away with devoting less than 1 percent of gross domestic product (GDP) to defense; some democratizing countries and aspiring democracies devote 10 percent or more of GDP to their military. The current stability and consensus politics in Japan is the product of often turbulent political disputes prior to democratization and in the years since democratization. Other countries will have to invest that same time in working through the contentious issues that sometimes destroy democracies in their infancy. Perhaps the Japanese brand of democracy and its economic miracle are among the few things that the Japanese will not be able to export successfully.

In looking for ways to adapt Western democracy to non-Western settings, the Japanese course has strengths and weaknesses. While many countries would welcome the economic achievements of Japan, it is not clear that they would want the political features of Japan's variation on Western democracy. Nor might they be eager to accept the socioeconomic peculiarities within which the Japanese political system thrives. What has worked well in Japan may not be as successful in other non-Western countries.

NOTES

[1]Takafusa Nakamura, *The Postwar Japanese Economy: Its Development and Structure,* trans. Jacqueline Kaminski (Tokyo: University of Tokyo Press, 1981), pp. 1–22.

[2]Edward J. Lincoln, *Japan: Facing Economic Maturity* (Washington, DC: Brookings Institution, 1988).

[3]See Ronald Dore, *Taking Japan Seriously: A Confucian Perspective on Leading Economic Issues* (Stanford, CA: Stanford University Press, 1987), pp. 183ff.

[4]Chalmers Johnson, *MITI and the Japanese Miracle: The Growth of Industrial Policy, 1925–1975* (Stanford, CA: Stanford University Press, 1982).

[5]See T. J. Pempel, *Regime Shift: Comparative Dynamics of the Japanese Political Economy* (Ithaca, NY: Cornell University Press, 1998).

[6]Lonny E. Carlile and Mark C. Tilton, "Is Japan Really Changing?" in Lonny E. Carlile and Mark C. Tilton, eds. *Is Japan Really Changing? Regulatory Reform and the Japanese Economy* (Ithaca, NY: Cornell University Press, 1998), p. 209.

[7]Johnson, *MITI and the Japanese Miracle,* pp. 34–35; 316.

[8]Peter J. Herzog, *Japan's Pseudo-Democracy* (New York: New York University Press, 1993), pp. 16–18.

[9]See the comic-book-style critique of Shotaro Ishinomori, *Japan Inc.: An Introduction to Japanese Economics (The Comic Book),* trans. Betsey Scheiner (Berkeley and Los Angeles: University of California Press, 1988).

[10]J. Mark Ramseyer and Frances McCall Rosenbluth, *Japan's Political Marketplace* (Cambridge, MA: Harvard University Press, 1993).

[11]Pempel, *Regime Shift,* p. 151.

[12]Pempel, *Regime Shift,* pp. 206–219. On the differences between welfare in the U.S. and Japan, see G. Esping-Anderson, "Hybrid or Unique: The Japanese Welfare State Between Europe and America," *Journal of European Social Policy* 7 (No. 3, 1997): 179–189.

[13]Dore, *Taking Japan Seriously,* p. 204.

[14]Kent E. Calder, *Crisis and Compensation: Public Policy and Political Stability in Japan, 1949–1986* (Princeton, NJ: Princeton University Press, 1988).

[15]Frank K. Upham, *Law and Social Change in Postwar Japan* (Cambridge, MA: Harvard University Press, 1987).

[16]Gavan McCormack and Yoshio Sugimoto, "Democracy and Japan," in *Democracy in Contemporary Japan,* ed. Gavan McCormack and Yoshio Sugimoto (Armonk, NY: M. E. Sharpe, 1986), p. 15.

[17]See Iwao Sumiko, *The Japanese Woman: Traditional Image and Changing Reality* (New York: The Free Press, 1994).

JAPAN: SELECTED BIBLIOGRAPHY

Kent E. Calder, *Crisis and Compensation: Public Policy and Political Stability in Japan, 1949–1986* (Princeton: Princeton University Press, 1988).

Lonny E. Carlile and Mark C. Tilton, eds., *Is Japan Really Changing Its Ways? Regulatory Reform and the Japanese Economy* (Washington, DC: The Brookings Institution, 1998).

Armand Clesse et al., *The Vitality of Japan: Sources of National Strength and Weakness* (New York: St. Martin's Press, 1997).

Gerald L. Curtis *The Japanese Way of Politics* (New York: Columbia University Press, 1988).

Scott C. Flanagan et al., *The Japanese Voter* (New Haven, CT: Yale University Press, 1991).

Shelton Garon, *Molding Japanese Minds: The State in Everyday Life* (Princeton, NJ: Princeton University Press, 1997).

Kenji Hayao, *The Japanese Prime Minister and Public Policy* (Pittsburgh: University of Pittsburgh Press, 1993).

Chikio Hayashi and Yasumasa Kuroda, *Japanese Culture in Comparative Perspective* (Westport, CT: Praeger, 1997).

Timothy Hoye, *Japanese Politics: Fixed and Floating Worlds* (Upper Saddle River, NJ: Prentice Hall, 1999).

Ronald J. Hrebenar, ed., *The Japanese Party System,* 2nd ed. (Boulder, CO: Westview, 1992).

Chalmers Johnson, *Japan: Who Governs? The Rise of the Developmental State* (New York: W. W. Norton, 1995).

Harold R. Kerbo and John A. McKinstry, *Who Rules Japan?: The Inner Circles of Economic and Political Power* (Westport, CT: Praeger, 1995).

B. C. Koh, *Japan's Administrative Elite* (Berkeley: University of California Press, 1989).

Fumie Kumagai and Donna J. Keyser, *Unmasking Japan Today: The Impact of Traditional Values on Modern Japanese Society* (Westport, CT: Praeger, 1996).

Curtis H. Martin and Bruce Stonach, *Politics East and West: A Comparison of Japanese and British Political Culture* (Armonk, VT: Sharpe, 1992).

Tim Megarry, ed., *The Making of Modern Japan: A Reader* (Dartford, England: Greenwich University Press, 1995).

Peter R. Moody, Jr., *Tradition and Modernization in China and Japan* (Belmont, CA: Wadsworth, 1995).

Ian Neary, *Leaders and Leadership in Japan* (Richmond, Surrey: Japan Library, 1996).

T. J. Pempel, *Regime Shift: Comparative Dynamics of the Japanese Political Economy* (Ithaca, NY: Cornell University Press, 1998).

Susan J. Pharr, "Public Trust and Democracy in Japan," in Joseph S. Nye, Philip D. Zelikov, and David C. King, eds., *Why People Don't Trust Government* (Cambridge, MA: Harvard University Press, 1997).

Susan J. Pharr and Ellis S. Krauss, eds., *Media and Politics in Japan* (Honolulu, HI: University of Hawaii Press, 1996).

Lucian W. Pye, *Asian Power and Politics: The Cultural Dimensions of Authority* (Cambridge: The Belknap Press of Harvard University, 1985).

J. Mark Ramseyer and Frances McCall Rosenbluth, *Japan's Political Marketplace* (Cambridge, MA: Harvard University Press, 1997).

Steven R. Reed, *Making Common Sense of Japan* (Pittsburgh: University of Pittsburgh Press, 1993).

Edwin O. Reischauer and Maius B. Jansen, *The Japanese Today: Change and Continuity* (Cambridge: MA: Belknap Press, 1995).

Dennis B. Smith, *Japan Since 1945: The Rise of an Economic Superpower* (New York: St. Martin's Press, 1995).

J. A. A. Stockwin, et al., *Dynamic and Immobilist Politics in Japan* (Honolulu: University of Hawaii Press, 1988).

Yoshio Sugimoto, *An Introduction to Japanese Society* (New York: Cambridge University Press, 1997).

Iwao Sumiko, *The Japanese Woman: Traditional Image and Changing Reality* (New York: Free Press, 1994).

Frank K. Upham, *Law and Social Change in Postwar Japan* (Cambridge, MA: Harvard University Press, 1987).

Ann Waswo, *Modern Japanese Society, 1868–1994* (New York: Oxford University Press, 1996).

David Williams, *Japan: Beyond the End of History* (London: Routledge, 1994).

Karel van Wolferen, *The Enigma of Japanese Power* (New York: Alfred A. Knopf, 1989).

Chapter 31

China's History
and Political Culture*

A fundamental factor in understanding China is the relationship between the land and its people. China's total land area is about 3.7 million square miles, slightly larger than that of the United States. However, about 85 to 90 percent of China's more than 1.2 billion people live and work on only one-sixth of this area. The remaining land is mostly hilly and mountainous. Unlike the United States, only 15 to 20 percent of China's land area is cultivable, and much of this land has been used intensively for centuries.

In addition to the limited land area for cultivation, the climatic conditions compound the problem of food production for a vast population. The uneven rate of precipitation is one example. Rainfall comes to most parts of China in the spring and summer, usually in torrential

downpours. It decreases from south to north. Average annual rainfall is about 60 to 80 inches for South China and less than 10 inches for the northwest. The fertile Yangtze River valley receives about 40 to 60 inches, while most of northern China, receives about 25 inches annually.

If the torrential downpours from the rainy season are not channeled into reservoirs, a serious water shortage may result that can ultimately affect the livelihood of millions of people. The successive downpours during the rainy season can cause flooding in China's two major river systems, the Yangtze (3900 miles) and the Yellow (3600 miles) and their tributaries. The Yellow River, known as "China's Sorrow" for centuries, has caused devastating floods. It has flooded fifteen hundred times in a period of 2000 years. The silt-laden waters of the Yellow River have changed course at least twenty-six times. The Yellow River normally carries 57 pounds of mud per cubic yard; but when it rises after a torrential downpour its mud-carrying capacity can reach as much as 900 pounds.[1] In one flood, the Yellow River overflowed its banks in a northern province, inundating towns and cities with a loss of life estimated at close to 1 million. In 1981, heavy rains

*James C. F. Wang, University of Hawaii at Hilo, authored the original version of this section on China. Grateful acknowledgment is hereby given for permission to use material from James C. F. Wang, *Contemporary Chinese Politics: An Introduction,* (Englewood Cliffs, NJ: Prentice-Hall 1980), and from James C. F. Wang, *Contemporary Chinese Politics: An Introduction,* 2nd ed., (Englewood Cliffs, NJ: Prentice-Hall 1985).

PEOPLE'S REPUBLIC OF CHINA

in late July and August caused the Yangtze River to flood over 65 percent of the counties in the southwestern province of Sichuan, leaving 1¹/₂ million people homeless. Chinese scientists have estimated that each year 250 million tons of earth are washed into the Yangtze's three main tributaries.[2] One study showed that for the period between 206 BC to AD 1911 there were a total of 1621 floods and 1392 droughts that brought endless sorrow to the Chinese people.[3]

More recently, in 1998, flooding in northeast China killed thousands of people, left millions homeless, and inundated millions of acres of crop land and a large part of China's largest oil field, causing over $25 billion in economic losses. But flooding is only part of the problem faced by agriculture in China. In northern China, some 550 million people, more than twice the population of the United States, suffer from a persistent water shortage. Four hundred, i.e., nearly two-thirds of China's 666 cities do not have enough water. The Yellow River, for centuries the source of devastating floods, has been running dry every year since 1985. While during the 1990s floods have accounted for economic losses averaging $10 billion a year, water shortages cost China $35 billion annually. Part of the problem is population growth—700 million since 1949; another is the concentration of the Chinese population on the farmland adjacent to China's rivers; and, finally, higher living standards, which have resulted in an increase of per capita water consumption due to the introduction of flush toilets, showers, and washing machines in most urban households.[4]

The limited amount of land available for cultivation, the frequency of flood and drought, the effects of urbanization, and the enormous size of the population dictate that the mobilization of its productive forces to feed its people is the primary task of China. This basic problem of population pressure on limited land for cultivation has plagued China for many centuries—certainly since its population doubled between 1740 and 1790 and its increase by another third during the next fifty years, resulting in a dramatic change in the historic man-land ratio and a substantial weakening of the fabric of Chinese society.[5] The functions of government and in many respects the very performance of government have involved what John Fairbank described as the control of "the land, the manpower, and the water supply" for this agrarian society.[6]

It should be noted, however, that, even before the Industrial Revolution in Europe, China was a land of great cities. At the beginning of the nineteenth century, China could lay claim to six of the world's largest cities. Yet a century and a half later China had many of the characteristics of a peasant society. While accurate statistics are difficult to come by, in 1949, when communism came to China, only about 10 percent of the population were urban. Although in many respects an agent of modernization, communism in China, as in the Soviet Union, contrary to the Marxist script, did little to eradicate "the differences between town and country." With 32 percent of its population classified as urban in 1997, it is evident that China, half a century after the communist takeover, still remains in the throes of the transformation from a peasant society into a modern industrial nation. At the same time, the ongoing process of urbanization, expected to reach 55 percent by the year 2025, will undoubtedly put enormous additional pressure on the limited land resources of the world's most populous country.[7]

HISTORICAL LEGACIES AND TRADITIONAL POLITICAL CULTURE

The Confucian Orthodoxy and Tradition

For over 2000 years, Confucianism, China's orthodox ideology before the 1911 Revolution, was "the chief subject of study" by scholars and the officialdom. As a body of political philosophy and a social code of ethics, the term Confucianism, as pointed out by John Fairbank, is "as broad and various as Christianity." As an ideology it has undergone many changes during the 2000 years of Chinese history. But, in spite of its ups and downs during the long course of China's cultural history, Confucianism demonstrated great tenacity. Although China under communism has succeeded in inducing fundamental changes, many of the Confucian ideas of governance still influence this essentially agrarian society. Some argue that the personality cult of Mao, the code of behavior for the party cadres, and the institution of self-criticism are basically Confucian in nature.[8] During the decade of the Cultural Revolution (1966–76), Confucianism was fiercely denounced as the root of all evils in China. In the 1980s, Confucianism was regarded as a "valuable national legacy" that needs to be restudied.

What are the basic tenets of Confucianism? To what extent have the Confucian traditions influenced China's political culture? First, Confucianism stressed the cultivation of a moral or virtuous individual. Cultivation of the spiritual aspects of conduct applied to the ruler as well as the ruled. The emperor and the civil service were expected to set high moral standards of conduct and benevolence as examples for the people to follow. When the ruler possessed impeccable virtues and moral standards, Confucius and his

The Great Wall in China, first built in the third century BC to keep China isolated (1982). *(Photographer/Source:* Michael Heron/AP/Wide World Photos)

disciples argued, the government need rely only on moral force; no coercive force would be needed to rule. This is the cardinal Confucian principle of "government by goodness" or "goodness produces power." In 1982, the need for high moral standards was stressed as a force for shaping attitudes and conduct. Hu Yaobang, the party's general secretary, called for the development of "socialist spiritual civilization" that embraces not only the raising of higher education and scientific training standards but also of "ideological, political and moral standards."[9] Hu's definition of a "socialist spiritual civilization" was much closer to Confucianism than Marxism:

> In essence, it consists of, above all, revolutionary ideals, morality and discipline. All Party members and other advanced persons in our society must continuously propagate advanced ideas and set an example by their own deeds so as to inspire more and more members of our society to become working people with lofty ideals, moral integrity, education and a sense of discipline.[10]

Second, Confucianism was basically authoritarian. This orthodox ideology emphasized the paramount need for accepting and obeying the established order, the centralized power of the emperor. Authoritarian rule was reinforced by the "mandate of heaven" theory, which provided that the emperor's rule was legitimate as long as it was good or unless things went wrong—heaven's anger and displeasure being manifested in the form of floods or droughts. Acceptance of authority was ingrained in the personality makeup of the Chinese through centuries of inculcation of this aspect of Confucianism.

Third, Confucianism proclaimed that the "government of goodness" could come about only if all citizens knew their roles and how to conduct themselves accordingly. Confucianism was a set of ethical codes designed to regulate the relationships between ruler and subject, father and son, friend and neighbor, husband and wife, and brother and brother. Strict observance of the complex web of this social code promoted collective societal norms and conformity, and it deemphasized individuality. Thus individual self-discipline was stressed at all times: one must be correct in one's moral conduct if others were to be expected to do likewise. This was the foundation on which social harmony rested.

Fourth, as an ideology Confucianism was elitist. "Government by goodness" or "government by moral prestige" could only be transmitted through study and learning by those who had a superior intellect and financial resources and by those who held positions of importance in society and government. From this there emerged the traditional concept of a ruling class, the Confucian scholar-gentry-officialdom. It was this class of elites that not only perpetuated the orthodoxy but actually governed the populace.

The Dynastic System and the Emperor Cult

Historically, the Chinese emperor ruled absolutely over his subjects. His power and legitimacy to rule the empire were based on the mythological belief that he was the "Son of Heaven" with a divine mandate to rule the earth. The "mandate of heaven" was legitimate so long as the emperor ruled righteously and maintained harmony within Chinese society and between society and nature. Rituals and symbols were designed to perpetuate the prestige and charisma of the emperor, and also to symbolize the divine nature of imperial rule. Preferences for imperial symbols persisted long after the 1911 Revolution that ended the Chinese empire.

Attempts to cultivate a "personality cult" or "emperor cult" were evident in Nationalist China in the rituals and symbols devised for Dr. Sun Yat-sen and Chiang Kai-shek.[11] And one of the more interesting aspects of de-Maoization has been the criticism made by the Chinese Communist Party (CCP) under Deng Xiaoping's leadership that Mao engaged in a "personality cult" and ruled the state autocratically as though he were the emperor.[12]

Of course, an emperor could be overthrown and replaced by another. The right to rebel against a tyrannical ruler was a corollary to the "mandate of heaven" theory. Rebellion became accepted in Chinese history if the emperor failed to maintain harmony or allowed widespread famine to occur

from lack of flood control and inadequate irrigation systems. However, rebellion was legitimate only if it succeeded, according to Charles Fitzgerald, a noted British scholar of Chinese history. Each successful regime became a new dynasty. Chinese history, the longest continuous recorded history in the world, is basically a record of twenty-four histories of imperial rule.

Each dynasty was established either by a successful rebellion or through invasions by either the Mongols or the Manchus from outside the Great Wall. Rebellions were generally either peasant uprisings exploited by some military figure or direct military insurrections. Each of the twenty-four dynasties was said to have followed a pattern of development known as the *dynastic cycle:* (1) establishment of a new virtuous and benevolent rule; (2) a period of intellectual rejuvenation; (3) an era of corruption or misrule; (4) the occurrence of uncontrolled natural calamities, such as floods and/or droughts; and finally, (5) overthrow of the regime by rebellion or invasions. The gigantic earthquake that shook Beijing in September 1976, prior to Mao's death, was viewed by many traditionalists as an omen of dynastic change.

SCHOLAR–GENTRY OFFICIALDOM: THE BUREAUCRATIC STATE

As the officially sanctioned ideology, Confucianism conditioned and controlled the minds of those who governed China; it became the undisputed "orthodox doctrine of the imperial state."[13] The teachings of the venerable sage served to legitimize the dynastic system. Traditional Confucian ideology made its greatest impact on the ruling elites. It left an "ideological vacuum" among the peasants, the bulk of the population then as now, who were more concerned with the burden of taxes levied by the rulers and the hardships of life than with theories of government.[14] The orthodox ideology was perpetuated by the Confucian education given to young men of means.

While the dynasties rose and fell, the actual administration of state affairs was vested in the hands of a civil bureaucracy. Under the imperial system, the government officials, the mandarins, dominated the political and economic life in China. The mandarins were those individuals who held positions of power and ruled the empire in the name of the emperor by virtue of imperial degrees obtained by successfully passing the civil service examination. A state civil service based on competence, merit, and professionalism was China's unique contribution to the world of bureaucracy. Much of the civil service examination for imperial degree candidates tested their knowledge and understanding of Confucian teachings.

Three types of competitive examination for the civil service were held at three intervals: the initial certification, the provincial examinations, and the final imperial examination in the capital. Only successful candidates for the initial certification were permitted to take the provincial examination, which qualified those who passed it to be appointed to lower-level government service. Only those who successfully passed the imperial examination were appointed to higher government posts as the emperor's ministers and counselors. Lucian Pye estimates that only 24,874 received the highest imperial degree during the 276 years of the Ming Dynasty from 1368 to 1644.[15]

Members of the civil service came almost solely from the wealthy landholding class, whose members had the resources to provide extended education for their sons. Imperial appointments to positions of power and prestige enabled the mandarins to acquire fortunes in landholdings for themselves and their families. They constituted the small privileged upper class of Confucian scholars in the traditional Chinese agrarian society. The size of the civil service ranged from 10,000 to about 40,000.[16] These scholar-gentry officials wielded enormous arbitrary power over their subjects, the vast majority of whom were illiterate peasants living in the countryside.

A typical magistrate for a Chinese county, according to one study, was responsible for the lives and well-being of about a quarter of a million subjects.[17] The magistrate, therefore, had to seek the cooperation and support of the large landholders to administer the county on behalf of the emperor and the central administration in Beijing. This administrative setup illustrates the gulf that existed between the educated elite and the illiterate peasants and indicates the hierarchical structure of Chinese imperial rule.

The Chinese bureaucracy was classified into ranks and grades, each with a special set of privileges and a compensation scale. A voluminous flow of official documents and memoranda moved up and down the hierarchical ladder. At each level of the hierarchy a certain prescribed form and literary style had to be observed—a multiplication of bureaucratic jargon. To control the huge bureaucracy, the emperor designated special censors in the various levels of the government to report on the conduct of public officials. The provincial governor or the top man in a branch of the central bureaucracy in Beijing could become a bottleneck in the policy initiation and implementation process. At the lowest level of administration—the Chinese county—all important decisions affecting the community were made by the elites with the blessing of the magistrate. These decisions were often disregarded or were contrary to the wishes of the earth-bound peasants, who constituted the majority. Arbitrary decision making, unresponsive to the uneducated masses in the villages, remains to this day a basic problem in the relationship between the leaders and the led in China. In traditional Chinese politics, as in modern China, the elites or officials exercised control over the mass of peasants.

COLLECTIVE PRINCIPLES IN TRADITIONAL CHINA

When examining the collective aspects of contemporary China under communism, one should bear in mind that China traditionally has been a collective society. The key to that collective society was the family system in which an individual's moral well-being, beliefs, and attitudes were dictated by the Confucian code of ethics. Moreover, economic security and political functions were all influenced strongly by the social system of families and kinship relations.[18] Few social organizations existed outside the family kinship.

The traditional Chinese society was basically paternalistic. The head of the family was held responsible and accountable for the behavior of individuals in the group as well as for the group's collective duties to the state, such as taxes and military service. A candidate who passed the imperial examination gave honor and prestige to the family as a whole. Punishment for crimes and wrongdoings against society were the responsibility of the family rather than the state. Government officials were viewed as parents who looked after the needs of the children, the people. The collective mold under Chinese communism is, in many respects, according to Lucian Pye, the continuation of the traditional "theory of collective responsibility."[19] Responsibility and control over constituent members of agricultural communes and production or office units are variations of the collective responsibility concept.

MILITARISM

Militarism has always played an important role in Chinese politics. Each dynasty employed military force to attain power. Although a new dynasty was legitimized under the Confucian precepts, each new ruler would be required to see to it that military power would remain under centralized control—that is, the military must be subject to the control of the central civil bureaucracy. The military has consistently served as "the ultimate power" and "the normal arbiter in the distribution of power and in the establishment of policy," according to Martin Wilbur.[20] To a large extent, modern Chinese political development has been influenced by the power of armies, on the one hand, and by the technique in the use of armies and in military organization, on the other.

For decades prior to the unification effort undertaken by the Chinese Nationalists in 1926, a system of regional military separatism dominated the political scene in China. Under the system, independent military-political groupings, each occupying one or more provinces, functioned as separate political entities and engaged in internecine warfare with each other in order to preserve their own separate regions and to prevent their rivals from establishing a unified and centralized political system. That contemporary China has been plagued by the problem of control of armies is really an understatement. It is largely by military means and through military

organization and technique that the Chinese Nationalists tried, and the Chinese communists succeeded, in reestablishing a "unified hierarchical and centralized political system."[21] The military thus constitutes a dominant group in society, and the military institution has played a dominant role in political development.[22]

The military has always occupied a special position in Chinese communist society. The Chinese Communist Party, for a long time before 1949, was the army. The party membership grew from the 20,000 Long March survivors in 1936 to over 1.2 million in 1945. Over 1 million of the total membership in 1945 constituted the military supply system.[23] These people were regular members of either the army or the party, working without salary and under a military type of discipline. Robert Tucker has labeled this unique system of militarizing the party as military communism to distinguish it from all other forms of communism.[24] It has been evident in recent years that the party leadership has depended upon party members in the army to carry on political work, to restore order, and to use the army as a coercive instrument in the contest for political power and succession.

THE REVOLUTION OF 1911

The collapse of the traditional Chinese political system in 1911 ushered in a period of revolutionary changes that are still going on today. Before discussing the revolution, it will be necessary to review briefly why the traditional imperial system collapsed and why a revolution took place in 1911.

Internal Decay and Rebellion

First, the dynastic cycle was once again nearing its end. The Manchu Dynasty had experienced considerable internal decline by the eighteenth century. Corruption among the civil bureaucracy that administered the empire became rampant during the later reign of Emperor Chien-lung. A bloody rebellion against the Manchus and against taxes took place in 1796, led by a fanatical secret society, the "White Lotus." The rebellion was finally brought under control after a new emperor had restored discipline among the imperial forces. Although the rebellion of 1796 was poorly organized and led, this challenge to the mandate to rule by the foreign Manchus was "an omen of dynastic decline."

Other signs of internal decay and decline were found in the evasion of taxes by the landed gentry and the widespread misuse or outright theft of funds allocated for public works projects, such as flood control and dike repair. The disastrous flood of the Yellow River in 1854, caused mainly by broken dikes following years of neglect and disrepair, devastated the countryside and caused widespread loss of life.

The Manchu Dynasty's mandate to rule was shaken to its foundation by the Taiping Rebellion (1850–64). This uprising was led by a Confucian scholar who failed to pass the civil service examinations three times and was said to have been under the influence of the early Western missionaries to China. He evidently had read translated biblical passages and declared himself a brother of Jesus. At the height of the rebellion, Taiping armies held half the Manchu empire and established its capital in Nanjing. Taiping leaders sought to build an egalitarian society with the abolition of monetary and commodity exchange, state ownership of land, and distribution of land to the peasants who tilled it. The rebellion was finally suppressed by the Manchu's newly restructured military organization, with technical assistance from foreign experts. The rebellion failed to receive support from the Confucian scholar-officialdom, a prerequisite for any successful rebellion. Its failure was also attributable to internal feuding among the Taiping leaders. Although the Manchu empire was saved, its ability to govern China was very seriously undermined.

Western Impact

While the Manchu Dynasty was confronting internal rebellions in the countryside, it had to deal with the demands of Western merchants and missionaries to keep China's door open for trade and diplomatic contact. Traditional Chinese policy toward Westerners was to keep them isolated in a corner of a port city, such as Canton, in order to restrict commerce and contact. Diplomatic

relations on the basis of sovereign equality was considered unacceptable to the Chinese, who traditionally looked upon foreigners as "barbarians." The Mongol and Manchu invaders had not made any lasting impact on Chinese civilization. Instead the conquerors were assimilated by the superior Chinese civilization. China under the Mongols and the Manchus was still governed and administered by the Confucian scholars in accordance with the sage's humanistic teachings. Until the 1840s, China did not feel threatened by the West and its dynamic civilization. But the Opium War of 1839–42, fought largely over cultural misunderstandings, not only paved the way for Western imperialism's entry into China, but also jolted Chinese civilization and encroached on the empire's territorial integrity. Thereafter China was forced by superior Western firepower to sign a series of unequal treaties under which territorial concessions and spheres of influence were granted to European powers.

In the eyes of the Chinese, the Manchu empire's inability to repel foreign imperialists had irreparably damaged the empire's prestige. Each confrontation with the European powers resulted in further defeat and humiliation for the empire. Meanwhile, unrest and rebellion reigned in the countryside, caused largely by the pressure of an ever-expanding population on the limited land. China's population had doubled between 1740 and 1790 and increased by another third by 1840. With limited land for cultivation, the population expansion only further aggravated the plight brought on by uncontrolled floods and droughts. The cost of suppressing the Taiping Rebellion added to the financial crisis of the empire. Each unequal treaty China was forced to sign contained war indemnity to a foreign power. Opium trade was also draining China's treasury in the lopsided trade pattern favoring the British. Uprisings and rebellion in the countryside made it fashionable for the populace to defy the imperial authorities over tax collection and law and order in general. In a desperate effort to raise additional revenue to meet the empire's mounting financial burden, government positions were put up for sale to the highest bidder.

With the empire now on the verge of collapse, conservative Confucian scholars initiated a "self-strengthening" movement, a sort of half-measured modernization in military science and technology. Reformers also sought to strengthen the old Chinese empire by making changes in traditional institutions, such as the examination system and the military establishment. But the optimism of the reformers was dashed when China sustained her greatest humiliation— defeat by Japan in 1895. This defeat convinced some that reform alone could not possibly save the empire and marked the beginning of the idea of revolutionary change to overthrow the traditional imperial system.

The Coming of the 1911 Revolution

In 1894, Dr. Sun Yat-sen founded a small secret society among overseas Chinese for the purpose of overthrowing the decaying Manchu Dynasty. As a revolutionary with a price on his head, Sun was forced to operate and organize abroad much of the time. After many years of hard work in southeast Asia, Japan, and Hawaii, Sun's movement took hold among the educated young Chinese abroad. In 1905, four hundred of Sun's followers gathered in Japan to form the first viable revolutionary movement, the Tung Meng Hui.[25] The members took a solemn oath to bring down the alien Manchu empire and to replace it with a Chinese republic. Ten different attempts were organized and financed by the group, headquartered variously in Tokyo and Hanoi, to strike down the vulnerable Manchu rule by assassinating imperial officials. As these revolutionary attempts failed, one by one, and more revolutionaries lost their lives, the movement became demoralized and ran low on funds. On October 10, 1911, an eleventh attempt was made. It resulted in a successful uprising by discontented and dissatisfied provincial officials, merchants, and imperial army commanders. The Manchu emperor abdicated, and shortly thereafter the Chinese imperial dynastic system came to an end.

While Dr. Sun's revolutionary movement, comprised largely of students, youth, and overseas Chinese, gave impetus and momentum to the revolution, it was not the force that brought down the empire. It was the new imperial army, headed by Yuan Shih-kai, that forced the abdication. Yuan Shih-kai assumed the power of the government immediately after the abdication and stayed on to become the first president of the Chinese republic under an agreement with Dr. Sun, who had little bargaining power. The new republic floundered from the start. Very few Chinese had any real understanding of Western democracy. All the Chinese political traditions and institutions were designed for imperial rule and therefore were ill-suited for constitutional democracy. Yuan Shih-kai increasingly disregarded the constitution and finally attempted to establish himself as emperor. The Chinese nation disintegrated as the new government proved incapable of commanding allegiance from the people in the midst of mounting domestic problems and the constant meddling in Chinese internal affairs by European powers and Japan. Yuan's death in 1916 marked the final collapse of the central government's effective authority.[26]

The Failure of the Nationalist Revolution

After 1911 China was in a process of disintegration; it was a nation in utter chaos. The main pillars that once had supported Chinese civilization had collapsed. There was no viable replacement for the Manchu imperial rule. The orthodox Confucian ideology was no longer the acceptable basis for legitimacy. The traditional civil service examination, the mechanism that had perpetuated the Confucian orthodoxy, was abolished in 1905 for its intellectual sterility and administrative corruption. The ancient Chinese civilization was beset on all fronts by the superior technology of the West. Soon China entered the era of warlordism (1916–36) as effective central control disappeared. When strongman Yuan Shih-kai died in 1916, some of his officers and others with sufficient power seized control of various regions. These territories were controlled by the warlords, who maintained private armies manned with conscripted peasants, to protect and extend their provincial domains. Even Sun Yat-sen and his followers had to seek refuge under the protection of the warlord in Canton. Sun's revolutionary program at this time called for the eventual establishment of constitutional government in three stages: first, unification of the nation through elimination of warlordism by military force and termination of foreign intervention in China;

second, a period of political tutelage to prepare the people for democratic government; and third, the enactment of a constitution by the people. Neither the European powers nor the warlords paid any attention to Dr. Sun, who had become disillusioned and desperate for a way to save China from further disintegration.

The political turmoil in China provided the impetus for an intellectual awakening. In 1919, this intellectual ferment culminated in the May Fourth Movement, instigated by high school and university students and their teachers to search for a model for building a new China. The May Fourth Movement led to reform of the written Chinese language, from the archaic classical style to the use of the vernacular, or everyday spoken form. It also introduced the study of Western science, technology, and political ideologies, including Marxism. The movement was closely tied in with demonstrations by university students against foreign intervention in Chinese affairs and against warlordism. These activities gave impetus to the new nationalistic and patriotic feeling emerging among the general population.

It was in this atmosphere of ferment and feelings of anger, humiliation, and disillusionment that a nationalist revolution took form. Dr. Sun fled from the southern warlord in Canton to Shanghai in 1922. There he was contacted by Adolph Joffe, an agent of the Communist Third International (the Comintern), who offered assistance to the Chinese revolutionary movement. Sun accepted the offer and signed an agreement to receive—from the Soviet Union through the Comintern—personnel to reorganize Sun's ineffective political party along the lines of the Communist Party of the Soviet Union and limited arms and training in Soviet military schools for members of the revolutionary armies to be organized by Dr. Sun's followers. In addition, the agreement called for an alliance with the infant Chinese Communist Party under the new National People's Party (the Nationalists), the *Guomindang*. A military academy was established in Whampoa, not far from the city of Canton, to train an officer corps to lead the newly recruited armies. Although Dr. Sun died in 1925, a military expedition was launched in 1926 to unify China by defeating the warlords. News of the expedition did unify the people with

nationalistic feelings and aroused it against foreign imperialism.

The expedition was launched under an uneasy alliance between Sun's followers, who were receiving financial backing from merchants in coastal cities and from large landowners in the countryside, and the members of the Chinese Communist Party, controlled by the Comintern. By March of 1927, the new nationalist government had come to be dominated by the left-wing elements of the Guomindang and the communists with headquarters in Wuhan in central China. When the expedition had gained control of eastern China on its push north, Chiang Kai-shek, commander of the revolutionary armies and successor to Sun Yat-sen, decided to end the internal schism between the Left and Right by first eliminating members of the Chinese Communist Party within the revolutionary movement. In April 1927, communists in the cities under Chiang's control were massacred in a lightning strike. This surprise blow, known as the Shanghai Massacre, was so effective that it practically decimated the communist ranks. Chiang also expelled the Soviet advisers from China. Then in Nanjing he established the nationalist government, which was recognized by most nations as the legitimate government of China in the 1940s. The remaining Chinese communists sought refuge in the mountainous regions in central China.

During the decade of Guomindang rule from 1927 to 1937, modest progress was made in many areas of modernization, initiated by the Nationalists under the leadership of Chiang Kai-shek and his Western-trained advisers and administrators. For the first time, China had a modern governmental structure. As soon as the major provincial warlords were eliminated or coopted into the system, the transportation and industrial facilities were improved and expanded in the area. Earnest attempts were made to expand elementary school education and to provide political indoctrination for the young. Most important, from Chiang's point of view, was the building of a more efficient and dedicated modern army for a host of purposes, including the eventual elimination of warlords and the communist guerrillas operating in mountainous areas of central China, as well as protecting China's borders from foreign attack.

There were glaring negative features in the Nationalist balance sheet. First, no real efforts were made to provide progressive economic and social programs to improve the lot of the people. Land reform measures to alleviate the plight of the peasants remained mostly on paper. Second, the regime alienated the intellectuals by its repressive measures against them in the guise of purging any elements of communist influence from their ranks. Third, enormous expenditures from the national treasury were devoted to the "extermination" of the Chinese communists operating in remote mountain regions. The Nationalists steadfastly refused to seek a nonmilitary solution to the problem of insurrection by the communists. Nor were they willing to seek consultation with other political groups, let alone share political power with other elements of Chinese society to pave the way for termination of their "tutelage rule." The Guomindang's modest accomplishments in nation building were soon obliterated by its obsession to eliminate all opposition.

Time was not on the side of the Nationalists. In 1931, when they had achieved some measure of national unification and modernization in the midst of waging encirclement campaigns against the communist guerrilla forces, the Japanese militarists annexed resource-rich Manchuria and made advances into northern China, inside the Great Wall. The Nationalist regime faced a hard choice in allocating its limited resources between the Japanese aggressors and the communist insurgents. In the early 1930s Chiang's strategy was to rapidly annihilate the communist guerrilla forces and then to face the Japanese. However, rising public sentiment, expressed in frequent demonstrations, demanded that the regime prevent further territorial losses to the Japanese, and in December 1936, Chiang was forced to join in a united front with the Chinese communists to fight the Japanese.

THE RISE OF CHINESE COMMUNISM: THE NEW ORTHODOXY

Although Marxism was introduced in China about the time of World War I, this ideology, which called for revolution by an urban proletariat under mature capitalism, elicited little attention. Fabian socialism—progressive and social change through gradual constitutional means, developed in England in 1884—became the most popular liberal ideology from the West. For example, Dr. Sun's program incorporated socialist planks, including nationalization of land, a welfare state, and a planned economy. Interest in Marxism increased among Chinese intellectuals after the 1917 Bolshevik Revolution in Russia. They saw in Lenin's revolution a relevant solution to China's political and economic problems. The keen interest in Bolshevism also reflected disillusion with Western democracy as a model for Chinese development. In addition, it expressed Chinese bitterness over the imperialist activities of the Western democracies in China.

The early Chinese Marxists and the founders of the Chinese Communist party were leading intellectuals in Beijing National University (Beita). In 1918, Li Dazhao, the university's head librarian, formed a Marxist study group to which many young students, including a library assistant named Mao Zedong, were attracted. These young students were more interested in learning how to make a revolution than in theorizing about Marxism. With some urging from Comintern agents, the Chinese Communist Party (CCP) was formed on July 1, 1921. The group of thirteen intellectuals and revolutionaries, representing a total of fifty-seven members, were called together by Chen Duxiu, who became the first secretary general. Meetings for the first two party congresses were held secretly in the French concession in Shanghai to prevent harassment from the police. This was the very modest beginning of the party and the movement that took root in later years.

For the first 6 years of the CCP's existence, 1921–27, the movement was under the control and direction of the Third International, or the Comintern. The Comintern had been formed in 1919 at the insistence of Lenin, who wanted a new international organization, controlled by Moscow, to provide direction for all proletarian parties and to promote antiimperialist revolutions throughout the world. Moscow directed and controlled the CCP and its leadership through Soviet Comintern agents who came to China with financial aid and military materiel. The leadership of the CCP before 1934, with few exceptions, was in the hands of the "returned Chinese bolsheviks," trained for party work in Moscow under the sponsorship of the Comintern.

The Comintern's doctrine insisted that revolutions in colonial areas must be based on industrial workers. Its strategy called for the participation of nonproletarian elements, such as the bourgeoisie, in a united front alliance to lead national revolutions. The manifestos adopted by four consecutive CCP congresses, from 1922 to 1925, echoed the Comintern line, calling for a revolutionary alliance with the landlord- and merchant-based Guomindang, Dr. Sun's Nationalist Party. This Comintern strategy, which limited the communist base to urban industrial workers and called for individual communists to join the Guomindang under a united front, enhanced the CCP's growth as a viable political party during its early years.

By 1927, the united front alliance had become unworkable. Chiang Kai-shek's power as commander in chief and head of the Guomindang was threatened by leftist elements in control of the revolutionary government, which was supported by the communists. As pointed out earlier, Chiang decided to purge the communists from his organization in the famous "Shanghai Massacre" and to set up a rival government in Nanjing. Not long after, the leftist-dominated Wuhan government also turned on the communists when it became known that the Comintern, under direct orders from Stalin, had instructed the CCP to eliminate the landlord elements and militarists in order to transform the alliance into a new revolutionary force. This also turned out to be a bloody mass execution of the communists who were caught.

Instead of admitting the mistake of his China policy, Stalin blamed the CCP leaders for their failure to prepare the workers in Wuhan for action.[27] Partly as a rebuttal to criticism raised by Leon Trotsky, Stalin ordered the Comintern agents in China to plan a series of armed insurrections in the hope that quick victories would silence any criticism of the failure of his united front policy.[28] On August 1, 1927, now celebrated as founding day of the People's Liberation Army, Zhou Enlai and Zhu De led a mutiny of communist troops within the Guomindang forces in Nanchang in central China. After occupying the city briefly, the communists were forced to seek refuge as guerrillas in the hills of eastern Guangdong province. The CCP also authorized a

number of Autumn Harvest Uprisings in the fall of 1927 in central and southern China. One of these was led by Mao Zedong in his home province of Hunan.

These uprisings were ill-fated misadventures that ended in defeat and brought heavy losses to the already decimated CCP ranks. When Mao and his group sought refuge in the mountain stronghold of Chingkanshan on the Hunan-Jiangxi border in central China, he repudiated the Comintern-inspired strategy. As a reprimand, Mao was dismissed briefly from his membership of the Politburo, the executive and policy-making body of the party.

After the united front between the CCP and the Guomindang broke down, the Chinese communist movement split into two areas of operation; one in the cities as an underground movement, with close links to the Comintern; the other in rural areas as experimental soviets, operating almost autonomously and feuding constantly with the Comintern advisers. By the end of 1930, the party had been driven out of the cities, and only pockets of guerilla bands operated in remote mountain regions of central and southern China, and in northern Shaanxi. The plight of the CCP was evidenced by the fact that its central committee had to operate underground in Shanghai's foreign concessions and the Sixth Party Congress had to meet in Moscow in 1928. The leadership of the party was still in the hands of the returned Bolsheviks who adhered to the Comintern policies. In a last attempt to recapture an urban base for a proletarian revolution, the CCP leadership, under Li Lisan, launched an attack from the rural bases in the summer of 1930, with the objective of capturing a number of cities on the Changjiang (Yangtze) River. Like previous Comintern-instigated misadventures, this one also ended in failure, with the small bases in rural mountain regions under blockade by Chiang Kai-shek's forces. The Chinese communists' future at this juncture seemed bleak.[29]

THE RISE OF MAO ZEDONG AND MILITARY COMMUNISM

The future of the Chinese movement hinged on the survival of the small pockets of experimental soviets in the remote rural areas, mostly in central and southern China. The CCP's decision, in the fall of 1931, to establish a Chinese Soviet Republic, which would unite the scattered bases, was both a political necessity and an admission that a revolution based on an urban proletariat was no longer possible in China. Thus, by 1931 when the CCP's central committee moved from urban Shanghai to the rural Jiangxi soviet, a decade-long quarrel within the Chinese communist movement—regarding the theoretical correctness of a revolutionary strategy based on the peasants—officially ended. The foremost proponent of a peasant base was the leader of the Jiangxi soviet, Mao Zedong.

James Hsiung points out that Mao had developed a strategy for victory during the 6 years he operated the Jiangxi guerilla base. Besides the need for a highly disciplined united party, Mao's strategy contained three indispensable ingredients: (1) the development of a strong and mobile peasant-based Red Army for a protracted armed struggle; (2) the selection of a strategic terrain for military operations; and (3) the establishment of a self-sufficient economic base in the Red Army-controlled soviet areas to provide manpower and supplies for the armed struggle.[30] Mao believed that a highly disciplined party could only be built by a recruitment policy that would draw into the party the tough and dedicated guerilla soldiers of the Red Army, who were predominantly poor peasants. The party became "militarized" as Mao began to build a new base for revolution.[31]

The Guomindang intensified its attack against the guerilla base in its fifth and most extensive military campaign, which included an effective blockade that deprived the guerilla base of outside supplies, particularly salt. By 1934 the guerilla base had to be abandoned. The communists broke out of the Guomindang encirclement and moved the surviving forces, numbering not more than 150,000, westward and then north to the Great Wall. This was the legendary Long March of more than 6000 miles over treacherous terrain of high mountains and rivers, amid ambushes from warlords, the Guomindang troops, and hostile minorities en route.[32] In October 1935, after almost a year's march, the greatly reduced forces of about 20,000 survivors arrived in Yanan in the northwestern province of Shaanxi and established

a new base for guerrilla operations. By this time a stormy Politburo meeting, held in Zunyi in southwest Guizhou Province in January 1935, had selected Mao as the undisputed leader of the CCP, including the cells operating in some urban areas, mainly industrial centers such as Shanghai and Wuhan. This marked the end of Comintern dominance and the beginning of Mao's supremacy as the CCP's political and military leader. It lasted for over 40 years, until his death in 1976.

CONCLUSION

For over 2000 years the dominant political culture for China was the Confucian orthodoxy. The traditional Chinese political culture was basically authoritarian, elitist, and establishment-oriented. The orthodoxy was perpetuated by the scholar-gentry officialdom who monopolized the educational system and the civil bureaucracy. Other ingredients of the traditional Chinese political system included a strong filial collectivist orientation and a centralized government revolving around the personality cult of the emperor. Militarism played a pivotal role in the dynastic changes, as it does still today.

The Chinese revolution that began in 1911 reflected to a large extent the impact of the West. Yet, as in Russia, Western democracy and constitutional government were little understood by the Chinese and could not be used as a model. China was searching for a direction and a way out of chaos. Not until almost a decade after the abdication of the Manchu emperor was there any intellectual ferment in search of a suitable new orthodoxy to replace the old. Chinese intellectuals discovered Marxism in particular and socialism in general in their desperate quest for a new China. Even Marxism did not make very much of an impression on Chinese intellectuals prior to the 1919 Bolshevik revolution under Lenin. The initial support and aid given by Lenin and Stalin to the Chinese Nationalist revolution yielded few tangible results.

The Nationalist revolution, 1927–37, in the end deteriorated into a military dictatorship guided mostly by a revival of traditional Confucian precepts and mixed with modernizing programs brought back by those educated in the West. The Nationalists failed to provide relief and tangible solutions for the agrarian plight in the countryside during their rule on the Chinese mainland. On the other hand, the Chinese communist movement gained ground in China's rural interior by experimenting with land reforms with varied degrees of intensity.

Its eventual success can be attributed to the propagation of a new all-embracing ideology, Marxism-Leninism and Mao's Thought. It established an elaborate system of organizational networks for implementing its socialist programs, which initially were designed almost exclusively to improve the welfare of the peasantry. These organizational networks were staffed by a dedicated, loyal, obedient, and professional corps of party cadres, the backbone of the Chinese communist bureaucracy.

For about 40 years one man, Mao Zedong, was the undisputed authoritative voice and symbol of a new China. Mao, like past Chinese imperial rulers, represented virtue and goodness; he could do no wrong as the "personality cult" was built up by his disciples. Mao's Thought, Marxist ideology, and the manifold legacy of Confucianism provided the backbone of China's public philosophy. Mao had been the architect of the great dramas of modern China: the Revolution and "Liberation" from the despotism of the emperor system, the Great Leap Forward, and the Cultural Revolution. When he died in 1976, Mao, like Stalin in 1953, left an ideological vacuum. Maoism, like Stalinism, could not survive its creator. The failure of both ideologies to improve the daily lives of their people and the increasingly evident bankruptcy of the communist vision made change inevitable in both countries.

Under Deng Xiaoping various reforms were initiated, including a return to family farming; major Marxist precepts were abandoned, and—instead of Mao's "iron rice bowl" concept—the slogan "To get rich is glorious" was proclaimed. Chinese nationalism was resurrected, as Maoism was more or less unceremoniously abandoned. Unlike the Soviet Union, the emphasis in China was on economic reform. The limits of political change became apparent when the Chinese army ruthlessly massacred unarmed students in Tiananmen Square on June 3–4, 1989. Perhaps in the long run, the most important consequence of Mao's death and de-Maoization was the end of the belief in the infallibility of one leader.[33]

NOTES

[1]*Hawaii Tribune-Herald,* October 4, 1981, p. 9.

[2]*Beijing Review* 31 (August 3, 1981): 4–5.

[3]Shan-yu Yao, "The Chronological and Seasonal Distribution of Flood and Droughts in Chinese History, 206 B.C.–A.D. 1911," *Harvard Journal of Asiatic Studies,* 7 (1942): 275.

[4]*AP,* August 21, 1998; *Washington Post,* October 4, 1998.

[5]Lucian W. Pye, *China: An Introduction* (Boston: Little, Brown and Company, 1972), p. 81.

[6]John Fairbank, *The United States and China,* rev. ed. (New York: Viking Press, 1962), p. 48.

[7]John K. Fairbank, Merle Goldman, *China: A New History* (Cambridge, MA: The Belknap Press of Harvard University Press, 1998), enl. ed., pp. 357ff.; Kang Chao, *Agricultural Production in Communist China, 1945–1965* (Madison, WI: The University of Wisconsin, 1970), pp. 3–4; "Urbanization Across the Globe," at www.zpg.org/number.htm (3/24/99). In December 1998, a senior Chinese official predicted that China will have 800 cities by the year 2000 ("China's Urbanization Accelerated by Development," at www.skali.com.my/business/rtl/199812/16/rtl19981216_04.html).

[8]Fred Hung, "Some Observations on Confucian Ideology," in Goodwin C. Chu and Francis L. K. Hsu's *Moving a Mountain: Cultural Changes in China* (Honolulu: University Press of Hawaii, 1979), p. 423.

[9]Kuang Yaming, "Appraisal of Confucius: Why? How?" *Beijing Review* 22 (May 30, 1983): 22–24.

[10]"Creating a New Situation in All Fields of Socialist Modernization," *Beijing Review* 37 (September 13, 1982): 21.

[11]Ping-ti Ho, "Salient Aspects of China's Heritage," in Ping-ti Ho and Tang Tsou, eds., *China in Crisis,* vol. 1, bk. 1 (Chicago: University of Chicago Press, 1968), p. 17.

[12]"The Correct Concept of Individual Role in History," *People's Daily,* July 4, 1980, p. 1.

[13]Charles Fitzgerald, *Revolution in China* (New York: Holt, Rinehart and Winston, 1952), p. 23.

[14]Kung-chuan Hsiao, *Rural China: Imperial Control in the Nineteenth Century* (Seattle: University of Washington Press, 1960), pp. 253–254.

[15]Lucian Pye, *China: An Introduction,* 2nd ed. (Boston: Little, Brown and Company, 1972). p. 68.

[16]Pye, *China: An Introduction,* p. 71; and John Fairbank, *The United States and China,* rev. ed. (New York: Viking Press, 1962), p. 103.

[17]Fairbank, *The United States and China,* p. 103.

[18]C. K. Yang, *The Chinese Family in the Communist Revolution* (Cambridge, MA: M.I.T. Press, 1959).

[19]Pye, *China: An Introduction,* p. 72.

[20]Martin Wilbur, "Military Separatism and the Process of Reunification under the Nationalist Regime, 1922–1937," in Ho Piting and Tang Tsou, eds., *China in Crisis,* vol. 1, bk. 1 (Chicago: University of Chicago, 1968) p. 203.

[21]Wilbur, "Military Separatism and the Process of Reunification," p. 203.

[22]Ibid.

[23]John M. H. Lindbeck, "Transformation in the Chinese Communist Party," in Donald Treadgold, ed., *Soviet and Chinese Communism: Similarities and Differences* (Seattle: University of Washington, 1967), p. 25.

[24]Robert C. Tucker, "On the Contemporary Study of Communism," *World Politics* 19 (January 1967): 242–257.

[25]Fairbank, *The United States and China,* p. 191.

[26]Fitzgerald, *Revolution in China,* p. 38; and Fairbank, *The United States and China,* pp. 197–198.

[27]See Franklin Houn, *A Short History of Chinese Communism* (Englewood Cliffs, NJ: Prentice-Hall, 1967) pp. 21–33.

[28]Ibid., pp. 35–38.

[29]For an interesting perspective on the early history of the Chinese communists and their relations with the Communist International, see Conrad Brandt, *Stalin's Failure in China, 1924–1927* (Cambridge, MA: Harvard University Press, 1958).

[30]James Hsiung, *Ideology and Practice: The Evolution of Chinese Communism* (New York: Praeger Publishers, 1970), pp. 61–62.

[31]Lindbeck, "Transformation in the Chinese Communist Party," p. 76; and Stuart Schram, "Mao Tsetung and the Chinese Political Equilibrium," *Government and Opposition* 4 (Winter 1969): 141–142.

[32]James Hsiung, *Ideology and Practice,* pp. 45–46; Dick Wilson, *The Long March 1935: The Epic of Chinese Communism's Survival* (New York: Avon Books, 1973); and Edward E. Rice, *Mao's Way* (Berkeley, CA: University of California Press, 1972), pp. 83–88.

[33]For China's "Time of Troubles" after Mao's death, see Ross Terrill, *China in Our Time: The People of China From the Communist Victory to Tiananmen Square and Beyond* (New York: Simon & Schuster, 1992), pp. 147ff.; John K. Fairbank, Merle Goldman, *op. cit.,* pp. 406ff.; Orville Schell, David Shambaugh, ed., *The China Reader: The Reform Era* (New York: Vintage Books, 1999).

Chapter 32

The Social Setting of Politics in China

FAMILY STRUCTURE

The basic unit in Chinese society has always been the family. As pointed out earlier, the traditional family, as a social institution, influenced every aspect of an individual's life—from physical and moral well-being to economic security. The family system invariably extended beyond the nuclear unit into the kinship circles including the clan and village structure. In the traditional family, the father was the autocrat and exercised control and domination over everyone else's life and behavior. In other words, it was essentially a male- and age-dominated agrarian society. Life for a Chinese peasant family in a rural village followed closely what Fairbank calls "the rhythm of seasons and crops, of birth, marriage, and death."[1]

The introduction of new ideas from the West after the 1911 revolution created a "family revolution" in the urban family structure. C. K. Yang, the sociologist, points out that the family revolution that occurred after 1911 advocated equality of women in the family, marriage based on free choice, and free association between the sexes.[2] As the Confucian orthodoxy weakened, the urban family system underwent some significant changes in the 1920s and 1930s: challenges to the Confucian code of ethics, increased contact between the sexes, and nuclear families as a model in contrast to the extended family system. Both the Nationalists and Chinese communists made contributions to the family revolution in social relations that took place during the three decades before 1949.

Since 1949, several attempts have been made to define the role of the family in China. The enactment of the 1950 marriage law sought to "neutralize" the traditional power of the family by making marriage a matter of mutual consent and a civil act through registration with the civil authority instead of the family elders. Under the new marriage law, divorce became legal if both parties consent or through legal proceedings if contested. Traditional or feudal practices of concubinage and dowry were prohibited. However in rural areas today, marriage is still largely by arrangement through a third party go-between within the village or across the village lines. The practice of dowry in the form of material goods or money is still widespread in rural areas.

The Great Leap of 1958 temporarily disrupted the normal rhythm of family life when women

413

joined the vast labor force in building dams or similar earth-moving projects required by the mass mobilization. The harsh practice of separating the family by requiring members to live in dormitories and eat in huge dining halls was terminated after brief experimentation in some cases. In the early 1960s the traditional way of life in rural areas was the focus of concern. As the Socialist Education Campaign (1962–65) revealed, many traditional practices such as arranged marriage, dowry, bride price, and extravagant banquets for marriages, reappeared. While the Cultural Revolution brought violent attacks on the traditional authority of the family through accusations by the young against their parents or relatives, the family as an institution in the rural areas remained unbroken.

Despite the collectivized commune programs for the rural areas, the family remains a key unit in today's rural economy. In fact, since Mao's death and the demise of the radicals, rural families, under the "responsibility system," have been allowed to produce what they consider best to increase their income from sideline production on their private plots; these incentive measures are now considered a necessary adjunct to the socialist economy. Production teams now can enter into contracts with the peasant families for specific quotas of output. One widely practiced type of contract in rural areas known as *Baochan Daohu* ("to fix farm output quota for each household") permits a commune to make land available to each household, usually consisting of four to five members of a family. Under the arrangement, the household and the production team in the commune sign a contract fixing the quota for which the household is responsible. In another model, land can be contracted by the production team to a family on a per capita basis.

The family household not only must meet the state procurement requirements, but also must assume full responsibility for managing the land and all of its obligations to the collective. After deducting the various cost items for the state and the collective, the remainder of the earnings go to the family unit. While the responsibility system for the peasants has contributed to the growth of rural incomes, it has also created some problems in rural social development. One problem is the dropout rate for school-age children in rural areas

where many parents feel that it is more profitable to take their children out of school and make them work in the fields in order to increase production. Teachers in rural schools also prefer to work on the farm, where they can receive better rewards than in the classrooms. As a result, the educational gap between the rural and urban sectors has further widened.

In the cities, however, the change has been from extended families to nuclear families. A recent study showed that in the urban areas there has been a gradual decline in the number of married women living with their husbands' families as traditionally was the case. Also there has been an increase in the number of couples who live separately as nuclear families.[3]

In urban areas the traditional role of the social insurance function of the family has been, to a large extent, taken over by one's work unit, the *danwei*. An industrial worker or an office worker in the cities must be dependent on the danwei daily for needs such as housing and coupons for food and clothing, in addition to the salary and subsidies he or she receives from the work units. Everyone in China today is identified and referred to by the work unit or *danwei* to which he or she belongs.

Faced with an increasingly serious problem of overpopulation and an annual population growth of 15 million, China has implemented a family planning policy since the mid-1970s, which limits couples living in urban areas to one child. Couples living in some rural areas were allowed to have two children—if the first child was a girl or if they paid a fine for a second child. Since the initiation of this policy, the birthrate in China has steadily decreased—from 34.1 per 1,000 in 1969 to 16.4 in 1997, which is well below the world average of 25.0. It stands to reason that this rate will further decline because of urbanization.

THE SEARCH FOR A DEVELOPMENT MODEL

When the CCP came to power in 1949, its alternatives for economic development were rather limited. Its priority task was to rehabilitate the war-torn economy and the immediate implementation of its promise to the peasants for some form of land redistribution.

Land Reform: Basic Change
in the Countryside

By far the most important program enacted by the new regime, from 1950 to 1953, was agrarian reform. Land redistribution, a basic plank in the CCP program, had been carried out in the early Soviet phase in the Jiangxi border areas, and later in the northwest, with varying degrees of intensity. In 1949, when the CCP took over the country, some 500 million people were living in the rural villages. The land tenure system was such that "half the cultivated land was owned by less than one-tenth of the farm population, while two-thirds of the population owned less than one-fifth."[4] This serious problem of uneven land distribution was further aggravated by the large number of landless tenants who had to pay exorbitant annual rents, as high as 60 percent of their production. The 1950 Agrarian Reform Law was basically a mild reform measure that permitted rich peasants to retain their land and property (Article 6), and landlords to retain the land for their own use (Article 10). The land redistribution was completed in 1952 when 113 million acres, plus draft animals and farm implements, were distributed to over 300 million landless peasants.[5]

It soon became obvious that land redistribution was not going to solve the basic agrarian problem. The millions of new landowning peasants realized very quickly that their plots were too small to produce even enough to feed their families. The individual peasants simply did not have the means to acquire modern tools, much less to build irrigation projects. Having committed themselves to the party's cause by participating in the land redistribution, the peasants had to accept the party's new appeal for mutual aid teams, the pooling together of draft animals, implements, and shared labor.

In 1953–54, the mutual aid teams gave way to larger and more complicated cooperative ventures, the mandatory agricultural producers' cooperatives (APCs). An agricultural producers' cooperative was, in essence, a unified management of farm production. The individual peasants pooled their land, draft animals, implements, and houses in return for shares in the enterprise. Detailed accounting was kept, and after deductions were made for expenses incurred and taxes to be

paid, income was distributed to the members on the basis of their contributions, stated in terms of shares. While the movement was voluntary, the party conducted massive campaigns to persuade and sometimes to coerce peasants to join the APCs. Although an overwhelming majority of the peasants had joined the cooperatives by 1957, official accounts show resistance to the program. In some parts of the country peasants deliberately consumed what they produced to avoid forced delivery to government purchasing agencies.[6]

The APCs enabled the peasants to better utilize resources and labor. During the slack seasons, surplus labor could be mobilized easily to carry on small-scale irrigation works, such as making ditches, ponds, and dams. Combined surplus labor could reclaim land through irrigation and reforestation. The APCs certainly allowed the peasants to realize greater savings and investment. Even more important was the sharing of the risks of crop failure. Individual peasants no longer had to face the possibility of bankruptcy if crops failed. But there were also many problems inherent in the APCs: Many peasants were too poor to contribute funds to the cooperatives; there was a lack of qualified technical personnel, such as accountants, among the illiterate peasantry to provide efficient management; peasants were frequently unhappy when centralized purchasing and marketing operations were imposed on the cooperatives by the state, leading to intensified animosity toward the party and a reluctance to cooperate.[7]

Industrial Development:
The Stalinist Model

By 1953 the regime had completed the immediate tasks of rehabilitating the war-torn economy and consolidating its control over the nation. With the end of the Korean war, the regime was confident enough to embark on a rapid industrialization program. The approach selected was the Stalinist strategy of long-term centralized planning, which was perceived as a proven socialistic model that had enabled the Soviet Union to emerge from World War II as the second most powerful nation in the world. For ideological reasons it was the only logical strategy comprehensible to the Chinese communists at the time, particularly in view of the emerging bipolarization of the world into Soviet and Western orbits. The pragmatic Chinese were aware of the benefits in Soviet aid, in terms of both financial and technical assistance, which would be forthcoming to promote this model.[8]

Fundamental to the Stalinist model was the rapid buildup of the heavy industry sector through the concentrated allocation of investment into capital goods industries. The model also called for highly centralized decision making at the top to determine targets and quotas to be fulfilled by the various economic sectors.[9] In many ways, this strategy required basic structural change in the agricultural sector, from which the bulk of savings for investment must come. The introduction of agricultural producers' cooperatives was a necessary step in this structural change to accumulate these savings through increased agricultural production and controlled consumption. The First 5-Year Plan allocated 58 percent of the $20 billion investment fund to capital goods for heavy industries.[10] The bulk of these investment funds was financed by the Chinese themselves.

The Soviet Union made considerable contributions in the form of technical assistance, construction, and equipment of 154 modern industrial plants—which were paid for by the Chinese—and the training of Chinese technicians. In June 1960 Soviet-trained Chinese technicians numbered about 10,000, when Soviet aid was suddenly withdrawn. By 1957, when the First 5-Year Plan was completed, it had brought an annual growth rate of 8 percent to China's economic development,[11] an impressive achievement by any standard. In addition, the First 5-Year Plan made a lasting investment in education (130,000 engineers graduated) and public health (the control of such communicable diseases as cholera and typhoid, which formerly plagued the Chinese people).[12]

The First 5-Year Plan also had a number of drawbacks. First, the plan was rather costly when one considers that the bulk of the $20 billion in investments came from the Chinese. Second, the plan required large forced savings from the agricultural sector. Third, the Stalinist model placed undue concentration of investment in such heavy industries as steel, at the expense not only of agriculture but also of light and consumer-goods industries. Fourth, the model required a high de-

gree of centralization and the development of an elaborate bureaucratic structure to implement, control, and check the plan according to fixed targets and quotas. Fifth, since planning and implementation of the model emphasized the roles of technocrats, engineers, and plant managers, it neglected the need to politicize the millions of uneducated and tradition-oriented peasants to the rapid construction of an industrial socialist state.

After an agonizing reappraisal of the First 5-Year Plan, Mao and his followers launched the Great Leap Forward in an attempt to obtain a faster rate of growth and to develop a socialist economic model more suited to China's conditions and needs.

THE GREAT LEAP: MAO'S ALTERNATIVE TO THE STALINIST MODEL

Under the Great Leap Forward, the regime mobilized the creative enthusiasm of the Chinese masses for economic growth and industrialization in the same way it had mobilized them for the communist revolution.[13] The Great Leap substituted China's most plentiful resource, manpower, for capital goods in the same way the communists had successfully substituted committed men for modern weapons during the guerrilla and civil war days. The unemployed were to be put to work, and the employed were to work much harder, under military discipline, to make the gigantic leap to become an industrial power through the widespread use of labor-intensive, small-scale production. The emphasis was placed on the techniques of mass mobilization.

During this period some statistics on increased production were based on exaggeration and fabrication. Millions of tons of pig iron, much substandard and all a long way from being steel, were produced by backyard furnaces. Pig iron accumulated along railways, which could not possibly handle its movement, causing a serious bottleneck in the entire transport system.[14] In 1958, when the Great Leap and commune programs were launched, there was a good harvest. In 1959, heavy floods and drought laid waste to almost half of the cultivable land. Then in 1960, floods, drought, and pests ravaged millions of acres. To make matters worse, the Soviets withdrew all their technicians and advisers from China in June 1960 because of their disagreement over the development strategy. The drastic reduction in agricultural production stalled the drive for rapid development of industry. Famine was averted by the imposition of rationing in the communes and by large purchases of grain from abroad.

The Great Leap ended in failure, for the program merely promoted "excessive targets" with cadres issuing arbitrary decisions. In 1981 Mao was criticized by the pragmatic reformers as the person responsible for the mistakes committed in the Great Leap program. Mao was criticized for "smugness" and "arrogance"; he was charged with being impatient, looking for "quick results" and ignoring economic realities.[15]

THE CULTURAL REVOLUTION: A RADICAL REVERSAL OF ORDERLY DEVELOPMENT

During the early 1960s, China's economic policy shifted to a more orderly development program. Policy debate and dissension among the top leaders now focused on two alternative development strategies: The left, led by Mao, demanded mass mobilization for crash programs, while the moderates called for orderly planning with more modest growth targets. The debate culminated in the Cultural Revolution upheaval when the pendulum again swung to the left.

The Cultural Revolution was an attempt by Mao and the radicals to maintain their view of a continuing revolution. It began in August 1966 with mass criticism and purges of top party and military leaders. As the revolution spread, Red Guard youths, Mao's "revolutionary successors," led by the radicals, conducted criticism sessions and purges throughout the country. Large numbers of leaders and intellectuals were sent to the countryside for political education and manual labor.

During this period of chaos and violence, many regular party and government operations came to a standstill. Finally, in January 1967, the People's Liberation Army was called out to restore order and to establish revolutionary committees to fill the power vacuum. This was

Mao's last great campaign, although the moderates did not gain full political control and restore the former party and governmental structure completely until after his death in 1976.

MIXTURE OF PLANNED ECONOMY AND MARKET SOCIALISM

Following the Cultural Revolution, China once again returned to a period of relaxation in ideology and moderation in economic development. Capitalist market forces were introduced into the planned economy.

By 1980–81 thousands of state enterprises were subjected to "market socialism" experimentation through the introduction of the following reform measures:[16]

1. State-owned factories were allowed to produce for market demand as long as they fulfilled the assigned state quota.
2. State-owned enterprises were given the freedom to purchase needed raw material through the market, rather than remaining dependent on central allocation.
3. Prices for the products were to be set by the supply and demand mechanism.

In other words, for these concerns microeconomic decisions on production would be governed by market forces, not the state plan. All state-owned enterprises were to be responsible for their own profit and loss.

Addressing the NPC delegates in 1981, Premier Zhao explained the proper relation between the planned economy and market regulations as follows: In the case of

> . . . enterprises in the key branches of the economy or products vital to the economy . . . , production is organized under state plans which are mandatory in nature; [in the case of] numerous small enterprises or individual producers, for which it is inconvenient or impossible to enforce unified planning and management . . . , production is organized according to changing market conditions and within the limits permitted by the state plan.[17]

Thus, it was under the strategy of a planned economy with market regulations that China

Table 32–1   China's Sixth Five-Year Plan, 1981–85

	1980	1985	Percent Increase
Grain (million tons)	320.0	360.0	12.3%
Cotton (million tons)	2.7	3.6	33.0
Yarn (million tons)	2.9	3.5	22.8
Sugar (million tons)	2.5	4.3	67.3
Coal (million tons)	620.1	700.0	12.9
Steel (million tons)	37.1	39.0	5.0
Electricity (million kw)	300.6	362.0	20.4
Import (million yuan)[a]	29.1	45.3	55.6
Export (million yuan)	27.2	40.2	48.1
Total Import and Export (million yuan)	56.3	85.5	52.0
Education/Science/Technology (million yuan)	57.5	96.7	68.0
Gross Value of Industrial and Agricultural Products (million yuan)	715,900.0	871,000.0	21.8

[a]One Yuan = $0.60.

Source: Zhao Ziyang, "Report on the Sixth Five-Year-Plan," *Beijing Review* 51 (December 20, 1982): 11.

launched its Sixth 5-Year Plan (1981–85) in November 1982.[18] As can be seen from Table 32–1, the plan was a modest one in that it called for steady but slow economic growth. As such, it presented a correction of the tendency of Chinese economic planners to be overly ambitious in setting production targets. The modernization program launched in 1978, soon after Mao's death, represented, in the view of the reformers led by Deng Xiaoping, unrealistic projections reminiscent of what happened during the Great Leap in 1958. Moreover by 1978 China had experienced a serious budget deficit problem caused by the overly ambitious 1978 programs, which required the outlay of investment funds for development projects that practically exhausted China's financial resources. Thus the growth rate set by the Sixth 5-Year Plan was a modest annual rate of 4 percent over the five-year period.

In late 1978 the Chinese leadership began to shift from the Soviet-style centrally planned economy to a more flexible one with some market elements. In agriculture, collectivization was replaced by the system of household responsibility, local officials and industrial plant managers were given greater authority, a wide variety of small-scale enterprise in services and light industry was permitted, and foreign market controls were relaxed, resulting in an increase of trade and joint ventures. This policy shift proved to be very successful: Within a decade, China's industrial output more than tripled and there were major advances in agriculture as well.

SOCIAL STRUCTURE AND GROUP CONFLICTS

The Chinese social structure is made up of broad occupational groups: peasants, industrial workers, party/government bureaucrats, intellectuals, military, and students. Each of the occupational groups possesses a certain amount of political influence in society and articulates its vested interests. In the following sections we shall discuss briefly the characteristics of each of the occupational groups and the source of conflict that exists between them.

Peasants and Industrial Workers

In 1997 peasants constituted about 68 percent of China's population of over 1.1 billion. The rural peasants' primary concern is the ability to cultivate the land by individual families under the contract system with the commune. Their desire to be able to sell their sideline products in the free market is their second most important interest. They want basically the continuance of these practices, which have yielded increased income for their families. Also, they would like their children to have access to expanded educational opportunities.

In traditional as well as today's China noticeable disparity has existed between the rural and urban sectors. While the life of a peasant has become better because of the "responsibility system" introduced by the economic reform in the countryside, the peasants' standard of living is still lagging behind the urban workers. Social and economic change for these two groups may become the source of conflict in politics if one group continues to receive economic benefits at the expense of the other. The rural and urban disparity in China can be seen at many levels: education, income, health care, consumer goods availability, and recreational facilities.

For example, in 1981 many urban primary schools provided 6 years of education for children between the ages of 7 and 12, while rural schools offered only 4 to 5 years. Generally speaking, rural primary education is of poor quality when compared with the urban schools. Some Chinese educators have called for compulsory 6 years of primary education in rural schools to allow students to master some 2000 characters to eradicate illiteracy, which in 1985 was estimated at 25 percent for the total population. Opportunities beyond primary school are even more disparate.

For five decades, the government of China has been involved in an all-out battle against illiteracy. Before the 1949 Revolution, 80 percent of the population could not read or write. In 1982, 44.5 percent of the population age 25 and over had no schooling or an incomplete primary education; 32.7 percent had completed junior secondary, and 16.1 percent had completed senior secondary education; only 1.1 percent had a postsecondary education. In 1990, the illiteracy rate was down to 20.6 percent, that is, some 220 million people, 92 percent of whom were rural residents. In spite of the progress that has been made, the fight against illiteracy is an uphill battle—two million teenagers reach the age of 15 every year without being able to read or write. The goal of the government is to achieve a literacy rate of 85 percent in the countryside and 90 percent in the cities.[19]

The high priority given by the government to education is reflected in the figures for the seventh 5-Year Plan (1986–90) released at the end of 1990. During this period, state budget allocations for education increased by an average of 15.5 percent a year. In 1990, the central government, which funds nearly 80 percent of the total expenditures for education in China, invested 12.4 percent of its total budget in education, supporting in particular applied education—vocational-technical education, agricultural training, and adult education.[20]

During the Cultural Revolution, only those youths from a "revolutionary social background"—workers, peasants, and those who had volunteered to work with the peasants—could have the opportunity for higher education. This policy was designed to prevent the educational elites from dominating political and social life and to provide social equality through educational opportunity.[21] This policy of educational equality was rejected by the new pragmatic leaders who came to power soon after Mao's death in 1976.

Most urban areas have embarked on the redevelopment of special academically oriented secondary schools, known as "key schools," first established in the 1950s. These "key schools" provide quality education by receiving special government funds and recruiting the best-trained teachers. Students selected for the "key schools" generally are the best qualified intellectually and will go on to receive a university education.

The difference in the standard of living between the urban and rural population in China has remained. As in the former Soviet Union, the postrevolutionary regime in China did not succeed in eradicating the "difference between town and country" postulated by Karl Marx as one of the conditions for the development of communism. Before the 1980s the ratio of urban to rural income was about 2:1. The lower standard of living in the countryside was obvious to any Western traveler in China in the 1970s, when travel there once again became possible. Since 1978, China has achieved remarkable economic growth, especially in industrial production, which increased at an average annual rate of 11 percent during 1978–88 and in 1992 registered a growth rate of 20.8 percent. In overall terms, the gross domestic product of China increased by an average of more than 7 percent between 1988 and 1992. While the incomes of both peasants and urban residents rose steadily during this period, the differential in rural and urban incomes remained about 2:1, although it has narrowed.[22]

Economic reforms aimed at providing incentives for urban workers and peasants through the introduction of the "responsibility system" have decreased, but not eliminated, the disparities between the sectors. Nevertheless, as indicated by a grassroots survey of Chinese farmers in 1992, there is confidence and optimism in the countryside. In the perception of the overwhelming majority, rural living standards had improved significantly (45.2 percent), or somewhat (52.7 percent). A majority (66.4 percent) expressed confidence that the country could give its rural population a relatively comfortable life by the year 2000, while 28 percent were uncertain, and only 5.4 percent indicated their lack of confidence. Expectation of increased rural development was indicated by 81.7 percent, and 81.5 percent expressed confidence that the contract responsibility system would continue.[23]

A compensating factor for the peasants is that they can now keep all income earned from the private plot and sideline production. The industrial workers receive free health care and can purchase daily necessities at low prices with ration cards and coupons. In addition, the state subsidizes food, clothing, housing, and transportation for urban workers. Industrial workers also receive old age pension, labor insurance, and other welfare entitlements. Only in 1982 did some peasants in a few well-off provinces and municipalities begin to receive pensions when they reached age 60 for women and 65 for men.[24]

Industrial workers also have more job opportunities and a wider array of consumer goods available to them than the peasants. A wage earner in urban areas can take advantages of the recreational facilities, such as parks, and cultural activities. For recreation the peasants depend mainly on radios and occasional movies. While the industrial workers may be able to purchase a TV set, peasants depend on TV sets owned by the brigade or production team in the communes. There have been stories about rich and wealthy peasants who own TV sets and trucks. But these have been extreme cases used for publicity purposes.

A recent study suggests that—in spite of the rural background of the Chinese Communist Party and the People's Liberation Army, as well as the rural origins of the Chinese revolutionary elite, including Mao Zedong and Deng Xiaoping—China did not escape the general pattern of revolution and socialist development leading to social and cultural disadvantages for the rural population. One of the ironies of the Chinese revolution is that the rural revolutionaries, who were determined to eradicate the "differences between town and country," ended up institutionalizing the urban-rural gap, thus creating—in Marxist terms—an antagonistic contradiction that remains today and complicates any attempt to democratize the most populous country on earth. As the author of the study puts it, "China is still characterized essentially by a two-caste system, with fundamental distinctions in the lives and opportunities of the people born into each caste and relatively little appreciation and understanding between the two."[25]

Party/Government Bureaucrats: The Cadres

Chinese cadres, the *ganbu*—the bureaucrats who are in leadership or administrative positions in an organizational setup—are the elites. The top elites are senior cadres in the party and government. The intermediate level bureaucrats are the middle-level functionaries who staff the various party and government offices. Then there are the basic level cadres who must deal directly with the masses. On the basis of their employment, the cadres are divided into three broad general categories: state, local, and military. Each group has its own salary classification system with ranks and grades similar to civil service systems in noncommunist countries. Urban state cadres have a system with 24 grades, while local cadres have 26 grades.

Local cadres at the commune level or below are paid directly by the organizations they work for. As in the former USSR, this ranking system also is associated with status, privileges, and the degree of upward mobility in the career ladder. A cadre's rank, particularly at the state level, is determined not necessarily by length of service or seniority but frequently by educational background, expertise, or technical competence. Those cadres who have served the party before the revolution and the war against Japan naturally command more prestige than those who joined after the liberation in 1949. During the Cultural Revolution the term "veteran cadres" was widely used to denote cadres who had acquired administrative experience in managing party and government affairs prior to the Cultural Revolution.

It is difficult to obtain precise figures for the total number of state, local, and military cadres in China today. We know that in 1958 there were about 8 million state cadres, or one state leader for every eighty persons in China. If we use the ratio of 1:80 as a basis for a rough estimate, the total number of state cadres may now be over 14 million.[26] This figure does not include the millions of cadres at the local level and in the military, and it includes only some of the more than 50 million party members, many of whom are cadres. The leadership nucleus in China may well total 60 million cadres. These are the Chinese elites who must provide leadership for the masses.

Cadres are a special class in Chinese society. Like their counterparts in the former Soviet Union, they enjoy special privileges which set them apart from the masses. Thus we may generalize that China is still the type of society that is highly stratified in terms of, in A. Doak Barnett's words, "status and hierarchy" and the submission to authority. The special status and privileges accorded to the party/government cadres are in direct contradiction to the ideological stress for egalitarianism, a basic Marxist tenet. The problem of special privileges and material comforts for party and government cadres can best be seen by Chen Yun's talk at a high-level work conference:

> . . . For transportation, we travel by car and do not have to walk; for housing, we have luxurious Western style buildings. . . . Who among you comrades present here does not have an air conditioner, a washing machine, and a refrigerator in your house? Take the TV set, for example, please raise your hand if the one in your house is not imported from some foreign country.[27]

High-level cadres and members of their families not only have access to goods and services not available to ordinary citizens, but they also have access to foreign magazines and movies. Chen Yun also indicated that the children of higher cadres were the first ones to go abroad to study once the door was opened to the West in 1977. As a special privileged class, party and government cadres have been reluctant to give up any of these special prerogatives.

The Intellectuals

In 1998 there were nearly 25 million intellectuals in China. By definition, anyone who has had more than a secondary education is an intellectual. Thus, a teacher, a university professor, a technician, an economist or an engineer, or a writer would be called an intellectual. In most societies this group of people who possess knowledge and skill is generally treated with respect and valued as a precious human resource. In China this was not the case between 1957 and 1978. In 1957 Chinese intellectuals were labeled as "rightists" or "counterrevolutionary" and therefore not to be trusted. Their persecution and vilification lasted through the Cultural Revolution decade (1965–76). They were not considered productive members of the socialist society.

Since one of the most important assets of intellectuals is the possession of knowledge, information, and skill, efforts have been made since 1977 to correct the "leftist" mistake in their treatment. Better treatment of the intellectuals is also dictated by the hard reality of putting into service the brainpower of the intellectuals for the successful implementation of the modernization programs. The problems the Chinese must deal with regarding intellectuals are: (1) treating them as part of the working class, not as some alien elements in society; (2) utilizing fully their special knowledge and skill; (3) providing them with better wages, particularly teachers as a group; and (4) providing adequate housing and improvement in their working conditions. Many intellectuals are still suspect because of the lingering fear of "bourgeois academic authority" among the people after years of the radicals' propaganda and vilification against the group.

Youth and Students

As a group Chinese youth and students want more or less the same things their counterparts in most other countries want: good jobs, material goods, and a future to look forward to as they grow up and mature. Having played a dominant role during the Cultural Revolution decade, Chinese youth and students of today are more skeptical about marching behind any ideological banner. In fact, a chief characteristic of China's youth and students of today is their disillusion about communism as preached by Marx, Lenin, and Mao Zedong. In the late 1970s their discontent and unrest was expressed via demonstrations, wall posters, and disruption of city traffic. Although these feelings of discontent have been suppressed by the authorities since the "Democracy Wall" movement (see Chapter 36 of this section), the underlying problems of this group remain.

One of the problems facing youth is unemployment within their ranks. It is common to find thousands upon thousands of young people between the ages of 22–35 jobless in cities. Some years ago, approximately 75 percent of the secondary school graduates in the city of Shanghai could not find jobs. While it is true that the relaxed policy of permitting individual enterprises to operate in the urban areas has relieved some of the pressure of joblessness for the young, the unemployed urban youth are still a source of dissent in China today. The youths of China have entered the period of "awakening" after having gone through the periods of "blind faith" and "skepticism." It is in the awakening state that the young are seeking answers to their practical problems for which Chinese socialism does not seem to have the answers.

Not surprisingly, in China as elsewhere, it was the students who became the conscience of the nation. In April 1989, still believing in the possibility of enlightened party leadership, they appealed to the party leaders to implement the long-promised anticorruption campaign and democratic reforms and launched what they called a "patriotic democratic movement." Although their aim was clearly to democratize the Chinese political system, not to destroy it, it was branded a "conspiracy" and "turmoil" by the leadership. Evidently alarmed by the sympathy shown by other segments of the population for the students' cause and frightened by the prospect of a Chinese Solidarity Movement, China's leaders showed no hesitation in using brutal force to put down a massive but peaceful demonstration in Tiananmen Square on June 3–4, killing hundreds and perhaps thousands of Beijing citizens. As decisively as the students, their sympathizers, and innocent bystanders were crushed by the tanks of the People's Liberation Army, there is little doubt that their movement has left an indelible imprint. If authoritarian government has a tradition extending over more than a thousand years, so does protest against corruption and inefficiency.

The Military

The 3 million soldiers and officers of the People's Liberation Army (PLA) have always been considered an influential group in Chinese politics. Mao's rise to power was to a large extent helped by the military organization he developed, dating back to the Jiangxi guerrilla days in the 1930s. On the eve of and during the Cultural Revolution and its aftermath, the military was not only the most prestigious organizational establishment in China but the most influential politically. In the past the party leadership depended upon party members in the military to carry on political work, to restore order, and to use the PLA as a coercive instrument in the contest for political power and succession.

Members of the military establishment have been considered the most prestigious in society. Their recruitment and compensation system are the most efficient and most professional in China. In many ways the military personnel in China constitutes a distinct class in the social hierarchy. Not only do members of the PLA receive special privileges, but their families and close relatives also receive these same honors, prestige, and privileges. For many poor peasants, entry into the military ranks is a means of achieving upward social mobility. Since the military as a group has been molded and nurtured by Mao, it is considered the ardent adherent of Mao's revolutionary ideas. Some of the PLA old guard were said to constitute the opposition faction to Deng Xiaoping's economic reforms. (More on the military establishment will be found in Chapter 35.)

CULTURAL PLURALISM: CHINA'S ETHNIC MINORITIES

Like Russia, China has a number of national minorities along its frontiers. But China's ethnic minorities do not present a constant source of tension, except for occasional disturbances in the northwestern regions and in Tibet or Xinjiang. In theory China, like Russia, adheres to a policy of "regional autonomy" in areas where national mi-

Table 32-2 China's National Minorities

National Minorities	Areas of Distribution	1982[a]	1990[b]	Growth Rate in %
1. Zhuang	Guangxi, Yunnan, Guangdong, Guizhou	13,378,162	15,489,630	15.70%
2. Hui	Ningxia, Gansu, Henan, Xingjiang, Qinghai, Yunnan, Hebei, Shandong, Anhui, Liaoning, Beijing, Inner Mongolia, Heilongjiang, Tianjin, Jilin, Shaanxi	7,219,352	8,602,978	19.04
3. Uygur	Xinjiang, Hunan	5,957,112	7,214,431	20.99
4. Yi	Sichuan, Yunnan, Guizhou, Guangxi	5,453,448	6,572,173	20.43
5. Miao	Guizhou, Yunnan, Hunan, Guangxi, Sichuan, Guangdong, Hubei	5,030,897	7,3098,035	46.89
6. Manchu	Liaoning, Heilongjiang, Jilin, Hebei, Beijing, Inner Mongolia	4,299,159	9,821,180	128.18
7. Tibetan	Tibet, Sichuan, Qinghai, Gansu, Yunnan	3,870,068	4,593,330	18.57
8. Mongolian	Inner Mongolia, Xinjiang, Liaoning, Jilin, Heilongjiang, Qinghai, Hebei, Henan, Gansu, Yunnan	3,411,657	4,806,849	40.68
9. Tujia	Hunan, Hubei, Sichuan	2,832,743	5,704,223	101.23
10. Bouyei	Guizhou	2,120,469	2,545,059	19.91
11. Korean	Jilin, Heilongjiang, Liaoning, Inner Mongolia	1,763,870	1,920,597	8.73
12. Dong	Guizhou, Hunan, Guangxi	1,425,100	2,514,014	76.26
13. Yao	Guangxi, Hunan, Yunnan, Guangdong, Guizhou	1,402,676	2,134,013	52.03
14. Bai	Yunnan	1,131,124	1,594,827	40.88
15. Hani	Yunnan	1,058,836	1,253,952	18.36
16. Kazak	Xinjiang, Gansu, Qinghai	907,582	1,111,718	22.38
17. Dai	Yunnan	839,797	1,025,128	21.95
18. Li	Guangdong	817,562	1,110,900	35.76
19. Lisu	Yunnan, Sichuan	480,960	574,856	19.52
20. She	Fujian, Zhejiang, Jiangxi, Guangdong, Anhui	368,832	630,378	70.91

[a]According to the third national census of July 1, 1982, China's total population was 1,031,882,511 and that of the 29 mainland provinces, municipalities, and autonomous regions was 1,003,937,078. The population of the Han nationality was 936,703,824, making up 93.3 percent of the country's total, and that of the national minorities 67,233,254 or 6.7 percent of the total. Compared with statistics of the second national census in 1964, the population of the Han nationality increased 43.8 percent and that of the national minorities increased 68.4 percent.

[b]According to the 1990 census, China's population was 1,133,682,501, with the dominant Han accounting for 1,042,482,187 (91.9 percent) and the minority nationalities for 91,200,314 (8.1 percent) of the total population.

Source: Beijing Review, 26: 21 (May 23, 1983): 19–20; *ibid.,* 33:52 (Dec. 24, 1990): 34.

norities live in compact communities. In 1997 China's administrative subdivisions included 5 autonomous regions, 23 provinces (including Taiwan, which China claims as one of its provinces), 4 centrally-administered municipalities, and 1 special administrative region (Hong Kong, the former British Crown Colony, which China regained on July 1, 1997). The five autonomous regions are Inner Mongolia in the northeast, Xinjiang in the west, Guangxi in the southwest, Ningxia in the northwest, and Tibet. The Han people accounted for over 91 percent of the total

population, while China's 55 ethnic minorities—over 111 million—made up the balance. Table 32-2 lists the 20 largest national minorities, their population, growth rate, and areas of distribution.

An extremely important element in understanding China's policies toward minorities is that over 90 percent of China's border areas with neighboring countries are inhabited by these minority people. The border dispute between China and the former Soviet Union inevitably reminded us that the disputed areas are inhabited by Manchus, Mongolians, Uygurs, Kazakhs, and

Koreans. China's relations with Laos, Cambodia, and Vietnam bring to mind the minority people of Zhuang, Yi, Miao, and Bouyei in the autonomous region of Guangxi and provinces of Yunnan and Guizhou. The border dispute between India and China involves the Tibetans living in Chinese territory in Xizang, Sichuan, and Qinghai. Changes in China's minority policies in recent years have been influenced, to a large extent, by concerns for the security of its border areas.[28]

When the People's Republic of China was established in October 1949, the regime followed a policy that can best be described as one of gradualism and pluralism. Primarily for the purpose of a united front to consolidate control of the nation immediately after the civil war, minority customs and habits were tolerated in regions inhabited by minorities. Compromises were made to include as political leaders prominent minority elites of feudal origin in the newly formed autonomous areas for the minority nationalities. At the same time, modern transportation and communication networks were constructed to link the autonomous regions with the adjacent centers of political and economic power populated by the Chinese. The nomadic Mongols in pastoral areas were exempt from the application of land reform measures. The concept and practices of class struggle, so prevalent in other parts of China, were purposefully muted when applied to minority regions. However, no serious attempts were made to assimilate the national minorities into the main throes of the revolutionary movement in other parts of China.

The period of the Great Leap ushered in a rapid change in policies toward the national minorities. For the period of 1956 to 1968, the policy shifted from gradualism and pluralism to one of radical assimilation. For the first time, the Chinese spoken language was introduced in the minority areas. Training of minority cadres intensified. More important, socialist reforms, such as cooperatives and communization were introduced. The campaign against the rightists was also extended in the minority areas, aimed at those who advocated local nationalism. These policies of assimilation resulted in tension and violent clashes in the early 1960s between the Hans (Chinese) and the minority groups, particularly in Xizang and Xinjiang. It was precisely because of these disturbances in the minority

areas that the assimilation programs were relaxed in the mid-1960s, prior to the Cultural Revolution. Radical assimilation programs in certain minority areas were disbanded.

The slowdown did not last long. The Cultural Revolution brought back the radical line of assimilation for minority groups. Many prominent minority leaders in the border areas were subject to purges and vilification by the Red Guards, who were encouraged by the radicals. Ulanhu of Inner Mongolia, Li Qingchuan of Xizang, and Wang Enmao of Xinjiang were purged by the time the Cultural Revolution ran its full course from 1966 to 1968.[29]

But the Sino-Soviet border dispute, according to Lucian Pye, made the Chinese realize the necessity of winning over the minority groups for reasons of national security.[30] The policy of assimilation was again modified to provide for diversity. In addition to having minority nationalities learn Chinese, the Chinese cadres were asked to learn the minority language. Minority customs, dress, music, and dance were encouraged as expressions of ethnic diversity. It was within this policy of pluralism and diversity in the post–Cultural Revolution era that we began to see an increase in the representation of China's minority groups in party and government organs.

Both the constitutions of 1954 and its revisions in 1978 and 1982 provide identical detailed provisions for self-government in autonomous regions, in marked contrast to the brevity of such provisions in the 1975 constitution. This can be interpreted as a return to the policy of pluralism and gradualism. The people's congresses, as local organs of self-government for the autonomous regions, can make special regulations in light of the distinctive characteristics of the national minorities in these areas. This concept of diversity and pluralism was not mentioned in the 1975 constitution. In addition, the 1954, 1978, and 1982 constitutions mandated the local organs of self-government in these minority areas to employ their own ethnic language in the performance of their duties. This represents a marked departure from past policies of assimilation, which urged the use of the Chinese language, both written and spoken, as the official medium of communication.

There has been increased recognition of minority groups in both the party and the government. Special efforts evidently were made to recruit new party members from the minority regions. Figures show that from 1964 to 1973 over 140,000 new members from the minority areas were admitted into the party.[31] There is no precise breakdown of party membership distribution over the various autonomous regions, but there appears to have been a steady increase in party membership. Three minority leaders (Wei Guoqing, a Zhuang; Seypidin, an Uygur; and Ulanhu, a Mongol) were elected to the presidium of the Eleventh Party Congress, and thirteen minority representatives were elected to the Eleventh Central Committee (seven full and six alternate members).

Thirteen national minority leaders representing eight national minority groups were elected to full membership of the Twelfth Central Committee in 1982. Sixteen other minority leaders were elected to alternate membership. National minority leaders have held key government positions in various autonomous regions. For example, the chairman for the standing committees of the people's congresses for the autonomous regions of Xinjiang, Tibet, Gangxi, and Ningxia were leading cadres of national minorities.[32] At the national level, Ulanhu, a Mongol, was elected to the vice presidency for the Republic in June 1983.

Despite the increase in political participation and representation by the national minorities in the party and government, tensions and conflict still exist in Tibet and the Xinjiang Autonomous Regions, where Chinese Moslems constitute the majority. For example, we find that problems for Xinjiang—which shares its border with the former Soviet Union and now with the newly independent states of Tajikistan, Kyrgyzstan, and Kazakhstan—are mainly in four areas. First, the region has been under the strong influence of the Cultural Revolution radicals. There has been some foot-dragging by the local authorities in implementing the new party line and economic reforms launched by Deng Xiaoping and his pragmatic reformers. Several top Chinese leaders, including Deng, made inspection trips to the region in 1981. These led to the reappointment of Wang Enmao, a 20-year party overlord for the region before the Cultural Revolution, as the party's first secretary. Wang's return to the troubled region was designed to reestablish

political stability and bolster China's defense measures designed to cope with the Soviet Union's military might across the border.

Second, there evidently has been a strong desire on the part of the ethnic groups, who constitute the vast majority of the region's population of about 12 million, to be free to manage their own affairs. There are more than 7 million Moslem Uygurs, Kazakhs, Kirghiz, Uzbeks, and Tajiks compared with only 4 million Chinese in the region. At issue is the right of these Central Asian Moslems to practice their religion without interference. These ethnic groups want to establish their own communities in accordance with Islamic code and beliefs under the religious leadership of the imam, who is also a political leader.

Chinese efforts to integrate the Moslem groups have failed in the past, and the policy of assimilation has generated ill feelings toward the party authorities and Chinese "chauvinism." The Moslem communities have opposed the use of Latin script, introduced by the Chinese authorities in the late 1950s for writing their Uygur and Kazakh languages, instead of Arabic script. It was not until 1981 that the Latin script was replaced officially by Arabic. There also have been race and/or religious riots against the Chinese authorities. In 1962 there was a mass exodus of *Kazakhs* from the Ili district in Xinjiang to the Soviet Union across the border. The Chinese have since prevented such crossings by tightly sealing the border. The presence of large contingents of Chinese soldiers tends to increase the tension in Xinjiang.

Third, the unrest of urbanized educated Chinese youth "sent-down" to remote Xinjiang during the Cultural Revolution decade has been a thorn in the side of the Chinese authorities. At one time there were as many as 1 million Chinese youths from urban areas sent to work in state farms and reclamation projects in the region. Among the reasons for sending the city-bred youths to Xinjiang may have been a hidden policy of populating the remote region with more Chinese. Many youths have since settled down in Xinjiang, married local girls, and obtained responsible jobs. But many others have been unhappy and want to be returned to their cities. In desperation, they have staged riots and demonstrations to bring attention to their plight.

Chinese policy toward the national minorities since 1978 has been one of relaxing state control over the political and economic affairs in the autonomous regions. This policy calls for encouraging the recruitment and training of minority people as cadres. Chinese national leaders now seem to recognize that it is legitimate to demand the preservation of minority culture and "local nationalism" in terms of the right to self-rule. Until the new policy has taken root and has been implemented successfully, one cannot expect to see a reduction in tension and conflict in some parts of culturally pluralistic China.

NOTES

[1]John Fairbank, *The United States and China,* rev. ed. (New York: Viking Press, 1962), p. 32.

[2]C. K. Yang, "The Chinese Family in the Communist Revolution," as reprinted in Yung Wei, *Communist China: A System-Functional Reader* (Columbus, OH: Charles E. Merrill Publishing Company, 1972), p. 121.

[3]"Urban Family Structures and Their Change," *Beijing Review* 9 (February 28, 1983), pp. 25–29.

[4]E. Stuart Kirby, "Agrarian Problems and Peasantry," in Frank N. Trager and William Henderson, eds. *Communist China, 1949–1969: A Twenty-Year Appraisal* (New York: New York University Press, 1970), p. 160.

[5]Franklin Houn, *A Short History of Chinese Communism,* (Englewood Cliffs, NJ: Prentice Hall, 1967), p. 159.

[6]Ibid., p. 164; and Kirby, "Agrarian Problems and Peasantry," p. 162.

[7]See the official documents dealing with the debate over the cooperatives in Robert R. Bowie and John K. Fairbank, *Communist China, 1955–1959: Policy Documents with Analysis* (Cambridge, MA: Harvard University Press, 1965), pp. 92–126.

[8]Discussion of the First Five-Year Plan is based on the following sources: Alexander Eckstein, *China's Economic Revolution* (London and New York: Cambridge University Press, 1977), pp. 31–66; E. L. Wheelwright and Bruce McFarlane, *The Chinese Road to Socialism: Economics of the Cultural Revolution* (New York: Monthly Review Press, 1970), pp. 31–65; and Houn, *A Short History of Chinese Communism,* pp. 177–85.

[9]Houn, *A Short History of Chinese Communism,* pp. 178–79; Wheelwright and McFarlane, *The Chinese Road to Socialism,* p. 35.

[10]Houn, *A Short History of Chinese Communism,* pp. 178–79.

[11]Ibid., pp. 178–79.

[12]Wheelwright and McFarlane, *The Chinese Road to Socialism,* p. 36.

[13]Discussion in this section on the Great Leap program is based on these sources: Houn, *A Short History of Chinese Communism,* pp. 181–82; Fairbank, *The United States and China,* pp. 369–75; Eckstein, *China's Economic Revolution,* pp. 54–65; Roderick MacFarquhar, *The Origin of the Cultural Revolution: The Contradictions among the People, 1956–1957* (New York: Columbia University Press, 1974), pp. 57–74; and Hsiung, *Ideology and Practice,* pp. 185–99.

[14]Byung-joon Ahn, *Chinese Politics and the Cultural Revolution: Dynamics of Policy Processes* (Seattle and London: University of Washington Press, 1976), pp. 31–47.

[15]Huang Kecheng, "How to Assess Chairman Mao and Mao Zedong Thought," *Beijing Review* 17 (April 17, 1981): 22.

[16]See David Bonavia, "Peking Watch" in *China Trade Report,* August 1982, p. 2, and *Beijing Review* 12 (March 12, 1982): 12.

[17]"The Present Economic Situation and the Principles for Future Economic Construction," *Beijing Review* 51 (December 21, 1951) p. 26.

[18]"Report on the Sixth Five-Year Plan," pp. 10–35.

[19]*China Today* 39, no. 10 (October 1990): 48, cited in *China Facts and Figures Annual* [subsequently cited as CHIFFA] (Gulf Breeze, FL: Academic International Press, 1992), vol. 14, p. 352; *1994 Britannica Book of the Year* (Chicago: Encyclopedia, 1994), p. 584.

[20]CHIFFA, vol. 14, p. 350.

[21]David Lampton, "New 'Revolution' in China's Social Policy," *Problems of Communism* 22 (September–December 1979): 30.

[22]Central Intelligence Agency, *The World Factbook 1993* (Washington, DC: U.S. Government, 1993), p. 81; Central Intelligence Agency, *Handbook of Economic Statistics, 1993* (Washington: U.S. Government, 1993), p. 26; Joseph Fewsmith, "Economic Reform in China, in Ilpyong J. Kim and Jane Shapiro Zacek, eds., *Reform and Transformation in Communist Systems: Comparative Perspectives* (New York: Paragon House, 1991), p. 143; Martin King Whyte, "Inequality and Stratification in China," *China Quarterly* 64 (December 1975): 684–711.

[23]CHIFFA, vol. 17, p. 213.

[24]*Beijing Review* 40 (October 2, 1982), p. 8.

[25]Martin King Whyte, "City vs. Countryside in China's Development," *Problems of Post-Communism* 43 (January–February 1996): 20.

[26]See James C. F. Wang, *Contemporary Chinese Politics,* 1st ed. (Englewood Cliffs, NJ: Prentice-Hall, 1980), p. 119. Also see Hong-Yung Lee, "Deng Xiaoping's Reform of the Chinese Bureaucracy," *Journal of Northeast Asian Studies* 1 (June 1982): 21–35.

[27]Text of Chen Yun's speech at the CCP Central Committee Work Conference in *Issues and Studies* 16 (April 1980), p. 82.

[28]Lucian W. Pye, "China: Ethnic Minorities and National Security," *Current Science: Developments in the People's Republic of China* 14 (December 1976): 7–10.

[29]For China's policies toward the minority groups from 1957–1969, see June T. Dreyer, *China's Forty Millions* (Cambridge, MA: Harvard University Press, 1976), pp. 140–259; "China's Quest for a Socialist Solution," *Problems of Communism* 24 (September–October 1975): 49–62.

[30]Pye, "China: Ethnic Minorities," pp. 9–10.

[31]"New Party Members—A Dynamic Force," *Peking Review* 27 (July 6, 1973): 6–7.

[32]"Minority Leader Cadres in Various Provinces and Autonomous Regions," *Beijing Review* 10 (March 10, 1980): 23.

Chapter 33

China's Political Framework

In Western democracies a state constitution is generally considered sacred and inviolable. The Constitution is to be upheld by all branches of the government, and no one is above it. In some democracies, such as the United States, only the courts can interpret the constitution. Times and circumstances may change, but the constitution remains as it is unless it has been properly amended through the complicated process provided in the constitution.

There have been four different constitutions for the People's Republic of China (PRC) since 1954 when the first constitution was adopted. China's fourth constitution was adopted in December 1982, 6 years after the downfall of the radical Gang of Four and the death of Mao. In practice, constitutional changes for the PRC have occurred when a new power group had emerged or a new power base had been established. The 1954 Constitution presumably created a People's Democratic Dictatorship and was representative of "socialist legality," a phrase denoting the legal responsibility of the dictatorial state to its citizens. The 1954 Constitution was modeled on the 1936 Soviet Constitution. While the 1936 Soviet Constitution lasted for over 40 years and was

replaced in 1977, China's 1954 Constitution lasted less than 12 years. The Cultural Revolution launched in 1966 reduced the document to a heap of useless paper and rendered all its provisions meaningless, including the governmental structure established under it.

At the end of the Cultural Revolution the radicals led by Mao's wife, Jiang Qing, emerged as the dominant power. They adopted a new constitution representing the new power base and incorporating the ideology of the Cultural Revolution. The death of Mao and the arrest of radical leaders in 1976 brought to power a more moderate group of leaders. In 1978 China's new leaders produced the third constitution, which brought back some of the provisions contained in the 1954 Constitution but in general was supportive of the Cultural Revolution and Mao's policies. Then a power struggle took place during the period from 1978 to 1982, which culminated in the ascendancy of Deng Xiaoping and his pragmatic reformers.

For the fourth time a new constitution was drafted and finally adopted in December 1982. Peng Zhen, vice-chairman of the constitution revision committee, explained that a new constitution had to be drafted in order to represent a "period of important historical change" under which the mistakes of the Cultural Revolution must be rectified by "a series of new correct principles and policies." The 1978 Constitution "no longer conforms to present realities or meets the needs of the life of the state," and thus "all-around revision is necessary."

THE 1982 CONSTITUTION

We are told that the 1982 Constitution was the product of more than two years of work by the Committee for Revision of the Constitution, which was established in September 1980 by the Fifth National People's Congress. The Constitution's revised draft was circulated within party and government circles for debate and discussion. Reportedly, over 7 million speakers commented on the draft at millions of meetings held across the nation. The review produced over 1 million suggestions for revision. The final version of the draft was adopted by the Fifth National People's Congress at its session on December 4, 1982. The new Sixth National People's Congress, which met in June 1983, was elected, organized, and conducted under the provisions of the 1982 Constitution.

One major change in the 1982 Constitution was the deletion of lavish praise for Mao and references to the Cultural Revolution in the preamble. Instead, the 1982 Constitution affirms adherence to the four fundamental principles of Chinese socialism: the people's dictatorship, Marxism-Leninism and Mao's Thought, the socialist road, and the leadership of the Chinese Communist Party (CCP).

Articles 79–81 provided for the election of a president for the Republic, a position omitted by the 1975 and 1978 Constitutions in deference to Mao's long opposition to the idea of a chief of state in competition with the party chairman. Another new feature was the establishment of the State Military Council to provide direction for the armed forces. The 1982 Constitution restricted the role of rural people's communes to economic management in rural areas and terminated their responsibilities in local government.

The 1982 Constitution is said to have made a significant improvement over the previous constitutions because of its restrictions of the role of the party in its powers and functions in the state organs. For example, Article 2 of the 1978 Constitution stipulated clearly that "The Chinese Communist Party is the core of leadership of the whole Chinese people. The working class exercises leadership over the state through its vanguard, the Communist Party of China." No such reference is found in the 1982 Constitution. But this omission does not mean that the party's power has been reduced by the constitution. In fact, it may be greater since the present state constitution fails to define the party's powers in relation to the state organs.

On the surface it is true that the 1982 Constitution theoretically attempts to prevent the party from interfering in the decisions of the National People's Congress regarding the appointment of a premier and other members of the central government, but in practice it is highly questionable whether the party plays no role at all in the choice of top government officials since it is the fountainhead and source of all political power in China. Irrespective of the provisions stated in the constitution, there cannot be any independent political power. One must bear in mind that the party controls and directs the machinery of state through an interlocking system of party personnel and a party structure parallel to that of the state organs. It may be true that the interlocking system at present is not so widespread as it once was. For example, Hu Yaobang, the party's general secretary, held no high government position. However, the premier and his two vice premiers (Wan Li and Yao Yilin) for the State Council were also members of the Chinese Politburo. To a greater extent than in the former Soviet Union, Politburo members were also put in charge of major governmental ministries: state planning, restructuring the economic system, science and technology, and foreign trade. A majority of the state ministers and vice ministers were members of the party's Central Committee elected in September 1982.

The area of ambiguous change concerns the control of China's armed forces. While the 1978 Constitution, in Article 19, stated specifically that the chairman of the party's Central Committee commands the nation's armed forces, the 1982 Constitution, in Articles 93 and 94, places the armed forces under the command of the chairman of the Central Military Commission—which is theoretically responsible to the National People's Congress. However, there is some confusion as to whether the party's powerful committee on military affairs supersedes the constitutional provision stated here. There is really no clear delineation of the two organs in terms of their respective power, except the vague explanation that

> The draft of the revised Constitution not only confirms the leading role of the Chinese Communist Party in state political life but also stipulates that the Party must carry out activities within the extent of the Constitution and the Law. . . . Therefore, the Party's leadership over the armed forces could not be taken to mean that the armed forces do not belong to the state.[1]

The 1982 Constitution contains 22 articles dealing with fundamental rights and duties of citizens, such as the equality of all citizens before the law, inviolability of the dignity of the person, and prohibition of extralegal detention of citizens. Article 35 briefly states that "Citizens of the People's Republic of China enjoy freedom of speech, of the press, of assembly, of association, of procession and of demonstration." This new article was a revised version of Article 45 of the 1978 Constitution, which provided citizens the right to "speak out freely, air their views fully, hold great debates, and write big-character posters." After a short flurry of wall posters put up by the young dissidents during the "democracy wall" movement in 1978–79 under the guarantees of the 1978 Constitution, China's pragmatic reformers led by Deng Xiaoping saw these rights being used as weapons by ultra-leftists to advance their aims. The wall posters were viewed by the leaders as instruments used by dissenters to incite "anarchism" and "factionalism." Thus the rights to "speak out freely, air their views fully, hold great debates, and write big character posters" were deleted from the 1982 Constitution.

The extent to which the rights guaranteed in Article 35 can be exercised is, in fact, limited by Article 54. That provision lays down a set of conditions under which citizens have the duty and responsibility "to safeguard the security, honor and interest of the motherland; they must not commit acts detrimental to the security, honor and interests of the motherland." Moreover, Article 51 states that the rights guaranteed by Article 35 "may not infringe upon the interests of the state, of society and of the collective, or upon the lawful freedoms and rights of other citizens." This means that stern and repressive measures may be taken by the state to suppress any dissident engaging in "counterrevolutionary" activities. A dissident cannot take his or her case to a Chinese court to challenge the constitutionality of the suppressive measures imposed by the party through the state apparatus. Thus, formal constitutional arrangements are merely instruments of the Chinese Communist party. The locus of decision making resides in the party, not the government, in China.

One of the results of the Beijing Massacre on Tiananmen Square was that it served as a graphic reminder of the hollowness of the constitutional guarantees of human rights and civil liberties. The mere declaration by Deng Xiaoping that the student movement was "not an ordinary student movement but a turmoil" was sufficient to render these provisions meaningless.

THE GOVERNMENT

The government of the People's Republic of China consists essentially of the following levels of structure:

1. A unicameral national parliamentary body known as the National People's Congress (NPC)
2. A central government known as the State Council, which administers national affairs through a host of ministries and commissions, staffed by a bureaucracy or the cadres system
3. Provincial and local governments and people's congresses
4. A court system

Figure 33–1 (on page 430) presents the governmental structure of the People's Republic of China as provided by the 1982 Constitution.

THE NATIONAL PARLIAMENT: THE NATIONAL PEOPLE'S CONGRESS (NPC)

The NPC is the highest government organ and has constitutional duties similar to those of many parliamentary bodies in other nations. It is

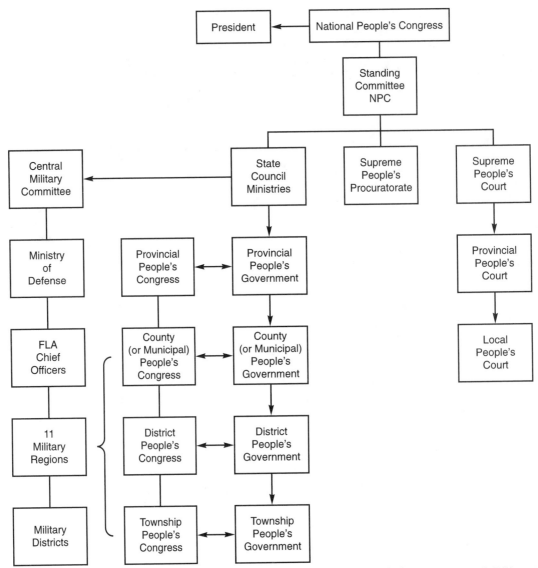

Figure 33–1   Governmental Structure of People's Republic of China, 1982 Constitution (*Source:* James C. F. Wang, *Contemporary Chinese Politics,* 2nd ed. [Englewood Cliffs, NJ: Prentice-Hall, 1985], p. 110. By permission of the publisher.)

empowered to amend the constitution, to make laws, and to supervise their enforcement. Upon recommendation of the president of the People's Republic, the NPC designates, and may remove, the premier and other members of the State Council and elect the president of the Supreme People's Court and chief procurator of the Supreme People's Procuratorate (equivalent to the combined role of a prosecutor and public defender). These structural relationships are reflected in Figure 33–1.

In accordance with the election law adopted by the Fifth NPC in December 1982, the Sixth NPC, convened in June 1983, had a ratio of one deputy, or delegate, for every 1.04 million people in rural areas and one for every 130,000 people in the urban areas. Sparsely populated provinces and autonomous regions, however, were entitled to no less than fifteen deputies each.

The size of the NPC has varied significantly—from 1226 members in 1954 to 3459 in 1978. It then declined slightly to 2978 in 1983 and 1988. The Eighth NPC, elected in March 1993, had 2977 members. The current Ninth NPC, elected in September 1997, a few months after Hong Kong became part of China again, has 2979 members, including 36 deputies elected in Hong Kong. The former British Crown Colony was incorporated into China as the Hong Kong Special Administrative Region, with its own economic and political system, its own executive, an appointed Provisional Legislative Council, and a multiparty system.

As the Supreme Soviet in the former USSR, the NPC has been broadly representative of different occupational groups: cadres, workers and peasants, intellectuals, members of the eight officially recognized minor parties which accept the leadership of the Chinese Communist Party (CCP), the military, and even the overseas Chinese. The enormous size of the NPC has sometimes been cited as evidence that it was never intended to function as a genuine deliberative body, but rather as a "rubber stamp" for the CCP. However, while in the past the NPC has generally enacted legislation of importance only after it had been approved by the CCP leadership, there are signs that it is gradually emerging as a more powerful legislative body intent upon promoting "a more open and consultative political system in China"—albeit at the rate of "glacial velocity."[2] At least the NPC has played an increasingly important role in the policy-making and legislative process in the recent past; it has made more active use of its right of legislative initiative and, party discipline notwithstanding, its members have shown a greater inclination to voice disagreement with top party leaders and the NPC leadership over proposed legislation; and, finally, the NPC has demonstrated greater sensitivity to social interests.

The NPC is mandated by the 1982 Constitution to meet at least once a year. Its annual session in the national capital in Beijing usually lasts for about 2 weeks. When it is not in session, its permanent body, the Standing Committee, acts on behalf of the congress. The NPC's Standing Committee is comparable to the Presidium of the former USSR Supreme Soviet as the continuous functioning organ. The Chinese Standing Committee of the NPC has a membership of 153, and is thus almost four times as large as its counterpart in the former Soviet Union, the USSR Presidium of the Supreme Soviet with 39 members. Under the 1982 Constitution the NPC's Standing Committee has the power to interpret the constitution, to enact or amend statutes, to adjust plans for national economic and social development, to annul local government regulations, to supervise the central government's administrative organs, and to appoint and remove court personnel as well as diplomatic envoys abroad.

The Sixth NPC introduced a system of committees, to be supervised by the Standing Committee, to examine problems in law, economics and finance, education, minority affairs, science and technology, and overseas Chinese affairs. There was also increased consultation between the Sixth NPC and the delegates to the Peoples Political Consultative Conference (CPPCC) through which inputs can now be made to the committee sessions of the NPC. Some speculate that the CPPCC might someday emerge as an upper house in the present basically unicameral setup. Certainly, the NPC's responsibility to adjust national economic plans, as provided by the 1982 Constitution, has placed it at the center in terms of prominence, if not importance. Thus, the NPC is more important than was the USSR Supreme Soviet, yet far less significant than the parliamentary bodies in Britain, France, or the Federal Republic of Germany.

The 1982 Constitution added new powers to the Standing Committee—for example, to enforce martial law in the event of domestic disturbance. Article 67 states that the NPC's Standing Committee may declare martial law either for the country as a whole or for a particular province, autonomous region, or municipality directly under the central government. Hypothetically, measures for suppression of domestic disturbance can now be constitutionally instituted and enforced. Presumably the NPC, through its Standing Committee, could suppress upheavals similar to the Cultural Revolution, if it wants to exert its constitutional obligation in the event of a national crisis situation. On the other hand, this provision may provide an avenue through which factional groups within the party and government leadership could very well seize power by suppressing the opposition forces in a power contest.

THE STATE COUNCIL AND CENTRAL GOVERNMENT EXECUTIVE ORGANS

The State Council, the nation's highest executive organ, administers the government through functional ministries and commissions. The constitution stipulates that the State Council be comprised of a premier, vice premiers, and heads of national ministries and commissions. The State Council may also include others, such as vice ministers. The membership of the State Council has varied, ranging from a low of thirty to over one hundred in the past. As the government expanded over the years, the number of ministries and commissions peaked at forty-nine just before the Cultural Rev-

olution. Subsequent administrative reform reduced the number of ministries and commissions supervised by the State Council from ninety-eight to forty, mainly through the merging of functions and staff. Personnel in the State Council was reduced from 49,000 to 32,000.[3] In 1998 the State Council consisted of sixteen officials: the premier, six vice-premiers, eight state councillors, and a secretary-general.

The State Council directly supervises the work of nine commissions, twenty-nine ministries and four ministerial-level organs (see Box below), eighteen administrations and offices, and fourteen institutions. It also directs the work of twenty-nine economic organizations, dealing with such industries as aviation, armaments, shipbuilding, and electronics, as well as agriculture, banking and insurance.[4]

Since the full State Council is too large for effective decision making, this role has in practice been assumed by an inner cabinet of the premier and his vice premiers.[5] In 1994 the inner cabinet consisted of a premier, four vice premiers, eight

---

THE STATE COUNCIL

Commissions

Economic and Trade
Education
Family Planning
Nationalities Affairs
Physical Culture and Sports
Planning
Restructuring of the Economy
Science and Technology
Science, Technology, and
    Industry for National Defense

Ministerial-Level Organs

People's Bank of China
Auditing Administration
Civil Aviation Administration
    of China
State General Bureau of Taxation

Ministries

Agriculture
Chemical Industry
Civil Affairs
Coal Industry
Communications
Construction
Culture
Electronics
Finance
Foreign Affairs
Foreign Trade and Economic
    Cooperation
Forestry
Geology and Mineral Resources
Internal Trade
Justice

Labor
Machine Building
Metallurgical Industry
National Defense
Personnel
Posts and Telecommunications
Power Industry
Public Health
Public Security
Radio, Film and Television
Railways
State Security
Supervision
Water Resources

State Council senior counselors, and a secretary general for the office of the State Council.

Doak Barnett has described the State Council aptly as the "command headquarters" for a network of bureaus and agencies staffed by cadres who administer and coordinate the government's programs at the provincial and local levels.[6] The degree of centralization of authority has fluctuated over the regime's history. During the First 5-Year Plan from 1953 to 1957, the ministries had enormous power over the provincial authorities in terms of quota fulfillment, allocation of resources, and management of such enterprises as factories and mines. The increasing complexity of coordinating the economy and gravitation of power to the individual ministries, the "ministerial autarchy," led to numerous problems and a continuing debate over centralization versus decentralization, according to Parris Chang.[7] In 1957, during the Great Leap, decentralization was instituted by giving the provinces authority to administer and coordinate consumer-goods-oriented industries. The decentralization of the Great Leap hampered central planning and resulted in inefficiency. Following the failure of the Great Leap, a modified version of centralization was adopted until the Cultural Revolution ushered in another period of decentralization.[8] With the reestablishment of planning operations and the emphasis on research and development under the Sixth 5-Year Plan (1981–85), approved by the Fifth NPC in December 1982, the pendulum once again swung back to more centralization. Generally speaking, however, the basic trend of the post-Mao reforms under Deng Xiaoping has been toward decentralization. Although the Leninist principle of democratic centralism as the foundation of the Chinese party-state has not been abandoned, a number of limited political reforms introduced by Deng Xiaoping after he returned to power in late 1978 created a basis for political change. These reforms sought to establish new norms and to institutionalize decision-making procedures designed to prevent the recurrence of another Cultural Revolution and a return to the kind of personal dictatorship characteristic of the Mao era. More specifically, Deng and his supporters introduced regulations that effectively limited the concentration of political power in the hands of one person or a few individuals. They established

term limits for government leaders (but not party leaders)—e.g., two five-year terms for prime ministers. Furthermore, they also tried to separate the functions of the party and the state, assigning the identification of national priorities and policy goals to the party while leaving policy formulation and implementation to the government. Finally, under the leadership of Hu Yaobang, party theoreticians were encouraged to revise the Chinese version of Marxism-Leninism to make it a more flexible, less dogmatic, and thus more useful instrument in the hands of the reformers.[9]

GOVERNMENT STRUCTURE AT THE LOCAL LEVEL

At the local and regional level, China is administered through 22 provinces, 5 autonomous regions, 4 municipalities (Beijing, Chongqing, Shanghai, and Tianjin), and 1 special administrative region (Hong Kong). The five autonomous regions of Inner Mongolia, Ningxia, Xinjiang, Guangxi, and Xizang (Tibet) are located on China's periphery and border on foreign countries. As mentioned earlier, they are inhabited by minority groups. The provinces and autonomous regions are listed in Table 33–1. It should be noted that China considers Taiwan as its twenty-third province.[10]

The Constitution of 1982 specifies three layers of local political power: provinces and autonomous regions, cities and counties, and townships. Since then the actual structure of local and regional government has become more complex. In 1991 there were four levels: provincial, prefectural, county, and township. Municipalities, other than the three then administered at the central level, were administered at the prefectural or county level.[11] The source of constitutional power at these levels is the people's congress. We must keep in mind that deputies of the provincial people's congresses are indirectly elected by people's congresses at the next lower level. Eligible voters at the lower level of government (in this case, the township) directly elect only the deputies to the county-level people's congress. Deputies to the provincial congress are elected for a 5-year term; deputies to the township and county congresses are elected for 3-year terms.

Table 33-1 Centrally Administered Subdivisions of China

No.	Units at the Provincial Level Total: 30	Capital	Area (1000 sq. km.) 9600	Population (1997) 1,227,740,000	Units at the Prefectural Level 208	Cities 230	Units at the County Level 2,136	Districts Under the Cities 514
1	Beijing		16.8	12,590,000			9	10
2	Tianjin		11.3	9,480,000			5	13
3	Hebei Prov.	Shijiazhuang	180+	64,840,009	10	10	139	39
4	Shanxi Prov.	Taiyuan	156	25,291,389	7	7	101	15
5	Inner Mongolian Autonomous Region	Hohhot	1200	19,274,279	9	10	79	13
6	Liaoning Prov.	Shenyang	140+	35,721,693	2	13	45	42
7	Jilin Prov.	Changchun	180+	22,560,053	4	9	37	9
8	Heilongjiang Prov.	Harbin	460+	32,665,546	7	12	66	61
9	Shanghai		6.2	11,859,748			10	12
10	Jiangsu Prov.	Nanjing	100+	60,521,114	7	11	64	33
11	Zhejiang Prov.	Hangzhou	100+	38,884,603	7	9	62	13
12	Anhui Prov.	Hefei	130+	49,665,724	8	12	70	34
13	Fujian Prov.	Fuzhou	120+	32,610,000	7	7	61	10
14	Jiangxi Prov.	Nanchang	160+	41,050,000	6	10	81	16
15	Shandong Prov.	Jinan	150+	87,380,000	9	9	106	21
16	Henan Prov.	Zengzhou	167	91,720,000	10	17	111	34
17	Hubei Prov.	Wuhan	180+	58,250,000	8	11	73	13
18	Hunan Prov.	Changsha	210	64,280,000	11	14	89	22
19	Guangdong Prov.	Guangzhou	210+	69,610,000	9	14	96	18
20	Guangxi Zhuang Autonomous Region	Nanning	230+	45,890,000	8	7	80	17
21	Sichuan Prov.	Chengdu	560+	84,280,000	14	13	182	22
22	Guizhou Prov.	Guiyang	170+	35,550,000	7	5	79	5
23	Yunnan Prov.	Kunming	390+	40,420,000	15	6	123	4
24	Tibet Autonomous Region	Lhasa	1200+	2,400,000	5	1	71	1
25	Shaanxi Prov.	Xian	200	35,430,000	7	6	91	11
26	Gansu Prov.	Lanzhou	450	24,670,000	10	5	73	6
27	Qinghai Prov.	Xining	720+	4,880,000	7	2	37	4
28	Ningxia Hui Autonomous Region	Yinchuan	60+	5,210,000	2	2	16	7
29	Xinjiang Uygur Autonomous Region	Urumqi	1600+	16,890,000	12	8	80	9
30	Hong Kong Special Administrative Region		1,092	6,310,000				

Source: "Administrative Divisions of the People's Republic of China," *Beijing Review,* January 3, 1983, p. 35. www.chinatoday.com/city/a.htm. (4/15/99).

434

It would be wrong to assume that the people's congresses at the various local levels are legislative bodies. However, Article 99 of the 1982 Constitution does authorize the local people's congresses to "adopt and issue resolutions." Their main responsibilities lie in six major areas:

1. To enact local statutes according to local conditions (authorized by the Organic Law of Local People's Congress and Local Government in January 1979)
2. To ensure the observance and implementation of the state constitution, the statutes, and administrative rules
3. To approve plans for economic development and budgets at the county level and above
4. To elect or recall governors, mayors, and chiefs for the counties and townships
5. To elect and recall judges and procurators
6. To maintain public order

RURAL TOWNSHIPS

From 1958 until 1982, the commune officially served two functions: It was the grassroots government below the county level and the collective economic management unit. This combination of government administrative and economic management functions created a number of problems.[12] Many of the problems stemmed from the over-concentration of decision-making powers in the hands of a few commune leaders. Difficulties arose in particular when the commune, in its role as a governmental administrator, interfered in the activities of the production teams. Zhao Ziyang's experiments with local government in three counties in the Sichuan province indicated that the separation of government administration from economic management in communes improved both economic activity and "the people's democratic life."[13] Specifically, the new local structure for the rural areas permitted a greater degree of independent management of the rural economy.

Formerly, the cadres at the commune centers held too many positions; it was practically impossible for them to devote much of their limited energy to economic activities. Too often these commune cadres had to spend most of their time supervising governmental affairs, such as planning, finances, and taxation for the communes with insufficient time left to supervise production. In addition there was a pressing need for a separate and more effective local government organization to discharge responsibilities in the area of dispute mediation, public security maintenance, tax collection, and welfare distribution in rural areas.

The 1982 Constitution reestablished the township government that existed before 1958 as the local grassroots government and limited the commune system to the status of an economic management unit. Under the new local government arrangement, the township people's congress elects the township people's government. Administration of law, education, public health, and family planning are the exclusive responsibilities of the township people's government. By January 1983, sixty-nine counties in thirteen provinces, including the municipality of Beijing, had instituted experiments to transfer the local governmental functions from the communes to the townships. By the end of 1983, over 12,780 township people's governments formed as the basic level of local government in rural China.[14] Twelve years later, in 1995, there were 29,800 township governments, 17,300 town governments, and 740,200 village committees.[15]

URBAN LOCAL GOVERNMENT

There are two types of municipalities in China. One type includes the important urban centers—Beijing, Chongqing, Shanghai, and Tianjin—administered directly by the central government. The other type includes subdivisions of the provincial governments.

A municipal government of a city like Beijing or Guangzhou is administered by the municipal people's government, elected by the municipal people's congress. As a municipal government, the people's government for the city must supervise a large number of functional departments or bureaus dealing with law and order, finance, trade, economic enterprises, and industries located within the city limits. We also find in these cities subdivisions of state organs, such as the people's court, the procuratorate, and the public security bureau for social control and law and order. Because of the size of some of the larger municipalities, the administration of the municipal government is subdivided into districts. The municipality of Beijing, with a total population of more than 12 million, is divided into numerous districts and counties as administrative subunits. Each district has a district people's congress that elects a district people's government as the executive organ for district affairs.

Within each district of a city there are numerous neighborhood committees which are, in the words of the 1982 Constitution (Article 111) "mass organizations of self-management at the grassroot level." There are thousands of neighborhood committees in Beijing city which serve as arms of district government within the city. Each neighborhood committee has a staff of trained cadres whose work is to mobilize and provide political education for the residents in the area. Generally, a neighborhood committee has 2500 to 3000 residents.

The neighborhood committees perform a variety of functions, including organizing workers, teachers, and students in the neighborhood for political study and work; organizing and managing small factories in the neighborhood; providing social welfare services, such as nurseries and dining halls, to supplement those provided by the cities; and administering health, educational, and cultural programs. These committees also perform surveillance activities in cooperation with the public security units in the area.[16] The success of social and political control in China is dependent upon the surveillance activities of the neighborhood groups. In that sense they have performed very well as a control mechanism.

Below the neighborhood committee are the self-governing units of the resident groups organized and staffed voluntarily by the residents. A typical resident group has about 20 families, or approximately 100 persons.

THE COURTS: FUNCTIONS AND STRUCTURE

The 1982 Constitution provides that judicial authority for the state be exercised by three judicial organs: the people's courts, the people's procuratorates, and the public security bureaus. The Supreme People's Court is responsible and

accountable to the NPC and its Standing Committee. It supervises the administration of justice of the local people's courts and the special people's courts. The local people's courts are at the provincial, county, and district levels. The local people's courts at the higher levels supervise the administration of justice of the people's courts at lower levels. The local people's courts are responsible and accountable to the local people's congresses at the various levels of local government. Article 125 of the 1982 Constitution stipulates that all cases handled by the people's courts must be open and that the accused has the right to defense.

When legal reforms were introduced in 1978, 3100 local people's courts were established at four levels: basic people's courts at the district and county level, intermediate people's courts at the municipal level, higher people's courts at provincial and autonomous region level, and the Supreme People's Court at the national level. Each of the basic people's courts has a civil and criminal division presided over by a judge. At the intermediate and higher levels, an economic division was added to help process cases that may involve economics and finance.

Alongside the court system is a parallel system of people's procuratorates, headed by the Supreme People's Procuratorate, which is responsible to the NPC and supervises the local procuratorates at the various levels. The system of procuracy is rooted both in the Chinese imperial practices and in the Napoleonic civil code, which was used in part in the former Soviet Union and many other continental European nations in their legal systems.[17] The procurator serves the dual functions of prosecuting attorney and public defender during a trial. The procurator also is responsible for monitoring and reviewing the government organs, including the courts, to provide a legal check on the civil bureaucracy.[18] The procuratorate is responsible for authorizing the arrests of criminals and counterrevolutionaries. In other words, the procuratorate examines charges brought by the public security bureau (the police) and decides whether to bring the case before a court for trial. This institution has many of the same functions as the procuracy had in the USSR.

As part of political and economic reform in the post-Mao era, a criminal code and procedure was promulgated for the first time in 1980. The code contains some 192 articles in eight major areas. These were offenses concerning counter-revolutionary activities, public security, socialist economic order, rights of citizens, property, public order, marriage and the family, and malfeasance. Principal penalties for offenses include public surveillance, detention, fixed term of imprisonment, and death. The death sentence is reserved for adults who committed the most heinous crimes; exception is made for pregnant women.[19] Productive labor and reeducation are stressed for detainees and prisoners.

Although the new criminal code represented China's effort to develop "a more predictable and equitable" criminal justice system,[20] the inclusion of "counterrevolutionary" as a criminal offense is a legacy of the Cultural Revolution. The code defines the term "counterrevolutionary" not merely as a thought a person might have at a given moment against the socialist system; it also must involve an "overt act." It should be pointed out that a large number of those placed under detention during the Cultural Revolution were accused of committing "counterrevolutionary" offenses under a law enacted in 1951 that remains in force today in spite of the new criminal code procedure.[21]

The legal reforms introduced by the pragmatic leaders represent an attempt to establish a "creditable legal system," designed to restore the people's respect for law after more than a decade of lawlessness. But these efforts have been marred by the harsh and ruthless treatment of criminals. Mass executions conducted by the police throughout China in August and September 1983 raise serious questions not only about China's legal creditability but the issue of human rights as well. The episode of mass executions and arrest of criminals leads one to wonder about the willingness of the present regime to establish a "creditable legal system" in China. As we have seen, the treatment of political dissidents, notably in the case of the student prodemocracy movement in 1989, raises similar questions.

POLITICAL REFORM

Since 1949 China has developed as a "socialist democracy." Unlike Russia and the fledgling "democracies" in Eastern Europe, China has not yet made the transition from single-party rule to a competitive, multiparty system. Government accountability to the people has not yet been anchored in the Constitution, let alone been institutionalized. As a result, the right and ability of Chinese citizens to question authority remains limited at best. "Rights" are still the prerogative of the government to dispense, not the attribute of the people to assert. In many respects, China remains a society ruled from the top, not governed with the consent and participation of its citizens, a society ruled by men, not by law.

Yet, taking the measure of contemporary China against its centuries-long tradition of authoritarian government, one cannot help but note the significant changes that have taken place in the Chinese political system since 1949—and especially since 1979 when a reform-oriented leadership under Deng Xiaoping began to chart a new course. The economic decentralization and deregulation measures of the 1980s and 1990s have produced a significant increase in the political leverage of the regions vis-à-vis the center. The deconcentration of power that has taken place has effectively undermined the former monopoly of power of the central government and the CCP, and, more specifically, their power over citizens and institutions at the regional and local level. These significant developments have taken place within the framework of the existing political institutions, which is one reason why their magnitude and significance have frequently been overlooked. Contemporary China, for some time, has offered the spectacle of a society of rapid cultural change and extraordinary institutional continuity, especially at the national level.

In the sphere of culture and in their personal lives, the Chinese today enjoy a relatively great measure of freedom, tolerance, and openness. Indeed, the level of personal freedom in present-day China may well be greater than anyone living in China today has ever experienced.[22] Because of their greater economic freedom and prosperity, the Chinese, who have the benefit of political stability, may well be better positioned to pursue their own interests than the citizens in most, if not all, of the formerly socialist countries.

In the end, the Chinese political leaders may not have a choice in the matter. There is evidence that China, for all practical purposes, has largely divested itself of the ideological straightjacket of

Marxism-Leninism-Mao Zedong Thought. New attitudes toward political authority, political engagement, and citizenship are emerging—at least in Beijing, and economic reform, among other things, has produced a new business class.[23] The suppression of the pro-democracy movement notwithstanding, there appears to be increasing public support for a more open and democratic political system, even among segments of the political elite. Thus, two decades of economic liberalization and improved living standards may well lead to more extensive political reforms and, ultimately, democratization.[24] But if this, indeed, is the trajectory China will follow in its development during the years ahead, progress is likely to be slow. China has not yet had competitive, multicandidate elections at the national level. Such basic democratic principles as political tolerance and equality are alien to its traditional culture. To put it differently, it is a stupendous distance from the "mandate of heaven" to the "mandate of the people."

Increasingly, the democratic forms of China's government, especially at the local and regional level, are being filled with real democratic content. The institutions that were designed to create the appearance or facade of democracy have changed little or not at all in form, but their content is different: They have begun to function democratically. As in the former Soviet Union under Gorbachev, the beginnings of genuine democracy have come to China through election reforms. The Election Law adopted in 1979 provided for multicandidate, direct elections of delegates up to the county people's congresses, the right of provincial congresses to pass local legislation, and a nominating process more open to popular participation. It also created the basis for the supervision of county-level government operations by standing committees of the county people's congress that operate when the congresses are not in session. In 1987 the NPC went a step further and replaced the old election system for CCP members at the local level with free and direct elections of CCP leaders by local constituents. The leaders elected under this system have learned in the meantime that their best chance for reelection is through responsiveness to their local constituents rather than through exemplary obedience to CCP directives from the center.

In short, in spite of the still-awesome power of the central authorities, new political forces have been created at the local and regional level in China. More specifically, there are now local and regional leaders who are learning (and in a good many cases have already learned) to make their own decisions and to accept responsibility for them—to govern, instead of merely implementing decisions handed down from the center. These leaders, so trained, will constitute a vital and critical element in the democratization of China, if, indeed, it occurs.

In the meantime, China, the most populous country on earth, is still ruled primarily from the top, on the basis of the 1982 Constitution, which, among other things, explicitly prohibits the right to strike and deprives the people of effective institutionalized control over the formulation of general policy. The evidence suggests that the Chinese leadership is committed to democratization only as a means to an end—that end being economic modernization. The question is whether in time the Chinese leaders and elites will cease to perceive the democratic process and democratic institutions as mere instruments, and come to regard them as values in themselves.

NOTES

[1] Hu Sheng, "On the Revision of the Constitution," *Beijing Review* 18 (May 3, 1982): 16.

[2] Murray Scot Tanner and Chen Ke, "Breaking the Vicious Cycles: The Emergence of China's National People's Congress," *Problems of Post-Communism*, 45, no. 3 (1998), p. 29.

[3] "The Present Economic Situation and the Principles for Future Economic Construction," *Beijing Review* 51 (December 21, 1981): 4.

[4] James Mulvenon, ed., *China Facts and Figures Annual. Handbook* (Gulf Breeze, FL: Academic International Press, 1998), pp. 11–15.

[5] Donald Klein, "The State Council and the Cultural Revolution," *China Quarterly* 35 (July–September), 1968): 78–95. Also see John P. Burns, "Reforming China's Bureaucracy, 1979–1982," *Asian Survey* 23 (June 1983): 707–714.

[6] *Cadres, Bureaucracy, and Political Power in Communist China* (New York: Columbia University Press, 1967), pp. 3–17.

[7] Parris Chang, *Power and Politics in China* (University Park and London: Pennsylvania Sate University Press, 1974), p. 50.

[8] See also Chang, *Power and Politics in China*, pp. 63–64, 106–108; Doak Barnett, *Uncertain Passage: China's Transition to the Post-Mao Era* (Washington, DC: The Brookings Institution, 1974), pp. 136–143.

[9]Fairbank and Goldman, *China: A New History,* pp. 419ff.

[10]Jie Chen and Yang Zhong, "Defining the Political System of Post-Deng China: Emerging Public Support for a Democratic Political System," *Problems of Post-Communism,* 45 (January–February 1998), pp. 30–42.

[11]CHIFFA [*China Facts and Figures Annual*], vol. 16, p. 6.

[12]"Important Changes in the System of People's Communes," *Beijing Review* 29 (April 19, 1982): 13–15.

[13]"Reestablishment of Township Experiment in Sichuan," *Ta Kung Pao Weekly Supplement* (Hongkong), June 17, 1982: p. 2.

[14]"12,000 Township Governments Restored," *Beijing Review* 46 (November 1983): 5.

[15]CHIFFA, vol. 23, 1998, p. 10.

[16]"City Dwellers and Neighborhood Committee," *Beijing Review* 44 (November 3, 1980): 19–25; and John Roderick, "Kumming Housewife Helps Govern China," reprinted in *Honolulu Star-Bulletin,* October 29, 1981: p. 8.

[17]See Frank Pestana, "Law in the People's Republic of China," *Asian Studies Occasional Report* 1 (Arizona State University, June 1975): 2; Victor Li, "The Role of Law in Communist China," *China Quarterly* 44 (October–December 1970): 70–110; and George Gingurgs and Arthur Stahnake, "The People's Procuratorate in Communist China: The Institutional Ascendant, 1954–1957," *China Quarterly* 34 (April–June 1968): 82–132.

[18]Gingurgs and Stahnake, "The People's Procuratorate," pp. 90–91.

[19]For more information about China's criminal code and procedure, see *Beijing Review* 33 (August 17, 1979): 16–27; *Beijing Review* 23 (June 9, 1980): 17–26; *Beijing Review* 44 (November 3, 1980): 17–28; Hungdah Chiu, "China's New Legal System," *Current History* 459 (September 1980): 29–32; Fox Butterfield, "China's New Criminal Code," *New York Times* Service as reprinted in *Honolulu Star-Bulletin,* July 20, 1979, p. A–19; Takashi Oka, "China's Penchant for a Penal Code," *Christian Science Monitor,* September 3, 1980, p. 3; and Stanley B. Lubman, "Emerging Functions of Normal Legal Institutions in China's Modernization," in *China Under the Four Modernization—Part 2: Selected Papers, Joint Economic Committee, Congress of the United States* (Washington, DC: U.S. Government Printing Office, 1982), pp. 235–285.

[20]Chiv, "China's New Legal System," p. 32.

[21]Ibid., p. 31.

[22]Suzanne Ogden, "The Changing Content of China's Democratic Socialist Institutions," in Ilpyong J. Kim and Jane Shapiro Zacek, eds., *Establishing Democratic Rule: The Reemergence of Local Governments in Post-Authoritarian Systems* (Washington, DC: In Depth Books, 1993), p. 140.

[23]Kristen Parris, "Entrepreneurship and Citizenship in China," *Problems of Post-Communism,* vol. 46 (January–February 1999), pp. 43–61.

[24]Jie Chen and Yang Zhong, "Defining the Political System of Post-Deng China: Emerging Support for a Democratic Political System," *Problems of Post-Communism,* vol. 46 (January–February 1998), pp. 30–42.

Chapter 34

Mass Participation and Political Socialization in China

A unique feature in Chinese political life has been the high degree of mandatory and nonvoluntary participation in a variety of political activities. As in the case of the former USSR, few Chinese citizens can escape from this participation. Practically, there is almost no exception to this uniform practice because every Chinese belongs to and is under the control of some sort of organizational unit. It is the responsibility of these organizational units to provide a steady diet of political education to their members. In fact, the Chinese communist movement owes a great deal of its success to the ability to get the populace organized.

Although the political activities vary, they are invariably designed to help the party execute its policies and programs. The mass participation and mobilization techniques, developed through many years of experience dating back to the guerrilla days in the 1930s, are based on the concept of the mass line formulated by Mao Zedong. This concept can be summarized as a process by which the leaders (cadres) seek mandatory compliance from the masses. In practice, it is a process of "mutual education of leaders and led," by which unity among the masses is achieved on a given issue, and through which the masses can lend

their overwhelming support by participating in the implementation of the decision.[1] Participation in Chinese politics involves three sets of actors—the top leadership at the Politburo level, the cadres at the middle level, and the masses at the bottom—and a host of actions, which include listening, learning, reacting, summing up, interpreting or reinterpreting changing attitudes, and decision making.

Although Mao has been criticized posthumously for his policy mistakes in his later years, his mass line concept has been enshrined in the 1982 Constitution, which states: "All state organs and functionaries must rely on the support of the people, keep close touch with them, heed their opinions and suggestions, accept their supervision and work hard to serve them.[2] Citizen participation in political activities is always accompanied by political messages formulated by the party for the purpose of mass persuasion and acceptance or political action. The Chinese masses, both rural and urban, are constantly being exposed to the networks of the political communication system: controlled mass media in the form of newspapers, radio broadcasts, and wall posters; the organization units to which the masses in one way or another become attached; and the "small group" or *xiaozu,* into which the masses have been organized and through which mass mobilization efforts are achieved.

ELECTIONS

While voting in elections may be the single most important act of citizen participation in Western democracies, it is only one form of legally approved political action for the people of China. The election process in China differs from that in Western democracies in several crucial respects.

First, the CCP manages the electoral process at all levels. Most important is the CCP control of the election committees, which prepare approved slates of candidates for all elective offices from the national to the basic level. Before 1980, these slates presented only one candidate for each office and thus determined the outcome of the election. Since 1980, it has been possible for more than one candidate to run for a local office in China. However, in a subsequent election provincial party authorities interfered by deleting a candidate from the final list of nominees because he openly declared himself a nonbeliever in Marxism.[3]

Second, local county elections for people's congresses may now involve campaign rallies with speeches by candidates. The new election process among the masses is used as a vehicle to arouse interest and heighten the political consciousness among the people.

Third, in 1979–81, direct elections by secret ballot were held at the county and township level. By 1981 it was reported that 95 percent of the 2756 local governments at the county level and below had elected people's congresses and other local government officials.[4]

Fourth, while the frequency of elections is prescribed by law, the legal schedule seldom has been followed in practice. Accounts published by the Chinese for the 1980 county level elections indicate that the typical local election process involves the following procedures.[5]

The first step is to establish electoral districts for a county. In 1979–81, election districts were designated in accordance with the following criteria: communes with populations between 5000 and 20,000, production brigades with populations between 5000 and 8000, and industrial units with requisite populations within the county. The local county and township governments decided their own ratios of population per deputy. For example, Tongxiang county in Zhejiang province established a ratio of one rural county deputy for every 1600 people and one township deputy for every 400 people.[6]

The second step in the local election process is to publicize the election laws, particularly reforms introduced in 1979: direct election at the county level and below, secret ballot, a requirement of a 50 percent majority to win, and the mandate that there must be more candidates than the number of elective offices on the ballot. Publicity about the election laws is carried out by agitation and propaganda teams dispatched to villages and towns, by radio and wall posters, and by small study groups.

The third step involves the registration of eligible voters. Everyone who is a citizen and at least 18 years old has the right to vote or be a candidate for election, except those who have been deprived of political rights by law.

The fourth step in the election process is the nomination of candidates. The CCP, other minor "democratic parties," and the mass organizations are permitted to nominate candidates for election. A voter or a deputy can nominate candidates if seconded by three other persons. At this stage the list of candidates is announced and circulated publicly and "consultations" are held among the voters' groups within the electoral districts. The purpose of "consultations" is to allow the various groups, including the CCP, to screen out candidates and narrow the list to manageable proportions so that only the preferred candidates are presented for final balloting. In one case in a rural county during the 1979–81 election there were more than 6000 nominations for 500 deputy seats in the preliminary round. The list finally was narrowed down to between 750 and 1000.[7] At this stage a voter could raise objection to anyone on the list. Of course, a large proportion of those on the list were party members.[8]

Next, the actual campaign for votes is initiated by the candidates and the voting groups who nominated them. Information about candidates is printed and distributed among the various groups of voters and broadcast over the radio. Posters are hung on public bulletin boards throughout the district. Finally, on election day, balloting is held within the various electoral districts. Election day in China usually has been a festive day, accompanied by fireworks and the beating of gongs. After the ballots are counted, the newly elected deputies make speeches at meetings called by the elections committee.

MASS ORGANIZATIONS

In China, literally millions of people participate daily in politics as members of a myriad of "mass organizations." These mass organizations have been described by Doak Barnett as the "organizational matrix" of the party's rule over the masses.[9] Like the mass organizations in the former Soviet Union, they serve not only as institutions for political education but also as what Lenin termed the "transmission belts" for party policy. They are used as vehicles to gain support for policies and to mobilize the masses for implementing policies. The enormous membership and widespread extension of the networks from these mass organizations assure participation in political action by millions of adults and youths.

All these mass organizations are formed on the basis of special interest or occupation and serve as "bridges and links" between the party and the masses.[10] The three largest and most active of these organizations are the Communist Youth League (CYL), the All-China Federation of Trade Unions, and the All-China Women's Federation.

The Communist Youth League (CYL) of China reported a membership of over 56 million in 1993. Some 2.7 million of the CYL members recruited between 1978 and 1982 were admitted into the CCP membership. Like the Komosomol in the former Soviet Union, the CYL serves as a reservoir for the recruitment of new party members. In addition, the CYL provides political and ideological education for a large number of China's youth. Also, a great many of the party's leaders have come up from the ranks of the CYL.[11] Hu Yaobang, later the party's general secretary, was the head of the CYL for many years.

Many secondary school students still consider it necessary to join the CYL in order to ensure entrance to universities. Every other day the CYL publishes a journal, *China Youth,* which generally reflects the party's views on youth and their problems.[12]

The All-China Federation of Trade Unions, founded in 1922, the largest mass organization in the industrial centers, was most active prior to the Cultural Revolution. That upheaval disrupted the functioning of this workers' mass organization to such an extent that by January 1967 it was dissolved at both the national and the local levels. Many of the union leaders were purged by the Red Guards and were charged with being followers of the Liu Shaoqi line—that is, opposed to the class struggle and emphasizing expertise in production.[13]

The Federation was not revived until 1978, when Deng Xiaoping and other key pragmatic party leaders urged that the Trade Union Federation (1) support the party's programs for modernization and labor discipline, and (2) observe the return to the system of decision making by factory managers.[14] In 1992 the Chinese Federation of Trade Unions reportedly had 104 million members, organized in 610,000 units or branches at the local level, in cities and towns. In the rural areas of China, fewer than 20,000 enterprises had trade unions, with a total membership of only 2.9 million. At the 1983 national conference, Li Xiannian, the newly elected president of the People's Republic and a key member of the party's Politburo, told the delegates that "Trade unions must make persistent efforts to give workers education in the basic theories of Marxism-Leninism and Mao Zedong Thought, and in patriotism, collectivism, socialism and communism."[15]

The All-China Women's Federation once had a membership of close to 100 million, but ceased to function as a mass organization in 1967 during the Cultural Revolution. The basic function of the women's federation was to mobilize women in support of the various programs initiated by the party. Since women "shouldered half the sky," as the Chinese are fond of saying, this mass organization played an important role in the past in helping to obtain support for party programs and policies and in providing political education for its vast membership.

SMALL STUDY GROUPS

No discussion of mass participation in China is adequate without a close examination of the small group.[16] Across China, cadres in offices, workers in factories, peasants in communes, students in schools, soldiers in the armed forces, and residents in neighborhood and street committees are organized in small groups, known as the *xiaozu*. Also, everyone in China is identified and referred to by the units *(danwei)* in which they work and belong.[17] A xiaozu is generally a political study group formed within an office or factory. A danwei is the organizational unit to which one is assigned for work purposes. Usually the small groups are formed from the members of the lowest organizational unit in factories, offices, and communes.[18] Frequently, an entire class in a school, even at the primary level, becomes a small group.[19]

It is a common practice to have representatives of the mass organizations, such as a peasants' association, a trade union, or the Communist Youth League, work with the party committee at the lowest level to organize these small groups. The most important activity of the small groups, as mentioned before, is political study. A small group may begin its political study with the reading of works by Marx, Lenin, or Mao. From mid-1983 to the end of 1986, the termination point of party membership reregistration (weeding out process), all small groups had to devote time to the study of the Selective Works of Deng Xiaoping, a collection of key speeches made by China's then most important leader. Past experiences have shown a great deal of boredom and disinterest during small group discussions. By 1992, however, the nationwide Friday afternoon "political study" sessions required in urban work units reportedly had lost most, if not all, of their traditional political education focus. They were largely concerned with administrative matters and dealt with Deng Xiaoping's January 1992 mandate "to experiment" in their own work units.

MASS CAMPAIGNS

A mass campaign in China can be defined as a movement, conceived at the top, that encourages and promotes active participation by the masses in collective action for the purpose of mobilizing support for or against a particular policy or program. Rarely has an important policy or program been launched without a mass campaign to support it. It is generally easy to detect the launching of a mass campaign. Since all mass campaigns require the active participation of the masses, the signal, or message, for the start of the campaign must be conveyed either in heavily couched ideological language or in "coded names" form, as Lucian Pye has described.[20] The signal is sent through newspaper editorials or in statements made by key party leaders and displayed in newspaper headlines. First, an important speech, made by a key leader, accompanied by an editorial highlighting the major themes, is disseminated. Soon slogans capturing the key ideas of the campaign, as outlined in the published speech or editorial, appear in the masthead of newspapers, on walls, and on banners in communes and factories. These articles and editorials become a basic source material for small group discussion and study.

During the Cultural Revolution, activists in universities and high schools displayed their wall posters *(daizibao)* to pinpoint a particular theme or target to be struggled against in a campaign. Photographic displays or exhibits illustrating key leaders' ideas also appear in prominent locations. It has become a standard practice, for instance, for the government-owned and controlled printing corporation, the Xinhua Bookstore, to display photo exhibits outside the walls of its branch stores all over China.

Next, massive public rallies and demonstrations are staged. In these campaign kickoffs, leading national, provincial, and local party and government cadres make repetitive speeches, outlining the purpose and targets for the campaign and exhorting the masses to participate and demonstrate their enthusiastic support.

Before 1976 public rallies and demonstrations were followed by intensive study in small groups. Generally speaking, small group meetings tended to become more numerous during a mass campaign. As the campaign intensified, the small group study in various basic units also became tense, particularly when the stage of criticism and self-criticism was reached.

Mass campaigns have been institutionalized and have become an indispensable part of contemporary political life. The fact that there have been more than seventy campaigns waged at the national level since the founding of the republic in 1949 testifies to the frequency of their occurrence—an average of two per year. Charles Cell has classified mass campaigns into three basic groupings:[21]

1. Campaigns waged on politics and economic development programs, frequently aimed at instituting basic changes

2. Ideological campaigns waged primarily to bring about social reforms or to induce new social values among the populace

3. Campaigns waged to weaken or eliminate groups or individuals who were considered enemies of the people, such as landlords, counterrevolutionaries, and rightist elements

Some major mass campaigns, however, cannot readily be classified into any of these categories because of the multiplicity of themes. The Great Proletarian Cultural Revolution of 1966–68 is such a campaign. However, the pragmatic leaders now in power have indicated that large-scale mass campaigns will not be undertaken in the future. They argue that the large-scale class struggles after 1953 were wrong and harmful to China's socialist system. The Spiritual Pollution Campaign of 1983–84—an effort to attack foreign life styles, values, and fashions, and to ward off "bourgeois influences"—may well have been the last great effort on the part of the CCP to enforce puritanical communist standards, and it ended in failure.

WALL POSTERS

Wall posters, as a form of political communication closely associated with mass campaigns, have been common in major urban centers in China since the Cultural Revolution. Political messages written by hand on paper of various sizes and colors have been posted on walls and sidewalks in China as a form of protest since the days of the emperors. During imperial times this form of petition to redress wrongs was considered a right of the people, but, of course, the petitioner risked the consequences of arrest or physical abuse from the authorities.

During the guerrilla days, the Chinese communist movement made wall posters a channel through which party members voiced their criticisms or complaints about inner party affairs. Wall posters were institutionalized in the 1950s when numerous mass campaigns were waged periodically, particularly the 1957 antirightist mass campaign. Initially the 1957 campaign called for free criticism of the regime under the slogan of "letting a hundred flowers bloom." But when the intellectuals finally responded to the call by pointing out ills and defects in the Chinese communist system, they became the target for attack. They were labeled "rightists" and "counterrevolutionaries" and subjected to purges and vilification. The behavior and thinking of the intellectuals were exposed in wall posters. It was then fashionable for anyone to put up a character poster on a wall or bulletin board of the work place for the purpose of exposing a colleague or superior for his or her wrong political views, bad personal behavior, or even private life.

Public exposure via wall posters reached its height during the Cultural Revolution, when party leaders were attacked by wall posters on information deliberately provided by the radical leaders close to Mao. Libelous and malicious charges were frequently made, and the attackers were not required to reveal their identities. This method of making malicious statements against others via wall posters gave the authors license to slander.

Too often the contents of these posters were merely unsubstantiated rumors or sheer hearsay, but once posted they caused irreparable damage to the persons under attack. Since China is a closed society, wall-postering frequently gave outsiders insights about policy debates or ongoing inner party struggles among the top leaders. A large portion of what we learned about the early phase of the Cultural Revolution came from wall posters tacked up by the feuding Red Guards. Occasionally wall posters—if they were spontaneous expressions without any manipulation from anywhere and by any authority—did represent possibly a sort of barometer for reading public opinion. But in the final analysis, all wall poster campaigns, like all mass campaigns of the past, have been abruptly terminated when the authorities call for a halt. The flurry of free expression exhibited on the "democracy walls" in 1978–79 in Beijing was abruptly halted in March 1979 by the authorities on the ground that it went too far in criticizing the leaders and the communist system.

With the major proponents of large-scale mass campaigns—Mao and the Gang of Four—removed from the political scene, what can we expect of mass campaigns in the future?

One answer seems to be that from time to time, mass campaigns will be waged to promote active support for or against a particular policy. What is not certain is how mass campaigns will be limited in scope so that they will not escalate into nationwide nightmares. The problem of a large-scale campaign is best illustrated by the short-lived "spiritual pollution" campaign launched from October 1983 to January 1984.[22]

The spiritual pollution campaign had its origin in Deng Xiaoping's speech at the second session of Twelfth CCP Central Committee, held in October 1983. Deng expressed his concern over the Western books, films, music, and audio/video recording tapes (which were regarded as vulgar even in Western countries) that accompanied the "open door," or "openness to the West" policy. (See Chapter 36 for more detail.) He issued a blunt warning that, unless some action was taken, the corrupt Western bourgeois culture would soon corrode China's youth.

Following Deng's speech on spiritual pollution, a set of regulations was issued by the Beijing Municipal Government prohibiting, among many other things, long hair and mustaches on males and lipstick or jewelry on females. Within a short span of a few months, the campaign against spiritual pollution escalated into a mass campaign reminiscent of the 1957 antirightist campaign against the intellectuals. Party propaganda officials spoke about keeping the "bourgeois liberalization" trends out by putting on screens "to let in the fresh air but keep the insects out." By November offices, schools, and factories held weekly study sessions, which failed to generate much enthusiasm. There were outright confiscations of publications, videotapes, and films with "pornographic content" representing the "decadent capitalist" life-style. Liberal Marxist views were attacked in the mass media because these questioned the validity of socialism.

By the end of 1983 and the first month of 1984 a brake was applied to the spiritual pollution campaign before it escalated into a full-scale mass campaign nationwide. There were several reasons why it was halted. First, the campaign against things Western as bourgeois had affected the confidence of foreign investors—particularly those from the West—about China's ability to keep its door open. More important, perhaps, was the impact the spiritual pollution campaign, if allowed to run its normal course, would have on the economic reform so crucial to China's modernization. Hu Yaobang, then the party chief, told Western reporters that the Chinese propaganda apparatus had failed to limit the campaign as prescribed by the top leaders. The campaign was supposed to be confined to discussion and criticism within the literary, artistic, and ideological circles. But in this case, either the limit was not very clearly communicated to local party officials or its prescribed parameters were overrun. Thus it escalated into a nationwide mass campaign. The brakes were applied in order to make necessary corrections and deviations. But the spiritual pollution campaign is a case in point—an illustration of the inherent problem of mass campaigns. The mass campaign has been a favorite instrument used by communist regimes to mobilize the masses. However, in no other communist country, including the former Soviet Union, has the mass campaign played as important a role in politics as in China.

INTEREST GROUPS

One of the important developments in post-Mao China is the erosion of ideological homogeneity and a significant increase in socioeconomic and cultural pluralism, as manifested in the establishment of numerous culture and leisure associations, professional associations, production and trade associations, as well as associations representing new socioeconomic groups. Beginning in the mid-1980s, there was also a significant increase in the formation of issue-oriented groups, which, by their very nature, are potentially more threatening to the political regime in China. By 1996, some 200,000 organizations were officially registered in the PRC.

Interest groups, like political parties, are an essential component in a democratic polity. They serve both to support and constrain the state in a democracy and constitute an important part of the viable civil society that is one of the hallmarks of a democracy. In order for them to play this crucial role, however, they must be independent of state control, i.e., they must be autonomous. China's interest groups, numerous as they are by now, do not meet this requirement. While government control of private business and professional associations has decreased and the state has continued to relax its control of cultural life (less censorship, greater tolerance of foreign influences), issue-oriented associations have been subjected to tighter state control, including the possible mandatory inclusion of party committees in their organizational structure.

In China, politically important interest groups have not yet emerged from state control to function independently, let alone to pursue their own agendas in opposition to the state. Shaped by Confucian ideals and principles, China lacks a tradition of rights against the state. While the idea of natural rights being vested in people at birth is slowly gaining acceptance in China, many Chinese continue to perceive individual rights as being granted by the state.[23] Perhaps most important, since in the Confucian perspective the state and society cannot be separated, they find it difficult to regard autonomous social institutions at the national level as legitimate.

PROSPECTS FOR DEMOCRACY

Historical experience suggests that the introduction of free market institutions in a society generally leads to the democratization of its political system. While the former communist countries in Eastern Europe are now testing whether this historical relationship can be reversed, the prospects for democratization in China remain unclear. Unlike in Russia and Eastern Europe, the transition process in China has involved rapid marketization, but slow political reform. Since 1978, the economic reforms undertaken by Deng Xiaoping and his followers have brought about the transformation of the former state-controlled

and centralized economy into a more market-oriented system with a substantial and growing private sector. This new type of economy, moreover, has been very successful in generating economic growth and greater prosperity, especially for the urban citizens in China. Yet since the Tiananmen Square incident in 1989 and the demise of communist regimes in Eastern Europe and the USSR, Chinese leaders have been even more reluctant to promote political liberalization and democratization, emphasizing instead economic development as the first and foremost national priority. As a result, the most populous country on earth, at the end of 1998, was still among the 50 of the world's 191 countries in the world and among the 10 of the 38 countries in Asia that deny their citizens basic rights and civil liberties and are, therefore, considered to be "unfree."[24]

China's dramatic economic development—13 percent growth in GNP, and 9 percent over a decade—is misleading in many respects. To begin with, the aggregate figures translate into rather low per capita incomes. According to government figures, 80 million people in China are living on less than $35 a year. There are also pronounced regional differences in economic development. What is important is that the achievements in overall economic growth have not been matched by progress in political reforms. In its present configuration, the economy is still a hybrid of central planning and elements of the market economy. On the other hand, one can clearly recognize the beginnings of the formation of a civil society in China and the political impact of market institutions.[25] Furthermore, there is evidence of continued intellectual ferment and the existence of democratic elements in the Chinese Communist Party and the military. There is the powerful example of successful democracies in close proximity to China and, since mid-1997—the example of Hong Kong, now a domestic influence.[26] Given its present trajectory of development and assuming increasing socioeconomic pluralism, the long-term prospects for democratization in China appear to be quite good. In the end, China may prove that "Confucian democracy" is not, as argued by Samuel P. Huntington, a "contradiction in terms."[27]

NOTES

[1]See Jack Gray and Patrick Cavendish, *Chinese Communism in Crisis: Maoism and the Cultural Revolution* (New York: Holt, Rinehart and Winston, 1978); and John W. Lewis, *Leadership in Communist China* (Ithaca, NY: Cornell University Press, 1963), p. 70.

[2]Article 27 of "The Constitution of the PRC," *Beijing Review* 25 (December 27, 1982): 15.

[3]See Fox Butterfield, *China: Alive in the Bitter Sea,* pp. 421–422. Laing Heng subsequently left China for the United States with his wife, Judy Shapiro. They wrote a biography, *Son of the Revolution* (New York: Knopf, 1983).

[4]"Election at the County Level," *Beijing Review* 5 (February 1, 1982): 18. Also see Brantly Womack, "The 1980 County-Level Elections in China: Experiment in Democratic Modernization," *Asian Survey* 22 (March 1982): 261–277.

[5]For Chinese coverage of elections, see "Election of Deputies of a County People's Congress," *Beijing Review* 8 (February 25, 1980): 11–19; 18 (May 4, 1981): 5; and 5 (February 1, 1982): 13–19.

[6]"Election of Deputies to a County People's Congress," p. 14.

[7]Ibid., pp. 16–17.

[8]Womack, "The 1980 County-Level Elections in China, p. 269.

[9]Doak Barnett, *Communist China: The Early Years, 1949–55* (New York: Holt, Rinehart and Winston, 1964), p. 30.

[10]"The PRC's New Labor Organization and Management Policy," *Current Scene* 15, nos. 11–12 (November–December 1977): 18–23; and Ni Chih-fu, "Basic Principle for Trade Union Work in the New Period," *Peking Review* 44 (November 3, 1978): 7–13, 24.

[11]"Communist Youth League Congress Opens," *Beijing Review* 52 (December 27, 1982): 4.

[12]See *China: Alive in the Bitter Sea,* pp. 142–143; *From the Center of the Earth,* pp. 172–173; and *Coming Alive: China After Mao,* pp. 210, 322–324.

[13]See *Peking Review* 4 (January 26, 1968): 7. Also see "China's Trade Union—An Interview with Chen Yu, Vice-Chairman of All-China Federation of Trade Unions," *China Reconstructs* 28, no. 5 (May 1979): 9–12.

[14]"Greeting the Great Task," *Peking Review* 42 (October 20, 1978): 5–8; and Chih-fu, "Basic Principle for Trade Union Work," pp. 10–13.

[15]*Beijing Review* 44 (October 31, 1981): 5.

[16]For an in-depth study of small groups, see Martin King Whyte, *Small Groups and Political Rituals in China* (Berkeley, CA: University of California Press, 1974); also see James Townsend, *Political Participation in Communist China* (Berkeley, CA: University of California Press, 1969): pp. 174–176.

[17]For a more recent account of the small groups, see Butterfield, *China: Alive in the Bitter Sea,* pp. 40–42 and *The Chinese,* pp. 45–46.

[18]Whyte, *Small Groups and Political Rituals in China,* p. 172; and *China: Alive in the Bitter Sea,* pp. 40–42 and 323–326.

[19]Whyte, *Small Groups and Political Rituals in China,* p. 105.

[20]Pye, "Communications and Chinese Political Cultures," *Asian Survey* 18 (March 1978): 228–230.

[21]See Charles P. Cell, "Making the Revolution Work: Mass Mobilization Campaigns in the People's Republic of China," Ph.D. dissertation, University of Michigan, 1973, pp. 26–28.

[22]For a good discussion of the "spiritual pollution" campaign, see Thomas B. Gold, "Just in Time!: China Battles Spiritual Pollution on the Eve of 1984," *Asian Survey* 24 (September 1984): 948–974; and David Bonavia, "Curbing the Zealots," *Far Eastern Economic Review,* December 15, 1983, p. 23.

[23]Kristen Parris, "Entrepreneurship and Citizenship in China," *Problems of Post-Communism,* vol. 46 (January–February 1999), pp. 43–61.

[24]Adrian Karatnycky, "The Decline of Illiberal Democracy," *Journal of Democracy,* vol. 10 (January 1999), pp. 112–125.

[25]Gordon White, Jude Howell, and Shang Xiaoyuan, *In Search of Civil Society: Market Reform and Social Change in Contemporary China* (Oxford: Clarendon Press, 1996).

[26]Martin C. M. Lee, "The Hong Kong Example," *Journal of Democracy,* vol. 9 (October 1998), pp. 4–8; Fang Jue, "A Program of Democracy," ibid., pp. 9–19; and Mao Yushi, "Liberalism, Equal Status, and Human Rights," ibid., pp. 20–23.

[27]Andrew Scobell, "After Deng, What? Reconsidering the Prospects for a Democratic Transition in China," *Problems of Post-Communism,* vol. 44 (September–October 1997), pp. 22–31; Samuel P. Huntington, "Democracy's Third Wave," *Journal of Democracy,* vol. 2 (Spring 1991), p. 24; Francis Fukuyama, "Confucianism and Democracy," ibid., vol. 6 (April 1995), pp. 20–33.

Chapter 35

China's Political Leadership

When one speaks of political leadership in the People's Republic of China, one refers essentially to the political leadership of the Chinese Communist party. In 1980 China's foremost leader Deng Xiaoping lectured the party leaders as follows:

> . . . The work of the government is, of course, done under the political leadership of the Party. The strengthening of government work means the strengthening of the Party's leadership.[1]

The Chinese Communist party exercises its leadership role in three principal ways. First, the central organs of the party, the Central Committee and its Politburo, initiate and formulate policies and programs for the state as a whole. In Chinese terminology, it is the party's leading organs that must establish the "correct party line." Second, the party provides supervision and coordination through its apparatuses at all levels of political and economic activities. Third, party members, over 58 million in 1997, penetrate levels of political, economic, social, and educational life, and they are looked up to by the rest of the populace as models to be emulated and leaders

to be followed. The Chinese Communist party claims that "without Party leadership, there would be no socialist system."

Looking at the Chinese political, or party, leadership as a whole, we may characterize the nature of the leadership by the following generalizations.

First, it is the top echelon of the party leadership that in essence initiates and defines policies and programs. Thus, a handful of individuals at the top of the pyramid are the real movers and shakers in the Chinese political system.

Second, the concentration of decision-making power in the hands of a few is supported by the hierarchical structure of the Chinese Communist party.

Third, there has been a high degree of instability among the Chinese top leadership. Under Mao's long rule—about 40 years—over the party, many top leaders arrived at the pinnacle of power only to be toppled later by purges and shifts in party policies. The turbulent years of the Cultural Revolution (1966–76) represented the most unstable period for both the Chinese political system and its leadership. Deng Xiaoping, China's top leader after Mao's death in September 1996, was removed twice from party and government positions during the Cultural Revolution decade. Twice apparent successors to Mao's leadership were purged, and one of them died under mysterious circumstances. Then, following Mao's death, the top radical leaders, led by Mao's wife, Jiang Qing, were arrested, tried, and imprisoned in a dramatic leadership change. These shifts in the top leadership correlate directly with changes in the direction or emphasis of the party line. Thus a change in party direction has invariably involved leadership shifts.

Political leadership instability in China is also the direct consequence of factionalism among the leadership. The top leadership in China has always been beset with factionalism.[2] Lucian Pye postulates that the dynamics of Chinese politics is a continuous tension that exists among the top elite between the need for consensus and the need for "particularistic relationships" that tend to produce factions.[3] Generational differences, geographic affinity, institutional affiliation, power strength, and personal association with in-groups are the factors that contribute to factionalism, according to Pye. Both Lucian Pye and Parris Chang point out in their studies that Chinese factionalism is neither "ideologically oriented" nor "policy-oriented." Rather, it is the elite's personal relationships or ties with each other that serve as "the glue" which cements the factions together.[4] Parris Chang developed a Chinese leadership factional scheme to show the dominance of the Deng group in coalition with the groups associated with the "Elder Statesmen" group of septuagenarians.[5] Deng Xiaoping and his close associates by 1982 had emerged as the dominant faction in Chinese politics. Key members of the Deng faction—Hu Yaobang, Zhao Ziyang, and Wang Li, who were still in their mid-60s—had become the first-line decision makers.

Fourth, the top echelon of the Chinese political leadership has been dominated by guerrilla revolutionaries of the older generation.

Considerable data has been compiled by scholars in the West on the elites of China, particularly on members of the Eighth and Ninth Central Committees and their Politburos.[6] One of the most comprehensive studies of the Eighth and Ninth Central Committees found that the members were largely from China's interior and

rural areas, generally had received less formal education than most modern elites, were predominantly administrative cadres of a generalist type, and were mostly past their middle years.[7] The average age for the Twelfth Central Committee in 1982 was between 65 and 66.[8]

After the death of Mao, China was ruled by a collective leadership consisting of men who helped Mao seize power in 1949. Forty years later, after the crushing of the pro-democracy movement in Tiananmen Square, this Old Guard consisted of eight men who ranged in age from 80 to 87. Deng Xiaoping, the de facto chief of state and head of government, was 85 years old. The average age of the gerontocratic oligarchy was close to 83 years. While the General Secretary of the Chinese Communist Party Central Committee, Jiang Zemin, at 63, and the premier, Li Peng, at 61, were some twenty years younger, real power was still in the hands of the men who took part in the legendary Long March.

Table 35–1 presents a frequency tabulation of characteristics of the twenty-eight members of the Politburo elected by the Twelfth Party Congress in 1982. Over 71 percent of the Politburo members were over 70, and the average age was about 74. Only 25 percent of the Politburo elected in 1982 were considered young (60 to 70 years of age). Two women—Deng Yingchao and Chen Muhua—were elected to this top policy-making body in 1982. Over 67 percent of the members came from the provinces in central, north, and eastern China. A summary of primary occupational background and institutional affiliation reveals that the largest representation, almost 40 percent, was from a dominantly military background, upholding the tradition from the revolutionary days when the party was the army. However, only five of the twenty-eight Politburo members were active military commanders. The next two largest groups, almost 18 percent each, were top administrators in the central government and leaders in scientific/technology ministries. These three categories combined—totaling 85 percent—represented the vast majority of decision makers who held important central administrative positions in the party and government. Very few active provincial party secretaries were elected to the Politburo in 1982. Two came from minority nationality backgrounds: Wei Guoqing

Table 35–1   Characteristics of the Chinese Top Elite Politburo Members Elected by the Twelfth Party Congress, 1982

	Number	Percentage of Total		Number	Percentage of Total
Age			*Occupational Background*		
80 and over	6	21.4%	Provincial	4	14.3%
70s	14	50.0	Central Party Apparatus/State		
60s	7	25.0	Apparatus	5	17.8
50s	1	3.6	Military/Public Security	11	39.3
40s	—	—	Economic Specialists/Scien-		
	28 (Average: 74)		tific Academic/Intellectual		
			Workers	5	17.8
Sex			Peasants	1	3.6
Male	26	92.9	Mass Organizations	—	—
Female	2	7.1		2	7.1
	28			28	
Nationality					
Chinese	26	92.9			
National Minorities	2	7.1			
	28				
Geographic Origin					
Central	11	39.3			
East	4	14.3			
North	4	14.3			
Northeast	1	3.6			
Northwest	—	—			
South	2	7.1			
Southwest	5	17.8			
Tokyo	1	3.6			
	28				

Source: Compilation is based on the following: Donald Klein and Anne B. Clark, *Biographic Dictionary of Chinese Communism, 1921–1965,* vols. 1 and 2 (Cambridge, MA: Harvard University Press, 1971); *Who's Who in Communist China* (Hong Kong: Union Research Institute, 1970); *Ming Pao Daily* (Hong Kong), September 11, 1982, p. 1; *Ta Kung Pao Weekly Supplement* (Hong Kong), September 16, 1982, p. 3; and *China Trade Report* 20 (July 1982): 12–13. See James C. F. Wang, *Contemporary Chinese Politics: An Introduction,* 2nd ed. (Englewood Cliffs, NJ: Prentice-Hall, 1985), p. 128.

(Zhuang) and Ulanhu (Mongol) had been party veterans with strong provincial ties.

THE TOP LEADERSHIP ELECTED IN 1992

The Fourteenth National Congress of the CCP in 1992 elected a Central Committee consisting of 189 full members and 140 alternate members. Among the full members were 12 women and 14 representatives of national minorities. The size of the Central Committee (full and alternate members) increased from 285 in 1987 to 329 in 1992. In the 1992 Central Committee, 55 (29.1 percent) of the full members were newly elected, 28 (14.8 percent) were promoted from alternate to full membership, 1 was promoted in 1989, 40 (21.2 percent) were elected at the Thirteenth CCP Congress in 1987, 39 (20.7 percent) at the National Party Conference in 1985, 18 (9.5 percent) at the Twelfth CCP Congress in 1982, and 8 (4.2 percent) were members already before 1982. Of the newly elected members of the 1992 Central Committee (full and alternate), 3.4 percent came from the central party apparatus, 20.8 percent from the central government, 22.5 percent from the army, 21.9 percent from the local party apparatus, and 23.0 percent from the local government apparatus.

THE TOP LEADERSHIP ELECTED IN 1997

The Fifteenth National Congress of the CCP in 1997 elected a Central Committee consisting of 193 full members and 151 alternate members. The size of the Central Committee (full and alternate members) increased from 329 in 1992 to 344 in 1997. In the 1997 Central Committee 61 (32 percent) of the full members were newly elected, 45 (23 percent) were promoted from alternate to full membership, and 84 (45 percent) were reelected. The size of the Politburo, including alternate members, increased from 23 in 1992 to 24 in 1997; the size of its Standing Committee remained the same (7 members). At the time of its election, the age range in the 1997 Politburo was from 71 to 53; the average age was 63 years; the median age was 64. Although this top leadership group was by no means young compared to similar elites in Western countries, it was quite young by Chinese standards and especially in comparison to the Politburo elected in 1982, whose average age was 74. The oldest person on the Politburo elected in 1997 was Jiang Zemin, the general secretary of the CCP Central Committee and, since 1993, the president of China.

As in the past, the Central Committee includes representation from the central party apparatus, the regional and local party apparatus, the military, the central, regional, and local government apparatus, the mass organizations, key newspapers and news agencies, and so on. In short, like the CPSU Central Committee in the former Soviet Union, its membership reads like a who's who among the politically powerful in China. The 1997 Central Committee, however, includes only 23 women—8 full members (compared to 12 in 1992) and 15 alternate members. China's national minorities are represented by 13 full members and 21 alternate members.[9]

Addressing the Fifteenth Party Congress in September 1997, President Jiang Zemin described the Chinese Communist Party as the "core of the leadership of the people of all nationalities in China" and emphasized its role as the "vanguard of the working class." While affirming China's policy of "opening up to the outside world and developing a socialist market economy," he also called for the improvement and development of "democratic centralism" and emphasized that the authority of the Central Committee must be safeguarded. He issued a stern warning to the party against the possible danger of self-destruction through corruption within its ranks and extolled the importance of "Deng Xiaoping Theory" as "a new powerful ideological weapon that will enable our Party to understand the world and to change it."[10]

ELITE CONFLICT AT THE CENTER

Elite conflict at the center produced by factionalism has been a dominant feature of Chinese politics. The presence of so many aged leaders in the top elite (as revealed, for example, in the profile study of the Politburo)—leaders who have blocked the advancement of middle-aged and younger ones—virtually guarantees the emergence of new party factions and new personal allegiances. The old pattern of major factions, or "constellations of party leaders," along the lines of diehard Maoists, old guards, and pragmatic reformers, gave way to new alignments, as the leaders disagreed over the speed, intensity, and consequences of economic reform and liberalization. In the 1980s, a struggle ensued between a moderate faction that favored limited restructuring of the economic system and a smaller role for a market economy, and the radical reformers, led by Deng Xiaoping, who favored fundamental—that is, structural—reforms of the economy and greater reliance on market forces.[11] In the end, however, the radical reformers were not prepared to press ahead with the much-needed political reforms—reforms that could have paved the way for further economic restructuring and, most likely, would have prevented the tragic events in Tiananmen Square in June 1989.

ELITE RECRUITMENT: MEMBERSHIP IN THE CCP

Since 1921 the CCP has grown from 57 members to over 58 million, or 4.7 percent of China's present population of 1.2 billion. This means that party membership has increased more than twelvefold from 4.4 million in 1949. In 1969, when the turmoil of the Cultural Revolution subsided, party membership stood at 20 million. By the time of the Fifteenth Party Congress, it had increased to 58 million, i.e., it had nearly tripled. This means that close to two-thirds of the party members joined the CCP after the Cultural Revolution—and over half of these were recruited and admitted since 1978, when China embarked upon structural reform of its economy under the leadership of Deng Xiaoping.[12]

In 1977, at the time of the Eleventh Party Congress after Mao's death, it was officially admitted that there was a serious problem in party organization and discipline, which resulted from the rapid recruitment of so many party members by the Gang of Four. Marshal Ye, then a vice chairman of the party, bluntly indicated that the radicals had recruited a large number of new party members in accordance with their own standards. What Ye was demanding was tighter requirements for party membership.

Initially the party relied mainly on urban intellectuals for membership. A dramatic change took place in 1945 when membership recruitment shifted from intellectuals to peasants who became the backbone of the guerrilla armies. In the 1950s party membership recruitment again shifted back to the intellectuals and those who possessed technical skills. Then came the Cultural Revolution decade (1966–76) when recruitment emphasis was placed on personal allegiance to the radical leaders and strict adherence to Mao's radical ideas. After 1978 there was a sharp increase in recruitment of party membership from among intellectuals, particularly scientists and persons with technical knowledge, who in the past were discriminated against for being either politically unreliable or for having complex social backgrounds. The trend to recruit more intellectuals and technocrats into the party membership continued, and a campaign for weeding out the deadwood or undesirables followed. A 1983 Central Committee decision stated that:

> . . . the stress of recruiting new Party members at present should be laid on the workers and staff members working in the front line of industry, transport and communications, finance and trade,

young peasants, PLA soldiers and officers, intellectuals in all trades and professions and students in the universities and colleges and secondary technical schools . . . Closed-doorism should be avoided, and hasty admission into the Party without going through the necessary procedures is forbidden.[13]

These requirements for membership listed in the 1982 Party Constitution stated that a candidate: (1) must show adequate ideological preparation in the study of Marxism-Leninism and Mao's Thought; (2) must bear personal hardship and work selflessly for the public interest; (3) must be ready to execute party decisions and observe party discipline; (4) must not engage in factionalism; (5) must be ready to admit mistakes and shortcomings and engage in self-criticism; (6) must follow the mass line by maintaining close ties with the people; (7) must play an exemplary vanguard role; and (8) must be ready to defend the country in times of danger. In addition, the 1982 Party Constitution, in Article 3, stressed that party members are to work not only "selflessly" but "absolutely never use public office for personal gains or benefits." This provision certainly expressed the party's concern over the widespread outbreak of corruption among party members in recent years. The Constitution of the CCP, partly amended by the Fifteenth Party Congress in 1997, lists essentially the same requirements for membership, but adds the conscientious study of Deng Xiaoping Theory as an additional requirement (Art. 3.1).

Party recruitment in the 1980s continued to be beset with problems, despite the crackdown on the "crash admittance" so widely practiced during the Cultural Revolution and its immediate aftermath. Two readily identifiable problems were how to weed out unfit or unqualified party members and how to upgrade party members' professionalism and competence as China moved toward modernization. In a speech to a conference of party cadres in January 1980, Deng Xiaoping stressed that too many party members were simply unqualified.[14] He deplored their preoccupation with acquiring social privileges instead of focusing on serving the people.

Although no attempts were made to implicate all those party members admitted during the

Cultural Revolution, about 15.6 million (more than one-third of the total membership) evidently were selected as targets for rectification.[15] Hu Yaobang told the 1982 Party Congress that beginning in mid-1983, for a period of three years until 1986, concerted efforts would be made to weed out the undesirable and unqualified party members. The method to be used for the housecleaning was to be the reregistration of all party members.[16] The requirements for membership stated in the 1982 Party Constitution were to be used to measure qualifications of party members who had been "rabble-rousers" during the Cultural Revolution, who had practiced factionalism, or who had instigated armed violence. Hu Yaobang indicated that "those who failed to meet the requirements for membership after education shall be expelled from the party or asked to withdraw from it.[17] Also targeted for expulsion from party membership were those who had committed economic crimes, such as bribery, embezzlement, and smuggling. The total number targeted for expulsion by 1986 has been estimated at as high as 2 million.[18]

The problem of upgrading the competence and professionalism of party members is a much harder task to accomplish. The 1982 Party Constitution contains a special chapter on party cadres. Article 34 states that party cadres (leaders) must possess both political integrity and professional competence. But the fact remains that perhaps as many as 50 percent of the 18 million party and government cadres at the state level have a minimal education equivalent to that of an American junior high school education.[19] The level is probably even lower among cadres at the party's basic organizational level in the countryside. Even at the party's central and provincial organizational levels, there is a dire need for trained and skilled administrators and managers.

Some efforts have been made to upgrade party cadres' professional competence. Cadres younger than 40 with only a junior middle school education (the equivalent of American eighth grade) have been sent to specialized party schools for 3 years on a rotation basis. The ultimate goal in upgrading party cadres is to provide leaders at every level of the party who are "revolutionized, youthful, intellectualized, and expert."[20] Considering the sheer numbers of party cadres who are

undereducated and in need of professional training, the task is an enormous one indeed.

In 1991 the CCP membership increased by 1,636,000. Of these new members, 740,000 (45.2 percent) were classified as workers, peasants, herdsmen, and fishermen; 283,000 (17.3 percent) as specialists and technicians; and 51,000 (3.11 percent) as students. Approximately two-thirds (67 percent) of the new members were below 35 years of age, and 66 percent had a senior secondary school level education or above.[21]

STRUCTURE OF THE CCP

The structure of the Chinese Communist Party is typically hierarchical and pyramidal. At the base is the lowest level of party organization known as the primary party units or cells. These are the party branches in "factories, shops, schools, city neighborhoods, people's communes, cooperatives, farms, town, companies of the People's Liberation Army and other basic units." There are more than 2 million party branches or cells at the lowest level. It is at this level that the functions of the party are carried out: membership recruitment, ideological study and training, party discipline inspection, and the maintenance of close ties with the masses. In short, the party committees at the lowest level direct party work and are responsible for general policy. More important, they also control assignment of personnel at the local level.

The second layer of party organs are the provincial party congresses and committees. The 1982 Party Constitution mandates that party congresses from provincial levels and autonomous regions be held once every 5 years. The provincial party congresses elect provincial party committees which are responsible for supervision and direction over five basic areas: (1) organization and control of the party in the provinces; (2) economic activities in agriculture, industry, finance, and trade; (3) capital construction of heavy industries; (4) mobilization of women and youth; and (5) research for policy development.

Since the provincial party committees and their subordinate basic-level party units within the province are responsible for the implementation of party policies, they hold a unique position within the party structure. The first secretary of the provincial party committee wields an enormous amount of power. Provincial party secretaries on occasion have deliberately refused to carry out directives from the party center.[22] During the post-Mao era, provincial party secretaries have been allowed to initiate and experiment with new programs. As a provincial secretary for Sichuan province, former Premier Zhao Ziyang established his reputation as a reform-oriented party leader by boldly experimenting with new incentive programs in agriculture and industry. These incentive programs later became the models for the nation in the 1980s. The power of the provincial party secretaries is both reflected and enhanced by their participation in central party affairs.

At the apex of the pyramidal party structure are the central level organizations: the National Party Congress, the Central Committee, and finally the Politburo, the apex of the apex. These are the national party organs that provide direction and supervision of the Chinese Communist party as a whole.

THE NATIONAL PARTY CONGRESS

In conformity with the tradition of a Leninist party, the CCP, on paper, vests its supreme authority in the National Party Congress. Since its founding in 1921, there have been fifteen such congresses; the latest, (as of this writing) the Fifteenth Party Congress, was convened in September 1997. By tradition a new National Party Congress must be convened every 5 years. The party charter adopted by the 1982 Party Congress stipulated that the party congress may be convened if more than one-third of the provincial party organizations request it. Since the party congress generally meets in a perfunctory manner to approve party policies and programs recommended by the Central Committee, its sessions have been short, a week or two in duration. The National Party Congress has a large membership. The 1992 Fourteenth Party Congress had 1,991 delegates. This indicates clearly that the Party Congress is not really a deliberating body with actual power. Delegates to the National Party Congress are presumably selected at the provin-

cial levels to reflect the "constellation of power" at the center. It is very possible that the powers at the center as well as at the provincial level engage in slate-making. The process of packing the congress at the various levels of the party organization to represent factionalized leaders has occurred. Wang Hungwen, one of the arrested radical leaders from Shanghai, was accused of pressuring his close supporters to run for the position of delegate for the Tenth Party Congress. It was revealed in 1968 that delegates to the Second through the Seventh Party Congress had been appointed.[23]

For the 1982 election, the Central Committee instructed that delegates were to be elected "by secret ballot after full consultation at party congresses" at every level of the party structure. For the first time, the instructions stipulated that "the number of candidates shall be greater than the number of delegates to be elected."[24] This was an attempt to democratize the party's election process.

A major task of the National Party Congress is to select the new Central Committee. Selection is perhaps not the proper term to describe the actual process involved: a preliminary list of those to become members of the Central Committee is usually drawn up by the key leaders in the hierarchy, and then the list is presented to the Party Congress for formal ratification. It was reported at the 1982 Twelfth Party Congress, delegates were given colored computer cards listing the names of all nominees for the Central Committee; they were permitted to delete names on the list during the balloting. For the first time delegates also were permitted to write in names not on the nomination list.[25]

Some students of Chinese politics have pointed out that, in addition to the important tasks of ratification of the party constitution and election of the Central Committee, the Party Congress accepts and reviews political reports from party leaders.[26] Reports presented at the National Party Congress have been published, and one can infer policy shifts and program emphasis from them. Since the Central Committee debates are never published except for occasional communiqués summarizing policy formulations and personnel changes, reports of the National Party Congress provide a unique source of information providing some insight into the issues and programs of concern to the party.

For example, on September 1, 1982, the political report delivered by Hu Yaobang, then the party's new general secretary, to the Twelfth Party Congress outlined the party's long-term strategy for quadrupling China's industrial and agricultural production through science and technology. Hu proposed that the following steps must be taken to revitalize the party: the restoration of inner party discipline, the placement of younger and more competent cadres in leadership positions, and the reregistration of party members (designed to ferret out remnants of the radical left) to be completed by 1986.[27]

Similarly, in 1992, Jiang Zemin, general secretary of the CCP and president of China, in his political report to the Fourteenth Party Congress, advocated the acceleration of reform and opening to the outside world and endorsed the intensification of market forces, including reform of the distribution and insurance systems, as well as change in the functions of government.[28] At the Fifteenth Party Congress in 1997, the most important themes, as reflected in President Jiang Zemin's report to the Congress, were the need to promote younger and more highly qualified cadres, corruption within the CCP, reform of the state-owned enterprises (SOE), and the importance of Deng Xiaoping Theory as "a new scientific system of the theory of building socialism with Chinese characteristics."[29] Translated into concrete policies, this means an end to the gerontocracy at the top leadership level, a reduction of the influence of the older conservatives in the CCP and their replacement with younger, more reform-minded cadres, and the consolidation of President Jiang Zemin's position as the top leader. Since more than half of the industrial production and almost all of the urban workers in the PRC still depend on the state-owned enterprises, their reform is necessary if the present policy of "reform and opening to the outside world," initiated by Deng Xiaoping in 1978, is to be continued. Corruption within the CCP has been a major problem in recent years. The seriousness of Jiang Zemin's resolve to deal with this issue was illustrated not only by his lengthy remarks on the subject in his report to the Congress, but also by the fact that, one week before the Congress opened,

Chen Xitong, the former head of the CCP party organization in Beijing, was handed over for criminal prosecution on charges of corruption. Finally, by embracing so explicitly the policies of Deng Xiaoping, his predecessor, he not only endowed himself with legitimacy as the successor of the great "paramount leader," but also made clear his determination to steer a middle course between the moderates and hardliners in the CCP.

There has always been a great deal of fanfare and publicity focused on the party congress. This is more than mere public relations work by the party. The convocation of the congress serves as a rallying point for the party members and for the populace in general. It creates a feeling of participation in the important decisions of the party among the delegates themselves, many of whom come from very humble backgrounds and remote regions of China. It instills in them what Franklin Houn calls the "sense of commitment" to and unity with their leaders and the party.[30] In 1982, television programs focused on the proceedings of the 1982 Party Congress for the first time. Provincial and local stations broadcast many feature programs about the party, including new songs composed for the occasion.

THE CENTRAL COMMITTEE

The party constitution vests in the Central Committee the supreme power to govern party affairs and to enact party policies when the Party Congress is not in session. As in the case of the CPSU Central Committee, with a still larger membership, the large size of the Central Committee makes it an unwieldy body for policy making. Although the Central Committee as a collective body rarely initiates party policy, it must approve or endorse policies, programs, and major changes in membership in leading central organs.

There are several reasons that the membership of the Central Committee has increased to the present enormous proportions. First, increased membership in the Central Committee reflects the phenomenal growth of the party membership as a whole since the Cultural Revolution. Second, like its counterpart in the former Soviet Union, membership in the former Central Committee has been used as a reward for loyal service to the party and to the government. Pre-eminent scholars and scientists have been recognized and elevated to Central Committee membership.

With a few exceptions, the Central Committee usually holds annual plenary sessions, either with its own full and alternate members in attendance, or with non-Central Committee members as well, in enlarged sessions. Chairman Mao frequently called these enlarged sessions to ram through some of his policies that did not really have majority support in the Central Committee. These regularized plenums of the Central Committee are the forums through which party and state policies and programs are discussed and ratified.

THE POLITBURO AND ITS STANDING COMMITTEE

The Leninist principle of democratic centralism calls for decision-making power of the party to be vested in a small number of key leaders who occupy positions at the apex of the power structure, the Political Bureau (Politburo). The formal language in the party constitution does not reveal the actual power of this top command for the CCP. The party constitutions of 1969, 1973, 1977, 1982, and 1997 simply stipulated that the Politburo shall be elected by the Central Committee in full session and shall act in its behalf when the Central Committee is not in session. Day-to-day work of the Politburo is carried out by its Standing Committee, the apex of the pyramidal structure of the party.[31] In essence, it is the Politburo and its Standing Committee that possess "boundless" power over the general policies of the party and all important matters of the regime that affect the government organs.[32] It is the Politburo that selects top personnel to direct the vast apparatus of the party, the government, and the military.

The Politburo holds frequent meetings; discussion is said to be frank and unrestrained. It has been compared to a corporate board of directors.[33] Decisions of the Politburo are generally reached by the group's consensus after thorough discussion of the available alternatives.

Of the 22 members of the Politburo elected in 1982, 9 were new faces. The new members were recognized capable party and government administrators; a majority of them, at one time or another, were associated with either Deng Xiaoping or Hu Yaobang. However, the Politburo elected in 1982 was best described as a "gerontocracy" with the average age of its members over 72. It was a leadership group that in terms of its age structure was not unlike the Soviet Politburo before the succession of Gorbachev as general secretary of the CPSU, in which 5 members were over 80 years old. In the extensive leadership shakeup in September 1985, 10 of the 24 members of the Politburo were ousted and replaced by younger men. Thus, the rejuvenation of the political leadership is one of the things the two communist giants had in common as they moved into the second half of the 1980s.

The 1997 Fifteenth Party Congress elected 24 members to the Politburo: 22 full and 2 alternate members. The 1956 Party Constitution introduced the concept of the "apex of the apex": the formation of the Standing Committee of the Politburo, which became the top ruling clique. In many instances the Standing Committee makes decisions without even consulting the Politburo. The membership of the Standing Committee has varied from five to nine. The 1997 Party Congress elected a seven-member Standing Committee. The average age of this committee, the apex of the apex in decision making, was 65.4. The youngest member of the Standing Committee was 55, the oldest—71, two members were 69, and the other members were 66, 65, and 63.

CENTRAL PARTY SECRETARIAT

The Central Committee and its Politburo are serviced by a host of centralized organs, responsible for executing party policies and managing party affairs. Some of this machinery deals with the routine matters of party organization, propaganda, and united front work. However, the principal central party organ has been the Central Secretariat, the nerve center of the party.

The Central Secretariat, as it existed from 1956–66, was the administrative and staff agency that supervised the party's numerous functional departments, paralleling the functional ministries of the central government. The total number of these central party functional departments may once have reached more than eighteen. Membership of the Central Secretariat was not fixed; it ranged from 6 to 11 top-ranking Central Committee members. For over a decade in the late 1950s and early 1960s, the Central Secretariat was under the control of Deng Xiaoping, who served as its general secretary. Deng and the members of the Central Secretariat used the machinery to make or influence many important party decisions. In the aftermath of the Cultural Revolution, the Central Secretariat, as a formal unit, was abandoned, probably at the insistence of Mao, who felt that it had overstepped its authority. From then until 1977 or 1978, the administrative functions of the party secretariat were absorbed by the General Office for the Politburo, headed by Politburo member Wang Dongxing. In 1978 a newly elected Politburo member, Hu Yaobang, a trusted protégé of Deng Xiaoping, was appointed as secretary-general of the Central Secretariat, which has been reestablished in its pre-Cultural Revolution form.

The reinstitution of a general secretariat and the abolition of the post of party chairman may be viewed as an obvious rejection of Mao's practice of "over-concentration of personal power" in the party. Daily work of the party or the Central Committee was supervised by the Central Secretariat headed by Hu Yaobang, who in turn was assisted by eleven other members, four of whom were concurrently members of the Politburo. The 1982 Party Constitution made it clear that the daily work of the Central Committee would be carried out by the Central Secretariat under the overall direction of the Politburo and its Standing Committee. Article 21 of the 1982 Party Constitution stipulates that the general secretary must be a member of the Standing Committee of the Politburo and that it is his responsibility to convene its meetings. The reestablishment of the Central Secretariat and its general secretary represented a distinct party reform demanded by the pragmatic leaders in the post-Mao era.

In the early 1980s, the Central Secretariat consisted of seven major departments:[34] organization, propaganda, united front work, liaison office with the fraternal parties abroad, publications of the Red Flag and the People's Daily, a policy research office, and party schools. It was known

to meet twice a week behind the red walls of the Zhongnanhai, a part of the former imperial palace and now both party headquarters and the seat of the central government, the State Council. Members of the Central Secretariat, elected by the National Party Congress, can initiate and formulate policies on anything they wish. The Central Secretariat has invited leaders from industry, commerce, agriculture, science, and education to the Zhongnanhai to brief its members on current development or problems. In addition, it processes a large volume of mail received from party cells and branches, as well as from the public.

By 1997, the organization of the Central Secretariat had become more complex through the addition of a number of commissions (for discipline inspection, politics and law, comprehensive management, protection of party secrets), committees (for central organization, central guidance on ethical and cultural construction), work committees (for organs under the Central Committee, central government organs), and offices (for party research, documents research), as well as leading groups (for rural work, party building, Taiwan affairs, and so forth).[35]

BUREAUCRACY: THE CADRES SYSTEM

The Chinese party and government bureaucracy is collectively known as the cadres, or *ganpu,* which denotes positions of leadership and responsibility in various party and government organizational units. Generally there are three layers of cadres: the top party and government leaders, such as Deng Xiaoping, Jiang Zemin, Chou En-lai, and Mao Zedong; the middle-level ministerial or provincial administrators; and the basic-level leaders who have immediate and direct contact with the masses. Not every cadre is a party member, nor is every party member a cadre. In short, cadres are the officials who staff the various party and government bureaucracies and have authority to conduct party or government business. When we use the term "elite" in discussing Chinese politics, it generally refers to the cadres at various levels.

On the basis of their employment, the cadres are divided into three broad categories: state, local, and military. Each group has its own salary classification system with ranks and grades, similar to civil service systems in noncommunist countries. Urban state cadres have a system with 24 grades, while local cadres have 26 grades. Local cadres at the commune level or below are paid directly by the organizations for which they work. This ranking system also is associated with status, privileges, and the degree of upward mobility in the career ladder.

There are approximately 10 million party cadres who constitute essentially the "party leadership" *(dang ganpu)* in the command structure of the party. Party cadres not only serve collectively as an important cog in the vast control mechanism in Chinese society, they must also be able and willing to implement party policies. As bureaucrats they are entrenched in their position and are reluctant to make changes. There is now open admission that there are really serious problems in the party cadres system. One of the problems lies in the slow pace at which the party cadres have accepted the new party line that calls for "correcting all erroneous 'Left' and 'Right' tendencies"—meaning the abandoning of their radical thinking of the Cultural Revolution days. Another problem has been the widespread practice of seeking personal gains and privileges from their positions of power. There is a long list of indictments against the entrenched work style of party cadres, which became a major target in the inner party campaign of purge and rectification. The Central Committee decision on party consolidation (rectification or purge) states:

> They ask the Party for higher positions and better treatment. They openly violate financial regulations and discipline, sabotage state plans, violate state economic policies and illegally retain taxes and profits; they invent all sorts of pretexts to squander, waste and occupy state and collective funds and property. With regard to the distribution of housing, the increase in wages and many other matters—such as the employment, education, promotion, job assignments and changing from rural residence registration to urban residence registration for their children, relatives and friends as well as foreign affairs work—they take advantage provided by their work and personal relations to seek special privileges, violate the law and discipline, and encroach upon the interests of state and the masses.[36]

As mentioned earlier, a 3-year campaign for housecleaning and reregistration of party members was instituted in mid-1983 to eliminate corruption and incompetence. However, this effort to purge the undesirables represents the perennial problem of how to monitor the bureaucracy and the monitors themselves.[37]

Another problem for the Chinese bureaucracy is the "defective personnel management system." Like the top leadership, the Chinese bureaucracy is overloaded with aged personnel. The bureaucracy is not only aged but deficient in education and professional competence. An important reform introduced by Deng was to place leadership positions in the hands of those who are "staunch revolutionaries, younger in age, better educated and technically competent." Reform leaders urged a greater emphasis on cadre utilization and promotion according to formal education attained and skill acquired. But the task of upgrading cadres' competence and training is a formidable one indeed when one considers the fact that a substantial portion of the bureaucracy has only the equivalent of a primary or, at best, junior high school education.

Since 1978 bureaucratic practices have been under constant attack by reform leaders at the center and in the media. One manifestation of bureaucratic behavior is inertia and the inability to make decisions. The practice of foot-dragging is more evident at the middle and lower echelons of the party and governmental organizations. Some foot-dragging by middle echelon bureaucrats may also be attributed to their opposition to Deng's reform measures. There is the traditional tendency for the cadres in organizational units to be devoted to rules and regulations and to exhibit what Deng called obstinacy, timidity, and an air of infallibility. These evils of bureaucracy are magnified further by too many organs and too many administrative units in different chains of command that require extraordinary mechanisms for control and coordination.

Chinese bureaucracy is, however, undergoing organizational reforms designed to streamline its operations in order to meet the needs of modernization. One of the first reforms was the reorganization of the central government establishment: the State Council and its administrative ministries and commissions. To streamline the ministerial structure of the State Council, the total number of ministries and commissions was reduced from 98 to 41, mainly through the merging of functions and staff. Personnel for the State Council was reduced from 49,000 to 32,000. The reform focused on the dismantling of the "overload" system that existed in the economic bureaucracy. For instance, the new State Economic Commission is the result of a merger of six separate ministries and commissions dealing with agriculture, machine building, energy, building material, transportation, railroads, finance, and the national economic plan. Typically the bloated economic bureaucracies have a "low capacity" to plan realistically. Work for these agencies is hampered by inadequate and unreliable data. Then there is the problem of lack of personnel trained in statistics gathering and analysis. Rapid development of skilled personnel for the economic bureaucracies is a top priority in the reform programs.

Finally about 1 percent of the 20 million cadres in the party/government bureaucracy are said to be "leftist" in orientation. These 200,000 cadres are the middle-level functionaries who came into power during the Cultural Revolution and thus are middle-aged and not subject to retirement for some time to come. If, in the process of inner party rectification and reregistration of party membership, they should lose their power and position, they could well emerge as a force or as a faction that would be difficult to deal with for years to come.

MILITARY LEADERSHIP

The Chinese military establishment has been called the "linchpin of power" in Chinese politics.[38] The military, up to the end of the Cultural Revolution decade (1965–76), played a dominant role at the central and provincial levels of party and government. Since the military has occupied a special position in Chinese politics, it is perhaps useful to discuss (1) its traditional role in politics; (2) efforts made by Deng Xiaoping to reduce that role; (3) its opposition to Deng's reform measures; and (4) the existence of factionalism within the military establishment that may contribute to political instability.

Dating back to 1935 when Mao assumed the political leadership over the military at the Zunyi conference, the military, now collectively known as the People's Liberation Army (PLA), has been viewed as "the repository of Mao's Thought" and as "the generator and legitimizer" of Chinese communist ideology.[39] For some time the military was the ideal model, a paradigm, for the nation as a whole to emulate. For a long time, Mao was the chairman of the party's Military Affairs Commission, which supervised the administration of the armed forces and made all decisions affecting the military.

Events of the Cultural Revolution and the arrest of the radical leaders in 1976 catapulted the military into a dominant role in politics. One aspect of its dominance can be seen from the military's representation on the party's Central Committee. Approximately 31 percent of the regular members of the Eleventh Central Committee, elected in 1977, were representatives of the PLA. Of the sixty-two PLA representatives on the Eleventh Central Committee, fifty-five (or 27 percent) were active PLA commanders and political commissars from regional and provincial commands. Military representatives declined in the full membership of the Twelfth Central Committee, elected in 1982, but they still accounted for 22 percent of the total membership. The military, together with the representation of the party/government administrators and technocrats, constituted more than 74 percent of the total full membership of 210 on the Twelfth Central Committee.[40]

However the military's traditional role as the guardian of ideological purity and as an active participant in Chinese politics has been reduced as the result of efforts by the reformers, led by Deng, to restrict its role to national security exclusively.[41] Restricting the military's role to national defense would provide less opportunity for it to participate or intervene in politics. Specifically, Deng Xiaoping and his reformers downplayed and deemphasized the image of the military as the most reliable organizational instrument—a popular symbol of the Cultural Revolution days.

The PLA's functions for internal security, such as guarding the bridges and running the railroads, have been turned over to other appropriate agencies. The 1982 State Constitution provided for a state commission for military affairs with the ultimate intention of placing the military establishment under the control of the state, rather than the party—a move designed to "divide the channels" for military intervention at the center.[42]

Because of the key role which the PLA played in the evolution of Chinese communism, the role of the military in Chinese politics has always been very prominent—certainly much more so than that of the military in Soviet politics. During 1985 there were indications that the civilian leadership in both China and the Soviet Union sought to limit the influence of the military in decision making at the national level. In one of the PRC's most extensive leadership shake-ups ever in September 1985, a number of high-ranking military officials were removed from the CCP Politburo and the CCP Central Committee, including Marshal Ye Jianying, one of the six members of the Politburo's Standing Committee.

Military opposition to Deng's reform policies seems to center in the ground forces of the PLA. It is here that one finds the bastion of Mao's Thought and defenders of the military's traditional role in Chinese politics. Military traditionalists, or "political military leaders," a term used by Alastair Johnston, constitute the core of opponents to Deng Xiaoping and his reform-minded supporters. They dislike the open rejection of Mao's values for a socialist China by the reformers. They see the various reform measures introduced by Deng as evidence of the present leadership's repudiation of Maoist values cherished by many for a long time. Military dissidents are fearful of the increasing corroding influence of the West on Chinese youth and society as China opens its doors to the West under Deng's policy to attract foreign investments and technology. They resent the establishment of "capitalist enclaves," or the special economic zones, bordering Hong Kong and Macao where bourgeois life-styles are evident and may be easily emulated.[43] There seems to be no doubt that these military traditionalists fought unsuccessfully against Deng's controversial plan to demobilize 25 percent or about one million of the numerical strength of the PLA in 1985 in order to provide efficiency and reduce the bloated military staff personnel.

Reform in agriculture under the responsibility system of the individual household has

alarmed the "military traditionalists" because the increased economic prosperity in the countryside has made recruitment for military service less attractive—one must bear in mind that traditionally the military relied on the peasantry for recruitment into the services. Moreover, considerable grumbling within the lower echelons of the officer corps indicates that many would prefer to return to the countryside and participate in the new economic prosperity, rather than stay in the military services.

However Deng and his associates did have the support of the "military modernizers," the professionals in the PLA.[44] Roughly 1.5 million of the 3.5 million in the PLA were in the defense industries, defense related research and development programs, and the military academies.[45] Deng Xiaoping's commitment to military modernization and the upgrading of military education and skills provided the rationale for support from those military leaders who wanted to strengthen Chinese military combat capacity and to acquire needed modern sophisticated weaponry. They were in favor of promoting younger or middle-aged officers to senior command positions based on skill, knowledge, and educational level attained.[46] They accepted Deng's call for limiting the military's role in politics as a necessary tradeoff for the leadership's commitment to military modernization. The military professional leaders were willing to have a percentage limit imposed on membership in the party from the military ranks. That reform measure was designed to reduce the PLA's involvement in party politics in the future.

In the end Deng was successful in reducing the military's role in politics. Yet one cannot rule out the reemergence of the traditional military role in Chinese politics if there is a prolonged and unresolved leadership conflict and instability at the center. For in the last analysis, the military is the final arbiter in a contest for power.

NOTES

[1]"On the Reform of the System of Party and State Leadership," *Selected Works of Deng Xiaoping (Deng Xiaoping Wenxuan): 1975–1982* (Beijing: People Publishing House, 1983), p. 294. English translation is from *Beijing Review* 41 (October 10, 1983): 21.

[2]See Lucian W. Pye, *The Dynamics of Factions and Consensus in Chinese Politics* (Santa Monica: Rand Corporation, 1980); Parris H. Chang, "Deng's Turbulent Quest," *Problems of Communism* 30 (January–February 1981): 1–21; and "The Last Stand of Deng's Revolution," *Journal of Northeast Asian Studies* 1–2 (June 1982): 3–20.

[3]Pye, *The Dynamics of Factions and Consensus in Chinese Politics,* pp. 5–6.

[4]Ibid., p. 6.

[5]Chang, "Deng's Turbulent Quest," p. 8.

[6]Robert Scalapino, ed., *Elites in the People's Republic of China* (Seattle: University of Washington Press, 1972).

[7]Robert Scalapino, "The Transition in Chinese Party Leadership: A Comparison of Eighth and Ninth Central Committees," in ibid., pp. 67–148.

[8]Hong-yung Lee, "China's 12th Central Committee: Rehabilitated Cadres and Technocrats," *Asian Survey* 23, no. 6 (June 1983): 683.

[9]The actual representation of women among the full and alternate members of the 1997 CCP Central Committee may be slightly higher. Full information about all members was not given in the source on which these figures are based. (CHIFFA, vol. 23, pp. 36–50.)

[10]CHIFFA, vol. 23, pp. 36–50, 76–78.

[11]Harry Harding, "Reform in China: A Mid-Course Assessment," *Journal of Northeast Asian Studies* 3 (Summer 1984), pp. 8–9.

[12]On membership development of the CCP, cf. James C. F. Wang, *Contemporary Chinese Politics: An Introduction* (Englewood Cliffs, NJ: Prentice-Hall, Inc., 1980), p. 82; the membership figure for 1997 is taken from Jiang Jemin's Party Congress Report in CHIFFA, vol. 23, p. 77.

[13]"The Decision of the Central Committee of the CCP on Party Consolidation," *Beijing Review* 42 (October 17, 1983): x–xi.

[14]See "Important Talk by Deng Xiaoping," *Ming Pao Daily* (Hongkong), March 5, 1980, p. 1.

[15]Song Renqiong, "Use the New Party Constitution to Educate New Members," *Hongqi (Red Flag)* 24 (December 16, 1982): 15.

[16]Hu Yaobang, "Create a New Situation in All Fields of Socialist Modernization: Report to the 12th National Congress of the CPP, September 1, 1982," *Beijing Review* 37 (September 13, 1982): 38.

[17]Ibid., p. 38.

[18]*Ming Pao Daily* (Hongkong), October 7, 1982, p. 1.

[19]See Song Renquiong, "Building the Revolutionized, Youthful, Intellectualized and Specialized Cadres Forces," *Hongqi* 19 (October 1, 1982): 14.

[20]Ibid., p. 14.

[21]CHIFFA, vol. 17, p. 36.

[22]See Parris Chang, *Power and Policy in China* (University Park, PA, and London: Pennsylvania State University Press, 1974), p. 184.

[23]*Renmin Ribao,* March 1, 1977 and *Ming Pao Daily* (Hongkong), March 3, 1977, p. 3, and *Survey of Chinese Mainland Press,* no. 4097 (January 11, 1968): 1–4.

[24]"Resolution on the Convening of the 12th Party Congress," *Beijing Review* 10 (March 10, 1980): 11.

[25]Lo Bing, "Inside View of the Elections at the 12th Party Congress," *Cheng Ming* (Hongkong) 60 (October 1982): 7.

[26]Franklin Houn, *A Short History of Chinese Communism,* p. 93.

[27]Yaobang, "Create a New Situation in All Fields of Socialist Modernization," pp. 11–40.

[28]*Beijing Review,* October 19–25, 1992.

[29]CHIFFA, vol. 23, p. 56.

[30]Houn, *A Short History of Chinese Communism,* p. 87.

[31]Art. 22 of the 1997 CCP Constitution, in CHIFFA, vol. 23, p. 29.

[32]Houn, *A Short History of Chinese Communism,* p. 89.

[33]"Board of Directors, China, Inc.," *Far Eastern Economic Review,* September 2, 1977: 9.

[34]"The Central Committee's Secretariat and Its Work," *Beijing Review* 19 (May 11, 1981): 21.

[35]CHIFFA, vol. 23, p. 36.

[36]"The Decision of the Central Committee of the CCP on Party Consolidation," p. iv.

[37]Ibid., p. viii.

[38]"China's Army: Linchpin of Power in Peking," *U.S. News & World Report,* October 1, 1984, p. 34.

[39]See Alastair I. Johnston, "Changing Party-Army Relations in China, 1979–1984," *Asian Survey* 24, no. 10 (October 1984): 1015.

[40]James C. F. Wang, *Contemporary Chinese Politics: An Introduction,* 2nd ed. (Englewood Cliffs, NJ: Prentice-Hall, 1985), pp. 174–175.

[41]Johnston, "Changing Army Relations in China, 1979–1984," p. 1018; also "China's Army: Linchpin of Power in Peking," *U.S. News & World Report,* October 1, 1984, p. 34; and V. G. Kulkarni, "A Retreat from Power," *Far Eastern Economic Review,* April 7, 1983, pp. 20–21.

[42]Johnston, "Changing Army Relations in China, 1979–1984," p. 1021; and Wang, *Contemporary Chinese Politics,* p. 159.

[43]For an excellent discussion of dissent in the military, see Ellis Joffe, "Party and Military in China: Professionalism in Command?" *Problems of Communism* 32 (September–October 1983): 48–63. Also see Harry Harding, "Reform in China," pp. 9 and 19–20.

[44]Johnston, "Changing Army Relations in China, 1979–1984," p. 1022.

[45]This figure is given by Johnston in ibid., p. 1022.

[46]See Wang, *Contemporary Chinese Politics,* pp. 176–177; and Joffe, "Party and Military in China," pp. 60–61.

Chapter 36

China's Political Performance

The long-term goal of the People's Republic of China since 1949 has been the rapid industrialization of an economically backward country. It is perhaps useful to review very briefly the development strategies employed to arrive at that basic objective and the outcomes in economic development.

During the initial period, 1949–52, the regime's main concern was to seek rapid economic recovery and rehabilitation after a long period of war with Japan and the civil strife that followed immediately after the end of World War II. In agriculture, it embarked on a fundamental land reform system by redistributing land to the landless peasants and by eliminating the land-gentry class in the countryside. Major industries were nationalized, but the managerial and technical personnel of the old capitalist system were treated cautiously. Whenever possible they were co-opted and their expertise and services were used.

For the next 5 years, 1953–58, the Stalinist strategy of centralized planning with emphasis on the rapid development of heavy industries was employed. During this period, modest gains were made in agricultural production capacity, and agricultural cooperatives were introduced to speed up growth. Significant increases were made in the output of steel, coal, cement, electric power, and machinery. However, living standards for the period were basically Spartan despite improvements in employment opportunities and food consumption.

Then in 1958 the regime embarked on a disastrous strategy of mass mobilization, known as the Great Leap, when orderly planning was abandoned from 1958 to 1960. In its drive to double industrial output, tremendous strains and stresses were imposed on the economic system. Enthusiasm for the commune program introduced in 1958 was fanned by unrealistic ideological fervor and by bumper crops in 1959. Then poor weather conditions developed in 1960, causing floods and droughts and near starvation. In the industrial sector, unrealistic output quotas for the factories resulted in breakdowns and products of inferior quality. For the first time since 1949, political dissension erupted within the ranks of the Chinese top leadership on the question of a suitable economic development strategy.

The ill-conceived Great Leap strategy was followed by a period of readjustment and recovery from 1961 to 1965. The egalitarian aspects of the commune program were abandoned and a policy allowing private plots for the peasants was permitted, which, aided by good weather, resulted in increased agricultural output. Rational management was reintroduced in the factories, and increased investment in oil and electrical machinery laid a more solid foundation for possible industrial growth. Living standards, however, remained at a low level. Then the pendulum again swung to radicalism under the banner of the Cultural Revolution. Agricultural production continued to grow at a slow pace, but industrial output was disrupted and showed significant decline, particularly for 1967–68. The Cultural Revolution decade, 1966–76, also severely disrupted education. Politically it was a period of instability and internal dissension. Just prior to Mao's death another period of recovery, from 1976 to 1978, was ushered in. This period was characterized not only by political instability but also by a marked shift in development strategy that called for innovative programs based on incentives for both agricultural and industrial production.

SOCIOECONOMIC POLICIES AND PERFORMANCE

The reversal from a mass-mobilization-oriented strategy to a comprehensive and orderly planning strategy for modernization occurred at the beginning of 1975 when Premier Zhou proposed a two-stage development for China's national economy: a comprehensive industrial system by 1980, and a comprehensive modernization program in agriculture, industry, national defense, and science and technology by the year 2000.[1] The radicals were set to attack any action that would restore "bourgeois rights." Yao Wenyuan, the radicals' theoretical spokesman, authored an article in the party's theoretical journal *Hongqi (Red Flag),* in which he raised at least four major points of disagreement with Zhou on the development of the economy.[2] First, Yao argued that a gap existed between the workers and peasants, between town and country, and between mental and manual labor, and that these differences must be removed or polarization and inequality would inevitably result. A comprehensive program for national economic development eventually would place the elite technocrats in a position of power and prestige and thus widen these gaps in society. Second, Yao argued that once the technocrats were in power, they would "restore capitalism in the superstructure" and would redistribute capital and power according to mental power and skills, rather than on the basis of "each according to his work." Third, Yao attacked the plan for reintroducing material incentives to induce workers and peasants to produce more in the name of modernization. Wage incentives to "lure the workers" to Yao represented the corrupt practice of the bourgeois right. Fourth, Yao labeled the rationale for increasing agricultural and industrial production as nothing but a scheme to "undermine the socialist collective economy."

Zhou's pragmatic planners wanted to step up production on the ground that the peasants needed food and clothing. To the radicals, as expressed by Yao, the very idea of introducing material incentives in order to spur production was to alter the nature of the commune system, which was based on "the socialist collective economy." The debate ended with the death of Mao and the arrest of the radical leaders in 1976. After the arrest of the Gang of Four, Hua Guofeng reintroduced Zhou Enlai's comprehensive plan for modernization and brought Deng Xiaoping back to revive his guidelines for accelerated industrial and scientific development.

Hua presented a detailed set of development plans to the Fifth National People's Congress in March 1978. The program consisted of two interrelated plans, comparable to Premier Zhou's 1975 two-stage development plan: a 10-year, short-term development plan, and a 23-year, long-term, comprehensive plan. The short-term plan called for 400 million metric tons of grain production, a 60 million ton capacity for steel production, and an overall 10 percent per year increase in industrial production by 1985.[3] The 10-year plan called for at least "eighty-five percent mechanization in all major processes of farm work" in the communes. The 10-year plan was to be followed by a series of 5-year plans to push China "into the front ranks of the world economy."[4] The plan also included large open-pit coal mines, oil field pipelines, modern iron and steel complexes, chemical fertilizer plants, farm machinery plants, and railway construction.

By the spring of 1979 it became obvious that the 1978 modernization plan needed revision. To understand China's economic readjustment from 1979 to 1981, we need to take a brief look at the economic problems that surfaced soon after the 1978 modernization plan was launched.[5] First, there was the key issue of industry versus agriculture. The orthodox Stalinist strategy of economic development with emphasis on heavy industry invariably placed hardship on the agricultural sector. A leading Chinese economist pointed out that between 1949 and 1978 heavy industry increased by more than 90 percent compared to a mere 2.4 percent increase in agriculture.[6] The immediate consequence of a slow growth rate in agricultural output was China's dependence on grain purchases from abroad. Second, there was the issue of heavy versus light industries. Because of the emphasis on investment in heavy industry, investment in light and consumer industries was insufficient to allow this sector to produce enough goods to meet the people's daily needs. In other words, "market supplies for the main light industrial goods have all along fallen short of needs."[7]

Third, the Chinese experience had shown that in the development of heavy industry excessive stress was placed on the development of metallurgical, machine-building, and processing industries. Energy resources development (coal and electric power) and transport facilities were neglected in the process. This resulted eventually in a critical energy shortage, and transportation and communications services remained backward. An example of this problem was the Baoshan steel complex.[8] When this giant complex was almost completed in 1979, the Chinese discovered that there was not enough power available to turn the steel rolling mills and that a new port was needed to handle the ores imported from Brazil and Australia. Fourth, heavy industrial development required large-scale investment in capital construction projects. Too often these projects' requirements far exceeded the available manpower, machinery, finances, and material resources that the economy could provide. The numerous projects under development during 1978–79 almost exhausted China's financial resources. Finally, there was the need to upgrade the efficiency of management in Chinese

enterprises. Most Chinese factories were either overequipped with machines or overstaffed. Most of the plants were not operating at full capacity.

In June 1979 a series of urgent measures to readjust the modernization program by retrenchment was enacted.[9] First, the priority light and consumer industries were given equal, if not greater, emphasis than heavy industry. The overambitious plan for 60 million metric tons of steel by 1985 was revised downward to 45 million metric tons. Energy and power industries were scheduled to be developed and expanded more rapidly. Capital construction projects for heavy industries were curtailed so that large amounts of investment funds would be freed. Second, the structure for economic management was overhauled. Enterprises were given the real decision-making power and initiative.

The old concept of "egalitarian tendency" had to be discarded so that those who had demonstrated success would be given authority and reward. Provinces and localities were given increased power in planning, financing, and foreign trade. Third, factory managers were given power in the operation of the plants in order to spur production. Managers were permitted to set prices for their own products. They also had to apply to the banks to borrow operating funds and pay interest. Fourth, all enterprises were required to produce quality products.

This austere readjustment program was to span the 3-year period from 1979 to 1981. Reform measures in the economy would slow down China's growth rate from 12 percent in 1978 to about 7 percent in 1979 and to just over 5 percent in 1980.[10] These scaled-down goals represented the admission that they had gone ahead "too fast" and were forced to apply the brakes.[11]

The 1979 economic readjustment and reforms were intended to correct two basic problems: the overemphasis in the investment and accumulation of heavy industries, discussed earlier, and the need for incentives to spur production. China's leading economists and planners, such as Chen Yun, a Politburo member and former director of state planning, and Xue Muqiao, an advisor to state planning, argued that the "scale of economic construction must be commensurate with the nation's capabilities" and that the state should commit a substantial investment expenditure on capital construction in heavy industries only when the people's standard of living had displayed marked improvement.[12] Chen Yun was quoted as saying that the distribution of the limited supply of raw materials should be given first to those "that ensure the production of people's daily necessities."[13]

The development strategy shift from heavy to light industries was made not only because of the need to provide consumer goods for the exploding population, but also for more expedient reasons. Heavy industries tend to consume an enormous quantity of energy resources. Light industries require less energy and also provide more jobs. It was pointed out that in China a 1 percent shift in the ratio from heavy to light industries saves 6 million tons of coal.[14] In addition, light industries produce China's export goods, which earn needed foreign exchange.

The economic development of China since 1949 offers a sharp contrast to the massive and consistent commitment to the growth of heavy industry in the former Soviet Union. However, despite the frequent zig-zags in China's development strategy, its overall economic growth record since 1949 has not been a poor one when compared with most of the developing countries of the world. Its economy has been able to sustain the rapidly growing population, the largest in the world, and lay a solid foundation for future growth.[15]

China specialist Arthur Ashbrook, using 1957, the last year of China's First 5-Year Plan, as a base year, has estimated China's economic growth rate from 1958 to 1980 as follows:[16]

	Gross Rate (%)
Gross National Product	5–6%
Industrial Production	9%
Agricultural Production	2–3%
Population	2%

Ashbrook also points out that the pattern of China's economic growth is rather typical of communist countries in that there has always been a higher rate of growth for industrial output and investment than for agriculture and consumer goods.[17] As we mentioned, it was not until 1979

that China's development strategy shifted from heavy to light industries in order to provide more consumer goods for the rapidly expanding population.

Since 1979 the economy of China has registered remarkable growth, thanks to the economic reforms and the open-door policy. The replacement of collective farming with the contract responsibility system, the revival of private business in urban areas, price reform, the granting of greater autonomy to local authorities and state enterprises, and the encouragement of foreign trade through the open-door policy have added up to a successful strategy for economic growth. Growing at an annual rate of 9.6 percent between 1979 and 1988, and 7.2 percent between 1989 and 1992, the Chinese economy performed very well—even when compared to the other leading East Asian economies, such as South Korea, Singapore, and Taiwan. Consumer goods, especially electric household appliances, have become more available. China's economy has benefited from over $10 billion in foreign investment.

There is no doubt that the economic reforms in the PRC have been effective. Growing at 8 percent during 1981–1990 and at more than 10 percent during 1991–1996, China's gross national product quadrupled in two decades (1978–1997). By 1996, China had overtaken Japan by a comfortable margin and become the world's second largest economy. It ranked first in the world in total grain production, wheat production, and rough rice production, and second—in primary energy production and electricity production. Given these trends, China seems poised to become the world's largest economy sometime in the 21st century.[18]

The economic future of China, however, depends on the ability of the government to control population growth. In recent years, China's population control program has been weakened by the deterioration of the authority of cadres in the countryside. Furthermore, the government must find ways of dealing more effectively with corruption and other economic crimes. As in post-Communist Russia, tax collection from individuals, businesses, and the provinces remains a problem. While the official unemployment rate is only 4 percent, the real rate is probably in the range of 8–10 percent.[19] There is large-scale unemployment and underemployment in rural China. Reportedly 60 to 100 million rural workers drift back and forth between villages and cities in an attempt to secure at least part-time employment in order to stay alive. China also faces serious environmental problems, including air pollution, decreasing water resources, especially in the north, and the significant loss of arable land due to economic development and soil erosion. Finally, it stands to reason that in the long run the increasingly decentralized economic system will prove to be incompatible with a political system that remains highly centralized.

LIVING STANDARDS AND CONSUMPTION LEVELS

While reliable statistics on wages and income in China are difficult to obtain, especially for the first three decades of communist rule, due to defective construction and design or recalcitrance on the part of the authorities, sufficient information is now available to make possible a meaningful, if not always accurate, assessment of the development of living standards. Both China's modernization effort and its increasing participation in international organizations, such as the U.N., the IMF, the World Bank, and the World Health Organization, have forced the Chinese government to make available more detailed and sophisticated statistics on a variety of subjects.

PEASANT INCOME

The available data suggest that there has been a significant improvement in the income of peasants, who in 1997 still accounted for more than two-thirds of China's population. For example, average net income for peasant households more than doubled between 1978 and 1982. Among the reasons for this improvement were the economic reforms introduced in 1978, in particular the responsibility or incentive system, which allowed peasant families to enter into individual contracts with production teams for the production of agricultural products, under their own management. Under this system, peasants were allowed to retain any earnings from production in excess of the state quota. Moreover, the new system also permitted peasants to engage in "sideline production" from their private plots. As in the case of the "private" garden plots of farmers in the former Soviet Union, "sideline production" responded especially vigorously to the new incentives.

Unfortunately the peasants are spending their incomes for consumption items, such as housing, rather than for investment in tools and supplies. The peasants' eagerness to consume may be influenced by their fear of a reversal of the present agricultural policy in the future. Furthermore, because agricultural research has not been a high priority for the Chinese government and agriculture is not highly capitalized, productivity is low in comparison especially with the Western European countries.

Note that while from 1978 to 1982 the average income from collectives reportedly rose some 63 percent, the income from sideline production was up 348 percent, and for other nonborrowing sources income increased 340 percent. While the 1982 figures are overstated in terms of real income due to inflation and perhaps statistical problems, it seems clear that incentive programs are indeed boosting peasant income. Rural income growth is also attributed to the higher prices paid to the peasants for the goods they produce.

There are also significant regional differences in peasant income and the differences between rich and poor peasant households. Peasant households on the outskirts of the cities tend to earn more since they can specialize in pig farming and vegetable gardening, which bring good cash income. Some regions such as Gansu in the northwest and Guizhou in the southwest tend to be poor agricultural provinces. Peasant households in resource-rich communes can earn two or three times more than the ones in the poor regions. But the overall trend in peasant household income is on the rise, compared to 1978 prior to the reform in agriculture.

With few exceptions, agriculture has been a major problem area in communist economies. During the post-Mao era, the People's Republic of China showed much greater flexibility in its agricultural policy than the former Soviet Union and was much more successful in achieving agricultural self-sufficiency. While the Soviet Union became the world's largest net importer of food products, China in recent years has been able to export food.

URBAN WORKER WAGES

The total Chinese nonagricultural labor force came to 293 million workers out of a total labor force of more than 623 million (in 1995).[20] For a long time the Chinese wage system for urban workers was designed to encourage quantitative rather than qualitative output. From 1958 to the end of the Cultural Revolution, the emphasis was on egalitarianism regardless of one's initiative or skill. Out of this concept emerged the system of the "iron rice bowl" which provided the workers with job security and a frozen wage system that permitted a wage disparity between the maximum and minimum pay of 1:3, according to W. Klatt's calculation.[21]

One of the first tangible economic reforms introduced by Deng Xiaoping in 1977 was a wage increase for about half of the urban workers who were on the bottom of the wage scale in order to reduce the disparity between high and low wage earners. A subsequent wage increase in 1978 was designed to reward the skilled workers and supervisory and managerial personnel. Since then wages for urban workers have been adjusted upward by the reform policy of bonuses and piecework payments.

Urban wage earners also receive other benefits, such as free health service, almost free primary education for their children and subsidized housing at nominal cost. In addition, urban workers receive retirement pensions from the state based on seniority and the final year's wages. Subsidies for urban workers have risen so sharply that in 1983–84 about 20 percent of China's national income was allocated to provide state subsidies for the urban workers and their families.

The introduction of wage reform in terms of bonuses and raises in the basic pay scale has resulted not only in rising expectations for more and better consumer goods but higher retail and consumer prices or inflation as well. According to CIA estimates, the rate of inflation for consumer prices was 19.5 percent in 1989, but dropped to 2.8 percent in 1997.[22] A large proportion of the income of urban workers must be spent for food, according to recent official statistics. W. Klatt has estimated the proportion of food consumption in workers' income in four countries: 20 percent in the United States, 30 percent in Japan, 50 percent in the Soviet Union, and about 60 percent in China.[23]

In 1992 the Comfortable Living Standards Unit of the State Bureau of Statistics published a number of indicators for a national comfortable living standard. It called for a per capita GNP of 2,400 yuan, which, based on 1990, would require almost doubling the GNP. A national comfortable living standard, furthermore, would require an annual per capita income of 1,400 yuan. These are ambitious goals, but they are not unattainable. At the annual meeting of the World Economic Forum in Davos, Switzerland, in 1992, then Premier Li Peng was able to announce that the first part of China's long-term development program—to double China's 1980 GNP in 10 years in order to provide the Chinese people with adequate food and clothing—was achieved in the 1980s. The next goal will be to double the GNP once again to enable the Chinese people to live a comfortable life by the year 2000. The third step in the strategy calls for increasing the per capita GNP in the subsequent 3–5 decades to the point where China would join the ranks of a medium-level developed country.[24]

Clearly, economic development and modernization has become the top priority for the Chinese government. The reforms enacted by the Chinese government have not only effectively ended China's isolation from the rest of the world (and especially the West), but they have resulted in economic growth and increased prosperity, a higher standard of living, and a more positive and hopeful outlook of its people. With only 7 percent of the world's total cultivated land, China has managed to feed 22 percent of the world's population—no small accomplishment by any measure. However, an essential requirement for China's long-term economic viability is an effective population control program. Unfortunately, resistance by the population, changes in the policy of the central government, and the loss of authority by rural authorities in the recent past have combined to weaken the government's efforts to keep population growth under control.

OPEN DOOR POLICY AND SPECIAL ECONOMIC ZONES

Of the reforms instituted by Deng Xiaoping and his pragmatic reformers, the policy of opening China's doors to foreign investment initiated in 1978 has been one of the most significant departures from the decades of largely self-imposed diplomatic isolation and ideological rigidity under Mao. A central feature of the new open door—or "open economic"—policy has been the experimentation with special economic zones (SEZs). Within a year of the announcement of the open door policy, four southern coastal cities—Shezhen, Zhuhai, and Shantou in Guangdong province and Xiamen in Fujian province— were designated as SEZs to engage in free trade.

The basic objective of the open door policy is not merely to seek economic cooperation in terms of trade with foreign nations; the 1978 communiqué of the third plenum of the Eleventh Central Committee made it quite clear that a basic objective of the open door policy was to strive to "adopt the world's advanced technology and equipment." Technology as defined by the Chinese also implies management and marketing skills and knowhow.

The geographic locations for the SEZs were selected to attract foreign capital and technological knowhow. Shenzhen SEZ is adjacent to the world's fourth largest financial center, Hong Kong, a British crown colony until 1997. Zhuhai borders the Portuguese colony of Macao. In addition both Guangdong and Fujian provinces have been the traditional areas through which foreign contacts were made and thus are considered more open to the outside world than the hinterland regions of China.

Both provinces also had been the original domiciles of the overseas Chinese who migrated to Southeast Asia, the Pacific, and the west coast of the United States. Certainly Hong Kong and Macao have large, dynamic overseas Chinese business communities. China experts P. S. Ho and Ralph Huenemann have pointed out that the close proximity of overseas Chinese capital and technological skills was a very important, if not dominant, consideration in selecting Shenzhen and Zhuhai as SEZs.[25]

There also were political considerations in the establishment of the SEZs.[26] First are international concerns. Considerable suspicion still exists in the outside world about China's open door policy. Foremost in the minds of potential investors is the fear of expropriations of capital plants and equipment. The SEZs can serve as showcases to demonstrate that China will honor its guarantees. By Chinese law and regulation, foreign investments in the SEZs are protected from expropriation.

Second are internal political concerns. The functions of the SEZs have been defined most broadly by economist Xi Dixin, director of the Institute of Economics of the Chinese Academy of Social Sciences:

1. To serve as the bridge for the learning of advanced "techniques and scientific methods of management" through the encouragement of foreign capital investment
2. To promote competition between regions in the areas of efficient production and market demand
3. To generate and absorb large amounts of foreign exchange
4. To provide laboratories, or "experimental units," for economic reform
5. To create employment for the jobless young

Additionally then, the zones were designed as self-contained entities, isolated from the rest of China, to serve as experimental laboratories where the impact of modernization and various reform policies could be observed without causing undue repercussions to the rest of the nation.

In October 1984 China expanded the open door policy by designating 14 additional coastal cities for increased contacts with the outside world, with the expectation that these cities should "strive to import advanced technology from abroad and adopt effective measures to draw foreign investment." Investment in the newly opened coastal cities is encouraged because China needs foreign investors to "set up technology-and-knowledge-intensive productive projects" and to upgrade its obsolete industries.

POLITICAL STABILITY AND SUCCESSION

The Cultural Revolution decade, 1966–76, witnessed the growth of "parochialization" in the party and government cadres system—that is, the replacement of able and experienced leaders by less educated and more radicalized ideologues. More than 15 million, or about 40 percent, of the 39.6 million party members were recruited during the Cultural Revolution. These cadres were really "parochial political newcomers" whose loyalty to the top leaders, known as the Gang of Four, and to Lin Biao, was more important than their education or competence.

Perhaps the gravest indictment that can be leveled against the Cultural Revolution was the human loss caused by the radicals' witch-hunting escapades. Many party veterans at that time were accused of being "rightist" or "counterrevolutionary." The denounced were subjected to beatings, imprisonment, loss of jobs, and banishment to remote rural areas to do menial labor. During the 1981 trial of the Gang of Four, it was revealed that 729,511 persons had been persecuted, including a sizable number of ranking party and state officials. Of that group, about 34,000 died.[27] In 1978 more than 100,000 victims of false accusations and persecution were rehabilitated and exonerated. Deng Xiaoping, who emerged as China's top leader in the post-Mao period, was personally convinced that as many as 2.9 million persons had been victims of persecution during the Cultural Revolution decade.[28]

While the pre-Cultural Revolution leaders of the party and government in China were mostly urban intellectuals who had gone through the baptism by fire of guerrilla warfare, the "parochial political newcomers" of the Cultural Revolution decade were even less educated, lacked revolutionary fervor, and were woefully deficient in ideological understanding. Their rise to power during the Cultural Revolution came as a result of their political activism in the streets and in factional infighting. Some members of the "parochial political newcomers" have since been accused of not only making errors in embracing "ultra-Left" tendencies, but also constantly seeking personal gain by using their position and power.

The CCP's general secretary's indictment of these party members in 1983 revealed the extent of the leadership problem: "They ignore the law, protect and shield criminals, and they even take a direct part in unlawful activities such as smuggled goods, corruption, accepting bribes and profiteering."[29] The 1983–86 purge or reregistration of party membership was designed to weed out the three types of persons who were admitted into the party during the Cultural Revolution decade: (1) those who rose to positions of power simply by blindly following the Gang of Four; (2) those who engage in factionalist cliques; and (3) those who engaged in persecuting others and extorting confessions from their victims by torture. These purges by a national mass campaign invariably resulted in a larger measure of political instability.

While periodic purges via mass campaigns have been symptoms of political instability that have characterized the Chinese political system since the mid-1950s, a basic cause for leadership instability has been factionalism within the top leadership. In an earlier chapter on Chinese political leadership mention was made of the continuing tension among the top echelon of China's elite between the need for consensus and what Lucian Pye describes as the need for "particularistic relationships" which encourage the formation of factions or in-group association on the basis of personal attachment.

During the Cultural Revolution old party veterans who disagreed with Mao and aligned themselves with Liu Shaoqi and Deng Xiaoping were purged. The dominant faction that controlled the Cultural Revolution, the so-called Gang of Four, was led by Mao's wife in temporary alliance with the Lin Biao military faction. By 1971 Lin Biao's group was purged after Lin's death—reportedly in a plane crash—following an alleged abortive coup against Mao. The return of Deng Xiaoping in 1977 to a position of power also brought back the purged veterans and victims of the Cultural Revolution. It was this group and Deng's close associates that gained the upper hand. But before they could assume complete control in 1982, a purge had to be engineered to eliminate the remnants of the Cultural Revolution collaborators from the top leadership.

The succession to leadership in the party has never been smooth and orderly since the CCP came to power in 1949. Mao ruled autocratically and relentlessly for over 40 years. In the mid-1950s he and the party designated the then vice chairman of the party, Liu Shaoqi, as his successor. Liu was purged in the early phase of the Cultural Revolution and died for lack of medical care while under house arrest. Then in 1969, as

Mao approached old age, a successor was again designated. The party charter named Lin Biao as the successor. Two years later, Lin also perished. When Mao died in September 1976, a compromise choice had to be made while the moderates and the radicals contended for power. Hua Guofeng temporarily became Mao's successor as party chairman and premier, only to be removed by the Deng forces in 1980.

From the standpoint of power base and choice, Deng Xiaoping would have been the party chairman and premier in the early 1980s. But Deng wisely insisted that the top leadership must be passed on to the younger generation and saw to it that his younger protégés Hu Yaobang and Zhao Ziyang were elevated to positions of power in the party and government. Being over 80 years of age already, Deng Xiaoping told many that he would like to retire in 1985—which, however, did not happen. As it turned out, plans for his succession did not materialize. Under pressure from party hardliners and senior leaders, he was forced to abandon his designated successors: Hu Yaobang, a close comrade-in-arms (in early 1987), and Zhao Ziyang, a consummate pragmatist and skillful administrator (in June 1989).

In the aftermath of the Tiananmen Square incident, it appeared, Deng's power base declined further, but he never lost control. And the expectations of many "China watchers" notwithstanding, with the appointment of Jiang Zemin as the new general secretary of the Chinese Communist Party and Li Peng as the new premier, the reform era in Chinese politics did not come to an end. On the contrary! Under the leadership of President Jiang Zemin, reform policies in China have not only continued, but have broadened and intensified. Against the opposition of mostly older conservatives, known as "leftists" in Chinese politics today, who argue that the present reform course and the "opening up" of China to the world will undermine the role of the CCP and lead to political instability, Jiang Zemin has aligned himself with the "friends of change," seeking to bring the dynamics of Chinese society in harmony with the demands of globalization. By cautiously supporting a third "emancipation of the mind" period and allowing a greater degree of political expression, he has clearly indicated his determination to distance himself from the China of Tiananmen and to leave his own mark on the history of his country. Through a series of deft political maneuvers, he secured the replacement of Qiao Shi, the chairman of the National People's Congress (NPC) and the third-ranking member of the Politburo Standing Committee, as well as Li Peng, who had served two terms as prime minister, thus clearing the way for a far-reaching organization of the CCP and the government. The CCP Central Committee elected in 1997 is younger, better educated and more highly trained than any of its predecessors—and 60 percent of its 193 members are newly appointed. On the government side, Jiang Zemin not only secured the appointment of the extremely popular Zhu Rongij as the new prime minister, but also NPC endorsement of a sweeping plan calling for the reduction of the number of departments of the State Council from 40 to 29 and the reduction of the central state bureaucracy by 50 percent by the end of 1998, with similar cuts projected for the provincial and county-level bureaucracies over the next two years. Taken together, these developments suggest that—the pledge of "holding high" the "great banner of Deng Xiaoping Theory" at the Fifteenth Party Congress in 1997 notwithstanding—we may be witnessing the onset of an increasingly distinctive Jiang Zemin era.

If present trends continue, its hallmarks may well be the continued reduction of state control, further economic modernization, and a gradual transition to a more democratic order. Two hundred billion dollars sin foreign investments, a multitude of foreign-funded ventures, a growing private sector accounting already for approximately one-third of the Chinese economy, and the introduction of private housing, among other things, will transform the nature of Chinese society. At the grassroots level, "village democracy" is already being practiced by approximately two-thirds of the Chinese population living in the rural areas. Once it spills over into the cities, China's transition to democracy will be difficult to prevent—even with its most eloquent advocates, such as Fan Lizhi, Liu Binyan, Wang Dan, and Wei Jingshen, in exile. It remains to be seen, however, what impact the rising nationalism, including among the young, will have on the future trajectory of Chinese politics.

HUMAN RIGHTS AND DISSENT

The relaxation that began in 1978 made it possible for Chinese dissidents to surface openly, a phenomenon that intrigued Western observers. The dissident movement could be observed in the daily posting of handwritten messages on a brick wall in downtown Beijing. Later, this wall came to be known as "democracy wall." A study of the wall posters that appeared for the period between November 1978 and December 1979 revealed several areas of concern. Initially there was the condemnation of political persecution under Mao's rule. Then there were appeals for redress of personal grievances inflicted upon those who were persecuted during the Cultural Revolution. Finally, there were advocacies of human rights, democracy, and justice.[30]

The democracy wall movement entered a new phase early in December 1978. In addition to candid expressions in support of sexual freedom and human rights, some criticisms of Deng Xiaoping appeared. At that time Deng withdrew his support for the posters, changed his earlier stand, and expressed disapproval of their criticism of the socialist system.

During December 1978 activists associated with the democracy wall movement became dissatisfied with the limited success of their posters and looked for ways to expand the campaign for democracy and human rights. They formed dissident organizations and study groups with names such as Enlightenment Society, China Human Rights Alliance, and the Thaw Society. Each published its own underground journals and offered them for sale at the democracy wall. Most publications were poorly produced. Nevertheless, some of the underground publications soon attracted worldwide attention, as American, British, Canadian, and French reporters were given copies for overseas consumption. Excerpts from underground journals, such as *Beijing Spring,* obviously inspired by the 1968 "Prague Spring" in Czechoslovakia, *April Fifth Forum,* derived from the demonstration at the Tiananmen on April 5, 1976, and *Tansuo (Exploration),*[31] were translated and published in the foreign press all over the world.

The appearance of these underground journals and the topics they discussed (freedom of speech, democracy, law and justice, human rights, and modernization of science and technology) were reminiscent of the 1919 May Fourth Movement 60 years earlier. The new movement spread to many provinces and cities in China. It also tried to forge an alliance with the many protest groups formed by demobilized soldiers and peasants who came to Beijing in increasing numbers. Then China launched its border war with Vietnam. Pressures now mounted for Deng Xiaoping to curb the dissident movement.

As the new regime was in the process of deciding to ban the posting of criticisms of socialism in China on the democracy wall, a leading young dissident, Wei Jingsheng, launched a personal attack on Deng in a special issue of his underground journal, *Tansuo (Exploration).* Wei's writings criticized Marxism-Leninism and Mao's thought and advocated the abandonment of the socialist system for China. Wei was arrested on March 29, 1979, along with thirty other young dissidents. In the one-day trial session in October, he was sentenced to 15 years imprisonment for supplying military intelligence to Western reporters, slandering Marxism-Leninism, and agitating for the overthrow of the socialist system in China. The brutal suppression of the students' prodemocracy movement in Tiananmen Square in 1989 was thus part of a long-established tradition of human rights violations.

Despite the passage of the criminal code in 1979, the new Chinese legal system still does not provide protection against arbitrary arrest and unfair trial. Amnesty International in 1984 published a long list of human rights violations by the Chinese, including detention and arrest of persons for purely nonviolent expression of their opinions and beliefs. The model case Amnesty International adopted was that of Fu Yueha, an unemployed woman, then 31 years of age, who was arrested in 1979 for allegedly helping the poor peasants organize their demonstration in Beijing for an end to hunger. After spending $2\frac{1}{2}$ years in prison, she was charged with disrupting the public order. After a confession forced by beating, Fu was sentenced to 2 more years in prison and upon release was sent to a labor camp for reeducation.

Although China has signed the International Covenant of Civil and Political Rights, its record

Beijing university students demonstrate in Tiananmen Square, May 20, 1989, in support of political reforms.
(*Photographer/Source:* AP/Wide World Photos)

of observing human rights leaves much to be desired. Considering freedom of assembly, equality under the law, protection from terror, social freedoms, and equality of opportunity, the *Far Eastern Economic Review,* in 1992, gave China the lowest ranking in the area of civil rights (along with Burma, North Korea, and Laos), and in the area of political freedom (along with Burma, North Korea, and Vietnam).[32] On the fifth anniversary of the massacre on Tiananmen Square, then Prime Minister Li Peng announced new security regulations that equated political discussions outside the party line with sabotage. The fabrication or distortion of facts and contact with hostile institutions, such as the foreign press, the decree made clear, could result in long prison sentences.

A report released in January 1997 by the U.S. Department of State makes clear that, recent Chinese legislation and commitments notwithstanding, serious problems in the observance of human rights continue to persist in such areas as the following: political and other extrajudicial killings; the enforced or involuntary disappearance of political activists and Tibetans; torture and other cruel, inhuman, or degrading treatment or punishment; arbitrary arrest, detention, or exile; denial of a fair and public trial; the unauthorized removal of organs from executed prisoners; the denial of freedom of speech; and many others.[33] The findings of this report are echoed by Amnesty International in testimony before the U.S. Congress on January 20, 1999, which, among other things, points out that, according to China's own statistics, nearly a quarter of a million persons are subjected to "re-education through labor." Frequently employed against dissidents, this form of administrative detention for up to three years is imposed by local government committees without any legal charge or trial. The report also points out that more prisoners are executed in China than in the rest of the world combined.[34]

The 10th anniversary of the Tiananmen Massacre on June 4, 1999 passed quietly in Beijing. There were no large-scale demonstrations. The vast majority of Chinese citizens in the capital went about their daily routine as if this date had no meaning or significance for them. But Tiananmen has not been forgotten. During the week of the 10th anniversary, the relatives of 105 of the victims took the unprecedented step of filing a lawsuit demanding a criminal investigation.[35] Eventually the Chinese people and their leaders will have to address the question of what happened in Tiananmen Square in June 1989 and why. They will have to recognize that important social, economic, and political issues cannot be effectively discussed if public debate is stifled by party censorship and that the "emancipation of the mind" is impossible without the existence of a variety of different viewpoints and their toleration. The question is whether such toleration is possible in China without systemic change.

Clearly, important changes have already taken place since 1989. China has become much more open to the outside world. Its economy is more market-oriented and more independent of the government. The political and intellectual atmosphere is very different from what it was, and so is the political leadership. But improvements in policies dealing with human rights thus far seem to be largely the result of international pressure. The release of Wei Jingsheng and Wang Dan and the legal reforms that have been enacted are cases in point. While they are a step in the right direction, they have occurred in an environment in which tolerance of political dissent remains extremely limited and politics are perceived as a zero-sum contest.

NOTES

[1]"Report on the Work of the Government," *Peking Review* 4 (January 24, 1975): 23.

[2]Yao Wenyuan, "On the Social Basis of the Lin Biao Anti-Party Clique," *Hongqi* 3 (1975), as translated in *Peking Review* 10 (March 7, 1975): 5–10.

[3]"Report on the Work of the Government," *Peking Review* 10 (March 10, 1978): 19.

[4]Ibid.

[5]"Readjusting the National Economy: Why and How?" *Beijing Review* 26 (June 29, 1979): 13–22.

[6]*China Trade Report,* April 1980, p. 9.

[7]"Readjusting the National Economy," p. 14.

[8]*Ming Pao Daily* (Hongkong), June 14, 1979, p. 1. Also see Martin Weil, "The Baoshan Steel Mill: A Symbol of Change in China's Industrial Development Strategy," in *China Under the Four Modernizations, Part 1, Selected Papers Submitted to the Joint Economic Committee, Congress of the United States* (Washington, DC: Government Printing Office, 1982), pp. 365–391.

[9]"Report on the Work of Government," *Beijing Review* 27 (July 6, 1979): 12–20. Also see *Far Eastern Economic Review,* October 5, 1979: 78–80.

[10]See Lowell Dittmer, "China in 1981: Reform, Readjustment, Rectification," *Asian Survey* 22, no. 2 (January 1982): 35.

[11]Interview with Huang Hua, then China's minister for foreign affairs, in Peter Stursberg, "Restructuring China Policy in the Wake of Chairman Mao," *Canadian Journal of World Affairs,* May–June 1981, p. 5.

[12]"Further Economic Readjustment: A Break with 'Leftist' Thinking," *Beijing Review* 12 (March 23, 1981): 27.

[13]Ibid., p. 28.

[14]*Asianweek,* February 20, 1981, p. 33.

[15]See Arthur G. Ashbrook, Jr., "China: Economic Modernization and Long-Term Performance," in *China Under the Four Modernizations,* p. 104.

[16]Ibid., p. 105.

[17]Ibid.

[18]CIA, *Handbook of International Economic Statistics* (Washington, DC: Central Intelligence Agency, 1997), pp. 20–22; CIA, *The World Factbook 1998* (Washington, DC: Central Intelligence Agency, 1998), at www.odci.gov/cia.

[19]Ibid.

[20]Ibid.

[21]W. Klatt, "The Staff of Life: Living Standards in China, 1977–81," *China Quarterly* 93 (March 1983): 20.

[22]*Beijing Review* 17 (April 24, 1982), 18; CIA, *The World Factbook* 1990, p. 64; ibid., 1993 edition, p. 81.

[23]Klatt, "The Staff of Life: Living Standards in China," p. 23.

[24]CHIFFA, vol. 17, p. 453; *Beijing Review,* February 17–23, 1992.

[25]Samuel P. S. Ho and Ralph W. Haenemann, *China's Open Door Policy: The Quest for Foreign Technology and Capital,* (Vancouver: University of British Columbia Press, 1984), pp. 49–52.

[26]See James C. F. Wang, "Capitalist Enclaves on Chinese Soil: The Special Economic Zones of Shenzhen and Zhuhai," paper given at Annual Meeting of the Southwestern Political Science Association, March 20–23; 1985, Houston, Texas.

[27]*A Great Trial in Chinese History* (New York: Pergamon Press, 1981), pp. 20–21.

[28]See Fox Butterfield, *China: Alive in the Bitter Sea* (New York: Times Books, 1982), p. 349.

[29]The Decision of the Central Committee at the CCP on Party Consolidation," *Beijing Review* 42 (October 17, 1983): iv.

[30]See Kjeld Erik Brodsguard, "The Democracy Wall Movement in China, 1978–1979: Opposition Movements, Wall Posters Campaign, and Underground Journals," *Asian Survey* 20, no. 7 (July 1981): 747–774.

[31]"The Democracy Wall Movement in China, 1978–1979"; and Melinda Liu, "Wei and the Fifth Modernization," *Far Eastern Economic Review*, November 27, 1979; 22–23.

[32]*Far Eastern Economic Review*, June 25, 1992, and July 2, 1992.

[33]U.S. Department of State, "China Country Report on Human Rights Practices for 1996," at www.usis.usemb.se/human/china.html (2/23/99).

[34]"Human Rights in China." Amnesty International Testimony before the Congress of the United States, House Committee on International Relations, January 20, 1999, at www.amnestyusa.org.ailib/aipub/1999/ASA/kumar01201999.html (2/22/99).

[35]"China after Tiananmen: Ten Years On," *The Economist*, June 15, 1999, p. 41.

CHINA: SELECTED BIBLIOGRAPHY

Byung-Joon Ahn, *Chinese Politics and the Cultural Revolution: Dynamics of Policy Processes* (Seattle: University of Washington Press, 1976).

Richard Baum, *Prelude to Revolution: Mao, the Party and the Peasant Question* (New York: Columbia University Press, 1975).

Richard Bernstein, and Ross H. Munro, *The Coming Conflict with China* (New York: Vintage Books, 1998).

John K. Fairbank, and Merle Goldman, *China: A New History* (Cambridge: Harvard University Press, 1998).

Lee Feigon, *China Rising: The Meaning of Tiananmen* (Chicago: Ivan Dee, 1990).

John Fraser, *The Chinese: Portrait of a People* (New York: Summit Books, 1980).

Maurice Freedman, *The Study of Chinese Society* (Stanford, CA: Stanford University Press, 1979).

David S. Goodman, *Deng Xiaoping: A Political Biography* (London and New York: Routledge: 1994).

Harry Harding, *Organizing China: The Problem of Bureaucracy, 1949–1970* (Stanford, CA: Stanford University Press, 1981).

Harold C. Hinton, ed., *The People's Republic of China: A Handbook* (Boulder, CO: Westview Press, 1979).

Francis L. K. Hsu, *Under the Ancestor's Shadow: Kinship, Personality, and Social Mobility in China* (Stanford, CA: Stanford University Press, 1967).

Willem van Kemenade, *China, Hong-Kong, Taiwan, Inc.* (New York: Vintage Books: 1998).

Nicholas D. Kristof, and Sheryl Wudunn, *China Awakes: The Struggle for the Soul of a Rising Power* (New York: Vintage Books, 1995).

Hong Yung Lee, *The Politics of the Chinese Cultural Revolution: A Case Study* (Berkeley: University of California Press, 1978).

Perry Link, *Evening Chats in Beijing* (New York: W. W. Norton & Co., 1992).

Alan P. L. Liu, *Political Culture and Group Conflict in China* (Santa Barbara, CA: Clio Books, 1976).

Roderick MacFarquhar, *The Origins of the Cultural Revolution* (New York: Columbia University Press: 1974).

Steven W. Mosher, *China Misperceived: American Illusions and Chinese Reality* (N.p.: A New Republic Book/Basic Books, 1990).

David Mozingo, *State and Society in Contemporary China* (Ithaca, NY: Cornell University Press, 1983).

Michel Oksenberg, Lawrence R. Sullivan, and Marc Lambert, (eds.), *Beijing Spring 1989, Confrontation and Conflict: The Basic Documents* (Armonk, NY: M. E. Sharpe, 1990).

Shu-tse Peng, *The Chinese Communist Party in Power* (New York: Monad Press, 1980).

Harrison Salisbury, *The New Emperors: China in the Era of Mao and Deng* (New York: Avon Books, 1992).

Orville Schell, and David Shambaugh, *The China Reader: The Reform Era* (New York: Vintage Books, 1998).

Ross Terrill, *China in Our Time* (New York: A Touchstone Book, 1993).

Jeffrey N. Wasserstrom and Elizabeth J. Perry, eds., *Popular Protest and Political Culture in Modern China: Learning from 1989* (Boulder, CO: Westview, 1992).

Robert Weil, *Red Cat, White Cat: China and the Contradictions of Market Socialism* (New York: Monthly Review Press, 1996).

Margery Wolf, *Revolution Postponed: Women in Contemporary China* (Stanford, CA: Stanford University Press, 1985).

Chapter 37

Historical Roots
of Divided Nigeria

Speaking for my generation, our attitude was that we were on the threshold of not only rediscovering ourselves as a people but of transforming ourselves in a way which would astound the colonial powers who had held us down for so long. . . . We would not, at the time, envisage any power stopping us. It took a while to realize that the internal hazards were our principal enemy. So largely, those promises have not been fulfilled.[1]

In 1960, as it achieved independence from Britain, many observers expected Nigeria to be one of the most likely prospects for a stable, democratic government among the many newly independent and about-to-be independent countries of Africa. The new Nigerian constitution was patterned on the Westminster form of parliamentary democracy that had worked so well in providing effective government in Britain and other former British colonies. Nigeria was one of the few newly independent states to emerge from colonial rule with a genuine multiparty system essential to the democratic selection of political leaders. It had a large number of British-educated leaders who had gained valuable political experience during the colonial era. It was the most populous country in Africa and had important

natural and human resources on which to base a growing economy. Indeed, from most viewpoints, Nigeria's future as an independent state appeared bright.

Six years later, this dream turned into the nightmare of military rule and then civil war. The imported parliamentary framework was unable to cope with the country's divisive forces; the multiparty system accentuated regional and ethnic differences; conflict over the pattern and location of economic development further divided the country. Eventually, when the Eastern Region sought to secede and form an independent state to be called Biafra, a tragic civil war took over a million lives.

PRECOLONIAL NIGERIA

As is the case in many other former colonial states, modern Nigeria does not correspond to any historical political unit. Its frontiers were established by European powers to fit the whims of colonial administrators and international politics rather than to conform to the boundaries of human geography. Modern Nigeria is, in fact, a

NIGERIA

consolidation of many ethnic groups, each of which has its own distinctive political history and background.

In northern Nigeria, the Hausa, Fulani, and Kanuri peoples came under the influence of Islamic cultures centuries ago. Situated on the fringes of the great desert, trans-Saharan traders selling goods for a prosperous Muslim world came about 700 A.D. in search of ivory, leather, ostrich feathers, and non-Moslems for slaves. Eventually, the peoples of northern Nigeria accepted Islam and became part of several well-developed Muslim empires. One of these empires, the Kanem-Borno empire, which

emerged in the ninth and tenth centuries and reached its peak in the middle of the thirteenth century, was centered in what is now northeastern Nigeria and Chad. Elsewhere in northern Nigeria small city-states developed among the Hausa peoples. Among the most important of these were Katsina, Zaria, Gobir, and Kano. As the rulers of these city-states accepted Islam, so did their peoples, spreading a common culture throughout Hausaland. The various political units had ties with the Islamic world and participated in the sixteenth-century conflict between the Sultan of Morocco and the Ottoman Sultan at Istanbul for the leadership of Islam.

The city-states and empires of northern Nigeria acquired well-developed bureaucracies to provide centralized rule. These were not modern civil services based on rational principles, efficiency, and open recruitment of skilled personnel; they were nevertheless impressive organizations for their time. Despite the common religion and culture, there was no unified political structure in northern Nigeria, since the separate city-states remained largely autonomous and occasionally battled each other. The political heritage of northern Nigeria is one of decentralized autocratic rule through hereditary emirs. Eligibility for positions of political and social status was conferred by birth and was viewed by the Hausas as a "gift of Allah."[2]

In the eighteenth and nineteenth centuries, Hausaland came under the control of the Fulanis, another Islamic people. During the centuries of Hausa predominance, the Fulanis had been nomadic cattle herders, although some Fulanis had risen to prominent positions in Hausa royal courts. As the Hausa empire declined and pagan religions reemerged in the eighteenth century, the Fulanis launched a holy war, or *jihad,* to reestablish Islam. By the middle of the nineteenth century, a Fulani empire stretched across all of what is now northern Nigeria and into Chad and Cameroon. The empire was made up of numerous semiautonomous emirates united by their common acceptance of the religious leadership of the Sultan of Sokoto and by the rule in most of these emirates of a Fulani aristocracy. Fulani rule established one of the most centralized kingdoms in Africa and a rigid class hierarchy. Together these political features "inculcated habits and attitudes of political deference and subordination" in the peoples of northern Nigeria.[3]

Dense tropical forests and the diseases carried by the tsetse fly blocked expansion of Islam into the southern portions of what we now call Nigeria. In the southwestern region, two related kingdoms developed among the Yoruba peoples. There is no written history of these kingdoms so the origins of the Yoruba and their governments are obscure, but we know the kingdoms flourished between the fifteenth and nineteenth centuries. The kingdoms of Yoruba and Benin were highly centralized and effective. They were, however, vulnerable to European incursions because of their proximity to the coast.

By the fifteenth century, Portuguese traders had established outposts along the West African coast, including one in the Benin port of Gwato. Over the next 400 years, some 24 million slaves were exported from West Africa. Nigerian ports were so heavily involved in the slave trade that Nigeria became known as the Slave Coast. At the height of the slave trade, some 22,000 slaves a year were shipped from Nigerian ports.[4] The people sold as slaves were often captives from the numerous civil wars that swept Yorubaland during this period. Other slaves were thieves whose punishment was to be sold into slavery. Nigerians who were shipped to America as slaves lost their ethnic identities, but many American blacks have their origins in Yorubaland.[5]

Among the Yorubas, political institutions were not as centralized nor as highly developed as in the north. There was somewhat broader participation in the political decision-making processes. Yoruba leaders were selected from clan elders. The chiefs participated in a council that selected the *oba* or king. Traditionally, the chiefs emerged because of their lineage or birth rather than because of their own achievements. In the twentieth century, however, the title of chief has been accorded to individuals who have distinguished themselves by their service to their communities.[6] Politics in Yorubaland soon became a principal means for upward social mobility.[7]

In southeastern Nigeria, there were numerous groups of people who later became known as the Ibos. Dense tropical forests in this region protected these tribes from outsiders and even reduced contacts among the Ibo tribal and clan groups. It was only in modern times when these groups came in contact with outsiders— Europeans, Yorubas, and Hausa-Fulanis—that they began to identify themselves as Ibos or as a single people.[8] There is no record of a common political unit among the Ibo people prior to the arrival of the Europeans. Each clan or village unit was autonomous and had few political ties with other Ibo groups. Each had its own dialect, religion, and legends on group origins. Typically, the largest political unit in Iboland was the village.[9]

Political power was always decentralized in the Eastern Region, with each Ibo village enjoying considerable autonomy. Among the Ibos, political participation was open to many. At the local level, political power was rarely autocratic and was usually shared by much of the community, including the women. Some Ibo villages did not even have chiefs; in these areas village elders formed a collective political leadership.

This brief summary of the political backgrounds and values of the three principal communal groups illustrates the variety of political legacies that modern Nigeria inherited. Beyond these major groups there were dozens of other ethnic groups, each with its own distinctive political culture and traditions. These varied peoples eventually were amalgamated under colonial rule into a single state. The separate political histories and values affected the ways in which the peoples of Nigeria responded to European colonization. The northern peoples—with a well-developed culture and political structure—resisted European influence and changes. The Ibos, and to a lesser degree the Yorubas, were more vulnerable to Western ideas.

COLONIAL ERA

British influence in Western Africa dates at least to early in the nineteenth century. Britain had outlawed slave trade in 1807. Out of the desire to control others engaged in slave trade—on moral grounds or on the practical ground of preventing others from benefiting from a lucrative business the British no longer wished to exploit—the British stationed a naval squadron off the coast of West Africa. Eventually, the British began to promote other trade and to support missionary work in the coastal areas of Nigeria.

Initial contacts seem to have been motivated by a European notion of "civilizing" Africa through control of slavery and the abolition of human sacrifice rather than by the need for natural resources. But the British did develop an extensive market for Nigerian palm oil. As their political and economic interests in Nigeria expanded, the British formally acquired control over the area. Lagos became a British colony in 1861; all of Yorubaland became a British protectorate in 1888, with Iboland added to what was called the Niger Coast Protectorate in 1893. Northern Nigeria resisted British penetration and it was not until the conquest of Sokoto in 1903 that the sultans

and emirs of the north accepted British rule. The irrationality of colonial-era world politics is well illustrated in this case since part of Hausaland, one of the more developed precolonial political entities in Africa, ended up in the British colony and the rest under French rule in the colony eventually known as Niger.[10] The British incorporated the impoverished and remote northern region primarily to prevent the French from adding it to their African holdings.[11] The colony acquired its name from the African correspondent of the *Times* of London, who invented the term "Nigeria" as a convenient means of identifying the diverse peoples and regions that had been added to the empire. By 1914, the colony had the name and approximate borders of modern Nigeria.

The British used an indirect form of rule in Nigeria and other colonies. Unlike the French, who set up entirely new political orders in their colonies, the British preferred to rule through existing native political institutions. The British colonial administrators calculated that one European officer could not control more than one or two hundred subjects. With Nigeria's population at the time well over 10 million, direct imperial rule would require a vast army of colonial officers. Nigeria was not a rich colony and could not provide sufficient revenue to support such an apparatus.

Thus, the British opted for indirect rule through existing, indigenous political institutions. In Nigeria, the British negotiated with the northern emirs and sultans, the Yoruba royalty, and Ibo leaders, offering them local self-rule and British support for their positions in exchange for the native leaders' acceptance of general British guidelines and acknowledgment of Britain's supremacy. In some cases, this meant that the British propped up otherwise decaying traditional institutions. In others, it simply reinforced the power of traditional rulers.

The British saw this as the most efficient way to rule their far-flung empire. Indirect rule allowed them to protect their economic interests and British nationals without having to expend large amounts of money and manpower to set up local governments. It also minimized British involvement in local politics. In Nigeria, a British governor-general supervised the whole colony with the assistance of two British lieutenant-governors, one for the north and the other for the south. These British colonial leaders exercised much of their control through the native leaders.

As a consequence of this indirect rule, there was considerable variation in programs and policies in the different parts of Nigeria depending upon the local leaders and situations. Indirect rule permitted the maintenance and sometimes even the reinforcement of traditional political and social power structures. For example, in northern Nigeria, the emirs were able to win British agreement to respect their Islamic religion and legal system in exchange for their declarations of fealty to the British Crown. Furthermore, British support for the emirs' political positions and prerogatives enhanced the power and legitimacy of these traditional leaders.

The indirect pattern of colonial rule accentuated regional differences in Nigeria. The southern areas, because of their proximity to the coast and their less-developed religions, were more vulnerable to European influence. European missionaries brought Christianity to these peoples and found acceptance since the indigenous religions were not resistant to the new religious beliefs and practices. In the north, missionary work was limited by the agreement to respect Islam and by the highly developed religion already in place.

Since missionaries and not the colonial state operated the schools, the southern peoples soon became better educated than the northerners. The Ibos and Yorubas became more westernized and better able to deal with the British colonial rulers and with western economic matters than the more traditional northerners. Hence, economic development proceeded more rapidly in the south, and native leaders in Nigeria were more often southerners than northerners.

INDEPENDENCE

Nigeria's efforts to achieve independence from British rule began almost as soon as the colony was consolidated in 1914. Woodrow Wilson's call for self-determination of all peoples in the Fourteen Points that Americans sought in the First World War inspired hopes for self-rule in the colonial areas of Africa and Asia as well as in the Balkan states of Europe. In Nigeria, this hope was quickly picked up by the European-trained teachers, clerks, merchants, doctors, and lawyers. As early as the 1920s, nationalist groups seeking home rule and later independence had begun operating. Among the early leaders of the independence movement was Herbert Macauley. The grandson of the first black bishop in the Anglican Church, Macauley studied in England and returned to Nigeria as a colonial civil servant. He soon launched himself into politics and in 1923 founded the Nigerian National Democratic Party (NNDP).

The NNDP was one of the first Nigerian political movements to advocate independence from Britain. By the mid-1930s, it was challenged by a new and more militant nationalist movement led by Nnamdi Azikiwe, the Nigerian Youth Movement. Regional and ethnic differences were soon evident in the various independence movements. Eventually, separate nationalist groups developed in each area: the Ibo-dominated National Council of Nigeria and the Cameroons (NCNC—known as the National Congress of Nigerian Citizens after independence) in the southeast; the Yoruba-led Action Group in the southwest; and the Northern Peoples' Congress (NPC) among the Hausa-Fulani peoples of the north.

Even in their efforts to oppose British imperial rule these groups found it difficult to unite. Each movement became involved in political struggles in its own region and defended regional interests in national politics. As the British began to devolve political authority to native politicians after World War II, the competition among educated Nigerians who wanted the new positions of power and prestige increased. Aspiring leaders recognized that their best source of support would come from their own ethnic group. This heightened the ethnic rivalries and made demands for independence more strident. As one writer notes, in the early electoral contests "tribalism was the dominant note; but when appealing to the people for support, the competing parties strove to outdo each other in the use of nationalist slogans."[12]

The NPC was markedly less enthusiastic about immediate independence than were the NCNC or Action Group. Northerners recognized that with only a few university graduates and only

2000 elementary school graduates, the north would not be able to govern even in their own region if the British left, and they certainly would be overwhelmed by southerners in national politics.[13] In 1954 the NPC refused to support a motion in the advisory legislative council calling for full independence in 2 years. When the NPC delegates left the hall, an angry crowd of nationalists harassed them. A few days later, mobs in the north sought revenge for this indignity by attacking southerners living in northern cities.

The British experimented with a variety of legislative councils and advisory bodies to deflect appeals for Nigerian independence. Separate councils were organized in each region and later a national council was established in Lagos. These quasi-legislative bodies had limited power and served generally as advisory councils to the British-appointed governor-general. They did provide a forum for Nigerians to present their needs and their demands for independence. They also gave experience to Nigerian politicians in preparation for self-rule.

Nigerians were also recruited to serve in the colonial civil service and the military. Unfortunately, once again the consequence was to heighten regional and ethnic rivalries. It was the better-educated and westernized southerners who filled most of the posts in preindependence government bodies. Northerners became involved in national politics later than did the others and were disadvantaged in competing for civil service and military jobs because they lacked European education. Northerners resented this and saw it as evidence of discrimination against them by the Ibos and Yorubas as well as by the British.

By the mid-1950s, Britain had agreed to grant independence to its Nigerian colony after a brief transition period. In October 1960, Nigeria became an independent state, one of 17 former African colonies to win independence that year. The constitution of this First Nigerian Republic was based on British parliamentary government with a prime minister and cabinet dependent upon the support of a majority of parliament. However, unlike the centralized British state, Nigeria had a federal structure of three "states": the Northern, Eastern, and Western Regions.[14] Each region had considerable autonomy and controlled the national civil service operating in its region.

The new democratic political system soon proved inadequate to meet the challenge of unifying and developing Nigeria. With the various political parties speaking for regional and ethnic interests, parliamentary government failed. As one Nigerian observer notes, parliamentary government cannot function where "parties are devoted not to working out those means which are most conducive to an accepted national end but to discovering the extent that the constitutional means can be used to further particular, i.e., regional or ethnic ends."[15] Nigerians talked about their government in terms of "chop, chop politics," meaning efforts by ethnic-based parties to assure an equal distribution of the nation's resources among the different ethnic groups. The problem with chop, chop politics was that the emphasis was on cutting up the economic cake with no reciprocal emphasis on baking it.[16] A new Nigerian middle class developed and became obviously wealthy while the vast majority of Nigerians saw little improvement in their lives. Corruption was widespread and the new democratic government soon lost its legitimacy in the eyes of many Nigerians.

Equally important as a source of the growing political crisis in Nigeria was the inability of the new regime to preserve domestic order. Political brinkmanship on the part of all the major parties brought tensions and periodic violence. Disputes broke out over a 1962 census which indicated that the population of the north far exceeded that of all the rest of Nigeria. Southerners, fearful that the census would result in political dominance by the more traditional and allegedly more authoritarian northerners, challenged the accuracy of the census. Northerners saw this as an attempt by southerners to perpetuate their control of the national government. There were periodic incidents of ethnic violence such as attacks on Ibos in northern cities and the Tiv uprising of 1964–66. Election campaigns were accompanied by violence and results of the elections were regularly denounced as fraudulent or rigged. By the end of 1965, unrest and violence were common throughout Nigeria. In the Western Region, a near-total breakdown of law and order provided the immediate cause for the military to step in and throw out the civilian government.

Nigeria's vast oil deposits offer an important source of foreign income not available to most other developing countries. Critics allege that much of this income is wasted as a result of widespread corruption. (*Photographer/ Source:* United Nations)

THE MILITARY IN POWER

Nigeria has been ruled by military regimes for 29 of its 40 years of independence. The frequency of military coups and regime changes have made Nigeria among the least stable states in Africa (see Table 37–1). The first coup came in January 1966, six years after independence. A group of young Ibo military officers attempted a coup, assassinating the prime minister, several other leading government figures, and the majority of all military officers above the rank of major. The remaining members of the government asked a surviving senior military officer, Major General Johnson Aguyi-Ironsi, to take over the government. The coup leaders surrendered but Ironsi suspended the constitution, ending the First Republic. He then organized a new military regime under his own leadership. It does not appear in retrospect that the initial coup was motivated directly by ethnic considerations. But the leaders of the abortive coup were Ibos, and Ibo political leaders—by design or accident—escaped assassination while political leaders from other ethnic groups were killed. Furthermore, the ultimate beneficiary of the coup, General Ironsi, was also an Ibo.

All this led many northerners to interpret the coup in ethnic terms. Northerners also believed the coup was an attempt to counter the growing political influence of their region. Five months later, Ironsi announced a new constitution that created a centralized government and bureaucracy. Northerners responded immediately and violently. Rioters in northern cities attacked Ibos and produced hundreds of casualties. In July 1966, a new military coup led by northern officers resulted in Ironsi's assassination and the overthrow of his government. Northern army men took revenge

Table 37–1   Important Landmarks in Nigerian History

1400s	Portuguese slave trade begins
1861	Lagos becomes a British colony
1888–1901	Various parts of what is now Nigeria brought under British colonial rule
1950	Constitutional Council begins deliberations on self-government in Nigeria
1951	Administrative regions set up along ethnic lines in the North, West, and East
1960	Nigeria gains independence and establishes the First Republic
1966	First military coups bring military-dominated government with General Yakubu Gowon as eventual leader
1967–1970	Biafran Civil War
1974	General Gowon ousted in coup that brought into power military leaders committed to a rapid transition to civilian government
1979–1983	Second Nigerian Republic with civilian rule under President Shehu Shagari
1983	Military coup ousts the Second Republic and installs General Muhammed Buhari
1985	Military coup ousts Buhari and replaces him with General Ibrahim Babangida as the new military leader
1992–1993	New political parties organized and elections held in preparation for the return to civilian rule
1993	Babangida declares presidential election to be invalid. Turns rule over to a civilian, Ernest Shonekan, to prepare new elections. Within weeks Shonekan is overthrown and General Sani Abacha becomes the new dictator
1998	Abacha dies of heart attack. New military leader, Abdulsalami Abubakar, plans rapid return to civilian rule
1999	Olusegun Obasanjo elected president and democracy is restored under the Third Republic

for the murder of their fellow countrymen 6 months earlier by executing Ibo officers and soldiers. Eventually, Lieutenant Colonel Yakubu Gowon emerged as the new military ruler of Nigeria.

Gowon was a Tiv, a minority ethnic group in the north. He had the confidence of the northern people but not of the Ibos. After the July 1966 coup, northerners continued their battles against Ibo influence by attacking Ibos living in the north. An estimated 10,000 Ibos were killed in riots and massacres that the Gowon government was not able to prevent. Ibos living in the north fled to their homeland, creating millions of refugees. In the south, and especially in the Eastern Region, there was retaliation against the smaller number of northern immigrants living there and these peoples were forced to leave for the north.

In the Eastern Region, the military governor, Lieutenant Colonel Odumegwu Ojukwu, began to ignore the central government and to act independently. On May 30, 1967, Ojukwu declared the secession of the Eastern Region and the formation of a new, independent Republic of Biafra. Gowon's government regarded this as a rebellion and directed the military to suppress it. By early 1968, Nigerian troops occupied the coastal portions of Biafra and cut off the remaining rebel forces from outside supplies. It took nearly two more years and over 600,000 deaths before Ojukwu fled the country and the last of the rebels surrendered.[17]

The Biafrans fought in desperation because they believed that the northern Muslims were bent on genocide of the Christianized Ibo people. These fears were real among the Ibos but greatly exaggerated.

After Biafra's surrender in 1970, the Gowon government avoided retaliation against the rebel forces or the Ibo people. A general amnesty freed from punishment all those who fought against the Nigerian army with the exception of a few leaders who served short prison sentences. This conciliatory approach by the Gowon government to the Ibos was an important first step in healing the ethnic divisions that had compromised Nigeria's debut as a new country.

While ethnic tensions declined after 1970, there were still occasional episodes of political turmoil. In July 1975, a military coup overthrew General Gowon for failing to fulfill his promise to return the country to civilian government. General Murtala Mohammed headed the new military regime and began drafting a new constitution for a civilian government. A countercoup against this regime failed but not before Mohammed was assassinated. He was replaced as head of state by Lieutenant General Olusegun Obasanjo. Obasanjo continued the preparations for the return to civilian government. On October 1, 1979, a new democratic constitution took effect and the military stepped back out of politics. This Second Nigerian Republic lasted only 4 years, with a military coup returning the military to power on December 31, 1983.

The coup occurred in a growing economic crisis produced by the drastic fall in the country's petroleum revenues. The loss of these revenues meant ambitious development plans had to be abandoned, sometimes in the middle of construction. Perhaps even more important in understanding why the military returned to politics in 1983 was the corruption of the political leaders both in the accumulation of personal fortunes and in widespread electoral fraud during the 1983 elections.

The new military regime, headed by Brigadier-General Muhammed Buhari, dissolved the institutions of the Second Republic and instituted a new era of military rule. In August 1985, a coup once again toppled the Buhari regime and replaced him with another military leader, Major-General Ibrahim Babangida. The Babangida regime began preparations for a return to civilian rule under the military's tutelage. By the end of the 1980s, parties were authorized and some local-level elections were held in preparation for a planned return to civilian rule in 1993. However, the parties were ephemeral and lacked public support. While the military regime moved toward a planned transition to democracy, it hindered the creation of the underlying supports that a democratic government would need to survive.[18]

Legislative elections were held in 1992 and a presidential election in 1993. The presidential election was supposed to result in the transfer of power from the military to civilians and the beginning of Nigeria's Third Republic. The two candidates—one a Northern Muslim, the other a Yoruba Muslim—had the approval of the military, but during the campaign the Yoruba candidate, Moshood K. O. Abiola, demonstrated more independence from the military than expected. When early results from the election suggested that Abiola would win, General Babingida halted the counting of the ballots and declared the

election invalid. In the face of mounting opposition, Babingida resigned and turned power over to a civilian leader, Ernest Shonekan, who was supposed to prepare for new presidential elections. However, Shonekan was overturned within weeks by a new military coup.

The new military leader, General Sani Abacha, gave little hope that the process of democratization would be renewed in the immediate future. He too refused to recognize the validity of the presidential election and eventually jailed the apparent winner of that election, Moshood Abiola. The military's hold on politics was increased; the legislative bodies that had earlier been elected were abolished and all political activity barred. Civil rights, generally respected by prior Nigerian military dictators, were drastically curtailed. The Abacha regime soon encountered stiff opposition from advocates of democracy. A general strike calling for the restoration of democracy paralyzed the nation during the summer of 1994. But Abacha arrested strike leaders, dissolved the leadership of striking unions, and successfully broke the strike. Abacha's rule was characterized by the most oppressive dictatorship in Nigeria's post-independence.[19] It was also more turbulent and violent than any time since the early 1960s. The Abacha era was a time of "predatory rule" due to the willingness of all in power to plunder the national treasury and because of Abacha's ruthlessness.[20] In the face of protests from ethnic groups, labor unions, intellectuals, dissidents in the army, and others, Abacha ruled heavy-handedly until his death of natural causes in June 1998. He was succeeded by another military leader, General Abdulsalami Abubakar. Abubakar immediately loosened controls over civil liberties and freed many political prisoners jailed by his predecessor. Abubakar pledged to return Nigeria to full civilian rule within a year. His promise was honored and the formation of political parties and conduct of local, congressional, and eventually presidential elections proceeded free of military interference.

In May 1999, civilian rule returned, albeit under the presidency of a former military leader, Olusegun Obasanjo. Obasanjo had been Nigeria's leader in the mid-1970s and worked diligently for the establishment of the Second Republic. Later he retired from military service and was accused by Abacha of trying to over-throw him. He spent three years in Abacha's pris-ons. His election as a civilian president in 1999 was fair and democratic. Even with a former gen-eral and military leader as the president, Nige-ria's government was civilian rather than military in form for the first time in nearly 17 years.

THE PAST AND MODERN NIGERIA

In 1937, the Nigerian nationalist leader Nnamdi Azikiwe called for the rebirth of Africa and evoked the vision of a new Africa where the dis-graces and divisions of the past could be forgot-ten.[21] Independence and self-rule would pave the way to breaking the bonds of poverty and over-coming ethnic divisions.

The first 4 decades of independence in Nige-ria failed to see the dawning of the new age. Lega-cies from the past—both from precolonial and colonial eras—brought ethnic conflict and vio-lence into the independent state of Nigeria. The difficulties of ruling a large and diverse country were too much for the fragile democratic struc-tures of the First Republic established in 1960. The military's efforts to achieve a more unified country and a more workable political framework are still uncertain of success. The advent of the Second Republic in 1979 offered renewed hope for progress toward Azikiwe's dream of a New Africa. But the failure of this second attempt at democracy proved that the historical problems that destroyed the first effort of this renaissance had not yet been overcome. The return of civilian rule in 1999 offers the possibility that Nigeria's rebirth may see the fulfillment of a vision of an Africa free from the disgraces and divisions of the past in the new century.

NOTES

[1]Wole Soyinka, Nigerian playwright, poet, and novelist, in *New York Times Book Review,* 23 June 1985.

[2]M. G. Smith, *The Economy of Hausa Communities of Zaria* (London: HMSO, 1955), p. 93.

[3]James S. Coleman, *Nigeria: Background to Nationalism* (Berkeley: University of California Press, 1960), p. 39.

[4]Michael Crowder, *The Story of Nigeria,* 4th ed. (London: Faber and Faber, 1978), p. 53.

[5]See Alex Haley, *Roots* (New York: Doubleday, 1978).

[6]Richard L. Sklar, *Nigerian Political Parties: Power in an Emergent African Nation* (Princeton, NJ: Princeton University Press, 1963), pp. 11–12.

[7]Oshomha Imoagene, *Social Mobility in Emergent Soci-ety: A Study of the New Elite in Western Nigeria* (Canberra: Australian National University, 1976), pp. 1–37.

[8]Robert Melson and Howard Wolpe, "Modernization and the Politics of Communalism: A Theoretical Perspective," in Melson and Wolpe, eds. *Nigeria: Modernization and the Pol-itics of Communalism* (Lansing: Michigan State University Press, 1971).

[9]Coleman, *Nigeria,* p. 30.

[10]William F. S. Miles, *Hausaland Divided: Colonialism and Independence in Nigeria and Niger* (Ithaca, NY: Cornell University Press, 1994).

[11]Robert Heussler, *British in Northern Nigeria* (London: Oxford University Press, 1968).

[12]James S. Coleman, "The Ibo and Yoruba Strands in Nigerian Nationalism," in Melson and Wolpe, *Nigeria,* p. 90.

[13]Crowder, *The Story of Nigeria,* p. 241.

[14]Shortly after independence a fourth state, the Midwest-ern Region, was created in the south.

[15]Moyibi Amoda, "Background to the Conflict: A Sum-mary of Nigeria's Political History from 1914 to 1964," in Josep Okpaku, ed. *Nigeria: Dilemma of Nationhood: An African Analysis of the Biafran Conflict* (Westport, CT: Green-wood Press, 1972), pp. 15–16.

[16]Okwudiba Nnoli, "The Nigerian-Biafra Conflict: A Po-litical Analysis," in Okpaku, *Nigeria,* pp. 121, 149.

[17]An accurate figure on the casualties in the Biafran war is elusive. The figure of 600,000 is given by John de St. Jorre, *The Brothers' War: Biafra and Nigeria* (Boston: Houghton Mifflin, 1972), p. 412.

[18]Julius Ihonvbere and Olufemi Vaughan, "Nigeria: Democracy and Civil Society: the Nigerian Transition Pro-gramme 1985–1993," in John A. Wiseman, ed., *Democracy and Political Change in Sub-Saharan Africa* (London: Rout-ledge, 1995).

[19]Peter Lewis, Barnett R. Rubin, and Pearl T. Robinson, *Stabilizing Nigeria: Sanctions, Incentives, and Support for Civil Society* (New York: The Council on Foreign Relations and The Century Foundation, 1998).

[20]Peter M. Lewis, "An End to the Permanent Transition?" *Journal of Democracy* 10 (January 1999): 145ff.

[21]Nnamdi Azikiwe, *Renascent Africa* (London: Frank Cass, 1968).

Chapter 38

Social Cleavages
and Nigerian Politics

One of the major problems for all modern countries is the need to integrate different social and cultural groups residing within their boundaries. This task of political integration involves creating a sense of belonging to a single political unit among the various social categories that are found in a country. It means development of a loyalty to a national entity that is superior to primordial ties to clan, religion, or ethnic group. It is a continuing political process, involving agreement on a national language or languages, acceptance of a uniform set of political symbols that evoke emotional support for the state and feelings of patriotism (a flag, national anthem, heroes, martyrs), and the building of new loyalties to the state.

In later stages of integration, it means the promotion of national unity among the various social class strata. In short, political integration is the process whereby loyalties and attachments to religious, linguistic, regional, social class, or racial groups are weakened and attachment to a broader political unit—the nation-state—is promoted as the object of the individual's ultimate political loyalty.

The newly independent state of Nigeria faced a major problem in political integration. Its historical legacy gave modern politicians a state divided by serious social and cultural differences. The social tensions soon proved far beyond the capacity of the still fragile political institutions and untrained leaders. Military rule and civil war were the consequences of the collapse of the state as it faced the multiple social divisions. The most important division, and the one that ultimately exploded in civil war, was the division into separate ethnic groups. Other divisions in Nigerian society—class, region, religion, language—generally reinforced rather than cut across these ethnic cleavages.

The major problem of political integration in Nigeria has been the overcoming of the ethnic divisions and the creation of loyalties to a Nigerian political unit. One African observer argues that the underlying problem is "the fact that national politics was introduced into Nigeria at a time when the individual had no attachment, or had no reason in fact for any commitment, to national government."[1]

ETHNICITY AND POLITICS

Nigeria includes within its borders three of the most populous ethnic groups in Africa: the Hausa-Fulani, the Ibo, and the Yoruba. There are also several hundred other ethnic or linguistic groups ranging in size from several million to a few thousand. The largest group, the Hausa-Fulani people of the north, is really two separate ethnic groups that speak the same language (Hausa). The Fulani people conquered the Hausa in the nineteenth century and then gradually became assimilated into the Hausa culture.[2] But families still trace their lineage back to either Hausa or Fulani ancestors. The differences among the Hausa-Fulani, Ibo, and Yoruba are manifold, including religion, language, cultural traditions, and social and occupational patterns. Writing of the various ethnic groups in modern Nigeria, one prominent political leader noted: "It is a mistake to designate them as 'tribes.' Each of them is a nation by itself with many tribes and clans. There is as much difference between them as there is between Germans, English, Russians, and Turks, for instance."[3]

The extent to which individuals identify themselves with a particular ethnic group varies considerably. For many Nigerians, the basic focal point of self-identification in relation to society as a whole is with the family, kinsmen, or the hometown village. In eastern Nigeria, where Ibo villages were isolated by dense tropical forest, a sense of identity beyond the village and family to an Ibo ethnic group did not develop until after contacts were made with outsiders in relatively recent decades.[4] Even as ties developed to the broader ethnic group, Ibos and other Nigerian peoples retained their primordial attachments to the clan and home town.

The greater mobility of peoples in modern times has increased contacts between individuals from different communal groups. Inevitably, these contacts sometimes produced conflict between the native residents of a town or village and the newcomers, even if they were from the same ethnic group. Thus, even within the same ethnic groups, there are tensions produced by continuing attachments to even more fundamental social groups such as villages, clans, and families.

The pattern of ethnic conflict in Nigeria is complicated by the interaction of at least two types of conflict. The most evident is the tension among the major ethnic groups: the Hausa-Fulani, Ibo, and Yoruba. The conflict among these groups has dominated Nigerian politics since before independence. A second source of tension is the conflict between the large ethnic groups, individually and collectively, and the hundreds of smaller ethnic groups residing alongside them. To some extent, the smaller ethnic groups became pawns in the broader battles of the large groups, joining one side or the other of the major ethnic-linked conflicts. But the smaller groups also seek to protect their own distinctiveness and autonomy. This often means hostility to the large ethnic groups closest to them, and thus most menacing to their independence, even if there are racial and cultural similarities with the larger group.

The source of ethnic conflict, whether it is between the major groups or between larger groups and smaller minority groups, is not found in bigotry and prejudice. The real heart of ethnic conflict in Nigeria is that "hostility derives not from ethnic differences but from competition between different peoples for wealth and power."[5] Politicians from each group seek to obtain greater political power and economic benefits for their own people rather than seeking the good of a united Nigeria.

A major political manifestation of ethnicity is the alignment of ethnic groups behind political leaders coming from their own ethnic group. During the first republic (1960–66), political parties became closely linked with separate ethnic groups. Even parties that had originated as national independence movements during the colonial years and that had attempted to unite all Nigerians regardless of ethnic background evolved into political parties drawing their support and leadership primarily from a single ethnic group. Thus, the National Council of Nigeria and the Cameroons was organized as a national independence movement appealing to all Nigerians to unite against British rule but ended up as a party based on the Ibo people (the National Congress of Nigerian Citizens NCNC). The Northern Peoples' Congress (NPC) emerged to defend the interests of the Hausa-Fulani peoples and the Action Group developed in the west as a Yoruba alternative.

All these parties sought initial support beyond their own ethnic groups, but with diminishing success. Where they did succeed in attracting other ethnic groups' votes was from among minority peoples outside their own regions who voted for a party other than that of the regional majority. For example, the NCNC, with its base among the Ibos in the east, garnered many votes in the west and midwest among minority groups who wanted to defend themselves against the Yorubas and Yoruba-dominated Action Group.[6] There were some doctrinal and policy differences among these parties, but voters distinguished between them on the basis of their ethnic identification. They generally opted to vote "for their own kind" rather than for a specific doctrine or set of policies.

Since the parties were closely tied to particular ethnic groups, their electoral strategies focused not so much on broadening their base to include new social categories but rather on how to mobilize the seemingly fixed group of supporters in order to maximize turnout. For instance, it was not likely that the Ibo-led NCNC could attract many Yoruba votes so they worked instead to increase voter turnout among the Ibos and minority groups hostile to the Yorubas. Often the best way to increase turnout was to heighten the fear of electoral defeat by warning their voters about the consequences should the other party or ethnic group win the election. In the extreme, it meant telling your supporters that the other side's victory would mean genocide. Unfortunately, in the last years before the military coups of 1966, this fear of genocide was sometimes used as an electoral ploy. Obviously, such electoral appeals increased tension among the ethnic groups and often led to violence during and after the campaigns. It was eventually evident that the parties were exploiting ethnic tensions and hatreds for their own ends. Because of the parties' contributions to ethnic tensions and violence, one of the first acts of the military government after the coup of January 1966 was to disband the parties.

A second political manifestation of ethnicity and communalism is found in the recruitment of political leaders. Traditional leaders, chiefs and emirs, continue to be prominent within Nigeria's leadership. In part, this was the product of Britain's indirect form of colonial rule that had placed these traditional ethnic leaders in positions of prominence during the colonial era. However, strong traditions of loyalty to clan and village remain important in Nigerian life and further this communal trend in recruiting political leaders. Individuals brought into public office by election or appointment use their influence to find jobs or government contracts for members of their extended families, clans, villages, or ethnic groups. Often they are the sons of chiefs or clan leaders and feel a strong obligation toward their own. This loyalty to primordial groups prevails over the presumed commitment to recruit public officials on the basis of ability or achievement.

Finally, ethnicity produced violence and conflict with which the political system had to deal. Rivalries, fears, and animosities among the various ethnic groups periodically led to violence. Ethnic associations or unions were formed to protect the interests of the ethnic group. In many instances, especially in large cities outside the group's usual homeland, these ethnic unions became active in politics.[7] Conflict between these unions was especially dangerous where large numbers of immigrants from one ethnic group had established themselves in areas dominated by rival groups. The presence of the outsiders, particularly if they were financially successful in the new area, annoyed the native people; the outsiders' presence became the explanations for all the problems of the community. As social tensions rose, the natives would attack the immigrants and the government would be hard-pressed to protect the embattled minority. This happened repeatedly in the first 5 years of independence. The most violent incidents took place in northern cities, where native residents rioted against Ibo immigrants. But northerners living in southern cities such as Port Harcourt and Imo River were victims of retaliatory racial rioting.

As we saw in Chapter 37, the growing ethnic tensions in Nigeria eventually ended the First Republic, brought two bloody military coups, and a civil war. The Biafran war was one of attrition producing starvation of children and the elderly. When Biafra did surrender, Nigerian leaders avoided harsh treatment of the Ibo people and leaders. The result was an "outstandingly successful reconciliation" of the Ibo people and leadership that still serves as an example to other divided African countries.[8]

The violence of 1966–70 alerted everyone in Nigeria to the need for cooperation in order to avoid its recurrence. There has been a general revulsion against ethnic violence that seems to discourage appeals to ethnicity and extremism in contemporary Nigerian politics. The conciliatory treatment accorded Ibos involved in the Biafran civil war aided the reintegration of this people and reduced the risk of Ibo sentiments for revenge.

Nigeria's leaders are aware that ethnicity remains a possible source of tension and violence. They have generally avoided raising ethnic issues out of fear of the consequences of renewed communal conflict. The danger of renewed ethnic tensions tends to be greater during democratic eras—when political discussion is open and restrictions on speech are minimal—than when under military rule. However, in 1994, General Abacha's regime tried to blame the Yorubas for the strikes, riots, and demonstrations against his autocratic rule. He also contended that the southerners were on the offensive to limit the influence of the north. In fact, opposition was more general than that, with opposition to Abacha's unusually harsh rule coming from all quarters. Nigerians everywhere opposed the strict limits on civil liberties that Abacha imposed.

Abacha's willingness to invoke ethnic loyalties in response to his political troubles was an ominous sign in a country still divided along ethnic lines. Even more seriously, Abacha proceeded to remove southern military leaders, cabinet ministers, state-level political leaders, and heads of state-owned corporations and replaced them with northerners. Southern concerns about domination by the north have grown dramatically and talk of secession returned for the first time since Biafra's defeat.

After Abacha's sudden death in 1998, his military replacement, Abdulsalami Abubakar, sought to conciliate ethnic tensions. The elections of 1999 at all levels marked a quick reduction in the level of ethnic conflict and demonstrated that when not motivated by demagogic leaders, the Nigerian peoples wanted to get along. Ethnicity remains, however, an important factor in

virtually all aspects of Nigerian society. For example, a family living and working in a state other than their native state may not be able to get their children into secondary schools of the state where they now live. Such problems reinforce identification to ethnic roots and hinder the development of a sense of being Nigerian.

REGIONAL CLEAVAGES

Nigeria inherited from its colonial period an administrative and federal structure based on three regions, each of which corresponded with the homeland and population center of one of the three major ethnic groups: the Northern Region of the Hausa-Fulani; the Eastern Region in Iboland; and the Western Region in Yorubaland. Shortly after independence, the Nigerian parliament created a fourth state, the Midwestern Region, to accommodate the interests of minority groups in the Western Region. Because these regions coincided with the ethnic groups, regional loyalties simply reinforced the ethnic divisions.

Only in the Northern Region did regional identity as such become important. Islam served to unite the peoples of the north despite the diversity of ethnic origins and served to distinguish them collectively from southerners. Northern political leaders encouraged regional unity in order to counter the threat of domination by better-educated southerners. With a larger population than the other regions combined, northern politicians felt they were entitled to a greater say in Nigerian national politics. To achieve this goal, they sought to unify all northerners regardless of their ethnic backgrounds. Thus, the NPC adopted as a slogan: "One North, One People irrespective of religion, race, or tribe." One northern politician is quoted as saying: "We had to teach the people to hate southerners; to look on them as people depriving them of their rights, in order to win them over."[9]

Regional politics became a source of political tension as each region attempted to use its power in the national government to extract the most material benefits for itself. Even the issue of population size of each region became a major political battle because of the possible reallocation among the regions of political power and

Table 38–1   Regional Disparities in Nigeria (North = 1.0)

	North	East	West	Midwest	Lagos
Education (1965)					
Enrollment in elementary school	1.0	5.1	4.7	8.1	8.6
University output of students	1.0	11.5	9.5	10.7	1.9
Transportation (1965)					
Length of all tarred roads	1.0	1.2	3.4	4.1	2.0
Health (1964)					
Hospital beds	1.0	2.1	1.2	2.5	4.8
Regional government expenses (1965–1966)					
Total current	1.0	1.4	2.1	2.5	—
Total capital	1.0	2.2	2.4	3.8	—

Source: Adapted from Victor P. Kiejomaoh, "The Economics of the Nigerian Conflict," in Joseph Okpaku, ed., *Nigeria: Dilemma of Nationhood: An African Analysis of the Biafran Conflict* (Westport, CT: Greenwood Press, 1972), p. 319.

governmental resources as a result of accurate census data.

On several occasions in the 1960s and 1970s, attempts to conduct censuses were dropped or their results discarded because of powerful tensions surrounding the potential consequences of the new information and because of accusations that the censuses were rigged by one region or the other. Finally, in 1991 a census set the population of Nigeria at 88.5 million people. However, there are widespread suspicions among Nigerians and outside observers that the census grossly undercounted Ibos and Yorubas and that the actual total population exceeds 100 million.

In the first years of independence, regional differences and rivalries contributed to the pattern of political instability and decay. Each region had its own political structure—a regional assembly, premier, and cabinet of ministers—which fostered regional awareness. Because each regional government had different resources and its own priorities in using its resources, governmental services varied sharply from one region to the next.

The disparities were greatest between the Northern Region on the one hand and all three southern regions on the other. This is illustrated in Table 38–1. The table makes adjustment for population differences between the regions. It suggests, for example, that for every northern student in elementary school, there were five eastern pupils attending school. The data in that table are old; it is difficult to obtain such figures now because of the highly sensitive nature of the issue and the passions that the north-south divide produces. Some equalization has occurred but the inequities between north and south remain important. The federal government became an arena for attempts to redress these regional imbalances by allocating more federal funds to the north. Southerners, whose stronger economies provided more of the federal government's tax resources, resisted these efforts to redistribute the nation's resources to favor other less-developed regions. The consequences were heightened regional conflict which reinforced and aggravated the already serious ethnic tensions.

After the quelling of the Biafran uprising, the military government attempted to reduce regional cleavages. It broke up the old regions inherited from the colonial period into a larger number of smaller states. The idea was to diffuse regional and ethnic tensions by creating several states from each of the main ethnic groups and other states for homelands of smaller ethnic groups. Regions would lose some of their identity as states within a region competed. Multiple states were also expected to lessen ethnic loyalties since there would be several Ibo states, several Yoruba states, and so on. In the new multiple state federal union, traditional regions would compete with each other for funds from the federal government. The number of states grew from 4 in 1963, 12 in 1976, 20 in 1979, 30 by 1991, and to 36 in 1999. This fragmentation diminished some regional loyalties but at the cost of stimulating greater infighting among the states over federal resources.

Despite efforts to combat regionalism, the north-south division remains in place. Indeed, these regional animosities increased after 1993. Sani Abacha's military regime was much more "northern" in composition than had been earlier military and civilian regimes. Southern resentments grew especially as Abacha tried to reinforce his authority by claiming that dissidents were southerners. As opposition continued, Abacha further reduced the numbers of southerners in government and military positions. And there are still important social and economic tensions between north and south. Northerners still feel less equal than others in the amount and quality of government services they receive and in their overall level of economic development. Southerners continue to complain bitterly and sometimes violently against the redistribution of wealth produced in their part of Nigeria to the northern states.

Nigeria remains divided despite the efforts to break down regionalism. The multiplication of states has in fact done little to address the regional problem or the ethnic tensions that are intimately linked to regionalism. One observer points to the "insidious trend" produced by 40 years of Nigeria's tinkering with its regions:

> . . . the increasing segmentation of its policy, a purely distributive approach to federalism, a politicization of ethnicity, the hardening (on a bipolar mode) of tensions and conflicts, and, ultimately, a shrinking concern for the preservation of the country as a meaningful entity.[10]

RELIGIOUS CONFLICT

Nigerians are the most religious people in the world. Eighty-nine percent of Nigerians attend Church at least once a week. This figure is more meaningful when compared with the weekly church attendance of other countries in this textbook: 27 percent in Britain, 21 percent in France, 14 percent in the western part of Germany, 2 percent in Russia, and 3 percent in Japan. With religion this important in the lives of Nigerians, it is not surprising that religion has important political manifestations.

We have already noted the important political and social consequences of differing religious heritages in the north and south. Religious differences between the Muslim north and the Christian south continue to pose important challenges to national unity. There are also occasional tensions among the various Christian religions and between Christianity and indigenous animistic religions. In the western states, the Yorubas are divided between Christians and Muslims. Harmony prevails largely because of the moderation of adherents to both faiths and their desire to live peaceably together.

Religion has also had a direct impact on a number of political debates. One of these disputes, dating back to before independence, is whether or not the national government should recognize the Sharia courts. These are traditional Islamic courts whose legal system is based on Islamic religious principles and whose jurists are religious figures rather than individuals trained in Western law. Such Sharia courts form the basic legal structure in much of northern Nigeria. The particularly sensitive issue is the jurisdiction of these religious courts over non-Muslims living in the north. So far, no regime, military or civilian, has definitively resolved this highly emotional question.

Another issue is Nigeria's association with Islamic organizations. In 1986, the military ruler, General Babangida, decreed Nigeria's full membership in the Organization of Islamic Conference, an international grouping of Islamic states. Many in the south opposed the action and felt that it compromised Nigeria's commitment to a secular state without ties to any one religion.[11] Concern about growing influence of Islam in Nigerian national politics grew throughout the 1990s as successive military leaders turned increasingly to northerners to fill government positions.

In the past 15 years, there has been conflict between Muslims and Christians living in the north and between various strains of Islam. Some of these clashes have resulted in deaths. There have been many incidents involving looting and burning of churches and mosques in the north. Many of these clashes pitted Muslim sects against each other; others involved conflict between

Muslims and Christian immigrants from the south. Christians living in the predominantly Muslim north have come to sense strong religious discrimination against them. They have responded with a more aggressive fundamentalist Christianity that heightens the tensions, especially when they build their churches near Islamic mosques or organize high-profile religious crusades in northern cities.

The continued problems of religious discrimination and violence in the north is another source of political tension and instability in Nigeria. The overall political significance of this religious violence is limited because the episodes are isolated clashes that are over in a day or two and unrelated to each other.[12] But the frequency and the extent of violence of these episodes is of growing concern for the new civilian government. In January and February 2000, there were violent protests in several northern states. Christians took to the streets against the imposition of Islamic law even though the Islamic code would only be used with Muslims. Over 400 people were killed in these clashes. President Obasanjo has the benefit of being both a Muslim and a southerner. That will help him maintain support in both Christian and Muslim communities.

SOCIAL CLASS

In every society, there is competition among various groups over the distribution of benefits produced by that society's economy. Classical and Marxist interpreters have examined this competition mainly in terms of rivalries among social classes. Such an approach is wholly inadequate in interpreting Nigerian society and politics. It is not that there are no social classes in Nigeria.[13] Social class distinctions are present and are becoming more pronounced as the economy and society develop. But the class-oriented approach is inadequate in Nigeria because ethnic and regional competition has tended to prevail over social class divisions. Even within the ethnic communities, the salient social divisions have been along family lineage, age, and gender lines rather than along wealth or occupation lines.[14]

Awareness of belonging to a social class (or class consciousness) is poorly developed in modern Nigeria.[15] Most social tensions have been diverted into ethnic and regional conflicts rather than overt class conflict.[16] A new class of blue-collar workers is emerging as industrial growth continues. Most of these workers are recent immigrants to the industrial centers from rural Nigeria. Working and living alongside peoples from other ethnic backgrounds, it might be expected that they would develop some sense of common identity as workers. But this does not appear to have occurred yet. The recent immigrant workers usually retain loyalties to their communal or ethnic groups rather than identify themselves as part of a pan-Nigerian working class.

The integrative nature of African ethnic societies holds ethnic people together even after they move to the city. Communal norms lead those who prosper to share their success with an extended family and those from the individual's home village. This sense of attachment to old ethnic or familial units inhibits the development of a culture of poverty in African urban centers similar to the socially explosive cultures of poverty found in Latin American urban areas. Nigerians have not developed a sense of working-class solidarity against an oppressive capitalist system. Indeed, most workers sense themselves as better off in their new industrial jobs than were their peasant fathers. Some even see these workers as forming a "labor aristocracy" over the peasants and other disadvantaged groups.[17]

The working class constitutes only a small portion of the total working population. About 40 percent of the Nigerian workforce is still engaged in agriculture. The peasants are divided by different farming practices according to the varied geography, climate, and social traditions in Nigeria. Like the workers, Nigerian peasants lack a sense of common unity with each other. They also do not seem to feel oppressed even though the majority of farmers are small peasants so poor they can barely provide for their own needs. But they do have small plots of land of their own.

Discontented elements can always leave farming for jobs in the cities rather than staying in the countryside to organize discontent. Before meaningful improvements can be made in the living conditions in rural areas, major government investments will have to be made in the infrastructure of rural Nigeria through rural electrification, highway and road construction, and new educational and health services.[18]

There are few signs of political action on the part of peasantry. Their lower levels of literacy and often remote location make it difficult to mobilize the peasants for political causes. No political party, past or present, has directed its appeal primarily to the farmers, although many have included agrarian reforms in their platforms. Nor do farmers seem to have directed their votes to any single party. Periodically, there are isolated peasant rebellions. The most important was the "Agbekoya," a rural protest against high taxes and inadequate government services that brought widespread unrest and violence to western Nigeria in 1968–69.

The middle and upper classes enjoy disproportionate benefits and live very comfortable lives that contrast sharply with the poor living conditions of the workers and peasants. There is thus the basis in actual differences between the poor and the rich for the development of sharp social class cleavages and tensions. But so far, few Nigerians perceive social class as important in explaining their problems or the inequalities in society.[19] There are two factors that reduce tensions that might be expected to develop out of this large gap between the impoverished masses and a small, privileged elite. First, the elite is a new one that has emerged only in the past one or two generations. As a result, most members of the middle and upper classes are individuals from modest backgrounds who have risen socially and economically because of their own merit and achievement. The elite is largely composed of those who were able to get an education and rise through the ranks of the military, the bureaucracy, or a business.

Second, and because the elite is new, individuals in the privileged strata still have social ties and interaction with lower status people.[20] The members of the elite still have friends from their families, clans, villages, or ethnic groups who are not in the elite. They mix with each other in social settings, and the elite members feel economic and social obligations toward their nonelite acquaintances.

Both the Ibo and the Yoruba traditional societies were relatively open, offering upward social mobility to all those with talent and drive.[21]

Few restrictions or privileges were accorded on the basis of lineage or clan. Skilled individuals were able to compete openly for positions of authority and leadership. This traditional emphasis on the importance of individual achievement continues in modern Nigeria. There appears to be widespread belief in equal opportunity and the idea that the individual's status and privilege should be determined by ability and achievement.

There is the danger that this upward social mobility will not continue. It has been possible because of Nigeria's relatively rapid economic growth and development. Indeed, the economic crisis of the last 15 years has damaged social class relationships. While all classes have been affected by economic decline, shortages of essential products, and unemployment, the working class has been particularly hard hit. International bodies, notably the International Monetary Fund (IMF), have pressured successive Nigerian governments to cut government expenses, increase taxes, and privatize industry and business in order to retain foreign loans. These economic reforms may make sense in international financial markets, but they have brought much suffering to the Nigerian people.

There is also the possibility that the openness of Nigerian society will not continue now that there is a new elite present. Independence from Britain resulted in a sudden and vast opening of opportunities for upwardly mobile Nigerians. Europeans who had filled the upper ranks of the bureaucracy and military officer corps were replaced by a new native elite.

Whether or not this new elite will establish itself and restrict access to its ranks to its own sons and daughters is still uncertain. The achievement-oriented cultures of Nigeria would seem to reduce this danger. But if social mobility should appear to be blocked, the widely accepted achievement ethos may well accentuate social discontent among those who feel they are being denied their just opportunity for advancement.

Unlike in many countries where the elite derives its wealth from private industry or commerce, much of the Nigerian privileged class is employed by the state in the civil service or in government-owned industries. The gap between these employees of the state and the blue-collar worker is enormous. This inequality is a heritage from the colonial era; civil servants' salaries are based on international standards, while the workers are paid according to African conditions. If class tensions rise in the future, there will be no cushion of a private elite to absorb class hostility; the government's privileged class will be the likely target and with it the government and state themselves. The accumulation of enormous fortunes by high-ranking politicians and corruption and profiteering at all levels discredit both civilian and military governments.

There have been very few political manifestations of social class so far in Nigeria. Efforts to develop political parties appealing across ethnic lines to social classes for electoral support were unsuccessful in the First Republic. None of the political parties that emerged after 1979 sought support along class lines. The new parties emerging in 1999 are similarly lacking in social class differentiations or appeals. The trade union movement has remained weak politically and in labor-management relations. There is no doubt potential for political expressions of social class conflicts, but so far these have been avoided by the political focus on regionalism and ethnicity.

A DIVIDED SOCIETY

Nigerians see their ethnic identities as Ibos, Yorubas, or Hausas as more salient in political conflicts than their identification of themselves as peasants, workers, or middle class. The governments, both military and civilian, have deliberately sought to disentangle politics and ethnicity. The violence of the past demonstrated the dangers of ethnic politics. Because of the close link between ethnicity and regionalism, the government and politicians have also avoided appealing to regional loyalties. The Abacha regime (1993–1998) represented a deviation from this tradition of avoiding fomenting ethnic and regional tensions.

There is substantial overlap of the religious, regional, and ethnic divisions. As a result, these cleavages tend to reinforce each other and thus raise tensions and heighten the threat to political stability. This is an example of the coinciding cleavage patterns that we discussed in the introduction. Tensions are more easily controlled

when the social cleavages overlap or criss-cross each other. So far, there is no indication that other social divisions—whether they be social classes, urban-rural cleavages, or ideological differences—are emerging to offset or moderate ethnicity as a basis for meaningful political distinctions. Certainly, there are cleavages that may eventually emerge as important political guideposts, especially socioeconomic divisions. Communal and ethnic ties continue to provide the principal political cue for most Nigerians.

NOTES

[1]Peter P. Ekeh, "Citizenship and Political Conflict: A Summary of Nigeria's Political History from 1914 to 1964," in Joseph Okpaku, ed., N*igeria: Dilemma of Nationhood: An African Analysis of the Biafran Conflict* (Westport, CT: Greenwood Press, 1972), p. 91.

[2]William F. S. Miles, *Hausaland Divided: Colonialism and Independence in Nigeria and Niger* (Ithaca, NY: Cornell University Press, 1994), pp. 42–47.

[3]Orafemi Awolowo, *Pathways to Nigerian Freedom* (London: Faber and Faber, 1946), p. 48.

[4]Robert Melson and Howard Wolpe, "Modernization and the Politics of Communalism: A Theoretical Perspective," in Robert Melson and Howard Wolpe, eds., *Nigeria: Modernization and the Politics of Communalism* (Lansing: Michigan State University Press, 1971).

[5]P. C. Lloyd, "The Ethnic Background to the Nigerian Civil War," in Keith Panter-Brick, ed., *Nigerian Politics and Military Rule: Prelude to Civil War* (London: Institute of Commonwealth Studies, 1970), pp. 1–13.

[6]See John P. Mackintosh, *Nigerian Government and Politics: Prelude to the Revolution* (Evanston, IL: Northwestern University Press, 1966), pp. 508–544.

[7]Audrey Smock, *Ibo Politics: The Role of Ethnic Unions in Eastern Nigeria* (Cambridge, MA: Harvard University Press, 1971).

[8]Daniel C. Bach, "Indigeneity, Ethnicity, and Federalism," in Larry Diamond, Anthony Kirk-Greene, and Oyeleye Oyediran, eds., *Transition Without End: Nigerian Politics and Civil Society Under Babangida* (Boulder, CO: Lynne Rienner, 1997), p. 333.

[9]M. J. Dent, "Tarka and the Tiv: A Perspective on Nigerian Federation," in Melson and Wolpe, *Nigeria*, p. 452.

[10]Bach, "Indigeneity, Ethnicity, and Federalism," p. 346.

[11]Rotimi T. Suberu, "Religion and Politics: A View from the South," in Diamond, et al., *Transition Without End.*

[12]Omar Farouk Ibrahim, "Religion and Politics: A View from the South," in Diamond, et al., *Transition Without End.*

[13]For an argument supporting the importance of class in African societies, see Immanuel Wallerstein, "Class and Class Struggle in Africa," *Monthly Review,* February 1975.

[14]Larry Diamond, *Class, Ethnicity, and Democracy in Nigeria: The Failure of the First Republic* (Syracuse, NY: Syracuse University Press, 1988).

[15]Peter C. Lloyd, *Power and Independence: Urban Africans' Perceptions of Social Inequality* (London: Routledge & Kegan Paul, 1974).

[16]Otwin Marenin, "The Nigerian State as Process and Manager; A Conceptualization," *Comparative Politics* 20 (January 1988): 215–232.

[17]R. Sandbrook and R. Cohen, eds., *The Development of an African Working Class* (Toronto: Toronto University Press, 1976).

[18]O. O. Lapido and A. A. Adesimi, "Income Distribution in the Rural Sector," in Henry Bienen and V. P. Diejomoah, eds., *The Political Economy of Income Distribution in Nigeria* (New York: Holmes and Meier, 1981), pp. 299–322.

[19]Donald G. Morrison, "Inequalities of Social Rewards: Realities and Perceptions in Nigeria," in Binen and Diejomoah, *The Political Economy of Income Distribution.*

[20]Robin Luckham, *The Nigerian Military: A Sociological Analysis of Authority and Revolt, 1960–67* (Cambridge, England: Cambridge University Press, 1971), pp. 112–113.

[21]See R. A. LeVine, *Dreams and Deeds: Achievement Motivation in Nigeria* (Chicago: University of Chicago Press, 1966), p. 40; and Oshomha Imoagene, *Social Mobility in Emergent Society: A Study of the New Elite in Western Nigeria* (Canberra, Australia: Changing African Family Project Series, Monograph No. 2, 1976), pp. 293–294.

Chapter 39

The Nigerian Political Framework

On May 5, 1999, General Abdulsalami Abubakar signed into law a new constitution for Nigeria. Its contents were still secret when the transfer to civilian rule occurred three weeks later. This marked the fourth constitution since Nigeria became an independent country in 1960. But much of the intervening 39 years involved dictatorial rule by the military with little regard to any constitution.

The country began with a parliamentary structure patterned on the British Westminister model coupled with an unBritish federalism to conform with its regional and ethnic subdivisions. This First Republic lasted only 5 years. It was succeeded by 13 years of military rule where decision making took place in an ad hoc manner without the existence of a constitutional document.

During this period, changes in government leaders occurred as a result of coups or assassinations rather than through an established pattern for rotating leadership. A new civilian constitution was implemented at the end of 1979. Its framers hoped to resolve some of the country's social divisions and political problems through constitutional engineering. The new system, patterned

openly on the American presidential and federal structure, was also influenced by the constitutional failures of the First Republic. Specifically, the 1979 constitution was designed to reduce the ethnic and regional conflicts that had seemed to be reinforced by the First Republic's political institutions. The Second Republic proved successful in avoiding the ethnic turmoil that had destroyed the First Republic, but it failed when its leaders became enmeshed in corruption, electoral fraud, and economic mismanagement. A coup on New Year's eve 1983 brought the suspension of the constitution and a new era of military rule. Five years later, in 1989, a new constitution was announced but never implemented. It was supposed to guide the civilian regime of the Third Republic, but its birth was aborted by the unsuccessful presidential elections of 1993. The most recent episode of constitution drafting occurred in 1998 and 1999 while the military prepared the country for the return to civilian rule. That regime was to be shaped by a constitution drafted in secrecy by the military with no public or civilian input. The new civilian president, Olusegun Obasanjo, started his term with a virtually unknown constitution.

THE FIRST REPUBLIC

One of the principal legacies of the colonial era to the newly independent Nigeria was a constitution patterned on the British parliamentary system of government. The center of Nigerian political power was the Federal Parliament with two chambers: the directly elected House of Representatives and the indirectly elected Senate, whose members were appointed, as in the U.S. Senate before 1913, by the state legislatures. While technically known as the upper house, the Senate's powers were less than those of the House of Representatives since it could not initiate money bills and could only delay for a maximum of six months any other bills it opposed.

It was a typical parliamentary system with a president elected by parliament and a prime minister and government accountable to the House of Representatives. The prime minister was selected by the House of Representatives and was responsible to that body. A vote of censure by the House would require the prime minister to step down. The absence of a single party majority in the House and the tense relations between parties meant that the prime minister's position was always tenuous and difficult.

The greatest source of difficulty came through the arrangements for a federal system. Three of the four states were based on the homelands of the great nations composing Nigeria. As each of the regions tried to increase its hold on the federal government and divert more federal resources in its direction, political conflict intensified. At the same time, ethnic tensions, reinforced by the fact that they coincided with political divisions, grew to the point of explosion. In this setting, the institutions of the First Republic failed. Paralyzed by the divided parliament, they were unable to check the rising ethnic and political tensions.[1]

THE SECOND REPUBLIC

The 1979 constitution drew upon American experience in establishing the relationship among the various branches of the federal government. The instability and ineffectiveness of government during the First Republic disenchanted many Nigerians with the parliamentary structures of that first constitution. Those charged with the task of devising an entirely new set of political institutions engaged in constitutional engineering in order to remedy the faults of the earlier parliamentary democracy and, more important, to seek constitutional forms to manage ethnic conflict.[2] For example, a single executive, combining both these responsibilities in a single office as in the presidential system, would contribute to integrating the diverse peoples and cultures of Nigeria into a single nation.[3] Nigeria, many felt, needed a strong executive able to act even if it lacked a cohesive majority in the legislature.

Ethnic, regional, and political pluralism in Nigeria made it unlikely that there would be the firm legislative majority that parliamentary systems require to operate well. In addition, parliamentary systems encourage the solidifying of the line between government supporters and its opposition. Some Nigerians thought that a presidential system would facilitate the development of shifting coalitions in the legislature—majorities that would change with the issues and over time—that would prevent the formation of an opposition force unable to do anything but attack the government.

Drawing heavily on American practice and principle, the drafters proposed a constitution calling for presidential government based on a president directly elected by the people. The president was elected for a 4-year term of office with the possibility of reelection for an additional 4-year term. A major concern of those drafting the constitution was to prevent the election to the presidency of any candidate with blatantly ethnic or sectional appeal. The presidential election procedure specified that the presidential candidate must select a vice presidential running mate with a different ethnic background. To be elected, the presidential candidate had to receive more votes than any other candidate and win at least 25 percent of the votes in two-thirds of the states. This assured that the president would have at least a minimal level of support from a large part of the country.

The 1979 civilian constitution granted broad powers to the president as at once head of state, head of government, and commander-in-chief of the armed forces. The president named the ministers who headed the various government departments; the president was obligated, however, to appoint at least one minister from each state in the federation and all appointees were subject to confirmation by a simple majority vote in the Senate. In practice, the president also felt it politically prudent to balance ethnic groups in cabinet appointments and to seek to broaden legislative support by including leaders from other parties in the cabinet. The first president, Shehu Shagari, proved to be an effective leader. His major weakness, which ultimately brought about his fall, was his inability to control the rampant corruption that spread in the ranks of his administration and his political party. It destroyed much of his popularity and left him in prison after the military toppled the Second Republic.

The National Assembly in Nigeria was the equivalent to the American Congress. As in the United States, this legislative body was bicameral with a Senate and a House of Representatives. The Senate had 95 members, five senators from each of the nineteen states serving 4-year terms of office. The House of Representatives had 450 members elected from single-member districts by a simple majority. Members of the House of Representatives also served 4-year terms. The basic lawmaking procedures were similar to those in the United States.

Powerful and independent legislative bodies are rare in the Third World. Even when there are constitutional governments as opposed to military rule or dictatorships, legislatures in developing countries are often fragile institutions that either fail completely or become rubber stamps for the political initiatives of the executive. The Nigerian National Assembly maintained its independence until the military dissolved it in 1984. Lively negotiations between the president and legislators and among legislators were necessary to develop successful majority coalitions for major legislative proposals.

The 1979 constitution established a Supreme Court with power to resolve the built-in conflicts of a presidential system where an independent executive faced a powerful and autonomous legislature. The court had the additional responsibility of resolving disputes among states and between states and the federal government. As the ultimate appellate court, the Supreme Court was also supposed to ensure the enforcement of the human rights listed in the constitution. As in the United States, the president appointed the Supreme Court justices subject to confirmation by the Senate. The Supreme Court had powers of judicial review by which it could declare void duly enacted legislation that conflicted with the constitution. It also had the duty of resolving legal conflicts between the states. The Nigerian Supreme Court established itself as an effective and independent restraint on the federal government.

CHOP, CHOP POLITICS

The need to rebuild constantly shifting legislative coalitions fit well with the traditions of Nigerian politics. The Nigerian equivalent of the American practices of "log-rolling" and "pork barrel legislation" is known as "chop, chop" politics. To build a majority, those guiding the legislation through the National Assembly had to make deals with individual legislators to win their support. Often these arguments involved adding provisions that would give new government services or programs to the constituents or friends of the key legislators. Sometimes votes were purchased by outside interests through bribes.

Chop, chop politics built majorities and got laws through legislative roadblocks but also led to the inefficient allocation of government resources and to widespread corruption. This often blatant corruption in high places contributed to the regime's loss of public support. Control over the allocation of public funds and the receipt of private bribes combined to make legislators very wealthy people. In addition, the costs of the legislators' salaries, staffs, offices, housing, and other perquisites ran into the hundreds of millions of dollars. In times of economic hardship, these expenses make this kind of democracy very expensive for a struggling Third World country.

The court also began to defend human rights against politically motivated attempts to infringe upon basic liberties. The Supreme Court continued to operate throughout the 1980s and early 1990s as an appellate court for civil and criminal cases. However, under military rule, the Court was not able to expand on its earlier moves toward becoming a check on the federal government's power.

GOVERNMENT UNDER THE MILITARY

Immediately after the military seized power on December 31, 1983, the new military leadership suspended the constitution of the Second Republic. Unlike the situation at the time of the 1966 coup, the institutions were still functioning but they had been discredited by the corrupt actions of the officials filling these institutions. Irregularities in the 1983 national elections had eroded the legitimacy of the majority party. Rampant corruption at all levels and in all parties had destroyed the public's confidence in public officials and politicians.

The new military regime set up in 1984 by General Muhammed Buhari resembled closely earlier military regimes in Nigeria. The key political body was the Supreme Military Council (SMC). Its members included the military chiefs of staff, officers of key elite military corps, and other senior military officers. Its composition was carefully balanced to reflect the ethnic and regional interests of the nation. The SMC named the Head of the Federal Military Government, Muhammed Buhari, and the other top governmental officials. It was the final arbiter on all national issues. The SMC was first organized in 1966 as a means of governing the country after the overthrow of the First Republic. It dissolved itself in 1979 to make way for the civilian regime. It was reorganized early in 1984 as the executive body for the new military regime headed by General Buhari. The head of the military government chaired the SMC and was designated commander-in-chief of the armed forces. He was granted full legislative and executive powers and ruled by decree. The decrees had the effect of laws.[4]

The August 1985 coup brought a change in the pattern of military rule. The SMC, which had been the major governmental organ during all earlier periods of military rule, was dissolved and replaced by the Armed Forces Ruling Council (AFRC). This body had twenty-eight members, all drawn from the military, and was headed by General Babangida. General Babangida soon had himself named as president of the republic. He was the first military leader to assume that title.

The military lacks both the disposition and the personnel to govern alone. The AFRC appointed a Federal Executive Council with powers much like those of the cabinet in parliamentary regimes. The Council was chaired by the head of the military government; other council members headed government departments. Some ministers were recruited from the military officer corps but most were civilians. Some were senior civil servants. Just before the transition to civilian rule in 1999, the Federal Executive Council was chaired by General Abubakar. There were 32 ministries, about a third of which were led by military officers.

Another major political institution was the National Council of State made up of the state military governors. Its task was the coordination of state and national economic and social policies. At all levels of government, military rule accords greater decision-making power and broader responsibilities to the civil servants. In the last analysis, of course, the military still controls politics. It is the military that coopts civilians into the government, not the reverse. The civilians, whether traditional leaders, civil servants, or one-time politicians, serve at the pleasure of the military leaders.

From 1985 to 1999, these three military-dominated bodies ruled Nigeria under three separate military dictators: Generals Babangida, Abacha, and Abubakar. As is typical with military governments, there was a good deal of flexibility in the pattern of decision making. Sometimes the AFRC would issue a decree peremptorily with little consultation or discussion; other times the decision was reached only after consulting key individuals or groups interested in the decision. Sometimes the decision was left to the appropriate minister or state level official; in other cases the AFRC acted itself. Many routine

In May 1999, the Nigerian military returned power to a civilian government headed by Olusegun Obasanjo. The new Third Republic inherited many social, economic, and ethnic problems that had worsened under military rule. (*Photographer/Source:* AP/Wide World Photos)

decisions were left to bureaucrats or traditional leaders. This ad hoc nature of decision-making suggests the absence of any institutionalized governmental routine even on an informal, unwritten basis.

THE THIRD REPUBLIC

A new constitution was written in 1989, but it was still-born with the failure of the transition to civilian rule in 1993.[5] The Third Republic finally came into existence in 1999 with a new constitution written by the outgoing military regime. The drafting of the Second Republic's 1979 constitution had proceeded openly and slowly with many opportunities for citizen participation. In contrast to "the extensive and broad-based process of public reflection and debate" that produced the constitution of the Second Republic,[6] secrecy surrounded the military's constitutional revisions

for the Third Republic and continued right up to the transition of power three weeks after the promulgation of the constitution. The constitution was promulgated in May 1999, but its contents were not divulged until after the transition to civilian rule.

The 1999 constitution draws heavily on the 1979 constitution. Indeed, the new constitution is primarily a document that addresses some of the minor problems that had become evident in the operation of the 1979 constitution between 1979 and 1983. For example, the 1999 constitution requires key political officials to file financial disclosure statements in an attempt to control the corruption that has undermined earlier civilian and military leadership. The new constitution continues the presidential system. The president is elected for a four-year term with a limit of two terms. As in 1979, rules for the presidential election require broad support around the country to prevent the election of a leader with only regional support. The key political powers are exercised by the president. President Olusegun Obasanjo made full use of those powers early in his term of office, reversing by presidential decrees actions taken by the military government in its waning months in office.

The legislative branch of Nigerian national government is made up of two chambers: the House of Representatives and the Senate. The House of Representatives has 360 members who serve four-year terms; the Senate has 109 members who also serve for four years. Both bodies are popularly elected. It remains to be seen if the new National Assembly will become the active legislative body that its 1979 predecessor had been. As the new regime starts up, it is still too soon to assess the impact of the Supreme Court, which had played a significant role in Second Republic politics. First, it must overcome the restraints on its actions imposed by the military regimes from 1983–1999.

One of the most sensitive legal questions in Nigeria is the problem of integrating two different legal traditions. In the north, the well-developed Islamic culture produced a distinctive judicial system based on Islamic law. In the south, there was no deeply entrenched legal tradition, and English common law became the basis of the judicial system there. After independence the two legal systems continued to coexist since the federal structure permits the maintenance of separate state court systems based on local legal tradition. There are some problems with two radically different legal systems in the same country: specific legal codes differ dramatically from north to south; Islamic law codifies discrimination against women and non-Muslims; non-Muslims living in the north may find themselves before courts from which non-Muslim jurists are barred.

The major controversy has been the issue of how to handle appeals from Islamic courts (called Sharia courts) to the federal appellate courts. The 1979 constitution created a single Federal Court of Appeals but provided that the personnel of the court may change depending upon the origin of the appeal. If it comes from a Sharia court, the panel must include at least three judges learned in the traditions of Islamic law; if it comes from

common law courts, the panel must include at least three judges trained in common law.

Defenders of Islamic law were dissatisfied with this compromise and feared that it would mean interference in Islamic judicial proceedings. Non-Muslims were also displeased with the possibility of falling under the jurisdiction of the Islamic courts if they lived or did business in the north. The ill-fated 1989 constitution tried to address this issue by limiting the jurisdiction of Sharia courts only to Muslims. Some have speculated that the provisions on this very sensitive issue is why the military kept the 1999 constitution secret until the transfer of power to civilians.

As we have seen in other contexts, "constitutional engineering" to come up with an exact set of institutions and practices that will resolve deep-seated societal problems are often unsuccessful. Constitutional engineering succeeded in postwar Germany and Japan, providing those countries with a solid base for democracy. But there were many other factors such as the impact of total military defeat followed by economic "miracles" that helped along these two examples of constitutional engineering. Rewriting the constitution to solve the problems of chronic political instability worked in France with the establishment of the Fifth Republic in 1958. It remains to be seen if efforts to make democracy work by a new constitution will succeed in Nigeria. Certainly the task is a large one given the ethnic, religious, regional, and economic challenges that the new civilian government faces in the new century.[7]

FEDERALISM

Nigeria's social geography with three great nations, each with its own language, culture, political institutions, and history, located in a specific region made the federal framework more appealing than a centralized unitary state.[8] By recognizing and maintaining regional political differences, British indirect colonial rule reinforced this social and political geographic pattern. Thus, there is little disagreement over the need for a federal structure. The specific nature of this federalism, however, has been a constant source of political tension since the preindependence era.

THE CAPITAL CITY OF ABUJA

When Nigeria won independence, its capital was designated as Lagos, the largest city in the country. In the mid-1970s, the government decided that Lagos was too crowded, too polluted, and too much tied to one ethnic group, the Yorubas, than was desirable for the capital of a country aspiring to be the leader of Africa. A new site was selected about 300 miles north of Lagos where a new capital, Abuja, would be built. The scheme was inspired in part by Brazil's construction of its new capital, Brasilia, near the geographic center of that vast country. Abuja is located near the geographical center of Nigeria. It is in a sparsely populated region away from the core of any of the three principal nationality groups.

The move of the federal government to the new capital progressed very slowly. The transfer of government office buildings was to have begun in 1982, but construction had barely started at that time. It was not until 1991 that the president established his official offices in Abuja. By the end of the 1990s, the new capital was in use, but many ministries and other government offices remain in Lagos. Housing for government employees, retail enterprises, and other amenities are still in short supply.

The government has invested over $10 billion in building the new capital. It has achieved ethnic neutrality. And the pace of life in Abuja is quieter. In contrast to the crowded streets of Lagos, the broad avenues of Abuja are more often filled with herds of cattle than with automobiles.

The number of states and the powers they should exercise have been important and decisive issues. As Nigeria acquired independence in 1960 it assumed a federal framework with a national government and three regional governments. Soon after independence a fourth state, the Midwestern State, was created between the Eastern and Western Regions to accommodate the large numbers of ethnic minority groups in the area. The creation of new states continued under military and civilian regimes. By the return of civilian rule in 1999, Nigeria had 36 states and one federal district as the federal capital: Abuja.

The basic notion was sound. Political leaders wanted to avoid the confrontation of ethnically based states by dividing them and creating new states that might be dominated by minority groups.[9] In this way, several Hausa states would compete against each other as well as against multiple Ibo, Yoruba, and other states.

The multiplication of states has certain appeal, especially to minority political and ethnic groups that might find their influence enhanced in smaller states.[10] Civil servants approved because of the increased opportunity for their advancement with the creation of new state bureaucracies. But the financial burdens of creating the new states and equipping them with buildings, legislative bodies, and universities were staggering.

The central issue underlying federal-state issues has been the allocation of resources. Nearly all taxes and all other government funds including oil royalties come to the federal government. It then redistributes these funds among the states.

There was little consensus on how these funds ought to have been distributed. Even the census figures on population by region were suspect; so it was difficult to find equitable criteria for dividing the federal government's money among the four regions. Very soon, political disputes over allocations to the states added to the already severe ethnic/regional differences. With the states corresponding closely to the homelands of the major ethnic groups, these battles over federal funds accentuated ethnic tensions. Some regions paid more in taxes to the federal government than they received back in services or federal subsidies. The governments of these regions, and their taxpayers, resented such reallocations of "their" money to less-developed areas of the country.

How much each state should receive in these funds and in government development activities has been a hotly contested political issue that reflects both inter-ethnic and intra-ethnic conflicts. As a result, federalism has only provided a new form of ethnic and regional conflict. Federalism brings perpetual battles over dividing up the federal government's revenues and resources among the various states.[11] The states all lack significant revenues of their own and instead rely on what the federal government gives them to run their state governments and to pay for their programs.

With nearly all tax resources going to the federal government, a crucial political issue is the division of these funds between federal, state, and local governments. Once the overall ratio between levels of government is established, there are further disputes over how the funds designated for the states should be divided up among the nineteen state governments. Since 1979, the criteria for allocations among the states included population, area, and oil production of the state. But these criteria are disputed by several states, which claim that other factors, such as overall level of development, ought to be considered. Debates on the allocation of money to the states are among the most impassioned and sometimes explosive discussions in national politics.

Each state is to be governed by a popularly elected state legislative body and governor. But these state governments have had little life. During the Second Republic (1979–1983), the state governments were busy establishing themselves and in most cases diverting public funds into the hands of those elected to govern. With the military's return to power in 1983, the popularly elected state governments were abolished. The military ruling council appointed a governor, a military officer, in each state. The military governor then selected a council of civilian and military officials to assist in administering the state government's affairs. The elected legislatures were closed down, but some military governors met regularly with the state councils of obas, chiefs, or emirs for advice and counsel.[12] A National Council of State made up of the state military governors and the national military leadership coordinated state and federal activities. In general, the military governments at the state level continued to exercise the same responsibilities as did their civilian predecessors. The military leaders accepted the federal framework as necessary and desirable. The Abacha regime, however, exercised far more central control over Nigeria from 1993 to 1998 than did earlier military regimes.

Civilian rule in the states began at the same time as the transition to civilian rule at the federal level in May 1999. Earlier elections had put in place state assemblies and governors. The fact that most governors and state assemblies, except those from Yoruba, are in the hands of the same party as President Obasanjo should facilitate cooperation between federal aud state political leaders. But how federalism will function in the Third Republic is still to be determined.

Federalism has the indisputable merit of permitting the continuation of social, economic, and political differences within a country that has diverse cultural and historical traditions. With Nigeria's ethnic and cultural diversity, it is hard to conceive of any alternative to federalism as a means of dividing power among the levels of government. The individual state governments have the ability to accommodate special regional and ethnic requirements. The large number of governmental units required by federalism brings government closer to the people and helps to prevent the sense of remoteness from government that is often found in centralized countries and especially in centralized developing countries. The creation of new states out of the original four regions has reduced the risk of secession in Nigeria and moderates the confrontation along ethnic and regional lines of the three great nations that make up modern Nigeria.

The federal framework adopted by Nigeria in its 1979 constitution was openly patterned on U.S. federalism. It responded to the need to accommodate regional differences in a diverse country. But it was also specifically designed to contribute to the easing of the ethnic conflicts that tore Nigeria apart in the 1960s. There must always be some skepticism about the ability of any institutional arrangement to solve profound social cleavages. Often, when the institutions ignore social cleavages or are not in harmony with the prevailing political attitudes of the people, they simply cannot function.

In the case of Nigeria, federalism, when it is allowed to operate, builds upon existing differences within ethnic groups and between the large groups and minority ethnic groups as a basis for the states. It does not eliminate ethnic rivalries but creates new rivalries within each group and with other groups which deflect political attention and conflict from the central battle among Hausa-Fulani, Ibos, and Yorubas. As one observer notes, "Nigerian federalism has been reasonably (even remarkably) effective in breaking up the hegemony of Nigeria's largest ethnic groups, decentralizing ethnic conflict, dispersing development, fostering cross-cutting cleavages, and in general containing the powerful centrifugal forces inherent in Nigeria's ethnic composition."[13]

CONCLUSION

Political scientists and historians have explored at length the relationship between a country's political culture and social structures on the one hand and its political institutions on the other. They have probed the degree to which the political and social settings affect the operation of specific political institutions and conversely the effects of the institutions on the political behavior and society. For some, political institutions are a "dependent variable" in that they are produced or explained by the sociopolitical setting. For others, the political framework is the "independent variable" that shapes the social and political world. The relationship between setting and political institutions is by no means simple, and experience in several countries suggests that it differs from one country to the next and even from one time to another in the same country.

Britain, for example, has a long-established pattern of political behavior and socioeconomic structures that have produced particular political institutions and practices. In other countries, such as the Soviet Union, a set of political institutions shaped the political culture and society. In France, the prevailing environment seems to have produced the institutions of the Third and Fourth Republics but the French Fifth Republic represented the imposition of new institutions that have reshaped political behavior and even the socioeconomic setting.

At times, reformers have tried to alter society and politics by changing the political framework. The record of such "constitutional engineering" is mixed. After World War I, Germany was endowed with a model democratic constitution but the grafting on of this democratic political structure to an unreformed imperial society failed. The fruits of this unsuccessful blend was a system that permitted Hitler to come to power legally. On the other hand, in the same country another democratic constitution was imposed by occupying powers after World War II and the result was a successful democratic government. All this is of interest because the Nigerian Third Republic, beginning in 1999, represents an attempt to remedy political and social problems in Nigeria through the device of a new constitution. The constitution was intended by its drafters to respond to some of the political, regional, social, and political troubles that plagued the earlier experiences in constitutional government.

The preamble to the 1999 constitution states: "We the people of the Federal Republic of Nigeria, having firmly and solemnly resolved to live in unity and harmony as one indivisible and indissolvable sovereign nation . . . do hereby make, enact, and give to ourselves the following constitution." In fact, the Nigerian people did not write the constitution; it was drafted under the tutelage of the military by a body of experts selected by the military. Nor did the people approve the constitution; there was no popular referendum on the constitution; the military enacted it through fiat. The military rulers were sincerely committed to turning power over to democratic civilian government and to staying out of politics once the change was made. The constitutional document they approved was technically well drafted. The crucial question was whether this document or any other such document could be made to work when imposed on a people that did not participate in its adoption and on a political setting that may not be conducive to its successful operation. Post–World War II Germany provides an example of a successful imposed democratic constitution, but there are many more examples of unsuccessful attempts to establish democratic government through constitutional engineering.

The Nigerian Second Republic (1979–1993) ended in failure not because its institutions failed to function well. It failed because of the personal greed and corruption of many of those who won elected office. Pervasive corruption, economic mismanagement, growing political violence, and staggering electoral fraud in the first elections under the Second Republic undermined the legitimacy of these institutions.[14] When the military returned to power, it was greeted by near euphoria from Nigerian citizens fed up with the waste, ineffectiveness, corruption, and arrogance of the civilian leaders.

We are now witnessing yet another attempt to install democratic, civilian political institutions and practices in Nigeria. How well the institutions of the Third Republic will cope with Nigeria's long-standing social and economic problems is uncertain. It is certain that the institutions alone will not do the job. There is also a need for democratic citizens exercising their civic rights, for meaningful political parties that can give political rather than ethnic options to the voters, and for the emergence of those attitudes among citizens and followers that will foster democratic attitudes and support democratic institutions.

NOTES

[1] For a history of the First Republic, see Larry Diamond, *Class, Ethnicity and Democracy in Nigeria: The Failure of the First Republic* (Syracuse, NY: Syracuse University Press, 1988).

[2] John A. A. Ayade, "Ethnic Management in the 1979 Nigerian Constitution," *Publius: The Journal of Federalism* 16 (Spring 1986): 73–90.

[3] E. Alex Gboyega, "The Making of the Nigerian Constitution," in Oyeleye Oyediran, ed., *Nigerian Government and Politics Under Military Rule 1966–1979* (New York: St. Martin's, 1979), p. 247.

[4] On policy making under military rule, see Henry Bienen,

"Military Rule and Political Process: Nigerian Examples," *Comparative Politics* 10 (January 1978): 205–226.

[5] Rafiu A. Akindele, "The Constituent Assembly and the 1989 Constitution," in Larry Diamond, Anthony Kirk-Greene, and Oyeleye Oyediran, eds., *Transition Without End: Nigerian Politics and Civil Society Under Babangida* (Boulder, CO: Lynne Rienner, 1997).

[6] Crawford Young. "Africa: An Interim Report," *Journal of Democracy* 7 (July 1996): 56.

[7] See the pessimistic assessments of one observer in Anthony Kirk-Greene, "The Remedial Imperatives of the Nigerian Constitution, 1922–1992," in Diamond, Kirk-Greene, and Obasanjo, *Transition Without End*, pp. 47–50.

[8] Egite S. Oyovbaire, *Federalism in Nigeria* (New York: St. Martin's, 1984).

[9] See L'Adele Jinadu, "Federalism, the Consociational State and Ethnic Conflict in Nigeria," *Publius: The Journal of Federalism* 16 (Spring 1986): 71–100.

[10] Dean E. McHenry, Jr., "Stability of the Federal System in Nigeria: Elite Attitudes at the Constituent Assembly and the Creation of New States," *Publius: The Journal of Federalism* 16 (Spring 1986): 91–112.

[11] S. Egite Oyovbaire, "The Politics of Revenue Allocation," in Keith Panter-Brick, ed., *Soldiers and Oil: The Political Transformation of Nigeria* (London: Frank Cass, 1978).

[12] J. Isawa Elaigwu, "Nigerian Federalism Under Civilian and Military Regimes," *Publius* 18 (Winter 1988): 173–188.

[13] Larry Diamond, "Nigeria in Search of Democracy," *Foreign Affairs* 68 (Spring 1984): 921.

[14] Tom Forest, "The Political Economy of Civil Rule and Economic Crisis in Nigeria (1979–1984)," *Review of African Political Economy* 35 (1986): 4–26; and Richard A. Joseph, *Democracy and Prebendal Politics in Nigeria: The Rise and Fall of the Second Republic* (Cambridge, England: Cambridge University Press, 1987), pp. 153–183.

Chapter 40

Political Participation in Nigeria

In many developing countries, political participation is a luxury in the sense that it is not available to many individuals who live at or near the subsistence level and who must devote all their time and energy to the struggle for existence. This is true of many Nigerians. Much of the population is engaged in subsistence farming that requires a total effort on the part of the family simply to meet its most essential needs.

Most Nigerians live in rural areas, sometimes isolated from the influence of the central government. Only a comparatively small section of the population has sufficient time for politics.

Illiteracy poses another obstacle to participation; some 47 percent of Nigerians are unable to read and write. There are several hundred distinct languages and dialects in use among Nigerians. Many Nigerians cannot speak English, the country's official language. As we have already seen, allegiances to communal and ethnic groups often have higher priority in Nigeria than do loyalties to the national political system. All of these factors are obstacles to developing widespread citizen involvement in national politics.

Nigeria, like other developing countries, faces a dilemma in finding a desirable level of citizen

political involvement. Too little participation may hinder economic and social development since the talents and energy of the population must be engaged if Nigeria wants to accomplish the economic development and social modernization its leaders promise. Furthermore, the creation of effective political institutions is usually contingent upon the involvement of citizens in these institutions. Political parties, for example, strengthen themselves and the political system as they recruit members and involve them in the political process.

On the other hand, too much participation may be destabilizing. The tensions produced by socioeconomic change and political development may result in protests, demonstrations, riots, violence, and other forms of political activism that are difficult if not impossible for fragile new political institutions to control.

Too rapid social and economic modernization—in education, urbanization, mass communications, industrialization, economic growth, and a rising standard of living—may produce anomie, or the collapse of social norms and values. Mass political participation in such an atmosphere may result in violence and the destruction of existing political institutions. Some argue that political stability and order is enhanced in those countries where political institutions develop first and then participation is expanded only when these institutions have become capable of handling the new participants.[1]

The crisis of Nigerian democracy in the early 1960s illustrates the dangers of excessive participation. With independence, Nigerians mobilized to defend their interests in the new political system. Political leaders exploited ethnic and regional fears to mobilize large numbers who had limited prior political experience. Extremist rhetoric instilling fears of genocide brought millions into politics but also produced violence. The new political institutions proved too fragile to cope with the multiple demands presented by the new participants and with the violence produced by the racial tensions. Public order collapsed in the Western Region; riots and violent demonstrations were frequent occurrences elsewhere. As a result, the military eventually stepped in to reestablish order.

After 13 years of military rule that permitted only limited citizen political participation, the civilians took over again in 1979 with a new set of political institutions. As political life revived under the Second Republic, however, it was soon evident that Nigerians still took their politics very seriously—perhaps too seriously. During the 1983 election campaign, intense party rivalries replaced the old ethnic cleavages and provoked political violence and electoral fraud. Growing fears of this chaos explain in part the enthusiastic welcome the military received when it intervened in December 1983 to end the political turmoil and the democratic system that had permitted it.

The return of the military in 1983 brought an end to partisan politics, but it did not end citizen participation. The usual pattern of clientelism continued even under the stiff anticorruption policies of the military regimes. Students, factory workers, civil servants, and others pressured the military governments to obtain benefits or desired policy changes. In the early 1990s, Nigerians intensified their political involvement as the Babangida military regime moved toward restoring civilian rule. When that shift failed in 1993, Nigerians resisted the return of the military and the

harsh rule of General Abacha with politically motivated strikes, riots, and uprisings. When the transition to civilian rule finally did occur in 1999, the Nigerians were again ready to resume their roles as full participants in the political process.

THE CITIZEN IN POLITICS

Nigerians appear to love politics and they engage in politics with enthusiasm. This political zeal is difficult to restrain and often leads to violence and disorder. A prominent Nigerian political scientist has captured the problem of citizen politics in Nigeria.

> We are intoxicated with politics. The premium on political power is so high that we are prone to take the most extreme measures in order to win and maintain political power, our energy tends to be channelled into the struggle for power to the detriment of economically productive effort, and we habitually seek political solutions to virtually every problem. Such are the manifestations of the overpoliticization of social life in Nigeria.[2]

As politics becomes warfare, the state decays and the military steps in to suppress all political action. Such was the case when the military intervened in 1966, 1983, and 1993.

The natural enthusiasm Nigerians have for politics is reflected in colorful and exciting political meetings and rallies. This often results in disorderly election campaigns and vote-rigging by overeager partisans. The opportunities for political action have been limited by long years of controlled participation when the military has ruled. When the military relaxes these controls or when there is a short-lived experience with democracy, the people explode in tumultuous political action. The disorder discredits democracy and provides excuses for renewed military intervention. The pattern of brief periods of exuberant politics followed by long years of repression has prevented the development of more orderly and effective patterns of citizen involvement.

Political participation in Nigeria is often a risky undertaking. Agitation under military rule can result in imprisonment or loss of employment. Short-lived democratic eras allow participation but those who do become involved may pay for it later when the military returns to power. Many politicians from the Second Republic were jailed after the 1983 coup. When steps were taken in the late 1980s toward a new democratic experience, the military banned the participation of all those who had been involved in the politics of the Second Republic, even in relatively minor ways. After the aborted 1993 elections, many of those who had taken active parts in the attempts to move toward civilian rule were jailed by the Abacha regime. Such patterns of on and off participation and the later punishment of those who do participate even when it is legal are powerful disincentives to public involvement in politics.

What citizen political activity does occur is concentrated in the urban areas among the more educated sections of the population. Less educated and rural Nigerians are generally left on the periphery of politics. A carpenter expressed well this isolation of the uneducated from politics: "In Nigeria the ordinary people are suppressed and their wants cannot be made known to the government, especially if you have no education."[3] With an illiteracy rate of 47 percent, many Nigerians have limited ability to play a meaningful political role.

Often, Nigerians seek to influence politics or seek relief from a problem with the bureaucracy indirectly through the use of middlemen or brokers. These brokers are individuals who have established personal networks or contacts with government officials and civil servants. The networks may be developed through the brokers' economic or work experience or they may stem from common educational backgrounds in the same schools. Individual citizens who need help in dealing with the bureaucracy will seek the intervention of one of these political brokers, whom they may know because of family ties, ethnic backgrounds, or a common hometown. The brokers use their personal ties and their superior knowledge of how the system works to help their friends or relatives. The importance of these informal brokers illustrates the continued political role of the primordial communal ties in modern Nigeria.

In a similar manner, ethnic and clan leaders still exercise political influence and serve as important political intermediaries. Traditional leaders no longer dominate formal positions of political power but they still have an aura of authority that gives them political influence. Political leaders still seek the advice and support of village leaders and the elders even though they do not feel compelled to always follow the advice they receive. The continued importance of traditional leaders is particularly marked in northern Nigeria,[4] but it also is evident in other parts of the country.

There is the expectation that political involvement brings economic advantage not only to the individual but to friends, family members, and those who come from the same village. This is reflected in three principles accepted widely in Nigeria:[5] (1) backers of the group in power can expect rewards in the form of contracts for government projects; (2) those benefiting from such material advantages from political power are expected to pass on some of the benefits to others from their family, clan, and community; and (3) this process helps those in power stay there because "they are at the fountainhead of wealth." To Western eyes, such a system suggests nepotism and corruption. Indeed, there is often abuse of the system and diversion of government resources into private hands. But the system is well entrenched in long-established practices and helps solidify and perpetuate the communal ties valued by Nigerians. That an individual might profit from government responsibilities is seen as natural. The celebrated Nigerian novelist Chinua Achebe captures this well as he describes a group awaiting the arrival of an important government minister:

> Tell them that this man had used his position to enrich himself and they would ask you . . . if you thought that a sensible man would spit out the juicy morsel that good fortune placed in his mouth.[6]

But the benefits were not simply personal; those in positions of influence are expected to help their friends and extended families. In another episode, Achebe presents a young man encouraged to take a post in the civil service because "our people must press for their fair share of the national cake."[7]

Even before independence, there was a well-established tradition of political protest and violence when less dramatic means of redressing grievances were unsuccessful.[8] The use of political violence continued after independence both during civilian and military rule. Perhaps surprisingly, much of this violence is not due to ethnic differences. Nigerians in all parts of the country traditionally have resorted to protest and violence because of economic or political discontent unlinked to ethnic divisions. Thus, there have been riots or violent demonstrations over taxes, bureaucratic rules, salary increases, agricultural prices, education reforms, and so on since independence. While this proclivity to political violence can be destabilizing, some see it also as an obstacle to the establishment of an authoritarian one-party state in Nigeria. One author writes: "This demonstrated ability to 'make things hot' for upper and especially middle level leaders who overstep the power people think they should have may well further the democratic process in the country."[9]

The most recent demonstration of the Nigerians' willingness to engage in political protest came in the early 1990s. After the Babangida regime voided the presidential elections held in June 1993, people from all across the country took to the streets to oppose the military's actions and to call for a return to civilian rule and democracy. The unrest continued for several weeks and contributed to General Babangida's decision to resign and appoint an interim civilian leader. That proved no solution to the problems and yet another military coup brought General Abacha to power.

Abacha's heavy-handed rule temporarily quelled the rebellion. But in June 1994, when the purported winner of the 1993 election, Chief Moshood Abiola, declared himself president, he was promptly arrested. New demonstrations occurred and a broad-based prodemocracy movement, the National Democratic Coalition, emerged. In July a long strike calling for Abiola's release and inauguration as president added to the political turmoil. The strike began with petroleum workers but spread through much of southern Nigeria among industrial and white-collar workers and professionals such as educators and doctors. Protests, strikes, and uprisings continued in Nigeria up to the transition to civilian rule in May 1999. The new civilian government of President Obasanjo may inherit the oppositional

kind of participation that has characterized Nigeria's eras of military rule. If protest and opposition prevail, they might convey the sense of a weak state under the civilians, undermine the legitimacy of the Third Republic, and provide an excuse for another military intervention.

Nigerians need to be able to do more than oppose. Nigerians seem much better at resisting authoritarian rule than in supporting democratic government. To oppose authoritarianism is only part of the solution. As one writer notes:

> . . . unwillingness to abide authoritarian domination is a positive cultural value attribute for democracy only when it is supplemented by other attributes, including tolerance, patience, political efficacy, willingness to compromise, and respect for the rules of the democratic game.[10]

Military regimes have dominated Nigeria's history of independence. They are not very good at teaching democratic values or practices. It is not surprising that as their country turns again to a democratic regime, Nigerians still lack the political culture of attitudes, values, and orientations that support democracy.

VOTING

Electoral politics under the First Republic (1960–66) had promoted instability and violence. Political campaigns heightened tensions between ethnic groups within and across regions as each party sought to maximize its turnout through extremist rhetoric. The last elections in the Western Region resulted in the near-total breakdown of public order and provided the pretext for the military's intervention into politics. For nearly 15 years while the military ruled, there were no elections of any kind in Nigeria. The military appointed all officials at the local and national levels.

Voter turnout in the years immediately after independence was high. Under the Second Republic (1979–83), however, turnout ranged from 30 to 54 percent of the registered vote in local, state, and national elections. When Nigerians next had the chance to vote for a civilian president in 1993, turnout is estimated to have reached only 30 percent of registered voters.[11]

Virtually every election in Nigeria since 1960 has been plagued with charges of voting fraud and corruption. Most of these accusations have some basis in fact. The physical problems of organizing elections in a country the size of Nigeria create one set of problems. Many polling places are in remote places without electricity, telephones, or other links to the Federal Election Commission charged with assuring honest elections.

The 1993 presidential elections marked some improvement over this record. A new set of primary elections in March 1993 achieved such order that one observer noted that it was "probably one of the most decent set of elections in [Nigeria's] history."[12] There were nonetheless many examples of "vote-buying and sometimes sordid horse-trading."[13] While most international observers declared the June 1993 presidential election to be fair, General Babangida disagreed and annulled the elections on the grounds that both the primaries and the actual election were rigged. There were abuses and irregularities; more unsettling was the reemergence of ethnicity in the campaign and its aftermath.

In late 1998 and early 1999, elections were held in anticipation of the resumption of civilian rule in May 1999. Electoral turnout in the state elections, local elections, and elections for members of the National Assembly was low. Only the presidential election, coming as the culmination of a series of elections for local governments, senators, and representatives, mobilized large numbers of Nigerian voters. The presidential election produced a lively debate among the supporters of the two candidates. After several aborted elections, many voters, however, were still wary of whether or not the 1998 and 1999 elections would mean anything. All of these elections, however, were deemed by foreign observers as fair and free from the fraud that had discredited earlier Nigerian elections.[14] Most important, the elections resulted in a democratic selection of leaders for the transition to the Third Republic.

Nigeria's abysmal record with elections is worrisome. Democracy is founded on free and competitive elections. Repeated problems with electoral fraud have discredited electoral politics in Nigeria. In addition, the inability to avoid ethnic and religious themes in the campaigns makes elections a dangerous time when old sectarian cleavages are reopened and deepened. As a result, elections—usually the key to modern representative democracy—may place obstacles on the path to democracy in Nigeria.

PARTICIPATION AND STABILITY IN NIGERIA

The alternation from extreme politicization during civilian rule and total repression of political action under military rule is understandable. Nigerians enjoy politics. When restraints are removed, they engage in it with zeal and eventually this produces excesses and violence. The violence and disorder precipitate military action and repression. The tragedy is that the repetition of the pattern several times in the 40 years of Nigerian independence has prevented the development of more normal and orderly forms of political involvement.

The challenge for the new democratically elected leaders of the Third Republic is to build on the Nigerians' natural zeal for politics while developing political institutions that can channel and respond to the citizens' demands. Over time, the regime must hope that citizens will develop those political cultural attributes that will support democracy: trust, patience, tolerance, and a sense of political efficacy. This will be difficult for a country trying to reinstall democratic institutions and at the same time forced to address the serious economic crisis and social tensions that Nigeria faces at the start of the twenty-first century.

WOMEN IN POLITICS

The role of women in Nigerian society has varied in the past from one region to another. In the north, prevailing Islamic traditions kept women in clearly secondary social and political roles. Northern Nigerian women had no part in making community decisions and were totally subject to their husbands. Under Islamic law, women were not regarded as legal persons. In contrast, women had important economic and political roles in both the Yoruba and Ibo traditional societies. Village or ethnic group councils, although led by male elders or chiefs, often solicited the views of women on issues affecting the community. Southern women traders dominated the market places and acquired economic importance. They were often able to use their economic power to influence politics.[15] Occasionally, women traders even resorted to violence to protest political decisions against their interests, as in the 1929 Aba "Women's War" against colonial taxes and in the 1958 riots over the introduction of school fees.

These regional differences persist in modern Nigeria. In the north women were not allowed the vote until the 1979 election, and even when they were finally able to vote, continued influence of Islamic principles required separate lines for women voters at right angles to the male lines.[16] Elsewhere in Nigeria women appear to be as interested or more interested in politics than men. They feel free to express their own political opinions rather than repeating those of their husbands. A comparative study of political participation in several countries suggests that Nigerian women are as politically active as women in Austria and Japan and much more active than women in India.[17]

Many women hoped for a greater political role in the return to civilian rule expected in 1993 and were disillusioned by the even smaller role allowed them under the Abacha regime. Women had a prominent place in the democratic movement that emerged after the annulment of the 1993 presidential election. However, prejudice against women in politics is still present and makes it difficult for a woman to win elected office.

INTEREST GROUP POLITICS

In many Third World countries interest groups are poorly organized and attract few members compared to similar organizations in Western democratic countries. In Nigeria this is not the case. A comparative study of political participation in seven countries found a greater proportion of southern Nigerians belonging to politically active interest groups than was found in more highly developed countries including Japan, the Netherlands, and the United States.[18] Another study found 75 percent of southern Nigerian

women and 80 percent of the men were members of at least one voluntary association.[19]

Many studies of democratization suggest that a key to success in building durable democracies is the presence of what is called a "civil society." A civil society is one where many voluntary associations allow citizens to learn to interact with each other, to develop trust, to learn compromise, and to organize participation in the broader polity. These associations serve to limit government by involving citizens in social, economic, and political activities. Nigeria has always had a potential strong point for building democracy in this African country because of the well-developed set of voluntary associations.

Some of these associations, however, had divisive consequences. Before independence and for a decade or more afterwards, the most prominent groups in Nigeria were the ethnic associations. Membership in these bodies was more common than affiliation with economic interest groups such as trade unions or employers' associations. These ethnic organizations have been especially important in growing urban areas where recent immigrants would turn to their respective ethnic associations for social ties, economic support, and defense of common ethnic interests.

The ethnic organizations became involved in regional and national politics and contributed to the racial tensions that tore apart the First Republic. When the military took over in 1966, it clamped down on the political action of ethnic associations and sought to reduce their memberships. With the return of civilian rule in 1979, the ethnic organizations enjoyed greater freedom of action but they did not regain the political importance that they had in the early 1960s. The ethnic organizations that still function concentrate their action on mutual aid and community development rather than on national politics.

Farm Groups

Farmers remain the largest occupational group in Nigeria composing an estimated 60–65 percent of the workforce. They lack a powerful association to express their political interests. Organizing the farmers for political or economic action is complicated by the variance in farming needs in different parts of the country. Farmers range from the peasants of northern Nigeria who remain firmly under the grip of traditional overlords to successful cocoa farmers to well-to-do large landowners. There are also large social and economic differences between traditional and more modern farmers that make cooperation difficult. With such varied interests and concerns, Nigeria's agricultural producers have had difficulty in organizing for common political action.

Even without an effective organization, farm interests must be taken into account by government leaders. The population is still overwhelmingly rural, and agricultural production is vital to the economy. In the past, government neglect of farm interests has provoked rural uprisings; several such episodes occurred during military rule to remind the generals of the dangers of failing to take care of the farmers. Democratic governments, facing the additional threat of penalties at the polls from the large farm population, are likely to pay heed to rural interests even without the presence of a powerful farmers' association.

Trade Unions

Trade unions have developed slowly in modern Nigeria. Industrial workers make up only a small proportion of the economically active population, so the base for recruitment remains small. Ethnic divisions hampered early efforts at unionization; the ethnic and communal loyalty was usually stronger than the sense of working-class solidarity. Under military rule, strikes and most other forms of union work action have been illegal. The military government tried to control the labor movement by creating a central labor organization known as the Nigerian Labour Congress (NLC). This central union was supposed to coordinate all trade union activity. The government created bargaining frameworks that were to settle disputes and to prevent labor unrest from turning into strikes. Despite these efforts, there have been periodic wildcat strikes and union-led work stoppages that succeeded in gaining some limited concessions for workers.

The unions remain weak in terms of membership, both in absolute numbers and in extent of unionization of potential members. All trade unions combined have only about 500,000 members in a country with a population in excess of 80 million. There are ideological divisions within the NLC. Despite efforts to overcome ethnic divisions, communal cleavages are also present in the labor movement. Finally, the weakness of the labor movement is compounded by the fact that the strongest work force, the oil workers, have their own union—the National Union of Petroleum and Gas Workers (NUPENG)—and reject calls for solidarity with the NLC. Such divisions were manifested in the labor-led struggle for democracy in July and August 1993. The strongest backing for the movement came from the oil workers' union. It was joined by some parts of the NLC, but unions in the north and many in Ibo states failed to join in the general strike. Such divisions contributed to the failure of the prodemocracy movement.

The military has tolerated some local and limited strikes where the objectives are clearly economic gains for the workers. However, successive military regimes have crushed strikes, especially those that seemed to take on political dimensions. On several occasions, the military has stepped in, dissolved the NLC and the NUPENG leaderships, and imposed new leaders more amenable to cooperation with the state. For example, the military dissolved the NLC leadership in 1988 when the unions launched an attack on the government's austerity policy. The NLC distributed posters and brochures opposing the government's attempts to cut benefits, freeze salaries, and increase revenues in the midst of Nigeria's deep economic crisis. In some cases, the trade unions succeeded in winning as when the government increased the minimum wage and rescinded cuts in welfare programs. But these victories were temporary as the struggling economy declined so that the results of these gains were nullified by inflation and deterioration of services.

After the failed attempt to restore democracy in 1993, there were several major strikes to challenge the voiding of the presidential election and to contest Abacha's authoritarian rule. Abacha imprisoned many labor leaders from both the oil workers' unions and eventually even the more timid leaders from the NLC.

The Nigerian labor movement's political weakness and lack of political access force it into reacting against government actions rather than contributing positive ideas to policy discussion. The unions must resort to protest because they are not consulted earlier in the policy-making process. Yet government is the principal interlocutor of the trade unions. The government itself is the largest employer in Nigeria; the overwhelming majority of union members work for federal or local government units. This immediately politicizes labor union activity, since the unions must pressure government not only for general policy changes but also for improved salaries and working conditions. With few privileged points of access to policy makers, the labor movement uses direct action through strikes and demonstrations to press its demands on government.

Business and Employers' Groups

Much less is known about the political impact of business and industrial interests. It might be expected that business influences in politics are strong because of the ease with which business can claim that its interests are those of the state given the government's preoccupation with developing the economy. Often the Nigerian government forms partnerships with private companies, both foreign and domestic, in order to develop a desired economic activity. This obviously leaves the government open to influence from private industry and business. In general, business seems to restrict its demands on government to fairly narrow concerns such as the granting of a license or concession rather than seeking to influence broader policy issues.

By far the most important business influence is that wielded by international investors. The Nigerian state owns its oil resources but foreign companies do the exploring, drilling, pumping, and refining while paying royalties to the government. These companies enjoy vast influence over Nigerian policy making that affects their industry in any way. In addition, foreign bankers and international bodies such as the World Bank and the International Monetary Fund often dictate social and economic policies as conditions for new loan guarantees or investments. Limits on government spending, economic restructuring, higher taxes, and fewer social programs are often the demands of these international interests. Such policies may accommodate the needs of the foreign investors but they are often detrimental to the interests of Nigerians.

The trading associations, especially the market women, have considerable influence over policies directly affecting them. Their overall political power is reduced by their traditional view of politics, which leads them to seek particular favors from individual politicians rather than to develop more enduring access into the political system in order to change government policies in a broader sense.[20]

Political influence of employer interests was long limited by the importance of foreigners in the business community. During the 1970s the military government decreed that foreigners could not engage in certain economic activities and must have Nigerian partners in other activities. Another stimulus toward the development of a Nigerian business community came in the early 1990s when the state began to privatize some of the enterprises that it owned. This promoted the growth of an indigenous business community that may well mean increased political influence for commercial and industrial interests.

Influence of Interest Group Politics

Interest group political influence in Nigerian politics does not appear to be great. There are few statutory bodies, such as the corporatist structures in Germany, to bring about the formal contact of government and interest group representatives in policy-making roles. Loose party discipline in the legislative bodies (when they operate) makes legislatures vulnerable to lobbying activities of interest groups. But there is little evidence to suggest that interest groups have yet developed the capability of exploiting their opportunities. Most seem to rely on traditional politics in the form of personal contacts with kinsmen or home village friends in attempting to extract particularistic favors from government. Beyond these narrow favors, much of the other interest group activity is negative in the sense of protest or opposition to policies already adopted by government. The regimes in power from 1983 to 1999 were even less vulnerable to interest group pressure. Their authoritarian nature and their willingness to use coercion to limit strikers or other groups opposing their policies limited the field of action for most interest groups.

Civil Society

In spite of their troubled history, Nigerians have always had strong longings for democracy in their country. In the mid-1990s, an active prodemocracy movement developed in Nigeria even under the oppressive rule of General Abacha. The movement began among supporters of Moshood K. Abiola, the presumed victor in the 1993 presidential election that was annulled by the military. It gradually drew in others who were committed to democracy: students, educators, lawyers and judges, trade unionists, human rights activists, journalists, and others.[21] The National Democratic Coalition (NADECO) emerged as an umbrella organization to coordinate and focus the activities of the various groups and individuals working for democracy. The prodemocracy coalition was cross-class and interethnic with representatives and groups from all parts of the country and all kinds of Nigerians. But its center in Lagos enabled the Abacha government to label it as "Yoruba" and to use that as a means of rallying other ethnic groups, especially northerners, to support its repression of the prodemocracy groups.[22] Hundreds of prodemocracy activists were jailed by Abacha's regime. The movement did not die but it waned as it appeared that Abacha was set to turn his military dictatorship into a civilian but still dictatorial regime.

When Abacha died in 1998, the new military ruler, General Abdulsalami Abubakar, renewed the promise of a prompt return to civilian rule. The democracy groups reemerged and pressed Abubakar to avoid delays or thwarting his pledge to turn the government over to an elected civilian government by May 1999. Now that the transition to democracy has occurred, there are concerns that the prodemocracy movement will fragment to pursue narrow interests of those who worked together to achieve democratic rule. For all their love of democracy, Nigerians also have a history of "democratic" politicians who destroy democracy by their personal avarice, concern for jobs and benefits rather than for national policy, communal and ethnic commitments, and excesses once in office. The proof of the depth and durability

of Nigeria's civil society will be the ability of the Third Republic to attract politicians willing to preserve democracy rather than personal perquisites.

POLITICAL PARTIES

When Nigeria achieved independence from Britain, many Western observers were particularly optimistic about its future because Nigeria was the only newly independent African country to start self-government with what most regarded as the prerequisite for democracy: a multiparty system permitting interparty competition and free elections. These hopes turned to disappointment as the parties' competition became extreme and election campaigns were accompanied by interparty violence. There was a political party identified with each region and ethnic group: the Action Group in the west among the Yoruba people; the National Congress of Nigerian Citizens (NCNC) in the east among the Ibos; and the Northern Peoples' Congress (NPC) in the north among the Hausa-Fulani peoples.

With a solid political base in one ethnic community, each party exploited ethnic and regional tensions for its own political benefit. The parties were a major contributing factor to the collapse of public order that brought the military into politics and ended the First Republic. Once the military took over in 1966, the new military leaders immediately disbanded the parties and barred organization of any new ones. Only in the last phases of the transition to civilian rule 12 years later did the Supreme Military Council (SMC) permit parties to reorganize.

The Party System of Nigeria's Second Republic

Five parties eventually emerged to seek influence in the Second Republic. A number of northern politicians formed the National Party of Nigeria (NPN). Many of its leaders had earlier played important parts in the old NPC. Within the NPN there were six candidates for the party's 1979 presidential nomination. After a lively contest, Alhaji Shehu Shagari emerged as the NPN presidential candidate and party leader. The other four parties developed around the presidential aspirants outside the NPN. Chief Obafemi Awolowo, a leader of the independence movement and former leader of the Action Group, organized the Unity Party of Nigeria (UPN) and became its presidential candidate. Dr. Nnamdi Azikiwe, another independence leader, founder of the NCNC, and former president of Nigeria before the military era, became the presidential candidate of the Nigerian People's Party (NPP). One element of the NPP rejected the Azikiwe nomination and split off to form the Great Nigerian People's Party (GNPP). This party nominated a Muslim, Alhaji Waziri Ibrahim, as its presidential candidate. Finally, the People's Redemption Party (PRP) was a break-off from the NPN. Its leader, Alhaji Aminu Kano, had a long reputation for challenging Hausa-Fulani rule in the north and felt his ideas were ignored by the more conservative NPN.

All parties avoided blatantly ethnic or regional appeals in both the 1979 and 1983 elections. Each party attempted to present ethnically balanced tickets for the positions at stake in the state and national elections. This ticket-balancing, referred to as "zoning" by the Nigerians, was often extensive and delicate. For example, the NPN reserved the presidential nomination for a northerner but stipulated that its vice presidential candidate would be an Ibo, its party chairman a Yoruba, and its nominee for Senate president someone from a minority ethnic group.

For a voter seeking to make a choice among rival party candidates, the party programs offered little variety despite the number of candidates.

Personality, regional and ethnic loyalties, and religious affiliations were all more important factors in distinguishing the parties of the Second Republic than their positions on policies for governing Nigeria. While their programs were basically similar in content, the parties were nevertheless polarized by personal rivalries and only partially disguised ethnic fears. This polarization meant that even though policy differences were not great, compromise and moderation were difficult to achieve.

Even though parties avoided ethnic appeals, in the end Nigerian voters still seemed determined to "vote for their own kind."[23] One party, the National Party of Nigeria, did emerge from the 1979 elections with a national following (see Table 40–1). To its strong base in the north, the NPN added important strength from minority ethnic groups in the South. The NPN's presidential candidate took 33.8 percent of the overall, nationwide vote—more than any other candidate—and was declared president. Finishing first or second in eighteen out of nineteen states, Shagari not only came in first in the north but also won more votes than any other candidate in seven southern states. The NPN also won House seats from sixteen states and Senate seats from twelve states. No other party came close to this national base of political support. Using the slogan "One Nigeria, One Nation," the NPN further broadened its appeal in 1983 by launching energetic efforts to establish the party in areas outside its natural ethnic base. The National Party of Nigeria emerged triumphant from the 1983 elections with the reelection of President Shagari, a solid

Table 40–1   Results in the 1979 and 1983 Elections of Nigeria's Second Republic

	Seats in Federal Senate (%)		Seats in Federal House of Representatives (%)		Governorships Won (%)		Presidential Vote (%)	
	1979	1983	1979	1983	1979	1983	1979	1983
NPN	37.9%	64.7%	37.4%	59.1%	36.7%	68.4%	33.8%	46.0%
UPN	29.5	14.1	24.4	8.1	26.3	15.8	29.2	30.1
NPP	16.8	14.1	17.4	10.6	15.8	10.5	16.8	13.6
PRP	7.4	5.9	10.9	9.0	10.5	5.3	10.3	6.8
GNPP	8.4	1.2	9.6	—	10.5	—	10.0	2.5

majority in both houses of the National Assembly, and over two-thirds of the governors. But the accusations of voter fraud that followed, tarnished this electoral success and ultimately undermined the legitimacy of Shagari's party and the Second Republic itself.

In 1984, the Buhari military regime moved quickly to suppress all political party activities. The parties were disbanded; new ones were forbidden. Party offices, records, and supplies were seized by the new military government. Many party leaders ended up in jail, not for their political persuasions but because they were accused, often accurately, of corruption and profiteering. Beyond the parties' tarnished reputations for dishonesty, the military leadership also disliked the perpetuation of old ethnic alignments. While overt ethnic themes were avoided, the party system of the Second Republic basically reproduced the trifold ethnic divisions of Hausas, Ibos, and Yorubas in a three-party system. There were few civilians who mourned the military's disbanding of the party system. In northern villages, youths put up signs in the early 1980s warning all parties to stay out.[24] The venality of their leaders and their proclivity to violence and disorder had discredited them before the military banned them.

Generals Making Parties, 1986–1998

After the fall of the Second Republic at the end of 1983, an era of military rule began in Nigeria that lasted over 15 years. The generals often talked about returning power to civilians but they proved reluctant to do so. By the late 1980s, however, the military leadership began preparations for the return to civilian rule by renewing political parties. The generals made clear that they wanted an entirely new party system and wanted to be strongly involved in the creation of the new parties. They established a National Electoral Commission (NEC) to supervise the formation of new parties. The NEC invited aspiring politicians to propose new parties and thirteen were proposed. However, the military saw in these "pre-parties" many of the same people and problems as in the discredited party system of the Second Republic: leaders with tainted reputations, ethnic and regional sectarianism, and lack of discipline. The Armed Forces Ruling Council

(AFRC), headed by General Babangida, stepped in directly and banned all of these aspiring parties. Instead, the AFRC created on its own two new parties: the National Republican Convention (NRC) and the Social Democratic Party (SDP). To ensure that the other pre-parties disappeared, police sealed their offices and enforced the ban by arresting any of their leaders who continued political activities.

The new NRC and SDP were to be entirely free of past associations with any earlier political organizations. Anyone who had participated in politics during the First or Second Republics was prohibited from joining or leading new political movements. All candidates had to be cleared by the National Electoral Commission and had to establish that they had no prior political tie. The NEC sought to synthesize programs for the parties from the manifestos of the 13 pre-parties. The National Republican Convention was given a platform situating it slightly to the right of center; the Social Democratic party was placed just to the left of center. The NEC then began the task of clearing tens of thousands of prospective candidates for the two parties in preparation for the first partisan elections in 1991. Within a few months of their organization, Nigerians were already beginning to see the National Republicans as a northern and Islamic party and the Social Democrats as southern and Christian.

This method of party building produced two artificial parties with no basis in existing political or social patterns. The ban on politicians with prior involvement in the First and Second Republics left the new parties without competent leaders. As a result, the new parties lacked the ability to cue voters to their preferences or to draw upon the popularity of older leaders as a means of establishing their identities and building a following.

The resulting 1993 presidential election was disastrous. It resulted in a complicated tangle of ethnic, regional, and religious loyalties and rivalries that were barely disguised at the beginning and openly expressed by the end. For example, the SDP candidate, Moshood Abiola, was a Yoruba but Muslim. He found difficulty in winning the confidence of the north, which largely favored the NRC candidate and faced hostility in the south from Christians and Ibos who did not want to be ruled by a Yoruba Muslim. As election day neared, a disgruntled SDP Ibo, who was disqualified from running himself but who nevertheless enjoyed an insider position with the military regime, led the campaign to void the election.

The election took place under the cloud of a last-minute effort by Babangida to cancel the election. While Babangida tried to stop the counting of ballots, independent and international sources showed Abiola with 58 percent of the vote and majorities in 19 states and Abuja.[25] He won majorities in 4 of 11 northern states (including the NRC candidate's home state of Kano). Abiola had 33 percent of the vote or more in twenty-eight states, well beyond the requirement that a successful candidate demonstrate cross-regional support by having a third of the vote in at least 20 states. However, General Babangida annulled the presidential elections. He then disbanded the parties he had created and arrested many of their leaders. Party life again came to an abrupt halt in Nigeria.

Efforts by General Sani Abacha to establish yet another party system a few years later were even more artificial. Under international and domestic pressures, Abacha talked about restoring democracy and finally agreed to do so by 1998. To this end, Abacha oversaw the creation of five new political parties in October 1996. The parties had little basis in political or social reality. Most of those earlier involved in Nigerian politics were deliberately excluded. The prodemocracy movement was not represented in the new parties. One opposition leader denounced the new parties as "five fingers of the same leprous hand."[26] These new parties provided candidates for the local and state elections that were supposedly designed to begin the transition to civilian rule. The lack of public interest in these parties was manifest in the very low turnout for these elections: 15 percent for state government elections in December 1997 and under 5 percent in the April 1998 elections for the National Assembly.[27] In April 1998, presidential nominating conventions were held by the five parties and all nominated General Abacha as candidate for the August presidential elections. This all-but-certain "coronation" of Abacha was averted only because of Abacha's sudden death by a heart attack in June 1998. The Abacha transition to his own version of "civilian rule" was ended as a new military leader, General Abdulsalami Abubakar, took power. The five parties he had created quickly fell apart.

The Political Parties of the Nigerian Third Republic

From the first days of his rule, General Abubakar promised a return to civilian rule by 1999. He kept that promise, turning power over to a democratically elected, civilian regime less than a year after he assumed power. His regime oversaw the creation of new political parties but allowed much greater latitude to the civilian politicians as they set up their new parties. Participation in the new parties was open to opposition and prodemocracy groups. The new parties seem to have taken hold, at least initially. They were able to generate real public support evidenced by growing turnout in the elections that brought about the transition to civilian rule in May 1999.

In quick order, three political parties emerged. The three parties differ little in ideological positions. The 1999 election campaigns at all levels rarely addressed specific policy commitments. Instead, they built on regional, ethnic, and personality loyalties.

The People's Democratic party (PDP) emerged almost immediately as the party with the broadest national appeal. It developed a strong organization with offices and supporters throughout all regions of Nigeria. It enjoyed the support of retired military officers, northerners, and many Ibo southerners as well. The PDP selected General Olusegun Obasanjo as its presidential candidate. Obasanjo is a former military leader who presided over a military regime from 1976–1979, the first military regime to pass power back to the civilians. He was imprisoned by General Abacha during the mid-1990s. He is a Yoruba Christian, but his own people do not trust him because of his ties to military officers in the north. During the election campaign, Obasanjo promised further economic deregulation and privatization of state-owned enterprises. He also more vaguely promised increased expenditures on education and health. In the 1999 elections, the PDP

Table 40-2   Political Parties in the Nigerian Third Republic, 1999

	Percentage Vote in the Presidential Election	Percentage of Seats in National Assembly*	Senate*
People's Democratic Party (PDP)	62.8%	57.2%	54.1%
All People's Party (APP)	} 37.2	{ 20.6	26.6
Alliance for Democracy (AD)		18.9	18.3

*Partial results for the National Assembly. There were 12 vacancies in the House and 1 in the Senate.

emerged as the clear winner at all levels (see Table 40–2).

The Yorubas organized their own party, the Alliance for Democracy (AD). In its campaigns, the AD stressed its independence from the military. More so than the other two parties, the AD became the rallying point for many of the prodemocracy groups that had mobilized after 1993. The Alliance for Democracy claimed a more "progressive" program but as was the case with the PDP and APP, it gave little specific detail to its proposals. The AD too issued vague calls for economic reforms and new efforts to respond to Nigeria's social needs. Underlying this campaign, however, was the AD's clear advocacy of the interest of the Yorubas. It had little electoral appeal beyond southwest Nigeria but there, in Yorubaland, it was very strong.

The All People's party (APP) has its political roots in the north and lacks the national appeal of the PDP. There was some evidence that the APP became the political base for some supporters of the former military dictator, Sani Abacha. The APP formed a coalition with the AD for the presidential election. It called for support of the AD's Olu Falae, a Yoruba and former federal finance minister. It was a strange coalition given the fact that the two parties seemed to bring together the bitterest of rivals during the Abacha era. Despite occasional stress, the coalition held together reasonably well through the presidential election. On its own, the APP did well in state and National Assembly elections in parts of the north. But it was unable to rally its supporters behind Falae in the presidential election.

These three new parties offered Nigerians choices in the elections of 1998 and 1999. They do not have, however, clear bases in Nigerian society. The key to the consolidation of democracy in Nigeria will be the success of these parties in defining clear alternatives, recruiting able and honest politicians, and establishing loyalties among the voters. That will take time.

Political Parties and Democratization in Nigeria

Political parties play a key role in representative democracy because they organize elections and offer voters options between different ways of approaching public policy matters. Nigeria illustrates how difficult it can be to develop and institutionalize parties that can in fact present governing alternatives.

Since its independence in 1960, Nigeria has had two different sets of problems with parties: (1) too many divisive parties and (2) the absence of parties. The first problem is the disruptiveness of divisive and irresponsible political parties. In the past, such parties have been a major part of the problems of civilian government in Nigeria. They have accentuated ethnic and regional divisions, contributed to political violence, and recruited dishonest and corrupt politicians. Multiple parties are needed for the competition that is an essential part of democracy. But party divisions heighten already serious cleavages and party competition leads to violence and corruption. The resulting chaos destroys the legitimacy of the state and raises doubt about democracy.

Many scholars see advantages in single party systems during the early phases of political development. But the problem is transforming that single party rule into a competitive and responsive system. The experience of the Communist Party in China demonstrates the ability of a disciplined single party to mobilize efforts to modernize a traditional society, but it offers little hope for the development of a responsive system, much less a democratic one.

This first illness in Nigerian parties has produced the second: the frequent intervention of the military followed by the disappearance of parties. A situation where there are no parties makes the restoration of democracy and civilian rule very difficult. Parties are the means by which representative democracy are able to work. Even effective dictatorships need parties to organize and mobilize public support for the regime. In the absence of parties or with ineffective parties, political disorder and chaos are likely. Parties are the single most important set of institutions in the development of effective and durable political systems. They develop, channel, and extend political participation of individual citizens. They provide goals and direction to the state and recruit and train future political leaders.

The failure of Nigerian parties has thus seriously handicapped the process of political development in the country. Political parties have been a source of problem throughout the history of independent Nigeria. During the First Republic they promoted ethnic violence; they discredited the Second Republic with corruption and disorderly elections. One of the main challenges facing Nigeria's Third Republic is the need to build and institutionalize democratic and competitive political parties that will offer responsible and honest political leaders.

CONCLUSION

The expansion of political participation needs to be balanced with the development of political institutions capable of organizing and channelling this participation if instability is to be avoided. In most cases, military regimes are very poor at maintaining such a balance.[28] The Nigerian military regime did not prove to be an exception to this general rule. In 1979 and 1993, the transitions to democracy were faulted by the military's interference and refusal to allow full participation and unfettered party development. But the blame was shared by civilian politicians who seemed more interested in personal gain and regional and

communal interests than in building a new Nigerian democracy. As the new century begins, Nigeria has the democracy that its people want. It is now up to the citizens and their political leaders to foster those attitudes and sets of behavior that will allow that democracy to flourish.

There is no doubt that one of Nigeria's greatest resources is its people. They are interested in politics and in reshaping the future of their country. The challenge for the new civilian leaders of the Third Republic is to mobilize the citizenry for constructive involvement in the country's political processes. Expanded opportunities for citizen involvement, more vital interest groups, and an orderly and honest set of parties are all essential to effective and stable political participation.

NOTES

[1] Samuel P. Huntington, *Political Order in Changing Societies* (New Haven, CT: Yale University Press, 1968).

[2] Claude Ake, cited in *West Africa,* May 26, 1981, pp. 1162–1163.

[3] Margaret Peil, *Nigerian Politics: The People's View* (London: Cassell, 1976), p. 149.

[4] C. S. Whitaker, Jr., *The Politics of Tradition: Continuity and Change in Northern Nigeria* (Princeton, NJ: Princeton University Press, 1970).

[5] Richard A. Joseph, *Democracy and Prebendal Politics in Nigeria: The Rise and Fall of the Second Republic* (Cambridge, England: Cambridge University Press, 1987), p. 1.

[6] Chinua Achebe, *A Man of the People* (Garden City, NY: Doubleday, 1969), p. 2.

[7] Ibid., p. 11.

[8] See for example, B. A. Williams and A. H. Walsh, *Urban Government for Metropolitan Lagos* (New York: Praeger, 1968), p. 28; and K. W. J. Post and G. D. Jenkins, *The Price of Liberty: Personality and Politics in Colonial Nigeria* (London: Cambridge University Press, 1973).

[9] Peil, *Nigerian Politics,* p. 177.

[10] Adigun Agbaje, "Mobilizing for a New Political Culture," in Larry Diamond, Anthony Kirk-Greene, and Oyeleye Oyediran, eds., *Transition Without End: Nigerian Politics and Civil Society Under Babangida* (Boulder, CO: Lynne Rienner, 1997), p. 158. (Agbaje attributes this idea to Larry Diamond.)

[11] Rotimi T. Suberu, "The Democratic Recession in Nigeria," *Current History,* May 1994, p. 215.

[12] *West Africa* 5, April, 1993.

[13] Suberu, "The Democratic Recession in Nigeria," p. 215.

[14] *New York Times,* 1 March 1999.

[15] See Margaret Peil, "Female Roles in West African Towns," in *Changing Social Structure in Ghana* (London: Oxford University Press, 1975).

[16]Barbara Callaway, "Women and Political Participation in Kano City," *Comparative Politics* 19 (July 1987): 379–393.

[17]Norman H. Nie et al., "Political Participation and the Life Cycle," *Comparative Politics* 6 (April 1974): 319–340.

[18]Sidney Verba et al., *Participation and Political Equality: A Seven-Nation Comparison* (London, England: Cambridge University Press, 1978), p. 101.

[19]Piel, *Nigerian Politics,* p. 162.

[20]Pauline H. Baker, *Urbanization and Political Change: The Politics of Lagos, 1917–1967* (Berkeley: University of California Press, 1974), pp. 241–243.

[21]Adebayo O. Olukoshi, "Associational Life," in Diamond, et al., *Transition Without End.*

[22]Peter M. Lewis, "An End to the Permanent Transition?" *Journal of Democracy* 10 (January 1999): 141–156.

[23]Olatunde B. J. Ojo, "The Impact of Personality and Ethnicity on the Nigerian Election of 1979," *Africa Today*, 1981, pp. 47–58.

[24]William Miles, Elections in *Nigeria: A Grassroots Perspective* (Boulder, CO: Lynne Reinner, 1988).

[25]Suberu, "The Democratic Resession in Nigeria," p. 213.

[26]Cited in Lewis, "An End to the Permanent Transition?" p. 150.

[27]Ibid., p. 150.

[28]Huntington, *Political Order in Changing Societies.*

Chapter 41

Political Elites in Developing Nigeria

In Nigeria, as in many developing countries, the pool of available leaders is small because much of the population lacks formal education and thus the skills for modern political leadership. Those individuals who do receive an education, and especially those who are able to go abroad for university training in Europe or the United States, are eagerly sought for leadership positions in politics, government administration, schools, the military, and private business and industry. The competition for the services of these educated individuals often reduces the number of leaders interested in the uncertain and sometimes risky career of a politician. Nevertheless, politics remains an attractive career option for many Nigerians who see politics as an "open ticket to wealth and fame."[1]

The need for skillful political leaders is particularly great in Nigeria. The divided Nigerian society makes it important that there be highly competent leaders who can cooperate with each other to hold the country together. This cooperation requires leaders who are willing to avoid exploiting social cleavages, especially ethnic and regional divisions, even if there appears to be political advantage in invoking these emotional is-

sues. During the First Republic leaders of this kind were not often found in key political positions. In those first troubled years of independence, political leaders often played up regional and ethnic divisions for the political gain of their parties. The political bickering of the leaders and their exploitation of social cleavages paved the way to broader political violence among the population in general.[2] Similar problems destroyed the Second Republic. The new institutions were well designed, but the leaders were not willing to abide by them. Now, with the return again to civilian rule, the new democratically elected leaders will need to do what their predecessors did not: provide the country with a set of honest, equitable, and able leaders.

POLITICAL LEADERS

There are two types of political leaders in contemporary Nigeria: those who have achieved their positions through their own efforts and those who have obtained political influence due to their traditional village, clan, or religious positions. Leaders who have risen through their own achievements are often those who have received an education and then see politics as a way for rapid upward mobility. The traditional leaders, while often highly educated, hold their positions due to hereditary or religious rights. In many cases, these traditional leaders hold elected office; in other cases they exercise indirect but powerful influence over politics from outside the formal governmental institutions. Under the First Republic, traditional leaders sat as ex officio members in the indirectly elected Senate. Under the Second Republic, traditional leaders were no longer granted automatic membership, but many of these same village, ethnic, and religious leaders won popular election to federal and state-level offices.

The political power of the traditional leaders was enhanced by the British form of indirect colonial rule, which left these rulers in power and often buttressed them against modernizing trends. More recently, military rule also reinforced traditional leadership because the military leaders dismissed all elected politicians and relied often on traditional leaders for local-level political support. Even after the return to civilian government in the early 1980s, the traditional rulers remained very powerful political forces. This was true especially in the Islamic north, but also in the urbanized and presumably modern setting of Lagos where the oba of Lagos continued to exercise traditional prerogatives with both ceremonial and real political influence. These leaders cling tenaciously to their powers. For example, in the early 1980s, when a progressive governor of a northern state dared to challenge the influence of the local emir, the reaction was swift and violent: rioting, the burning of the governor's mansion, and the sacking of his party's headquarters. Ultimately, the governor was driven out of office.

The return to military rule in 1983 brought renewed importance to the traditional leaders, especially at the state and local levels. With the abolition of elected legislatures, the traditional rulers were often convened in council by the military governors to seek counsel on state and local matters. Babangida attempted to reduce the influence of traditional leaders because of the likelihood that their prominence would reintroduce regional and ethnic tensions during the transition to civilian rule. He rescinded earlier plans to give traditional leaders additional political preroga-

tives after 1992. Further restrictions on the traditional leaders came under General Abacha. More so than earlier military dictators, he concentrated political power at all levels into the hands of a small group of loyal military officers.

With the resumption of civilian rule, traditional leaders are reemerging as important power brokers. In many cases, they have run for and won elected offices. In other cases, they are counted on to deliver the votes from their supporters to the designated candidate. Much of the presidential campaign in 1999 involved visits by the candidates or their representatives to the traditional rulers to gain their endorsements and support.

It is possible that the prominent political role of traditional leaders is a transitional feature that will gradually wane over the years as modern, achievement-based leaders increase in number and in power. For the time being, these traditional rulers retain important political power and show little disposition to surrender it. Communal and clan loyalties remain powerful social factors among the population in general and are likely to reinforce traditional political leaders for the foreseeable future.

Nigeria is plagued by another leadership problem common to developing countries. Both traditional and modern leaders are set apart from the rest of the population. The gap between leaders and followers is due in part to the privileged economic status of the political leaders. It is also a product of the better education of the elite compared to the typical Nigerian. The leaders have accepted the values and practices of a modern and urban society while the rest of the society remains overwhelmingly rural and traditional. It is not simply that the leaders have more privileges and status, but that they have different views of the world. Some of the gap between leaders and the rest of the population is bridged by the informal familial and communal ties that link elite members with ordinary citizens from their extended families or villages.

Patron-client networks further reduce the distance. Political leaders (patrons) establish a body of followers (clients) who organize political support for their patron in exchange for material advantages. In exchange for political assistance, clients receive practical rewards such as government contracts, jobs, educational opportunities, or even food and clothing. Patrons at one level have clients who are patrons to a lower level of clients and so on. These networks form a pyramid of patron-client relations that link the political elite with the grassroots, although often at the cost of inefficient allocation of government resources. In the eyes of Western observers, such patron-client relations and family ties smack of corruption and nepotism. But these practices are not alien to traditional Nigerian customs and norms, which stress the importance of caring for one's family and fellow villagers, of exchanging gifts for services, and of doing favors to show deference to elders or traditional leaders.[3]

During the Second Republic, politicians generally avoided the ethnic demagoguery of the earlier era of civilian government. But their venality brought the fall of Nigeria's second democratic experiment. As the most important avenue for social and economic upward mobility, politics attracted many individuals who were more interested in enriching themselves and their kin than they were in building a new country. Through the extraction of bribes, the sale of government services and contracts, the misappropriation of public funds, and outright theft, politicians at all levels of the political system accumulated enormous private fortunes in a very short time. When the military stepped in at the end of 1983, the public warmly welcomed the fall of the discredited democratic regime and the arrest of its corrupt politicians.

Politicians also shared responsibility for the failure of the transition to civilian rule in 1993. Their willingness to bring ethnic, regional, and religious differences into the election campaign inflamed the always dangerous sectarian tensions. When the military interfered repeatedly in the electoral process from the time of the creation of the parties until the presidential primaries, the parties failed to act in unison. Instead, each party tried to draw advantage from the military's role. Finally, when Babangida voided the presidential election, the politicians failed to unite against that affront to democracy. A united front to defend democracy and civilian rule against the military very probably would have forced the generals to retreat. But NRC governors from all northern states and SDP governors in several eastern states applauded the military fiat that prevented the seating of the duly elected Yoruba SDP presidential candidate.

Western observers are often shocked by political corruption in Nigeria and other developing countries. We in the West, however, need to remember that widespread collusion between moneyed people and politicians has characterized our own countries' development and continues to taint politicians' reputations today. In addition, it should be pointed out that corruption can have certain positive effects. In some countries, but not Nigeria, party control over government contracts and services has permitted the growth of strong parties needed for political development. Bribes to political friends can reduce the frustrations of dealing with an otherwise unresponsive bureaucracy. All this is not to excuse corruption but to point out that development can take place alongside extensive political corruption if the levels of corruption are not so great as to destroy the legitimacy of the regime, as happened in the 1980s and 1990s in Nigeria.

Earlier experiences with democracy in Nigeria demonstrate the problems of building democracy without a leadership committed to fair play, respect for minorities, and honest management of state resources. A Nigerian scholar noted that the 1993 fiasco and the failure of the political leaders to unite against the military illustrate "the futility of trying to build democracy without true democrats." As a new democratic government takes Nigeria into the new century the recruiting of good leaders will be the secret to the success or failure of the venture.

BUREAUCRACY

At independence, Nigeria inherited a large and well-organized bureaucracy. There was no effort to change the basic administrative structures. There was, however, a strong desire to change the personnel at the top of the bureaucracy. Most of the senior positions were filled at the time with Britons or Indians. A first priority was the "Nigerianization" of the civil service: the replacement of the "expatriates" (foreigners) in public office with native Nigerians. As desirable as such a process might seem at first glance, Nigerianization antagonized relations among the ethnic communities. Northerners were much less enthusiastic about removing the foreigners than were southerners.

Recruitment regulations restricted the selection of senior civil servants to those Nigerians who had received formal educational degrees and even advanced university education. The better-educated southerners thus began to fill most senior civil service positions to the dismay of northerners. Northerners viewed this as discriminatory; they were particularly unhappy to see southerners take top positions even in the northern bureaucracy. In their view, Nigerianization simply meant the shift from one set of foreign rulers to a new set of equally "foreign" masters. To counter the growing influence of southerners in the civil service, the northerners organized "northernization" committees to promote the access of their people into the civil service. Despite these efforts, northerners still filled less than 1 percent of the senior posts in the federal civil service at the time of independence.[4]

Unequal access to positions in the civil service remains a major problem. In the 1980s and 1990s, successive military regimes replaced older, professional, senior civil servants with senior military officers and personal cronies. The usual justification was bureaucratic reform but the overall effect was to increase the presence of northerners in the bureaucracy.[5] By the late 1990s, southern resentments against the civil service had reached extreme levels. When the new civilian government took office in 1999, it faced the challenge of restoring the ethnic balance in the public service. In the climate of aggravated ethnic tensions, perceived discrimination builds pressures for greater regional autonomy or outright secession.

The Nigerian civil service has always been a large one. At independence, government employees and employees of state-controlled public corporations made up in excess of 63 percent of the nonagricultural working force. Even now, nearly half the nonrural workforce is employed by the government. The absolute size of the bureaucracy has grown rapidly, especially during the period when the military was in power. Another source of the growing bureaucracy was the creation of new states. Each new state had to create its own agencies and educational system. For example, in one year, the number of universities

in Nigeria went from six to eleven. This brought a vast expansion in the size of the public service. Once in place, civil servants and their posts are difficult to remove. Thus, the size of the bureaucracy continued to grow through the 1990s.

Maintaining political control over such a large and unwieldy bureaucracy has always been a problem. Prior to independence, British attempts to impose their brand of administrative neutrality and loyalty were thwarted by the tendency of Nigerian civil servants to feel justified in subverting a colonial system in order to suit local needs. This quite natural reaction against foreign masters contributed to the development of an independent and even disloyal attitude of civil servants toward those who were supposed to give them political direction.

The strength, independence, and power of the civil servants expanded enormously during the years that the military controlled Nigerian politics. Army officers have little skill in administration and even less expertise in the technicalities of public policies. They tended to rely heavily on the professional civil servants both in overseeing the bureaucracy and in providing information for policy decisions. In the last year of military rule, General Abubakar removed many of the military ministers and replaced them with civil servants. He tried to shift more responsibility for policy making into the hands of the career civil servants. However, a major problem was that much of the senior ranks of the civil servants was then filled with military-appointed cronies from the earlier "reforms." In effect, a dyarchy was established between the military rulers and the bureaucracy. The two groups dominated the political process and ruled together. Ultimate power remained with the military leaders, but the bureaucrats made most of the routine policy decisions and influenced even the major policy orientations in ways they had not been able to do under the civilian government. Eventually the civil servants became enmeshed in the factional politics within the military.

Over the last 15 years, the Nigerian bureaucracy lost its earlier reputation as modern civil service. Older, professional civil servants trained in western notions of bureaucracy were replaced by the friends of the military leadership. The replacements were less able and less honest. Many milked the public treasury and accumulated large fortunes. As the economic crisis worsened, lower-level bureaucrats left the civil service when they went months without pay—or compensated for the lack of pay by demanding bribes for the most routine actions. "What do you have for me?" is a common refrain used by customs officers at the airports, postal employees, building permit officials, and so on. At the same time that they gouge the public for bribes, the bureaucrats behaved badly toward those they were supposed to serve. The bureaucracy is seen as a white man's institution left over from colonialism. The middle-level civil servants, with whom most citizens are likely to have contact, are often condescending, peremptory, and rude in dealing with the public.

Much of the public views civil servants as corrupt and as having chosen their careers more because they saw the bureaucracy as a means for personal gain and improved mobility than because they wanted to serve the state. On several occasions in the 1980s and late 1990s civil servants were imprisoned, accused of often massive corruption. But graft and fraud continue to permeate the Nigerian bureaucracy.

It is important to note that the whole notion of bureaucracy differs from the Western notion of a body devoted to the impartial administration of government policy. Nigerians see bureaucracy "as a tool for the execution not of national objectives, but for the satisfaction and fulfillment of social and ethnic obligations (kinship ties, ethnic loyalties)." With such a conception of the bureaucracy it is not surprising that for many Nigerians ". . .

he is a hero who can successfully defraud and appropriate public service resources."[6]

The new civilian regime faces real challenges in restoring ethnic balance, public confidence, efficiency, and honesty to the tattered remnants of what was once an effective civil service. President Obasanjo and his government will also need to restore political control over a bureaucracy that has been politicized and free to do what it willed for almost two decades. Such control is necessary since democratic accountability depends on civil servants who obey political leaders, who are in turn elected by the public. Civil service reform is difficult everywhere; it is likely to be particularly challenging for the new democratic government in Nigeria.

THE MILITARY

The military has been the principal political actor in Nigeria's 40 years of independence. It ruled outright for 28 years and lurked on the sidelines as a powerful watchdog during the 12 years of civilian rule. By 1994, Nigeria had experienced six successful military coups; there were at least another six to eight abortive coups, including one in February 1976 that nonetheless changed the military dictator when General Murtala Muhammed, the chief of state at the time was assassinated (see Table 41–1).

The causes of the coups vary widely.[7] The 1966 coups were motivated by ethnic rivalries and civil disorder. Other coups were the result of rivalries within the military. General Gowon was overthrown after nine years in office in what was

Table 41–1   Military Coups in Nigeria, 1960–99

Date	Military Ruler	Ousted Leadership
January 1966	Johnson Aguyie Ironsi	Overthrew First Republic
July 1966	Yakabu Gowon	Ousted Ironsi regime
July 1975	Murtala Mohammed	Ousted Gowon regime
February 1976	Olusegun Obasanjo	Replaced Mohammed, who was killed in an abortive coup
December 1983	Muhammed Buhari	Overthrew Second Republic
August 1985	Ibrahim Babangida	Ousted Buhari regime
November 1993	Sani Abacha	Toppled caretaker civilian rule of Ernest Shonekan

called a "corrective coup."[8] His fellow officers were critical of the corruption that had developed during Gowon's rule and of Gowon's slow progress in restoring civilian rule. The military overthrew the Second Republic because of rampant corruption among political leaders and a contested presidential election. The military was

> . . . swept into power on a deep tide of disillusionment and disgust with civilian politics. Its primary purpose appears overwhelmingly to have been national salvation, not personal aggrandizement.[9]

Buhari was toppled in 1985 by his fellow generals as a result of internal military politics. Some officers felt that his rule was too heavy-handed, too slow in moving to restore civilian rule, and inept in managing the economy. Finally, General Sani Abacha seized power in 1993 when civil unrest, rising ethnic and religious tensions, economic collapse, and widespread corruption seemed to threaten the very existence of the state.

Thus, whenever the country encounters economic crisis, political violence, excessive corruption, or electoral fraud, the military steps in. A political coup is the "normal" way to respond to political problems and a solution often welcomed by the people. The pattern of repeated coups sets a tradition that will be very difficult to overcome once civilian rule is reestablished. The military will always be on the sidelines, watching, ready to intervene when it feels necessary.

This summary of military intervention demonstrates that the military in Nigeria, and in many other countries where the military frequently takes over the government, is not unified or homogeneous. Regional, ethnic, ideological, and personal rivalries split the Nigerian military as they split the civilian political leadership. On occasion, these divisions produced coups or attempted coups even while the military held power. As a result, the military dictator often tries to purchase the loyalty of other military officers with pay raises, public contracts, and generous retirement programs. There are also the celebrated "brown envelopes" of cash passed on to senior officers on their birthdays, religious holidays, marriages of their children, and so on.[10] From 1993–1998, General Abacha added the stick to the incentive system by periodic jailing of very senior officers, including General Olusegun Obsanjo, a past and future head of state.

The mechanics of a coup are quite simple, as illustrated by the coup that toppled the Second Republic. Late in the night on December 31, 1983, military units seized key government

---

THE KADUNA MAFIA

In the northern city of Kaduna the elite of the Nigerian military enjoys retirement in high style. The city was founded by the British, who made it their northern center of what they called Nigeria. After independence, Kaduna became the site of the new state's military academy. More recently it has become a comfortable military retirement community for senior ranking officers.

In a country plagued with poverty and suffering, life in Kaduna can be pleasant. Traces of the old colonial past are found in the plush Polo Club and Rugby Club. The retired officers, primarily from the north, still have the love of horses coming from their horse-riding culture of the past. The retirees may be too old to play much themselves, but they can enjoy watching the country's best polo players in comfort and grumble about the overall state of affairs.

While the military ruled, Kaduna was the center of political debate and occasionally plotting. As civilian rule is reestablished, it remains to be seen if the "Kaduna mafia" (as it is known in the south) can be kept out of politics. The words of one retired colonel indicate the challenge that the civilian leadership will have in keeping the military securely in the barracks or in Kaduna:

> I am not going to stand by and see anyone exclude me from my country. To say now that we need a clean break from the military—there is no clean break. . . . It is most unfair and most painful to have people lump us together and say we are incompetent because we are the military. . . At 56 and condemned! No way! No way![11]

offices, radio-television stations, and airports. President Shagari was arrested after a brief battle between his personal guards and the army units sent to arrest him. Similar operations in federal ministries and state capitals assured a quick victory for the conspiring officers. Within a few hours, the military had complete control of Africa's most populous country with only a handful of casualties and few shots fired. The New Year's eve coup of 1983 ended Nigeria's second experiment with democracy and ushered in an additional 16 years of military dictatorship.

How the Military Rules

Although the military rulers have the ability to govern in an authoritarian manner, on most occasions they have avoided doing so in Nigeria. They consult traditional leaders and civil servants and other presumably influential individuals. Nevertheless, the military leaders often prove to be unresponsive to "signals from below" such as newspaper editorials, letters to the editor, and "murmurings" in the market places, taverns, and other public forums. Indeed, the failure to provide for representation of the general public and organized groups is one of the great weaknesses of Nigerian military government.

There is a lively debate among political scientists about the ability of military regimes to contribute to political and economic modernization. Some see military governments as able to organize a developing country's efforts at modernization. The military is better able to do this than others because of its ability to impose political order in otherwise tumultuous settings. It can provide discipline, organization, and hierarchical control that civilians often find elusive as they seek to govern and change their societies. Because of the armed forces' concern for a strong economy as a support for national defense and to finance the purchase of the latest military hardware, military governments are viewed as having a greater dedication to modernization than civilian governments. Their authoritarian nature also makes it easier for modernizers to ignore the opposition of those attached to traditional social patterns.

Others challenge this optimistic view of the military as modernizers. They claim that in practice, when the military rules, the generals inevitably divert a larger share of the national wealth to the armed forces. Much of the increased defense expenditure goes for the purchase of military equipment from abroad. This investment in foreign military hardware robs the domestic economy of important resources that otherwise might have been used to promote economic growth at home. More important, critics of the military's role as a modernizer point to the inability of the military to develop the effective political institutions, especially those institutions like political parties that organize broader citizen participation—that is, the very institutions that are needed for political development.

Nigerian experience does not resolve this debate over the positive or negative contributions of military rule. But in the case of Nigeria, there have been more negative than positive effects on modernization. Military rule in the 1970s coincided with important economic gains, but these gains are attributable to the exploitation of the country's oil resources and rising petroleum prices rather than the military's economic control. In the 1980s and 1990s, military rule did not stop the country's economic decline. Nor did the generals prove any more resistant to corruption than had the civilian politicians and bureaucrats of the Second Republic. Under military rule, the army grew to one of the largest and best equipped on the continent. It still absorbs a substantial portion of the country's economic resources. In addition, shifts in the world economy, notably the apparent economic competitive advantages of free economies and open societies, made military dictatorship in Nigeria a clear liability to the country in resolving its economic problems. To achieve real economic progress Nigeria needs "government officials to adhere to strict standards of public service and accountability" and the rule of law, characteristics not often found in military rulers.[12]

Beyond the question of the military's contribution to economic development is the issue of the military's ability to promote political development. Inevitably, military rule is authoritarian. It has done little to promote healthy forms of political participation, durable political institutions, or government responsiveness to citizens' concerns. The military does have the capability of enforcing order on a restive society. The military regime of General Gowon succeeded in rapidly defusing ethnic and regional tensions after the Biafran war. His conciliatory position toward the secessionist Ibos made it possible to very rapidly reintegrate this people into a more united Nigerian nation. The firm rule of the military restored order to those parts of the country torn by political strife in the last years of the First Republic, a task that the civilian leaders had failed to fulfill.

The military's record in the 1980s and 1990s was less positive. Its officers rapidly became entangled in the corruption that had prompted the military to intervene in 1983. The military regime proved unable to eliminate and sometimes even to control the growing religious divisions within the country. Finally, and perhaps most ominous, the military after 1993 seemed willing to evoke ethnic tensions to justify its reneging on the pledge of civilian rule.

Back to the Barracks

The key problem in military rule is how to make the transition back to civilian government when everyone, even the armed forces, feels that should occur. The first delayed and then failed transition to democracy in the early 1990s in Nigeria illustrates the difficulty of getting the military out of politics once it has entered. There is often strong sentiment among military officers to get out of politics and "return to the barracks." They recognize that governing diverts the military from its primary task of defending national security. Military leaders often worry, and correctly so, that their involvement in politics will entice their fellow officers into corruption that will discredit the military. Such impulses reinforce feelings in the general public that the military should not remain in political power. On the other hand, the entanglement in government strengthens the military officers' vested interests in staying in power.

When the military decides it is time to return government to civilians it often tries to control the circumstances of that change and to leave itself with tools to control politics even after they have returned to the barracks. That was the case with the Nigerian military in the 1990s. Nigerian military leaders seem to have wanted to return to the barracks, but they did not trust the civilians to handle the nation's problems. When 1993

elections seemed likely to produce a president that the military feared it could not control, the generals refused to relinquish political power.

In Nigeria, the two eras of transition proved to be long: 13 years between the First and Second Republics, 16 years between the Second and Third Republics. In both transitions, the military played a tutelary role in the rebuilding of democracy.[13] The military oversaw the creation, more accurately the imposition of new party systems, monitored elections, and directed the writing or rewriting of the constitution.

As a result of the military's role in preparing the way for civilian rule in 1979, public interest in the transition to democratic rule was minimal. There was no great popular movement for democracy. Nor was there in the failed transition to civilian government in 1993. The military's dominance of the democratization process offered little place for involvement of the citizenry in general. This was not the case in the 1999 transition. The military's tutelage was still omnipresent in forming the party system, conducting elections, and revising the constitution. But there was growing public insistence that the military step aside for civilian and democratic government. The oppressive nature of Abacha's rule and frustrations from the aborted presidential election in 1993 created a prodemocracy movement.[14] While it enjoyed its greatest strength from the professional and intellectual circles, the movement also had a mass base. First Abacha and then Abubakar faced considerable pressure to restore civilian rule.[15] There were large-scale demonstrations and smaller acts of sabotage that showed the growing impatience with seemingly permanent military rule. If the new civilian regime can maintain this public enthusiasm, it will be able to endure. The military rarely undertakes a coup against a popular government.

In 1999, the Nigerian military returned to the barracks and political control passed to an elected civilian government. Of course, the big question is whether or not the military will indeed stay out of politics. One Nigerian scholar notes that the problem facing the Third Republic is

> whether soldiers, who have been used to enjoying certain perquisites and privileges of political power, and who have been accustomed to being treated like

lords as the politicians before them would be content with the drab and unprestigious life of the barracks.[16]

A lot of the future of democratic rule depends on how the civilian government fares. If it is able to make progress, even slow progress in addressing Nigeria's economic and social problems, the military may stay out of politics. In some ways, the fact that President Obasanjo is a former military general and ruler may assist in keeping the military content. At the beginning of his tenure, he enjoys the confidence of the military. He remains close friends with many in the "Kaduna mafia" and may listen to their advice if only to keep them from feeling too isolated from power.

However, Obasanjo is no more a proxy for military rule from behind the scenes than Dwight Eisenhower was in the United States. In his inaugural address, Obasanjo was surprisingly critical of the preceding military regimes. One of his first acts in office was to suspend all contracts made by the Abubakar government in its last months. Many of them were to military figures. Within a month of his installation, Obasanjo forced 29 senior officers into retirement. He seized hundreds of millions of dollars from these and other associates of Abacha. It was a good strategy to act so soon against the military. Now his continued mastery of the ship of state depends on his ability to produce policy decisions that will ease Nigeria's many socioeconomic problems.

NOTES

[1]Margaret Peil, *Nigerian Politics: The People's View* (London: Cassell, 1976), p. 178.

[2]Kenneth Post and Mighael Vickers, *Structure and Conflict in Nigeria 1960–1966* (London: Heinemann, 1973), pp. 234–236.

[3]Rotimi T. Suberu, "The Democratic Recession in Nigeria," *Current History,* May 1994, p. 217.

[4]Taylor Cole, "Bureaucracy in Transition," in Archibald Callaway et al., *The Nigerian Political Scene* (Durham, NC: Duke University Press, 1962).

[5]Ladipo Adamolekun, "Transforming the Civil Service," in Larry Diamond, Anthony Kirk-Greene, and Oyeleye Oyediran, eds., *Transition Without End: Nigerian Politics and Civil Society Under Babangida* (Boulder, CO: Lynne Rienner, 1997).

[6]Fidelis C. Okoli, "The Dilemmas of Premature Bureaucratization in the New States of Africa: The Case of Nigeria," *African Studies Review* 23 (September 1980): 12.

[7]For a good general treatment of why the military intervenes, see Samuel E. Finer, *Man on Horseback: The Role of the Military in Politics,* 2nd ed. (Harmondsworth, England: Penguin, 1976). For specific studies of the Nigerian military's actions, see S. K. Panter-Brick, ed., *Nigerian Politics and Military Rule: Prelude to the Civil War* (London: Athlone Press, 1970.

[8]M. J. Dent, "Corrective Government: Military Rule in Perspective," in Keith Panter-Brick, ed;, *Soldiers and Oil: The Political Transformation of Nigeria* (London: Frank Cass, 1978), pp. 101–137.

[9]Larry Diamond, "Nigeria in Search of Democracy," *Foreign Affairs* 62 (Spring 1984): 905.

[10]J. 'Bayo Adekanye, "The Military," in Diamond, et al., *Transition Without End,* p. 63.

[11]*New York Times,* 3 February 1999.

[12]Adebayo Adedeji, "An Alternative for Africa," *Journal of Democracy* 5 (October 1994): 122.

[13]Richard A. Joseph, "Democracy Under Military Tutelage: Crisis and Consensus in the Nigerian 1979 Election," *Comparative Politics* 14 (October 1981): 75–100.

[14]Adebayo O. Olukoshi, "Associational Life," in Diamond, et al., *Transition Without End.*

[15]Peter M. Lewis, "Nigeria: An End to the Permanent Transition?" *Journal of Democracy* 10 (January 1999): 141–156.

[16]Adekanye, "The Military," p. 77.

Chapter 42

Nigerian Political Performance

What would happen if I were to push my way to the front and up on the palm-leaf-festooned dais, wrench the microphone from the greasy hands of that babbling buffoon and tell the whole people . . . that the great man they had come to hear . . . was an honorable Thief. But of course they knew that already. No single man and woman there that afternoon was a stranger to that news . . . and because they all knew, if I were to march up to the dais now and announce it they would simply laugh at me and say: What a fool![1]

These words from a novel by one of Nigeria's leading writers betray the disillusionment of the country's intellectual elite with the corruption and ineffectiveness of postindependence government. But the evaluation of how well a political system is performing is always highly subjective since there are no broadly agreed upon standards of what constitutes a "good" political system. Evaluators are left to determine on their own the criteria and measures for good political performance. The resulting assessments reflect the evaluator's biases and judgments. It is particularly difficult to make such evaluations of a Third World country where political values and aspirations are likely to be quite different from those

of observers in Western industrialized democracies. Inevitably, the developing country is judged by how far along the road of Westernization it is, with the assumption that a Western type modern state is a universal goal. Such is not the case. Many Third World countries have cultures with entirely different priorities than do Western industrial societies. In such settings, a "livable" state may not be one with a rapid economic growth rate or large-scale industrialization but rather a state where there is less emphasis on foreign industry, loans, and technology and greater attention to the agricultural sector, a concern for social equality even at the cost of slower economic growth, and a preference for informal training rather than formal education. The chaotic conditions in Africa in the 1990s have provoked a renewed concern among African intellectuals for seeking genuine African models for development and democracy.[2]

Until such a model is defined and implementation begun, however, it is likely that Nigeria and other African states will be evaluated by the rest of the world—and also by themselves—according to Western models of modernity. Irrespective of the nature of the regime, virtually all Third

World countries aspire to develop their economies. Both for informed citizens and public officials economic success is a prime indicator of the government's effectiveness. In new states recently freed from colonial rule, such as Nigeria, the desire for national independence includes the need to develop the economy through industrialization.[3] This "modernization imperative" leads the political elites in these countries to stress economic growth and industrialization even where the traditional cultures and values might favor other avenues of political development.

Another pitfall in the evaluation of Third World countries is the problem of finding reliable data on key measures of economic performance, social trends and change, and political attitudes. It is often difficult to find statistics even on the basics. For example, in Nigeria there is no reliable census data to give accurate information on the size of the population, its geographic distribution, age structures, or life span. Where statistics are available, they are often unreliable. Thus, in a survey of Nigeria, a respected London news magazine warned: "This is the first survey published by *The Economist* in which every single number is probably wrong. There is no accurate information about Nigeria."[4]

With these caveats on the dangers of imposing Western values and measures on a still traditional society and on the unreliability of even the best data available, we will nevertheless undertake an evaluation of the political performance of the regimes in Nigeria. Readers are encouraged to view these evaluations with particular skepticism and to attempt to form their own judgments on the successes and failures of this new country.

ECONOMIC DEVELOPMENT

Nigeria ought to be economically sound. With vast petroleum resources, Nigeria is the world's sixth largest oil producer. The large deposits of high quality, low sulphur petroleum lie along and off the shores of southeastern Nigeria in the delta of the Niger River. New deposits are still being discovered. Nigeria ought to have enough oil for domestic purposes and exports well into the new century. Gas reserves, perhaps even more important than the oil deposits, have only recently been exploited. The irony is that with all this oil wealth, Nigeria is on the brink of economic collapse with over $29 billion of foreign debt, a gross national product that has dropped by 50 percent since 1983, and a crumbling infrastructure of public utilities, roads, railways, airports, and seaports.

During the 1970s, oil's potential for economic growth was demonstrated as petroleum production and exports increased rapidly giving Nigeria an annual growth rate of 8 percent. Six large multinational oil companies have developed Nigeria's oil industry, with Dutch-based Shell Oil Company the largest. But the Nigerian government has a majority ownership in the industry and receives vast amounts of royalty payments. The state-owned Nigerian National Petroleum Corporation takes 60 percent of all profits. The relationship between the government and the oil companies is close, with government officials skimming off fortunes for their personal use. For example, General Abacha and a small coterie of his followers are believed to have diverted $2.5 billion in oil revenues to their own uses. But it is not just one set of leaders; the pillaging of the Nigerian economy by those who rule has continued through successive civilian and military regimes.[5]

Oil provides 95 percent of export revenues and about 90 percent of government revenues. Any economy that is so highly concentrated in one industry faces risks. Those risks are especially important when the single product is a natural resource. Markets for natural resources are highly volatile and unpredictable even for one as essential as oil. Prices and demand fluctuate wildly, making it difficult for economic planners to predict future revenues and production. For example, oil production in Nigeria grew very rapidly during the 1970s to the point that daily production reached 2.1 million barrels a day by 1980. Projecting future oil sale receipts on the basis of these trends, the government launched an ambitious national development plan for using oil revenue to promote agriculture, education, and transportation.

Then the worldwide economic recession hit, reducing demand for oil; oil producers dropped their prices, diverting Nigeria's customers to other lower-cost sources of oil. Oil production in Nigeria plummeted from 2.1 million barrels a day in the summer of 1980 to only 500,000 barrels a day

GAS LINES IN OIL-RICH NIGERIA

One of the great ironies of recent years is that despite their vast oil resources, Nigerians have frequently faced gas shortages and very high fuel costs. The reasons are political. In the 1970s and 1980s, Nigeria took steps to develop its own refineries to meet domestic needs. However, political leaders of successive regimes allowed these refineries to deteriorate and to eventually stop production. Today, of four refineries, two are closed and the other two operate at about 50 percent capacity despite very strong domestic demands. The leaders have allowed this to occur because they found an important way to reward themselves and their friends. They made enormous amounts of money by selling or owning import licenses for refined oil products and thereby controlling fuel costs. As a result, gasoline shortages are frequently severe and fuel prices are very high. At the end of 1998, a gallon of gas sold for almost $7 in much of Nigeria. Black marketeering and fuel smuggling have become rampant.

Handling volatile fuels in this manner is dangerous. In October 1998, fuel thieves broke open the pipeline from the south to Kaduna to pirate gasoline. A huge crowd had assembled over three days to get their share of the spewing fuel. Eventually, a spark ignited the gasoline. The explosion and massive fireball killed over 700 people, many of them children and women scavenging gas from puddles to resell.

a year later. The loss of oil income endangered the ambitious and costly development plans and left Nigeria with some serious trade deficits and foreign loans to pay off. Since 1981, oil production has increased slowly, but the possibility of radical changes in the natural resource markets weakens economic planning and puts long-term investment programs in very great difficulty. The success in oil has not spilled over to other economic areas. Petroleum exports account for over 95 percent of Nigerian exports. As a result, the country's economy is extraordinarily vulnerable to fluctuations in the world oil market.

Another problem with oil-related development is that it does not lead to balanced economic growth. Most of the investments in drilling and refinery equipment go to pay for the importing of foreign manufactured goods and services. For example, in 1970 oil companies spent some $182 million (U.S. dollars), but less than 10 percent of this amount went to Nigeria-controlled companies for materials produced in Nigeria with a large Nigerian ownership. Most of the oil is still exported in its crude form for refining elsewhere. This means that Nigeria misses out on the profits of refining its oil in its own refineries and exports less valuable crude.

In addition to these structural and economic problems, politics contributed to the failure to prosper from the country's oil wealth. Collaboration between the Nigerian government and the oil industry has brought vast corruption. One estimate puts the amount of oil revenues squandered through "contract cronyism and corruption" over the past 25 years at an incredible $250 billion.[6] This has discredited and delegitimized successive civilian and military regimes. Overwhelming public deception with any and all political leaders is a heavy legacy from this corruption that the new civilian regime inherits.

Close ties between oil companies, notably Shell Oil Company, and the government have allowed exploitation without concern for environmental protection. There are few environmental regulations and those that exist were easily waived in response to bribes or payoffs. Today, much of the air, land, and waters of the Niger delta region, once Nigeria's most fertile region, are contaminated.

Finally, the close intertwining of oil and the state have produced problems of distributing the benefits from the industry throughout the country.[7] The oil resources are concentrated in a half-dozen states in southeastern and south central Nigeria. Over the decades, the federal government has struggled with the task of dividing the oil revenues between itself and the states and among all states. The resulting political conflicts pit north against south and one state against others. Political squabbling over oil money has fed already dangerous regional and ethnic conflicts. All over Nigeria, government officials want a share of the oil money since oil provides over 90 percent of the country's revenues. They see oil revenue as the key to their state's economic development and their ability to provide services to their peoples.

The peoples of the delta region, especially the Ijaw and Ogoni, feel that their wealth has been stripped from them. In spite of their region's oil wealth, they are among the poorest in Nigeria. They feel that the regime's failure to allow them to benefit from "their" oil wealth is a continued sanction for their attempted secession in the 1960s. Peoples in the oil-rich region see themselves as losing in two ways: first the loss of "their" natural resource and second the destruction of their land by the pollution of rapid and unregulated oil exploitation. In recent years they have rebelled, seizing pipelines, occupying pump stations, and sabotaging other oil facilities. The first ethnic incident that the new democratic Third Republic faced was an uprising in the delta region within days of its installation. It is likely to face more such challenges in the coming years.

Industrial Development

Beyond the oil industry, which is more of an extractive industry than a manufacturing one, industrial development has moved only slowly. Since independence, Nigerians have sought to develop their own iron and steel industry, an industry regarded widely as the keystone of a modern, independent economy. Development of such an industry requires foreign expertise and financial assistance, and several foreign governments considered and then abandoned plans to build an iron and steel complex in Nigeria. Eventually, the Soviet Union agreed to help build one in Ajaokuta, near the confluence of the Niger and Benue rivers. The new plant, the largest in Africa, began operation in 1985. But by the end of the decade the Ajaokuta steel factory was operating at a very reduced level due to both economic and technological problems.

Heavy industrial plants are scattered and often are subsidiaries of foreign firms. For example,

Peugeot and Volkswagen automobiles are assembled in Nigerian plants for delivery throughout sub-Saharan Africa. However, the economic crisis of the 1980s cut sharply into the production of such plants. The Peugeot plant was assembling 270 vehicles a day at the end of the 1970s; its production had fallen to only 10 a day at the end of the 1980s. Volkswagen production dipped from 50,000 cars a year to only 5,000. Many other factories that seemed promising are producing well below half of their capacity.

Over the past decade, the infrastructure that once seemed among the best in Africa has deteriorated. Roads, electrical generators, and telecommunications have gone undeveloped and poorly maintained.

In a country of over 115 million inhabitants, there are fewer than 350,000 telephones. Postal service is slow and unreliable. Highways and railroads are still few in number and nearly always in poor repair. Many parts of the country are still without electricity. Where there is electricity, there are frequent power outages that disrupt production as well as people's lives. Nigerians have altered the acronym for the state-owned National Electric Power Authority—NEPA—to stand instead for "never expect power again."

Without modern transportation and communication, industrial growth outside already developed and sometimes overdeveloped urban areas is uneconomical. Over the past decade, the country's infrastructure has been allowed to deteriorate. Roads, railroads, ports, thermo- and hydroelectric generators, and other public utilities are worse than they were in the 1980s as those who could plundered the government's coffers rather than maintain or expand public utilities. The key supports for industrial growth are now missing. The new civilian regime faces the enormous task of rebuilding this infrastructure at a time of economic depression and vast external debts.

Neocolonialism

Inherent in the dependence on foreign investment and technical know-how is the threat of a new economic colonialism to replace the old imperial colonialism. Foreigners profit more from Nigerian petroleum than do Nigerians; they seem to exercise undue influence over economic and financial decisions by Nigeria's industry and even its government. Nigerians often feel that their national institutions are disregarded by the foreign firms doing business in their country. They resent the economic and political influence that these firms are able to exercise. They are able to point to numerous examples of such interference. Fifteen years of fruitless negotiating with foreign countries over the construction of an iron and steel complex, viewed by Nigerians as an essential element in their economic independence, offered proof to many Nigerians that these countries were thwarting their desires for true independence. Phillips Petroleum's unexpected and unexplained withdrawal from an international consortium building a natural gas liquification plant demonstrated the unreliable nature of multinational corporations. In the 1980s, the unilateral cancellation of commitments to purchase Nigerian petroleum by multinational oil companies provided further evidence of foreign firms' failure to keep their agreements with Third World countries.

To promote greater control over the economy, successive Nigerian governments, both civil and military, pressed for nationalization, indigenization, and Nigerianization of business undertakings in Nigeria. Nationalization means the bringing under public or government ownership of certain existing or projected industries. In most cases, the Nigerian government has acquired majority holdings, or total ownership, in a number of key economic enterprises: banking, insurance, mining, public utilities, natural gas, petrochemicals, fertilizers, and iron and steel. Indigenization assures private Nigerian businessmen participation or control over certain economic activities. Nigerianization means the replacement of foreign ("expatriate") personnel in key economic positions with native Nigerians.

The results of these efforts were mixed. Even firms where the government holds majority ownership seemed to act independently. Oil firms are sometimes criticized by Nigerians for following sales or pricing policies that are more responsive to the minority multinational oil company's interests than to the needs of the majority shareholding Nigerian government. Indigenization ran into delays as the number of Nigerians interested

in buying out foreign owners was not large and the money available for such transactions was limited. Nigerians sometimes served as front men for foreign economic interests in order to comply at least on the surface with indigenization requirements. Nigerianization also met with limited success. Sometimes, as at the Peugeot plant, foreign firms negotiated exceptions from the rules. Overall, there was little indication of an exodus out of Nigeria of displaced expatriates.

Under pressure from international financial institutions such as the World Bank and the International Monetary Fund, Nigeria began to reverse some of these policies in the 1990s. Nearly 100 state-owned enterprises were sold to private investors but this privatization steered clear of the major enterprises and affected only 2 percent of the state's share of the economy. Unlike in Britain and France where privatization produced important new sources of revenue for the government, in Nigeria, any income from privatization seems to have disappeared, probably into the hands of corrupt officials. Foreign ownership of industry is still limited to 40 percent of any single enterprise in manufacturing, energy, and banking. The impediments to investment in Nigerian industry in the form of rules, bureaucratic red-tape, and corruption discourage all but the hardiest of foreign investors.

Despite its oil wealth, Nigeria faces a dilemma common to all the developing world. It does not have enough capital to finance the construction of the needed infrastructure and industrial base that it hopes will give it a modern industrial economy. It must therefore turn to foreign economic interests. As it accepts foreign help, it risks losing control over the economy and even the country's fiscal policies. The foreign interests, which include private multinational corporations, international banks, and foreign countries, acquire the ability to influence and even dictate the policies and politics of Nigeria and other such countries, bringing the fear of a neocolonialist domination.

Agriculture

The oil revolution and the growth of new industries overshadow the fact that agriculture still remains the basis of the Nigerian economy. About 54 percent of the working population is engaged in farming. Agriculture accounts for approximately 40 percent of the gross national product, down from over 60 percent of the GNP as recently as 1960. Despite its agricultural wealth, Nigeria has seen its rural economy founder in the past 25 years. Until recently, Nigeria was self-sufficient in food production. Cocoa, cotton, palm oil, and other commodities were Nigeria's principal exports. Now many of these agricultural exports have declined. By the 1980s, Nigeria had become an importer of agricultural products, with food amounting to approximately 15 percent of the total imports each year. Fertilizer is in short supply. Production is up but struggles to keep up with a growing population. Shortages of basic commodities are common.

The poor performance of agriculture is due to a large number of problems, many of them beyond the ability of any government to remedy. Climatic problems have reduced the arable land as prolonged drought in much of central Africa has pushed the Sahara Desert southward toward northern Nigeria. Nigeria has not experienced the critical famine that has plagued other countries bordering the Sahara. It is farther from the region affected by desertification, although some sections of northern Nigeria have experienced problems.

In the south, the problem is just the opposite: tropical rains have eroded the topsoil in areas near rainforests. Most farmers are illiterate and lack knowledge of soil conservation, fertilizer use, and improved seeds. They are often wedded to traditional farming techniques and resist efforts to teach them new ways. The farms are scattered and remote from population centers, making rapid distribution of farm goods difficult. Traditional marketing practices are inefficient and result in large profits for middle-men. On occasion, these agricultural problems are exacerbated through extensive hoarding by profiteers, creating food shortages and very high prices for staple foods such as rice and sugar.

Modern Nigerian governments inherited a complicated mixture of traditional landholding patterns. In a few areas, land was owned by individuals. Some large cocoa and rubber plantations developed during the colonial era and survived after independence. The dominant land tenure form was communally owned farmlands controlled by the village or clan leaders in southern Nigeria

and by local governments in northern Nigeria. Families were allocated use of this communal land according to their needs. Often the same plots remained in the hands of the same family for several generations, but the title to the land officially belonged to the community.

Whatever the ownership, the vast majority of farms in Nigeria were small plots barely large enough to provide for the needs of the families working them. In 1978 the military issued a decree transferring ownership of all land to the state governments. The purpose was to break up some large privately held farms, to improve access to farmland for landless farmers, and to avoid land speculation. Those using the land for farming were entitled to continue doing so rent-free. One early problem was that government ownership of the land made it impossible for farmers to use the land as collateral for loans needed to purchase the seeds, fertilizer, or equipment needed to improve their production.[8]

A "green revolution" in the 1980s produced only limited progress. The government intended to invest in agro-based industries and to promote the use of fertilizer, improved seeds, farm implements, and tractors. Despite the government's commitment to this reform, the green revolution faltered from the start. Much of the money devoted to rural reform was absorbed by an urban bureaucracy and spent on offices in the cities to run the "revolution." The economic problems brought on by the oil glut of the early 1980s slowed investment in agriculture. Farmers resisted the use of new techniques; plans for tractor pools failed; land clearance and irrigation projects moved ahead very slowly if at all. There is often talk about the urgent need for change but very little action. One problem is that nearly all talk of reform is couched in terms of large-scale agriculture that has little effect on the predominant small peasant for whom such grandiose plans are far beyond their means or their skills.

The problems of the green revolution illustrate some of the key economic difficulties confronting Nigeria. The economy remains closely linked to the world petroleum market; reduction in oil revenues threaten performance and progress throughout the economy. The large government bureaucracy charged with administering the economy consumes much of the money available to promote development in maintaining itself.

Modern techniques and change encounter resistance from poorly educated people still attached to familiar and traditional values.

SOCIAL AND HUMAN DEVELOPMENT

Nigeria, like many other countries recently embarking on the path to economic modernization, is a country of remarkable contrasts. In the small villages life goes on little affected by the country's changes. The majority of Nigerians still live in huts in small villages with traditional values and practices still dominant. In sharp contrast is life in the large cities where the modern economy is evident. Here the problems are those of the industrial countries: overcrowded cities, polluted air, high crime rates, housing shortages with jammed government-subsidized apartment complexes and slums and shanty towns inhabited by recent immigrants from the villages, inadequate health and sanitary facilities, inadequate schooling opportunities, massive traffic jams, and an extremely high cost of living. The government, situated in the urban setting and preoccupied with the task of building modern industry, often neglects the problems of the majority of the population still living in a more traditional setting and life pattern.

Nigeria has made efforts to meet the needs of its people. The prolonged political and economic crisis of the last 15 years has compromised those efforts. Health clinics lack staff and medications; less than 40 percent of Nigerians have access to potable water; sewage systems in urban areas have decayed from overuse and undermaintenance and in most rural areas there are no sewers; retirement benefits are restricted to military officers and a few senior civil servants. The state simply cannot afford social welfare programs that are expected in the developed world.

Education

With illiteracy handicapping approximately 50 percent of the population, all Nigerian governments have attempted to promote educational opportunities. The people are eager for education and see it as a means of personal upward social mobility. Even northerners, who once rejected Western education offered by Christian missionaries, now recognize the importance of education. Regional differences nevertheless remain, with more southern than northern children enrolled in schools, especially beyond the primary level. These variations are due not only to the differing cultures, but also to the fact that northern people are often widely dispersed. It is much more difficult to provide educational opportunities for dispersed or nomadic groups.

Since 1976 the government has promised universal, free primary education for all Nigerians. The resulting explosion in the student population is illustrated in Table 42–1. Despite this commitment, only 50 percent of eligible children were enrolled in primary schools at the end of the 1980s. Secondary schools and universities are now tuition-free, but they often require residence away from home—an expense many modest income families find impossible to bear. The rapid growth in the number of students at all levels has strained the educational system to the breaking point. Schools are greatly overcrowded and often situated in temporary accommodations while new classrooms are under construction. There are far too few teachers and their training is often inadequate. While these problems are real and urgent, increased enrollments offer hope that illiteracy will be overcome in the future.

Secondary and higher education still remain the privilege of only a small handful of the population. Most Nigerian youths must leave school for work at the end of primary education. The removal of tuition in 1979 eliminated some of the financial burden of going beyond primary education.

There are approximately 20 universities in operation, with more planned. The growth in the university system—seven were established in a single year—resulted in uneven quality of education. There are not enough professors for all the universities; many expatriates have been hired to fill the teaching staffs.[9] Over the past few years, the universities have been disrupted by political disturbances and by student or faculty strikes protesting inadequate resources and facilities. Another problem in higher education is the graduation of large numbers of liberal arts students and very few of the engineers, agronomists, biologists, geologists, and other scientists needed to support economic development.

Nigerians have a strong commitment to education. Since independence in 1960, many new universities have been created in Nigeria. The universities now provide a large number of able young people to assist their young nation's economic development. *(Photographer/Source:* United Nations)

Health

Modern health services are limited in Nigeria. In the mid-1990s, there was only one doctor for every 4,496 people and one hospital bed per 1,070 people. (In comparison, in the United States, the figures are one doctor per 243 persons and one hospital bed per 365 persons.) An infant born in Nigeria had a life expectancy of only 54

years in 1998, an improvement of 11 years over life expectancy in 1982. There are still important problems. Infant mortality is high; health standards and services vary greatly from the poor conditions in rural areas and the north to much better health and more modern facilities in southern urban settings; malnutrition remains a serious problem with the Lagos University Hospital reporting malnutrition a primary factor in one out of ten deaths in the 1980s.

All of these statistics are unfavorable in comparison with developed democratic countries, but they are not unusual in countries at the same stage of economic development as Nigeria. The government has plans to increase medical personnel and hospitals but actual achievements in these domains have lagged well behind the targets. At present, the country simply does not have the resources to train the needed doctors and nurses and build hospitals across the land.

Table 42–1   Growth in Students Enrolled
in Nigerian Schools

	1960	1979
Primary schools	2,900,000	10,200,000
Secondary schools	135,000	1,700,000
Higher education	1,400	53,000

Source: Christian Science Monitor, 4 January 1982.

With the help of international health organizations, the government has succeeded in carrying out successful vaccination programs against smallpox and malaria. Beyond these preventive efforts, government medical programs have thus far touched the lives of only a small portion of the population. The AIDS epidemic has hit hard in Nigeria overwhelming the ability of the medical profession to provide appropriate treatment. It affects all parts of the population. Prevention programs and AIDS awareness training are inadequate. It will be the major public health issue in the next decade.

Social Welfare Programs

A country such as Nigeria that is still struggling with the problems of providing basic education and health care for its people cannot be expected to offer the same social welfare benefits as the more established industrial states. For the present, government expenditures are devoted to promoting future economic growth rather than to social programs. Old age assistance, unemployment and disability insurance, social security, and other social welfare programs are not available to most Nigerians. Usually the only ones to benefit from these programs, where they exist at all, are government civil servants and the employees of large, foreign companies with private insurance programs.

Most Nigerians seek protection from periods of hardship and care in old age from traditional family and clan ties. Couples assure themselves of shelter in their old age by having lots of children who will care for them. Family ties remain strong and the extended family is still important not only in caring for the elderly but also in providing help to brothers, sisters, cousins, and whomever in finding jobs or in enduring times of economic difficulties.

Civilian and military governments have pledged to promote greater social and economic quality. The results have been meager. As we have already seen, there are vast differences between a small, wealthy, and privileged elite and the overwhelming majority of the population. The oil boom only deepened the economic disparities between the urban and rural populations.[10] Often government programs to promote egalitarianism seem to result in the further concentration of wealth. Moves to indigenize economic enterprises in order to give more Nigerians a share of their economy resulted instead in the enriching of an already well-to-do business elite. What made this even more objectionable was the fact that these privileged individuals benefited from low-interest government loans to buy out foreigners and thus enhance their personal fortunes. In so doing, the government indirectly subsidized the private acquisition of capital and the private gains of a handful of wealthy businessmen. In another area, the government land tenure decree transferring ownership of all land to the state governments was designed to open up greater access to land. It instead increased problems for farmers seeking to borrow the money they needed to run their farms.

POLITICAL STABILITY

Another point of evaluation in a country's performance is the regime's ability to provide order and stability. The concern for political stability is not always paramount; sometimes, especially in developing countries, the desire for change is so desperate that it overrides interest in a stable political setting. The fall of the Second Republic illustrates this. Westerners had a difficult time understanding why the public reacted so favorably to the military's seizure of power and the destruction of a democratic government. Economic dislocations, severe shortages of basic food commodities, shocking examples of corruption, and a violent and fraudulent election period all contributed to a widely shared public feeling that anything would be better than a continuation of this faulty democracy. In more ordinary settings, people desire stability and predictability in their political system. So it is appropriate to examine several dimensions affecting the stability of Nigerian governments.

One such issue is the economic well-being of the country. The economy brings both strength and weakness to Nigeria. At the end of the century, the Nigerian economy was worse than ever. The people attribute this to the state's mismanagement of the economy. As a consequence, there is widespread alienation and disaffection with any kind of government, civilian or military. The new Third Republic will have to work hard to regain the public's confidence in economic matters. Foreign penetration of the economy and the sense of colonial subservience to developed countries is often blamed on weak and ineffective government. In recent years, the informed public has been particularly hostile to the limitations imposed by the IMF and international lenders and the acceptance of these limits by their government. Economic inequality is great and appears to be growing, but traditional family and communal ties for the present link the new elite with the masses.

Much of the impoverished population lives in remote villages. Such potentially disaffected citizens are not easily mobilized against the government because they remain illiterate and uninformed about the government's actions or lack of action. To the extent that they are informed about politics, they get their information from family members or neighbors who have an education and who have made it in the new Nigeria. When these people vote or engage in other political acts, it is usually at the instigation of their literate family members or friends who are part of the privileged strata of society. This tends to limit the potential for revolt in the less advantaged sections of the population.

We have seen how public repugnance toward the rampant corruption in political circles helped destroy the legitimacy of the Second Republic and force the military out of politics. There is nonetheless considerable tolerance of corruption. While all condemn corruption, it is widely accepted as part of life and seen as normal. The attitude often seems to be "everyone does it; so what?" Sharing access to government jobs with friends and family members is regarded as nepotism in Western societies, but as normal and even as moral or desirable in Nigeria. Such activities have always been present, and they are likely to trouble the current civilian government just as they did previous military regimes. What made corruption a political issue recently has been the sheer enormity of the public funds diverted to private hands during the 1990s. The new democratic government can build its legitimacy if it is able to first punish those who robbed the state while the military ruled and then keep civilian

politicians from continuing the military's corrupt practices.

Perhaps the most troubling aspect of democratic Nigerian politics is the extent of political violence and the polemical nature of political rhetoric. During civilian eras there were frequent incidents of political violence linked to one or the other political parties. Political rivals were denounced as thieves and traitors rather than just as rascals. This violence and extremist rhetoric brought political instability. It was such political violence that produced the breakdown of public order in the mid-1960s and brought the military into politics. The same pattern returned in 1979–83. The election campaign of 1993 was orderly, but there were serious disruptions after the military voided the results of that election. The short-lived Shonekan "interim national government" in 1993 suffered too because of its ineptitude in handling political violence. Nigerians accept more political violence than do the British, French, Germans, or Japanese. But the inability of a regime to maintain public order leads to military intervention. Much of the success of the Third Republic will depend upon the ability of civilian government to control ethnic, regional, and religious violence and to restore order to crime-ridden urban areas.

HUMAN RIGHTS

Nigeria has had one of the most positive records on human rights in all of Africa. Even after the Biafran civil war, there were very few people detained and most of those few were released within a year or so of the end of hostilities. The military rule has usually been an authoritarian one but an enlightened one as far as respect for civil liberties is concerned. There have been some restrictions on political activities but little political repression. In many Third World countries, political arrests, assassinations and disappearance of political enemies, and the torture of dissidents are unfortunately normal politics. Such has not been the case in Nigeria. Under both military and civilian regimes, there have been virtually no incidents of state terror where the power of the state is used to intimidate or suppress political rivals.

In the aftermath of the troubled 1993 elections, the Babangida and Abacha military dictatorships jailed several hundred people on political grounds. Indeed, under General Sani Abacha Nigeria experienced the worst abuses of human rights in its history. The military used violence to quell the disturbances with the result that several hundred people died in political disturbances in 1993 and 1994. Others were jailed for lengthy periods without trial. Party leaders, journalists, and union leaders were among the victims of this political repression. Many were held indefinitely without formal charges. When the courts ordered against Abacha's actions, they were ignored. The right of habeas corpus effectively disappeared for political prisoners during the Abacha era. Political rivals were arrested and several prominent opposition politicians were executed. The wife of the person believed to have been elected president in 1993, Kudirat Abiola, was assassinated. Human rights abuses under Abacha were so numerous and egregious that Nigeria's membership in the British Commonwealth of Nations was suspended.

The Abacha era was a break with the usual respect for basic civil liberties. After his death in 1998, the new military dictator, General Abubakar, released most of those imprisoned during Abacha's rule. The press regained its usual freedom and liveliness. Opposition groups were able to express their views without fear of being charged with treason. When Abubakar turned power over to President Obasanjo less than a year after Abacha's death, full civil and political liberties were restored.

The criminal law system works well and accords the accused basic rights to defend themselves. Human rights advocates express indignation at the relatively frequent recourse to the death penalty for civil crimes. Not only are violent crimes such as murder and armed robbery punished by public execution, the military government has recently extended capital punishment to drug traffickers. In addition, southern Nigerians often complain about the harsh punishments meted out by the Sharia courts in the north to both Muslim and non-Muslim accused.

Nigeria's era of economic growth resulted in the influx of a large number of immigrant workers from surrounding and poorer African countries. As the economy worsened, tolerance of these immigrants declined. The government was anxious to get rid of these immigrants to ease unemployment among its own citizens. As we have seen in Britain, France, and Germany, this is by no means an unusual problem. But the Nigerian response contrasted markedly with the modest efforts of the Western European countries to encourage repatriation of their immigrant workers.

The SMC issued a decree in 1985 ordering vast numbers of illegal immigrants to leave the country within a specified period under threat of arrest and physical expulsion by the military. The peremptory nature of the decree and the short time allowed to the immigrants as well as the expulsion itself aroused criticism throughout the world and especially from Nigeria's neighbors, who had to receive refugees or serve as transit points for them. But among Nigerians, the move was generally welcomed.

The press usually provides an independent and often highly critical view of government action. The written press—newspapers, magazines, and other published materials—gives readers wide-ranging political views. It is regarded as "the most outspoken, volatile, witty, and free in Black Africa."[11] Television and radio are government-owned and -operated. This does not prevent the electronic media from presenting unbiased political news or from taking an independent and often critical view of government actions.

On occasion, the military has reacted against the openness of the Nigerian press. In 1984, the Buhari regime issued a decree limiting freedom of the press and spelling out penalties for criticism of the government. The most egregious attacks on the press, however, came in 1994 when the Abacha regime closed down three major publications and ordered them to remain closed for at least six months.

Overall, the pattern of human rights in Nigeria is mixed. Compared to the other countries explored in this volume, Nigeria has the worst record for human rights in the 1990s with the sole exception of China. This bad record was already improving under the military rule of General Abubakar and it is expected to end under the new civilian government. Nigeria's ethnic and religious diversity set limits on the ability of any regime to impose its will without risking civil war. In addition, society is becoming increasingly complex and pluralist with relations around the world that place formal and informal limits on the arbitrary rule by its leaders.

CONCLUSION

Oil revenues made Nigeria a comparatively rich developing country. This wealth did not prove to be a panacea for all ills. The sudden inflow of oil money fueled inflation and encouraged too rapid development. The growth of industry and commerce nearly overwhelmed the existing communications and transportation infrastructure. It led to many of the problems of the industrialized world: congestion, overpopulation, and pollution in the large cities, especially Lagos. Development was not planned or directed; it simply occurred, resulting in economic, social, and political dislocations. Then came the collapse of the world oil market. Within a decade, Nigeria had fallen from a middle-income to a low-income developing country. Ambitious plans for economic and social development had to be scrapped. Heavy foreign debts weighed down the country's future. Of greater importance, the economic collapse undermined support for the civilian government and helped pave the way for renewed military rule.

Perhaps the most serious economic problem remains agriculture. The population still is essentially agrarian and the country has the potential and the need for important agricultural production. In recent years, agriculture has not kept pace with the expanding population. With a current population growth of approximately 3.5 percent a year, Nigeria is expected to double its population to 200 million by early in the new century. Food production is far from keeping up with population growth. So far government attempts to achieve a green revolution have met with only limited success.

Some critics of economic development in the third world complain that western notions of economic development need not be imposed everywhere. They argue that many cultures place higher values on other things than the consumer-oriented, market economies of the developed world. They see, for example, more potential in grass-roots, community-based economic changes drawn from traditional practices and values than in the top-down economic modernization and industrialization based on western models.[12] This may be true, but in most cases, and clearly in the case of Nigeria, the vision of what economic development means is not imposed by the outside. Nigerians define their economic goals in terms of what is happening in developed countries. Whatever their cultural heritage, they want the same consumer goodies that people have elsewhere in the world. In an era when modern communications technologies bring people together and spread information widely and rapidly, it is difficult to keep people from wanting the same advantages and living standards as enjoyed by others. A regime that tried to lower or change these expectations would not survive in a democratic setting.

Politics have been turbulent under both civilian regimes. Until the dangers of over-politicization are mastered, the military will always have a prominent role. The political enthusiasm of Nigerians seems incompatible with the authoritarianism of its lengthy military regimes. But that very enthusiasm makes the transition to democracy so troublesome.

Forty years ago, Nigeria was one of many African countries to gain its independence from colonial masters from afar. Now, as one Nigerian notes, it is necessary for Nigeria and the rest of Africa is to seek a "second independence this time from the indigenous leadership whose economic mismanagement, together with brutal repression, have made mere survival all but impossible."[13] Another Nigerian intellectual, Adebayo Adedeji, argues for the need of a new form of democracy for Africa that goes beyond the electorally oriented democracy of the Western world.

> Democratization in Africa will be sustainable only if it comes as an integral part of the transformation of the continent's political and socioeconomic structures. . . . Imitative democracy . . . will lead the continent and its people nowhere. In fact, it will only make things worse. . . .[14]

Of course, this only compounds the challenge to Nigerians, especially since the vision of such African democratic forms remains so vague.

As a new popularly elected civilian government took power in May 1999, there was no great optimism about its future. It faces enormous economic and social problems. More fundamental is the issue of what kind of democracy. So far, the unique African version of democracy has not emerged. As in the past, the new democracy starts with the Western assumptions of representative democracy through competitive elections. The 1998 and 1999 elections proved again that Nigerian parties cannot escape the ethnic sectarianism that produces violence in their own country and wherever else parties assume an ethnic basis. Elections in Nigeria seem too vulnerable to corruption and too ready an occasion for enthusiastic supporters to go beyond the bounds of legitimate activities. Democracy will have little appeal to Nigerians if it leads to government that is unable to face the complex economic challenges and the ethnic and religious tensions in Nigerian society.

Adedeji expresses hope more than confidence when he states that by looking into its past Africa can find new models for democracy from "Africa's historical mosaic of economies and modes of social organization."[15] This search will always be hindered by popular expectations among Nigerians already established by exposure to Western democracy. Will people believe that a new form of democracy without party-based elections is democratic? Will people accept a different set of human rights than those embodied in Western democracies?

Indeed, the search for models of democracy in Africa's past may itself be an error. Other Nigerian intellectuals see that past as more of a problem than a source of new democracy. Chinua Achebe asks in his novel, *Anthills of the Savannah,* "What must a people do to appease an embittered history?"[16] The dilemma of identifying an appropriate form for African democracy will continue. And it will always be hindered by popular expectations based on what democracy is in the West.

NOTES

[1]Chinua Achebe, *A Man of the People* (New York: John Day, 1966), pp. 130–131.

[2]Claude Ake, "The Unique Case of African Democracy," *International Affairs* 69 (April 1993): 239–244; and Adebayo Adedeji, "An Alternative for Africa," *Journal of Democracy* 5 (October 1994): 119–132.

[3]Baldev Ray Nayar, "Political Mainsprings of Economic Planning in the New Nations: The Modernization Imperative versus Social Mobilization," *Comparative Politics* 6 (April 1974): 341–367,

[4]*The Economist,* 23 January 1982.

[5]See the bitter critique by Nigeria's Nobel Prize winning author, Wole Soyinka, *The Open Sore of a Continent: A Personal Narrative of the Nigerian Crisis* (New York: Oxford University Press, 1996).

[6]*Financial Times* (London), 28 May 1999.

[7]Augustine Ikein and Comfort Briggs-Anigboh, *Oil and Fiscal Federalism in Nigeria: The Political Economy of Resource Allocation in a Developing Country* (Aldershot, England: Ashgate, 1999).

[8]O. Teriba, "Financial Institutions, Financial Markets, and Income Distribution," in Henry Bienen and V. P. Diejomaoh, eds., *The Political Economy of Income Distribution in Nigeria* (New York: Holmes & Meier, 1981), pp. 496–497.

[9]See the sharp criticism of the universities in Julius O. Ihonvbere, *Nigeria: The Politics of Adjustment to Democracy* (New Brunswick, NJ: Transaction Books, 1994).

[10]Bienen, "Political Economics of Income Distribution in Nigeria," in Bienen and Diejomaoh, *The Political Economy of Income Distribution in Nigeria,* pp. 1–27.

[11]Guy Arnold, *Modern Nigeria* (London: Longman, 1977) p. 163.

[12]See, for example, the interesting examples of community-based development described in Adebayo Adedeji, ed., *Nigeria: Renewal From the Roots: the Struggle for Democratic Development* (New York: St. Martin's, 1997).

[13]Ake, "The Unique Case of African Democracy," p. 240.

[14]Adedeji, "An Alternative for Africa," pp. 127, 128.

[15]Ibid., p. 131.s

[16]Chinua Achebe, *Anthills of the Savannah* (New York: Anchor Books, 1989).

NIGERIA: SELECTED BIBLIOGRAPHY

Adebayo Adedeji, ed., *Africa Within the World: Beyond Dispossession and Dependence* (London, Zed Books, 1993).

Adebayo Adedeji, ed., *Nigeria: Renewal From the Roots: the Struggle for Democratic Development* (New York: St. Martin's, 1997).

Guy Arnold, *Modern Nigeria* (London: Longman, 1977).

Henry Bienen, *The Political Conflict and Economic Change in Nigeria* (London: Frank Cass, 1985).

Michael Crowder, *The Story of Nigeria,* 4th ed. (London: Faber and Faber, 1978).

Basil Davidson, *The Black Man's Burden: Africa and the Curse of the Nation-State* (New York: Times Books, 1992).

Larry Diamond, *Class, Ethnicity and Democracy in Nigeria: The Failure of the First Republic* (Syracuse, NY: Syracuse University Press, 1988).

Larry Diamond, Juan Linz, and Seymour Martin Lipset, eds., *Democracy in Developing Countries,* Volume Two: *Africa* (Boulder, CO: Lynne Rienner, 1988).

Larry Diamond, Anthony Kirk-Greene, and Oyeleye Oyediran, eds., *Transition Without End: Nigerian Politics and Civil Society Under Babangida* (Boulder, CO: Lynne Rienner, 1997).

Billy Dudley, A*n Introduction to Nigerian Government and Politics* (Bloomington, IN: Indiana University Press, 1982).

Ibrahim A. Gambari, *Theory and Reality in Foreign Policy Making: Nigeria After the Second Republic* (Atlantic Highlands, NJ: Humanities Press, 1990).

Julius O. Ihonvbere, *Nigeria: The Politics of Adjustment to Democracy* (New Brunswick, NJ: Transaction Books, 1994).

Augustine Ikein and Comfort Briggs-Anigboh, *Oil and Fiscal Federalism in Nigeria: The Political Economy of Resource Allocation in a Developing Country* (Aldershot, England; Ashgate, 1999).

Richard A. Joseph, *Democracy and Prebendal Politics in Nigeria: The Rise and Fall of the Second Republic* (Cambridge, England: Cambridge University Press, 1987).

Peter Lewis, Barnett R. Rubin, and Pearl T. Robinson, *Stabilizing Nigeria: Sanctions, Incentives, and Support for Civil Society* (New York: The Council on Foreign Relations and The Century Foundation, 1998).

William Miles, *Elections in Nigeria: A Grassroots Perspective* (Boulder, CO: Lynne Rienner, 1988).

William Miles, *Hausaland Divided: Colonialism and Independence in Nigeria and Niger* (Ithaca, NY: Cornell University Press, 1994).

Keith Panter-Brick, ed., *Soldiers and Oil: The Political Transformation of Nigeria* (London: Frank Cass, 1978).

Margaret Peil, *Nigerian Politics: The People's View* (London: Cassell, 1976).

Wole Soyinka, *The Open Sore of a Continent: A Personal Narrative of the Nigerian Crisis* (New York: Oxford University Press, 1996).

C. S. Whitaker, *The Politics of Tradition: Continuity and Change in Northern Nigeria* (Princeton, NJ: Princeton University Press, 1970).

Howard Wolpe, *Urban Politics in Nigeria* (Berkeley: University of California Press, 1974).

Index